The Oxford Guide to
FINANCIAL MODELING

The Oxford Guide to FINANCIAL MODELING

Applications for Capital Markets, Corporate Finance, Risk Management, and Financial Institutions

Thomas S. Y. Ho

Sang Bin Lee

OXFORD
UNIVERSITY PRESS

2004

OXFORD
UNIVERSITY PRESS

Oxford   New York
Auckland   Bangkok   Buenos Aires   Cape Town   Chennai
Dar es Salaam   Delhi   Hong Kong   Istanbul   Karachi   Kolkata
Kuala Lumpur   Madrid   Melbourne   Mexico City   Mumbai   Nairobi
São Paulo   Shanghai   Taipei   Tokyo   Toronto

Copyright © 2004 by Thomas S. Y. Ho and Sang Bin Lee

Published by Oxford University Press, Inc.
198 Madison Avenue, New York, New York, 10016
www.oup.com

Oxford is a registered trademark of Oxford University Press

Library of Congress Cataloging-in-Publication Data

Ho, Thomas S. Y.
The Oxford guide to financial modeling : applications for capital markets, corporate finance,
risk management and financial institutions / by Thomas Ho and Sang Bin Lee.
p. cm.
Includes bibliographical references.
ISBN 0-19-516962-X
1. Finance.   2. Finance—Case studies.   3. Derivative securities.   4. Derivative securities—
Case studies.   5. Corporations—Finance.   6. Corporations—Finance—Case studies.   I. Title:
Financial modeling.   II. Yi, Sang-bin.   III. Title.
HG173 .H5815 2004
332'.01'1—dc22   2003018741

9 8 7 6 5 4 3 2 1

Printed in the United States of America
on acid-free paper

In the middle of writing this book, the tragic events of September 11, 2001, occurred. When we looked out from our office, which was covered with gray ash, and saw the collapsed World Trade Center and the devastation of Ground Zero, we came to realize there is no effort that is too small to strengthen the awareness of peace among peoples. We dedicate this book to world peace.

Preface

With more than 20 years of financial experience each, we have seen financial modeling play an ever-increasing role in financial markets. Option models were introduced to trading floors in the 1970s. Interest rate models were widely used in the 1980s for fixed-income securities. At the same time, the growth of financial products in this period led to the prevalent use of financial models in asset management. In the 1990s, financial models became indispensable tools for fast-growing risk management practices.

Starting with our earliest involvement, we considered financial modeling to be the art of finding the best quantitative solution to a business problem. Financial models are fast becoming indispensable decision-support tools for trading, portfolio management, risk management, corporate financing, financial planning, regulation, and so on. But what is financial modeling? What are the financial concepts (theories) behind the mathematical algorithms? How do we build financial models to provide business solutions? This book is written to answer these questions and to address the needs of both practitioners and educators in finance.

This book is the outcome of our experiences in both the academic and the corporate worlds. These experiences include researching, teaching, developing, and implementing the financial models that are the focus of this book. Throughout our academic careers, we have spent much of our time developing valuation models for financial securities and testing them empirically. We teach financial modeling in our academic classes as a scientific discipline, emphasizing the thinking process that is required to properly develop and use them. As practitioners, we have worked with the investment departments of financial institutions in areas of asset/liability management, corporate management, trading, and risk management. These experiences have enabled us to gain insight into how various financial models can be and should be used in practice.

We are aware of no other book that successfully ties the thought processes and applications of the financial models together and describes them as one process which provides business solutions. Generally, financial textbooks segment the world of finance into "investments," "financial institutions," "corporate finance," and "securities analysis," and in so doing they rarely emphasize the relationships between the subjects. Recently, courses in financial engineering programs have evolved a fundamental raison d'être more rooted in mathematics than in financial theories. The "practitioners' books" tend to focus on the how-to approach, as if there is always a manual for solving a financial problem. Surely, to understand financial modeling, don't we first need or want to see an overview of the process, with a balanced perspective across the main disciplines of finance? This book is written to fill this void.

Once a graduate from a prestigious business school was overheard saying, "Financial modeling is really quite simple. It is just about different variations of the Black–Scholes model." Such a remark must have aroused a deep sense of disappointment and fear in academics and practitioners alike. As academics, we are proud to have participated in the successful growth of the subject of financial modeling, but this person reduced all the accomplishments to "just different variations of the Black–Scholes model." As practitioners and educators in quantitative research, we fear that our financial engineers too often focus on alternative mathematical models and not often enough on the thinking process of modeling. As a result of emphasizing the techniques and not understanding the broader context of a business problem, they may provide an erroneous or irrelevant solution. Users of financial models must understand that financial modeling is a process for providing business solutions. This process begins with understanding the business problem and posing the appropriate statement of the problem within the context of a quantitative analytical framework by specifying the assumptions of the model. Next, a theory or model is developed to address the problem. The model is then applied to the business solution with empirical evidence.

Despite the prevalent use and growing importance of financial models, most publications are devoted to describing specific models, such as those for stocks, bonds, or options, or to their specific applications, such as arbitrage trading and portfolio management. Few books describe the financial principles behind the models and tie the models to business solutions. But those who employ financial models should know how each model should be used as part of a whole. Otherwise, the potential use of models and the development of modeling will be significantly limited. A key motivation for writing this book is to describe financial modeling in this broader context. To understand such a broader context, we believe one needs to understand financial problems in a coherent framework.

It is our belief that financial modeling can only become more important to our financial system. Although financial modeling is critical to so many aspects of our financial system, such as trading, hedge fund investments, and risk management, corporate management is only *beginning* to use financial models. In our experience, few models are integrated into the management of a firm, yet the use of financial models in corporate management has vast potential.

There are at least two reasons for the slow adoption of financial modeling in corporate finance. A distinct failure to relate how valuations can be used in practice in classrooms, and how research can be directed to practical problems in corporate finance, is one reason. Another reason is that prevailing financial models have not been extended to deal with corporate financial management issues, and thus fail to reach the attention of the corporate senior management. For these reasons, there is a need for a book to explain the significant value of financial modeling applying to capital markets and corporate finance. It is our hope that this book will serve this need well.

About the Book

Theme and Organization

The essential premise of this book is that theory and practice are equally important in describing financial modeling. We try to strike a balance in our discussions between the theories that provide foundations for financial models and the institutional details that provide the context for applications of the models.

We present the financial models of stock and bond options, exotic options, investment-grade and high-yield bonds, convertible bonds, mortgage-backed securities, and liabilities of financial institutions. We also describe the applications of the models to corporate finance, and we relate the models to financial statements, risk management for an enterprise, and asset/liability management with illiquid instruments. The business model and the corporate model are used to provide the analyses.

The book presents the progression of the financial models from option pricing in the securities markets to firm valuation in corporate finance, following a format that emphasizes the three aspects of a model: the set of assumptions, the model specification, and the model applications.

- The *set of assumptions* describes the conceptual ideas behind the model, the circumstances that the model may be applicable to, and the problem that the model seeks to evolve. In going through the assumptions of the models, readers gain insight into the thought process behind the model.
- The *model specification* is the mathematical description of the model showing how input data are used to produce the quantitative results predicted by the model. The specification may be presented as a mathematical formula or as a step-by-step procedure of building a model.
- *Model applications* show how each model is used or should be used in practice. The financial models described in this book can further our understanding of financial theories, and have direct and important applications in business.

Black and Scholes's seminal 1973 article, "The Pricing of Options and Corporate Liabilities," is a milestone in the development of financial models. It proposed a new paradigm for valuing options and anticipated that the methodology can be extended to corporate liabilities, as the title indicates. The organization of this book follows the flow of thoughts suggested by that paper and is divided into three parts.

Part I, "Options," starts with the portfolio theory and ends with a broad array of valuation models of derivatives. The valuation models described include equity, bonds, and their options. Empirical results are provided to support the validity of these models and the implications of the models are discussed.

Part II, "Corporate Liabilities," extends option pricing to corporate liabilities and the applications of the model to the balance sheet items: corporate bonds, high-yield securities, mortgage-backed bonds, convertible securities and other bond types, and the liabilities of financial institutions. These items are less liquid; some have no liquid market, if they are tradable at all. Yet the theory argues that the contingent claim theory remains applicable to them. The valuation model is then shown to have important implications for the management of a firm's balance sheet.

Part III, "Corporate Finance," further extends the analysis to valuing any firm. The analysis argues that a firm itself can be viewed as a security, a contingent claim on its uncertain revenues. The valuation model is then used to describe corporate financial strategies. The empirical testing of the model is provided. More important, the model of a firm enables us to evaluate the effectiveness of some corporate financial decisions in increasing shareholders' value.

The formation of each building block is as self-contained as possible. Each chapter presents the models and their usefulness in providing economic insights. Empirical evidence and applications of the model are then provided. The appendix to each chapter is integral to the book. The appendices provide the proofs and technical details necessary for financial engineering. In many ways, they are as important as the text to the flow of ideas of the book. Because the more technical aspects of the book are presented in appendices, however, readers can appreciate the thought development in the main text without being distracted by equations. At the same time, financial engineers are encouraged to treat the appendices as part of the book.

The Chapters

Each chapter begins by introducing a practical problem. The financial models that provide solutions to the problem are then described. The chapter concludes with how the models can be applied. Whenever possible, we build each model upon the previous models so that all the models are specified in one consistent framework and can all work together as one decision-support tool.

The models are introduced in chapters 1–14 and provide solutions to progressively more complicated and general problems. These models are described as essential steps to address business solutions. The remaining chapters describe how the system of financial models can be used in a broader context in risk management, corporate financial planning, asset and liability management, and regulatory policy issues.

New and unpublished models by the authors can be found throughout the book.

- In chapters 5 and 6 we describe a multifactor arbitrage-free interest rate model that has a number of advantages over the current state-of-the-art interest rate models.
- In chapter 7 we describe a general multifactor risk model that can be used for valuating securities which are subject to multiple risk sources and for building the business models of a firm.
- In chapter 8 we describe the pathwise value approach to implement static hedging.
- In chapter 11 we study the fair valuation models of financial institutions' liabilities and their applications.
- In chapters 12 and 14 we describe a model of a firm that treats the firm as a contingent claim on its business risk, and its fixed operating cost as a long-term liability. The model has a number of new applications, including one that enables equity analysts to conduct peer group analysis and to identify the strategic value of a firm.
- In chapter 13 we propose a high-yield bond model that incorporates the firm's business model, providing a more realistic credit risk model that takes the firm's fixed costs, business risks, and strategic value into account.
- In chapter 15 we introduce process engineering from the perspective of risk management and valuation.
- In chapter 16 we provide an integrated business model and corporate model of a firm with GAAP and fair value financial statements.
- In chapter 17 we provide a VaR measure for securities not for trading.
- In chapter 19 we provide a description of forward measures in the binomial lattice context.

Emphasis on Practical Usability

The book provides at once a useful overview and challenging ideas of financial models to both students and professionals in finance, and advocates using financial modeling to meet some of the current challenges in financial markets and corporate entities. Specifically, the book urges corporate financial managers to use corporate models more systematically to formulate corporate strategies, manage enterprise risks as a business process, and determine optimal financial decisions for their firms. Furthermore, we intend the book to be a tool for practitioners in the securities markets. Traders and portfolio managers can use the models for their decision-support systems. Financial managers will find the book useful, and many will appreciate the inclusion of new and as yet unpublished financial models. Financial engineers may find our binomial lattice approach to expound the continuous time theory useful. We hope that readers can enjoy the book from different perspectives and at different technical levels.

Because of the nature of the material on financial models, the book presents many results as mathematical formulations. In order to make the text more enjoyable and avoid distraction by equations, we give special attention to explaining the mathematical models and defer the more rigorous mathematical derivations to the appendices and to the epilogue.

An interested reader can go to the website www.thomasho.com to gain deeper understanding of the financial models. At the site, some Excel financial models are available. Interested readers can build and test the models described in this book using Excel, and they can submit their models to the site. Readers also can use the forum to discuss the models. The website also provides server-based models for readers to gain insights into the applications of the models, as well as PowerPoint descriptions of the chapters. Students can use the question banks on the chapters for studying.

To further evaluate the theoretical discussions to practical experiences, the book describes some of the experiences of one of the authors (T. H.) as anecdotes. Presented at the end of most chapters, they provide background information to the relevance and applicability of the theories in practice.

Intended Audience

This book can be used in MBA programs, specifically in courses on derivatives, fixed-income securities, and corporate finance. It covers the subjects of a typical program and enables students to understand how each subject fits in a broader perspective of finance. It can also be used in the final year of an MBA program in a course on applications of financial theories, allowing students the opportunity to tie the theoretical framework of securities valuation to cases of corporate finance.

Because it focuses on corporate issues as well as securities valuation, the book can be used in risk management courses, where the emphasis is not only on risk measures methodology but also on the framework of analysis of "enterprise risks." The book can also be used in financial institutions courses, for which it provides a general context of the issues specific to financial institutions, which are described in chapters 16 and 17. Students can better understand the relevance and implementation issues of fair value financial reporting.

Considering the growing importance of financial modeling to businesses, we believe financial modeling should be a course offered in the MBA curriculum. This book can be used as the text for such a course. It treats the models rigorously, deriving most of the results. For this reason, the book can be used in the graduate courses offered in business schools and mathematics departments on mathematical finance or financial engineering. For these courses, it covers the financial theories and practical applications of the models.

This book addresses a broad range of professionals' needs. We attempt to link corporate finance and securities market theories together, and to tie financial engineering to the financial principles to convey the importance of financial modeling applications to corporate managers. Financial managers, corporate planning managers, investment professionals, treasurers, and risk managers will find this book applicable to their work. It can be used for in-house training programs; attendees can appreciate a broad view of the work of "quants," bridging the gap between the research department and the users of quantitative research, such as the sales department and senior management. The sales staff can better understand client needs, and senior management can relate quantitative results to the firm's financial performance.

Portions of this book can be used by professionals including actuarial professionals, bankers, risk managers, accountants, and investment managers for their professional advancement. To these groups this book offers a perspective on each profession as an integral part of the finance profession, not as an isolated entity. Specifically, management can better appreciate the "fair value" accounting concepts. Managers are presented with the option to "open the hood" and look into the black box that calculates the fair value numbers. And, we hope, they can fully appreciate the work of financial engineers and learn how to put the financial models into practice.

The book should appeal to a general reader interested in finance and financial modeling. It is written so that a reader can skip the mathematical formalism and still appreciate the importance and essentials of financial models. At the same time, Ph.D.s in mathematics can treat the appendices containing mathematical derivations as the main part of the book, while reading how the models are formulated and applied.

Reference

Black, F. and M. Scholes, 1973. The pricing of options and corporate liabilities. *Journal of Political Economy*, 81, 637–654.

Acknowledgments

We are indebted to the former clients and staff of Global Advanced Technology Corporation. Its former clients were our teachers in the real world. In particular, we would like to thank Tony Kao of General Motors Corporation, who has given us guidance in our research since our NYU days; we are still working on our "Ho, Lee, Kao" model. We thank Tom McAvity of Scottish Annuity, who assisted us in developing many of the conceptual ideas in the book. We thank Gerd Stabbert, Kin Tam, and Alex Scheitlin of Metropolitan Life, who assisted extensively with this book, teaching us endless institutional details and business objectives. We thank Edwin Betz of TIAA-CREF and Marsha Wallace of Worldwide Asset Liability Management, who taught us much about life insurance products and assisted us extensively in preparing chapter 11. We thank Lars Soderlind of Risk Ciceron for his inputs on risk management. We thank Hideki Sakura of Nomura Securities for providing us their equity research. We would like to thank Chuck Lucas and Victor Marsh of Market Risk Management, American International Group (AIG) for providing support to the project. Special thanks go to Blessing Mudavanhu and Yuan Su, who gave much assistance in the preparation of the manuscript. We thank Marlys Appleton and Susan Ma of AIG, Eric Anderson of Enron Corporation, and Ronald Singer of Houston University for their comments on the early versions of the manuscript. They assisted in the research on interest rate modeling and corporate models, and provided valuable comments. We want to thank the Owen School of Vanderbilt University, which provided an initial research grant to support this work, and Hans Stoll in particular for his continual encouragement and stimulating ideas over the past 20 years. We thank the Stern School of New York University for providing an excellent research environment for our work. In particular, we thank Ned Elton for his generous support of our research ideas and efforts since one of the authors' first day at work. Without Vanderbilt University and New York University support, this book would not have a sound academic base.

We are grateful to the research team at Hanyang University, Korea, who provided invaluable assistance in research and analysis. Especially, we are thankful for the help of Jaeuk Khil, Inho Kim, Kyou Yung Kim, and Sang-Gyung Jun, professors at Hanyang University. We are indebted to four graduate students: Yoon Seok Choi, Hanki Seong, Junghoon Soo, and Ji Hyun Lee. Yoon and Hanki worked with us tirelessly throughout the writing of the book, commenting, researching, and building software programs for the project. Their efforts were crucial to the completion of the book. We are also grateful to Tommy Liu, Laura Leung, and Glen Swafford for their extraordinary editorial assistance in the early drafts of the manuscript.

We thank the staff of Oxford University Press for their active support of this project. In particular, we thank Paul Donnelly, the editor, for his encouragement and his many insightful suggestions.

Contents

Model List

Models are defined here to have a mathematical measure, whose validity depends on the assumptions made

PART I

DERIVATIVES VALUATION

1

Introduction: Discounted Cash Flow Method

Financial modeling is an important methodology used by managers at all levels for the purpose of providing business solutions. The process must begin with understanding the business objectives and specifying the economic concepts on which the model is based. Some of the fundamental economic concepts are present-value measures, efficient capital market, perfect capital market, and risk-averse behavior. These concepts lead to the formulation of the discounted cash flow method as a basic approach to valuing financial instruments.

Today, financial models find broad applications in managing financial and nonfinancial corporations. Their importance can only increase over time as both system technologies and financial technologies continue to change our financial markets and the management of firms. Traders apply the financial models to trading securities; analysts use the models to analyze stocks and bonds; portfolio strategists use them to position their investment portfolios; corporations use them to simulate financial and strategic planning. Financial models seem to be everywhere, but what, exactly, are they? Why do we need them?

To answer these questions, we first illustrate the relationships between financial models and financial problems with some real-life examples. We will examine three financial cases: the JP Morgan Company and SK Securities Company agreement, Starbucks Coffee Japan, and Orange County, California. These examples, which involve many management issues, were chosen to illustrate the broad applications of financial models in asset management, corporate investments, and the treasury management of a municipality. Relating financial models to these situations requires a framework of analysis, building the financial models in a coherent way to analyze the problem. The development of a financial model is important for making corporate financial decisions. This chapter will provide an overview of the framework of analysis as the first step in building financial models.

A significant management issue that we will discuss concerning financial models is valuation. It is essential to determine the present and future value of investments. But what valuation methodology should be used? In this chapter, we will examine the discounted cash flow method, then discuss the relevance of the valuation and how it relates to risk. How does our level of risk tolerance affect our investments? Using the discounted cash flow model, how do we determine our rates of return? We will see that a financial model can help us determine our rates of return in order to profit from our investment decisions.

1.1 Examples of Financial Issues

Below are examples of financial issues that have implications for the broader context of the economy. These issues are highlighted in this chapter to give the reader a taste of what's coming; they will be revisited in later chapters for full explanations and solutions.

JP Morgan Company and SK Securities Company

Early in January 1997, JP Morgan offered SK Securities a seemingly attractive investment proposal: if SK Securities invested in the fund, it could realize 3 percent or 4 percent returns in excess of the Korean bond yields. In addition, SK Securities could receive another 3 percent if they utilized a structured derivative trading program designed by JP Morgan.

On January 29, 1997, SK Securities established the Diamond Fund in Labuan, Malaysia. It raised $35 million denominated in Korean won from several Korean institutional investors and borrowed $53 million denominated in Japanese yen from JP Morgan. The Diamond Fund invested $88 million in bonds denominated in Indonesian rupiah. This trade could leave SK Securities exposed to both yen and rupiah foreign exchange rate risk. To hedge the foreign exchange risks, SK Securities implemented a hedging program designed by JP Morgan.

SK Securities anticipated realizing an annual 20.225 percent rate of return on this investment. But that did not happen. By June 1999, the investment was sustaining significant losses; the Diamond Fund was obligated to pay over $257 million to JP Morgan, thereby threatening the viability of SK Securities, one of the major investment banks in Korea. The case was finally settled out of court, with SK Securities arguing that JP Morgan misrepresented the risk of the investment.

Financial engineering is a powerful tool for structured investments. However, we must bear in mind that the tool has to be used appropriately and we must appreciate its limitations, the assumptions made in the financial models. Clearly, this case demonstrates that financial engineering can be used to exploit market opportunities to provide excess returns, but at the same time we must be aware of the risks so that we can avoid unanticipated losses.

What are the risks when financial engineering is implemented in the investments? How are these financing structures designed? We will show how the use of financial models can determine the risk exposure of structured financing and how to manage such risks. This case exemplifies the prevalent use of financial models in the securities market.

Starbucks Coffee Japan

When we take a stroll on the Ginza in Tokyo, and walk into Starbucks Coffee for a cup of coffee, have we ever wondered how Starbucks, the chain based in Seattle, Washington, expanded to Japan?

In the early 1990s, the entrepreneur Yuji Tsunoda repeatedly sent letters and E-mails, and made telephone calls, to Starbucks' CEO, Howard Schultz, suggesting that Starbucks be introduced in Japan. His persistence led to a joint venture, initially in Tokyo, to introduce and market Starbucks coffee to Japanese consumers.

Founded in October 1995, the company followed the Starbucks Coffee business model, targeting a specific market segment. New stores were added annually to continue aggressive growth. The company went public in October 2001, at a market valuation of

¥90 billion with more than 200 stores. The company's development strategy goes beyond the design of the storefront and the making of the coffee. Corporate finance is at work, dealing with returns on the investments, mechanisms of raising capital, and sharing of profits.

When a store opens, a financial analyst can estimate the customer flow, total purchases, profit margin, and profitability, and make financial projections. Using spreadsheets for capital budgeting is a familiar practice in finance. But how do entrepreneurs make strategic decisions, not knowing where the 200 stores will be, without even doing the spreadsheet analysis? How does a corporation assign a value to a strategy when specific plans are not made?

We will show that strategic investment decisions are considered to be real options. These options can be valued, and strategies can be formulated to maximize these values. This new frontier of financial research promises to have broad applications for corporate finance.

Orange County, California

In December 1994, TV viewers learned that Orange County, in southern California, had declared default. The county treasurer, Robert Citron, was responsible for overseeing a $7.5 billion investment pool for 187 government participants, including 34 cities and 38 school districts. The county reported a financial loss of $1.7 billion, then the largest financial loss ever reported.

The news coverage reported that the investment pool was leveraged from the original $7.5 billion to exceed $20 billion. The investment strategies had been gaining 2 percent over the market rates for several years.

But in one month, the investment pool collapsed and Orange County had no reserves to continue to operate, even though the county was one of the wealthiest in the country. The collapse should not have been a complete surprise, considering that the investment strategies were not particularly complex. The portfolio strategies were criticized by Mr. Citron's political opponent in the election that had been held a few months earlier. Although the risks were publicized, voters chose to ignore the warnings and had to bear the consequences.

The default had broad implications: the school system, water companies, and many municipalities suffered investment losses by participating in the pool. The default led to downgrading of California bond ratings, and as a result the state of California had to borrow at a higher cost for all its bonds.

The default imposed social costs and became the center of many political, social, and economic discussions. Would it have been possible to implement procedures, change regulations, or take legal actions without fully understanding the risks and valuation of these investment strategies? Furthermore, how could a management control process for an elected official who managed over $20 billion, using somewhat complicated financial instruments such as reverse repurchase agreements, be put in place? We will discuss the use of financial models to measure and monitor risks, and we will demonstrate how investment risks must be managed as a process. We will show that financial models play an important role in the management of a corporation, where the business processes should be modeled for management purposes.

1.2   Financial Models

In the above examples, JP Morgan and SK Securities investment strategies were based on financial models used to evaluate the trade-off in risk and returns in financial markets. Financial models are tools used for making investment strategies. The examples show the importance of developing the appropriate financial models for the purpose and understanding the assumptions used in each financial model. In recent years significant progress has been made in building and using financial models for trading and investments. Financial models have been developed to determine the relationships of cross currencies, interest rate movements, equity market risks, and a wide range of securities valuation models. These models are then used to identify the investment values of the securities, formulate trading strategies, and evaluate risks of trading positions. The list of applications is extensive. There are few firms in the securities industry that do not rely on some kind of financial model in their operation.

The example of Starbucks Japan shows that the use of financial models is not confined to the securities industry. Corporate financial managers can use them to make strategic investment decisions. For example, let us take the case of Starbucks Coffee launching in Japan. In corporate finance, financial models are tools used to determine the valuation of a strategic investment by the marketplace. Corporate managers make decisions maximizing the shareholders' value based on stock valuation increases. Through extension of the financial model applications and formulations from the capital market to corporate finance, corporate decisions become an integral part of the capital markets. When we extend the applications of financial valuation models to analyze a strategic investment decision, there are many factors that need to be taken into account. A corporate manager may even argue that there is no value in making a list of them; instead, many decisions need to be made with a "business instinct." Maybe such an assertion is correct, but a framework to formalize the problem should be an important tool for corporate management. Financial models can help corporate management to build a framework. For this reason, financial models play a significant role in the optimal functioning of the markets.

The Orange County case shows that financial models are not simply a black box that determines the values of securities or strategic decisions. Financial models do not need to be "only" algorithms that determine values of securities or decisions. The failure of the Orange County investment was not for lack of financial modeling. It was the lack of an investment process. Managing a $20 billion portfolio of assets is not just a matter of determining the value of a portfolio; it is a process of decision-making. An investment process involves monitoring the capital markets, valuing securities, formulating expectations of market directions, executing the trades, and many other activities. Financial models play a crucial role in measuring the performances of the phases of an investment or other financial process. Their use in the management of a firm, in risk management, and in other business activities can significantly enhance the functioning of a business entity.

Defining a Financial Model

This book will cover the broad applications of a financial model. But first we need to define "financial model," since the term is interpreted differently in various contexts. For our purpose, financial models have three parts: (1) the set of economic assumptions, (2) the quantification of the model, and (3) applications of the model.

1. Economic assumptions

A *model* is a simplified description of a real situation. Its purpose is to provide insights into the functioning of markets, firms, or financial processes. To make a complex problem abstract, we establish a set of assumptions, a model. Often, these assumptions may not seem realistic. The reasonableness of the assumptions is not the main concern, but the reasonableness of the model's results is. Does the model give us better insights into the financial process? Does the model provide a testable hypothesis? Are its results consistent with empirical findings? These are the criteria to measure the importance of a financial model.

Milton Friedman[1] wrote, "[T]he relevant question to ask about the 'assumptions' of a theory is not whether they are descriptively 'realistic,' for they never are, but whether they are sufficiently good approximations for the purpose in hand. And this question can be answered only by seeing whether the theory works, which means whether it yields sufficiently accurate predictions."[2]

For each financial model, we make a set of assumptions, and these assumptions have varying degrees of importance for the purpose in hand. We can separate the assumptions into two types. On the one hand, some assumptions are technical in nature. They are made to present a concept elegantly and precisely, but they do not significantly affect the basic idea of the model. For example, in this book, we choose to assume that all individuals trade at the end of a period. This assumption is referred to as a *discrete time model*. The fact that everyone trades continuously or discretely does not affect the model results for our purposes. If we assume a *continuous time model*, research can show that the results would be similar. And therefore the distinction between a discrete time model and a continuous time model is a technical point. On the other hand, there are the economic assumptions. Some economic assumptions are held as *first principles*, which means that they are fundamental in describing the basic nature of the people and the markets. For example, we assume that all individuals maximize their happiness level, and that increasing wealth leads to an increase in happiness. Some economic assumptions may seem heroic, appearing unreasonable in that everyone is rational and maximizes wealth all the time. Yet, these assumptions are important because they provide sufficiently accurate predictions, and some financial models do have predictive value even though they sometimes depend on heroic economic assumptions. Thus, developing financial models is an art, offering a scientific challenge.

By deriving financial models based on empirically proven or theoretically sound basic assumptions, we are assured that they are derived from first principles. Thus, we know that all the models belonging to the same set of assumptions will be consistent with each other. This book seeks to present a set of financial models used in capital markets and corporate finance by assuming that each model has the same consistent framework of analysis, which will enable readers to gain insights into financial systems in one coherent view.

We will present two types of models: normative and positive.[3] *Normative models* are prescriptive. They offer us the most favorable way to achieve our objectives. Most finance students find these models useful because they provide a step-by-step way of achieving a goal. *Positive models*, on the other hand, describe the financial world as seen through the prism of financial models. These models provide useful insights into how markets function, leading us to what we can see at the equilibrium point. Readers can gain insights into the financial markets via the positive theories.

2. Quantification of the economic models

Financial models described in this book must be quantitative. The purpose of the book is not only to provide insights into financial markets, but also to describe financial models based on the first principles in economic theories that provide quantifications in our financial analysis.

The financial models are formulated such that they can use input data to calculate security prices, determine valuations of decisions, and measure the performance of each phase of a business process. Furthermore, they are described in such a way that, at least in principle, they can be implemented and have direct implications for finance in practice. While some economic theories are important in providing insights to further understand the economy, our concerns in this book are to build a system of financial models that provide applications to the problems in hand.

3. Applications of the models

The final aspect of the financial models is their applications to finance. Models are developed to solve specific problems. Their usefulness is therefore measured by their ability to do so. Therefore, in a description of any model, we first have to state the problems that it seeks to solve and then determine its ability to solve them. Describing a financial model without showing its applications would have minimal value for our purpose.

There are different types of applications. Some models are used to provide hypotheses about our world that can be tested empirically. Other models are proposed as tools for financial management. There are models that identify the salient features of complex problems and to indicate how these problems may be solved.

Financial modeling is a process that starts with understanding the business problem, then moves to specifying the assumptions, implementing the models, and applying the models. But the process does not stop with the applications. The model's results and applications should be monitored and the assumptions of the model should be continually evaluated. Therefore financial modeling is a cycle of activities. (See figure 1.1.)

4. Other aspects of financial modeling

There are other aspects of financial modeling that we do not cover. One type of financial model is *subjective modeling*, which seeks to abstract complex problems to deal with a

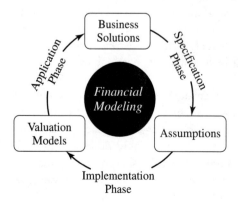

Figure 1.1 Financial model cycle. Financial modeling is a process to solve the business problems. To address the business problems, we specify the assumptions, implement the models and apply the models to solve the business problems. Since the model results and applications should be monitored and the assumptions should be continuously evaluated, financial modeling is a cycle of activities.

purpose in hand. These models are not derived from first principles. They are derived by rules or ideas that may contradict the basic principles of finance or economic theories. These models are often found at trading desks, where they are used to predict the markets. We will not dwell on these models. However, the book will provide some examples of such models in regulatory rules, risk measures of rating agencies, and other real-world models. For example, in chapter 16, we describe the regulatory rules in valuing reserves of annuities or the equity of a firm. From the perspective of the economic principles, these models can be best described as ad hoc. Nevertheless, they are real in the sense that they affect our way of making financial decisions.

Another class of model that we do not cover is *financial engineering models*,[4] which are particularly concerned with implementation issues: How can we devise efficient algorithms in solving differential equations? How can we estimate the financial models from the observed data? What are the numerical methods in solving for an optimal solution? Research in such financial engineering models has grown into a vibrant discipline. The financial models provided in this book prove the basic economic thoughts behind the models and link these ideas to mathematical formulations. But in applications there are many specific details that must be considered. These details may be institutional: the tax codes, the trading conventions, the data that are available, and more. The financial models in this book must be, and can be, extended to financial engineering models that incorporate such details.

We must consider the engineering aspect of modeling. As we extend a stylized model to incorporate the details of reality, implementation and computing become increasingly more challenging. There are many numerical issues that a system must confront, including errors in numerical approximations, stability of a large system, and methodologies in solving equations. While such financial engineering implementation is beyond the scope of this book, it is important to note the role that these models play in taking financial models to the operational level.

We must, however, know the limitations of financial modeling. They are only models. Their usefulness depends on the robustness in yielding sufficiently accurate predictions. In financial markets a lot of data are available for testing the models. And the models have to be judged by their empirical validity.

1.3 Basics of Modeling: Present Value and Measures of Risk

Let us review basic financial concepts so that our description of a valuation framework is self-contained. The first basic tool that any financial economist must use is the present-value method. Simply put, the value of $1.00 at a future date is less than $1.00 today. If the values were the same, then the promise of $1.00 in the future would be exchanged at $1.00 today. Investing the proceeds in an interest-bearing account will yield interest income in addition to the $1.00 principal. In that case everyone would rather invest $1.00 in an interest-bearing account than buy the promised future payment of $1.00.

Present Value

In general, there is no question about the discount of a future payment to a smaller present value. This is called the time value of money. But what is the appropriate discount rate? If the future payment is certain, with no risk of not receiving the promised payment in full, then the discount rate should be close to the market interest rate, referred to as the risk-free rate. If the promised payment at the payment date T, which is also the expected payment in this certainty case, is CF_T, the annually compounding risk-free rate is r_f, and the number of years to the payment date is T, then the present value, PV, is given by

$$PV = \frac{CF_T}{(1 + r_f)^T} \tag{1.1}$$

Where r_f captures the *time value of money*. Market-determined interest rates relate the value of a future payment to the present value because the market interest rate enables us to invest our cash, which equals the discounted value, and realize the same future payment.

Consider the following example. We have $100 in our pocket. The bank is offering 10 percent interest at the annual rate. If we leave the cash with the bank, in one year the bank account will grow to $110. Now consider the reverse. If we have a promissory note that pays $110 one year from now, then it should be worth $100 (= 110/(1.1)) today. Therefore the interest rate relates the future payment to the present value.

Generally, when we receive multiple payments over T years, the present value is calculated by

$$PV = \frac{CF_1}{(1 + r_f)} + \frac{CF_2}{(1 + r_f)^2} + \cdots + \frac{CF_T}{(1 + r_f)^T} \tag{1.2}$$

We say PV is the present value of the cash flows $CF_1, CF_2, \cdots, CF_T$.

Preference and Utility Function of Wealth

The present value of a payment is more complicated when the cash flow is uncertain. This complexity can be illustrated by von Neumann and Morgenstern's thought experiment.[5] Suppose we have subjects recruited from a university campus for an experiment. There is a way to measure happiness by registering the behavior of the pulse. After sitting the subject down, we give him $10 as a gift. Should we expect any measure of increase in happiness? We can suppose that the subject would not feel sad about it. He should be happier. This is called a marginal increase in utility. "Utility" is a conceptual construct that measures one's happiness in relation to some factor, and in this case we measure the happiness in relation to wealth. Thus far the experiment is not very exciting.

Next we pay the subject $20, then $30, then $100, and finally $1000. Each gift should lead to an increase in the utility. But if we plot the utility against the increase in wealth, we see that the utility increases, but at a gradually decreasing rate. This graph is called the utility function. That is, after receiving $1000, an additional $10 would lead to an increase in utility, but at a lower level than at the beginning of the experiment. This behavior is called decreasing marginal utility of wealth.

An example of a utility function of wealth is given below:

$$U(W) = \frac{W^\gamma}{\gamma} \tag{1.3}$$

where W is the wealth level and γ is a constant between 0 and 1 ($0 < \gamma < 1$). Then we can see that

$$\frac{dU}{dW} = W^{\gamma-1} > 0 \text{ and } \frac{d^2U}{dW^2} = (\gamma - 1)W^{\gamma-2} < 0 \qquad (1.4)$$

The first inequality denotes increasing marginal utility and the second denotes decreasing marginal utility. If we believe that an individual has a utility function which increases with wealth but decreases at the margin with wealth, then, von Neumann and Morgenstern conclude, that individual must be *risk-averse*. The reason is given below.

Suppose we present a subject with a gambling opportunity. The subject flips a coin, and if it lands "heads," the subject receives $100; if it lands "tails," the subject receives nothing. We assume a fair coin, with a 50–50 chance of landing heads or tails. But the subject has a choice. He can play the game, or not play the game and still collect $50. We leave a $50 bill on the table.

The expected utility of wealth in playing the game, using the above utility function (assuming $\gamma = 0.5$), is

$$E[U(W)] = 0.5 \times \frac{\sqrt{100}}{0.5} + 0.5 \times \frac{\sqrt{0}}{0.5} = 10$$

The utility of receiving $50 is

$$U(50) = \frac{\sqrt{50}}{0.5} \cong 14.14$$

Mathematics shows that the subject would take the $50 and not play the game because the utility of certain wealth ($50) is higher than that in playing the game. In general, the subject would prefer the certain payment to the uncertain payment, if the expected payment and the payment with certainty are the same. The reason is straightforward. We have already shown experimentally that the subject has an increase in utility with an increase in wealth, but the increase cannot compensate for the loss of the equal amount of wealth, because of the decreasing marginal utility. For this reason, playing and losing the game would lead to a lower utility than taking the expected payoff, $50. Such behavior causes us to say that the subject is risk-averse. Risk thus far is defined as uncertainty, and is measured by the standard deviation. (See figure 1.2.)

This argument shows that an investor requires a higher expected return for a riskier project, where the risk is measured by the standard deviation of the return. Thus, there are alternative investments to which the investor is indifferent because they have higher expected returns that compensate for the risks acceptable to the investor. This combination of risk and return plots the *indifference curve* for the investor.

Given a set of investment opportunities that have a range of expected returns and risks, the investor would choose the investment that maximizes his utility value. Mathematically, that investment would lie on the tangent point for the line of investment opportunities and an indifference curve of the individual. It is a straight line because the risk-free rate is not correlated with a risky asset, and therefore, if we invest a proportion ω in the risky asset and $(1 - \omega)$ in the risk-free asset, the expected return is the weighted sum of the expected returns of the risky asset and the risk-free asset. Similarly, the risk of the portfolio is simply the ω proportion of the standard deviation of the risky asset.

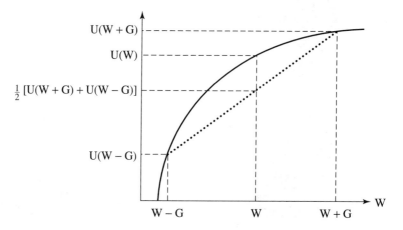

Figure 1.2 Concave utility function. The utility function increases at a gradually decreasing rate. Therefore the first derivative is positive and the second derivative is negative. The risk-averse investor prefers a certain payment to a risky payment. Even though the expected value of the risky payment is equal to the certain payment, $U(W)$ is greater than $1/2[U(W + G) + U(W - G)]$, which is the expected utility of the risky payment. The expected value of $W + G$ and $W - G$ with equal probability is W, which is equal to the certain wealth, W.

That means that any proportion ω leads to a point on the straight line. A graphical representation of this decision-making process is depicted in figure 1.3.

Discounted Cash Flow Method

Recent financial research literature tends to claim that all individuals are risk-averse, and therefore we do not need to analyze the specification of the utility function of an

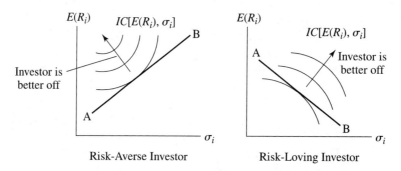

Figure 1.3 A risk-return relationship for risk-averse investors and risk-loving investors. The y-axis is the expected return and the x-axis is the standard deviation of an investment. The indifference curves (IC) represent the trade-offs between risk and returns for the risk-averse and risk-loving investors. The risk-averse investor requires higher returns to compensate for an increase in risk, while the risk-loving investor accepts a lower return for higher risk. Both investors prefer higher expected returns. Line AB indicates how expected returns and standard deviations are related. In the left figure, the line slope is positive, which means that there is an inverse relationship between expected returns and standard deviations. In other words, risk-averse investors should be compensated with higher expected rate of returns for bearing more risk. The opposite interpretation can be applied to the right figure.

individual, but assume that he has a certain preference. The standard preference we assume is that he maximizes the expected return for a given risk level or minimizes the risk for a given expected return. If an individual requires additional expected returns for the risk taken, this expected premium is called the *risk premium*.

Formally, we can summarize the above discussions as follows. If receipt of the payment is risky, then the appropriate discount rate for the expected (not the promised) payment $\widetilde{CF}_T$ is different from the risk-free interest rate. By definition, those who make such investments demand a higher discount rate (or lower present value) for risky payments. The present value of the expected payment adjusted for this risk aversion is PV', where

$$PV' = \frac{E\left[\widetilde{CF}_T\right]}{(1+\rho)^T} \tag{1.5}$$

and we expect that

$$\pi = \rho - r_f > 0 \tag{1.6}$$

Risk premium (π) is the additional investment return demanded by the investor to compensate for the risks. The premium can be measured by the spread between the discount rate for the risky assets ρ and for the risk-free asset r_f. Generally, we have the expected value of a risky cash flow, $E\left[\widetilde{CF}_1\right], E\left[\widetilde{CF}_2\right], \cdots, E\left[\widetilde{CF}_T\right]$, where each payment is made at the end of a period, say one year.

The value of the cash flow is

$$PV' = \frac{E\left[\widetilde{CF}_1\right]}{(1+\rho)} + \frac{E\left[\widetilde{CF}_2\right]}{(1+\rho)^2} + \cdots + \frac{E\left[\widetilde{CF}_T\right]}{(1+\rho)^T} \tag{1.7}$$

The above equation is called the *discounted cash flow method*. The present-value concept enables us to value assets with uncertain returns. Moreover, the present-value methodology begins with estimating the expected value of the risky asset at the end of the time horizon. Then we determine the discount rate, taking the time value and risk premium into account. The present value is the discounted expected value.

Note that the discounted cash flow method equation (1.7) can be used in a different way. Suppose the asset is traded in the marketplace and we can observe the market price of the risky asset, PV'. An investor can anticipate the expected payment of the risky assets, $\widetilde{CF}$. Now, we can use equation (1.7) and solve for ρ. That is, the investor can use equation (1.7) to determine the present value of a risky asset by stating the required rate of return of the asset ρ, or, alternatively, to determine the market discount rate of the risky asset by using the observed market price.

It is important to note that at market equilibrium, the expected return of a risky asset must be equal to its required return. For example, when the market has concerns with inherent risks of technology stocks, investors may require a higher return from stocks such as ABC.com. The ABC.com price would fall until its expected return at the new price level the same as the required return. If the expected rate of return of the risky asset is lower than the required rate of return, investors will think that the risky asset is not providing enough return for the risks. Therefore, the price will fall until the asset's expected return equals the required rate of return. Conversely, if the expected rate of return is higher than the required rate of return, the price will rise, since investors believe the asset has good value. In the capital market, traders say, "There are no bad bonds, only bad prices." The price should adjust to the level at which expected return equals the required return.

The discounted cash flow method is used widely for its simplicity. When we invest in a home, evaluate the trade-off between buying and leasing a car, or lend money, we can use the discounted cash flow method. The method entails determining the expected cash flow of the project and discounting it by a rate that is the sum of the risk premium and the market interest rate.

1.4   Summary

Financial models convey different meanings to different people. For the purpose of this book, financial models are derived from a set of economic assumptions that enables us to quantify our analysis. These models may be valuation models or risk models. They are derived from the principles of financial economics and have direct applications to financial markets.

The two most important tenets of financial analysis are the time value of money and the risk premium. In this chapter, we have discussed risk aversion. Investors are interested in maximizing their funds and minimizing their risk. They require a risk premium when investing in risky assets. We have discussed the most basic methodology in valuing risky securities, the discounted cash flow method.

The discounted cash flow is the simplest way of assigning a value to a risky stream of payments. As a result, it is used for valuation in many financial situations. It relates the expected payments to their value. The discount rate is the internal rates of returns of the expected future payments and their present value. In the following chapters we will see how it is applicable to valuing stocks, bonds, and firms. But will it need to be adjusted to develop a different model? In the next chapter, we shall see how the discounted cash flow method is applied to stock valuation.

Notes

1. M. Friedman, *Essays in Positive Economics* (Chicago: University of Chicago Press, 1966). Friedman received the 1976 Nobel Prize in economics.

2. The Standard Capital Asset Pricing model (CAPM), whose assumptions seem to be less realistic than those of the non-Standard CAPM, yields more accurate results than the non-Standard CAPM. We will talk about CAPM in chapter 2.

3. According to Friedman, positive economics has to do with "what is," while normative economics has to do with "what ought to be." Therefore, normative economics tends to be subjective, value laden, and emotional in its presentation.

4. One example of financial engineering models is numerical procedures such as the Monte Carlo simulation to solve the partial differential equation. We will describe such methods briefly in chapter 4.

5. J. Von Neumann and O. Morgenstern, *Theory of Games and Economic Behavior* (Princeton, NJ: Princeton University Press, 1980).

References

Copeland, T. E., T. Koller, and J. Murrin, 1990. *Valuation: Measuring and Managing the Value of Companies.* John Wiley and Sons, New York.

Damodaran, A. 2002. *Investment Valuation*, 2nd ed. John Wiley & Sons, New York.

Friedman, M. 1966. *Essays in Positive Economics.* University of Chicago Press, Chicago.

Von Neumann, J., and O. Morgenstern. 1980. *Theory of Games and Economic Behavior.* Princeton University Press, Princeton, NJ.

2

Equity Market:
The Capital Asset Pricing Model

The Capital Asset Pricing model, an important tool in financial modeling, is used to calculate the required rate of return of risky assets. Specifically, it asserts that the risk premium of a risky asset is determined by its systematic risks and it provides a method to value equity securities. More generally, it provides a methodology to analyze the value of risky securities and emphasizes the importance of portfolio diversification to determine the risk premium.

At the heart of financial theory is the study of the time value of money in relation to the risk premium. If we lived in a world without risk, much of finance would be reduced to the bookkeeping of cash flows, paying taxes, distributing profits, covering expenses, and reporting returns. In other words, the study of finance would be better described as accounting. However, we do live in a world where risk changes the time value of money. Individuals grapple with the risks of capital investments and ventures with one fundamental preference in mind: the value of $1.00 should be more today than it will be tomorrow; a $1.00 certain payment should worth more than a $1.00 uncertain payment. But exactly how much more is the question that fuels financial research.

The valuation of a risky asset is a central theme in finance. The valuations of stocks, bonds, currencies, insurance policies, capital investments, portfolios, and pension funds are just some of the examples that involve the question. As a result, many corporate, investment, and financial decisions are related to this question.

If the world lacked financial theories, the following prescriptive solution could be used to value a risky payment of $1.00. First, estimate the expected payment. Then assign a risk premium—for instance, 4 percent—commensurate with the riskiness of the investment. Add this premium to the cost of borrowing and use this rate to discount the expected payment. This intuitive and direct approach is similar to that used in operational research and accounting, where the risk premium is exogenously specified, and is not, in general, derived from financial economic principles.

However, there may be a flaw within the prescriptive solution because, for example, not all projects with uncertain cash flows require a risk premium in the marketplace. Who should decide on this risk premium for the market price? How should this risk premium be decided in the capital market? Financial theories provide the solutions to these questions. This chapter suggests a positive theory, predicting what this risk premium should be in equilibrium.

Specifically, this chapter will begin with a description of the major financial markets. Then our discussion will cover the perfect capital market assumptions and the efficient capital market theory. We will introduce the Markowitz theory of portfolio diversification to underscore Sharpe's Capital Asset Pricing model, which provides a methodology for valuing any risky financial asset. Ultimately, we will see how the Capital Asset Pricing model will have broad financial applications, including the specification of the stock valuation model.

2.1   Real and Financial Sectors

Assets are foundations of an economy. Buildings, roads, bridges, and factories are examples of assets. They are often called *tangible assets* because they have a physical presence and have been made for specific functions or have the ability to produce physical goods. Gold, oil, natural gas, and wheat are examples of other types of tangible assets, often referred to as *commodities* because they are more homogeneous in nature and can be bought and sold more easily.

Many manufacturing economies are evolving into service economies using the latter's know-how as the driving force. Thus, *intangible assets* like branding and intellectual properties are fast becoming equal partners to tangible assets. For example, the value of a software company is not determined by the value of the buildings or the campus. The values are determined by its know-how and knowledge of technologies. On-line retailing companies' values are based in large part on their accumulated knowledge of individuals' buying behaviors.

Both tangible or intangible assets are called *real assets* because they produce goods and services for an economy. The term is somewhat unfortunate because it implies that when an asset is not real, it is imaginary or secondary in the economy. "Imaginary" assets are called *financial assets* (or securities), and it could not be further from the truth that they are less important and more fictitious than real assets.

Securities are financial claims, such as stocks and bonds, as long as they are traded. Stocks represent ownerships of corporations, and they have claims to corporations' earnings. Bonds are contractual claims to specific payments over time. A bondholder typically requires principal and interest payments from the borrower. Stocks, bonds, and other securities are contracts between the parties involved, and these contracts can be customized to the requirements of the transaction. Since they are agreements among parties, they are less "real" but not less important to an economy.

Financial assets can be claims on tangible assets that impose a corporate structure— a legal corporate entity assigning roles and responsibilities of individuals—over the tangible assets. These financial assets can be traded in parallel with their underlying real assets. Gold mine shares are traded along with the gold. Shares of development companies are traded as buildings that are bought and sold. Financial assets can also be claims on intangible assets like branding, intellectual properties, ideas, and knowledge of a corporation. Then the stock value of the corporation is the value of the intangible assets.

Financial assets such as stocks (or equity) of corporations are means of assigning values to real assets, which are the bricks and mortar of knowledge and intellectual properties. Financial services, legal and health services, and large segments of our economy have values that are not based on tangible assets. But, like tangible assets, they can be monetized by securities such as stocks and bonds. Financial assets provide a way to value all real assets.

There is another important attribute of securities. Since they are in essence contracts that can be designed for their intended use, they can be designed to facilitate transactions. In that sense, financial assets become perfect commodities. The contracts can be standardized and monitored, scaled for any size of transaction. Transaction costs can be minimized and the markets for financial assets can be designed to be as frictionless as possible, since a transaction involving financial assets is relatively straightforward.

In order to facilitate our discussion of financial sectors, we first need to discuss the basic securities and their derivatives as distinct financial sectors. For each sector, we will discuss its instruments and their markets. Later in the book, we will relate the real assets to the financial assets. We will build the models that demonstrate how optimal investment decisions on real assets are affected by financial values, as well as how the values of the financial claims are determined by the investment decisions. Real and financial assets, while distinct from each other, are not competitive but complementary. We will first consider stocks and stock markets.

2.2   Stocks and Stock Markets

There are two major types of stock markets: the spot market and the futures/forward markets. We will describe the institutional structure of these markets, and how the securities are traded in them, in the following sections.

Spot Market

Spot markets are markets where monetary transactions are made by investors who pay for financial or real assets. A corporation is an entity with a charter that specifies the rights and obligations of its shareholders. Shareholders are the owners of the corporation, and therefore they own all of its real assets. Common stocks represent the equity (or an ownership position) of the corporation. Typically, each share represents one vote of a shareholder to amend the charter or on other corporate decisions required by the charter. Each share also represents a pro rata portion of the value of the corporation.

The charter of a corporation may specify how the corporation is organized. As owners of the corporation, shareholders have the ultimate control over its management. Their interests are represented by the board of directors, which in turn controls the senior management of the corporation. For our purpose, senior management has two branches: financial and nonfinancial. Financial management is responsible for the corporation's finances, such as dividend payout, capital budgeting, funding of projects, share issuance, and financial reporting. Nonfinancial management is concerned with the real asset management, such as production, operations, and marketing. A corporation may own a portfolio of corporations. The economics (but not the legality) of the relationship between the parent company and its subsidiaries is similar to that of the headquarters with its lines of businesses (or branches) in terms of control and profit flows.

Shareholders derive their returns from ownership in two ways: dividends and *capital gains (or losses)*. Dividends may take the form of cash payments (cash dividends) or additional shares (stock dividends). In the latter case, shareholders are given a number of new shares as dividends. The number of shares owned by a shareholder will increase, but the portion of the equity holding in the corporation may remain the same. Often, dividends are paid quarterly if any dividend is declared. Dividend payments are not obligations to the shareholders; corporations do not have to pay dividends. The actual amount paid per share is often announced ahead of the dividend payment date. The date that dividends are announced is the *announcement date*, and the date after dividends are paid is the *ex-dividend date*. The total dividends paid during the fiscal year, divided by the stock price at the closing of the market, is called the *dividend yield*. Often presented as a percent, dividend yield measures the annual expected return to the shareholders in term of dividends.

Typically, shareholders expect to derive the main portion of their returns from holding the shares through the capital gain or price appreciation. The ownership of most stocks can be transferred. The transfer is a transaction between a buyer and a seller at an agreed-upon price. The difference between the selling price and the original price is called capital gain (or loss). Since the price at which it will be sold is unknown to the buyer when the stock is originally bought, stock returns are risky. Since price appreciation can best be realized by the transfer of ownership, change in ownership of stocks is an important part of the ownership of a corporation.

A transaction is seldom conducted between just two individuals, the buyer and the seller. Transactions are conducted in a network of activities called the *securities markets*. Today, securities markets are somewhat abstract. They are quite unlike flea markets, where physical goods are sold and prices are established. They are also unlike auctions, where auctioneers let bidders determine the transaction price. The economic principles of securities markets may be similar to these real sector markets, but the process is quite different.

There are two major types of markets: the *primary* and the *secondary*. The primary market handles the initial sales of securities. When a corporation is first established and shares are sold to the initial investors, those transactions are conducted in the primary market. They often involve investment bankers acting as intermediaries, setting the subscription prices of the stock and placing the shares sold at the set price with investors. When the shares are traded after the initial placement, the transactions are conducted in the secondary market. In the secondary market, there is another network of activities. Perhaps stock exchanges bear the closest resemblance to a flea market.

A stock exchange is organized in a physical location where trades are transacted. The prices of the trades are reported as the transaction prices. The New York Stock Exchange conducts the transactions using a *specialist* system. Each stock is assigned to a specialist individual or firm. The specialist is responsible for maintaining orderly price movements, to ensure that the stock does not skyrocket or plummet, as well as the liquidity of the stock, if there is a transaction. At any time, unless there is a trading halt, the specialist provides the bid price and the ask price. The specialist is willing to buy at the bid price and to sell at the ask price. Needless to say, the ask price should always be higher than the bid price. Otherwise, the specialist would like to buy and sell to himself. The specialist should not indicate to the market that he would like to buy at a price higher than the price at which he is willing to sell. Everyone wants to buy low and sell high.

When an investor uses a *market order* to buy, the trade is executed at the specialist's ask price. Conversely, when an investor sells, the transaction price is the specialist's bid price. As a result, an investor tends to buy at a higher ask price and sell at a lower bid price. In a *round-trip trade*, which is instantaneous execution of buy and sell trades, the cost of transacting to the investor is the difference between the bid and ask prices, referred to as the *bid-ask spread*.

But the specialist is only a node in this network of trading activities that define the secondary market. *Upstairs dealers* are dealers who place their orders to the stock exchange to provide liquidity to any imbalance of supply and demand of shares; they stand ready to buy and sell shares, making a profit in the process. There are *brokers* who seek out buyers and sellers, providing the services for a fee. There are also portfolio managers, hedge funds, and other investors, including individual investors.

A market that has no central location and no specialists to maintain the trading of each stock is an *over-the-counter (OTC) market*. Traders or *market makers* offer to trade from their offices, which may be anywhere. By and large, the competitive forces of the quotes ensure that the transaction prices and the bid-ask quotes are fair and reasonable. Dealers submit their bid-ask quotes to compete for the order flows, and in the process the bid-ask spread is tightened to its competitive equilibrium level. The National Association of Securities Dealers Automated Quotation (NASDAQ) System is an OTC market.

More recently, we have seen dramatic growth in electronic communications networks (ECN). Under U.S. securities law, ECNs disseminate quotes.[1] These electronic systems enable subscribers to post their limit orders so that they can be displayed to other market participants. Instinet, Island, and Archipelago are ECNs. Since they also offer executions, these ECNs should be more appropriately classified as alternative trading systems.[2] In essence, they offer an open limit order book for the market.

For the most part, all markets rely on both competitive forces and regulations to ensure that prices are fair and equitable. The specialist of an exchange is often acting as a broker for the orders from upstairs or floor dealers. The specialist must compete with other dealers for the order flows. The market makers of an OTC market quotes must follow guidelines to ensure the orderly functioning of the market even in the absence of a specialist. All organized markets (exchanges or OTC) have rules and regulations for all participants to ensure orderliness and competitiveness.

Through the efficient trading of stocks, we derive the continual establishment of stock prices. These are called *real-time prices*. Real-time prices do not imply that we have a transaction at any moment in establishing the price. But we do have bid—ask quotes for most stocks at any time, by and large determined by market competition. One convention is to use the midquote (the average of the bid-ask quotes) as the price of the stock at any time. At the close of the market, the *closing price*, the last transaction price of the trading session, is established. The price is the continual market valuation of the corporation.

Economic theory suggests that these prices are determined by the supply and demand of the securities. What are the supply and demand curves for a stock? What determines these buying and selling orders and how they are transacted, leading to the prices that are reported? Moreover, since these prices suggest that we can buy and sell any securities at any time, can we profit from the information? What does it tell us about the markets? What does it take to understand these issues? Einstein seems to have had an answer.

One day, Einstein was enjoying his walk near Princeton. He came across another hiker and he asked, "What is your IQ?" "400" was the response. They had a very enlightening discussion on mathematics. Then he came across another hiker. "What's your IQ?" Einstein asked. "300" was the response. They had a wonderful discussion on physics. When Einstein ran into a third hiker and asked the same question, the response was "100." Then Einstein mumbled, "Oh, how is the stock market?" Did Einstein really think that there was not much to know about the market? Or did he already know something that we have taken 50 years to find out about market efficiency? Einstein developed a random walk model to describe the total randomness of the movements of tiny particles in water. This model will be used extensively in later chapters of this book for securities price movements.

Futures and Forward Markets

A *forward contract* is an agreement between a buyer and a seller. They agree on a future expiration date and the contract price on the underlying asset. There is no exchange of money or goods at the initial agreement. At the expiration date, the buyer will take delivery of the underlying asset at the contract price.

Futures contracts are basically the same as forward contracts, except that they are traded on exchanges with daily marking to market. The futures contract may have a new contract price at the end of the trading session. If the contract price has increased, the seller pays the buyer the difference, and if the contract price falls, the buyer pays the seller the price change. The futures exchange establishes the contract prices and intermediates the payments.

For the equity market, the exchange-traded futures contracts are all based on indices, such as the S&P 500 Index, the Nikkei 225 stock average, and the FT-SE 100 Index. Futures of an index are contracts that have an expiration date, and on the expiration date, the futures price is the index price; no physical delivery is required. Roughly speaking, the futures price represents the market expectation of the index value at the expiration of the contract.

Since the only difference between futures and forwards is the *marking to market* feature that leads to daily reinvestment or borrowing of cash, interest rate risk would lead to the different pricing of futures and forwards. If we ignore the interest rate risk, futures and forwards should have the same value. Since most futures contracts are relatively short-term, expiring in less than one year, this assumption is often used. Therefore, the futures are often priced as forward contracts. If the spot stock price is S and the forward or futures price is F, then the present value of F at the risk-free rate net of the dividend yield must equal S. Or the forward price is the future stock price growing at the risk-free rate net of the dividend yield. This is an arbitrage condition when the dividend yield is equal to 0 for simplicity.

$$F = S(1 + r_f)^T \qquad (2.1)$$

The arbitrage mechanism is given as follows. Suppose the forward price is higher than $S(1 + r_f)^T$. The arbitrageur would sell the forward contract, borrow cash (which is equal to S at the risk-free rate r_f), and buy the stock. On the delivery date, the arbitrageur would deliver the stock and collect the forward price. After repaying the loan, the remainder is the profit. Since this profit is risk-free, a guaranteed payment, the profit is called an arbitrage profit.

Similarly, when the forward price is below $S(1 + r_f)^T$, the arbitrageur would buy the forward contract. Simultaneously, he would short the stock and invest the proceeds at the risk-free rate. On the delivery date, the arbitrageur would use the invested proceeds to buy the stock at the forward price. The stock is then used to cover the short position. The difference between the investment at the risk-free rate and the forward price is the arbitrage profit. The arbitrage mechanism would continue until the forward price and the stock price would align according to equation (2.1).

2.3   Perfect Capital Market

In general, stocks, Treasury securities, and swap markets have minimal frictions in trading relative to other securities. Market participants have access to the market information, and they can submit their supply and demand curves (or their propensity to trade) to the market. Trading is a price discovery process. It allows the market to establish the price that clears the market, so that supply equals demand. By way of contrast, consider a transaction involving an office building. This transaction has more friction and involves information-gathering; and the price determined may fail to reflect the value of the building that properly clears the demand and supply of such a building for all potential traders.

Financial sector markets are distinct from real sector markets because trading is quite frictionless. The set of assumptions is a description of the ideal capital markets proposed by Miller and Modigliani.[3] Some of their work will be discussed in part III of the book. This model is called the *Perfect Capital Market* model. The model envisions that the capital market is frictionless in the following sense: A market is defined as a place where many sellers and many buyers exchange their securities, and a perfect capital market is a place where many buyers and many sellers exchange their securities in a frictionless environment with the following characteristics.

All financial claims are perfectly divisible.

We can buy or sell any fraction of a security. There is no minimum quantity to buy or sell that restricts sellers' or buyers' desire to trade. From a modeling point of view, this is a technicality. If we do not make this assumption, we will have to keep track of the transaction sizes. This simplifying assumption may affect the model result slightly, but would not change the basic insight on the factors affecting the equilibrium price.

There are no transaction costs.

Transaction costs include broker fees, asset management fees, phone calls to make a transaction, and bid-ask spreads. In many ways, they affect the model results and the implications on the markets. For example, without transaction costs, there is a chance that the economy will have no financial intermediaries, such as banks and insurance companies. After all, if there were no transaction costs, why would an economy have financial intermediaries? This assumption is made to understand the impact of transaction costs on the analysis. We make this assumption because the *portfolio theory*, which is applied to constructing an optimal investment portfolio and understanding the implications of the optimal portfolio on the pricing of securities, is not really concerned with the role of banks and other institutions and does not affect how we construct a portfolio. This assumption will be relaxed later in the book.

There are no taxes.

In financial research, an assumption like "there are no taxes" is described as "heroic." Clearly we all have to pay taxes, and taxes affect the way we construct a portfolio. This "simplifying" assumption enables us first to understand the solution without taxes and later to improve the model to analyze how each aspect of taxes affects the results.

The market is competitive.

One single buyer or seller cannot influence the market price, because there are so many sellers and buyers. This assumption is indispensable. Imagine that the financial world has a central bank that decides on the fairness of stocks' values. Then the portfolio theory will have to be quite different. It will focus more on predicting the central bank's decisions and less on the functioning of the markets and the price discovery process when assets are bought and sold. Our market is sufficiently competitive that this assumption is clearly both realistic and important.

There is no limit on short selling.

Short selling refers to selling a security without owning it. Usually an investor short-sells a security when he believes that its price will fall over a certain time horizon. The mechanism of short selling can be described as follows. The investor borrows the security, promising to return it to the owner at some future date. The investor then sells the security in the open market. Over a period of time, if the security price has fallen, the investor can buy back the security and return it to the original owner. The difference between the first sale price and the purchase price when the security is bought back is the profit to the short seller. In practice, the broker typically implements the transactions. An investor just has to place the order to the broker.

There are many restrictions on short selling. Investors need to have margins (collaterals like cash) to maintain a short position. And there are fees for short selling. However, both of these constraints may not be of consequence to large asset management funds or large corporations. There may be some short-selling constraints in our capital market, and such constraints may affect the market equilibriums. Research continues to investigate how this assumption affects the model.

Information is symmetric.

We assume information symmetry—that is, all market participants have the same information available to value assets. Otherwise, we may face complex issues such as dead-weight loss caused by information asymmetry. In chapter 14 we will discuss the impact of modulating this assumption. With incomplete information, the signaling theory will suggest how the results will be affected.

Investors are rational with increasing utility of wealth but decreasing marginal utility of wealth (risk-averse).

All market participants seek risk-adjusted profits. Investors will always invest in a project with higher returns, given two projects having the same risks. This assumption is clearly both reasonable and important. Financial researchers cannot imagine a world where investors do not like higher profits, given the same risks. This investors' preference is often described as increasing utility of wealth. In other words, the richer the investor, the happier the investor is. But the increase in happiness decreases with higher wealth level. The behavior is shown to be equivalent to risk aversion, as we discussed in chapter 1.

This is not true with gamblers, of course. Gamblers spend money to take risks, even though spending the money clearly leads to a negative expected return. But gamblers are enjoying the game, and are not really investing. The similar point has to be made about philanthropists. Giving more money to others makes philanthropists happier. They take happiness in things other than money. Financial research is about the happiness of possessing money.

For this reason, we assume all market participants are risk-averse but may have different levels of risk aversion.

2.4   Efficient Capital Market Hypothesis

We now assume a certain behavior of the investors in a frictionless market (or perfect capital market). Suppose the investors have all the available information on the corporation, and understand its real processes and their implications to an investor's return. Furthermore, they continually adjust their investment portfolios to reflect real-time prices and changing preferences. Then the trading price will fully reflect the present value of the future cash flows generated from the firm to the investors. When we arrive at this state of things, we say the capital market is efficient.

But an efficient market definition requires the specification of "available information." There are several forms of efficiency, depending on the information set. *Weak-form efficiency* is defined by the information set that is only the history of prices and returns. A market is weak-form-efficient if it is impossible to realize abnormal profits by using only past prices. For example, if investors can follow price trends to realize abnormal excess returns, then the market is not weak-form-efficient. *Semi-strong-form efficiency* includes all publicly available information. For example, if investors can realize abnormal excess returns using the published financial statements, then the market is not semi-strong-form-efficient. *Strong-form efficiency* includes all information known to any market participant (both public and private information). It is difficult to prove or reject because the set of private information is difficult to specify.

Empirical evidence tends to support the view that the U.S. financial markets are at least weak-form-efficient. That is, using only technical analysis by price charts to predict momentum, supports, and breakout, it is very difficult to realize abnormal returns. Research also supports semi-strong-form efficiency by showing that corporate announcements, accounting information, and other public information are instantly incorporated in stock prices. Testing strong-form efficiency is difficult because the definition of "private information" is ambiguous. After all, how can information not available to the public be incorporated in the market? If the information unavailable to the public is incorporated in the market, that would be considered insider trading. While we can have empirical evidence to support an efficient capital market hypothesis, there is no way to prove market efficiency, for there are innumerable types of public information and ways to use them. We can only have evidence to reject the view that the market is not efficient.

The implications of an *efficient capital market* are significant. An efficient capital market ensures us that corporate actions such as real investments, dividend payment, and other decisions are fully reflected in the stock price. In an efficient capital market, the capital market is integrated with the real sector values. (See figure 2.1.)

We have two measures of market performance: efficiency and completeness. Efficient markets and *complete markets* deal with different aspects of the market. The efficient market emphasizes how much information has been incorporated into prices. The complete market emphasizes the availability of securities for market participants to trade in order

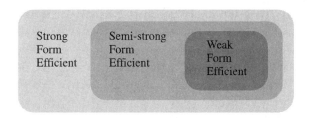

Figure 2.1 The relationship among three forms of efficient markets. The weak-form-efficient market reflects past information, such as prices. The semi-strong-efficient market reflect publicly available information, such as dividend announcements. The strong-form-efficient market reflects all information, including private information. Therefore, the strong-form-efficient market is also a semi-strong-form-efficient market, and the semi-strong-form-efficient market is also a weak-form-efficient market. However, the reverse does not hold.

to reveal their preferences to the marketplace. They can do so by hedging their portfolios or taking risky positions. A complete market enables all market participants to transact, and an efficient market ensures that the prices clear the market supply and demand. At market equilibrium, no trading occurs and every investor is content with his portfolio holdings. At such a time, the expected return of a security must equal its required return.

2.5   Diversification

H. M. Markowitz was the first to show that not all risky assets require a risk premium even if we are all risk-averse.[4] He applied this diversification theory to portfolio management. *Diversification* is defined as the lowering of risks by holding multiple risky assets. That is, a portfolio of risky assets may have less risk than an individual risky asset.

Consider a simple example. Suppose that an individual has $100. He takes a gamble flipping a coin. He can double his bet if it lands on heads, or lose it all if it lands on tails. The two outcomes, head and tail, have an equal probability. If he bets all $100 on one flip of the coin, the expected outcome would be $100, but the standard deviation is $100. If he spreads the risks to two flips, betting $50 each time, the outcomes and the probabilities are given below:

	Head/Head	*Head/Tail*	*Tail/Tail*
Probability	0.25	0.5	0.25
Outcome	$200	$100	0

The expected outcome is $100 $= 0.25 \times \$200 + 0.5 \times \$100 + 0.25 \times \$0$. The standard deviation is

$$\$70.71 = \sqrt{0.25 \times (\$200 - \$100)^2 + 0.5 \times (\$100 - \$100)^2 + 0.25 \times (\$0 - \$100)^2}.$$

The expected outcome is $100, but the standard deviation is reduced to $70.71 from $100 by spreading the risks over two flips. The individual can spread the risks further by 100 flips of the coin with a $1.00 bet on each. In this case, the standard deviation, which is the square root of the number of flips times the standard deviation of the payoff of each flip, becomes almost negligible: $10 $(= \sqrt{100} \times 1)$. The reason for this is that 100 flips of the coin are independent of each other, and each flip of the coin has the same standard deviation. If we apply this logic to the two flips example, we have 70.71(= \sqrt{2} \times \$50)$, which is the same as above. Intuitively, with many bets made at the same time, the number of heads is approximately the same as the number of tails, and therefore the gains and the losses tend to balance each other, resulting in minimal risks. Not all diversification can lead to eliminating all risks. The crucial assumption made in this example is that there is no correlation between the outcome of one flip of a coin and another.

The assertion that a portfolio of risky assets may have less risk than any individual risky asset is also used in practice. Imagine that a casino has numerous slot machines. The risk of winning at a slot machine is exciting to the gambler, a source of enjoyment. But the returns to the casino owner in playing against these gamblers are basically risk-free. The risks to each gambler are diversified in aggregate for the casino owner. From the casino owner's perspective, slot machines have no risk and no risk premium. The casino does not require a risk premium to discount the revenues from each slot machine, even though the gambling profit for each machine is uncertain.

We now extend this idea to portfolio management. Let us consider a security—a stock. The stock price can take on a range of values with assigned probabilities at the end of a time horizon, say one year. This is called the probability distribution. We will use this probability distribution to specify the risks and returns of a stock, and then to derive a strategy to minimize the portfolio risk while maximizing the portfolio returns. Two common distributions that financial research often uses are normal distribution and lognormal distributions. Since they represent the stock returns, we no longer assume that these distributions are uncorrelated. Stock returns in general are positively correlated with each other.[5]

Normal distribution is symmetrical and lognormal distribution is asymmetrical. These distributions are defined by the mean and standard deviations. The mean shifts the distributions to higher or lower values. The standard deviations change the dispersion of the distributions. (See figure 2.2.)

Stock returns are defined as the proportional change in price over a time horizon (say one year), minus 1.

$$\text{Stock returns} = \frac{S(T)}{S(0)} - 1$$

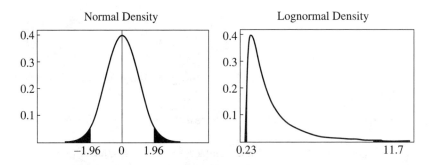

Figure 2.2 Normal and lognormal distributions with a mean and a standard deviation. The means and standard deviations of the two distributions are (0,1) and (0.5,1) respectively. The probability that a normally distributed variable falls beyond 1.96 or less than −1.96 is 2.5% each. The probability that a log normally distributed variable has a value more than 11.7 or less than 0.23 is 5% each. Since the normal distribution is symmetric, the left red area is the same shape as the right red area. This is not the case for the lognormal distribution.

where $S(T)$ is the stock price at the end of the period and $S(0)$ is the stock price at the initial date. We assume that there are no dividends or other returns during this holding period. Stock prices are often modeled as lognormal because the lognormal distribution does not allow negative stock prices, whereas the normal distribution does allow the possibility. For cases where the outcomes are fairly symmetrical, normal distributions are used because they have many desirable properties. We will be clear about which distribution we use in our description of risks.

Risks or uncertainties are central to financial research. For this reason, these probability distributions are used extensively in this book. Whenever a variable (say the returns of a stock) is assigned as a distribution, it represents a range of outcomes with their assigned probabilities, and the variable is not just one number but many possible numbers. The distribution can be reduced to one number when we take the expectation of the distribution or the standard deviation of the distribution.

Markowitz began his analysis with the perfect capital market assumptions. The investor has a specific investment horizon, say one year. At the end of the period, the investor calculates the worth of the portfolio and decides his level of happiness with the gain/loss via the utility. Assume that there are many securities in a perfect capital market.

Under these assumptions, the investor would construct a mean variance analysis. He would try to construct a portfolio and calculate its expected returns and standard deviation. The optimal portfolio would be the one that gives the highest expected returns for a risk level that is acceptable to the given risk tolerance.

The Markowitz model provides a prescriptive solution to the investment problem. In this case, we are told how to construct the optimal portfolio for ourselves. Markowitz's approach is called a normative theory or a prescriptive theory. His message is clear. An individual stock has a lot of risk. A better approach to investment is to take a portfolio approach. The importance of the portfolio approach is diversification. Therefore not all the risk of an individual stock is relevant to investment. Some of the individual stock risk can be diversified away, but some cannot. As we noted earlier, in the presence of correlations, stock risks can no longer be entirely eliminated by diversification.

Suppose we hold a portfolio of stocks whose returns are independent of each other; when one stock rises, no one can infer how the other stocks will behave. If we spread our investments across these stocks by investing 1/n in each of the n stocks, and if there are many stocks, then the risks cancel out each other. The resulting portfolio has no risks. However, stock returns are not all independent of each other, and therefore a portfolio can never be designed such that the risks are all diversified away. The risk of stock returns can be minimized by carefully selecting stocks. Part of stock risks can be diversified, and therefore the appropriate discount rate or the required rate of return of the stock should be based on the risk that cannot be diversified. The risk that cannot be diversified away is called *systematic risk* or *market risk*. The risk that can be diversified away is called the *residual (or unsystematic) risk*. (See figure 2.3.)

What are the implications of diversification? Diversification is a way of reducing risk by forming a portfolio of individual stocks. Therefore, we can see that an individual stock has two types of risk, depending on whether the stock belongs to a portfolio or stands alone. When the stock stands alone, we can measure its risk by the standard deviation. However, when the stock is a part of a portfolio, we can measure the risk of the stock by how much the stock contributes to the portfolio risk. The portfolio risk is less than the summation over the risk of the individual stocks in the portfolio. The reason for this is the diversification effect. To quantify how much the stock contributes to the portfolio

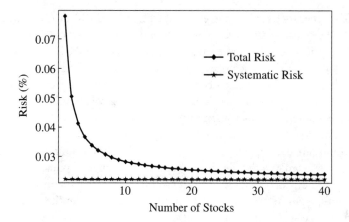

Figure 2.3 Effects of portfolio size on average portfolio risk for daily stock returns. We randomly sample 40 stocks from November 11, 2002, to February 5, 2003. The firms included in the sample are CVS Corp., Adobe System, Delphi Corp., Moody's Corp., Ford Motor Co., and Apollo Group. The data source is http://finance.yahoo.com. The X-axis and Y-axis represent the number of stocks and the daily volatility of the portfolio respectively. The figure shows that the protfolio risk decreases with the number of stocks in the portfolio. But the portfolio risk cannot be eliminated completely. The minimum level of the portfolio risk is call the market risk. This figure shows that as we put 30 stocks or more in the portfolio, the portfolio risk (0.024878%) is very close to the market risk (0.0223695%). This means that we can diversify away most of individual stock risk by forming a portfolio of 30 stocks.

risk, we use a covariance between the stock's returns and the portfolio returns rather than a standard deviation.

To explain why the covariance is an appropriate measure when the stock is part of a portfolio, we use a simple example of two stocks, A and B. Stock A and stock B have σ_A and σ_B for their stand-alone risk. When we form a portfolio with them, we have the portfolio risk $\sqrt{\omega_A^2\sigma_A^2 + 2\omega_A\omega_B\sigma_{A,B} + \omega_B^2\sigma_B^2}$, where $\sigma_{A,B}$ is a covariance between stock A and stock B and $\omega_A(\omega_B)$ is a weight of stock A(stock B). We manipulate the portfolio risk as follows to see that the covariance is a proper measure.

$$\begin{aligned}
\sigma_P^2 &= \omega_A^2\sigma_A^2 + 2\omega_A\omega_B\sigma_{A,B} + \omega_B^2\sigma_B^2 \\
&= \omega_A^2\sigma_A^2 + \omega_A\omega_B\sigma_{A,B} + \omega_A\omega_B\sigma_{A,B} + \omega_B^2\sigma_B^2 \\
&= \omega_A(\omega_A\sigma_A^2 + \omega_B\sigma_{A,B}) + \omega_B(\omega_A\sigma_{A,B} + \omega_B\sigma_B^2) \\
&= \omega_A \times \sigma_{A,P} + \omega_B \times \sigma_{B,P}
\end{aligned}$$

When we manipulate the above equation, we substitute $\sigma_{A,P}(\sigma_{B,P})$ for $\omega_A\sigma_A^2 + \omega_A\sigma_{A,B}$ $(\omega_A\sigma_{A,B} + \omega_B\sigma_B^2)$.[6] We see that the covariance between stock A (stock B) and the portfolio constitutes the portfolio risk. Therefore, stock A's risk when it is part of the portfolio can be measured by the covariance, which is a marginal increase of the portfolio risk due to stock A. When we marginally increase stock A's weight, we see that the portfolio risk increases by $\sigma_{A,P}$.

The most important implication of diversification is that the risk of a stock to the investor should not be the standard deviation of the stock returns. The risk premium assigned to the stock is therefore not related to the standard deviation, but it should be related to the marginal increase of the risk to the portfolio when we add the stock. In other words, the risk premium assigned to a stock is related to the marginal increase in the risk the stock contributes to the portfolio.

2.6   Capital Asset Pricing Model (CAPM)

The Markowitz theory generally applies to any portfolio of risky assets: slot machines, real estate, commodities, anything risky. The normative approach of Markowitz's method almost provides a prescription for constructing an optimal portfolio of risky assets. To construct an optimal portfolio of stocks, we need to know the variances and covariances, and their expected returns, of the stocks. Using an optimization algorithm, we can find the optimal portfolio that provides the highest expected returns for a given level of risk. A collection of the optimal portfolios constitutes the efficient frontier. Once we have an *efficient frontier*, the next question would be which point on the efficient frontier will be selected as an optimal portfolio of risky assets and what will be an equilibrium price of a risky asset if investors behave optimally to maximize their expectation, given their risk preference. In other words, what would be the relationship between the risk and the expected return of risky assets in the mean-variance world? The *Capital Asset Pricing model* (CAPM) is proposed to answer the above question.

Sharpe continues this line of argument to provide a positive theory, CAPM.[7] He takes the next steps from where Markowitz left off, adding two assumptions to the perfect capital market assumptions. First, he assumes that all investors have the same one-period horizon, and borrow and lend at the same risk-free rate. Second, all market participants have the same information at the same time. This way, no one has private information or better information. They have homogeneous expectations in that they all agree with the forecasts of risks and expected returns of the risky assets.

Given these assumptions, Sharpe argues that in Markowitz's world, everyone should use all the stocks traded in the market and go through the optimization process as Markowitz would envision. All the investors would maximize the returns for their optimal level of risk. In equilibrium, when all the trades are completed, there will be a special set of portfolios deserving more attention—the *efficient portfolios* of risky assets, those with the highest returns for each level of risk.

If we put all the expected returns and the standard deviations of all the portfolios on a diagram plotting the risk and return trade-off, we will see that the locus of the efficient frontier is a curve (see figure 2.4). Now, use a ruler and draw a straight line between the risk-free rate and the tangent point on the efficient frontier of risky assets. This line, called the *capital market line*, is optimal for everyone, even better than the efficient frontier of risky assets. This means that along the capital market line, the portfolio achieves a higher return for the same risks. A point on this capital market line can be reached by holding a combination of the tangent portfolio and the risk-free asset. The higher the proportion invested in the tangent portfolio, the closer the point is to the tangent portfolio. The lower the proportion invested in the tangent portfolio, the closer the point is to the risk-free asset. That means everyone should hold the tangent portfolio on the efficient frontier of risky assets and the risk-free rate.

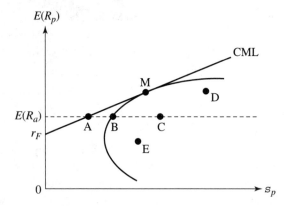

Figure 2.4 Capital Market Line. The efficient frontier is the portfolio of stocks that offers the highest expected returns for a given risk level. The capital market line (CML) is the line tangent to the efficient frontier from the risk-free asset. The capital market line, which should represent the optimal portfolio for all risk-averse investors, is a combination of the market portfolio and the risk-free asset. Portfolio A is efficient, whereas portfolio B is not efficient even though it is on the minimum variance set of risky assets. Portfolio C also is not efficient, because it has more risk than portfolio A even though they yield the same expected return. Portfolios D and E are not efficient, because they are inside the efficient frontier.

To illustrate, consider the following numerical example. Suppose we have five stocks, and calculate their historical returns and standard deviations from their historical returns. The results are presented below.

Stock	A	B	C	D	E
Returns (%)	10	10	10	12	8
Standard deviation	0.3	0.4	0.6	0.8	0.5

Let us assume that the historical returns are appropriate estimates of the expected returns of the stock; then we can plot these numbers with returns on the y-axis and the standard deviations on the x-axis. These plots show the feasible set of the risk and returns trade-off.

A risk-averse investor would hold the tangent portfolio and a large position in risk-free investments. A less risk-averse investor would hold a larger tangent portfolio and less risk-free investments. An even less risk-averse investor would borrow at the risk-free rate to invest in the tangent portfolio—buying the tangent portfolio at the margin. This result, often referred to as the *Separation Theorem*, refers to the theoretical result that investors' portfolios differ only by the proportion of their holdings in the risk-free asset and the tangent portfolio. In a way, this result is very counterintuitive. It seems to suggest that everyone holds the same portfolio of stocks, differing only in the allocation of their risk-free investments and the tangent portfolio. However, the result is not as surprising as it might at first appear. After all, we assume that everyone is the same except for their risk aversion, and therefore there is no reason for the theory to predict many different optimal portfolios. Risk aversion decides on the trade-off of the tangent portfolio's higher expected returns and corresponding higher risk in relation to the risk-free rate.

If everyone holds the tangent portfolio, then that portfolio must be the actual observed portfolio in the stock market—a portfolio consists of all the stocks in the market, with the portfolio weight of each stock being the proportion of its capitalization (the stock price times the number of shares outstanding) to the value of the market. This portfolio is a *market portfolio*. Since CAPM is an equilibrium model where the market demand for a risky asset should be equal to the market supply of the risky asset, we should impose the market-clearing condition to derive CAPM. We know that every investor holds the same portfolio of risky assets, the tangent portfolio, regardless of the degree of risk preference. Since the market demand for a risky asset should be equal to the market supply of the risky asset and every investor holds the identical portfolio of risky assets, the identical portfolio should be the market portfolio. Otherwise, we cannot have the market-clearing condition.

Now, every investor holds the market portfolio. To measure the risk of an individual stock in the market portfolio, we should calculate the covariance between the individual stock and the market portfolio. The variance of the market portfolio is given in equation (2.2), where σ_M^2 is the variance of the market portfolio and N is the total number of stocks in the market portfolio.

$$\sigma_M^2 = \omega_1 \operatorname{cov}(\tilde{R}_1, \tilde{R}_M) + \omega_2 \operatorname{cov}(\tilde{R}_2, \tilde{R}_M) + \cdots + \omega_N \operatorname{cov}(\tilde{R}_N, \tilde{R}_M) \qquad (2.2)$$

If we divide the both sides of equation (2.2) by σ_M^2, we have

$$1 = \omega_1 \frac{\operatorname{cov}(\tilde{R}_1, \tilde{R}_M)}{\sigma_M^2} + \omega_2 \frac{\operatorname{cov}(\tilde{R}_2, \tilde{R}_M)}{\sigma_M^2} + \cdots + \omega_N \frac{\operatorname{cov}(\tilde{R}_N, \tilde{R}_M)}{\sigma_M^2}$$

$$= \omega_1 \beta_1 + \omega_2 \beta_2 + \cdots + \omega_N \beta_N$$

where $\beta_i = \frac{\operatorname{cov}(\tilde{R}_i, \tilde{R}_M)}{\sigma_M^2}$, $i = 1, \cdots, N$

Dividing by σ_M^2 is a kind of normalization. Since the covariance is a measure of the systematic risk, β is also the measure of the systematic risk, because it is the covariance divided by the same number for all the risky assets, σ_M^2. In particular, when the risky asset is the market portfolio itself, the β, according to the definition, is 1.

Now we can calculate the expected return of a stock and its systematic risk, which is β. The relationship between the expected return and β is linear, simply a mathematical derivation.[8] It is called the *security market line*.

To the extent that all individuals hold similar views on the market and there are no fundamental differences among individuals, CAPM is an approximation to the real world. The weight of the theory can be verified empirically.

2.7   Beta—The Systematic Risk

We now extend this thought process another step further. We have not done any empirical tests, nor do we have any evidence to support any part of the theory. We are just following the argument to its logical conclusion.

First let us introduce the definition of *index fund*. Index funds are stock portfolios available to any investor. They are constructed to mimic the market portfolios, such as Standard and Poor's (S&P) 500. These portfolios have returns similar to the market portfolio, and investors can invest in an index fund as if they were buying a stock. They do not have to select many stocks and manage them.

Consider a particular stock. Its uncertain returns can be broken into two parts: one moves in step with the market and the other is totally unrelated to the market. Under the CAPM assumptions, there is only one factor in the capital market—the market portfolio risk. Only this risk factor is systematic; all other risks become diversifiable. Then any stock can be thought of as a portfolio of an index fund, risk-free rate, and a noise term. To isolate the noises from the rest of the portfolio, we can use a line of best fit to the scattered plots of the stock returns and the market returns. The slope of this line specifies the sensitivity of the stock returns to the market portfolio returns. (See figure 2.5.)

If we assume the risk premium of the market to be $\pi(= E[R_M] - r_f)$, then the risk premium of the stock must be $\beta \times \pi$. Therefore, the expected return of the stock is linearly related to the systematic risk of the stock, β. The plot of the expected returns of risky assets against the risky assets' βs is called the security market line. Then the required expected return of the risky asset is given by the Capital Asset Pricing model:

$$E[R_i] = r_f + \beta_i(E[R_M] - r_f) \qquad (2.3)$$

This result yields a number of important insights on the pricing of securities. Consider an asset which has positive returns when the market falls and has negative returns when the market rises. There are few stocks like this, if any. Such a stock would have a negative β. The stock would have an expected return less than the risk-free rate, even though the stock is risky. An investor would wish to hold such a stock even though the stock has an

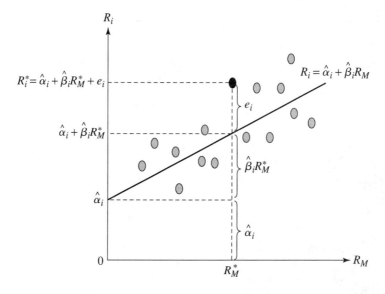

Figure 2.5 Line of best fit to determine β. A scatter plot of the observed (monthly) returns of a stock and the market portfolio over a period of time, say five years. Market returns are on the x-axis and the stock returns on the y-axis. β of the stock is the slope of the line which best fits to the scattered plots. The β determines the risk premium of the stock according to the Capital Asset Pricing model.

expected return less than the risk-free rate because it can lower the portfolio risk. The model is consistent with the arbitrage argument. Suppose we set up a trust where we have a small portfolio of stocks. We then issue shares of the portfolio. This construct is identical to setting up a mutual fund as a closed-end fund. The β of the share is the same as the portfolio β. According to the CAPM, the expected return for the stock with the portfolio β is exactly the expected return of the portfolio.

The importance of the CAPM in finance is that it provides a systematic way to calculate the required rate of return on risky assets. The market reaches its equilibrium when the required rate of return equals the expected rate of return. For this reason, the CAPM can also be used to calculate the required rate of return on risky assets. This required rate of return is based on the market valuation.

The general methodology in valuing a risky asset is to follow the valuation procedure as we would a recipe in a cookbook. First, we estimate the expected cash flows of risky assets for the investors. Second, we estimate the β of the risky assets. Third, we apply the CAPM to determine the required rate of return on the asset. Finally, we use the required rate of return to discount the expected cash flows in order to determine the present value, which is the value of the asset. (See figure 2.6.)

2.8 The Stock Model–Dividend Discount Model

This section derives a valuation model of a stock. To simplify the exposition, let us assume that the stock pays steady dividends, and the value of the stock is the present value of all the dividends that we can receive from the stock. Of course, in principle,

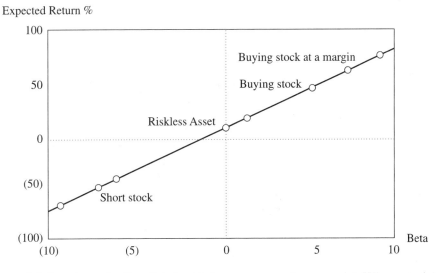

Figure 2.6 Security market line: Relationship between expected return and β. When a stock is part of a portfolio, the individual stock risk can be defined as an additional risk which the stock adds to the portfolio risk. We can quantify the additional risk as a covariance of the stock with the portfolio, which is referred to as β risk. When the covariance of the stock with the portfolio is positive, we have positive β, and vice versa. The β of the risk-free asset is 0, and for the asset with positive (negative) β, the expected rate of return is above (below) the risk-free rate of return.

a firm can retain all the earnings all the time and reinvest them without paying any dividends. The stock would still be valuable even though the firm pays no dividends. In this case, we can still assume that at some time the firm will distribute its value.

In this case, the stock price is the present value of all the future dividends. Let us further suppose that the stock's dividends grow at a constant rate g.

$$div(n + 1) = div(n)(1 + g) \qquad (2.4)$$

Let us assume that the required rate of return is R_{req}. Then the stock price is

$$S = \frac{div(1)}{(1 + R_{req})} + \frac{div(1)(1 + g)}{(1 + R_{req})^2} + \frac{div(1)(1 + g)^2}{(1 + R_{req})^3} + \cdots \qquad (2.5)$$

This equation can be simplified to

$$S = \frac{div(1)}{(R_{req} - g)} \qquad (2.6)$$

The required rate of return of a stock must equal the expected rate of return at market equilibrium. Given the risk of the stock, if the market requires the stock to provide a rate of return of at least R_{req}, which is greater than the expected return, then the stock price would fall because the stock is not expected to provide the return needed. When the price is sufficiently low and the expected rate rises to equal the required rate of return, we have reached equilibrium. Since the required rate of return of the stock can be specified by the CAPM, we therefore have a valuation model for a stock.

In general, dividends do not grow at a constant rate. Often, forecasts of dividends are provided for the next several years. This is accomplished by using the forecasts of the future earnings and a constant dividend payout ratio to determine the dividends. We then assume that at some future date, the dividends will grow at a constant rate. Then the model can be written as

$$S = PV(\text{forecast dividends over T periods}) + \frac{div(T + 1)}{(R_{req} - g)(1 + R_{req})^T} \qquad (2.7)$$

PV (forecast dividends over T periods) is the present value of the projected dividends over a projected horizon of T years. The projected horizon is usually decided by analysts depending on the availability of information on the dividends, goodness of the forecast, and other information on the firms and the markets. This discount rate, used to determine the present value of the projected dividends, is the required rate of return of the equity or the expected return of equity, which is R_{req}.

For example, when div(1) = \$2.00, the growth rate (g) for next three years = 18%, the growth rate (g) from the fourth year = 6%, and the required rate of return (R_{req}) = 16%,

$$PV(\text{forecast dividends over 3 periods}) = \frac{2}{1.16} + \frac{2 \times 1.18}{1.16^2} + \frac{2 \times 1.18^2}{1.16^3} = 5.262$$

$$S(3) = \frac{div(4)}{R_{req} - g} = \frac{2 \times 1.18^2 \times 1.06}{0.16 - 0.06} = 29.519$$

$$S(0) = 5.262 + \frac{29.519}{1.16^3} = 24.174$$

2.9 An Application of the Capital Asset Pricing Model in Investment Services

The CAPM has broad applications to investment services. We provide one simple example here. According to the CAPM, the most efficient portfolio is the market portfolio. Market portfolios are often taken to be Standard and Poor's 500 (S&P) market index or some other broad-based index. Mutual funds are constructed to replicate these market indices. There are many closed-end funds that replicate these broad-based indices. These funds seek to minimize the management fees and hence to minimize the transaction costs. At the same time their returns should closely match the broad-based indices that often have many stocks. (S&P has 500 stocks.)

Exchange traded funds are traded like a stock on the exchange. Investors can buy the market portfolio by just buying these stocks. (SPY stands for the Standard and Poor's Stock index and QQQ stands for NASDAQ index.) As a result of the CAPM, these funds are made available to investors so that they can optimize their own portfolios.

2.10 Empirical Tests of the Capital Asset Pricing Model

Suppose that we have never heard of the CAPM and we are investing in the stock market. The CAPM may sound like a theory that must be erroneous, given all the unrealistic assumptions that have been made to derive the results. But model assumptions are made to highlight the essence of the problem. The theoretical results can be quite intuitively appealing and the model in principle can be tested.

Since the theory predicts that all investors have a market portfolio, and as long as the market portfolio is on the efficient frontier, we have a linear relationship between βs calculated using the market portfolio on the efficient frontier and the expected return. Therefore, the CAPM can be empirically tested by showing that the market portfolio is efficient. However, the empirical results have been mixed in supporting the theory.

The CAPM tells us that all investors hold an efficient portfolio in the expected return and standard deviation space. Since the market portfolio is the weighted average of each investor's efficient portfolio, it should be efficient. This is the most important prediction we could make from the Capital Asset Pricing model. Once the market portfolio is positioned on the efficient set, the linear and positively sloped security market line in the β and expected return space automatically follows mathematically.

To empirically test whether the CAPM is valid, all we have to do is see whether the market portfolio is on the efficient set. However, researchers such as Black, Jensen, and Scholes (BJS) (1972) and Fama and Macbeth (FM) (1974) have tested the Capital Asset Pricing model indirectly, by testing the properties of the security market line. For example, they empirically tested whether the intercept of the security market line was the rate of return on a risk-free bond, as predicted by the CAPM.

They used a two-pass regression technique. In the first pass, they conducted a time-series regression to estimate the *security's characteristic line*. They regressed the time-series return data of the market portfolio against each security's time-series return data, which is called the security's characteristic line. The slope of this characteristic line is the estimate of the security's β. The second pass regression is cross-sectional, estimated βs from the first pass are regressed against average returns of corresponding securities. The estimated line from the second pass is called the security market line. Then the researchers tried to determine whether the properties of the security market line were consistent with the CAPM predictions about the security market line.

At first glance, their empirical results appeared to support the CAPM; however, in 1977 Richard Roll criticized the two-pass empirical methodology by claiming that the empirical results of BJS and FM were tautological—they would follow even in the case where CAPM does not hold. In other words, regardless of how the expected return and the β have been related in the real world, it is possible to obtain results which BJS and FM derived in the two-pass methodology. If it is true, we have not empirically tested whether the relationship between expected return and β would hold in the real world, as the CAPM claims. More important than Roll's criticism is that since the only CAPM prediction is that the market portfolio is on the efficient set in the expected return and standard deviation space, it is important to observe the market portfolio to test the CAPM. However, since the market portfolio contains all the risky assets, such as real estate and human capital, in the economy, it would be almost impossible to observe the market portfolio. If we cannot observe the market portfolio, it logically follows that the CAPM cannot be tested.

Stambaugh (1982) conducted a sensitivity analysis to determine whether expanding the type of investments in the market portfolio has a significant impact on the empirical results of the CAPM. For this purpose, he initially included only stocks on the New York Stock Exchange in the market portfolio. Then he added corporate and government bonds. Finally, he expanded to real estate and durable consumer goods to see how the empirical results of the CAPM would change depending on how he expanded the type of risky assets for the market portfolio. Even though he reported that the conclusions were not significantly affected by expanding the asset composition, we may argue that the risky assets he considered are still a small fraction of all the risky assets that we should include in the market portfolio if it should contain all the risky assets in the world.

Even though many researchers argue that CAPM is dead because empirical evidence has not given strong support to the theory, the CAPM remains an important concept in finance. It provides a framework for determining the trade-off between risk and returns, and is intuitive for two reasons.

First, suppose that we have no idea how stocks will fluctuate and we are investing in the stock market. The best way to invest in stocks would be to invest in many stocks rather than one stock. Diversification works when we are confronted with risk or uncertainty. The key point that CAPM is making (as Markowitz pointed out) is that diversification always pays off. Therefore, investors should hold a portfolio of stocks, and the natural portfolio is the market portfolio.

Second, since investors are holding a portfolio, an individual stock's risk level should be measured by how much risk the stock is contributing to the overall portfolio risk. In this sense, we can break down the individual stock's risk into two parts: diversifiable risk and nondiversifiable risk. The market should compensate risk-averse investors for holding risk. However, it should not compensate investors for holding risks which they can easily diversify away by forming a portfolio.

2.11 Summary

The discount rate is an important tool in valuation. Time value and risk premiums are two important components of the discount rate. Any individual's required risk premium may differ from the market risk premium. Markowitz introduced the concept of diversification in a portfolio of risky assets where risks can be laid off. Therefore, the appropriate discount rate should be based on systematic risks that cannot be diversified.

Given the perfect capital market, all investors would hold a portfolio. The result shows that they must all hold the same risky portfolio with the risk-free rate, known as the Separation Theorem. The risk premium is the required expected return in excess of the risk-free rate. The CAPM shows that the risk premium is the β times the risk premium of the market portfolio. The CAPM is a systematic way of calculating the required rates of return of risky assets. This in turn allows investors to use the required rate to discount the expected cash flow in order to determine the present value of their assets. Furthermore, this theory may be empirically verified, though some financial economists suggest that it is not testable. Indeed, the theory has led to extensive theoretical and empirical research in subsequent years.

Today, stock analysts routinely apply the dividend discount model to evaluate stock valuation. In their analyses, they provide a methodology to determine the β of a stock. They use their proprietary models to determine the projected dividends of the stock. The dividend discount model is then applied. Betas are also widely used to measure the risk of the stock and for hedging purposes. For this reason, βs are provided in many stock analytical reports, and have become a standard tool in stock portfolio management, risk measures, and performance measures.

The CAPM has established a standard of what a financial theory should be and has became a pillar of modern finance. It epitomizes modern financial theories. Using a market equilibrium portfolio, the CAPM changes the way we think about portfolio investment in a fundamental way. It argues that investment is not just about stock picking or normative portfolio construction. We may accept the equilibrium market concept and take the market solution as given. This model has enabled us to derive these logical conclusions. The CAPM has laid a scientific basis for modern finance.

Devoting one chapter of the book to the CAPM can never do the subject justice. However, this book is not about investment. Our focus is on financial modeling. Nevertheless, the CAPM is the bedrock of many modern financial theories, and we cannot understate its broad implications in our discussion of financial modeling.

The CAPM has set a high standard for subsequent financial theories. Some groundbreaking research has met its standards and has important implications. This research begins with a deeper understanding of each security and specific capital markets. Chapter 3 will start such an exploration with some of the most important markets.

Appendix A. Expectations and Standard Deviations

We define an expected value and a variance. They represent the average outcome and a measure of dispersion, respectively.

Definition of the expected value:

$$E(R_i) = \sum_{j=1}^{M} \frac{R_{ij}}{M} \text{ when the outcomes are equally likely}$$

$$= \sum_{j=1}^{M} P_{ij} R_{ij} \text{ when the outcomes are not equally likely}$$

Definition of the variance:

$$\sigma_i^2 = \sum_{j=1}^{M} \frac{\left[R_{ij} - E(R_i) \right]^2}{M} \text{ when the outcomes are equally likely}$$

$$= \sum_{j=1}^{M} P_{ij} \left[R_{ij} - E(R_i) \right]^2 \text{ when the outcomes are not equally likely}$$

where M = the number of outcomes; R_{ij} = the jth possible outcome for the return on security i; and P_{ij} = the probability of the jth outcome for the return on security i.

Appendix B. A Summary of the CAPM

Here, we will explain how to derive CAPM in a descriptive way. To calculate βs, we regress the security's time-series returns against the portfolio's time-series returns. Usually we use the market portfolio returns as an independent variable in the regression. Property I says that as long as we have a minimum-variance portfolio return as an independent variable in the regression, we have a linear relationship between the β and the expected return of the security. (See Figure 2.7.)

Assumptions

1. Investors can choose portfolios based on expected return and standard deviation.
2. All investors have homogeneous expectations about expected returns, standard deviations of stocks, and correlation coefficients among stocks.
3. The market is competitive and perfect.

Derivation

1. Since investors have homogeneous expectations about the mean and standard deviation, all investors face the same efficient frontier. Furthermore, the same risk-free rate of return confronted by investors on top of the same efficient frontier makes all investors have the same portfolio of risky assets. This is called the Separation Theorem.

2. Since all investors have the same portfolio of risky assets, that portfolio should be the market portfolio. Otherwise, we cannot have an equilibrium where the demand is equal to the supply.

3. Since all investors have the market portfolio, which is a well-diversified portfolio, all investors have only systematic risk. β is a measure of systematic risk.

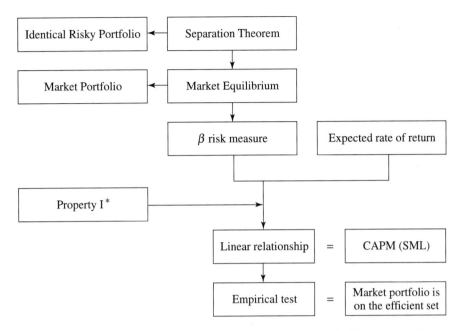

Figure 2.7 Capital Asset Pricing model systematic diagram. *Property I: Given a group of securities, there should exist a linear relationship between the β and the expected return of the securities if and only if the βs of the securities have been calculated using a minimum-variance portfolio. In other words, when we calculate the stock βs based on the minimum-variance portfolio and plot the expected returns against the corresponding βs of each stock, we have a linear relationship between the expected returns and the βs. However, we do not have a linear relationship if we calculate the stock βs based on a portfolio which is not the minimum-variance portfolio of each.

4. Since CAPM is a pricing model, it is concerned with the relationship between β and expected return. According to Property I, we can see that the relationship is linear. The linear relationship between β and the expected return is called the security market line.

5. Even though we can consult a book for a formal proof of Property I,[9] we will try to understand Property I by deriving the security market line from the efficient set mathematics.

To determine the efficient frontier when short sales as well as riskless lending and borrowing are allowed, we maximize the objective function:

$$\theta = \frac{E[R_M] - r_f}{\sigma_M} \text{ subject to } \sum_{i=1}^{N} \omega_i = 1$$

Since $E[R_M] = \sum_{i=1}^{N} \omega_i E[R_i]$ and $\sigma_M^2 = \sum_{i=1}^{N}\sum_{j=1}^{N} \omega_i^2 \omega_j^2 \rho_{i,j} \sigma_i \sigma_j$, substituting them into

the objective function yields $\theta = \left[\sum_{i=1}^{N} \omega_i (E[R]_i - r_f)\right]\left[\sum_{i=1}^{N}\sum_{j=1}^{N} \omega_i^2 \omega_j^2 \rho_{i,j} \sigma_i \sigma_j\right]^{-\frac{1}{2}}$.

Taking the first derivative of the objective function with respect to ω_i where $i = 1, \cdots, N$ and equating them to 0 yields[10]

$$- \left[\lambda \omega_i \sigma_i^2 + \sum_{\substack{j=1 \\ i \neq j}}^{N} \lambda \omega_j \sigma_{i,j} \right] + (E[R_i] - r_f) = 0 \qquad (2.8)$$

where $\lambda = \dfrac{\sum\limits_{i=1}^{N} \omega_i (E[R_i] - r_f)}{\sum\limits_{i=1}^{N} \sum\limits_{j=1}^{N} \omega_i^2 \omega_j^2 \rho_{i,j} \sigma_i \sigma_j} = \dfrac{E[R_M] - r_f}{\sigma_M^2}$. σ_M^2 denotes the variance of the market portfolio.

Simplifying equation (2.8) using $\sigma_{i,M} = \omega_i \sigma_i^2 + \sum\limits_{\substack{j=1 \\ i \neq j}}^{N} \omega_j \sigma_{i,j}$ yields $E[R_i] - r_f = $

$\dfrac{E[R_M] - r_f}{\sigma_M^2} \cdot \sigma_{i,M}$. Further rearranging yields $E[R_i] = r_f + \dfrac{\sigma_{i,M}}{\sigma_M^2}(E[R_M] - r_f) = r_f + \beta_i(E[R_M] - r_f)$, using $\beta_i = \dfrac{\sigma_{i,M}}{\sigma_M^2}$, which is the security market line.

If we arrange equation (2.8) to get $\dfrac{E[R_i] - r_f}{\beta_i} = E[R_M] - r_f$, we see that $\dfrac{E[R_i] - r_f}{\beta_i}$ is a slope of stock i on the expected return and β plane. Furthermore, the slope of each stock is identical and constant across the stocks. Therefore, the relationship between the expected return and β is linear as long as we calculate β based on the portfolio on the efficient frontier. In other words, as long as investors hold the market portfolio, which is on the efficient frontier, the relationship between the expected return and β should be linear. If the market portfolio is not on the efficient frontier, we cannot have the linear relationship. The linear relationship is a result of the optimization process where investors minimize the risk given the expected return.

6. To test whether CAPM holds in the real world, all we have to do is to see whether the market portfolio is on the efficient frontier, because once it is, we have a linear relationship between the expected return and β risk, which we can see from Property I. Traditionally we empirically tested whether the intercept of the security market line is the risk-free rate; the security market line is linear; or the slope of the security market line is equal to $(E[R_M] - r_f)$. However, once the market portfolio is on the efficient frontier, the above facts automatically hold. That is why we only have to check whether the market portfolio is on the efficient frontier to empirically test CAPM.

Notes

1. U.S. Securities and Exchange Commission. Order execution obligations, release no. 34-37619A (1996).

2. U.S. Securities and Exchange Commission. Regulation of exchanges and alternative trading system, release no. 34-40760 (1998).

3. Merton Miller and Franco Modigliani, professors at the University of Chicago, received the Nobel Prize in economics in 1990 and 1985, respectively.

4. For this work, Harry Markowitz received the Nobel Prize in economics in 1990.

5. A random variable Y is defined to be normally distributed if its density is given by $f(y; \mu, \sigma^2) = \frac{1}{\sqrt{2\pi\sigma^2}} \exp\{\frac{-(y-\mu)^2}{2\sigma^2}\}$. The mean and variance of Y are μ and σ^2, respectively. Let X be a positive random variable and let a new random variable Y be defined as $Y = \log_e X$. If Y has a normal distribution, then X is said to have a lognormal distribution. The density of a lognormal distribution is $f(x; \mu, \sigma^2) = \frac{1}{x\sqrt{2\pi\sigma^2}} \exp\{-\frac{1}{2\sigma^2}(\log_e x - \mu)^2\}$ where $-\infty < \mu < \infty$ and $\sigma > 0$.

The mean and variance of X are $e^{\mu+\frac{1}{2}\sigma^2}$ and $e^{2\mu+2\sigma^2}-e^{2\mu+\sigma^2}$, respectively. Intuitively, the random variable X is lognormally distributed if $\log_e X$ is normally distributed.

6. The average risk of a portfolio made up of k securities out of the market portfolio is

$$\overline{\sigma}^2 = \frac{1}{k}\overline{\sigma}_i^2 + \frac{k-1}{k}\overline{\sigma}_{ij}.$$

where $\overline{\sigma}_i^2$ = the average of variance of all the individual stocks which comprise the market portfolio, and $\overline{\sigma}_{ij}$ = the average of covariance of all the individual stocks which comprise the market portfolio.

Here we assume that the market portfolio consists of 40 different stocks. To understand how we derive the formula, we illustrate that the formula holds when the market portfolio consists of four stocks and we select three stocks out of four stocks to form the portfolio. Assume that the market portfolio consists of four stocks which are A, B, C, and D. We choose 3 stocks from the market portfolio and invest 1/3 in each stock. The number of the three-stock-portfolios is $\binom{4}{3}$ and the average risk of those portfolios is

$$\overline{\sigma}_k^2 = \frac{\sigma_{ABC}^2 + \sigma_{BCD}^2 + \sigma_{CDA}^2 + \sigma_{DAB}^2}{4} \quad \text{when } k = 3$$

where

$$\sigma_{ABC}^2 = \frac{1}{9}\cdot\sigma_A^2 + \frac{1}{9}\cdot\sigma_B^2 + \frac{1}{9}\cdot\sigma_C^2 + \frac{2}{9}\cdot(\sigma_{AB} + \sigma_{BC} + \sigma_{CA})$$

$$\sigma_{BCD}^2 = \frac{1}{9}\cdot\sigma_B^2 + \frac{1}{9}\cdot\sigma_C^2 + \frac{1}{9}\cdot\sigma_D^2 + \frac{2}{9}\cdot(\sigma_{BC} + \sigma_{CD} + \sigma_{DA})$$

$$\sigma_{CDA}^2 = \frac{1}{9}\cdot\sigma_C^2 + \frac{1}{9}\cdot\sigma_D^2 + \frac{1}{9}\cdot\sigma_A^2 + \frac{2}{9}\cdot(\sigma_{CD} + \sigma_{DA} + \sigma_{AC})$$

$$\sigma_{DAB}^2 = \frac{1}{9}\cdot\sigma_D^2 + \frac{1}{9}\cdot\sigma_A^2 + \frac{1}{9}\cdot\sigma_B^2 + \frac{2}{9}\cdot(\sigma_{DA} + \sigma_{AB} + \sigma_{DB})$$

Therefore,

$$\overline{\sigma}_k^2 = \frac{1}{3}\cdot\frac{(\sigma_A^2 + \sigma_B^2 + \sigma_C^2 + \sigma_D^2)}{4} + \frac{2}{3}\cdot\frac{2\,(\sigma_{AB} + \sigma_{AC} + \sigma_{AD} + \sigma_{BC} + \sigma_{BD} + \sigma_{CD})}{12}$$

$$= \frac{1}{3}\cdot\overline{\sigma}_i^2 + \frac{2}{3}\cdot\overline{\sigma}_{ij}$$

7.
$$\sigma_{A,P} = Cov(\tilde{R}_A, \tilde{R}_P) = Cov(\tilde{R}_A, \omega_A\tilde{R}_A + \omega_B\tilde{R}_B) = Cov(\tilde{R}_A, \omega_A\tilde{R}_A) + Cov(\tilde{R}_A, \omega_B\tilde{R}_B)$$

$$= \omega_A \times Cov(\tilde{R}_A, \tilde{R}_A) + \omega_B \times Cov(\tilde{R}_A, \tilde{R}_B) = \omega_A \times \sigma_A^2 + \omega_B \times \sigma_{A,B}$$

8. William Sharpe, a professor at Stanford University, extended Markowitz's diversification theory to a market equilibrium theory. In 1990 he received the Nobel Prize in economics for this theory.

9. See Robert A. Haugen, *Modern Investment Theory*, 5th ed. (Englewood Cliffs, NJ: Prentice-Hall, 2000), pp. 114–116.

10. Ibid. Property I here is Property II in Haugen's book.

11. For the more detailed derivation, consult E. J. Elton et al., *Modern Portfolio Theory and Investment Analysis*, 6th ed. (New York: John Wiley and Sons, 2003).

References

Black, F., M. Jensen, and M. Scholes. 1972. *The Capital Asset Pricing Model: Some Empirical Tests, Studies in the Theory of Capital Markets*, Praeger, New York.

Elton, E. J., M. J. Gruber, S. J. Brown, and W. Goetzmann. 2003. *Modern Portfolio Theory and Investment Analysis*, 6th ed. John Wiley and Sons, New York.

Elton, E. J., M. J. Gruber, and M. D. Padberg. 1976. Simple criteria for optimal portfolio selection. *Journal of Finance*, 31, no. 5, 1341–1357.

Fama, E. F. 1970. Efficient capital markets: A review of theory and empirical work. *Journal of Finance*, 25, no. 5, 383–417.

Fama, E. F. 1991. Efficient capital markets: II. *Journal of Finance*, 46, no. 5, 1575–1617.

Fama, E. F., and J. Macbeth. 1984. Risk, return and equilibrium: Empirical test. *Journal of Political Economy*, 81, 607–636.

Gordon, J. A. 1993. Short selling and efficient sets. *Journal of Finance*, 48, no. 4, 1497–1506.

Haugen, R. A. 2000. *Modern Investment Theory*, 5th ed. Prentice-Hall, Englewood Cliffs, NJ.

Markowitz, H. M. 1952. Portfolio selection. *Journal of Finance*, 7, no. 1, 77–91.

Modigliani, F., and M. Miller. 1958. The cost of capital, corporation finance and the theory of investment. *American Economic Review*, 48, 267–297.

Modigliani, F., and M. Miller. 1963. Corporate income taxes and the cost of capital: A correction. *American Economic Review*, 53, no. 3, 433–443.

Mossin, J. 1966. Equilibrium in a capital asset market. *Econometrica*, 34, no. 4, 768–783.

Roll, R. 1977. A critique of the asset pricing theory's tests: Part 1. On past and potential testability of the theory. *Journal of Financial Economics*, 4, no. 2, 129–176.

Sharpe, W. F. 1964. Capital asset prices: A theory of market equilibrium under conditions of risk. *Journal of Finance*, 19, no. 3, 425–442.

Stambaugh, R. 1982. On the exclusion of assets from tests of the two-parameter model: A sensitivity analysis. *Journal of Financial Economics*, 10, 237–268.

Statman, M. 1987. How many stocks make a diversified portfolio? *Journal of Financial and Quantitative Analysis*, 22, no. 3, September, 353–363.

Tobin, J. 1958. Liquidity preference as behavior towards risk. *Review of Economic Studies*, 26, no. 1, 65–86.

Tobin, J. 1965. The theory of portfolio selection. In *The Theory of Interest Rates*, ed. F. H. Hahn and F. P. R. Brechling. London: Macmillan.

3

Bond Markets: The Bond Model

Considered the cornerstone model for establishing valuation of fixed-income securities, the bond model applies the law of one price to value a cash flow using the observed yield curve. Specifically, the model suggests that cash flows can be replicated by a portfolio of zero-coupon bonds, and therefore the value of the cash flows should be the same as that of the portfolio. The bond model has wide applications to fixed-income securities markets. Fixed-income securities valuation methods described in the following chapters are refinements or extensions of this bond model.

Financial sectors are directly affected by the interest rate. As described by the discounted cash flow model in chapter 1, the present-value concept depends on the market interest rate level. Bond markets, stock markets, futures and forward markets, and commodity markets are all affected by the interest rate level.

Interest rates are also important to the real sector of the economy. They affect the levels at which people consume or invest. If we all prefer to save more for the future and consume less today, interest rates will fall. Interest rates are also related to the economy's productivity. If the economy is productive and has a high rate of return for providing goods and services that we can consume in the future, we will be more likely to invest, sacrificing today's consumption for tomorrow's enjoyment. Thus the interest rate would rise, reflecting the productivity of the economy.

The interest rate is related to the quantity of money. The quantity of money affects the inflation rate, which in turns affects the interest rate level. If the government printed a large amount of paper money and gave it to everyone, this increase in the quantity of money simply would lead to a higher price level, or inflation. With the shrinking purchasing power of $1.00, the market would demand higher interest rates. The higher interest rates would in turn affect everyone's desire to save as opposed to consume or firm's investment decisions and production plans. Monetary authorities or central banks consider interest rates to be a key tool in their management of the economy by influencing the interest rate level.

The financial instrument that reflects the interest rate level is a bond (often called a fixed-income security). A bond has a cash flow, stated payments at future dates, specified in a contract. The buyer pays for the bond at its price, and receives the future contractual payments.

Since interest rates are important to financial markets and to the real economy, bonds play a critical role in financial analysis; the valuation of bonds is an important part of financial theory. The valuation of bonds enables the market to price individual, corporate, and government borrowings.

However, given that the market interest rate is uncertain, and bonds in general have uncertain values over a holding period, can we view a bond as a risky asset and measure its β, so that we can apply the Capital Asset Pricing model (CAPM) to determine the risk premium? The answer, in general, is no. Using the estimation of β is too inaccurate for many practical applications in bond pricing. As an alternative to the CAPM, we can apply the methodology of the bond model. We can determine the bond price more accurately by measuring the time value of money inferred from the capital market. Then the observed time value of money can be used to determine the present value (or the price) of a bond.

In order to grasp the principles of a bond market, we need to begin with the basics of bond mathematics, which will be used to study the Treasury securities market and the swap market. These markets enable us to examine the yield curve and its movements over time. We will examine how the bond model is then used to study the forward and futures contracts. Finally, we will discuss the measure of risk, duration, and convexity of the bonds.

3.1   Bond Mathematics

A bond is a financial contract to receive specified payments over time. These payments are usually called principal and interest (or coupons).

Principal and coupons

A bond is often specified by the *coupons* and the *principal*. The coupons usually represent regular, periodic payments to the holder. Principal (often called the face value) is the sum that is promised to be repaid by the borrower to the lender. The coupon amount or interest is calculated as a percent of the principal. That percentage is referred to as the coupon rate. For an investor, the key determination in buying a bond is the return on the investment, which is the combination of the coupons and principal. Together, we call these cash flows. One relevant distinction between coupons and principal is tax. The coupons are subject to income tax. The appreciation of the price is subject to the capital gains tax.

The time until the final payment of a bond is called the *maturity*. The price of the bond is the price the bond transacted in the market, as in the case of a stock. The price quoted is often considered a percent of the principal amount, and therefore a bond price is quoted with the face value based on 100. In general, the terms and conditions of a bond that specify the future payments can be varied, and there are only broad guidelines. Since these payments are often specified as fixed-amount promised payments over time, bonds are more appropriately called *fixed-income securities*. Fixed-income securities that have no maturity (or infinite time to maturity) are called *perpetual bonds*.

Accrued interest

Accrued interest is an accounting entity that amortizes the coupon payment over the period between two coupon dates. The accrued interest at any time t is calculated to be the portion of the next coupon payment such that the proportion of the accrued interest to the next coupon payment is the time lapse from the last coupon date to the time interval between the last and the next coupon dates. The *quoted price* (also called the clean price) is the price at which the bond will be bought or sold, and the amount transacted is the quoted price plus the accrued interest. This amount is called the *invoice price* (or the dirty price). The invoice price is the true economic value of the bond. For example, consider the value of a bond one day before the maturity date. The annual coupon rate is 10% and the principal is 100. The total payment at the maturity date is therefore 110. Since the accrued interest is 10, the quoted price, which is the present value of the bond net of the accrued interest, is 100 ($= 110 - 10$).

The quoted price is a market convention and not the economic value of the bond. Why do we not quote a bond price incorporating the accrued interest? Suppose the yield curve is flat. When the bond is sold, the coupon rate will be the same as the market interest rate and the price is par (100). Suppose the interest rate has not changed for the entire year. The invoice price will rise to the coupon payment and then drop immediately to reflect the coupon payment, whereas the quoted price will remain constant, appropriately reflecting the constant interest rate. When we quote a bond price at par (or 100), we can infer the market interest rate from the coupon rate. However, if we use the invoice price, we have to take the accrued interest into account before we can make such an inference.

Yield

Yield measures the rate of return of a bond. There are several yield measures. The most commonly used measure is called *yield to maturity*. It is the internal rate of return of a bond. More specifically, the yield to maturity is given by

$$Invoice\ Price = \frac{coupon}{(1 + YTM)} + \frac{coupon}{(1 + YTM)^2} + \cdots + \frac{coupon + principal}{(1 + YTM)^T} \quad (3.1)$$

where YTM is the yield to maturity.

The above equation refers to the coupon being paid annually. But in the United States many bonds have coupons paid semiannually. In that case, the formula is

$$Invoice\ Price = \frac{coupon/2}{(1 + YTM/2)} + \frac{coupon/2}{(1 + YTM/2)^2} + \cdots + \frac{coupon/2 + principal}{(1 + YTM/2)^{2T}}$$

This yield to maturity is semiannual compounding and is called the bond yield.

The coupon payment period does not have to be semiannual. It can be daily, monthly, or some other regular period. The yield to maturity can be defined as daily compounding or monthly compounding. When a bond has a continuously compounding yield, then the continuously compounding yield r over a term T for a $1.00 payment at time T is given by

$$Price = \exp(-rT)$$

It is important to specify the compounding period of the yield that is quoted. For example, a bond that has a 10% monthly compounding rate has a higher return than a bond quoted 10% at an annual compounding rate.

When the yield to maturity equals the coupon rate, the bond price is the same as the principal (the face) value. In this case, we say that the bond is trading at par. If the yield to maturity is higher than the coupon rate, the bond price is below par. In this case, we say the bond is trading at discount. Finally, when the bond yield to maturity is below the coupon rate, the bond price will exceed the par price and we say that the bond is trading at premium.

An increase in the yield will result in a lower bond price, and a fall in the yield will lead to an increase in the bond price. The bond price is negatively related to the yield. These relationships are direct results from the yield to maturity in equation (3.1).

For the perpetual bond (also called the consol bond), which has no maturity, the bond price is related to the coupon rate and the yield to maturity, the time value of money, in a simple way. The perpetual bond price is given by

$$Price = \frac{annual\ coupon}{YTM} \tag{3.2}$$

The yield to maturity of a perpetual bond can be considered the yield of a bond with the longest maturity that one can observe in the market.

3.2   Bonds and Bond Markets

Money Markets

Money markets are investments with a short time value of money, ranging from daily to annual rates. There are quite a few markets providing different rates, depending on the borrowers and lenders. The followings are some examples of money market instruments. The *London Interbank Offered Rate* (LIBOR) is the British Bankers Association average of interbank offered rates for dollar deposits in the London market, based on quotations at major banks. This market is very active, and the LIBOR rates are often considered the benchmarks for the time value of money. The *prime rate* is the base rate on corporate loans. These rates should be higher than the LIBOR rates with the same term to maturity because they represent the lending rates of the banks. The *discount rate* is the charge on loans to depository institutions by the Federal Reserve banks. This rate represents an administered rate, a rate not fully representing the market supply of and demand for funds. *Federal funds* are reserves traded among commercial banks for overnight use. Commercial banks use federal funds to manage their short-term liquidity needs. *Commercial paper* consists of short-term unsecured promissory notes issued by corporations. They are sold in the open market, typically with maturity less than a year. *Bankers' acceptances* are negotiable, bank-backed business credit instruments that typically finance an import order. The *overnight repurchase rate* (repo) is the dealer financing rate for overnight sale and repurchase of Treasury securities. Each rate indicates the required returns for the risk and time value of money for each market segment. For example, consider the money market rates on February 7, 2002, in table 3.1. The LIBOR (annualized) rates show that the interest rates increase with the term. The discount rate, federal funds, and repo rates are annualized daily rates.

Treasury Securities

Treasury securities are fixed-income securities and have three submarkets: bills, notes, and bonds. *Bills* are discount instruments (which have no coupon payments) with a maturity of less than one year at issuance. They are important to the money markets for their size in the market and their creditworthiness. *Treasury notes* are fixed-income securities with coupons paid semiannually and a maturity of less than ten years at issuance. *Bonds* are similar to notes and have a maturity of 30 years at issuance. Some

Table 3.1 Money Market Rates on
February 7, 2002

Money Market Rates	Rate (%)
LIBOR (month)	
1	1.84
3	1.90
6	2.02
12	2.42
Discount rate	1.24
Fed Funds	1.50
Repo	1.68
Banker's acceptance	1.86
Prime rate	4.75

Money markets refer to investments with a short
time value of money, ranging from daily to annual rates. The LIBOR rates are increasing with
the term. The discount rate, Fed Fund, and Repo
rates are annualized daily rates. Each rate indicates the required returns for the risk and time
value of money for each market segment.

Treasury bonds have call features such that the Treasury can call (buy back) the bonds at
par over the five years before maturity. The call feature gives the Treasury some control
over the scheduling of the bonds' principal payments coming due. Some recent bond
issues (since 1997) have the principal linked to the inflation rate. These bonds are called
Treasury inflation protection securities, or TIPS. The principal of the bond is adjusted by
the semiannual inflation rate. Therefore the principal of the bond at time T is the initial
principal amount compounded at the published inflation rate at semiannual intervals.
The coupon payments are based on the fixed coupon rate on the adjusted principal
amount. When the inflation rate is high, the bond pays higher coupons and higher
adjusted principal at maturity. Therefore these bonds offer a hedge against inflation for
the investors.

There is an active secondary market. There are over 300 types of Treasury securities
outstanding in the market that participants can buy or sell. As of 2001, the Treasury
markets have had a value of over $3 trillion. The market is very liquid, particularly for
some of the recent issues. These issues are called *on-the-run issues*. For such issues, a $10
million trade would not have much (if any) impact on the market because many market
participants stand ready to trade these securities. However, an investor can buy as little
as $10,000 of the bonds without incurring significant transaction costs. Since Treasury
notes and bonds are sold at a coupon rate such that the market price is 100% of the
principal (that is, the bonds are sold at 100 or par), these bonds' yields are benchmarks
for the market to infer the time value of money. These yields are called the *par rates*. The
plot of these par rates against their maturities is called the *par yield curve*. The par yield
curve therefore defines the yields of par bonds for different times to maturity.

Some of these coupon issues (notes and bonds) are held by the U.S. Treasury, and are
then "stripped" into coupons and principal payments. Each payment becomes a zero-
coupon bond. The zero-coupon bonds have no coupon payments, just one payment at
maturity. These bonds appeal to investors who need to have a particular payment at a
specific time. This market is called the STRIPS market. In February 1985, the Treasury
began its *Separate Trading of Registered Interest and Principal of Securities* (STRIPS)
program, which facilitated the stripping of designated Treasury securities.

In general, the Treasury markets (including the STRIPS market) are assumed to have no default risks. Considering that most bonds are liquid, they become the standard for measuring the time value of money.

When a bond is quoted as traded at par, it means that the bond price is 100. When the price is above 100, the bond is called premium, and when the price is below 100, the bond is discount. Treasury bills do not pay any interest, and they are always traded at discount. The same observation applies to the STRIPS bonds (zero-coupon bonds).

The yield curve observed from the STRIPS market is the *market-observed spot curve*, and the prices of the STRIPS bonds form the *discount function*. By convention, the discount function is quoted on the basis of a face value of 1 (not 100, as in the case of the STRIPS bond prices). The STRIPS prices can be used to price Treasury bonds because a Treasury coupon bond can be viewed as a portfolio of STRIPS bonds. Each coupon payment and its principal is a zero-coupon bond. Each zero-coupon bond can be valued by using the observed STRIPS bond prices (the discount function). The portfolio value can be calculated by summing the values of all the STRIPS bonds. This portfolio value should be close to the observed coupon bond price.

There is a reason for this observed closeness of the prices. The market allows for arbitrage between the Treasury markets and the STRIPS markets. When the Treasury bond (note) is priced below the fair price, dealers can buy these (*cheap*) bonds and strip them to sell the coupons and principals at the observed higher price. The stripping will continue until the fair price and the quoted price are aligned again. Conversely, if the bond price is traded above the fair price, the dealers can "reconstitute" the bond by buying the STRIPS bonds. The portfolio of STRIPS bonds replicates the actual bond. Then the portfolio can be sold as a bond.

Other Bonds

The issuers can be quite varied. Corporations are often borrowers, promising the investors coupons and principals. Such bonds are called corporate bonds. Typically, bondholders do not have claims on any real assets or corporate entities. They are not subject to any charter of a corporation, nor are they directly rewarded by the returns of the real sector and real processes, as stockholders are.

Municipalities' borrowings are called *municipal bonds*. Bonds that use real estate properties as collateral are called *mortgages*. Some bonds' coupons and principals are derived from a portfolio of other bonds. These bonds are called *pass-through certificates*, suggesting that the cash flows are just passed from one type of bond to other bonds, changing the bond characteristics in the process.

Most bonds are traded in the OTC markets. (Some corporate bonds are traded on the New York Stock Exchange, but the market is less liquid.) Understanding the terms and conditions of each bond type and their markets will be the subjects of chapters 8–10. This chapter will describe the government bond market, the U.S. Treasury Securities market.

3.3   Swap Markets

A *swap* is an over-the-counter instrument that is not issued by any corporation or government agency. It is an exchange of payments between two parties. These payments are interest payments that may be based on a floating rate or a fixed rate, on the same amount of principal and maturity. *Floating rates* are short-term interest rates which may be daily (for example, 2 percent above the fed fund rate), accruing over time and paid monthly or semiannually. A *fixed rate* is a coupon rate fixed to the end of the contract. As a result, only the interests (floating and fixed) are exchanged, since the principals are the same on both sides of the swap. The maturity (or the term of the agreement) is called the *tenor*. The principal is called the *notional amount*, since it will never result in a payment.

Vanilla swap refers to a swap where one party pays a standard floating rate (for example, daily LIBOR) and receives a fixed rate, as described above, without any embedded options or contingencies, or any nonstandard fixed or floating payments. A vanilla swap has two components: (1) borrowing at the short-term rate, "short term funding," and (2) buying a fixed-rate bond. Therefore, entering into a vanilla swap is equivalent to securing short-term funding and investing in a bond. For this reason, the fixed rate for a given tenor of the swap (time to the termination of a swap) reflects the term structure of interest rates in the capital market. When the parties are highly rated (have minimal default risk), the *swap rates* can be used as a benchmark for the time value of money. Since the swap rate is the coupon rate determined for the fixed payments, it refers to the rate on the notional amount such that if we view the fixed payments as a bond, the market value of the bond is par. Swap rates are equivalent to the par rates of the bond market, and the swap curve is the par curve in the swap market.

Not all swaps are vanilla. Since swaps are agreements between two parties in the over-the-counter market, there is no standardization of designs. The fixed payment can be a *bullet payment* (a bond that accrues all the interest to be paid at the termination date), or an amortization schedule, or coupon-paying but with nonstandardized payment dates.

Unlike bonds, a swap has no multiple borrowers or lenders, only parties who exchange the cash flows. Such arrangements offer significant flexibility in the design. The terms and conditions of each swap are summarized in a confirm sheet, which includes the names of the parties, the notional amount, specifications of the exchange of payments, and the termination date.

Swap markets are very liquid in the United States. Swaps can be arranged in large notional amounts (in billions of dollars) continually. In countries where there is no national debt or that have fairly short-term national debt, swap rates are often used as benchmarks for the time value of money. Indeed, the swap rates for bullet payments build the spot curve for the market.

3.4 Economics of the Yield Curve

Yield Curves

A *spot curve* is defined as the relationship between the required rate of return of $1.00 invested over a time horizon T. It is represented by $r(T)$, and it measures the time value of money required by the market. There are several ways to construct the yield curve.[1] We will describe three ways to construct the theoretical yield curves for Treasuries, depending on which bonds we include in the construction. The candidates are Treasury STRIPS, on-the-run Treasury issues, and all Treasury coupon securities and bills.

The STRIPS market is one practical measure of the spot curve. U.S. Treasury securities are bonds that best approximate the theoretical construct of "default-free" bonds. The probability that the U.S. government will default on its debt is perceived as negligible at present. As long as the U.S. Treasury can print more money, the government's debt obligations can be repaid. The Treasury spot curves are important to the fixed-income markets in pricing other bonds because of Treasury bonds' liquidity and creditworthiness. (See figure 3.1.)

The plot of the yields to maturity of the Treasury securities outstanding in the marketplace against their maturities is called the *nominal yield curve*. Since each bond has both the coupons and the principal payments, the nominal yield curve is only an approximation of the time value of money, since it does not precisely specify the present value of $1.00 at time T.

Another commonly used yield curve is the *par curve*. The par curve is used for the most closely watched bonds, the on-the-run issues. These are the most recently issued Treasury bills, notes, and bonds. These bonds are the most actively traded, and their movements represent the market's view of the equilibrium values of the bonds. Since these Treasury securities are the most recently issued and they are issued at par (except for the bills), their yields are close to their coupon rates. If we construct a yield curve by linearly interpolating the yields to maturity of these par bonds, the yield curve will represent the time value of money best represented at any one time by these most actively traded bonds. This yield curve is called the par curve.

The market has established the convention of quoting the price as a spread off the Treasury rate. For example, a bond may be quoted as 100 basis point off the ten-year Treasury, meaning that the bond yield to maturity is the yield to maturity of the ten-year on-the-run Treasury bond, plus 100 basis points. For this reason, the par curve is important on trading floors. We will show in section 3.7 how the par curve, the spot yield curve, and the nominal yield curve are related mathematically.

The bonds are continually traded and the prices are continually updated. Therefore, the yield curve fluctuates in an uncertain fashion over time. But two bonds with similar maturities cannot have price movements independent of each other. The yield of T year

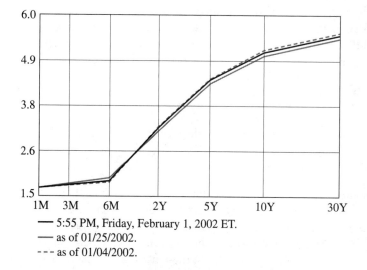

Figure 3.1 Treasure market spot curve. Since the Treasury market is a liquid market with no default risks, its spot curve is often used as a benchmark for time value of money. Here, yield curves at different points in time show how yield curves fluctuate over time.
Source: http://www.bondmarkets.com

bond should be similar to that of a bond with maturity T year plus one month. After all, the time value of money represents the market participants' preferences for returns over a time horizon, and therefore, the time value of money should be a smooth function related to the time to maturity.

If the yield $r(T)$ is constant and not dependent on the time to maturity T, we say that the spot yield curve is flat. If $r(T)$ rises (falls) with time T, we say the curve is a upward (downward)-sloping curve. The shape of the curve depicts the market supply and demand for funds over time.

In recent years, as a result of the U.S. government's effort to retire the national debt, the Treasury securities market has become smaller and, in some of the maturity spectrum, less liquid. At times the spot yield may fail to reflect the market supply of and demand for funds over time for lack of liquidity in part of the yield curve. An alternative benchmark to measure the time value of money is the swap market.

The swap market is a highly liquid market. Further, many countries do not have a liquid government bond market with longer maturities; their debts have maturities extending only one year. The swap curve becomes a necessary market benchmark for these countries. However, since swaps are contracts arranged between two parties, and the market swap rates are gathered by the market from the global financial institutions, there is a possibility that credit risks may affect these swap rates. The choice of the benchmark bonds to determine the yield curve and the choice of yield curve (spot curve or par curve) depend on the applications of the yield curve.

Real Rate and Nominal Rate

The interest rates of the yield curves that we have discussed so far are called *nominal rates*. These are the yields of the bonds or the interest that we receive on our investments. Our study focuses on the nominal interest rate, which has two components: inflation and the real rate. The *real rate* reflects the real sector, where there is no impact of money on the purchase of goods. If the economy has higher productivity, investment increases and consumption falls. In addition to the real rate, the inflation rate affects the nominal interest rate. When we expect a higher inflation rate, the nominal interest rate will increase. This is summarized by the Fisher equation, stated as

$$nominal\ interest\ rate = real\ rate + expected\ inflation\ rate \qquad (3.3)$$

The Fisher equation is particularly relevant for the long-term rate. The short-term rate is often affected by government monetary policy. For example, when the market expects persistent recession (hence low inflation and real rate), the long-term rate will fall. At this point the government may seek to lower the interest rate by using short-term instruments, which directly affects the cost of funds to the banks. For example, the monetary authority uses the *discount window* (central banks provide short-term liquidity needs of banks) and *open market operations* (central banks buy and sell government securities in the secondary markets) to lend or to buy short-term bonds, and such trading may affect the market short-term rates. In this case, the yield curve will fall, but the short-term rate will fall faster. Such was the case in the United States during the period 1990–1992.

Conversely, the market may experience a high inflation rate, resulting in a high long-term rate. The government may combat the inflation via lowering the money supply.

It may then raise the short-term rate higher. In this case, the yield curve will move up, but the short-term rate will move up faster. This movement will result in an inverted (downward-sloping) yield curve. Such was the case in the United States during the period of 1975–1978. (See figure 3.2.)

Expectation hypothesis

The movement of the yield curve should be dependent on market expectations. When market participants anticipate that the interest rate will rise, the long-term yield of bonds should rise. Suppose we predict that the one-year rate will rise in one year; then the two-year bond yield should rise to reflect the market expectation. The new two-year rate should rise by an amount such that the investor rolling over the one-year bond has the same expected return as one locking in the two-year returns.

Establishing notations is in order at this point. We denote the t year interest rate prevailing at time 0 as $r_{0,t}$. Extending this notation to future periods, we denote the $T^* - t$ year interest rate prevailing at time t as r_{t,T^*}. In other words, r_{t,T^*} is the interest rate that will be applied during the period from t to T^*, where t and T^* denote the times. Then the expectation hypothesis asserts that

$$(1 + r_{0,1})(1 + E(\tilde{r}_{1,2})) = (1 + r_{0,2})^2 \tag{3.4}$$

The left-hand side of the equation represents the investment of $1.00 at the one-year interest rate in the first year and reinvested in the second year at the prevailing one-year rate. One expects that the total return should equal the return of investing in a two-year bond compounded at the two-year rate over two years. For example, let the one-year and two-year interest rates be 6% and 7%, respectively. Then the implied expected one-year rate, one year from now $E(\tilde{r}_{1,2})$, is solved from the following equation:

$$1.06 \times (1 + E(\tilde{r}_{1,2})) = 1.07^2 \text{ or } E(\tilde{r}_{1,2}) = 8.01\%$$

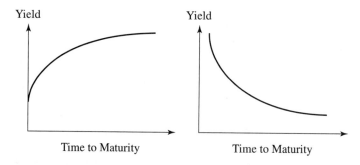

Figure 3.2 Yield curve shapes. Yield curves are upward- or downward-sloping, depending on factors such as the market supply of and demand for funds. Various interpretations have been put forward to explain why the yield curves are upward- or downward-sloping. For example, if the yield curve is downward-sloping, we expect that the spot rates in the future will decrease, according to the expectation hypothesis. However, this is not always the case for the liquidity premium hypothesis.

Liquidity premium hypothesis

The U.S. Treasury bond market has bonds that mature in 30 years. One may argue that most investors have an investment horizon much shorter than 30 years. For investors to hold these bonds, they will demand a higher return for taking the price risks, in case the yield curve changes and they sell the bond at the prevailing (uncertain) price. Therefore, they should be compensated with an additional return, called the *liquidity premium*. In such a case, the yield curve should generally be upward-sloping, reflecting the liquidity premium that increases with maturity.

Preferred habitat hypothesis

Preferred habitat refers to the segment of the yield curve that each investor occupies. Typically, banks tend to hold short-term securities because their deposit accounts and other fundings are short-term. Life insurance companies hold long-term bonds because their liabilities are life policies, which often require insurers to make payments in a fairly distant future, such as 40 years. To ensure that the investments can support these obligations, life insurers often seek to buy long-term bonds. The change in supply and demand of a type of bond within each segment will prompt the yield curve to change its shape if there is a preferred habitat effect.

3.5   The Bond Model

The market becomes efficient because market participants trade in a way which assures that the prices fully reflect the underlying value. The arbitrage mechanism is particularly important in this trading process to assure market efficiency.

Short selling is part of the arbitrage mechanism. When a security is underpriced, investors will buy the security. The buy orders will continue until the price rises to the level at which the security is no longer underpriced. When a security is underpriced, we say that it is cheap; if it is overpriced, it is rich. When a security is rich, investors will sell the security. But the investor who is aware that the security is rich may not own the security to sell. Short selling allows such an investor to make use of his private information. The security can first be borrowed, with the investor being obligated to return it over a time horizon. After borrowing the security, the investor sells it in the market and reinvests the proceeds. If the investor is correct about the security's price movement, and the price falls within this time horizon, then he can buy back the security at a lower price. The security is returned, and the profit is the difference between the sold price and the buy price.

Arbitrage opportunity occurs in a situation where two or more identical securities are priced differently. Then the investor will buy the cheap security and sell short the rich security as much as possible. The trade does not require capital, since the investment in the cheap security is always equal to the proceeds from the short selling net of the arbitrage profits. Arbitrage trade therefore ensures that two identical securities have the same price. The arbitrage profit is risk-free. Furthermore, the arbitrage depends only on the relative values of two securities, and not on their value relative to the true investment value. A consequence of the availability of the arbitrage mechanism is the law of one price.

Figure 3.3 The relationship between no arbitrage and law of one price. No arbitrage opportunity is represented by the phrase "no free lunch." The law of one price means that the same price will be assigned to the same securities. The law of one price does not imply no arbitrage opportunity. For example, assume that the price of two identical stocks is −$10. Since we assigned the same price to two identical securities, the law of one price clearly holds. However, since the price is negative, we have an arbitrage opportunity. In this case, we would hold the stock (since we are paid to hold it) and wait to profit from the captial gains on it since there is limited liability on the firm (and hence the stock).

The *law of one price* states that if two securities have the same cash flows, they should have the same price. More to the point, if the law of one price does not hold, there will be an arbitrage opportunity, which cannot exist in an efficient capital market. The law of one price should hold in an efficient capital market. (See figure 3.3.)

Model Assumptions

We assume that the bond market is *complete* by asserting that it has default-free discount bonds traded at all maturities. A discount bond with maturity T is a bond that pays $1.00 at time T. The bond market is complete because under this assumption any default-free, fixed-income security is a portfolio of discount bonds that are traded in the market.

Let $P(T)$ be the price of a discount bond with maturity T years with $1.00 principal. $P(T)$ as a function of maturity T is called a discount function. For example, the prices of the STRIPS bonds divided by 100 in the Treasury bond market form a discount function. The prices of the bullet payment (single payment without coupons) swaps can be used as a discount function for the same reason the the STRIPS prices are used for the spot curve. The bullet payments enable an investor to identify the time value of money.

We define the yield $r_{0,T}$ to be

$$P(T) = \frac{1}{(1 + r_{0,T})^T} \qquad (3.5)$$

where $r_{0,T}$ is a function of T and is called the spot (yield) curve based on annual compounding.

Let us assume that the law of one price holds. If we can estimate the discount function at any moment, then given any cash flow, we can determine its present value by viewing the cash flow as a portfolio of payments. The present value of each payment can be calculated because we know the present value of $1.00 and that present value is the discount factor. Now, according to the law of one price, the present value of the cash flow is simply the sum of the present values of all the payments. As a result, we can replicate a portfolio of zero-coupon bonds such that the bond portfolio has the same cash flow as the bond. The bond price must therefore be equal to the value of the portfolio. (See figure 3.4.)

$$Price = \frac{coupon}{2} \times P(0.5) + \frac{coupon}{2} \times P(1) + \cdots + (\frac{coupon}{2} + principal) \times P(T) \ (3.6)$$

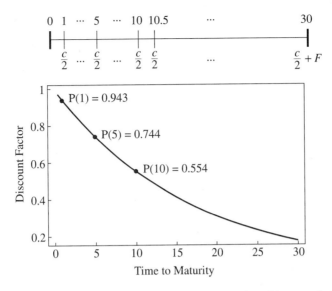

Figure 3.4 Bond pricing. Since the bond price is the present value of future cash flow, we need a discount function and future cash flow of the bond to calculate the price. The numbers above and below the time line in the upper diagram represent the time and the corresponding cash flow, respectively. The discount function indicates the time value of money. The bond price is the sum of cash flows discounted by the corresponding discount function.

where $P(i)$ is the discount function and i denotes the time to the payment.

The above discussion can be summarized by the bond model shown below. Suppose a bond has coupon and principal payments $CF(i)$ every year i until maturity year T. Then the value of the bond is

The Bond Model $$B = \sum_{i=1}^{T} P(i) \times CF(i)$$ (3.7)

The discount function is the set of present-value discount factors inferred from the capital market by observing the traded prices of the discount bonds. These factors measure the time value of money in the capital market and can be used as benchmark values for other fixed-income securities. The time value of money can be represented by the discount function or by the spot yield curve.

Let us take a numerical example. Consider the following zero-coupon bonds.

Price	Maturity (years)	Yield to maturity	Discount factor
90	1	0.1111	0.9
80	2	0.118	0.8
70	3	0.1262	0.7

Suppose we have a bond maturing in three years with coupon rate of 10 percent. Can we calculate the price?

The cash flow for each year is shown below.

Term	1	2	3
Coupon	10	10	10
Principal			100
Cash flow	10	10	110

The price, by the law of one price, is

$$Price(P) = 10 \times 0.9 + 10 \times 0.8 + 110 \times 0.7$$

$$= 94 \qquad (3.8)$$

If a bond is trading below the fair value, we can buy and then resell it as three separate zero-coupon bonds. If the bond is trading above the fair price, we can buy the zero-coupon bonds, repackage them, and sell them on the coupon bond market. This method assumes that the law of one price holds.

The law of one price used in equation (3.8) can be explained quite intuitively. Suppose that we walk into a grocery store and note that apples are 50 cents each, oranges are 40 cents each, and mangoes are a dollar each. Later, we see a fruit basket with five apples, six oranges, and seven mangoes. What would be a guess for the price of the fruit basket? An educated guess would be $11.90 ($= 0.5 \times 5 + 0.4 \times 6 + 1.0 \times 7$). Every day the STRIPS market determines the price of $1.00 for each maturity date. Therefore, if we have a stream of future promised payments, we can use the market prices from the STRIPS market to determine the value of the payments, just as we used the prices of the fruit in the grocery store. Of course, thus far we are assuming that the payments have the creditworthiness of the U.S. government. (We will deal with the pricing of credit risk in chapter 8.)

3.6   Forward Prices and Forward Rates

Bond markets are often called cash markets because investors buy the bonds at the time of the transaction. By way of contrast, a forward or futures bond market determines the bond price at a future delivery.

Futures and Forward Contracts

Interest rate futures and *forward contracts* are financial contracts similar to those for equity indices. Interest rate futures are traded on the exchange that ensures the marking to market mechanism. Interest rate forwards are traded in the over-the-counter markets without any marking to market. The interest rate futures' and forwards' underlying assets are interest rate sensitive. Examples of exchange-traded interest rate futures are Treasury bond futures, Treasury note futures (five-year and two-year Treasury note futures), and Eurodollar futures.

Unlike the index futures, bond futures have deliverable assets: the corresponding bonds. Since the market needs to assure that there is liquidity in the market, the seller of a futures contract can deliver any bond in the deliverable basket of bonds. The basket is determined by the futures exchange, through defining the bonds to be included in the basket.

Futures and forward contracts are not priced in the same way because of the daily marking to market in a futures contract. When there is money exchanged at the end of each day, the cash has to be reinvested, and this reinvestment is subject to uncertain interest rate levels. However, a forward contract does not necessarily have any money change hands during the life of the contract. For this reason, it is valued differently, but typically the differences in prices are quite small relative to the price risks.

A forward contract of a bond is the agreement to deliver a bond with time to maturity T at a future date T^* (the termination date) at a price stated in the agreement. Note that when we "buy" a forward contract, there is no exchange of money at the time of the agreement. Only at the termination date there is an exchange where the buyer pays the agreed-upon price (the forward price) and receives the T time to maturity bond. This exchange will not take place even when there is a significant change in market interest rate during this period before the termination date.

Given the forward price, we can calculate the yield of the bond. Suppose we buy a $1.00 T^*-year bond. At maturity T^*, we will receive the principal and interest. If we also have a forward contract that requires us to buy the T-year bond for which the maturity date of the contract is T^*, then at year $T^* + T$, we will receive the total of the interest and principal reinvested at the forward rate. The main point is that by holding a T^*-year bond and a T-year forward contract with a delivery date at year T^*, we can assure a fixed return, which has to be the return of the $T^* + T$ year bond. (See table 3.2.)

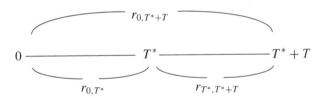

In other words, the law of one price suggests that if we know the yields of $T^* + T$ year and T^* year bonds, we can determine the yield of the forward contract (the *forward rate*.) Therefore, given the spot curve, we can determine the forward rate, the interest rate that we will receive on the forward contract. Now if we assume that there is only one possible way for the yield curve to move in the future (that there is no uncertainty), then the yield curve must move according to the forward curve. In that sense, the forward

Table 3.2 Forward contract pricing model

Time	0	T^*	$T^* + T$
Holding a T^*-year bond	$-P(T^*)$	$coupon + principal =$ $P(T^*)(1 + r_{0,T^*})^{T^*}$	
Holding a T-year forward contract with a delivery date at year T^*		$-(coupon + principal)$	$(coupon + principal)$ $\cdot (1 + r_{T^*,T^*+T})^T$
Cash Flow	$-P(T^*)$	0	$P(T^*)(1 + r_{0,T^*})^{T^*}$ $\cdot (1 + r_{T^*,T^*+T})^T$

The cash flow at time $T^* + T$ is $P(T^*)(1 + r_{0,T^*})^{T^*}(1 + r_{T^*,T^*+T})^T = P(T^*)(1 + r_{0,T^*+T})^{T^*+T}$ by no arbitrage condition.

rate is the "expected rate" from the market. The relationship between the forward rate and the spot rate is often called the expectation hypothesis.

The above discussion is summarized by the forward contract pricing model.

$$P(T^* + T) = P(T^*)F(T^*, T) \tag{3.9}$$

$F(T^*, T)$ is the forward price, with a delivery date at time T^*, delivering a bond with face value 1 and time to maturity T. Equation (3.9) is important because it shows that the discount function (or the spot yield curve) can determine the forward price. This observation will be used extensively in chapter 5, in deriving interest rate models.

The above equation can be expressed as in terms of rates:

$$\frac{1}{(1 + r_{0,T^*+T})^{T^*+T}} = \frac{1}{(1 + r_{0,T^*})^{T^*}} \times \frac{1}{(1 + r_{T^*,T^*+T})^{T}} \tag{3.10}$$

where r_{T^*,T^*+T} is the forward rate with a delivery date at time T^*.

A specific forward rate with special importance is the one-period forward rate, r_{T^*,T^*+1}. This is the one-period forward rate T^* periods from the present. Given these relationships, we have the following results that are useful in fixed-income analytics.

$$\frac{1}{(1 + r_{0,T^*+1})^{T^*+1}} = \frac{1}{(1 + r_{0,T^*})^{T^*}} \times \frac{1}{(1 + r_{T^*,T^*+1})} \tag{3.11}$$

$$1 + r_{T^*,T^*+1} = \frac{(1 + r_{0,T^*+1})^{T^*+1}}{(1 + r_{0,T^*})^{T^*}} = (\frac{1 + r_{0,T^*+1}}{1 + r_{0,T^*}})^{T^*}(1 + r_{0,T^*+1})$$

$$r_{0,T^*+1} > r_{0,T^*} \Leftrightarrow r_{T^*,T^*+1} > r_{0,T^*+1}$$

$$r_{0,T^*+1} < r_{0,T^*} \Leftrightarrow r_{T^*,T^*+1} < r_{0,T^*+1}$$

That is, if the spot curve is upward-sloping, then the one-period forward rate exceeds the yield of the bond with maturity $T^* + 1$. Conversely, if the spot curve is downward-sloping, then the one-period forward rate is lower than the yield of the bond with maturity $T^* + 1$.

Forward rates and spot rates are related. For a flat spot curve, the one-period forward rate is constant and is the same as the spot rate. The forward rate rises for an upward-sloping spot curve and the forward rate falls for a downward-sloping spot curve. (See figure 3.5.)

Note that the one-period forward rate with a delivery date at time 1 is in fact

$$r_{1,2} = \frac{(1 + r_{0,2})^2}{(1 + r_{0,1})} - 1 \tag{3.12}$$

Here, $r_{1,2}$ is the one-period forward rate with a delivery date at time 1; $r_{0,2}$ is the two-year rate (or yield of the two-period bond); and $r_{0,1}$ is the one-year rate.

Thus, if equation (3.4) holds, then the forward rate (which is simply calculated from the observed yield curve) equals the expected future spot rate. When the expected future one-period spot rate equals the forward rate, we say that the *local expectation hypothesis* holds. Unfortunately, this hypothesis defies simple testing. There is no easy way to ask the market participants what they think the future spot rates will be and compare their

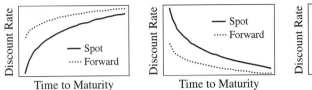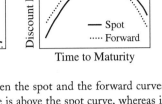

Figure 3.5 Forward and spot rates. The relationship between the spot and the forward curves is that if the spot curve is upward-sloping, the forward curve is above the spot curve, whereas if the spot curve is downward-sloping, the forward curve is below the spot curve. Therefore, the forward curve crosses from above the highest point of the spot curve according to the rightmost panel. By analogy, the spot rate could be treated as if it were an average batting average and the forward rate as if it were a marginal batting average. (The marginal batting average is a batting average in the current game.) If the marginal batting average is larger than the average batting average, the average batting average including the current game will be rising, and vice versa.

expected numbers with the forward rates. But the hypothesis does provide us with some guidelines to why the yield curve moves.

If the expectation hypothesis is true, then an upward-sloping yield curve can be interpreted as predicting rising interest rates and the future yield curve can be specified exactly by the forward curve. Similarly, the downward-sloping curve would predict falling interest rates. To the extent that the forward curve does predict the future yield curve, the expected return of a bond over a time horizon must be the same as the return of the risk-free bond over that period. The movement of this short-term rate is therefore dependent on the shape of the yield curve.

We assume the following upward-sloping yield curve for illustration purposes. We can determine the forward yield curve according to equation (3.12).

Maturity (T)	1	2	3
Spot rate (%)	$r_{0,1} = 8\%$	$r_{0,2} = 9\%$	$r_{0,3} = 10\%$
Forward rate	$r_{1,2} = 10.01\%$	$r_{1,3} = 11.01\%$	N/A
Forward rate	$r_{2,3} = 12.03\%$	N/A	N/A

$$r_{1,2} = \frac{(1 + r_{0,2})^2}{(1 + r_{0,1})} - 1 = \frac{(1.09)^2}{1.08} - 1 \cong 10.01\%$$

$$r_{1,3} = \sqrt{\frac{(1 + r_{0,3})^3}{(1 + r_{0,1})}} - 1 = \sqrt{\frac{(1.1)^3}{(1.08)}} - 1 \cong 11.01\%$$

$$r_{2,3} = \frac{(1 + r_{0,3})^3}{(1 + r_{0,2})^2} - 1 = \frac{(1.1)^3}{(1.09)^2} - 1 \cong 12.03\%$$

Specifically, under the expectation hypothesis, the yield curve at time 1 will be the forward yield curve implied by the current yield curve. The return on each bond for the one-year holding period is 8%. The implied forward one-year rate (i.e., $r_{1,2} = 10.01\%$) is the one-year spot rate at year 1.

The return of the one-year zero-coupon bond over one year is

$$\left(100 \div \frac{100}{1+r_{0,1}}\right) - 1 = \left(100 \div \frac{100}{1+0.08}\right) - 1 = 8\%$$

The return of the two-year zero-coupon bond over one year is

$$\left(\frac{100}{1+r_{1,2}} \div \frac{100}{(1+r_{0,2})^2}\right) - 1 = \left(\frac{100}{1+0.1001} \div \frac{100}{(1+0.09)^2}\right) - 1 = 8\%$$

The return of the three-year zero-coupon bond over one year is

$$\left(\frac{100}{(1+r_{1,3})^2} \div \frac{100}{(1+r_{0,3})^3}\right) - 1 = \left(\frac{100}{(1+0.1101)^2} \div \frac{100}{(1+0.1)^3}\right) - 1 = 8\%$$

This numerical example shows that the return of a bond on the yield curve over one year is always the one-year rate (the risk-free rate over the year) if the forward curve prevails at the end of the first period.

However, if the spot rate curve at year 1 is different from the forward curve, the return on each bond for the one-year holding period is not 8%. To show that the return over the one-year holding period is not 8%, we assume that the spot rate curve at year 1 is a horizontal yield curve at 9.5%. Then the return of a one-year zero-coupon bond over one year is

$$\left(100 \div \frac{100}{1+0.08}\right) - 1 = 8\%$$

The return of a two-year zero-coupon bond over one year is

$$\left(\frac{100}{1+0.095} \div \frac{100}{(1+0.09)^2}\right) - 1 \cong 8.5\%$$

The return of a three-year zero-coupon bond over one year is

$$\left(\frac{100}{(1+0.095)^2} \div \frac{100}{(1+0.1)^3}\right) - 1 \cong 11.01\%$$

The returns of the two-year and the three-year zero-coupon bonds are different from the one-period risk-free interest rate of 8%.

Forward rate movement

Let us consider a money market forward contract expiring at time T^*. A one-month Eurodollar forward contract is an example when it agrees on the price of a one-month discount Eurodollar payment for a forward delivery. Suppose, at time 0, we have a particular shape of a yield curve. We all agree on this for the next month. There is no uncertainty. When the yield curve moves according to the market anticipation, this forward rate should not move at all. If today we all believe that the one-month borrowing rate will be 10% for the year 2005 and one year later, if there is no new information (no uncertainty), then there is no reason for the forward rate to change. It will still be 10%.

More formally, let us denote the discount curve as $P(T)$. Let the forward contract price that delivers a T-year maturity bond at time T^* be denoted by $F(T^*, T)$[2].

$$F(T^*, T) = \frac{P(T^* + T)}{P(T^*)} \tag{3.13}$$

Now suppose that after time t, the new discount function is the same as the forward discount function implied by today's discount function.

$$P^*(T) = \frac{P(t + T)}{P(t)} \tag{3.13a}$$

Further suppose that after time t, the time to expiration of the contract is now $(T^* - t)$, and therefore the forward contract price at time t is $F^*(t, T^*, T)$. By equation (3.13), we can rewrite the equation as

$$F^*(t, T^*, T) = \frac{P^*(T^* + T - t)}{P^*(T^* - t)}$$

By using equation (3.13a) to relate P^* to P, we can derive

$$F^*(t, T^*, T) = \frac{P^*(T^* + T - t)}{P^*(T^* - t)}$$
$$= \frac{P(t + T^* + T - t)}{P(t)} \bigg/ \frac{P(t + T^* - t)}{P(t)} = \frac{P(T^* + T)}{P(T^*)}$$

But by the definition of the forward price, we have

$$\frac{P(T^* + T)}{P(T^*)} = F(T^*, T)$$

Therefore, we have $F^* = F$. That means the forward contract price remains unchanged as long as the prevailing yield curve is the forward curve. Therefore, a change of the forward price is not the result of a change in the spot curve, but rather the deviation of the spot curve from the forward curve.

The following numerical example is offered as illustration. Consider a flat yield curve where the interest rate is 6%. The discount factors for the one-year, two-year, and three-year terms are 0.9433, 0.8899, and 0.8396, respectively. Therefore the forward contract price that delivers the one-year maturity bond at year 2 is 0.9433 (= 0.8396/0.8899) by equation (3.13). Here T^* is 2 and T is 1. Suppose the future discount function at year 1 is the same as the forward discount function implied by today's discount function (equation [3.13a]). The time elapsed, t, is 1. The forward discount function at year 1, which is implied by today's discount function, is given by the one-year discount factor, 0.9433 (= 0.8899/0.9433) and the two-year discount factor, 0.8899 (= 0.8396/0.9433). Given this forward discount function, the one-year forward contract is 0.9433 (= 0.8899/0.9433), and therefore the one-year forward contract price has not changed over the first period, as long as the prevailing discount function is the forward discount function.

3.7   Bond Analysis

Cheap/Rich Analysis

The bond model provides a systematic approach to analyze values of Treasury securities. For simplicity, we will ignore the TIPS and callable Treasury bonds, so that the securities that we will use are Treasury securities with simple cash flows. A simplified method can be described as follows. Consider all the STRIPS bond closing prices on a particular day, the evaluation date, and order them according to their maturities.

Maturity	U.S. STRIPS Type	Bid Price
Aug 02	ci	99 24/32
Aug 02	np	99 23/32
⋮	⋮	⋮
Nov 02	ci	99 14/32
Nov 11	ci	61 02/32

(ci indicates that the bond is stripped from the coupons, and np indicates that the bond is stripped from the principal.) The maturities of the STRIPS bonds extend to 2011.

The observed discount function is specified by the bid prices divided by 100. One can use the midmarket prices, depending on the purpose of the analysis. For marking to market of a trading book, the bid prices are often used to represent the prices of selling the positions.

We can apply a standard statistical curve-fitting methodology to represent the observed discount function. To illustrate, we can specify the discount function to be a polynomial:

$$P(T) = a + bT + cT^2 + dT^3 \qquad (3.14)$$

where T is the maturity. We can now fit the polynomial $P(T)$ to the observed discount function. Specifically, we initially use $a = b = c = d = 1$ in equation (3.14) and determine the theoretical STRIPS prices for each maturity. Let the pricing error ε_i be the observed price net of the theoretical price for each bond i. Consider a penalty function

$$F(a, b, c, d) = \sum \varepsilon_i^2$$

Now we use a nonlinear optimal search algorithm to determine a set of coefficients $a, b, c,$ and d, such that the penalty function is minimized. That is, we search for a discount function that best fits the observed spot prices, assigning the same weight to each bond in the fitting process. This optimal set of coefficients determines the theoretical discount function.

In practice, alternative functions can be used for different purposes. There are many functional forms that can be used to fit the observed data, and this subject is treated in most numerical analysis textbooks. One common function is the cubic spline function. A cubic spline function is defined by a set of knot points t_i—say the key rate terms, one, two, three, five, seven, and ten years. Then the *cubic spline function* is defined as

$$P(t) = 1 + at + bt^2 + ct^3 + a_1 \max\left[(t - t_1)^3, 0\right]$$
$$+ a_2 \max\left[(t - t_2)^3, 0\right] + \cdots + a_n \max\left[(t - t_n)^3, 0\right]$$

where a, b, c, $a_i (i = 1, \cdots, n)$ are constants to be estimated. The advantage of the cubic function is its flexibility to take on any shape. The choice of the number of knot points depends on the trade-off between attaining a low penalty function value and a better control of the shape of the yield curve. A larger number of knot points may lead to a better fit of the data but also to an unappealing shape of the theoretical spot curve. Typically, five knot points may be appropriate.

Any Treasury bonds or notes can be represented by the cash flow, and the bond model, along with the fitted discount function, can determine a theoretical bond price. The observed bond price net of the theoretical bond price is called the *cheap/rich value*. For example, when a bond's observed price is 101, while using the bond model determines the price to be 102, we say that the bond is trading "cheap" by $1.00. If the same bond has an observed price of 104, then we say that the bond is trading rich. To the extent that the bond model is correct, one would seek to sell the rich bond and buy the cheap bond.

The fitted discount function enables us to compare the value of the bond with other bonds of similar marketability and creditworthiness. Cheap/rich analysis is a useful way to evaluate the value of a bond. It is important to note that the discount function is estimated from the STRIPS bond market. If a bond is rich, that means, in principle, that its quoted price is higher than the portfolio of STRIPS bonds that have similar cash flows. Conversely, if a bond is cheap, the quoted price is lower than the value of a portfolio of STRIPS bonds with a similar cash flow. In principle, the arbitrage mechanism would keep the cheap/rich values small; therefore the fitted function can approximate the discount function well, and the theoretical prices can represent the market prices well.

Spot Yield Curve, Par Yield Curve, and Nominal Yield Curve

Now we can relate the par yield curve and the spot curve. More generally, we can think of the par curve as the relationship of the coupon rate of a par bond with maturity T to its maturity. Then we note that we can derive a par curve from the spot yield curve, or vice versa. Let $P(i)$ be the discount function, the present value of $1.00 with maturity t, derived from the spot yield curve, and let *coupon(t)* be the coupon payment of a par bond with maturity t and $1.00 par. Then, by the bond model, we have

$$1 = (coupon(1) + 1)P(1)$$

$$1 = coupon(2)P(1) + (coupon(2) + 1)P(2)$$

$$1 = coupon(3)P(1) + coupon(3)P(2) + (coupon(3) + 1)P(3)$$

The above system of equations can be extended analogously to any number of coupon periods. This system of equations shows that given the numbers $P(i)$, we can derive *coupon(i)* and vice versa. This method is often called bootstrapping.

Given the observed Treasury bill, note, and bond prices, we can use a similar method to determine the underlying spot yield curve. Specifically, if we rank all the Treasury securities by their maturities, we can write the following system of equations:

$$price(1) = (coupon(1) + 1)P(1)$$

$$price(2) = coupon(2)P(1) + (coupon(2) + 1)P(2)$$

$$price(3) = coupon(3)P(1) + coupon(3)P(2) + (coupon(3) + 1)P(3)$$

where $price(i)$ is the observed invoice prices of the bonds. In principle, given the above equations and the inputs of $coupon(i)$ and $price(i)$, we can solve for $P(i)$. However, in practice, the coupon dates of the bonds are not the same. The coupons are not all paid in June and December, for example. But dealing with this problem is quite straightforward. We can assume that $P(i)$ has a functional form, such as a polynomial or a cubic spline, as described above, and we can use the above system of equations to estimate the coefficients of the functions, employing an optimal search routine. This estimated discount function (and hence the yield curve) is sometimes called the *implied spot curve*. This is the curve that represents the time value of money estimated from all the coupon issues of the Treasury markets as opposed to observed from the traded prices of the STRIPS market.

Considering that the Treasury markets are quite efficient, the estimated spot yield curves and the observed STRIPS curve should be quite similar, though their differences may be important for trading purposes.

Durations

Perhaps the most commonly used analytical measure for bonds is the duration. The terminology "duration" is somewhat misleading and is a source of confusion in many instances. Duration, sometimes called effective duration, is defined as the price sensitivity of a bond to a parallel shift of the spot curve, where the spot yield is typically assumed to be semiannual compounding. The (*effective*) duration is defined as

$$\frac{\Delta P}{P} = -effective\ duration \times \Delta\ spot\ yield \tag{3.15}$$

For a default-free zero-coupon bond, the duration is approximately the same as the maturity of the zero-coupon bond. For example, for a zero-coupon bond with maturity T, the price P is given by

$$P = \frac{1}{(1 + r_{0.5}/2)^{2T}}$$

where $r_{0.5}$ is a semiannually compounding rate.

When we apply equation (3.15) by letting the Δspot yield be a small change in the interest rate $r_{0.5}$, we can derive the duration by differentiating P with respect to $r_{0.5}$ and have

$$Duration = \frac{T}{(1 + r_{0.5}/2)} \tag{3.16}$$

where $r_{0.5}$ can be called the yield of the bond. The term $1 + r_{0.5}/2$ is a modifier that is required to calculate the duration. Duration is the price sensitivity of a bond to the spot yield change. But the spot yield can be specified as an annual compounding yield, a semiannually compounding yield, a monthly, or even a daily compounding yield. Surely, a 1% change of a daily compounding yield has a larger impact on the bond price than a 1% change in the annual compounding yield. $(1 + r_{0.5}/2)$ is used to adjust for a semiannual compounding. In general, the modifier is $1 + r_{1/n}/n$ where n is the number of periods used in one year.

For example, suppose a zero-coupon bond has a maturity of ten years and the semi-annual compounding yield is 6%. The duration is 9.708 $(= 10/(1.03))$. The price of the bond is $100/(1 + r_{0.5}/2)^{20}$. For a special case, cash has zero duration, and by convention the price of the cash is 100.

	Zero-coupon Bond	Cash
Maturity (years)	10	0
Spot yield (semiannual compounding)	6%	—
Price	55.36	100
Duration	9.708	0

That means that when the spot yield curve falls 1% (or equivalently stated, by convention, drops 100 basis points) in a parallel fashion, the bond price will rise 9.708%. The change of the interest rate level does not affect the cash. That is, the cash has zero duration.

The duration measure has a very convenient property. The duration of a portfolio is the weighted average durations of each bond, where the weights are defined as the proportion of the bond market value to the portfolio market value. That is,

$$Duration_P = \sum_i \left(\frac{B_i}{P} \right) Duration_i \qquad (3.17)$$

where $Duration_P$ and $Duration_i$ are the durations of the portfolio and bond i, respectively. B_i is the market value of the bond position and P is the portfolio value, such that the sum of B_i is the portfolio value P.

Continuing the above numerical example, if the portfolio has $10 million in bonds and $20 million in cash, then the portfolio value is $30 million and the duration is 3.236 years (9.708/3).

We can think of any bond with specified cash flows as a portfolio of zero-coupon bonds. Following the above argument, the duration of the bond is very close to the weighted average life of the bond. The weighted average life of a bond is called the *Macauley duration*. This figure is very helpful in providing insight into bond behavior. For example, for a ten-year coupon bond with an average life of six years, a 1 percentage point shift upward in the interest rate will lead to an approximately 6% drop in value. However, we must recognize the limitation of this link between the life of a bond and its duration. The link is true for bonds without embedded options. We will discuss the duration measure for option-embedded bonds in chapter 6.

What does the duration mean for a bond with no embedded options? Suppose we have a bond with two payments: $100 in one year and $100 in five years. And suppose that the duration of the bond is 2.8 years. Suppose the interest rates fall instantaneously in a parallel fashion by 1 percentage point and remain constant for the subsequent years. The first $100 will have to be reinvested at a lower market rate (lowered by 1%), while the second $100 will have a higher present value because of the lower interest rate. The duration is like a fulcrum balancing the capital gains from the five-year payment and loss of reinvestment of the one-year payment. The duration is the break-even point in the sense that after 2.8 years, when we liquidate the bond position, the unrealized capital gains from the five-year payment exactly offset the loss of the reinvestment interest payment of the one-year payment. Duration is calculated to find this point in time. If the investment horizon of the investor is 2.8 years, then this shift of interest rates does not affect his portfolio value when he liquidates the position.

Duration is a useful measure for managing the interest rate risks of an investment portfolio. For swaps and bond trading, where the positions can have positive or negative value, a measure of proportional change in the portfolio value or a swap value has little meaning. For those purposes, dollar duration is used. Dollar duration is defined to measure the dollar change in value with a parallel shift of the spot yield curve. In this case, one can measure the dollar duration of any trading position. The position is hedged when the dollar duration is 0 and the value is unchanged with a small change in interest rates. Dollar duration is related to duration in a simple manner for a bond or an option.

$$\$ \, Duration = Duration \times Value \tag{3.18}$$

Dollar duration is measured in dollars and is the value sensitivity of the bond portfolio to the yield curve. By market convention, a similar measure of risk is also used, called the *price value of a basis point* or PV 01. The "01" refers to a 1 basis point shift of the yield curve, and value 01 is the change in the bond price or portfolio value by 1 basis point shift of the yield curve. Thus dollar duration and value 01 are related by

$$Value \; 01 = \$ \, Duration \times 0.0001 \tag{3.19}$$

Continuing the above numerical example:

	$ Duration
Cash	0
Bond position	$97.08 million
Portfolio	$97.08 million
PV 01	$9,708

Note that the bond position and the portfolio have the same dollar durations. This is because the cash does not contribute any price risk to changes in the interest rates.

Modified duration

Another duration measure is the *modified duration*. As we have discussed, the price and the yield to maturity of a bond are mathematically related. Yield to maturity is the internal rate of return of a bond's cash flows. The price has the same informational content as the yield. They are just two ways of expressing the value of a bond. The price is the present value of the bond's cash flows. The yield is the return of the bond over its life. Modified duration is the price sensitivity to the changes in the yield to maturity.

$$\frac{\Delta P}{P} = -modified\ duration \times \Delta\ yield\ to\ maturity \qquad (3.20)$$

Often we want to know a small change of price in relation to a small change of yield. Maybe the investor is interested in knowing how the price quote may be affected by a small change in the yield. Modified duration relates the small change of the yield to maturity to the change in the bond price. For example, a bond has a modified duration of five years. We are told that the yield to maturity of the bond is 7%. If the yield to maturity increases to 8%, then the bond price will fall by 5%.

The mathematical relationship can be derived from the price yield formula. For a bond without any embedded options, the formula is similar to that of the weighted average life of the bond where the weights are the present value of the payments discounted at the yield.

Key rate duration

The yield curve does not always make parallel shifts, whereby each interest rate moves by x basis points along the entire yield curve. This is the underlying assumption of the use of the effective duration to measure the risk of a bond. In reality, the yield curve makes many types of movements. A measure of the price sensitivity to the yield curve risk, which is the impact of the uncertain yield curve movement on the price of the bond, is called the key rate duration. The key rate duration is the proportional change in the bond price in response to a small change in the key rate. The dollar key rate duration is defined as the dollar change in value with a small shift of the key rate.

A spot yield curve is a continuous function of the maturity. We need to represent the movement of this yield curve by a finite set of points. One approach is to use the terms of the on-the-run issues of the Treasury markets. As explained before, the on-the-run bond or note issues are the most watched securities in representing the spot yield curve movements. They are three-month, six-month, 12-month, two-year, three-year, five-year, seven-year, and ten-year. The Treasury recently stopped issuing 30-year bonds. To measure the yield curve sensitivity, we should add 20- and 30-year rates. If we can identify bond price sensitivities to these key rate movements, we in principle can capture the price risk of the bonds.

Using this observation, we can now define an ith key rate shift to be a rise of 10 basis points at the ith key rate. Now we need to describe the changes of the other interest rates, given the change of one key rate. We assume that the size of the shift decreases linearly on both sides of the ith key rate, reaching 0 at the $(i - 1)$th and $(i + 1)$th key terms. (See figure 3.6.)

Figure 3.6 illustrates the upward shift of key rates at one-year, and five-year terms and a downward shift at the 30-year term; there is no shift in the rest of the terms.

Then the ith *key rate duration*, $KRD(i)$ is defined as

$$\frac{\Delta P}{P} = -KRD(i) \cdot \Delta r(i) \qquad (3.21)$$

where the ith key rate shift is represented by $\Delta r(i)$.

One useful property of the key rate duration is that the sum of key rate durations is the duration. We can therefore think of key rate durations as a decomposition of a duration number. More generally, we can add any subset of the key rate durations as a

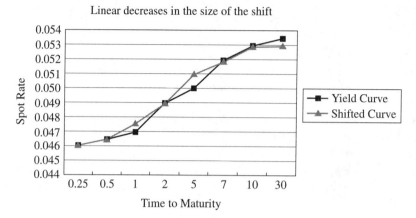

Figure 3.6 Yield curve and Shifted curve. This illustrates the upward shifts of key rates at year 1 and year 5. In addition to the upward shifts at year 1 and year 5, the figure also shows a downward shift at the 30-year term. However, there are no shifts on the 0.25, 0.5, 2, 7, and 10-year terms. If an upward or a downward shift occurs at a certain term, we draw a straight line connecting the upward or downward shift point to the adjacent terms to denote how the adjacent rates will be changed due to the shift.

measure of interest rate risk to a particular segment of the yield curve. For example, we can use the sum of the first three key rate durations to measure a bond's sensitivity to the short-term segment of the yield curve. Another useful property of key rate duration is that the key rate duration of a portfolio of bonds and options is the weighted average of the key rate durations of all the securities in the portfolio weighted by the proportion of the value of the bond or option position in the portfolio.

Consider a zero-coupon bond with T year maturity. The bond price is not affected by any change in the key rates except those that lead to a change in the spot curve at the T year term. This is somewhat nonintuitive at first glance. Suppose an investor is holding a long-term zero-coupon bond, and the short-term interest rates have just shifted. The bond price should not be affected, since the bond pricing model shows that the bond price is determined by discounting the bond's cash flows at the long-term interest rates rather than the short-term interest rate. For clarity, assume that the T year term is a key rate. Then the key rate durations are all 0 except for the Tth year key rate. The key rate duration of this key rate is the duration of the bond $T/(1 + r_{0,T})$, where $r_{0,T}$ is the Tth year spot rate. The key rate duration is the same as the duration in this case because the sum of key rate durations must equal the duration number.

For a leveraged position, where the position involves shorting or borrowing of securities, such as in swaps, the value of the position may not be positive and can at times have a zero or negative value. In such a case the measure of exposure is the *dollar key rate duration* $\$KRD(i)$, as defined by

$$\Delta P = -\$KRD(i) \cdot \Delta r(i)$$

Present value 01 is defined analogously, as the dollar change in value for 1 basis point change in each key rate.

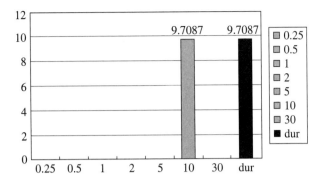

Figure 3.7 Duration and key rate duration of a zero-coupon bond. This shows that the sum of the key rate durations is equal to the duration. The duration of a zero-coupon bond is 9.7087. Its key rate duration is 9.7087 at the 10-year term because there is no cash flow except the 10-year term.

Key rate duration profile refers to the relationship of the key rate durations and the key rates. For example, consider the key rate duration profile of the bond discussed above in figure 3.7.

Convexity

Bond prices do not change proportionally to the shift in the interest rate as specified by the effective duration. As the spot curve falls, a bond value may increase at an accelerated or decelerated rate. Convexity provides a measure of such an acceleration or deceleration to better describe the behavior of the bond price in relation to the changing yield curve. *Convexity* is defined as

$$Convexity = \frac{1}{2}\left(\frac{d^2P}{dr^2}\right)/P \qquad (3.22)$$

where P is the bond price and r is the interest rate. For example, consider a zero-coupon bond with maturity T and a semiannually compounding market yield of $r_{0.5}$. Then

$$P = \frac{1}{(1 + r_{0.5}/2)^{2T}} \qquad (3.23)$$

A straightforward calculation shows that the convexity of such a bond is

$$Convexity = \frac{1}{4} \times \frac{T(2T + 1)}{(1 + r_{0.5}/2)^2} \qquad (3.24)$$

In general, when a bond has embedded options or the yield curve is not flat, both effective duration and convexity do not have simple mathematical expressions like the ones shown above. In practice, both effective duration and convexity are numerically simulated, using a valuation model of a bond.

The estimated convexity value can be given by

$$Convexity = \frac{1}{2} \frac{[P(\Delta) - 2P + P(-\Delta)]}{\Delta^2} \frac{1}{P}$$

where $P(\Delta)$, $P(-\Delta)$ are the bond prices with the spot curve shifted by Δ up and down, respectively.

Given the definition of convexity, it can be shown that the changes of a bond value can be approximated by the duration and convexity as follows:

$$\Delta P = -Duration \cdot P \cdot \Delta r_{0.5} + Convexity \cdot P \cdot (\Delta r_{0.5})^2 \qquad (3.25)$$

The above equation holds even for bonds with embedded options, not just for bonds with fixed cash flows. This relationship of the change in price to the change in interest rates, using duration and convexity, is derived by using a Taylor expansion of P as a function of interest rate r. Using the above numerical example, we have cash with a convexity of 0, a bond position with a convexity of 49.486, and a portfolio with a convexity of 16.49 ($= 49.486 \times 10/30$).

The change in bond price as a function of a parallel shift of interest rates is

$$\Delta P = -9.708 \times 55.36 \Delta r_{0.5} + 49.486 \times 55.36 \Delta r_{0.5}^2$$

For example, if the yield curve shifts 2% or 200 basis points upward, then $\Delta r_{0.5}$ is 0.02, and the change of the bond price is

$$\Delta P = -9.708 \times 55.36 \times 0.02 + 49.486 \times 55.36 \times (0.02)^2 \cong -9.65$$

That means that if the yield curve rises 200 basis points, the bond would drop in price from \$55.36 to \$45.71, as approximated by using duration and convexity.

Performance Profile

Performance profile depicts the value of a bond over a range of instantaneous parallel movements of the interest rate level. The performance profile can clearly depict how the behavior of the bond price changes with the level of interest rates. For a bond with a positive duration, the price will fall as the interest rate increases, and therefore the performance profile of the bond will have a negatively sloped curve. The curvature of the performance profile is related to the convexity of the bond. The higher the convexity of the bond, the higher is the curvature of the performance profile, with an accelerated increase in the price as the interest rate falls.

The performance profile is particularly useful for understanding the interest rate exposure of a bond portfolio position. If the bond portfolio is not sensitive to the interest rate parallel movement, then the performance profile will be horizontal. (See figure 3.8.)

3.8   Applications of the Bond Analytics

In this section, we present two applications using the bond analytics described. One refers to a commonly used bond trading strategy called "barbell trade," and the other is the use of key rate duration to manage an enhanced indexed Treasury portfolio.

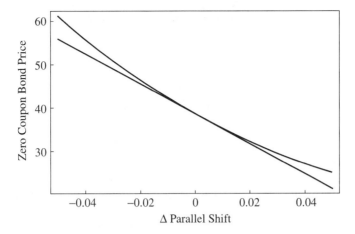

Figure 3.8 Performance profiles of a bond. We plot the prices of a zero-coupon bond against parallel shifts of interest rates from −5% to 5% with an interval of 1 basis point. The face value is $100 and the maturity is 10 years hence. The current yield curve is 10% flat. The blue line is a zero-coupon bond profile and the red line is a tangent line at the no shift point, where the yield is 10%. Since the curve is above the straight line, the bond profile is convex rather than concave. In other words, the appreciating amount of the bond when the rate goes down is larger than the depreciating amount when the rate goes up. In this sense, the more convex a bond is, the more valuable it is, other things being equal.

A Barbell Trade

A *barbell position* refers to buying bond positions with short-term bonds and long-term bonds while selling medium-term bonds such that the net portfolio position is 0. The dollar duration of the barbell position is also 0. The combination of the use of short-term bonds and long-term bonds (hence the name "barbell") leads to a higher convexity in the buy position than in the sell position. The reason that the barbell has a higher convexity will be explained below. As a result, the barbell position leads to positive returns when the yield curve rises or falls in a parallel way.

Assume that the market has a flat yield curve at 6%. Consider an example of a barbell trade: holding a bond position of $100 in a one-year zero-coupon bond and $100 in a five-year zero-coupon bond and shorting $200 in a 2.999-year-zero coupon bond.

	Bond position value	*Maturity*	*Duration*	*Convexity*
A	$100	1	0.9708	0.7069
B	$100	5	4.8543	12.9606
Total	$200	3	2.9125	6.8337
Short-selling	$200	2.999	2.9125	4.9486

The holding portfolio value as a function of parallel shifts of the yield curve is given by

$$\Delta V(holding) = -2.9125 \times 200 \times \Delta r_{0.5} + 6.8337 \times 200 \times \Delta r_{0.5}^2$$

Similarly, the short-selling position value is given by

$$\Delta V\,(short\ selling) = -2.9125 \times 200 \times \Delta r_{0.5} + 4.9486 \times 200 \times \Delta r_{0.5}^2$$

The net position is given by

$$\Delta V = \Delta V\,(holding) - \Delta V\,(short\ selling)$$
$$= 377.02 \Delta r_{0.5}^2$$

For example, if the spot yield curve shifts 100 basis point up or down, then $\Delta r_{0.5} = 0.01$, and the profit is $\Delta V = \$0.0377$.

This description of the barbell trade, according to the above equation, seems to suggest that the bond position can realize profits as long as the yield curve moves up or down. Of course it is not always possible to attain a position where only profitable situations occur. If the medium-term rate falls more relative to the short-term and long-term rates, then the barbell trade will realize a loss.

If we analyze the barbell position, we should find positive dollar key rate durations at the one- and five-year terms and a negative dollar key rate at the 2.999-year term. The dollar key rate durations for the terms are given below.

Year	Dollar key rate duration $\times$ 0.0001 = PV 01
1	$0.9708 \times 100 \times 0.0001 = 0.009708$
2.999	$-2.9125 \times 200 \times 0.0001 = -0.05825$
5	$4.8543 \times 100 \times 0.0001 = 0.04854$
Total	0

Since the net dollar key rate duration is 0, the price of the barbell position is insensitive to the parallel shifts of the spot yield curve. However, for example, a fall of 1 basis point at the 2.999-year rate, while the other rates remain unchanged, would lead to a loss of $0.05825. Indeed, there are many possible yield curve movements that may lead to losses in holding the barbell position. This trade is designed to bet on parallel yield curve movements.

Replicating a Treasury index—passive portfolio management

In bond portfolio management, asset managers may offer a portfolio managed against a Treasury bond index. A *Treasury bond index* is defined as a portfolio constructed from all the Treasury notes and bonds outstanding, subject to some liquidity constraints on each bond issue. Asset managers offer to manage a client investment that will mimic the Treasury index monthly total returns. Such management style is called *passive* because the asset management is not actively seeking to provide high returns for the clients but passively reacting to the performance of the bond index.

Suppose the investment is $100 million. The size of the investment would prohibit the portfolio manager from buying all the Treasury bonds and notes outstanding in proportion to each bond's outstanding amount relative to the total Treasury securities market. Also, given the size of the investment, the transaction costs would be prohibitive.

A commonly used approach to this problem is to choose various characteristics of the index and then determine the value of the Treasury bond position as a proportion of the outstanding amount that has those characteristics. Such characteristics may be the coupon rate range, maturity range, and yield range. The portfolio can then be constructed to replicate the Treasury index by matching the portfolio values to each of the cells. For example, according to the Treasury index, the proportion of bonds that have yields 5%–5.5%, coupon rates 6.0%–6.5%, and maturities of three to five years is 10%. Then the replicating portfolio can be constructed by assigning 10% of the investment to bonds that satisfy the above criteria.

Much of the risk of the Treasury index return is driven by the changing shape and level of the yield curve. Another approach is to use key rate duration. McCoy (1993) uses a portfolio of 12 bonds that match the key rate durations of the Treasury index at the beginning of the month, and continually revises the portfolio at the end of the month. He empirically tests the strategy using historical data from January 1990 to December 1990. The test shows that the average absolute difference in returns was only 2 basis points. He then tests various strategies for enhancing the portfolio returns, including choosing cheap bonds. The return generated by various strategies ranges from 22 basis points to 238 basis points. Of course, we have to note that the test was conducted with observed bond prices; transaction costs have not been properly accounted for. In any case, the test does show that controlling the risk of yield curve movements is important in managing a bond, particularly a Treasury bond, portfolio.

3.9 Law of One Price: An Arbitrage Trade and Fair Value Analysis

My first lesson in applying the law of one price was a rude awakening. By 1986, Wall Street had started paying attention to quantitative research in building financial models. The time is also considered the prehistory of financial engineering because Wall Street had not decided how quantitative research could be used.

That year I was invited by the head of fixed-income research to present a bond valuation methodology to the Treasury bond trading department. In a corner of the trading floor there was a conference room with a long conference table. I sat at one of the table facing the head of the Treasury bond trading department and looking down two rows of traders.

After a polite introduction by the head of fixed-income research, I proceeded to discuss research on Treasury bonds, with the prices they provided me. Applying the yield curve estimation method discussed in this section, together with an analysis of the callable bonds (to be discussed in chapter 8), I dramatically showed that there were arbitrage opportunities for the traders. The long bonds were trading a full 4–5% off the fair price. I demonstrated how the arbitrage profits could be made in a way similar to that described in this chapter. I was pleased with my research.

At the end of the presentation, silence fell. Everyone was waiting for the head of Treasury bond trading to comment and thank me for my excellent effort. He stood up in due course, in front of the screen where my results were displayed. In a dramatic fashion, he stretched out his arm, showing his white sleeves and cuffs. His thumb pointed *down*. In equally dramatic fashion, he sat down and said, "All my traders can price the key bonds within 5 cents [0.05%]." He then dismissed everyone.

I walked out to the elevators with the head of fixed-income research. We were both disappointed, no doubt. As he shook hands with me, he said, "That guy [the head of Treasury bond trading] knows nothing."

The word "arbitrage" has different interpretations, depending on the context. Traders, or more appropriately "market makers," seek arbitrage profits over a short holding period. The market prices to the traders are the prices offered by other traders. The arbitrage trade according to the law of one price often is not an arbitrage at all for traders. The convergence may take weeks, months, or even years, never mind the days that the traders want to wait.

Arbitrage conditions affect the price relationships across selected securities. But precisely how these conditions are held depends on the arbitrage mechanism available to the markets or the structure of the markets. There may be deviations from the arbitrage conditions in the marketplace because of transaction costs or lack of an effective arbitrage mechanism. This deviation is called the *arbitrage band*.

Exploiting the difference of the market price from the theoretical price, taking the arbitrage band into account, is profitable, too. Often such trades are implemented by hedged funds which can have a much longer holding period. The law of one price is ensured not just by traders but also by many market participants. Today, traders and strategists often work closely to exploit these arbitrage opportunities. Trading floors have highly automated, sophisticated Treasury bond pricing systems.

Arbitrage opportunities were interpreted differently by the head of fixed-income research and the head of Treasury bond trading. Little did I know I would be back on the trading floor to prove my view of an arbitrage opportunity within a year by strategizing Treasury bond trading.

3.10 Summary

In contrast to the Capital Asset Pricing model in valuing risky assets, described in chapter 2, the bond model does not require an estimation of β for the bonds. Instead, this approach uses the observed values of the yield curve to value bonds.

A yield curve measures the time value of money required in the capital market. When time value increases, the yield curve rises and bond prices will fall. The price and yield of a bond have an inverse relationship. Since bonds are continually traded, the yield curve will fluctuate in an uncertain fashion over time. However, the movement of the yield curve should be dependent on market expectations. When the interest rate is anticipated to rise, then the long-term yield of bonds should rise.

When bonds are "stripped" into coupons and principal payments and each payment becomes a zero-coupon bond, the market is called the STRIPS market. It was presented in this chapter to provide a constructive method to specify the yield curve. The yield curve that is observed from the STRIPS market is the market-observed spot curve.

To ensure that the market is efficient during the trading process, bond prices need to reflect bonds' underlying value. One market mechanism that is particularly important in this trading process is the arbitrage mechanism. It enables the financial market to maintain the law of one price. If we assume the law of one price, we can derive the bond model, which enables us to value securities in a bond market or swap market. The law of one price allows us to use the discount function (derived from the spot curve) to determine the bond market. If we know the set of present-value discount factors (the discount function) observed during the trading of STRIPS bonds, we can determine the present value of a cash flow by viewing the cash flow as a portfolio of payments. Hence we can value the bonds.

The bond model has broad implications for fixed-income securities valuation. Using the bond model, we can determine the risk measures of bonds, including duration, convexity, and key rate duration. These risk measures enable us to implement bond portfolio strategies and risk management. Further, the bond model enables us to take the observed market time value of money as the starting point and value other bonds relative to the observed yield curve, an approach used widely in fixed-income securities valuation, a subject that will be discussed in chapter 6 of this book.

The bond model is applied extensively in bond trading. Much research has been devoted to developing accurate estimation procedures to determine the underlying spot curve, monitoring the spot curve movements continually in the market, and identifying arbitrage opportunities. Indeed, the bond model, or the estimation of the spot curve, is often viewed as the foundation in building trading valuation models of fixed-income securities and bond portfolio management systems. The following chapters will continue with the discussion of developing valuation models that are based on the bond model described in this chapter.

Appendix A. Taylor Expansion

Taylor expansion plays an important role in understanding the concepts of duration and convexity because they are the first and second derivative terms in the Taylor expansion. The Taylor expansion is concerned with how the function will be approximated in the neighborhood of a certain point. Specifically, we have a function, $f(x)$. We want to approximate the function at $x + \Delta$, which is around a given point, x. According to the Taylor expansion formula, we have the following expression:

$$f(x + \Delta) = f(x) + \frac{1}{1!} \cdot f^1(x) \cdot \Delta + \frac{1}{2!} \cdot f^2(x) \cdot \Delta^2 + \frac{1}{3!}$$

$$\cdot f^3(x) \cdot \Delta^3 + \cdots + \frac{1}{i!} \cdot f^i(x) \cdot \Delta^i + \cdots$$

$$= \sum_{i=0}^{\infty} \frac{1}{i!} \cdot f^i(x) \cdot \Delta^i$$

where $f^i(x)$ is the ith derivative of $f(x)$ with respect to x.

In figure 3.9, given x and $f(x)$, we approximate $f(x + \Delta)$ with $f(x)$ and its derivatives. Since the first derivative can be interpreted as a slope, $f^1(x) \cdot \Delta$ can be added to $f(x)$. We can interpret the second derivative in a similar way. Since we have denoted the first and second derivatives, the combined effect from the higher derivatives will be denoted as the remainder in figure 3.9.

As a numerical example, we assume that $f(x) = x^3 + x^2 + x + 1$ and $x = 1.5$. Furthermore, we approximate the function when $\Delta = 0.5$, which means that $x + \Delta = 2.0$. The values added to $f(1.5)$ due to the first derivative and the second derivative are 5.375 and 1.375, respectively. We still have an error of 0.125 because we have taken care of up to the second derivative. (See figure 3.10.)

$$f(x + \Delta) = f(x) + \frac{1}{1!} \cdot f^1(x) \cdot \Delta + \frac{1}{2!} \cdot f^2(x) \cdot \Delta^2 + R$$

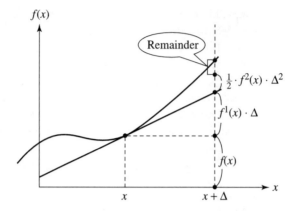

Figure 3.9 Graphical representation of the Taylor approximation.

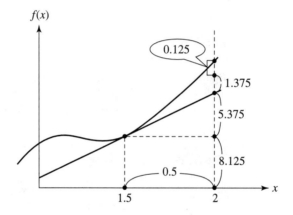

Figure 3.10 Numerical example of the Taylor expansion.

$$f(2) = f(1.5) + \frac{1}{1!} \cdot f^1(1.5) \cdot 0.5 + \frac{1}{2!} \cdot f^2(1.5) \cdot 0.5^2 + R$$

$$15 = 8.125 + 5.375 + 1.375 + 0.125$$

Appendix B. The Derivation of Macaulay Duration and Convexity

We know that the bond price can be represented as

$$B = \sum_{t=1}^{N} \frac{CF_t}{(1 + YTM)^t} = \sum_{t=1}^{N} CF_t \cdot (1 + YTM)^{-t}$$

where B-bond price; CF_t = Cash flow at time t including coupons and principal; YTM = Yield to maturity; N = number of cash flows; t = time.

By applying the Taylor expansion to the bond price, we can obtain:

$$dB \cong \frac{\partial B}{\partial YTM} dYTM + \frac{1}{2} \cdot \frac{\partial^2 B}{\partial YTM^2} dYTM^2$$

$$= -Duration_{Mod} \cdot B \cdot dYTM + Convexity \cdot B \cdot dYTM^2 \qquad (3.26)$$

First, taking the first derivative, multiplying by (B/B) and factoring out the constant $B/(1 + YTM)$, we can derive the duration measure from the first derivative.

$$\frac{\partial B}{\partial YTM} = \sum_{t=1}^{N}(-t \cdot CF_t \cdot (1 + YTM)^{-t-1})$$

$$= \frac{B}{(1 + YTM)} \cdot \frac{\sum_{t=1}^{N}(-t \cdot CF_t/(1 + YTM)^t)}{B} \qquad (3.27)$$

$$= \frac{B}{(1 + YTM)} \cdot (-Duration_{Mac})$$

$$= B \cdot (-Duration_{Mod})$$

where $Duration_{Mac}$ denotes Macaulay Duration; $Duration_{Mod}$ denotes Modified Duration; $Duration_{Mod} = \frac{Duration_{Mac}}{1+YTM}$.

Second, taking the second derivative, multiplying by (B/B) and factoring out the constant, B, we can derive the convexity measure from the second derivative.

$$\frac{1}{2} \cdot \frac{\partial^2 B}{\partial YTM^2} = \frac{1}{2} \cdot \frac{\partial}{\partial YTM}\left(\frac{\partial P}{\partial YTM}\right) = \frac{1}{2} \cdot \sum_{t=1}^{N}\left((-t - 1) \cdot (-t) \cdot CF_t \cdot (1 + YTM)^{-t-2}\right)$$

$$= \frac{1}{2} \cdot \sum_{t=1}^{N}\left(\frac{CF_t \cdot t \cdot (t + 1)}{(1 + YTM)^t(1 + YTM)^2}\right)$$

$$= B \cdot \left(\frac{1}{2} \cdot \frac{1}{(1 + YTM)^2} \cdot \frac{\sum_{t=1}^{N}(CF_t \cdot t \cdot (t + 1)/(1 + YTM)^t)}{B}\right)$$

$$= B \cdot Convexity \qquad (3.28)$$

Appendix C. Duration and Convexity in Measuring Price Sensitivity

The Macaulay duration or effective duration is based on three assumptions about yield curve movements: parallel, infinitesimal, and instantaneous shifts. Since they are restrictive to the point that the Macaulay duration does not reflect the realities, the subsequent research presents three possible remedies to relax the three restrictive assumptions. To

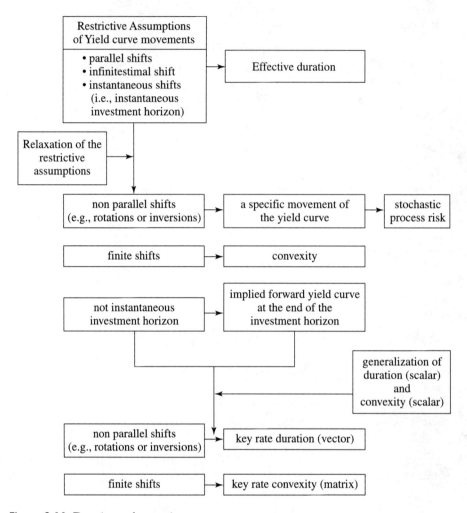

Figure 3.11 Duration and convexity.

incorporate nonparallel shifts such as rotations or inversions, we should specify how the yield curve moves in a nonparallel way and derive durations accordingly. The problem of this approach is that the yield curve should move as we have specified to make the durations a useful tool in bond management. Otherwise, we will have a bigger discrepancy in estimating bond return sensitivity based on a certain type of yield movement. Sometimes, it would be better to use Macaulay duration when the actual yield curve shifts are contrary to what we have assumed. This is called specification risk in the current literature. To take care of finite shifts, we usually calculate convexity in addition to duration, because convexity is the second derivative and the second derivative will add more accuracy in a Taylor expansion. If the yield curve does not move instantaneously such that the yield curve moves at the end of a investment horizon, yield curve shifts should be measured by the shifts of the yield curve from the implied forward curve on the horizon date rather than the spot yield curve. The rationale behind this is that if the yield curve on the horizon date is the implied forward curve, then all the default-free bonds will have the same total return, which is the risk-free return over the horizon period.

Even though the subsequent research relaxes the three assumptions, we still have the specification risk. The key rate duration has been forwarded to handle the specification risk. Since the key rate duration should be expressed as a vector rather than a scalar, the key rate convexity should be a $(n \times n)$ matrix, where n is the number of key rates used in determining the vector of the key rate duration. Only in the special case, where we use a parallel shift to determine the effective duration, is the convexity a scalar.

Notes

1. Generally speaking, the yield curve is defined as the relationship between the yields on bonds with or without coupons and their maturities. The spot yield curve is defined as the relationship between the yields on zero-coupon default-free bonds and their maturities. The spot yield curve correctly represents the time value of money.

2. Since $F(T^*, T)$ is the forward price at time 0, it can be denoted $F(0, T^*, T)$.

References

Bierwag, G. O. 1977. Immunization, duration and the term structure of interest rates, *Journal of Financial and Quantitative Analysis*, 12, 725–742.

Bierwag, G. O., G. G. Kaufman, and C. Khang. 1978. Duration and bond portfolio analysis: An overview. *Journal of Financial and Quantitative Analysis*, 13, 671–681.

Carleton, W. T., and I. A. Cooper. 1976. Estimation and uses of the term structure of interest rates. *Journal of Finance*, 31, 1067–1083.

Cox, J. C., J. E. Ingersoll, and S. A. Ross. 1979. Duration and the measurement of basis risk. *Journal of Business*, 52, 51–61.

Cox, J. C., J. E. Ingersoll, and S. A. Ross. 1981. The relationship between forward prices and futures prices. *Journal of Financial Economics*, 9, 321–346.

Duffee, G. R. 1998. The relation between treasury yields and corporate bond yield spreads. *Journal of Finance*, 53, no. 6, 2225–2241.

Fong, H. G., and O. Vasicek. 1983. The trade-off between return and risk in immunized portfolios. *Financial Analysts Journal*, 39, no. 5, 73–78.

Ho, T. S. Y. 1992. Key rate duration: A measure of interest rate risks exposure. *Journal of Fixed Income*, 2, no. 2, 29–44.

Jarrow, R. A., and G. S. Oldfield. 1981. Forward contracts and futures contracts. *Journal of Financial Economics*, 9, 373–382.

Longstaff, F. A. 2000. Arbitrage and the expectations hypothesis. *Journal of Finance*, 55, 989–994.

Macaulay, F. R. 1938. *Some Theoretical Problems Suggested by the Movements of Interest Rates, Bond Yields and Stock Prices in the United States since 1856.* Washington, D.C.: National Bureau of Economic Research.

McCoy, W. F. 1993. Enhancing the returns of a replicating portfolio. In Thomas S. Y. Ho, ed., *Fixed-Income Portfolio Management: Issues and Solutions.* Homewood, Ill.: Business One Irwin.

Morgan, I. G., and E. H. Neave. 1993. A discrete time model for pricing treasury bills, forward, and futures contracts. *Astin Bulletin*, 23, no. 1, 3–22.

Further Readings

Forsgren, A. 1998. A note on maximum smoothness approximation of forward interest rates. Working Paper. London: Royal Institute of Technology.

Jordan, B. D., R. D. Jorgensen, and D. A. Kuipers. 2000. The relative pricing of U.S. Treasury STRIPS: Empirical evidence. *Journal of Financial Economics*, 56, 89–123.

4

Equity Options:
The Black–Scholes Model

The Black–Scholes model is widely used in option trading for pricing as well as for formulating trading strategies to replicate options, hedge stock positions, and demonstrate product innovations. The model asserts that when a derivative can be replicated by a dynamic hedging strategy using the underlying securities, we can value such a derivative by a "risk-neutral" method, assuming the underlying security follows a risk-free drift and the expected cash flow is discounted along the risk-free yield curve. This valuation approach is also called a relative valuation model to emphasize that a derivative can be valued relative value to the underlying asset's observed value.

Option pricing is an important subject. Stock options are traded on the exchanges. Many financial contracts contain options that cannot be detached and traded separately. These options are called *embedded options*. Many financial contracts have contingency features such that the holder has the right to pay for an installment of the cost at a future date as a more complex form of an option.

For these reasons, investors and corporations alike are interested in a methodology for valuing options. But what approach can we use to determine their worth? How can we determine the appropriate required expected returns or discount rate? What is the appropriate risk premium for holding an option? If we use the Capital Asset Pricing model to value an option, how do we determine the β of an option when β may change over time, depending on the stock price level?

Unfortunately, methodologies like the Capital Asset Pricing model are too imprecise to determine the value of options, since the estimation of the β can have significant errors. A new approach is needed to value an option.

This chapter explains how the Black–Scholes model (1973) provides such a solution.[1] The Black–Scholes model exploits a key feature of an option: its uncertain payments at the expiration date are specified by the prevailing stock price, and therefore the option must move in tandem with the stock at all times. When the stock price rises, the call option price rises; when the stock price falls, the call option price also falls. The Black–Scholes model applies the law of one price to suggest that any option can be replicated by a portfolio of the underlying stock and a short-term risk-free asset. Thus, the cost of replicating the portfolio is, in fact, the option price.

This chapter begins with a description of an option and a brief overview of the basic types of options. We then derive the Black–Scholes option pricing model to highlight the insight gained from this new "dynamic hedging approach" versus the Capital Asset Pricing model or discounted cash flow method. We will then discuss how the option model can be applied to the option trading market.

4.1   Description of an Option

A *European call option* on a stock gives the holder the right to buy the underlying stock at a fixed price at a specified time. For example, a holder of a Microsoft call option can buy Microsoft at a fixed price, the strike price of $60 on the expiration day (say March 30 of this year). On the expiration date, if Microsoft is trading at $70, the call option holder would exercise the call option; buying the Microsoft stock for $60, $10 below the market. However, if the Microsoft stock trades at $50 on the expiration date, the holder would simply let the option expire, because the investor would not buy the Microsoft stock at a price $10 higher than the price traded in the market. The holder therefore has the option to exercise his right whenever it is to his advantage.

Obviously, an investor would consider buying a call option when he thinks that the stock will rise in value—for example, the Microsoft stock rising to $70 by the end of March. However, if he thinks that the Microsoft price will fall to $50, then he needs to consider another security, a put option. A *European put option* on a stock gives the holder the right to sell (not buy) the underlying stock at the strike price on the expiration date. In this case, if the Microsoft stock trades at $50 at the expiration, the put option would be worth $10. But if Microsoft stock trades at $60, the put option would expire worthless.

In what ways are options different from stocks? Given that a security is called an "option," we may think that the central difference between a stock and an option is that options give the holder the right—not the obligation—to do something. There is a choice built into the terms and conditions of the option security. This choice is a feature of an option, but it is not the central matter. After all, why wouldn't a rational investor exercise a call option when the stock price is above the strike price at expiration? Conversely, why would the rational investor want to buy that stock at a price higher than the market price by exercising a call option when the stock price is below the strike price? These same questions can be raised for the put options.

A rational investor always follows an optimal exercise rule at expiration to maximize his returns. Therefore, in pricing an option, under the rational behavior of the holder of the option, we can think of an option as a security that pays the stock price net of the strike price whenever the stock price is above the strike price at expiration, and otherwise pays nothing. A payment rule, based on the prevailing stock price, for the option holder is specified on the expiration date. This rule is important in defining the option.

In order to discuss how these payoff rules affect the option prices, we need to review option terminologies. An option security is usually called an option contract. Option prices are often called *option premiums*. We say a buyer holds the contract while the seller writes the contract. Time to expiration is the length of time to the expiration date. *Nearby contracts* refer to options with a short time to expiration. The risk of the underlying stock price returns is measured by the standard deviation of the returns, called the *stock volatility*. The intrinsic value is the value of the option if the option were to be exercised immediately. The *intrinsic value* of a call option is the underlying stock price net of the strike price if the netting is positive. Otherwise it is 0. For a put option, the intrinsic value is the strike price net of the underlying stock price, if the difference is positive. Otherwise it is 0. An option is said to be *at the money* if the underlying stock is trading around the strike price; it is *in the money* if the intrinsic value is positive; and it is *out of the money* when the intrinsic value is 0.

The *payoff diagram* is defined as the payment to the option holder on the expiration date. For the call option, the payoff is given by

$$C_T = Max\,[S_T - X, 0] \qquad (4.1)$$

where C_T is the call price or the payoff to the call option on the expiration date, T; S_T is the underlying stock price on the expiration date, T; and X is the strike price.

For the put option, the payoff is given by

$$P_T = Max\,[X - S_T, 0] \tag{4.2}$$

where P_T is the put option price at the expiration date.

Equations (4.1) and (4.2) and are called *terminal conditions of the options* because they specify the payout at the expiration date. Call and put stock options have particularly simple payout specifications.

Call options provide the upside return but protect the downside risk, losing, at most, the initial investment should the stock price fall. Similarly, the put option offers the upside return when the stock price falls and downside protection when the stock price rises.

4.2 Institutional Framework

Exchange-traded stock options are contracts between two parties. There are as many holders of the contracts as there are sellers. The number of contracts sold (and bought) for a particular security is called the *open interest*. Options can be traded on stock, forwards and futures, commodities, and other financial securities. In the United States, the exchange-traded options are American options, referring to the feature that the option holder can exercise the option at any time before the expiration date. We will discuss this feature in more detail in chapter 7.

Exchange-traded options on stocks such as the Nasdaq-100 Index Tracking Stock, Microsoft, Cisco Systems, and Citigroup are traded on the American Stock Exchange;[2] index options such as the Dow Jones Industrial Average Call and Put, on the Chicago Board of Trade.[3] There are also over-the counter options customized for specific needs. For example, on February 4, 2002, Microsoft was trading at 62.66. Table 4.1 gives the call option and put option prices for the strike price 60, for each expiration date.

In Table 4.1, the intrinsic values of the March call and put contracts are 2.66 (= Max[62.66 − 60, 0]) and 0. The prices show that the market trades the call option

Table 4.1 The Market Closing
Microsoft Option Prices for 2/4/2002
for Strike 60 at 62.66

Month	Call	Put
March	3.4	0.7
April	4.4	1.7
July	5.4	2.7

On February 4, 2002, Microsoft was trading at 62.66. For the strike price 60, the call and put premiums are given. Since the call options are in the money, the call premiums are larger than the intrinsic value. The differences between the call premiums and the intrinsic value are the time values. As time to maturity increases, the time value increases.

at a price exceeding the intrinsic price by 0.84 (=3.40–2.66) for the possible higher returns when the Microsoft price rises (of course weighing the possible loss of the entire premium of 3.40 if the price falls instead). For the put option, the market assigns 0.70 for the probability that Microsoft falls below 60 by the end of March.

The time to expiration of these exchange-traded stock options is typically less than a year. The exchange-traded options with longer expiration are called *LEAPS* (long-term equity anticipation securities). For example, on February 4, 2002, the call and put options of Microsoft LEAPS expiring in January 2003 are reported to be traded at 11.60 and 6.50, respectively. We can see that the premiums of both call and put options increase with the time to expiration compared with the option prices in table 4.1, reflecting the higher likelihood of these options expiring with higher expected returns as the time of expiration lengthens.

4.3 Put–Call Parity

A European call option, a European put option with the same strike price and expiration date, and the underlying stock are not independent of each other. In fact, any one of them can be replicated by the other two securities: the call option is a combination of the stock and the put option, and the put option is a portfolio of the stock and call option. This relationship is called the *put-call parity*, first proposed by Stoll (1969).

Let C and P be the prices of the call and put options, respectively. The options are European and have the same strike price, X, and the same underlying stock, S. Let the continuously compounding risk-free rate be r and the time to expiration T. Then the following relationship must hold.

$$C - P = S - PV(X) \qquad (4.3)$$

where $PV(X)$ is equal to $e^{-rT}X$, discounting the strike price at the risk-free rate.

In order to demonstrate that the put–call parity is correct, we need to consider the payoffs, at expiration of a portfolio, of holding the call option and shorting the put option. The payoff of the portfolio is given by

$$Y = Max\,[S_T - X, 0] - Max\,[X - S_T, 0] \qquad (4.4)$$

Now consider the case when the stock price exceeds the strike price at expiration. In this case, at expiration, $Max\,[S_T - X, 0] = S_T - X$ while $Max\,[X - S_T, 0] = 0$. Therefore, the payout of the portfolio is $Y = S_T - X$.

When the stock price is below the strike price at expiration, the payout Y is also equal to $S_T - X$. This means that the portfolio holding a long position in a call option and writing a put option with the same exercise price and maturity date has the same value as holding the underlying stock and owing the strike price in cash, for all the possible values of the stock price at the expiration date.

The put–call parity can be explained graphically. Consider a portfolio consisting of a long call and a short put (see figure 4.1).

The stock price is 62.66, and the strike price of the call and the put is 60. The present value of the exercise price is 59.96. The call premium is 3.4 and the put premium is 0.7. Since the put–call parity can be expressed such that (long a call + short a put) is equal

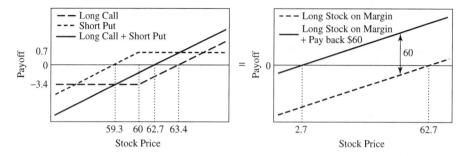

Figure 4.1 Put–call parity. The stock price is 62.66, and the strike price of the call and the put options is 60. The present value of the exercise price is 59.96. The call premium is 3.4 and the put premium is 0.7. The left panel shows the profile of a portfolio consisting of longing a call and shorting a put. Since the profile shows the cash flow at time T, the —— line indicates the cash flow of the call at maturity against various stock prices at maturity. The −− line can be represented in a similar way. The combined cash flow is a 45° stright line which crosses the horizontal line originating at 0 when the stock price is 62.7. The right panel shows the profile of a portfolio of longing a stock and shorting a risk-free asset (i.e., borrowing). The - - - line in the right panel indicates the profile of longing the stock when we have bought the stock at 62.66 by borrowing at 59.96. Since the principal amount with interest should be paid back at maturity, the red dotted line shifts downward by 60.

to (long a stock + risk-free borrowing), the cash flow at maturity of longing the call and shorting the put is equal to that of longing the stock combined with risk-free borrowing. The left panel in figure 4.1 represents the cash flow at maturity when we have a portfolio which consists of longing a call and shorting a put. The right panel in figure 4.1 indicates the cash flow at maturity when we long a stock by borrowing the present value of an exercise price.

The put–call parity can be explained intuitively. We have mentioned that call options offer the upside returns while protecting the downside risk, and shorting the put options means that we are exposed to the downside risk with a truncated upside. When we combine the two positions, we have both upside gain and downside risks of a stock without any protection. This means that we have the risk of a stock.

The simplicity of the put–call parity result often disguises its important implications. First, any analysis of the call option, including its pricing, can extend directly to the put option. Consider the numerical example of the Microsoft March contracts. The traded options allow holders to exercise the options early, while the put–call parity does not allow options to have such a feature. We will ignore the value of early exercise until we revisit this issue in chapter 7. Since the stock, the put, and the call are 62.66, 0.70, and 3.40, respectively, we have

$$S + P - C = 62.66 + 0.70 - 3.40 = 59.96$$

The value 59.96 is the present value of the exercise price 60, where the discount rate will be the short-term funding costs for the arbitrage trading over the period from February 4 until the expiration date. This formula must take the bid–ask spreads (the price difference between the highest bid price and the lowest ask price) set by the market makers and other transaction costs into account, and in practice, the arbitrage-free models can be approximately correct only within a band around the theoretical price. Within such a band, an arbitrage position cannot be profitable because of all the transactions in implementing the trade. In most cases, these bands are quite narrow.

This numerical example illustrates that the prices of the put option, the call option, and the stock must be aligned according to the put–call parity; otherwise, arbitrage opportunities would occur. The alignment should be within the bid–ask spread or within the cost of an arbitrage.

Second, the put–call parity prescribes a straightforward *static hedging strategy*. Suppose an investor is holding an illiquid call option. He would not want to be exposed to the market risk. Using the put–call parity, he can sell both the underlying stock and the corresponding put option, and invest the proceeds at a risk-free rate of return. The net position would result in a risk-free position. This hedge position is static in the sense that the position does not have to be revised until the expiration date, when the entire position can be liquidated.

4.4   The Main Insight of the Black–Scholes Model

Prior to 1973 there had been many attempts to value options. The general approach was to use a risk and return framework, applying the discounted cash flow method. First, we determine the expected return of the underlying stock. Then we determine the expected payoff of the option at the expiration date. As a result, the option price is the present value of the expected payoff. However, determining the appropriate discount rate is difficult when we use this approach.

This methodology can be applied to primary securities such as stocks, as seen in the dividend discount model. However, because by definition the value of derivative securities depends on the underlying securities and the underlying securities' prices are changing on a real-time basis, the continual change of risks inherent in derivative securities prohibits a rigorous valuation model from determining the appropriate discount rate.

To overcome this difficulty, Black and Scholes devised a way to neutralize the risk inherent in options. Since this risk is driven by the stock, we can eliminate the risks of the option by taking the opposite position in the stock. There should be a specific ratio between the stock and option positions such that the risks of the stock and the option exactly cancel each other. This argument's main issue concerns a search for the combination such that the portfolio has no risks. This combination is referred to as "the *hedge ratio*" or the Greek letter delta (Δ) in the current literature.

Construction of a Binomial Lattice of Stock Prices

Previous chapters have provided a model of financial markets, the perfect capital market. The model specifies the rules for trading a security, the behavior of the investors, and a trading mechanism—the arbitrage mechanism. Now we proceed to describe a basic model that enables us to value securities.

We assume a discrete time model where all trading occurs at regular intervals. All investors make their decisions at the same time, including revising their portfolio and adjusting for their expectations. The market clears at these time intervals at one price for each security. Let the times of trading be denoted by *n*. For clarity of exposition, we assume that each time interval is one year. In practice, depending on the purpose of the modeling, the time interval can be daily for most instruments.

This section formulates the model that describes the uncertainties. The model is described by flipping a coin: head (up state) and tail (down state) are the "outcomes," with their corresponding probabilities. We will assume that the probability of the up state is q, and of the down state, $(1 - q)$.

The flip of a coin can be considered an event with two possible outcomes. After each event, an outcome is determined, and each successive event has another two possible outcomes. All of the possible future outcomes can be illustrated in a "tree" that maps all the possible paths of a random walk. We say the tree is "recombining" if an up state followed by a down state equals a down state followed by an up state.

Forcing the tree to recombine reduces the number of nodes. If the tree does not recombine, each node will have another two outcomes after each period. In N periods, there will be 2^N nodes at time N. That is, the number of states at any time N grows exponentially with the number of periods N. However, in a binomial lattice (*a recombining tree*), the number of states is only $(N + 1)$. There are significantly fewer states to manage in a binomial lattice model. By forcing the tree to recombine, we have constructed a binomial lattice.

This binomial lattice is a random walk. At any time n, there are $(n+1)$ possible states of the world. Each state is denoted by i. We refer to the ith state at time n as the node (n, i). At the initial node, we can calculate the probability of reaching any node (n, i) for a particular n, a probability distribution that is called *binomial distribution*. We get a distribution of the likelihood of the position of the point. Given the probability distributions and the outcomes, expected values and standard deviations of future uncertain outcomes can be calculated.

For example, let the price of a stock be S. In the up state, the price becomes S_u, and in the down state, S_d. Consider only one step. The expected price is

$$E[S] = qS_u + (1 - q)S_d \qquad (4.5)$$

and the standard deviation σ is

$$\sigma^2 = q(S_u - E[S])^2 + (1 - q)(S_d - E[S])^2. \qquad (4.6)$$

Consider an example of a binomial process of a stock price. To this end, we assume that the stock price follows a multiplicative binomial process. During a time period, the stock goes up to uS or down to dS. The initial stock price is 100 and the time to maturity is four years. The continuously compounding risk-free rate of return, r, is 5%. The stock volatility is 20%. (See appendix D for how to derive u, d, r, and p, given the continuously compounding risk-free rate of return and the volatility.) Figure 4.2 shows a binomial stock price process.

The expected values and standard deviations of the stock price at each year are given in table 4.2. As time passes, the expected value and the standard deviation increase. The reason for the increasing expected value is due to the upward probability, which is greater than 0.5. The reason for the increasing volatility is that the difference between the highest and the lowest stock price is increasing as we go further in the future, which is an inherent property of the binomial process.

Note that since the rate of return is measured by the continuously compounding rate, the expected annual return over one year is 5.127% ($= \exp(0.05) - 1$), which is greater than 5%.

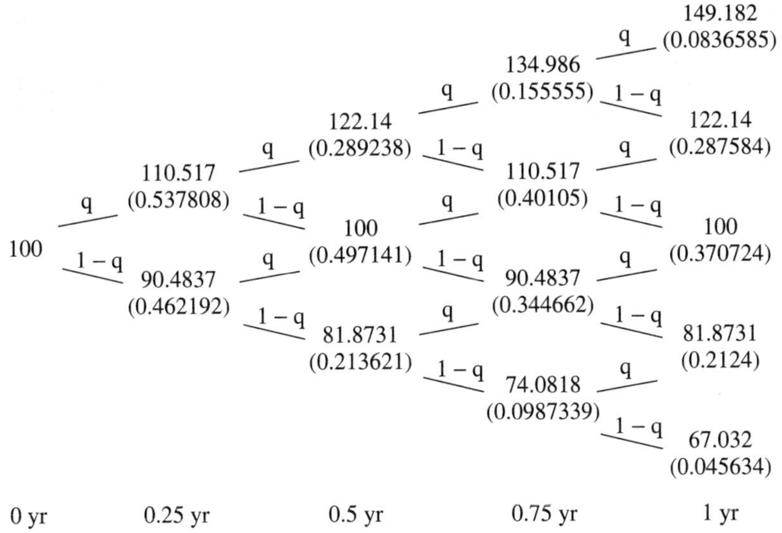

Figure 4.2 A binomial stock price process. The value of the stock price is denoted at each node with the probability of arriving at the node, which is in parentheses. The continuously compounding risk-free rate of return (r) is 5% and the volatility is 20%. The initial stock price is 100, the time to maturity (T) is one year and m is equal to 4.

$$u = \exp\left\{\sigma\sqrt{\frac{1}{m}}\right\} = 1.10517, d = \frac{1}{u} = 0.904837, \text{ and } p = \frac{\exp\left[\frac{r}{m}\right] - d}{u - d} = 0.537808$$

Table 4.2 The mean and volatility of the binomial stock price process

Time (year)	0	0.25	0.5	0.75	1
Expected Value	100	101.258	102.532	103.821	105.127
Standard Deviation	0	9.988	14.3376	17.824	20.8911

As time passes by, the volatility increases because we expect more uncertainty at later periods.

The binomial lattice in modeling risk has a number of interesting properties. This process is a Markov process. That is, at each node, the possible outcomes are independent of how the price arrives at that node. The Markov property is frequently used in finance, and many financial models have the Markov property. The formal definition of the *Markov property* is that the conditional distribution of $\tilde{S}(T)$, given information up until t (where $t < T$), depends only on $S(t)$. Even though the formal definition of Markov is a little bit unfriendly, the intuition behind Markov is straightforward. If we assume that stock prices have the Markov property, we simply say that we need only today's stock price to guess tomorrow's stock price. We do not have to collect past prices, because information contained in the price history is already incorporated into today's stock price. In this case, t is today and T is tomorrow. The amount of information we can extract to predict tomorrow's stock price is the same regardless of whether we collect the price history or only look at today's stock price.

The Markov property is related to the efficient market hypothesis, which says that stock prices instantaneously reflect information. As long as stock prices instantaneously reflect information under the efficient market hypothesis, we cannot squeeze more information from the price history, and we can only use today's price to predict tomorrow's price.

The Dynamic Hedging Argument

Section 4.3 demonstrated how we can replicate a call option using a put option and the underlying stock. This section will show that we can replicate the call option using the underlying stock and the risk-free investment only at each node on the binomial lattice tree. Different from the put–call parity, this hedging requires a continual revision of our portfolio of stock and risk-free position at each node. This continual revision of a portfolio is called *dynamic hedging*.

Let me give a numerical example to intuitively explain the seemingly complex idea. Let us assume that there are three securities in a one-period and two-states setting. Security A at time 0 is $55 and its value at time 1 is $75 when the weather at time 1 is sunny and $35 when the weather at time 1 is rainy. We further assume that the sunny weather and the rainy weather are mutually exclusive—only one of them will occur at time period 1. Security B's value is $35 when the weather at time 1 is sunny and $75 when the weather at time 1 is rainy. Note that the payoffs of securities A and B directly offset each other in their outcomes. (See figure 4.3.)

Finally, the risk-free rate of return over one period is 10%, which means that the price of the risk-free asset at time 0 is $100 when its value at time 1 is $110, regardless of the weather at that time. Let this risk-free asset be called Security C. The problem we are facing now is how much we should pay to buy Stock B at time period 0.

Our first observation is that Stock A and Stock B are risky assets because their cash flow at time 1 depends on the weather at time 1. Security C is a risk-free asset because its cash flow is the same regardless of the weather. However, if you add one share of Security A to one share of Security B, it is equal to the share of Security C, which is risk-free ($75 + $35 = $110). The portfolio value at time 1 is $110, regardless of the weather at time 1. Since the portfolio of Security A and Security B is risk-free, its value

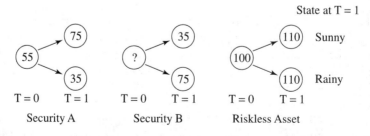

Figure 4.3 The portfolio outcomes. The price of security A goes to 75 when the weather is sunny at time 1 and to 35 when it is rainy at time 1. The price of security B goes to 35 when it is sunny at time 1 and to 75 when it is rainy at time 1. The risk-free rate of one period is 10%. When we form a portfolio by combining one share of security A with one share of security B, we will have a risk-free portfolio, even though we put together risky securities. This is a basic idea behind option pricing.

at time 0 is 100 when we apply the law of one price. Therefore, the price of one share of security A and one share of security B must equal 100 (since the portfolio value is the sum of its components). This argument leads us to conclude that the price of security B at time period 0 is \$45 (= \$100 − \$55).

Let us continue with this example. If the price of Security B happens to be \$50 and not \$45, what will happen? Since Security B's price is greater than \$45, we have an arbitrage opportunity. We sell one share of Security B and one share of Security A. This sale provides \$105. Now we buy security C for \$100, leaving us a cash inflow of \$5. What is nice for the arbitrageur is that the cash flow at time 1 is always 0, regardless of the sunny or rainy weather. The payout of Security C, \$110, can be used to meet the uncertain obligated payments of Securities A and B. Arbitrage trading will continue until the selling pressures of A and B lead to falls in their prices until we reach a new price level where there is no arbitrage opportunity. Similarly, if Security B is trading below 45 (say 40), we will buy Securities A and B and sell Security C.

Interestingly, we have priced security B without making any assumptions about the probability of having the sunny or rainy weather at time 1. Furthermore, we do not need to know the expected rate of return of Security A. Not having to know the likelihood of sunny or rainy weather at time 1 is surprising, because, using the discounted cash flow method, we need to know the probabilities to determine the expected value and the risks. However, when we use an arbitrage argument, probability distribution is irrelevant for pricing purposes.

Derivation of the Black–Scholes (Discrete Time) Model

The Black–Scholes option pricing model is derived in a continuous time framework by solving a stochastic differential equation. (The result is provided in appendix A of this chapter.) Here, we provide the model, often called the Cox, Ross, and Rubinstein model (1979) or the Rendleman and Bartter model (1979), in discrete time. The discrete time model is more intuitive to explain and may offer a flexible approach to valuing a broad range of securities.

Before we begin developing the pricing model, we will state the assumptions of the model:

1. The stock follows a multiplicative binomial process. During a time period, its price goes up to uS or down to dS, where $d < e^r < u$.
2. The stock volatility is constant. Stock risk is the only source of risk for the purpose of valuing the options.
3. The continuously compounding risk-free interest rate is constant at r. In this section, we will automatically assume a flat yield curve with all the forward rates being the same.
4. The market is perfect, with no frictions such as transaction costs, and the market is efficient, the prices fully reflecting all available market information. There are no short selling constraints.
5. The call option has a strike price X and time to expiration n.

First we derive the binomial option pricing model in a simple one-period case. We begin by assuming a binomial stock process. The second step determines the payoff one period hence, which is the maturity date in this example. Once the stock process is given, we can easily calculate the payoff by the boundary condition of the option. We construct a *levered portfolio* consisting of the stock and the option to duplicate the option payoff at the maturity date. We call the duplicating portfolio the levered portfolio because we buy the stock on margin. Since the option has the same cash flows as the levered portfolio, the option value at this period should be equal to the cost of constructing the levered portfolio to avoid any arbitrage opportunities. Alternatively, we can create a risk-free portfolio to price the option. We now elaborate the method in four steps.

Step 1   **Step 1**

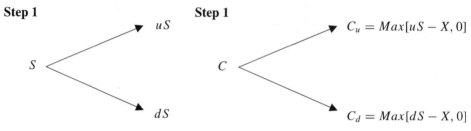

Step 1

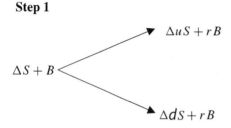

In step 1, we construct a binomial lattice of the stock, where u and d are defined by the volatility of the stock and r is the continuously compounding risk-free rate as specified in figure 4.2. In step 2, we consider one period before the expiration of the option. At the expiration date, we know the payoffs of the options, as specified in equation (4.1) and (4.2).

In step 3, we construct a levered portfolio by holding Δ shares of stock and a risk-free asset B to duplicate the cash flow of the European call option.

$$\Delta uS + e^r B = C_u$$

$$\Delta dS + e^r B = C_d$$

By solving the two equations, we get

$$\Delta = \frac{C_u - C_d}{uS - dS} > 0 \tag{4.7}$$

Substituting $\frac{C_u - C_d}{uS - dS}$ for Δ in equation (4.7), we get $B = \frac{C_d u - C_u d}{e^r (u-d)}$.

In step 4, since we know B and Δ, we can solve for C by substituting $\Delta S + B = C$ in the equation. We have $C = \frac{pC_u + (1-p)C_d}{e^r}$, where $p = \frac{e^r - d}{u - d}$, $1 - p = \frac{u - e^r}{u - d}$.

Note that we have not used the subjective view of the expected return of the stock or the subjective view of the probability of the stock's outcomes. p is defined by the stock lattice and is called the risk-neutral probability, which we will discuss further later. The formulas in step 4 are applied to each node of the option lattice. As long as we know the payoff of the option at the expiration date, we can apply the formulas recursively and solve for all the option prices at all the nodes in the lattice.

To provide a clearer explanation of this dynamic hedging, we can derive the same binomial option pricing model by constructing an alternative hedging using a risk-free hedging portfolio.

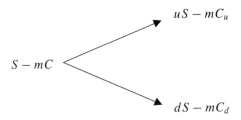

In step 3', a risk-free hedge portfolio of longing one share of S and shorting m shares of C should be risk-free by construction; the cash flow at the up state should be the same as the cash flow at the down state.

$$uS - mC_u = dS - mC_d \qquad (4.8)$$

Simplifying the above equation, we get $m = \frac{uS-dS}{C_u-C_d} = \frac{1}{\Delta}$

In step 4', substituting $\frac{uS-dS}{C_u-C_d}$ into m in equation (4.8) and using the fact that the risk-fee cash flow should be discounted at the risk-free rate, we have

$$S - mC = \frac{uS - mC_u}{e^r} = \frac{dS - mC_d}{e^r}$$

Simplifying the above expressions, we have the same binomial option pricing model as step 4.

$$C = \frac{pC_u + (1-p)C_d}{e^r}, \; p = \frac{e^r - d}{u - d}, 1 - p = \frac{u - e^r}{u - d}$$

Note that p can be interpreted as a probability because it is less than 1 and greater than 0. Therefore, the expression for C can be interpreted as the present value of the expected payoff of the option. If we extend this construction of the option value recursively from one period to two periods and to n periods, as we will explain further in the following section, the expression for the option value is given below.

$$C = \frac{1}{e^{r \cdot n}} \sum_{i=0}^{n} \binom{n}{i}^{i} p(1-p)^{n-i} Max\left[0, u^i d^{n-i} S - X\right]$$

where $\binom{n}{i} = \frac{n!}{(n-i)!i!}$ is the binomial factor. This is the discrete time option pricing model. $Max\left[0, u^i d^{\tau-i} S - X\right]$ is the terminal condition of the European call option for each state i, and $e^{-r \cdot n}$ is the present value factor, using the risk-free rate. The main insight of the Black–Scholes model is that the option price C can be interpreted as the discounted expected value of the payoff of the option at expiration under the risk-neutral probability p. For this reason, if we construct the stock lattice according to figure 4.2, which is based on the risk-neutral probability, and determine the option prices on that lattice, we can derive the option price according to the option pricing model. We will discuss the specific valuation methodologies next, using these insights.

4.5   Valuation Methods

1. Backward Substitution Valuation Method

The idea of the pricing methodology is intuitive. The binomial lattice enables us to itemize all the relevant information for valuing the option at each node. Each node specifies the state and time of the world, as in figure 4.2. First, the price of the option is specified at the terminal date by the payoff rule of the option. Take a node one period before the terminal date. At that time and state, we know the risk-neutral expected value of the option. In other words, we know the perfect hedge, using the stock and bond to replicate the option. The cost of the replicating portfolio is the option price, where we also have proved that the price is, in fact, the expected risk-neutral value of the option discounted back at the risk-free rate. Using this argument, we can determine all the option prices for all the states of the world at the time one period from the terminal date.

Let us consider the time two periods from the terminal date. We can repeat the same argument. This time, since we know all the option prices at the time 1 period from the terminal date, we can calculate the expected risk-neutral values. Then we discount back at the risk-free rate to determine the option prices for all the states of the world for two periods from the terminal date.

We can determine the option price recursively, always one period back at each iteration. In repeating the process, we will arrive at the initial date, and the price of the option at that point is the price of the option at present, the price that we seek to determine. This procedure of pricing the option is called *backward substitutions*. (See figure 4.4.)

Consider a numerical example, using the lattice depicted in figure 4.2. Consider a call option expiring at the end of year 1 with a strike price of 100 (at the money). The results are shown in figure 4.5.

2. Risk-neutral valuation approach—closed form solution

Now consider the risk-neutral option lattice. This lattice is based on the risk-neutral stock lattice by assuming that the stock has a risk-free return, as if all market participants are risk-neutral. We can make this assumption because in the dynamic hedging argument, we never use any notion of risk aversion or risk premiums. Arbitrage arguments are preference-free.

We repeatedly apply this arbitrage argument at each node of the lattice. If we know the exact payout on the expiration date for each stock price, we should know the option price one step before the expiration date that would ensure the portfolio value's having a risk-free rate. If we know the values of the option at the nodes one step before the expiration for all the stock values, then we can calculate the option price for each stock price two steps before the expiration. If we continue that thought process, we can determine the option price.

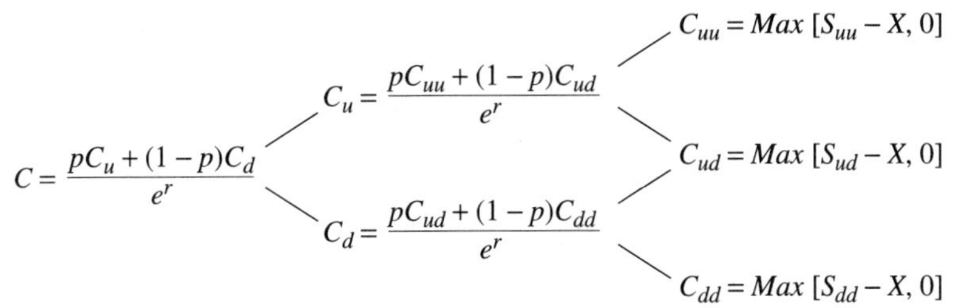

$$C = \frac{pC_u + (1-p)C_d}{e^r}$$

$$C_u = \frac{pC_{uu} + (1-p)C_{ud}}{e^r}$$

$$C_d = \frac{pC_{ud} + (1-p)C_{dd}}{e^r}$$

$$C_{uu} = Max\,[S_{uu} - X, 0]$$

$$C_{ud} = Max\,[S_{ud} - X, 0]$$

$$C_{dd} = Max\,[S_{dd} - X, 0]$$

$$u = \exp\left\{\sigma\sqrt{\frac{1}{m}}\right\}, \quad d = \frac{1}{u}, \quad p = \frac{\exp[\frac{r}{m}] - d}{u - d}$$

Figure 4.4 Payoffs of the option at the nodes in a binomial lattice. Stock prices are assumed to go up and down by the factors u and d, respectively. The European call option on the stock matures at period 2 with strike price X. At period 2, the option has an intrinsic value. At period 1, the option value is the expected value discounted by the risk-free rate. To calculate the expected value, we use the risk-neutral probabilities, p, rather than actual probabilities. Under risk-neutral probabilities, all the securities have the same rate of return, which is the risk-free rate regardless of the risk level they might assume. σ is the stock volatility. u and d are the upward movement and downward movement factors, r is the continuously compounding risk-free interest rate. p is risk-neutral probability. m is the number of subperiods partitioned in a period. Since r and σ are measured for one period, we have to adjust accordingly when we divide one period into m subperiods.

Therefore, in this procedure, any investor would agree on the option price, independent of his risk aversion. The pricing is preference-free. If the valuation is preference-free, then we can assume that the stock price movement is determined by the risk-neutral market participant. That means we can assume that everyone is risk-neutral and all risky assets, both the underlying stock and its options, have risk-free expected returns.

Since the stock movement is assumed to be following a random walk with risk-neutral probabilities, the stock price at the terminal date is

$$S_{n,i} = Su^i d^{n-i}$$

where $n =$ discrete time and $i =$ the number of upward movements.

Given these stock terminal values, we can determine the option payoff at the terminal date. And, in turn, given the value of the option at each node at the terminal date, we can calculate the expected value using the risk-neutral probabilities p. The expected value is

$$\text{risk-neutral expected call option payoff} = \sum_{i=0}^{n} Max\left[Su^i d^{n-i} - X, 0\right]\binom{n}{i}p^i(1-p)^{n-i}$$

The price of the option, being the present value of the expected value discounted at the risk-free rate, is therefore

Cox-Ross-Rubinstein model

$$C = e^{-r\cdot n}\sum_{i=0}^{n} Max\left[Su^i d^{n-i} - X, 0\right]\binom{n}{i}p^i(1-p)^{n-i} \tag{4.9}$$

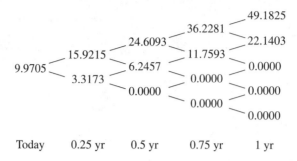

| Today | 0.25 yr | 0.5 yr | 0.75 yr | 1 yr |

Figure 4.5 A risk-neutral binomial lattice for the option price. Given the same binomial stock price process as in figure 4.2, we calculate the binomial call option price process. The continuously compounding risk-free rate and the initial stock price are the same as in figure 4.2 and are adjusted accordingly by partitioning the one period into four subperiods. The parameters are

$$u = \exp\left\{\sigma\sqrt{\frac{1}{m}}\right\} = 1.10517, d = \frac{1}{u} = 0.904837, S = 100, \sigma = 0.2, r = 0.05, T = 1$$

$$p = \frac{\exp\left[\frac{r}{m}\right] - d}{u - d} = 0.537808, 1 - p = 0.462192$$

At maturity, the call option prices are the intrinsic values. When rolled back by one subperiod, the call option price is the expected value discounted by the one-subperiod risk-free interest rate. For example, at 0.75 year and the highest node, the expected value is $49.182580 \times 537808 + 22.1403 \times 0.462192$. If we discount the expected value by the one-subperiod risk-free rate, which is 1.01258, we have 36.2281, which is the call option value at the node. The option values at the other nodes will be calculated in a similar manner. If we roll back to the initial period, we have 9.97052 as the current call option price.

where r is the risk-free rate for the one-period step size. (See table 4.3.)

The Black–Scholes model is usually expressed in a form where the step size converges to 0. In the limit, equation (4.9) becomes

the Black–Scholes model $\qquad C = SN(d_1) - Xe^{-rT}N(d_2)$ $\qquad\qquad$ (4.10)

where

$$d_1 = \frac{\ln(S/X) + (r + \sigma^2/2)T}{\sigma\sqrt{T}}, \qquad d_2 = d_1 - \sigma\sqrt{T}$$

$N(\cdot)$ is the cumulative normal distribution

The derivation of the model is provided in appendix A. The interpretation of the Black–Scholes model is the same as that for discrete time. The option value is the expected value of the option payoff discounted at the risk-free rate. The expected option payoff is determined by a stock process that follows a lognormal distribution, with a drift at the risk-free rate and a constant volatility.

Table 4.3 Option payoffs and corresponding Binomial Probabilities in Cox-Ross-Rubinstein model

(1) *Number of upward movements*	0	1	2	3	4	*Sum*
(2) Payoffs Max[S-X,0]	0.0000	0.0000	0.0000	22.1403	49.1825	—
(3) Binomial coefficients	1	4	6	4	1	16
(4) Binomial probabilities	0.0456	0.0531	0.0618	0.0719	0.0837	—
(3) × (4)	0.0456	0.2124	0.3707	0.2876	0.0837	1.0000
(5) Expected Payoffs (2) × (3) × (4)	0.0000	0.0000	0.0000	6.3672	4.1145	10.4817

Call option value can be obtained by calculating the expected value at maturity (year 1) and discounting the expected value by the risk-free rate over four subperiods. 10.4817 is the expected value at year 1. The call option value, 9.97052, can be obtained by discounting. 10.4817 with $\exp\{\frac{r}{m} \cdot 4\} = 1.01258^4 = 1.05127$. The sum of the probabilities is one. The sum of all the binomial coefficients equals the total number of paths, which is $16 (= 2^4)$.

3. Pathwise Methodology

We can view the lattice from another perspective. A lattice is a representation of many possible scenarios. In fact, there are 2^N scenarios, exhausting all the possibilities of the price paths of the stock if the terminal discrete period is N. We can then analyze the behavior of an option, scenario by scenario. A path on a lattice (a scenario) is a vector of events starting from the initial state. A path is denoted by $(+, -, +, \ldots)$, where "+" means the stock moves up and "−" means that the stock moves down. We analyze a scenario in order to understand what happens when a stock takes a specific path in the lattice. It does not matter whether the path is taken in the risk-neutral lattice or the true lattice,[4] because the node values are the same regardless of the lattice. Once the path is specified in the stock lattice, the paths are also specified in the option lattices. In other words, while there are four lattices, a scenario path is well defined in all the lattices (as will be further explained in section 4.6).

A *pathwise value* is the present value of the cash flow based on the risk-neutral lattice discounted over each period at the risk-free rate. The probability assigned to each pathwise value is the probability calculated using the risk-neutral probability: $p^i (1 - p)^{N-i}$, where p is the risk-neutral probability, N is the final period, and i is the number of up states for that scenario.

Numerical Example of the Pathwise Values

Table 4.4 shows that the mean value of the pathwise values is the same as that determined by the backward substitution approach. The pathwise value is the risk-adjusted present value of the payoffs along each scenario.

As shown in appendix C, the option price is the mean of the pathwise values of the risk-neutral lattice. That means the value of an option is the mean of the present values of the option cash flows for all the scenarios. When we pay for an option, we are in fact paying for the mean of all possible outcomes. We have constructed the pathwise values from the risk-neutral lattice.

The pathwise approach enables the approximate construction of any option as a combination of options. This can be achieved by seeking a combination of options

Table 4.4 European option pricing by path-wise valuation

Scenarios	(1) Payoffs	(2) Probabilities	(3) Discount	(1) × (2) × (3)
{0, 0, 0, 0}	0.00000	0.0456	0.95123	0.00000
{0, 0, 0, 1}	0.00000	0.0531	0.95123	0.00000
{0, 0, 1, 0}	0.00000	0.0531	0.95123	0.00000
{0, 0, 1, 1}	0.00000	0.0618	0.95123	0.00000
{0, 1, 0, 0}	0.00000	0.0531	0.95123	0.00000
{0, 1, 0, 1}	0.00000	0.0618	0.95123	0.00000
{0, 1, 1, 0}	0.00000	0.0618	0.95123	0.00000
{0, 1, 1, 1}	22.14028	0.0719	0.95123	1.51416
{1, 0, 0, 0}	0.00000	0.0531	0.95123	0.00000
{1, 0, 0, 1}	0.00000	0.0618	0.95123	0.00000
{1, 0, 1, 0}	0.00000	0.0618	0.95123	0.00000
{1, 0, 1, 1}	22.14028	0.0719	0.95123	1.51416
{1, 1, 0, 0}	0.00000	0.0618	0.95123	0.00000
{1, 1, 0, 1}	22.14028	0.0719	0.95123	1.51416
{1, 1, 1, 0}	22.14028	0.0719	0.95123	1.51416
{1, 1, 1, 1}	49.18247	0.0837	0.95123	3.91387
Sum		1.0000		9.97052

The scenarios consist of ones or zeros which represent the upward movements and downward movements, respectively. The payoffs are the call option value at maturity when we follow the corresponding scenarios. If we multiply the payoffs by the corresponding probabilities and discount them with the appropriate discount factors, we have the path-wise value for each path. If we sum up the path-wise values, we have the call option price, 9.97052, which is the same as the two previous methods (Figure 4.5 and Table 4.3).

that have the same pathwise values. Consider a special case of a portfolio of options whose pathwise values are all 0. In this case, if we follow one particular scenario over time, we will have cash inflows and outflows. When the cash flows of the portfolio of options along a scenario are invested (or borrowed) at the risk-free rate, at any future date and state of the world the terminal value is always 0 under each scenario because the pathwise value is 0. Therefore, if we can construct a portfolio of options such that the portfolio has the same pathwise values as those of another option, then the portfolio of options is equivalent to that particular option in the sense that the terminal values in all the scenarios are the same, allowing for borrowing and investing at the risk-free rate. Furthermore, if the pathwise values are constant, then the security is equivalent to cash or the risk-free asset.

4.6 Relationships of Risk-Neutral and Market Binomial Lattices

It is important to remember that when we are using the risk-neutral probabilities, the expected values or distributions of values are not the true distributions. This interplay between the market lattice and the risk-neutral lattice is always a source of confusion. To avoid this confusion, we introduce two separate lattices: the market lattice and the risk-neutral lattice. The prices of all securities at each node in the market lattice should be the same as those of the corresponding node in the risk neutral lattice. The two lattices differ in the probabilities assigned to the model.

In much of financial research, we concentrate on the pricing, and not the market distributions of the values. After all, this is the most important feature of the relative valuation approach, which says that we do not need to know the expected return or the required return of the underlying stock, and that we can price the option relative to the stock.

For this reason, we often ignore the market lattice and use the risk-neutral lattice's probabilities. We will be interested in the relationship between the market distribution and the risk-neutral distribution in chapter 14 on the corporate model. Here we need to introduce the lattices. (See figure 4.6.)

Given the underlying security (for example, a stock), we can determine its expected returns and volatilities, and the market probability, q. These parameters will enable us to construct the risk-averse binomial lattice in figure 4.6.

From the risk-averse binomial model, we can construct the risk-neutral binomial lattice of the stock using the risk-free rate of drift, r, and the risk-neutral probability, p. On the risk-neutral binomial lattice, we can determine the lattice for the option at each node, given the terminal conditions. From the risk-neutral binomial lattice of the option, we can now derive the risk-averse binomial lattice of the option by the transformation of the risk-neutral probability p to the market probability q.

The four lattices are risk-averse stock lattice, risk-neutral stock lattice, risk-averse option lattice, and risk-neutral option lattice. A node (n, i) represents the same instant of time and state. For this reason, the stock prices of each node in the true lattice and in the risk-neutral lattice are the same. They are the same because in the construction, we only change the probabilities from market to risk-neutral. The outcomes remain the same for each node. Similarly, the option prices at each node on the risk-averse option lattice and on the risk-neutral option lattice are the same.

The difference between the risk-averse lattice and the risk-neutral lattice is the probabilities. The risk-averse lattice uses the market probabilities that assure the expected returns, and volatilities allow for risk premiums.

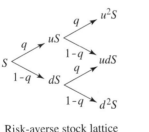

Risk-averse stock lattice

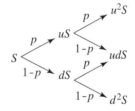

Risk-neutral stock lattice

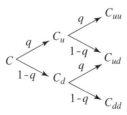

Risk-averse option lattice

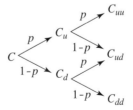

Risk-neutral option lattice

Figure 4.6 Risk-averse vs. risk-neutral lattices. The only difference between the actual world and the risk-neutral wold is the specification of the probability; q is the actual probability and p is the risk-neutral probability.

4.7   Option Behavior and the Sensitivity Analysis

Five key variables affect option prices—the underlying price, the volatility (standard deviation of returns), the risk-free rate, the exercise price, and the time to maturity. How each variable affects an option price when the other four variables are constant is called the *comparative statics*. Understanding the comparative statics is important for investors who wish to gain more insight into how option strategies should be formulated when responding to a rapidly changing market environment. (See figures 4.7 and 4.8.)

Delta is defined as the sensitivity of the option price to the stock price; Δ indicates a small change.

$$Delta = \frac{\Delta C}{\Delta S} \tag{4.11}$$

Delta also measures the number of stocks we need to short to hedge a call option. The hedge ratio enables traders or other market professionals to hedge any option position at the evaluation time. Or they can use the hedge ratio to determine the number of options to be used to hedge a stock position. We need to add "at the evaluation time" to emphasize that the replicating portfolio has to be continually revised. This strategy is called dynamic hedging. (See figure 4.9.)

Gamma is the ratio of the change of delta to the change in the stock price. It measures the extent to which the option price does not move in step with the underlying stock price. An important aspect of an option is that the option returns have high potential positive returns with the downside loss protected. Such a payout must lead to the option price not moving in step with the underlying stock price. An option with a large gamma would suggest that the option has significant downside protection relative to the potential positive returns.

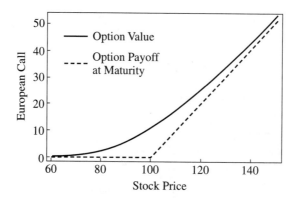

Figure 4.7 The stock price is between $60 and $150. The exercise price is $100. The stock volatility (standard deviation) is 0.5. The continuously compounding risk-free rate is 10%. The time to maturity is 0.25 year. We have partitioned 0.25 year into 20 subperiods to generate a smooth European call option profile by a binomial option pricing model. The European call option value converges to the 45° line originating from the present value of the exercise price when the stock price goes up. It implies that the higher the stock price goes, the more similar the two price movements will be. The solid line indicates the option value and the broken line indicates the payoff at maturity.

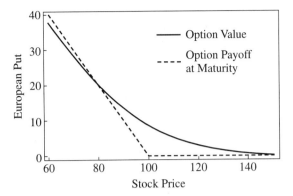

Figure 4.8 Simulation of the European put option value for a range of stock prices. The stock price is between $60 and $150. The exercise price is $100. The stock volatility is 0.5. The continuously compounding risk-free rate is 10%. The time to maturity is 0.25 year. We have partitioned 0.25 year into 20 subperiods to generate a smooth European put option profile by a binomial option pricing model. The European put option value converges to the 45° line originating from the present value of the exercise price when the stock price goes down. It implies that the lower the stock price, the more similar the two price movements will be. The stock and the options would move in step. The line indicates the option value, and the dotted line indicates the payoff at maturity.

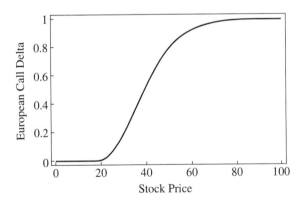

Figure 4.9 Delta surface. The stock price is between $0 and $100. The exercise price is $45. The stock volatility (standard deviation) is 0.3. The continuously compounding risk-free rate is 10%. The time to maturity is one year. We have partitioned one year into 50 subperiods to generate a smooth European call option delta profile by the binomial option pricing. Delta is a measure that shows how the European call option changes given a unit change of the underlying stock price. As the stock price goes up, delta converges to 1, which implies that the amount of price change is the same regardless of the stock or the European call option. Therefore, deep-in-the-money options behave as if they were stocks.

$$\Gamma = \frac{\Delta delta}{\Delta S} \tag{4.12}$$

Vega is the sensitivity of the option price to a small change in volatility. It occurs in an option because of the gamma in the option: the higher the volatility of the stock, the more the gamma of the option will stand to gain, because the holder will have both an accelerated gain and a protected downside. For this reason, the option value will rise with increase in volatility.

$$Vega = \frac{\Delta C}{\Delta \sigma} \tag{4.13}$$

Theta is the time decay, which is the change in the option price over a short period of time, assuming the other variables (including the stock price) do not change. As time to maturity decreases, the opportunity of benefiting from the downside protection or gain on the upside return decreases. Therefore, the option value decays.

$$\Theta = \frac{\Delta C}{\Delta t} \tag{4.14}$$

Gamma (Γ) and theta (Θ) are related concepts. Since an option provides downside protection, the option must have positive gamma. Given a high positive gamma, the option should have a higher expected return when the stock volatility becomes higher. This effect is counterbalanced by the time decay such that a *delta-neutral portfolio* should have a risk-free return. For this reason, gamma and theta should be related. The relationship is given by

$$\Theta + \frac{1}{2}\sigma^2 S^2 \Gamma = r\Pi \tag{4.15}$$

given that the portfolio is delta-neutral (i.e., the option is delta-hedged by the stock) and the portfolio value is Π. (See appendix B for the derivation.)

4.8   Extensions of the Black–Scholes Model

The Black–Scholes model presented in this chapter was proposed by Rendleman and Bartter (1979) and Cox, Ross, and Rubinstein (1979). The original model presented by Black and Scholes (1973) was formulated in a continuous time world, where all individuals can trade the option at any time continuously. The model presented has ignored some of the details in option contracts in practice. But these details can be captured in most cases by simple adjustments to the basic model. The following are some examples.

Discrete Time Versus Continuous Time Models

The Black–Scholes model explicitly assumes that the continuously compounded rates of return of the stock are normally distributed with a constant mean and variance. Therefore, the stock price at period T in the future is lognormally distributed. To understand this, we need to make two observations. First, the future stock price is equal to $S_0 \exp[\mu_S \cdot T]$, where μ_S is the continuously compounded stock return and a normally distributed variable by assumption. Second, if we take a logarithm over a random variable and the resulting random variable exhibits a normal distribution, we can say that the random variable is lognormally distributed. For example, a random variable $\tilde{x}$ is lognormally distributed if the logarithm of $\tilde{x}$ is normally distributed. We have the equation $\ln S_T = \ln S_0 + \mu_S \cdot T$. Since $\ln S_0$ is constant and μ_S is normally distributed, S_T is lognormally distributed by definition.

We choose the parameters of a binomial distribution, in the limit, which will converge to a given lognormal distribution (see appendix D for the specifications of the parameters). To this end, we assume one period, and the interval of one period is partitioned into m subintervals so that as m tends to infinity, the binomial distribution will converge to the given lognormal distribution.

Since we can specify the lognormal distribution and the binomial distribution with the respective mean and variance, we can match the mean and variance of the binomial distribution with those of the lognormal distribution for approximation purposes. Therefore, given the lognormal mean and variance, we can express the mean and variance of the binomial distribution in terms of the mean and variance of the lognormal distribution and the number of partitions.

By constructing the binomial distribution, we can accommodate various features, such as an early exercise where the option holders have the right to exercise at any time before the expiration date, which cannot be incorporated by the Black–Scholes closed-form solution.

The Black–Scholes model explicitly assumes that the stock price is a continuous time state variable that will move only infinitesimal increments over any infinitesimal time interval. Therefore, the resulting sample path of the stock price is continuous. Moreover, it assumes that the continuously compounded rates of return of the stock are normally distributed with a constant mean and variance, so that we can derive the intuitively appealing closed-form solution.

Time-Varying Stock Volatilities and the Jump Process

One may criticize the lognormal stock price distribution assumption used thus far by arguing that it is unlikely that the stock volatilities are constant over time. The second criticism is focused on the assumption of continuous stock price movements.

Obviously, the volatility of the stock returns is not constant through time, so the constant variance of the lognormal distribution in the Black–Scholes model can be extended to incorporate a time-varying variance. Cox (1975) derived a call option model that explicitly assumes a nonstationary variance of stock returns where the variance of stock returns depends on the stock price level. Because of this dependency of the variance on the stock price level, the distribution is nonstationary.

As we saw on Black Monday, when the stock market fell precipitously, losing 30 percent of the capitalization in two days in October 1987, stock prices often exhibit sudden, large movements. Cox and Ross (1976) were the first authors to analyze the possibility of valuing options under the assumption that the underlying asset follows a continuous-time jump process.

Term Structure of Interest Rates and Interest Rate Risks

The Black–Scholes model assumes a flat and constant term structure of interest rates. If the interest rate risk is negligibly small relative to the stock risks but the yield curve is not flat, adjusting the Black–Scholes model is quite straightforward. At each node point on the binomial lattice, we can assume that the one period discount rate is the one-period forward rate, not the fixed constant rate used in the Black–Scholes model.

The Black–Scholes model also assumes only the stock price risk. This is obviously a restrictive assumption, since unexpected interest rate shifts can be a major source of uncertainty for the valuation of a long dated option; the time value of money for long dated securities is often an important source of risk.

Merton (1973) was the first to explicitly derive a European call option that incorporated a stochastic interest rate. Following the standard approach to constructing an arbitrage portfolio with the call option, the default-free discount bond, and the stock, Merton derived a partial differential equation whose solution is the price of a European call that is subject to both stock price and interest rate uncertainty. We will consider this problem explicitly in chapter 7.

Dividend-Paying Stock

Thus far we have ignored the impact of the stock dividends on the option price. Clearly, the dividends affect the option price. Consider a long dated call option with a time to expiration of ten years to demonstrate the issue. The option holder in this case would not receive any of the dividends that are paid to the stockholders. For this reason, the call option price should be lower with a higher dividend payout.

One measure of dividend payout is the dividend yield, the annual dividend payment per share divided by the stock price. For each period, the dividend yield plus the yield on the capital gain (capital gain/stock price) is the total return of the stock. Therefore, to price an option of a dividend-paying stock, we need to make just a minor adjustment in the above model.

In setting up the stock lattice as in figure 4.2, we now require the stock drift to be the risk-free rate net of the dividend yield, so that the stock drift is biased downward by the dividend payment. Then we apply the backward substitution procedure or the risk-neutral valuation approach, using this binomial lattice. However, the present value, discounting the expected value, is determined by using the risk-free rate, and not the risk-free rate net of the dividend yields. The same methodology applies to the put options or other types of the options that we will discuss in chapter 7.

4.9   Option Pricing Procedure and Analytic Framework

This section summarizes the methods proposed in the previous section through a step-by-step procedure building the pricing models and the analytical framework. The formulas below are based on the continuously compounding risk-free rate r and stock volatility σ given for the specified step size.

Step 1. Set up a risk-neutral binomial lattice given the stock price, the volatility σ over one period, and the step size.

$$S(n+1, i+1) = S(n, i)e^{\sigma}$$
$$S(n+1, i) = S(n, i)e^{-\sigma} \tag{4.16}$$

Step 2. Let r be the risk-free rate, and the risk neutral probability p for the upward movement is given by

$$p = (e^{r} - e^{-\sigma})/(e^{\sigma} - e^{-\sigma}) \tag{4.17}$$

Step 3. Determine the terminal conditions and roll back to determine the option price in the risk-neutral option lattice. The terminal conditions are payoffs of the options at the expiration date as specified by the stock prices and the option payout rules at the nodes on the expiration date.

Step 4. Sensitivities are determined by applying the model repeatedly. A small change is made to a parameter, x, of the model, denoted by Δx. The parameter may be the stock price, the time to expiration, the volatility, the risk-free rate, and so on. The small change of the parameter will lead to a corresponding small change in the option price ΔC. Sensitivity is defined as the ratio of the small changes, $\Delta C/\Delta x$. By definition, the sensitivity measure is dependent on the choice of "small change," which may be 1 percent or less of the parameter. But the value of the option is related to the parameters such that the sensitivity measures are quite insensitive to the size of the "small change" as long as the change is small.

Step 5. Pathwise values can be determined by discounting the payout at the risk-free rate in the risk-neutral lattice. The associated probability of a pathwise value is calculated by $p^i(1-p)^{N-i}$, where N is the final time period for the scenario and i is the number of upward movements along that path.

The number of possible paths in the binomial lattice is astronomical in practice. Much of financial research on options consists of searching for a practical solution to the problem. One common methodology is to begin with the risk-neutral probability such that the upward movement has the same probability as a downward movement. Then all the scenarios have the same probability. Next, we use a random number generator and randomly take the paths in the lattice. Assuming that a sample of these paths is a good representation of all the paths, we calculate the pathwise value of this sample and take an average. The average value is the option price. This methodology is called a Monte Carlo simulation. A description of the Monte Carlo simulation is in appendix E.

Our main objective is to provide the principles behind option pricing and their applications. We therefore introduce the concept of pathwise values to provide insight into the valuation models of options.

4.10 Applications of Option Models

Option Trading

The basic idea of using an option is to provide protection on the downside risk. If the investor believes the stock price will rise, buying a call option will enable the holder to realize higher returns if the stock rises. However, the holder always has the maximum loss of only the initial investment, because an investor cannot lose more than he pays for an asset. Similarly, if the investor believes the stock will fall, he can buy a put option.

A *covered call* refers to writing a call option while holding the underlying stock. The investor (or corporation) receives the premium, often treated as income to the firm. When the stock price falls below the strike price at expiration, the covered call position will have only the stock position. If the stock price rises above the strike price at expiration, the option holder will exercise the option, and the investor (or corporation) will receive the strike price, losing the position in the stock. When comparing a covered call position against holding the stock alone, the investor is capping the upside of the stock position to the strike price while still bearing all the downside risk of the stock. In return, the investor (or corporation) receives the premiums up front as income.

Options offer effective ways to implement different investment strategies. Equivalent strategies using only stocks and bonds can be prohibitively expensive in terms of the transaction costs. One popular use of a put option is as "insurance." If we are concerned with the stock portfolio losing significant value when the market falls, put options can be bought to protect the downside of the portfolio.

We must remember that time decay, gamma (curvature to the price risk), and vega (sensitivity to the volatility risk) are interrelated for a particular option. An option with high gamma may also have high vega risk. Therefore a portfolio of options may be needed to satisfy the requirements of an option strategy.

An Option Strategy—A Straddle

There are many option strategies. We will discuss one particular strategy to illustrate how the financial model is used to analyze the effectiveness of an option strategy. If the investor thinks that the market will move significantly, but is unsure of which direction, he can buy the volatility. In this case, the investor buys a call and a put with the same strike price. This position is called a straddle. A straddle enables the holder to profit from a significant upward or downward move of the stock, or an increase in the stock's volatility. However, if the stock does not move significantly, the position will lose value in the time decay. Therefore, if we plot the value of the straddle against the stock price level, the straddle performance profile is a u-shape with the minimum point at the current stock price.

Figure 4.10 shows that the delta of the straddle is 0 at the current stock price; thus the price of the straddle reaches its lowest value at the current price, and the value increases if the stock price either increases or decreases significantly. When the stock price is high, the call option is significantly in-the-money and the put option is significantly out-of-the-money. For this reason, the delta of the straddle is the same as that of the deep in-the-money call option; that is, delta equals 1. Conversely, when the stock price is low, the put option is deep-in-the-money and the call option is out-of-the-money, and the delta becomes −1.

As expected, the gamma of the straddle is highest at the current stock price. After all, the purpose of the straddle is to capture the accelerated increase in value as the stock price increases or decreases. As we explained before, the vega and gamma are similar because they both capture the value of the option in relation to the stock volatility. Figure 4.10 shows that the straddle vega and straddle gamma behave very similarly.

Implied Volatility

The stock volatility is often estimated from the historical stock returns. The volatility is the standard deviation of the time series of the stock returns. However, such a measure of the risk of the stock is dependent on the historical experience and is not forward-looking. If we believe that the stock has a higher risk in the future than that in the past, then this approach may not be correct.

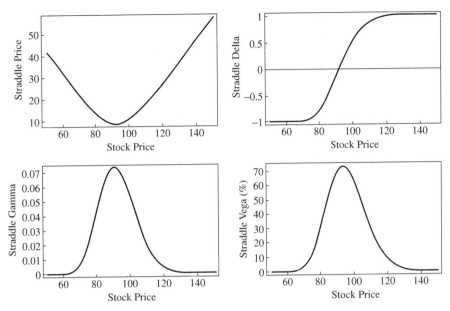

Figure 4.10 Profile delta, gamma, and vega of the straddle over a range of stock prices. The straddle consists of longing one call and one put with the same strike price. The purpose of the straddle is to capture the accelerated increase in value as the stock price deviates from the current price level, regardless of the direction. The stock price range is from 50 to 150. The stock volatility is 12%. The maturity is one year. The continuously compounding risk-free rate is 8%. We have partitioned one period into 50 subperiods for accuracy purposes. The delta of the straddle is 0 at the current stock price, which means that the straddle price reaches its lowest value at the current stock price, and the straddle price increases if the stock price either increases or decreases significantly. When the stock price is high, the call option is significantly in-the-money and the put option is significantly out-of-the-money. Since the delta of a deep in-the-money call option converges to 1 and that of a significantly out-of-the-money put option is almost 0, the delta of the straddle is the same as that of the deep in-the-money call option, which is 1. Exactly the reverse interpretation holds when the stock price is low. As expected, the gamma of the straddle is highest at the current stock price.

A stock option offers an alternative approach to measuring the stock volatility on a forward-looking basis. We can use the Black–Scholes model to determine the volatility as an input to the model such that model option price equals the observed option price. This volatility measure is called the *implied volatility*.

Consider a stock that has different options, put and call with different strike prices and expiration dates. The prices of these options should be determined by the volatility of the stock. Therefore, we can use the Black–Scholes model to determine the stock volatility that best fits the observed option prices. Using the best fitted volatility to determine the model prices of the option, we can determine the deviation of the observed prices from the model prices. In this approach we do not rely on the historical estimation of the stock volatility but use the stock's implied volatility, derived from the market observed option prices. When we use this approach, we say that we have calibrated the model to the observed prices. This calibration procedure is a practical method of using financial models that do not depend on the historical experience. We will revisit the calibration methodology in chapter 6.

4.11   Accounting for Employee Stock Options

The option pricing model may also be used for financial reporting. *Employee stock options* are options, usually call options, issued to a firm's employees as part of their compensation. Usually these options are vested: the employees cannot exercise them for a certain period (for example, three years) and they must be employed by the company at the time of exercising the options.

In recent years, there has been an increased use of stock options as compensation for corporate employees. It has been suggested that the issuance of these options enables the firm to align employees' goal with that of the shareholders: maximization of the shareholders' value. There are other possible reasons. Direct compensation to employees is an expense that directly affects the net income of the firm. If the firm seeks to preserve capital for growth, it has the incentive to issue stock options to employees. These options usually expire in from one year to ten years. The strike price is usually higher than or equal to the prevailing stock price at issuance. There is usually no market for these options. At expiration, the employee can elect to exercise the option and buy the firm's stocks at the strike price.

The impact of option compensation leads to the discussion of financial reporting of employee stock options. Since the shareholders have to bear the costs of these options, how should employee stock options be accounted for in financial reporting?

Under APB opinion no. 25, compensation expense arising from employee stock options consists of the excess of the market value of the stock over the exercise price of the option on the grant date. If the exercise price equals or is higher than the market value of the stock on the grant date, no compensation expense is recognized. That means, from a financial reporting perspective, the cost of issuing employee stock options is not directly recognized.

It has been argued that financial reporting does not have to recognize such an expense because investors can also consider the impact on the share values on a fully diluted basis, something that is reported. That means investors can assume that all the options will be exercised, and therefore the shares outstanding include the employee stock options, resulting in a dilution.

But the impact on stockholders' value using fully diluted analysis would overstate the impact of employee stock options on the firm. Using the fully diluted approach, the impact would not be related to the market volatility, the time to expiration, the level of the strike price (as long as the strike price is above the stock price at the grant date), and all other market parameters such as the interest rate and the stock price level. In short, the measure would be so imprecise that it encourages the firm to structure the employee stock option in a way that will optimize the presentation of the financial statements.

Another approach is to use the Black–Scholes model to determine the option prices. This approach may lead to a significant departure from the basic principles of accounting. The employee stock option prices would be marked to market, reflecting the changing market environment. Indeed, in 1993, the Financial Accounting Standards Board tried to mandate the expensing of options, but was unsuccessful because of the opposition to the idea. More recently, Boeing, Coca-Cola, and Winn-Dixie Stores have been among the important U.S. corporations that have begun to expense employee stock options. They retain investment banks to value the options. The options are valued by using financial models because they are not traded in the market. When the options are issued, their value is treated as an expense, thus affecting the earnings.

Clearly, employee stock options are important to financial reporting. The *Wall Street Journal* (July 15, 2002) reported that the estimated percentages declines in earnings per share for 2002 if stock options were expensed: information technology, 70 percent; telecom, 12 percent. FAS 123 suggests that an option valuation model be used to determine the employee option value, which should be reported to adjust the net income.

4.12 Intuitive Explanations of the Behavior of an Equity Option

Paul O'Neill was the chairman of Alcoa, the world's largest aluminum concern, before becoming the secretary of the Treasury. According to the *New York Times Magazine* of January 13, 2002,[5] when he left the company, he had options for almost 4 million shares of stock. "Taking the Treasury job meant walking away from the bigger part of his Alcoa-based fortune . . . giving up his stock options."

This was a matter of concern to Mr. O'Neill. He felt that he should get his children's permission to give up this fortune in order to serve his country. He believed that he would never be able to spend all the money from the stock options, and therefore he was effectively giving up his children's money.

The *New York Times* continued, "Interestingly, he calculated the value of these options at $250 million. Well established pricing models value these options at roughly $25 million. O'Neill got his number using financial assumptions about how high Alcoa stock was likely to go in the next 10 years."

He told his children that they would be giving up $250 million. Fortunately for the nation, he said that his children did not care. Later, the reporter did verify the episode with one of his children. The important part of the anecdote was that the children really did not care, whether $250 million or $25 million. And Mr. O'Neill became secretary of the Treasury.

A pragmatic reader can argue that this anecdote is playing with words. The "value" of the option can be interpreted as the present value or cash equivalent today, commonly referred to as fair value. Or "value" can be interpreted as the simulated value over a long-term horizon, giving a value under a certain scenario.

To some, "fair value" has no meaning. The usual argument goes as follows: No one can take these options to the securities market to exchange them for $25 million. We have seen that all the standard models have to make some assumption about the volatilities, and there is no agreed-upon price.

The proponent of the fair value approach would argue that simulating a future possible value is, without a doubt, erroneous. Suppose the children were given $25 million cash, but the government said, "Since you can buy $25 million worth of Alcoa stock options, the value of the cash is really $250 million, and accordingly the gift tax should be based on $250 million." This argument is so preposterous that we all discard it as nonsense. But valuing an option based on a scenario is no different than valuing any asset (bonds, stocks, pensions) based on a scenario.

This anecdote underscores several of the fundamental issues in option pricing. First, the discount rate of an option payoff is not a simple and easily understood number like a risk-free rate with a constant premium. The discount rate has to depend on all the characteristics of the option, and any casual method that we use for bonds and stocks can lead to large errors in option pricing. The simulated value may be $250 million, but the appropriate discount rate for the option can be so high that the present value is $25 million.

Second, while financial theory proposes valuation models, we need to accept that valuation does not have to be a price that can convert a security to cash. "Fair value" is a concept that has to be accepted before it can be used for financial reporting. Financial reporting can be in the form of a financial statement in the annual report or verbal statement of an estate's value. The debate of "fair value accounting" that we will visit in chapter 11 is as much a debate on the valuation methodology as a debate on concept.

We are a bit ahead of ourselves in this valuation issue. But Mr. O'Neill's option pricing method is not a minor episode in his living room. Valuing options under some "reasonable" set of assumptions is more common a practice than one would hope. The unfortunate part of the story is that most "reasonable" assumptions are far from reasonable, as this anecdote shows. We hope this book can make this issue clear as we proceed.

4.13 Summary

Options are extensively used in financial markets and their valuation has broad applications. We have explained that five key variables affect option prices: the underlying price, the volatility (standard deviation of returns), the risk-free rate, the exercise price, and the time to maturity. We have shown that an option has special characteristics. In comparison with a stock, an option is priced relative to an underlying security. And relative to the underlying security, an option offers downside protection measured by gamma. Related to the gamma, the option value is changed by a change in the volatility of the underlying security, even if the security value remains unchanged.

However, the pricing of an option is complicated because there is no simple method of determining the discount rate of the expected cash flows. Therefore, applying the discounted cash flow approach will lead to an erroneous discount rate. Implementing the Capital Asset Pricing model will be complicated since the appropriate β for an option is difficult to estimate because it changes on a real-time basis.

In this chapter, we have presented the Black–Scholes model, which provides a relatively simple model for pricing options. The methodology of the option pricing model shows that we do not need to know the equilibrium discount rate for the option. The price is determined by continually revising the hedge, using the underlying securities. The model shows that an option can have characteristics different from the stock. The gamma of a call option measures the acceleration of the increase in price when the stock price rises and the deceleration when the stock price falls. Time decay measures the fall in the option price when the stock price remains unchanged over time.

The Black–Scholes model introduces the concept of dynamic replication. It proposes that options can be replicated dynamically, using the risk-free rate and the underlying securities. By the law of one price, the option value can be determined as the cost of replication.

The Black–Scholes model is widely used in option trading, not only in pricing but also in formulating trading strategies to replicate options, hedge stock positions, and provide product innovations for corporate management. More recently, the Black-Scholes model has been used for financial reporting.

The contribution of the Black–Scholes model goes beyond providing a valuation formula for an option. The valuation approach is a key to unlock the door to better understanding of the valuation of many securities and financial decisions, from options to bonds, from valuation of a balance sheet to corporate finance, and even to the option's underlying stock. The underlying stock is an option itself, as we will discuss in chapter 13.

Also, the impact of the Black–Scholes model goes beyond the stock option market. We will see that the basic insights of the model can be used in many major financial markets. One important assumption we use in this chapter is that there is no interest rate risk. Chapter 5 will focus the analysis on options related to interest rate risks. As we have discussed, interest rate risk differs from stock risks in two fundamental ways. First, interest rate is not a security, and therefore one cannot determine the hedge in a straightforward manner. Second, interest rate movement has to take the yield curve shape and movements into account. We will discuss these issues chapter 5.

Appendix A. Derivation of the Black–Scholes Continuous Time Model Using Different Numeraires

We derive the Black–Scholes Model by using two different numeraires. The first is a one-period risk-free rate and the second is the stock price itself. We normalize all the assets, such as the stock or the call option, with the numeraire because we can construct a martingale process by normalizing. Once we express the option price as an expected value of the payoff at maturity date, we can derive the Black–Scholes model in a straightforward manner whose mathematical derivation is shown in appendixes A1 and A2. Basically, we need economic reasoning to express the option price in terms of the expected value of the payoff at maturity. Once we do that, the rest of the job is algebra to calculate the expected value.

First, we assume a stochastic process for a stock and a deterministic risk-free process. Second, we can choose the one of two numeraire candidates. If we choose the one-period risk-free asset, we divide the stock price by the one-period risk-free bond price. In this case, the normalized bond price is always 1. Third, by applying Ito's lemma,[6] we can derive the stochastic process for the normalized asset prices, which is also called the relative price process. Fourth, we identify the equivalent martingale measure by applying Girsanov's theorem.[7] By analogy, identifying the equivalent martingale measure is equal to calculating a risk-neutral probability in the binomial option pricing model. When applying the risk-neutral probability, we can convert a risky asset such as an option into a risk-free asset. If we can convert the option into the risk-free asset by the risk-neutral probability, we can evaluate the option price by calculating the expected value using the risk-neutral probability and discounting it at the risk-free rate. We can do exactly the same thing with the continuous case. By identifying the equivalent martingale measure, we can convert the relative price process into a martingale. By the definition of the martingale process, we can express the option price as the expected value of payoff at maturity.

There are two assets, money market account and stock

$$dS = \mu S dt + \sigma S dW$$

$dB = rBdt$

We can use two kinds of numeraires

$S'_t = \frac{S_t}{B_t}$ $B'_t = \frac{B_t}{S_t}$

We can obtain the relative price processes using the Ito lemma

$dS' = (\mu - r)\, S'dt + \sigma S' dW$ $dB' = (r - \mu + \sigma^2)\, B'dt - \sigma B' dW$

To identify the equivalent martingale measures, we can apply Girsanov's Theorem

For $dW = dW^B - \left(\frac{\mu - r}{\sigma}\right) dt$ we obtain the new measure Q^B, where the process S' follows

For $dW = dW^S + \left(\frac{r - \mu + r^2}{\sigma}\right) dt$ we obtain the new measure Q^S, where the process B' follows $dB' = (r - \mu + \sigma^2)\, B'dt - \sigma B' \left(dW^s + \frac{r - \mu + 0^2}{\sigma} dt\right) = -\sigma B' dW^s$, which is a martingale. Under the measure Q^s the prize process $1/S$ follows

$d\frac{1}{S} = (-\mu + \sigma^2)\frac{1}{S} dt - \sigma\frac{1}{S}\left(dW^S + \left(\frac{r-\mu}{\sigma} + \sigma\right) dt\right) = -r\frac{1}{S} dt - \sigma\frac{1}{S} dW^S$

$dS' = (\mu - r)\, S'dt + \sigma S' \left(dW^B - \frac{\mu - r}{\sigma} dt\right)$
$= \sigma S' dW^B$

Under the measure Q^B, the original price process S follows the process

$dS = \mu S dt + \sigma S \left(dW^B - \frac{\mu - r}{\sigma} dt\right)$
$= rSdt + \sigma S dW^B$

The solution to the above SDE can be expressed as

$S_t = S_0 \exp\left\{\left(r - \frac{1}{2}\sigma^2\right)t + \sigma W_t^B\right\}$ $\frac{1}{S_t} = \frac{1}{S_0}\exp\left\{\left(-r - \frac{1}{2}\sigma^2\right)t - \sigma W_t^S\right\}$

where $W_t^B \sim N(0, t)$ or   where $W_t^S \sim N(0, t)$ or

$\ln S_t = \ln S_0 + \left(r - \frac{\sigma^2}{2}\right)t + \sigma W_t^B$ $\ln S_t = \ln S_0 + \left(r + \frac{\sigma^2}{2}\right)t + \sigma W_t^S$

Now we define

$Z = \dfrac{\ln S_t - \ln S_0 - \left(r - \frac{\sigma^2}{2}\right)t}{\sigma\sqrt{t}} \sim N(0, 1)$ $Z = \dfrac{\ln S_t - \ln S_0 - \left(r + \frac{\sigma^2}{2}\right)t}{\sigma\sqrt{t}} \sim N(0, 1)$

$n(z) = \frac{1}{\sqrt{2\pi}}e^{-\frac{z^2}{2}}$ $n(Z) = \frac{1}{\sqrt{2\pi}}e^{-\frac{Z^2}{2}}$

$S_t = \exp\left\{Z\sigma\sqrt{t} + \left(r - \frac{\sigma^2}{2}\right)t + \ln S_0\right\}$ $S_t = \exp\left\{Z\sigma\sqrt{t} + \left(r + \frac{\sigma^2}{2}\right)t + \ln S_0\right\}$

From the martingale property, we know that[8]

$C_0 = E^B\left[Max\left(S_T - K, 0\right)/B_T\right]$ $C_0 = S_0 \cdot E^s\left[Max\left(S_T - K, 0\right)/S_T\right]$

$= B_T^{-1}E^B\left[(S_T - K)^+\right]$ $= S_0 \cdot E^s\left[\left(1 - \frac{K}{S_T}\right)^+\right]$

$= B_T^{-1}E^B\left[\left(e^{Z\sigma\sqrt{T} + \left(r - \frac{\sigma^2}{2}\right)T + \ln S_0} - K\right)^+\right]$ $= S_0 \cdot E^s\left[\left(1 - Ke^{-Z\sigma\sqrt{T} - \left(r + \frac{\sigma^2}{2}\right)T - \ln S_0}\right)^+\right]$

Appendix A1. Derivation of the Black–Scholes Continuous Time Model Using the Stock as a Numeraire

Define

$$Z = \frac{\ln S_T - \left(r - \frac{\sigma^2}{2}\right)T - \ln S_0}{\sigma\sqrt{T}} \sim N(0, 1)$$

$$n(Z) = \frac{1}{\sqrt{2\pi}}e^{-\frac{z^2}{2}}$$

$$S_T = e^{Z\sigma\sqrt{T} + \left(r - \frac{\sigma^2}{2}\right)T + \ln S_0}$$

And

$$E^B\left[(S_T - K)^+\right] = E^B\left[\left(e^{Z\sigma\sqrt{T}+\left(r-\frac{\sigma^2}{2}\right)T+\ln S_0} - K\right)^+\right]$$

$$= \int_{\frac{\ln(K/S_0)-\left(r-\frac{\sigma^2}{2}\right)T}{\sigma\sqrt{T}}}^{\infty} e^{Z\sigma\sqrt{T}+\left(r-\frac{\sigma^2}{2}\right)T+\ln S_0} n(Z)dZ - K\int_{\frac{\ln(K/S_0)-\left(r-\frac{\sigma^2}{2}\right)T}{\sigma\sqrt{T}}}^{\infty} n(Z)dZ$$

Therefore, $\left(e^{Z\sigma\sqrt{T}+\left(r-\frac{\sigma^2}{2}\right)T+\ln S_0} > K \Leftrightarrow Z > \dfrac{\ln(K/S_0) - \left(r-\frac{\sigma^2}{2}\right)T}{\sigma\sqrt{T}}\right)$

$$= e^{rT+\ln S_0}\int_{\frac{\ln(K/S_0)-\left(r-\frac{\sigma^2}{2}\right)T}{\sigma\sqrt{T}}}^{\infty} n(Z-\sigma\sqrt{T})dZ - K\int_{\frac{\ln(K/S_0)-\left(r-\frac{\sigma^2}{2}\right)T}{\sigma\sqrt{T}}}^{\infty} n(Z)dZ$$

Let $Z - \sigma\sqrt{T} = x$

$$E^B\left[(S_T - K)^+\right] =$$

$$e^{rT+\ln S_0}\int_{\frac{\ln(K/S_0)-\left(r-\frac{\sigma^2}{2}\right)T-\sigma^2 T}{\sigma\sqrt{T}}}^{\infty} n(x)dx - K\int_{\frac{\ln(K/S_0)-\left(r-\frac{\sigma^2}{2}\right)T}{\sigma\sqrt{T}}}^{\infty} n(Z)dZ \tag{4.18}$$

The first term on the right-hand side of equation (4.18)

$$= e^{rT+\ln S_0}\int_{\frac{\ln(K/S_0)-\left(r-\frac{\sigma^2}{2}\right)T-\sigma^2 T}{\sigma\sqrt{T}}}^{\infty} n(x)dx = e^{rT+\ln S_0}\left(1 - \int_{-\infty}^{\frac{\ln(K/S_0)-\left(r+\frac{\sigma^2}{2}\right)T}{\sigma\sqrt{T}}} n(x)dx\right)$$

$$= e^{rT+\ln S_0}\left(1 - \int_{-\infty}^{-\frac{\ln(S_0/K)+\left(r+\frac{\sigma^2}{2}\right)T}{\sigma\sqrt{T}}} n(x)dx\right) = e^{rT+\ln S_0}N\left(\frac{\ln(S_0/K)+\left(r+\frac{\sigma^2}{2}\right)T}{\sigma\sqrt{T}}\right)$$

The second term on the right-hand side of equation (4.18)

$$= K\int_{\frac{\ln(K/S_0)-\left(r-\frac{\sigma^2}{2}\right)T}{\sigma\sqrt{T}}}^{\infty} n(Z)dZ = K\left(1 - \int_{-\infty}^{\frac{\ln(K/S_0)-\left(r-\frac{\sigma^2}{2}\right)T}{\sigma\sqrt{T}}} n(Z)dZ\right)$$

$$= K \cdot N\left(\frac{\ln(S_0/K)+\left(r-\frac{\sigma^2}{2}\right)T}{\sigma\sqrt{T}}\right)$$

If we arrange those two terms,

$$E^B\left[(S_T - K)^+\right] = e^{rT+\ln S_0}N\left(\frac{\ln(S_0/K)+(r+\frac{\sigma^2}{2})T}{\sigma\sqrt{T}}\right) - KN\left(\frac{\ln(S_0/K)+\left(r-\frac{\sigma^2}{2}\right)T}{\sigma\sqrt{T}}\right)$$

Therefore,

$$C_0 = e^{-rT} E^B \left[(S_T - K)^+ \right] = S_0 N(d_1) - K e^{-rT} N(d_2) \tag{4.19}$$

where

$$d_1 = \frac{\ln (S_0/K) + \left(r + \frac{\sigma^2}{2} \right) T}{\sigma \sqrt{T}}, d_2 = \frac{\ln (S_0/K) + \left(r - \frac{\sigma^2}{2} \right) T}{\sigma \sqrt{T}}$$

Appendix A2. Derivation of the Black–Scholes Continuous Time Model Using a Money Market Account as a Numeraire

$$C_0 = S_0 \cdot E^s \left[Max \left(1 - \frac{K}{S_T}, 0 \right) \right]$$

$$= S_0 \cdot E^s \left[\left(1 - \frac{K}{S_T} \right)^+ \right]$$

$$= S_0 \cdot E^s \left[\left(1 - K e^{-Z\sigma\sqrt{T} - \left(r + \frac{\sigma^2}{2} \right) T - \ln S_0} \right)^+ \right]$$

$$= \int_{\frac{\ln\left(\frac{K}{S_0}\right) - \left(r + \frac{\sigma^2}{2}\right)T}{\sigma\sqrt{T}}}^{\infty} n(Z)dZ - K \int_{\frac{\ln\left(\frac{K}{S_0}\right) - \left(r + \frac{\sigma^2}{2}\right)T}{\sigma\sqrt{T}}}^{\infty} e^{-Z\sigma\sqrt{T} - \left(r + \frac{\sigma^2}{2} \right) T - \ln S_0} n(Z)dZ$$

Therefore, $\left(1 - K e^{-Z\sigma\sqrt{T} - \left(r + \frac{\sigma^2}{2} \right) T - \ln S_0} > 0 \Leftrightarrow Z > \frac{\ln \left(\frac{K}{S_0} \right) - \left(r + \frac{\sigma^2}{2} \right) T}{\sigma \sqrt{T}} \right)$.

Let $Z + \sigma \sqrt{T} = x$

$$E^s \left[\left(1 - K e^{-Z\sigma\sqrt{T} - \left(r + \frac{\sigma^2}{2} \right) T - \ln S_0} \right)^+ \right]$$

$$= \int_{\frac{\ln\left(\frac{K}{S_0}\right) - \left(r + \frac{\sigma^2}{2}\right)T}{\sigma\sqrt{T}}}^{\infty} n(Z)dZ - \frac{K e^{-rT}}{S_0} \int_{\frac{\ln\left(\frac{K}{S_0}\right) - \left(r - \frac{\sigma^2}{2}\right)T}{\sigma\sqrt{T}}}^{\infty} n(x)dx \tag{4.20}$$

The first term on the right-hand side of equation (4.20)

$$\int_{\frac{\ln\left(\frac{K}{S_0}\right) - \left(r + \frac{\sigma^2}{2}\right)T}{\sigma\sqrt{T}}}^{\infty} n(Z)\, dZ = \left(1 - \int_{-\infty}^{\frac{\ln\left(\frac{K}{S_0}\right) - \left(r + \frac{\sigma^2}{2}\right)T}{\sigma\sqrt{T}}} n(Z)\, dZ \right) = \left(1 - \int_{-\infty}^{-\frac{\ln\left(\frac{S_0}{K}\right) + \left(r + \frac{\sigma^2}{2}\right)T}{\sigma\sqrt{T}}} n(Z)\, dZ \right)$$

$$= N \left(\frac{\ln \left(\frac{S_0}{K} \right) + \left(r + \frac{\sigma^2}{2} \right) T}{\sigma \sqrt{T}} \right) = N(d_1)$$

The second term on the right-hand side of equation (4.20)

$$\frac{Ke^{-rT}}{S_0}\left(\int_{\frac{\ln\left(\frac{K}{S_0}\right)-\left(r-\frac{\sigma^2}{2}\right)T}{\sigma\sqrt{T}}}^{\infty} n\,(x)\,dx\right) = \frac{Ke^{-rT}}{S_0}\left(1 - \int_{-\infty}^{\frac{\ln\left(\frac{K}{S_0}\right)-\left(r-\frac{\sigma^2}{2}\right)\cdot T}{\sigma\sqrt{T}}} n\,(x)\,dx\right)$$

$$= \frac{Ke^{-rT}}{S_0}\left(1 - \int_{-\infty}^{-\frac{\ln\frac{S_0}{K}+\left(r-\frac{\sigma^2}{2}\right)\cdot T}{\sigma\sqrt{T}}} n\,(x)\,dx\right)$$

$$= \frac{Ke^{-rT}}{S_0}N\left(\frac{\ln\left(\frac{S_0}{K}\right) + \left(r - \frac{\sigma^2}{2}\right)T}{\sigma\sqrt{T}}\right)$$

$$= \frac{Ke^{-rT}}{S_0}N\,(d_2)$$

Therefore,

$$E^s\left[\left(1 - Ke^{-Z\sigma\sqrt{T}-\left(r+\frac{\sigma^2}{2}\right)T-\ln S_0}\right)^+\right] = N\,(d_1) - \frac{Ke^{-rT}}{S_0}N\,(d_2)$$

$$S_0 \cdot E^s\left[\left(1 - Ke^{-Z\sigma\sqrt{T}-\left(r+\frac{\sigma^2}{2}\right)T-\ln S_0}\right)^+\right] = S_0 \cdot N\,(d_1) - Ke^{-rT}N\,(d_2)$$

Q.E.D.

Appendix B. The Relationship Between the Time Decay and the Gamma of a Delta-Neutral Portfolio

The price of a single derivative dependent on a nondividend-paying stock must satisfy the differential equation $rSC_S + C_t + \frac{1}{2}\sigma^2 S^2 C_{SS} = rC$.

It follows that the value of a portfolio of such derivatives, f, also satisfies the differential equation

$$\frac{\partial f}{\partial t} + rS\frac{\partial f}{\partial S} + \frac{1}{2}\sigma^2 S^2\frac{\partial^2 f}{\partial S^2} = rf \qquad (4.21)$$

Because

$$\Theta = \frac{\partial f}{\partial t}, \Delta = \frac{\partial f}{\partial S}, \Gamma = \frac{\partial^2 f}{\partial S^2}$$

it follows that

$$\Theta + rS\Delta + \frac{1}{2}\sigma^2 S^2\Gamma = rf \qquad (4.22)$$

For a delta-neutral portfolio, $\Delta = 0$ and

$$\Theta + \frac{1}{2}\sigma^2 S^2 \Gamma = rf \tag{4.23}$$

Appendix C. Pathwise Valuation

The option price is the mean of the pathwise values of the risk-neutral lattice.

Proof: We assume S, u, d, p, n, X, r as usual. We prove by induction. When the option maturity is 1, the option value is

$$\frac{p \cdot Max\,[uS - X, 0] + (1 - p) \cdot Max\,[dS - X, 0]}{e^r}.$$

The number of paths at period 1 is two. When we represent an upward movement and a downward movement by {1} and {0}, respectively, the paths at period 1 are {1} and {0}, because we have only an upward movement or a downward movement at period 1. The pathwise value of {1} is $\frac{Max[uS-X,0]}{e^r}$, and that of {0} is $\frac{Max[dS-X,0]}{e^r}$. Therefore, the mean of two pathwise values is equal to the option values.

When we assume that the $k - 1$ period option price is equal to the mean of the pathwise values, we will show that the k period option price is equal to the mean of the pathwise values. The $k - 1$ period option represents the option which matures at period $k - 1$, and the k period option can be defined similarly. For this purpose, we calculate the k period option value at each node of period $k - 1$ by backward substitution and the mean of pathwise values. If two values are same at each node of period $k - 1$, we can show that the k period option price is equal to the mean of the pathwise values.

From a node of period $k-1$ where the stock price is $u^j d^{k-1-j} S$ or j upward movement has occurred, the stock price will be $u^{j+1} d^{k-j-1} S$ or $u^j d^{k-j} S$ at period k, depending on whether the movement is upward or downward. Therefore, the k period option value at this node of period $k - 1$ is

$$\frac{p \cdot Max\left[u^{j+1} d^{k-j-1} S - X, 0\right] + (1 - p) \cdot Max\left[u^j d^{k-j} S - X, 0\right]}{e^r}.$$

Furthermore, the probability of getting stock price $u^j d^{k-1-j} S$ at period $k - 1$ is $\binom{k-1}{j} p^j (1 - p)^{k-1-j}$. If we multiply the k period option value at the node of period $k - 1$ by the probability, we will get the marginal option value contributed by that particular node to the overall k period option prices.

The total number of paths at period $k - 1$ is 2 to the power of $k - 1$, and it will be twice that at period k, because each path at period $k - 1$ generates two paths at period k. From the node of period $k - 1$, one path has the $u^{j+1} d^{k-j-1} S$ stock price and the other path has the $u^j d^{k-j} S$ stock price at period k.

We know that there are $\binom{k-1}{j}$ paths which have $u^j d^{k-1-j} S$ at period $k - 1$, and each path at period $k - 1$ has the value of $\frac{p \cdot Max[u^{j+1} d^{k-j-1} S - X,0] + (1-p) \cdot Max[u^j d^{k-j} S - X,0]}{e^r}$, which is exactly the value obtained with the backward substitution. Furthermore, the probability of those paths is $\binom{k-1}{j} p^j (1 - p)^{k-1-j}$.

Therefore, the option value and the mean of the pathwise values at period k are equal to each other.

Q.E.D.

Appendix D. Derivation of Discrete Time Parameters

The continuous time model can be derived from the discrete time model, as presented above, by taking the following transformation. m is the number of intervals subdividing a period. Parameters will be adjusted accordingly when we divide one period (e.g., one year) into m subperiods. When we take the limit as n tends toward infinity, the discrete time model will converge to the continuous time model.

Suppose that a stock return is lognormally distributed with mean μ and standard deviation σ. Let the variables be

$$S^* = \text{stock price in the binomial lattice}$$

$$S = \text{initial stock price in the binomial lattice}$$

$$u = \text{upward factor with probability } p$$

$$d = \text{downward factor with probability } (1 - p)$$

$$j = \text{the number of upward movements.}$$

$$j \sim B(n, p) = \text{random variable}$$

For example,

$$S^* = u^j d^{n-j} S$$

the number of time steps is $j + (n - j) = n$.

$$\log\left(\frac{S^*}{S}\right) = j \log(u) + (n - j) \log(d) \sim N(\mu, \sigma^2)$$

First, we can make two equations from the above example, for related mean and variance.

$$E\left[\log\left(\frac{S^*}{S}\right)\right] = E[j] \cdot \log\left(\frac{u}{d}\right) + n \cdot \log(d)$$

$$= n \cdot p \cdot \log\left(\frac{u}{d}\right) + n \cdot \log(d) = \mu \tag{4.24}$$

$$Var\left[\log\left(\frac{S^*}{S}\right)\right] = Var\left(j \cdot \log\left(\frac{u}{d}\right) + n \cdot \log(d)\right)$$

$$= n \cdot p \cdot (1 - p) \cdot \left[\log\left(\frac{u}{d}\right)\right]^2 = \sigma^2 \tag{4.25}$$

Second, we can obtain equation (4.26) from equations (4.24) and (4.25), using the binomial property.

$$n \times p \times \log\left(\frac{u}{d}\right) + n \times \log(d) = \mu$$

$$n \times p \times (1 - p) \times \left[\log\left(\frac{u}{d}\right)\right]^2 = \sigma^2 \tag{4.26}$$

In equation (4.26). There are three unknown variables—u, d, and p—but only two equations.

Cox, Ross, and Rubinstein (CRR, 1979) suggested $u \times d = 1$. It means "the jump sizes are equal."

$$u = exp\left[\sigma\sqrt{\frac{1}{n}}\right], d = exp\left[-\sigma\sqrt{\frac{1}{n}}\right] \text{ and } p = \frac{1}{2} + \frac{1}{2}\frac{\mu}{\sigma}\sqrt{\frac{1}{n}} \qquad (4.27)$$

Jarrow and Rudd (JR, 1983) suggested another constraint on equation (4.26): $p = (1 - p) = 0.5$. It means "equal probability."

$$\text{Let } p = \frac{1}{2}, \text{ then } u = exp\left[\mu\frac{1}{n} + \sigma\sqrt{\frac{1}{n}}\right], d = exp\left[\mu\frac{1}{n} - \sigma\sqrt{\frac{1}{n}}\right] \qquad (4.28)$$

Note that we have derived u, d, and p in the real world. However, we have to convert μ to $r - \sigma^2/2$ in the risk-neutral valuation. Therefore, equations (4.27) and (4.28) convert to (4.29) and (4.30), respectively.

CRR parameters

$$u = exp\left[\sigma\sqrt{\frac{1}{n}}\right], d = exp\left[-\sigma\sqrt{\frac{1}{n}}\right], p = \frac{1}{2} + \frac{1}{2}\frac{\left(r - \sigma^2/2\right)}{\sigma}\sqrt{\frac{1}{n}} \qquad (4.29)$$

JR parameters

$$p = \frac{1}{2}, u = exp\left[\left(r - \frac{\sigma^2}{2}\right)\frac{1}{n} + \sigma\sqrt{\frac{1}{n}}\right], d = exp\left[\left(r - \frac{\sigma^2}{2}\right)\frac{1}{n} - \sigma\sqrt{\frac{1}{n}}\right] \qquad (4.30)$$

Last, consider the probabilities. The probability, which makes the stock prices discounted by the one-period risk-free rate a martingale, is

$$exp\left(\frac{r}{n}\right) = pu + \left(1 - p\right)d = p\left(u - d\right) - d$$

$$p = \frac{exp\left(r/n\right) - d}{u - d} \qquad (4.31)$$

which we have used in the book. As $n \to \infty$, the difference between the p in equation (4.29) and in (4.31) converges to 0. (See figure 4.11.)

Appendix E. Monte Carlo Simulation and Finite Difference Method

We have shown that we can derive the Black–Scholes formula by resorting to the fact that the call option should satisfy the martingale property. In addition to the analytical solution, we can get the European call option value by numerical procedures. We should be concerned with them because we have many exotic options for which analytical solutions are not available. For example, to price American options, we have to depend

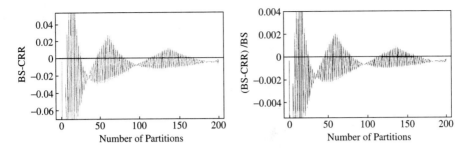

Figure 4.11 The convergence of the discrete CRR model to the continuous BS model. As the number of partitions grows, the differences between Black–Scholes and the binomial option pricing model converge to 0. Furthermore, the ratio differences between them also decrease as we have finer partitions. The stock price is 100 and the exercise price is 95. The stock volatility is 20%. The time to maturity is one year. The continuously compounding risk-free rate is 5%. The European call option price is 10.4506 by Black–Scholes.

on numerical solutions. Since we have already shown the binomial lattice approach, we will introduce the Monte Carlo simulation and the finite difference method.

Consider a European call option for illustration purposes. We assume constant interest rates. The European call option depends only on the stock price at maturity. We can value the European call option as follows.

First, simulate a random path of a stock in a risk-neutral world.

$$dS = rSdt + \sigma SdZ$$

$$d \ln S = \left(r - \frac{\sigma^2}{2} \right) dt + \sigma \, dZ$$

$$S(t + \Delta t) = S(t) \exp \left\{ \left(r - \frac{\sigma^2}{2} \right) \Delta t + \sigma \varepsilon \sqrt{\Delta t} \right\}$$

where ε is a random number generated from $N(0, 1)$

Second, determine the payoff at maturity.

Third, repeat the first two steps to get many payoffs at maturity from simulated random paths.

Fourth, calculate the mean of payoffs at maturity.

Fifth, discount the mean payoff to the present at the risk-free rate.

Figure 4.12 shows the distribution of stock prices at maturity with 100,000 simulations. We assume that the initial stock price is 100, the volatility is 0.2, the risk-free rate is 10 percent, and the time to maturity is one year. The graph shows that the distribution is similar to the lognormal distribution.

Figure 4.13 shows stock price paths. We assume that the initial stock price is 100, the volatility is 0.2 and the time to maturity is one year. From this graph, we can see that the stock prices exhibit a random walk.

We can directly solve the partial differential equation to get a European call option. The European call option should satisfy the partial differential equation if there is no arbitrage opportunity. Since there is no standard method to solve partial differential equations, we should depend on finite difference methods. The basic idea behind finite difference methods is that we divide the maximum stock price and the maturity time into

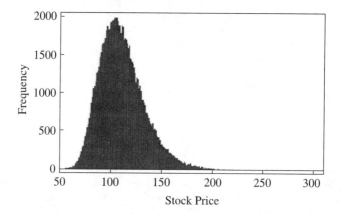

Figure 4.12 The histogram of stock prices at maturity generated by a Monte Carlo simulation.

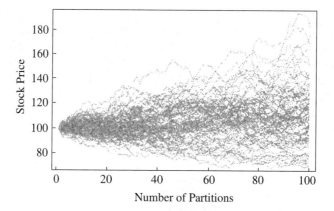

Figure 4.13 Stock price by Monte Carlo simulation. The number of scenarios and the number of sample points on a path is 100.

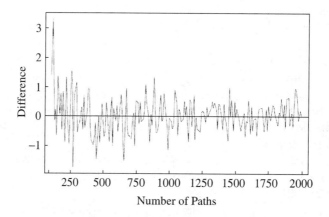

Figure 4.14 Monte Carlo simulation vs. Black–Scholes model. We increase the number of sample paths from 100 to 2000; one sample path is made up of 500 sample points. The European call option price calculated from the Monte Carlo simulation converges to the solution of the Black–Scholes model as we increase the number of sample paths in the Monte Carlo simulation.

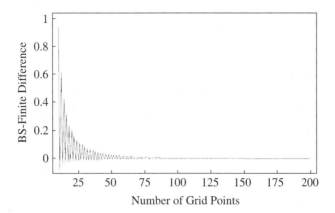

Figure 4.15 The finite difference method vs. the Black–Scholes model. This figure plots the difference of the European call option price by the Black–Scholes model and the explicit finite difference method against the number of grid points of the finite difference method from 10 to 200. The exercise price is 100, the volatility is 0.2, the risk-free rate is 0.1, and the time to maturity is one year.

equally spaced intervals and calculate the call price at each intersection from the maturity. Once we calculate the European call option values at maturity with $Max\,[S_T - K, 0]$ over the stock intervals, we can calculate the European call prices at one step before the maturity, because the partial differential equation tells us how two values are related to each other under the no-arbitrage opportunity.[9]

We compare European call option values from three different methods. Since the Black–Scholes model is the benchmark, we subtract two approximation methods—the Monte Carlo simulation and the finite difference method—from the Black–Scholes. We assume that the stock price is 100, the exercise price is 100, the volatility is 0.2, the risk-free rate is 0.1, and the time to maturity is one year. The Black–Scholes value is $13.2697. (See figures 4.14 and 4.15.)

Notes

1. For their research in option pricing, Myron Scholes and Robert Merton received the Nobel Prize for economics in 1997. Fischer Black passed away two years before the announcement.

2. Visit www.amex.com/ for further information.

3. Visit www.cbot.com/ for detailed information.

4. "True lattice" is used interchangeably with "risk-averse lattice."

5. Michael Lewis, *New York Times Magazine,* January 13, 2002.

6. We will derive Ito's lemma at length in chapter 19.

7. We will intuitively explain Girsanov's theorem in chapter 19.

8. Since we follow the four steps when we derive the binomial option pricing model, we can also develop the continuous counterpart on a parallel basis to express the option price as the expected value of payoff at maturity.

Step 1 $dS = \mu S dt + \sigma S dZ$

Step 2 $C = C\,(S, t)$. Applying Ito's lemma to dC, we have

$$dC = C_S dS + \frac{1}{2} C_{ss}\,(dS)^2 + C_t dt$$

$$= C_S \left(\mu S dt + \sigma S dZ \right) + \frac{1}{2} C_{SS} S^2 \sigma^2 dt + C_t dt$$

$$= \left(\mu S C_S + \frac{1}{2} \sigma^2 S^2 C_{SS} + C_t \right) dt + \sigma S C_S dZ$$

By longing C_S shares of the stock and shorting one share of the option, we can get rid of the uncertain part of the portfolio. The incremental change of the portfolio over an instant of time is $-C_t - \frac{1}{2} \sigma^2 S^2 C_{SS}$.

Step 3 $d \left(S \cdot C_S - C \right) = C_S \cdot dS - dC = \left(-C_t - \frac{1}{2} \sigma^2 S^2 C_{SS} \right) dt$

Since the portfolio has no uncertainty, its rate of return should be risk-free.

Step 4 $d \left(S \cdot C_S - C \right) = r \left(C_S S - C \right) dt = \left(-C_t - \frac{1}{2} \sigma^2 S^2 C_{SS} \right) dt$

$$r S C_S + C_t + \frac{1}{2} \sigma^2 S^2 C_{SS} = rC$$

From the Feynman-Kac formula, we know that $C_0 = E^{\widetilde{P}} \left[e^{-rT} Max \left[S_T - K, 0 \right] \right]$ is a solution that corresponds to the above partial differential equation.

9. The partial differential equation and boundary conditions are given as follows.

$$\frac{\partial f}{\partial t} + rS \frac{\partial f}{\partial S} + \frac{1}{2} \sigma^2 S^2 \frac{\partial^2 f}{\partial S^2} = rf$$

with boundary conditions

at final time T: $Max \left[S - X, 0 \right]$

at deep in the money: $\Delta_{Call} = \frac{\partial f}{\partial S} |_{S=S_{Max}} = 1$

at deep out of the money: $\Delta_{Call} = \frac{\partial f}{\partial S} |_{S=S_{Min}} = 0$

References

Beckers, S. 1980. The constant elasticity of variance model and its implications for option pricing. *Journal of Finance*, 35, 661–673.

Black, F., and M. Scholes. 1973. The pricing of options and corporate liabilities. *Journal of Political Economy*, 81, 637–654.

Brennan, M. J. 1979. The pricing of contingent claims in discrete time model. *Journal of Finance*, 34, 53–68.

Cox, J. C. 1975. Notes on option pricing. I: Constant elasticity of variance diffusions. Discussion paper, Graduate School of Business, Stanford University.

Cox, J. C. 1996. The constant elasticity of variance option pricing model. *Journal of Portfolio Management*, December, 15–17.

Cox, J. C., and S. Ross. 1976. The valuation of options for alternative stochastic processes. *Journal of Financial Economics*, 3, 145–166.

Cox, J. C., S. Ross, and M. Rubinstein. 1979. Option pricing: A simplified approach. *Journal of Financial Economics*, 7, 229–264.

Johnson, S. A., and Y. S. Tian. 2000. Indexed executive stock options. *Journal of Financial Economics*, 57, 35–64.

Merton, R. C. 1973. Theory of rational option pricing. *Bell Journal of Economics and Management Science*, 4, 141–183.

Rendleman, R. J., and B. R. Bartter. 1979. Two state option pricing. *Journal of Finance*, 34, no. 5, 1092–1110.

Stapleton, R. C., and M. G. Subrahmanyam. 1984. The valuation of options when asset returns are generated by a binomial process. *Journal of Finance*, 39, no. 5, 1525–1539.

Stoll, Hans R. 1969. The relationship between put and call option prices. *Journal of Finance*, 31, 319–332.

Sundaram, R. K. 1997. Equivalent martingale measures and risk-neutral pricing: An expository note. *Journal of Derivatives*, 5, no. 1, 85–98.

Further Readings

Amin, K. I., and V. K. Ng. 1993. Option valuation with systematic stochastic volatility. *Journal of Finance*, 48, no. 3, 881–910.

Ball, C. A., and A. Roma. 1994. Stochastic volatility option pricing. *Journal of Financial and Quantitative Analysis*, 29, no. 4, 589–607.

Breen, R., 1991. The accelerated binomial option pricing model. *Journal of Financial and Quantitative Analysis*, 26, no. 2, 153–164.

Britten-Jones, M., and A. Neuberger. 2000. Option prices, implied price processes, and stochastic volatility. *Journal of Finance*, 55, no. 2, 839–866.

Chung, S. L., and M. Shackleton. 2000. The binomial Black–Scholes model and the Greeks. Working paper, Lancaster University Management School.

Gao. B. 2000. Convergence rate of option prices from discrete- to continuous-time. Working paper, Kenan-Flagler Business School, University of North Carolina..

Hull. J., and A. White. 1987. The pricing of options on assets with stochastic volatilities. *Journal of Finance*, 42, no. 2, 281–300.

Hull, J., and A. White. 1990. Valuing derivative securities using the explicit finite difference method. *Journal of Financial and Quantitative Analysis*, 25, no. 1, 87–100.

Jackwerth, J. C. 1997. Generalized binomial trees. Working paper, Hass School of Business, University of California at Berkeley.

Jarrow, R. A., and A. Rudd. 1983. *Option Pricing*. Homewood, Ill.: Richard D. Irwin.

Leisen, D., and M. Reimer. 1996. Binomial models for option valuation-examining and improving convergence. *Applied Mathematical Finance*, 3, no. 4, 319–346.

Levy, H. 1985. Upper and lower bounds of put and call option value: Stochastic dominance approach. *Journal of Finance*, 40, no. 4, 1197–1218.

Longstaff, F. A. 1992. Option pricing and the martingale restriction. *Review of Financial Studies*, 8, no. 4, 1091–1124.

MacBeth, J. D., and L. J. Merville. 1979. An empirical examination of the Black–Scholes call option pricing model. *Journal of Finance*, 34, no. 5. 1173–1186.

MacBeth, J. D., and L. J. Merville. 1980. Tests of the Black–Scholes and Cox call option valuation models. *Journal of Finance*, 35, no. 2, 285–300.

Merton, R. C. 1976. The impact on option pricing of specification error in the underlying stock price distribution. *Journal of Finance*, 31, no. 2, 333–350.

Prigent, J. L., O. Renault, and O. Scaillet. 1999. An autoregressive conditional binomial option pricing model. Working paper, Department des Sciences Economiques, Universite Catholique de Louvain.

Robert, R. T., E. A. Brill, and R. B. Harriff. 1992. Pricing options on an asset with Bernoulli jump-diffusion returns. *Financial Review*, 27, no. 1, 59–79

Rubinstein, M. 1985. Nonparametric tests of alternative option pricing models using all reported trades and quotes on the 30 most active CBOE option classes from August 23, 1976 through August 31, 1978. *Journal of Finance*, 40, 455–480.

Stutzer, M. 1996. A simple nonparametric approach to derivative security valuation. *Journal of Finance*, 51, no. 5, 1633–1652.

5

Interest Rate Derivatives: Interest Rate Models

Interest rate models are important to financial modeling because they can be
used for valuing any financial instruments whose values are affected by interest rate
movements.Specifically, the arbitrage-free interest rate model is an extension of the
Black–Scholes model to value interest rate derivatives. The model valuation is
assured to be consistent with the observed yield curve in valuing interest rate
derivatives and providing accurate pricing of interest rate contingent claims, and
is widely used on trading floors, for portfolio management, and for other capital
market activities.

There are many examples of *interest rate derivatives* that are actively traded in over-the-counter markets and in organized exchanges. Caps, floors, Treasury bond options, Treasury bond futures options, Eurodollar futures options, and swaptions are just some examples of this important class of derivatives in financial markets. They are classified as "interest rate derivatives" because their stochastic movements are directly related to the interest rate movements in a way that is analogous to the stock option price that moves in step with the underlying stock price.

Chapter 4 presented a relative approach, the Black–Scholes model, to value a stock option. Can we use the Black–Scholes model to value interest rate options? Applying this technique to interest rate options would be difficult because we need to take into consideration the movements of the entire yield curve, and not just the price movements of one underlying asset (as in the stock option model). We can no longer assume that the bond price moves in a lognormal process to determine the price of a bond option. Nor can we assume that the entire yield curve follows a lognormal process to determine the price of the interest rate options. These lognormal assumptions are not consistent with the empirical evidence of the yield curve and bond price movements. Furthermore, they may not be consistent with the principles of finance, such as arbitrage-free conditions.

However, we can extend this relative valuation approach to interest rate derivatives by introducing a class of models called "interest rate models." The basic idea of these models is to specify interest rate movements such that all the interest rate derivatives can be valued-based on these movements, and there is no arbitrage opportunity among the derivatives' model prices.

Interest rate models have broad applications to financial engineering. In valuing all interest rate-sensitive securities, which are called interest rate contingent claims, we have a consistent framework to manage interest rate risks, enhance financial innovations, and invoke many other applications.

This chapter first presents an empirical analysis of historical yield curve movements, which conveys its relationship to interest rate models. Then we offer an overview of the interest rate models, providing the step-by-step procedure in building these models. We will then compare the models, showing how they should be used and highlighting their salient features.

5.1   Interest Rate Movements: Historical Experiences

Interest rate movements refer to the uncertain movements of the Treasury spot yield curve. Each STRIPS bond is considered a security. When the daily closing price is reported, the bond's yield to maturity can be calculated. The observed Treasury spot yield curve is the scattered plot of the yield to maturity against the maturity for all the STRIPS bonds. Since the spot yield curve is a representation of the time value of money, and the time value of money is related to the time to horizon in a continuous fashion, the scattered plots should be a continuous curve. Hence, we call the scattered plot a yield curve.

What are the dynamics of the spot yield curve? Let us consider the historical behavior of spot yield curve movements in relation to interest rate levels. The monthly spot yield curves from the beginning of 1994 until the end of 2001 are depicted in Figure 5.1.

As figure 5.1 shows, the spot yield curves can take on a number of shapes. When the yields of the bonds increase with the bonds' maturities, the yield curve is said to be upward-sloping. Conversely, when the yield decreases with maturity, the spot curve is called downward-sloping. Although not shown in figure 5.1, the early 1980s displayed a yield curve that was downward-sloping. In 1998, the yield curve was level or flat. In the early part of 2001, the yield curve was humped, with yields reaching the peak at the one-year maturity. Historically, the spot yield curve has continually changed its shape as well as its level.

The yield curve movement is concerned with the change of the yield curve shape over a relatively short time interval, say one month. Describing yield curve movements is

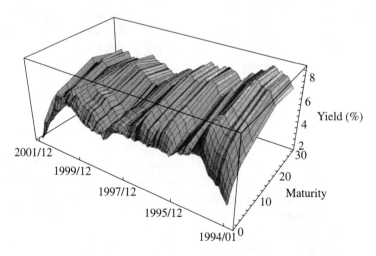

Figure 5.1 A time series diagram of monthly spot yield curve movements (1994.01–2001.12). The Treasury spot yield curve continually exhibits random movements, changing its level as well as its shape over the period from January 1994 to December 2001. Interest rate movement models are supposed to specify such movements; for example, to price bonds with option provisions or bond options. Since the data are par yields at key rate maturities of 0.25, 0.5, 1, 2, 3, 5, 7, 10, 20, and 30 years, we convert them into spot yields, assuming that par yields are semiannually paid coupon rates. For example, if a par yield at year 7 is 10%, we convert the par yield into a spot yield by assuming that the semiannually paid coupon rate is 10% and the bond price is at par. Data from http//:www.economagic.com/.

slightly more complicated than describing a stock movement. To describe the latter, we can decompose the stock movement into two parts: the expected drift or expected returns and the uncertain movement. The model is represented by

$$dS = \mu S dt + \sigma S dZ \tag{5.1}$$

where dS is a small movement for a short interval dt. μ is the instantaneous returns of the stock, and σ is the instantaneous standard deviation (or volatility) of the stock. dZ represents a small, uncertain movement specified by a normal distribution. The mean and the standard deviation of the normal distribution are 0 and $\sqrt{dt}$, respectively. The first term, called the drift term, represents the expected movement of the stock price. If the first term is 0, then the future stock price is expected to be the same as the present observed price. Of course, the realized stock price in the future can deviate from the initial stock price because of the uncertain stock price movement specified by the second term. The random term dZ can be viewed as a unit of risk, a normal distribution over an (infinitely) short interval.[1] The coefficient of dZ represents the volatility of the process. If this coefficient is 0, then the process has no risk and the stock price movement has no uncertainty.

But specifying the movement of the yield curve in a way that is similar to equation (5.1), is more problematic. Since a yield curve is determined by all the U.S. STRIPS bonds, its movement should be represented by the movements of all the bond prices. But the movements of all the bond prices are not independent of each other. They have to be correlated. The following empirical evidence may suggest how the yield curve movements may best be specified.

Lognormal Versus Normal Movements

The movements (often called the dynamics) of each interest rate of the spot yield curve can be specified as we have done for a stock. We can rewrite equation (5.1), replacing the stock price with a rate that is the yield to maturity of a zero-coupon bond of a specific maturity T. Thus we have

$$dr = \mu(r, t) r dt + r\sigma \, dZ \tag{5.2}$$

When a T year rate is assumed to follow the process specified by equation (5.2), we say that the interest rate follows a *lognormal process*, and equation (5.2) is called a lognormal model. In comparing equation (5.2) with equation (5.1), note that the drift term of the interest rate model is any function of the short-term interest rate r and time, while the lognormal model for stock tends to assume that the instantaneous stock return is a constant number. Therefore, the research literature of interest rate models has somewhat abused the language in calling equation (5.2) a lognormal model. The important point is that in a lognormal process, the volatility term is proportional to the interest rate level $r(t)$. When the interest rate level is high, we experience high interest rate volatility. When the interest rate level is low, we experience low interest rate volatility.

There is an alternative specification of the interest rate process, which the research literature calls the *normal process*. In the normal process, the volatility is independent of the interest rate level, and it is given below:

$$dr = \mu(r, t)dt + \sigma\, dZ \qquad (5.3)$$

Equation (5.3) is called the *normal model*. Note that the distinction made between the lognormal model and the normal model depends only on the volatility term. For a normal model, the interest rate fluctuates with a volatility independent of the interest rate level over a short interval. For a lognormal model, the interest rate has a volatility related to the interest rate level, in particular when the volatility becomes arbitrarily small when the interest rate level approaches 0. This way, the interest rates can never become negative. A lognormal process is written as

$$\frac{dr}{r} = \mu(r, t)dt + \sigma\, dZ \qquad (5.3a)$$

Historical observations have shown the yield curve movements to be both normal and lognormal, depending on the interest rate levels. Which model is more appropriate to describe interest rate movements, the normal or the lognormal? We need to evaluate the model from an empirical perspective. Using U.S. historical interest rates, the squared change of the interest rate over one month is plotted against the interest rate level. Figure 5.2 presents the scattered plots for 1-, 5-, 10-, and 20-year rates.

As Figure 5.2 indicates, over this time period the interest rate volatility has no

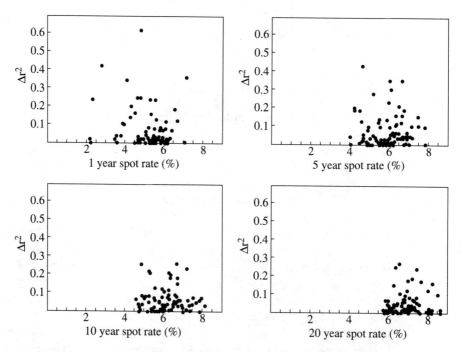

Figure 5.2 The relationship between the squared change of interest rate and the interest rate level. The interest rate levels are plotted against the squared changes in the monthly interest rates over the following month during the period from 1994 to 2001. The results do not indicate any specific relationship between the interest rate level and its volatility, which can be interpreted to suggest that the volatility does not depend on the interest level. If that is the case, we cannot reject the normal interest rate models.

relationship to the interest rate levels. If there were a positive relationship, we would see the higher volatility values related to higher interest rates. This result is consistent with Cheyette (1997),[2] who shows that the positive correlation between the interest rate volatility and the interest rate level is weak when the interest rate level is below 10 percent. However, when the interest rate level was high in the late 1970s and early 1980s, the interest rate volatility was also high, showing positive correlations during that period.

Interest Rate Correlations

We have discussed the dynamics of interest rates. Now let us consider the comovements of interest rates. Do interest rates move together in steps, such that they all rise or fall together?

While the yield curve in principle can take many shapes, historically, all the interest rates along the yield curve have been positively correlated. But the interest rates do not shift by the same amount. Their comovements can be investigated by evaluating the correlations of the interest rates, as presented in table 5.1.

The results show that all the correlations are positive, suggesting that all the interest rates tend to move in the same direction. The long rates, with terms over ten years, are highly correlated, meaning that the segment of the yield curve in a range of 10 to 30 years tends to move up and down together. The interest rates that are closer together along the yield curve have higher correlations.

Term Structure of Volatilities

Interest rate volatility is not the same for all interest rates along the yield curve. By convention, based on the lognormal model, the uncertainty of an interest rate is measured by the annualized standard deviation of the proportional change in a bond yield over a time interval (dt). For example, if the time interval is one month, then dt equals 1/12 year. This measure is called the interest rate volatility, and it is denoted by $\sigma(t, T)$, the

Table 5.1 Correlation Matrix of the Interest Rates

	0.25	0.5	1	2	3	5	7	10	20	30
0.25	1.000	0.936	0.837	0.701	0.630	0.533	0.443	0.377	0.087	0.083
0.5	0.936	1.000	0.938	0.832	0.770	0.675	0.587	0.509	0.224	0.154
1	0.837	0.938	1.000	0.940	0.895	0.816	0.731	0.654	0.379	0.291
2	0.701	0.832	0.940	1.000	0.989	0.950	0.898	0.832	0.573	0.426
3	0.630	0.770	0.895	0.989	1.000	0.980	0.945	0.887	0.649	0.493
5	0.533	0.675	0.816	0.950	0.980	1.000	0.982	0.946	0.736	0.595
7	0.443	0.587	0.731	0.898	0.945	0.982	1.000	0.976	0.821	0.670
10	0.377	0.509	0.654	0.832	0.887	0.946	0.976	1.000	0.863	0.750
20	0.087	0.224	0.379	0.573	0.649	0.736	0.821	0.863	1.000	0.867
30	0.083	0.154	0.291	0.426	0.493	0.595	0.670	0.750	0.867	1.000

The results show that all the correlations are positive so that all the interest rates tend to move in the same direction. The long rates (with terms over 10 years) are highly correlated, which means that the rates in the 10- to 30-year range tend to move up and down together. The interest rates that are closer together along the yield curves have higher correlations. However, the correlations of the short term rates and the long term rates are relatively low.

volatility of the Tth year rate at time t. More precisely, the volatility is the standard deviation of the proportional change in rate over a short interval, and it is given by

$$\sigma(t, T) = \sigma\left(\frac{\Delta r(t, T)}{r(t, T)}\right) \Big/ \sqrt{\Delta t} \qquad (5.4)$$

where $r(t, T)$ is the yield to maturity of the zero-coupon bond with time to maturity T at time t and Std.$(\cdot)$ is a standard deviation over dt. We can relate equation (5.4) to (5.3a) by the following algebraic manipulations. For a small time step, equation (5.3a) can be written as

$$\frac{\Delta r(t, T)}{r(t, T)} \cong \mu \Delta t + \sigma(t, T)\Delta Z$$

For sufficiently small Δt, we have

$$\sigma\left(\frac{\Delta r(t, T)}{r(t, T)}\right) \cong \sigma(t, T)\sqrt{\Delta t}$$

Rearranging the terms, we can express σ as equation (5.4) requires. Similarly, based on the normal model, the term structure of volatilities is given by

$$\sigma(t, T) = \sigma(\Delta r(t, T))/\sqrt{\Delta t} \qquad (5.5)$$

The relationship of the volatilities to the maturity is called the *term structure of volatilities*. The interest rate volatilities can be estimated using historical monthly data ($\Delta t = 1/12$). The standard deviations of the rates for 0.25, 0.5, 1, 2, 3, 5, 7, 10, 20, and 30 years are presented in table 5.2.

The historical term structure of volatilities shows that the short-term rates tend to have higher volatilities than the long-term rates, falling from 19.06 percent for the 0.25-year rate to 11.37 percent for the 30-year rate. The empirical results suggest that we cannot think of interest rate volatility as one number. It depends on the term of the interest rate in question.

Mean Reversion

Thus far the discussion has focused on the volatility term of the dynamics of the interest rates. Now we investigate the drift term. Research tends to argue that the yield curve cannot follow a random walk as a stock does, as in equation (5.1). The yields of Treasury

Table 5.2 Historical Term Structure of Volatilities: $\sigma(\Delta r(t)/r(t)) \cdot \sqrt{12}$

Term	0.25	0.5	1	2	3	5	7	10	20	30
Volatilities	0.1906	0.1908	0.1872	0.1891	0.1794	0.1632	0.1487	0.1402	0.1076	0.1137

The first row identifies the term of the yield and the second row reports the volatilities. The relationship of the volatilities with respect to the maturity is called the term structure of volatilities. The interest rate volatilities can be estimated using historical data reported in figure 5.1. The historical term structure of volatilities shows that the short term rates tend to have higher volatilities than the long term rates, falling from 19.06% for the 0.25-year rate to 11.37% for the 30-year rate.

bonds cannot rise and fall with the expected drift, yet be constant or a certain fixed proportion of the interest rate level. Since the nominal interest rate, which is what we are concerned with here, is decomposed into the real interest rate and the expected inflation rate, as stated in the Fisher equation (see chapter 3), the movements of the nominal rates can be analyzed by considering the movements of the real rates and the inflation rate. One may argue that the real rate cannot follow a random walk because it is related to all the individuals' time value of money in real terms. We tend to think the real interest rate is quite stable and does not follow a random walk. To the extent that we believe the government seeks to control the inflation rate, the inflation rate cannot follow a random walk either. Therefore, we cannot assume that the (nominal) interest rate follows a random walk.

One may conclude that the interest rates tend to fall when they are high and, conversely, tend to rise when they are low. This is a somewhat imprecise description of a yield curve's behavior; there will be a more precise description later in the chapter, where we will provide alternative interest rate models. Research literature calls the dynamics that describe this behavior of interest rates a *mean reversion process*.

5.2 The Three-Factor Yield Curve Movement Model

Litterman and Scheinkman (1991) proposed a three-factor yield curve movement model that summarizes the observations made in the previous section. The model states that the U.S. yield curve movement over a period is a combination of three independent movements: level, steepness, and curvature. These movements are obtained from the historical variance and covariance matrix of the interest rate movements. They are specified by the eigenvector of the variance–covariance matrix that has the highest eigenvalues.

We can solve for the n-dimensional eigenvector, **v** and the eigenvalue λ in the following matrix equation, using a standard linear algebra method.

$$A \times \mathbf{v} = \lambda \times \mathbf{v} \tag{5.6}$$

A is an $n \times n$ symmetric matrix of the variance—covariance matrix of n key historical interest rate changes over a specified time period. Linear algebra shows that there are n possible solutions to equation (5.6), and a λ is associated with each solution **v**. Often the eigenvectors are called the *principal components*.

Intuitively, the variance-covariance matrix is the variability of a set of random variables. We want to decompose the variability in terms of directions (how the yield curve should move) and corresponding amplitudes (the significance of this movement to explain the historical behavior). The direction of the interest rate movements can be expressed by eigenvectors and the amplitudes by eigenvalues.

Since we have ten key rates, we have ten eigenvectors and ten eigenvalues. The sum of ten eigenvalues is 0.607802, and the sum of three dominant eigenvalues is 0.593819. Therefore, the explanatory power of the three dominant eigenvalues is 0.593819/ 0.607802 = 97.7%. Specifically, the result shows that this three-factor yield curve movement model can explain over 97% of the historical yield curve movements, with the level movement explaining 77%, the steepness movement 17% and the curvature movement 3%.

The three movements are given in table 5.3, and the shifts are depicted in figure 5.3.

The level movement is represented by a shift of the yield curve up or down. The shift can be represented by a vector $\mathbf{v}(1)$, where the dimension of the vector is the number of key interest rates that represent the spot yield curve, and the entry of the vector is the shift of the key rate.

The steepness movement is represented by a nonparallel shift of the yield curve, where the shorter-term rates fall while the longer-term rates rise, or vice versa. This movement demonstrates that the yield curve can become steeper when the shift is positive or less

Table 5.3 The three yield curve movements: three dominant eigenvectors

| | *Time to Maturity* | | | | | | | | | |
	0.25	0.5	1	2	3	5	7	10	20	30
Level $\mathbf{v}(1)$	0.2247	0.2792	0.3346	0.3953	0.3951	0.3787	0.3507	0.3207	0.2162	0.1768
Steepness $\mathbf{v}(2)$	0.4607	0.4196	0.3078	0.1167	0.0164	−0.1135	−0.2137	−0.2817	−0.4300	−0.4245
Curvature $\mathbf{v}(3)$	0.4672	0.2628	0.0459	−0.2300	−0.2722	−0.2422	−0.1750	−0.0313	0.2352	0.6618

When we apply principal component analysis on the variance-covariance matrix from the historical movements of the yield curves, we get three dominant eigenvectors. The explanatory power of the three dominant eigenvectors is 97.7%. The first, second, and third eigenvector represent level, steepness, and curvature shifts, respectively.

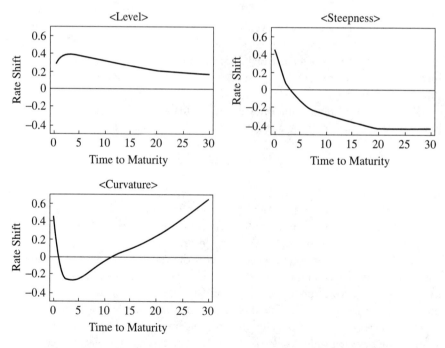

Figure 5.3 The three yield curve movements. The yield curve movements consist mainly of three forms; level, steepness, and curvature shifts. The level shifs represent parallel shifts over maturities. The steepness shifts represent nonparallel shifts of the yield curves, where the shorter-term rates fall while the longer-term rates rise, or vice versa. The curvature shifts are represented by shifts of three segments, where the short- and long-term segments of the yield curves rise while the middle-term segments fall, or vice versa. The three forms of shifts can explain over 97.7% of the historical yield curve movements.

steep when the shift is negative. This vector of shifts of all the key rates is represented by $\mathbf{v}(2)$.

The third movement, curvature, is represented by a shift of three segments of the spot yield curve. The short-term and the long-term segments rise while the middle segment falls, or vice versa. The vector of this movement is represented by $\mathbf{v}(3)$.

Intuitive Explanation of the Model

This methodology is the same as the factor model used in equity research to estimate multiple factors that explain the stock returns, extending from the one-factor model of the Capital Asset Pricing model. This model hypothesizes that a stock return is related only to the market risk which is a factor, and other uncertain price movements are simply diversifiable risks, a noise of the price movement. Subsequent research hypothesizes that there may be multiple factors affecting the stock price, including interest rate risks, industry/sector risks, and other macroeconomic uncertainties. Empirical methodologies are established to determine these factors.

For the U.S. Treasury bond market, the movement of a particular interest rate on the yield curve can be related to multiple factors or risk sources. With the empirical methodologies mentioned above, we can use these factors to represent the uncertain movements of the yield curve, which can give us insight into the movements of the spot yield curve.

With reference to the yield curve, the model supports the "preferred habitat" hypothesis, according to which different segments of market participants hold different parts of the yield curve. Banks tend to focus on short-term debt, while insurance companies are large buyers of long-term bonds. Banks tend to secure funding from deposit accounts and checking accounts, and invest the funding in loans, which tend to be short-term. Banks represent a large class of market participants that tend to buy and sell in shorter-term markets. The factors' movements are depicted in figure 5.3. The factors show that money market rates can fluctuate significantly, as depicted by the curvature movement, where the one-year short rate tends to move quite differently from the other rates.

As a result of the preferred habitat hypothesis, market participants tend to think of bonds with maturity longer than ten years as a class called "long bonds." Their yields therefore tend to move in step with each other. By considering the steepness movement, we can see that the shifts of the yields are very similar for all the bonds with maturities exceeding ten years.

The segment of the yield curve approximately from two to ten-years' maturity determines whether the yield curve is upward- or downward-sloping. The market tends to trade on the steepness of the curve, using bonds with maturities in the range of two to ten years. Figure 5.1 depicts the "steepness" factor, which agrees with this observation on the practice in the marketplace, showing the slope of the curve for a range of from two to ten years.

It is important to note that the model is estimated from U.S. Treasury bond market data. The movements can be quite different for government bond markets of other countries. In the United States, there is a significant long-term bond segment as well as a large money market with discount securities that have maturities of less than one year. For this reason, the yield curve movements are segmented into three movements. In other economies, we may find that the yield curve movements can be explained by just the level movement or the level and steepness movements of the yield curve because they have less sophisticated markets.

5.3   Equilibrium Models

The yield curve movement model described in the previous section is useful in specifying probable yield curve movements, but it cannot be used to value interest rate derivatives. What is needed in order to value interest rate derivatives? We will now examine the characteristics of an interest rate model.

First, consider pricing a *U.S. STRIPS bond option*. A bond option offers the holder the right to buy a specific U.S. STRIPS bond at the expiration date at a fixed price. Economists in the 1960s used the present-value method to price the bond option. They simulated interest rate scenarios based on an economic forecast to determine all the probabilities of interest rate levels at the expiration date. Then the expected payout of the bond option was calculated. Finally, the expected payment was discounted to determine the present value of the expected payment, the option price. However, the last step was the most difficult calculation. What was the appropriate discount rate? Would the discount rate be the observed rate from the yield curve? How would the forecast interest rate scenario be used to determine the discount rate? And should the risk premium be adjusted?

Interest Rate Models

Interest rate models seek to specify the interest rate movements such that we can develop a pricing methodology for an interest rate option. We will describe three such models.

The Cox–Ingersoll–Ross model

The Cox–Ingersoll–Ross (CIR, 1985) interest rate model is based on the productive processes of an economy. According to the model, every individual has to make the decision between consuming and investing his limited capital. Investing in the productive process may lead to higher consumption in the following period, but it will sacrifice consumption today. The individual must determine the optimal trade-off.

Now assume that the individual can borrow capital from and lend capital to another individual. Each person has to make economic choices. The interest rates reach the market equilibrium rate when no one needs to borrow or lend. The model can explain the interest rate movements in terms of an individual's preferences for investment and consumption, as well as the risks and returns of the productive processes of the economy.

As a result of the analysis, the model can show how the short-term interest rate is related to the risks of the productive processes of the economy. Assuming that an individual requires a premium on the long-term rate (called term premium), the model continues to show how the short-term rate can determine the entire term structure of interest rates and the valuation of interest rate contingent claims.

The CIR model $$dr = a(b - r)dt + \sigma \sqrt{r}dZ \qquad (5.7)$$

Cox–Ingersoll–Ross (1985) is one of the earlier attempts at modeling interest rate movements. The proposed equilibrium model extends from economic principles of interest rates. It assumes mean reversion of interest rates. As we discussed in section 5.1, mean reversion of interest rates means that when the short-term interest rate (r) is higher than the long-run interest rates (b), the short-term rate will fall, adjusting gradually to the long-run rate. Conversely, when the short-term interest rate is lower than the long-run rate, the short-term rate will rise gradually to the long-run rate. Note that the long-run interest rate is not the long-term rate. The long-term interest rate continuously moves stochastically, while the long-run rate is a theoretical construct which hypothesizes that the economy has a constant long-run interest rate to which interest rates converge over time. The constant (a) determines the speed of this adjustment. If (a) is high/low, the rate of adjustment to the long-term rate will be high/low. The CIR model is a lognormal model because the interest rate volatility is positively related to the interest rate level. The classification of lognormal and normal is based on the uncertain movement of the interest rate over a short period of time, as described above.

The Vasicek model

The second model was developed by O. Vasicek (1977). It is similar to the CIR model in that it assumes all interest rate contingent claims are based on short-term interest rates. The only difference is that the volatility is not assumed to be dependent on the interest rate level, and therefore it is a normal model.

The Vasicek model $\qquad dr = a(b - r)dt + \sigma\, dZ, (a > 0)$ $\qquad\qquad$ (5.8)

This model assumes that there is only one source of risk and is referred to as a one-factor model. This assumption implies that all bond prices depend on the movements of the rate (r), and that all bond prices move in tandem because of their dependence on one factor. At first, this assumption seems to be unrealistic because, as we have discussed, the yield curve seems to have many degrees of freedom in its movements. Therefore, how can we confine our yield curve to exhibit a *one-factor movement*?

Dybvig (1989), using the Litterman and Scheinkman (1991) findings discussed in section 5.2, shows that the one-factor model offers an appropriate first-order approximation for modeling the yield curve movement. Empirically, the dominant factor, the level movement, can explain much of the yield curve movements, and for the purpose of valuation, simplified models like those of Cox–Ingersoll–Ross and Vasicek may be justified. In other words, a one-factor model may be acceptable on an empirical basis.

Market price of risk

From a theoretical perspective, neither the Cox–Ingersoll–Ross nor the Vasicek model for interest rates is a direct extension of the Black–Scholes model for stocks. In these models, the bond values are not determined by risk-neutral valuation (as in the Black–Scholes model), discounting the cash flows at the (stochastic) risk-free rate (r). These one-factor interest rate models cannot use the Black–Scholes relative valuation technique because the risk factor (r) is not a security that can be bought and sold to implement a dynamic hedging strategy. Therefore, the bonds cannot be valued relative to the observed interest rate level (r).

In a world where the yield curve has only one risk factor (r), the arbitrage-free condition in the bond market imposes a condition on the drift (μ) and the risk (σ) for all the bonds. This condition is

$$\frac{\mu - r}{\sigma} = \lambda(r, t) \tag{5.9}$$

$\lambda(r, t)$ depends on the risk factor, r, and time, t. But more important, it is independent of the derivatives. Any derivatives depending on the risk factor must have the instantaneous drift μ and the risk σ related by equation (5.9), for the same λ. Equation (5.9) suggests that the excess returns over a short period per unit risk, measured by the standard deviation, are the same for all the derivatives on the risk source. For this reason, Cox–Ingersoll–Ross calls λ *market price of risk*, the excess return required for this risk factor per unit risk measure. The excess return ($\mu - r$) is the premium for bond returns, and is called the *term premium*.

Cox–Ingersoll–Ross (1981) and Abken (1990) provide a discussion comparing the concept of term premium with the traditional hypothesis of liquidity premium of the term structure and the preferred habitat effect. The term premium or the market price of risk cannot be determined within the context of the model. Additional assumptions have to be made about the economy and the behavior of market participants to provide deeper insight into the value of the market price of risks. Cox–Ingersoll–Ross proposes that when there is no market price of risk, or equivalently no term premium, the market assumes the local expectation hypothesis to hold. In this case, all the bonds would have the expected return of the short-term rate (r) over one period.

The Brennan and Schwartz two-factor model

For many purposes the one-factor model may not be appropriate to use as a valuation model. An interest rate spread option is one example that a one-factor model may not be adequate to value. The values of some securities depend on the changing interest rate spreads between the two-year rate and the ten-year rate. The one-factor model assumes that all the interest rates that move in tandem would eliminate the risk of the spread between the two-year and the ten-year rates.

One extension asserts that all the bond prices of all maturities are generated by the short-term interest rate and a long-term rate—the long-term rate being the consol bond, which has no maturity and whose rate represents the long-term rate. Versions of the two-factor models have been proposed by Brennan and Schwartz (1982), Richard (1978), and Longstaff and Schwartz (1992). The Brennan and Schwartz model is given below.

$$dr = a_1 + b_1(l - r)dt + r\sigma_1 dZ$$
$$dl = (a_2 + b_2 r + c_2 l)dt + l\sigma_2 dW \tag{5.10}$$

where r is the short-term rate and l is the consol rate (where a consol bond is a bond that pays a fixed coupon periodically into the future on a notional amount with no maturity); and σ_1 and σ_2 are the standard deviations of the short-term and consol rates, respectively. dZ and dW represent the risks which may be correlated. The parameters a_1, b_1, a_2, b_2, and c_2 are estimated from the historical data.

Given the interest rate models and one factor or two factors, and if we further assume some market price of risk (for example, Vasicek assumes a constant value for λ), then we can use a standard numerical analysis technique to determine the simulations in interest rates from the above differential equations. These interest rate scenarios can then determine the cash flows of the bonds or derivatives for each interest rate scenario. The mean of all the present values of cash flows under all the interest rate scenarios is the value of the bond or derivatives.[3] Alternatively, a bond or a derivative can be expressed as a solution to a differential equation (often called the *heat equation*) dependent on the interest rate model used.[4] Numerical methods are then often used to solve the differential equation to provide the bond or derivative value.

We assume that the spot interest rate follows the following stochastic differential equation.

$$dr = \mu(t, r)dt + \sigma(t, r)dZ \tag{5.11}$$

Since the functional forms of $\mu(t, r)$ and $\sigma(t, r)$ are general, the spot rate change can accommodate any term structure models. As we did in the Black–Scholes derivation, we consider the value V, which depends on time t and the spot interest rate r.

From Ito's lemma we obtain

$$dV = M(t, r)dt + \Omega(t, r)dZ$$
$$M(t, r) = V_t + \mu(t, r)V_r + \frac{1}{2}\sigma(t, r)^2 V_{rr} \tag{5.12}$$
$$\Omega(t, r) = \sigma(t, r)V_r$$

To construct a riskless portfolio, we should take a long position in V and a short position in the underlying asset for the stock option case. However, in the interest-contingent case, the underlying asset is the spot interest rate, which is not a traded asset. Therefore, we cannot directly apply the method we use when the underlying asset is a traded asset. The best way to hedge an interest rate contingent claim would be to use the other interest rate contingent claim rather than the underlying spot interest rate.

We form the risk-free portfolio with two interest rate contingent claims, V_1 and V_2, by taking a long position in V_1 and a short position in ΔV_2, where Δ is a hedging ratio. The value of the risk-free portfolio is $\Pi = V_1(t, r) - \Delta V_2(t, r)$, where V_1 and V_2 follow the process with coefficients M_1, Ω_1 and M_2, Ω_2, respectively. The change in the risk-free portfolio is given in equation (5.13).

$$d\Pi = (M_1(t, r) - \Delta M_2(t, r))dt + (\Omega_1(t, r) - \Delta\Omega_2(t, r))dZ \tag{5.13}$$

To make the stochastic term in $d\Pi$ disappear, Δ should be Ω_1/Ω_2. Since the portfolio has no stochastic term, the portfolio should earn the riskless return, which is the spot interest rate to avoid arbitrage opportunities.

$$d\Pi = r\Pi dt \tag{5.14}$$

Plugging (5.13) into (5.14) and rearranging terms leads to

$$\frac{M_1(t, r) - rV_1(t, r)}{\Omega_1(t, r)} = \frac{M_2(t, r) - rV_2(t, r)}{\Omega_2(t, r)}$$

This equality should hold for any interest contingent claims. Let $\lambda(t, r)$ denote the common value of the ratio, which is known as the market price of risk.

$$\frac{M(t, r) - rV(t, r)}{\Omega(t, r)} = \lambda(t, r) \tag{5.15}$$

Substituting (5.12) into (5.15) and rearranging terms gives

$$V_t + (\mu(t, r) - \lambda(t, r)\sigma(t, r))V_r + \frac{1}{2}\sigma(t, r)^2 V_{rr} - rV = 0 \tag{5.16}$$

We numerically solve the partial differential equation (5.16) to determine the interest rate contingent claims.

5.4   Arbitrage-Free Models

From the standard economic theory perspective, arbitrage-free modeling departs from the CIR approach. The main point of departure is sacrificing the economic theory by providing a model of the term structure of interest rates for a more accurate tool to value securities. Since the yield curve measures the agent's time value of money, the standard economic theory relates the interest rate movements to the dynamics of the economy. In contrast, arbitrage-free modeling assumes that the yield curve follows a random movement much like the model used to describe a stock price movement. We showed in chapter 4 that stock prices are assumed to be random, and such an assumption does not incorporate the modeling of the agent's behavior and the economy.

The Ho–Lee model

Ho and Lee (1986) take a different approach to modeling yield curve movements than do CIR and Vasicek. The *arbitrage-free interest rate model* uses the relative valuation of the Black–Scholes model. This concept becomes more complex in the interest rate theory. Arbitrage-free modeling argues, like the Black–Scholes model, that the valuation of interest rate contingent claims is based solely on the yield curve. Economic research focuses on understanding the inferences made from the yield curve shape and its movements. The arbitrage-free model omits all these fundamental issues; apparently ignoring part of the economic theory behind interest rate research. The model assumes that the yield curve moves in a way that is consistent with the arbitrage-free condition.

Let us assume that there is a perfect capital market in a discrete time world. But this time, the binomial model is applied to the yield curve movements. We assume the following:

1. Given the initial spot yield curve, the binomial lattice model requires that the yield curve can move only up and down.
2. The one-period interest rate volatility (the instantaneous volatility) is the same in all states of the world.

3. There is no arbitrage opportunity at any state of the world (at any node point on the binomial lattice).

Assumption (1) is a technical construct of the risk model. Assumption (2) is made simply for this example; it will be altered in the next section. Assumption (3), the arbitrage-free condition, is the most interesting and important. This condition imposes constraints on the yield curve movements.

Thus far, it seems that the extension is directly from the Black–Scholes model. But there is one problem: interest rate is not a security. We cannot buy and sell the one-period rate, though we can invest in the rate as the risk-free rate. Moreover, we cannot use the one-period rate to form an arbitrage argument, as the Black–Scholes model does with stock, since the one-period rate is the risk-free rate, which obviously cannot be the "underlying asset" as well. In an equity option, the stock is both the underlying instrument and the risk source or the risk driver.

Arbitrage-Free Hedging

The conceptual extension of the interest rate arbitrage-free model from the Black–Scholes model is introduction of the short-term interest rate as the risk source (or risk drive or state of the world). The Black–Scholes model's risk-neutral argument requires an underlying security and the risk-free rate. However, in the interest rate model, the risk-free rate is the risk source. One condition we want to impose on the interest rate movement is arbitrage-free, that is, the interest rate movements do not allow any possible arbitrage opportunity in holding a portfolio of bonds at any time. Research shows that the interest rate movements are arbitrage-free if the following two conditions hold:[5] (1) all the bonds at any time and state of the world have a risk-neutral expected return of the prevailing one-period rate, and (2) any bond on the initial yield curve has the risk-neutral expected return of the one-period interest rate of the initial yield curve. That is, for an interest rate movement to be arbitrage-free, there must be a probability assigned to each node of a tree such that all interest rate contingent claims have an expected risk-free return, which is the one-period rate. Note that this is the *risk-neutral probability*, whereas the market probability can be quite different.

Recombining Condition

For tractability of the model, we require the discount function to recombine in a binomial lattice. This requirement is similar to the Black–Scholes model: the yield curve making an upward movement and then a downward movement must have the same value as the yield curve that makes a downward movement and then an upward movement. The difference between the yield curve movement and the stock movement is that we need the entire discount function (or the yield curve), and not just one bond price, to be identical when they recombine.

Under these restrictions, we can derive all the possible solutions. Let us consider the simplest solution in order to to gain insight into these arbitrage-free models. Suppose the spot yield curve is flat. The spot curve can shift in a parallel fashion up and down. The binomial lattice represented is normal (or arithmetic) because the parallel shift of the curve is a fixed amount and not a proportion of the value at the node. The movements of the discount function can be represented by figure 5.4.

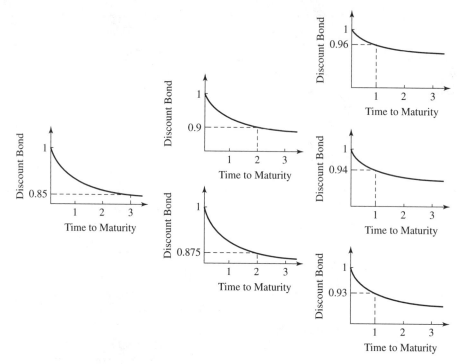

Figure 5.4 Arbitrage-free movements of the discount function. The discount function is depicted in each state and time in a binomial lattice. The discount function always originates from value 1. It increases in value in an up state but drops in value in a down state. Consider the three-period bond. Initially, its value is P(3). At time 1, it becomes a two-period bond, and its value can be either $P_1^1(2)$ or $P_0^1(2)$ at time 2, this bond becomes a one-period bond, and its value cannot deviate much from unity in any state of the world, and must converge to unity at maturity.

The purpose of the arbitrage-free model is not to determine the yield curve from any economic theory or to hypothesize that the yield curve should take particular shapes. The arbitrage-free model takes the yield curve (or the discount function) as given, and then hypothesizes the yield curve (or the discount function) movements in order to value other interest rate derivatives in relative terms. Using a dynamic hedging argument similar to the Black–Scholes model shows that we can assume the local expectation hypothesis to hold: the expected return of all the bonds over each time step is the risk-free rate, the one-period interest rate.

The Ho–Lee model is similar to the Vasicek model in that they are both normal models. The main difference, of course, is that the Ho–Lee model is specified to fit the yield curve, whereas the Vasicek model is developed to model the term structure of interest rates. For this reason, the Vasicek model has the unobservable parameter called term premium, and the yield curve derived from the Vasicek model is not the same as the observed yield curve in general. Unlike the Vasicek model, the arbitrage-free interest rate model does not require the term premium, which cannot be directly observed. Instead, the arbitrage-free interest model requires only the given observed yield curve to value bonds. Hence, the theoretical bond prices would be the same as those observed.

Specifically, let the initial discount function, the price of a zero-coupon bond with a face value of $1 and with maturity T, be denoted by $P(T)$. $P(T)$ may be observed from the STRIPS market. The yield of the bond $P(T)$ is denoted by $r(T)$. Let σ be the volatility of the interest rate. Interest rate volatility may be estimated from historical data. Then the price of a one-period bond $P_i^n(1)$ in time n and state i on the binomial lattice is given by

$$P_i^n(1) = 2\left[\frac{P(n+1)}{P(n)}\right] \cdot \frac{\delta^i}{(1+\delta^n)} \tag{5.17}$$

where

$P_i^n(1) =$ a one-period bond price at time period n and state i,

$\delta = e^{-2\cdot r(1)\cdot\sigma}$,

$\sigma =$ standard deviation of $\left(\dfrac{\Delta r(1)}{r(1)}\right)$.

Here, $-0.5\ln\delta$ is the standard deviation of the change of the interest rate over each step size, and σ is the standard deviation of the proportional change of the interest rate.

While equation (5.17) provides the bond price for one period at any state i and time n, the model also has closed-form solutions for bonds with any maturity at any node point on the lattice.

The derivation of the model is provided in appendix B. The basic idea of the derivation is quite simple, though the manipulation of the algebra is somewhat laborious. To derive the model, we need to determine the closed-form solution for $P_i^n(T)$, the price of a T year zero-coupon bond at time n and state i, such that under the risk-neutral probability 0.5, the expected return of a zero-coupon bond with any maturity, at any node point, equals the one-period risk-free rate. That is,

$$P_i^n(T) = 0.5P_i^n(1)\left\{P_i^{n+1}(T-1) + P_{i+1}^{n+1}(T-1)\right\} \tag{5.18}$$

and satisfies the initial observed yield curve condition:

$$P(T) = 0.5P(1)\left\{P_0^1(T-1) + P_1^1(T-1)\right\} \tag{5.19}$$

The above equations hold for any i, n, and T. Then the model is assured to be arbitrage-free, in that all bonds have the expected returns and the pricing consistent with the initial spot yield curve (or the discount function P(T)).

Equation (5.17) specifies the one-period bond price (and hence the one-period interest rate) on each node of the binomial lattice. For this reason, we say that the model is an *interest rate model*, since it specifies how the short-term interest rate movements are projected into the future.

Later in this chapter, we will show that once we can specify the one-period rate on a lattice, we can determine all the bond prices at each node point on the lattice by a backward substitution procedure similar to that used by the Black–Scholes model.

We can define the one-period rate to be

$$r_i^n(1) = -\ln P_i^n(1) \tag{5.20}$$

Using equation (5.20), we see that $r_i^n(1)$ can be expressed in three terms:

$$r_i^n(1)1 = \ln \frac{P(n)}{P(n+1)} + \ln \left(0.5 \left(\delta^{-\frac{n}{2}} + \delta^{\frac{n}{2}}\right)\right) + \left(\frac{n}{2} - i\right) \ln \delta \qquad (5.21)$$

The first term is the one period forward rate. That means, under the arbitrage-free interest rate movement model, we can think of the movement of the short-term rate as based on the forward rates. When there is no interest rate uncertainty, ($\delta = 1$), the second and third terms are equal to 0, and therefore the one-period-forward rates define the future spot rate arbitrage-free movements. This result is consistent with our discussion in chapter 3 on forward rates.

The last term specifies the cumulative upward and downward shifts of the rates after n periods. It is important to note that the sizes of all the shifts are the same, $\ln \delta$. That means the interest rate risk is independent of the level of the interest rate, and the interest rate follows a normal distribution.

The second term is both more difficult to explain and more important.[6] Let us consider a two-year bond. Assume that the yield curve is flat at 10 percent. The bond price is therefore 0.826446. After one year, the interest rate shifts to 20 percent or 0 percent with equal probability, just to exaggerate the problem a little bit. The expected price of the bond is now 0.916607 $\left(= \frac{1}{2} \times \left(\frac{1}{1.2}\right) + \frac{1}{2} \times \left(\frac{1}{1.0}\right)\right)$. The expected return of the bond over the first year is 0.109095 $\left(= \frac{0.916607}{0.826446} - 1\right)$. Therefore, even with a yield curve that is flat at 10 percent, the yield curve makes the shifts up or down with the same probability and the expected return of the bond exceeds 10 percent. The reason is straightforward: when the interest rate moves, the bond price does not move in step with it. This is simply a matter of bond yield calculation, where the yield is in the denominator. In chapter 3, we showed that bonds have positive convexity. When the yield curve makes a parallel shift up or down with equal probability, the expected bond price is higher than the prevailing bond price. After all, it is the positive convexity of a bond that motivates the barbell trades.

Since bonds have positive convexity, if the interest rate shifts up or down by the same amount (with equal probability) relative to the forward rate, the expected returns of the bonds would exceed the one-period interest rates. To maintain the arbitrage-free condition, such that the local expectation hypothesis holds, we require the interest rate to shift higher in both up and down movements, so that the expected returns are equal to the one-period interest rate. That is, the interest rate movements must be adjusted upward to correct for this convexity effect. This correction is the second term. Note that the second term, the *convexity adjustment* term, increases with the volatility.

A Numerical Illustration

For example, suppose the yield curve is 6% flat and the volatility is 15%.

$$P(n) = \frac{1}{1.06^n} \qquad (5.22)$$

and

$$\delta = e^{-2 \times 0.06 \times 0.15} = 0.982161 \qquad (5.23)$$

Then

$$P_i^n(1) = 2 \cdot \frac{1}{1.06} \frac{0.982161^i}{(1 + 0.982161^n)} \tag{5.24}$$

The Ho–Lee model captures many of the insights of arbitrage-free rate models. Because of its simplicity, it is useful for illustrating the salient features of arbitrage-free interest rate models. One shortcoming is that the interest rate movement does not exhibit any mean reversion process and the volatility of the one-period rate is constant at each node point. To be consistent with the historical behavior of the yield curve movements, the model should accept a term structure of volatilities as input. The following section will first describe how the interest rate model can be used to value interest rate contingent claims, and the section after that will seek to remedy this problem by describing a time-varying volatility model.

Interest rate derivative valuation and verification of the arbitrage-free property

We now consider using the interest rate model to value an interest rate contingent claim. Given an arbitrage-free interest rate model, the pricing of interest rate contingent claims is now relatively straightforward. The process is similar to that of pricing an equity option. We use the backward substitution procedure, starting from the terminal condition that specifies the value of the derivatives on the expiration date at each node point of the lattice. Then we determine the value of the derivative at each node point one period before that terminal date by discounting the risk-neutral expected value of the derivative (viewed from the node point where the derivative value is being calculated) at the prevailing one-period interest rate. The choice of the discount rate is the key in the development of the arbitrage-free rate model.

Unlike valuing an equity option in the binomial lattice, where the discount rate is the constant risk-free rate, in the case of uncertain interest rate movement, the one-period discount rate is determined by the interest rate model at the node point where the derivative value is being determined.

Once the derivative value is determined at all the node points one period before the terminal date, we can now determine the values of the derivatives at all the node points on the binomial lattice two periods before the terminal date, using the derivative values at the node point one period before the terminal date. We apply this procedure iteratively until we reach the initial date. This iterative procedure is identical to that of valuing the equity option. Therefore, the only difference between the equity option valuation and the interest rate derivative valuation is the use of a one-period discount rate in the backward substitution procedure. The equity option pricing uses a constant rate, while the interest rate derivative option pricing uses the prevailing one-period interest rate, as determined by the arbitrage-free interest rate model, at that node point.

The following binomial lattice of interest rates explains the backward substitution procedure for valuing a bond option. Suppose the bond option expires in two years. At the terminal date, the option holder has the right to buy a T-year zero-coupon bond at a strike price, X, given that the interest rate volatility is σ and the market discount function is $P(T)$. Suppose we use the Ho–Lee model and determine the one-period discount factor $P_i^n(1)$ as described above. The following steps are then taken to determine the bond option price.

Step 1. Determine the two-year bond value on the terminal date at each node point on the binomial lattice. This can be accomplished by applying equation (B.5.1) in appendix B, where we present the model that specifies zero-coupon bond prices at each node point on the lattice. These bond prices are denoted by $P_i^n(T)$, where T is the time to maturity (in this case, 2) of the bond at the terminal date; n is the terminal date; and i is the state of the world. Therefore, we can assign the price of the two-year bond at each node point, at the termination date.

Step 2. Determine the terminal condition on the binomial lattice. The value of the bond option at the terminal date is given by $Max[B[2, i, T] - X, 0]$.

Step 3. Apply backward substitution at each node. If we denote the discount rate at each node (n, i) by $r(n, i)$, then by definition of a discount factor, we have

$$P_i^n(1) = \frac{1}{1 + r(n, i)} \tag{5.25}$$

For the formulation of the Ho–Lee model presented, we assume that the risk-neutral probability (p) is 0.5. Using this probability, we can calculate the expected derivative values one period ahead and discount the expected value using the prevailing interest rate, as shown in figure 5.5.

As a special case, we can use the same procedure to value a T-year zero-coupon bond. To value a zero-coupon bond price, the terminal date is the maturity of the bond T. The terminal condition at time T is that the bond price value is \$1 for all the nodes at the terminal date. When we conduct the backward substitution procedure, the initial value should exactly match the input discount bond prices $P(T)$. This is the essence of an arbitrage-free interest rate movement model, in the sense that the model takes the yield curve (of the discount function) as given, and the model price of any zero-coupon bond in a way consistent with the input discount function. (See figure 5.6.)

There are two remarks that are important. First, note that given the one-period

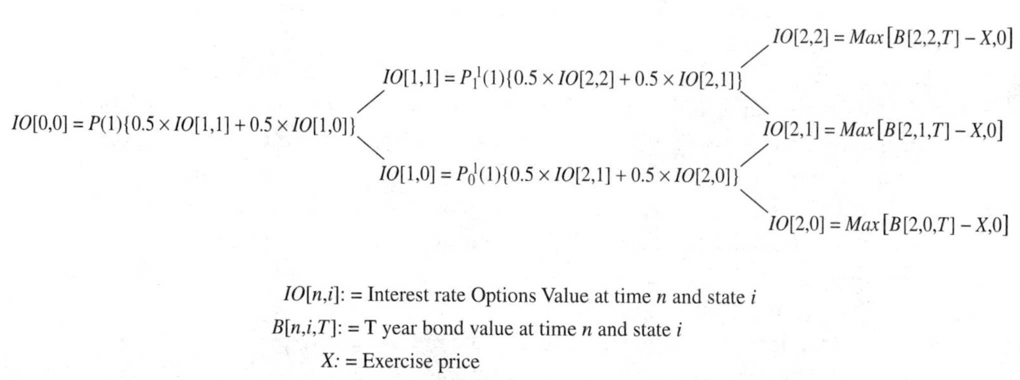

$$IO[2,2] = Max[B[2,2,T] - X,0]$$

$$IO[1,1] = P_1^1(1)\{0.5 \times IO[2,2] + 0.5 \times IO[2,1]\}$$

$$IO[0,0] = P(1)\{0.5 \times IO[1,1] + 0.5 \times IO[1,0]\}$$

$$IO[2,1] = Max[B[2,1,T] - X,0]$$

$$IO[1,0] = P_0^1(1)\{0.5 \times IO[2,1] + 0.5 \times IO[2,0]\}$$

$$IO[2,0] = Max[B[2,0,T] - X,0]$$

$IO[n,i]:$ = Interest rate Options Value at time n and state i

$B[n,i,T]:$ = T year bond value at time n and state i

$X:$ = Exercise price

Figure 5.5 Pricing the interest rate option by recursive methods. For the formulation of the Ho–Lee model, we assume that the risk-neutral probability is 0.5. We can calculate the expected derivative values one period ahead with 0.5 risk-neutral probability and discount the expected value at the prevailing interest rate. $IO[n, i]$ is a interest rate option at time n and state i. $B[n, i, t]$ is a T-year bond value at time n and state i. X is an exercise price.

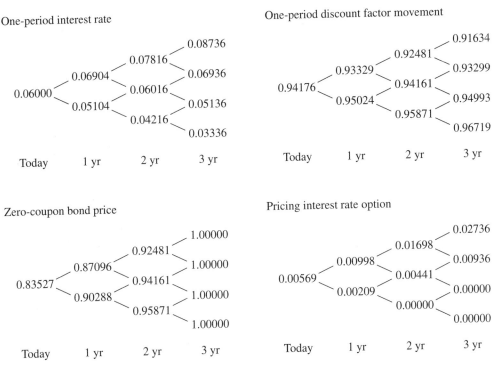

Figure 5.6 The one-period interest rate, discount function movements, zero-coupon bond price and interest rate contingent claim (cap), using the assumptions as stated above, 6% yield curve. The zero-coupon bond price which pays $1 for all nodes at the terminal date is 0.839619, which is the same as $P(3)(= 1/1 + 0.06)^3)$. This is the essence of the arbitrate-free interest rate model. The terminal condition of the interest rate option is $Max[r(3, i) - 0.06, 0]$, $i = \{0, 1, 2, 3\}$, where $r(n, i)$ is the one-period interest rate for time n and state i. The annual compounding rate is 6% and the volatility is 15%. The risk-neutral probability for upward movements is 0.5, the exercise price is 6%, and the notional amount is 1. The maturity of the option contract is three years. The one-period interest rates and corresponding one-period discount functions are shown in the figure. Based on them, the binomial lattice of interest rate options is represented in the subsequent diagram. At the highest state of year 3, the interst rate is 0.08736. If we subtract the exercise rate of 6% from the interest rate at that state and multiply the notional amount, we have the interest rate option value at the highest state of year 3.

arbitrage-free discount rates specified at all the node points on the binomial lattice, we can always determine the zero-coupon bond price at any node point, using the method described above. Or we can value any derivatives at any node point. Therefore, in principle, we do not need to use equation (B.5.1) in step 1 to specify the bond price at the node point. However, equation (B.5.1) does provide a closed-form solution that enhances the computational efficiency. The important point is that specifying the one-period interest rate movement is sufficient to determine all interest rate derivatives. Second, this procedure of valuing an interest rate derivative relies only on the one-period arbitrage-free rate assigned to the binomial lattice. Therefore, this procedure is appropriate for any arbitrage-free rate models (described below) that can assign the one-period interest rate to all the nodes on the binomial lattice.

Continuous time formulation of the Ho–Lee Model

To enable us to compare the Ho–Lee model with other interest rate models, it is convenient to express the models in a continuous time representation. If we let the step size of the binomial lattice become arbitrarily small, the interest rate model can be expressed in a continuous time formulation given as

$$dr = (f'(0, t) + \sigma^2 t)dt + \sigma dz \qquad (5.26)$$

where $f'(0, t)$ is the first derivative of $f(0, t)$ with respect to t. First we need to define the notation $f(t, T^*)$.

Let $f(t, T^*)$ be the instantaneous forward rate at time t with the forward delivery date T^*. In the discrete time modeling, we can think of the instantaneous forward rate $f(t, T^*)$ as the one-period forward rate with a delivery date T^* at the evaluation date t. Or we can think of this instantaneous forward rate as the forward rate of the daily money market rate for delivery on a date T^*, say on December 1, 2010.

Therefore $f(0, t)$ is the instantaneous forward rate at delivery date t (or, analogously, the one-period forward rate in the binomial lattice model, which is $\ln(P(t)/P(t + 1))$, where $P(t)$ is the initial observed discount function), as observed at the initial time. When the step size becomes small, the one-period forward rate becomes the instantaneous forward rate at the delivery date t. Given a discount function, if we want to know the forward daily rate at time t from now, that forward rate is $f(0, t)$.

Equation (5.26) says that the change of an arbitrage-free short-term interest rate $r(t)$ at a future time t is the sum of three components: (1) the change of instantaneous forward rate; (2) a drift as a result of the volatility (which we call the convexity drift), to assure that the arbitrage-free condition will hold, taking the convexity of bonds into account; (3) a random noise term. The result is very intuitive. The result says that if there is no interest rate risk (without the third component), then the interest rate has to change at time t as predicted by the change in the forward rate derived from the initial spot yield curve. This is in fact the expectation hypothesis explained in chapter 3. Since there is interest rate uncertainty, the Ho–Lee model specifies the risk to be an instantaneous normal distribution at time t. The third term therefore specifies the normal model, and other models may have different specifications. Under this specification of the risks, where we let the interest rate to go up or down symmetrically with mean 0, the convexity of the bonds would have an expected return higher than the instantaneous interest rate $r(t)$ because of the bond convexity. The second component is used to adjust for this effect.

The Extended Ho–Lee model

So far we have required the assumption of constant volatility at each node. Clearly this assumption contradicts the market reality. If we revisit the arguments made in the above section, we see that there is no reason for us to assume that the instantaneous volatility is constant. The volatility can differ at each period. The one-period volatilities can be set such that the model can take on any term structures of volatilities.

In the market, we observe that the term structure of volatilities is downward-sloping. That means the yields of the long-term bonds have a lower volatility than those of the shorter-term bonds. This observation has implications for the yield curve movements.

We assume that the initial yield curve is flat. When the yield curve shifts upward, the short-term rate will shift more than the long-term rate. Then the yield curve will be downward-sloping. In this case, according to the expectation hypothesis, the interest rates will fall. Similarly, in the down state, the short-term rate will fall more than the long-term rate. The yield curve will be upward-sloping. In this case, the yield curve will be expected to rise. This observation shows that a declining term structure of volatilities implies a mean reversion process of interest rates within the context of the model.

Term structure of volatilities

Before we can describe the interest rate models that can accept time-varying interest rate volatilities, we need to define some terms. There are two ways to express the term structure of volatilities: *forward volatilities* and *spot volatilities*.

Forward volatility is the volatility of the one-period forward rate in year n, for each $n = 1, 2, \cdots$. For example, if we say the forward volatility of the one-period rate in year n is 10%, that means the one-period rate in year n will have a volatility of 10%. When we allow for time-varying interest rate volatility, the one-period rate may have a lower volatility in year $n + 1$, and so on. We denote the term structure of forward volatilities by $\sigma^f(n)$, which is a function of n.

The term structure of spot volatilities, $\sigma^S(n)$, refers to the volatility of the nth-year rate of the spot curve for each $n = 1, 2, \cdots$. For example, when we reported the volatilities of the interest rates in section 5.1, the term structure of volatilities was based on the spot volatilities.

Model specifications: Forward volatilities and spot volatilities

The extended Ho–Lee model is a direct extension from the Ho–Lee model. Instead of describing the interest rate volatility using a constant δ, we begin with defining parameters $\delta(n)$ for each period n. If the model is specified by the forward volatilities $\sigma^f(n)$, the forward volatility over one step at time n, then $\delta(n)$ is defined by the following equation, where forward volatilities $= \sigma^f(n)$.

$$f(n) \cdot \sigma^f(n) = -0.5 \ln \delta(n) \qquad (5.27)$$

If the model is specified by the spot volatilities $\sigma(n, T)$, then the $\delta(n)$ are solved for from the following equation, where spot volatilities $= \sigma^S(n)$.

$$r(n) \cdot \sigma^s(n) = -\frac{0.5 \ln [\delta(n)\delta(n-1)\cdots\delta(1)]}{n} \qquad (5.28)$$

The reason for using the forward rate $f(n)$ in equation (5.27) and the spot rate $r(n)$ in equation (5.28) is that by convention, the interest rate volatilities are quoted as a proportion of the interest rate level. But a normal model measures interest rate risk by the absolute level, and therefore we need to make that adjustment.

Forward volatility is the volatility of the one-period rate n years from now, and the spot volatility is the yield of the n-year bond over one period where $n = 1, 2 \cdots$. As was discussed in chapter 3, the n-year bond rate is related to the one-period forward rates by the following equation:

$$(1 + r_{0,n})^n = (1 + r_{0,1})(1 + r_{1,2})(1 + r_{2,3}) \cdots (1 + r_{n-1,n})$$

That means the compounding returns of holding an n-year bond are the same as reinvesting in the one-period forward rate. This equation (5.28), provides the intuitive explanation of equation where the spot volatility is expressed as the geometric mean of the forward volatilities.

The extended Ho–Lee model for the one-period bond price movement is given by

$$P_i^n(1) = \left[\frac{P(n+1)}{P(n)} \right] \cdot \left[\frac{(1 + \delta_{n-1}\delta_{n-2} \cdots \delta_1) \cdots (1 + \delta_{n-1})2}{(1 + \delta_n \cdots \delta_1)(1 + \delta_n \cdots \delta_2) \cdots (1 + \delta_n)} \right] \cdot \delta_n^i \quad (5.29)$$

The interpretation of the model is similar to the Ho–Lee model. In comparing the two models, we note that the extended Ho–Lee model also is based on the forward rates, which are the first factor. Since the volatilities are time-varying, the model specifies the interest rate risk by the forward volatilities. The second factor adjusts for the convexity effect and, as expected, is somewhat more complicated. We will revisit the interpretation of this factor in the section "Continuous Time Representation." The third factor represents the interest rate uncertainties in the same way as the Ho–Lee model.

Numerical Example

Let us use a numerical example to illustrate the model. Assume a flat yield curve of 6%. The forward volatilities (and the derived δ_n) are presented in the following table.

Year	1	2	3	4	5
Volatility σ^f	0.1	0.09	0.08	0.07	0.06
δ_n	0.98807	0.98926	0.99045	0.99164	0.99283

The corresponding spot volatilities are 0.1, 0.095, 0.09, 0.085, and 0.08 years 1–5, respectively. The relationship between the spot volatility and the forward volatility is $f(n) \cdot \sigma^f(n+1) = (n+1) \cdot r(n+1) \cdot \sigma^s(n+1) - n \cdot r(n) \cdot \sigma^s(n)$. For example, $\sigma^f(2)$ can be calculated as follows:

$$(2 \cdot 0.06 \cdot \sigma^s(2) - 1 \cdot 0.06 \cdot \sigma^s(1))/0.06 = 2 \cdot 0.095 - 0.1 = 0.09$$

(See figure 5.7.)

Continuous time representation

Following the analysis used for the Ho–Lee model, we can derive the continuous time specification of the extended Ho–Lee model as shown below.

$$dr = \left(f'(0, t) + \sigma(t)^2 t + \frac{\sigma'(t)}{\sigma(t)} \left[r(t) - f(0, t) \right] \right) dt + \sigma(t)dZ \quad (5.30)$$

In comparing equations (5.30) and (5.26), we note the following differences. First, the central difference is the specification of the noise term, the last term of equation (5.30). We see that the uncertainty term depends on the rate volatility, which is not constant

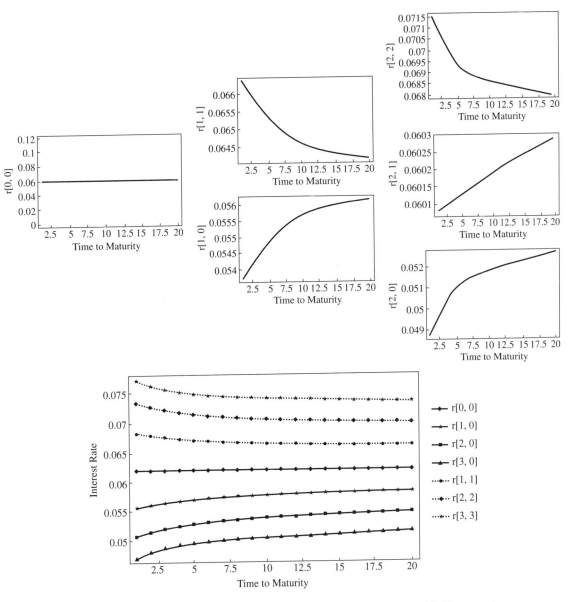

Figure 5.7 Arbitrage-free yield curve movement of extended Ho–Lee model: Time varying volatility. The extended Ho–Lee model is a one-factor term structure movement model with time-varying volatility. We assume a flat yield curve of 6% and the spot volatility is 0.1, 0.95, 0.09, 0.085, and 0.08 for 1, 2, 3, 4, and 5 years. Since we assume that the term structure of volatility exhibits a downward slope, we expect that the slope of the yield curve becomes flatter as time passes. The reason for this is that the short-term rates fluctuate more than the long-term rates, as indicated by the downward-sloping term structure of volatility. The upper panel shows how the yield curves move over time, and the lower panel shows the yield curve movements in one picture to compare with each other.

across time. That is, the extended model allows for a time-varying term structure of volatility. Second, we see that the extended Ho–Lee model has only one term more, $\frac{\sigma'(t)}{\sigma(t)} \left[r(t) - f(0, t) \right]$, then the Ho–Lee model.

The additional term specifies adjustments of the interest rate to the forward rate, as observed initially from the yield curve. Suppose that the term structure of volatility is downward-sloping; where the forward volatility declines with time, we have $\sigma'(t)$ negative. If the interest rate is lower than the forward rate, the interest rate will be adjusted upward. And conversely, if the interest rate is higher than the forward rate, then the interest rate will be adjusted downward. This is the essence of mean reversion, as induced by the term structure of volatilities. The speed of adjustment is the proportional change of the term structure of volatilities with time. For example, if the term structure of volatility has a functional form given by

$$\sigma(t) = be^{-\alpha t} + \sigma \qquad (5.31)$$

such that σ is the long-term forward volatility and $\sigma + b$ is the shortest-term volatility, which decays to the long-term forward volatility exponentially. Then the adjustment rate of the mean reversion process is $-\alpha (= \sigma'(t)/\sigma(t))$, if we further assume that the long-term forward volatility σ is 0.

The Ho–Lee n-factor Binomial Lattice model

As we have noted, all interest rates move with perfect correlation over each period for one-factor models. As a result, the yield curve cannot make a twist movement, whereby the short rate falls as the long rate rises, or vice versa. We have empirically observed that the yield curve can make a twist movement and parallel movement. Therefore, we need a multifactor model.

Before we can describe a two-factor model, we need to further extend the concept of the term structure of volatilities to the volatility surface. The volatility surface describes the volatilities of the entire yield curve into the future. We have discussed spot volatilities, which describe the yield curve volatilities over one period of time. We have also discussed the forward volatilities, which describe the volatilities of a rate one period into the future. Volatility surface describes the volatilities of all rates (the spot volatilities) and the volatilities of all the future rates (for example, the forward volatilities). The table below shows a representation of a *volatility surface*.

Volatility Surface in %				
Maturities (years)		1	2	3
Time horizon (years)	0	20	15	12
	1	18	14	11
	2	17	12	10

The first row represents the volatilities of one-year, two-year, and three-year rates as estimated today (the spot volatilities). The first column is the one-year rate volatilities for today, one year forward, and two years forward (the forward volatilities for the one-year rate). Now, consider any number in the table, say, the cell in column 2, row 2. The cell indicates that the two-year rate one year forward is 14%.

Given a two-factor interest rate model, we now seek to specify the interest rate movements such that the movements can best fit the volatility surface. The modeling approach of the Ho–Lee two-factor model adds further extension to the extended Ho–Lee model. First we describe the two-factor binomial lattice. In a one-factor interest rate binomial lattice, we assume the yield curve (alternatively represented by the discount function) follows a binomial movement, but they must recombine in the second step. That is, starting from any node in the lattice, the yield curve realized after an upward movement followed by a downward movement must be identical to that realized by a downward movement followed by an upward movement.

In a two-factor binomial lattice model, at any node point, the yield curve can take four possible movements. Each factor has two outcomes, and since there are two factors, we have four outcomes. These four outcomes can be represented by (uu), (ud), (du), (dd), where u represents "up" (or upward movement,) and d represents "down" (or downward movement). The first entry represents the movement of the first factor and the second entry represents that of the second factor. We can construct four node points from each node point of a two-factor binomial lattice. Starting from any node point, after one step, there are four possible outcomes. After another step, there are 16(= 4 × 4) possible outcomes. However, these 16 outcomes are not different from each other because of the recombining condition. (See table 5.4.)

Recombining must occur for each factor. Let (uu)(ud) mean a up-up movement followed by an up-down movement. We can analogously define all other movements. An example of a recombining requirement would be (uu)(ud) = (ud)(uu). (See figure 5.8.)

In this case, we keep the first factor movement the same for the left-hand side and the right-hand side (moving up in both periods), but the second factor must recombine. The left-hand side makes an upward movement followed by a downward movement, and the right-hand side makes a downward movement followed by an upward movement.

These recombining conditions reduce the 16 possible outcomes to 9 possible outcomes. The first factor can attain three possible states, $i = 0, 1, 2$; the second factor also can attain three possible states, $j = 0, 1, 2$. The combined possible states are represented by (i, j) for $i, j = 0, 1, 2$. Hence, these notations can represent all nine possible states. In general, after n steps, there are $(n + 1)^2$ possible states, and each state is represented by (i, j) for $i, j = 0, 1, \cdots n$.

Table 5.4 The numbers of nodes of the n-factor model

No. of nodes	Time						
	0	1	2	3	4	5	n
1 factor	1	2	3	4	5	6	$(n + 1)^1$
2 factor	1	4	9	16	25	36	$(n + 1)^2$
3 factor	1	8	27	64	125	216	$(n + 1)^3$
4 factor	1	16	81	256	625	1296	$(n + 1)^4$

When we generate 1 factor recombining binomial tree, the number of nodes at period n is $(n + 1)$, which linearly increases with the time period as compared to the 2^2 for the non-recombining tree. We can determine in a similar way when we have more than one factor.

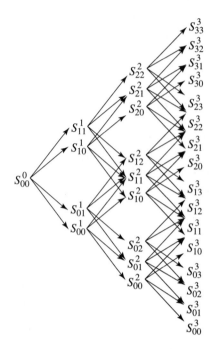

Figure 5.8 The recombining condition of the Ho–Lee two-factor model. A binomial lattice that results from generating a two-factor binomial tree. The superscript indicates the time period. The left and the right subscripts indicate the number of upward movements of the first factor and the second factor, respectively. The number of nodes at period 2 and period 3 are 9 and 16, respectively.

The Ho–Lee two-factor model asserts that there are two yield curve movements much like the empirical model of Litterman and Scheinkman. The first movement of the Litterman and Scheinkman model is represented by the extended Ho–Lee model with one specific term structure of volatilities, represented by $(\delta_1^1, \delta_2^1, \delta_3^1, \cdots, \delta_n^1)$. Similarly, the second factor is represented by another term structure of volatilities $(\delta_1^2, \delta_2^2, \delta_3^2, \cdots, \delta_n^2)$. The model then assures that the recombination of the two factor movements holds, resulting in a closed-form solution. (The *closed-form solution* is a solution that can be expressed in one equation rather than by an algorithm.) The closed-form solution is given below.

$$P_{i,j}^n(1) = \frac{P(n+1)}{P(n)} \times \frac{(1+\delta_{n-1}^1 \cdots \delta_1^1)(1+\delta_{n-1}^1 \cdots \delta_2^1)\cdots(1+\delta_{n-1}^1)2}{(1+\delta_n^1 \cdots \delta_1^1)(1+\delta_n^1 \cdots \delta_2^1)\cdots(1+\delta_n^1\delta_{n-1}^1)(1+\delta_n^1)} \times$$

$$\frac{(1+\delta_{n-1}^2 \cdots \delta_1^2)(1+\delta_{n-1}^2 \cdots \delta_2^2)\cdots(1+\delta_{n-1}^2)2}{(1+\delta_n^2 \cdots \delta_1^2)(1+\delta_n^2 \cdots \delta_2^2)\cdots(1+\delta_n^2\delta_{n-1}^2)(1+\delta_n^2)}(\delta_n^1)^i(\delta_n^2)^j \qquad (5.32)$$

The extension of a one-factor Ho–Lee model to a two-factor Ho–Lee model is surprisingly simple. Comparing the solution with the Ho–Lee model in equation (5.29), we see that for a two-factor model, we simply add the additional uncertainty term $(\delta_n^2)^j$ and its associated convexity drift term $\frac{(1+\delta_{n-1}^2 \cdots \delta_1^2)(1+\delta_{n-1}^2 \cdots \delta_2^2)\cdots(1+\delta_{n-1}^2)2}{(1+\delta_n^2 \cdots \delta_1^2)(1+\delta_n^2 \cdots \delta_2^2)\cdots(1+\delta_n^2\delta_{n-1}^2)(1+\delta_n^2)}$. (Note that the superscript of δ denotes the factor of the movements, and is not a mathematical power. (For example, $(\delta_n^2)^j$ denotes the second factor movement.) This result is intuitively clear.

We follow the insight of Litterman and Scheinkman's results on the term structure movements to interpret the two-factor Ho–Lee model. We assume that the yield curve can make several uncorrelated movements. Therefore, the only impact of each factor we add to the model is simply an adjustment for the convexity drift.

More important, we can specify any arbitrary number of factors to the model. The extension to an n-factor model is straightforward. We simply need to multiply the expression in equation (5.B.4) by the random movement and the convexity drift term. The probability of each outcome is $1/2^n$. Given the empirical results of estimating the yield curve movements, three-factor interest rate movements may suffice to value interest rate contingent claims for most cases.

The two-factor model can also be expressed as a continuous time model. The result is presented below. It shows that the general expression is a direct extension from the one-factor model.

$$dr = \left\{ f'(t) + |\sigma(t)|^2 t + \frac{|\sigma'(t)| \cos \phi(t)}{|\sigma(t)| \cos \theta(t)} \left[r - f(t) \right] \right\} dt + \sigma(t) dW \quad (5.33)$$

where $\theta(t)$ is the angle between the two vectors $\theta(t)$ and $X(t) + W(t)$, and $\phi(t)$ is the angle between the two vectors $\sigma'(t)$ and $X(t) + W(t)$.

$$\sigma(t) \bullet (X(t) + W(t)) = |\sigma(t)| \cdot |X(t) + W(t)| \cdot \cos \theta(t)$$

and

$$\sigma'(t) \bullet (X(t) + W(t)) = |\sigma'(t)| \cdot |X(t) + W(t)| \cdot \cos \phi(t)$$

$$X(t) = (\int_0^t \int_s^t \sigma_1(u) du ds, \int_0^t \int_s^t \sigma_2(u) du ds)$$

$$\sigma = (\sigma_1, \sigma_2)$$

$$\sigma' = (\sigma_1', \sigma_2')$$

$$W = (W_1, W_2)$$

For the numerical example below, we define the term structures of volatilities to be

$$\sigma^1(t) = 0.0396$$

$$\sigma^2(t) = 0.1158 e^{-0.6813t} + 0.0117$$

where t is measured in years.

That means we assume that first term structure of volatilities to be constant, similar to the Ho–Lee model. However, the yield curve has a second movement, where the short term volatilities are higher than the long-term volatilities. Equations (5.27) and (5.28) are used to derive $\delta(n)$ for each $n = 1, 2, 3, \cdots$, using the term of structures of volatilities specified above. (See figure 5.9.)

In chapter 6, we will discuss how the Ho–Lee two-factor or n-factor model can be fitted to the observed market prices of derivatives. These derivatives may be caps and floors, swaptions (American or European), or bond options (American and European). The term structures of volatilities are estimated so that the model can determine all the

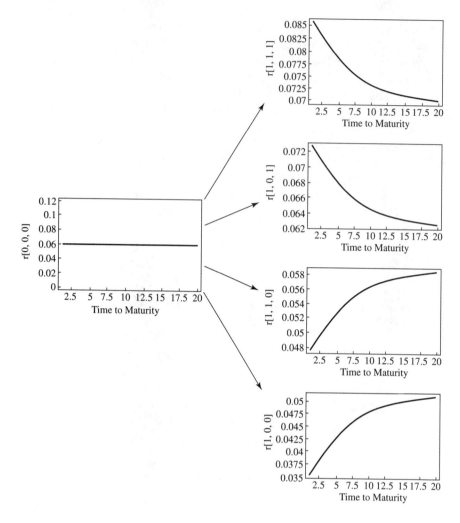

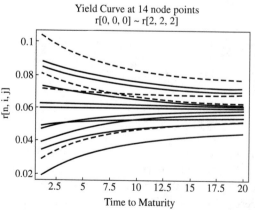

Figure 5.9 Arbitrage-free yield curve movement of the Ho–Lee two factor model. $r[n, i, j]$ is the interest rate when the time period is n, the state of factor 1 is i and the state of factor 2 is j. The Ho–Lee two-factor model is a two-factor term structure movement model with time-varying volatility. Since two independent factors are determining the yield curve shape, the rates along the yield curve are not necessarily perfectly correlated, in contrast to the one-factor models. We can observe that the future yield curves are crossing each other, which could not be seen in the one-factor term-structure movement model.

observed prices of the derivatives simultaneously. As illustrated above, σ^1 and σ^2 can be assumed to take a specific functional form and the coefficients of the functions can be estimated. For example, σ^1 can be assumed to be constant and σ^2 can be assumed to be an exponentially declining function. This procedure is called *calibration*.

Thus far, we have discussed a set of interest rate models that exhibit normal distributions, which does not reflect the relationship between the interest rate uncertain movements and the interest rate levels. The lognormal model ensures that the interest rate uncertain movement increases or decreases with the interest rate level. In particular, when interest rates continue to fall, the interest rate movement will continue to decrease. In this case, the interest rates cannot become negative, while the normal model often has scenarios where the interest rates can do so. An example of a lognormal model is the Black, Derman, and Toy (1990) model.

The Black–Derman–Toy Model

The Black–Derman–Toy (BDT) model is a binomial lattice model which assumes that the short-term interest rate follows a lognormal process. The model does not have a closed-form solution and can best be explained by describing the procedure to construct the short-term interest rate movements.

Valuation procedure

The BDT model uses a recombining lattice to determine a lognormal interest rate model. Further, the model can take the initial term structure of the interest rate as input, as well as the term structure of volatilities, as in the extended Ho–Lee model. The model is specified by an iterative construction that can be best illustrated with an example.

As inputs to the model, we begin with the given term structure of interest rates and the term structure of forward volatilities.

Maturity (years)	1	2	3	4	5
Yield (%)	6.0	7.0	8.0	9.5	10.0
Forward Volatility (%)	15.0	14.0	13.0	11.0	

On the lattice, initially we have a one-period rate, say, 6 percent. The lognormal model is determined by the following random walk at a node:

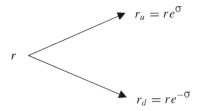

Note that, using the definition of r_u and r_d, we know

$$r_u = r_d e^{2\sigma} \qquad (5.34)$$

Step 1. Construct the lowest short-term rate for each period in the lattice. These rates are $r, r \cdot \exp\left[-\sigma(1)\right]\mu(1), r \cdot \exp\left[-\sigma(2)\right]\mu(2) \cdots$. Note that we do not know μ, the only parameter unknown at this point.

Step 2. Specify the short-term rates at all the nodes, using equation (5.34). We need to iteratively calculate the rate r_u, applying equation (5.34) repeatedly.

Step 3. Determine μ by a "bootstrap" approach. Search for the value $\mu(1)$ such that a two-year bond, given by the discount function $P(T)$, can be priced according to the market. Then we determine $\mu(2)$ such that $\mu(2)$ can price the three-year bond exactly according to the observed (or given) three-year bond price. This iterative procedure, called the bootstrap approach, can determine the lattice as desired.

We calculate the short rates by following the BDT procedure, given the yields and the instantaneous forward volatilities in the table above. Furthermore, using the same data, we generate the short rates with the extended Ho–Lee model for comparison proposes. (See figure 5.10.)

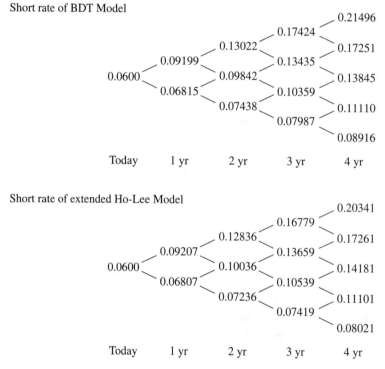

Figure 5.10 Short rates of BDT and extended Ho–Lee models. We use the same forward volatility given in Figure 5.9 to generate the one-period interest rates for the BDT and the extended Ho–Lee model. The BDT model is a lognormal model, and the extended Ho–Lee model is a normal model. Therefore, the way to calculate the forward volatility is different. For example, the first year forward volatility is 15%. For the BDT model, the first year forward volatility, 15%, can be calculated by Log[0.09199/0.06815]*0.5, where 0.09199 and 0.06815 are the one-period interest rate at time 1 and state 1, and at time 1 and state 0, respectively. For the extended Ho–Lee model, we have the same 15% forward volatility by (0.09207 − 0.06807)*0.5/0.08, where 0.08 is the forward rate and 0.09207 and 0.06807 are the one-period interest rates at time 1 on the extended Ho–Lee binomial lattice.

Continuous time representation

While there is no closed-form solution for the BDT model in a binomial lattice frame-work, we can compare the model with the Ho–Lee model.

$$d \log r = \left(\theta(t) - \frac{\sigma'(t)}{\sigma(t)} \log r \right) dt + \sigma(t)dW \qquad (5.35)$$

where $\theta(t), \sigma(T)$ are chosen to match the term structure of spot rates and the term structure of spot rate volatilities. Comparing this model with the extended Ho–Lee, we see that they are very similar. The main difference between the extended Ho–Lee and the BDT models is that the Ho–Lee has a closed-form solution in the binomial lattice, and the BDT does not have negative rates in all the scenarios.

Note that for a given yield curve shape, the forward rate can be negative. Consider a steep downward yield curve; the forward rates projected in the future can be negative. However, under the lognormal model construction, since the interest rates cannot be negative under all scenarios, the binomial lattice of the BDT model must have all the interest rates higher than the forward rates, whenever the forward rates are negative.

The Black–Karasinski (1991) model is an extension of the BDT model that allows for an explicit mean reversion process, assuming a long-term equilibrium rate that the short-term rate continually adjusts toward. The model assumes that there is a long-run equilibrium rate and that the spot interest rate seeks to adjust to the long-term equilibrium rate. The Black–Karasinski model decouples the adjustment rate ($\alpha(t)$) and the short-rate volatility term ($\frac{\sigma'(t)}{\sigma(t)}$).

$$d \log r = (\theta(t) - \alpha(t) \log r)dt + \sigma(t)dW$$

The Hull–White Model

The Hull–White model (1990) is a normal model that has an explicit term to capture the mean reversion of interest rates. It is similar to the Vasicek model, but is arbitrage-free. This approach enables the model to capture the term structure of volatilities by adjusting the adjustment rate of the short-term rate to the long-term equilibrium rate. The lattice model they propose is a trinomial model. This enables the model to adjust for the speed of adjustment, and it can be constructed such that the model has no negative interest rates in all scenarios.

The continuous time version of the model can be expressed as follows.

$$dr(t) = (\alpha(t) - \beta \cdot r(t)) \cdot dt + \sigma \cdot dW(t) \qquad (5.36)$$

where

$$\alpha(t) = \frac{\partial f(0, t)}{\partial T^*} + \beta \cdot f(0, t) + \frac{\sigma^2}{2\beta} \left(1 - e^{-2\beta t} \right)$$

β, σ: *constant*

We can see that the model is similar to the Vasicek model. The mean reversion process is assumed explicitly, such that the short-term rate seeks partial adjustments to the long-term rate. The forward volatility (σ) is constant such that reversion is not induced from the forward volatilities. This formulation also provides closed-form solutions to a coupon bond value at any point in time.

The Hull–White model can also be extended to a two-factor model (1994) that is arbitrage-free in a form similar to the Brennan and Schwartz model. Specifically, the model is specified by two simultaneous equations:

$$dr = [\theta(t) + u - ar]\, dt + \sigma_1 dW \tag{5.37}$$

$$du = -bu\, dt + \sigma_2 dZ \tag{5.38}$$

In this case, the short-term rate makes partial adjustments to the long-term rate, while the long-term rate follows a random movement. Using normal model properties, these models can derive closed-form solutions for many derivatives in the continuous time formulation.

5.5   A Comparison of Models

Interest rate modeling is a very active area of financial research. Though we have provided descriptions of some of the models, we have not covered many models that have contributed to the literature. The subject is too broad to be covered in one chapter, even a brief overview. Our purpose is to introduce interest rate models for the development of the material in this book. This overview provides a context of how interest rate models are chosen. Furthermore, it emphasizes that there is no single interest rate model that can be used for all purposes.

We have discussed some of the desirable features of interest rate models that can be used for valuing interest rate contingent claims and can capture the historical observations in the real world. These include the lognormal versus normal distribution behavior, mean reversion, and the number of factors. But on the implementation level, we must also consider some of the technical issues of the model features.

Modeling features

1. Continuous or discrete time is not a significant matter. We have discussed a model using a discrete time or a continuous time. In most cases, models can be converted from one version to the other. The continuous time model can offer insights into the model behavior as well as closed-form solutions. In most cases, however, discrete time models have to be used for implementation.

2. Recombining: the growth of computation intensity is linear with the number of steps of the one-factor binomial model. A recombining lattice enables us to price securities with the computation intensity growing linearly. If we use a simulation approach, the computing time grows exponentially. The computation speed is important in implementation.

3. Recombining lattice: optimization. Generating interest rate scenarios is only the first step in valuing a security. In the chapter 6, we will discuss how the model is used. The applications can involve making optimal decisions at each node point on the lattice. A recombining lattice enables us to determine the optimal solution more efficiently.

4. Clarity versus completeness. Often, interest rate modeling is only part of a "large" model. There are other risks, such as stock risks and currency risks. In modeling, we may need to find the trade-off between completeness and clarity of the model.

This chapter provides explicit solutions to lattice models with normal interest rates. Special attention is paid to these models because their formulation is appropriate for the purpose of this book. The reasons are (1) the approach can be explained without the use of differential equations or other mathematical tools in calculus; (2) this framework provides closed-form solutions to many derivatives, and therefore interested readers can develop many models (to be discussed in chapter 6) on their spread sheets or any other platforms in a more straightforward manner; (3) in the development of the firm model in part III of this book, Bellman optimization is used. Binomial lattice models provide the most straightforward solution to the optimization problem.

While the chapter has compared interest rate models, the presentation has suppressed the discussion of continuous time modeling, which has become the foundation of mathematical finance. In light of the importance of interest rate modeling in a continuous time framework, the material is described in chapter 19 so that interested readers can relate the material in this chapter to the continuous time framework.

To conclude the discussion of the models, table 5.5 shows how each model incorporates different features and how each captures the interest rate historical behavior.

5.6   Generalizations of Interest Rate Models

Readers who are not interested in interest rate models may skip the following sections. Their discussions are more technical, and they are not central to the development of the book. However, they do cover some of the more recent research in interest rate models.

There are interest rate models that provide much flexibility in modeling the movement of the yield curve. We will discuss three such models in this section, including the Heath–Jarrow–Morton model, which provides the mathematical relationship between the term structure of volatilities and the specification of the interest rate model,

Table 5.5 Summary of Term Structure Movements Models

Term structure movements model	Distribution		Factor		Mean reversion		
	Normal	Lognormal	1	2	Explicit MR	Implicit MR	Not MR
Vasicek	○		○		○		
Cox-Ingersoll-Ross		○	○		○		
Brennan-Schwartz		○		○	○		
Hull and White (extended Vasicek)	○		○		○		
Black-Karasinski		○	○		○		
Ho and Lee	○		○				○
Black-Derman-Toy		○	○			○	
Extended Ho and Lee	○		○			○	
Ho and Lee 2 factor	○			○		○	
Hull and White (extended CIR)		○	○		○		

The explicit mean reversion means that the mean reversion feature is explicit in the models. However, even though the implicit mean reversion has the mean reversion property due to changing volatility, the mean reversion feature is not explicit in the models.

which is expressed in terms of the instantaneous forward rate movement, and the Brace–Gatarek–Musiela/Jamshidian model, which assures that the interest rate model can fit the benchmark securities' prices without using the calibration of benchmark security prices procedure outlined in chapter 6.

Heath–Jarrow–Morton Model

Financial research often cites the Heath–Jarrow–Morton (HJM) model (1992) in valuing derivatives as a model that uses the forward rates instead of the spot interest rates. The model is also described as flexible, and can determine a broad range of interest rate movements.

Within the context of this book, the HJM model can be better understood if we consider it as a useful mathematical theorem or a model of interest rate models. The challenge to financial engineers is to specify an interest rate model that fits a list of desired properties, in addition to being arbitrage-free and consistent with the observed yield curve. HJM offers an approach to solve this problem. The theorem says that if we know the volatility surface, we can specify an arbitrage-free interest rate model.

Specifically, HJM shows that the volatility surface is the characterization of an arbitrage-free interest rate model. In order to focus on this volatility surface, HJM begins the analysis on the money market forward rates (or instantaneous forward rates). For the clarity of exposition, let us assume that we use a one-factor model.

Let $P(t, T^*)$ be the price of a zero-coupon bond at time t with a maturity date T^*. The risk-neutral process of these zero-coupon bonds requires that the expected returns of all the bonds be the same as the risk-free rate. We can represent this by the process

$$dP(t, T^*) = r(t)P(t, T^*)dt + \sigma^P(t, T^*)P(t, T^*)dZ \tag{5.39}$$

$f(t, T^*)$ is the instantaneous forward rate at time t with the forward delivery date T^*. In the discrete time modeling, we can think of the instantaneous forward rate $f(t, T^*)$ as the one period forward rate with a delivery date T^* at the evaluation date t.

Employing this instantaneous forward rate is useful because the uncertainty of this forward rate over the next day is independent of the shape of the yield curve, for the following reason. Using the yield curve, we can calculate the one day forward rate to be delivered on December 1, 2010. We expect to revise this forward rate, keeping the delivery date the same, the next day. But the change should not depend on the shape of the yield curve that we observe today. (This observation is discussed in chapter 3, section 3.6.) In fact, the price dynamics of the money market forward rates can be expressed as

$$df(t, T^*) = m(t, T^*)dt + \sigma(t, T^*)dZ \tag{5.40}$$

The theorem of HJM is that both $m(t, T^*)$ and $\sigma(t, T^*)$ can be expressed in terms of $\sigma^P(t, T^*)$. That means the volatility surface used to specify the bond price processes in equation (5.39) can in fact determine the entire instantaneous forward rate process. Specifically, HJM shows that the instantaneous interest rate process is

$$df(t, T^*) = \sigma^P(t, T^*)\sigma^P_{T^*}(t, T^*)dt - \sigma^P_{T^*}(t, T^*)dZ \tag{5.41}$$

where the subscript denotes a derivative.

Both the drift term and the volatility term for the instantaneous forward rate are determined by the bond volatilities. The short-term (instantaneous) interest rate is simply the short-term (instantaneous) forward rate that has the delivery date today. Or, more generally, the short-term interest rate at any time t is the short-term forward rate with the delivery date also at time t.

$$r(t) = f(t, t) \tag{5.42}$$

Therefore, to determine the arbitrage-free interest rate, given the volatility surface $\sigma(t, T^*)$, simply solve equation (5.41) for $f(t, T^*)$. We defer this to chapter 19 because the theorem is important to the interest rate literature, but it is not central to the development of the theme of this book. In order to continue the development of the financial models, we will discuss the model briefly in this section.

The implication of the HJM result is that financial engineers can now turn their attention to the choice of the volatility surface. The reason for this is that the interest rate model derived from the HJM formulation with the chosen volatility surface can best serve the requirements of the problem that the financial engineers are tackling. For example, the Ho–Lee model can be derived from the HJM formulation using different volatility surfaces. The Ho–Lee model in HJM terms can be written as

$$df(t, T^*) = \sigma^2 . (T^* - t)dt + \sigma dZ(t)$$

with

$$f(0, T^*) = r_0 - \frac{1}{2}\sigma^2 T^{*2} + \int_0^{T^*} \theta(s)ds$$

where $\theta(t) = \sigma^2 \cdot t + \frac{\partial f(0,t)}{\partial T^*}$ and $f(t, T^*)$ is the (continuously compounded) instantaneous forward rate at time t with calendar maturity T^*.

In HJM terms the Hull–White model can be written as

$$df(t, T^*) = \frac{\sigma^2}{\beta}(e^{-\beta(T^*-t)} - e^{-2\beta(T^*-t)})dt + \sigma \cdot e^{-\beta(T^*-t)}dW(t)$$

$$dr(t) = (\alpha(t) - \beta \cdot r(t)) \cdot dt + \sigma \cdot dW(t)$$

$\alpha(t)$: deterministic function of time given by

$$\alpha(t) = \frac{\partial f(0, t)}{\partial T^*} + \beta \cdot f(0, t) + \frac{\sigma^2}{2\beta}(1 - e^{-2\beta t})$$

β, σ : *constant*

The BDT model and other models described in this chapter can also be derived from the HJM formulation, using different volatility surfaces. For this reason, it can be ambiguous to report "using the HJM model for the valuation" without specifying the volatility surface that is used. Therefore, to say that HJM is an interest rate model limits the deeper applications of the HJM results.

Since the solutions to equation (5.41) are based in continuous time, the interest rate models derived by the HJM formulation are usually nonrecombining interest rate trees.

Therefore, to use the HJM model to value securities, we often need to use Monte Carlo simulations (as discussed in chapter 4, appendix D). Specifically, we may need to use Monte Carlo simulations to value even the benchmark securities when we calibrate the model, a process we will explain in the following chapter.

Longstaff–Santa-Clara–Schwartz "String" Model

Goldstein (2000), Santa-Clara and Sornette (2001), and Longstaff, Santa-Clara, and Schwartz (LSS; 2000) introduce the string models of the term structure. Here, we will follow the exposition of LSS. This model assumes all the points on the discount function to be independent risk factors. That means all the zero-coupon bonds that define the spot curve are independent risk sources. To maintain arbitrage-free movement, we only need to require that each bond have an expected return equal to the short-term rate. Specifically, we require that the bond price dynamics follow equation (5.43).

$$dP(t, T^*) = r(t)P(t, T^*)dt + \sigma(T^* - t)P(t, T^*)dZ(t, T^*) \qquad (5.43)$$

The volatilities and the correlations of the bond price return are calibrated to the observed term structure of volatilities and correlations. This model can then be used to iteratively simulate one period forward at a time. This method has the advantage of being flexible to fit any observed volatilities and correlations.

We begin with a discount function, and denote a zero-coupon bond with maturity T^* by $P(t, T^*)$, where t is the calendar time, T^* is the maturity date of the bond, and $r(t)$ is the risk-free rate. Let $\sigma(s)$ be the term structure of volatilities of proportional change in the bond price. This term structure of volatilities can be estimated from the term structure of spot volatilities and multiplied by the duration and the yield level.[7]

This model can generate arbitrage-free discount functions (and hence yield curves) going forward, and therefore is an interest rate simulation model. The string model is arbitrage-free in the sense that it fits the initial term structure exactly, and the expected return on all discount bonds is the spot rate under the risk-neutral measure. This model provides an intuitive and constructive approach to generate multiple risk factors and show the flexibility of the model to incorporate different volatility structures into the model, resulting in different arbitrage-free models. Hence, the model is flexible and can be easily implemented.

The model is no longer recombining, nor can it provide a closed-form solution to a derivative. The valuation is based on simulating the entire yield curve forward, one period at a time. The simulated yield curve is then used to determine the cash flows of the options. And the cash flow is then discounted back, using the one period interest rate, along this scenario path. The mean of the present values of the paths is the option value. These approaches, while more computing-intensive, have the advantage of being flexible, allowing the yield curve to take any shape.

The Brace–Gatarek–Musiela/Jamshidian Model (The LIBOR Market Model)

As we discussed earlier, for derivative trading in practice, we try to calibrate the interest rate model to value some of the benchmark securities, such as caps, floors, and swaptions. In using a relative valuation model, we accept the observed yield curve as the given time value of money, and we can also accept caps and floors or other interest rate options as given to determine the market volatility. A relative valuation model—or an arbitrage-free model—is a tool that values securities relative to benchmark securities, without making assumptions on the market supply and demand in determining the equilibrium market prices.

Is it possible to develop an interest rate model that automatically fits the yield curve and prices some of the benchmark securities, like caps and floors, exactly, without using the nonlinear search numerical methods? For example, can we specify an interest rate model such that the benchmark securities are priced exactly the same as those quoted in the market without using a calibration procedure that requires the nonlinear search numerical method?

An interest rate model that deals with this question is the Brace–Gatarek–Musiela/Jamshidian (BGM/J; 1997) model. The BGM/J model is a multifactor model that simulates future interest rates such that they are arbitrage-free, and when these interest rates are used to determine the zero-coupon bond prices and the benchmark securities of caps and floors or swaptions, the model prices are the same as those used as inputs to the model.

The BGM/J model is often called the market model because the inputs to the model are market quoted rates such as LIBOR rates or swap rates, not the instantaneous short rates or forward rates. Specifically, the BGM/J model provides LIBOR rates as inputs, and the Jamshidian model uses swap rates. For simplicity, we will discuss the LIBOR market model here.

LIBOR rates are defined as follows. Let Δ be the reset period. If the reset period is three months, then $\Delta = 0.25$. Let $k = 0, 1, 2, \cdots m$, where Δk are the reset dates of the LIBOR rate. The LIBOR at these reset dates is set to the market Δ period rate. Specifically, let $P(t, T^*)$ be the price of a zero-coupon bond at time t, maturing at calendar time T^*. Then the LIBOR rate at the kth reset date is given by

$$LIBOR = \frac{1}{\Delta} \left(\frac{1}{P(\Delta k, \Delta(k+1))} - 1 \right) \qquad (5.44)$$

While the derivation of the BGM/J model is based on the continuous time framework of HJM, for implementation purposes, the BGM/J model derives the process of the Δ-period forward LIBOR rates over discrete time with intervals defined by Δ. The BGM/J model begins with defining the forward LIBOR rate, using equation (5.44), as below:

$$L(t, T^*) = \frac{1}{\Delta} \left(\frac{P(t, T^*)}{P(t, T^* + \Delta)} - 1 \right) \qquad (5.45)$$

$L(t, T^*)$ is the Δ-period forward LIBOR rate at time t with the forward contract expiring at calendar time T^*. $P(t, T^*)$ is the price of the zero-coupon bond at time t for $1 payment at time T^*. Therefore the forward contract price is $\frac{P(t, T^*+\Delta)}{P(t, T^*)}$, as explained in chapter 3, and equation (5.45) shows that the LIBOR rate uses a simple accruing basis. This definition of the LIBOR rate is central for the market model approach. As we have noted, market prices like $P(t, T^*)$ are determined by the market activities, while the yield or rates are measured by the market convention. Equation defines the market convention of the LIBOR rate, using simple compounding for annualization, and equation (5.45) shows that the LIBOR rate can be expressed as a function of the market prices $P(t, T^*)$. The model can then be derived using stochastic calculus. This basic idea can be extended as any measure of yields under different market conventions. Bond yields and swap rates are among these market models.

It can be shown that the forward LIBOR rate $L(t, T^*)$ is specified by the stochastic differential equation

$$dL(t, T^*) =$$

$$L(t, T^*) \left[\sum_{j=t*}^{N^*} \frac{L(t, j\Delta)\Delta}{1 + L(t, j\Delta)\Delta} \Lambda(T^* - j\Delta)\Lambda(T^* - t)dt + \Lambda(T^* - t)dZ \right] \quad (5.46)$$

where t^* is the smallest integer such that $t^*\Delta$ is greater than t, and N^* is the number of reset periods to the delivery date T^* (i.e., $T^* = N^*\Delta$).

This equation leads to a discrete time model. Δ is the LIBOR rate reset period and is also the discrete time period. Indices k and j are integers $k, j = 0, 1, 2, \cdots m$, where $m\Delta$ denotes the time horizon of the analysis. Then $L(k, j)$ is the forward LIBOR rate at calendar time $j\Delta$ with the delivery date $k\Delta$. At the initial date for $j = 0$, given the initial observed discount function $P(\cdot)$, we have

$$L(k, 0) = \frac{1}{\Delta} \left(\frac{P(\Delta k)}{P(\Delta k + \Delta)} - 1 \right) \text{ for } k = 0, 1, 2, \cdots m$$

For the subsequent periods, $j = 1, 2, \cdots$, the forward LIBOR rates are defined recursively by equation (5.47).

$$L(k, j + 1) = \quad (5.47)$$

$$L(k, j) \exp \left[\left(\sum_{i=j+1}^{k} \frac{L(i, j)\Delta}{1 + L(i, j)\Delta} \Lambda_{i-j-1}\Lambda_{k-j-1} - \frac{\Lambda_{k-j-1}^2}{2} \right) \Delta + \Lambda_{k-j-1}\sqrt{\Delta}\tilde{Z} \right]$$

The Λ_i denotes the instantaneous volatility at time $i\Delta$ for $i = 1, 2, \cdots m$. It can be estimated from the volatilities used to value caplets in Black's model, which will be explained in chapter 6. Let σ_j be the Black volatility for the caplet that corresponds to the period between times Δj and $\Delta(j + 1)$. The Λ_i are calculated from equation (5.48), based on the observed σ_j for $j = 0, 1, 2, \cdots m$.

$$\sigma_j^2 j = \sum_{i=1}^{j} \Lambda_{j-i}^2 \quad (5.48)$$

$\tilde{Z}$ is the standardized normal distribution.

Equation (5.48) shows that the variance of the distribution on the jth period is the sum of the variances of the j periods. This is the property of a random walk process. Equation (5.47) can be explained intuitively. The term $\Lambda_{k-j-1}\sqrt{\Delta}\tilde{Z}$ reveals that the uncertainty depends on $(k - j - 1)$, which is the time to the delivery date of the forward. The term $\frac{\Lambda_{k-j-1}^2}{2}$ is the adjustment to the expected value of a lognormal distribution over a finite time period. $\frac{L(i, j)\Delta}{1 + L(i, j)\Delta}$ relates the LIBOR rate to arbitrage-free pricing.

The LIBOR rate is determined at the beginning of each reset period, but the interest payment of $L(i, j)\Delta$ is paid at the end of the period. To determine the present value at the beginning of the period when the uncertainty is resolved or when the arbitrage-free condition must hold, we need the denominator to discount the value. Finally, $\Lambda_{i-j-1}\Lambda_{k-j-1}$ is the convexity adjustment term that we discussed in the context of the extended Ho–Lee model. The LIBOR rate has to drift up as specified by this term to negate the higher expected returns due to the bond's positive convexity.

It is interesting to compare the BGM model with the extended Ho–Lee model. On the implementation level, both are discrete time models. Since the extended Ho–Lee model specifies the discount function at each node point, the LIBOR rate can be calculated at each node point using equation (5.44). In this sense, the two models are similar. However, the interest rate in the BGM model follows a lognormal process that is nonrecombining, while the extended Ho–Lee model's interest rate follows a normal model that is recombining.

The implementation of the model will be described in chapter 6. We will show, step by step, how the model is used to fit the term structure of interest rates and benchmark securities' prices.

5.7 Summary

In this chapter, we have examined different models to determine the value of interest rate options. Interest rate models are classified into economic models and arbitrage-free models that have distinctive features. The features that are important to the choice of the models are (1) lognormal versus normal models of interest rate movements, (2) recombining lattice models versus nonrecombining models, (3) one-factor versus multiple-factor models, and (4) the treatment of mean reversion of interest rates.

Unfortunately, specifying an interest rate model that can capture the observed interest rate movements is not an easy task. This chapter provided an overview of the interest rate models that are used in practice, with more emphasis on their conceptual differences and less on their technical differences.

The choice of the interest rate model to value interest rate derivatives should depend on the model's application. The model may be used as a trading tool to identify market mispricing and arbitrage opportunities. Or it may be used for portfolio analysis to determine portfolio interest rate exposures.

Traders often prefer models that offer them speed and an intuitive understanding of the formulation. They also need to know the values of their trades relative to benchmark securities that they continually follow. For these reasons relatively simple models are often required.

An arbitrage-free interest rate model may be preferred in managing a fixed-income portfolio or performing asset/liability management for a financial institution. In the arbitrage-free framework, all bonds have "expected risk-free returns." A consistent framework for valuing a broad range of fixed-income securities is helpful for portfolio managers to calibrate the portfolio value to the benchmark bonds that they observe. The choice of a one-factor or multiple-factor model, normal or lognormal, and other aspects depends on the nature of the portfolio.

In formulating portfolio strategies where the input of economic parameters is important, general equilibrium economic models may be more useful. These models can take the economic environment into account. Arbitrage-free models do well in interpolating values among observed values of benchmark securities. General equilibrium models enable us to extrapolate values. Since these models can relate the yield curve to the economic factors, we can better understand the interest rate behavior at times of liquidity trap or hyperinflation, and therefore we can value options in those economic scenarios.

Clearly, interest rate models are important to financial modeling in general. Interest rate models should be used for valuing any financial instruments whose values are affected by interest rate movements. The subsequent chapters of the book will show that interest rate models are integral parts of valuation models for corporate bonds, financial institutions' liabilities, balance sheet values, and values of corporations.

Appendix A. Yield Curve Movements Represented by the Principal Components

At any time t, the spot yield curve movement over a short interval dt can be represented by the change of the spot yield curve, which can be represented be a vector $v(t)$. Then the three-factor movement of the spot yield curve can be specified by equation (5.49).

$$\bar{y}(t) = \bar{a}(t) \cdot v(1) + \bar{b}(t) \cdot v(2) + \bar{c}(t) \cdot v(3) + \bar{e} \qquad (5.49)$$

where $\bar{a}$, $\bar{b}$, and $\bar{c}$ are uncorrelated normal distributions; $\bar{e}$ is the error term; and $\bar{y}(t)$ is the yield curve movement. For example, consider a yield curve that is flat initially. The next period, the yield curve takes on a different shape. The change is represented by $\bar{y}(t)$. According to the three-movement model, this change can be approximately decomposed into three movements: $v(1)$, $v(2)$, and $v(3)$. The weights assigned to each movement vary over time. Each yield curve change is a combination of a level, a steepness, and a curvature movement.

Note that if we use n key rates to represent the movement of the yield curve, then $\bar{y}(t), v(1), v(2)$, and $v(3)$ are vectors of dimension n. Now we proceed to estimate the distributions $a(t), b(t)$, and $c(t)$. Using the vectors $v(1), v(2)$, and $v(3)$, at each historical time t we can estimate the coefficients $a(t), b(t)$, and $c(t)$ such that equation (5.49) is the best fit. If we have a historical time series for $t = 1 \cdots m$, then we will estimate $a(t), b(t)$, and $c(t)$ for $t = 1 \cdots m$. As a result, we have derived the time series of these coefficients. Each time series enables us to estimate the mean and standard deviations, which then complete the specification of the model that describes the movements of the yield curve.

Appendix B. Derivation of the Ho–Lee, Extended Ho–Lee, and the Ho–Lee Two-Factor Models

For the Ho–Lee model, the closed-form solution for a T time to maturity bond at time n and state i is given by

$$P_i^n(T) = \frac{P(T+n)}{P(n)} \frac{(1 + \delta^{n-1})(1 + \delta^{n-2}) \cdots (1 + \delta)2}{(1 + \delta^{T+n-1})(1 + \delta^{T+n-2}) \cdots (1 + \delta^{T+1})(1 + \delta^T)} (\delta^T)^i \qquad (5.B.1)$$

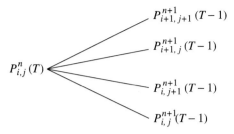

Figure 5.B.1 Basic building block of two-factor binomial tree.

To show that the model satisfies the arbitrage-free condition, we require that

$$P_i^n(T) = 0.5P_i^n(1)\{P_{i+1}^{n+1}(T-1) + P_i^{n+1}(T-1)\} \tag{5.B.2}$$

and satisfy the initial condition

$$P(T) = 0.5P(1)\{P_1^1(T-1) + P_0^1(T-1)\} \tag{5.B.3}$$

where $P(T)$ is the initial observed discount function. By substituting equation (5.B.1) into (5.B.2) and (5.B.3), we can see that the conditions are satisfied. In particular, if we let $T = 1$ in equation (5.B.1), we have derived the Ho–Lee model, equation (5.17).

For illustration, suppose $n = 1$; then equation (5.B.1) equals

$$P_i^1(T) = \frac{P(T+1)}{P(1)} \frac{2}{(1+\delta^T)}(\delta^T)^i$$

And when $n = 2$, equation (5.B.1) is

$$P_i^2(T) = \frac{P(T+2)}{P(2)} \frac{(1+\delta)2}{(1+\delta^{T+1})(1+\delta^T)}(\delta^T)^i$$

The expressions for other n values are derived analogously.

For the extended Ho–Lee model, the discount bond with time to maturity T at time n and state i is given by

$$P_i^n(T) = \tag{5.B.4}$$

$$\frac{P(T+n)(1+\delta_{n-1}\cdots\delta_1)(1+\delta_{n-1}\cdots\delta_2)\cdots(1+\delta_{n-1})2(\delta_{T+n-1}\cdots\delta_n)^i}{P(n)(1+\delta_{T+n-1}\cdots\delta_1)(1+\delta_{T+n-1}\cdots\delta_2)\cdots(1+\delta_{T+n-1}\cdots\delta_{n-1})(1+\delta_{T+n-1}\cdots\delta_n)}$$

By a direct substitution of (5.B.4) into equations (5.B.2) and (5.B.3), we can show that the solution satisfies both conditions.

For illustration, for $n = 1$, we have

$$P_i^1(T) = \frac{P(T+1)2(\delta_T\cdots\delta_1)^i}{P(1)(1+\delta_T\cdots\delta_1)}$$

And for $n = 2$, we have

$$P_i^2(T) = \frac{P(T+2)(1+\delta_1)2(\delta_{T+1}\cdots\delta_2)^i}{P(2)(1+\delta_{T+1}\cdots\delta_1)(1+\delta_{T+1}\cdots\delta_2)}$$

Note that the function

$$F(n, T) =$$

$$\frac{(1+\delta_{n-1}\cdots\delta_1)(1+\delta_{n-1}\cdots\delta_2)\cdots(1+\delta_{n-1})2}{(1+\delta_{T+n-1}\cdots\delta_1)(1+\delta_{T+n-1}\cdots\delta_2)\cdots(1+\delta_{T+n-1}\cdots\delta_{n-1})(1+\delta_{T+n-1}\cdots\delta_n)}$$

that represents the convexity adjustment is independent of i and the observed yield curve. For computational efficiency, we can first calculate

$$d(n) = \delta_{n-1}\cdots\delta_1 \text{ for all } n.$$

Then we compute the function $F(n, T)$. Finally, the discount function at any node point can be calculated quickly by introducing the remaining factors of the function $P_i^n(T)$.

Similarly, we can extend this argument to the n-factor model. Specifically, consider the two-factor model. The discount function with time to maturity T, at time n and state i, is given by

$$P_{i,j}^n(T) = \frac{P(T+n)}{P(n)} \times \qquad (5.B.5)$$

$$\frac{(1+\delta_{n-1}^1\cdots\delta_1^1)(1+\delta_{n-1}^1\cdots\delta_2^1)\cdots(1+\delta_{n-1}^1)2(\delta_{T+n-1}^1\cdots\delta_n^1)^i}{(1+\delta_{T+n-1}^1\cdots\delta_1^1)(1+\delta_{T+n-1}^1\cdots\delta_2^1)\cdots(1+\delta_{T+n-1}^1\cdots\delta_{n-1}^1)(1+\delta_{T+n-1}^1\cdots\delta_n^1)} \times$$

$$\frac{(1+\delta_{n-1}^2\cdots\delta_1^2)(1+\delta_{n-1}^2\cdots\delta_2^2)\cdots(1+\delta_{n-1}^2)2(\delta_{T+n-1}^2\cdots\delta_n^2)^j}{(1+\delta_{T+n-1}^2\cdots\delta_1^2)(1+\delta_{T+n-1}^2\cdots\delta_2^2)\cdots(1+\delta_{T+n-1}^2\cdots\delta_{n-1}^2)(1+\delta_{T+n-1}^2\cdots\delta_n^2)}$$

The arbitrage-free conditions for the two-factor model are

$$P_{i,j}^n(T) = \qquad (5.B.6)$$

$$0.25 P_{i,j}^n(1)\{P_{i+1,j+1}^{n+1}(T-1) + P_{i+1,j}^{n+1}(T-1) + P_{i,j+1}^{n+1}(T-1) + P_{i,j}^{n+1}(T-1)\}$$

$$P(T) =$$

$$0.25 P(1)\{P_{1,1}^1(T-1) + P_{1,0}^1(T-1) + P_{0,1}^1(T-1) + P_{0,0}^1(T-1)\} \qquad (5.B.7)$$

Equation (B.5.6) should be satisfied for any $n = 0, 1, 2, \cdots, T = 1, 2, \cdots$, and $i, j = 0, 1, 2, \cdots, n$.

The volatility structure of the model is generated by defining

$$P_{i,j}^n(T) = P_{0,0}^n(T) \cdot \alpha_1(n, T)^i \alpha_2(n, T)^j \qquad (5.B.8)$$

for all $n > 0$, $T > 0$, and all $i, j \geq 0$. The original Ho–Lee model assumed a one-factor model with factor α depending only on T.

By considering the nodes (i,j), $(i,j+1)$, $(i+1,j)$, $(i+1,j+1)$ at time n and the nodes (i,j), $(i,j+1)$, $(i,j+2)$, $(i+1,j)$, $(i+1,j+1)$, $(i+1,j+2)$, $(i+2,j)$, $(i+2,j+1)$, $(i+2,j+2)$ at time $(n+1)$ in equation (B.5.6), we deduce the following consistency condition, which guarantees that the tree is well defined as a recombining tree:

$$\frac{\alpha_1(n,T)}{\alpha_1(n,1)} = \alpha_1(n+1,T-1) \tag{5.B.9}$$

for all n, $T \geq 1$.

Note that the above equations can be solved with the input data $\delta_n^1 := \alpha_1(n,1)$, $\delta_n^2 := \alpha_2(n,1)$ for $n = 1, 2, \cdots$. The solution is given explicitly by

$$\alpha_1(n,T) = \frac{\alpha_1(1,T+n-1)}{\alpha_1(1,n-1)} = \delta_n^1 \delta_{n+1}^1 \cdots \delta_{T+n-1}^1 := d_{T+n-1,n}^1$$

$$\tag{5.B.10}$$

$$\alpha_2(n,T) = \frac{\alpha_2(1,T+n-1)}{\alpha_2(1,n-1)} = \delta_n^2 \delta_{n+1}^2 \cdots \delta_{T+n-1}^2 := d_{T+n-1,n}^2$$

where we define for $n > m$,

$$d_{n,m}^1 = \delta_n^1 \delta_{n-1}^1 \cdots \delta_{m+1}^1 \delta_m^1 \text{ and } d_{n,m}^2 = \delta_n^2 \delta_{n-1}^2 \cdots \delta_{m+1}^2 \delta_m^2 \tag{5.B.11}$$

Each move has the same risk-neutral probability, 1/4.

Proposition 5.B.1 The Closed-Form Solution for Bond Prices
    Let $P(T)$ be the initial discount function. Then the arbitrage-free movement of the discount function is given by

$$P_{i,j}^n(T) =$$

$$4\frac{P(T+n)}{P(n)} \left(\prod_{k=1}^{n} \frac{1+d_{n-1,k}^1}{1+d_{T+n-1,k}^1} \right) \left(\prod_{k=1}^{n} \frac{1+d_{n-1,k}^2}{1+d_{T+n-1,k}^2} \right) \left(d_{T+n-1,n}^1 \right)^i \left(d_{T+n-1,n}^2 \right)^j \tag{5.B.12}$$

where we set $d_{n-1,n}^1 = d_{n-1,n}^2 = 0$.
    Alternatively, it can be expressed as

$$P_{i,j}^n(T) = \frac{P(T+n)}{P(n)} \times$$

$$\left[\prod_{k=1}^{n} (G_{Tnk}^1)^{-1} \right] \left(d_{T+n-1,n}^1 \right)^{i-0.5n} \times \left[\prod_{l=1}^{n} (G_{Tnl}^2)^{-1} \right] \left(d_{T+n-1,n}^2 \right)^{j-0.5n} \tag{5.B.12a}$$

where

$$G_{Tnk}^1 = \left[\left(d_{T+n-1,n}^1 \right)^{-0.5} + \left(d_{T+n-1,n}^1 \right)^{0.5} \times d_{n-1,k}^1 \right] \Big/ \left(1 + d_{n-1,k}^1 \right)$$

$$G_{Tnl}^2 = \left[\left(d_{T+n-1,n}^2 \right)^{-0.5} + \left(d_{T+n-1,n}^2 \right)^{0.5} \times d_{n-1,l}^2 \right] \Big/ \left(1 + d_{n-1,l}^2 \right) \tag{5.B.13}$$

Proof:

From the construction we have

$$P_{i,j}^n(T) = P_{0,0}^n(T) \cdot \alpha_1(n, T)^i \alpha_2(n, T)^j = P_{0,0}^n(T) \cdot \left(d_{T+n-1,n}^1\right)^i \left(d_{T+n-1,n}^2\right)^j \quad (5.B.14)$$

Thus it suffices to check that

$$P_{0,0}^n(T) = 4\frac{P(T + n)}{P(n)} \left(\prod_{k=1}^{n} \frac{1 + d_{n-1,k}^1}{1 + d_{T+n-1,k}^1}\right) \left(\prod_{k=1}^{n} \frac{1 + d_{n-1,k}^2}{1 + d_{T+n-1,k}^2}\right) \quad (5.B.15)$$

We use mathematical induction. For $n = 1$, we have from equation (5.B.12) with $i = j = 0$ that

$$\frac{P(T + 1)}{P(1)} = \frac{1}{4}P_{0,0}^1(T)\left[1 + \alpha_1(1, T) + \alpha_2(1, T) + \alpha_1(1, T)\alpha_2(1, T)\right]$$

$$= \frac{1}{4}P_{0,0}^1(T)\left[1 + d_T^1\right]\left[1 + d_T^2\right] \quad (5.B.16)$$

Hence we get

$$P_{0,0}^1(T) = 4\frac{P(T + 1)}{P(1)} \frac{1}{\left[1 + d_T^1\right]\left[1 + d_T^2\right]} \quad (5.B.17)$$

Therefore the formula for $n = 1$ is valid. Now we suppose that the formula is satisfied for n, and we will check the formula for $n + 1$. From equation (5.B.6) we have

$$P_{i,j}^n(T + 1)/P_{i,j}^n(1) = \frac{1}{4}\left\{P_{i+1,j+1}^{n+1}(T) + P_{i+1,j}^{n+1}(T) + P_{i,j+1}^{n+1}(T) + P_{i,j}^{n+1}(T)\right\}$$

$$= \frac{1}{4}P_{0,0}^{n+1}(T) \left(d_{T+n,n+1}^1\right)^i \left(d_{T+n,n+1}^2\right)^j \left(1 + d_{T+n,n+1}^1\right) \left(1 + d_{T+n,n+1}^2\right) \quad (5.B.18)$$

By the induction hypothesis, we get

$$\frac{P_{i,j}^n(T + 1)}{P_{i,j}^n(1)} =$$

$$\frac{P(T + n + 1)}{P(n + 1)} \left(\prod_{k=1}^{n} \frac{1 + d_{n,k}^1}{1 + d_{T+n,k}^1}\right) \left(\prod_{k=1}^{n} \frac{1 + d_{n,k}^2}{1 + d_{T+n,k}^2}\right) \left(d_{T+n,n+1}^1\right)^i \left(d_{T+n,n+1}^2\right)^j \quad (5.B.19)$$

where we have used the fact $d_{T+n,n}/d_{n,n} = d_{T+n,n+1}$.

Substituting this into equation (5.B.18), we get

$$P_{0,0}^{n+1}(T) =$$

$$4\frac{P(T + n + 1)}{P(n + 1)} \left(\prod_{k=1}^{n} \frac{1 + d_{n,k}^1}{1 + d_{T+n,k}^1}\right) \left(\prod_{k=1}^{n} \frac{1 + d_{n,k}^2}{1 + d_{T+n,k}^2}\right) \frac{1}{\left(1 + d_{T+n,n+1}^1\right) \left(1 + d_{T+n,n+1}^2\right)}$$

$$= 4 \frac{P(T+n+1)}{P(n+1)} \left(\prod_{k=1}^{n+1} \frac{1+d_{n,k}^1}{1+d_{T+n,k}^1} \right) \left(\prod_{k=1}^{n+1} \frac{1+d_{n,k}^2}{1+d_{T+n,k}^2} \right) \qquad \text{(5.B.20)}$$

because $d_{n,n+1} = 0$ (by construction). This is the required formula for n + 1, and so the proof is complete.

Notes

1. Einstein first used the mathematical construct dZ to study the random movements of particles.

2. Oren Cheyette, "Interest Rate Models," in *Advances in Fixed Income Valuation, Modeling and Risk Management,* edited by Frank J. Fabozzi (Frank J. Fabozzi Associates, 1997).

3. After changing μ to r in the stochastic differential equation of bonds or after changing μ_r to $\mu_r - \lambda\sigma_r$ where μ_r, and $\lambda\sigma_r$ are drift and volatility of r, respectively.

4. The heat equation is a partial differential equation to describe the flow of heat in materials where its rate is proportional to the temperature gradient. The solution to the heat equation gives the temperature in the materials as a function of time and position. The heat equation is also called the diffusion equation, since the same equation can be used to describe the diffusion of quantities other than heat, such as stock prices or interest rates

5. J. M. Harrison, and D. M. Kreps, "Martingales and Arbitrage in Multi-period Securities Markets," *Journal of Economic Theory,* 20 (1979): 381–408.

6. We will describe the Heath–Jarrow–Morton model that analyzes this term in more detail in Chapter 6.

7. LSS proposed using the swaption prices.

References

Abken, P. A. 1990. Innovations in modeling the term structure of interest rates. *Economic Review,* 75, no. 4. Federal Reserve Bank of Atlanta July–August.

Baxter, M., and A. Rennie. 1996. *Financial Calculus.* Cambridge University Press, Cambridge U.K.

Black, F. 1995. Interest rates as options. *Journal of Finance,* 50, no. 5, 1371–1376.

Black, F., E. Derman, and W. Toy. 1990. A one-factor model of interest rates and its application to Treasury bond options. *Financial Analysts Journal,* 46, 33–39.

Black, F., and P. Karasinski. 1991. Bond and option pricing when short rates are lognormal. *Financial Analysts Journal,* 47, 52–59.

Brace, A., D. Gatarek, and M. Musiela. 1997. The market model of interest rate dynamics. *Mathematical Finance,* 7, 127–155.

Brennan, M. J., and E. S. Schwartz. 1979. A continuous time approach to the pricing of bonds. *Journal of Banking and Finance,* 3, 135–155.

Brennan, M. J., and E. S. Schwartz. 1982. An equilibrium model of bond pricing and a test of market efficiency. *Journal of Financial and Quantitative Analysis,* 17, 301–329.

Chen, R. R., and Scott L. 1992. Pricing interest rate options in a two factor Cox, Ingersoll and Ross model of the term structure. *Review of Financial Studies,* 5, 613–636.

Cheyette, Oren. 1997. "Interest rate models." In *Advances in Fixed Income Valuation, Modeling and Risk Management,* edited by Frank J. Fabozzi. Frank J. Fabozzi Associates. New Hope, Pennsylvania.

Cox, J. C., J. E. Ingersoll, Jr., and S. A. Ross. 1981. A reexamination of traditional hypothesis about the term structure of interest rates. *Journal of Finance,* 36, 769–799.

Cox, J. C., J. E. Ingersoll, Jr., and S. A. Ross. 1985. A theory of the term structure of interest rates. *Econometrica,* 53, 385–407.

Cox, J. C., S. A. Ross, and M. Rubinstein. 1979. Option pricing: A simplified approach. *Journal of Financial Economics*, 7, 229–263.

Das, S., and R. Sundaram. 2000. A discrete-time approach to arbitrage-free pricing of credit derivatives. *Management Science*, 46, 46–63.

Dothan, U. L. 1978. On the term structure of interest rates. *Journal of Financial Economics*, 6, 59–69.

Dybvig, P. H. 1989. Bond and Bond Option Pricing Based on the Current Term Structure. Working Paper, Washington University, Saint Louis.

Feller, W. 1951. Two singular diffusion problems. *Annals of Mathematics*, 54, 173–181.

Flesaker, B. 1993. Testing the Heath–Jarrow–Morton/Ho–Lee model of interest rate contingent claims pricing. *Journal of Financial and Quantitative Analysis*, 28, no. 4, 483–495.

Goldstein, R. 2000. The term structure of interest rates as a random field. *Review of Financial Studies*, 13, 365–384.

Goldys, B., M. Musiela, and D. Sondermann. 1996. Lognormality of Rates and Term Structure Models. Discussion paper no. B-394, Bonn University.

Golub, B., and M. Tilman. 1997. Measuring yield curve risk using principal component analysis, value at risk, and key rate durations. *Journal of Portfolio Management*, 23, no. 4, 72–84.

Grant, D., and G. Vora. 1999. Implementing no-arbitrage term structure of interest rate models in discrete time when interest rates are normally distributed. *Journal of Fixed Income*, 8, 85–98.

Harrison, J. M., and D. M. Kreps. 1979. Martingales and arbitrage in multi-period securities markets. *Journal of Economic Theory*, 20, 381–408.

Heath, D., R. Jarrow, and A. Morton. 1992. Bond pricing and the term structure of the interest rates: A new methodology. *Econometrica*, 60, 77–105.

Ho, T. S. Y. 1995. Evolution of interest rate models: A comparison. *Journal of Derivatives*, 2, no. 4, 9–20.

Ho, T. S. Y. 1999. Market valuation of liability: Transfer pricing, profit release and credit spread. In *Fair Value of Life Insurance Liability*, edited by Irwin T. Vandenhoof and Edward I. Altman, Kluwer Academic Publishers, Boston.

Ho, T. S. Y. 2000. A Closed-Form Binomial Interest Rate Model. Research paper, Owen School of Business Administration, Vanderbilt University.

Ho, T. S. Y., and S. Lee. 1986. Term structure movements and pricing of interest rate contingent claims. *Journal of Finance*, 41, 1011–1029.

Ho, T. S. Y., and S. Lee. 1990. Interest rate futures options and interest rate options. *Financial Review*, 25, no. 3, 345–370.

Hogan, M. 1993. Problems in certain two-factor term structure models. *Annals of Applied Probability*, 3, 576–581.

Hull, J., and A. White. 1990. Pricing interest-rate-derivative securities. *Review of Financial Studies*, 3, no. 4, 573–592.

Hull, J., and A. White. 1993. One-factor interest-rate models and the valuation of interest-rate derivative securities. *Journal of Financial and Quantitative Analysis*, 28, no. 2, 235–254.

Hull, J., and A. White. 1994. Numerical procedures for implementing term structure models II: Two-factor models. *Journal of Derivatives*, 12, no. 2, 37–48.

Jamshidian, F. 1989. An exact bond option formula. *Journal of Finance*, 44, 205–209.

Jamshidian, F. 1993. A simple class of square root interest rate models. *Applied Mathematical Finance*, 2, 61–72.

Langetieg, T. C. 1980. A multivariate model of the term structure. *Journal of Finance*, 35, 71–97.

Litterman, R., and J. A. Scheinkman. 1991. Common factors affecting bond returns. *Journal of Fixed Income*, 1, no. 1, 54–61.

Longstaff, F., P. Santa-Clara, and E. Schwartz. 2000. The Relative Valuation of Caps and Swaptions: Theory and Empirical Evidence. Working paper, The Anderson School of UCLA, September.

Longstaff, F. A., and E. S. Schwartz. 1992. Interest rate volatility and the term structure: A two-factor general equilibrium model. *Journal of Finance*, 47, 1259–1282.

Miltersen, K. R., K. Sandman, and D. Sondermann. 1997. Closed-form solutions for term structure derivatives with log-normal interest rates. *Journal of Finance*, 52 (March), 409–430.

Musiela, M., and M. Rutkowski. 1997. Continuous time term structure models: Forward measure approach. *Finance and Stochastics*, 1, 261–291.

Pearson, N., and T. Sun. 1994. Exploiting the conditional density in estimating the term structure: An application to the Cox, Ingersoll, and Ross model. *Journal of Finance*, 49, 1279–1304.

Rebonato, R. 1998. *Interest-rate Option Models*, 2nd ed. Wiley, Chichester.

Revuz, D., and M. Yor., 1991. *Continuous Martingales and Brownian Motion*. Springer-Verlag, Berlin.

Richard, S. 1978. An arbitrage model of the term structure of interest rates. *Journal of Financial Economics*, 6, 33–57.

Ritchken, P., and L. Sankarasubramanian. 1995. Volatility structure of forward rates, and the dynamics of the term structure. *Mathematical Finance*, 5, 55–72.

Rogers, L. C. G. 1995. Which model for term-structure of interest rates should one use? In *Mathematical Finance*, 65, 93–115.

Sandman, K., and D. Sondermann. 1993. A term structure model and the pricing of interest rate derivatives. *Review of Futures Markets*, 12, 391–423.

Sandman, K., D. Sondermann, and K. Miltersen. 1994. Closed-Form Term Structure Derivatives in a Heath-Jarrow-Morton Model with Log-normal Annually Compounded Interest Rates. Discussion paper no. B-285, Bonn University.

Santa-Clara, P., and D. Sornette. 2001. The dynamics of the forward interest rate curve with stochastic string shocks. *Review of Financial Studies*, 14, no. 1, 149–185.

Schaefer, S. M., and E. S. Schwartz. 1987. Time-dependent variance and pricing of bond options. *Journal of Finance*, 42, no. 5, 1113–1128.

Schlögl, E., and D. Sommer. 1997. Factor Models and the Shape of the Term Structure. Discussion paper no. B-395, Bonn University.

Sommer, D. 1996. Continuous Time Limits in the Generalized Ho–Lee Framework Under the Forward Measure. Discussion paper no. B-276, Bonn University.

Tuckman, Bruce. 2002. *Fixed Income Securities*. Wiley, New York.

Turnbull, S. M., and F. Milne. 1991. A simple approach to interest-rate option pricing. *Review of Financial Studies*, 4, no. 1, 87–120.

Vasicek, O. 1977. An equilibrium characterization of the term structure. *Journal of Financial Economics*, 5, 177–188.

Further Readings

Björk, T., G. Masi, Y. Kabanov, and W. Runggaldier. 1997. Towards a general theory of bond markets. *Finance and Stochastics*, 1, 141–174.

Chacko, G., and S. Das. 1999. Pricing Interest Rate Derivatives: A General Approach. Working paper, Harvard University.

Chan, K., G. Karolyi, F. Longstaff, and A. Sanders. 1992. The volatility of short-term interest rates: An empirical comparison of alternative models of the term structure of interest rates. *Journal of Finance*, 47, no. 3, 1209–1227.

Dybvig, P. H., and W. J. Marshall. 1995. Pricing Long Bonds: Pitfalls and Opportunities. Working papers, Orlin School of Business, Washington University in St. Louis.

6

Implied Volatility Surface:
Calibrating the Models

Calibration is a powerful technique that fits the relative valuation models to the benchmark securities market observed prices in order to value other securities, in a relative sense, to these benchmark securities. In particular, the method ensures that the arbitrage-free interest rate model is consistent with the observed market yield curve, the market volatility surface, and other benchmark securities' prices to determine the basis spreads. The concept and the general methodology are applied to markets beyond the interest rate markets, and they are the key tools in developing hedging and arbitrage strategies, and pricing methodologies. Later chapters will apply this method to a broad range of markets and applications.

The valuation of interest rate derivatives using an arbitrage-free interest rate model requires the inputs of the spot yield curve and the term structure of volatilities (or a volatility surface). We have discussed the importance of volatilities for option pricing. Without volatilities, options simply reduce to cash flows, which can be valued by the bond model. Volatilities affect the option value.

Chapter 5 described the valuation of options based on the term structure of volatilities or volatility surface that can be estimated from the observed time series of the bond yields. The approach is problematic because the historical estimation of the yield volatilities is backward-looking. The option value depends on future uncertainties and not on the volatility based on historical experience. The approach described in chapter 5 is appropriate only if we argue that the future uncertainty is the same as the historical uncertainty. But when the market anticipates higher uncertainty in the future—for example, when interest rates are subject to higher inflation rate uncertainty—how is such market anticipation measured in evaluating interest rate options?

We have seen that the Black–Scholes model enables us to quote a stock option value not by the option price but by the implied volatility, which is the stock volatility used by the Black–Scholes model to give the option price. We say XYZ option is traded at x percent volatility as a way to quote the price of the option via the Black–Scholes model. This price quote system has the advantage of expressing the option price in terms of the market's anticipation of the future risks. Can we quote bond options by the volatility value? This problem is much more complicated for interest rate options because we have seen that there are a number of interest rate option models. In order to agree on the quoted volatility to express the value of an option, we need to have models that the market will accept as the standard. How do we determine such models?

These are two questions that this chapter will address. This discussion will complete the study of valuing interest rate options, from how price quotes are made to how models can value an interest rate derivative. For the remainder of the chapter, we will apply the valuation models to analyze bond options and show how such financial models can be used as tools to formulate investment strategies.

6.1   Implied Volatility Surface and Benchmark Securities

Benchmark Securities

In chapter 3, we discussed the bond model, which uses the concept of the law of one price. A coupon bond is valued as a portfolio of a set of zero-coupon bonds. This set of zero-coupon bonds is then used as a benchmark to value any bonds expressed as a cash flow.

In chapter 4, we showed how a stock option can be priced relative to another option (a benchmark option) on the same stock. This approach uses the price of the benchmark option to determine the implied volatility of the stock via the Black–Scholes model. Then we use the implied volatility of the stock as input to the stock option that we seek to evaluate.

In both cases, we need to decide on *benchmark securities* that the valuation model is based on. The financial models that we have discussed are relative valuation models. They provide the value of a derivative based on the observed prices of a set of securities (the benchmarks). Therefore, to begin any valuation procedure, we need to determine the set of benchmark securities.

For interest rate derivatives, the market convention tends to use caps/floors, swaptions, and bond options as benchmarks because they are actively traded in the market. We can observe their prices traded in the market and use an interest rate model to provide a valuation of derivatives relative to these observed prices.

It is important to decide which benchmark securities are appropriate to value interest rate derivatives. We have to assume that benchmark securities are fairly priced by the market. If they are mispriced, then the valuation model would misprice all the securities. Thus, the benchmark securities tend to be chosen for their liquidity in the market with significant trading activities, so that the observed prices are considered fair in reflecting the market's view of future interest rate volatilities.

Calibration of the Interest Rate Model

The calibration of an interest rate model to the observed prices of a set of benchmark securities, like caps/floors and swaptions, is the determination of the set of the volatilities as input data for an interest rate model such that the model prices of the benchmark securities are best fitted to their observed market prices. In this approach, we do not use the historical experience of interest rate volatilities as inputs for an interest rate model. Instead, we use the implied volatilities, which are implied from the prices of the benchmark securities. Thus, the implied volatilities reflect the market's view of the future uncertainty and the interest rate derivatives are valued according to this view.

We have discussed the importance of time value of money. The yield curve is the foundation of valuation models and has broad implications for the economy. Arbitrage-free models are developed to take the yield curve as given, so that the pricing of any cash flows with no embedded options is assured to be consistent with the traditional present value approach to value the cash flow.

As the market becomes more complete with more actively traded interest rate contingent claims available and with their prices more widely disseminated, as in the case of caps/floors, the market becomes aware of the importance of the volatility surface.

That is, any interest rate contingent claims pricing should be aware of the market prices of the time value of money (the yield curve) and prices of the benchmark interest rate derivatives (the market volatility surface). The time value of money and prices of the derivatives should both be inputs for the arbitrage-free interest rate model.

Let $\sigma(T^*, T)$ be a volatility surface required by an interest rate model. For example, the model may require as inputs $\sigma(T^*, T)$, which may be the volatility of the Tth year spot rate T^* years from now, where T^* and T vary over a range of years. These volatilities are often displayed in two dimensions, and hence called a surface, as discussed in chapter 5.

Let us first assume a set of implied volatilities to be used for the interest rate model. We now use the model to calculate the theoretical prices of the benchmark securities in a procedure described in chapter 5. Next we assume a goodness of fit function, which may be the sum of the squares of the difference between the theoretical price V_i^* and the observed (or quoted) price V_i of all the benchmark securities. The goodness of fit function need not be simple summation of the differences: it can be weighted sums, where the weights ω_i are determined on a number of factors; perhaps we should be concerned with the percentage price difference and not the absolute price difference, and assign the weights to be the inverse of the quoted price; or perhaps we are concerned with the quality of the quoted price and assign higher weights to the benchmark securities that are more liquid.

The last step of the calibration is the nonlinear search for the volatilities as inputs to the interest rate model such that the goodness of fit function

$$\sum_{i=1}^{N} \omega_i \left(V_i - V_i^*\right)^2$$

is minimized—the differences between the benchmark market quotes (or prices) and the theoretical prices are smallest. This set of volatilities that gives the best fit is called the *implied volatility surface*. This approach is similar to that for estimating the spot yield curve from the observed bond prices, as explained in chapter 3, and the use of implied volatility of stock in chapter 4.

The concept of calibration is different from empirically estimating a model. For example, we can use historical observations of interest rates to estimate the parameters of the Cox–Ingersoll–Ross model or the Vasicek model. We then use the model to value the interest rate contingent claims. In these examples, the model is estimated from historical data, and the estimated model uses the market probability (the actual probability) and not the risk-neutral probabilities of an arbitrage-free model. Further, the model can be tested for its stability, in that the model should fit not only the historical data and its empirical robustness can be tested with updated data.

By contrast, in calibration the model is not estimated from the historical data, but from the observed prices in the market at the present time. The justification for using this benchmark approach for valuation is the essence of the *contingent claim theory* (or the relative valuation approach), which tells us precisely how a security's value is related to other benchmark securities' values. Therefore, the model is not tested by its empirical robustness. Indeed, in calibration, we continually adjust the implied volatility surface to fit the market prices, even though these adjustments contradict the assumptions of the model. In calibration, we assume a set of volatilities of interest rates in the future, but at the same time we allow the model to change these assumptions. From a theoretical perspective, we may argue that these models are not robust because the model is not internally consistent. But calibration does offer a practical approach to valuing securities.

We should also note that the risk-neutral probability estimated from the calibration is not the market probability. It is just a probability measure that fits the observed prices and cannot be used to infer the market perception of the uncertain movements of the interest rates.

6.2 Price Quotes of Benchmark Securities

One set of benchmark securities is a selection of bond options, caps and floors, and swaptions. In the market we can observe the prices for this set of benchmark securities. But by market convention, the prices of these securities are often quoted by the volatilities implied by a Black–Scholes model that is adjusted for each instrument. These models are called the *Black models*. Using them, we can convert the quoted volatility numbers to the benchmark securities prices.

Futures Options

To start the discussion of a *bond option*, let us consider the put and call exchange-traded options. For exchange interest rate options, they are all futures options. At the Chicago Board of Trade, the T-bond futures, T-note futures, and five-year Treasury note options are traded. Eurodollar futures options are traded on the Chicago Mercantile Exchange.

Let us consider the T-bond futures option for the following expiration dates with a strike price of 102. The implied volatilities are derived from the call option prices, using equation (6.1) (See table 6.1.)

The basic idea relating the benchmark derivatives prices to the volatility surface is the use of the Black model. In the valuation of a futures contract on a commodity or an equity, the Black model modifies the Black–Scholes model by replacing the stock price in the Black–Scholes model with the present value of the futures price, discounted by the risk-free rate from the time to expiration of the options.

The Black model for futures call options is given by:

$$C = P(T^*)\left[FN(d_1) - XN(d_2)\right]$$

$$d_1 = \frac{\ln(F/X) + \sigma^2 T^*/2}{\sigma\sqrt{T^*}} \tag{6.1}$$

$$d_2 = d_1 - \sigma\sqrt{T^*}$$

Table 6.1 Put and Call Options on T-Bond Futures

	Call Option	Put Option	Implied Volatility	Futures
March	1.7813	1.0078	0.0672	102.7813
	2.5313	2.9601	0.0974	101.5625

where

$$C = \text{the value of a European futures option}$$
$$P(T^*) = \text{price at time 0 of a zero-coupon bond paying \$1 at time } T^*$$
$$F = \text{the futures price at time 0}$$
$$X = \text{strike price of the option}$$
$$N(\cdot) = \text{the cumulative normal distribution}$$
$$\sigma = \text{annualized volatility of the futures price}$$

Similar to the Black–Scholes model, the futures price at the expiration date T^* is assumed to have a lognormal distribution. The following sections will apply this formula to the benchmark derivatives repeatedly, to define the implied volatilities of the volatility surface.

Bond Options

Like stock options, bond options give the holders the right—but not the obligation—to buy a bond at a fixed price on the expiration date (call option) or to sell at a fixed price on the expiration day (put option). Variations of these types of options are traded on the exchanges; they can be Treasury bond futures options, Treasury note futures options, or Euro futures options.

While the exchanges traded options are important, the understanding of valuing a bond option has much broader implications across many sectors of the economy, from insurance to banking, and from corporate finance to investments. The applications have important implications to a firm's strategies and an individual's decisions.

Valuing a bond option

Let us consider a simple call option to begin the discussion on interest rate contingent claims. Suppose we need to value a call option on a two-year, risk-free zero-coupon bond. The option expires in one year at a strike price of 90. If the one-year rate at expiration is 12%, then the option is out of the money, since the present value of 100 at the market rate of 12% is less than 90. If the rate is 9%, then the option is in the money, since the present value of 100 at the market rate of 9% is higher than 90. Can we use the Black–Scholes model to price this option, with the two-year zero-coupon bond as an underlying security? Yes, but it will be slightly complicated. The volatility of the bond is not constant, since it must decrease as the bond's maturity approaches. In fact, the volatility at maturity of the bond must be 0. We must consider time-varying volatilities in bond options.

Another complication concerns the underlying bond. If the call option is on a callable corporate bond, then the behavior of the volatility would be very difficult to model, because the callable corporate bond behavior is difficult to specify. To tackle this problem, we need to model the risk sources (the interest rate risk) and not the price risks—which, as a matter of fact, are dependent on interest rate risks

The Black model for a bond option

The Black model for pricing the bond option ignores these issues. The model uses the Black–Scholes model for bonds, assuming that the forward bond price has a lognormal distribution, like a stock, to derive the option price.

More specifically, let $B(T^* + T)$ be the price of a zero-coupon bond with maturity $T^* + T$. The Black model assumes the bond prices at T^*, denoted by $B_{T^*}(T^* + T)$ to have a lognormal distribution, where $\ln B_{T^*}(T^* + T)$ has a normal distribution with a mean of $F(T^*, T)$ and a standard deviation of $\sigma\sqrt{T}$. $F(T, T^*)$ represents a forward price of $B(T^* + T)$ for a forward contract with time to expiration T^*. Then the value of the call option is

$$C = P(T^*)\,[F(T^*, T)N(d_1) - XN(d_2)]$$

$$d_1 = \frac{\ln[F(T^*, T)/X] + \sigma^2 T^*/2}{\sigma\sqrt{T^*}} \qquad (6.2)$$

$$d_2 = d_1 - \sigma\sqrt{T^*}$$

where

$$C = \text{the value of a bond call option}$$

$$T^* = \text{the expiration date of the option}$$

$$T^* + T = \text{the maturity of the bond}$$

$$F(T^*, T) = \text{forward price of } B(T^* + T) \text{ for a forward contract with maturity } T^*$$

$$X = \text{strike price of the option}$$

$$P(T^*) = \text{price at time 0 of a zero-coupon bond paying \$1 at time } T^*$$

$$B_{T^*}(T) = \text{value of } B(T) \text{ at time } T^*$$

$$\sigma = \text{annualized volatility of the bond price at time } T^*$$

For example, the bond has a face value of 100, and maturity $T^* + T$ of ten years. Assume the yield curve to be flat at 10%, annual compounding rate. The bond price $B(T^* + T)$ is 38.55 ($= 100/(1.1)^{10}$). Suppose the expiration date of the option, T^*, is three years, and the forward price, $F(3, 7)$, is 51.31 ($= 100/(1.1)^7$). Suppose further that the strike price is 50, and the volatility is 15%. Then

$$d_1 = (\ln 1.0263 + 0.0337)/0.2598 = 0.2296)$$

$$d_2 = (\ln 1.0263 + 0.0337)/0.2598 - 0.2598 = -0.0301)$$

and

$$C = 0.7513 \times (51.31 \cdot N(0.2296) - 50 \cdot N(-0.0301))$$

Caps/Floors

A *cap* is a series of bond options, and each option is called a caplet. A caplet has one payout at the expiration date. If at expiration the current *n*-period rate is above the strike rate, the option pays the difference of the two rates (as an index), times a factor, to scale the actual payment. The maturity of the rate is usually the interval between two caplets. For example, a three-month LIBOR cap with two-year tenor (two years to the termination date), with a strike rate of 7%, has seven caplets. There is no caplet for the first three months, because we already know the three-month LIBOR rate for that period. Each caplet has an expiration date set on the "reset date" every three months, on a three-month zero-coupon bond. A caplet on a T-month LIBOR with *tenor* (maturity) at T^* with strike rate of x% is an option that pays the difference of the current T month LIBOR and the strike rate at the expiration date T^* in dollars.

Since a cap is a portfolio of caplets, the price of a cap must be the total cost of all the caplets. Suppose we label the current T month LIBOR as "stock"; if we apply the Black–Scholes model to these caplets, assuming that the caplet is a call option for a given price, we can determine the implied volatility. This is called the *Black volatility*. In the interest rate derivative market, cap and floor prices are often quoted in terms of Black volatilities. The implied volatilities derived from the Black volatilities are in fact the volatility of the term of the cap or floor at each reset date. For example, consider a series of caplets, with a reset period of three months. The volatilities are the volatilities of the three-month rate for terms at 3, 6, 9, 12, 15 $\cdots$ in increments of three months until the tenor of the cap.

The Black caplet price formula is given by

$$\text{caplet } C_k = L\delta_k P(t_{k+1})\left[F_k N(d_1) - R_X N(d_2)\right]$$

where

$$d_1 = \frac{\ln\left[F_k/R_X\right] + \sigma_k^2 t_k/2}{\sigma_k\sqrt{t_k}}$$

$$d_2 = d_1 - \sigma_k\sqrt{t_k}$$

(6.3)

where

T = a cap's total life

L = a principal

R_X = a cap rate expressed with a compounding frequency equal to the frequency of resets

t_k = reset dates:$t_1, t_2, \cdots, t_n, t_{n+1} = T$

F_k = the forward rate for the period between time t_k and t_{k+1} expressed with a compounding frequency equal to the frequency of resets

δ_k = the reset period $t_{k+1} - t_k$

σ_k = annualized volatility for the kth caplet

A flat volatility of a cap is a single volatility assumed for all the caplets of a cap. In this case, for a given price of a cap, there is a unique implied (flat) volatility number. Conversely, given a flat volatility, we can determine the price of the cap. Floors are similarly defined. If the rate falls below the strike rate of a floorlet, then the payment to the holder is the rate difference times a factor. An analogous situation occurs with the *floors*, where the market can also quote the price of a floor by its volatility number.

Swaptions

As described in chapter 3, a swap trade has two simultaneous payments between two parties. One party receives floating interest rate payments on a notional, say monthly, LIBOR rate on the notional amount, from the counterparty, and at the same time pays the same counterparty a fixed interest payment, say 7% on the same notional amount. This exchange of payments has a termination date, the tenor. The fixed-rate payments may be monthly, quarterly or semiannual. The fixed rate is called the swap rate. The exchange of payments can take many forms; the one just described, called a vanilla swap, is the most common.

We can think of a swap to pay a fixed rate and receive a floating rate as a portfolio holding a floating-rate bond and shorting a fixed-rate bond where both bonds have the same face value. If we consider the fixed side of a swap as a bond, where the notional amount is the face value, then the swap rate is the yield of the bond when the market value of the bond is par. That is, the market value of the fixed side of the swap trade equals the notional amount.

The holder of a *swaption* has the right at the expiration date to enter into a swap at a strike rate R_X, such that the holder can pay the fixed rate R_X when the prevailing swap rate R exceeds R_X, and pay the prevailing fixed rate R if it is lower than the strike rate. Let the notional amount be L, and if the prevailing swap rate exceeds the strike rate, the interest cost saved for one year is the interest differential times the notional, $L \times (R - R_X)$. If both R and R_X are expressed as having a compounding period of m times per year, then the saving from the swaption is a series of cash flows which is the same amount at each exchange of interest payments, and is equal to

$$\frac{L}{m} Max(R - R_X, 0)$$

m: the number of payments per year under the swap

L: principal or the notional amount

R, R_X: the prevailing swap rate and strike rate, respectively, for an n-year swap at the expiration of the swaption, expressed with a compounding period of m times per year.

Let us denote the payment dates as $t_1, t_2, \cdots, t_{m \cdot n}$, measured in years from today. Then the Black model states that if the swap rate at the expiration date has a lognormal distribution, where the log of the distribution has an annualized volatility of σ, then the value of the cash flow received at time t_i is

$$\frac{L}{m} P(t_i) \left[R_F N(d_1) - R_X N(d_2) \right]$$

where

$$d_1 = \frac{\ln[R_F/R_X] + \sigma^2 T^*/2}{\sigma\sqrt{T^*}}$$

$$d_2 = d_1 - \sigma\sqrt{T^*}$$

R_F is the forward swap rate, which is the forward rate, with the delivery date T^* and delivering a swap of tenor T.

$$T^* = \text{expiration of the swaption}$$

$$= \text{starting point of the underlying swap}$$

The total value of the swaption, which expires at time T^*, on a swap with tenor T, is

$$\text{swaption} = \sum_{i=1}^{mn} \frac{L}{m} P(t_i) [R_F N(d_1) - R_X N(d_2)]$$

$$= L \cdot A [R_F N(d_1) - R_X N(d_2)]$$

where

$$A = \frac{1}{m} \sum_{i=1}^{mn} P(t_i) : \text{the value of a contract that pays } 1/m \text{ at times } t_i, (1 \le i \le mn)$$

Once again, the price of the swaption determines the implied volatility and vice versa. Thus, a swaption price can be quoted by the implied volatilities. Note that this swaption is the same as the bond put option. At the expiration of a bond option, if the market rate exceeds the bond coupon rate, then the bond price must fall below the face value. Therefore, the swaption is in the money in exactly the same way that the bond put option is in the money. The Black model for the swaption assumes that the swap rate has a lognormal distribution at the expiration date, and the value of the swaption is the risk-neutral valuation based on the distribution of the swap rate.

Market Volatility Surface

We have discussed the Black models for pricing futures options, bond options, caplets, floorlets, and swaptions. There are several main characteristics of these models, and they are related.

First, they are closed-form solutions, in that with only the assumption of the lognormal distribution of the underlying risk, the model provides an exact value of the option for the assumed volatility.

Second, the volatility σ depends on two parameters: T^*, the expiration of the option, and $(T^* + T)$, the maturity (or tenor) of the underlying security. Sometimes we can think of the two parameters as being T^* and T, where T is the term or maturity of the bond to be delivered. For this reason, the volatilities of the market are presented by the volatility surface. The derivative market provides quotes of these benchmark securities in terms of this surface. Since they are commonly used as a quote sheet in the market, we call them a *market volatility surface*, as distinct from the implied volatility surface that is described in section 6.1. The implied volatility surface is the set of volatilities assumed within the interest rate model. Using these volatilities, the model values of the benchmark securities can best fit the market quoted price. The market volatility surface is a set of volatilities based on the Black models that assume the risk of the securities following lognormal distributions. The set of volatilities can be translated to the market prices of the benchmark securities.

Third, the Black models relax the assumptions of the Black–Scholes model to allow for interest rate risk, yet the models show that the formulation requires only minor adjustment to the original Black–Scholes model. Specifically, this model replaces the futures price of the commodity in the Black model of futures option (equation (6.1)) with the forward price of the bond. The simplicity hinges on the assumption that the log of the bond price, $\ln B_{T^*}(T)$, is a normal distribution with volatility $\sigma\sqrt{T^*}$; hence, the forward bond price also follows a lognormal process. Under this assumption, the Black models show that we can ignore all the interest rate uncertain movements from now until the expiration date, and further, we can discount the risk-neutral expected value by the T^* year discount factor, in the same spirit as the Black–Scholes model. We will reconcile this approach to the valuation approach, using the interest rate model where we need to conduct the backward substitution procedure to value the bond option, as described in chapter 5 later. A more detailed mathematical explanation is given in chapter 19.

The advantage of the model is that it provides a closed-form solution to the call option. Given the bond option price, we can calculate the implied volatility of the bond option the same way we calculate the implied volatility for stock options. Since the formula is closed-form—such that a valuation model can be expressed in the form of an equation—the implied volatility can be uniquely determined for any option price. As long as all the traders agree on using the Black model as the convention in pricing the option, traders can provide a price quote of a call option by giving the volatility number. For example, the quoted price of the call option of the above numerical example can be given as 15% volatility. Any trader can then calculate the exact price of the option.

Conversely, a trader may use his proprietary interest rate model, which may assume that the bond price distribution may not follow a lognormal distribution, and determine the call option price to be $x. He can then use the Black model to give a quote to the market based on the Black model, without revealing the precise assumptions he made to determine the call option price.

The advantage of quoting the value of options using the Black model implied volatility is that it enables the market to have a convention for measuring relative values of different options. It is a way for traders to compare the price of put options with call options, or options of bonds with different maturities or options with different expirations. This is similar to quoting the price of a bond by the yield. From the bond yield, we can determine the quoted price and the invoice price (or dirty price) that we pay or receive for the bond. The quote in yields enables us to compare the relative value of the bond to other bonds. Quoting in volatility has the same advantage for relative valuing of the options in the market.

For the following numerical example, we use a flat yield curve of 6% at continuously compounding rate. We assume a forward volatility curve in figure 6.1. These volatility curves will be used as inputs to illustrate the implementation of the models that will be discussed below. The caplets are assumed to have a tenor of three months with strike at 6%.

We have chosen the function $\sigma = (a + bt)\exp(-ct) + d$ to represent the volatility curve because this function decays exponentially and, when t is relatively small, the curve

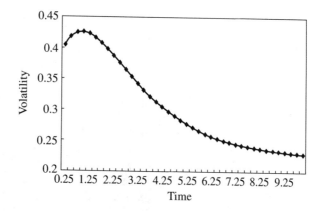

Figure 6.1 Caplet volatilities. This figure presents the estimated caplet volatilities represented by a function $\sigma = (a + bt)\exp(-ct) + d$. The function is calibrated to fit the quoted cap volatilities, given in the market volatility surface data in table 6.2. The function used for the calibration assumes an exponential decline, and allows for a hump in the early years of the curve.

Table 6.2 An Example of Market Volatility Surface: US Swaption vols on July 17, 2002

Option term (years)	Swap tenor (years)					Cap volatility
	1	3	5	7	10	
1	37.2	29.3	25.4	23.7	22.2	42.5
2	28.3	24.8	22.7	21.7	20.5	40.5
3	25.0	22.9	21.3	20.5	19.4	34.6
4	22.7	21.3	20.0	19.4	18.3	31.1
5	21.5	20.2	18.9	18.3	17.2	28.7
7	19.2	18.0	16.9	16.2	15.5	25.5
10	16.8	15.5	14.6	14.1	13.6	22.6

The market volatility depends on two parameters. One is the expiration of the option and the other is the maturity (or tenor) of the underlying asset, in this case, a swap. The derivative market provides quotes of the benchmark securities in terms of the surface.

may exhibit a hump, depending on the parameters a and b. This configuration of the volatility curve is observed in the market.

6.3   Valuation of Interest Rate Derivatives Using Market Benchmark Prices

By introducing the pricing convention of benchmark securities using the Black model, we can now summarize the methodology, step by step, in valuing an interest rate derivative using market benchmark prices.

Step 1. Determining the set of benchmark securities

The selection of benchmark securities depends on the purpose of the valuation. These securities should have tenors and other characteristics of the securities that we would like to value. They should have actively traded prices that are representative of the market assessment of their values. These prices may be determined by different traders, using different financial models and approaches in the market. Some firms may bet on interest rates falling and other firms may bet on interest rates rising. The aggregation of their views is expressed by the prices of benchmark securities, and these prices are expressed in terms of the market volatility surface as market price quotes.

Step 2. Calibration of the interest rate model

We first decide on the interest rate model that is most appropriate to value the derivative. A spot curve that can provide input to an interest rate model may be the swap curve or the Treasury rates. The choice is determined by how we would like to relatively value the derivatives. We use the Black models to translate the market volatility surface to the benchmark securities prices. (See figure 6.2.)

We now develop the valuation models of the benchmark securities as described in chapter 5, where these models are based on the arbitrage-free interest rate movement model. For example, these valuation models may be using backward substitution methods in determining the cap and swaption prices. Using these valuation models, we can determine the set of implied volatilities as input for the interest rate model that best fits the model prices of the benchmark securities to their observed prices, calculated in step 1. Once these implied volatilities are determined, we have calibrated the model.

Step 3. Valuing an interest rate derivative

Now we can apply the calibrated interest rate model to value an interest rate derivative, which may not be a benchmark security. In order to do so, we need to use the procedure discussed in chapter 5 to determine the terminal and boundary conditions on the binomial lattice for the interest rate derivative. Then we use the valuation model to determine the derivative value. Note that after we obtain the derivative value, we can continue to determine the sensitivities of the derivative value to small changes in market parameters, such as the interest rate level and the volatilities. We will discuss some of these sensitivities later in this chapter.

Schematically, we can view the interest rate contingent claims as valued according to the steps shown in figure 6.3.

In completing the discussion of the valuation procedure of interest rate derivatives, we now discuss the advantages of using the arbitrage-free interest rate model in valuing interest rate derivatives. Given a bond option, can we use the discounted cash flow

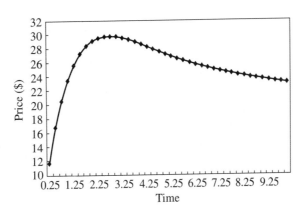

Figure 6.2 Caplet prices obtained using the Black model. The yield curve is 6% flat, the notional amount is 10,000 and the caplet tenor is three months.

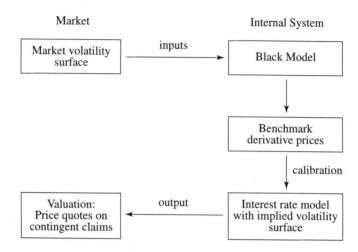

Figure 6.3 Valuation of interest rate derivatives using market benchmark prices.

method to determine the bond option price? Once again, the discounted cash flow method fails to provide an accurate discount rate for the expected cash flow of the bond option. For this reason, the discounted cash flow method is not used for pricing bond options in this chapter. We instead describe in this chapter how we use an interest rate model and calibrate it to some benchmark securities prices, and then use the model to value a bond option.

There are two other reasons why an arbitrage-free interest rate model is useful. The first reason is the use of benchmarks for accurate option pricing. Imagine you are a scientist in a laboratory, and you need to use a laser beam to target a tiny dot on a screen ten yards away. One direct way is trial and error. You may continually adjust the laser beam until it hits the target. However, there is another way. You can first set up the instrument so that you can adjust the position of the laser accurately. Next, you determine several reference points (benchmarks) on the screen and adjust the laser so that it targets the reference points. Then measure the target point relative to the positions of the reference points and use this information to adjust (calibrate) the laser beam. Now you can accurately estimate the position of the dot because your laser beam has been calibrated using benchmark points relative to your target. Furthermore, if the target point moves slightly, you can readjust the laser beam, using the reference points. Arbitrage-free models value any derivative relative to a set of benchmark securities. To the extent that the benchmark securities are appropriately priced, the relative valuation procedure can provide an accurate pricing method.

Another useful aspect of an arbitrage-free interest rate model is that the model relates all the bonds and all the options in one framework. We no longer have to trade a bond option quoting the volatility of that particular bond, as we would normally do if we treated a bond option like a stock option. Instead, we can quote the volatilities of the interest rates; then all interest rate contingent claims can be valued in one consistent framework. For these reasons, the study of interest rate modeling is actively seeking to provide an accurate and efficient framework to value a broad class of derivatives. When an interest rate contingent claim is valued by this calibration approach, the implication is that this interest rate contingent claim can be replicated by the bonds that determine the spot yield curve and the benchmark securities at a cost of buying this portfolio (which may have to be dynamically adjusted over time) equaling the theoretical value of the security.

For these reasons, in the valuation of the interest rate contingent claims, the volatilities surface is as important as the determination of the spot yield curve. The volatilities surface specifies how the market prices the volatilities at each moment in time, much as the spot yield curve specifies the market time value of money.

In the following section we illustrate the calibration procedure for different interest rate models. We consider the valuation of caplets' prices using forward volatilities in figure 6.1 and market caplet prices (implied by the Black model) in figure 6.2. We assume a flat rate of 6%.

6.4   Calibration of the Black–Derman–Toy Model

Up to now we have assumed that the term structure of volatility σ is known. We now discuss how it is determined so that the prices of the benchmark securities implied by the BDT model are the same as the Black–Scholes prices. We illustrate the calibration procedure, using caps with market parameters, as in section 6.3. Using three-month step sizes and at most ten-year maturity caps, we have 39 caplets as calibration instruments. We choose a term structure of forward volatilities from section 5.4, model 4, of the form

$$\sigma(t) = (a + bt)\exp(-ct) + d$$

where the volatility parameters a, b, c, and d are chosen via the calibration procedure. The next stage is to choose a goodness of fit measure. In this example we choose

$$\sum_{i=2}^{40}(V_i - V_i^*)^2$$

where V_i is the market price (obtained using the Black–Scholes model) of the ith caplet and V_i^* is the corresponding price given by the BDT model. Note tht the interest rates must also match the initial term structure.

Our objective is to use a nonlinear optimization routine to determine the volatility parameters $(a, b, c, d$ of the term structure of volatilities above) in order to minimize the goodness of fit measure. Figure 6.4 shows the implied volatility obtained using this calibration procedure. Note that since the BDT model is lognormal, the implied volatility should be the same as given forward volatility. The error depicted by figure 6.5 is primarily due to the step size used in this example; smaller step size will result in the same volatility functions.

As expected, the BDT model can be fitted to value the caplets quite well, using the term structure of volatilities. The inaccuracy of the model with a close expiration date results from the coarse step size of three months. For short dated derivatives, daily or weekly step size is more appropriate for the valuation models.

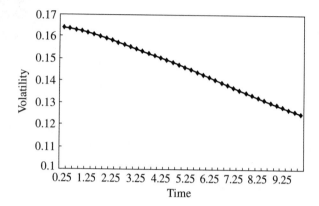

Figure 6.4 Implied volatility of the BDT model. This figure uses the functional form of the term structure of volatility defined above.

6.5   Calibration of the Ho–Lee Models

In this section we illustrate how the extended Ho–Lee and the two-factor Ho–Lee models can be calibrated to caplet prices obtained using figure 6.1. An extension to n factors directly follows the procedure outlined below. Using the implementation procedure outlined in chapter 5, the calibration procedure seeks to find an implied forward volatility function such that the extended Ho–Lee and two-factor Ho–Lee model prices match the market prices quoted using the Black model.

In the extended Ho–Lee case, the volatility function enters the model through $\delta(n)$, given by

$$\ln \delta(n) = -2f(n)\sigma(n)$$

where $f(n)$ are forward rates, in our example, equal to 6% for all n. We choose the functional form

$$\sigma(n) = (a + b.n)\exp(-c.n) + d$$

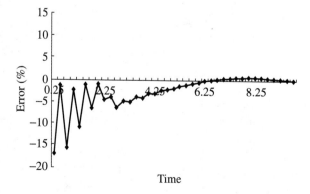

Figure 6.5 The percentage error of caplet prices obtained using the calibrated BDT model. The figure shows the percentage error for the calibrated quarterly step size BDT model.

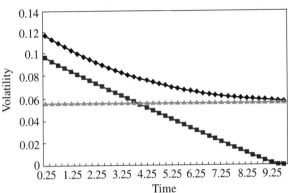

Figure 6.6 Implied volatilities of the extended Ho–Lee and the two-factor Ho–Lee models. This figure uses the functional forms of the term structure of volatilities defined above.

for the implied forward volatility. Using the goodness of fit function in section 6.4, we obtain the optimal implied volatility parameters, using a nonlinear optimization procedure. Figure 6.6 shows the implied volatilities resulting from the calibration procedure. The resulting implied volatilities are estimated from a normal model, and therefore they are different from the forward volatilities used as inputs in the Black model.

For the two-factor Ho–Lee model, we have

$$\ln \sigma^1(n) = -2f(n)\sigma^1(n) \quad \text{and} \quad \ln \delta^2(n) = -2f(n)\sigma^2(n)$$

For our calibration procedure we choose

$$\sigma^1(n) = (a + b.n)\exp(-c.n) + d \text{ and } \sigma^2(n) = e \text{ (a constant)}$$

Figures 6.6 and 6.7 show the implied volatilities and percentage errors of caplet prices obtained using the calibration procedure, respectively.

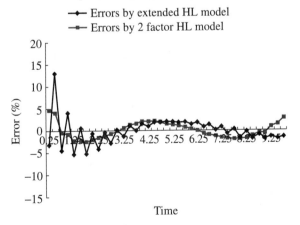

Figure 6.7 The percentage error of caplet prices obtained using the extended Ho–Lee model and the two-factor Ho–Lee model. The models use quarterly step sizes.

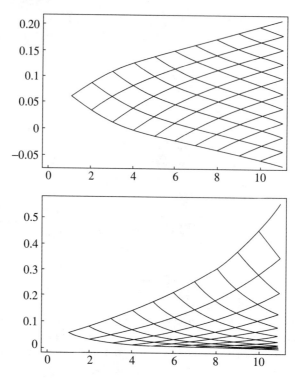

Figure 6.8 The interest rate trees of the extended HL model versus the BDT model. This figure shows the differences between the lognormal model (BDT model) and the normal model (extended Ho and Lee model). While the normal model exhibits negative interests, the lognormal model generates much higher interest rates as compared to the normal model. The volatility across the states in the normal model is constant, whereas the volatility across the states in the lognormal model decreases as the interst rates approach zero.

The results show that the Ho–Lee models can fit the caplet prices quite well. Since we use only caplet prices and not the complete volatility surface, the extended Ho–Lee model does as well as the two-factor Ho–Lee model. The result also shows that the implied volatilities as measured by normal models have magnitudes similar to those measured by the lognormal model.

For comparision purposes, we draw a binomial lattice for the extended HL model (normal model) and the BDT model (lognormal model) in figure 6.8.

6.6   Calibration of the Longstaff–Santa-Clara–Schwartz "String" Model

We showed in chapter 5 that the string model is given by

$$dP(t, T^*) = r(t)P(t, T^*)dt + \sigma(t, T^*)P(t, T^*)dZ \tag{6.4}$$

The string model is a multifactor model where $\sigma(t, T^*)P(t, T^*)dZ$ is the vector formed by stacking correlated individual terms $\sigma_i(t, T_i^*)P(t, T_i^*)dZ_i$.

The volatilities and the correlations of the bond price return are calibrated to the observed term structure of volatilities and correlations. In our example we use the correlation matrix in table 5.1.

The approach proposed by Longstaff, Santa-Clara, and Schwartz (2000) is to solve for the implied correlation structure of the model that best fits the observed market prices of our caplet market prices. Instead, we specify the correlation structure exogenously and seek a term structure volatility that best fits caplet market prices. Let $\sigma(s)$ be the term structure of volatilities of proportional change in the bond price. This term structure of volatilities can be estimated from the term structure of spot volatilities and multiplied by the duration.[1] Specifically, we can write

$$\sigma(t, T^*) = y(t, T^*)\sigma^*(T^* - t).(T^* - t) \qquad (6.5)$$

where $\sigma^*(\tau)$ is the estimated term structure of volatilities of the interest rates derived from the swaption, expiring over time Δ, with the tenor of the swap $\tau.y(t, T^*)$ is the yield of a bond at time t that matures at calendar time T^*. $y(t, T^*)\sigma^*(T^* - t)$ is the standard deviation of the yield of a bond with maturity $(T - t)$ at time t. Since the duration of the $(T - t)$ year bond is $(T - t)$, assuming continuous compounding of the measure of yields, the right-hand side of equation (6.5) is the standard deviation of the $(T - t)$ year bond, as required. If the yield is not measured on a continuously compounding basis, then a modifier is used, as described in chapter 3. The bond price dynamics follows

$$dP(t, T^*) = r(t)P(t, T^*)dt + \sigma(T^* - t)P(t, T^*)dZ(T^* - t). \qquad (6.6)$$

Now we can rewrite equation (6.6) in a discrete time formulation. Let us assume that the step size is Δ. Let $k, j = 0, 1, 2, \cdots, m$. For clarity of exposition, we abuse the notations by writing $P(k, j)$, $\sigma(i)$, and $r(k)$ to mean $P(k\Delta, j\Delta)$, $\sigma(i\Delta)$. and $r(k\Delta)$, respectively. Then equation (6.6) can be written as

$$P(k+1, j) = P(k, j) \exp\left[\left(r(k) - \frac{\sigma^2(j - k)}{2}\right)\Delta + \sigma(j - k)\sqrt{\Delta}Z(j - k)\right] \qquad (6.7)$$

where Z is a *Brownian motion* increment over a unit of time (i.e., a standard normal variate). $P(0, j)$ is the initial discount function, the price of a zero-coupon bond for each maturity j. Now, using equation (6.7), we can simulate the arbitrage-free discount function movements, $P(k, j)$, where k denotes the time dimension of the evolution of the discount function movement and j is the calendar time of the maturity of the bond—or, equivalently, $(j - k)$ is the remaining maturity of the bond. In particular, $P(k, k + 1)$ is the one-period bond price at time k, and $r(k) = -\ln P(k, k + 1)$ is the one-period interest rate.

In this simulation, for illustrative purposes, we set the step size at one year, $\Delta = 1$. To apply equation (6.7) iteratively, we first need to determine the initial discount function, which is derived from a flat initial yield curve assumption of 6%. Next we need to determine the Brownian process $Z(j - k)$ for each time j. This is accomplished by taking the following steps.

We use the following definitions:

$\mathbf{Z}$ = vector of $(Z(1), Z(2), Z(3), Z(4))$, $Z(i)$ is the price risk of a zero-coupon bond with i year maturity at the end of the period.

$\mathbf{Z}_{uncorr}$ = vector of uncorrelated standard normal variates in each step in table 5.1.

$\mathbf{M}$ = *Cholesky decomposition* of the correlation matrix of the zero-coupon bonds, which is the same as the correlation matrix of the spot yields in table 5.1. $\mathbf{M}$ is an $n \times n$ matrix, defined to be $\mathbf{M^T M} = \Sigma$, where $\mathbf{M^T}$ is the transpose of $\mathbf{M}$ and *Corr* is the correlation matrix of n risk sources. Then we have

$$\mathbf{Z} = \mathbf{M^T} \times \mathbf{Z}_{uncorr} \tag{6.8}$$

Using the correlation matrix

$$\Sigma = \begin{bmatrix} 1.000 & 0.940 & 0.895 & 0.856 \\ 0.940 & 1.000 & 0.989 & 0.970 \\ 0.895 & 0.989 & 1.000 & 0.990 \\ 0.856 & 0.970 & 0.990 & 1.000 \end{bmatrix}$$

extracted from table 5.1, we can derive

$$M^T = \begin{bmatrix} 1.0000 & 0.0000 & 0.0000 & 0.0000 \\ 0.9400 & 0.3412 & 0.0000 & 0.0000 \\ 0.8950 & 0.4329 & 0.1075 & 0.0000 \\ 0.8560 & 0.4847 & 0.1307 & 0.1235 \end{bmatrix}$$

Using a standardized normal distribution generator, we simulate the 16 uncorrelated numbers above (see table 6.3).

Using equation (6.8), we can now generate the correlated random outcomes for the string model. The main characteristic of the string model is the use of correlated risk sources for each period along the entire yield curve. For this numerical example, for each time step, we have five sources of uncertainties at the beginning. After each step, the yield curve is shorter by one period, and the number of uncertainties falls accordingly. To generate one discount function movement scenario, we have the random outcomes shown in table 6.4.

Now we proceed to determine the instantaneous volatilities of the bond price $\sigma(i)$ where i is the bond maturity. We begin with the observed spot volatilities quoted from the swaption market. $\sigma^*(T^* - t)$ is assumed as given by the first column in table 6.5. Thus, at period $k = 1$ the volatilities of bonds maturing at years $j = 2$ and $j = 3$ are given by $\sigma(1) = y(1) \times \sigma^*(1) \times 1 = 6.0\% \times 20\% = 1.2\%$ and

Table 6.3 Table of Random Draws

$$Z_{uncorr} = \begin{bmatrix} 0.1589 & 0.4049 & 0.3110 & 0.5212 \\ -2.3733 & 0.8001 & 0.5650 & \\ -0.9183 & -0.1906 & & \\ 0.7583 & & & \end{bmatrix}$$

Notice that at each successive time period we make one less random draw.

Table 6.4 Table of Uncertainties

T^*	t	1	2	3	4
1	$Z(1)$	0.1589	0.4049	0.3110	0.5212
2	$Z(2)$	−0.6603	0.6536	0.4851	
3	$Z(3)$	−0.9839	0.6883		
4	$Z(4)$	−1.0460			

$\sigma(2) = y(2) \times \sigma^*(2) \times 2 = 6.0\% \times 19\% \times 2 = 2.3\%$, respectively. The yield is from the previous period, $k = 0$. Table 6.5 is derived iteratively for $k = 1, 2, 3$, and 4. After deriving the column of volatilities for each k, we proceed to derive the zero-coupon bond prices.

The iterative process begins with the initial discount function presented in the first column, where $k = 0$. From the one-period bond price, we can calculate the one-period interest rate. Now, using the first column of the uncertainties and equation (6.7), we can derive the discount function for $k = 1$. (See table 6.6.)

Given the bond prices, we can determine the yields of the bonds by noting that the yield y is related to the bond price by $P = \exp(-yT)$, where T is the bond maturity. At $k = 1$, table 6.7 shows that the prices of bonds maturing at $j = 2$ and $j = 3$ are given by $0.943 = 0.887 \exp\left[0.06 − 0.012^2/2 + 0.012 \times 0.1589\right]$ and $0.873 = 0.835 \exp\left[0.06 − 0.023^2/2 + 0.023 \times 0.(−0.6603)\right]$, respectively.

Once again we repeat the process. We begin with table 6.4, period 2 (column 2). Using the new set of bond price uncertainties, we now compute the instantaneous volatilities of the bond in period 2, using the updated bond yields. Then we derive the discount function for period 2, using equation (6.7) again. We continue the process until we reach the period $k = 5$. The derived path of one period interest rates (6%, 5.82%, 7.25% 6.09%, 4.76%) is then used to determine the pathwise value of a security. Using the procedure

Table 6.5 Term Structure of Volatilities of Proportional Change in the Bond Price

t	1	2	3	4
$\sigma^*(1)\ 20\%\ \sigma(1-k)$				
$\sigma^*(2)\ 19\%\ \sigma(2-k)$	1.20 %			
$\sigma^*(3)\ 18\%\ \sigma(3-k)$	2.28 %	1.16 %		
$\sigma^*(4)\ 17\%\ \sigma(4-k)$	3.24 %	2.57 %	1.45 %	
$\sigma^*(5)\ 16\%\ \sigma(5-k)$	4.08 %	3.82 %	2.62 %	1.22 %

Table 6.6 Generating the Discount Function Movements $P(k,j)$

T^* \\ t	0	1	2	3	4	5
0	1.000					
1	0.942	1.000				
2	0.887	0.943	1.000			
3	0.835	0.873	0.930	1.000		
4	0.787	0.809	0.871	0.941	1.000	
5	0.741	0.753	0.819	0.892	0.954	1.000

t is the passage of time and T^* is the calendar time.

Table 6.7 Deriving the Yields from the Bond Prices, $P(r) = e^{-rt}$

t T^*	0	1	2	3	4
1 $y(1-k)$	6.0 %				
2 $y(2-k)$	6.0 %	5.82 %			
3 $y(3-k)$	6.0 %	6.77 %	7.25 %		
4 $y(4-k)$	6.0 %	7.08 %	6.89 %	6.09 %	
5 $y(5-k)$	6.0 %	7.08 %	6.65 %	5.73 %	4.76 %

t denotes the passage of time and T^* is the calendar time.

by now familiar to the reader, we take the mean of all the pathwise values, using a *Monte Carlo simulation* to determine the security value.

Thus far, we have assumed some observed term structures of volatilities from the swaption market. We can also conduct a nonlinear search for the best estimated term structure of volatilities by assuming the term structure has a certain functional form. Specifically, we assume that

$$\sigma^*(T^* - t) = (a + b(T^* - t)) \exp(-c(T^* - t)) + d \qquad (6.9)$$

and we can determine parameters a, b, c, and d, so that the model caplet prices fit the caplet market prices.

This procedure begins with specifying the discount function $P(T)$, using the prevailing zero-coupon bond prices at the initial date. We assume an initial term structure of volatilities by assuming values for a, b, and c for the specification of the term structure of volatilities. The correlations of the interest rates are based on the historical correlation matrix presented in table 5.1.

Using equation (6.4), we simulate the term structure of zero-coupon bond prices, which will be converted to forward rates in order to calculate the payoffs of the caplets. The value of $F(j+1,j) = \frac{1}{\Delta t} \left(\frac{1}{P(j+1,j)} - 1 \right)$ is the realized rate for the period between j and $j+1$, and this enables the caplet payoff at time $j+1$ to be calculated. This caplet payoff is discounted to time 0, using the one-period rates determined along the interest rate path. The estimated caplet value is the mean of the discounted payoffs. Now we use

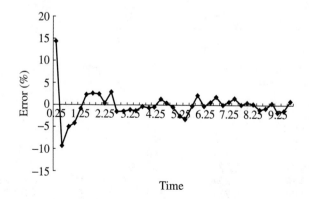

Figure 6.9 The percentage error of the string model caplet prices. The percentage error of caplet prices was obtained using the calibrated string model.

a nonlinear optimization procedure to search for the optimized parameters a, b, and c such that the caplet prices are best fitted to the valuation model. (See figure 6.9.)

The number of Monte Carlo simulations used is 1000, with quarterly step sizes. The result shows that the errors of the nearby caplets are higher because of the coarseness of the quarterly step size. Some errors can also be attributed to the Monte Carlo simulations that may require a higher number of simulations.

6.7 Calibration of the Brace–Gatarek–Musiela/Jamshidian Model (the LIBOR Market Model)

We implement a Monte Carlo process for the BGM/J model described in chapter 5 with quarterly step sizes. Table 6.8 shows the calibrated volatility obtained using table 5.1. First, we calculate instantaneous forward volatilities Λ_j, using $\sigma_j^2 j = \sum_{i=1}^{j} \Lambda_{i-1}^2$ where σ_j is the Black volatility for a caplet that corresponds to the jth period. These Black volatilities are specified in figure 6.1. In chapter 5, we showed that the forward LIBOR rates $L(k, j)$ are given by

$$L(k, j + 1) =$$

$$L(k, j) \exp \left[\left(\sum_{i=j+1}^{k} \frac{L(i, j) \Delta}{1 + L(i, j) \Delta} \Lambda_{i-j-1} \Lambda_{k-j-1} - \frac{\Lambda_{k-j-1}^2}{2} \right) \Delta + \Lambda_{k-j-1} \sqrt{\Delta} Z \right] \quad (6.10)$$

where Z is a random sample from a normal distribution with mean equal to 0 and variance equal to 1.

For illustrative purposes we consider the following example. The path of the forward LIBOR $L(t, j)$ rates is shown in table 6.8.

The column σ_j presents the observed volatilities observed from the caplets, using the Black model. Λ_{j-1} are the instantaneous volatilities derived from σ_j. For this example, the initial yield curve is flat 6%. Therefore, the forward one-period rate for each year k is also 6%. At the end of the first period, a random draw is taken, giving $Z = -1.162$ and the LIBOR rate at the next period,

$$4.81\% = 6\% \times \exp[0.057(20\%)(17.94\%)$$

$$+ 0.057(17.94\%)^2 - (17.94\%)^2/2 + 17.94\%(-1.162)]$$

Table 6.8 Generating the Forward LIBOR Movements, L(t,j)

t			0	1	2	3	4
	Z			-1.162	0.347	1.999	0.985
T^*	σ_j	Λ_{j-1}					
1	20 %	20 %	6.00 %				
2	19 %	17.94 %	6.00 %	4.81 %			
3	18 %	15.81 %	6.00 %	4.96 %	5.21 %		
4	17 %	13.56 %	6.00 %	5.10 %	5.35 %	7.56 %	
5	16 %	11.14 %	6.00 %	5.27 %	5.50 %	7.47 %	7.50 %

The reset period is assumed to be one year ($\Delta = 1$).

where $0.057 = \frac{6\%}{1+6\%}$. Using equation (6.10) repeatedly for $j = 1, 2, 3, 4, 5$, we derive the second column of the forward LIBOR rates for the period $k = 1$. Following this procedure, we can derive all the forward LIBOR rates as presented. Note that the forward LIBOR rates along the diagonal are in fact the simulated spot rates. These spot rates are the simulated LIBOR rates to be used for valuation. This interest rate path is then used for valuation in a way similar to other interest rate models.

In valuing the caplets, we use the interest rate path to calculate the payoff of the caplet. This caplet payoff is discounted to time 0 along the interest rate path to determine the pathwise value. Finally, the estimated caplet value is the mean of the discounted payoffs for 1,000 interest rate path simulations.

Figure 6.1 shows instantaneous forward volatilities calculated as inputs to the model. The errors of the BGM model are comparable to the other models. The main advantage of this approach is not requiring the nonlinear optimization procedure to calibrate the model to the caplet prices. Instead, the calibration of this *market model* is to calculate the instantaneous forward volatilities from the forward volatilities of the Black model before simulating the interest rate scenarios using the Monte Carlo procedure. (See figure 6.10.)

By contrast, the Black model can price one benchmark security at a time and is not an interest rate model, which is a general framework to value all interest rate contingent claims. All interest rate models that we have discussed require the calibration procedure to fit the benchmark securities' prices.

The BGM/J type of model assumes that the LIBOR rates and swap rates follow a lognormal distribution, as the Black model requires. Also, these models take the Black prices as given in much the same way as taking the spot yield curve as given. Therefore, these models are not constructed to evaluate the fair pricing of the caps/floors and swaptions. They take these securities' prices as given and cannot be used to value these securities. In this sense, these models are calibrated to the market prices without using the nonlinear search routines that are used in the Ho–Lee, BDT, Hull–White, and other models.

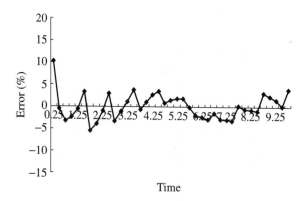

Figure 6.10 The percentage errors of the BGM/J caplet prices. Quarterly step sizes are used. The notional amount of the caplet prices is 10,000, and the initial yield curve is 6% flat.

6.8 Comparing the Black Models and the Interest Rate Models

The Black models provide a mathematical relationship between the bond option price and the interest rate volatility. Therefore, we can convert a given volatility number into the bond option price so that we can quote prices in terms of volatilities. This market convention is similar to that of a bond model, where we can quote a bond price relative to a yield curve. Although in reality we trade on the price of a bond, we quote the price in terms of a yield percentage. Similarly, we trade interest rate-sensitive securities based on the option price, but we convey the price in terms of the volatility number.

The basic idea of the Black model is simple: determine the expected value of the bond option on the expiration date of the option at year T^* and then discount that expected payment at the T^*-year risk-free rate to determine the present value.

The simplicity of this approach seems contradictory to our discussion of the valuation of the bond option in chapter 5. In that discussion, we proposed that we should first develop an arbitrage-free interest rate model, then determine all the bond prices at all the nodes at the expiration date. We did not suggest using one discount rate (the T^*-year rate) to discount the expected payment to determine the price. Instead, we applied the backward substitution approach to determine the value, resulting in lower discount rates for higher bond prices, and higher discount rates for lower bond prices. This is because, at the expiration date, the bond prices are higher when the current interest rates are low on the binomial lattice. Since we applied the backward substitution procedure to determine the prices, this approach does not have a simple closed-form solution of the bond option price, as in the case of the Black model.

Can both valuation models be correct? To analyze this question, we begin with an analysis of the pricing of futures and forward contracts, an issue that we ignored in earlier chapters. Previously we asserted that under interest rate uncertainty, the futures price differs from the corresponding forward price. This price difference is in fact the key to reconciling the different approaches of the Black model and the interest rate model.

Futures and Forward Contracts

The Ho–Lee model, though simple, can provide insights into some fundamental concepts in financial modeling. Let a bond forward contract be defined as a contract that takes delivery of a T-year zero-coupon bond at time T^* at the price $F(T^*, T)$. We have shown, using an arbitrage argument, the forward price of the bond forward contract,

$$F(T^*, T) = \frac{P(T^* + T)}{P(T^*)} \tag{6.11}$$

where $P(T)$ is the discount function observed in the market. We have also discussed that the futures contract is similar to that of the forward contract except that the futures contract requires marking to market, which means that any daily change in the futures price has to be settled immediately (daily) from the margin account. We have noted that the futures price is not the same as the forward price when there are interest rate risks; in other words, the difference in the prices is relative to interest rate risks. We can now apply the interest rate derivatives valuation procedure to determine the bond futures price in support of this assertion.

The terminal date of the futures contract is time T^*. The terminal condition is to specify the futures contract value at the terminal date. The values are the T-year zero-coupon bond value at each node point. Now we apply the backward substitution procedure. However, the futures contract does not require any initial investment to acquire. Therefore, there is no discount factor. The futures price at each node is simply the risk-neutral expectation of the futures price in the subsequent periods. By following this procedure, we can determine the futures price at the initial date.

Figure 6.11 provides a numerical example. Assume that we have a flat yield curve of 6%. The futures and forward contracts have the terminal date in five years and the deliverable bond at the terminal date is a three-year bond. Assume that the interest rate risk is 20%. The binomial lattice depicts the futures price. The results indeed show that the futures price is different from the forward price.

What does this result tell us about our model assumptions? There are several related implications of interest rate models, and some of these implications have been discussed before, but as isolated observations. An arbitrage-free model enables us to relate them in one analytical context.

We have noted that when there is no interest rate uncertainty, the expectation of interest rates at any future time is equal to the forward rates. This is obvious, because if there is no interest rate uncertainty, the future rates by definition do not deviate from the forward rates. But subject to uncertain interest rate movements, the forward bond price cannot be the expected bond price, based on the lattice's risk-neutral probability. Forward rates equaling the expected future rates and forward prices equaling the expected bond prices can be true only when there is no interest rate risk. And if there is no interest rate risk, "expectation" does not involve any probabilistic interpretation. The source of this discrepancy arises from the "convexity adjustment" in which a bond always has positive convexity.

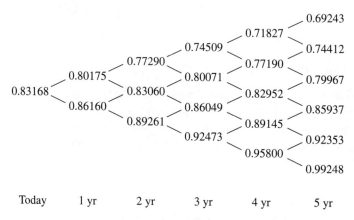

Today   1 yr   2 yr   3 yr   4 yr   5 yr

Figure 6.11 The Binomial lattice of interest rates futures prices. The binomial lattice provides a numerical example of how to calculate the future price. Assume that we have a flat yield curve of 6%. The futures and forward contracts have the terminal date in five years, and the deliverable bond at the terminal date is a three-year bond. Assume that the interest rate volatility is 20%. The binomial lattice depicts the valuation of the futures contract. The results indeed show that the futures contract price is different from the forward price. The futures price is 0.83168, whereas the forward price is 0.83527 ($e^{-0.06\times3}$).

Economic literature explains the expectation hypothesis in terms of the observed yield curve shape. Another way of understanding the interpretation is to consider the reinvestment in a money market account. Suppose we own a $(T^* + T)$-year zero-coupon bond, called bond A, that has a price $P(T^* + T)$. We have a T^*-year time horizon when we will need to liquidate our position. Suppose we know that the interest rate moves according to the arbitrage-free rate movement (say, the Ho–Lee model). Then at each node point, we can calculate the expected total return of bond A. The expected total return is the return of holding the bond one period, then selling the bond at the end of that period. The arbitrage-free condition would ensure that the expected total return of the bond is always the same as the risk-free one period return, at each node in the binomial lattice.

We may wonder, then, if the bond's total return at each node is the same as the current one-period risk-free rate, whether we may expect the expected bond price to equal the forward price. The result shows that the (risk-neutral) expected value of the bond price is not the forward price, but the futures price. This is somewhat disconcerting. We have shown that if we had a $(T^* + T)$-year bond, and if our time horizon is at T^* (for example, withdrawing the investment for retirement), we can always enter a forward contract to receive the forward price at time T^*. However, that forward price is not the expected value of the bond at time T^*. That means the expectation hypothesis cannot simultaneously hold for each time period and over an arbitrary time horizon. For this reason, Cox, Ingersoll, and Ross (1977) proposed the local expectation hypothesis, discussed in chapter 5, to ensure that there is no ambiguity of the term "expectation hypothesis." When interest rate movements satisfy the local expectation hypothesis, then the futures price is the expected bond price, not the forward price. Also, the forward price is not the expected value of the bond.

Let us provide a more formal analysis using the Ho–Lee model. Given a discount function $P(T)$, as we have discussed, the forward price that delivers a (T)-year bond at time T^* is given by

$$F(T^*, T) = \frac{P(T^* + T)}{P(T^*)} \tag{6.12}$$

To determine the futures price, we note that the futures prices at time T^* on the Ho–Lee lattice is given by

$$P(T^*, i; T) = \frac{P(T^* + T)}{P(T^*)} \cdot 2 \cdot \frac{\prod_{t=T}^{T+T^*-1} h(t)}{\prod_{t=1}^{T^*-1} h(t)} \cdot \delta^{T \cdot i} \tag{6.13}$$

where

$$h(t) = \frac{1}{1 + \delta^t} \tag{6.14}$$

Now we perform the backward substitution, using the futures prices at expiration of the contract as the terminal condition. In this backward substitution process, we do not use any discounting because these are futures prices. Let $f(T^*, T)$ denote the futures price at the initial time.

The solution is

$$f(T^*, T) = \alpha \cdot \frac{P(T^* + T)}{P(T^*)}, \ (\alpha < 1) \tag{6.15}$$

For example,

$$f(3, 2) = \alpha \cdot \frac{P(5)}{P(3)}$$

where

$$\alpha = \frac{(1 + \delta^2)^3}{4(\delta^2 - \delta + 1)(1 + \delta^4)}$$

If we replace the constant volatility, δ under the Ho–Lee model, with 0.99, then

$$\alpha = 0.999849 < 1$$
$$f(3, 2) = 0.999849 \cdot \frac{P(5)}{P(3)} < F(3, 2) = \frac{P(5)}{P(3)}$$

Now the futures price is less than the forward price. The reason is clear. Since futures contracts require daily marking to market, the profit and loss of the futures price changes result in reinvestment or borrowing at an uncertain short-term rate. When the short-term rate is positively correlated to the long-term rate, which is the yield of the bond to deliver at the expiration date, the futures contract realizes a profit if the interest rate falls, but the profit has to be invested at a lower rate. Similarly, when the futures contract realizes a loss, the loss has to be covered by borrowing at a higher interest rate. Therefore, the mark-to-market is adverse to the value of the contract. For this reason, the futures contract should be valued less than the forward contract.

$$f(T^*, T) < F(T^*, T) \tag{6.16}$$

The Black Model and an Arbitrage-free Rate Model

Given the insights provided above, we can now derive the Black model of a bond option from an interest rate model. In brief, the derivation proceeds as follows. (A more detailed explanation is given in chapter 19.) Use the Ho–Lee model to derive the $(T^* + T)$ periods zero-coupon bond value at each node point. This zero-coupon bond has a maturity of $(T^* + T)$ at the initial date and a maturity of (T) at the option terminal date. Now use these bond prices and the T^* period bond prices to determine the dynamic hedging that replicates the bond option at each node point, as shown in figure 6.12. This procedure is the same one used in the Cox–Ross–Rubinstein model for a stock option. In doing so, we can perform the backward substitution approach and derive the option value relative to the $(T^* + T)$-year bond. The bond option value formulated this way is the Black model.

The Black model can be interpreted as follows. It is an extension of the Black–Scholes model in such a way that it does not need to make any assumption about the short-term interest rate. The model shows that we can conduct the dynamic hedging with the $(T^* + T)$ bond and the T^* bond until the expiration date. Of course, the $(T^* + T)$-year

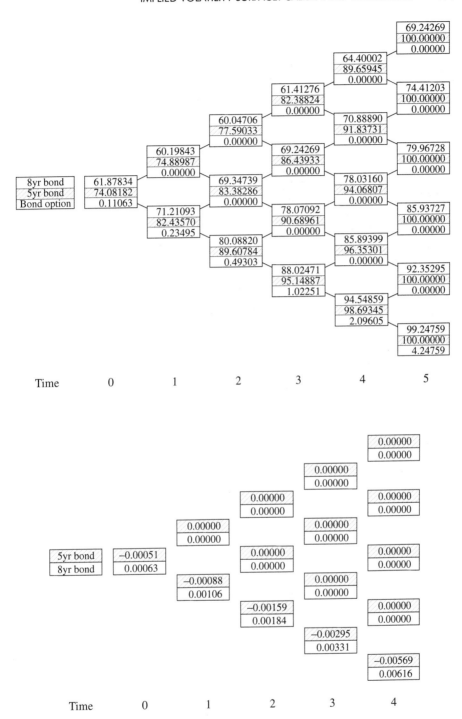

Figure 6.12 The portfolio lattice for dynamic hedging. We replicate a bond option with two bonds. The bond option has a maturity of 5 years and the underlying bond of the bond option is an 8-year bond. Since the bond option depends on the 5-year bond and 8-year bond, a portfolio of 5-year and 8-year bond duplicates the payoff of the bond option. The upper panel shows the bond price dynamics for a 5-year bond and 8-year bond as well as the bond option value at each node. The lower panel shows the dynamic hedge ratios.

bond price does not follow a simple binomial process like that of a stock, but we have shown that the interim movement of the stock price (or the bond price) does not affect the valuation of the option, only the distribution of the stock prices (or bond prices) at the expiration date that is relevant.

Since dynamic hedging uses the $(T^* + T)$-period bond and the T^*-period bond to replicate the bond options, the risk-neutral probabilities derived from the hedging are not the same as the risk-neutral probabilities of the interest rate model. For this reason, research literature refers to the probability used in the Black model as the forward measure.

This result provides the intuition behind the validity of the Black model. Since, on one hand, we use the forward price for the Black model, we are overstating the risk-neutral expected value of the bond prices at time T^*, because the risk-neutral expected value of the bond prices at time T^* is the futures price, which is less than the forward price. On the other hand, however, when we discount the future bond prices at time T^* by backward substitution, we discount the higher prices (the bond value is high when the interest rate is low) at lower interest rates and discount the lower bond prices at higher interest rates. Therefore, in the Black model, discounting all the interest rate scenarios at the same constant risk-free rate leads to understating the present value. Fortunately, these two effects balance each other, and the interest rate modeling approach agrees with the Black model valuation.

6.9   Applications of Interest Rate Models

A reasonable question to ask is How do I choose the appropriate interest rate model for a task at hand? In chapter 5, as well as in this chapter, we have introduced interest rate models in an order that follows the chronology of their discovery. Each interest rate model was proposed to solve new challenges. Now we should look back and discuss how the models fit together in order to solve financial modeling problems.

There are various categories of financial modeling problems. We will present problems and their solutions on different levels. On the highest level, understanding the term structure of interest rates (the yield curve) is important to economics. There is much research on the economic factors affecting interest rate levels and movements. Often these models are called *equilibrium models*. They study the supply of and demand for funds in the economy and determine the equilibrium solutions to the preferences of the economic agents. They enable us to understand how macroeconomics affects interest rates and how interest rates relate to government fiscal policies and other macroeconomic policies.

In financial markets, we are concerned with the valuation of interest rate contingent claims. The yield curve is used as a benchmark to value other securities. In this case, we use the arbitrage-free interest rate movement models. These models provide a more accurate pricing because they specify the contingent claim price relative to the yield curve. Such models are partial equilibrium models because they do not require any notion of equilibrium solution to the yield curve; only the arbitrage-free condition between the contingent claims and the yield curve is necessary.

Arbitrage-free interest rate models are also preference-free, independent of the market agents' preferences and their investment and consumption behavior. However, they need to be calibrated to fit the observed market volatilities in addition to the yield curve.

The market volatilities are represented by the prices of the benchmark securities, such as caps/floors, swaptions, and bond options.

Black models are closed-form models that provide the price of these benchmark securities given the volatility assumptions. Therefore, these models are ideal to use for market convention in quoting these benchmark securities in terms of the market volatilities. Black models provide the exact mathematical relationships between the market quote on volatilities and the value of the benchmark derivatives.

Given the market quote of the volatilities, the market models translate those quotes to the prices of the benchmark derivatives. Now the arbitrage-free interest rate models are calibrated to fit these benchmark derivative prices by solving for the implied volatility surface that is applicable to the interest rate model. Different interest rate models have (possibly only slightly) different implied volatility surfaces. For example, a lognormal interest rate model assumes that the benchmark derivative prices are derived from a lognormal interest rate movement. A normal interest rate model would assume that the interest rates follow normal distributions. Irrespective of the assumptions of the models, they all seek to value the benchmark derivatives accurately and to value other contingent claims relative to the benchmark derivatives' values.

Within the arbitrage-free interest rate models, we can choose from a selection of models, depending on the features of the models, as discussed in chapter 5, which provides two mathematical theorems that link the volatility surface to the interest rate models. The first theorem is the Heath–Jarrow–Morton (HJM) model, which provides an interest rate model as a solution to any volatility surface specified to the model. Therefore, HJM has reduced the problem of specifying an interest rate model to that of specifying the volatility surface. For a given volatility surface, HJM provides an interest rate model as a mathematical solution that has the implied volatility surface identical to the given volatility surface. For example, we saw in chapter 5 that the term structure of volatilities is consistent with the Ho–Lee model in the continuous time setting. Using this specification, we can derive the instantaneous forward rates simulated in the future, and those rates will be consistent with the Ho–Lee model in the continuous time framework.

However, the market provides the prices of the benchmark derivatives or the market volatility surface that is based on the Black models (for caps/floors, swaptions, etc.), and not a volatility surface based on a particular interest rate model. Therefore, we need to calibrate the implied volatility surface to the observed market prices. Calibrating the HJM interest rate model to the prices of the benchmark derivatives can be difficult because the HJM interest rate models are often nonrecombining. Using Monte Carlo simulations may lead to errors in the calibrating process.

The BGM/J model is the second mathematical theorem that provides a solution to the aforementioned problem. BGM/J shows that an interest rate model can be specified directly from the quoted volatility surface for a particular set of benchmark securities. The interest rate model is a multifactor model derived from continuous time analysis.

Interest rate models derived from HJM and BGM/J are continuous time models rather than binomial lattice models. Given a continuous time model, there is no specific procedure to provide a recombining lattice model. A binomial lattice models in the limit; as the step size of the lattice becomes arbitrarily small, it becomes a continuous time model, but the converse is not true in general. That is, there is no specific mathematical procedure that translates a continuous time model into a recombining binomial lattice. And there are advantages to using a recombining lattice model for particular purposes.

The most important attribute of recombining lattices is that they cover the states and time by the nodes in a way that is not computationally prohibitive. Therefore, we have a way to describe the contingent claim, its price, and its behavior at each node, and how the information of each node is related to other nodes. By contrast, when we simulate the interest rate movements as in the HJM, BGM/J, or string model, scenarios are generated, and at each point on a scenario, we know only where that point came from and where it will go. There is no analytical relationship between any point of one scenario and another point of another scenario. For this reason, we will show that it is more difficult to solve multiperiod optimal decisions in a tree that is not recombining. This attribute will be particularly useful later in this book. In corporate finance, we need to describe how corporate management makes optimal decisions that are related not only to the prevailing market realities but also to the management's past and future decisions. In other words, corporate optimal decisions cannot be made myopically, looking only at the outcome of the next step; decisions at all the nodes have to be made jointly. The use of the recombining feature of a lattice model will become more evident in the next chapters.

Given the relatively inexpensive computational power, the step size used for practical purposes can be made very small. Academic research may use monthly step size to price a five-year bond, for example. But in practice, the step size can be daily. The computational requirement is still manageable in most cases. Therefore the error of assuming a discrete outcome in the lattice model can be small.

For derivatives that require use of Monte Carlo simulations, the random scenarios can be generated from the lattice, as we have shown in the pathwise analysis. Therefore, a lattice can be viewed as a consistent valuation framework that can be used for selecting scenarios and for using backward substitution to value securities.

In summary, we list below some of the issues in relation to using a normal recombining lattice interest rate model.

1. Efficiency in calibrating to benchmark securities
   a. Since the lattice approach can value a broad range of derivatives (including American options, which we will discuss in chapter 7) accurately, we can use a broad range of derivatives to calibrate the model, instead of being confined to caps/floors and European swaptions.
   b. When a normal interest rate model is used, there is a concern with the probability of negative interest rates. This problem can be handled by using benchmark securities like floors with strike rate and price being 0 in calibrating the model. Fitting the interest rate model to ensure that the floors with 0 strike price have no value minimizes the importance of negative interest rate scenarios in derivatives pricing.
   c. It is interesting to note that there were times when some floors on yen rates with 0 strike rate had positive value, suggesting that the market perceived possible negative interest rate scenarios. A lognormal model that prohibits any possibility of negative interest rates would violate this observation in the market.
   d. Some Black models assume the bond price has a lognormal distribution. For example, if we extend the Black–Scholes model to the bond option model, we assume that the bond price follows a lognormal distribution. Then, since the log of the price is by definition proportional to the yield, we would implicitly assume that the interest rate is a normal process. Indeed, the string model suggested by Longstaff and Schwartz implicitly assumes that the interest rates follow a normal model and negative interest rate scenarios are possible.
   e. Finally, this probability measure is a risk-neutral measure and not the market prob-

ability measure. While the normal model allows for negative interest rates, it does not assign any real probability to those scenarios.

2. Consistency with simulations
   a. Random scenarios selected from the lattice can be ensured to be consistent with the pricing of the benchmark securities, because the interest rate model can be calibrated to all the benchmark securities' prices.
   b. For the above reason, we can use the recombining lattice to calibrate the interest rate model, and then use the lattice to determine the Monte Carlo simulations.

3. Simultaneous analysis of related decisions at all the nodes
   a. Since we can relate all the information at each node to information at all other nodes, we can formulate optimal decisions made at all the nodes of a lattice simultaneously, resulting in a global optimal solution.
   b. The main advantage of a normal model is that the interest rate model provides a closed-form solution of the term structure of interest rates at each node point. Since many decisions require the knowledge of the entire term structure, the model provides an efficient method to determine the optimal decisions.

6.10 Key Rate Duration and Dynamic Hedging

Duration

A valuation model of interest rate options or contingent claims enables us to develop the analytics of the securities, as we have done with stock options. The approach is very similar to stock options; they differ mainly in terminologies. Perhaps the most commonly used analytical measure for any interest rate contingent claim is the duration measure.

Duration is defined as the price sensitivity of an interest rate contingent claim to a parallel shift of the spot yield curve. Typically the spot yield curve is assumed to be semiannual compounding. Using an arbitrage-free interest rate model, we can simulate the duration of any interest rate contingent claim by shifting the spot yield curve (which is a model input) upward by a small amount, say five basis points.

As we have shown before, for a default-free zero-coupon bond, the duration turns out to be approximately the maturity. However, for a bond option, duration cannot be interpreted as maturity or time to expiration. For options, there is almost no relationship between the duration measure and the maturity or time to expiration. Indeed, for out-of-the-money call options, the duration can be very high—for example, 100 years. The duration for in-the-money call options approaches the duration of the underlying bond as the option becomes more in the money.

A similar analysis can be conducted for a put option. The bond put option has a negative duration. An out-of-the-money bond put option can have a duration of −100 years, and a deep in-the-money put bond option's duration almost equals the negative of the duration of the underlying bond.

Key Rate Duration

Since an arbitrage-free interest rate model takes the yield curve as given, we can input any shape of the yield curve to the interest rate model and the valuation can still be assured to be consistent with arbitrage-free conditions. Specifically, we can use the shifts of the key rates as inputs to the interest rate model. The *key rate duration* of a bond option is the negative price change of the bond option with the key rate shift divided by the option price and the size of the shift. This definition is the same as the one proposed in chapter 3. Here, we note that since an arbitrage-free interest rate model can take any yield curve as given, we can appropriately define the key rate duration of an interest rate contingent claim using an arbitrage-free interest rate model.

The Black–Scholes model prescribes a methodology in replicating a stock option using the delta as the hedge ratio. We can implement the key rate durations of an interest rate contingent claim to determine the deltas (or hedge ratios) using zero-coupon bonds to dynamically hedge the interest rate contingent claim. Specifically, given an interest rate contingent claim, we can calculate its key rate durations (KRD) for key rates $1, 2, 3, \cdots, N$. Let the price of the contingent claim be P. Let the duration of each zero-coupon bond with maturity T be $D(T)(= T/(1 + r(T)/2))$. Then the dollar amount we should hold to replicate the contingent claim for each zero-coupon bond is

$$X(i) = P \times \frac{KRD(i)}{D(i)} \text{ for } i = 1, 2, 3 \cdots, N$$

That is, given any small change in the ith key rate, the change in the zero-coupon bond value would equal the change in the price of the contingent claim attributed to the change in the key rate. The amount invested in cash is the price P net of all the investments in all the zero-coupon bonds. Cash in this case represents all the short-term payments not captured by the first key rate. The cash portion of the bond has no interest rate sensitivity and therefore is not captured by the equation above. The sum of KRD equals D. This portfolio replicates the interest rate contingent claims.

For example, we consider a call option on a ten-year zero-coupon bond. The option expiration date is five years and the initial yield curve is flat at 5%. The five-year key rate duration is -93.57 and the ten-year key rate duration is 196.67. Therefore the effective duration is 103.10. The call option price is \$1.58437. The durations of the five-year and ten-year zero-coupon bonds are 4.88 and 9.76, respectively. In this case, we sell \$ $-30.2952(= 1.58 \times -93.57/4.878)$ of five-year zero-coupon bonds and buy \$31.8507($= 1.58 \times 196.67/9.7561$) of ten-year bonds. The amount invested in cash is \$0.02887($= \$1.58437 - (31.8507 - 30.2952)$). The bond portfolio of the five-year bond and the ten-year bond replicates the call option over a short time interval. This bond portfolio will be revised, using the above procedure, at the end of this time interval.

Key rate durations of bonds and options

Let us consider some examples: a zero-coupon bond, a call option, and a put option. As we showed in chapter 3, the key rate durations of a T-year zero-coupon bond are all 0 except for the Tth year. That key rate duration is $T/(1 + r/2)$ year at the T year term.

Consider a floating-rate note bond. This bond has a principal of 100 maturing in T years. A floating rate note pays interest as follows. The interest is accrued at the daily LIBOR rate. The accrued amount is paid out at the end of the year. Typically, interest is accrued with a margin (an additional spread) to a short-term interest rate and the interest payments are made quarterly or semiannually.

Although the floating-rate note described above is a bond with interest and principal, its behavior is more like a cash account. The bond is not different from a cash account that accrues interest and withdraws cash at regular intervals. Therefore, for such a floating-rate note, the key rate duration is 0.

Consider a European bond call option. At the expiration date, the call option can buy a zero-coupon bond at the strike price X. The relative pricing model shows that the call option is equivalent to buying the zero-coupon bond on margin. More specifically, we are shorting a zero-coupon bond maturing at the expiration date and buying the underlying zero-coupon bond. It is similar to the replication for a forward contract. However, the hedge ratios to replicate the option are different from that of the forward contract. The ratio of the two bonds is continually adjusted so that the hedging position can replicate the option value. Following this argument, we see that all the key rate durations are 0 except for the key rate duration at the expiration date and the maturity of the bond. The key rate duration is negative at the expiration date and is positive at the maturity. While we all know options have high duration values (are sensitive to interest rate shifts), the result shows that an option typically has an even larger exposure to the bends of the spot curve. A drop in the key rate at the option expiration date with a rise in the rate at the maturity date would simultaneously compound the effect of interest rate risks on the option.

In a similar fashion, we can analyze the key rate durations of a put option. Put options can be replicated by shorting the underlying zero-coupon bond and holding a position of a zero-coupon bond maturing on the expiration date. Again, the ratio of the two bond positions is continually adjusted, depending on the bond values. Therefore the key rate duration of a put option at the expiration date is positive and the key rate duration at the maturity of the underlying bond is negative. (See figures 6.13 and 6.14.)

Dynamic Hedging

The importance of the equity option pricing model is based in large part on the specification of the delta. By specifying the replicating portfolio of an option, the market has a method to exploit any mispricing of an option. When an option is "mispriced," as judged by the Black–Scholes model, a trader can buy the option and sell the replicating portfolio, or vice versa, to realize an arbitrage profit. This can also be achieved

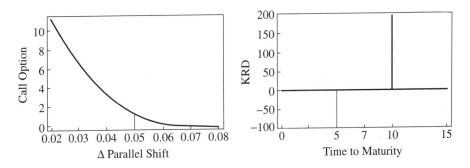

Figure 6.13 The bond call option profile and key rate duration. This figure depicts the performance profile and the key rate durations of a call option on a bond. The maturity of the underlying bond is year 10 and the option expiration date is year 5. The initial term structure is flat at 5%. The exercise price is $78 and the face value is $100. The key rate duration of the bond put option at the expiration date is negative, and the key rate duration at the maturity of the underlying bond is positive.

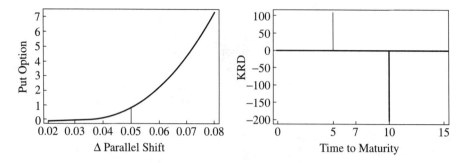

Figure 6.14 The bond put option profile and key rate duration. This figure depicts the performance profile and the key rate duration of a put option on a bond. The maturity of the underlying bond is year 10 and the option expiration date is year 5. The initial term structure is flat at 5%. The exercise price is $78 and the face value is $100. The key rate duration of the bond put option at the expiration date is positive, and the key rate duration at the maturity of the underlying bond is negative.

in the bond option market. But for an interest rate option, in most cases we cannot use only one bond. We need to use the entire yield curve to hedge the interest rate option.

To extend the concept of hedging to interest rate options, we need to use more than one sensitivity number (delta); we need a vector of numbers. Key rate duration is based on the understanding that the yield curve movements are influenced by benchmark bonds in the market. Benchmark bonds are bonds with certain maturities that the market follows. Other bond yields tend to follow a blend of the yields for these bonds. For example, two-year and three-year Treasury bonds are benchmark bonds because the U.S. Treasury issues them, and the market accepts them as benchmark bonds. A bond with a maturity of 2.5 years is often quoted with a yield having a spread relative to the average of the two-year and three-year bond yields.

Therefore the movement of an entire yield curve is greatly affected by the key rate movements. Given an option with calculated key rate durations, we can construct a portfolio of bonds with no embedded options such that it has the same key rate durations and the same value as the option. This portfolio must dynamically replicate the option. If we want to hedge the option, then we should short this replicating portfolio. Holding the option and the short position of the replicating portfolio would lead to a dynamic hedging strategy instead of a dynamic replicating strategy.

If any option is priced above the arbitrage-free valuation, in theory we should sell the option and long the replicating portfolio of bonds (or swaps) based on fair value. The difference between the option price and the fair value (which is the same as the cost of the replicating portfolio) is the arbitrage profit. Similarly, if the option price is below the fair value of the arbitrage-free valuation, then the model suggests that we buy the option and sell the replicating portfolio.

Convexity

Convexity, like the gamma of a stock option, measures the curvature of a price behavior. It is a historical accident that the converse of convexity is not concavity. There is no concavity. Therefore, we distinguish the option behavior as positive convexity or negative convexity. The measure is defined as

$$C = \frac{1}{2}\frac{\partial^2 P}{\partial r^2} \bigg/ P \tag{6.17}$$

The definition comes from the expression of a Taylor expansion.

$$\Delta P = -D \cdot P\Delta r + C \cdot P(\Delta r)^2 \tag{6.18}$$

A call option has positive duration because its value increases with the fall in interest rates. The option also has positive convexity. That means that when interest rates move up or down significantly, the option gains higher value than that predicted by the duration. The additional returns are attributed to the positive convexity.

A put option has negative duration because when interest rates fall, the option value falls along with them. However, since options always provide the holder with downside protection while offering upside returns, the put option also has positive convexity.

6.11   Pathwise Valuation and Decomposition of an Option

In Chapter 3 we discussed alternative methods to the backward substitution approach in pricing a European stock option, and in chapter 5 we introduced the backward substitution approach to price vanilla European bond options. Do we also have alternative methods for pricing these options with interest rate risks? The answer is yes.

As with an equity option, we can value a bond option by calculating the mean of all its pathwise values. Consider a binomial lattice of a one-factor interest rate model. For a simple explanation, we will consider only a one-factor model, even though extending to an n-factor model is straightforward. At each node point on the lattice, (n, i), the interest rate model assigns the one-period interest rate $r(n, i, 1)$ or the discount factor $P(n, i, 1) = 1/(1 + r(n, i, 1))$. An interest rate path is a path, $p(k)$, taken from the binomial lattice. A path is a possible interest rate scenario in which the yield curve may move up or down from each node, starting from the initial date and ending at the last node on the binomial lattice. Also, we can list all the possible scenarios in the binomial lattice of interest rate movements, and there are 2^N distinct paths in a binomial lattice with N steps. The complete set of interest rate paths of a binomial lattice is called the path space.

Now we have a representation of a bond or an interest rate derivative. Given an interest rate derivative or a bond along each interest rate path, we can assign a cash flow to the path. That means that on the condition that the interest rates take a particular scenario, we will realize the (nonstochastic) cash flow of the option. This set of cash flows for all the paths is a representation of the bond or the interest rate derivative.

For example, a five-year zero-coupon bond assigns $100 at the end of the fifth year for all the interest rate paths. If two bonds or interest rate derivatives have the same set of cash flows, then the two securities are identical as far as using the binomial lattice is concerned. This is because, in essence, the two have identical cash flows for any interest rate scenario that occurs within the context of the modeling framework.

For each path, we can now discount the cash flow along this scenario by the short-term rates $r(n, i)$ of the path. The present value, called the pathwise value, is denoted by

$PWV(k)$, where k denotes the index for the path. The pathwise value can be interpreted as the present value of the cash flow if such an interest rate scenario occurs. If two bonds (or derivatives) have the same set of pathwise values, then they are equivalent in the following sense: If we reinvest all the cash flows at the current interest rate at each node point, then the two securities will have the same value at the end of the interest rate paths (or the interest rate scenario). Further, the mean of the pathwise values (assuming that we take the risk-neutral probability to be 0.5, so that all scenarios are equally weighted) is the price of the securities as derived by the backward substitution method. These pathwise values provide a systematic way to decompose a derivative into its components.

Primary Decomposition

Consider the case when we apply an arbitrage-free interest rate model to value a security (a bond or an interest rate derivative) using a 0 volatility. We know that all the interest rate scenarios will be that of the forward rates. In this case, the cash flow assigned to the scenarios is that of the security, based on the condition that forward rates prevail at the future dates. That is, all the interest rates in the future are those specified by the forward rates.

We now determine the pathwise values of this cash flow, denoted by $PWV^p(k)$. The superscript p indicates that this set of pathwise values represents the *primary decomposition* of the security. Since this set of values is determined in the case of no interest rate volatility, if the set of pathwise values of the security differs from the set of the pathwise values of the cash flow, $PWV^p(k)$, then the security must have a cash flow for a particular interest rate path that is sensitive to uncertain interest rates, or the security has an embedded option.

Secondary Decomposition

Now consider the pathwise values of the security net of the pathwise values of the primary decomposition.

$$v(k) = PWV(k) - PWV^p(k) \quad \text{for each } k = 1, 2, \cdots, 2^N$$

This net value represents the deviations of the pathwise values of the security from the pathwise values of a cash flow. Now we can have a procedure to determine the decomposition of the derivatives. We do so by first calculating the pathwise values of the benchmark securities that we have selected to calibrate the interest rate risk model. Let these pathwise values be $PWV^j(k)$, for $j = 1, \cdots, M$, where M is the number of all the benchmark securities.

A decomposition can be established if we can determine a set of coefficients $a_j, j = 0, 1 \cdots, M$, such that

$$v(k) = a_0 + a_1 PWV^1(k) + a_2 PWV^2(k) + \cdots + a_M PWV^M(k) \text{ for each } k = 1, 2, \cdots, 2^N$$

This fitting can be achieved through linear regression, using $PWV^j(k)$ as independent variables. Each coefficient represents the number of each benchmark security needed for the decomposition. In general the equation above cannot hold exactly, and the goodness of the decomposition can be judged by the explanatory power of the regression. The intercept a_0 denotes the cash amount.

In summary, by using the arbitrage-free interest rate model, we can determine a decomposition of securities into a cash flow and a portfolio of the benchmark securities. The cash flow is determined by the primary decomposition, and the portfolio of the benchmark securities is determined by the *secondary decomposition*. This method is appropriate for securities that do not have primary decomposition. For example, floating-rate instruments are often decomposed into cash and caps and floors. Fixed-rate bonds are not appropriate benchmark securities.

Similar to the decomposition of an equity option, we assume that the pathwise values of the security are the same as those of the portfolio of securities determined in the decomposition. Then, if all the net cash flows are invested or borrowed at the current interest rate, then the accumulated values at the end of the horizon for all interest rate paths are the same for the securities and the portfolio. Pathwise values are a tool to represent a complex option, or an option-embedded bond, by a portfolio of benchmark options. In other words, we have a tool to decompose an option to other options that are considered the primary building blocks of derivatives.

6.12   Intuitive Explanation of the Bond Option Valuation

Similar to equity options, the development of the theoretical valuation of bond options can seem logical and reasonable, but the actual applications often lead to counterintuitive conclusions.

Consider the Treasury yield curve in December 1992, depicted in figure 6.15. The yield curve at the time was very positively steep. The understanding at the time was that the monetary policy sought to lower the interest rate in order to stimulate the economy. The Federal Reserve Bank lowered the bank rate, leading to a positively sloped curve. In

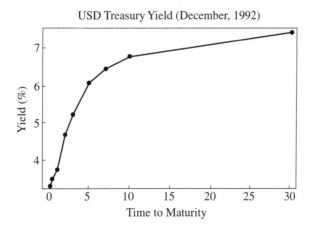

Figure 6.15 USD treasury constant maturity rate, December 1992 (monthly sample). This figure shows the USD yield curve in December 1992. At times it was very positively steep. The Federal Reserve Bank lowered the bank rate, leading to a positively sloped yield curve. Data from http://www.economagic.com/.

this situation, as chapter 2 shows, forward rates (calculated from the spot rates) increased rapidly. Many market participants did not consider forward rates close to reflecting the market expectation of future interest rates. The rapidly rising forward rates, or the positively steep spot yield curve, is simply a market "technical" factor, an imbalance of supply and demand.

However, an arbitrage-free pricing of a cap is based on the forward rate. In such a scenario, the likelihood of interest rates rising above the strike rates under risk-neutral pricing becomes very high. A market comparing such cap prices with the true expectation of the market view would find these caps trading very "rich." Anyone buying such a cap would be paying a high price for the unlikely event of interest rates rising so high in the future.

These investors would be willing to sell these caps even below the arbitrage-free pricing. On the opposite side of the trade, the buyer of these caps would dynamically hedge this cap position. The hedge would require the buying of long-term bonds and shorting the short-term bond. This exactly reflects the view that the long-term bonds have become a preferred investment. Therefore the "mispricing" of the option using an arbitrage-free model simply reflects the "mispricing" of the underlying spot curve. Any trading of the option differing from the arbitrage-free pricing would only lead to arbitrage opportunity for other market participants.

The arbitrage-free price is the fair price only in terms of arbitrage pricing. If we buy the cap at a price lower than the arbitrage-free price, that in itself does not provide a higher likelihood of positive returns. We are just betting against the view of the seller of the cap. We can profit from the trade only if we hedge against the cap position, using dynamic hedging strategy. If we do not hedge and wait for the cap price to converge to the arbitrage-free price, then the underlying yield curve can move and the uncertainty of the trading position can be quite risky.

6.13   Lecture on Convexity

At 7:30 P.M. on Tuesday, I took a deep breath before my lecture on duration and convexity in my class on fixed-income securities for second-year MBAs. I would go through durations during the first half of the lecture. What I dreaded was the second half of the lecture, on convexity. Using the equation where "convexity is defined as the second-order term of the Taylor expansion" never went well in class, especially on a Tuesday evening when the students were already tired. In the past, students had told me that they did not want to use calculus to explain convexity.

One year, some students complained to the associate dean about my convexity lecture. They stated that I never said the "Taylor expansion" was a prerequisite for the fixed-income securities course. When someone in the class asked me if the "second-order term" would be on the exam, there was almost a rebellion when I said yes.

Then how should I explain convexity? When the lecture reached the point that I had to explain convexity, I walked to one end of the lecture hall and said, "Imagine the interest rates are falling steadily. I am the bond price, and I have no convexity. You can see now the price is steadily rising." I walked steadily across the hall

Then I walked to the other side of the hall and said, "This bond has positive convexity." This time, I walked across the hall and accelerated my pace halfway through. "See, this is a great bond when the rates fall." Some giggles . . . some reactions.

Then I walked back to the other side of the hall. "This is a callable bond." I started walking, and then accelerated. As I approached the wall, I rapidly decelerated, raising my voice. "The bond has become negatively convex." I hit the wall gently. "I got called," I announced. The class laughed heartily.

My informal survey suggested that this class actually remembered the convexity concept. But I never could bring myself to do the performance again. The theatrical style was too draining for a research academic like myself.

6.14 Summary

This chapter considers an important issue in the implementation of an arbitrage-free interest rate model. The problem is to measure the future interest rate risks that determine the option price.

Often market-implied volatilities are used to deal with this issue; they are solved for by using benchmark securities prices. We discussed the market convention in the use of market models to provide the market quotes in terms of implied volatilities, as well as such conventions in more detail, with bond options, swaptions, and caps and floors.

We then showed the applications of the interest rate models. The valuation model is consistent with the replication using dynamic hedging, because the Black–Scholes model ensures that the stock option price can be used for determining the replicating portfolio. The analytics used to determine dynamic hedging portfolios are the key rate durations. We also showed that the valuation of interest rate contingent claims can be accomplished by using the pathwise values calculated from the interest rate model. The pathwise values can also be used in static hedging, as in the case of an equity option.

In chapters 3–5 we discussed the valuation of vanilla stock and bond options. However, in practice there are many types of options that cannot be priced by the straightforward backward substitution approach. Adjustments have to be made in this method to ensure that we can value a broad range of financial options, contingent on stock or interest rate risks. These variations of the methodology in valuing different types of options (often called exotic options) will be explored in chapter 7.

Note

1. LSS proposed using the swaption prices.

References

Aït-Sahalia, Y., and A. Lo. 2000. Nonparametric estimation of state-price densities implicit in financial asset prices. *Journal of Finance*, 53, 499–548.

Amin, K. I., and A. J. Morton. 1994. Implied volatility functions in arbitrage-free term structure models. *Journal of Financial Economics*, 35 (2), 141–180.

Andersen, L. 1999/2000. A simple approach to the pricing of Bermudan swaptions in the multifactor LIBOR market model. *Journal of Computational Finance*, 3 (2), 5–32.

Andersen, L., and J. Andreasen. 2000. Volatility skews and extensions of the LIBOR market model. *Applied Mathematical Finance*, 7, 1–32.

Black, F. 1976. The pricing of commodity contracts. *Journal of Financial Economics*, 3, 167–179.

Brace, A., D. Gatarek, and M. Musiela. 1997. The market model of interest rate dynamics. *Mathematical Finance*, 7, 127–155.

Chriss, N. 1996. Transatlantic trees. *RISK*, July, 45–48.

Das, S. R., and R. K. Sundaram. 1999. Of smiles and smirks: A term structure perspective. *Journal of Financial and Quantitative Analysis*, 34 (2), 211–240.

Derman, E. 1999. Regimes of volatility. *RISK*, April, 55–59.

Derman, E., and I. Kani. 1994a. Riding on a smile. *RISK*, February, 32–39.

Derman, E., and I. Kani. 1994b. The volatility smile and its implied tree. *Quantitative Strategies Research Notes* January, 1–20 (Goldman Sachs)

Dupire, B. 1994. Pricing with a smile. *RISK*, January, 18–20.

Goldstein, R. 2000. The term structure of interest rates as a random field. *Review of Financial Studies*, 13, 365–384.

Heath, D., R. Jarrow, and A. Morton. 1992. Bond pricing and the term structure of interest rates: A new methodology for contingent claims valuation. *Econometrica*, 60, 77–105.

Heath, D., R. Jarrow, A. Morton, and M. Spindel. 1993. Easier done than said. *RISK*, May, 77–80.

Heston, S. 1993. A closed-form solution for options with stochastic volatility with applications to bond and currency options. *Review of Financial Studies*, 6, 327–343.

Heynen, R., A. Kemna, and T. Vorst. 1994. Analysis of the term structure of implied volatilities. *Journal of Financial and Quantitative Analysis*, 29 (1), 31–56.

Hull, J., and A. White. 1987. The pricing of options on assets with stochastic volatilities. *Journal of Finance*, 42, 281–300.

Hull, J., and A. White. 2000. Forward rate volatilities, swap rate volatilities, and the implementation of the LIBOR market model. *Journal of Fixed Income*, 10 (2), 46–62.

Jamshidian, F. 1997. LIBOR and swap market models and measures. *Finance and Stochastics*, 1, 293–330.

Jäckel, P. 2000a. Non-recombining trees for the pricing of interest rate derivatives in the BGM/J framework. Working paper, Quantitative Research Centre, Royal Bank of Scotland.

Jäckel, P. 2000b. Monte Carlo in the BGM/J framework: Using a non-recombining tree to design a new pricing method for Bermudan swaptions. Working paper, *Quantitative Research Centre*, Royal Bank of Scotland.

Jäckel, P., and R. Rebonato. 2000. Linking caplet and swaption volatilities in a BGM/J framework: Approximate solutions. Working paper, Quantitative Research Centre, Royal Bank of Scotland.

Jackwerth, J. C. 1997. Generalized binomial trees. Working paper, University of California, Berkeley.

Jackwerth, J. C., and M. Rubinstein. 1996. Recovering probability distributions from option prices. *Journal of Finance*, 51, 1611–1631.

Longstaff, F., P. Santa-Clara, and E. Schwartz. 2000. The relative valuation of caps and swaptions: Theory and empirical evidence. Working paper, The Anderson School of UCLA, September.

Longstaff, F., and E. Schwartz. 2001. Valuing American options by simulation: A least squares approach. *Review of Financial Studies*, 14 (1), 113–147.

Rebonato, R. 1999. On the simultaneous calibration of multifactor lognormal interest rate models to black volatilities and to the correlation matrix. *Journal of Computational Finance*, 2 (4), 5–27.

Rosenberg, J. V. 2000. Implied volatility functions: A reprise. *Journal of Derivatives*, 7 (3), 51–64.

Rubinstein, M. 1994. Implied binomial trees. *Journal of Finance*, 49, 771–818.

Santa-Clara, P., and D. Sornette. 2001. The dynamics of the forward interest rate curve with stochastic string shocks. *Review of Financial Studies*, 14 (1), 149–185.

Shimko, D. 1993. Bounds of probability. *RISK*, 6, 33–37.

Further Readings

Aït-Sahalia, Y. 1996. Nonparametric pricing of interest rate derivative securities. *Econometrica*, 64 (3), 527–560.

Gatarek, D. 2000. Modelling without tears. *Risk*, 13, September, 20–24.

Lewicki, P., and M. Avellaneda. 1996. Pricing interest rate contingent claims in markets with uncertain volatilities. Working paper, Courant Institute of Mathematical Science, New York.

Pelsser, A. 2001. Mathematical foundation of convexity correction. Working paper, Erasmus University, Rotterdam.

Rebonato, R., and M. Joshi. 2001. A joint empirical and theoretical investigation of the models of deformation of swaption matrices: Implication for model choice. Working paper, Quantitative Research Centre, Royal Bank of Scotland.

Zhu, Y., and M. Avellaneda. 1998. A risk-neutral stochastic volatility model. *International Journal of Theoretical and Applied Finance*, 1 (2), 289–310.

7

Exotic Options: Bellman's Optimization, the Filtration Model, and the n-Factor Model

There is a broad range of derivatives in equities, interest rates, and currencies. We need a systematic approach to value them: (1) identify the derivatives as generic types, including European, American, Bermudan, or Asian options; (2) base the valuation method on five important techniques: backward substitutions, filtration model, Bellman optimization, pathwise method, and multifactor modeling. Using a general consistent framework of valuation enables us to develop portfolio strategies and enterprise risk management systems without being narrowly confined to single security pricing and analysis.

In previous chapters we have covered vanilla options regarding two main risk sources: stock price and interest rates. Specifically, we have considered European call and put options. These options, while simple in their terms and conditions, capture the salient features of an option. And the sources of risks that we have described enable us to understand a broad range of risk sources and how they affect option values and characteristics. The previous chapters have provided the principles behind the option pricing and the framework to analyze options we need to make the transition from theory to practical applications.

In practice, options are not simply European put and call options. Nor do options often have one underlying risk source (e.g., the stock price risk). There is a broad range of options. Finance is a social science, not a natural one. Options are made and designed every day, and they are not found in nature. Making an exhaustive list of possible options found in the market may be a futile exercise.

What is useful is to describe the types of options in terms of their economics. What are the designs in the options that make them valuable? What options can we use as building blocks for other options? Which options are similar in terms of their economics even though they have different names? These are the questions that this chapter will seek to answer.

Exotic options are options that are not standard—in our case, any options that are not European. Elsewhere, many option types are considered standard, and exotic options are options not commonly used. The purpose of this chapter is to provide an overview of different important features of options.

Options apply to any underlying asset, whether it is a stock, a bond, an exchange rate, or a stock index. The valuation methodology using binomial lattices is also basically the same for any of the underlying securities, as long as the derivative can be dynamically hedged by the underlying securities and relative valuation applies. "A European call option on an American call option on the maximum of GE and AIG digital" may seem like a string of words. This chapter will provide an explanation and a framework—like a recipe—to value such an option.

This chapter will describe some of the generic exotic options in a taxonomy that builds on increasing complexity in their features. These features are early exercise of the options (American) and look-back options (Asian). The three important valuation techniques that this chapter will use are (1) the Bellman dynamic programming method, (2) the filtration model, and (3) the multifactor model.

The Bellman dynamic programming method enables us to solve for the optimal early exercise rule, and the filtration model construction enables us to have some memory of what has happened in the past along a possible scenario path, so that we can value the options whose payoffs depend on historical information. The multifactor model will represent all the possible outcomes of multiple risk sources from the binomial lattice. We will see how these three valuation methods can be applied to pricing exotic options that have complicated payoffs resulting from multiple risk sources

7.1   Options with Alternative Payoffs at Expiration

European stock options or bond options have a relatively simple specification of the payoff at the terminal date; the payment is $Max\,[S_T - X, 0]$ for a call option. But the payoff can take alternative specifications. One example is a digital option (or binary option).

The *binary option* pays $\$Q$ if the underlying assets has a value above the strike price on the expiration date. There is no payment if the underlying asset has a value below the strike price. There are two main differences between a digital option and a European call option. First, the payoff function is discontinuous at the strike price for the digital option. That means that near the expiration, implementing a delta hedge will be difficult.

Second, the payoff of the digital option is truncated on the upside. The maximum payment is Q. For a deep-in-the-money option, the expected payoff in all likelihood will be a fixed payment of Q at expiration. Therefore, the option will behave like a bond.

Consider an option that is out of the money. As the stock value rises, the option value increases at an accelerated pace because the likelihood of being paid Q increases. We then have positive gamma. In this region, we will also have time decay effect.

As the stock price continues to rise, the positive gamma turns into a negative gamma. This is because a digital option has the payoff capped at Q. In this region, there is a significant downside risk that the option will pay nothing when the stock price falls, but there is a limited upside, capped at Q. As the stock price increases, the option value reaches its maximum of the present value of Q. As time passes, and if the stock price remains unchanged, the option will appreciate in value as the likelihood of receiving payment Q increases. (See figure 7.1.)

The valuation method is the same as the European option. We will roll back the value from the terminal date. We assume that the stock price is 100, the exercise price is 100, the stock volatility is 10%, the time to maturity is one year, the continuously compounding risk-free rate is 10%, and the number of partitions is six. (See figure 7.2.)

If we think that the underlying asset price will be above the strike price at expiration, we might buy either a European call or a digital call. The European call has upside potential, growing with the underlying asset price beyond the strike price, whereas the digital option can never pay off more than Q. If we expect the underlying asset to rise significantly, then we should buy the European call; otherwise, we should consider the

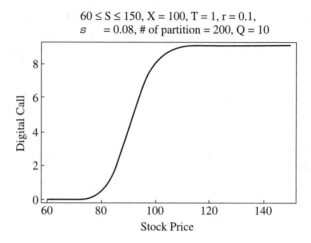

Figure 7-1 Performance profile of a digital option. The digital call option pays $10 (Q) if the stock price exceeds $100 (X) at time period 1; otherwise there is no payment. The standard call option pays $Max[S - X, 0]$ at time period 1. The stock price varies from 60 to 150 for simultion purposes. The continuously compounding risk-free rate is 10%. The stock volatility is 0.08. We partition one period into 200 sub-periods to enhance the accuracy.

digital call, which may cost less because it does not give the potentially high returns that are offered by the European call.

Digital options can be used as building blocks for European options. For example, suppose the European option has a strike price of $10. Then let us hold a portfolio of digital options, one option for each strike price: $10, $11, $12, ⋯, with $Q = \$1$. We can see that this portfolio of digital options has a payoff at the expiration similar to that of the European option. Therefore, in general, a portfolio of digital options with different strike prices with payoff Q can approximate a European option because its payoff schedule approximates that of the European option.

If we long a digital option and short another with a higher strike, it leads to a security that has a payoff for a range of stock prices. Using this combination of digital options, we can construct a broad range of payoffs for a portfolio of options. We can also create more gamma by increasing the number of digital options with increasing strike price. The payoff can be a power function like S^n to the payoff function at the expiration of the option, where S is the stock price and the n is some number. Therefore, this payment is no longer one-to-one with the stock price but a power of the stock price. Creating a high gamma leads to an accelerated positive payoff when the stock price rises. The holder can benefit more from the stock price increase.

7.2   Options with Boundary Conditions

Options may have conditions, called *boundary conditions*, imposed on the payoff from the initial date to the expiration date. An important example of this type of option is the barrier option. There are two kinds of barrier options. The *knockout* option is a European put or call option that ceases to exist when the underlying stock reaches the barrier (a prespecified stock level), which may be above or below the current stock price,

Stock Lattice

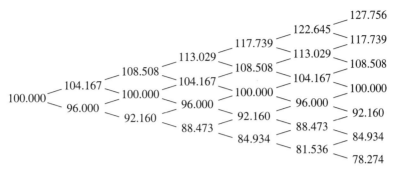

Digital Option Lattice

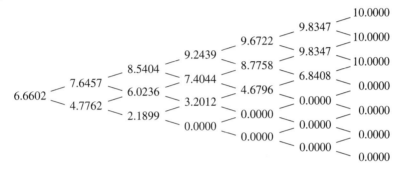

Figure 7-2 The binomial Lattice of a digital option. The binomial lattice of the stock prices is shown in the upper panel. We assume that the initial stock price is 100, the stock volatility is 10%, the time to maturity is 1 year, and the continuously compounding risk-free rate is 10%. Since the number of partitions is 6, we adjust the upward parameter, u, the downward parameter, d, and the risk-free rate over one sub-period to 1.04167, 0.959997, and 0.01681, respectively. The risk-neutral probability is 0.695573.

$$u = \exp\left\{\sigma\sqrt{\frac{1}{m}}\right\} = 1.04167, d = \frac{1}{u} = 0.959997, S = 100, \sigma = 0.1, r = 0.1, T = 1$$

$$p = \frac{\exp\left[\frac{r}{m}\right] - d}{u - d} = 0.695573, 1 - p - 0.304427, m = 6$$

The binomial lattice of the digital option is represented in the lower panel. At maturity, the digital option prices are Q if the stock prices exceed the exercise price. At one subperiod before the maturity, the digital option prices are determined by backward substitition. For example, we get 9.8347 by discounting the expected value with the risk-free rate over one subperiod. That is $(10 * 0.695573 + 10 * 0.304427)/1.01681$.

any time before the expiration. The *knock-in* option is a European option (put or call) which comes into existence whenever the underlying stock reaches the barrier any time before expiration.

The economic reason for the design of the barrier option is to allow the investor to buy or sell options at any stock price level, which is not subject to the current stock price. In the other words, we can activate or deactivate an option depending on the prevailing stock price over a horizon period.

The barrier option is the same as the European option except for one important feature: it depends on the path of the stock price. If a stock falls below the barrier and rises back to the initial value, the knockout option will have no value, because as soon as the stock reaches the barrier, the option expires. However, a European option value stays alive until the expiration date. Thus we can say that the barrier option is *path-dependent*. Similarly, for the knock-in option, if the stock falls below the barrier and rises back, the option will have value. However, if the stock price stays constant, the knock-in option has no value. Therefore, the knock-in option also is path-dependent.

Consider the following example. Let C be a European call option with strike price X and time to maturity T. Suppose that we have a knockout barrier at X (the strike price). Then the option pays nothing if the stock price falls below X at any time before expiration. Such a barrier option should be worth less than the equivalent European option. The barrier may be referred to as the absorption barrier, since the option expires when the stock price hits the barrier and the option is "absorbed."

We can use the rolling-back method on a binomial lattice to value such a barrier option. We assume that the option survives and is not absorbed until the expiration. We know the payoff, and we roll back to one step before expiration. For all the nodes (state and time) that the stock price falls below the strike, we let the option price be 0. Then we proceed to use backward substitution until we reach the initial time, and that is the price of the option. (See figures 7.3 and 7.4.)

The European knockout call option becomes a standard European call option whenever the underlying stock prices do not touch the barrier before expiration. The European knock-in call option becomes a standard European call option whenever the underlying stock prices reach the barrier before expiration. Since the probability that stock prices will or will not touch the barrier is 1, a portfolio of a European knockout call option and a European knock-in call option is a standard European call option.

$$\text{Knock-out} + \text{Knock-in} = \text{European Call Option}$$

If we want to have a call option when the stock price reaches a certain level, we can buy a knock-in option today. Thus, we have bought such a strategy at a fixed price. By contrast, if we buy the call option when the stock meets the price level, the option cost will be uncertain because the option price depends on when the stock price hits the barrier.

7.3   Options with the Early Exercise Feature (American) and the Bellman Optimization

Early exercise is a feature that allows the holder to exercise the option at any time before, and right up to, the expiration date, not just at the expiration date (as in the case of a European option). This type of option, called the *American option*, can apply to a call or put option.

An American option has an added feature that can only be valuable for the holder. The holder can always treat an American option as a European option without bothering to exercise early, and therefore an American option should be valued higher than or equal to the European option. The possibility of the early exercise feature having no value (that means the European option is priced identically to the American option) exists

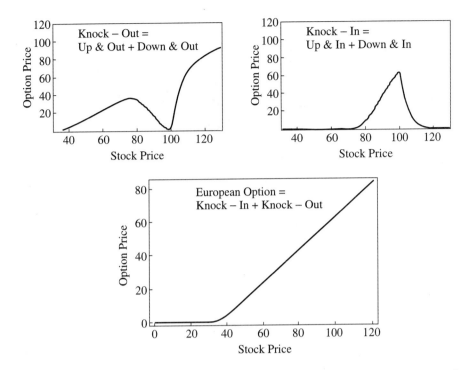

Figure 7-3 Performance profile of knock-in and knockout options. The European knockout call option becomes a standard European call option whenever the underlying stock price does not touch the barrier before expiration. If it touches, the European knockout call option is worthless even though the stock price is above the strike price at the maturity. The stock price varies from 30 to 130 for simulation purposes. The continuously compounding risk-free rate is 10%. The variance of the stock returns is 0.1. The time to maturity is 1 year. The knockout barrier is 100 and the strike price is 40. We partition one year into 100 subperiods to enhance the accuracy. The uper-left diagram shows two knockout options. One is up and out and the other is down and out. The up and out knockout option has value when the stock prices are below 100, which is the knockout barrier. The down and out knockout option has value when above 100, which is the knockout barrier. Similar interpretation can be given to the knock-in options in the upper-right diagram. If we combine the two options, we get the European option profile shown in the lower diagram.

because it is possible that for some options it is never profitable to exercise them early. For example, we will show that an American call option on a nondividend-paying stock should be priced like a Europe call option because there is no rational reason to exercise the option early.

One common variation of an American option is called the *Bermuda* option. A Bermuda option allows the holder to exercise the option at certain times, for example, at the end of each month or each week. Therefore, it is similar to an American option in that it can be exercised early—but only at specific dates, instead of at any time.

An American option is similar to a barrier option in terms of being path-dependent; the stock price may reach a level that makes early exercise desirable. It is different from a barrier option because the early exercise decision may not be a simple rule that is specified in the term sheet of the option. The exercise rule depends on the investor. Indeed, the American option introduces an important aspect to option decisions in finance. The

Stock Price Lattice

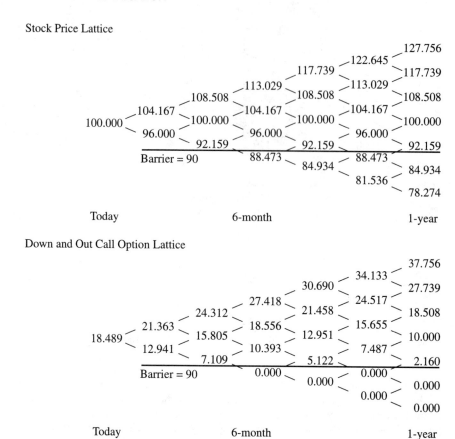

Down and Out Call Option Lattice

Figure 7-4 The binomial lattice for barrier option pricing (European knockout call option). The European knockout call option becomes a standard European call option whenever the underlying stock prices do not touch the barrier before expiration. The initial stock price is 100 and the barrier is 90. Therefore, if the stock price touches 90, the option will expire. The strike price is 90. As we can see in the second panel, the knockout option is nil below the stock price of 90, which is the barrier.

questions the American option poses are as follows: Is there an optimal early exercise rule that a rational investor should follow? If such a rule exists, what is it?

Understanding this optimal early exercise rule is central to pricing an American option. More important, the concept is applicable to many financial theories that can be used to model an individual's behavior in the capital market. For this reason, we will first discuss a mathematical concept introduced by Bellman. The decision rule is dynamic in the sense that it depends on the current state of the world: the stock price, time to expiration, and all the other market variables. Therefore the decision has to be revised continually—and hence is dynamic.

The pricing of American options requires an extra argument. The initial price of an American option must depend on its optimal exercise at any future time prior to the expiration date. We must consider all the stock price paths and the optimal exercise point, and discount the payoff at the risk-free rate to determine the present value. The option price is the highest of all the possible exercise rules. A rule such as "exercise when the stock price reaches a certain level at time t without any dip in the price history" may be included. The optimal exercise rule is to search for such a rule that maximizes the value of an option. This would be an enormous search. For example, we can search through the binomial tree and explore all the possible early exercise rules. Given that any exercise rule can determine an option price, we can in principle search for a solution. However, this search to determine the optimal value seems mathematically intractable.

The *Bellman optimization* procedure provides a very elegant solution to this problem. Bellman's argument proposes that if the option price is given by the optimal exercise strategy, then that strategy has to be optimal over any period. This means that at any time before expiration, the optimal exercise rule must assume that it will be used in the subsequent time steps.

Following Bellman's argument, we must therefore solve the problem backward. At time $(n-1)$, we need to decide whether we would exercise the option. The optimal rule, therefore, states that we should exercise the option if the payoff is higher than the option price. Therefore, the option price at each node is the maximum of the option payoff if exercised early at that node and the rolled-back option value. We repeat this procedure iteratively backward from step n-2 to step 0.

The results show that the Bellman optimal decision depends on the current option price, which is determined by the stock price and other parameters of the option model. The optimal rule takes the value of waiting into account. Since the option can be exercised only once, we need to consider the probability of future stock price movements. Bellman's solution takes all the future contingencies into consideration and decides what action is optimal at present, and it does not look only at the immediate future.

In an American call option on a stock that does not pay dividends, there should be no optimal early exercise. The option holder should never exercise the option early, because he is always better off selling the option than exercising it. This assertion can be derived as follows. First, note that the option price should always be above the stock price net of the present value of the strike price.

$$C > S - PV(X) > S - X \tag{7.1}$$

If not (i.e., $C \leq S - PV(X)$), we should buy the call option, short the stock, and invest the present value of the strike price at the risk-free rate. The net investment is the arbitrage profit, because the payoff at the expiration of this arbitrage position is always positive. At the expiration, the cash flow of the arbitrage position is $Max[S - X, 0] - S + X$, which is always positive or 0 regardless of S relative to X. It follows that the call option value at any time must exceed the stock price net the exercise price. Thus, at any node point on the binomial lattice, the call option price is never below the value of earlier exercise $(S - X)$, and hence there should be no early exercise.

However, this is not the case with put options. By the same argument made above, put options should always trade above the present value of the exercise price net of the stock price.

$$P > PV(X) - S \tag{7.2}$$

But in this case, it is possible for the put option to have a value less than the strike price (not the present value of the strike price) net of the stock price (i.e., $X - S > P > PV(X) - S$). In these instances, early exercise of the put option is optimal, because the put option holder will get $X - S$ by exercising the option. However, the put option

$60 \leq S \leq 150,\ X = 100,\ s = 0.5,$
$T = 0.25,\ r = 0.1,\ \#\ \text{of partitions} = 20$

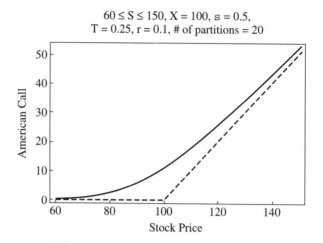

Figure 7-5 Performance profile of an American call option. The American call option has an early exercise feature that the holder can exercise before the expiration date, which is the only difference from the European counterpart. To properly price the American options, we should determine the early exercise boundary, which is not a simple job. However, since the American call option on nondividend-paying stocks will never exercise early, we price the American call option as if it were the European call option. The stock price varies from 60 to 150 for simulation purposes. The continuously compounding risk-free rate is 10%. The variance of the stock returns is 0.5. The time to maturity is 0.25 year. We partition a period of 0.25 year into 20 subperiods to enhance the accuracy.

holder will get P by selling it. Therefore, it is to his benefit to exercise early rather than sell it. (See figures 7.5–7.7.)

The value of the early exercise option of an American put option can be analyzed. Figure 7.8 plots of the American put option and the European put option.

Both the American put option and the dividend-paying American call option have values for early exercise. As we have shown, the put–call parity does not allow any possibility of early exercise, and therefore the parity condition does not hold for American options. Unfortunately, most options on the exchanges are American, and any put–call parity trading strategies have to take early optimal exercise into consideration.

An American option offering holders early exercise is valuable in many ways. In practice, there are times when there may be liquidity problems in the option market. Selling an option at an inappropriate time may be expensive. An American option offers flexibility to the holder.

Using a similar method, we can value the Bermuda put option. In this case, we apply the optimal decision rule only at the specified exercise dates. (See figure 7.9.)

An Intuitive Explanation of the Bellman Optimization Solution

Determining an optimal dynamic rule is very valuable for financial decisions. For this reason, an extended discussion of the intuition behind this optimization method is in order. The intuition can be related by using an anecdote.

A physicist sitting in his backyard saw an apple on the grass. An ant was crawling from the bottom of the apple to the top. The physicist picked up the apple, and traced

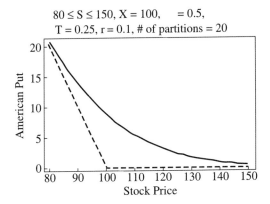

$80 \le S \le 150$, X = 100,   = 0.5,
T = 0.25, r = 0.1, # of partitions = 20

Figure 7-6 Performance profile of an American put option. The American put option has an early exercise feature that the holders can exercise before the expiration date, which is the only difference from European counterparts. To properly price American options, we should determine the early exercise boundary, which is not a simple job. For this reason, we do not have a closed-form solution for American put options. The stock price varies from 80 to 150 for simulation purposes. The continuously compounding risk-free rate is 10%. The variance of the stock returns is 0.5. The time to maturity is 0.25 year. We partition a period of 0.25 year into 20 subperiods to enhance the accuracy.

the path of the ant on the apple. Next he took a rubber band and anchored its ends at the beginning of the path and the end of the path. He found that the rubber band lay on top of the ant's path, demonstrating that the ant took the shortest distance between two points.

This was somewhat surprising to the physicist. How could an ant possibly know that it was taking the shortest path between two points far apart, when it could feel and see only a rather short distance? How should the ant make the decision for each step forward?

Consider the ant that is standing on the apple, pondering the next step. Bellman's optimization solution says that the ant should take the next step that has the shortest distance between the point where it took the last step the point where it will be in the next step. The ant has to make optimal local decisions. For a path that is optimal globally, from one point of the apple to another point far away, we must require the path to be optimal locally, ensuring that it is the shortest from the last step to the next step.

In pricing an option with an early optimal exercise feature, the thought process suggests that we solve the problem backward. We need to make an optimal decision at each point to attain the optimal solution at large. Like the ant, we always seek the optimal decision at each local point. On the binomial lattice, we always choose the optimal decision among all the alternatives at each node point.

7.4 Compound Options

A *compound option* acts on another option, and not on a stock. Stock risk is the only risk source for the compound option. The compound option of a stock can behave differently from other options. It tends to be more sensitive to the underlying stock price.

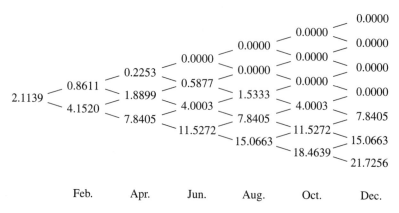

Feb.   Apr.   Jun.   Aug.   Oct.   Dec.

Figure 7-7 The binomial lattice of an American put option. The underlying stock prices are the same as before. The exercise price of the American put option is 100. At maturity, prices are determined by $Max[X - S_r, 0]$. The prices at the months before maturity are determined by comparing the intrinsic values of $Max[100 - S_t, 0]$ with the values of the backward substitution. For example, 11.5272 in June is determined by comparing $11.527 (= Max[100 - 88.473, 0])$ with $10.5321 (= (7.8405 * 0.61285 + 15.0663 * 0.38715)/1.01005)$. The continuously compounding risk-free rate is 6%.

Compound options can be a series of options, each option (choice) being an option on another option. These options can be put or call options.

One common compound option is the *retention option*. It has a series of strike prices. Instead of having an option to buy an asset (for example, stock) at a strike price X, a retention option offers the holder the opportunity to buy the asset in installments. However, if any installment payment is skipped, the holder loses the right to buy the asset. In other words, if we are offered an option to buy an asset, and we can pay for the asset in installments, and we can let the option expire, then this flexibility has value, and the value is the retention option price. We will revisit this issue in chapter 13, where this idea is used for designing contracts for product development.

The retention option is a compound option; the decision to exercise the first option to pay the first installment has to depend on the optimal decisions that one will be making for all the subsequent periods. For example, if the asset value is significantly higher than the first payment, we should pay the first installment. The retention option spreads out the buy decision into a series of options. Of course, we have to take the cost of all the installments into account.

The valuation of a compound option using a rollback method is the same as that of an American option or a Bermuda option. The valuation begins from the expiration date, assuming that all the installments have been paid to retain the option. Then backward substitution determines the option price on the expiration date of the last option. The terminal condition of the next option is the max [option prices strike prices, 0]. In rolling back the value of the options, we can determine the value of the option at the next expiration date. Then we will continue the backward substitution procedure until we reach the initial position.

By simulating the values of the retention option, we can compare the results with the European option. (See figures 7.10.)

In many instances, the cost of a purchase is spread over a period of time. Therefore

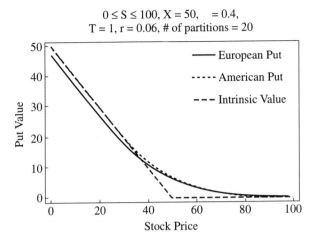

$$0 \le S \le 100, X = 50, \quad = 0.4,$$
$$T = 1, r = 0.06, \# \text{ of partitions} = 20$$

Figure 7-8 American put vs. European put option. The only difference between the American put option and the European put option is whether the option holders have the right to exercise early. Therefore, the price differential between them will reflect the early exercise premium. The early exercise premium is higher when the option are in-the-money rather than out-of-the money. The stock price varies from 0 to 100 for simulation purposes. The continuously compounding risk-free rate is 6% per period. The volatility of the stock return is 0.4. the time to maturity is 1 year. We partition one period into 20 subperiods to enhance the accuracy.

there are many compound options. In chapter 12 we will discuss the stock of a firm with coupon bonds outstanding. Since the shareholders have to pay the coupons every six months and the principal at the bond maturity date in order to retain ownership of the firm, the stock could be treated as a compound option.

7.5   Options with Look-back Features (Asian) and the Filtration Model

The *look-back option* offers the holder the right to receive the highest historical price of the stock or the prevailing stock price at the expiration. More generally, there is a class of options whose payoffs at expiration depend on some of the historical stock prices. Consider options such that the payout on the expiration date is an index not just of the current stock price (as it is in standard options) but of some of the historical stock prices as well. For example, a ratchet call option may have an index that is the highest stock price in the past week, and an Asian option, the average stock price over a historical period, such as last week. Ratchet and Asian options can have features that are similar to other options, with the exception of the index that is based on historical data. For example, they can be call or put, American or European, compound or not compound options.

Let us compare a *ratchet call option* where the index is the highest price in the past five trading days with a standard call option. Its price must be higher than that of the European call option, because the index is always higher than or equal to the stock price.

Let an *Asian option* indx be the average price of the past five trading days. It will have a lower price than the corresponding European call option, but not because the

Stock lattice

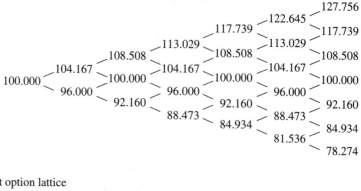

Bermuda put option lattice

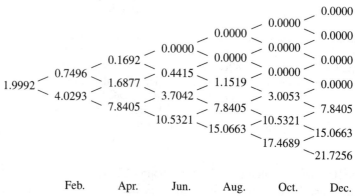

Feb.   Apr.   Jun.   Aug.   Oct.   Dec.

Figure 7-9 Binomial lattices of a Bermuda put option. In the Bermuda put option lattice the underlying stock prices are the same as those of the digital call option. The exercise months of the Bermuda put optionas are April, August, and December. At maturity, the Bermuda put options' prices are the intrinsic valus of $Max[X - S_T, 0]$. The prices at the exercise months except maturity are determined by comparing the intrinsic values at the nodes with the values determined by backward substitution. For example, in August we get 15.0663 by comparing the intrinsic value of $Max[100 - 84.934, 0]$ with the backward substitution value of 13.0862(= $(10.5321 \times 0.61285 + 17.4689 \times 0.38715)/1.01005$). The continuously compounding risk-free rate is 6%. The prices except in exercise months are determined only by backward substitution, because early exercise is not allowed.

average price is lower than that of the current price. The average price can be higher or lower than the current price. It is the volatility of the average price that matters. The volatility of the average price is lower than that of the stock price, which affects the price of an Asian option. Since the call option lowers the value of an option that has a lower volatility, Asian options become cheaper.

The look-back option requires the index to "remember" the historical experience. Therefore, the index is path-dependent; its level depends on the price path that the stock has traversed.

Consider the pricing of an Asian call option where the index is the average of the last period and the current price. The methodology can be extended to other look-back options. The valuation model has to take such a path-dependent feature into account. No longer can we just roll back the index. We must construct the movement of the

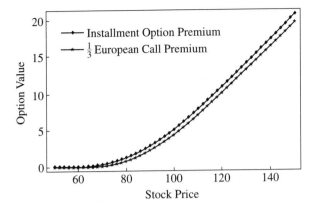

Figure 7-10 An installment option is a European option in which the premium is paid in a series of installments rather than being paid up-front. If all installments are paid, the holder has the corresponding European option, but the holder has the right to terminate payments on any payment date, in which case the option lapses with no further payments. In other words, the holder has a series of opportunities to decide whether he continues holding the option or terminates the option. The corresponding European option holder does not have this flexibility. Stock price varies between 50 and 150. The volatility of the underlying stock is 0.2 The time-to-maturities of both options are 1. The continuously compounding risk-free interest rate is 0.1. We assume 3 equal installment payments, i.e., one up-front payment and two interim payments of the same amount. We partition 1 year into 6 periods for convenience purposes. For example, when the initial stock price is 100, the equal installment premium is 5.06037, which is greater than one third of the corresponding European call price, 4.31009 (= 1/3 × 12.9303), the difference between them being the value of a put option on the call.

index from the stock price movement. In principle, we can conduct the rollback from a binomial tree structure. Given the complete tree of a stock movement, we can construct the index values for all the node points on the tree. Then we can calculate the payoff at the expiration date, and construct the rollback to determine the price. However, such an approach generally is not practical, because there is a large number of paths in the tree.

From the above discussion, we can see that the tree approach is not optimal in the use of computing time. Fortunately, the Asian option does not require the valuation model to remember the entire history of the stock movement. Therefore, the model needs to remember only the stock prices of the past two periods. In this sense, we can value an Asian option by keeping track of the past two periods.

A more practical approach is using a mathematical construct called a filtration model. The concept of *filtration* is widely used in mathematical finance, and we will discuss it in chapter 19. It refers to the information set that the valuation model requires at any time and state in the world. A filtration model introduced here is concerned with the specific construction of the information set at each node point of a lattice for a particular valuation model. In order to evaluate path-dependent securities in a binomial lattice, we need to track the history of each node, because each node has a different history. For example, the node (2,1) has two paths: {up, down} and {down, up}. A *filtration model* is a set of numbers assigned to each node in order to keep track of the state that the node has passed. We will call this set of numbers a *bundle*. This concept is borrowed from mathematics, where "bundle" denotes a set of information assigned at each point.

Stock lattice

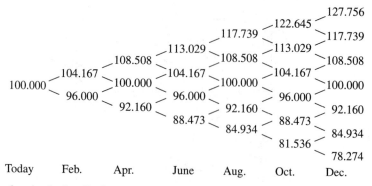

Today   Feb.   Apr.   June   Aug.   Oct.   Dec.

Compound option lattice: Backward Recursive Procedure 1

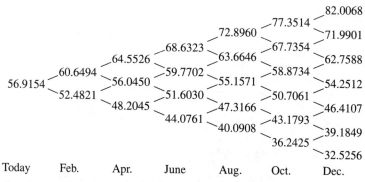

Today   Feb.   Apr.   June   Aug.   Oct.   Dec.

Compound option lattice: Backward Recursive Procedure 2

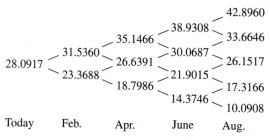

Today   Feb.   Apr.   June   Aug.

Compound option lattice: Backward Recursive Procedure 3

8.6643 — 11.7350 — 15.1466
                   — 6.6391
        — 4.0283 — 0.0000

Today   Feb.   Apr.

Figure 7-11 The lattices of a compound option. The exercise months of the compound call option are April, August, and December. The exercise prices of the exercise months are 20, 30, and 45.7488. The compound call option prices in December are $Max[S_T - 45.7488]$. The underlying asset of the compound call option is the stock, which is shown in the binomial stock lattice when we exercise in December. In August, the exercise price is 30 and the underlying asset is the call option, the maturity of which is December. The binomial lattice of the December call option is shown in the second panel. The second option value at the highest node in August, 42.8960, is determined by subtracting the exercise price of 30 from 72.8960. In April, the exercise price is 20 and the underlying asset is the call option, the maturity of which is August. The binomial lattice of the August call option is shown in the third panel. The third option value at the highest node in April, 15.1466, is determined by subtracting the exercise price of 20 from 35.1466.

The filtration model is a model in the sense that the specific construction does not need to be unique. We may have alternative filtration models to construct a valuation model of an option, depending on the option. There are no rules for designing a filtration model, but there may be guidelines for a model to provide efficient computation or mathematical elegance.

In this example, the filtration model over each node of the risk-neutral stock lattice has two numbers representing the index. The filtration model and the nodes of the lattice are depicted in figure 7.12. The upper number is the index value when the previous stock price is lower. The lower number is the index when the previous stock price is higher. Since the index values on the bundle depend on the stock price in the previous period, we can construct the lattice of the index movement, as illustrated in figure 7.12. In essence, there are two lattices constructed in the filtration model. They are derived from the stock tree, to use only the information that the valuation model requires.

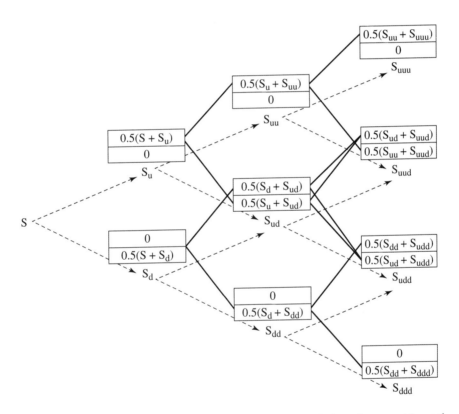

Figure 7-12 Filtration model of an Asian option. To evaluate path-dependent securities at the binomial lattice, we need to track the history of each node, because each node has a different history. For example, the node (2,1) has two paths: {up, down} and {down, up}. A practical approach is using a mathematical construct called a filtration model. A filtration model is a set of numbers assigned to each node in order to keep track of the state that the node has passed. In this diagram, the bundle over each node has two numbers representing the index. The upper number is the index value where the previous stock price is lower. The lower number is the index where the previous stock price is higher. Since the index values of the bundle depend on the stock price in the previous period, we can construct the lattice of the index movement with the edges of the lattice linking the nodes on the bundle. In essence there are two lattices constructed in the bundle. They are derived from the stock tree, which uses only the information that this valuation model requires.

For a European Asian option, the valuation procedure is quite straightforward. At the expiration date, we determine the payout of the option on each of the two lattices in the bundle. Then we roll back the values on both lattices, which are then combined in the initial node. For an American Asian option, we can compare the rolling-back option value with the intrinsic value. If the option value is lower than the intrinsic value, we replace the option value with the intrinsic value as we take the early exercise option.

Earlier we suggested that the ratchet call option has a higher value than the corresponding European call option, which in turn has a higher value than the European Asian option. The valuation model enables us to compare them. (See figures 7.13 and 7.14.)

Ratchet options are used because investors want to lock in the high-water mark, the highest value, of the stock attained from a specified time until expiration. Ratchet options protect the investors in case of a sudden drop in value because the payoff depends on the high-water mark of the stock and not on the stock price at expiration. Of course, the protection comes with a high premium; ratchet options are more expensive.

Asian options are used because many financial transactions depend on the average stock price rather than the closing stock price. An employee's option may depend on the annual closing price of the company stock. However, both sides of the option contract prefer an index which reflects the company stock prices over one year or some period longer than the last day of the year. Therefore, the employee's option would not be significantly subject to a one-day price movement of the stock. Using an average of a period of time is quite standard in such financial transactions. The cost of an Asian option is lower than the corresponding European option because of its lower volatility.

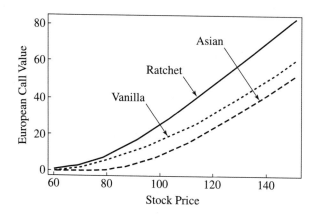

Figure 7-13 Comparing the Asian option and ratchet option with the European option. The Asian option and the ratchet option are path-dependent in the sense that the payout on the expiration date is an index, not just the current stock price, as in standard options. The index depends on the historical stock price. For example, a ratchet call option has an index that is the highest stock price over a past period and an Asian option is the average stock price over a historical period, such as last week. Asian options and ratchet options can be call or put, American or European, compound or not compound options. The stock price varies from 60 to 150 for simulation purposes. The risk-free rate is 10% per period. The variance of the stock returns is 0.3. The time to maturity is one year. We partition one period into 10 subperiods to enhance the accuracy. The ratchet call, the Asian call, and the European standard call have the same exercise price of 100. The ratchet call option is the most valuable among the three, followed by the European standard call and the Asian call option.

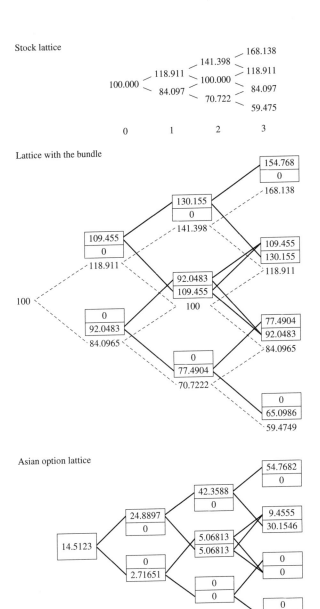

Figure 7-14 The lattices of the Asian option. The binomial lattice of the stock prices is shown in the uppermost panel. We assume that the initial stock price is 100, the stock volatility is 30%, the time to maturity is 1 year, and the continuously compounding risk-free rate is 10%. Since the number of partitions is 3, we adjust the upward parameter, u, the downward parameter, d, and the risk-free rate over one subperiod to 1.18911, 0.840965, and 0.0339, respectively. The risk-neutral probability is 0.55418.

$$u = \exp\left\{\sigma\sqrt{\frac{1}{m}}\right\} = 1.18911,\ d = \frac{1}{u} = 0.840965,\ S = 100,\ \sigma = 0.3,\ r = 0.1,\ T = 1$$

$$p = \frac{\exp\left[\frac{r}{m}\right] - d}{u - d} = 0.55418,\ 1 - p = 0.44518,\ m = 4$$

The binomial lattice of bundles and the corresponding Asian lattice are shown in the middle and lower panels.

7.6 Chooser Option

The *chooser option* is similar to a compound option in the sense that it is an option on options. Unlike a compound option, the chooser option does not let an option expire. The holder of a chooser option has the right to choose to have a call or a put option on the same underlying stock at a prespecified time. When the stock rises over the period, the holder will choose the call option because it will have a higher value than the put option. Conversely, if the stock value falls, the choice will be the put option.

The chooser option is similar to holding a *straddle*, a portfolio of put and call options sharing the same strike price. They are similar in that the option is not betting the stock will be bullish or bearish. But the chooser option does not pay for both options entirely. It maintains the flexibility of deciding which option to buy later. A straddle, however, pays for both options immediately. The chooser option should have a lower price.

The chooser option is conceptually different from other options discussed thus far. Unlike European options, the terminal payment depends on the decisions made previously. Unlike American options, the decision is binary (choosing a call option or a put option) rather than continually dealing with an early exercise option. The chooser option is closer to the Asian option in the sense that it has a (limited) memory, requiring the valuation to keep track of decisions that have already been made.

Using this insight, we can develop a valuation model of a chooser option using the filtration models as a limited memory device. We construct a filtration model of two states for each node. One state is assigned to the call option and the other is assigned to the put option. At the expiration date of the put and call options, we determine their payouts by applying the option payout formulas: call option, $Max[S_T - X, 0]$, put option, $Max[X - S_T, 0]$. Now use the backward substitution procedure and determine the put and call option values at the expiration date of the chooser option. The terminal condition of the chooser option is $Max[C, P]$, where C is the call option price and P is the put option price.

That is, at time t, we exercise the chooser option. The value of the nodes at time t is the maximum of the put or the call option prices for all the states of the world. Then the backward substitution methodology continues until it reaches the initial point. (See figures 7.15 and 7.16.)

We can now consider a more general solution to the chooser option—the *compound chooser option*. Consider an option which gives the holder the right to choose another chooser option or a call option at an expiration date t. Now we need to construct four binomial lattices: the stock underlying lattice, the call option for the first chooser option, and the put and call options for the second chooser option.

Roll back the put and call options from the expiration date of the second chooser option. Determine the terminal condition of the second chooser option. Then roll back the value to the expiration date of the first chooser option. Determine the terminal conditions for the first chooser option by comparing the values of the call option against the values of the second chooser option at the expiration date of the first chooser option. Now roll back the values to the valuation date. (See figures 7.17 and 7.18.)

The example illustrates that this approach is a general solution to option valuation. We can first construct the decision tree of the choices, then roll back the lattices, and then calculate the optimal solution. The decision tree in this case is given in figure 7.19.

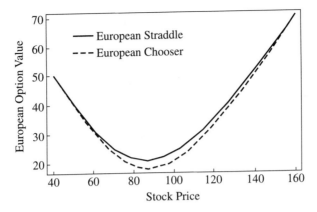

Figure 7-15 Performance profile comparing a straddle with a chooser option. The holder of a chooser option has the right to choose at a prespecified time to decide between a call or a put option on the same underlying stock. When the stock rises over the period, the hold will chose the call option because it will have a higher value than the put. Conversely, if the stock value falls, the choice will be the put. The chooser option is like holding a straddle, a portfolio of put and call options sharing the same strike price. The chooser option should have a lower price. The stock price varies from 40 to 160 for simulation purposes. The continuously compounding risk-free rate is 10%. The volatility of the stock returns is 0.3. The time to maturity of the chooser option is 0.5 year; that of European call and put options is 1 year. We partition one period into 20 subperiods to enhance the accuracy. The European straddle and the European chooser have the same exercise price of 100.

Since the compound chooser option is a chooser option on another chooser option, we have two chooser options. The first is an option to choose between a call and a put option, which are the underlying assets of the first chooser option and mature in December. The maturity date of the first chooser option is June. The second chooser option is an option to choose between the first chooser option and another call option. The maturity date of the second chooser option is April. The maturity date of the call, which is the underlying asset of the second chooser option, is June.

The basic idea of a chooser option is prevalent in many financial transactions. In corporate finance, the corporation often has the right to double up (speed up) the retirement of debt at certain dates, a bond feature that we will discuss further in chapter 8. The choice to double up is in essence a chooser option. We will study this problem further in chapter 8.

7.7 Multiple Risk Sources

All previous examples of options have depended on a single risk source. But there are many options that depend on several risk sources. For example, the *exchange option* offers the holder a payment at the expiration date of $Max[X, Y]$, where X and Y are different stock prices. This option offers the holder the higher of the two stocks (or any number of stocks in a basket). The *performance option* is the option that pays $Max[X - Y, 0]$. It is called a performance option is because we can think of Y as a stock index and X as a portfolio value. The option pays the asset manager when the portfolio outperforms the stock index. Typically, asset managers are not explicitly penalized in the incentive

Stock lattice

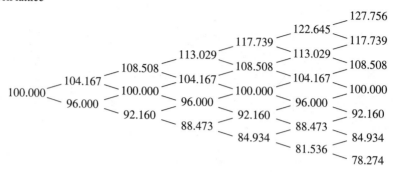

Chooser option lattice

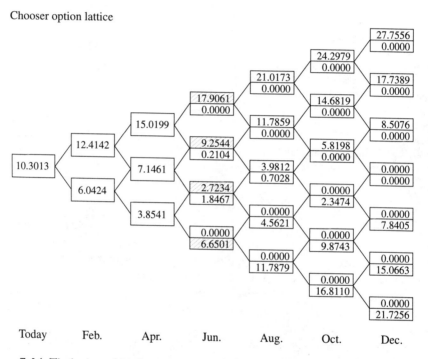

| Today | Feb. | Apr. | Jun. | Aug. | Oct. | Dec. |

Figure 7-16 The lattices of the chooser option. The binomial lattice of the stock prices is shown in the upper panel. We assume that the initial stock price is 100, the stock volatility is 10%, the time to maturity is 1 year, and the risk-free rate is 10%. Since the number of partitions is 6, we adjust the upward parameter, u, the downward parameter, d, and the risk-free rate over one subperiod to 1.04167, 0.95997, and 0.01681, respectively. The risk-neutral probability is 0.695573.

$$u = \exp\left\{\sigma\sqrt{\frac{1}{m}}\right\} = 1.04167, d = \frac{1}{u} = 0.959997, S = 100,$$

$$\sigma = 0.1, r = 0.1, T = 1, p = \frac{\exp\left[\frac{r}{m}\right] - d}{u - d} = 0.695573, 1 - p = 0.304427, m = 6$$

The upper value and the lower value of a bundle are a European call option and a European put option value, respectively. The terminal conditions for the European call and put options are $Max[S_T - X, 0]$ and $Max[X - S_T, 0]$ respectively. The maturity date of the chooser option is June. Since chooser holders choose the higher value between the call option and the put option in June, the terminal condition of the European chooser options is $Max[C, P]$, (shaded). From June to today, we apply backward substitution to get the current chooser option price.

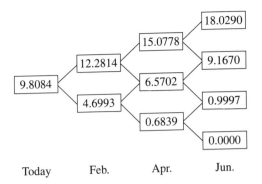

Figure 7-17 The second call option for the compound chooser option. The stock price is 100 and the exercise price is 95. The maturity date is December. The risk-free rate is 10%. Given the intrinsic values, $Max[S_{Dec} - 95, 0]$, at each state in December, we use the backward substitution procedure to determine the call option prices in June.

performance fee structure when the portfolio performance is below the benchmark, but are rewarded for outperforming the benchmark.

Consider an exchange option. Let us think of Y as an exchange rate, say the yen/dollar exchange at the current level of 130. Let X be a U.S stock quoted in yen, say ¥135. Then X/Y is the stock price in U.S. dollars. Now note that

$$Max[X, Y] = Y \times Max[X/Y, 1] \tag{7.3}$$

That means the payoff at the expiration date is the European call option of the U.S. stock in U.S. dollars with a strike price of $1. But the payment is made in yen, because we multiply the payoff by Y. We just need to multiply the European option value by the

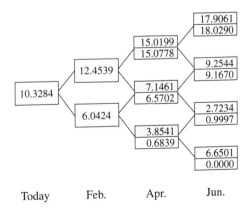

Figure 7-18 The compound chooser option lattice. The holder of the compound chooser option has the right to choose between the call option in figure 7.17 and the chooser option in figure 7.16. The upper values are the chooser options and the lower values are the call option values. Since the maturity date of the compound chooser option is April, the holder takes the higher value between them. For example, at the highest state in April the holder chooses 15.0778 rather than 15.0199. 12.4539 in February can be calculated by $(15.0778 \times 0.695573 + 7.1461 \times (1 - 0.695573))/1.01681$.

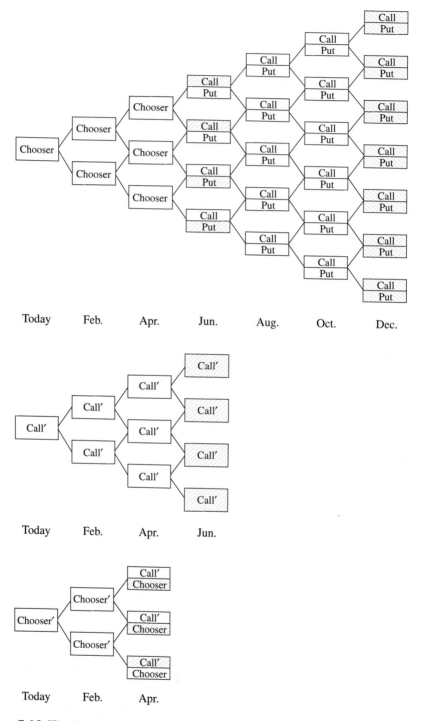

Figure 7-19 The decision tree of a compound chooser option.

exchange rate. This approach results in pricing a standard European option by changing the risk processes from X and Y to X/Y. While the problem is posed with multiple risk sources, the valuation requires only the standard European option pricing.

Consider a European exchange call option with two risk sources, $\widetilde{X}$ and $\widetilde{Y}$, such that the payoff at maturity, T, is $Max\,[X_T - Y_T, 0]$. The value at time t is denoted by $C(X_t, Y_t, t)$ where t is less than T. We can show that $\lambda C(X_t, Y_t, t) = C(\lambda X_t, \lambda Y_t, t)$, where λ is a constant number. This property indicates that the call option is linear homogeneous in $\widetilde{X}$ and $\widetilde{Y}$. Therefore, if we take $\widetilde{Y}$ as numeraire, the boundary condition will be $Y_T\,Max\left[\frac{X_T}{Y_T} - 1, 0\right]$ because of the linear homogeneous property. By taking $\widetilde{Y}$ as numeraire, we can reduce two risk sources to one, which is $\widetilde{X}_t/\widetilde{Y}_t$. Since we have only one risk source, we can apply the Black–Scholes option pricing model, which has five parameters to price the exchange option. In this case, $\widetilde{X}_t/\widetilde{Y}_t$ is the underlying asset. The maturity date is T. The exercise price is \$1. Since the numeraire is asset $\widetilde{Y}$, the risk-free rate is 0. The volatility of the underlying asset is $\sqrt{\sigma_X^2 + \sigma_Y^2 - 2\sigma_X \cdot \sigma_Y \cdot \rho_{X,Y}}$, where σ_X, σ_Y, and $\rho_{X,Y}$ are the standard deviation of asset $\widetilde{X}$, the standard deviation of asset $\widetilde{Y}$, and the correlation coefficient between asset $\widetilde{X}$ and asset $\widetilde{Y}$, respectively.

For the performance options, we just need to note that

$$Max\,[X - Y, 0] = Max\,[X, Y] - Y \tag{7.4}$$

Therefore the performance option is the exchange option value net of the value of Y. Once again, the problem of multiple risk sources is reduced to one of our standard option valuation problems with a single source of risk.

However, this is a special case where these transformations in equations (7.3) and (7.4) can be made. For example, in a *basket option*, where the option holder can choose the highest value of several stocks, we cannot reduce the problem to an option pricing problem with a single source of risks because not all multifactor models can be reduced to a one factor model. We now need to proceed to develop a framework to value options with multiple risk sources.

Let us consider a problem with two risk sources, X and Y. First, we need to construct a two-dimensional lattice from the lattices of X and Y. This can be done by building a node with four states instead of the two states of a one-dimensional lattice. The four states are all possible combinations of two sets of two states. (See figure 7.20.)

A two-dimensional lattice can then be constructed by ensuring that the paths recombine in the following step. This construction is repeated over n periods, building a lattice that resembles a pyramid.

Next we need to model the correlations of two risk sources. If we assign equal probabilities to all four states at each node, then the two processes will be independent. If we assign a higher probability to the states where both stocks rise and fall, then we require the stocks to be positively correlated. Conversely, if we let those states have lower probabilities, then the stocks are negatively correlated. That means the correlation of the stocks can be determined by the probabilities. Appendix B provides the precise specification of this n-factor lattice model.

This approach can be generalized to any number of dimensions and any number of risk sources. While the construction is difficult to visualize and depict, the algorithms

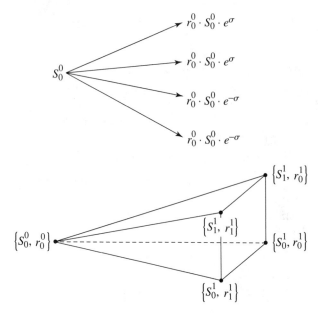

Figure 7-20 A node with four states. The upper diagram and the lower diagram represent a stock price process and a stock-interest rate process, respectively. The superscript and the subscript denote the time and the state, where state 1 and state 0 refer to an upward state and a downward state, respectively. Since each factor follows a binomial process, we have four nodes at time 1, which originated from one node at time 0. As shown in the upper diagram, the stock price is determined by two factors, the interest rate and the volatility inherent in the stock price.

are mechanically straightforward. The formulation, provided in appendix B, assigns probabilities to all the combinations of outcomes for multiple risk sources.

7.8 Constant Maturity Swap

Constant maturity swap is a swap between two parties such that the swap payment is based on the swap rate of a fixed term at each payment date. For example, the constant maturity swap receives a five-year swap rate and pays one-year LIBOR on an annual basis. In this case, at the anniversary date, the interest payment received is based on the prevailing five-year swap rate.

In order to understand the valuation of a constant maturity swap, we need to take into consideration that the bond pays a five-year rate. Consider a flat yield curve. If the bond pays annual interest based on the one-year rate, then the bond is simply a floating-rate note and the price should be par. But when the bond pays a five-year rate, should the bond be priced at par?

The lattice of five-year interest rates and one-year interest rates is generated by the Ho–Lee model for a six-year constant maturity swap contract with a flat yield curve of 10% and a volatility of 12%. The upper values in a bundle are five-year interest rates, and the lower values are one-year interest rates. (See figure 7.21.)

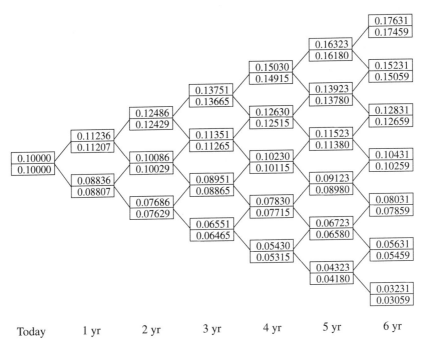

Today   1 yr   2 yr   3 yr   4 yr   5 yr   6 yr

Figure 7-21 A lattice for a five-year interest rate and a one-year interest rate. This figure depicts a lattice of a 5-year interest rate and a 1-year interest rate. The lattice of 5-year interest rates and 1-year interest rates is generated by the Ho–Lee model for a 6-year constant maturity swap contract with a flat yield curve of 10% and volatility of 12%. The upper values in a bundle are 5-year interest rates and the lower values are 1-year interest rates.

A lattice for a six-year constant maturity swap contract is given in figure 7.22. The underlying interest rates for the six-year constant maturity swap are five-year and one-year interest rates.

The valuation begins at the end of year 6. The differences of the payments are then rolled back, discounted at the prevailing one-period rate. Then we then add the differences of the payments to this discounted value at each node point. Now we proceed to roll back another step, again using the prevailing one-period rate. The process continues until we reach the initial value.

In this example, we start with a flat yield curve with the five-year rate being the same as the one-year rate. The forward five-year rates then also equal the corresponding one-year rates. However, the swap has a positive value. This is because the five-year bond has a higher convexity than the one-year bond. A convexity adjustment, as explained in chapter 5, leads to a positive constant maturity value.

The basic idea of a constant maturity swap is used in many financial contracts. Often, the interests on a short-term contract sold by a financial institution like a bank or an insurance company are based on the asset portfolio's performance. However, the portfolio may have a long duration. In this case, in essence, the financial contract pays the interests of a longer duration bond, even though the interest payments are adjusted over a short time interval. (We will revisit this issue in chapter 11, where we show some of the pension products that pay an interest rate based on the five-year swap rate, for example, but the interest rate is continually updated, like a floating-rate instrument.)

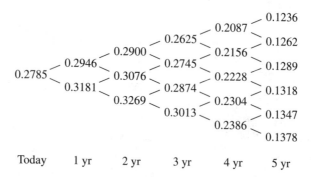

Today   1 yr   2 yr   3 yr   4 yr   5 yr

Figure 7-22 Six-year constant maturity swap contract. This figure depicts a lattice for a 6-year constant maturity swap contract. The underlying interest rates are 5-year and 1-year rates. At each node, we calculate $F \times [r(n, i, T) - r(n, i, t)]$ where $F = 100, T = 5, t = 1$, and $r(n, i, t) = t$ year interest rate at time n and state i. Once we determine the values at each node, we apply backward substitution to get the initial value at time 0 and state 0. The risk-neutral probability for an upward movement is 0.5. 0.2087 at time 4 can be obtained by $(((0.5 \times 0.1236 + 0.5 \times 0.1262) + 100 \times (0.15030 - 0.14915))/1.14915)$, where 0.15030 and 0.14915 are the 5-year interest and 1-year interest at time 5 and state 5, respectively.

7.9 Interest Rate Spread Option

The Treasury yield curve or the swap curve takes on different shapes over time. In chapter 5 we discussed yield curve movements that over time may flatten or become more upward-sloping or downward-sloping. We showed that this movement is quite prevalent. The three-factor movement model shows that parallel movements and steepening movements are the two most important components of any yield curve's changing shapes.

As of February 24, 2002, the spread between the two-year rate and the ten-year rate was 3.5%, where the spread is defined as the ten-year interest rate net of the two-year interest rate. This spread is very significant, considering that it exceeds the two-year rate level. The steepness of the curve is uncertain. One reason for the steepness of the curve may be the Fed's easing the money supply over the period by lowering the discount rate. But there is a risk that the Fed may tighten the money supply if the economy grows at a faster rate. In this scenario, the short-term rates would rise, leading to a lower spread. Or the economy could continue to weaken, leading to a lower long-term rate while the short-rate remains unchanged because the Fed will not raise the interest rates. In this case, the spread between the two-year rate and ten-year rate also would tighten.

The *spread option* is an option on the spread of two bonds. For example, consider the spread of a two-year bond with a yield of 3% and the 10-year bond with a yield of 5%. An option expiring in one year with strike of 2% pays a maximum of a multiplier times the spread measures in percent net of the strike, and 0 at expiration. The strike spread is the current bond spread between the ten-year and two-year bonds.

In summary, the payoff of the option at expiration is

$$X = Max\left[multiplier \times \{(yield A - yield B) - strike\}, 0\right] \qquad (7.5)$$

where the yields of bond A and bond B are yield A and yield B, respectively, and the multiplier is a number specified in the contract.

Clearly the spread option depends on the movement of two bonds. Also, the option can be hedged by the current 3-year and 11-year bonds. Since the option can be replicated by using dynamic hedging strategies of these two bonds, we should not be concerned with exactly how and why the observed yield spread changes. Maybe the Fed will tighten the money supply. Maybe recession will lower the rates. In any case, the valuation does not care. The main issue is to determine the cost of replicating the spread option using these two bonds, as long as the two bonds follow an arbitrage-free rate movement model.

Now consider the two-factor model and the nodes one year from the maturity date. At each node, we can calculate the yield spreads of the two bonds. Then we can determine the payments at each node. We then use backward substitution, which recursively determines the present values of the payments one period closer to the initial date, starting with the option payoffs at the expiration date, one year from now.

If the option has an early exercise feature (an American feature), we can use the same procedure by rolling back the value, but we need to compare the roll-backed values with the intrinsic value, taking the minimum or the maximum of the two values, depending on whether the option is a call option or a put option. (See figures 7.23 and 7.24.)

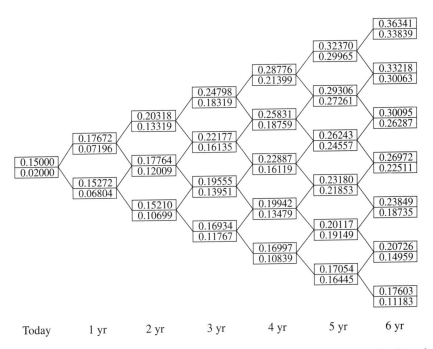

Figure 7-23 A lattice of a ten-year interest rate and two-year interest rate. We use the Extended Ho–Lee model to generate the lattice for an interest rate spread option. The initial yield curve is upward sloping, where the rates are rising from 1% at year 1 to 20% at year 16. The spot volatility curve is downward sloping, where the volatility is declining from 10% at year 1 to 6.6% at year 16. The upper values are 10-year intest rates and the lower values are 2-year interest rates.

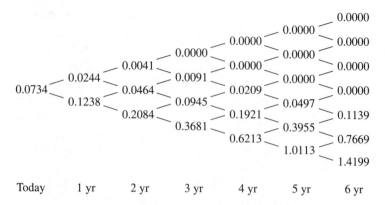

Today   1 yr   2 yr   3 yr   4 yr   5 yr   6 yr

Figure 7-24 A lattice for spread option pricing. The spread option payoff at the expiration is $Max[m \times (spread - X, 0]$ and the option values before the expiration are determined by backward substitution. The strike rate is 0.02 and the multiplier is 100. The spread can be obtained from figure 7.23.

7.10   Options on Forward/Futures Contracts

We discussed forward contracts and futures contracts in chapter 2. These contracts are agreements on a price and delivery date at time 0, with no money changing hands. For a forward contract, the buyer will buy a certain asset or commodity at the contract price, and the seller delivers the asset and receives the contract payment. The futures contract marks to market. That means that if the futures contract price changes the following day, say up by $1, the buyer receives $1 from the seller.

Let $F(n, T)$ denote the forward contract of a zero-coupon bond at time n for a T-year maturity bond. We have shown that the forward contract has to be

$$F(n, T) = \frac{P(T + n)}{P(n)} \tag{7.6}$$

The forward price can be determined by the law of one-price arbitrage argument. Since we can determine the discount function at each node point on a binomial lattice model, we can determine all the forward prices at each node point.

For the futures price, we need to determine the futures prices on the expiration date. The futures contract price must be equal to the bond price at the expiration date. The bond price is given by the interest rate arbitrage-free model. Now we apply backward substitution on the futures price. To avoid any arbitrage possibility, the rollback price is the expected price under risk-neutral probability. We can continue this process until we reach the initial point.

Chapters 5 and 6 noted that the futures price is slightly lower than the forward price. This is because when the futures' mark to market is positive, the interest rate is likely to have fallen. Perfect correlation between the futures price and the interest rate change is assured for the one-factor interest rate model. Therefore, the investment return is lowered. For this reason, the futures contract has a lower price than the forward contract.

In general, we can apply the procedure to value any futures and forward contracts on stocks or other risky assets, using a stock lattice or a stock lattice with interest rate risks. The procedure is the same for both contracts.

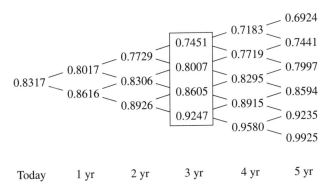

Today   1 yr   2 yr   3 yr   4 yr   5 yr

Figure 7-25 A binomial lattice for future prices. We assume that the term structure of interest rates follows the Ho–Lee model. The underlying aset of the futures contract is a 3-year bond. The maturity of the futures contract is year 5 and the maturity of the option contract on futures is year 3. Also we assume that the yield curve is 6% flat and the interest rate volatility is 20%. We calculate the 3-year bond prices at year 5 and then roll them back without discounting to calculate the futures prices at year 3. The futures prices at year 3 are 0.7451, 0.8007, 0.8605 and 0.9427. For example, 0.7451 can be obtained by $(0.6924 \times 0.25 + 0.7441 \times 0.5 + 0.7997 \times 0.25)$.

Once we have the futures and forward prices, we can price all the options on futures and forwards on the lattice because we can specify all the terminal conditions and boundary conditions. The terminal condition of a futures/forward call option is *Max [(future or forward price − strike price), 0]*, and of the put option is *Max [(strike price − futures or forward price), 0]*.

Numerical Example for the Option on a Futures Contract

We assume that the term structure of interest rates follows the Ho–Lee model. The underlying asset is a bond with three-year maturity. The maturity of the futures contract is the end of the fifth year period and the maturity of the option contract is the end of the third year. The exercise price is 0.01. We also assume that the yield curve is flat at 6% and the interest rate volatility is 20%. In the options on futures markets, the expiration dates of the options are set very close to the expiration of the futures contract, unlike this example. (Therefore, this example is constructed for illustration purposes.) (See figures 7.25 and 7.26.)

Numerical Example for the Option on a Forward Contract

Figures 7.27 and 7.28 show similar lattices for a forward contract. Again, this illustration is constructed for illustration purposes.

7.11   Commodity Options

Commodities are physical goods such as crude oil, wheat, pork bellies, precious metal (e.g., gold), and other nonfinancial goods. The difference between *commodity options* and financial options is that the physical good cannot be used for continual dynamic hedging, as in the Black–Scholes model, because there are carrying costs associated

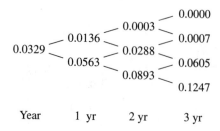

Year   1 yr   2 yr   3 yr

Figure 7-26 A binomial lattice for the option on a futures contract. The underlying asset is the futures contract given in figure 7.25. The exercise price is 0.8. The maturity date of the option on futures is year 3. After we specify the terminal conditions, we apply backward substitution to get the price of the option on futures at the initial node, which is 0.0329.

with commodities. In the case of wheat and other agricultural commodities, harvests and other factors affect the price. To the extent that we can capture all these factors and can implement dynamic hedging by forming a replicating portfolio of the commodity price change over each period, we can apply the relative valuation approach discussed in this chapter.

"*Normal backwardation*" and "*normal contango*" refer to the relationship between the expected spot price and the forward price. Under the theory of normal backwardation, the forward price is less than the expected spot price. Hence, the forward price has an upward drift. Hedgers tend to short the forward contract and pay speculators a return to offset their risks. The reverse is called contango. If there are futures prices on the

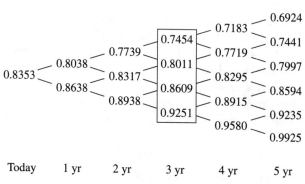

Today   1 yr   2 yr   3 yr   4 yr   5 yr

Figure 7-27 A lattice for the three-year forward prices. We assume that the term structure of interest rates follows the Ho–Lee model. The underlying asset of the forward contract is a 3-year bond. The maturity of the forward contract is year 5 and the maturity of the option contract on forward is year 3. Also we assume that the yield curve is 6% flat and the interest rate volatility is 20%. We calculate the forward prices at year 3 by $\frac{P(3,i,5)}{P(3,i,2)}$ where $i = 0, \cdots, 3$. The value of 5 in the numerator is the difference between year 3 and year 8. Year 8 is the maturity of the underlying asset of the forward contract. The value of 2 in the denominator is the difference between the option maturity and the forward contract maturity. $P(3, i, 5)$ is the price of a zero-coupon bond whose time at maturity is 5 at year 3 and state i. The node values except for year 3 are similarly calculated. For example, at year 2, we use $\frac{P(2,i,6)}{P(2,i,3)}$ where $i = 0, \cdots, 2$. To price an option on the forward contract described above, we need the forward prices at year 3.

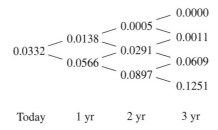

Today   1 yr   2 yr   3 yr

Figure 7-28 A binomial lattice for the option on a forward contract. The underlying asset is the forward contract given in figure 7.27. The exercise price is 0.8. The maturity date of the option on futures is year 3. After we specify the terminal conditions, we apply backward substitution to get the price of the option on the forward contract at the intitial node, which is 0.03321.

commodities, then the valuation of the options on the futures is the same as that for the financial options.

Precious Metals

Precious metals include gold, silver, and platinum. Since their storage costs are low and their physical composition does not change over time, we can securitize the physical commodity by realizing its cash value. In this case, an investor can lease the gold or silver. That is, the investor, the holder of the metal, can lend the metal to another party, who needs the physical commodity, at a rate called the lease rate. The investor will receive the metal in a specified period (say one year) together with a payment called the lease payment.

Over a horizon t, an investor can borrow cash, buy the gold, and sell the forward contract, which agrees to buy a specified amount of the precious metal at a fixed price, F. The investor can then lease the gold that he has bought. At the end of the period, the investor repays the loan $S(1 + r_f)$. He receives F for delivering the gold with the short position of the forward contract. He also receives the lease payment, $S \cdot l$. Or he can short the gold, buy the forward contract, and invest the cash in the capital market. Therefore the arbitrage payment has to hold.

$$F(t) + S \cdot l = S(1 + r_f)$$

$$\frac{F(t) - S}{S} + l = r_f$$

That is, the forward yield plus the lease rate must equal the market interest rate from the yield curve.

We can consider electricity as a commodity. Unlike precious metals, there is no storage for electricity. It has to be used when produced. Using the electricity spot price to value an electricity option would not be appropriate because the option pricing model that we have introduced requires continual hedging, and the hedging instruments (or securities) have to be reinvested continually. Since we cannot store the electricity, we cannot save it for future delivery, and therefore the valuation approach we take fails to price an electricity option by its relative price to the electricity spot price. A financial model that does not use the relative valuation approach has to be used instead. Such a financial model requires building the supply and demand for electricity and determining the electricity price. There is no standard model for these problems.

Weather Derivative

Weather derivatives are important contingent claims. There are several types of *weather derivatives*. The contract can be based on rain or snow accumulation. Perhaps the most popular weather derivatives are contingent claims on temperature. Energy companies are very concerned when there is uncertain fluctuation in temperatures. When the temperature is low, consumers increase the use of energy for heating, which increases the demand for heating oil and gas. When the temperature is high, the demand for electricity increases to run air-conditioning. Any unanticipated increase or decrease in demand for energy can affect the profitability of energy companies significantly. They may have to produce more energy to meet the unanticipated demand at a higher cost, without being able to pass the additional cost to the consumer in general.

The local weather station provides temperature measures. The deviations of temperature from a specific temperature may lead a consumer to switch from one source of energy to another. Research has shown that 67°F is a standard measure. A *degree-day* is the cumulative temperature differences between the average temperature of the day and 67°.

A degree-day is an objective and verifiable number that financial derivatives can use as a factor for designing contingent claims. *HDD* (heating degree-days) is the degrees below 67°F. *CDD* is cooling degree-days, the degrees above 67°F. The contract should specify the index (HDD or CDD), the strike price, the location, the reference of 67°, the period (March, April, May), the option type (put, call, collar, swap), and the payment based on the reference index. The underlying index for contracts is based on the cumulated degree-days over a stated period.

A degree-day is not a financial instrument, and therefore we cannot apply a straightforward risk-neutral pricing methodology to value this type of contract. Certainly, a direct application of the Black–Scholes model would not be appropriate because the degree-day, like electricity, is not a financial instrument or asset that we can use to hedge and form replicating portfolios. Therefore, the relative valuation modeling approach cannot be applied simply.

The weather derivatives and the electricity options show that the relative valuation model cannot be used for all derivatives. Relative valuation requires the construction of dynamic hedging to ensure that the risk of the derivative can be neutralized. If such a hedge does not exist, then relative valuation cannot be applied in general.

Cao and Wei (2002) propose an equilibrium valuation framework by generalizing the Lucas model to include the weather as a fundamental source of uncertainty in the economy. Specifically, they assume that the capital market has a utility function on consumption $U(W, t)$ as explained in chapter 1, where W is the uncertain wealth and t is the time horizon. The value of a security that has an uncertain payoff of $\tilde{q}_t$ based on the utility function is $X(t, T)$, where

$$X(t, T)\frac{dU(W(c), t)}{dc} = E_t\left(\frac{dU(\tilde{W}(c), T)\tilde{q}_t}{dc}\right)$$

That is, the marginal utility of wealth times the value of the security must equal the expected marginal utility of wealth of the security's payoff. This is because the impact on the utility of paying for the security at time t must equal the expected impact at time T, when the security gives the payoff. The Lucas model is an economic model of the wealth process W. The payoff $\tilde{q}_t$ is determined by the weather derivative in this case. From the equation, we can solve for $X(t, T)$, the price of the derivative.

More generally, when we cannot form arbitrage-free dynamic hedging strategies such that we can use the relative valuation approach, we may have to use a utility function based the valuation model. Since there is no accepted utility function for the economy or for the capital market, this method has less predictive power than the relative valuation approach that we have discussed so far.

7.12   An Overview of the Valuation Framework

A Valuation Procedure

Let us consider how one may value a European call option expiring at time T' with strike K' on an American call option on the maximum of stock A and stock B expiring at time T with strike K, where the stocks do not pay dividends. It is used here to illustrate how the valuation procedure described so far can value an option as complex as this somewhat strange one.

Step 1. We first construct a two-dimensional binomial lattice of two stocks, A and B. We will need to estimate the stocks' variances and covariances. The expected returns are the risk-free rates according to the arbitrage-free argument.

Step 2. At the expiration date T of the underlying option, we calculate the values

$$Y = Max\,[A, B] \tag{7.7}$$

for each node on the binomial lattice. A and B are the stock prices on the expiration date.

Step 3. Determine the payoff function of the option at each node of the two-dimensional lattice on the expiration date T. The payoff is

$$X = Max\,[Y - K, 0]$$

Step 4. Apply the backward substitution procedure and check for an early exercise condition at each node point. Let X^* be the substituted price. Then at each node we use the value

$$X = Max\,[X^*, Y - K] \tag{7.8}$$

This procedure stops when we reach the expiration date T' of the first option.

Step 5. Determine the terminal condition at time T' (or the payoff of the first option on the expiration date) by using

$$Z = Max\,[X - K', 0] \tag{7.9}$$

Step 6. Apply the backward substitution procedure to Z, starting from the expiration date of the option. Since this is a European option, we do not need to check for an early exercise condition. The option price is the price at the initial point.

Five Main Attributes of an Exotic Option

Beyond the European put or call options, the exotic options tend to have a combination of five important attributes: the early exercise option (American), path dependency (Asian), multiple risk sources, the compounding feature, and options with the cash flows based on the scenarios.

The technical tool to solve the early exercise option feature is to use the Bellman optimization procedure, which shows that we can solve the problem using backward substitution. The path dependency is related to using the information gathered along the historical scenario path. To keep track of the information, we use the filtration model. It is a model of the appropriate information set and the backward substitution procedure that is based on the historical data. For options on multiple sources of risks, we need an n-dimensional lattice to represent all the possible outcomes of the risk sources. This lattice can also capture the correlations of the risk factors. The compounding of options recognizes that an option's underlying asset is itself an option, and we can always apply backward substitution to value this and other options. Finally, if we know the cash flow of the option under all possible scenarios, we can enumerate all the scenarios and calculate the present values of the cash flows under each scenario, which is the pathwise value; the mean of these pathwise values is the value of the security. The technique used to solve this problem in practice is called the Monte Carlo simulation. The technical solution to value such an option is to iteratively define the terminal condition for each option. The summary is presented in the following table.

Salient features	*Method*
American	Bellman optimization
Asian	Filtration model
Multidimensional risk sources	N-factor model
Compounding	Multiple terminal conditions

7.13   Summary

This chapter has provided an overview of a broad range of options. While the discussion has surrounded mainly equity options, the same principles apply to interest rate options. The use of equity terminologies is simply for clarity of exposition. The market has American, Asian, and Bermuda options for bonds and currencies. The concepts, applications, and valuation methodologies are by and large the same for these risk sources.

The overview of these options serves several purposes. For users of financial derivatives, this range of options is a menu for designing investment or hedging strategies. These options have been designed to meet the needs for their economic values. Users can therefore learn about the successful products available from the market.

From a theoretical standpoint, this overview provides financial engineers with a tool kit to value a range of options that are not included in this chapter but that may be variations of the generic options discussed in the chapter.

We have introduced some important tools. The Bellman optimization shows that a rational pricing of an option can enable us to determine the early exercise rule of an American option. Its approach enables us to determine optimal decisions that can take all future contingencies and all future optimal decisions into account to determine the optimal decision today. We will rely on this powerful method in formulating the optimal corporate decisions in the chapters on corporate finance.

Another tool is filtration modeling. This approach enables us to deal with options using "memory." We have a set of information related to each node of the lattice, called a bundle. Lattices are built on the bundles that provide relevant information for valuation.

An appreciation of different types of options enables us to better understand the embedded options in bonds and other corporate liabilities. Options traded in OTC and exchange markets are important to the economy as measured by the size of the market and the trading activities. The options embedded in corporate securities, corporate bonds and other assets, are equally, if not more, important. Chapter 8 will develop the option pricing concept to value corporate bonds.

Appendix A. Optimal Early Exercise Using Simulations

Since the Bellman optimal solution suggests that we need to know all the possible future outcomes and subsequent optimal decisions before we can determine the present optimal decision, we have used the backward substitution approach to provide the optimal early exercise of options and the rational pricing of American options. However, if we use simulations of stock risk or interest rate risk, then at any future date the simulation can have only the history of the path. In that case, these methodologies have to be extended to deal with early exercise of options.

There is a significant amount of literature devoted to this problem. In general, these approaches use various methods to determine the early exercise boundary. See Bossaerts (1989), Tilley (1993), Barraquand and Martineau (1995), Averbukh (1997), Broadie and Glasserman (1997a, 1997b, 1997c), Broadie et al. (1997), Raymar and Zwecher (1997), Broadie et al. (1998), Carr (1998), Ibanez and Zapatero (2000), and Garcia (2000).

Longstaff and Schwartz (2001), Carriere (1996), and Tsitsiklis and Van Roy (1999) take another approach. At any node of the lattice, the backward substitution approach captures all the information backward to that node. At that node point, we can form an expectation of the value one period ahead and then compare the present value of that expected value with an early exercise decision, given the current stock price or the yield curve information. While we do not have the lattice to aggregate all the information in the simulation approach, we can use the simulations as sampling and estimate the conditional expected value as a function of the observed stock price or interest rate information. Using this empirically estimated function, we can then compare the present value of the expected value with the early exercise decision for each point on the simulated time paths at time t.

Appendix B. N Factor Lattice Model

Let us consider the problem is two parts. For the first part, we consider an n-dimensional random walk. We show how the joint probabilities can be changed such that the outcomes can capture the correlations. When there is no correlation, each risk factor will have a probability of an up or down move of 0.5. Part 2 will show how this result is used for n factor models

Part 1: N-Dimensional Random Walk

An n-factor model can be exemplified by taking an n-dimensional random walk using n coin throws to decide on the direction the person should walk.

First we illustrate the problem with $n = 2$ (two coins).

Each coin outcome is head (up) $= 1$, tail (down) $= -1$; hence the mean is 0 and std. $= 1$. (See table 7.1.)

$$\text{Corr}(1, 2) = \text{correlation} = 2p - 2(0.5 - p); \text{ hence } P = (1 + \text{Corr}(1, 2))/4.$$

The other probability is $0.5 - p = (1 - \text{Corr}(1, 2))/4$.

Q.E.D.

Extend the problem to three coins, using the same notations. (See table 7.2.)
Outcome (i, j) is the product of outcomes of coins i and j.
Now define the correlations:

$$\text{Corr}(1, 2) = 2p1 + 2p2 - 2p3 - 2(0.5 - p1 - p2 - p3) = 4p1 + 4p2 - 1$$

$$\text{Corr}(1, 3) = 2p1 - 2p2 + 3p3 - 2(0.5 - p1 - p2 - p3) = 4p1 + 4p3 - 1$$

$$\text{Corr}(2, 3) = 2p1 - 2p2 - 3p3 + 2(0.5 - p1 - p2 - p3) = -4p2 - 4p3 + 1$$

Table 7.1 Two-coin Outcomes

Event	Outcomes (product of the outcomes of the events)	Probability
UU	$1 * 1 = 1$	p
UD	$1 * (-1) = -1$	$0.5\text{-}p$
DU	$(-1) * 1 = -1$	$0.5\text{-}p$
DD	$(-1) * (-1) = 1$	p

Table 7.2 Three-coin Outcomes

Events	Outcome (12)	Outcome (13)	Outcome (23)	Probability
UUU	1	1	1	$p1$
UUD	1	-1	-1	$p2$
UDU	-1	1	-1	$p3$
UDD	-1	-1	1	$0.5 - p1 - p2 - p3$
DUU	-1	-1	1	$0.5 - p1 - p2 - p3$
DUD	-1	1	-1	$p3$
DDU	1	-1	-1	$p2$
DDD	1	1	1	$p1$

In matrix form

$$
\begin{pmatrix} 1 + Corr(12) \\ 1 + Corr(13) \\ -[1 + Corr(23)] \end{pmatrix} = \begin{pmatrix} 4 & 4 & 0 \\ 4 & 0 & 4 \\ 0 & 4 & 4 \end{pmatrix} \begin{pmatrix} p1 \\ p2 \\ p3 \end{pmatrix}
$$

Now, given $R(ij)$, invert the matrix and solve for pi's

For any n, the matrix will be a combinatorial of 2 out of n, $C(n, 2) \times C(n, 2)$, with non-0 entries (which is 4) in selecting two out of n elements of each row.

Q.E.D.

The problem with $n = 4$ is that this procedure can no longer provide an $n \times n$ matrix that one can invert. Therefore, one has to use a row reduction method to determine a solution, and the solution is not unique. The n-nomial approach is not a complete market.

Part 2: Application to n-factor Models

Consider a stock return model. We first implement the binomial model of the stock returns, using equal probability implementation to ensure that the upward movement and the downward movement at every node is 50%.[1]

Using the standard notations in the binomial model, we require the expected returns and the standard deviation of the movement at each node to be the specified values. We therefore have

$$
pu + (1 - p)d = \exp(\mu \Delta t)
$$

$$
\sqrt{p(1 - p)} \log(u/d) = \sigma \sqrt{\Delta t}
$$

When we require $p = 0.5$, as explained in chapter 4, appendix C, the equations become

$$
u + d = 2 \exp(\mu \Delta t)
$$

$$
\log(u/d) = 2\sigma \sqrt{\Delta t}
$$

We can now solve for u and d:

$$
u = 2 \exp(\mu \Delta t) \exp\left(2 \cdot \sigma \sqrt{\Delta t}\right) \bigg/ \left(\exp\left(2 \cdot \sigma \sqrt{\Delta t}\right) + 1\right)
$$

$$
d = 2 \exp(\mu \Delta t) \bigg/ \left(\exp\left(2 \cdot \sigma \sqrt{\Delta t}\right) + 1\right)
$$

Using this implementation for each risk source, we can specify the n-nomial model as we have discussed. Given the correlations of the risk factors, we can use the result of part 1 to specify the probabilities assigned to each node. When there are no correlations, the probabilities will be the same for all the outcomes.

The Ho–Lee model implementation is already based on the risk-neutral probability of 0.5%. Therefore we have both stock risk and interest rate risk; we only need to adjust the equal probability implementation to the stock returns and apply part 1 to generate the correlations among the risk sources.

Appendix C. A Numerical Example of Dynamic Programming

The problem we are facing is to find the least cost path from point A to point M, where the toll between two points is indicated in a circle. For example, if we travel from point A to point D, we have to pay a toll of $4. This problem could be solved by a brute-force method. We can enumerate all the paths from point A to point M shown in the lower panel of figure 7.29. If we add up all the tolls along the paths, we can determine the total toll for a specific path and choose the least cost path. However, we can solve this problem in an elegant way with Bellman's optimization. First, instead of mapping the optimal path from point A to point M, we can imagine that we are at the end of stage 4 (i.e., points K and L). To arrive at point M from points K and L, we have to pay $4 and $5, respectively. We denote the optimal tolls from K and L in parentheses below the points shown in the upper panel. Second, rolling back by one stage, we are at point I or J.

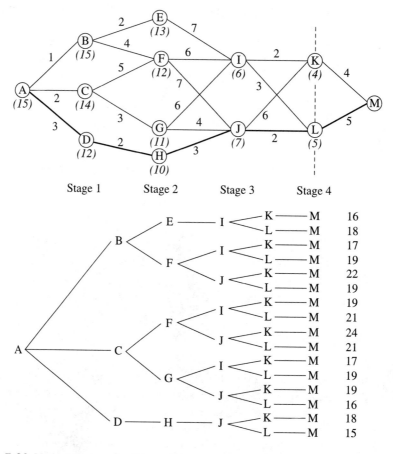

Figure 7-29 Numerical example of dynamic programming.

From point I, we can go to point K and point L. If we go to point K from point I, we pay $2. Since we pay a $4 toll from point K to point M, we know that the total toll from point I to M via point L is $6. If we go to point L from point I, we pay $3. Since we pay $5 from point L to point M, we know that the total toll from point I to point M via point L is $8. Therefore the optimal path from point I to point M is via point K rather than point L. We denote $6 below point I to indicate that $6 is the minimum toll from point I to point M. By the same argument, we can determine the least toll path from point J to point M, which is via point L, with the minimum toll of $7. Repeating the same backward procedure, we can calculate the least toll path from every point at each stage shown in the upper panel. From this panel, we can determine the optimal path by the backward procedure: which is ADHJLM, with the minimal toll of $15. We can confirm that two methods give us the same answer.

Note

1. Neil A. Chriss, *Black-Scholes and Beyond Option Pricing Models.* New York: McGraw-Hill. Chapter 6.

References

Alziary, B., Jean-Paul Decamps, and Pierre-Francois Koehl. 1997. A P.D.E. approach to Asian options: Analytical and numerical evidence. *Journal of Banking and Finance*, 21 (5), 613–640.

Babbs, S. 2000. Binomial valuation of lookback options. *Journal of Economic Dynamics & Control*, 24, 1499–1525.

Boyle, P. P. 1998. A lattice framework for options pricing with two state variables. *Journal of Financial and Quantitative Analysis*, 23 (1), 1–12.

Boyle, P. P., and J. S. H. Lau. 1994. Bumping up against the barrier with the binomial method. *Journal of Derivatives*, 1 (4), 6–14.

Boyle, P. P., and Y. S. Tian. 1999. Pricing lookback and barrier options under the CEV process. *Journal of Financial and Quantitative Analysis*, 34 (2), 241–264.

Boyle, P. P., and Y. K. Tse. 1990. An algorithm for computing values of options on the maximum or minimum of several assets. *Journal of Financial and Quantitative Analysis*, 25 (2), 215–227.

Brennan, M. J., and E. S. Schwartz. 1977. The valuation of American put options. *Journal of Finance*, 32 (2), 449–462.

Broadie, M., and P. Glasserman. 1997. A continuity correction for discrete barrier options. *Mathematical Finance*, 7 (4), 325–349.

Broadie, M., P. Glasserman, and S. G. Kou. 1998. Connecting discrete and continuous path-dependent options. *Finance and Stochastics*, 2, 1–28.

Cao, M., and J. Wei. 2002. Equilibrium value of weather devivative. Working paper, Joseph L. Rotman School of Management, University of Toronto.

Carr, P., and A. Chou. 1997. Hedging complex barrier options. Working paper, Computer Science Department, MIT.

Chalasani, P., S. Jha, F. Egriboyun, and A. Varikooty. 1999. A refined binomial lattice for pricing American Asian options. *Review of Derivatives Research*, 3 (1), 85–105.

Chriss, N. A. 1997. *Black–Scholes and Beyond Option Pricing Models.* New York: McGraw-Hill.

Conze, A., and R. Viswanathan. 1991. Path dependent options: The case of lookback options. *Journal of Finance*, 46, 1893–1907.

Geske, R. 1979. The valuation of compound options. *Journal of Economics*, 7, 63–81.

Goldman, M. B., H. B. Sosin, and M. A. Gatto. 1979. Path dependent options: Buy at the low, sell at the high. *Journal of Finance*, 34 (5), 1111–1127.

Johnson, H. 1987. Options on the maximum and minimum of several assets. *Journal of Financial and Quantitative Analysis*, 22 (3), 277–283.

Longstaff, F. A. 1990. The valuation of options on yields. *Journal of Financial Economics*, 26, 97–121.

Longstaff, F. A., P. Santa-Clara, and E. S. Schwartz. 2001. The relative valuation of interest rate caps and swaptions: Theory and empirical evidence. *Journal of Finance*, 56 (6), 2067–2110.

Omberg, E. 1987. A note on the convergence of binomial-pricing and compound-option models. *Journal of Finance*, 42 (2), 463–469.

Reimer, M., and K. Sandmann. 1995. A discrete time approach for European and American barrier options. Working paper, University of Bonn.

Rubinstein, M. 1990. Pay now, choose later. *RISK*, December, 13.

Rubinstein, M. 1991a. One for another, *RISK*, July–August, 30–32.

Rubinstein, M. 1991b. Options for the undecided. *RISK*, April, 43.

Rubinstein, M. 1995a. Double trouble. *RISK*, January, 73.

Rubinstein, M. 1995b. Somewhere over the rainbow. *RISK*, January, 63–66.

Rubinstein, M., and E. Reiner. 1991a. Breaking down the barriers. *RISK*, September, 28–35.

Rubinstein, M., and E. Reiner. 1991b. Unscrambling the binary code. *RISK*, October, 75–83.

Thompson, A. C. 1995. Valuation of path-dependent contingent claims with multiple exercise decision over time: The case of take-or-pay. *Journal of Financial and Quantitative Analysis*, 30 (2), 271–293.

Turnbull, S. M., and L. M. Wakeman. 1991. A quick algorithm for pricing European average options. *Journal of Financial and Quantitative Analysis*, 26 (3), 377–389.

Willard, G. A. 1997. Calculating prices and sensitivities for path-independent derivative securities in multifactor models. *Journal of Derivatives*, 5 (1), 45–61.

Further Readings

Ackert, L. F., and Y. S. Tian. 2001. Efficiency in index options markets and trading in stock baskets. *Journal of Banking and Finance*, 25 (9), 1607–1634.

Avellaneda, M., and R. Buff. 1997. Combinatorial implications of nonlinear uncertain volatility models: The case of barrier options. *Applied Mathematical Finance*, 6 (1), 1–18.

Averbukh, V. Z. 1997. Pricing American options using monte carlo simulation. Ph.D. dissertation, Cornell University.

Babsiri, M. E., and G. Noel. 1998. Simulating path-dependent options: A new approach. *Journal of Derivatives*, 6 (2), 65–83.

Barone-Adesi, G., and R. E. Whaley. 1987. Efficient analytic approximation of American option values. *Journal of Finance*, 42 (2), 301–320.

Barraquand, J., and D. Martineau. 1995. Numerical valuation of high dimensional multivariate American securities. *Journal of Financial and Quantitative Analysis*, 30 (3), 383–405.

Boassaerts, P. 1989. Simulation estimators of optimal early exercise. Working paper, Carnegie-Mellon University.

Boyle, P. P., J. Evinde, and S. Gibbs. 1989. Numerical evaluation of multivariate contingent claims. *Review of Financial Studies*, 2 (2), 241–250.

Broadie, M., and P. Glasserman. 1997b. Pricing American-style securities using simulation. *Journal of Economics and Control*, 21, 1323–1352

Broadie, M., and P. Glasserman. 1997c. A stochastic mesh method for pricing high-dimensional American options. Working paper, Columbia University.

Brodie, M., P. Glasserman, and G. Jain. 1997. Enhanced Monte Carlo estimates for American option prices. *Journal of Derivatives*, 5 (1), 25–44.

Carr, P. 1998. Randomization and the American put. *Review of Financial Studies*, 11 (3), 597–626.

Carriere, J. F. 1996. Valuation of the early-exercise price for options using simulation and non-parametric regression. *Insurance: Mathematical and Economics*, 19, 19–30.

Derman, E., I. Kanu, D. Ergener, and I. Badhan. 1995. Numerical methods for options with barriers. *GoldmanSachs Quantitative Strategies Research Notes*, May, 1995.

Dong-Hyun, Ahn, S. Figlewski, and B. Gao. 1999. Pricing discrete barrier options with an adaptive mesh model. *Journal of Derivatives*, 6 (4), 33–43.

Figlewski, S., and B. Gao. 1999. The adaptive mesh model: A new approach to efficient option pricing. *Journal of Financial Economics*, 53 (3), 313–351.

Forsyth, P. A., K. R. Vetzal, and R. Zvan. 1998. Convergence of lattice and PDE methods for pricing Asian options. Working paper, University of Waterloo (Canada).

Gao, B., Jz. Huang, and M. Subrahmanyam. 2000. The valuation of American barrier options using the decomposition technique. *Journal of Economic Dynamics & Control*, 24 (11), .

Garcia, D. 2000. A Monte Carlo method for pricing American options. Working paper, University of California at Berkeley.

Geske, R., and H. E. Johnson. 1984. The American put option valued analytically. *Journal of Finance*, 39 (5), 1511–1524.

Henderson, V., and R. Wojakowski. 2001. On the equivalence of floating and fixed-strike Asian options. Working paper, Lancaster University Management School.

Hyungsok, Ahn, A. Penauld, and P. Wilmott. 1998. Various passport options and their valuation. MFG Working paper, Oxford University.

Ibanez, A., and Zapatero, F. 2002. Monte Carlo valuation of American options through computation of the optimal exercise frontier. Working paper, Instituto Tecnológico Autónomo de México and University of Southern California.

In-Joon, Kim. 1990. The analytic valuation of American options. *Review of Financial Studies*, 3 (4), 547–572.

Joshi, M. S. 2001. Pricing discretely sampled path-dependent exotic options using replication methods. Working paper, Royal Bank of Scotland Group Risk.

Kane, A., and A. J. Marcus. 1986. Valuation and optimal exercise of the wild card option in the Treasury bond futures market. *Journal of Finance*, 41 (1), 195–207.

Kou, S. G. 2001. On pricing of discrete barrier options. Working paper, Columbia University.

Lemieux, C., and Pierre L'Ecuyer. 1998. Efficiency improvement by lattice rules for pricing Asian options. Working paper, IEEE Computer Society.

Lyuu, Y. D. 1998. Very fast algorithms for barrier option pricing and the ballot problem. *Journal of Derivatives*, 5 (3), 68–79.

Milevsky, M. A., and S. E. Posner. 1998. Asian options: The sum of lognormal and the reciprocal gamma distribution. *Journal of Financial and Quantitative Analysis*, 33 (3), 409–422.

Nielsen, J. A., and K. Sandmann. 1999. Pricing of Asian exchange rate options under stochastic interest rates as a sum of delayed payment options. Working paper, University of Bonn.

Raymar, B. R., and M. J. Zwecher. 1997. Monte Carlo estimation of American call options on the maximum of several stocks. *Journal of Derivatives*, 5 (1), 7–33.

San-Lin, Chung, M. Shackleton, and R. Wojakowski. 2000. Efficient quadratic approximation of floating strike Asian option values. Working paper, Lancaster University Management School.

Schmock, U., S. E. Shreve, and U. Wystup. 2002. Valuation of exotic options under shortselling constraints. *Finance and Stochastics*, 6 (1), 143–172.

Taksar, T. S. 1997. Analytical approximate solutions for the prices of American exotic options. Working paper, State University of New York at Stony Brook.

Tilley, J. A. 1993. Valuing American options in a path simulation model. *Transactions of the Society of Actuaries*, 45, 83–104.

Tsitsiklis, J., and B. Van Roy. 1999. Optimal stopping of Markov processes: Hilbert space theory, approximation of algorithms, and an application to pricing high dimensional financial derivatives. *IEEE Transactions of Automatic Control*, 44, 1840–1851.

CORPORATE LIABILITIES

8

Investment Grade Corporate Bonds: Option Adjusted Spreads

The option adjusted spread (OAS) method, used in a relative valuation context, is central to extending the valuation method for derivatives to balance sheet items. In using an option adjusted spread to allow for risk sources not explicitly modeled, we can extend the relative valuation models for the derivatives to a broader class of securities in the capital markets. OAS is widely used in fixed-income analytics for mortgage-backed securities, corporate bonds, and many other securities to identify the embedded option value and the market risk premiums.

Corporations borrow money by issuing bonds, which are debts. They can be bank loans or short-term funding, including commercial paper. Or they can be medium-term notes or private placements in which debts are issued to a restricted group of lenders. However, in this book, *corporate bonds* refer to public bond issues, available for any investor to buy and sell. This chapter will keep the discussion on credit risk to a minimum. The impact of the firm's likelihood of default on the bond's value will be discussed at greater length in chapter 9.

We have seen how the law of one price can be used to value any fixed cash flows based on the Treasury or swap curve. This bond model provides a consistent framework to measure the value of a bond. However, can the bond model in chapter 3 apply to corporate bonds, because they often have embedded options on interest rate risks? What valuation method can be applied to incorporate all the specifications of corporate bonds? The interest rate contingent claim method will enable us to compare bonds that may have vastly different provisions.

In order to see how this valuation framework can be applied, we will describe a corporate bond, Wal-Mart 8.57 2010, as an example. Each corporate bond has specific terms and conditions, covenants and provisions that are important for valuation purposes. Particular attention is given to value the call provision, the sinking fund provision, and the use of option adjusted spreads. The valuation approach enables us to value the embedded options in a bond by simultaneously taking the shape of the yield curve into account. The valuation approach can identify the appropriate bonds for comparison and can quantify the bond values relative to comparable bonds. A key element in this valuation approach is the use of the option adjusted spread, which is affected by the liquidity spread and the credit risk of the bond. The following sections further elaborate on these two factors affecting the bond value. We will discuss how to measure liquidity (or marketability) spread and the credit scoring methods that can provide a method to calculate the option adjusted spread.

The valuation model of a bond can be used for bond analysis. What analytical tools can be used in a valuation model for a corporate bond? We show that these tools will enable us to measure the bond's sensitivity to the interest rate risks and the risk of tightening or widening of the option adjusted spreads. These tools include key rate durations and option adjusted durations. The following section provides a numerical example of analyzing a Eurobond with a step-up coupon and a call provision, using the valuation model. Since this Eurobond can be separated into a swaption and a straight bond with a coupon and a principal, we can show that corporate bond pricing and the capital market pricing of derivatives must be governed by the market arbitrage condition. As a result, relative pricing or contingent claim pricing is not only theoretically robust but also a result of market practice. Finally, we will describe some applications of the valuation model and the bond analysis. These applications are important to portfolio management, asset and liability management, and risk management of financial institutions.

8.1   Describing a Corporate Bond

The corporate debt market is estimated to be $3.9 trillion,[1] approximately 21% of the entire U.S. debt market, which includes government securities, mortgages, municipal bonds, and consumer financing. Corporate debt is clearly a major sector in our fixed-income market. (See figure 8.1.)

Since the issuer of a corporate bond can be any type of firm, the bond does not have to adhere to any rigid format. There are some common bond types and designs, but there are also many varieties. The maturities can range from one day to 100 years. The coupons can be fixed or floating, changing according to a specified schedule. We will focus on the standard bond types in this chapter. Chapter 10 will discuss other innovations.

In order to have an overview of the salient features of a bond, we will review one example. Let us consider a typical description of a bond in the investment community. Wal-Mart Stores is the largest retailer in North America, operating discount department stores, wholesale clubs, and combination discount stores and supermarkets. The firm had a capitalization of $203 billion in 2000. The long-term debt level to the capitalization is 37%, showing that Wal-Mart has a significant debt outstanding, but the

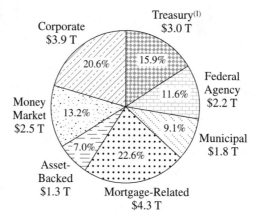

Total: $19.0 Trillion

[1] Includes marketable public debt

Figure 8-1 Outstanding bond market debt as of March 31, 2002*
[1]Includes marketable public debt.
*The Bond Market Association estimates
Sources: Federal Reserve System, U.S. Treasury, GNMA, FNMA, FHLMC.

debt is supported by much of the shareholders' value, since it is less than 40% of the capitalization.

One of the bonds is described as follows:

Wal-Mart Stores WMT 8.57 01/02/10

Issuer: Wal-Mart Stores, retail discount

Bond type: Pass-through certificate

Coupon: 8.57   Fixed S/A   30/360

Issue size: USD 160,023,000   Amount outstanding: USD 120,843,550

Call @ make whole

Pro rata sinking fund

An issuer's contractual terms reflect the market concerns at the time of issuance. These concerns range from existing interest rates and the probability of default on the bond to the supply of and demand for a particular bond type. After the issuance, the market may change (for example, the yield curve moves) but the agreement, as described above, will not. In the secondary market as well as in the primary market, participants need to evaluate the risks and rewards embedded in each corporate issue. We will proceed to discuss each item in the general description of the bond.

Identification, Issuer, Sector:

Wal-Mart Stores WMT 8.57 01/02/10

Retail discount

WMT 8.57 means that the Wal-Mart (WMT) bond has a coupon rate of 8.57%. The last principal payment is paid on January 2, 2010.

Corporate bonds are often referred to by their issuer's symbol, followed by the coupon rate and the maturity date. The industry sector of the issuer is often relevant because the bond's credit risk is related to the business risk of the sector. Firms in the same sector tend to have similar debt structures and bond features. The sector can indicate whether the bond is sensitive to economic downturns or interest rate levels. For these reasons, portfolio managers tend to use the information to diversify their risk exposure across the sectors. In managing a corporate bond portfolio, investing a significant amount in one sector is called the *concentration risk*. A portfolio manager typically avoids concentration risk, since the risk exposure will not be properly diversified. To diversify the credit risk, a portfolio manager seeks to lower the concentration risk in terms of any one firm or firms legally related to any one entity, and also to any market segment or industry sector.

Corporate financial managers decide on the bond maturities, types of coupon rates (floating versus fixed), principal payment schedules, and other debt terms and conditions. These decisions depend on two things. The first is the debt structure of the firm, which describes the debts that the firm has already sold. The second is the market conditions on the demand for and supply of the bonds for different maturity spectra and credit risk levels. Firms may seek long-term debt financing when their assets have long economic lives. For example, utility firms often use long-term debt to finance their capital investments. The decisions on using debt to fund the firm's operation or on the type of the bonds to add to the existing debt structure are complex financial theory problems. We will deal with this question at length starting in chapter 12. For now, we will focus on the analysis of corporate bonds that have been issued.

Bond Type: Pass-through Certificates

The WMT bond is a pass-through certificate, a claim on a certain portion of the cash flows from the assets in a trust. For example, a firm may package its accounts receivable as assets. A trust, a legal entity representing a firm, is set up. The portfolio of accounts receivable becomes the assets of the trust's balance sheet. Pass-through certificates are issued as liabilities to raise funds in order to buy the accounts receivable. The cash flows from the accounts receivable are then passed to the investors in the pass-through certificates. Then the firm replaces its accounts receivable with cash. We say that the firm has securitized the accounts receivable. That is, in general, the interest and principal on these assets in the trust account will support the payments of the pass-through certificates. Wal-Mart Stores' operational cash flows are not used to support the bond. That means the principal and interest payments are passed from the financial securities— in this case, the lease incomes—of Wal-Mart to these pass-through certificates. This type of bond is an *asset-backed security*.

There are many other bond types. Mortgage bonds are secured by real estate; *equipment bonds* are secured by the firm's equipment. Unsecured bonds, called *debentures*, are perhaps the most common bond type. Bonds sold through agents without the full disclosure required by the Securities and Exchange Commission are called *medium-term notes*, a misleading term. "Medium-term note" does not mean that the bond maturities are not long-term or short-term. The distinction is made for a legal reason. Since these bonds are sold directly to a specific, targeted group of general investors, they are not subject to full disclosure. *Public bonds*, which are available to all general investors, are required to provide a full disclosure.

Coupon description: 8.57   Fixed S/A   30/360

The bond is a fixed-rate bond that pays coupons on a semiannual basis determined by the annual coupon rate of 8.57% (4.285% of the outstanding principal for each six-month period). In general, the interest payment can be floating. That means it can be based on a market rate like the three-month LIBOR or the one-year Treasury rate plus an interest margin (additional spread amount). Floating-rate bonds enable the firm to borrow at short-term rates that continually adjust to the market, even though the maturity of the bond may be long. These rates are continually reset over time at regular intervals. The dates for the resets are called *reset dates*. For example, a one-year Treasury rate can be reset every month, but the interest may not be paid out monthly. In such cases, the interest accrues and is paid out over a longer time period. For example, it can accrue monthly and be paid out semiannually.

In the United States, most corporate bonds have semiannual coupon payments. Their use is of a market convention. Other bonds, like the mortgage-backed securities that we will discuss in chapter 10, pay interest monthly and many bonds sold in Europe pay annual coupons. Therefore, the frequency of interest or coupon payment is based more on the market convention than on any fundamental economic reasons.

The accrual convention 30/360 is based on counting every month as thirty days, twelve months a year, for most corporate bonds in the United States. That means the amount of accrued interest is the proportion of the number of days from the last coupon date to the 180 days of the semiannual coupon payment. When the amount of accrued interest is added to the quoted price, the combined amount is the actual price which investors pay or receive.

Issue size: USD 160,023,000; Amount Outstanding: USD 120,843,550

The *issue size* is important to an investor because it indicates the liquidity in the market. However, the amount outstanding in the marketplace decreases with time to maturity because of the *sinking fund provision*, which we will discuss below in more detail. Briefly, a sinking fund provision requires the firm to retire a specified amount of debt over the life of a bond. For this reason, the amount outstanding is not the same as the issue size. Moreover, the investor needs to know the amount outstanding to evaluate the liquidity of a bond in the marketplace. The larger the amount outstanding, the higher the likelihood of a bond being more widely held; therefore, there is more trading activity, which means that more buyers and sellers of a bond are available. WMT bonds have over $120 million outstanding, which should indicate that the bond is quite liquid.

Bond Call Provision: Call @ Make Whole

Firms have the option to call bonds. For a typical debenture, the *call provision* is represented by a call schedule that allows the corporation to buy back bonds at the call price at a specified date. When a bond is called, the firm pays the holders the call price and the accrued interest. Corporate bonds have precise *call schedules* stating the call prices at specific dates. Call schedules vary greatly. Typically, there is a first call date that stipulates the first date at which the bond is callable. A bond may be immediately callable, or it can be called at any time after the issuance. The first call price is often half the coupon rate in addition to the face value. For example, if the coupon rate of a bond is 10%, then the first call price is often 105. Then the call prices linearly decline to par (to 100, bond face value) some time before maturity or at maturity. If the call price reaches face value some time before maturity, its price will remain at par until maturity. For example, consider a ten-year bond with a 10% coupon rate. The first call price may be 105, effective immediately. The second year, the call price may be 104, then drop by 1 every year, reaching the call price of 100 in the fifth year. Then the call price will remain at 100 until maturity.

WMT's *call at make whole* is slightly more complicated. The make whole provision enables a firm to have control over the capital structure, but not the option of refinancing the bond when interest rates are favorable. This purpose is accomplished by requiring the firm to pay the investors a call price higher than they would otherwise receive independent of interest rate scenarios. This price is often set by discounting the bond cash flows at 5–15 basis points over the Treasury curve for investment grade, and 50 basis points for high-yield, bonds. Since such spreads are very low, judging by historical experience, in general calling bonds would be very expensive as measured by net present value. For example, consider an A rated bond. Its value is based on discount rates that are the Treasury rates plus, say, 50 basis points. If the bond has a make whole provision and the firm seeks to use the call provision, then the firm can buy back the bond at a price determined by the present value of the coupons and principal, using the discount rates of the Treasury rates plus, for example, five basis points. This price would be higher than the price of a bond which is otherwise identical except for the call provision.

Bonds may be called for managerial reasons. The firm may wish to retire some debt in order to lower the debt ratio and consequently increase the corporate bond rating. Or it may wish to have a simpler balance sheet to ready itself for merger and acquisition activities. Perhaps, in a merger and acquisition, the bonds have to be retired as one of the conditions. In such cases, investors may not suffer financially from the call because the call price may be significantly higher than an equivalent bond without the make whole call provision.

Bond Sinking Fund Provision: Pro Rata Sinking Fund

A sinking fund provision requires bonds to be retired over time according to a specified schedule. Sinking funds are designed so that the repayments are amortized over a period of time; these bonds are retired on a pro rata basis. That means investors will receive the coupons and a portion of the principal paid back over time, and this proportion is the same for all investors. For example, in this case, if the upcoming sinking fund is 10% of the outstanding amount, then each bondholder will receive 10% of the principal as an early payment. The proportion of the principal which remains outstanding to the amount issued is called the *factor*. For example, a bond's original issue amount is $100 million. After some years, a portion of the bonds has to be retired by the firm, and the outstanding amount in the market is $90 million. The bond factor is 0.9. The factor of the bond at issuance is 1, and it declines gradually until it reaches 0 at maturity. The factor of the WMT bond is $0.755161 (= 120,843,500/160,023,000)$.

In this case, the sinking fund is paid down semiannually in a slightly complicated way. This is because the schedule has to match the cash flows of the assets in the trust. (See table 8.1.)

The schedule continues until the maturity date. The last sinking fund payment can be quite small, since much of the debt will have been retired when we reach the last sinking fund payment. For this reason, the average weighted life of the bond can be significantly lower than is suggested by the maturity.

There are other sinking fund arrangements. For a debenture, typically there is no requirement for sinking funds for the first several years. After a deferment of a period, usually five years or more, a fixed amount of bonds must be retired at par to the trustee of the bond, who represents all the bondholders' interests. The trustee will ensure that the firm fulfills its sinking fund obligations. If such obligations are not fulfilled, then the

Table 8.1 Sinking Fund Amortization Schedule

Date	Amount
1/2/00	1,310,200
7/2/00	15,000
1/2/01	12,451,000
1/2/02	13,701,000
1/2/03	14,518,000
7/2/03	300,000
1/2/04	15,517,000
7/2/04	554,000
1/2/05	17,309,000
7/2/05	3,538,000

trustee may decide to declare the firm in default. The sinking fund provision requires the firm to retire the bond gradually over the life of the bond. This can be accomplished by the firm's buying back some of the outstanding bonds over time and surrendering them to the trustee. There are two ways to retire the bond in this manner. First, the firm that has issued the bond can buy back portions of the bond in the open market. Second, the firm can make payments to the trustee, who will then call the bonds back at par through a lottery in which bond certificate numbers are drawn at random, and the firm can retire those selected bonds. The number of bonds selected will equal the number determined by the sinking fund requirement. If the firm cannot satisfy the sinking fund obligation (i.e., cannot get the required number of bonds to surrender to the trustee), the firm is considered in default of the debt.

8.2   Valuation of a Bond

Price Quote in Terms of Yield

The price of WMT 8.57 10 is quoted at 114.4083 (6.25). The price quote is based on a percent of the principal. The yield (semiannually compounding) is 6.25%. The yield of a bond is calculated as the internal rate of return of the cash flow (coupon payments and sinking fund payments) given the price. It is important to note that the yield and price are mathematically related. For this reason, the yield of 6.25% and the price quote both indicate how the market values the bond.

There are alternative conventions in quoting a bond price. Another common convention is using the yield spread. Suppose the weighted average life of a bond is six years, and the yield of a Treasury seven-year on-the-run bond is 6%. Then the bond yield (or price quote) can be quoted as a spread in terms of basis points over the seven-year Treasury bond yield. For example, the spread may be quoted as 25 basis points, setting an arbitrary number. The 25 basis points is the yield spread to the nearest on-the-run Treasury bond. However, when the yield curve has a significant slope, a weighted average life of six years may no longer be comparable with the seven-year Treasury bond. In this case, we can have a blended rate as a benchmark comparison. The quote may be given as a spread from the linearly interpolated yields of two on-the-run Treasury bonds. Suppose another benchmark bond is the five-year Treasury bond with a yield of 5%. The blended yield for the six-year bond is 5.5%, which is the average of the seven-year on-the-run bond yield of 6% and the five-year Treasury bond yield of 5%. Using the yield spread of blended yields to determine the yield of the bond is often called *matrix pricing*. In matrix pricing, pricing or quoting a bond depends upon the market prices of actively traded bonds that reflect benchmark prices. Matrix pricing often does not depend on any financial modeling, but compares a bond against bonds similar in terms of their characteristics, such as maturity, coupon rate, sector, and rating.

For a callable bond with a call schedule, the yield to maturity does not represent the internal rate of return of holding a bond until maturity. This is because the maturity of the bond is no longer certain and the bond cash flow is not fixed. Rather, the yield to maturity depends on future interest rate scenarios. If the interest rate has fallen significantly and the bond is likely to be called, then the expected weighted average life of the bond will be shortened. As a result, the yield to maturity will entirely misstate the internal rate of return of the bond by still assuming that the bond will be held until maturity. For this reason, the bond price may be quoted as *yield to call*, which is the yield to the first call price. Alternatively, the bond price may be quoted as the *yield to worst*, which is the lowest yield number for all the possible call prices on the call schedule. The yield to worst is calculated by checking the yield for each call price along the call schedule to determine the lowest yield.

The central point in this discussion is that the price quote based on the yield spread is simply a market quote, a way to indicate the price. In contrast, the methodology that determines the appropriate present value of cash flows is called valuation. For the most part, the valuation of a bond (particularly an investment grade bond) is fundamentally different from valuing equity. A precise bond valuation model can explain much of the bond value. Unlike equity, bond values can be determined by comparing market prices of similar bonds. There are no empirically estimated parameters like beta or future estimates like earnings. For bonds, the cash flows are stated precisely and the discount rates can, by and large, be estimated. Developing an accurate bond valuation model is important because these models for investment grade bonds can provide a fairly accurate valuation of a bond in the market.

Callability

The call provision affects the value of the bond. It has a dual purpose. First, it allows a firm to buy back bonds at a fixed price, enabling it to have control over its capital structure. For example, the firm may wish to reduce the debt outstanding because it wants to increase its creditworthiness. Or, for some sinking fund bonds, the remaining issues outstanding toward maturity may be only a small amount with little or no liquidity. The firm may "sweep" the remaining bonds away from the market and repackage the debt into a larger issue. When the firm needs to retire the debt, for whatever reason, it may prefer not to rely on the capital market to provide the liquidity necessary to purchase the bonds in the market. This is because the bonds may not be purchased at a fair price. For example, *accumulators* (investors who hold the bonds in anticipation of the firm's buying them back) may require a significant premium on the intrinsic value of the bonds to sell back to the issuer. A call provision can provide a cap on the price in these situations.

There is another motivation for the call provision: when interest rates fall, the firm can sell more bonds at current lower rates and buy back the bonds at the call price. The call provision provides the firm a way to re-fund the debt at a lower interest cost. This re-funding provision in essence offers the firm a call option to buy back the bonds at a fixed price, where the underlying risk is that of the interest rates.

$$\text{Callable Bond Price} = \text{Non-callable Bond Price} - \text{Call Option Value} \qquad (8.1)$$

This equation shows that holding a callable bond is the same as holding a noncallable bond and shorting a call option. A fall in interest rates will lead to a higher price of the option-free bond, but part of that price increase is mitigated by the loss of the call option position.

We can also view the equation from an issuer's perspective. In issuing a callable bond, the firm has issued an option-free bond, but simultaneously has bought some call options of the bond. In doing so, the firm has the right to retire the bond at a fixed price, but at the cost of the option premium. The proceeds to the firm of selling the bonds are the present value of the option-free bond net of the option cost. The proceeds are therefore less than those of selling an option-free bond.

The callable bond price is equal to the noncallable bond price minus the call option value, as suggested by equation (8.1). Therefore, the callable bond price should be lower than that of the corresponding noncallable bond because the call option value is subtracted from the noncallable bond price. Alternatively stated, the yield of a callable bond should be higher than that of a noncallable bond.

To maintain managerial control over the ability to retire bonds without paying a higher yield for the interest rate option, some bonds are issued with a "no refunding restriction" for a certain period. For the period when the bond is nonrefundable, the firm is not allowed to buy back the bond for the stated purpose of reselling a bond at a lower interest rate. But there are many ways to re-fund a nonrefundable bond. After all, firms sell bonds (or take out loans) and buy back bonds quite often. For example, a firm can take out a bank loan and use part of the proceeds to call a bond with nonrefunding restrictions. It is quite difficult to identify a particular purpose of a debt issuance or a bank loan, since the firm does not need to specify the purpose of a particular borrowing. For this reason, the re-funding restriction generally has little economic value.

Sinking Fund

The sinking fund affects the bond value in two ways. In essence, a sinking fund specifies the timing of the principal repayments. Thus, the value of a sinking fund bond is affected by the shape of the yield curve. For example, consider two bonds with the same maturity T but one has a sinking fund schedule and the other does not. Now suppose the T-year interest rate rises, while other rates remain the same; then the price for the bond without the sinking fund would fall more than that of the bond with the sinking fund. This is because the bond with the sinking fund has more obligated payments in earlier years, and therefore its value is more sensitive to changes in the shorter-term interest rates than to changes in the T-year rate. Beyond the cash flow timing issue, there is the option aspect. The sinking fund option provision offers the issuer the ability to retire the sinking fund obligation by an open market purchase or by a lottery, essentially calling the sinking fund bond at par. This option affects the bond price because of the call at the par price; or the firm can buy back the sinking fund bond at par value. The annual or semiannual sinking fund operation is similar to a call schedule such that it offers the firm the ability to buy back the bonds at a fixed price. The differences are, first, that the call price of the sinking fund option is par, whereas the call price of the call provision is often above par. Second, and more important, the sinking fund option applies to only a portion of the bond at each sinking fund operation date; a call option applies to the entire issue. Thus, the sinking fund option is a series of call options on the bond issue. At each sinking fund date, the issuer has the choice to call back the sinking fund amount at par or buy back the bonds at the market price.

Some sinking funds have an additional feature called the *double-up option*. At each sinking fund date, the firm can retire the stated sinking fund amount or double that amount. Using the double-up option, bonds can be retired faster. But the choice is the same as that of the chooser option, allowing the holder to decide whether or not to exercise the double-up option. The valuation methodology is therefore the same as that for a chooser option.

Consider this example. For simplicity, we will assume that the bond has no call provision. It is a coupon bond with a three-year maturity and the principal value is $100. The bond has a double-up sinking fund provision of a $10 principal at the end of each year.

The double-up option decision has the structure of a tree. At the end of each year, the firm can decide whether or not to double up. When the double-up decision is made, the principal of the bond falls by $20. When no double-up decision is made, the principal amount falls by only $10, the sinking fund requirement. The decision tree is illustrated in figure 8.2.

We now construct an arbitrage-free interest rate binomial lattice model over three years, using a monthly (or annual) step size. At the terminal date of the third year, each node has a bundle of information consisting of four values that keep track of the historical events: the bond is doubled up or not doubled up in the first year, and the same two possibilities apply in the second year. The remaining principals at maturity are $60, $70, $70, and $80, as depicted in figure 8.2. In other words, at each maturity node we have four remaining principals for the bond with the double-up sinking fund provision, whereas we have only one principal for a straight bond. We calculate the bond price based on a par value of 100 for simplicity.

Since there are four cases, we will construct the backward substitution to derive the market value of the bond prices for each case, depending on the history of the doubling up of the sinking funds. Refer to the four cases in figure 8.2. First, let us consider case 1. For each node at the end of second year, the firm exercises the double-up. Let the market value of the bond with $1 face value at the end of the second year at state i have the value $B^*(i)$. This value is determined by rolling back the bond from the maturity date to the end of the second year. We will provide a numerical example of this valuation approach later in this chapter.

Credit Risk Ratings

Rating Agency	Moody's	S & P
Rating	Aa2	AA

Credit risk is one major determinant of bond value. A number of corporations, called rating agencies, provide ratings of the creditworthiness of issuers and issues. The credit-worthiness of a bond or an issuer is defined as the ability to pay the promised payment on time. There is no precise definition of the credit measure. The measure is not related only to the possible dollar amount of loss. The issuer may delay a payment by six months or may default on the entire principal. These rating agencies do not provide the public with their precise methodologies in evaluating creditworthiness, since the rating process is only partially quantitative. It also depends on the analysts' views on the management style and less tangible attributes.

Two major rating agencies are Standard and Poor's Corporation (S&P) and Moody's Investors Services, Inc. (Moody's). Their rating systems range from AAA to D (S & P) and Aaa to C (Moody's), in a way that is akin to grades for university students, except there are no Fs. Today, few corporations have the highest rating (AAA or Aaa). Most bonds (measured in dollar amount) at issuance carry a rating of A or AA. For example, in November 2001, 20.3% of the bonds sold were rated AA, and 59.1% were rated A.

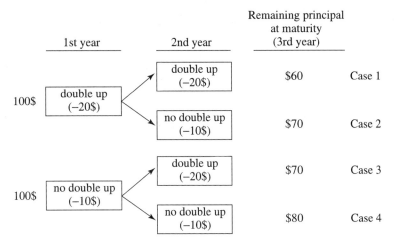

Figure 8-2 The double-up option. The double-up option decision has the structure of a tree. At the end of each year, the firm can decide whether or not to double-up. When the double-up decision is made, the principal of the bond falls by $20. When no double-up decision is made, the principal amount falls by only $10, the sinking fund requirement.

The remaining issues were rated lower. The WMT bond carries a Moody's rating of Aa2 and an S&P of AA.

Bonds with ratings below BBB (S&P) or Baa (Moody's) are considered *high yield or junk bonds*. These bonds are considered risky in terms of default. Bonds with ratings equal to or above BBB and Baa are called *investment grade*. The distinction can be important. Many pension funds and other asset managements are not allowed to hold junk bonds in their portfolios. A firm with a rating below investment grade cannot access a large portion of potential investors. Thus, ratings are important to corporate financial management.

The default risk of bonds with the same issuer may be different and the bonds can have different ratings. One main reason is that bonds may have different priority rules. The bond covenants state the obligations of the corporation to the investors. Among these obligations is the responsibility of the corporation to pay interest in a timely fashion, and to keep its corporate status high. The covenant also indicates under what conditions the firm will declare bankruptcy. A number of conditions may trigger bankruptcy. For example, the cross-default clause stipulates that the bond is in default if any other bond of the firm is in default. Some clauses specify courses of action that are contingent on the values of standardized financial ratios. For instance, a clause may give investors the right to prepayment of principal if the debt ratio exceeds a stated limit. If the firm cannot raise the funds to pay the principal, then the bond is in default.

At default, under Chapter 11 (which we will discuss at length in chapter 9), the firm is protected by the bankruptcy court. The bond trustees will be responsible for proposing a reorganization plan. Not all bonds are treated alike, because there are priority rules. Senior debentures will receive the promised payment first before the junior debt holders. Equity holders are the last to receive any payments. When such a rule is strictly followed, we say that the *absolute priority rule* is followed. That means the payments to different classes of bondholders, junior or senior debts, strictly follow the specifications in the bond covenants.

However, the absolute priority rule is not strictly followed in practice. The reorganization under the bankruptcy law allows for renegotiation among the bondholders and shareholders that seeks to maximize the values to the claimants. Sometimes the firm's value depends on the management in place, and the debt holders are better served if the management (who may own part of the equity) remains in the firm. As a result, the absolute priority rule is adjusted for this purpose. This is referred to as *strategic debt servicing* to underscore how debt holders accept an immediate loss by giving up a portion of the firm to the equity holders in exchange for the longer-term gain. The gain is realized when the management succeeds in increasing the firm's value.

The bond rating is important to bond valuation. A number of studies have provided us with an overview of the behavior of these ratings. Altman and Kao (1992) show that the ratings are serially correlated; a downrating is more likely to be followed by another downrating. Therefore, rating changes are not random walks, where the rating change depends on the firm's recent rating history. Furthermore, the probabilities of an upgrade or downgrade, called *rating transitions*, vary significantly over time. Modeling the changes of rating is quite difficult. Unlike market prices, ratings do not change in real time, continually adjusting to the market conditions. Ratings are derived, for the most part, from historical information. Hite and Warga (1997) show that rating changes by agencies often lag behind market information, as in bond prices and stock prices. And Ederington et al. (1987) also find that credit rating changes lag market pricing.

Option Adjusted Spread

The final part of the valuation of a corporate bond is tying the credit premiums, liquidity premiums, and the provision values together.

Now we apply the bond model to determine the theoretical bond price. *Option adjusted spread* (OAS) is the constant spread (in basis points) that we add to the spot curve such that when we apply the bond model based on the spot curve to the OAS, we have the theoretical price or the observed price. OAS is therefore the spread that provides the annual excess returns from the spot curve to compensate for the credit premium and the liquidity premium. The spread is option-adjusted such that we can isolate the values of the call and sinking fund provisions. The bond model incorporates the rational pricing of the interest rate option embedded in the bond. The average OAS of the comparable bonds may provide an indication of the appropriate OAS of the bond we are valuing. Using this average OAS, we can then use the bond model to value the bond.

There are many corporate bonds without embedded options. In those cases, by definition the OAS is the spread added to the spot curve in determining the present value of the promised payments of the bond.

As discussed before, corporate bonds can be classified under one of the following major sectors: utilities, transportation, financial, and industrial. Each sector's bonds possess different characteristics because each sector has different motives for issuing debt. Utility companies, for example, issue bonds to support power plants. Since the plants represent long-term assets, bonds of utility companies tend to have very long maturities. An AAA rated bond in one sector may provide a higher yield than another sector's AAA bond, given the same coupon, maturity, and provisions. This difference is attributable to unique, nonfinancial risk factors such as political or environmental issues (see figure 8.3).

Let us assume that the yield spreads approximate the option adjusted spreads for

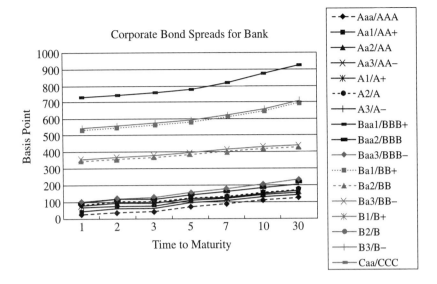

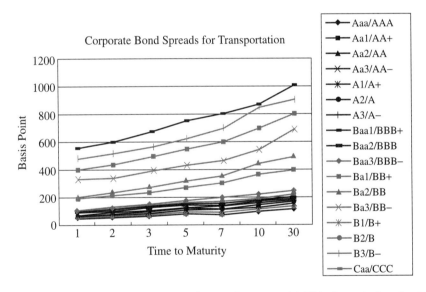

Figure 8-3 Yield spreads of the Corporate Sectors, June 21, 2002. This figure depicts the yield spreads between corporate bonds and Treasury bonds with comparable maturities. The yield spreads are plotted as functions of the maturity for different ratings, grouped under different sectors: bank, transportation, utility, industrial, and financials. The results show that the spread increases with maturity and the spread between two consecutive notches widens with the decrease in rating. Bonds with the same rating but in different sectors may have different yield spreads. This is true for all sectors. Source: http//:www.bondsonline.com/asp/corp/spreadfin.html.

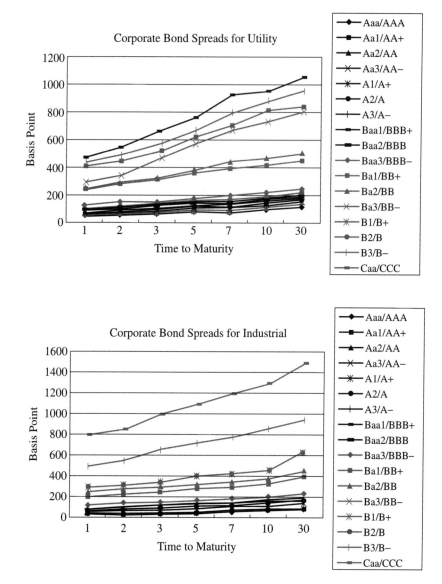

Figure 8-3 (cont.)

the purpose of this discussion. In recent years, most bonds have not had embedded options, and therefore this assumption should be quite reasonable. According to figure 8.3, we can make the following observations. The option adjusted spreads depend on the bond rating, the sector, and the maturity. More specifically, the spread increases with maturity. This may suggest that the likelihood of default increases with maturity or the marketability falls with longer maturity. Of course, one expects the spread to increase with a lower rating. But the spread between two rating notches accelerates as the rating falls. This observation suggests that bond pricing related to credit risk is not directly proportional to credit risk measures, such as debt ratios, profitability, and liquidity ratios. The complex relationship of the default risk of a bond to its value will be dealt with in more detail in chapter 9.

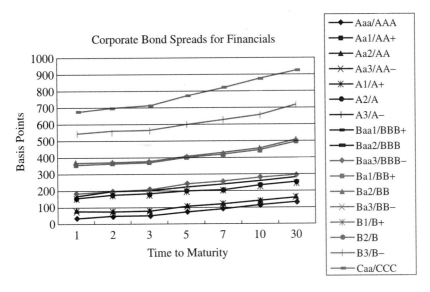

Figure 8-3 (cont.)

With lower rated bonds, the credit spread falls with longer maturity, in contrast to investment grade bonds, which are not shown in figure 8.3. The difference between lower rated bonds and investment grade bonds is the promised payments versus the expected payments. For lower rated bonds, investors do not expect to receive the promised coupons and principals, because the firm is likely to default on the promised payment—to such an extent that using the spread as an approximation is too crude to be useful. For example, consider a zero-coupon low rated bond. The investors do not expect to receive the full promised principal of the bond. Assume that they expect to receive only 50% of the principal when the bond matures. Then the bond price is determined by discounting $50 at the Treasury bond rate plus a risk premium. We assume that the yield curve is flat at 6% and the risk premium is 2%. The yield to maturity of the bond would assume the principal payment to be par, $100. The yield to maturity is the discount rate for $100 that equals the market price. The 10-year and 20-year low rated bond prices are $23.16 and $10.73, respectively. Furthermore, the yield to maturity is 15.75% for the 10-year bond and 11.81% for the 20-year bond. This simple numerical example shows that the yield to maturity falls with longer maturity.

Sarig and Warga (1989) studied the term structure of yield spread over three credit ratings—BBB, BB, and B/C. To isolate the credit risks from other factors, they considered only zero-coupon issues without any other provisions, such as callability, coupons, and sinking funds. Their results were interesting: BBB spreads were upward-sloping and the B/C bonds were downward-sloping. We will revisit these high-yield or low rated bonds in chapter 9.

The credit spread is also related to the shape of the yield curve. This is often attributed to the close relationship between the pricing of credit risk and the health of the economy. In credit-risk analysis, the most important systematic risk, one that affects a large segment of bonds, is the impact of a recession on the firm's ability to service the debt.

These spreads change, depending on the market supply and demand. During major economic events, such as the Asian crisis of 1997, the Russian economic crisis of 1998, or the tragedy of September 11, 2001, many investors seek to hold liquid and safe bonds such as Treasury securities. As a result, many investors sell corporate bonds and buy government bonds. This phenomenon, called *flight to quality*, leads to an increase in yield spreads. Is the increase in spread a result of increased default premium, risk premium for default, or liquidity premium? Unfortunately, there is no simple answer to this question. The uncertain changes in these spreads are called *basis risks*, referring to the changes of the relationships across sectors of asset classes. For example, the uncertainty of the spread between the utility sector and the industrial sector of the same rating is called the basis risk between the two sectors.

The basis risks of bonds having different ratings are positively correlated. When the spread of AAA to the Treasury curve widens, the spread of AA to the Treasury curve is also likely to widen. This suggests that the market assigns a credit risk premium which has two components: the expected losses from default and the risk premium for default. For this reason, when the market becomes more risk-averse with respect to the credit risk, corporate bonds will trade with a wider spread.

8.3   Numerical Examples

Consider a flat spot yield curve at 6.5%. Assume that the bond has an annual coupon payment of 7% and a maturity of six years.

Valuation of a Bond with No Embedded Options

The bond with a principal of $100 has an annual coupon payment of $7. Needless to say, the payment is $107 on the maturity date, which falls in the sixth year. The spot yield curve is flat at 6.5%. The bond value is therefore the present value of the coupon up to year 6, and the principal in year 6.

$$Bond\ Price = \left(\sum_{n=1}^{6} 7e^{-0.065 \cdot n} \right) + 100 \cdot e^{-0.065 \times 6} = 101.366 \qquad (8.2)$$

Valuation of a Callable Bond

Continuing with the above example, let us now assume that the bond has a call schedule with an immediately callable call price of $106, and the call price linearly declines to $100 for the last year. Therefore, the call price schedule is $106 at year 0, 105 at year 1, $\cdots$, $100 at maturity. For illustration purposes, we use the Ho–Lee one-factor model. Let us assume that the volatility is 15%, and the yield curve is flat at 6.5%. Therefore, the normal volatility σ is 0.15×0.065. Let the discount function be denoted by $P(T) = e^{-0.065T}$. The binomial annual discount rate $P(n, i, 1)$ is given below.

$$P(n, i, 1) = \frac{2P(n+1)}{P(n)} \frac{\delta^{n-i}}{(1 + \delta^n)}$$

$$\delta = \exp\{-2 \times 0.15 \times 0.065\} = 0.980689$$

For example, when the time period is 3 and the state is 3, $P(3, 3, 1)$ can be obtained by $2 \times \frac{e^{-0.065 \times 4}}{e^{-0.065 \times 3}} \times \frac{0.980688^{3-3}}{(1+0.980688^3)}$, which is 0.96447 in figure 8.4.

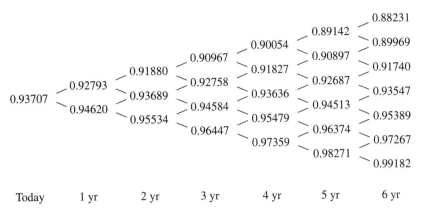

| Today | 1 yr | 2 yr | 3 yr | 4 yr | 5 yr | 6 yr |

Figure 8-4 Lattice of one-year pure discount bond prices. Each node denotes a one-year pure discount bond price. The one-year pure discount bond prices follow an arbitrage-free process. We have used the Ho–Lee model to generate the one-year pure discount bond prices. $P(n, i, 1)$ denotes a one-period discount bond price at time n and state i. At the initial node, $P(0, 0, 1)$ is $e^{-0.065} = 0.93707$.

Now we conduct the backward substitution procedure for the straight coupon bond. At maturity, the value is $107. The resulting lattice is given in figure 8.5.

Note that the arbitrage-free interest rate model ensures that the bond price determined by the backward substitution on the arbitrage-free rate movement model is the same as that determined by using the bond model. Now we apply the backward substitution procedure to determine the callable bond price. In this case, we conduct the backward substitution from the bond maturity date. At each step, we compare the bond price with the call price, and determine the value at each node by the following equation. (See figure 8.6.)

$$\text{bond price } (n, i) =$$
$$\text{Min} \left[\text{call price}, (0.5 \times \text{bond price } (n+1, i+1) + 0.5 \times \text{bond price } (n+1, i)) \times P(n, i, 1) \right] + \text{coupon}$$

Calculation of a Static Spread and an Option Adjusted Spread

We assume that the callable bond has credit risk and marketability risk. The bond price is assumed to be $99.5, which is less than the callable bond price shown in figure 8.6. The promised cash flows and the option-adjusted cash flows from the callable bond are given in figure 8.7. Since the callable bond pays a yearly coupon payment of $7 and the principal at maturity, the cash flow at each node before maturity is $7 and the cash flows at each state of the maturity date are $107. The state-dependent cash flows are determined according to when the call decision is made by the issuing company. Now, we search for an additional spread (OAS) to the one-year period rate given by figure 8.4 such that the theoretical bond price equals the observed bond price of $99.5. Assume an initial OAS of 50 basis points (bp). Using the backward substitution method and noting the nodes where the call option is exercised, we can determine the call boundary where the firm pays the call price, as depicted in figure 8.7, and the bond price at time 0.

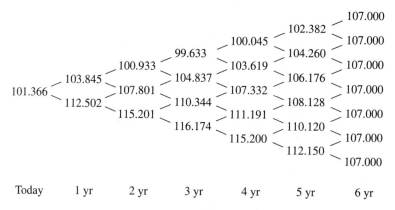

Figure 8-5 Lattice of the coupon bond price. Each node denotes the coupon bond prices. The annual coupon rate is 7% and the maturity date is year 6. The cash flow of each node at year 6 is $107 (= principal + annual coupon payment). By backward substitution from the maturity date to the initial node, we can calculate the coupon bond price of 101.366, which is identical to the bond price in equation (8.2). When the time period is 5 and the state is 5, 102.382 at period 5 can be obtained by $(107.0 \times 0.5 + 107.0 \times 0.5) \times 0.89142 - 0 + 7.0$, where 0.89142 is the one-period discount bond price at that node.

Now search for the OAS such that the bond price is 99.5. The OAS is then determined. This procedure affects the call boundary. The calculated static spread is 36.42bp and the option adjusted spread is 16.54bp. The static spread can be calculated by assuming that the cash flow of the callable bond is risk free and seeking the spread to backout the price. When the option-adjusted spread is 16.54bp, we have the call boundary shown in figure 8.7.

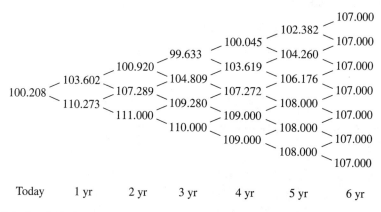

Figure 8-6 A callable bond price lattice. Each node denotes the callable bond price. The call price is $106 at the initial node and it linearly declines to $100 for the maturity year. When we conduct the backward substitution, we compare the bond price from the backward substitution with the call price and replace the bond price with the call price if the bond price exceeds the call price. When the time period is 5 and the state 5, 102.382 is obtained by $Min\,[95.382, 101.0] + 7.0$ where 95.382 is the backward-substituted bond value at the corresponding node in figure 8.5 and 7.0 is an annual coupon payment.

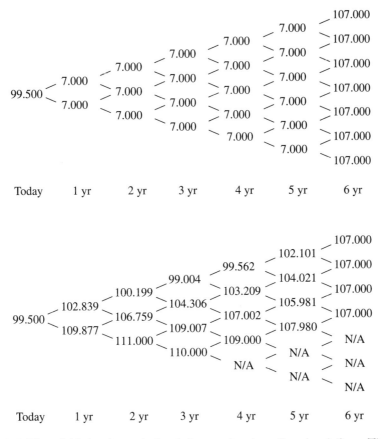

Figure 8-7 The callable bond promised cash flows and option adjusted cash flows. The upper lattice shows the promised cash flows and the lower lattice represents the state-dependent cash flows on the binomial lattice for the callable bond. The call boundary will be changed, depending on the discount curve. We depict the call boundary when the discount curve is flat at 6.6654% in the lower lattice. Even though the promised cash flows can be shown on a time line, we show them on the binomial lattice for comparison purposes.

Valuation of a Sinking Fund Bond with No Market Purchase Option and No Call Provision

Let us now consider the bond with a sinking fund schedule retiring $10 every year, starting the fourth year. Then the principal repayment and interest schedules are given as shown below.

Year	0	1	2	3	4	5	6
Principal to be retired each year	0	0	0	0	10	10	80
Outstanding amount at the beginning of each year	100	100	100	100	100	90	80
Remaining principal at the end of each year	100	100	100	100	90	80	0
Interests		100×0.07	100×0.07	100×0.07	100×0.07	90×0.07	80×0.07

The interests are calculated by multiplying the remaining principal by the coupon rate, which is the interest earned over the period on the remaining principal. The bond value is discounting this cash flow, which is the principal payments plus the interest, at the discount rate of 6.5%. The resulting bond value is 101.307.

$$7e^{-0.065} + 7e^{-0.065 \times 2} + 7e^{-0.065 \times 3} + 17e^{-0.065 \times 4} + 16e^{-0.065 \times 5} + 85.6e^{-0.065 \times 6}$$
$$= 101.307$$

Valuation of a Sinking Fund Bond with Delivery Option

We use the binomial lattice of interest rates above. Now we consider the terminal condition of the bond at maturity. The value of the bond is $80 \times (1.07)$. Now we start the backward substitution. When we retire the $10 face value, we use the market purchase price when the bond price is below par or exercise the sinking fund call at par when the market bond price is above the par price. The *par price* here refers to the principal remaining at the time and not to 100, although by market convention, par is often denoted by 100, to mean 100% of the remaining principal. The lattice of the bond value is given in figure 8.8.

Valuation of a Double-up Sinking Fund

In this example, we consider a sinking fund bond with a double-up option (which was explained in an earlier section). We have four cases, depending on when the firm will exercise the double-up option. The four cases are shown in figure 8.9.

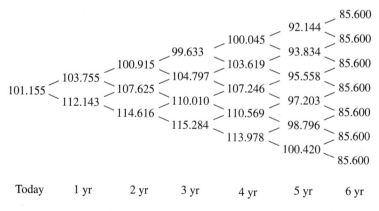

Today   1 yr   2 yr   3 yr   4 yr   5 yr   6 yr

Figure 8-8 Lattice of the sinking fund bond. The nodes represent the sinking fund bond prices. The sinking fund schedule is that the issuing firm will retire $10 for year 4 and year 5, respectively. Therefore the remaining principal at the maturity year (year 6) is $80. When we conduct the backward substitution, we apply the delivery option to see whether the issuing company buys the bonds at the market price or calls the bonds at par to fulfill the sinking fund obligation. $92.144 at year 5 can be obtained by $Min\left[85.6 \times 0.89142 \times \frac{9}{8}, 85.6 \times 0.89142 + 10\right] + 90 \times 0.07$. The first term in the bracket refers to buying the bonds at the market price and the second term represents calling the bonds at par. The company will choose the lesser of the two terms to maximize the firm's value. Since the outstanding principal between year 4 and year 5 is $90, we multiply the coupon rate by $90 to calculate the coupon payment. Other years, except for the sinking fund operation years, the coupon payment is $7.

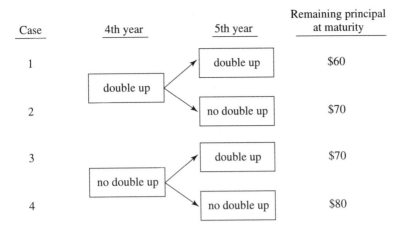

Case	4th year	5th year	Remaining principal at maturity
1	double up	double up	$60
2		no double up	$70
3	no double up	double up	$70
4		no double up	$80

Figure 8-9 The double-up sinking fund principal process

For cases 1 and 2, at the end of the fourth year the firm exercises the double-up option on the first sinking fund, and therefore at the beginning of the fifth year the remaining principal is $80. Since the firm has one more double-up option at the fifth year, the remaining principal at maturity is $60 when the firm exercises the double-up option or $70 when the firm does not. Now we construct the backward substitution procedure for these two cases and evaluate the bond with the double-up sinking fund provision. Specifically, we consider the minimum value of the two alternatives for the delivery option for each state in the world. Using minimum values, we can conduct the backward substitution to the end of the fourth year. The outstanding amount at the beginning of each year in case 1 and case 2 is [100,100,100,100,80,60] and [100,100,100,100,80,70], respectively. We can determine the outstanding amount at the beginning of each year in cases 3 and 4 in the same way. The binomial lattices for each case are given in figure 8.10.

Let us denote the entries in each lattice by $B^j(n, i)$, where j denotes the jth case, n is the period, and i is the state. Now we can decide on the optimal double-up option exercise rule at the end of year 5 by comparing the bond value at each node for the end of year 5 (second column from the right). We first consider the case where we elect a double-up option at the end of year 4, using cases 1 and 2. We do so by specifying the bond value for the end of year 5 to be

$$B^{1,2}(5, i) = Min\left[B^1(5, i), B^2(5, i)\right] \text{ for each } i = 0, 1, 2, 3, 4, 5$$

We then roll back the bond value $B^{1,2}(5, i)$ by one year, to the end of year 4. The value at each node for the end of year 4 is denoted by $B^{1,2}(4, i)$.

Similarly, we consider the double-up option decision at the end of year 5 conditional on the no double-up option decision made at the end of year 4, using cases 3 and 4. Once again, we take the minimum of the bond values at each node, in cases 3 and 4, at the end of year 5 (the second column from the right).

$$B^{3,4}(5, i) = Min\left[B^3(5, i), B^4(5, i)\right] \text{ for each } i = 0, 1, 2, 3, 4, 5$$

Using these optimized numbers, we roll back the bond value $B^{3,4}(5, i)$ by one year, to the end of year 4. The value at each node is denoted by $B^{3,4}(4, i)$.

Case 1. Elect to double up at the end of the 4th and 5th years

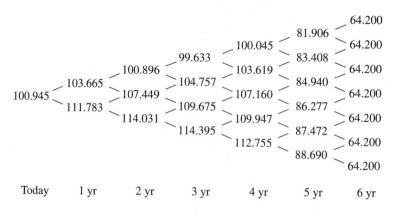

Today   1 yr   2 yr   3 yr   4 yr   5 yr   6 yr

Case 2. Elect to double up at the end of the 4th year and not the 5th year

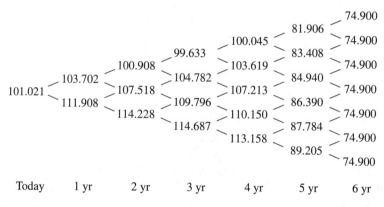

Today   1 yr   2 yr   3 yr   4 yr   5 yr   6 yr

Figure 8-10 The double-up sinking fund. The company with the double-up sinking fund has an option to double the sinking fund retirement amount. Therefore, it can retire up to 20 at the sinking fund operation years, which are years 4 and 5. Since the company has 2 sinking fund operation years, there are 4 cases. Each panel in the figure shows four corresponding cases. For example, the outstanding amounts at the beginning of each year in case 4 are $100, $100, $100, $100, $90, and $80. Once we determine the outstanding amount at the beginning of each year, we can apply the method to determine the bond value with a sinking fund provision in figure 8.8.

The appropriate value under the optimal decision at the end of year 4 is taking the minimum of the value of the bonds,

$$B(4, i) = Min\left[B^{1,2}(4, i), B^{3,4}(4, i)\right] \text{ for each } i = 0, 1, 2, 3, 4$$

This approach enables us to specify whether the firm should double up the payment at each node. Now we can roll back the bond value, adjusted for the coupon payments, from the fourth year to the initial date. (See figure 8.11.)

8.4 Liquidity (Marketability) Spread

For high rated bonds, say AAA, we tend to find a positive option adjusted spread. Given the low probability of default on these bonds, the spread may not be just the spread

Case 3. Elect not to double up in the 4th year but double up in the 5th year

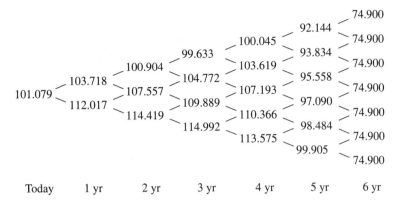

Case 4. Elect not to double up in both the 4th and 5th year

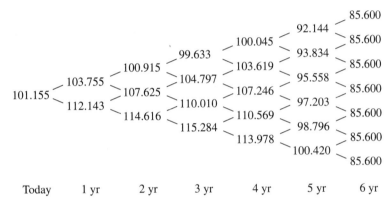

Figure 8-10 (continued)

required to compensate for credit risks. Part of this spread is often called the *liquidity spread*. "Liquidity" has different meanings in economic theory, as we discussed in the theory of interest rates, where "liquidity premium" refers to the preference of investors for shorter-term debt. Thus, some research prefers to relate this spread to the marketability of bonds.

Consider a zero-coupon bond, called an illiquid bond, that has no default risk and no embedded option. By the law of one price, we may compare the bond with the Treasury STRIPS bond that has the same maturity and principal. The value of the zero-coupon bond should be the same as that of the STRIPS bond.

However, Treasury bonds and STRIPS bonds are relatively liquid. There is a market for these bonds to be bought and sold at all times. Furthermore, the coupon bonds can be stripped to become STRIPS bonds, and the STRIPS bonds can be reconstituted to become coupon bonds. As we have explained, there is a market mechanism of reconstitution which makes the coupon bond and zero-coupon bond markets available to investors.

Such market liquidity may not be available to the holder of an illiquid bond. Consider a hedge fund holding an illiquid bond financed by a margin position. The hedge fund

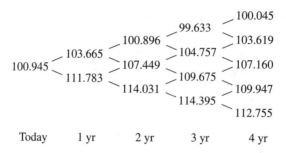

Figure 8-11 Lattice of the bond prices from the end of the fourth year to the starting date. The company decides on the optimal double-up exercise rule by comparing 4 different cases. For example, 112.755 at period 4 is obtained by taking the minimum values among the four cases. That is, $Min[112.755, 113.158, 113.575, 113.978]$, where the numbers in the brackets are from the four cases in figure 8.10.

may need to sell the bond for managerial reasons. For example, it may need to sell the bond to raise cash, or its leveraged position (the firm borrows to buy the bond) is triggered by the margin call on the bond when interest rates rise, leading to a fall in the bond price. When a liquidity investor needs to sell an illiquid bond, there is no market mechanism to ensure that the bond price is specified according to the law of one price at the time of sale. The investor cannot seek reconstitution with a corporate bond. That is, market liquidity is not assured.

An illiquid bond may be sold at a significant discount from the STRIPS bond price. The transaction price will depend on the market condition at the time. At times, there is a lack of demand for bonds; therefore, a bond may be sold at a steep discount. The uncertainty of having to sell a bond at a disadvantaged price is the liquidity risk or marketability risk of holding the bond.

The market price of an illiquid bond is not likely to be higher than the STRIPS bond price. If such a situation were to occur, the market would sell more illiquid bonds and buy the STRIPS bonds, leading to a lower illiquid bond price and a higher STRIPS bond price until the market reached an equilibrium.

Since the liquidity is one-sided when the investor runs the risk of selling the bond in a "fire sale," the holder will require an additional return for this liquidity risk; this additional return is measured on an annual basis by a spread called the liquidity spread. This liquidity spread is always positive, since the investor demands a higher return and the corporate bond will have a lower price than the STRIPS bond price.

The liquidity spread can be viewed as the premium of an option.[2] An illiquid bond has liquidity risks because the demand for it is not assured even when its price is below the price determined by the law of one price. For the liquidity investor, the liquidity risk can be mitigated in theory by buying a knock-in option. The underlying risk of the knock-in option is the liquidity risk, the uncertain variation of the liquidity spread. The strike price of the knock-in option is a specified liquidity spread. Whenever the spread exceeds the specified spread, the option swaps the bond for the equivalent STRIPS bond. The liquidity spread is indeed the premium of this knock-in option expressed in basis points. This analysis can be summarized by the following equation.

Default-free illiquid bond =

Treasury equivalent bond − knock-in option on liquidity

From this argument, we can see that the higher the liquidity risk or the liquidity spread volatility, the higher the liquidity spread.

Unfortunately, a bond seldom has only the liquidity risk. The liquidity risk is almost always confounded by default risk or other risk sources. We will later discuss U.S. government-backed mortgage securities. These bonds have negligible default risk but they have *prepayment risks*, where the mortgagors prepay their loans to the banks. Liquidity risks therefore cannot be separated from other risk sources, making the quantification of liquidity risk difficult.

To the extent that there is a liquidity premium such that liquidity investors are willing to accept the liquidity risk for the higher returns, the buy-and-hold investors will benefit from the extra returns without confronting the risks. These buy-and-hold investors can be insurance companies, banks, and pension funds where there are no mark to market requirements, so that they can hold the bonds until maturity without requiring the asset management to sell the bond. For these investors, the liquidity premium offers additional excess returns relative to the Treasury bond market.

8.5 Credit Scoring Approaches

The proposed bond valuation model requires a knowledge of the rating of bonds. The bond rating enables us to identify the appropriate option adjusted spread to be used in the model. However, many bonds are not rated because they are not traded and thus do not need a rating. We need a way to determine the comparable option adjusted spread to be used in the valuation model. One approach is to use financial ratios to compare the creditworthiness of the bonds. The option adjusted spreads can be determined from a sample of bonds which have the same or similar creditworthiness, and therefore we have a relative valuation of the bonds. From this sample, we can determine the appropriate option adjusted spread for the bond being evaluated.

One method to determine the creditworthiness of a firm with respect to a bond is *Altman's Z score*. The scoring system uses discriminant analysis to establish important factors that determine the likelihood of a firm's going bankrupt in the future. An example of an Altman's Z score is given by

$$Z = 1.4x_1 + 1.2x_2 + 3.3x_3 + 0.6x_4 + 1.0x_5 \qquad (8.3)$$

where

x_1 = working capital/total assets (percent)

x_2 = retained earnings/total assets (percent)

x_3 = earnings before interest and taxes/total assets (percent)

x_4 = market value of equity/total liabilities (percent)

x_5 = sales/total assets (percent)

The explanatory variables (x_i) can be calculated from the firm's financial statements, and the Z score can be determined. In this model, a score below 1.81 signifies serious credit problems, while a score above 3.0 indicates a healthy firm.

The model has to be adjusted for different sectors in order to be more accurate. For example, the financial sector may have a different specification, not only different coefficients but also different explanatory variables. It may have an explanatory variable based on sensitivity to interest rates, since its businesses are often sensitive to interest rate movements.

The main contribution of the Altman model is that it can provide a fairly accurate measure of bond credit scoring with the use of financial ratios.

8.6   Bond Analysis

Cheap/Rich Analysis

The bond model enables us to compare the value of the bond with other bonds of similar marketability and creditworthiness. The comparable bonds may have different provisions, maturities, and coupon rates. The bond valuation model described in this chapter takes these factors into account. The model then reduces the comparison to the OAS value. When a bond has a higher OAS than comparable bonds and the difference cannot be explained by the difference in liquidity premium and credit premiums, then the bond is "*cheap.*" That is, for the price quoted, the bond offers a higher return than its comparables. Alternatively, if the bond has a lower OAS than its comparables, it is "*rich.*" Cheap/rich analysis is a useful tool to evaluate the value of a bond. Using OAS as a measure of comparison is more precise and accurate than using yield to maturity. The shape of the yield curve and all the characteristics of the bonds are isolated in this OAS analysis. The value determined by using the bond model with an appropriate OAS is called the *fair value*. It is used to indicate the intrinsic value of a bond or the market-implied present value of the cash flows.

Effective duration

The effective duration (sometimes called the option adjusted duration) is defined by the following equation:

$$\frac{\Delta P}{P} = - \text{ effective duration} \times \Delta \text{spot yield} \tag{8.4}$$

A callable bond has an embedded call option. The effective duration is therefore lower than the corresponding bond without the call provision. For a premium callable bond, when the likelihood of being called is high, the effective duration will fall to 0. A sinking fund bond should have a shorter duration than a corresponding bond without such a provision. This is because the sinking fund provision leads to earlier payments to the investors.

Key rate duration

A key rate duration profile provides a measure of the price risk of the bond along the spot yield curve. The profiles in table 8.2 show the key rate durations of different bond types.

Table 8.2 Key Rate Duration Profiles

0.25	1	2	3	5	7	10	15	20	25	30	*dur*	*P*
−0.04	0.11	0.28	0.54	0.79	0.84	1.18	1.05	0.70	0.57	0.39	6.41	92.85
−0.04	0.08	0.21	0.44	0.77	0.95	1.47	1.44	1.02	0.94	0.77	8.05	85.43

A key rate duration profile provides a measure of the price risk of the bond along the yield curve. These key rate durations were reported in Ho (1992).

Figure 8.12 shows the key rate duration profile of AAA 30-year callable bonds. The first bond has a 9% coupon rate and the second has an 8% coupon rate.

A 9% coupon bond has a lower effective duration because higher coupon payments lead to a lower weighted average life. Furthermore, they also lead to the higher likelihood of a bond being called because it has a higher option value. In comparing the key rate duration profiles of the two bonds, it is clear that the bond with a higher coupon rate has less sensitivity to long-term rate movements. And since the sum of the key rate durations is equal to the effective duration number, the results show that much of the effective duration lowers with an increase in coupon rates, which arises from lower key rate duration numbers for the longer-term interest rates.

OAS duration

OAS duration measures the sensitivity of the bond price to a parallel shift of the option adjusted spread. A tightening of the OAS affects the bond value in two ways. That is,

$$OAS^* = OAS - \Delta$$

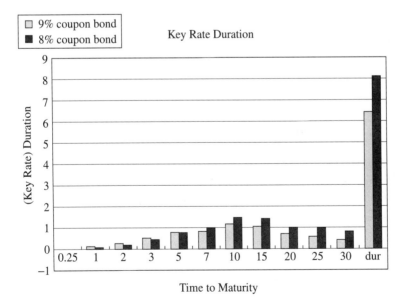

Figure 8-12 Key rate duration profile of AAA 30-year callable bonds. The bonds are AAA 30-year callable bonds with a 30-year maturity. The first bond has a 9% coupon rate and the second bond has an 8% coupon rate. A 9% coupon bond has a lower duration, because higher coupon payments lead to a lower weighted average life of the bond.

where OAS^* is the shifted OAS and Δ is the constant shift of the OAS used in the discounting at each node point. First, the discount rates used at each node of the binomial lattice in the valuation model are lowered, leading to a higher present value of the cash flow. Second, the bond is more likely to be called because of its higher value. For this reason, the bond sensitivity to the tightening of the OAS has the same effect on the bond price as the sensitivity of the bond to a parallel shift downward of the spot yield curve. The OAS duration provides such sensitivity measures. For a callable corporate bond, we have the following relationship:

$$\text{OAS duration} = \text{effective duration}$$

For a bond without the call provision, and having no embedded option, the impact of a OAS shift on the bond price must be the same as that of a shift of the spot yield curve. Therefore, the above equation also holds for bonds with no embedded options.

Convexity

In chapter 4, we discussed the measure of convexity. We showed that bond prices do not change in proportion to the shift in the interest rate as specified by the effective duration. Effective duration is only a first approximation of the true price movement of the bond. Convexity provides a measure for a better description of bond price movements in relation to shifts in interest rates.

When the bond price is low relative to the call prices, and the likelihood of a bond being called is small, the convexity of the bond is similar to that of a bond without a call provision. The convexity of this bond is positive.

Now consider a bond that is immediately callable. When the interest rate falls, the bond price rises and the likelihood of the bond's being called becomes high. When this happens, the convexity of the bond can become negative and remain negative until the bond is called. A callable bond's convexity is not always positive, nor is the convexity number constant. Both the effective duration and the convexity of a bond change with interest rate levels.

8.7 Numerical Example: Valuing a Eurobond Issue

Let us illustrate the valuation methodology of a corporate bond with a numerical example. Consider a new issue Eurobond on February 21, 2002. It was issued by a German bank with a face value of 50 million euros and has an annual coupon rate of 4.2%. On February 21, 2003, the bond can be called at par. If it is not called, the remaining life of the bond will pay a 4.6% annual coupon until the maturity of February 21, 2005.

This bond can be viewed as a step-up coupon bond with an initial interest rate of 4.2%, that steps up to 4.6% the following year. However, the issuer has a European call option on a two-year bond with a 4.6% coupon and a strike price at par. Therefore the bond has an embedded option affecting its value.

The steps to price the Eurobond are as follows:

Step 1. Specify the swap curve, which we assume to be 4% flat.

Step 2. Specify the volatility surface, applying the Ho–Lee two-factor model.

	1yr	2yr	3yr	4yr	5yr	20yr	30yr
$\sigma 1$	0.15	0.14	0.13	0.12	0.1	0.1	0.1
$\sigma 2$	0.1	0.1	0.1	0.1	0.1	0.1	0.1

Step 3. Construct the binomial lattice: we use the Ho–Lee two-factor model to generate the rates, as was discussed in chapter 6.

Step 4. Value by backward substitution.

We now construct a binomial lattice on the Eurobond, according to the procedure discussed in the chapter (see figure 8.13). The terminal condition determined on the maturity date in year 3 is the principal amount plus the 4.6% interest. This terminal condition is conditional on the bond never being called. In rolling back the value to year 1, given by $X(1, i)^*$, which is the backward substituted value, we determine the value of each node point to be

$$X(1, i) = Min\,[X(1, i)^*, 100]$$

We then add the interest rate of 4.2% to $X(1, i)$ at each node point and roll back to the initial value. We have assumed that the swap rate is the appropriate discount rate of the bond. If the bond credit risk requires a higher premium, we should add a spread to the swap rate in determining the present value at each node point.

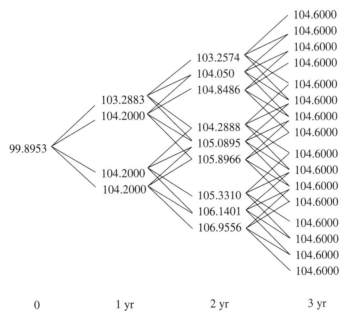

Figure 8-13 A binomial lattice of a Eurobond. We use the Ho–Lee two-factor model to generate the term structure of interest rates. We can calculate the callable bond price by backward substitution. 106.9556 at year 2 is obtained by 104.6 × 0.9785 + 4.60.9785 is the one-period discount function at the corresponding node. We can get 103.2883 at year 1 by Min[99.0883, 100]+ 4.2.99.0883 is a backward-substituted value by [103.2574 + 104.0498 + 104.2888 + 105.0895] × 0.25 × 0.9512 is also the one-period discount function at year 1 and state 3, which locates at the highest position for year 1.

The bond can be valued by three approaches:

1. We can use a term structure of volatilities calibrated from the prices of caps and floors as observed in the capital market, and use the arbitrage-free binomial lattice to determine the bond value, as we have shown above.
2. In the bond market, we often value a bond with an embedded option as a portfolio of a straight bond and an option. In this case, we can estimate the two-year euro rate volatility and value the bond option as the option to buy a two-year bond with an annual interest rate of 4.6% at the expiration date. The time to expiration is one year. The option can be priced using a binomial model, as explained in chapter 5. Then the callable bond value is the present value of the coupons and principal net of the call option value.
3. We have noted that a swaption is in fact a bond option because, in the bond option, we have an option to buy the underlying bond by paying the exercise price. The underlying bond and the exercise price could be treated as if they were the fixed-rate receiver and the floating-rate payer in the swaption, respectively. Therefore, we can directly observe the bond option value described in (2) by using the swaption market. The swaption is a cancelable swaption of a payer swap, with a fixed interest payment of 4.6%, expiring in one year. The Eurobond can in fact be viewed as a portfolio of a bond and a swaption.

8.8   Applications of Bond Analytics

Analytical tools are just that—tools. They are valuable only when they can assist the buyers and sellers in making their decisions. This section will provide some examples of how these tools may be used.

Total Return Approach

The most fundamental application is the fair value comparison. Cheap/rich analysis may be used to compare a bond value over time or across bonds. It may, for example, be the basis for a bond swap in which a portfolio manager sells a rich bond and buys a cheap bond, leaving the portfolio duration unchanged.

Key rate duration enables the portfolio manager to take directional bets. If the portfolio manager believes the yield curve will flatten from a steeply sloping yield curve, then he can bet that the short-term rate will rise and the long-term rate will fall. In this case, he can increase the long-term key rate duration and lower the short-term key rate duration of the bond portfolio.

Another approach that may add value to the total returns is to use the OAS durations. The portfolio manager may believe that the sector OAS must follow a mean reversion process. Therefore, at times the sector OAS may reach a maximum and then return to a lower level. In this case, he may lengthen the OAS duration when he believes that the sector has reached its highest level.

Managing Interest Rate Risk and Basis Risks

Portfolio managers may use the analytics to design a portfolio structure appropriate for portfolio benchmarks. The portfolio benchmarks may be a market index or a liability. Key rate durations can be used to control interest rate risks or to design the portfolio structure to expose all segments of the yield curve movements more evenly.

The *basis risk* is referred to as the changes in the OAS. In this case, we will apply a methodology similar to the key rate durations to the OAS durations. Using an OAS duration for each market sector (e.g., utilities and industrials), we can identify the risks that we are exposed to by each sector. And then we can formulate a risk management strategy.

Index Enhancement Strategy and Asset/Liability Management

Fixed-income managers provide investment services for their clients. They offer various investment strategies, often referred to as product. One product may be passive management. In this case, the investment manager seeks to invest in such a way that the total returns before fees replicate a chosen fixed-income benchmark portfolio. One common benchmark portfolio is called the *Lehman Index*. It is an index compiled by holding all the outstanding bonds in the Treasury, agency, corporate, and mortgage markets. Such an index is called a *broad-based index*. For a product called an *enhanced index*, the portfolio manager will try to outperform the index by a certain amount. Such asset management strategies are called managing against an index.

Managing against an index or an enhanced index is similar to doing just as well as the market or outperforming the market. This can be a challenge in fixed-income investment because there is no possibility of holding even a fraction of all the bonds in the market. There are too many bonds in the broad-based index. Further, most bonds are illiquid.

To manage against the corporate sector of a broad-based index, we have shown that we can use the key rate durations with fewer bond issues to mimic the benchmark portfolio in terms of interest rate risk sensitivities. If we then allocate the portion of bonds in each rating bucket and each sector bucket, such that we can control the basis risk of each sector using OAS duration, then we will be able to replicate the index by controlling most of the risk sources. Of course, there are other issues that have to be taken into account, including liquidity and transaction costs. When continually revising the replicating portfolio of the index, we have to control the transaction costs. Another issue is that the *rating bucket approach*, where we assign the same proportion of bonds in each rating group, may be too crude to control credit risk. Chapter 9 will deal with the credit risk in more detail.

For the enhanced index product, the portfolio management can concentrate on cheap bonds to "pick up" higher yields to outperform the benchmark. Using key rate durations and sector OAS analysis to control the risks, portfolio managers can use fewer bonds to replicate the market index. For this reason, we can exploit the cheap/rich analysis more effectively. If the portfolio has many bonds, we need to have a significant turnover, buying and selling many bonds to pick up the yield of the portfolio. As a result, the transaction costs can be high. The risk management methodology described here enables us to use fewer bonds to construct an enhanced index bond portfolio.

The assets of banks and insurance companies should be managed against their liabilities, which are the financial products that they sell: deposit accounts, insurance benefits to the policy holders, and so on. In these cases, the above discussion of managing against an index applies to their asset and liability management; their benchmark portfolios are their liabilities as opposed to market broad-based indices.

8.9 Explaining the Concept of the Arbitrage-free Condition on a Solemn Occasion

In 1986, there was much excitement in fixed-income research about using the arbitrage-free condition to value bonds: corporate bonds, mortgage-backed bonds, and collateralized mortgage obligations (CMOs), as we have discussed in this chapter. Market professionals were eager to learn about the state-of-the-art methods in financial modeling.

Professor Marti Calabi and I were keynote speakers at a corporate event in Tokyo. As we were being chauffeured to the Imperial Hotel for the conference, we started trading ideas about how to explain the arbitrage-free condition, an idea central to financial modeling. "I have this joke, which is really good," Marti said. Below is an abbreviated version of what he told me.

> A tax man caught a gambler counting his money in his home one day. "How did you make all this money?" demanded the tax man. "I gamble," replied the gambler. "No one can make money consistently by gambling," the tax man retorted. "Well, I can. In fact, I bet that your butt will turn green this time next week for $1,000," the gambler responded. "That's silly. OK, I'll take your bet." A week later, the tax man came back to see the gambler and showed him that he had not turned green, even agreeing to be examined in the sunlight near the window. "You win. Here is the $1,000," said the gambler. The tax man took the money and said, somewhat mystified, "But you are supposed to win all the time." The gambler shrugged his shoulders and said, "But I do. I had a bet with my neighbor for $2,000 that my tax man would undress for him today. You can see him from the window."

Marti was having a good time relating the joke, and added, "Arbitrage is about exploiting an event by taking in more money than giving out."

In horror, I begged Marti not to tell this joke. "Please, this event is very solemn. Your joke is too long, too complicated to translate, not to mention that it is somewhat crude."

"Don't worry," he said, "I have the PG version of this joke." He could not stop laughing.

The occasion was solemn indeed. Six hundred people were sitting quietly in an enormous hall—expressionless and motionless, pens and pads ready for taking notes. Marti was a small figure on the large stage. His face appeared on the large screen above him and on six large TV screens along the sides of the hall. He then proceeded with the joke. I sank in despair, shaking my head. At the end of his joke, most people laughed heartily, and some applauded.

Later, at the reception, Marti greeted me with pride. "I told you. My joke works on all occasions."

"Yes, but you did not hear the translator."

"What did she say?"

"She said, 'Professor Calabi just told a joke. Please laugh.'"

8.10 Summary

The investment grade corporate bond market is an important sector of the fixed-income market and is also important for corporations. The bonds have several distinctive features.

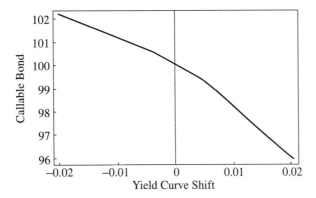

Figure 8-14 Performance profile of a Eurobond by the Ho–Lee two-factor model. We assume a parallel yield curve shift. When we parallel-shift the yield curve by 0.001, we have a callable bond performance profile. The bond has a negative convexity due to the embedded option.

Table 8.3 The Euro Bond Key Rate Duration

Key rate year	0.25	0.5	1	2	5	10	30	Parallel Shift
Key rate duration	0.00	0.00	0.76	0.48	0.23	0.00	0.00	1.47

Bond provisions allow for sinking funds and call provisions. These may be embedded in the bond and can be priced using option pricing methodologies. This chapter applies interest rate option modeling to corporate bond pricing. The bond model provides a consistent framework to measure bond value. The relative valuation approach enables us to compare bonds with different provisions, and we can still compare their value.

Unlike pure bond options, the corporate bond market has risks beyond interest rate risks. These are marketability risks and credit risks. For investment grade bonds, we assume these risks are relatively small. But their presence no longer enables us to arbitrage their contingent payments with the underlying bonds, the Treasury securities, or the swap payments. The cash flows of the corporate bonds are not perfect substitutes for the cash flows from the Treasury bonds or the swap payments because of the presence of default risk. Therefore the law of one price cannot hold precisely. To deal with this issue, we introduced a measure of option adjusted spread.

First, we isolated the embedded option values, in the form of call and sinking fund provisions, from the bond price. We determined the bond value without the embedded options and estimated a constant spread in excess of the Treasury spot rates to give that value. This spread is called the option adjusted spread (OAS). It varies from one sector to another, and is dependent on the rating and the maturity of a bond. Three steps are involved:

1. We show the Treasury equivalent cash flows.
2. We determine the bond theoretical price and the corresponding cash flows by the embedded options.
3. Given the cash flows and the market price, we can determine the OAS.

We did not specify a model that explains the behavior of the OAS effectively. We simply inferred the option adjusted spreads from the market prices, analogous to the approach used to determine the implied volatilities from the caps and floors in the swap markets.

Thus far, we have briefly discussed the importance of credit risk to the valuation of corporate bonds. We assume the credit risk to be small so that we can focus our analysis on the investment grade bonds. However, when the credit risk becomes significant, this approximation method, such as the option adjusted spread approach, will fail. In chapter 9 we will study the credit risks in more detail. We will show that a significantly different analytical framework is required to evaluate credit risks.

Appendix.   Callable Bond and Sinking Fund Bond Pricing

The interest movement model provides the framework to value callable, sinking fund, and callable-sinking fund bonds. In this chapter, these securities are viewed as contingent claims on discount bonds and are defined by their particular provisions. This section first specifies the assumptions about these bond provisions, then proceeds to derive the valuation model of each of these securities.

To develop the bond model, we assume the following:

A. 1. The market is frictionless. There are no taxes and no transaction costs, and all securities are perfectly divisible.

A. 2. The market clears at a discrete point in time, t_n, for $n = 0, 1, 2, \cdots$ separated by a regular interval, Δ, with the initial time denoted by t_0. It follows that we can write $t_n = n\Delta$ for $n = 0, 1, 2, \cdots$.

We define a discount bond of maturity T to be a bond that pays \$1 at the end of the Tth period, with no other payments to its holder.

A. 3. The bond market is complete. There exists a discount bond for each maturity $t_n (n = 0, 1, 2, \cdots)$.

A. 4. At each time (t_n), there is a finite number of states of the world. For state (i), we denote the equilibrium price of the discount bond of maturity T by $P_i^n(T)$, a function that relates the price of a discount bond to its maturity. This function is called the discount function. Within the context of the model, the discount function completely describes the term structure of interest rates of the ith state at t_n. The function $P_i^n(T)$ must satisfy several properties. It must be positive because it represents asset value and also, by definition,

$$P_i^n(0) = 1 \tag{8.5}$$

$$\lim_{T \to \infty} P_i^n(T) = 0 \tag{8.6}$$

A. 5. The firm that issues the corporate bonds faces no (negligible) bankruptcy risk. Shareholders seek to maximize the equity value of the firm, under perfect capital market assumptions (the Modigliani–Miller paradigm).

Before we derive the pricing models, we first present the following proposition that is useful for subsequent analysis. It is analogous to the continuous arbitrage argument.

Risk-Neutral Pricing Proposition

Consider any asset B that can be bought and sold in a frictionless market environment described by assumptions A.1–A.5. Suppose that in the nth period, at the ith state, the asset value is $B(n, i)$. Further suppose that it can attain the values $B(n + 1, i + 1)$ and $B(n + 1, i)$ in an up state and a down state, respectively. In the subsequent period, then, under the arbitrage-free assumption, the following equation must hold:

$$B(n, i) = 0.5 \left[B(n + 1, i + 1) + B(n + 1, i) \right] P_i^n(1) \tag{8.7}$$

where

$$P_i^n(1) = \frac{P(n + 1)}{P(n)} \frac{2\delta^{n-i}}{(1 + \delta^n)} \tag{8.8}$$

Equation (8.7) shows that at any time n and in any state i, the asset value is the expected value of the asset at the end of the period, discounted by the risk-free rate for that period. The expected value is calculated as if the local expectation hypothesis holds. Therefore, the result is analogous to the risk-neutral valuation approach.

Callable Bond

A callable bond is a coupon bond with a call provision which allows the issuer to retire the bond at a predetermined price. The bond is specified by the maturity, T; the coupon payments, c; and the call schedule, k. We will denote the initial callable bond price by B_c and the price in the ith state and the nth period by $B_c(n, i)$.

C. 1. We assume, for each bond, that the investor receives the principal, assumed to be $1 at maturity, T, and a fixed coupon payment, c, at the end of each period.

C. 2. For the first $(I - 1)$ periods, the issuer cannot call the bonds. In subsequent periods, the issuer can retire bond issues at any time, but at a predetermined price, the call price. The call price depends on the time to maturity, and this call schedule is represented by a vector $k = (k_1, \cdots, k_T)$ where k_i is the call price in the ith period. Consistent with current practice, we assume k_T equals the principal value. I is the first call date.

C. 3. The firm's optimal call policy entails minimizing the bond value. Following Ingersoll 1977, we assume that bonds are called whenever the bond price equals or exceeds the call price.

We now employ the backward substitution approach to value the callable bond, applying assumptions C. 1–C. 3 to each time period. At maturity, the bond price is $(1 + c)$. Therefore, rolling back one period, $(n = T - 1)$, the bond price is the present value of $(1 + c)$ discounted by the one-period discount bond rate. That is, in state i,

$$X_c(T - 1, i) = (1 + c)P_i^{T-1}(1)$$

But, if $X_c(T - 1, i) > k_{T-1}$, by C. 3 the bond will be called, and the bond price will be

$$B_c^*(T - 1, i) = Min\left[X_c(T - 1, i), k_{T-1} \right]$$

Independent of whether or not the bonds are called, the firm must make the coupon payment for the $(T - 1)$th period. Hence the bond marking-to-market value is

$$B_c(T - 1, i) = B_c^*(T - 1, i) + c$$

The risk-neutral pricing proposition enables us to value the callable bond recursively. At $T - 2$, equation (8.7) shows that the bond price in state i, if not called, is

$$X_c(T - 2, i) = 0.5 [B_c(T - 1, i + 1) + B_c(T - 1, i)] P_i^{T-2}(1)$$

Imposing the call condition, we have

$$B_c^*(T - 2, i) = Min [X_c(T - 2, i), k_{T-2}]$$

and consequently the mark-to-market value is

$$B_c(T - 2, i) = B_c^*(T - 2, i) + c$$

In general, for any period n, the callable bond price for par value of \$1 is determined by the following recursive formulas:

$$X_c(n, i) = 0.5 [B_c(n + 1, i + 1) + B_c(n + 1, i)] P_i^n(1) \tag{8.9}$$

$$B_c(n, i) = Min [X_c(n, i), k_n] + c \tag{8.10}$$

These formulas determine the unique callable bond price, B_c, at the initial time, $n = 0$.

Sinking Fund Bond

A sinking fund bond, denoted by B_s, is a coupon bond with a sinking fund provision, which, on the one hand, obligates the firm (the issuer) to amortize a portion of the bond prior to maturity. On the other hand, it gives the firm an option to satisfy this amortization requirement either by purchasing the bonds to be redeemed from the market or by calling the bonds via a sinking fund call. We make the following assumptions.

S. 1. Since a portion of the bond must be retired over the lifetime of the bond, the par value of bonds outstanding at any time is predetermined by the amortization schedule. Let F_i denote the outstanding amount at the beginning of each period i, for $i = 0, \cdots, T$, where T is the maturity of the bond. Then, at the end of period i, the amount of bonds which must be retired is given by $F_i^* = F_i - F_{i+1}$. The amortization rate is defined as the portion of the bond outstanding to be retired prior to maturity, and is therefore specified as

$$A = \frac{F_0 - F_T}{F_0}$$

For simplicity, we let $F_T = 1$. Note that for some i, we may have $F_i = F_{(i+1)}$. In such a case, there is no sinking fund operation at the end of the ith period.

S. 2. Coupons are paid at the end of each period. Let c denote the coupon for each bond per period n, and it follows that the coupon payment to the investment at the end of the ith period is cF_i.

S. 3. The sinking fund call price is assumed to be the par value. At the sinking fund operation, following Ho and Singer (1984), we assume that the firm seeks to minimize the bond value given by A. 5.

S. 4. The bond market is competitive.

Once again we employ the backward substitution approach to value the sinking fund bond, applying S. 1–S. 4 to each time period. Let the sinking fund bond price initially be B_s and the value in state i at time n be $B_s(n, i)$. At maturity (T), the bond value is $F_T(1 + c)$. At time ($T − 1$), the value of the unredeemed bond is the present value of $F_T(1 + c)$ discounted at the one-period discount bond rate.

Therefore, in the ith state, the value is

$$X_s(T − 1, i) = F_T(1 + c)P_i^{(T−1)}(1)$$

It follows that an instant prior to the sinking fund operation, in the absence of the sinking fund call, the bond value is

$$X_s(T − 1, i) = F_T(1 + c)P_i^{(T−1)}(1)$$

Since the firm seeks to minimize value, $X_s(T − 1, i)$ must be compared against the value of the payment when the bond is called. Consequently, the sinking fund bond value is

$$B_s^*(T − 1, i) = Min\left[\frac{F_{T−1}}{F_T}X_s(T − 1, i), (F_{T−1} − F_T) + X_s(T − 1, i)\right]$$

But at the end of period ($T − 1$), the firm must pay out the coupon payment, $cF_{T−1}$. Therefore the mark-to-market value of the bond at time ($T − 1$) in the ith state is

$$B_s(T − 1, i) = B_s^*(T − 1, i) + cF_{T−1}$$

Now we can determine the sinking fund bond value recursively. Suppose we know the values of $X_s(j, i)$ for all $j > n + 1$ and for all states i. By the risk-neutral pricing proposition, we can determine the sinking fund bond value immediately after the sinking fund operation. It is given by

$$X_s(n, i) = 0.5\left[B_s(n + 1, i + 1) + B_s(n + 1, i)\right]P_i^n(1) \text{ for each state } i$$

Just prior to the sinking fund operation, and in the absence of a sinking fund call, the bond value is

$$X_s^*(n, i) = \frac{F_n}{F_{n+1}}X_s(n, i)$$

Applying the optimal strategy to the sinking fund operation, the bond value becomes

$$B_s^*(n, i) = Min\left[\frac{F_n}{F_{n+1}}X_s(n, i), (F_n − F_{n+1}) + X_s(n, i)\right]$$

Now, including the coupon payment, the mark-to-market value is

$$B_s(n, i) = B_s^*(n, i) + cF_n$$

In general, for any period n, the sinking fund bond price for par value of $1 is determined by

$$X_s(n, i) = 0.5 \left[B_s(n + 1, i + 1) + B_s(n + 1, i) \right] P_i^n(1) \tag{8.11}$$

$$B_s(n, i) = Min \left[\frac{1}{F_{n+1}} X_s(n, i), (1 - \frac{F_{n+1}}{F_n}) + \frac{1}{F_n} X_s(n, i) \right] + cFn \tag{8.12}$$

Equations (8.11) and (8.12) complete the recursive relationships required to price the sinking fund bond, B_s at the initial time, where $n = 0$.

Notes

1. According to Bond Market Association, *Research Quarterly*, May 2002.
2. The idea that the liquidity spread can be viewed as an option was suggested by Myron Scholes.

References

Altman, E. 1968. Financial ratios, discriminant analysis and the prediction of corporate bankruptcy. *Journal of Finance*, 23, 589–609.

Altman, E., and D. L. Kao. 1992(a). Rating drift in high yield bonds. *Journal of Fixed Income*, March, 15–20.

Altman, E., and D. L. Kao. 1992(b). The implications of corporate bond rating drift. *Financial Analysts Journal*, May/June, 64–75.

Brennan, M. J., and E. S. Schwartz. 1977. Savings bonds, retractable bonds and callable bonds. *Journal of Financial Economics*, 5, 67–88.

Carayannopoulos, P. 1995. The mispricing of U.S. Treasury callable bonds. *Journal of Futures Markets*, 15 (8), 861–879.

Courtadon, G. 1982. The pricing of options on default-free bonds. *Journal of Financial and Quantitative Analysis*, 17 (1), 75–100.

Cox, J. C., J. E. Ingersoll, and S. Ross. 1979. Duration and the measurement of basis risk. *Journal of Business*, 52, 51–61.

Duffee, G. R. 1998. The relation between Treasury yields and corporate bond yield spreads. *Journal of Finance*, 53 (6), 2225–2241.

Ederington, L., J. Yawitz, and B. Roberts. 1987. The informational content of bond ratings. *Journal of Financial Research*, 10 (3), 211–226.

Harrison M. J. and D. M. Kreps, 1979, Martingales and Arbitrage in Multi-period Securities Markets. *Journal of Economic Theory*, Vol. 20, 381–408.

Hite, G., and A. Warga. 1997. The effect of bond rating changes on bond price performance. *Financial Analysts Journal*, 53 (3), 35–51.

Ho, T. S. Y. 1990, *Strategic Fixed-Income Investment*, Dow Jones-Irwin, Homewood, Illinois.

Ho, T. S. Y., 1994, *Fixed-Income Investment, Resecent Research*, Irwin Professional Publishing, Burr Ridge, IL.

Ho. T. S. Y., and R. F. Singer, 1984, The Value of Corporate Debt with a Sinking-Fund Provision, *Journal of Business*, Vol. 57, Iss. 3, 315–336.

Ho, T. S. Y. 1992. Key rate durations: Measures of interest rate risks. *Journal of Fixed Income*, 2 (2), 19–44.

Ingersol, J., Jr., 1977, An Examination of Corporate Call Policies on Convertible Securities, *Journal of Finance*, Vol. 32, 463–478.

Ingersoll, J., Jr., J. Sketon, and R. Weil. 1978. Duration forty years later. *Journal of Financial and Quantitative Analysis*, 13, 627–650.

Jarrow, R., 2002, *Modelling Fixed Income Securities and Interest Rate Options*, 2nd ed., Stanford University Press, Stanford, CA.

Kwan, S. 1996. Firm-specific information and the correlation between individual stocks and bonds. *Journal of Financial Economics*, 40, 63–80.

Leland, H. E. 1994. Corporate debt value, bond covenants, and optimal capital structure. *Journal of Finance*, 49, 1213–1252.

Litterman, R., and T. Iben. 1991. Corporate bond valuation and the term structure of credit spread. *Journal of Portfolio Management*, Spring, 52–64.

Nunn, K. P., Jr., J. Hill, and T. Schneeweis. 1986. Corporate bond price data sources and return/risk measurement. *Journal of Financial and Quantitative Analysis*, 21 (2), 197–208.

Rendleman, R. J., Jr., and B. J. Bartter. 1980. The pricing of options on debt securities. *Journal of Financial and Quantitative Analysis*, 15 (1), 11–24.

Sarig, O., and A. Warga. 1989. Bond price data and bond market liquidity. *Journal of Financial and Quantitative Analysis*, 24 (3), 367–378.

Sarig, O., and A. Warga. 1989. The risk structure of interest rates: Some empirical estimates. *Journal of Finance*, 44 (5), 1351–1360.

Further Readings

Elton, E., and M. Gruber. 2000. Factors affecting the valuation of corporate bonds. Working paper, New York University.

Elton, E., M. Gruber, D. Agrawal, and C. Mann. 2001. Explaining the rate spread on corporate bonds. *Journal of Finance*, 56 (1), 247–278.

Falkenstein, E., and J. Hanweck. 1996. Minimizing basis risk from nonparallel shifts in the yield curve. *Journal of Fixed Income*, 6 (1), 60–68.

Falkenstein, E., and J. Hanweck. 1997. Minimizing basis risk from nonparallel shifts in the yield curve, part II: Principal components. *Journal of Fixed Income*, 7 (1), 85–90.

Kliger, D., and O. Sarig. 2000. The information value of bond ratings. *Journal of Finance*, 55 (6), 2879–2902.

Reitano, R. 1996. Non-parallel yield curve shifts and stochastic immunization. *Journal of Portfolio Management*, Winter.

9

High-Yield Corporate Bonds: The Structural Models

The credit risk of a corporate liability is an important concern to market participants: portfolio managers, treasurers, loan managers, and many others. Financial models have contributed significantly to determining the credit risk premium of a bond. The Merton model provides a basic framework to model credit risks, tying the firm value to the valuation of the claims on the firm's value. The model asserts that a bond with credit risk is a risk-free model with a short position of a put option on the firm value. This idea has broad implications for the analysis of credit risks of corporate bonds. Many extensions of this basic model have been proposed to provide a broad range of business solutions.

Credit risk is an important determinant of the value of a corporate bond. It is important because credit risk is prevalent in corporate bonds and may affect the bond value significantly. Few corporate entities (if any) have investment grade ratings which could match the creditworthiness of the U.S. government. One can then say all corporate bond issues have credits risks that vary by a matter of degrees. Many firms have such significant credit risk that they are on the verge of bankruptcy. In this case, their bonds are trading at a fraction of their principal value.

A high-yield bond has a rating lower than investment grade—lower than S&P BBB or Moody's Baa. These bonds may be issued with a low rating or be original investment grade bonds which have been rated downward. The latter are called *fallen angels*. (This chapter however does not deal with high-yield bonds whose risk is related to the country risk.)

Understanding the valuation of the high-yield bond is important because the high-yield bond market plays an important role in corporate financing. Many public and private companies can gain access to bond financing through the high-yield bond market.

High-yield bonds can be traded in the over-the-counter market, but many of them do not have market liquidity. Many lower rating bonds are traded under private arrangements; there are numerous loans, syndications, and structured products that are subject to significant credit risks. Understanding the modeling of credit risks of public bonds will enable us to evaluate a broad spectrum of bonds on the balance sheets of firms.

Valuing the credit risk of a bond poses a particular challenge because the characteristics of a high-yield bond vary greatly. An investor in a BB rating bond may evaluate the bond by its contractual terms, such as its coupons and principals. An investor in a C or D rated bond is more concerned with the outcomes of a bankruptcy reorganization plan, which in turns depends more on the business risk of the firm and less on the bond's contractual obligations.

Chapter 8 proposed a methodology to value the credit risk of a bond. The method suggests that you must first calculate an average of the option adjusted spreads of benchmark bonds with a particular rating in an industry sector. Then any bond belonging to that rating and sector can be valued, using the average option adjusted spread.

But can this approach be useful for high-yield bonds? Unlike investment-grade bonds, the yield spreads of high-yield bonds vary greatly, even within the same rating. This is because the credit risk is such a significant component of value for a high-yield bond that an average of the option adjusted spreads can no longer approximate the bond's required return to compensate for the credit risk. An alternative approach must take the default process and business risks into consideration.

This chapter will begin with an example of a high-yield bond illustrating salient features that are needed for valuation. We then describe the default proceedings and their impact on a bond value. The description of the institutional framework of bankruptcy will establish the foundation of the valuation models. Then we will describe three methodologies in valuing the credit risks of bonds: the actuarial model, the reduced form, and structural models. We will discuss the structural models in more detail to study the implications of absolute priority rules on bond values. We will use a numerical example to illustrate the use of these models to value a high-yield bond.

9.1   An Example of a High-Yield Bond

Let us consider a high-yield bond of McLeodUSA, Inc., quoted in Nasdaq National Market System as MCLDQ. McLeodUSA provides communication services, including local services in the Southwest, Northwest, and Rocky Mountain states, and long-distance and data services nationwide. On December 3, 2001, the company filed a prenegotiated plan of reorganization through a Chapter 11 bankruptcy petition. On February 11, 2002, the stock was traded at 0.15.

Let us use September 20, 2001 as our evaluation date. We begin the analysis with the quarterly balance sheet, which is summarized by the following major items:

Balance Sheet ($billion)

Current assets	0.4	Current liabilities	0.7
Net fixed assets	2.7	Long-term debt	3.7
Net goodwill	1.1	Others	0.2
Others	0.6	Equity	0.2
Total assets	4.8	Total liabilities and equity	4.8

On a book value basis, the firm has a minimal equity of $200 million to support the debt of $3.7 billion. Furthermore, a significant part of the total asset is a net goodwill of $1.1 billion, as a result of its acquisitions. Therefore there are not enough tangible and liquid assets to support the debt.

The business model of the communication company is not generating enough cash flows to support the operating costs, and is certainly not sufficient to support the interest costs. The income statement below shows that the company was incurring significant losses. (EBT is earnings before tax.)

Income Statement ($billion)

Revenue	0.450
Gross profit	0.179
Operating income	(3.082)
EBT	(3.108)
Net income	(3.108)

We now turn our attention from the analysis of the financial statements to the debt structure. The above analysis clearly shows that the firm has significant credit risk. Its credit risk leads to the evaluation of the potential loss of the bond values, which is the default risk of each bond in the debt structure. In order to analyze the default risk, we need to begin with a description of the debt structure. To value the default risk of a high yield bond, we must value the bond not in isolation, but within the context of all the firm's financial obligations. The debt structure is summarized in tables 9.1 and 9.2.

The summary shows that there are eight bonds in the structure. The first row in table 9.1 presents the identifiers of the bonds. The second row presents the coupon rates. The third row shows that all the bonds have a fixed coupon rate except 07-1, which has step-up coupons. The fourth row presents the exact maturity dates. The numbers show that the maturities vary over a relatively tight maturity spectrum from 2007 to 2009. All the bonds were rated CCC1 at the time. All the bonds have the same semiannual interest payment frequency and are callable (make whole call) except for 09-1. The total bond face value is $2.935 million in table 9.2. We calculated this number based on table 19.1. The debt structure shows that all the bonds have the same priority, (belong to the same class).

The debt structure provides us with some insight into the credit risk of the firm and the valuation of the bonds. No bond in the debt structure will mature within 12 months. The default of the firm in the next 12 months will not be triggered by any of the bond's maturing, but may be triggered by the drain of cash in operating costs or the coupon payments of the bonds. The bank loans also may trigger default. But the presence of these bonds may exhaust any debt capacity of the firm, and may even restrict the firm's access to equity external funding in the capital market.

The income statement and balance sheet describing the size of the debt in par value and annual income alone cannot properly determine the credit risk of a firm. Such information only suggests that at the liquidation of the firm, the bonds may suffer significant loss in principals, and the firm's internal cash flow is not sufficient to support the operating costs. But the firm may have the potential to be very profitable in the future. For this reason, the firm may have access to the capital market for equity or debt funding, and as a result the probability of defaulting on the existing bonds may be low. To evaluate the firm's ability to use external financing to manage its credit risk, we now turn our attention to its market total capitalization.

A firm's market total capitalization, in academic literature, is usually called the *firm value*, denoted by V. The value represents the market valuation of the firm as a going concern. On the one hand, it is the present value of the free cash flows of the firm. On the other hand, it is the value of all the claims on the firm. In the case of McLeodUSA, there are only two claims, the stockholders and the bondholders. The claims of the stockholders are *capitalization*, the product of the stock price and the number of shares outstanding (denoted by S). The claim of the debts is the market value of the debt (denoted by D) By definition of market valuation, the present value of the free cash flows of the firm must be equal to all the claims on the firm's value.

$$V = S + D \qquad (9.1)$$

Now, let us evaluate the credit risk of McLeodUSA as a going concern. On June 1, 2001, the stock was traded at $5.22. The number of shares outstanding was 611,990,000. Therefore the capitalization was $3.195 billion. The eight bond prices and the respective

Table 9.1 Debt Structure of McLeodUSA

Issuer	McLeodUSA 07–1	McLeodUSA 07–2	McLeodUSA 08–1	McLeodUSA 08–2	McLeodUSA 08–3	McLeodUSA 09–1	McLeodUSA 09–2	McLeodUSA 09–3
Coupon Rate	10.50	9.25	8.38	12.00	9.50	11.38	8.13	11.50
Coupon Type	STEP CPN[1]	Fixed	Fixed	Fixed	Fixed	Fixed	Fixed	Fixed
Maturity	20070301	20070715	20080315	20080715	20081101	20090101	20090215	20090501
Rating	CCC1	CCC1	CCC1	CCC1	CCC1	CCC1	CCC1	CCC1
Frequency	2	2	2	2	2	2	2	2
Maturity Type	CALLABLE	CALLABLE	CALLABLE	CALLABLE	CALLABLE	NORMAL	CALLABLE	CALLABLE
Outstanding[2]	500,000.00	225,000.00	300,000.00	150,000.0	300,000.00	750,000.00	500,000.00	210,000.00

[1]Step-up coupon.

[2]Outstanding amount.

Table 9.2 Call Schedule of the Corporate Debt Securities

McLeodUSA 07-1		McLeodUSA 07-2		McLeodUSA 08-1		McLeodUSA 08-2	
call date	call price	call date	call price	call date	call price	call date	Call price
20020301	105.250	20020715	104.625	20030315	104.188	20030715	106.000
20030301	103.500	20030715	103.083	20040315	102.792	20040715	104.000
20040301	101.750	20040715	101.542	20050315	101.396	20050715	102.000
20050301	100.000	20050715	100.000	20060315	100.000	20060715	100.000

McLeodUSA 08-3		McLeodUSA 09-1		McLeodUSA 09-2		McLeodUSA 09-3	
call date	call price	call date	call price	call date	call price	call date	Call price
20031101	106.750	N/A	N/A	20040215	104.063	20040501	105.750
20041101	105.400	N/A	N/A	20050215	102.708	20050501	103.834
20051101	104.050	N/A	N/A	20060215	101.354	20060501	101.917
20061101	102.700	N/A	N/A	20070215	100.000	20070501	100.000
20071101	101.350	N/A	N/A				

outstanding par amounts (given in parentheses) are 65.99 ($500 million), 70.6 ($225 million), 64.75 ($300 million), 101.56 ($150 million), 67.5 ($300 million), 74.75 ($750 milion), 64.8 ($500 million), and 74.5 ($210 million). The market value of debt is $2.079 billion. The firm value, the sum of the capitalization and the debt value, is $5.274 billion. Thus the present value of all the free cash flows generated by McLeodUSA to determine the firm value is only $5.274 billion. Since market total capitalization depends on the market price of risk on the firm's future profits, it has a high volatility. The probability that the value will fall below the par value (or the face value) of the bonds, $2.935 billion, over a short horizon (say one year) can be very high. Therefore, the credit risk of the firm is high.

The discussion above provides us with an overview of the credit analysis of a firm, starting from the financial statements, to the terms and conditions of the debt structure, and then to the market valuation of the firm as a going concern. The example also illustrates the challenges in developing a valuation model for high yield bonds.

You can assume that a valuation model of high yield bonds must be an extension of the model for investment grade bonds because as credit risk decreases, high yield bonds have the same ratings as investment grade bonds. However, the high yield bond cannot be an interest rate-contingent claim, whereas the investment grade bond can be the interest rate contingent claim. The high yield bond must depend on the debt structure, the business risk, and all the issues that we have discussed above. This chapter will present some of the models that deal with these challenges.

The example also illustrates the many possible applications of a high yield bond valuation model. A high yield bond market tends to be less liquid than the investment grade bond market because of the bonds' higher credit risk. The quoted bond prices are often indications of the bond value. In these cases, the quoted prices cannot be used for larger transaction sizes and may not even reflect the equilibrium price, which may be established when there is a larger transaction volume. A valuation model can provide a systematic approach to determine the fair value of the bonds, for the purpose of managing the risk of a bond portfolio, marking to market of a high yield bond portfolio, and many other practical applications of bond portfolio management.

9.2   Institutional Framework of Bankruptcy and Bankruptcy Proceedings

We begin with an overview of the institutional framework of bankruptcy and bankruptcy proceedings. The bankruptcy framework describes the principles behind the rules of bankruptcy, and the proceedings show the actual functions of the bankruptcy. Bankruptcy determines the payments to each of the bondholders, the shareholders, and other claimants of the firm's assets or future earnings. Therefore, it is the logical starting point to understand the valuation of a high yield bond.

A Bond Indenture

Corporations tend to issue a number of debts, which may be publicly sold and/or privately placed. The portfolio of debt of the corporation is called the *debt structure*. It may consist of bank notes, private loans, and public debts. The portfolio may have long-term bonds and short-term bonds, and each of the bonds may have its own provisions and covenants. Therefore there may be several classes of creditors: secured and unsecured (*secured creditors* have the debt secured by some assets of the firm), and junior and senior (the *senior creditors* have higher priority to the claims than the junior creditors).

Bankruptcies are often triggered by the failure to meet the obligations of any bond in the debt structure. These triggers are specified in the bond contract, called the *indenture*, agreed upon between the bondholders and the shareholders. More specifically, the indenture has two separate agreements. The first part, called the *covenant*, states the obligations of the borrower. A violation of the covenant triggers default. The second part explains what happens in the event of default.

While the shareholders and bondholders can negotiate the agreement in any form, the bond indentures tend to converge on some industry standards. These standards follow a certain format and language for ease of interpretation of the intent and implementation of the agreements. These standards are called *boilerplate*. Some of the standard terms are described below.

The covenant addresses the main concerns of bondholders. It explains the bondholders' privileges and restrictions of their rights. Bondholders want to ensure that equity holders remain as junior claimants to the firm's assets by limiting the shareholders' cash dividends and to prevent the firm's assets from being passed to any classes subordinate to the senior bondholders. They also want to keep down the number of claimants in their class or senior to their class in the future, so that the risk of the bond is not adversely affected—the increase of such claimants would lead to a higher probability of default. Consequently, these claimants will either share the firm's assets with them or have a higher priority in their claims to the firm's assets.

Any substantial breach of the covenants will lead to default. As a result, the *acceleration clause* requires the firm to pay not just the coupon but the principal. The *cross default* on a bond states that the bond is in default if the firm defaults on any bond in the debt structure. The cross default clause will accelerates the other debts' payments (e.g., the principals and unpaid coupons).

The second part of the indenture describes the implication of default. The bonds in the capital structure may be of several classes. Some are more senior than others, as specified in the bond covenants. Each bond class has a representative for all the bondholders, called the *trustee*. The trustee oversees the agreement made between the borrowers and lenders and is also responsible for exerting the rights of the bondholders in the event of default. The rights may vary according to the priority rules specified in the indenture.

The absolute priority rules specify the order of payment in the event of bankruptcy. Senior debt holders have the right to receive their payments before junior debt holders. These rules are usually applied when a firm files for Chapter 13, the liquidation of a firm, where the firm's assets are sold and distributed to all the claimants. The equity holders decide whether or not they want to liquidate the firm.

Default Proceedings

In the event of default, equity holders can choose not to liquidate. If a firm's value is based on marketable assets, it may plan to pursue a liquidation of all the assets and, in practice, the absolute priority rule would be carried out. However, if the firm's value depends on the management and relationships with clients, it would not make sense to liquidate. For example, liquidating a consulting company would yield little value to the bondholders. It is important for the management team (who often hold shares) to remain in order to maintain the firm's value.

There are other alternative actions a firm can take in the event of default. Equity holders can seek protection under the bankruptcy court procedure. Or they can initiate an out of court settlement. In this case, even if there is a settlement, the equity holders may still petition for Chapter 11 protection for a court approval of such a plan.

Chapter 11 provides protection of the firm's assets and its ability to function as a going concern while reorganizing its capital structure. The bankruptcy proceeding under Chapter 11 is a negotiation based on a certain framework. A bankruptcy court does not dictate a solution, nor does a bond indenture have any written or prespecified solution. Chapter 11 offers legal protection for a firm in default to have the opportunity to reorganize so that the firm can emerge from the bankruptcy proceeding as a viable, going concern while satisfying all the claimants in the event of default. However, bankruptcy proceedings can be complicated, involving negotiations that seek to maximize the firm's value.

The Reorganization Plan

The bankruptcy court oversees the management of the firm. Under its protection, the management of the firm will continue to function as a going concern. The bankruptcy court also oversees the reorganization plan. Usually the senior debt holders will present the plan. The reorganization becomes a negotiating process. Its end result is to propose a reorganization plan that can gain the approval of all the claimants, including the equity holders and the bankruptcy court.

The principle behind the plan should be that the firm can function without envisioning another bankruptcy. The plan has to be timely to minimize bankruptcy costs, ensuring that the management will avoid making highly risky investments with negative net present values, hoping to avoid losing all the equity value. The bankruptcy court needs to approve the plan that the classes agree on. More important, it needs the firm to be viable as a going concern. The court seeks to lower the probability of the firm's declaring bankruptcy in the near future.

In the event of reorganization, the senior debt holders play an important role. They are often responsible for proposing a reorganization plan. A reorganization does not necessarily result in following the provisions as strictly stated in the priority rules. Senior debt holders have the most right to be paid in full. In fact, equity holders may retain a portion of their equity and not give all the shares to the bondholders. In such a case, the bondholders may realize a higher return than what they would be able to receive under liquidation. Senior debt holders would receive less to ensure that the firm's value is maximized by taking into consideration the preservation of the management or seeking better management, maintaining the client base, and the tax implications.

The plan may propose the deferment of the senior debt payments, or permit satisfying the claims by paying with securities other than cash: subordinated debt, preferred shares, or common shares. The plan must be accepted by all the impaired classes, and the votes within each class have to be accepted by half of the votes represented by a two-thirds majority of debt value. Finally, the court has to approve the plan.

When the classes cannot agree on a plan, the court can designate a class to be "not in good faith" because it is not exerting its best effort to support a reorganization plan that is considered workable by the court. For this reason, the court can "cram down" on the dissenting minority, in essence overruling their disagreement.

If the negotiations fail (that is, an agreement cannot be reached to the satisfaction of either party), the final option is to convert from a Chapter 11 filing to a Chapter 13 liquidation of the company.

Since the reorganization plan is about "who will get what," it clearly affects the valuation of a high yield bond. The plan affects the bond values in two ways: the value of the firm post reorganization and the negotiating positions of each class of creditors. If the plan leads to a higher valuation of the firm, then the holders of high yield bond will likely receive more for their claims. After all, the payments to the bondholders must come from the valuation of the reorganized firm. If the bondholders are in a stronger position to negotiate, the bond value can be enhanced. For example, if the firm value is based more on assets with marketability and less on management know-how, the bondholders have a stronger negotiating position against the management team. These two aspects are not independent of each other; they are related because the firm's value and the source of the value affect the negotiations.

At bankruptcy, there are other claimants to the firm's value. According to the priority rules, taxes owed to the government have the first claim. Then the wages and benefits of the workers have the second claim, which has a higher priority than the debt holders. The benefits to the employees can trigger the default of the firm. The mechanism of the trigger works as follows. When the pension fund is underfunded beyond a limit, the firm is obligated to inject more funding. We will discuss the pension plan in more detail in chapter 11. When the firm fails to inject the funds, the pension liability can force to the firm to declare bankruptcy.

The *Pension Benefits Guarantee Corporation* (*PBGC*) is a federal government agency that insures private defined benefit pension plans. It can protect the pension liability by making the firm meet the obligations. It can also take over the pension plan and assume fiduciary duties. This decision depends on the negotiating positions of the firm and PBGC. Every firm has to pay insurance premiums to PBGC.

9.3   The Fisher Model

All corporate bonds have credit risks. The distinction between the high yield bonds and the investment grade bonds is based on their exposure levels to the default risk. To formulate a model of credit risk, we will begin with the investment grade bonds. As we discussed in the context of WMT 8.25, the size of the amount outstanding may affect the yield spread. Fisher (1959) provides some indications of the determinants of the yield spreads. The precise specification of the model can be updated because the debt market has changed beyond recognition since the 1960s. However, the basic idea provides important insights.

The model uses historical data and estimates the important factors that determine the bond yields. Both the independent and the dependent variables are expressed in natural log, where the dependent variable is the yield spread (the yield of the bond net the yield of the Treasury bond with a similar maturity). The independent variables are earnings variability, X_1; time without default X_2; equity/debt ratio X_3; and market value of debt, X_4.

X_1 = the ratio of standard deviation of the firm's net income to the average net income

X_2 = the number of years that the firm has been operating without a default

X_3 = the capitalization (market value of equity) to the par value of all the firm's debts

X_4 = the market value of the bond as a proxy for the marketability of the bond issue.

$$\text{Yield spread} = 0.987 + 0.307X_1 - 0.253X_2 - 0.537X_3 - 0.275X_4 \qquad (9.2)$$

The coefficients of the model are estimated from the historical data. The model shows that the earnings variability adversely affects the bond value; a 1% increase in earnings variability would lead to a 0.307% increase in the yield spread. Similarly, other variables can be explained intuitively.

The model is useful to gain insight into the determinants of the bond yield spreads. It is also simple to derive, and is intuitive in its explanation. Furthermore, it can provide us with a foundation from which to probe deeper into the valuation of a bond with credit risks. It can prompt us to further question the specifications of the valuation, leading us to a more comprehensive view of the model. For example, how should the probability of default be explicitly reflected in the valuation model? The next model provides a solution.

9.4   An Actuarial Model

A *default premium* is defined as the difference between the promised yield and the expected yield. Consider a bond maturing in a year with a promised payment of $100, but the expected payment is only $50. Assume the market is willing to pay $50 for the bond (in order to keep the arithmetic simple). This assumption is of course unrealistic, because the bond should be priced below the expected value for the time value of money, if not for risk premium. The *promised yield* is 100% and the expected yield is 0. The promised yield is the yield based on the promised coupon and principal payments. But as a result of default, the expected payments of the bonds may be less than the promised amount.

To begin the investigation of default experiences, we first describe the mortality of individuals in actuarial sciences. Mortality is analogous to a firm's default. For a given population, we first group the population by cohorts: female, male, smokers, nonsmokers. Then we collect the death experiences of the population. From the experiences, we can calculate the conditional probability of death and survival rate for each cohort of each age group. This compilation is called the *mortality table*. From it we can derive the risk of selling insurance to an individual.

The *actuarial approach* to default, proposed by Pye (1974), follows a similar argument. Of course, we have to stretch our imagination to think of a person as a bond or vice versa, since such an idea sounds preposterous. With a person, there is a biological factor; most mortality tables cease at age 100. Firms have no biological termination date, even if investors have an investment horizon of less than ten years for most practical purposes. The actuarial approach to bond valuation is not to model a bond as an individual, but to borrow the methodology of using historical data to help us forecast the future and price the default premium. The focus is on the methodology and not on the modeling or the assumptions of the model.

Here, we present a model similar to Pye's. The model assumes that the marginal probability of default each year is constant, p_d. In the event of default, the bondholders realize a proportion of the face value, λ, the recovery ratio. If there is no default, the bondholders receive the risk-free rate r_f plus the default premium (π). Since we want to relate the expected returns of bonds to the probability of default, we will first derive a model which assumes that the investors are risk-neutral and we do not have any risk premium. This way, the default premium is simply the expected loss of the bond due to default. We have

$$\frac{1}{1 + r_f + \pi} = \frac{p_d \cdot \lambda + (1 - p_d)}{1 + r_f} \tag{9.3}$$

By rearranging the terms, we have

$$\frac{1}{1 + r_f + \pi} = \frac{1 - (1 - \lambda) \cdot p_d}{1 + r_f} \tag{9.4}$$

Therefore, we have

$$1 + \frac{\pi}{(1 + r_f)} = \frac{1}{1 - (1 - \lambda) \cdot p_d} \tag{9.5}$$

To further simplify, we have

$$\pi = \frac{(1 + r_f) \cdot (1 - \lambda) \cdot p_d}{1 - (1 - \lambda) \cdot p_d} \tag{9.6}$$

This elegant model shows more precisely how the increase in probability of default or a lower recovery ratio would lead to higher default premium.

In comparison to the Fisher model, it is important to note that the Pye model focuses on the default premium. The observed yield spread, according to Fisher model, is also determined by the marketability and the investors' risk aversion. The actuarial model provides deeper insight into a component of the yield spread, and such insights can be very useful in deciding how reasonable the observed market option adjusted spreads are. The Fisher model and the Pye model offer a baseline to measure whether the market is overestimating or underestimating the credit risks based on the observed level of the option adjusted spreads.

9.5   Historical Experience and Estimation of the Parameters of Default Models

Default Rate and Mortality Rate

The actuarial model suggests that we need to estimate the probability of default and the recovery rate of a bond. One approach to determine the probability of default is to follow the methodology used in measuring the mortality rate of a person.

The most basic element of a mortality table is the death rate, measured by the number of deaths per 1,000 population. The first question we confront with bonds is how to measure the default rate. Unlike a person, where death is well defined, it is less clear to how to measure bond default as an event. Should default (1) measure the proportion of the number of defaults (as events) at the end of the period against the total number of firms at the beginning of the period? Or (2) should it measure the face value of defaults in relation to the total amount of face value at the beginning of the period? For the measure of default rate, we have two possibilities.

If approach (1) is used, the default rate is influenced by many small debts. If approach (2) is used, the default rate is influenced by the experiences of large debt issues. Therefore the choice between the two approaches depends on the application. If the purpose of the model is to determine the likelihood of default of a sample of bonds, then approach (1) is preferred because the sample is based upon a cross-section of firms and not biased by the large historical default cases. If the purpose of the model is to measure the default by the dollar amount of a bond portfolio that has a spectrum of bonds, including those of large corporations, approach (2) would be more applicable.

Default Table

For the mortality table, we have the cumulative probability of default or the conditional probabilities. Cumulative probability measures the probability of a bond's surviving for a certain number of years. Given the cumulative probability, we can calculate the conditional probabilities, showing that likelihood of a default in one year is conditional on the firm surviving a certain number of years. These studies use extensive historical data and following the "life cycle" of the bond from the day of issuance.

The time-series data (historical default data of the bonds outstanding in the market) are relatively short—because many bonds do not go into default—when compared with the mortality table. These default tables lack the extensive data that mortality tables have to support the results.

Similar to mortality tables, which group the subjects into categories by sex and habits, default tables group bond categories by the sectors of the markets (e.g., utilities, industrial, financial, and others). In addition, default tables can categorize bonds by their credit rating, which is similar to the measures of health levels in mortality tables.

The default table provides the probability of default as a function of the age of the bond and the bond rating at its issuance. It is comparable to a mortality table, although they have distinctive differences. They are both used to determine the probability of future experiences: default and death.

Recovery Rates by Industry

The other estimate needed for the actuarial model is the *recovery ratio* or *recovery rate*. The recovery ratio is defined as the proportion of the amount received by the creditor emerging from bankruptcy to the par amount. The empirical results show that the recovery rate can vary significantly from one bond to another. As expected, the senior debt holders can receive more than the junior debt holders because they have higher priority claims to the firm's assets.

There are many measures of the recovery rate. We can observe it directly, since it is reported in bankruptcies. But this observation will be based on book value. For example, according to a workout plan, the bondholders may surrender x% of their claims. Then $(1 - x)$ is the recovery ratio, and is based on the par value of the bonds. In order to measure value based on market valuation, some research suggests using trading prices one month after default as the recovery rate. The assumption behind this approach is that the value of the debt after the bankruptcy is the market-determined recovery to the creditor emerging from bankruptcy. Using a one-month lag enables the market to determine the equilibrium price such that the price is not affected by frictions in the market mechanism. For example, the illiquidity of trading of the bonds immediately after bankruptcy may lead to market quotes not reflecting the true market supply of and demand for the bond.

Altman and Kishore (1996) used 25 years of defaults in the United States to determine the recovery ratio to be 40% on average. The senior debt recovers 45% of the face value, while the junior debt recovers only 30%.[1] That means in the event of default, senior debt holders may lose about 55% of the par value, while the junior debt holders may lose over 70%. As the model indicates, these losses are not equal to some gains by other claimants. These losses mean that the firm value can no longer cover 100% of the original investments by the bondholders. In practice, the investors who provided the capital infusion for the reorganization of the firm may end up holding the majority of the firm's value as their condition for supplying the new capital.

The recovery ratio is shown to be related to the state of the economy. In particular, the recovery ratio is low at times of high GDP growth rate. One may argue that the debt holders are more willing to recover less in order to expedite the default procedure in a robust economy. The sooner the firm in default becomes operational, the higher the likelihood that it can repay the outstanding debt. Firms like utilities, with more stable income and tangible assets backing the long-term debt, tend to have higher recovery ratios.

There are many other factors affecting the recovery ratio, such as the direct bankruptcy costs. The higher the direct bankruptcy costs, the less the firm value can be allocated for the recovery. Warner (1977) reports that the direct cost of bankruptcy is 5% of the firm's value. Altman and Spivack (1983) estimated that the cost be 2–15%. Alderson and Betker (1995) show that the cost of reorganization is 13–62%, including indirect costs such as the loss of clients, termination of potentially profitable business, failing to exploit profitable new business opportunities because of the oversight of the bankruptcy court, and losing valuable human resources as some employees may leave the company. This shows that the direct cost alone has a large variation in its estimates, and the estimate of the indirect costs has even a wider margin for error.

Another important factor affecting the recovery ratio is the deviation from the absolute priority rule. When a significant portion of the value of the firm is required to pay for the management or new capital infusion, there is much less for the outstanding bondholders.

The last main reason for the variations of the recovery ratio is the specification of the bond covenant. The recovery rate should depend on the covenant triggering default. Most trustees of the bonds do not declare the firm in default until it cannot meet its obligations. Also, they do not declare the firm in default based on forecasts of its ability to repay. For this reason, when a firm defaults, the recovery ratio depends on what is left for the bondholders at the time. We will revisit this view later, in the description of the structural model. For the time being, let us assume that when the firm defaults, the bondholders recover a portion of the face value.

Credit Risk Migration

The determination of credit risk migration depends on the use of historical data. Using historical data, we can also determine the probability of the rating's migration from one rating to the other. Using historical data this way is analogous to determining the likelihood of a person's health improving or deteriorating in one year. This is called the *transition matrix*. (See table 9.3.)

Consider the cell on the first row and the third column. The value 0.68 means that there is a probability of 0.68% that an AAA bond may lower the rating to A by the end of the year. Other entries of the matrix are defined similarly.

The example shows that the likelihood of a high rating bond falling several notches down in one year is possible but not probable. The matrix is not symmetrical. That means that the likelihood of downgrading is not the same as that of upgrading.

The usefulness of the transitional matrix is that if we perform a matrix multiplication of itself, the resulting matrix is the transition matrix for a two-year period. Another matrix multiplication would be for three years, and so on. Therefore, specifying a transition

Table 9.3 Transition Matrix

Initial Rating	AAA	AA	A	BBB	BB	B	CCC	Default
AAA	90.81	8.33	0.68	0.06	0.12	0.000	0.000	0.000
AA	0.70	90.65	7.79	0.64	0.06	0.14	0.02	0.00
A	0.09	2.27	91.05	5.52	0.74	0.26	0.01	0.06
BBB	0.02	0.33	5.95	86.93	5.30	1.17	0.12	0.18
BB	0.03	0.14	0.67	7.73	80.53	8.84	1.00	1.06
B	0.00	0.11	0.24	0.43	6.48	83.46	4.07	5.20
CCC	0.22	0.00	0.22	1.30	2.38	11.24	64.86	19.79
Default	0.00	0.00	0.00	0.00	0.00	0.00	0.00	100.00

Source: Standard and Poor's Credit Week, April 15, 1996.

matrix over a period enables us to specify the transitional matrix that can estimate a bond's rating shift over any time horizon. (See table 9.4.)

For illustration purposes, we derived a simplified one-period transition matrix from the original transition matrix. We chose AAA and AA and put other ratings into the Others category. The probability of other ratings would be $1 - \text{Prob(AAA)} - \text{Prob(AA)}$. Once we have the 3×3 simplified one-period transition matrix, we can calculate the two-period transition matrix by squaring the one-period transition matrix. We can calculate the three-period transition matrix by multiplying the one-period transition matrix by the two-period transition matrix. 0.825959 at the northwest corner of the two-period transition matrix represents that AAA firms will remain the same category in two years with the probability of 82.5959 percent. The other numbers can be interpreted in similar ways.

Underlying this property is the assumption that the one-period transitional matrix is Markov, meaning that the matrix measures the probability of future rating changes, and these probabilities have no memories independent of the rating of the bonds' previous years. As we saw in chapter 8, this property is not supported by the empirical observations of Altman and Kao (1992). But the use of the transition matrix can be a practical approximation.

Table 9.4 Transition Matrix Over One, Two and Three Periods

Assume the one-period transition matrix for AAA, AA, and others is

$$\Xi = \begin{bmatrix} 0.9081 & 0.0833 & 0.0086 \\ 0.0070 & 0.9065 & 0.0865 \\ 0.0840 & 0.0102 & 0.9049 \end{bmatrix}$$

Two-period transition matrix

$$\Xi\Xi = \begin{bmatrix} 0.825959 & 0.151244 & 0.022797 \\ 0.002005 & 0.823208 & 0.156746 \\ 0.153995 & 0.255484 & 0.820456 \end{bmatrix}$$

Three-period transition matrix

$$\Xi\Xi\Xi = \begin{bmatrix} 0.753047 & 0.206317 & 0.040815 \\ 0.037274 & 0.749506 & 0.213220 \\ 0.209679 & 0.044356 & 0.745968 \end{bmatrix}$$

We have modified the transition matrix to generate a multiperiod transition matrix. First, we derived a simplified one-period transition matrix from the original transition matrix. We chose AAA and AA, and put other ratings into Others category. The probability of other ratings would be 1-Prob(AAA)-Prob(AA). Once we have the 3×3 simplified one-period transition matrix, we can calculate the two-period transition matrix by squaring the one-period transition matrix. We can calculate the three-period transition matrix by multiplying the one-period transition matrix by the two-period transition matrix. 0.825959 at the northwest corner of the two-period transition matrix represents that AAA firms will remain in the same AAA category in two years with the probability of 82.5959%. The other numbers can be interpreted in similar ways.

9.6   The Reduced Form Models

Based on the historical estimates of the probability of default and the recovery ratio, we can now formulate valuation models that extend from the Pye (actuarial) model. To begin, the Pye model is static. Given the probabilities, we can calculate the expected values. The model does not specify any stochastic process, which enables us to measure the risk and returns over a time horizon.

The Jarrow–Turnbull model (1995) assumes that default is an event. The mathematical formulation used to study default as an event is similar to that which is used to study the durability of a lightbulb. The lightbulb has a finite life. The death of a lightbulb is an event. Measurements can be made to determine the average life span of a lightbulb, but the event can occur at any time. The mathematical model for such a stochastic process is called Poisson jumps. Jarrow and Turnbull use Poisson jumps to develop the model of the behavior of a bond, assuming risk-neutral pricing.

The model can be expressed quite simply as

$$B(t, T) = P(t, T)\left[(1 - p_d(t, T)) + p_d(t, T)\lambda\right] \qquad (9.7)$$

By rearranging, we derive

$$B(t, T) = P(t, T) - P(t, T)(1 - \lambda)p_d(t, T) \qquad (9.8)$$

where $B(t, T)$ and $P(t, T)$ are the bond values at time t and with maturity T, with default risk and without default risk, respectively. $p_d(t, T)$ is the probability of default at time t for a bond with maturity T, and λ is the recovery rate.

The usefulness of the model clearly lies in its simplicity, making full use of the historical estimates of the recovery ratios and probability of default. The mathematics of the Poisson process is then used to determine the bond value distribution and the bond returns process. The simplicity enables us to understand the implications of the default risks and the losses from default on the bond valuation.

The Jarrow–Lando–Turnbull model (JLT, 1997) incorporates the transition matrix into the bond valuation model. The idea is the same as the Jarrow–Turnbull model in modeling default as an event, but instead of using a mathematical description of the likelihood of a default, JLT uses the transition matrix to solve for the default event. This extension enables us to view the transition of the rating changes as a process that leads to default. In doing so, we can make use of the additional information of the estimation of the credit transitional matrices and provide additional information on the bond value via the bond rating changes. Specifically, the rating transition matrix can be used in two ways. For a given bond of a certain rating, we can determine the probability of reaching rating D (default) in one year. Once we square the one-period transition matrix, we can determine the probability of default in two years. If we continue this process, we can determine all the conditional probabilities of default over the life of the bond.

Another approach is to use the transition matrices to determine the probability distribution of the ratings of a bond with a certain initial rating. By noting the option adjusted spread for each rating group, we can then calculate the bond value over the time horizon for the given attained rating. Therefore, we have a distribution of the bond values. This approach enables us to determine the risk of the bond over a horizon. This method is then used to calculate the bond value at risk (VaR), which we will discuss in chapter 15.

The Duffie–Singleton model (1999) extends the JLT model to incorporate stochastic spreads. This model further assumes that the market price of risk of default also changes stochastically. Therefore, instead of discounting the uncertain bond payments (as a result of default) at a risk-free rate, Duffie–Singleton model assumes this discount rate is also stochastic. This extension can incorporate all the uncertain factors that drive the risk of a bond with credit risks.

Thus far, we can see that the models find their roots in the actuarial models, driven by the parameters estimated from historical data. However, the use of financial theory, like option pricing and capital structure models, is limited. The models are not used in any direct and important way. The default is exogenously specified, and the firm's uncertain value follows a specified process. Default is reduced to an event determined by a process without any agents' optimal decisions, providing a simple modeling approach to default, but perhaps unable to capture some of the economics of default in depicting the agents' optimal decisions.

The Ericsson–Reneby (2002) model incorporates firm risk more explicitly than the models described thus far. It considers the equity of a firm as a knockout option on the firm's value. The underlying asset of the knockout option is the value of the firm. The debt is then the firm's value net of the equity. Or the debt can be the knock-in option. In previous models, there is no default trigger point. The Ericsson–Renely model assumes that the bond covenant has an explicit default trigger point, driven by the risk of the firm's value, and that there is a specified default trigger value or strike price of the knockout options. Whenever the firm's value falls below the default trigger value, the equity holders will be given a call option on the firm's value at the expiration with the strike price of the face value of the debt. The use of the default trigger point leads to the possibility of the firm's defaulting before the maturity of the bonds.

These models are called *reduced form models* because they relate the bond value to historical estimates, and do not depend on detailed information on the firm: its capital structure, the bond covenants, size of issues, and so on. They do not endogenize the recovery rate, but use the historical estimates as given. They are driven by historical data and therefore cannot distinguish one firm from another. The strengths of these models are in their simplicity and tractability. We can use historical data to price the bonds, but the simplicity comes with a cost. Much of the information on the firm is not incorporated in the valuation. These methods are useful for pricing default risks when there is not very much information on the firm, or when there is a large portfolio analysis where a relatively rough estimate of the value of each bond is sufficient.

9.7 The Structural Model

In contrast to the reduced form model, the *structural model* is concerned with relating the bond value to the firm's business risk and its capital and debt structures, at the time of evaluating the bond. Structural models provide a detailed financial modeling of credit risks of a debt, spelling out more precisely the determinants of its value or of the recovery ratios and probability of defaults.

The Merton model (1974) provides the foundation of this approach. It applies the Black–Scholes model to corporate bond pricing. Beyond the perfect capital market assumption, valuing the corporate debt with credit risk requires further assumptions on the corporation's financial policy. This approach does not require the investors to know the profitability of the firm and its market expected rate of return; we need to know only the firm's value. Using a relative valuation approach, the firm's profitability and other attributes are captured by the firm's value.

The following assumptions are made:

1. There is no interest rate risk, with a constant risk-free rate of r. We will see that this assumption can be relaxed in a straightforward manner.
2. The firm's value V follows a lognormal process with an annualized volatility σ_V, for simplicity in an arbitrage-free binomial lattice, with m steps per year.
3. The firm pays a dividend at a portion of its firm value.
4. The debt structure is a zero-coupon bond with maturity T, and therefore the number of steps of the lattice is $n = T \times m$, where m is the number of steps per year.
5. Default is reorganization, not liquidation. At default, the bondholders take over the firm from the equity holder.
6. The firm is in default when the equity value is 0.
7. The bondholders take over the firm with no bankruptcy costs.
8. In the Miller–Modigliani world, which we will describe in more detail later, the firm value is independent of the capital structure and financial policies. Therefore, the firm value can be kept independent from the default and bond valuation.

Then, following the notations of chapter 4, we have

Cox-Ross-Rubinstein model:

$$S = \frac{1}{e^{rT}} \sum_{i=0}^{n} Max\left[Vu^i d^{n-i} - F, 0\right] \binom{n}{i} p^i (1-p)^{n-i} \tag{9.9}$$

$$u = \exp\left\{\sigma\sqrt{\frac{1}{m}}\right\}, d = \frac{1}{u}, p = \frac{\exp[\frac{r}{m}] - d}{u - d}$$

S is the capitalization of the firm or the shareholders' value, and V is the firm value. F is the face value of the debt. The bond value D is the firm's value net of the capitalization value, that is,

$$D = V - S \tag{9.10}$$

The crux of the model assumptions is a perfect capital market. The firm's value can be assumed to follow a lognormal stochastic process, and its value is not affected by the level of debt. (This assertion is supported by the Miller–Modigliani theory, which we will discuss in chapter 12.) All financial claims on the firm, such as stocks and bonds, are contingent claims on the firm's value.

The model suggests that the stock of the levered firm should behave like a stock option, and the bond is a portfolio of longing a risk-free bond and shorting a put option. Using the contingent claim valuation approach, the model can determine the appropriate discount rate for the credit risk, using the valuation of the firm. Specifically, a bond is viewed as

$$\text{defaultable bond} = \text{risk free bond} - \text{put option on the firm} \tag{9.11}$$

Since this is a contingent claim valuation model, the valuation approach depends on the price and not on the discount rate. Instead of focusing on the appropriate yield spread, we now turn to the valuation of the put option.

Another important departure from the other models is that the recovery rate is stochastic and endogenized. We can no longer assume that the recovery rate is a historical observation that can be applied to all the bonds in a certain group. The recovery ratio in a structural model is uncertain, depending on the outcome. According to the Merton model, the recovery ratio is the firm's value at default on the day of the maturity of the bond. More precisely, when the firm's value is below the bond face value on the maturity date, the debt holders receive only the remaining firm value, which is uncertain at any time before the maturity date. The recovery rate for each industry must depend on the debt structure of its sector.

Given the model assumptions and the mechanism used to describe the valuation of an option, the valuation of a bond according to the Merton model is straightforward. We can use the backward substitution approach on a binomial lattice. This approach enables us to incorporate other bond features, such as the call and sinking fund provisions that were discussed in chapter 8, into the model. The structural model proposes that a bond is holding a short position in a put option. This approach enables us to value many items on the balance sheet and on corporate securities. An important contribution of the structural model is its ability to integrate the firm's risk to the bond valuation, and solve for the default trigger points using the option pricing theory. Much subsequent research has sought to exploit this insight.

The Black–Cox model uses the Merton model to study the valuation of junior and senior debts according to the absolute priority rule. They wanted to study the allocation of risk among the classes of bonds. In order to do so, they had to view all the classes of claims as options on the firm's value with different payments at maturity. The risk-neutral pricing approach (or the relative valuation approach) enabled them to solve for the appropriate value of each claim on the firm's value, relative to the firm's value. If the discount cash flow method is used, we will have to calculate the expected payment for each claimant and determine the appropriate discount rate for each claim, given its risks. Without a framework to determine the relationship between the risk and the market risk premium, we cannot evaluate the allocation of risk and value to all the claimants to the firm's value. This is exactly what a relative valuation framework seeks to accomplish.

There are many extensions of the models. Most of these models introduce stochastic interest rates. These extensions are motivated by the empirical evidence demonstrating that the shapes of the yield curve and interest rate levels are important factors relating to the number of defaults.

For example, Shimko et al. (1993) developed a model with stochastic interest rates using the Vasicek (1977) normal interest rate model in specifying the short-term interest rates, as described in chapter 5. The credit spreads of the bonds can be derived from the model, and they found that the credit spreads increase with the interest rate volatility, as well as when there is a correlation between the interest rate risks and the firm value risk. This model result can be explained intuitively. When there is interest rate risk, especially when the interest rate risk is positively correlated with the firm's value risk, the defaultable bond's embedded option's value will increase, leading to a higher credit spread.

These models assume that default occurs only when the firm cannot meet its debt obligations. Since these models also assume that debt is a zero-coupon bond with only one payment, then the firm can default at only one time—bond maturity. This requirement is unpleasant because many defaults do not happen only at the maturities of the bonds. Often the bondholders are protected by *safety covenants* written in the bond indenture. These safety covenants protect the bondholders for the life of the bond by conditions that trigger the firm to accelerate the principal payments to the bondholders. For example, some of the firm's financial ratios cannot fall below certain criteria—for instance, the debt ratio cannot exceed a certain level or the market capitalization cannot be lower than some number. The following models assume a default trigger barrier where the firms default whenever they hit the barrier. The Longstaff–Schwartz model (1995, p. 792, assumption 4) allows the firm to default whenever its value falls below a barrier $K(t)$. This approach combines the Merton model with the default trigger approach. This way, they could use the estimated recovery ratio, and do not have to assume default is triggered at maturity and there is no default before maturity.

Saá-Requejo and Santa-Clara (1999) allow for stochastic strike price X, and Briys and de Varenne (1997) allow the barrier to be related to the market value of debt. In a way, these models are similar to the reduced form model of Ericsson and Renely, in that the default condition is almost specified by the model, particularly the barrier $K(t)$, and less by the debt structure of the firm, the interactions of the shareholders' optimal strategy in declaring default, and the bondholders' ability to protect their investments.

Therefore, these models consider a defaultable bond to be a portfolio of risk-free bonds net of a barrier option.

$$\text{defaultable bond} = \text{risk-free bond} - \text{barrier option}$$

By contrast, the Kim–Ramaswamy–Sundaresan model (1993) allows for stochastic interest rates, and the bondholders get a portion of the face value at default. The bankruptcy condition is based on the lack of cash flow to meet obligations. They define the default trigger point as a net cash flow at the boundary, when the firm cannot pay the interest and dividend. Their assumption is motivated by the observed default experience and tends to be triggered by the lack of cash flow to meet the debt obligations.

Specifically, they assume that at default, the bondholders receive $Min[\delta(t), B_t, V^*]$, where B_t is the value of an otherwise identical bond, V^* is the value of the firm at the time of default, and it is specified by a lognormal binomial lattice of a firm value $V(n, i)$ for time n and state i, and $\delta(t)$ is a discount of the risk-free bond value. The most important contribution of the model is the use of the free cash flows of the firm. The model assumes that the free cash flow generated by the firm at each node is a constant fraction of the firm's value. Therefore, the free cash flow $f(n, i)$ is given by

$$f(n, i) = \beta \cdot V(n, i) \text{ where } \beta \text{ is a constant}$$

The default trigger is specified by $f(n, i) < c(n, i)$, where $c(n, i)$ is the coupon payment on the debt at time n and state i. Therefore the cash flow to the bondholders at each time and state (each node point on the lattice) is defined. Using the backward substitution approach and the risk-neutral probability, we can determine the bond value. Since the recovery rate depends on the negotiation in default, debt holders should not receive the full amount. Leland (1994) develops a model that seeks to determine the default boundary $X(V < X)$ by incorporating the negotiation model to solve for the optimal decision of the shareholders in declaring bankruptcy.

As we have seen in earlier chapters, integrating interest rate risks to the stock risk in a binomial lattice is fairly straightforward. Most of these models seek to analyze the bond behavior under interest rate risks not by simulations but by analytical solutions. Therefore, they need to simplify the interest rate process so that they can determine tractable solutions to the problems. Thus they tend to use normal interest rate models.

For some of the models, the link between the firm's capital structure and the risk of the bond default is the measure of the likelihood of a knockout event as the firm's value reaches the default trigger boundary. The link is rather tenuous, and the distinction between the structural model and the reduced form models becomes blurred. The following models are more consistent with the spirit of a structural model. They do not assume such an exogenous default trigger barrier and a recovery ratio.

9.8 Valuation of a Debt Package Using a Compound Option Model

Geske (1977) and Geske and Johnson (1984) show that the equity of a firm with a coupon-paying bond or a bond with a sinking fund is a compound option. In order to analyze the risk of a bond, we have to value the debt package first. Because of the cross default clause, any bond risk has to be considered within the context of the debt package.

The description of all the bonds, their covenants, their provisions, and their maturities, is called a debt structure. The argument shows that in order to understand the default risk of a bond, we need to know the entire debt structure. This is clear from the default process and the prevalent use of the cross default clause in the bond covenant. From the bond package, we can determine the promised cash flows of the entire debt structure, including the coupon payments.

When the firm is obligated to pay the first payment of the debt, which may be the coupon, the principal, or both, we assume that the firm cannot sell its capital assets or use its liquid financial assets to meet the obligation. Instead, the firm must go to the capital market to raise either equity or debt to finance the payments. When the firm uses capital to finance the first payment, the ability to raise the needed amount has to depend on the total debt outstanding. If the present value of debt outstanding plus the first payment is higher than of the firm's value, then the equity holder will declare the firm in default. The shareholders will not be able to raise the capital via equity market or to refinance the payment with another debt. This argument applies to the following payment and to all subsequent payments. As a result, the equity is a compound option on the firm's value. Each bond payment, coupon or principal, is the strike price of a call option to buy another option.

When an equity is viewed as a compound option, the firm can default before the maturity and the default is triggered by a cash obligation, similar to the Kim–Ramaswamy–Sundaresan model. But the firm's value can exceed (and usually does exceed) the cash requirement in the compound option model. The firm declares default because the remaining debt forbids it to raise more capital to meet the immediate obligations. This is an important distinction because the compound option approach in fact models the recovery ratio by showing how the design of the debt structure, the payment schedules, affects the probability of default and the recovery ratio. More important, the model closely resembles the way firms generally declare defaults.

By way of contrast, a model using knockout options relies on bonds having protective covenants, which require the firm to declare default as soon as some market value measure (for example, capitalization value) falls below some book value. Such bond covenants do not seem to be widely used or enforced.

Valuing a Debt Within a Debt Structure

Ho and Singer (1982) extend the concept of the structural model of a bond to a package of bonds where the implications of the absolute priority rules are analyzed. The relative values of the junior and senior debt are affected by three confounding factors: priority rules, the term structure of credit risk, and the coupon level.

To study the impact of the debt structure on the bond valuation, Ho and Singer retain all the assumptions made in the Merton model, except that they modify the assumption on the debt structure. The assumptions made about the debt structure are the following:

1. The debt structure has two zero-coupon bonds: a long-term bond with maturity T_L and face value F_L, and a short-term bond with maturity T_s and face value F_s.
2. The bond covenant specifies that the senior debt has the absolute priority to take over the firm's assets or value at the time of default. And there are two possible cases: (a) The long-term debt is senior to the short-term debt and (b) the short-term debt is senior to the long term-debt.

When bonds are in the same class in the capital structure, at bankruptcy they are paid according to their proportion of face value. However, when the absolute priority rule applies, the credit risks for the senior debt holders and the junior debt holders are different, and risk is further complicated by their maturities.

Under the absolute priority rule, the senior debt valuation would consider both the junior debt and the equity as one class. The presence of junior debt should not affect the senior debt value. Thus, the value of the senior debt can be valued as "debt" and the package of the junior debt and equity can be considered "equity." We can then apply the compound option model to determine the debt and equity values of the firm, and the senior debt value can be determined

Specifically, let us consider the case where the long-term debt is senior to the short-term debt. In this case, the long-term debt valuation can ignore the presence of the short-term debt because, from the perspective of the long-term debt holders, the junior debt holders and the equity holders belong to the same class of claimants in the event of default—both junior to them. For this reason, the long-term debt value is given by using equations (9.9) and (9.10):

$D(senior\ long\text{-}term) =$

$$V - \frac{1}{e^{r \cdot T_L}} \sum_{i=0}^{T_L} Max \left[Vu^i d^{T_L - i} - F_L, 0 \right] \binom{T_L}{i} p^i (1-p)^{T_L - i} \qquad (9.12)$$

To determine the junior debt value, we consider the package of the senior debt and junior debt as "debt" and the equity as "equity" in the compound option model. This valuation enables us to determine the value of the portfolio of senior and junior debt. Then the junior debt can be valued as the debt package value net of the senior debt value.

Specifically, in this case, first we need to determine the value of the debt package, using Geske's compound option model. At time T_S and state k, the capitalization value (the shareholders' value) before the short-term debt payment is given by (see figure 9.1)

$$S_k^* = \frac{1}{e^{r \cdot (T_L - T_S)}} \sum_{i=k}^{k+(T_L-T_S)} Max\left[Vu^i d^{T_L - i} - F_L, 0 \right] \binom{T_L}{i} p^i (1-p)^{T_L - i} \quad (9.13)$$

The firm will default if the capitalization is negative after paying for the short-term debt face value. Therefore the shareholders' value should be

$$S_k = Max\left[S_k^* - F_S, 0 \right] \quad (9.14)$$

Given this terminal condition for the shareholders' value and using the backward substitution, we can determine the shareholders' value, S, given by

$$S = \frac{1}{e^{r \cdot T_S}} \sum_{k=0}^{T_S} S_k \binom{T_L}{i} p^k (1-p)^{T_S - k} \quad (9.15)$$

Therefore the value of the debt package is

$$D(debt\ package) = V - S \quad (9.16)$$

But the debt package value must be the sum of the senior and junior debt. Therefore, the junior short-term debt is given by

$$D(junior\ short\ term) = D(debt\ package) - D(senior\ long\text{-}term) \quad (9.17)$$

To understand the impact of these factors on the bond value, let us consider the case when we have junior short-term debt and senior long-term debt. For illustrative purposes, let us assume that there are priority rules in the McLeodUSA bonds. This assumption is made for illustrative purposes—the actual bonds do not have such priority

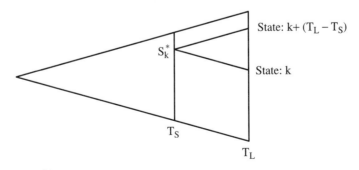

Figure 9-1 The capitalization value at state k and time T_S. T_L is a maturity date of the senior long-term bond. T_S is a maturity date of the junior short-term bond. S_k^* is the stock value at T_S after the stockholders exercise their option at T_L. Therefore S_k^* is the expected value over the terminal conditions from state k to state $k + (T_L - T_S)$ at T_L, discounted at the risk-free rate for the period between T_L and T_S.

rules. We then study the bond values as the firm value increases from 0 to a high value of $3 billion. Let us consider three segments in this spectrum of the firm values. (See figure 9.2.)

When the firm's value is low relative to the face value of the debt, the default risk is significant. The senior debt must have a lower risk than the junior debt. When the firm's value increases, the probability of default of the short-term debt decreases faster than that of the long-term debt. The short-term debt being senior to the long-term debt, the default risk of the short-term debt is allocated to the long-term debt. When the value of the firm becomes high, the long-term debt increases its value more rapidly.

By this argument, we can see that if the long-term debt is junior to the short-term debt, then the long-term bond should always have a higher risk than the short-term bond. On the other hand, if the long-term bond is senior to the short-term bond, then the risk allocation between the long-term bond and short-term bond is more complicated.

The complication arises because default risk increases with the term to maturity. But when the long-term debt is senior to the short-term debt, part of the default risk is allocated to the short-term debt. The short-term debt may have significant default risk when the firm's value is low, as depicted in figure 9.2, for the firm value less than 0.2. As the firm's value increases, the short-term debt value increases slowly relative to the senior long-term debt, as depicted by the firm value ranging from 0.2 to 1 in figure 9.2. Only when the firm value becomes high does the short-term debt value increase rapidly.

Most corporations have a debt structure in which the short-term debts have priority over the long-term debt. Bank loans and other short-term financing are usually secured, while the debentures tend to be longer terms with lower priority. In the presence of a

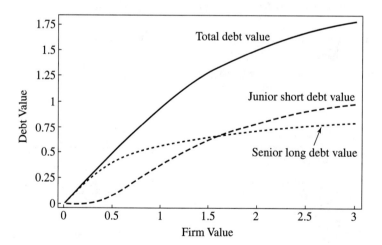

Figure 9-2 Profile of short-term junior and long-term senior debt. The total face values of the long-term bonds and the short-term bonds are 1.175 and 0.781, respectively. We assume that the junior short bonds have a time to maturity of 9, 13.5, 21.5, and 25.5 months, and the senior long senior bonds have a time to maturity of 89, 91, 92.5, and 95 months. We assume the time to maturities of the bonds as above in order to have a big gap between two maturities for illustration purposes. One interesting result of the simulation is that when the firm value increases from 0 to 0.2, the senior debt takes most of the increase. The junior debt has a positive gamma and then a negative gamma as the firm value increases.

large amount of debentures outstanding relative to its value, the firm may not be able to roll over bank loans or other short-term financing even though its total capitalization value exceeds the immediate obligation payments. This is because the firm will default if its value net of the long-term debt value is less than the immediate obligated payments. In other words, the first option of a compound option may expire out of the money. This is the evidence of the validity of the use of compound options to value the debt in order to capture the impact of long-term bonds on the short-term financing capacity of a firm.

However, long-term debt can be senior to short-term debt. In section 9.2, we described the rule at the bankruptcy court. In this rule, the pension liability has a higher priority than the debt of the firm. Since the pension liability has much longer maturity, the debts should be considered junior obligations to the pension liabilities. We will also show in chapter 12 that the fixed cost of an ongoing concern can be viewed as a perpetual senior debt. With a significant presence of fixed costs, both the bonds, which are junior to the fixed costs, and the equity can be greatly affected. In this case, we will see that the debt has positive gamma that turns into negative gamma as the firm's value increases, as described in this chapter. In chapter 12, we will discuss in more detail how the cost structure of the operation of a firm can be viewed as a debt structure, and how operating leverage is related to financial leverage. The results in this section will provide insights into the valuation of a firm, something that we will discuss in chapters 12.

9.9 Empirical Evidence

Many empirical studies have been conducted to test the financial models described above. Jones et al. (1984) used the monthly prices for the traded debt of 27 companies from 1975 to 1981 to test the Merton model. The results showed that the market prices of defaultable bonds tend to have higher spreads than those predicted by the model. The results suggest that the Merton model does not price the default risks sufficiently. To remedy this problem Zhou (1997) extended the Merton model to jump the process so that the model can be better explained by the observed data.

Empirical results show that there seems to be an additional risk premium added to the non-investment grade bonds (Fons, 1987; Altman, 1989; Jarrow et al. 1997; Barnhill et al., 2000). However, the empirical estimation of the premium may not be attributed to the credit risk alone. The spread may be the result of the lack of market liquidity.

Other approaches do not test the Merton model directly, but test its implications. The structural model also relates the probability of default (measured in the risk-neutral measure) to the firm's leverage, volatility, and the bond maturity. These are the attributes used in bond rating, similar to Altman's Z score. Therefore, we can use the structural model to estimate the default probability in a risk-neutral measure, and the model can provide the likelihood of bond rating change. Deliandis and Geske (1999) show that the risk-neutral rating transition probabilities derived from the structural pricing model are similar to those calculated from the historical data.

Ogden (1987) uses the data of individual bonds to determine the parameters that may explain the spread variations. The results show that the model can explain 60% of spread variations. Specifically, the test shows that the stochastic interest rate is important as an explanatory variable and the firm size adds explanatory power. That is, the size of the firm tends to lower the credit spread.

9.10   A Review of the High Yield Bond Models

Despite significant progress made in contingent claim pricing theories, such as the proposal of the Merton model in 1974, few risky bond models are successfully implemented. We have seen many models proposed, but empirically no model can measure up to the successes of other contingent claim models in other areas.

The modeling approaches for investment grade bonds, interest rate, and equity derivatives are widely used for their accuracy in valuations. While we have seen many interest rate models presented, they have been designed to meet special requirements, such as satisfying lognormal distribution or normal distribution, one-factor or multiple-factor interest rate risk, and other features that we have described. They are all, by and large, practical; they can be used with success in valuing and managing interest rate risks. However, this is not the case with high yield bond models. Credit risk models are less widely used and less precise for valuing high yield bonds. This simply emphasizes the complexity in modeling a high yield bond.

High yield bond analysis is often reported as an extension of the analysis of investment grade bonds. This is unfortunate, because a high yield bond is, after all, a security that encompasses both equity and fixed income. When a firm can meet its debt obligations, the bond is a fixed income. When the firm defaults, the bond shares the risk of the equity. A high yield bond is a hybrid security of fixed-income security and equity.

If we think we can simplify the problem by arguing that the debt is a contingent claim on the firm's value, then we must model (1) the contract between the bondholders and stockholders properly and (2) the underlying firm value movements. But neither model is simple.

To model the contract between the stockholders and bondholders, we must model the bankruptcy proceedings and the debt structure, both of which depend on the industry and sector type. Since the bankruptcy proceedings, as described earlier, involve negotiations of the claimants and the valuation of the underlying businesses, the modeling of such a process must necessarily be complicated. Further, in some bankruptcies, there may be over a hundred creditors, and understanding the implications of the contracts can be a difficult task.

Merton assumes that the underlying firm value follows a random walk. We doubt that this assumption is valid in most cases. We will show in later chapters that the fixed operating costs can be viewed as a perpetual senior debt of a firm that has no financial leverage. In addition, the firm also has embedded real options, options to deploy capital investment. We will show, in fact, that the Merton firm value is itself a complicated compound option and not a security with constant volatility and expected returns. We can only conclude that a valuation of a high yield corporate bond must require the understanding of the business risk of the firm as the equity valuation of the firm.

Wall Street has understood that valuing a high yield bond must be treated as partly equity research, and not a direct extension of fixed-income research. The valuation of a low rating bond must take into account the debt structure, industry standards, and other fundamentals of a firm used in equity research. This is the approach that we will take in chapter 12.

We have described the credit risk models, moving from investment grade bonds to defaulting bonds. This progression is summarized as follows. The simplest extension we described is the Pye model, using an actuarial approach to quantify the credit risks.

Poisson processes and transition matrix models extend the actuarial model to describe the risk of the bond at any future time.

Then there is a set of models that view a bond with embedded barrier options. For these models, default is the result of the underlying risky asset (i.e., the firm's value) hitting a default trigger barrier. A defaultable bond is a bond with a short position in a barrier option. The use of a barrier option, assuming that there is a default trigger point, sees that the debt structure has covenants which trigger the firm to default. However, bondholders who can trigger the default because of the barrier option also anticipate the possible outcomes of the bankruptcy procedure. Therefore, the bondholders in essence have to continually renegotiate with the management before using the trigger. Prespecifying the default trigger barrier would ignore the negotiating process between the bondholders and stockholders. Also, the use of the model would require the knowledge of the default trigger barriers.

The Merton model, in contrast, views the bond as a risk-free bond that has sold a put option. And the Geske model views any coupon bonds or debt package in the context of a compound option. Since coupon payments are almost continuously paid, the model in essence specifies the default trigger barrier in the sense that the firm is continuously tested for its viability as a going concern, checking if the capital market is willing to finance the firm to pay its coupons.

9.11 Analysis of the McLeodUSA Bond

In this section we will value the McLeodUSA debt package using the structural model, specifically the compound option model.

Methodology

Step 1. Specify the spot yield curve.

We assume that the spot yield curve on June 1, 2001, is flat at 4.938 percent.

Step 2. Construct the firm's value binomial lattice.

McLeodUSA does not pay dividends. We construct the nondividend-paying stock lattice. We assume some initial volatility σ_V and initial firm value V.

Step 3. Construct the cash flows of the debt structure.

We consider all the bonds as one debt package. Using a perfect capital market assumption, we do not make any distinctions between coupon interest and principal. Together they are the cash flows that McLeodUSA is obligated to pay the creditors.

Step 4. Determine the debt value by an iterative process.

Let the value of the firm be V, capitalization of the firm, S, and the market value of the debt package, D. By definition of the firm value, the total capitalization of the firm is the sum of equity and debt.

$$V = S + D \qquad (9.18)$$

The value of the debt package is

$$D = V - S \qquad (9.19)$$

S is the number of shares outstanding times the share price. But V has to be estimated. Often, the total capitalization of a firm is approximated by the sum of the capitalization and the book value of debt. For high yield bonds, the market value of debt can be significantly different from the book value. For this reason, we cannot use this approximation. And we need to solve for V.

We treat the capitalization S as a compound option on the underlying asset V. Following the standard valuation procedure, we assume that V has an expected return of the risk-free rate, with a volatility of σ_V. Both V and σ_V are unknowns at this point. There are two relationships: (1) the stock option valuation, using the compound option model, as a function of the firm's value; (2) the stock volatility as a function of the firm's value and its volatility. Therefore, using the capitalization value and its historical volatility of 131 percent as the initial starting point of the iterative search, we can determine the firm value V and its volatility σ_V.

Results

The observed capitalization of McLeodUSA is $3.195 billion. The observed bond package value is $2.079 billion. The firm (market) value is the sum of capitalization and market debt value, which is $5.274 billion.

Using a theoretical model, we determine the firm's value, debt value, and volatility. These values are determined using a relative valuation model based on the observed capitalization (equity market value) S. The estimated debt value is $1.920 billion and the firm's value is $ 5.118 billion. The theoretical results are quite close to the observed values. The error is only $159 million, or 7.6% for the debt. The model also provides an estimated firm volatility of 93.5%.

To illustrate the use of a structural model to determine the bond value, we employ a relatively simple model and ignore a number of factors that may also affect the bond value. We have assumed the absolute priority rule. Maybe there are more payments to the equity holder if the bond value is lowered further. We have not assumed any liquidity spread, which would lower the bond price. We have also ignored any of the make whole call provision values. However, the value of such an option is negligible.

All these factors suggest that the bond price should be lower. This implies that the volatility should be lower than 93.5%.

9.12   Analysis of Credit Risk

Analytical Results

Figure 9.3 is a plot of the capitalization against the bond package value compared with the simulated results. The result shows a reasonable fit of the simulated values and the observed values. In particular, it shows that the bond price falls in step with the stock value. But the bond price falls precipitously when the capitalization falls below a certain level. The observed bond prices seem to fall faster than the simulated results. An explanation is proposed in chapter 13, where we will discuss the impact of the firm's fixed operating costs on bond and stock price behavior. (See also figure 9.4.)

Elasticity is defined as the ratio of the proportional change in the market value of equity or the market value of debt to proportional change in the firm's value. It can be

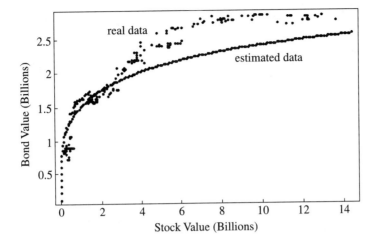

Figure 9-3 Stock value vs. bond value of McLeod USA. We plot bond value against stock value in terms of actual data versus theoretical values. We collected data of McLeodUSA's debt package and stock for the period 1/5/2001 to 2/22/2002. We also calculated the theoretical values of a stock and debt package using Merton's model, augmented by the compound option pricing model.

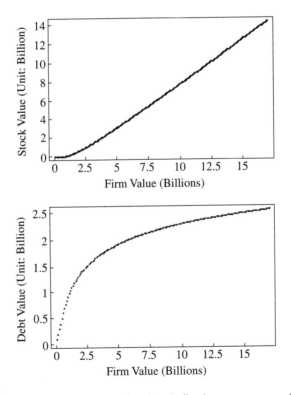

Figure 9-4 Performance profile of the bond and capitalization over a range of firm values. We plot stock value and bond value against the firm value. We collected data of McLeodUSA's debt package and stock for the period 1/5/2001 to 2/22/2002. We also calculated the theoretical value of a stock and debt package using Merton's model, augmented by the compound option pricing model.

simulated from the valuation models. The elasticity of equity to the firm's value at the current price is calculated to be 1.423 and 0.302 for the bond package.

This means that for any 1% fall in the firm's value, the equity will fall by 142.3% and the debt will fall by 30.2%. However, the elasticities for both equity and bonds increase with the falling value of the firm. Particularly when the firm's value reaches the $2 billion level, the face value of the debt the sensitivities of the changes of values of both equity and bonds will increase significantly as the firm's value falls.

Following Up

At the beginning of the chapter, we described McLeodUSA, evaluated in September. The evaluation showed that the firm had significant credit risks. Soon after September, the firm conducted a major restructuring, terminating many unprofitable units and projects, and sold off some of its assets. However, the restructuring came too late. In late January, the firm filed for bankruptcy protection. It was a prepackaged plan. Forstmann Little & Co. would inject $175 million in capital, and the plan would eliminate 95% of the outstanding debt. The shares last traded on January 30 at 0.18.

On April 17, 2002, the firm announced that the reorganization plan had become effective, and emerged from bankruptcy protection. From September to January, the stock price had fallen precipitously. Over this wide range of the stock price, the model described in this section provides the corresponding bond values, tracking those observed values quite closely.

On June 19, 2002, the *Wall Street Journal* reported the implications of the bankruptcy. Table 9.5 provides a summary.

The bankruptcy lasted from January 2002 until mid-April 2002, and the company emerged as a viable entity. With capital infusion, the capital structure was reorganized. While the stockholders and the bondholders sustained significant losses, the stockholders did not lose all their investments and the bondholders received a recovery ratio less than the historical upper limit of 30%. More important, the debt load was lowered such that the firm could generate free cash flows and minimize the loss of clients.

Table 9.5 A Summary of the Implication of the Bankruptcy

	Pre-bankruptcy	Post-bankruptcy
Debt	$ 3.964 billion	$ 0.965 billion
Original sharedholders' share	76%	17%
Senior secured debt	—	received 100%
Debentures	$ 0.14 per $1	$ 0.21–$ 0.23 per $1 + stock/warrants $0.55
Stock price	$0.15	$0.55
Cash reserve	$ 140 million	access to $ 120 million line of credit
Forstmann Little position	15%	60%
Number of customers	441,830	469,572

9.13 Summary

This chapter has extended chapter 8 by describing a bond that is subject to default risks. It began with a description of the bankruptcy proceedings, a legal process of reorganizing the firms, mainly its capital structure. It is relevant for the discussion of this chapter, which is concerned with bonds that are confronted with high probabilities of default.

However, this book is about the economic values of financial assets. We have noted that many reorganizations are completed before filing bankruptcy. Therefore the important aspect of the bankruptcy court is to provide an efficient means to help firms to reorganize and continue to provide economic outputs for the economy. To determine the value of financial assets, the important feature remains the optimal reorganization of the capital structure. Credit risk models described in this chapter are developed in order to capture these salient features of a high yield bond.

Academic literature discusses credit risk models in terms of the actuarial models, reduced form models, and structural models as alternative approaches to valuing high yield bonds.

A high yield bond is a very complex security. If the purpose is to extend the investment grade model to better understand the high yield securities, then the actuarial model offers a reasonable extrapolation to BB bonds, for example. An actuarial model can clearly identify the default premium of each bond, which makes it easier to specify the credit spread for each bond. It enables us to determine the default spread so we do not need to rely on the average of the market segment or rating group.

If we need a model to estimate the default risk impact on a bond, then the reduced form model may offer us some insights and measurements. It describes a stochastic process for the default risks, enabling us to quantify the distributions of the bond values.

But to gain insights into the most important feature of a high yield bond, as a hybrid of equity and fixed-income securities, and the appropriation of firm value for its claimants under bankruptcy proceedings, the structural model framework (or contingent claim valuation) should be used. As we explained earlier, a contingent claim valuation provides the appropriate discount rate for the risks, something that the actuarial models or reduced form models do not achieve because the option pricing model is not directly applied.

While we have described the high yield bond model, focusing only on the firm's business risk, and have ignored the interest rate risks, the extension of the structural model as a contingent claim on both firm risk and interest rate risk is straightforward and important. In the earlier chapters, we described the model for both interest rate risks and stock risk. Using such a multiple-factor model, as described in chapter 5, we can directly extend the analysis to this chapter.

In conclusion, we observe that the models thus far have focused on the claims against the firm's value. But another important contributor to the likelihood of default is the operating costs. A high operating leverage has the effect on the risk of the stock and the default risk similar to that of a high financial leverage. A model that ignores the operating leverage would not yield a better understanding of the valuation of high yield bonds. For example, in the presence of significant fixed operating costs, within the context of the structural model, the firm's value does not follow a simple random walk. And the change of the stochastic process of the firm's value has significant implications for the analysis of the high yield bond. In the following chapters, we will investigate alternative models to those described in this chapter and their implications for pricing high yield bonds.

Note

1. We might question why the senior debt does not recover in full when the junior debt recovers. One reason is that the priority rule is not followed. Another reason is that this is an average. Some junior debt may lose everything and some receive the full par amount.

References

Alderson, M., and B. Betker. 1995. Liquidation costs and capital structure. *Journal of Financial Economics*, 39 (1), (September), 45–69.

Altman, E. I. 1984. A further empirical investigation of the bankruptcy cost question. *Journal of Finance*, 39 (4), 1067–1090.

Altman, E. I. 1987. The anatomy of the high-yield bond market. *Financial Analysts Journal*, 43 (4), 12–25.

Altman, E. I. 1989. Measuring corporate bond mortality and performance. *Journal of Finance*, 44, 909–922.

Altman, E. I. 1993. Defaulted bonds: Demand, supply and performance. *Financial Analysts Journal*, 49 (3), 55–60

Altman, E. I. and J. Spivack, 1983, Predicting bankruptcy: the value line relative financial strength system vs. the zeta bankruptcy classification approach, *Financial Analysts Jurnal*, 39 (6), 60–67.

Altman, E. I., and V. Kishore. 1996. Almost everything you wanted to know about recoveries on defaulted bonds. *Financial Analysts Journal*, November–December, 57–64.

Altman, E. I. and D. L. Kao, 1992, The implications of corporate bonds ratings drift, *Financial Analysts Journal*, 48 (3), 65–75.

Anderson, R., and S. Sundaresan. 1996. Design and valuation of debt contracts. *Review of Financial Studies*, 9, 37–68.

Anderson, R., and S. Sundaresan. 2000. A comparative study of structural models of corporate bond yields: An exploratory investigation. *Journal of Banking and Finance*, 24, 255–269.

Asquith, P., R. Gertner, and D. Scharfstein. 1994. Anatomy of financial distress: An examination of junk-bond issuers. *Quarterly Journal of Economics*, 109 (3), 625–657.

Asquith, P., D. W. Mullins, Jr., and E. D. Wolff. 1989. Original issue of high yield bonds: Aging analyses of defaults, exchanges, and calls. *Journal of Finance*, 44 (4), 923–952.

Barnhill, T., Jr., M. Barnhill, F. L. Joutz, and W. F. Maxwell. 2000. Factors affecting the yields on noninvestment grade bond indices: A cointegration analysis. *Journal of Empirical Finance*, 7 (1), 57–86.

Black, F., and J. Cox. 1976. Valuing corporate securities: Some effects of bond indenture provisions. *Journal of Finance*, 31, 351–367.

Blume, M. E., D. B. Keim, and S. A. Patel. 1991. Returns and volatility of low-grade bonds. *Journal of Finance*, 4 (1), 49–74.

Briys, E., and F. de Varenne. 1997. Valuing risky fixed rate debt: An extension. *Journal of Financial and Quantitative Analysis*, 32 (2), 239–248.

Brown, K. C., and D. J. Smith. 1993. Default risk and innovations in the design of interest rate swaps. *Financial Management*, 22 (2), 94–105.

Cathcart, L., and L. El-Jahei. 1998. Valuation of defaultable bonds. *The Journal of Fixed Income*, 8 (1), 65–78.

Chance, D. M. 1990. Default risk and the duration of zero-coupon bonds. *Journal of Finance*, 45, 265–274.

Collin-Dufresne, P., and R. Goldstein. 2001. Do credit spreads reflect stationary leverage ratios? *Journal of Finance*, 56 (5), 1929–1958.

Collin-Dufresne, P., R. Goldstein, and S. Martin. 2001. The determinants of credit spread changes. *Journal of Finance*, 56 (6), 2177–2208.

Cooper, I., and M. Martin. 1996. Default risk and derivative products. *Applied Mathematical Finance*, 3, 53–74.

Cornell, B., and K. Green. 1991. The investment performance of low-grade bond funds. *Journal of Finance*, 46 (1), 29–48.

Cossin, D., and H. Pirotte. 2001. *Advanced Credit Risk Analysis*. London: John Wiley & Sons.

Dammon, R. M., K. B. Dunn, and C. S. Spatt. 1993. The relative pricing of high-yield debt: The case of RJR Nabisco Holdings Capital Corporation. *American Economic Review*, 83 (5), 1090–1111.

Das, S. R., and P. Tufano. 1996. Pricing credit-sensitive debt when interest rates, credit ratings and credit spreads are stochastic. *Journal of Financial Engineering*, 5 (2), 161–198.

Delianedis, G., and R. Geske. 1999. Credit risk and risk neutral default probabilities: Information about rating migrations and defaults. Working paper, The Anderson School, UCLA.

Duffee, G. R. 1996. Estimating the price of default risk. Working paper, Federal Reserve Board.

Duffie, D. 2001. Term structures of credit spreads with incomplete accounting information. *Econometrica*, 69 (3), 633–664.

Duffie, D., and K. J. Singleton. 1999. Modeling term structures of defaultable bonds. *Review of Financial Studies*, 12, 687–720.

Elton, E., M. Gruber, D. Agrawal, and C. Mann. 2001. Explaining the rate spread on corporate bonds. *Journal of Finance*, 56 (1), 247–277.

Ericsson, J., and J. Reneby. 1998. A framework for valuing corporate securities. *Applied Mathematical Finance*, 5 (3), 143–163.

Ericsson, J., and J. Reneby. 2002. Estimating structural bond pricing model. Working paper, McGill University.

Fisher, L. 1959. Determinants of risk premiums of corporate bonds. *Journal of Political Economy*, 67 (3), 217–237.

Fons, J. S. 1987. The default premium and corporate bond experience. *Journal of Finance*, 42 (1), 81–97.

Foss, G. W. 1995. Quantifying risk in the corporate bond market. *Financial Analysts Journal*, March–April, 29–34.

Geske, R. 1977. The valuation of corporate liabilities as compound options. *Journal of Financial and Quantitative Analysis*, 12, 541–552.

Geske, R., and H. Johnson. 1984. The valuation of corporate liabilities as compound options: A correction. *Journal of Financial and Quantitative Analysis*, 19, 231–232.

Helwege, J. 1999. How long do junk bonds spend in default? *Journal of Finance* 54 (1), 341–357.

Helwege, J., and Christopher M. Turner. 1999. The slope of the credit yield curve for speculative-grade issuers. *Journal of Finance*, 54 (5), 1869–1884.

Ho, T., and R. Singer. 1982. Bond indenture provisions and the risk of corporate debt. *Journal of Finance*, 41, 375–406.

Hui, C. H., and C. F. Lo. 2000. A note on risky bond valuation. *International Journal of Theoretical and Applied Finance*, 3 (3), 575–580.

Hull, J., and A. White. 1985. The impact of default risk on the prices of options and other derivative securities. *Journal of Banking and Finance*, 19, 299–322.

Hurley, W. J., and L. D. Johnson. 1996. On the pricing of bond default risk. *The Journal of Portfolio Management*, Winter, 66-70.

Jarrow, R., D. Lando, and S. Turnbull. 1997. A Markov model for the term structure of credit spreads. *Review of Financial Studies*, 10, 481–523.

Jarrow, R., and S. M. Turnbull. 1995. Pricing derivatives on financial securities subject to credit risk. *Journal of Finance*, 50, 53–86.

Jones, E. P., S. P. Mason, and E. Rosenfeld. 1984. Contingent claims analysis of corporate capital structures: An empirical investigation. *Journal of Finance*, 39, 611–625.

Kim, I. J., K. Ramaswamy, and S. Sundaresan. 1993. Does default risk in coupons affect the valuation of corporate bonds? *Financial Management*, 22, 117–131.

Leland, H. 1994. Corporate debt value, bond covenants, and optimal capital structure. *Journal of Finance*, 49, 1213–1252.

Leland, H., and K. Toft. 1996. Optimal capital structure, endogenous bankruptcy, and the term structure of credit spreads. *Journal of Finance*, 51, 987–1019.

Longstaff, F. A., and E. M. Schwartz. 1995. A simple approach to valuing risky fixed and floating rate debt. *Journal of Finance*, 50 (3), 789–819.

Madan, D., and H. Unal. 2000. A two-factor hazard rate model for pricing risky debt and the term structure of credit spreads. *Journal of Financial and Quantitative Analysis*, 35 (1), 43–65.

Mella-Barral, P., and W. Perraudin. 1997. Strategic debt service. *Journal of Finance*, 52, 531–556.

Mella-Barral, P., and P. Tychon. 1996. Default risk in asset pricing. Working paper, London School of Economics.

Merton, R. C. 1974. On the pricing of corporate debt: The risk structure of interest rates. *Journal of Finance*, 29, 449–470.

Miikka, T. 1999. A comparison of bond pricing models in the pricing of credit risk. Working paper, Indiana University.

Nickell, P., W. Perraudin, and S. Varotto. 2001. Ratings versus equity-based credit risk modelling: An empirical analysis. *Bank of England, Quarterly Bulletin*.

Ogden, J. 1987. Determinants of the rating and yields on corporate bonds: Tests of the contingent claims model. *Journal of Financial Research*, 10 (4), 329–340.

Patel, J. B., D. A. Envans, and J. E. Burnett. 1998. Junk bond behavior with daily returns and business cycles. *Journal of Financial Research*, 21 (4), 407–418.

Pye, G. 1974. Gauging the default premium. *Financial Analysts Journal*, 30 (1), 49–69.

Rocardo J. R. 1998. Default risk, yield spreads, and time to maturity. *Journal of Financial and Quantitative Analysis*, 23 (1), 111–117.

Saá-Requejo, J., and P. Santa-Clara. 1999. Bond pricing with default risk. Working paper, University of California at Los Angeles.

Schonbucher, P. J. 1997. Term structure modelling of defaultable bonds. Working paper, London School of Economics.

Shimko, D., N. Tejima, and D. Deventer. 1993. The pricing of risky debt when interest rate are stochastic. *Journal of Fixed Income*, 3 (2), 58–65.

Skinner, F. S. 1994. A trinomial model of bonds with default risk. *Financial Analysts Journal*, March–April, 73–78.

Sorensen, E. H., and T. F. Bollier. 1994. Pricing swap default risk. *Financial Analysts Journal*, May–June, 23–33.

Vasicek, O. 1977. An equilibrium characterization of the term structure. *Journal of Financial Economics 5*, 177–188.

Vu, J. D. 1998. The effect of junk bond defaults on common stock returns. *Financial Review*, 33, 47–60.

Ward, D. J., and G. L. Griepentrog. 1993. Risk and return in defaulted bonds. *Financial Analysts Journal*, 49 (3), 61–65.

Warner, J. B. 1977. Bankruptcy costs: Some evidence. *Journal of Finance*, 32 (2), 337–347.

Zhou, C. 1997. *A Jump-Diffusion Approach to Modeling Credit Risk and Valuing Defaultable Securities*. Finance and Economics Discussion Series. Washington, DC: Federal Reserve Board.

Further Readings

Das, S., and R. Sundaram. 1999. A discrete-time approach to arbitrage-free pricing of credit derivatives. *Management Science*, 46 (1), 46–63.

Duffie, D., and D. Lando. 2000. Term structures of credit spreads with incomplete accounting information. *Econometrica*, 69, 633–664.

Jarrow, R., D. Deventer, and X. Wang. 2002. A robust test of merton's structural model for credit risk. Working paper, Kamakura Corporation.

Kiesel, R., W. Perraudin, and A. Taylor. 2001. The structure of credit risk: Spread volatility and ratings transitions. Bank of England, Quarterly Bulletin.

Krahnen, J., and M. Weber. 2001. Generally accepted rating principles: A primer. *Journal of Banking and Finance*, 25, 3–23.

Lando, D. 1998. On Cox processes and credit risky securities. Working paper, University of Copenhagen.

Madan, D. 2000. Pricing the risks of default. Working paper, University of Maryland.

10

Convertibles, MBS/CMO, and Other Bonds: The Behavioral Models

---

Mortgages, convertible bonds, and credit derivatives are examples of many instruments which can be approximated as contingent claims. Even though they cannot be perfectly replicated by other market instruments, because they are subjected to risk sources beyond the market risks, we can use empirically estimated behavioral models of the relevant market participants to build financial models of these securities. Using these behavioral models, we can further extend the relative valuation approach to value securities that are almost contingent claims on market risks.

We have discussed many types of fixed-income securities, such as Treasury securities and corporate bonds, in the previous chapters. This chapter mainly describes three other types: convertible bonds, mortgage-backed securities (pass-throughs), and collateralized mortgage obligations. Convertible bonds are corporate bonds that offer bondholders the option to convert their bonds to shares of the firm. Mortgage-backed securities are securitized portfolios of homeowners' mortgages. *Collateralized mortgage obligations* are structured securities backed by mortgage-backed securities and other collateralized mortgage obligations.

These bond types are important segments of the bond market with a significant amount outstanding in U.S. bond markets. They have special features that satisfy specific needs of the corporate borrowers and the investors. An overview of these types of bonds can provide us with a better understanding of the bond markets.

These markets demonstrate the importance of financial innovations to the growth of bond markets. They also show that the design of bonds is a dynamic process driven by market demands, and these designs often involve embedded options. These embedded options cannot be analyzed by the standard yield to maturity measures, and financial models have to be used to value and analyze them.

These bond types introduce another aspect of financial modeling that has not been discussed until this chapter: the integration of behavioral models to financial modeling. *Behavioral models* are empirically estimated models that describe the behavior of the agents in the market that affects the bond value. The models for the convertible bonds and the mortgages require specifications of the behavior of the investors and the borrowers, in addition to the modeling of risk sources (stock or interest rate risks). The convertible bond valuation requires modeling the borrower's strategy in forcing a conversion, and the mortgage-backed securities valuation requires a modeling of the mortgagors' prepayment behavior. As a result, these models are confronted with greater modeling risks.

This chapter begins with a discussion of convertible bonds, showing how equity risk, firm risk, and bond features are integrated into one valuation framework. We continue to discuss mortgage-backed securities to show how the modeling of consumer behavior can be used for valuing this large and liquid market. Financial innovations in collateralized mortgage obligations are then discussed. The chapter concludes with descriptions of some other fixed-income innovations and some fixed-income management strategies.

The purpose of this chapter is similar to that of chapter 7; we will present the progression of the thought process in developing the valuation models. Each bond type poses a new challenge to the basic relative valuation approach. Each solution to the problem provides a deeper understanding of the relative valuation tool and its applications. From this new level of understanding, we meet the next new challenge.

10.1 Convertible Bonds

Corporations raise capital through the sale of equities and bonds. They also raise capital through a hybrid security of stocks and bonds called convertible bonds. Often, a *convertible bond* is described as a bond with a warrant, a long-dated call option that is issued by a company on its own stock, attached. While the statement is fairly true, taking this claim at face value can be misleading. This section will explain how some of the bond provisions affect the bond value in such a way that a convertible bond cannot be viewed as a bond with an attached warrant.

Overview

The convertible bond market is an important segment of the fixed-income sector. A convertible bond is a bond with an embedded call option on the company's stock. It offers the holder the option to convert the bond into a specific number of shares of the firm, usually at any time up to the maturity of the bond.

Typically, the face value of the bond is assumed to be 1000. The *conversion ratio, CR,* is the number of shares that the face value of the bond can convert into. The *conversion price CP*, is the stock price, at which the converted equity holding equals the par value of the bond. That is,

$$CP \cdot CR = 1000 \qquad (10.1)$$

The *parity, CV* (the *conversion value*), is the value of the bond at the face value if the bondholder decides to convert. It is equivalent to the equity worth of the convertible bond. Therefore the parity is the product of the conversion ratio and the stock price, S:

$$CV = CR \cdot S \qquad (10.2)$$

The *investment value* of the bond (I) is the value of the bond, ignoring the possibility of converting it to equity. The investment value is therefore the underlying bond value, which is the present value of the bond cash flow (coupon and principal) adjusted for the credit risk, the sinking fund provision, and other bond-related issues.

The conversion is an addition to the other features of corporate bonds that are briefly restated below:

1. The call provision that allows the firm to buy back bonds at prespecified prices
2. The sinking fund requirement that obligates the firm to redeem the bonds over a period of time
3. The put option that gives the investor the right to sell the bonds back to the firm at predetermined prices.

As we have explained, these features often dramatically affect the behavior and value of a bond. Although similar to nonconvertible corporate bonds, convertible bonds represent a spectrum of vastly different securities. Because convertibles are hybrids of bonds and stocks, they must inherit all the complexities of the underlying instruments and behave in an often complicated fashion as a mix of two securities. While convertible securities may offer many opportunities for investing and for formulating portfolio strategies, they are also relatively complicated to analyze. Thus, the purpose of this chapter is to provide a basic framework for analyzing these securities, given their diverse characteristics. This section offers an analytical framework that will enable bond issuers and investors to deal with these difficulties in a systematic fashion.

Basic Framework

This section will describe the basic assumptions of the model. The approach we will take here is the standard framework for studying securities pricing. Since our concern is to derive the fair value of a convertible bond, we will need to consider the determining factors of the bond price in a specific way. We will take the perfect capital market assumption.

We will ignore all types of transaction costs: the commissions, the bid-ask spreads, the issuance costs, and all the explicit costs. In essence, we want to determine the bond price if the market is functioning perfectly (i.e., the fair value).

These assumptions will enable us to focus our discussion on the options aspect of the pricing problem. We will ignore issues such as tax implications of the convertible, marketability of the issues, and corporate strategies. While we recognize that these issues are important to bond pricing, they are beyond the scope of this chapter.

An Illustrative Example

There are many terms and notations used to describe a convertible bond. We will discuss them by examining a particular bond.

Amazon.com is an E-commerce/products company based in Seattle. On January 15, 2002, Amazon 4.75 (coupon rate) of maturity 2009 was trading at 507.556 (yield = 12.92). The Moody rating was Caa2. The par amount was 1000; the conversion ratio, 12.816; and the conversion price, 78.027. The stock was trading at 10.240. The parity was 131.236. The bond was callable at 103.325 in 2002, declining to par on maturity.

The market capitalization was $3,810.470 million. The debt structure had two private placements, and three convertible bonds. Three of them were

Coupon	Maturity	Amount (mil)	Type
10	5/1/08	264	callable
4.75	2/1/09	1249.81	convertible
6.875	2/16/10	690	convertible

Valuation of a Convertible Bond

A convertible bond is similar to a corporate bond in that it has a maturity, coupon payments, and face value. We can use the investment grade corporate bond model with the spot yield curve to value a convertible bond.

The example illustrates several important aspects of a convertible bond differing from a corporate bond in their valuation. First, the latent warrant on the bond offers equity returns to the investor while the downside is protected by the face value of the bond. Second, the call provision that leads to the forced conversion of the bond reduces the interest payout by the firm. Unlike the call provision of a corporate bond, the optimal call must be exercised taking stock volatility into account, which we will explain further later in this section. Third, many convertible bonds in the United States do not have high creditworthiness. Credit risks have to be taken into account. Finally, when the convertible bond issue is relatively large compared to the firm size, the effect of dilution has to be taken into account. Even though these aspects are important to a convertible bond, there are other features peculiar to particular convertible bonds. Understanding how these features are valued provides us with a methodology to value many bond types. We will discuss each of these aspects.

Latent warrant

A warrant is a long-dated call option on a stock. A convertible bond can be thought of as a straight bond that has a coupon and principal with a warrant that expires at the bond's maturity. The exercise price of the warrant is the principal value of the convertible bond. This warrant embedded in a convertible bond is called a *latent warrant*. If the stock price rises above the principal at the bond's maturity, the convertible bondholder will exercise the warrant to convert the bond into stock. If the stock falls below the principal amount at the bond's maturity, the convertible bondholder will let the warrant expire worthless, and receives the principal payment.

The latent warrant is an American call option on a stock that may pay a dividend. But typically, even if the firm pays the dividend, it is less than the interest from the bond. There is no incentive for the convertible bondholder to convert, exchanging the bond for stock at any time, even if the latent warrant is very much in the money, because convertible bond value always exceeds the conversion value. For the same reason, if the stock does not pay a dividend, there is no early exercise of an American call option. The latent warrant is indeed a long-dated call option. (See figure 10.1–10.3.)

Call provision and forced conversion

Similar to the call provision of a corporate bond, the optimal exercise of the call option depends on the stock level and the time to expiration—much like an American call. The main difference is that at any given time the convertible bond depends not only on the interest rate level but also on the stock price level because it is a hybrid of a bond and a stock. When the firm calls the convertible bond, the bondholders may choose to convert the bonds to equity instead of surrendering them for the cash payment at the call price. The value of the bond at the time of converting to shares is called the conversion value.

In valuing the convertible bond, we may use the binomial lattice. Given the terminal condition, when we roll back on the binomial lattice, the firm will call the convertible bond whenever its price is above the call price.

However, the convertible bond price when the bond is called is not necessarily the call price. The bond value is the maximum of the call price and the conversion value. Interest rates may have fallen to the extent that it is advantageous for the firm to call the bond to refinance at lower interest rates. When the bondholders are expected not to

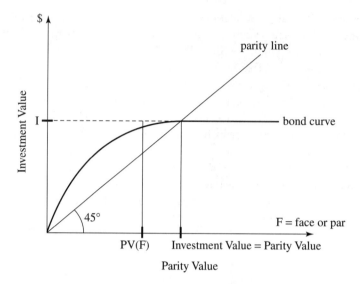

Figure 10-1 Bond curve and parity line. The bond curve depicts the behavior of a bond. The 45° line through the origin is called the parity line. It represents the convertible bond value at the instant the bond is converted to equity (conversion value). Since we can decompose the convertible bond value into the bond value and the latent warrant, the bond value converges to the risk-free bond as stock prices increase. On the 45° line, the investment value is equal to the parity value.

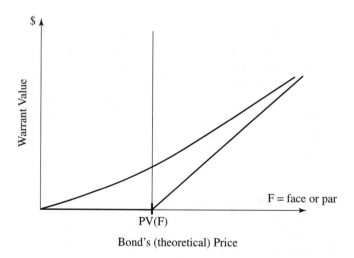

Figure 10-2 Warrant curve. Standard option theory shows that the minimum warrant value is the 45° line that intersects the x-axis at the present value of the exercise price (the present value of the par value, in our case). Given this argument, we can sketch the warrant curve. Since a warrant is a call option with a strike price of face value, we see that the warrant diagram looks like the call option on a stock.

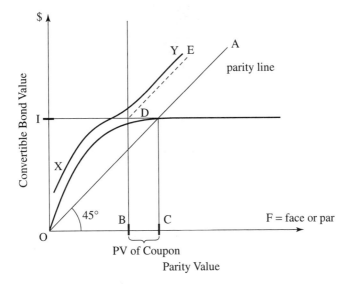

Figure 10-3 Composition of the convertible bond value. The convertible bond is the sum of the bond curve and the warrant curve. Here it is represented where the curve x, y represents the convertible bond value. The line OA is the parity line. However, when the parity value is high, the convertible bond value does not converge to the parity line. Instead, it converges to the parallel line DE. The distance of point D from the y-axis (it is the same as OB) is the present value of the face value of the bond. Since the bond value, or the investment value, is the sum of the present value of the face value and the coupon value, it follows that the distance between the parity value and the line DE is the present value of the coupon.

convert the bonds to equity and receive the call price, the bond will be valued at the call price. However, in the event the stock has risen to the extent that when a firm calls the bond, the bondholders will prefer to convert the bonds to stocks and not surrender the bonds at the call price, then the bond will trade at the conversion value. In this case, we say that the firm seeks to effect a *forced conversion*, forcing the bondholders to convert the convertible bond to stock by calling the bond. The investors will not surrender the bond at the call price because the conversion is more advantageous to them.

There is an additional minor adjustment to the model to take into account. It pertains to the desire of the firm's management to be sure that the bondholders convert the bonds to equity without having a chance to choose surrendering the bond at the call price. When they choose surrendering the bond at the call price, the firm must raise cash to pay the call price. However, if they convert to equity, the firm does not have to be prepared to raise cash. Whether the investors choose surrendering or not depends on how the stock price behaves during the period between the announcement date and the effective call date. When the conversion value is less than the call price on the effective call date, the investors choose surrendering the bond at the call price. Even though the call announcement is made by the firm when the conversion value is greater than the call price, the firm cannot be sure that the conversion value will still be greater than the call price on the effective call date. Therefore, the call should be made when the convertible bond price is above an effective call price—when the effective call price exceeds the call price by an amount equaling, for example, one standard deviation of the stock price volatility. The spread between the effective call price and the stated call price depends on the trade-off between the likelihood that the stock will fall to a level at which the bondholders will surrender the bonds instead of converting them into stock during the period between the announcement date and the effective call date, and the cost of delay in a forced conversion.

$$\text{effective call} = \text{call price} + \text{factor}$$

Suppose the stated call price is 104 percent. Let us define the *critical parity value* to be the parity value at which the firm will optimally exercise the forced conversion. At this critical parity value, the cash value to retire the debt via the call is $1040 (= 104 percent of 1000 par). The convertible bond is forced to convert, and therefore its value equals the conversion value. Assume that the stock volatility is 35 percent annually. The time period between the conversion decision made by the investors and the announcement of the calling of the bond by the issuer is typically 30 days (one month). Therefore, the stock volatility over one month is $0.35/\sqrt{12}$. Suppose that the firm's financial management requires at least one standard deviation for the stock price to be above the stock price that defines the cash value to retire the debt via the call (i.e., $1040); then the increase in the parity value (or the stock price, since the parity value is proportional to the stock price) required above $1040 is $105.078 (= $(0.35/\sqrt{12}) \times 1040$). The effective call is the call decision that is triggered by this higher parity value. The factor is $105.078 = (0.35/\sqrt{12} \times 1040)$ (see figure 10.4).

The determination of the factor and the effective call price is considered a behavioral model, because the derivation of the model is not based on a precise optimization of economic gains by the financial management of the firm. We have not taken into

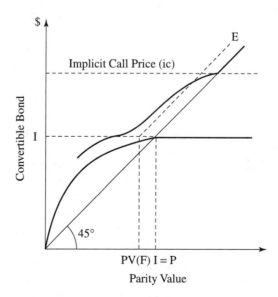

Figure 10-4 Effect of the implicit call price. Here, we see that the convertible bond value must be capped by the implicit call price. As the parity value rises, the convertible bond value rises in step. But as the convertible bond value approaches the implicit call price, the market will anticipate the firm's calling the bond, and the bondholders will convert the bonds to the parity value.

consideration the transaction costs for the firm to prepare to pay the investors cash or new shares, or any other economic reasons for the firm's delay in exercising the option explicitly to solve for the effective call. A factor is simply proposed to reflect the "inefficiency" for the firm in exercising the option, and the model proposes that the inefficiency depends on the stock price volatility.

Credit Risk

To incorporate the credit risk, we use the firm value, and not the stock value, as the underlying risk source, following the approach of the Merton structural model for credit risk. At the terminal date, the convertible bond value is given by the Max[conversion value, Min[the principal, firm value]]. Min[the principal, firm value] is supposed to take care of credit risk for pricing purposes.

The condition for default and the implications of default follow from the assumptions of the structural model described in chapter 9. The firm may default at any time. It defaults when the convertible bond value exceeds the firm value, which means the firm's liability is higher than its value. At default, we assume that the convertible bondholders take over the ownership of the firm, and the convertible bond price is then the firm value.

If the firm does not default on the bond, it may call the bond when the convertible bond price exceeds the effective call price. The value of the convertible bond price at the time of call is the Max [conversion value, call price].

$$\text{bond price} = \text{Max[conversion value, call price]}$$

Dilution

When conversion occurs, the firm issues new shares to convertible bondholders. Issuance of new shares leads to an increased number of outstanding shares. After the conversion, the stock price is the firm value divided by the total shares outstanding, including the newly issued shares. The increase of the number of shares outstanding is said to dilute the value of each share. Therefore we need to adjust the model for the effect of dilution. The convertible bond should be priced as if the firm has issued all the new shares, and the convertible bond should be priced based on the diluted shares.

To make this adjustment, we assume that there are m number of shares outstanding before the conversion takes place, and n number of additional shares after the conversion; then the conversion value of the convertible bond is $\frac{n}{m+n}V$, where V is the firm value. This is the only adjustment for the effect of dilution. In the presence of dilution, we should think of the conversion value as a portion of the firm value and not the value of stock price times the number of shares in conversion. This is because the firm value is independent of the convertible bond price while the stock price is not. For this reason, we can specify the binomial process of the firm value and use the binomial lattice to determine the convertible bond value.

Analysis

We now apply the models to the convertible bonds of Amazon. We will discuss the impact of each aspect on a bond value. There are several aspects in the valuation of Amazon convertible bonds. First, we consider the default risk of the bond, the potential loss of value of the bond, an aspect which is similar to a high yield bond. For the default risk, we use the structural model where the firm defaults when its value falls below the face value of the bond, and the bondholders take over the firm value in the event of default.

The second effect is the dilution effect, discussed above. It lowers the conversion value of the bond, and hence the convertible bond value is the price according to the diluted shares. The third effect is the impact of the forced conversion. (See figure 10.5.)

At maturity, the conversion decision takes the default risk and dilution effect into account. Therefore, we have three different cases to evaluate the convertible bond at maturity. First, if the firm value is less than face value plus the coupon amount, the bondholders will take over the firm, which means that the convertible bond value is the firm value. Second, if the firm value is greater than the face value plus the coupon amount but less than $\frac{m+n}{n}F$ when n is the number of additional shares after the conversion and m is the number of stock shares before conversion, the convertible bondholders will receive the face value plus the coupon amount, because it will not be beneficial to exercise the convertible option. Third, if the firm value is greater than $\frac{m+n}{n}F$, the convertible bondholders will exercise their convertible option. Whenever the conversion option is exercised, additional shares will be issued, which leads to a dilution effect. To accommodate the dilution effect, we should adjust stock prices because the conversion price is less than the stock prices. Once we determine the convertible bond values at maturity, we employ the backward substitution. Since we have call options, default conditions, and convertible options, we should compare the backward-substituted convertible bond

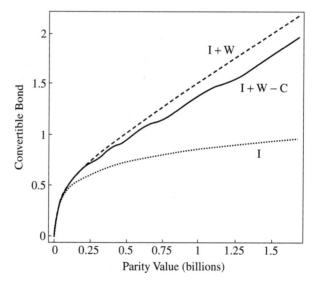

Figure 10-5 Amazon.com performance profile and the impact of each feature on the bond value. We assume a flat yield curve of 3%, and the risk premium for Caa2 is 5%. In the presence of the call provision, the convertible bond has three components. CB = I + W − C where I is the investment value, W is the latent warrant, and C is the call provision. The figure shows lines corresponding to I, I + W, and I + W − C. The differences between line I and line I + W are the latent warrant value. The differences between line I + W and line I + W − C are the call provision values. The investment value reflects the default risk, because the investment values approach the risk-free bond as the stock price increases.

value with the effective call value, firm value, and conversion value to determine the optimal exercise of those options.

In figure 10.5, the result shows that when the parity value rises from 0 to 0.1 billion, the convertible bond value increases quickly; this is because the convertible bond behaves like a bond. With the increase in the parity, the firm value and the bond price both increase. Around the parity of 0.75 billion, the convertible bond has a positive gamma because the convertible bond offers the upside returns to the holders and protection against downside loss when the parity value falls (but does not fall so much that the bond begins to face default risks). Above the 1 billion parity value, the convertible bond faces the effective call price, and beyond that effective call price, it behaves like a stock.

Behavior of a Convertible Bond: A Summary

If the stock value drops, the investor, at worst, will still receive the coupons and principal. As a result, the downside risk of the investment is protected against.

In short, the convertible bond offers upside returns and downside protection. The investor, in essence, is holding a straight bond and a warrant. A warrant is an instrument that provides the holder with the right to purchase a specified number of shares of a stock at a specified price. Although this is a useful way of thinking about a convertible bond, it does not accurately describe most of the convertible bonds traded in the U.S. market.

There are other structures of convertible bonds. For example, liquid yield options are noninterest-bearing convertible debt issues. For this convertible bond, the underlying bond is a zero-coupon bond. If the issue converts, the issuer will in effect have sold a tax-deductible equity. At conversion, the investor converts all the accrued interest and the principal to common equity, giving up the cash coupons for the equity, while the accrued interest can be deducted as interest expense by the issuer. As a result, from the issuers' perspective, the implied interest costs are tax-deductible, and the issuers may find such an issuance tax efficient.

10.2 Mortgage-Backed Securities (Pass-through Certificates)

The mortgage-backed securities market is a significant segment of U.S. fixed-income markets. *Mortgage-backed securities* are securities backed by a pool of individuals home mortgages. A *mortgage pool* is a portfolio of mortgages collected under certain guidelines. The pool is put into a trust, and bonds are issued as claims against the portfolio. These bonds are referred to as *pass-throughs*, in that they simply pass the interest and principal collected from all the mortgagors and pass them to the bondholders on a pro rata basis. That is, the bond represents a percent of the original pool, and the interest and principal that the bondholder receives each month will be based on that percentage.

The mortgage-backed securities market is broad and diverse, with many variations. This chapter will focus only on the basic valuation principles of these securities. We will not dwell on the complex and intricate bond arithmetic, such as calculations of yields, prepayment speeds, and day count conventions. We emphasize two aspects of the market: (1) embedded options in these securities and (2) different bond types that can be derived from these mortgage-backed pass-throughs. For this reason, the pass-throughs and all the bonds derived from them are often generically called derivatives.

Agency and Nonagency Deals

The Government National Mortgage Association (GNMA), the Federal National Mortgage Association (FNMA), and the Federal Home Loan Mortgage Association Corporation (FHLMC) are three major government agencies that are responsible for providing mortgages to homeowners. The mortgage pass-throughs that originate from these government agencies are called *agency deals*. The mortgage pass-throughs that originate from private corporations are called *whole loans*.

The GNMA mortgage-backed securities program has over $600 billion of securities outstanding. These securities are backed by mortgage loans and mortgage-backed securities themselves. The process of originating a GNMA pool (or a GNMA pass-through) begins with a mortgage bank, which acts as a dealer taking principal risks. That means they do not just act as a broker. They buy mortgages and sell out of the position at an uncertain price. They assemble the mortgages (usually under certain guidelines) from banks or financial companies that provide mortgages to homeowners. When the pool reaches a certain size, say $500 million, the bankers structure the pool as a trust. The trust will then pass to GNMA for insurance (which will be elaborated later). After GNMA's approval, the pool is sold to investment banks. The investment banks in turn sell shares of the pool to investors through their distributive networks. Investors may be portfolio managers, insurance companies and other financial institutions.

Now we follow through this process from the payment point of view. The payment begins with a homeowner, the mortgagor. The mortgagor pays the bank, the lender of the mortgage (the mortgagee), the monthly interest payment and the scheduled principal paydown. The mortgagee takes a portion of the interest payment (not principal) as a servicing fee. At this point, the bank is not really the lender. The bank is acting as servicer (or intermediary), collecting the payments and keeping track of all the paperwork. The net payment goes to GNMA. GNMA also takes a portion of the interest (not principal) as insurance and passes the rest of the amount to trusts. Then the trusts distribute the payments to all the investors (see figure 10.6).

What happens to the insurance? U.S. mortgages allow mortgagors to prepay the mortgage in part or in whole at any time, at par. There is usually no penalty for mortgagors to prepay. In this case, the total amount, including the entire principal, will be passed to the investors. For that month, the investors will note that more principal has been paid down. This paydown of principal is measured by a factor (the proportion of the principal remaining to the original face value). At issuance, the factor is 1, and it decreases over time to 0, when all the mortgagors retire their debts. When many mortgagors pay down the principals in one particular month, the factor will fall faster. However, when a mortgagor defaults and cannot make the monthly payment, the missing payment affects the investors' returns on their investments. That is, the investors are subject to the credit risks of the mortgagors. To eliminate this risk, GNMA steps in. Using its insurance pool, the funds collected from the insurance fees taken from the payments, GNMA makes whole that monthly payment, paying the investors the promised interest and principal in full. If the mortgagor defaults on the payment, GNMA will pay the entire principal amount. The investor will receive the paydown as if the mortgagor had prepaid. The investor cannot distinguish whether the paydown is a result of a prepayment by a mortgagor or a make whole by GNMA. There is no reason for the investor to care. In essence, GNMA steps into this process as a guarantor of the creditworthiness of mortgagors to the investors.

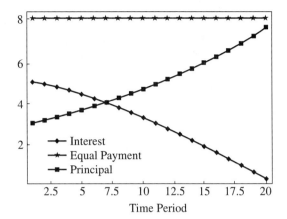

Figure 10-6 Level payments on mortgage loans. This figure shows how the interest payments and the principal payments behave over the life of the loan when the loan is paid in equal installments. To this end, we assume a flat 10% yield curve and 10% annual interest. The interest is paid semiannually. The term of the loan is 10 years and the principal is $100. The level payment is 8.02426.

Are agency pass-throughs safe from credit risk? There are two layers of insurance. First, GNMA capital is supporting the credit risk. Second, GNMA as a corporation has the full backing of the U.S. government. The security of the GNMA corporation compared with Treasury bonds is a matter of some legal discussions, but certainly the general understanding is that the corporation is sufficiently safe. For this reason, agency deals are often sold as being "as safe as U.S. government securities."

Prepayment Risk and the Prepayment Model

"Safety" has to be properly defined. In credit analysis, safety applies to the loss of principal and interest. However, when mortgagors do not prepay according to the payment schedule, there is a risk, or uncertainty, of the cash flow of the mortgage pass-through. Some of that risk is almost inconsequential, but some is significant.

When a mortgagor sells a home because of job relocation or has an urge to be rid of all debt, the mortgage may be prepaid. There are many mortgages in a pool, and on average there is always a certain level of prepayment. This average is quite stable because of the diversification effect, if we assume that all mortgagors act quite independently of each other in their prepayment, selling their houses, reducing their debt, and other reasons. When the pool is large, we can estimate the proportion of mortgagors who will prepay each month. We can determine the historical monthly prepayment as a portion of the face value outstanding for each pool. In this empirical investigation, we can take into account geographic distribution, coupon distribution, and other attributes of the mortgages.

Now consider a mortgage pool of 30-year fixed-rate mortgages. When the interest rate falls significantly, and particularly when talk shows and newspapers suggest that the time is ripe for refinancing—prepay the entire mortgage and take another mortgage with a lower rate—many mortgagors will prepay. As a result, the investors will have to reinvest the payments in lower interest rates, resulting in a loss of interest that they would have received if the mortgagors had not refinanced.

The crux of the argument is that mortgagors have a call option on the mortgages, similar to a callable corporate bond where the issuer (the borrower) can call back the bond and terminate the agreement. On mortgages, the mortgagor (the borrower) can call the mortgage at par (with no call premium) at any time. On the flip side, we can see that the investor has sold a call option. This option clearly has value to the mortgagors and costs to the investors. The investors demand a higher coupon rate (or interest costs) to compensate for the options that they have offered to the mortgagors for such pass-through securities.

From the above discussion, the principle behind valuing a mortgage pass-through is related to the valuation of a call option. But we cannot directly apply the callable corporate bond procedure because for a corporate bond, the financial manager usually is "rational," focusing only on the maximization of wealth. Rational behavior is used here in the context of financial theory. All agents are rational when they always seek the highest returns among all the investment alternatives.

But mortgagors have many motives for prepayment other than refinancing; they are not only seeking to maximize their wealth only. To determine the value of the embedded call option in mortgages, we need to model the behavior of the mortgagor. This model is commonly called the *prepayment model*. Prepayment models are estimated from historical data of mortgagors' prepayment behavior. Some of the factors that are commonly cited as the main reasons for the prepayment are the following:

1. Seasonality—There are more prepayments in late spring because there are more home sales; families usually want to settle into a new home during the summer, before school starts.
2. Seasoning and aging—There is usually very little prepayment with a new mortgage pool. The prepayment speed gradually increases for two years. Conversely, for an aged pool, there are very few prepayments because the remaining mortgagors tend not to move.
3. Interest spread between the new mortgage rate and the mortgagor's present mortgage rate—When the new mortgage rate is lower than the mortgage rate of the pool, particularly when the rate has fallen over 200 basis points, the mortgagors will likely refinance.
4. Burnout—A pool that has gone through a low interest rate period is more likely to have less prepayment risk than a pool that has not gone through such a period. Mortgagors who are alert and ready to refinance their mortgages are not likely to remain in this pool because they have prepaid already. This pool is called *burnout*.
5. Slope of the yield curve—Historical data show that the slope of the yield curve is a factor in deciding refinancing behavior. This observation may be explained by the mortgagors' alternatives in refinancing. They can refinance at an adjustable rate with interest costs based on the short-term rate. When the yield curve is upward-sloping, they may refinance their fixed-rate mortages with adjustable-rate mortgages, leading to an increase in refinancing.

Using historical data, the prepayment model can be specified. Given the prepayment model, we can determine the cash flows of the pass-through under different scenarios. The mortgage pass-through model is then specified.

The prepayment model is a behavioral model in that we use historical experiences to hypothesize how mortgagors behave. The model does not solve for mortgagors' optimal prepayment decisions from economic principles. Instead, the prepayment model assumes that mortgagors are "myopic," in that they make their prepayment decisions without simulating the future outcomes or conducting dynamic optimization strategies which take future uncertainties and optimal decisions into account (e.g., the Bellman solution). They simply follow some rules based on the prevailing economic realities.

The prepayment model is important in valuing mortgage-backed securities because it specifies the value of the embedded option in mortgage-backed securities. The prepayment model captures the mortgagors' behavior.

First consider a homeowner's mortgage. The mortgagor can refinance when the interest rates fall to a level that enables him to refinance optimally or to retire the debt at the par price, since there is no prepayment premium. In this case, a mortgage is similar to the callable corporate bond. For a mortgage, the borrower (the mortgagor) has the option to retire the debt at par. For this reason, we can express the mortgage as a combination of an option-free bond and an embedded option, as we have done for the callable corporate bond.

$$\text{Mortgage} = \text{option-free bond} - \text{a bond call option}$$

For mortgage-backed securities where we have a portfolio of mortgages, the embedded options can be viewed slightly differently. A higher prepayment rate, associated with falling interest rates (called prepayment risk to the investors), is detrimental to the investors. This cost to investors is equivalent to their holding a short position in an interest rate floor. In other words, when the interest rate falls, mortgagors can save the difference between the lower interest rate and the fixed mortgage rate by prepaying the mortgage, which is tantamount to holding the interest rate floor. Conversely, a lower prepayment rate is related to rising interest rates (called extension risk to the investors). This delay of prepayment also is detrimental to the investors, because they cannot reinvest the prepayment that they would receive at a higher market interest rates. The extension risk results in the investment being locked into fixed-interest payments lower than the market reinvestment rate for a longer period of time. The investors have a short position of a cap whereby they will sustain a loss when interest rates rise, particularly beyond a certain rate. The reason for this is that the mortgagors will not pay interest rates higher than the fixed mortgage interest rates. This can be summarized by the following equation.

$$\text{Mortgage-backed securities} = \text{option-free bond} - \text{a floor} - \text{a cap}$$

The above discussion suggests that we can be slightly more specific about bond options. To capture both the extension risk and the prepayment risk, the investors have in fact sold both caps and floors to the mortgagors. As interest rates continue to fall or rise, the impact of the extension risk and prepayment risk on the bond value begins to lessen, and the burnout effect starts to affect the bond behavior. For this reason, we can think of the mortgage-backed securities as having sold a cap but bought back a more out-of-the money cap. These options replicate the impact of extension risk on the mortgages. Also, the mortgage-backed securities have sold a floor but bought back a more out-of-the-money floor. These options replicate the impact of prepayment risks on the mortgages. The result is summarized below:

Mortgage-backed securities

= option-free bond − a floor + out-of-the-money floor

− *a cap* + out-of-the-money *cap*

The expression above can be made more specifically after our discussion of the valuation models of mortgage-backed securities, in the following section.

PSA Methods and Embedded Options

In the previous chapters, we have discussed the yield to maturity of a bond extensively because the measure is used widely in fixed-income markets, despite its many defects in properly measuring the returns of a bond. For a bond with a coupon rate and maturity, the yield to maturity can be calculated as the internal rate of return of the coupon and principal cash flows.

For mortgage-backed securities, there are two aspects that we need to address before an internal rate of return concept can be used. First, the principal of the mortgage is amortized over the life of the obligation, such that the cash flow of the mortgage interest and the principal payments together is level over time. The yield of the mortgage should therefore be the internal rates of return of the cash flow. This aspect of the mortgage does not pose any problem to the definition of a yield. After all, it is the same as that of a sinking fund bond in the corporate bond market, where bonds are required to be retired over time according to a specified schedule on a pro rata basis. Obviously, a mortgage amortizes the principal over a payment schedule.

The second aspect, however, is more complicated and the discussion is more involved. In the United States, since there is no penalty for prepayment, the prepayment risk can be significant. The average life of mortgage-backed securities is shortened by the prepayments. In the early years after mortgage-backed securities were introduced to the market, research found two empirical facts regarding the prepayment behavior. First, the prepayments tended to be a proportion of the remaining principals outstanding. Second, there was little prepayment when the mortgage was taken down recently. Mortgagors tend not to refinance in the early years of their mortgages. Both observations seem reasonable. Prepayments should be related to the size of the mortgage pool; when a pool size increases, more mortgages are expected to be prepaid. Also, if you consider all the expenses that are needed to take down a mortgage, the likelihood of an immediate prepayment should be low. The Public Securities Association (PSA) determined a convention whose results are summarized by a PSA formula. A mortgage-backed pool that has a 100 PSA means that the prepayment speed, defined as the annual principal amount prepaid divided by the amount outstanding at the beginning of the period, increases linearly to 6% in 30 months and stays constant for the remaining life of the pool. (See figure 10.7.)

If a mortgage pool has a higher prepayment speed, say twice that of the 100 PSA pool, then it is said to have a 200 PSA. In general, a mortgage pool speed is measured as a percent of the 100 PSA. For any mortgage pool, if the mortgage prepayment speed is quoted, the yield of the projected cash flow can be calculated from a given price. This yield measure is called the *static yield* because we assume that the prepayment experience will be that of the quoted prepayment speed.

There are some interesting characteristics of the static yields. They have to be quoted along with the PSA assumption. The yield is based on the speed assumption of the trader. Also, one expects that the static yield has a different value than the yield of the Treasury bond with a comparable weighted average life. There are several reasons for this difference, even though GNMA and other government agency pools have few, if any, credit risks. One reason is that the projected cash flows of a mortgage pool and the Treasury bonds are very different, even if they have a similar weighted average life. The

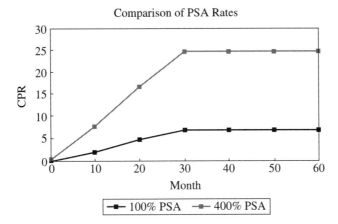

Figure 10-7 PSA rates. Prepayment rates are commonly expressed in three different ways: SMM, CPR, and PSA. Single Monthly Mortality (SMM) is a prepayment rate which measures the percentage of dollars prepaid in any month, expressed as a percentage of the expected mortgage balance. SMM is expressed mathematically by the following equation:

$$\text{SMM} = 100 \times \frac{(\text{Scheduled Balance} - \text{Actual Balance})}{\text{Scheduled Balance}}$$

The Conditional Prepayment Rate (CPR) is a percentage prepayment rate which relates the percentage of the outstanding balance prepaid on an annual basis. CPR is expressed mathematically as

$$CPR = 100 \times \left(1 - \left(1 - \frac{SMM}{100,}\right)^{12}\right)$$

Finally, *PSA* is a market convention adopted by the Public Securities Association in the mid-1980s in which prepayment rates, expressed in CPR, are assumed to follow a standard path over time. A 100% PSA curve implies that the prepayment rate starts at 0.2% in the first month, and then rises by 0.2% in each month until month 30, when it levels out at 6%.

cash flow pattern of a mortgage pool must take into account the principal amortization and the PSA speed. Another reason is that the static approach of PSA cannot capture the embedded option value. Since the embedded option is detrimental to the investors, in that the mortgage falls in value when the interest rate rises or falls, it should lead to a higher yield of the bond. The final related reason is the model risk of the mortgage pool. The prepayment behavior is assumed in the model, and therefore there are some model risks involved. As a result, the arbitrage relationship between the Treasury bond market and the mortgage market is not perfect, resulting in basis risks (changes in the relationship due to fluctuations in the option-adjusted spread) between the two markets.

The bond arithmetic gives a precise bond price for a given PSA and yield. When a bond manager evaluates a particular mortgage pool, he takes its coupon rate, the age of the pool, the factor indicating how much the pool has been paid down, and types of mortgages into account, and decides on the speed of prepayment and the appropriate yield for the bond. Using the PSA and the yield of the bond, the bond manager can then decide on the price. In this sense, PSA may be viewed as a valuation model. But there are of course many limitations to this approach. More appropriately, PSA should be viewed only as a market convention, a common measure of prepayment speed for the market. A financial model should capture the prepayment behavior more precisely.

Monte Carlo Simulations

To value mortgage-backed securities with embedded options appropriately, one popular approach is to use Monte Carlo simulations. We have shown that the value of a bond can be determined as the average of the present value of the cash flows along the interest rate paths, for all the possible interest rate paths in the binomial lattice. In other words, if we can enumerate all the possible scenario interest rate paths, and determine the bond cash flows for each path, then the average of the present values of these cash flows (the average of the pathwise values) is the bond price.

Given a particular scenario and prepayment model, we can determine the cash flows of the mortgages. Once again, this is bond arithmetic. At each point in time along the interest rate scenario, the mortgage terms and conditions determine the interest and the principal the investor should receive.

However, enumerating all the possible interest rate paths is problematic. There are just too many possible paths. A random sampling of these scenarios can provide one solution. But these scenarios do not have to be selected purely at random. There is much research conducted on the subject of finding intelligent ways to select a sample. However, we are not concerned with this issue here, even though it is certainly important in financial engineering.

Another approach in valuing a mortgage pool is to recognize any mortgage pool as a portfolio of mortgages. We have discussed the valuation of a mortgage where a mortgagor exercises the call option optimally. The approach can treat a mortgage like a callable bond. The mortgagor considers the final payment of the mortgage at the maturity date as if there were no prepayment. Then, using the backward substitution approach, the mortgagor determines the optimal exercise decision in calling the mortgage at par. When the mortgage reaches the initial date in the backward substitution procedure, the value determined is the value of the mortgage when the mortgagor's prepayment decision is optimal. We call this a *high prepayment efficiency*.

However, not all mortgagors exercise their options efficiently. We can assume that there is a distribution of mortgagors with a varying degree of implicit transaction costs involved in prepayments. We can assume some mortgagors will prepay irrespective of the interest rate level. Then a mortgage pool is a portfolio of all such mortgages. The precise distribution of these mortgagors has to be estimated from historical data or implied from market prices.

Using either the Monte Carlo simulation model or viewing a mortgage pool as a portfolio of mortgages, along with the prepayment model and the arbitrage-free interest rate model, we have completed the description of valuation models for mortgage-backed securities. Similar to the discussion of corporate bonds, for a particular mortgage pool, given the price, we can determine the spread off the Treasury spot curve such that the mortgage pool value (as determined by the valuation model) equals the quoted price of the mortgage pool. This spread is the option adjusted spread for the mortgage pool. A corporate bond, which may have a call provision or a sinking fund provision, is quite different from a mortgage pool in terms of cash flow characteristics and embedded options. But option adjusted spread has isolated all these features in its valuation, and thus we can compare the corporate bond and mortgage-backed securities using the option adjusted spread. This is something that a static yield of a mortgage pool cannot provide.

10.3 Collateralized Mortgage Obligations (CMO)

The financial innovation of pass-through securities has had a tremendous impact on the financial market. The introduction of these securities has benefited homeowners in their access to capital because mortgagors can access the capital market for the mortgages via the pass-throughs. This innovation was followed by another development that dramatically changed the financial markets in the following years, collateralized mortgage obligations (CMO).

Individual mortgages are used in a trust to create pass-throughs. Investment banks assemble a portfolio of mortgage pass-through pools, which are the assets of a trust. The claims on these assets are CMOs, which are backed by pass-throughs. The main innovative feature of pass-through securities is that they generate different classes of claims. The advantages of segmenting a bond into different classes will be discussed below. These classes are called *tranches*, a French word for slice.

Different packaging of these tranches creates different CMOs. There is no limit to the number of designs of the deals. Some specific examples of CMOs are described at the end of the chapter. The design is driven by market demands because the cost of producing different designs is relatively small. However, there is still a need for some standardization for marketability. Some of the more common structures are discussed below.

Interest Only and Principal Only (IO/PO)

The *interest-only (IO)* investor will receive only monthly interests of the mortgage pass-through. The *principal-only (PO)* investor will receive only the principal of the pass-through monthly.

A mortgagor pays down the principal slowly at the beginning and accelerates the paydown in the latter years. For this reason, much of the scheduled principal payment is deferred until years later and the PO that pays the principal payments to the investor has a longer weighted average life. Conversely, since the early payments of a mortgage consist mostly of interest, and the IO pays the interest portions of the mortgage payments to the investors, the IO has a shorter weighted average life. In separating the pass-through into two classes—the PO and IO polarize the weighted average lives of the CMO bonds—investors are given more choices to fit their needs. IO and PO also have significant embedded options, which lengthen the PO duration and shorten the IO duration.

Consider an extreme scenario when all mortgagors prepay. PO investors would receive all the payments in full immediately, and that would be a windfall to them. On the other hand, the IO value becomes 0, since there is no interest to be paid in the future. In another scenario, if all the mortgagors decide never to prepay, then the IO investors will enjoy their interest payments for a much longer time while the PO payments will be deferred for many years.

When IO and PO stand alone, each become riskier than when they are combined. When they combine and make whole the pass-through, their individual risks are mitigated. Moreover, the risks are initiated from the call option embedded in the pass-through. That means IO and PO have significant options. PO has an embedded call option (in a long position). The option increases the price and hence lowers the yield. IO has an embedded short call option, lowering the price and increasing the yield.

When IO and PO are recombined, we can construct the mortgage-backed bond. Hence, the following arbitrage condition must hold (see figure 10.8):

$$MBS = IO + PO$$

The above result shows that the principal-only bond has a higher and positive duration, with a more negatively sloped performance profile. The interest-only bond has a negative duration with a positively sloped performance profile. For the interest-only bond, when the interest rate falls, the bond value falls, unlike a Treasury bond or any typical corporate bond.

Sequential Structure

The classic vanilla structure enables investors to buy bonds with the weighted average life that they prefer. It is a five-tranche deal, and each tranche has its own embedded options. These tranches are labeled A, B, C, D, and Z. Each tranche is structured to look like a vanilla corporate bond, with a fixed coupon rate and a sinking fund schedule. A, B, C, and D all have sinking funds and fixed coupon payments. Z is an accrual bond with no coupon payments and its interest is accrued, but it is a sinking fund bond. Therefore, each bond has its own coupon and its principal repayment schedule, a sinking fund schedule.

Each bond is paid down by a priority rule. Every month, the interests and principals

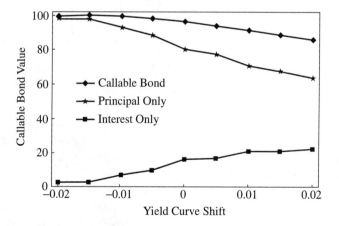

Figure 10-8 Callable bond, principal only, and interest only. This figure shows the performance profiles of a callable bond, a principal-only bond (PO), and an interest-only bond (IO) for illustration purposes. The PO and IO receive the principal and the interests of the callable bond, respectively. We choose the callable bond rather than mortgage-backed securities (MBS) as an underlying bond of PO and IO, because the callable bond has characteristics similar to MBS. The initial term structure is 4% flat. The term structure has been shifted by 50 basis points to show how those bonds are behaving as interest rates increase. We can see that the IO increases as the interest rate goes up, in contrast to the PO. Needless to say, the sum of PO and IO is the callable bond.

from the mortgage pass-throughs are used to pay down the scheduled payments of all the bonds, their coupon and principal. If the prepayments are much faster than anticipated, bond A's principal will be paid down first. After bond A is paid down entirely, bond B stands next in line to absorb all the early payments. Bond C is next in line, and so on.

If the prepayment is slower than anticipated, then all the bonds' interests will be paid first. The principal paydown will be deferred, but bond A's principal will always be paid down before B, and B before C, and so on. Z will be paid down when all other bonds have been paid down.

Finally, there is the residual bond. A residual bond is the remaining cash flow from the mortgage pass-through bonds in a trust. For example, a CMO is a trust certificate. That means the CMO bonds are usually overcollateralized and it is expected that, when all the CMO bonds are paid down, there will still be some mortgage pass-through bonds left in the trust. The residual bonds are the residual cash flows. The residual bondholders are in fact the shareholders of the trust, and receive the remaining assets in the trust after all the liabilities have been paid down.

Planned Amortization Class (PAC)

We have discussed that agency mortgage-backed securities have negligible default risks but may have significant prepayment risks. Can we design a CMO such that one bond class can also have negligible prepayment risk? Yes. This class of bonds is called the *planned amortization class* (*PAC*).

PAC bonds have a planned amortization schedule stating precisely the principals that will be paid down over a period of time. The proportion of PAC bonds to the entire package of mortgage-backed bonds varies significantly. Let us assume that the proportion is 30%. The other tranches, the non-PAC bonds, in the deal are called *supporting tranches*. Bonds are designated PAC or non-PAC in the structuring of a CMO. The design is often driven by the supply and demand of the marketplace for the type of bonds that need to be created.

When the prepayment speed is faster than expected, the supporting tranches' principals will be paid down before the PAC bonds. If the prepayment speed slows down, then the supporting tranches will not be paid down and are deferred to let the principals of the PAC bonds to be paid down according to the plan. In other words, supporting tranches are used to ensure that PAC bonds are not affected by uncertain prepayments.

Other CMO Bonds

With the innovation of CMO tranches, the designs of the bonds are unlimited. The basic idea is to use mortgage pass-through bonds, and rearrange the cash flows so that each cash flow is directed to a different class of buyers.

For example, buyers such as banks want to hold floating-rate instruments in their portfolio because their liabilities tend to be of short duration. One can even generate floating-rate notes out of a portfolio of fixed-rate mortgage-backed securities. The approach is to first determine an amortization schedule of the principal of the floating rate tranche. Then we determine the floating-rate index, say 1 month LIBOR rate plus 20 basis points. This index determines the interst payments of the tranche. Clearly, we cannot be obligated to pay the interests at any rate level because the bonds are supported by the fixed rate bonds. If 1 month LIBOR rate becomes very high, the total interest payments may exceed the interest incomes of the fixed-rate collateral bonds. Therefore, these bonds have caps and floors on the interest rates in their terms and conditions. Also, these floating-rate bonds must have companion bonds, so that the floating-rate bonds together with the companion bonds become the mortgage-backed pass-through.

In structuring a floating-rate bond inside a pass-through, we must have a companion bond that neutralizes the floating-rate risk of the bond. This companion bond is called the inverse floater. When the interest rate (LIBOR in this case) rises, the inverse floater has a formula of a form $(a^* - r)$ such that the bond pays a lower interest rate, where a^* is a constant number decided in the structuring of the deal and r is the specified interest rate (e.g., 3 month LIBOR). Conversely, when the interest rate falls, inverse floaters will pay higher interest rates. An inverse floater bond and a floating-rate bond become a fixed-rate bond. Inverse floaters have very interesting properties. When interest rates fall, fixed-rate bonds rise in value because the discount rates on their fixed interest payments are lowered. For inverse floaters, their interest payments actually increase in this scenario, and therefore their values should rise even faster. This means that they have a high duration and positive convexity. Inverse floaters are useful for asset managers to capture the falling rate scenario.

The Cow Graph

It can be confusing to study collateralized mortgage obligations since there are many financial innovations that create different bond types. Further, one has to ask how these innovations enhance the economy, especially when we take all the structuring fees and bond sales commissions into account. What is the business purpose of creating these bonds?

Consider going to a steak restaurant. A restaurant in New York City would typically charge $35 for a 14-ounce steak. If we go to a cattle auction, we would find that $900 can buy an 1,100-pound beef cow. One has to be struck by the spread between the source of meat and the end product served in the restaurant.

Let us now go to a butcher shop. You will often see a "cow graph" on the wall, with white lines on the black hide identifying the parts of the cow: flank steak, rump roast, brisket, standing rib, and so on. Customers buy the cuts they want. The sum of the cost of the parts is much more than the cost of the individual animal. Customers prefer to pay higher prices because they get what they need. (See figure 10.9.)

Mortgage-backed securities provide the sources of cash flows for financial engineers to rearrange assets and resell the final products to the customers. In rearranging the cash flows, we can reallocate the embedded options or create embedded options to fit the needs of the portfolio managers. The growth of collateralized mortgage obligations markets and related markets, such as the asset-backed securities market and whole loan markets, show the importance of the role of the butcher shops in delivering the appropriate products to the end customers.

10.4   Other Bonds

Dual Currency Bonds

This bond pays interests in one currency and principal in another. For example, a dual currency bond may pay coupon in yen and the principal in U.S. dollars. It can be driven

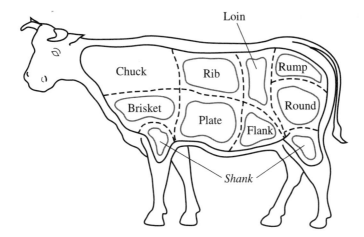

Figure 10-9 The cow graph. We can think of many examples in the real world where the sum of the parts is more valuable than the whole. Consider stripping, a process to create synthetic zero-coupon bonds by decomposing a coupon bond, because the coupon bond is a portfolio of zero-coupon bonds. Since people prefer a zero-coupon bond to a coupon bond, stripping the coupon bond into zero-coupon bonds is profitable. The same argument is applicable to the cow diagram.

by the tax code and accounting of some countries, depending on their treatment of the bond book value and income (whether the exchange rate is based on the historical book value or marking to market to the changing level of the exchange rate). Indexed currency option notes allow issuers to pay reduced principal at maturity if the specified foreign currency appreciates sufficiently relative to the domestic currency. (See figure 10.10.)

Floating-rate Note

The floating-rate note is a note that pays interest reset at regular intervals. The vanilla floating rate note's interest rate is adjusted to the market rate, say LIBOR, plus a margin, say 50 basis points. In so doing, the floating-rate note should always be traded close to par at all the reset dates. Such may not be the case if the liquidity spread widens or the rating of the issuer changes. In these cases, the floating-rate bonds may trade at a discount, even at the reset dates.

However, the interest rate reset does not need to be the prevailing market rate with the same term. There are several variations.

1. The reset rate is based on a term other than the reset period. A monthly reset floating rate can be paid over a one-year rate.
2. The rate can be a formula depending on a floating-rate index. The index can be a swap rate of a particular tenor.
3. The formula may be *inverse floating*, meaning that if the market rate goes up, the interest rate falls.

Rating-sensitive notes are floating-rate notes in which a floating rate resets with a spread off LIBOR, but the spread depends on the rating.

An oil-interest indexed dual currency bond is a bond when the principal is indexed to the yen and the semi-annual coupon payment is indexed to crude oil (e.g., max[$34, two barrels of crude oil]). The maturity of the bond is 5 years. The cash flow of the bond is

||

This bond can be decomposed into three parts: a straight bond, 10 call options on 2 barrels of crude oil, and a 5-year forward contract with the forward price of 140 ¥/$.

Buying a straight bond

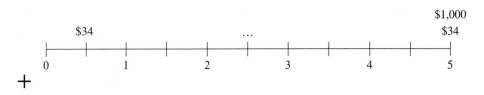

+

Buying 10 call options on 2 barrels of crude oil

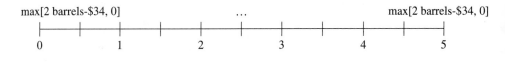

+

Buying a 5-year currency forward contract with the forward price of 140 ¥/$

Money unit = $; Underlying asset = ¥0

Figure 10-10 Oil interest indexed dual-currency bond

Spread-Protected Debt Securities and Credit-Sensitive Bonds

Spread-protected debt securities can be redeemed on a specified date prior to maturity, at the option of the holders. The redemption price is equal to the present value of the remaining promised payment discounted at a rate equal to a specified Treasury benchmark yield plus a fixed spread. This feature offers protection to the investor against a possible deteriorating of the creditworthiness of the bond. When the bond has a higher default risk, the investors can exercise the option to ensure that they receive a payment with a credit spread no wider than that specified in the provision.

A *credit-sensitive bond* is a bond with the coupon rate related to the bond rating. The issuers show their confidence in their firm by issuing these bonds, which have a coupon rate that is not fixed until the maturity of the bond, but depends on the bond rating. As the bond rating falls, the coupon rate will increase by a prespecified schedule. When these bonds were first issued, the design was motivated by market demand. The investors had concerns about the issuer's credit and wanted to be compensated if the rating fell. However, if the firm's financial health deteriorates, credit-sensitive bonds add more financial pressure for the firm.

These two bond types are related to the credit risk of the issuer. The models discussed in chapter 9 are often used to value these securities. As we have seen, modeling credit risk is complex, to say the least, and these bonds are also difficult to model. Their valuation must be related to the operations and profitability of the issuers. Therefore, to better understand the valuation of these bonds, we cannot simply view them as another type market securities, but securities tied to corporate finance. In chapter 13, after we discuss the firm valuation and corporate finance, we will revisit the modeling of these bonds.

Surety Bonds

Surety bonds are property and casualty insurance contracts. The insurance covers the fulfillment of an obligation. There are three parties involved: the surety is the insurance company that sells the contract. The insurance company receives the premium and pays the coverage when the obligation is not fulfilled. The surety guarantees the performance of the obligation that one party (the principal) owes to the other party (the obligee).

The obligations can vary significantly. For example, there are bonds on the performance of a principal in accordance with the terms and conditions of a contract, and bonds on payments for labor and materials to subcontractors. There are bonds for public officials to protect the public against loss of funds due to fraud and failures of the officials. There are surety bonds covering the securities industry, specific to its business risks. In short, surety bonds are contingent claims of the events, payments to the policyholders should certain events occur, and the prices of such contingent claims are the insurance premiums.

For example, at the time of Enron's default, a number of insurers had to pay the coverage of surety bonds because Enron, the principal, could not finish the projects that were being undertaken by outside firms. These firms were the obligees which had financial stakes in the completion of their respective projects. The surety bonds served them well in hedging against Enron's default.

We should note that surety bonds are a product offered by insurance companies. They are not corporate bonds whose issuers seek to raise capital from the capital markets. The insurance companies sell surety bonds that seek profits. We classify these bonds as "liabilities" of financial institutions, and we will cover them in chapter 11. However, they are bondlike from the modeling perspective, and they are in essence an exchange of promised cash flows.

Another important point to note is that the risk of the surety bonds is, in general, not capital market-based. The main sources of risk are the uncertainties that projects will be completed. For this reason, as we noted in chapter 7, in general we cannot use the relative valuation approach to determine the value of these bonds. They are not contingent claims on the stock risks, interest rate risks, or other capital market risks. Their risks usually cannot be hedged and must have their market price of risks. For this reason, there is no general acceptable methodology to value all these bonds. We have to evaluate them as individual cases.

10.5   Credit Derivatives

In recent years, there has been a significant growth in credit derivatives. These have been used to hedge the credit risks of a corporate bond portfolio, to generate income for the seller of credit risk protection, and to gain access for corporate funding to a broader group of investors. Asset management, hedging funds, arbitrage trading companies, insurance companies, banks, and other financial institutions are active participants as counterparties in these derivatives. Further, there are continual innovations in the product developments in this growth area. Financial modeling plays a significant role in the development of this market, and the models are being refined to meet the market demands. We will give an overview of these derivatives and the financial models being employed to nalyze them.

Product Descriptions

Credit derivatives include all the derivatives related to (though not exclusively) credit risk. There are many types of credit derivatives. Their basic building blocks are the "single name products." These derivatives are traded based on the credit risk of a particular bond. We will discuss three generic types here. Perhaps the simplest example of such a derivative is the credit default swap (CDS).

The confirm sheet or term sheet of a credit default swap first identifies the reference entity or the reference obligation—for example, Unisys bond. Then we identify the counterparties of the swap. They are the protection seller and the protection buyer. The protection buyer may be an asset management fund that seeks protection against the credit risk of the reference entity. The buyer pays a premium periodically, often quarterly, to the seller, say 60 basis points on the notional amount. Today, the most actively traded credit default swap has a term to expiration of five years, and the typical notional amount is $10 million. At any time before the termination of the swap, the seller pays the buyer if a credit event occurs. The credit event may be filing for bankruptcy protection or debt restructuring. In such case, the seller pays the par amount of the bond equaling the notional amount and receives the bond from the buyer for the same par amount. The swap terminates after this exchange.

Another commonly used credit derivative is the *total return swap*. In this case, the asset manager may want to get rid of the credit risk of a bond in the portfolio. He can be the total return payer, paying the counterparty (the total return receiver), the coupons and the capital gains (loss) over the term of the swap. In return, he receives an agreed-upon spread off the LIBOR rate. In essence, the swap provides the asset manager with a hedge against the credit risk of the bond. Unlike the credit default swap, there is no physical exchange at the end of the swap. The exchange of payments depends on the marking to market of the bond value.

Credit-linked notes (CLN) extend the concept of the credit default swap by using a special-purpose vehicle as a counterparty to the credit protection buyer. The special-purpose vehicle is an entity that sells credit-linked notes to investors. The funds raised are used to buy high quality bonds. These assets are then used to support the credit protection sold. Therefore, the periodic inflows of funds to the special-purpose vehicle are the premiums received from the credit protection buyer and the coupons from the collateral high quality bonds. In the event of default, the special-purpose vehicle uses the collateral to settle the payments with the credit protection buyer. Such net cash flows of the special-purpose vehicle are passed to the investors, the buyers of the credit-linked notes. In essence, credit-linked notes are bonds with credit default swap as an overlay, and the investors pay for the collaterals so that the special-purpose vehicle can be a seller of credit default swaps.

$$CLN = CDS + Bond$$

Such an arrangement enables investors to participate in the returns and the risks of a credit event without having to be dealers in the derivative markets.

The concept of credit-linked notes can now be further extended to the collateralized debt obligations, collateralized loan obligations, or other package of bonds. The collateralized obligations are not single name derivatives. Like the collateralized mortgage obligations that we discussed earlier, the credit collateralized obligations begin with a special-purpose vehicle that holds the reference assets, which may be bonds, loans, or credit default swaps. Then the special-purpose vehicle sells tranches to the investors, as with the CMOs, where priority rules are predetermined.

The tranches are called the senior tranche, the mezzanine tranche, and the equity. The senior tranches have the highest priority to receive the interests and principals. The mezzanine tranche has second priorty, and equity supports all the other tranches. Given this priority rule, we can determine the "waterfall" of the cash flow payments. The senior tranche has the highest priority in receiving the full interest payments, then the remaining interests pay the mezzanine tranche, and the equity receives the remaining interest payments. Under this general framework, many types of collateralized obligations based on credit risk can be designed. For example, the reference assets can be extended to managed funds or hedge funds. Different cash flow patterns to the tranches can be triggered by different credit events. One example of a trigger can be described as follows. When the interest payments to a particular tranche are impaired, the event triggers the bonds in that tranche to be repaid at par immediately. There can be as many obligation structures as there are in CMOs.

Valuation Models

The general framework to value credit derivatives is the same as that to value a high yield bond. In both cases, we need to identify the state when the default event occurs, the payments at the event, and the appropriate discount rate for the event. One common approach taken in valuing credit derivatives is the use of the actuarial approach that was discussed in chapter 9.

Consider a credit default swap, for example. Given the reference entity of a credit default swap, we can determine the survival rate of the bond, where the survival rate is defined as the probability that the bond will not default until time t. The drop in the survival rate from time t to $t + 1$ therefore is the probability of default for year t. If we also assume a recovery ratio, then the credit protection seller will pay the amount $(1 -$ recovery ratio) for each dollar of the notional amount at time t. If we further assume that we know the appropriate discount rate for the expected cash flow for the term of the swap, the present value can be calculated. This approach has the advantage of being simple, but it also suffers from a number of limitations.

First, the historical estimations of the recovery rate and the survival rate are not stable over time. They vary significantly, depending on the period of the historical data used. Further, given the change of the market structure, the macroeconomic environment, the firm's capital structure, and other factors, there is a lack of support for the view that the past is a good predictor of the future. Second, in essence, this approach is an application of the discount cash flow method applying to the credit derivatives. There is no theoretical basis for determining the appropriate discount rate for the expected cash flow generated by the default event. If we consider a high yield bond as a risk-free bond with shorting a put option on the firm value, as proposed by the Merton model, then we will appreciate that the discount rate which should be used to value the put option is complex as well as crucial. As we noted in chapter 2, since the put option is likely to have a negative beta, the discount rate may be lower than the risk-free rate. In chapter 13, we will revisit these issues.

10.6   Managing a CMO Portfolio

PACs That Fit Portfolio Needs: Using Key Rate Durations

Analyzing PACs

Consider FNMA 93-5, which is a pass-through issued in 1993. The deal, priced on December 9, 1992, at 200 PSA, is backed by FNMA 7.5s (GWAC 7.97%) and settled on January 29, 1993. GWAC is the gross weighted average coupon rate of the deal, the interest rates paid by the mortgagors. It is the GWAC that is relevant to the prepayment behavior of the mortgagors. The pass-through pays a coupon rate of 7.5%. The spread between the GWAC and the coupon rate of the deal pays for the credit insurance of the pass-throughs and the transaction costs, as was explained above. The deal has 15 tranches, of which 13 are PAC/TACs. (PAC is Planned Amortization Class and TAC is Target Amortization Class.) TACs are same as PACs except that they are protected against either the prepayment risk (call risk) or the extension risks, but not both (as in the case of PACs). The PACs are supported by 21% of the deal.

Table 10.1 describes three PACs in further details. Tranches C, G, and H are relatively large pieces of the deal. Since they have different coupon rates, the PAC-IOs strip out more coupons from the front tranches and therefore absorb more call risk from Tranche C than Tranche H. The effective collars are the PSA prepayment speeds that determine a band. The band is represented by the lowest and the highest PSA speeds. As long as the prepayment experience falls within this band, the PAC should be protected against the

Table 10.1 Characteristics of three PACs

Tranche	Size (MM)	Coupon	WAL(yr)	Effective Collar	Amort Window
C	55.6	6.25	3.5	92-336	'96-'97
G	60.0	7.15	8.0	86-276	'00-'02
H	79.1	7.50	11.2	63-276	'02-'08

WAL denotes the weighted average life; the amortization window is the time period where the PAC bonds pay down the principal payments, according to the plan.

prepayment risk and the extension risk. Any PSA speeds outside this band will lead to the PAC bond's not paying the interests and principals according to the plan. However, over time, the band changes. In this case, the effective collars of the PACs have drifted slightly since its issuance, but remain relatively wide. Finally, the amortization windows, the period between the projected first principal payment and the last projected principal payment, range from one to six years. The PACs are often viewed as default-free bonds with an amortization schedule, but they do have some prepayment or extension risks.

Yield attribution of PACs

Given the price and the PSA speed that determines the projected cash flows, we can determine the internal rates of returns. We calculate a yield that is referred to as the static yield. The static yield is then broken down into its components. The results are given in table 10.2. The pricing speed used is 200 PSA, and the analytics are based on March 5, 1993, prices. The yield attribution approach takes the shape of the yield curve and the PAC windows into account. There are three components of the yield. First is the yield of the projected cash flow, based on the Treasury curve. That means we calculate the value of the cash flow, then use this value to determine the internal rate of return. This is called the Treasury equivalent yield. Next is the option cost. The embedded option in the bond depresses the bond price, and hence increases the yield. This change of the yield is the option cost. The third component is the option adjusted spread (OAS), which we have discussed at length in chapter 8. The OAS numbers reflect the net returns to the investors. In general, the sum of these three components does not equal the static yield. This is because the PSA used in determining the expected prepayment is not the same as that used in the prepayment model. The difference measures the goodness of the PSA assumption.

Consider table 10.2, which measures the yield attribution of the bonds. The first column describes the bond. Usually the alphabetic order suggests the order of the maturities. The second column is the quote spread. For example, the C tranche is trading 75

Table 10.2 Yield Attribution of PACs

Tranche	Yield spread	Price	Static yield {(1) + (2) + (3)}	(1) TSY yield	(2) Option cost	(3) OAS
C	75/3 yr	103-15	5.08	4.68	0.02	0.38
G	85/7 yr	405-01	6.34	5.80	0.08	0.46
H	102/10 yr	104-31	6.89	6.11	0.10	0.67

Note: TSY yield-Treasury yields

Table 10.3 The Key Rate Durations of Each Bond

Tranche	0.25	1	2	3	5	7	10	15
C	0.01	0.06	0.13	2.19	0.66	—	—	—
G	0.02	0.07	0.14	0.32	0.60	3.37	1.13	—
H	0.02	0.07	0.15	0.32	0.54	1.19	3.54	1.01

basis points over the three-year bond. In all cases the option cost is low, with the highest of 102 basis point for the H tranche. This result suggests that all the PAC bonds are quite well protected. The result also shows that PACs are not without prepayment or extension risks. Finally, the result suggests that tranche H has the highest option risk in the bond but offers the highest returns as measured by OAS. If the model is correct and if we hedge the bonds appropriately, this bond will release 67 basis points annually for the investors.

The key rate duration profile (the plot of the key rate durations versus terms) of bond H is presented in table 10.3. The profile shows that the key rate durations start out small and increase with the term until around ten years. They are low initially because the bond pays only interest during this period. They increase with longer terms because the values of payments with longer terms are more sensitive to rate shifts.

While PAC bonds are protected from prepayment and extension risks, using duration (and not key rate duration) to manage the PAC bond interest rate risks may not be sufficient. This is because the PAC bonds may have complex cash flow patterns. Further, the protection of the prepayment and extension risks may not be effective. Using key rate duration, we can identify more precisely how the yield curve affects each bond or the portfolio of the PAC bonds.

Analyze the Duration of a Z Tranche

The Z tranche accrues interest and offers no cash flow before the first principal payment date. As a result, the Z tranche has a long duration.

Consider FNMA 92-77. The deal was priced on April 1, 1992, at 185 PSA. The deal size is $750.1 million with no PACs. ZA is the last tranche, with size $33.1 million. The collateral is 30-year 8.5%.

First, compare the analytics of ZA (assuming 195 PSA and priced at par) with the 10- and 30-year Treasuries. The calculations in table 10.4 are based on July 31, 1992, numbers.

The window of ZA spans from 10 to 30 years. Using the comparable yield to this cash flow, the yield of ZA exceeds the benchmark Treasury by 89 basis points. Of this

Table 10.4 Bond Characteristics

Description	ZA	10-year TSY	30-year TSY
Coupon Rate	8.0%	7.5%	8.0%
Window	4/2007–1/2022	—	—
Price	Par	105.62	106.47
Yield	8.10%	6.71%	7.45%
Spread	89 bpt	—	—
Option Cost	44 bpt	—	—
OAS	45 bpt	—	—

spread, 44 basis points are attributable to option and 45 to OAS. Considering that AAA industrials are trading at only a 32 basis point spread, ZA's OAS is relatively high. In addition, ZA offers long duration, shown in table 10.5.

ZA's duration is longer than that of the 30-year Treasury, even though the WAL is shorter. This is because ZA accrues the interest at a fixed rate and in essence is a zero-coupon bond. However, the collateral prepayments lower the convexity, which remains positive though less than that of the 30-year. An equal dollar-weighted position in ZA and the 10-year has a duration (10.98 years) comparable to the thirty-year.

Note that Z bonds have both a long duration and a significant embedded option value, even though the convexity is positive.

Decomposition of a CMO Bond

Often in a general description of bonds in research and fixed-income securities books, mortgage-backed securities and collateralized mortgage obligations are described as "option embedded bonds." That labeling is made to convey the idea that the cash flows of the bonds are uncertain, and often implies that the bonds are risky. But what are these options? Are they call options or put options? What are their strike prices and expiration dates? Are their cash flows just uncertain, or are they related to risk factors, so that we can value the options relative to the underlying risks? Within the context of the discussions of this book, we can and should be more precise about the phrase "option embedded" bonds, because if we can identify these embedded options, we can better hedge the risks, then the risk of the bond can be managed, and the bond can have different implications for the bond portfolio management.

One approach to identify the option embedded in a collateralized mortgage obligation is to use the decomposition method explained in section 6.11. The method and the results (Ho and Chen, 1997) are illustrated below.

The analysis seeks to determine the decomposition of a collateralized mortgage obligations tranche, FH 1747:Q. The bond is a fixed 8% coupon bond maturing in December 2003. The bond is a support tranche bearing much prepayment risk allocated from the PAC tranches of the deal. The collaterals are FHLMC 30-year with a net weighted average coupon of 8%.

The analysis is based on January 9, 1995, and the price at the time was $92.09. In simulating the bond cash flows, the weighted average life of the cash flows is shortened in a simulation with low interest rates, indicating the prepayment risk. The cash flows also lengthen in a simulation with high interest rates, indicating that the bond has extension risks. Can we determine the embedded options that can capture these prepayment and extension risks? Prepayment risks are the risks of mortgagors paying down the principals when interest rates fall, while the extension risks are the risks of the mortgagors of not paying down the principals when the interest rates rise.

Table 10.5 Risk Analysis

	ZA	10-year TSY	30-year TSY
WAL	19.57 years	10 years	30 years
Effective Duration	15.10 years	6.77 years	10.94 years
Convexity	1.23	0.60	2.02

We now use the decomposition method explained in chapter 6 to analyze the bonds. In this decomposition, we select the caps and floors as benchmark securities. Specifically, we select the caps with their strikes above the forward rates and the floors with their strikes below the forward rates. This way, the benchmark securities are out-of-the money options.

The primary decomposition is conducted to determine the cash flows, replicated by Treasury bonds, of the CMO bond under the scenario where the forward rates prevail. Then the pathwise values of the benchmark securities are used to replicate the pathwise values of the CMO bond net of the pathwise values of the replicating Treasury securities portfolio.

The results are presented below:

$$FHLMC\ 1747Q = -1.258\text{cash} + TSY - 1.458C(95 - 18,\ 8.17\%)$$
$$- 8.325F(95 - 08, 6.45\%) + 6.461F(95 - 08,\ 6.87\%)$$

where TSY denotes the Treasury securities replicating portfolio; F and C denote the floors and caps, respectively; the first parameter denotes the start date and the termination date, and the second entry is the strike of the cap or floor.

The coefficients represent the number of caps and floors that should be bought to make the decomposition. The explanatory power of the decomposition is 96.88%; that means the decomposition can explain 96.88% of the variations of the pathwise values. The research uses stratified sampling, meaning that the scenarios are chosen over a large possible span of the interest rate scenarios, rather than a random sampling.

The selling of caps indicates the presence of extension risks, as we discussed in the previous section. Extension risks lead to losses for the investors when the interest rate rises above a certain level, similar to holding a cap in a short position. The floors indicate the prepayment risks. This decomposition measures the size and the specifications of the embedded options. Further, note that a floor is bought with a lower strike price. That floor is used to capture the burnout effects. When interest rates continue to fall, the impact on the prepayment lessens with the burnout effect, and therefore the floor with the lower strike price is bought to mitigate this effect. When interest rates continue to rise, the opposite argument can be made for the cap with the higher strike price.

Concluding Thoughts

We should make a few observations regarding these examples of using financial models to manage a fixed-income portfolio. These models clearly show the importance of embedded options in mortgage-backed securities and collateralized mortgage obligations. The embedded options have two types of risks: the extension risk and the prepayment risks. The extension risk refers to mortgagors who delay their prepayment of their mortgages as the result of an increase in interest rates. Prepayment risk refers to the mortgagors exercising their prepayment option early as the result of falling interest rates. Valuation models are used to determine the value of these options, and as a result, we can determine the appropriate yield required to hold the bonds.

These bonds are traded with the yields quoted. The yield numbers cannot properly describe whether the bonds are cheap or rich. In the presence of an embedded option, we need to use financial modeling to determine the fair value of the bonds, taking the value of the embedded option into account.

Financial models are useful to portfolio managers even if the portfolio managers follow a buy and hold strategy. If they do not intend to sell the bonds, but to hold them until all the principal is received, one may argue that they do not need financial models to analyze the bonds. However, such is not the case. First, the financial model enables portfolio managers to evaluate whether the bonds are trading fairly, given the embedded options. Second, the managers can calculate the durations of the bonds so that they can evaluate the reinvestment risks of all the interim cash flows. If a collateralized mortgage obligation bond is quoted with a weighted average life of N years, the portfolio manager still needs to know under what condition the bonds may be prepaid earlier than the stated weighted average life. Third, duration and key rate durations are the tools which should be used to ensure the reinvestment risks are managed, to mark the bonds to market. Since many of these bonds are not actively traded, there are no accurate price quotes for them continually in the market. To determine the marking to market value for risk management purposes or regulatory purposes, financial models are used.

For total return portfolio managers, financial models are important tools. In total return asset management, managers need to simulate the impact of the yield curve movements of the bond, the prepayment behavior affecting the bond value, or the impact of the basis risks (changes in the option adjusted spread) on the bond value. Using these simulations they can then take the bond positions whose return over a period, typically one month, can be evaluated. In sum, the model allows them to do the prospective as well as the retrospective analysis of each portfolio position taken.

10.7 Summary

In previous chapters we have described corporate bonds. We viewed them as contingent claims and developed the valuation model for corporate bonds that have provisions (which are interest rate derivatives) and default risks. These models are specified such that we assume investors or borrowers are acting optimally, whether they are calling the bonds or declaring default. Their optimal decisions are solved within the context of the relative valuation model.

However, there are many bond types whose behavior does not depend on the optimal behavior of the investors or the borrowers. We assume that they do not act "optimally" in a strict sense of the word, in that they do not seek to optimize value. In an actual life situation, maybe the investors or the borrowers act suboptimally because they have other goals beyond maximizing their wealth. The description of such behavior is called the behavioral model.

Specifically, this chapter has described convertible bonds and mortgage-backed securities. In convertible bonds, there is the feature of forced conversion, whereby the issuer seeks to call the bonds with the intent of forcing the investors to convert their bonds to shares of the firm, and not to surrender the bonds for cash at the call price. In this case, we model the behavior of the issuer in making that decision without solving for the optimal strategy. For mortgage-backed securities, the behavioral model is more complex. Historical experiences of mortgagors are used to estimate the prepayment model to describe the factors that affect their prepayment decisions. The prepayment model is then integrated into the arbitrage-free interest rate model. Together, the two models provide the valuation model of the mortgage-backed securities.

This chapter also has described one important aspect of financial engineering: financial product innovations. We have shown how investment banks can create different types of securities to satisfy the needs of the market. Using financial engineering, they can create a large fixed-income securities market, a collateralized mortgage obligations market that has a wide range of bond characteristics which target portfolio managers' requirements.

Thus far, we have dealt extensively with corporate liabilities in general. Corporations borrow funds by selling corporate bonds and convertible bonds. While mortgages are liabilities to individuals, the CMOs are liabilities of the trusts that have MBS as assets. There are other corporate liabilities. Many financial institutions sell financial contracts; for example, time deposits, insurance contracts. These contracts may be viewed as "securities," and we may be able to value them as derivatives. However, these financial contracts have no markets and have little common standards across institutions. And of course they have their specific product risks, like mortality risks for life insurance product. Further, since there is no trading of such contracts, there may be limited use of an "economic" valuation of these contracts. Yet, the use of relative valuation model to determine the value of these contracts is at present a very active area of research for practical applications. These are some of the topics that we will discuss in chapter 11, drawing upon many of the concepts described thus far.

References

Asquith, P., and D. W. Mullims, Jr. 1991. Convertible debt: Corporate call policy and voluntary conversion. *Journal of Finance*, 46 (4), 1273–1289.

Brennan, M. J., and E. S. Schwartz. 1977. Convertible bonds: Valuation and optimal strategies for call and conversion. *Journal of Finance*, 32 (5), 1699–1715.

Davidson, A. S., T. S. Y. Ho, and Y. C. Lim. 1994. Collateralized mortgage obligations. *Probus*.

Fabozzi, F. 1997. *Advances in Fixed Income Valuation Modeling and Risk Management*, edited by Frank J. Fabozzi, New Hope, Penn., Wiley.

Ho, T. S. Y., and M. Z. H. Chen. 1996. *Arbitrage-free Bond Canonical Decomposition*. in *Fixed Income Solution*, edited by T. S. Y. Ho, Homewood, Ill., Irwin.

Ingersoll, J. E. 1976. A contingent-claims valuation of convertible securities. *Journal of Financial Economics*, 4, 289–322.

Ingersoll, J. E. 1977. An examination of corporate call policies on convertible securities. *Journal of Finance*, 32 (2), 463–478.

Lavely, J. A. 1971. Comparative usage of bond-warrant and convertible bond issues. *Journal of Finance*, 26 (3), 796–797.

Mayers, D. 1998. Why firms issue convertible bonds: The matching of financial and real investment options. *Journal of Financial Economics*, 47 (1), 83–102.

Further Readings

Cheyette, O. 1996. Implied prepayment. *Journal of Portfolio Management*, 23 (1), 107–115.

Kang, J. K., and Y. W. Lee. 1986. The pricing of convertible debt offerings. *Journal of Financial Economics*, 41, 231–248.

Kremer, J. W., and R. L. Roenfeldt. 1992. Warrant pricing: Jump-diffusion vs. Black–Scholes. *Journal of Financial and Quantitative Analysis*, 28 (2), 255–272.

Schwarz, E. S., and W. N. Torous. 1992. Prepayment, default, and the valuation of mortgage pass-through securities. *Journal of Business*, 65 (2), 221–239.

Takahashi, A., T. Kobayashi, and N. Nakagawa. 2001. Pricing convertible bonds with credit risk: A Duffie–Singleton approach. Working paper, Faculty of Economics, University of Tokyo.

Tsiveriotis, K., and C. Fernandes. 1998. Valuing convertible bonds with credit risk. *Journal of Fixed Income*, September, 95–102.

11

Financial Institutions' Liabilities: Required Option Adjusted Spread

Liabilities of financial institutions are examples of a vast segment of the capital markets that are nontradable. Using the required option adjusted spread (ROAS) off the transfer pricing curve, we can extend the relative valuation model to determine the economic values of these instruments. Such "fair value" of these balance sheet items is therefore based on the market values of the benchmark securities which are established as references to the liability value. This fair value financial modeling has tremendous implications for financial reporting, asset/liability management, corporate governance, performance metrics, risk management, and many other business processes.

Financial institutions are issuers of a broad range of financial contracts. Banks' savings, such as time deposits and savings accounts, are examples of financial contracts. Property and casualty insurers' financial products may include auto insurance and workers' compensation insurance. Life insurer's policies, such as term insurance and whole life insurance, are also examples of financial contracts. Corporations are obligated to pay benefits to retired employees. They are often called the "liabilities."

These are only some examples of financial contracts that financial institutions sell to customers to raise funds. They sell these financial contracts and invest the proceeds, deriving profits from the spread (returns of the investments net of the funding costs). These contracts are different from the corporate debt of financial institutions because they are not capital market securities; they have no active markets and no transaction prices except at issuance. They are similar to private placements, an arrangement made between a seller and a buyer. Their designs are often specific to their issuers, and they are also subject to different regulations on financial disclosure and management. Of course, these liabilities also have their own risk drivers. For example, the deposit accounts have withdrawal risks; property and casualty insurance carries general insurance risks; life products have mortality risks. These specific risk sources are also important in defining the characteristics of these liabilities.

In this chapter, the focus will be on the nature of liabilities without a capital market and their specific risk sources, the main characteristics that distinguish them from other capital market securities. This chapter notes that policyholders cannot buy and sell insurance policies in secondary markets; they have to buy them from insurance companies. Also banks, do not trade deposit accounts in the banking system because time deposits are not financial contracts that can be traded.

Since these contracts do not have a market in which to trade, these liabilities have to be serviced by financial institutions for the contract life. Some of the bank liabilities may be securitized (bundled and sold to the securities markets). Some insurance liabilities may be reinsured or sold. Although liabilities can be sold, their main distinctions from capital market securities are (1) their lack of marketability and (2) their unique product risks.

The term "liabilities" must be defined within the context of this book. Liabilities in this chapter are referred to as the liabilities of financial institutions. Note that a liability to one firm is an asset to another party. Any security that is bought by an investor has to be sold by a firm. Bonds are liabilities to the issuers but assets to the investors.

This chapter continues to expand the use of the contingent claims valuation approach to liabilities. This extension represents an important progress in our understanding of the valuation methodology. The use of a general approach of relative valuation in financial modeling is no longer confined to tradable securities. It can even be used for illiquid securities which have no secondary markets. The relative valuation model can be used for financial contracts that have no markets at all.

In this case, when there are no market prices and no trading, what is used to determine the "market value" of a liability? How do we determine benchmark securities to determine the relative valuation? How do we know that the model value is correct when there are no traded values to verify? These are some of the questions that this chapter will focus on.

This chapter will begin with a discussion of the differences between book value and fair value of a liability. We will then describe the margin required to determine the value of a liability. After setting the assumptions of a liability model, we will describe specific models for a range of liabilities of banks, property and casualty insurance, life insurance, and pension liabilities. We will conclude with some applications of financial models of the liabilities.

11.1 Balance Sheet Analysis—Book Value

Liabilities can be found in the balance sheets of financial institutions. Liabilities, in this chapter, refer to the financial products sold by these firms as part of their business because this is a way to borrow money for their investments. We are therefore addressing only the balance sheet items that have cash flows. We will not be addressing accrual items such as deferred acquisition costs. *Deferred acquisition costs* are accounting means of delaying the recognition of up-front expenses, but this chapter deals instead with the actual expense cash flows as they arise. We shall not address bonds, debentures, or other forms of funding from capital markets. These items are dealt with in other chapters that discuss the securities in the capital market.

Under generally accepted accounting principles (GAAP), the value of these liabilities is represented by book value on the balance sheet in the firm's annual (or quarterly) financial statements. The book value tends to be a measure of historical amortization cost, and is not sensitive to the changing capital markets and market prices of risks.

For example, the core accounts of banks (demand deposit accounts and money market accounts) are valued according to the amount deposited in the banks. When deposits are made to the bank and are then invested in loans, the bank liability and the loan item increase by the same amount. However, if interest rate rates fall subsequently, both book values on the balance sheets are not affected. Furthermore, if there is a "flight to quality" phenomenon in the capital markets when markets discount credit risk at a higher rate, the balance sheet also remains unchanged.

The same concept is true with insurers. In general insurance (often called property and casualty insurance), the insurance sold is reported on a book value basis in the form of reserves for future losses. The premiums collected and invested are reported as assets. Details of these calculations will be discussed later in this chapter. In essence, the actuaries estimate the possible losses. They then calculate the present value of this estimated loss. Generally, a zero discount rate is used, and therefore the present value is the estimated amount not discounted by the time value of money.

The life insurer's treatment of financial disclosure of liabilities is similar to that of general insurance, except that a nonzero discount rate is generally used in the present-value calculations of life insurers. After an insurance contract is sold, the premium is invested and the investments are reported as an asset. Insurance companies represent the present value of their liabilities net of the present value of future premiums as reserves. Using industry guidelines, reserves are calculated, adjusting for the discount rate and other aspects of the products. But these guidelines do not need to reflect the market view of the present value. Guidelines for the discount rate do not continually change with the market reality.

One may argue that this book value treatment of financial contracts on the balance sheets of financial institutions is reasonable if financial institutions can be viewed as conducting their businesses like any manufacturing business or utilities firm. The financial institutions' assets are treated like factories or power plants that produce products and generate revenues. Their liabilities allow them to finance the acquisition of assets. If the amortized book value is stable and close to the economic value, then the book value approach assures standardization of reporting across market sectors, ensuring comparability of the financial analysis.

But in recent years, dramatic changes have taken place in the financial services sector. The paradigm has changed. With the growth of capital markets, banks, insurance companies, and their customers are all closely tied to the bond markets, stock markets, and derivative markets. And these markets have become more volatile. As a result, some of the financial institutions' funding costs and investment returns have high market volatilities, affecting their profitability. Often, the book value can no longer reflect the economic value of the balance sheet. The financial sector is now confronted with the challenge of deciding how to report the value of the items in their balance sheet.

One solution is to report the fair value of liabilities, which can better represent their market value even when there is no market for these financial contracts. The balance sheet of a financial institution can be considered a portfolio of financial securities. Then a financial institution can be likened to a hedge fund, holding assets in a leveraged position and providing profits to its investors. We can therefore mark to market the entire balance sheet of a financial institution and measure the total return of the balance sheet, as is presently required of asset management portfolios or hedge funds.

There are many possible methods of deciding the fair value of liabilities that have been proposed for different purposes. The financial reporting may be used for accounting, financial disclosure, risk reporting, or internal management. This is a subject of much current debate, and these issues will be discussed in chapter 16. This chapter focuses on the methodologies used in calculating the fair value of liabilities, and this discussion will have important implications for the financial industry in the near future.

11.2   Fair Values

From a financial disclosure point of view, investors would like to see the present value of their liabilities measured in economic terms to reflect the continually changing market realities for a number of reasons. The fair value of the liabilities would represent what the financial institutions would owe the investors if these liabilities were sold in the market.

When the present value of the assets is less than the present value of the liabilities, then it can be concluded that the liquidation of the firm would lead to the failure to prepay the liability. The fair value of a liability refers to this general concept of present value.

While there are general agreements on the definition of the fair value of a liability, there are differences in the precise valuation methodology. Even so, the variations of the proposed approaches require the following steps.

Determining the Transfer Pricing

To realize a fair value of both assets and liabilities, a consistent framework of analysis is needed across a possible broad range of maturities. Therefore, to accomplish any valuation, we should begin with the time value of money. What is the appropriate time value of money, the base yield curve or discount function for discounting any cash flows?

A financial institution may measure the present value of a cash flow using a transfer pricing curve to measure the time value of money. The *transfer pricing curve* is the spot curve that determines the internal benchmark for present-value calculations. Since most banks' Treasury departments use the swap market for funding operations, the transfer pricing curve is the LIBOR for the shorter end of the maturity spectrum and the swap curve for maturities beyond one year. For example, a bank may receive funds from a certificate of deposit account at a lower interest rate of 3.5% at a six-month maturity and invest the deposits in a loan at 6% with a two-year maturity. For simplicity, we will ignore the credit risk of the bank and the investments in this discussion. (We will deal with the credit risk issue later.) The interest margin is 2.5%. However, this spread between the interest income and the funding cost is not gained without risks because of the yield curve risk, whose shape can change unexpectedly. To determine the gain on a risk-adjusted basis, we can in principle hedge both the certificate of deposit and the loans with the six-month and two-year swaps, taking a long position in the six-month rate and short in the two-year rate. The hedge would require a spread of the two-year rate and the six-month rate determined by the transfer pricing curve, which in this case would be the swap curve. If the spread between the six-month and the two-year rates is 2%, then the hedge costs 2% annually. The risk-adjusted interest margin is 0.5% (= interest margin 2.5% − spread 2%) would be risk-free.

In using the transfer pricing curve as the base curve for the time value of money, we can determine the present values of all the cash flows, and therefore we can compare the asset and liability values on one consistent basis. In particular, we can determine the asset value net of the liability value, which we call equity in the banking sector. Equity is a measure of solvency for a bank.

Suppose a financial institution is on the verge of default due to the lack of cash to meet immediate cash payment obligations, and has to decide to liquidate its assets. If a financial institution sells all its assets and buys back liabilities at market competitive prices, then the equity value is the net cash position (the liquidation value). Therefore, a significantly positive equity value implies that there are sufficient assets supporting the liabilities in a liquidation scenario, such that the financial institution can meet the obligations of the liabilities to its customers, even if there are no new sales in the future. The financial institution remains solvent. Negative equity means that when the firm liquidates, there are not enough assets to pay for the value of the liabilities.

There is an alternative intuitive explanation of the positive equity. When all the items on the balance sheet are fair valued, using an arbitrage-free valuation framework (which we will discuss in this chapter), then there should be a hedging strategy such that the financial institution will always remain solvent if we let the balance sheet run off (that is, assuming there are no new sales). Conversely, if the equity is negative, on a runoff basis there will always be scenarios that the financial institution would be insolvent, and there is no hedging strategy that can eliminate this risk. For these reasons, a positive equity is a desirable measure of the solvency of a financial institution.

For life insurance companies, using the transfer pricing curve is fairly complicated. For regulatory and other reasons, life insurance companies are much less active in the swap or other derivative markets. Typically, the swap curve is not generally part of the insurer's operation in any significant way relative to the banks. Insurers may consider other alternatives, such as the Treasury curve or a curve based on the firm's rating (such as the AA financial curve). We will discuss the criteria for the choice of the transfer pricing curve next.

It is important to specify the stated purpose of the transfer pricing curve. The curve is the base curve to determine discount rates for the time value of money, such that as the yield curve changes, the transfer pricing curve can appropriately reflect such market realities to both sides of the balance sheet. Other risk premiums (or margins)—such as credit risks, product risks, and liquidity risks for both assets and liabilities—are captured in their spreads off this transfer pricing curve. (We will discuss the precise adjustments of these spreads to the transfer pricing curve later.) The transfer pricing curve should be chosen from the market for its liquidity in the interest rate risk management operations of the firm. For this reason, one should consider primarily the Treasury curve or the swap curve. The choice between the two standard market benchmarks, or some other benchmark, will depend on the firm's operations.

Required Margin

In previous chapters, assets were revealed to have an option adjusted spread to capture a number of factors affecting their appropriate discount rate beyond that of the time value of money. These factors may be the liquidity (or marketability) spread, credit risk, and risks other than credit and interest rates, such as prepayment risk.

For the bank sector, typically the fair value is defined for liabilities with no adjustments for these factors. This is a common practice in banking. It may perhaps be difficult to measure the appropriate option adjusted spread for the liquidity spread or the errors of the modeling of the withdrawal risk. As a result, the present values of banks' liabilities are defined by discounting the projected cash flows along the transfer pricing curve. Later in this chapter, we will discuss how the option adjusted spread of a bank product can be estimated by means of a transfer pricing curve, using as the measure the required option adjusted spread of equation (11.1).

However, the spread adjustment is more complicated for life insurers. The main difference for life insurance products is their long(er) durations. Life insurance products can have a life of over 50 years. When the cash flow is discounted at 0.5%, below the transfer pricing curve, the resulting change in present value can be significant. (We will illustrate the issue below.)

Consider a single-premium liability, with the policyholder making one payment at the initial date and receiving the benefits in 30 years. If the funding cost[1] of the cash flows is secured at 0.5 percent below the transfer pricing curve, and the cash flows are discounted along the transfer pricing curve to determine the fair value, then the liability value is approximately 15% ($\cong 0.5\% \times 30$) lower than the premium value. Or we can report an immediate gain of 15%. If we report the immediate gain in the fair value accounting, the gain is called the *gain-on-sale*. The rationale behind the gain-on-sale in measuring profitability is that in the fair value calculation, we assume that a set of assets which is precisely matched to our liabilities can yield the returns specified according to the transfer pricing curve. If we invest 85% of the premium at the transfer pricing curve, then we will have the exact future value to meet the liability obligations. Therefore, if the cost of funding is 0.5% below the matched investment returns for 30 years, then the profits, in present value, would be 15% of the premium.

However, this approach to measuring profits requires a number of assumptions. The cost of funding usually entails some risks that cannot be hedged or diversified. In such cases, the gain-on-sale approach does not allow for reserves for future risks. This approach risks reporting profits that may not be realized. This is particularly the case if we use the AA financial/industrial yield curve (as opposed to using the Treasury or swap curve) as the transfer pricing curve for reporting profits. In this case, we are assuming that investments can continually outperform the Treasury curve, providing investment returns exceeding the AA financial/industrial yield curve.

An alternative approach to the gain-on-sale approach is the *profit release approach*. In a profit release, the discount rate is the transfer pricing curve less a spread that reflects the risks and other factors pertinent to the liability. In this case, the profit on the sale of the liability is released continually, and the profit is the spread that is specified.[2] Note that if the product has a very short duration, the gain-on-sale value for each dollar of premium is much smaller, and the difference between the gain on sale and the profit release is small. Perhaps for this reason, banks typically (as an approximation) use the gain-on-sale approach in determining the fair value of liabilities.

Consider a simple numerical example of a single-premium product for illustration. Suppose an insurer sells a policy that is expected to have a claim of $100 at the end of the fifth year. The premium received at the time of sale, net of all the sales costs, is $100. Suppose the transfer pricing curve is 6% flat in the next five years. Then the discount rate of the policy that equates the future claims to the premium value is 0%. The required spread is therefore $-6\%(= 0\% - 6\%)$. That means that if the investment of the premium is expected to yield 6% every year, then the policy will release a profit of 6% annually. This numerical example clearly explains the reasons for using the profit release approach. The liability payment fair value in this approach is determined by the discount rate of 0%. Therefore, the fair value of the liability is expected to be $100 every year. On the investment side, since the investment return on the $100 premium is 6%, the profit release is therefore 6%. By way of contrast, the gain on sale of this policy is the premium net of the present value of the claim, equaling $100 \cdot \left(1 - \frac{1}{1.06^5}\right)$. (See figure 11.1.)

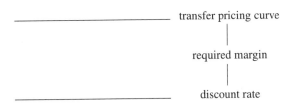

Figure 11.1 The spread structure

When the financial contract has embedded options, the specification of the required spread is extended to the option adjusted spread. The specification of the option adjusted spread for the liability is the same as the option adjusted spread for an asset. It is the constant spread off the transfer pricing curve such that the present value of the cash flows or the fair value of the cash flows, using an arbitrage-free model based on the transfer pricing curve plus the constant spread, equals the market value of the financial contract.

More precisely, let V be the market observed value of the financial contract. Let $V^*(r_f(t))$ be the arbitrage-free model value of the financial contract based on a time value curve $r_f(t)$. Let $r_f(t)$ be the transfer pricing curve, and oas be the option adjusted spread. Then, the oas must satisfy the equation

$$V = V^*(r_f(t) + oas) \qquad (11.1)$$

The option adjusted spread of an asset is the additional annual return for the investor over the life of the asset due to the embedded option. For this reason, the spread for a liability is the same as the required return for the investment needed to cover the additional liability obligations. The additional gain for the investor is the required financing cost for the borrower.

However, unlike mortgage-backed securities and other tradable assets, determining the option adjusted spread may not be simple for liabilities because there is no available capital market to estimate the prevailing market spreads. One approach is to determine the option adjusted spread at the initial sale. The option adjusted spread can be the spread that equates the fair value to the initial premium value. By this definition, the fair value of the liability must equal to the initial premium value at the time of sale. Therefore, in this case, there is no gain-on-sale to be reported. Instead, the profits will be released over the life of the product according to the spread. This spread is called the *required option adjusted spread* (ROAS; see Ho et al., 1995). As illustrated numerically above, the ROAS is −6 percent.

When the premium received is lower than the present value of the future cash flows discounted along the transfer pricing curve, the discount rate of the cash flow has to be higher to ensure that the premium equals the present value of the cash flow. The additional spread, the ROAS, is positive. It is the required excess returns of the investments above the transfer pricing curve so that the product is sold profitably. When the ROAS is negative, the product will release the profit annually at the rate specified by the absolute value of ROAS over the life of the liability, if the investment return is always the transfer pricing rate. It is important to note that since many of the insurance liabilities are very long dated, their investments tend to have long maturities with little liquidity. For this reason, their investments may have a positive option adjusted spread to compensate for their illiquidity, as we discussed in chapter 8. As long as the positive option adjusted spread of the investments exceeds the ROAS of the liabilities, the liability is profitable.

The ROAS may be kept the same for the life of the product, and the spread is used to calculate the fair value of the product or liability in subsequent periods. Or the ROAS can be adjusted over time, as the product pricing changes. Specifically, as the product gains more market acceptance and the spread tightens, the ROAS should be adjusted, using the prevailing spread of the new issues to reflect the market reality. The choice of the precise procedure will depend on the product and the firm. In some cases, there are no comparable products in the market to determine the ROAS, and thus there are no benchmarks to guide the adjustments to the ROAS over time. In this case, adjusting the ROAS over time based on market benchmarks can be difficult to implement. This becomes more an implementation issue.

There are several components of the ROAS, including the credit risk of the insurer, the liquidity, the risk of expenses in maintaining and servicing the sale, mortality risk, and morbidity risk. Each risk source may have a margin to compensate for the risk. For example, the mortality risk may require an additional spread of x basis points of profits to bear the risk. ROAS is the sum of these margins. For internal management, the profit released from the ROAS may be further decomposed to better appreciate the sources of the profits. This can be accomplished by using the model to determine the attribution of the returns, showing the sources of profits generated from the margins of the risk sources.

Credit Risks

Credit risk, here, is not about the assets, but the credit risk of the financial institutions, the firms that sold the liabilities. By the definition of fair value, when the credit rating of the financial institution falls, and to the extent that the credit risk affects the funding costs of the liabilities, the fair value measure should capture the fall in value of the liability.

The ROAS approach described above clearly captures such credit risks. When the financial institution's credit rating falls, for example, the certificates of deposit will have to bear higher interest rates, leading to a lower profit release; or the insurance policy will have a lower insurance rate or lower premium charged to customers. However, such an approach raises some concerns. First, it can be argued that if fair valuation is used, financial institutions may have an incentive to lower the liability value by acquiring a higher debt ratio, because the higher debt ratio leads the decrease in the financial institution's credit rating. This effect is explained below.

Since equity is defined as the total asset value net of the total liability on the balance sheet, the financial institution's equity value increases with a lower credit rating, holding everything else constant. Therefore, we are led to a fairly nonintuitive and unsettling result. In corporate finance (as we discussed in chapter 12), this phenomenon is called the *wealth transfer* between the shareholders and bondholders with an increase in debt. Once the shareholders have assured the funding from the bondholders, the fall in the firm value is partially borne by the bondholders, rather than by the shareholders alone. That is, the policyholders or bank customers must also bear some of the business risk. This phenomenon is generally true with any capital structure, and is not specific only to the financial institutions' liabilities. The solution to the problem is not to change the definition of the fair value of a liability, but to ensure that shareholders cannot effect a wealth transfer. Indeed, regulators and other agencies have devoted many resources to safeguard the solvency of financial institutions so that they protect the liabilities, which we will discuss later.

Second, another seemingly nonintuitive result of fair valuation of the liability, using the ROAS approach, is the sale price of the liability. Suppose a low rating financial institution has arranged for a portion of its liability to be assumed by a higher rating institution by paying the other firm a sum in cash. That sale value should be higher than the fair value of the liability on the books of the original insurer. As a result, the customer now has less credit risk with other firms supporting the credit. The increase in value is simply a wealth transfer from the financial institution to the customers (and the price of this wealth transfer is equivalent to the price of a credit enhancement). Of course, there would be no wealth transfer if the sale price is the original fair value (when the liability is held by the another low credit firm).

Having discussed these issues with regard to credit risk, it is important to note that credit risk in general is low for these liabilities. There are different types of insurance covering the credit risk of liabilities to ensure confidence in customers and to avoid a "run on the bank." The insurance companies in each state tend to have a fund that stands by to provide liquidity to any insurance company that suffers insolvency. Therefore, even when financial institutions have a low credit rating, the liabilities may still maintain high creditworthiness. In the event of default, the liability has much higher creditworthiness than the debentures and other capital market funding in the capital structure, because the liability is considered the senior debt to all other debts on the financial institution's balance sheet. The financial institution must meet the obligations of the insurance policy before the debt payoff of the company. The impact of credit risk on the liabilities' value should be a concern, and should be captured as a component of the ROAS. This component however should be less than the credit spread assigned to the firm's debentures.

In summary, the ROAS is the excess returns of the asset that the asset investment must attain so that the liability is sold at a breakeven price. Therefore the ROAS is adjusted off the transfer pricing curve such that the fair value equals the initial premium values. Hence we have

$$\text{discount rate} = \text{transfer pricing} + \text{ROAS} \qquad (11.1a)$$

The ROAS can be attributed to three main components: the credit spread, the profit release and product risk margins. To the extent that the financial institution can measure the appropriate market credit spread for the liability and the product risk margins, then we can measure the profit release. Credit spread is the additional cost of funding for the credit risk of the financial institution. The product risk margins are margins charged for the specific risks of the products.

$$\text{ROAS} = \text{credit spread} - \text{profit release} - \text{product risk margins} \qquad (11.1b)$$

For example, consider the single-premium product above. If we assume that the expected cost is properly measured and that no product risk margin is required and the firm has no credit risk for the product, then the ROAS is -6%. That means, according to equation (11.1b), that the profit release is 6%, as expected.

11.3 Liability Modeling

Consider the following assumptions regarding liabilities and the financial institutions that sell them (see Merton, 1999). Liabilities are defined as the products sold by financial institutions, such as banks and insurance companies. They differ from assets in a number of ways.

1. The lenders expect their money to be safe. Lenders do not want to accept credit

risk. In general, bank customers and insurance policyholders who buy the liabilities are less motivated by the higher returns to compensate for the credit risk of the financial institutions compared with securities market pricing. They are adverse to credit risks. To the extent that the credit risk of the financial institution becomes important, the use of the required option adjusted spread is sufficient to capture the problem in assigning a higher spread, as explained above.

2. Opaqueness to customers. In general, lenders do not behave like bondholders, having the need to oversee a financial institution's management or trying to change the management. Bank customers in general cannot be well informed on the bank's operations and the details of the portfolio. For this reason, they can only assume a bank's creditworthiness based on simple measures such as its credit rating. Therefore, banks need to prove that they are dependable by consistently providing security for bank deposits. This is an important departure from the perfect capital market assumption. If the perfect capital market condition were to hold, there would be no financial institutions as we know them. Financial institutions are intermediaries that invest their customers' savings accounts in loans and in the capital market. In a perfect capital market where there are no transaction costs, financial institutions have no means to derive profits from their services. With such market imperfections, the management of a financial institution is quite opaque to the lenders of their liabilities.

3. There exists a competitive market. The market is competitive in pricing and in product design. As a result of competitive pricing, a thin profit margin exists for any errors in forecasting future business outcomes. In this market, financial institutions act as *atomistic agents* (agents with no market power) that cannot set market prices.

The implication of the assumption (1) is that regulators and financial institutions have the incentive to ensure that these liabilities will have minimal default risk and will have a high recovery ratio should default occur. Assumption (2) suggests that the liabilities are illiquid and it is difficult for a capital market to assign fair values to them because of their opaqueness. Assumption (3) suggests that the pricing of products is always competitive, and therefore the basic ideas of financial modeling that are described in this book should be appropriate. Further, an appropriate measure of the profitability of products and implementation of asset–liability management are important issues to financial institutions.

In order to describe the characteristics of liabilities and the methodology used in their valuation, assumptions are made: a transfer pricing curve, a term structure of volatilities (or a volatility surface) observed in capital markets, and the contingent claims valuation methodology, along with the ROAS, will be applied to determine the fair value.

In many ways, this application of the contingent claim method to value a liability represents a number of extensions of concepts from the previous chapters. These are some of the challenges that we will face.

1. Assets and liabilities are intricately linked. Some of the liabilities are intricately linked to assets. Unlike assets, some liabilities have cash flows defined not by terms and conditions but by the investment strategies of the firm. We will provide examples of such liabilities (e.g., SPDA) later. Therefore, we need a method to sever these linkages between assets and liabilities.

2. A very long-dated duration. As indicated before, some of the liabilities have a product life much longer than those in the capital markets. How can the time value of money be determined when we cannot observe the market discount rate?

3. No market for trading. As discussed before, there is no market for trading. Except in some cases, trading can exist when an insurer sells a block of business to another company. A portfolio of liabilities would be considered a block of business.

4. Complex financial reporting requirements are mostly based on historical experiences. Financial reporting requires firms to disclose their holdings on their balance sheets. The financial disclosures are mostly based on the book values of liabilities, which are determined by complex rules. To the extent that often we need to reconcile the fair value of a liability to its book value, this process can be quite complicated.

5. Unpredictable consumer behavior. In mortgage-backed securities and other capital market assets, consumer behavior is predicted by the use of extensive databases, whereas financial institutions do not disclose the experiences of consumer behavior of liability investors. For this reason, there is always a lack of data to predict the consumers' behavior.

6. Expenses. Often expenses of sales (e.g., commissions for the sales offices and the salesperson) are very significant. Maintenance expenses include the costs of servicing the liabilities, maintaining the accounts of each client, and providing reports and payments, if any. Overhead costs are all the fixed costs in managing the business. Some of these expenses should be included in the calculation of the fair value because these are the costs associated with the funding.

To describe how these issues are addressed in practice, we will consider some specific examples in the following sections.

11.4 Bank Liabilities

Banks act as financial intermediaries who take customers' deposits and subsequently invest in assets that offer higher returns than the cost of funds (the interest paid to the customers and the expenses of maintaining the accounts). They offer liquidity to customers so that they can withdraw funds at any time; they offer security for customers' deposits because some deposits are federally insured; they provide transactional services with economic efficiencies, such as check clearing and loan servicing. By providing a range of services to capture the customer base, banks tend to offer a range of savings and time deposit accounts and other investment instruments.

There are several types of bank liabilities. *Personal demand deposit accounts* (DDAs) are checking accounts for individual customers, and *commercial deposit accounts* are for corporations. They do not pay interest, but provide services and liquidity, cash on demand, for the customers.

Negotiable order of withdrawal accounts (NOW accounts) are transaction accounts offered to noncorporate customers. Transaction accounts are interest-bearing checking accounts. Transactions can be made fairly easily because customers can withdraw money on demand. However, NOW accounts differ from traditional checking accounts because a minimum deposit is required to receive interest. If it is not maintained, interest will not be paid and the account will function like a traditional DDA.

Passbook savings accounts are less liquid than demand deposit and NOW accounts. They are not checking accounts, and customers need to be at a branch of the bank to withdraw funds.

A *money market deposit account* (MMDA) is a product introduced to compete with money market mutual funds. The bank provides liquidity to the customers, allowing a checking account that provides interest. However, there are restrictions in an MMDA. There is a minimum balance requirement and there are limits to the number of checks written per period and a limited number of transfers that can be made.

Certificates of deposit (CD) have a fixed maturity and a face value. The maturities may range from two weeks to eight years. The interest rates are fixed, and customers can roll over and automatically buy another CD as they mature.

Bank Rates

Bank rates are interest rates offered by the bank to its customers. A higher bank rate will encourage customers to deposit more savings. By adjusting the bank rate, a bank can attract new customers and deter withdrawals of funds. The bank rates tend to be different from market rates in a number of respects. First, they do not tend to change continually, like LIBOR rates or other capital market rates. The bank sets its interest rates and they tend to stay the same until the market changes sufficiently to require the bank to adjust its rates.

The bank rates may depend on market rates such as the LIBOR rate and Treasury securities rates. When the market rates fall, the banks also lower their rates; otherwise their cost of funds from deposit and saving accounts would be higher than their investment returns. When the market rates rise, banks raise their rates so that customers will not withdraw funds from the bank to invest in the market. However, bank rates, particularly the savings account rates, typically tend to remain constant and then adjust to the market in a jump of 10 basis points or more. Depending on the country and the sector, the rates may also depend on government administered rates, such as housing rates or other discount rates of government agencies.

Finally, the rates depend significantly on competitors' rates or rates of competing products. It is important to note that customers seek other services, as mentioned above, from the bank and therefore bank rates do not necessarily affect the depositors' behavior directly, even though the bank may offer personalized services and a convenient location for transactions. There are considerations, other than the bank rates, that attract deposits for the bank.

Behavioral Model

We do not quite understand all the reasons why customers withdraw funds from an account. Their seemingly random withdrawals have to be described by a behavioral model. Typically, banks keep records of their customer's deposits and withdrawal patterns. The historical behavior data are compiled and analyzed. Statistical analysis is used to determine the relationships within the behavioral patterns in a way that is similar to developing the prepayment models of mortgage-backed securities. Determining the relationships between the withdrawal behavior and interest rate risks, along with bank rates and other explanatory factors, is an integral part of the valuation model.

The cash flow can be determined on a runoff basis, which can be interpreted as no new sales coming in; therefore, banks keep track of how much money goes out. In other words, all deposits from new customers are assumed to be new borrowing. Even though we consider the liabilities on a runoff basis, it doesn't mean that deposit accounts are declining all the time because customers are withdrawing money. The deposit account value may increase because the old customer can raise the level of deposits.

A Valuation Model

A number of research papers have provided valuation models of bank liabilities. Their approaches can be exemplified by O'Brien (2000), whose paper proposes a contingent claim valuation model for the NOW account and MMDA. To value these nonmaturing accounts, two interrelated issues must be taken into consideration: (1) the relationship of the deposit rate and the depositors' desired balances, and (2) the relationship of the deposit rate and the market interest rates. The model is presented below.

$$dR_t^D = a(br_t - c - R_{t-1}^D)dt + \sigma \, dZ_t \tag{11.2}$$

R_t^D is the deposit rate set at time t; r_t is the market short-term rate, assumed to be a monthly rate; σ is the standard deviation of the random noise of the deposit rate; and dZ represents the random noise. The parameters, a, b, and c can be estimated from the historical data of the deposit rates and the market interest rate. Equation (11.2) is a partial adjustment model. The deposit rate tries to converge to the equilibrium rate, which is related to a market rate r_t. The adjustment rate, a, is asymmetric. The bank is more likely to lower its rate when the market rates have fallen than to raise its rates when the market has risen. Therefore, the adjustment rate depends on whether $s = (br_t - c - R_{t-1}^D) > 0$ or < 0. The adjustment to the target rate is faster if the target rate is below the current deposit rate (i.e., $s < 0$). Conversely, the adjustment rate is slower if the target rate is above the current deposit rate (i.e., $s > 0$). This model assumes that the deposit rate changes continually with the market rates. This is usually not the case. The deposit rate tends to move a small jump at a time and to stay constant at other times.[3] We can define a as follows:

$$a = \left\{ \begin{array}{ll} a^+ & \text{if } \ s > 0 \\ a^- & \text{if } \ s < 0 \end{array} \right\}$$
$$0 < a^+ < a^-$$

Let the level of deposits be D_t. Then we assume that

$$\log D_t = a_1 + a_2(R_t - R_t^D) + a_3 \log y_t + a_4 \log(D_{t-1}) + e_t \tag{11.3}$$

The depositors' desired level (equation (11.3)) is hypothesized to be related to the interest rate spread between the deposit rate and market rate, the national income y, and the lag deposit level. The model uses the national income as the external factor that affects the growth in deposits. This assumption can be replaced by other factors related to each bank and its clients' behavior.

Both equations can be estimated from historical data. Equation (11.2) relates the market rate and the deposit rate. We can obtain a time series of both the market rates and the deposit rates. Using a regression of the time series, we can estimate the coefficients of equation (11.2). Similarly, for equation (11.3), using the time series of the deposit level, the deposit rate, the market rate, and the national income, we can estimate the coefficients of the equation.

The specification of the model (the coefficients of the equations) will depend on the account, the client base and the bank. For example, some core accounts can have a deposit rate that can be very low and insensitive to the market rates. Then the adjustment rate will be very low. For some accounts, withdrawal begins after Thanksgiving; the cash is taken to buy holiday presents. The deposit increases after the New Year, when annual bonus payments have been made. To include the seasonality effect, we can follow the method used in the prepayment model. We can have an additional term in equation (11.3) where the deposit rate also depends on the calendar time, specifically, the month.

The model considers the nonmaturing account as a contingent claim on the interest rate. The cash flows generated from the model need to be determined. Let f be the reserve ratio, the proportion of any deposit that has to be put aside as a noninterest-bearing reserve. Let D be the deposit level, R^D the deposit rate, and c the cost of maintaining \$1 of deposit per unit time. Initially, the deposit is $D(0)$. The outflow payment for reserve is $f - D(0)$. At the end of the period and of subsequent periods, the total payments (CF) are of the form

$$CF_t = (R^D_{t-1} + c_{t-1})D_{t-1} - (1 - f)dD_t \qquad (11.4)$$

Since r_t is an arbitrage-free market short-term interest rate, which may be a transfer pricing rate, the value of the account as a contingent claim on r_t can be determined. We assume that the market interest rate follows a one-factor interest rate model with a term structure of volatilities.

The results show that the present value of the future cash flows from the deposit account decreases as the interest rates increase (see figure 11.2.). The value of the account V to the bank is therefore the initial deposit amount $D(0)$ net of the present value of the future cash outflows $PV(\widetilde{CF}_t)$.

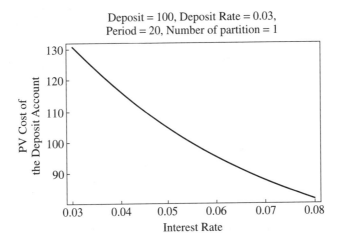

Deposit = 100, Deposit Rate = 0.03, Period = 20, Number of partition = 1

Figure 11.2 The present value cost of a deposit account. We assume that we receive a \$100 deposit at time 0 to generate the level of deposits according to equation (11.3). The coefficients of a_1, a_2, a_3, and a_4 in equation (11.3) are 0.909, −1.653, 0, and 0.85 respectively, using the coefficients estimated in O'Brien. We use the Ho–Lee model to generate the arbitrage-free short-term market rate, r_t. We assume that $b = 0.7, c = 0$ and an adjustment coefficient $a = 0.5$ in equation (11.2). The annual maintenance costs C and the reserve ratio f in equation (11.4) are 0.015 and 0.02, respectively. The initial flat term structure varies from 0.03 to 0.08. We assume that the deposit is withdrawn at year 20.

$$V = D(0) - PV\left(\widetilde{CF_t}\right) \tag{11.5}$$

The product is profitable if V is positive and unprofitable if V is negative. The result shows that if we take the future deposits into account, given the assumed parameters, the deposit account is profitable when interest rate levels are above 5.5 percent. The model can be used to determine the optimal deposit rate-setting strategy that will maximize V. The model can also be used to determine the key rate durations of the liability and other sensitivity measures.

11.5 Property and Casualty Insurance

Property and casualty insurance companies sell insurance to individuals and institutions to cover costs incurred as the result of unanticipated events. The insurance may cover property losses due to fire and theft (property insurance). The insurance may cover bodily injury (casualty insurance). There are standard lines of insurance, such as auto insurance. Or insurance companies may underwrite special kinds of insurance for unusual events, such as insurance against kidnapping. Insurance companies specialize in evaluating risks and have the scale of economy to diversify the risks by selling insurance covering uncorrelated risks. Thus, they collect a fee for removing (sometimes partially) the risks from their customers. For example, we discussed the surety bond in chapter 10. Surety bonds remove the risks from project owners who may not be able to secure the completion of a project by the contractors. After the unsystematic risks have been diversified by writing a broad range of insurance policies to any customers, the insurance contract, from the insurer's perspective, may behave in a way similar to a bond, in that the expected cash outflow to pay for the insurance coverage has negligible remaining risks. This is likened to the casino's perspective on slot machines, as described in chapter 2. In practice, of course not all the unsystematic risks can always be diversified, and we have the residual risks, which are considered the product risks.

Insurance Products

Property and liability insurance underwriting is concerned with providing compensation to policyholders for unforeseen events, man-made or natural disasters alike. Fire is a major part of the insurance. Other causes of loss can be windstorm, hurricanes, tornadoes, and earthquakes.

The largest segment of insurance is auto insurance. An underwriter decides on a premium based on a number of factors that may result in claims. These include the age of operator, the type of automobile, particular uses of the automobile for pleasure or for work, driving record, territory where the automobile is used, gender, occupation, personal characteristics, and physical condition of the automobile.

The second largest segment is worker compensation insurance. This insurance pays compensation for death, injuries, or occupational diseases that occur in the course of employment. Benefits include death benefits, disability income, medical expenses, and rehabilitation expenses as required by the workers' compensation law.

Book value treatment

While insurers sell a range of products to different market segments, the general description of an insurance product is similar for all of them. In part, such standardization is a result of financial reporting regulations, using the book value.

Premiums An insurance contract begins with *underwriting*, the process of determining the insurance rate (or premium) for the specified coverage. The insurer may use an agency writer or a direct writer. The *underwriters* are the insurer's agents who evaluate the risks and determine the premium charged to the customer. *Commissions* are then paid to the broker who sells the insurance contract.

The insurance company may then purchase reinsurance from another company so that the insurer retains only part of the risks in case there is an event with very severe loss and part of this loss is passed to the reinsurer. The premium paid to the reinsurer is called the *ceded amount*, and the premium net of the ceded amount is called the *net premium written*.

On a balance sheet, a significant component of the asset is called the *unearned premium*, the portion of the premium received by the insurer that has to be retained to cover the remaining term of the contract. The net premium written is added to the unearned premium on the asset side of the balance sheet. Reserves for possible losses are added to the liability side of the balance sheet. Then earned premium is defined as

Earned premiums = fall in unearned premiums + written premiums for the year.

Premiums are earned over the coverage period, so not all the written premium can be reported as income immediately, even though the cash payment for the premium has been received.

This accounting of underwriting income can be illustrated with a numerical example. Consider an insurer that begins its business at time 0. At the beginning of each period, which may be three months, the insurer sells $10 million of insurance, collecting the premium immediately, and the policy covers two periods. The insurer sells the insurance for two periods. For simplicity, let us assume that there are no reported losses in the next three periods.

At time 0, the premium written is $10 million and the unearned premium is also $10 million. At the end of the first period, $5 of the premium is earned. Therefore the remaining unearned premium is $5 million.

At the beginning of period 1, another $10 million premium is sold. Therefore the total unearned premium is $15 million, and it follows that the change in unearned premium is −$5 million. The premium written is $10 million and the earned premium is $5 million. Hence the above identity is verified.

At the end of period 1, then unearned premium is $5 million, and therefore at the beginning of period 2, together with another $10 million premium sold, the unearned premium is now $15 million. The change of unearned premium over the past period is 0. The written premium is $10 million and the premium earned is also $10—$5 million earned on the premium sold two periods ago and another $5 million earned on the premium sold in the previous period. Again the above identity holds.

If no incident occurs over the duration of the coverage, the entire net premium written is realized as revenues. If an incident incurs for property insurance, the settlement in general can be timely, because the value of the damage, and the cost of repair or replacement, can be determined quickly. However, for casualty insurance, the losses may not be determined immediately. Some claims may have to be settled in court, and the actual payments may be made years later. Therefore, losses and loss adjustment expenses incurred, which are the estimates of the losses, are reported in the income statements as costs against the incomes from the premium.

Insurance companies invest the net premium paid by the investors. Typically, property and casualty companies tend to invest a large part of their portfolio in fairly liquid assets, in case major incidents occur and they have to pay the coverages for the losses.

Loss Exposures   An analysis of the insurance liability begins with measuring liability loss exposures. One measure is the *loss frequency*, which is defined as the number of events that are likely to occur within some time interval. Another is *loss severity*, which is the estimate of the losses caused by an occurrence. An example of an occurrence that involves loss is an injured worker who may receive weekly income for life due to an accident on the job. Catastrophic losses have low frequency and high severity. Therefore the total dollar loss is defined as

$$\text{Total dollar loss} = \text{loss frequency} \times \text{loss severity}$$

Since this information is based on forecasts, a measure of the credibility of the loss prediction is needed. An important part of loss reserve analysis is the case reserve. Case reserves are reserves established on each individual claim. The reserve is dependent on the line of insurance. Often after an incident occurs, the policyholder may not make a claim immediately. Then an item in the reserve has to reflect the pending claims, the IBNR (incurred but not yet reported). The balance of the reserve is for losses that have been reported.

$$\text{Reserve} = \text{IBNR} + \text{reported loss}$$

Expenses   Expenses are all the expenses incurred in the underwriting and maintenance of the policies, and legal expenses. They may be paid when the premium is sold, as in the commission expenses, or years later, as legal expenses after an incident. After an incident occurs, the insurer can decide on the extent of the expenses that have already been allocated and how much has not been allocated. These two items are called *allocated loss adjustment expenses* and *unallocated loss adjustment expenses*, respectively. The reserves on the financial reporting can then be adjusted.

Fair value analysis

The financial modeling of property and casualty liabilities is primarily statistical, using historical data. The state of the economy and the inflation rate may be used to adjust for the potential liabilities of the claims. The development pattern of the claims is estimated for each product line of the company, but for the most part the model is based on statistical estimation. The statistical method is similar across all products.

Step 1. Premiums   Assume that premiums are paid annually. Then the insurer calculates the net premium after the commissions and ceded amount (premium paid for reinsurance) are determined. The net premium represents the proceeds to the insurer that can be used for investments.

Step 2. Loss Analysis   Losses include claims frequency, medical and indemnity severity, and loss adjustment expenses, including fixed and variable components. The main components are frequency of claims, the average cost of medical care and indemnity per claim, the amount of allocated loss adjustment expenses (either per claim or per dollar of loss of indemnity), and the amount of unallocated loss adjustment expenses. For example, for workers' compensation, the loss is the indemnity loss and the medical loss.

The main tool for analyzing the expected losses is the *development triangle*. It refers to the loss incurred and the increase in loss over time, and is estimated from the historical experience. Consider incidents incurred in 1980. The historical record would show the expenses and losses paid for the incidents from the subsequent year (1981), until the current year (1990). Similarly, we consider the incidents incurred in 1981 and then the payouts in the subsequent years. This record, displayed as a "triangle," indicates how $1 of loss incurred may result in a payout ratio over time, at least from the historical perspective.

A numerical example of a development triangle of historical losses (in millions of dollars) incurred is given below.

1980	1981	1982	1983	1984	⋯	1990
112	98	83	75	63	⋯	3
	128	90	81	70	⋯	2
		130	100	80	⋯	2
			101	90	⋯	2
				102	⋯	2
						2

The long tail of a product development loss refers to the loss extended over time. The historical records of the development triangle can be used as a basis to project the expected loss over time, which may be as long as ten years. For general insurance, such as workers' compensation, as discussed above, the settlement may take several years, perhaps more than ten years. These expenses include the cost of litigation and the settlement, which are called *development costs*. For such long periods of settlement the risk should include the inflation risk, since the legal costs are based on the prevailing legal rates, which will depend on the inflation rates. The inflation risk is related to the interest rate risk, as was described in chapter 3 concerning the Fisher equation. The relationship to the interest rate level can be estimated using historical data.

Using the development triangle, actuaries can estimate the payout of the claims on average, and which is called the *development pattern of claims*. For example, assuming an inflation scenario (which is based in part on the interest rate scenario), the historical experience may project that x_i% of the coverage is paid out each ith year for the next 15 years. The payments would include the indemnity and the cost of litigation adjusted for inflation.

Step 3. Persistence and the Behavioral Model   Since most insurance premiums cover only one year, the insurer expects a high degree of persistence, the tendency for policyholders to renew the insurance. For example, most drivers renew their auto insurance with the same insurer every year without much hesitation. Few drivers actively seek the best rates and services at every renewal date. Furthermore, the premium does not adjust to the market interest rates continually. For these reasons, the cash inflow stream can be quite stable over many years.

The persistence behavior depends on the type of policy. For example, in workers' compensation, the projected premium is affected by setting the premium level and the exposure base, which in turn is based on the number of insured employees and changes in wages due to inflation. Using historical experience, we can develop the behavioral model of the customers in their persistence behavior. We can estimate the renewal rate per year, under different interest rate or inflation rate scenarios.

Now, given the persistence model, projecting the amount of premium sold in an in-force business (i.e., assuming no new customers but allowing the present customers to renew their insurance), and the loss development pattern that projects the payout amount, we can combine the cash inflows and outflows to the insurer.

Step 4. Discounting   Under each inflation and interest rate scenario, the associated cash flow can be determined. Using an arbitrage-free interest rate model, we can determine the present value of the cash flow for each interest rate scenario. Using the now familiar methodology of averaging all the pathwise values of the simulation, the present value of the cash flows is determined. By specifying the appropriate required option adjusted spread (ROAS), the fair value of the liability can be calculated. This approach can be repeated for each product line.

The cash flow projected is a combination of the inflows of premiums and out flows of loss payments.

Remarks

While general insurance tends to be perceived as a short-term contract because the premium coverage is often only one year, from a financial modeling perspective, the contract may indeed have a long duration. The following example illustrates the long tail nature of some of the products. On February 8, 2002, the *Wall Street Journal* reported that AIG had increased the reserves for claims pending from a 1994 California earthquake. Eight years after the event, insurers were still adjusting the loss reserves!

Performance measures: fair value approach and the book value approach

For financial reporting (the book value approach), profitability of an insurer depends on underwriting profits and net investment income. Underwriting profit is measured by the premium earned net of expenses and losses. Therefore the profitability is related to the *expense ratio* and the *loss ratio*. The expense ratio is the ratio of all expenses to the net premium written, and the loss ratio is the ratio of losses and adjustment expenses incurred to the net premiums earned.

The sum of the two ratios is the *combined ratio*. The underwriting profitability is (1− the combined ratio). If the combined ratio is 0.95, that roughly means that for every dollar of premium earned, 95 cents pays for all the costs, and the insurer retains 5 cents profit. In actuality, the insurer's profit is much higher because the premiums are invested. If the investment return is 6%, then the total profit on a $1 premium would be 11% (= 5%+6%).

This performance measure is unique to property and casualty insurers, in that the industry maintains a 0 discount rate, ignoring the time value of money for their reserves. The expected cost of $1 million to be paid in ten years may be reported as a $1 million loss today. Perhaps the development period is over ten years, but in general the reserve does not take discounting of future payments into account.

11.6   Life Insurance Products

Life insurance companies provide insurance to cover the economic consequences that occur upon the death of an individual, called the insured life. Unlike property and casualty insurance, the benefit is often known in advance, or it is specified in the contract how the benefits are determined, since the purchaser of the policy selects the amount of coverage desired and there is no assessment of cost in the event that a claim occurs.

Before describing types of insurance products available for different purposes and modeling these financial contracts as tradable securities, we must first briefly discuss the process by which a typical insurance company sells and manages a policy.

Sales

The sales process for life insurance differs from most financial products. When a contract (called a policy) is offered to an applicant and the applicant accepts the offer, the insurer and the new policyholder enter a long-term contractual relationship. The policyholder makes payments (called premiums) to commence and maintain coverage. The policyholder has the right to terminate the policy at any time, but the insurer's obligations under the contract remain until the policyholder terminates the policy. The policyholder terminates the policy when the term of coverage is reached or the death of the insured life occurs. This differs from the production and sale of tangible goods, where the delivery of the finished product is typically the final step of the product cycle. For life insurance, the sale is the beginning of the "production process."

The insurance industry often says that life insurance is sold, not bought. Compared with homeowner's insurance or automobile insurance, where coverage is often required as a mortgage stipulation or by statute, selling a life policy takes extraordinary effort. There are several types of sales organizations (also called distribution systems or channels). Distribution systems include salaried employees of the insurance company, captive agents, general agency systems, insurance brokers, stockbrokers, bank sales, direct marketing (mail and television advertising) and Internet sites. The most familiar distribution entity is the insurance agent. In the most generic sense, an agent is a person or corporation appointed by an insurance company to sell its products. An agent (even a captive agent) is considered an independent contractor, not an employee of the insurer. The agent receives compensation in the form of commissions (a percentage of the premiums).

Net Premiums

The cost of building and maintaining distribution channels is a significant expense to most insurance organizations. In addition to the direct sales expense, other acquisition costs are incurred before the insurer receives any premium. The insurer underwrites the policy (i.e., examines the application, including the health of the insured life and the financial reasons for insurance, to determine whether the application constitutes an acceptable risk and if so, to determine the premium appropriate to the risk). The financial status of the individual can be related to the effect of adverse selection. For example, a wealthy individual can self-insure, but his private information on his health may prompt him to buy insurance.

Most life insurance companies and multiline insurers separate insurance management from investment management. The business unit of insurance operations collects premiums, pays commissions, and records the transactions. A liability called a reserve is established on the balance sheet of the insurer, reflecting the current value of the future obligations on each policy. These obligations are offset by the current value of expected premiums (net of expenses) that will be collected in the future.

Reserves

A reserve is a somewhat confusing term because it is not consistent with other sectors' accounting terminology. The *reserve* is in fact the insurance liability book value. There is no market for trading policies. The policies cannot even be returned to the policyholders, as we noted above. The insurer must carry this policy on its balance sheet for many years—possibly over 80 years if the holder buys an insurance policy at age 20 and lives to be 100. When the policy has been sold and has not terminated, it is said to be in the in-force business. Insurance policies just sold are referred to as new sales.

Each insurance company is required to pay expenses that include agent commissions, insurance business unit expenses, insurance benefits, and shareholder dividends. After direct expenses from the acquisition and maintenance of the business are paid, the remaining amount is available for investment; hence, the premium must be invested. Insurers rely on investment income to support the product expenses and profit objectives. In addition to direct expenses, product revenues must provide for allocated overhead expenses, investment management fees, corporate charges for use of capital, and the risks embedded in the contracts. All of this culminates in a complex cost allocation accounting.

Investment of the Net Premiums

Asset managers generally follow guidelines that reflect regulatory capital requirements and the expectations of rating agencies. Investments in risky assets require a higher capital base—more assets relative to the reserve. Each year net investment income is reported in the financial statements of the insurer or the corporate entity that owns it. Net investment income is the realized gain and the interest received during the year, net of all investment expenses. The interest income net of expenses is called the *net interest income*, a number often considered important because the realized gain is considered opportunistic. Firms believe that analysts and rating agencies prefer the firm's net investment income to consist of mostly interest income and not capital gains.

Capital gains tend to represent opportunistic investment gains and not the robustness of the business model. Some companies include noncash items as investment income—for example, realized capital gains and losses may be amortized over a period of years.

Business Processes

A firm is required to satisfy many aspects of the administrative process in order to properly issue an insurance policy. It has to manage assets and liabilities in a way that complies with the requirements of the regulators. Financial reporting has to be done appropriately. Also, the firm must manage the expectations of rating agencies and stock analysts over a long horizon where the reserve is not priced by the market but is often determined by rules specified by the regulators.

The design of a proper business process is a challenging task. Moreover, competition among insurance companies results in thin profit margins. These profit margins may reward innovators of new products that satisfy market needs. If they do, the insurers can reap above the market profits (rents). However, these product designs can be copied in a short period of time. Thus, when competition is present among companies, and they scramble to copy and create innovative designs so as to one-up each other, the prices will be lowered accordingly.

Insurance products are generally administered separately according to the line of business that is differentiated by the type of risk class. The line is drawn between group products and individual products. *Group insurance* is issued to a group of people under a master policy. Generally, the policyholder is a corporation and the insured people are the employees of the corporation. *Individual insurance*, on the other hand, is sold on an individual basis. The policyholder (owner) may be a corporation, but separate policies are required for each insured life.

A secondary subdivision by line of business is between life insurance and annuities. *Life insurance* is paid upon the death of the insured person and provides financial protection in case of premature death. An *annuity*, on the other hand, pays a monthly benefit as long as the insured person (called the annuitant) is alive, providing protection against extreme longevity (living beyond one's assets). Annuities are popular retirement vehicles. Funding a meaningful monthly benefit requires a significant premium, because benefits will usually be paid for many years. Thus insurers developed a contract that provides for an accumulation period to build up funds and a payout period within the same contract. These contracts, called deferred annuities, have seen remarkable sales growth in recent years. They are generally available as single premium or flexible premium contracts, where the flexible premiums are paid over time. Single premium immediate annuities are contracts that do not have an accumulation period, and they only provide periodic payments.

Primary Risk Sources

The concern of any insurer is to make adequate provision for the risks inherent in the business. For insurance production, profits will emerge only to the extent that the business performs in accordance with certain expectations of revenues, benefit payments, and expenses. Premiums over the life of the business depend on the rate at which policyholders choose to renew coverage each year (or, equivalently, the rate at which policyholders lapse their policies). Recovery of acquisition expenses, therefore, requires low lapse rates for several years. Revenues also depend on investment income, and thus projection of interest rates is inherent in product profitability. Claim costs rely on projections of mortality rates. For some products, claim costs increase when the in-force business ages and profitability may fall short of expectations if the in-force business does not terminate quickly enough. Finally, operating expenses are subject to variations based on changing productivity levels and general inflation trends.

In summary, the primary risks embedded in life insurance products are mortality, voluntary termination rates (also called lapse rates), persistence, interest rates, expenses, and inflation. We will discuss these risks in turn.

Since life policies are insurance products for the event of death, clearly one major concern is the mortality risk. Typically, actuaries believe the risks have to be well diversified over many policies, and on average the death claims are considered quite predictable—except for insured lives over age 80. The expected death claims are calculated from mortality tables compiled by companies on the basis of their underwriting guidelines and past experience. This is generally regarded as proprietary information, although intercompany mortality experience of several large companies is published by the Society of Actuaries.

Several factors affect the expected mortality of an individual. Age and sex are well-known factors—mortality rates are typically higher as age increases, and female mortality is typically lower than male mortality. Other factors may change these simple relationships, however. Insurers classify insurance applications by "lifestyle"—the choice of an individual to pursue activities that increase the likelihood of a claim. Markers of a risky lifestyle include use of tobacco products, motor vehicle violations, and "hazardous" recreational pursuits such as piloting a small aircraft. Insurers also classify applications for health risks. This classification process divides the insurance population into relatively homogeneous risk classes. The insurance rates vary by risk class so that the cost of insurance is related to the riskiness of the protection.

The mortality characteristics of a risk class will change over time, but once the policy is issued, the risk class cannot be changed by the insurer. On one hand, the insured person's health may deteriorate. On the other hand, if a risk factor changes for the better—for example, if the insured stops using tobacco products—the insured will drop coverage at the expensive charges for that risk class. As a result, the insurance coverage must take this adverse selection bias into account. Hence, the mortality of a risk class also depends on the length of time that the insurance coverage has been in force. The longer the coverage has been in effect, the higher the impact of adverse selection bias on the product.

Lapse risk is the rate at which policyholders voluntarily terminate their contract. However, like holders of callable bonds, they tend not to exercise these options optimally. The lapse experience—historical behavior of the policyholders—is usually analyzed to predict the policyholders' behavior. Using historical data, statistical methods are developed to measure the lapse rate relative to the levels of the surrender charges, market factors, and crediting rates (the interest returns given to the policyholders), all of which may affect the policyholders' decisions regarding lapsing. The estimated statistical model is then applied to the in-force business and new sales. We will describe some of these models for specific insurance products.

A policyholder can lapse at any time. Part of the lapse risk is adverse selection.

A policyholder may not lapse because he has private information not available to the insurer. He may have health complications, for example. The insurer has to sufficiently ensure that many policyholders do not lapse too soon after the purchase because the insurer has to cover the expenses of acquiring the policy and the cost of adverse selection bias. The acquisition cost includes commissions, underwriting, and other processing costs. On products that feature cash surrender values, the insurer may impose a penalty on any withdrawal, called a *surrender charge*, during the early policy years. A surrender charge recovers all or some of the acquisition cost from lapsing policyholders, and may deter lapsing during the surrender charge period. Not surprisingly, the surrender charge schedule is similar to the call schedule of a bond, with higher surrender charge in the early years. Some policies allow partial withdrawal up to a certain amount of the account value (say 10%) without penalty.

Given the long-term nature of liabilities, the interest rate risk can be significant. The duration of the liabilities can be so long that few assets have the duration to match the liabilities. Since inflation rates change over time, some long-term disability claims paid are related to the cost of living. For these products, inflation risk is a concern.

This overview underscores the challenges in valuing liabilities. On the one hand, an insurance policy is similar to an asset such as mortgage-backed securities with prepayment risk, interest rate risk, and options. On the other hand, insurance policies have no observed prices and are very long dated. How should we value these policies? We will discuss a representative sample of these insurance products that suggests how they should be valued, and hence managed, in the following sections.

Guaranteed Investment Contract

Perhaps the simplest insurance investment product is the guaranteed investment contract (GIC). Policyholders pay the face value to the insurer. The insurer can then guarantee a fixed interest rate over a term of one to ten years. The interest is generally accrued and paid at the termination date. In essence, the insurance company has issued a zero-coupon bond to the customer. Since the product design is relatively simple, insurers tend to compete for the funding by offering a competitive rate. The rate must also depend on the rating of the insurer. The higher the rating, the lower the interest rate required (or the lower the funding cost to the insurer.) Sometimes, the customers may not buy the GIC immediately. The customer, a plan, may wait until everyone in the group covered by the plan has made the contributions to his retirement. In these cases, the insurer may offer a GIC with a window period during which the funds are to be accumulated. Thus, the GIC is similar to a forward contract, where the payment is exchanged during the window period and at the termination date.

A GIC is one of the few insurance products that have daily market quotes, and therefore it has more market liquidity than other insurance products whose yields are tied closely to the Treasury spot curve. The fair value of a GIC would be discounted by the spot curve (transfer pricing curve of the firm) and would use the ROAS of the firm to determine the spread. The expenses for this product tend to be small. GICs are the insurance product that comes closest to representing a capital market security, and as a result they are often managed like a capital market instrument by the insurance companies.

Structured Settlement

When judgments are made in court, plaintiffs may be awarded a stream of payments. Or, after a lottery, the winners receive an annuity over 10, 25, or more years. Typically, the court or the lottery management auctions the annuity business to insurance companies, since neither the defendant in court nor the state government is in the business of managing money, particularly in administering a stream of payments for many years. When a court case results in a settlement, the defendant pays a lump sum to an insurance company that is responsible for paying the plaintiff in installments, as stated in the settlement. Similarly, after a lottery, the state government collects the income and pays a portion of the income to the winning insurance company in an auction. The winner of the auction receives a lump sum payment up front and is responsible for the long-term payments to the lottery winner. The state government collects the income net of the lump sum for the insurance company as the proceeds for the state government.

In general, these liabilities can be priced as a cash flow with a required option adjusted spread, by assuming some long-term interest rate that extends beyond the Treasury yield curve or the swap curve. This product is rather problematic to manage because the cash flow extends out where few bonds can match the payments. The duration of a structured settlement can be much longer than the bonds insurance companies can buy. In this case, their liabilities (commitments to a lottery winner, for example) are much longer than their assets. If interest rates fall over time, the reinvestments of the assets, at the prevailing lower market interest rates, will not be able to cover the liability payments. Insurance companies can use a short-term liability such as a GIC, along with the structured settlement, as one portfolio of liabilities. If it does so, the weighted average duration of the liability portfolio becomes shorter, and the company can then invest in assets such that it can manage the durations of the assets and liabilities in a way discussed in chapter 3. This way we can have a combined liability that may have a more manageable duration. But this portfolio has a characteristic of the barbell portfolio discussed in chapter 3, showing its sensitivity to the yield curve risk as measured by key rate duration, even though the portfolio is duration-matched by the assets.

SPDA: Individual Annuity

Annuities represent the reverse of life insurance. Instead of building up funds, annuities involve different contractual methods of liquidating a fund. The basic type is a *single-premium deferred annuity* (SPDA),[4] in which the policyholder pays a premium (single premium) to the insurance company. The company then credits a rate to the account. Usually, there is a minimum guaranteed rate. The account value then grows at the crediting rate, which is generally reset each year. In the event of death, the policyholder is paid the account value. The policyholder can also turn the account value into an annuity, requiring the insurer to pay a fixed amount every year for rest of the life of the policyholder. Beyond age 59.5, the policyholder can turn the policy into an annuity without the excise tax. But policyholders can generally annuitize before age 59.5 as well. But turning the SPDA into an annuity is very infrequent. More often, the policyholders withdraw the cash value of their funds when they need additional liquidity or when they believe that they can attain higher returns by investments other than the SPDA. Often the policy offers a guaranteed rate of return. The rate is assumed to be 3 percent.

The commission for an annuity, in general, is about 4%–6% or higher. Should the policyholder wish to withdraw the money from the account value, then there is a penalty during the first several years, often seven years, which is called a *surrender charge*. The surrender charge is often based on a schedule that declines to zero over time.

Fair valuation assumptions

For illustration, we will describe the valuation of an SPDA by considering a cell. A *cell* is a representative collection of policies that have similar or the same characteristics. The commonly used characteristics are age, sex, *issue age* (years since the issuance of the policy). We will consider a policy issued to a male age 50 on 1/1/2002. Historically, SPDA finds more willing buyers who are older than age 55, when saving for retirement becomes a growing concern.

The initial premium is assumed to be $100. On the day of purchase, the policyholder pays the premium for the contract. The insurance company receives the premium and pays the commissions. Some commissions are trailing, with a portion paid the following year. This feature is not assumed here. The commission is assumed to be 6%.

The interest rate paid to the policyholder as accruals to his account value is called the *crediting rate*. It is affected by the competition and is reset annually.

Suppose the current market crediting rate (the target rate) is based on the market yield of a portfolio that replicates the market broad-based index, which has a duration of five years. The target rate is modeled as the yield of a five-year constant maturity Treasury swap (CMT) minus 75 basis points. The renewal rate, or the new crediting rate for the in-force block, is the partial adjustment rate, adjusting 50 percent annually to the target rate, with a minimum guarantee of 4 percent. The crediting rate is reset annually. This discussion is summarized by the equations below.

Initial rate = initial five-year CMT = 0.052 (bond equivalent yield)

Target rate = current five-year CMT − 0.0075

Renewal rate = $Max \left[0.04, 0.5 \times \text{target rate} + 0.5 \times \text{prior crediting rate} \right]$

Reset frequency = annually

The lapsing behavior has to be modeled, in part using historical experience of the data on lapsing. Lapsing affects the duration of the product and introduces uncertainty to its profitability. There is the base lapse rate, where we assume that there is always some lapsing. The lapsing is also affected by factors such as the surrender charge and the spread between the target market rate and the insurer's rate.

We assume that the percentage lapse rate is given by an arc tan function in the variable x, which is equal to the market rate less the crediting rate and surrender charge. Functions other than the arc tan can be used to reflect the lapse behavior.

Policyholder surrender behavior is modeled by assuming the lapse rate to equal

$$A + 0.01575 \times \arctan \left[220 \times (\text{current 5-year CMT} - \right.$$
$$\left. \text{Current Crediting Rate} - \text{Current SC}/3) - 3.3 \right]$$

where

$$A = \begin{cases} 0.12 & \text{if } SC > 0 \\ 0.17 & \text{if } SC = 0 \end{cases}$$

where SC is the surrender charge, which is a time schedule. Typically, the schedule starts with a high charge of, say, 6% and declines linearly to 0% over five to seven years. These are percentages based on the account value, the amount received by the policyholder upon surrender. (See figure 11.3.)

This specification of the lapse function ensures that there is a base lapse rate at which, irrespective of the crediting rate, some policyholders always seek to lapse. This base lapse rate (A) increases when there is no surrender charge. The model seeks to show that the lapse experience increases with a wider spread (market rate − the crediting rate), but the lapse rates are bounded below by the base rate and bounded above by some maximum lapse rate. All the parameters (numbers in the lapse functions) are estimated from historical experience.

The lapse function is similar to the prepayment model of mortgage-backed securities in its use of historical experience to estimate its parameters. The lapse function is the behavioral model that each insurer estimates from its own database to better understand its customers, offering a product that fits their needs at a competitive but profitable price.

The cost structure is important and complex. There is an expense assigned to each policy that includes a maintenance cost based on the face value (typically 0.20% annually).

Fair valuation procedure

Given the assumptions above, we now proceed to the algorithm in determining the fair value of the SPDA.[5] For this purpose, we assume that the initial term structure is flat at 6%. The SMDA terminates at year 4 for simplicity. Since we use the extended Ho–Lee model, we assume the following spot volatility structure. (See figure 11.4.)

Year	1	2	3	4	5
Spot Volatility	0.1	0.095	0.9	0.085	0.8

Once the lattice is generated, cash flows can be generated along each interest path, using

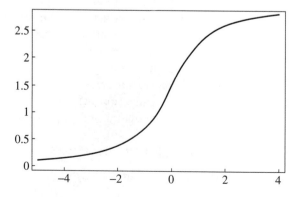

Figure 11.3 Arctan function. The arctan function is often used to model the lapse rate.

One-year interest lattice

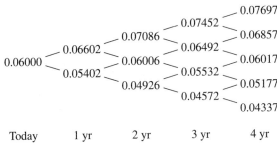

Five-year constant maturity swap rate

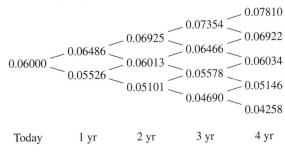

Figure 11.4 The one-year interest and the five-year constant maturity swap rate

the crediting rate, lapse function, and expenses. In this case, there are 16 (2^4) interest rate paths.

Step 1. Initialization   We begin with the face value, $100. The account value is assumed to be the face value at the beginning. At the end of the year, the crediting rate is determined by the crediting function, and the account value is adjusted to the credited amount.

Since we model the crediting rate as *Max* [0.04, 0.5 × target rate + 0.5 × prior credit rate], the crediting rate for each path, based on the five-year constant maturity swap rate given above, is shown in table 11.1.

Step 2. Determining the Maintenance and Expenses   Maintenance charges and expenses are deducted from the account value. Then we determine the lapse payment at the end of the year after adding the credited amount to the account value and deducting the expenses and charges. In taking the mortality rate into account, we can also determine the amount paid out. The remaining population of the account is then noted. We set the initial population at 1.

Step 3. Simulating Net Cash Flows   The cash outflow is the sum of the lapse payments, death payments, and expenses. It is determined for each interest rate scenario. We

Table 11.1 Scenarios and Crediting Rate

Scenario	Crediting rate
{0, 0, 0, 0}	{5.91, 5.34 4.85, 4.39}
{0, 0, 0, 1}	{5.91, 5.34 4.85, 4.39}
{0, 0, 1, 0}	{5.91, 5.34 4.85, 4.84}
{0, 0, 1, 1}	{5.91, 5.34 4.85, 4.84}
{0, 1, 0, 0}	{5.91, 5.34 5.30, 5.07}
{0, 1, 0, 1}	{5.91, 5.34 5.30, 5.07}
{0, 1, 1, 0}	{5.91, 5.34 5.30, 5.51}
{0, 1, 1, 1}	{5.91, 5.34 5.30, 5.51}
{1, 0, 0, 0}	{5.91, 5.82 5.54, 5.19}
{1, 0, 0, 1}	{5.91, 5.82 5.54, 5.19}
{1, 0, 1, 0}	{5.91, 5.82 5.54, 5.63}
{1, 0, 1, 1}	{5.91, 5.82 5.54, 5.63}
{1, 1, 0, 0}	{5.91, 5.82 6.00, 5.86}
{1, 1, 0, 1}	{5.91, 5.82 6.00, 5.86}
{1, 1, 1, 0}	{5.91, 5.82 6.00, 6.30}
{1, 1, 1, 1}	{5.91, 5.82 6.00, 6.30}

assume that the maintenance charges and the expenses are 0 for simplicity, and we model the lapse function as

$$A + 0.01575 \times \arctan\left[220 \times (\text{Current 5-year CMT} - \right.$$

$$\left. \text{Current Crediting Rate} - \text{Current SC}/3) - 3.3\right]$$

where

$$A = \begin{cases} 0.12 & \text{if } SC > 0 \\ 0.17 & \text{if } SC = 0 \end{cases},$$

The lapse rate and the lapse cash flow cash flow for each path are shown in table 11.2.

Table 11.2 Scenarios, Lapse Rates, and Lapse Cash Flows

Scenario	Lapse rate	Lapse cash flow
{0, 0, 0, 0}	{9.73, 9.79, 9.89, 15.09}	{10.31, 9.86, 9.42, 89.60}
{0, 0, 0, 1}	{9.73, 9.79, 9.89, 15.09}	{10.31, 9.86, 9.42, 89.60}
{0, 0, 1, 0}	{9.73, 9.79, 9.89, 15.38}	{10.31, 9.86, 9.42, 89.98}
{0, 0, 1, 1}	{9.73, 9.79, 9.89, 15.38}	{10.31, 9.86, 9.42, 89.98}
{0, 1, 0, 0}	{9.73, 9.79, 10.02, 15.21}	{10.31, 9.86, 9.57, 90.46}
{0, 1, 0, 1}	{9.73, 9.79, 10.02, 15.21}	{10.31, 9.86, 9.57, 90.46}
{0, 1, 1, 0}	{9.73, 9.79, 10.02, 15.62}	{10.31, 9.86, 9.57, 90.84}
{0, 1, 1, 1}	{9.73, 9.79, 10.02, 15.62}	{10.31, 9.86, 9.57, 90.84}
{1, 0, 0, 0}	{9.73, 9.85, 9.94, 15.14}	{10.31, 9.97, 9.57, 91.19}
{1, 0, 0, 1}	{9.73, 9.85, 9.94, 15.14}	{10.31, 9.97, 9.57, 91.19}
{1, 0, 1, 0}	{9.73, 9.85, 9.94, 15.47}	{10.31, 9.97, 9.57, 91.57}
{1, 0, 1, 1}	{9.73, 9.85, 9.94, 15.47}	{10.31, 9.97, 9.57, 91.57}
{1, 1, 0, 0}	{9.73, 9.85, 10.08, 15.27}	{10.31, 9.97, 9.74, 92.02}
{1, 1, 0, 1}	{9.73, 9.85, 10.08, 15.27}	{10.31, 9.97, 9.74, 92.02}
{1, 1, 1, 0}	{9.73, 9.85, 10.08, 15.77}	{10.31, 9.97, 9.74, 92.41}
{1, 1, 1, 1}	{9.73, 9.85, 10.08, 15.77}	{10.31, 9.97, 9.74, 92.41}

Step 4. Present Valuing the Cash Flows   Now use an arbitrage-free rate movement model to determine the fair value of the SPDA. We illustrate this with one path where the one-year interest rate rises and falls alternately. The scenario can be represented by {1, 0, 1, 0} where 1 denotes the rising case and 0 denotes the falling case. (See table 11.3.)

The one-year and five-year rates are derived with the extended Ho–Lee model. Lapse cash flow is determined by the lapse rate of the remaining in force, where the initial in force is 100 and the in force accrues at the crediting rate. The lapse cash flow at year 2, \$9.97, can be obtained as ($100 \times (1.0 + 0.0591) - \$10.31) \times (1.0 + 0.05827) \times 0.0985$ where 0.0591 and 0.05827 are the crediting rates at year 1 and year 2, respectively. 0.0985 is the lapse rate at year 1. \$10.31 is the lapse cash flow at year 1. The other lapse cash flows can be determined similarly. Discount rate is the one-year rate plus 0.75 percent, the credit spread. However, we assume ROAS to be 0. We will use the net proceeds to solve for ROAS at the time of sale. Present value factor at year n is $\exp[-\text{discount rate}(1) - \text{discount rate}(2) \cdots - \text{discount rate}(n)]$. Pathwise value is the present value of the lapse cash flow using the discount factors. Once the cash flows are generated, we can calculate their present value along each path. The present values are called pathwise values. The average of the pathwise values is the fair value. The fair value of the SPDA is \$95.2.

Now we consider the valuation of the SPDA at the time of sale. Assume that the proceeds are 98.5. ROAS is then determined to assure that the fair value equals the net premium received. In other words, ROAS is determined as the basis point spread that is required to net off the transfer rate such that the average of the pathwise value is 98.5. The ROAS is kept constant when we revalue the SPDA portfolio over a period of time, say every month or quarter, depending on the firm's management process. The result of the analysis is that such a spread is 12.5 basis points. Using the definition of profit release, we can calculate it to be 87.5 basis points. Duration is determined in relation to the proportional change in the market value of the SPDA with a shift of the yield curve by 10 basis points, keeping the credit spread and profit release constant. Duration is shown to be 0.34234 year. That is, a parallel rise of the yield curve of 10 basis point would lead to a reduction of the SPDA value by 0.34234%. These results are summarized below.

Premium	Initial cost	Net Proceeds	Profit Release	Credit Spread	ROAS	Duration
100	1.5%	98.5	87.50 bpt	0.75%	−0.125%	0.34234

Table 11.3 Present Value of the Cash Flows

Year	0	1	2	3	4
1-year rate	6.00%	6.60%	6.01%	6.49%	6.02%
5-year rate	6.00%	6.49%	6.01%	6.47%	6.03%
Crediting rate	5.91%	5.82%	5.54%	5.63%	n/a
Lapse rate	9.73%	9.85%	9.94%	15.47%	n/a
Lapse cash flow	—	10.31	9.97	9.57	91.57
In force	100	95.61	91.20	86.69	91.57
Discount rate	6.75%	7.35%	6.76%	7.24%	6.77%
Discount factor	1	0.9347	0.8685	0.8117	0.7550
Present value	—	9.63	8.65	7.77	69.14
Pathwise value	**95.20**				

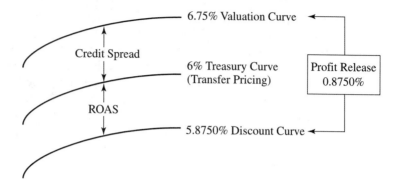

Figure 11.5 Components of spreads

The results can also be summarized by the components of the spreads. (See figure 11.5.)

Remarks

The description of the SPDA serves several purposes in this chapter. First, the arbitrage-free financial modeling can be applicable to nontraded financial instruments. Because the customers' lapse behavior is assumed to be dynamic, reacting to the spread between the crediting rate and the market rate, SPDA has an embedded option in which the insurer has sold an interest rate option to the policyholders. In using the fair value approach, we can identify the value and the risk of the embedded options under alternative crediting rate strategies. Second, the description shows that the crediting rate strategy can be approximated by market securities like constant maturity swaps, which have been described in earlier chapters. We have shown that the policyholders stand to benefit from the convexity charge of the constant maturity swap. The convexity of the constant maturity swap provides a higher expected return under interest rate uncertainty. The insurer can use the fair value approach to manage a somewhat complex asset/liability mismatching in interest rate risks. Third, this example shows how fair valuation can identify the profitability of the insurance product in economic terms, as opposed to book value terms. The use of ROAS is to isolate all these embedded option effects, and determine the profit release from the sale of the product over time.

Finally, there are many products similar to SPDA, and the description above illustrates the importance of the use of fair valuation and how fair values can be determined. For example, a product similar to SPDA is the flexible premium deferred annuity. As the name suggests, this product is similar to SPDA in that the annuity is deferred, but the premium is not paid in one payment. Instead, the policyholders can pay the premium in installments.

Variable Annuity

A variable annuity is a savings product that has grown significantly in recent years. At present, the total amount outstanding is approaching $1 trillion. The *Wall Street*

Journal devotes a large part of a page to reporting all the variable annuities available in the market. Major insurance companies have offered variations of this product to their customers. These products can be described by the following characteristics.

The insurance company acts as an asset manager for the policyholder. Asset management offers choices of funds to switch to, including fixed income and equity, and many types of funds within each category. Asset management fees can vary significantly from one variable annuity to another, and from fund to fund within a variable annuity. Since the insurer is acting as an asset manager, the variable annuity product is often reported in a separate account rather than in the general account of the firm's liabilities and assets. For the separate account, the policyholders in principle own the assets, and the insurance company is only managing the funds on their behalf.

Often there are age-dependent guarantees provided in the annuities. They may guarantee that at a certain future date (say in ten years) the account value will at least equal the initial premium. This variable annuity is said to have a *guaranteed minimum account value*. There are also minimum guarantees of the payment at death. When a policyholder lapses, he receives the account value of the annuity, but if he dies, the variable annuity may have a guaranteed minimum payment. This feature is called the *guaranteed minimum death benefit*. Another guarantee has a ratcheting feature guaranteeing the highest historical value of the account value at the anniversary dates over the period from the start date to the time of death, akin to a look-back option. This is an example of the *guaranteed minimum income benefit*. Another variable annuity allows the policyholder to partially withdraw from the account value at the book value, in essence offering the policyholder an American put option. This type of guarantee is called the *guaranteed minimum withdrawal benefit*. These are just some of the option features available in variable annuities. They are embedded in the annuities, instead of traded as derivatives in capital markets, but we will show that the same relative valuation methodology used to determine such options (look-back options, American options, European options) in chapter 7 applies to such insurance liabilities.

When the policyholder lapses, he receives only the account value, and may pay a surrender charge for early withdrawal. There is usually no surrender charge after a certain number of years (typically seven years.) Management fees and fees to cover the costs of guarantees, profits to the insurer, and expenses are all deducted from the account value, as in the case of the SPDA.

The guaranteed mortality death benefit is a put option on the account value offered to the policyholder. Of course, the policyholder has to die in order for the benefits to be collected. These options have a very long period to expiration. When a 60-year-old policyholder invests in a variable annuity, the life expectancy can be another 20 years or more.

Is the valuation correct even when the policyholders cannot optimally exercise these options, since benefits are paid only in the event of death? This confusion is caused by the term "option." To be more accurate, the guaranteed death benefits should be called "contingent claims." In the valuation of guaranteed benefits, the product features are valued as a contingent claim of the equity. The policyholders do exercise their options optimally. The "option" is "exercised" at death. For this reason, the guarantee is better termed a contingent claim and the relative valuation method applies.

Valuation procedure

The valuation procedure is similar to that of the SPDA. We begin with the face value F. Assuming that the asset funds are based on a stock index, we can determine the particular index return by using a path in the binomial lattice of a stock return. The account value at the end of the year is then calculated. Given the new index level, the guaranteed minimum death benefit (GMDB) is updated. If the GMDB is simply guaranteeing the face value, then it will remain equal to the face value F if the index level is low enough so that the GMDB is less than the face value. If the GMDB has a ratcheting feature, then we update it to the highest account value experienced up to that point in time.

Next, we deduct the charges from the account value. Charges include maintenance and expenses, along with charges for the GMDB. Then, as in the valuation procedure, we determine the lapse payment and the death payments, and update the remaining population in the portfolio. Add all the cash outflows at the end of each year, and generate the cash outflow for a stock index scenario in the binomial lattice. The average of the pathwise values determines the ROAS of the product. Fixing the ROAS over a time interval, as discussed above, the fair value of the variable annuity in the subsequent times can now be determined.

Remarks

Since the death benefits and other options can result in significant costs to the insurer, asset and liability management is needed to manage the guarantees written in the variable annuities. A valuation model, as described above, can be used for the quantification and the management of the guarantees. The above discussion illustrates that in the insurance market, there are many examples of "exotic" options, with significant option value, being long-dated together with significant outstanding face value.

Term Insurance

Term insurance, including group term, is the most widely held type of insurance contract. Term insurance pays a death benefit in the event of the death of the insured during the coverage period. The coverage period can vary from one to 40 years or even longer. The most popular term policies provide level death benefits with 10 or 20 years of level premiums. The popularity of term insurance stems from the low cost of protection and guaranteed premium rates that are common on individually sold policies. Sales of this product by brokers and independent agents are very sensitive to price. This means the insurer has to offer a competitive price in the marketplace to generate sales, resulting in a narrow profit margin. To remain profitable, close control over benefit payments and expenses is necessary.

To keep rates low, companies have introduced several tiers of risk classes with different premium rates. Elaborate underwriting, or risk classification, enables the insurer to stratify policyholders into different premium classes. Commissions to the sales force can run 85% of the first year's premium or more in the case of a general agent. Since this also covers agency overhead (rent, equipment, and support staff), much less is actually available to the sales agent.

The valuation model seems relatively straightforward at first glance. For an individual who buys a term insurance policy, the mortality table calculates the present value of the death benefits and the expenses. We then calculate the option adjusted spread (more appropriately the spread, since there is no option) that matches this present value of the cash outflows to the net premium. If we use a fixed spread off the spot curve for the subsequent period (before adjusting to a new required option adjusted spread) and apply the bond pricing model, we have a method to determine the fair value of the term insurance.

But term insurance is not just for one year. Policyholders have overwhelmingly opted for guaranteed premium rates, despite substantial discounts for accepting nonguaranteed premium rates. These are, in fact, forward contracts. Therefore, the value of the in-force business must take these future premiums into account. The in-force business will be projected to have a declining face value as the policyholders are assumed not to renew the contracts over time. The resulting liability can have a very high duration—sensitivity to the interest rate risks—usually associated with forward contracts. This will be discussed further in the section on whole life insurance, which is valued in the same way.

For example, suppose a term insurance policy has $10 premiums for $100,000 coverage. At time $t = 0$, we collect a $10 premium. Let us assume the persistency rate to be 90%. Then at beginning of the second year, we receive a $9 premium and an expected payout of $90,000 \times$ death rate at the end of the second year. This second year sale is equivalent to a one-year forward contract to deliver a one-year bond. The block of business of the term insurance is therefore like a series of forward contracts.

Immediate Annuity

An *immediate annuity* is somewhat like the opposite of term insurance. With term insurance, the policyholder pays a premium at the beginning and receives the death benefits at death. An immediate annuity pays a specified amount every year until death. The benefit of the immediate annuity is that it eliminates the risk of outliving the savings. That means an individual in retirement may need to draw down the principal of his savings when living expenses exceed the interest earned by the savings. In such cases, there may be a risk of exhausting the savings before death.

While receiving a fixed amount from the insurer may assure income until death, we have to note that the amount is the nominal amount, not factoring in the risk of inflation. Typically, a person does not buy an immediate annuity when he still has earning power. There is no reason to pay for the insurance and then receive the annuity while the person is still generating income for savings. For this reason, the immediate annuity is usually bought by people reaching retirement age.

Whole Life

Whole life provides protection to the policyholder for as long as the insured lives. The premiums are higher than term premiums for two reasons: (1) insurance is more expensive at the end of life (particularly after age 70) because of the higher mortality rate, and (2) the long-term nature of the whole life contract requires more conservative assumptions as the basis for guaranteed premiums than are used for term insurance. As experience emerges that is more favorable than the conservative basis underlying the premiums, "excess" profits are generated relative to profits that would emerge under premiums based on more realistic assumptions. Most whole life policies return "excess premiums" in the form of policyholder dividends. They are called *participating policies* because the policy-holder participates in the experience of the policy. There are very few nonparticipating policies. Individuals receive the face value of the life insurance contract on death. The premiums are usually level payments.

Policyholder dividends are a critical part of the whole life policy in the competitive sales environment. The policyholder has the option of receiving the dividend in cash; paying the annual premium payment and leaving the dividends with the insurer (accumulating with interest each year); or purchasing additional insurance. The last option is very popular in sales situations, since the reinvestment of dividends in the contract allows greater growth in cash value. Policyholder dividends are not subject to income tax, since they are a return of "excess" premiums. The buildup of cash value in a whole life insurance policy is not subject to income tax unless the policy is surrendered.

The premium is higher than the cost of insurance during the early policy years, resulting in positive cash flows. In later years, the cost of insurance exceeds the premiums and the deficit must be funded from the accumulation of the earlier gains. The funds set aside for this purpose are called the *policy reserves*, and the process of determining reserves is called *valuation*. Reserves do not recognize the actual experience of the policy, but follow conservative standards defined in state laws governing insurance. To protect policyholders who have developed significant reserves by paying premiums for several years, state laws also mandate that whole life insurance provide *nonforfeiture benefits*, or cash values, payable when the policyholder voluntarily terminates the policy. The calculation of the cash value is based on an actuarial formula which in simple terms is accumulated premiums less the theoretical cost of insurance and an allowance for acquisition expenses amortized over the premium-paying years.

The policyholder does not need to surrender the policy to access the cash value. He can borrow against the cash value. The policy loan interest rate may be a variable rate defined by a market index, or a fixed rate defined in the contract. The dividends usually reflect the policy loans, because loan interest is part of the investment income of the company. Historically, policy loans were low yielding assets relative to the rest of the insurer's portfolio. With 8% policy loan rates on some contracts, this is not universally true today.

The valuation of whole life insurance is similar to that of term insurance. The conservative premium is not all profit to the insurer, since the cash amount will be paid to the insured. The value of the product is the net of the present value of the policy premiums and the death benefits.

Universal Life

Universal life is a flexible premium policy that allows the insured to change the death benefit from time to time, in contrast to traditional policies that maintain premiums at a given level over a fixed contract period.

A *premium load*, or *front-end load*, is a charge the insurer deducts to cover a portion of the operating expenses. The balance of the premium is allocated to a policyholder account. This is an interest-bearing account with a minimum guaranteed rate (e.g., as 3%; interest in excess of the guaranteed amount is credited to the policyholder account. The excess interest may reflect a portfolio rate or new money rates (or some combination of the two). The portfolio rate is the yield of the portfolio that supports the life product (less a spread), and the new money rate is the prevailing market rate for similar policies.

Charges are deducted from the policyholder account for the cost of insurance (the cost of the death benefits) and for expenses which include the administrative maintenance costs.

Since premiums are deposited in a policyholder account, they function differently from whole life premiums, which are pure revenue to the insurer. Revenues of universal life products come from taking a portion of the premium as revenue, called *expense loading on premiums*; investment income earned in excess of interest credited to the policyholder account (interest rate spread); and revenues deducted from the account value for cost of death benefits and expenses. Most insurers impose a surrender charge (which is a source of revenue) to protect against lapses before the recovery of acquisition expenses.

A policy loan feature similar to the whole life loan feature is available to the policyholders. Since the policy loan interest rate can be quite different from the earned rate on other assets, the interest credited to the policyholder account is computed separately for "borrowed" and "unborrowed" amounts.

Premiums are flexible, and the crediting rate is a partial adjusted rate similar to the SPDA. Surrender charges are calculated as the surrender charge schedule (for example, linearly declining from $x\%$ to 0% over a time horizon of T years) times the specified face amount (in units).

As an illustration of the structure of a universal life policy, consider a policy with a face amount of $100,000 and a yearly premium of $1,000. Table 11.4 illustrates the different cost elements, and clearly demonstrates the "unbundling" of the "bundled" insurance contract. This table is purely illustrative and is not based on any product in the market.

Referring to table 11.4, we assume that the policyholder pays $1,000 each year to the account. $50 is deducted from the premium as "premium charges" when the premium is paid. Policy account charges are the amount taken from the account value for the maintenance costs, and cost of insurance is the cost that covers the death benefits. Both deductions are taken from the account monthly. For simplicity, we assume that the amounts are deducted at the end of the year. Interest is the amount credited to the

Table 11.4 The "Unbundling" of an Insurance Contract

						End of Year Values		
Policy Year	Premium Paid	Premium Charges	Policy Account Charges	Cost of Insurance	Interest	Account Value	Surrender Charge	Cash Surrender Value
1	1,000	50	60	200	59	749	4,500	0
2	1,000	50	60	220	111	1,530	4,200	0
3	1,000	50	60	240	165	2,345	3,900	0
4	1,000	50	60	260	221	3,196	3,600	0
5	1,000	50	60	280	280	4,086	3,300	786
6	1,000	50	60	300	342	5,018	3,000	2,018
7	1,000	50	60	320	406	5,994	2,700	3,294
8	1,000	50	60	340	474	7,018	2,400	4,618
9	1,000	50	60	360	545	8,093	2,100	5,993
10	1,000	50	60	380	619	9,222	1,800	7,422

The first number under Account Value, 749, can be obtained by (premium paid − premium charges − policy account charges − cost of insurance + interest), the account value at year 1. The account value at each subsequent year is defined in a similar way. The second number, 1530, is a sum of the account value at year 1 and the account value at year 2. The cash surrender value is Max[account value − surrender charge, 0].

account value, paid at the end of the period. Therefore the account value at the beginning of the year is the sum of the account value at the end of the previous year and premiums paid. And the account value at the end of the year is the account value at the beginning of the same year, net of premium charges, policy account charges, and cost of insurance, plus the interest. Surrender charges are specified in the contract. If the policyholder wants to lapse, then amount that he can take is Max(account value − surrender charge, 0).

The annual report is a statement of accounting of all transactions for the policy year, including the closing policyholder account value (the value of the policy to the hlder) and the cash surrender value (account value net of the surrender charges). Policyholders can easily observe the difference, and are more likely to lapse after the surrender charge period, when there are no charges imposed in surrendering, even if the difference is minimal. Disclosure of the interest crediting rate increases the propensity of policyholders to borrow or surrender when new money rates increase and the crediting rate does not increase proportionately. In this environment, the policyholders feels that their policy is not earning the market rate, and they would surrender, terminating the policy.

Modeling the economic value of universal life should recognize the positive correlation between interest rate changes and policyholder behavior, such as premium paid over time, lapse rates, and policy loan utilization. Modeling this explicitly provides an analytical tool for creating or validating interest rate crediting strategies that reflect current economic conditions appropriately.

Policy loan utilization, expressed as a percentage, is assumed to be

$$Loan = 100 \times Max\left[0.50, Min\left[0.15, 0.15 + A \times (5 \text{ year } CMT - CR)\right]\right]$$

where $A = 5$ or 10. That is, the percent of loans taken out of the cash value is assumed to be at least 15%. The greater the spread of the market rate net of the crediting rate, the higher the loan utilization rate. But there is a maximum utilization of 50%. These relationships are usually estimated from the historical data. The market rate is the five-year constant maturity Treasury rate (that is, the five-year prevailing Treasury bond rate), as explained in chapters 3 and 7. We use a rather simple model to illustrate the salient features of the product. The policy loan utilization may depend on a market rate more complex than that described, a constant five-year rate.

An important difference between universal life and whole life is the dynamic premium flows. The policyholder can increase or decrease the premium contributions every year. One possible model of this behavior is given below.

Dynamic premium =

$$\text{base premium} \times Max\left[0.50, \{1.20 - 25 \times (5 \text{ year } CMT - CR)\}\right] \quad (11.6)$$

Referring to equation (11.6), the model assumes the policyholder has a base premium level. The new premium is at least 50% of the base premium. But the new premium amount increases with the crediting rate relative to the market rate, and in this case the market rate is assumed to be the five-year CMT rate. If the policy pays the market rate, the policyholder will contribute 120% of the base premium. If the crediting rate exceeds the market rate, the new premium can be even higher. These factors may be added to the model, but the creation of fair value works the same as for the whole life insurance model.

Variable Universal Life

This type of policy is the same as universal life, except that the assets can be invested in equity and the returns to the policyholders are specifically related to the returns on the assets, as opposed to being determined by a formula-driven crediting strategy. Thus, the death benefits vary according to the performance of the assets of the underlying contracts. Therefore, once the policyholder transfers assets to equities, the risk of investment performance is carried entirely by the policyholder. For a universal life contract, the insurer guarantees a minimum rate of return. Universal life policies that were designed and marketed in an era of high interest rates, such as the 1970s and 1980s, may have guarantees that became meaningful (valuable to the policyholder and risky to the insurer) in the interest rate climate of the 1990s. These guarantees cannot be ignored in valuation.

Another difference between universal life and variable universal life is the regulatory governance. Universal life is subject to the laws of state governments and the regulations of state insurance departments. VUL is subject to these regulations as well, but because the assets can be invested in equity, it is considered an investment and subject also to regulations of the Securities and Exchange Commission, a regulatory arm of the federal government. For this reason, surrender charges, which are considered an expense load, are subject to limits based on the premiums paid, like an investment product, rather than on the units of insurance purchased, as in some insurance products. Compensation is subject to federal limits as well, and is disclosed in the prospectus that must be delivered before a sale can be made.

Taxonomy of the Products

We have covered a range of life insurance products in this chapter. The main issue is to combine the mortality table and the lapse behavior of the policyholders to simulate the future cash flows. The cash flows are then used to determine the fair value by means of the arbitrage-free models. Different insurance products are combinations of different basic characteristics of a life insurance product. These characteristics are summarized below.

1. Insurance inflows can be flexible, fixed for multiple periods, or single premium
2. Investments (tax-deferred investment fund). Most insurance products offer the policyholders returns depending on the firm's investments; though the structure of these returns varies by product. Some products have account value that depends on the crediting rate generated from the investment portfolio; some policies have cash value that depends on dividends that usually have a target rate; and some have cash values that depend on the separate account where the insurer manages the asset on the policyholders' behalf, collecting management fees.
3. Payout methods. Insurance products have different means to provide payouts to the policyholders. One is providing dividends to their cash accounts. Another is allowing the policyholders to annuitize at retirement. Policyholders can borrow against their cash value; these loans are called *policy loans*. Or policyholders can lapse, withdraw from the account, or have benefits paid at their death.
4. Guarantees and features. Insurance products offer different guarantees, as well as minimum investment guarantees. For example, SPDA offers a minimum guarantee of crediting rate, and a variable annuity offers guaranteed minimum death benefits.

11.7   Pension Liabilities

Employers provide pension benefits to their employees via pension plans. A *pension plan* is a financial arrangement between two parties: the sponsors and the participants. Under the agreement, the sponsors make periodic payments into an investment fund, called the pension fund. The fund provides the capital for retirement benefits as part of the compensation for the employees' services to the firm. The participants are the employees who provide the services to the firm and receive the pension benefits. The manager of the fund is called the *trustee*.

There are two types of pension plans: *defined contribution* and *defined benefits*. In a defined contribution plan, the participants bear all the risks of the performance of the pension fund. The sponsor deposits the funds into an investment fund for the employees, according to the agreement. The cost of the pension plan to the sponsor is relatively simple to determine because the contribution to the fund and the cost can be treated as part of the compensation package for the employees' services, a component similar to salaries.

By way of contrast, a defined benefit plan obligates the sponsor to agreed pension payments in the future. Usually an employee is entitled to receive a pension payment, an anuuity, in retirement after a certain period of service at the firm. After a certain number of years of service, the employee has the right to receive earned pension benefits even if he leaves the firm. Such benefits are *vested*. *Nonvested benefits* are therefore obligations to the firm depending on whether the employee remains with the firm. These future obligations to meet the funding of pension benefits are pension liabilities to the firm.

There are several present-value measures of this pension liability to the firm. The simplest is called the *vested benefit obligations* (VBO). It is the present value of the pension benefits, assuming the same pay level of the employees. *Accumulated benefit obligations* (ABO) extend from VBO. They include the nonvested benefits, but at the present pay level. Estimating ABO is more complicated because we have to estimate the likelihood of the participants forefeiting the pension benefits by leaving the firm. Further complicating the determination the present value of the pension benefits is incorporation of the projected pay increase. This measure requires an estimate of the future pay level, which requires the estimate of the future inflation rate and other economic assumptions that may affect the future salaries. This present-value measure is called *projected benefit obligations* (PBO).

The discount rate for determining pension liabilities for PBO or ABO is approximately the yield of a 20-year AA-rated bond. Since the pension benefits are cash outflows for the sponsor starting from the retirement of the participants, the liability often has long durations—typically 15 years. The pension actuaries are responsible for determining the PBO and ABO values for the sponsors.

The pension liability is not treated independently on the balance sheet. The PBO or ABO is tied to the value of the pension fund assets. Today, a typical pension fund portfolio has an allocation of 60% in equity and 40% in debt. The duration of the debt in the asset portfolio tends to be medium-term. As a result, there is a significant mismatch in market risks between the assets and liabilities. The assets have significant equity risk and the liabilities have significant duration risks. However, these risks are not reflected entirely in the balance sheet because for most firms, the value of the assets is based on the calculated value in accordance with the accounting rules and not on the fair value.

We then consider the net value of the assets and the pension liability value expressed as PBO or ABO. When the net value is positive, the pension plan is overfunded; when it is negative, the plan is underfunded. This funding number goes into balance sheet information.

The pension income item that appears in the income statement is more complicated. The complication arises from both the assets and the liabilities. We will deal with the assets first. If we use the actual returns of the assets in the pension fund—defined as the income from the interest, dividends, and any unrealized or realized capital gain of the pension fund portfolio over the accounting year—then the pension income will result in a volatile earning number for the firm. As was explained above, the mismatch of risks of the pension assets and liabilities is significant. In order to smooth the income, the firm can report an "expected return" for the portfolio. The expected return is an estimate of the long-run return of the portfolio. For example, a typical pension fund has an asset allocation of 60% equity and 40% debt. The reported expected return may be 7%. Then the implied equity return will be 8.3% and the debt return 5%. The assumed return on assets affects only the reported income of pension investment. It reflects the average rate of earnings expected on the funds invested or to be invested.

On the liability side, we decompose the charges to three components: *service cost, interest cost,* and *amortization.* Service cost is the increase of PBO attributable to employee service during the period. These projected benefits depend on a number of assumptions that include the changes in the firm's number of employees, changes in overall compensation, and any changes in the actuarial assumptions (e.g., life expectancy, employee turnover, and rate of salary increases). Some estimate may even assume future renegotiation of union contracts.

Interest cost is the growth in PBO during a reporting period. It is the product of the discount rate and the PBO at the beginning of the period. The discount rate is the same as the one used in determining the present value of the PBO.

Amortization is used to smooth the reported pension income. It includes the amortization of gains/losses, the cumulative difference between expected and actual returns on assets, and/or changes in obligations. It is not required if the net recognized gain or loss at the beginning of the period is within a minimum range. The limit is 10% of the greater of the PBO and the fair value of the plan assets at the beginning of the period.

To illustrate, let us consider the following calculation of the pension investment income. Consider a pension benefit of an employee. He has 15 years until retirement, and the benefit pays an annuity of $1000 per year for ten years. Suppose that the discount rate is determined by the actuary to be 8%. Then the service cost is the present value of ten payments of $1000 starting in 15 years. The present value is determined by the use of the discount rate of 8%.

Suppose further that the value of the pension liabilities is $100 million and of pension assets, $200 million where the asset value exceeds the liability value. And let us assume that the expected return on plan assets is 9% and the discount rate for the obligation is 6%. Then

Expected return on asset $200 × 9%

Interest cost $100 × 6%

Pension investment income is the expected return on asset—the service cost net of interest cost.

By way of contrast, in fair valuation we determine the pension assets and liabilities separately. The asset portfolio value can be determined using the financial models discussed thus far for assets without liquid market prices. Otherwise, market prices are used. For the liability portfolio, we would use a transfer pricing curve to determine the present value of the liability cash flows. The fair value approach would provide mark to market value information on the combined value of assets and liabilities, allowing the sponsor to better understand the overfunding or underfunding as determined by the capital market. The variations of the overfunding/underfunding value also provides the sponsors with the appropriate measure of risks that the pension plan has introduced to the firm's capitalization. The pension income as measured by the fair valuation approach is the total return of both the assets and the liabilities over the period, taking all the realized and unrealized capital gains or losses into account.

One reason for the slow adoption of the fair value approach is that this accounting method may lead to significant volatility of the firm's reported earnings. In this case, it has been argued that the sponsors would use less equity in their pension funds, and longer term debt to reduce the mismatch of the asset and liability risks. As a result, the investment of the pension funds would be shorter-term focused and would not take a longer horizon. We will revisit this debate on fair value account in chapter 16.

11.8 Applications of the Financial Models to Liability Management

Pricing

Actuarial pricing is the approach taken to decide on the premium charged on a product with a particular design such that the insurer can be assured that the product can be sold profitably. The required spread for shareholders' return is often used in product pricing. Typically, the cash flows of the product (e.g., SPDA, variable annuity, whole life) are projected, and then the net cash flows from the assets and liabilities are discounted at the shareholders' required rate of returns. This present value must exceed the required surplus, the capital required to support the product, in order to be considered profitable.

To the extent that the liability can be replicated by capital market instruments, we have shown in this chapter that the liability can be valued using the relative valuation methodology. And the profitability of the liability can then be evaluated. The relative valuation methodology that we have discussed is often called the risk-neutral valuation. We assume that the interest rate movements are arbitrage-free, such that all default-free bonds have expected returns equaling the risk-free rate. Similarly, all equity returns also equal the risk-free rate. Then the present values of stochastic cash flows of the liabilities are determined by being discounted at the risk free rate.

Therefore, the actuarial pricing methodology differs from the risk-neutral valuation by the use of market probabilities versus the use of risk-neutral probabilities. Chapter 4 described the differences of market probabilities and risk neutral probabilities. For this reason, if the "required rate of returns of the shareholders on the product is chosen appropriately, the actuarial pricing method provides the same fair value of the liability. This observation is made by Babbel, Gold and Merrill (2002) and Girard (1999)

Use of Market Analytics

When we have a consistent methodology to value the liabilities relative to the traded securities in the capital markets, we can utilize the same set of analytical tools for both sides of the balance sheet of financial institutions.

For managing interest rate risks, we can use effective durations to measure the sensitivities of the assets and the liabilities, and as a result we can determine the impact of the interest rate risks on the firm's equity—the asset value net of the liability value as measured by fair value (or economic value, and not book value). The use of key rate durations enables us to implement more precisely the hedging strategies or risk management strategies to deal with the changing shapes of the yield curve. As discussed in chapter 6, when interest rate volatilities are high or the dynamic hedging positions are not revised frequently enough, convexities should also be used in managing interest rate risks. Similarly, delta and gamma measures calculated from the fair value model of the liabilities should be used for managing the equity risks.

The use of pathwise values of both the assets and liabilities enables us to determine the type of embedded options in liabilities more precisely, so that we can use the assets to hedge the liabilities. Thus ensuring the sale of liabilities can release more predictable profits to the shareholders. This pathwise hedging methodology was discussed in section 6.11, with an example given in section 10.6.

The use of OAS durations for the assets and ROAS durations for liabilities enables us to determine the risks of each market segments and product segment on the balance sheet. These durations can then be used to study the diversification effect of investing in different capital market segment and its impact on the product mix that the insurer sells.

In summary, in the previous chapters we have reviewed many capital market strategies in pricing and management of assets. These techniques can be used for liabilities, and the main benefit is enabling senior management to integrate product design and management with capital market instruments. As a result, insurers can better manage the risks of the liability portfolio and sell their products at more appropriate prices.

11.9 "Not If, But When"

In early 1992, I was invited to explain arbitrage-free valuation to a senior executive of a major life insurance company. In one hour, I went from the Black–Scholes model to the valuation of SPDAs to the management of risks.

At that time, the book value approach was the standard in valuing many insurance products for financial reporting purposes. Thus it would be considered radical to contemplate valuing insurance products using a fair value approach for accounting purposes. From a market valuation perspective, armed with contingent claims valuation tools, many actuarial professionals would like to imagine that it would be more appropriate to use fair value than liability reserves.

And in fact this approach is more consistent with many existing pricing models and asset and liability management (ALM) models. However, for accounting purposes, this is not the norm. In a more subtle way, we have seen that embedded options cannot be measured by a historical, accrued experience approach. Further, the term "reserve" can have multiple meanings. It can be defined as the value of the liability, and at other times it can be interpreted to mean the "conservative estimate" of the cost, albeit that measure may not be conservative at all because the discounting methodologies often are not determined by market prices.

For these reasons, one would tend to agree with some actuarial professionals that it is not a matter of if, but a matter of when, fair value financial reporting will be accepted. Following the thought process from the Black–Scholes model to the SPDA model would be meaningful and practical. At least, that was what I thought.

At the end, the senior executive looked at me, and his eyes were as motionless as his face. After a long pause, he said, "You seem to speak in a different language. There is no link from what I do to what you said." A long silence prevailed. His assistant came to the rescue with a positive spin: "Maybe we have planted some valuable seeds in our subconsciousness."

Unfortunately, insurance products are complex and nontradable, often have very long maturities, and are highly regulated. They have many risk attributes that differ from a Treasury bond or a swap. Yet fair valuation believers seem to agree that fair value accounting will ultimately become the insurance financial reporting standard. But when? When I asked my actuarial friend about this issue of "when," he checked his mortality tables and pondered aloud: "In my lifetime?"

As I learned in subsequent years, the difficulties of applying the fair value approach to actuarial operational procedures are not only a matter of accepting the concepts of market valuation. There are other regulatory impediments that are rigid enough to deter us from implementing fair values. The standardization of performance measures requires any use of a fair value approach to be consistent with the prevailing measures of profitability—which often is not possible. There is also a lack of incentives for change. Many of the products are long-dated and the values are based on book accounting. There aren't many managers who are concerned with the performance of the business or profitability of a product over a 10–20 year planning period. Often they are more concerned with the reported book profit. In chapter 16, we will revisit some of these issues again.

11.10 Summary

This chapter has provided an overview of valuing liabilities. The main aspects distinguishing liabilities from assets are the lack of markets, the lack of prices, and the very long-term duration. For this reason, we propose that the valuation of liabilities should be based on a transfer pricing curve and financial modeling should incorporate behavioral models.

This chapter also has shown that contingent claim valuation is important not only to value securities in capital markets, but also to many financial instruments on the balance sheets. We have shown that savings and deposit accounts are option embedded because the customers' withdrawal and deposit behaviors are affected by interest rate levels. We have shown that property and casualty development costs are dependent on the inflation rate, which is correlated to the interest rate risks. Life insurance policies, fixed and variable annuities, and other life products are nontraded financial instruments that have both interest rates and equity embedded options. Contingent claims valuation models can be applied to these nontraded financial instruments.

A required option adjusted spread must be introduced so that profits can be released over time. In the absence of market prices, there needs to be a systematic procedure to value liabilities. The ability to value each item on a balance sheet means that we must have a procedure to value the entire balance sheet. Then we can analyze the holdings or equity of the firm.

This chapter reached another milestone of the book. We have covered the valuation methodologies for a broad range of instruments. If the reader now opens the *Wall Street Journal*, section C, "Money and Investing," he can turn to the last pages devoted to the market prices of securities and find that nearly all the securities reported there have been discussed. We have discussed Treasury bonds, notes, and bills. Also reported are the U.S. Treasury STRIPS and inflation-linked bonds. We have discussed the government agency bonds, Fannie Mae and Freddie Mac issues. For interest rate derivatives, we have discussed Treasury bonds and notes, LIBOR and Euro futures, bond options, CMO sequentials, PACs, guaranteed investment contracts, high yield bonds, variable annuities, leaps, index funds, index options, and corporate bonds. We have shown how different fixed-income sectors are related and how embedded options in these financial instruments affect their value and behavior. Therefore, the price quotes reported every day should not behave like random numbers drawn from an urn, as if capital markets were like lotteries. We have identified the economic relationships of these prices, and these relationships in turn have been described by the financial models presented in previous chapters.

There has not been a discussion of tax-exempt bonds and the municipal bonds. These bonds are tangential to the interests of this book and have been omitted for the time being. At the same time, there have been discussions of many instruments that are not reported in the *Wall Street Journal* because these instruments, such as liabilities, are not traded in the exchanges and over-the-counter markets.

We have not dealt with equity in detail. Equity is intimately related to corporate finance, which concerns the valuation of a firm. We propose that the firm is a contingent claim on the business risk. For this reason, equity also can be viewed as contingent claims on the business risks. Part III of the book will take a departure from valuing the securities in the marketplace and focus on the management of a firm. However, we will revisit the issue of valuing equity after our discussion on corporate finance. Looking ahead, the ability to value the balance sheet, and hence the equity value of the firm, is not to say we can value the firm. The value of a going firm has to include the future sales; this problem will be tackled in chapter 12.

Notes

1. The funding cost is a rate of return on the part of the policyholder.

2. For example, the spread is 1 percent for the 30-year liability. By the profit release approach, we will get 1 percent profit over 30 years. However, we will get the present value of the 1 percent spread over 30 years at the initial period according to the gain-on-sale approach.

3. The adjustment of the model to accommodate this observation is straightforward.

4. The SPDA model is based on Ho (2000). The equations on page 391, 392, 394, and 402 are taken from Hohmann (1995).

5. Further explanations and a numerical example are given in Ho (1999).

References

Babbel, D., and C. Merrill. 2000. *Valuation of Interest-sensitive Financial Instruments,* rev. ed. New Hope, PA: Society of Actuaries, Frank J. Fabozzi Associates.

Babbel, D., and C. Merrill. 1998. Economic valuation models for insurers. *North American Actuarial Journal*, 2 (3), 1–17.

Babbel, D., J. Gold, and C. Merrill. 2001. Valuation of insurance liabilities: The bullet GIC as an Example. *Risk and Rewards*, February, 1, 4–7.

Beeson, M. 1998. Objectives of financial statement measurements, session 73: Fair value of insurance liabilities. *Society of Actuaries, Spring Meeting*. Maui, June 15–17.

Doll, D. 1997. Liabilities valuation. In *Fair Value of Liabilities*, E. Altman and I. T. Vanderhoof, eds. Burr Ridge, Ill.: Irwin.

Embrecht, P. 2000. Actuarial vs. financial pricing of insurance. *Journal of Risk Finance*, 1 (4), 17–26.

Giraldi, C., et al. 2000. Insurance optional. *RISK*, 87–90, April.

Girard, L. 1996. Fair valuation of liabilities—Are the appraisal and option pricing methods really different? *Risk and Rewards*, 25 (March), 1, 5–7.

Girard, L. 2000. Market value of insurance liabilities: Reconciling the actuarial appraisal and option pricing methods. *North American Actuarial Journal*, 4 (1), 31–49.

Grosen, A., and P. L. Jorgensen. 1999. Fair valuation of life insurance liabilities: The impact of interest rate guarantees, surrender options, and bonus policies. Working paper, Aarhus University, Denmark.

Ho, T. S. Y. 2000. Market valuation of liability: Transfer pricing, profit release and credit spread. In *The Fair Value of Insurance Business*, Irwin T. Vanderhoof and Edward I. Altman, eds. Amsterdam: Kluwer.

Ho, T. S. Y., A. Scheitlin, and K. Tam. 1995. Total return approach to performance measurement. In *The Financial Dynamics of the Insurance Industry*, E. I. Altman and I. T. Vanderhoof, eds. Burr Ridge, Ill.: Irwin.

Hohmann, J. 1995. Fair value of life insurance company liabilities. Working paper. American Academy of Actuaries, Washington, DC.

Koltisko, J. 2000. Market value of liabilities. Presentation at the Society of Actuaries, San Diego.

Merton, R. 1999. In *Theory of Risk Capital in Financial Firms—The New Corporate Finance Where Theory Meets Practice*, Donald H. Chew, Jr., ed., 2nd ed. New York: McGraw-Hill.

O'Brien, J. M. 2000. Estimating the value and interest rate risk of interest-bearing transactions deposits. Research paper, Federal Reserve System.

Reitano, R. R. 1997. Two paradigms for the market value of liabilities. *North American Actuarial Journal*, 1 (4), 104–129.

Wallace, M. 1997. Performance measurement using transfer-pricing. Working Paper, Transamerica Corp.

Wallace, M. 1999. Fair value accounting for financial liabilities. In *The Fair Value of Insurance Business*, 153–190, Amsterdam: Irwin T. Vandenhoof and Edward I. Altman, eds..

PART III

CORPORATE FINANCE

12

Valuation of a Firm: The Business Model

Corporate management begins with understanding the firm's business model. A business model can be described as a contingent claim on the business risk by stating the underlying risks of the business, the cost structure (variable and fixed costs) of the business, and the allocation of the operating income to the claimants. The approach is an extension of the Merton model to include the operating leverage. Such a financial modeling of a firm enables us to appropriately determine the expected returns of equity; to explore arbitrage opportunities between equity and bond pricing; to determine the relative value of equities in similar market sectors; and to implement other equity portfolio valuation and strategies. In essence, financial modeling of the business model provides a framework to analyze equities as contingent claims, which has broad implications.

A firm is an economic entity that has three major components: an *organization struc-ture* consisting of its owner, managers, and employees; a *production process* that gen-erates goods and services; and a *financial process* that provides financing for projects and distributions of revenues to its stakeholders. The production and financial processes to-gether is called the *business process*. A firm can provide services such as brokerage or travel, or it can manufacture widgets, or it can produce intangible assets such as know-how to develop patents. A firm can have many different statuses, ranging from a startup company that is building its first client base, to a mature company that is experiencing steady, recurring revenue, to a struggling company on the brink of bankruptcy. All these firms have a management organization, a production process and a financial process.

The organization structure has a charter that defines the roles and responsibilities of the managers and shareholders. The managers are the agents who act on behalf of the shareholders. Sometimes the shareholders manage the firm themselves, rather than hire managers. Therefore, the managers and the shareholders are not mutually exclusive. The organization structure further specifies how the business units are related to each other and are managed by the headquarters.

The production process generates goods and services to the economy. In chapter 2, we discussed that corporations or firms are fundamental units for real sectors, and the production process describes all the activities involved in producing the goods. For example, consider a manufacturer that makes widgets. Its production process involves the inputs of raw materials, the making of widgets, and the distribution of the final product.

The financial process managed by the chief financial officer has two major compo-nents: financing and corporate finance. Financing seeks external or internal funding for projects or for the production processes. Corporate finance deals with the distributions of the funds to its stakeholders. For example, the firm has a *capital structure*, which specifies the relationships of all the claims on the firm's assets and profits. The capital structure determines the proportion of the stockholders' and bondholders' claims on the firm. The bondholders have various types of bonds, such as floating-rate notes, fixed coupon bonds, short-term obligations, and long-term debentures. Corporate finance determines the mix of these claims.

A business model describes the three components of the firm and shows how they contribute values to the shareholders. The specification of the business model for a firm is important because it explains the business objective of the firm and the economic reasons for its existence. The business model ties the real sector (the production process) and the financial sector (the financial process) together. This chapter begins to build the links between the production and financial processes by developing a business model of a firm. Such a business model enables us to determine the relationships between the business process and the value of the financial claims on the firm.

How are the risks of generating profits transferred to shareholders and other claimants in the capital structure? How are the claims and shares valued? What do we mean by the links between the financial assets and real assets within the context of a firm? How, precisely, do financial assets complement the real assets? These questions are related to the valuation of the firm and the financial claims on its values.

This chapter will first describe the salient features of a firm and steps to determine a firm's value. Then we discuss some of the standard methodologies to determine the value of a firm. We then describe the MM theory that allows us to use the discounted free cash flow method, which is an application of the DCF method in valuing securities. Finally, we describe a contingent claim valuation model of a firm and show that it can have important implications in securities valuation and in capital investment decisions.

In sum, firm valuation has broad implications for many aspects of capital markets and corporate finance. It is the focus of much research and is the subject of this chapter.

12.1   Descriptions of a Firm

The method of valuating a firm has to take into consideration that firm's business processes. For instance, mining companies' values are based, in large part, on the commodities' values. Barrick Gold is the second largest gold producer in North America. The company has a capitalization (market value of equity) of $5.6 billion. It produces 4–5 million oz at a cash cost of $145/oz. But the market price of gold changes with the market supply and demand, thus affecting the firm's value. Utility companies require significant capital outlays to produce their outputs, whose prices may be regulated. For example, CINergy Corp. has over 1.4 million customers for electricity and 0.5 million for gas in Ohio, Indiana, and Kentucky. The firm has a capitalization of $4.8 billion. It has projected significant construction expenditures of $2.0 billion through 2004, and its net income is $400 million.

The firm's value may not be tangible resource-based. Financial institutions derive much of their incomes from servicing large balance sheets of financial assets and liabilities. For example, the Federal National Mortgage Association, more commonly known as Fannie Mae, is a government-sponsored enterprise that functions to increase the availability of mortgage credit for home buyers. Its capitalization is $69.8 billion, with total assets of $575 billion and a relatively low book equity value of $16 billion. It must manage its large portfolio as part of the business. Retail chain companies leverage on their chain stores for their distributions. For example, Wal-Mart is the largest retailer in North America, operating mainly a chain of 3000 discount stores. It has a capitalization of $203 billion and its success is based on efficient operation.

Firms may not have stable income but still command high valuation. Technology companies expense a significant portion of their revenues in research and developments.

Amgen is the world's largest independent biotechnology company, with a capitalization of $64.8 billion. Its research and development spending is $823 million (or 24.6% of revenue), and its net income is $1 billion.

Clearly, these firms are not alike; they provide different services to the economy. The firm value of each business depends on its functions. Each firm has its own way of organizing its business to generate profits. Moreover, each firm requires its own business model because it has its own risk and return profiles. In order to analyze firms, we need to have a consistent framework to compare their business models so that there is a relative valuation procedure across the firms. In other words, in order to compare two firms that have different business models, we need to determine how the business model affects each firm's values.

To determine the value of a firm, we can follow the following steps:

1. Business model. The business model is concerned with the means by which the firm generates profits. It describes the nature of the business and the strategies of the management.
2. Competitive advantages and profitability. The profitability of the business model is evaluated within the context of its competitive advantage. The business environment and its competitors are important in defining the value of the firm. The competitiveness of the business or the growth potential in the market should be analyzed. The competitiveness of the firm within its sector is an important factor in evaluating the viability of its business model.
3. Financial analysis and forecasts. Financial analysis is the first step in the quantification of the description and valuation of the firm. The most basic sources of information are the balance sheets, income statements, retained earning statements, and uses and sources of funds statements. Then financial ratios are used to compare the performance and valuation of the firms. The financial analysis, on one hand, provides validation of the business model, and on the other hand, provides a framework to project the returns to the shareholders or generally to the claimants on the firms.
4. Valuation. In order to value the firm, the forecasts of sales and the firm's profitability will be provided. Furthermore, the risks embedded in the business model are described.

Starbucks Coffee Japan—An Illustration

We will use Starbucks Coffee Japan to illustrate the above four steps.[1]

Business model

Starbucks Coffee Japan is a joint venture of Starbucks Corp. based in Seattle, Washington, and Sazaby Inc., Japan. It has pioneered the development of the specialty coffee shop in Japan. The company opened its first outlet on the Ginza, in Tokyo, in August 1996 and had grown to 226 outlets by the end of March 2001.

The business model is based on three salient features. First, it defines the standard for specialty coffee shops to maintain a high profit margin; second, it develops brand recognition to increase customer base and return on investment; third, it integrates Sazaby's local management with Starbucks Corp. global merchandising know-how.

Competitive advantage and profitability

In Japan there were nine national specialty coffee shop chains with 1,428 stores, in the fiscal year ending in 2001. The total coffee shop market is ¥1.3 trillion but has been declining steadily since the end of fiscal year 1999, with total sales down 4.4 percent. The specialty coffee market has only about 5 percent of ¥1.3 trillion, but it has grown by 15–20 percent a year. Starbucks Coffee Japan offers a range of specialty coffees in a different environment—an alternative lifestyle.

The main competitors' price for coffee is significantly lower, ¥180 versus ¥280 per cup. Starbucks Coffee Japan has a higher profit margin. Its success must rely on the uniqueness of its brand and merchandising in creating a new market.

Financial analysis and forecasts

The high fixed cost reflects the initial cost of building a management system for the company. It is expected that the fixed cost will not increase in a significantly in the coming years, because the management feels that infrastructure of the firm has been built and therefore no significant overhead costs will be required in the future. Starbucks Coffee Japan differs from some other chain stores because it is not a franchise; it does not license its stores or share profits with its managers. Instead, Starbucks Coffee Japan owns all of the branches, and it pays a local manager to run each store. As a result, the fixed costs are kept high relative to the firm's sales while keeping variable costs low. This, in turn, generates a high operating leverage. If sales are high, profits will be significant. But if the sales are low and the profit is negative, Starbucks is still obligated to pay fixed costs. (See table 12.1.)

For this reason, the profit margin will increase while the *gross profit margin* of 71.16 percent will remain high. The company has been reporting losses since the founding of the company and so there have been no tax payments.

The balance sheet is relatively straightforward, reflecting the growth stage of the firm. It has a significant investment position that is to be used for capital expenditures. The investments are mainly rent deposits and reserves. The fixed assets are mainly stores, mostly in Tokyo, that sell the products. The funding is mostly equity injected by the joint venture partners. (See table 12.2.)

Valuation

In 2002, Starbucks Coffee Japan had an initial public offering of ¥90.88 billion. There are 1.42 million shares outstanding and the share price at the evaluation date is ¥64,000.

Table 12.1 Income Statement of Starbucks Coffee Japan

Income Statement 2001	(billion ¥)
Sales	29.13
Cost of sales	8.40
SG&A expenses	19.16
Operating Profit	1.57
Nonoperating income	−0.15
Pretax profit	1.42
Tax and interests	−0.02
Profit	1.44

Note: The data are based on March 2001.

Table 12.2 Balance Sheet of Starbucks Japan

Balance Sheet 2001	(billon ¥)
Current assets	4.62
Fixed assets	6.84
Investments	6.79
Intangible assets	0.14
Total assets	18.39
Current liabilities	6.78
Long term debt	5.96
Equity	5.65
Total liabilities & equity	18.39

Note: The data are based on March 2001.

Therefore the *market capitalization*, (the market value of the equity, which is the product of the number of shares outstanding and the share price) is ¥90.88 billion.

The *total capitalization* is the market value of the equity plus the market value of the debt. It represents the value of the firm, which is the present value of the earnings of the firm. The market value of debt is ¥7.528 billion and the total capitalization is ¥98.408 billion. Therefore, the liabilities to the shareholders' equity are only 8.28% (=7.528/90.88).

Starbucks Coffee Japan has made a profit of only ¥1.44 billion after spending ¥19.16 billion on overhead costs. However, its valuation is based on forecasts of the future, and the driving factor is the sales growth. The growth is estimated to be 24.5% over 1–5 years and 6.5% over 5–10 years. The growth is primarily driven by the opening of new stores. Presently there are 273 stores (20% of the market), and this figure is expected to grow by 120–130 stores/year. The annual capital expenditure is ¥9 billion, with the cost per store ¥75 million and the annual sales/store ¥170 million. It is argued that the company can maintain this aggressive growth rate even though the present market size is limited. The model assumes that Starbucks Coffee Japan is successfully establishing its specialty coffee to create a new market.

This brief overview generates two related issues. First, how can the management of the firm increase the shareholders' value? Second, how should the investment community value the firm? The first question relates to corporate finance, concerning capital budgeting (when to incur capital investment), optimal capital structure (how to raise funding, by debt or by equity) and related issues. The second question relates to securities analysis. These are the subjects that we will turn to now.

12.2 Traditional Firm Valuation Methodologies

For clarity of the discussion, we will assume that the firm that we are concerned with is publicly traded, so that it provides more financial information and the stock prices are available to the public. Therefore, we can observe the stock price. The firm can access the capital market and can issue new shares or bonds to raise funds. The value of a firm is also called the total capitalization. The value is based on market value determined by publicly traded prices and not on book value, which is derived from historical prices. Total capitalization is the sum of the market values of equity, bonds, preferred stocks, and other claims on the firm. Since total capitalization is the present value of all the claims on the firm, the value must be the present value of all the free cash flows of the firm generated from the business model to pass to all the claimants of the firm.

Traditional methodologies are based on comparing financial ratios with other firms in the peer group. For example, the stock price may be determined by assuming that the price/earnings ratio (P/E ratio) should be the same for comparable firms. Or, for firms such as banks, where a significant portion of the value of the balance sheet represents the value of financial instruments, the ratio of the market value to book value of the stock is used to compare the relative values of the stocks. If two firms are similar in all respects, then one may think that their market-to-book values are the same. These approaches rely on the accuracy of financial ratios and the validity of deciding the comparables. This ad hoc nature of the methodology, though commonly used, lacks the ability to capture the salient features of the firm to determine its stock value more accurately.

Another common traditional valuation methodology that is not based on financial ratio comparison is the dividend discount model that was discussed in chapter 2. The dividend discount model projects the firm's dividend payouts into the future and discounts the dividend cash flows at the cost of equity. The present-value number is the equity value of the company. This approach assumes that we can accurately estimate dividend payouts and the cost of equity.

The cost of equity is the required rate of return of the stock. As has been discussed, the required return of the stock should be the same as the expected return of the stock at the market equilibrium. The expected return of the stock should be the risk-free rate plus a market premium for risk. To determine the risk premium, we can use the Capital Asset Pricing model. This method is illustrated below.

Consider a firm that has the following balance sheet and income statements.[2] (See table 12.3.)

Suppose that the firm is expected to have no growth, and all financial statements remain the same every year, which means that the firm pays the $10 dividend forever.

In our model we will assume that the gross profit margin is the ratio of the gross profit (revenues net of cost of goods sold) to the revenue, which is 83%. Let us assume that the marginal tax rate is 30%.

Given the risk-free rate, r_f, the expected rate of the market portfolio, $\overline{R}_M$, and the beta, β, which are input parameters for the Capital Asset Pricing model, we can calculate the cost of equity, K_e, which is 10%.

$$K_e = r_f + \beta(\overline{R}_M - r_f) = 10\% \tag{12.1}$$

Using the dividend discount model, the capitalization value (market value of equity) is[3]

$$S = \frac{dividend}{K_e} = \frac{\$10}{0.1} = \$100 \tag{12.2}$$

There are many merits to this approach in contrast to other valuation approaches that use financial ratios for comparison. The model is based on the analysis of cash flows of the firm. The approach also uses a discount rate that properly adjusts for the risk premium.

However, there are also drawbacks to using this methodology. Dividends may not be easy to project for some of the growth firms. Dividends are decided by the management and may not properly reflect the free cash flows of the company. Since the stock beta is

Table 12.3 Financial Statements

Income Statement	
Sales	300
Cost of Sales	50
Gross Profit	250
Selling & General Administrative Expense	100
Depreciation	20
EBIT	130
Interest Cost	86
Other Income	0
Pretax income	44
Tax	15
Provisions	0
NI	29
Retained Earnings Statement	
NI	29
Dividends	10
Chg in Retained Earnings	19

Balance Sheet			
Cash	100	Current Liabilities	100
Other Current Assets	500	Long Term Debt	1000
Current Assets	600	Total Liabilities	1100
Capital Assets	600	Equity	500
Other Assets	400		
Total Assets	1600	Total Liabilities & Equity	1600

determined by the historical data, this method may not be able to capture the change in the risk of the stock in the future. To improve the dividend discount model, another method that relates more directly to the operations of the firm is necessary.

12.3 Corporate Financial Decisions and Firm Value Maximization

Enhancing Shareholders' Value

Shareholders are owners of a corporation, whether they are employees or managers, and whether they have a small fraction of the shares outstanding or a majority of the shares.

Managers are individuals who manage the corporation, the production process, the employees, and clients. They are responsible for the welfare of the stakeholders of the corporation. These stakeholders include clients, employees, the community, the government, the vendors, and (last but not least) the shareholders. Indeed, the role of management is a complex one, since the managers are responsible for many aspects of a firm. For the purpose of this book, we will assume that the objective of the management is to maximize the current shareholders' value.

An alternative to this objective is the maximization of the stakeholders' value. In order to describe such an alternative objective, we need to propose relative performance measures other than the equity values of the firm to reflect the broader context of the goals of the firm. These measures can be related to security of employment, social responsibilities, and environmental protection. However, we chose the maximization of the shareholders' value as an objective for the firm for a number of reasons. Firms seem to maximize shareholders' value for the reasons suggested by Copeland et al. (2000).

In recent years, it has been more prevalent for the goal of the management to be the maximization of the shareholders' value. This observation is supported by the increased use of equity-based compensation to the firm's management. This type of compensation is used to encourage an alignment between the goals of the shareholders and those of the management. Shareholders are also taking an active role in the management of firms. Institutional investors are increasingly vocal in their views regarding management. In the past, they were more passive; if they did not like the management, they would simply sell the stock. More recently, if the institutional investors are not satisfied with the management, they round up as many shareholders as they can get to vote the management out. Furthermore, if management is not actively maximizing the shareholders' value, then some shareholders buy shares with borrowed funds to gain control of the firm. Once they control the firm, they replace the management. This is what we call *leveraged buyout*, often used to replace the management of undervalued firms.

Management of the firm is a complex function that must take many conflicting issues into account. However, narrowly stating that the management should only maximize the shareholders' value may often oversimplify their goal, although using this assumption for our discussion in this book is appropriate because, after all, this book's emphasis is on finance. If we incorporate other goals of the firm to derive optimal corporate financial results, we would be dealing with complex social issues. Copeland et al. (2000) suggest that the maximization of the shareholders' value in fact does have broader implications than benefiting the shareholders in a narrow sense. They suggest that healthier firms seem to perform well for their employees, vendors, and clients. A profitable firm benefits a broad range of constituents, since the profits are often indirectly shared by the stakeholders. Furthermore, with the growing equity ownership, a firm's profitability leads to wealth creation in the economy. For these reasons, the maximization of the shareholders' value not only is practiced in corporate management but also is an appropriate goal for the economy at large.

Since the corporation is publicly traded, the shareholders' value is the current share value, which is the wealth that the shareholders have in the corporation. Most corporate decisions will lead to future profits or at least result in implicit benefits to the corporation. However, such benefits can be realized by the stock price. Using a measurable, metriclike share value enables us to align the goals of all shareholders with those of the management.

Business Processes to Enhance the Shareholders' Value

Corporate decisions are based on a business model. A business model is the design of a business that will generate profits to the shareholders. Business processes describe the range of activities that a corporation must carry out to implement the business model. The shareholders' value is the present value of all the expected profits accrued to the owners of the corporation. The business model, the business processes, and the shareholders' value are interrelated.

For example, consider a community bank. The business model of the bank may be to borrow money at a low rate by creating deposit accounts and to invest the deposits in assets with higher returns. The investment income net of the borrowing cost and the administrative cost is the profit. The model will ensure that the profits are high enough to compensate for the risks.

To implement this business model, there are many different activities—the business process. There are account managers to manage the deposits, loan officers to invest, asset and liability managers to manage the balance sheets, and a chief financial officer to manage the funding and the profits, just to name a few. The success of the design of the business model and the implementations of business processes are measured by the shareholders' value.

One important challenge is to assure that the business processes are logical, all working together to enhance the shareholders' value. How can we measure the performance of each management decision by its contribution to the shareholders' value? How can we design the business processes that will best implement a business model? These are the questions that this book seeks to answer. One approach is to use an integrated financial model, which is based on the theory of relative valuation.

12.4 Miller–Modigliani Theories

A standard tool in making corporate financial decisions is the net present value methodology. Corporate decisions may range from capital budgeting and optimal debt level to optimal dividend payments. In principle, the decision can be made depending on whether the present value of the benefit net of the present value of the cost is positive or negative. When the net present value is positive, the management will accept the project, because the shareholders' value is enhanced by the amount of the net present value that will result from taking the project. In practice, the problem is determining the discount rate. The discount rate is not simply the opportunity cost of the funding or the borrowing cost in the narrow sense. We must adjust for the risk of the cash flows to determine an appropriate discount rate. Determining the risk-adjusted discount rate is a nontrivial task. Furthermore, when the risk changes over time, which is the usual case, determining the risk-adjusted discount rate will be much more difficult.

The shareholders' value is a capital market concept. The market continually determines the value of future cash flows. Therefore, to enhance the shareholders' value, we must first identify which factors are playing a major role when the market evaluates future cash flows from the stock. These factors must include the interest rate level and the cash flow's risk. Once we identify these factors, we should determine how they are affecting the discount rate in order to calculate the net present value. However, there is no simple way to determine the relationship between these factors and the discount rate in a coherent way.

In practice, many corporations have established discount rates for all their corporate decisions. This discount rate, often called the cost of capital, is defined as the weighted sum of the required return of the stockholders and that of the bondholders if there are no other claims on the firm except for the stocks and bonds. Many corporations are aware that this cost of capital should be adjusted for different corporate investment decisions since not all corporate investments have the same risk. Is there a systematic approach to make such adjustments? Can we use more debt to retire outstanding shares, so as to increase shareholders' value?

Modigliani and Miller (1958) were the first to provide insights into the relationships between the operations of the firm in the real sector and the corporate financial decisions in the financial sector. Their theories enable us to formulate the theory of a firm, which is concerned with how the firm should be valued. The theory suggests that in order to determine the values of stocks, bonds, or other claims on the firm, we should determine the firm value.

The Miller–Modigliani Theory, Proposition I

The Miller and Modigliani (MM) theory (1958) has provided the foundation for corporate finance for over 40 years. We have touched upon the MM theory twice earlier in the book, without analyzing the theory. It is first presented in chapter 1, where it is related to the perfect capital market assumptions. We then mentioned the MM theory to value the high yield bonds using the structural model in chapter 9, where we assert that the firm value is independent of the firm's capital structure.

The MM theory uses the law of one price and the arbitrage mechanism to show that the value of a firm is independent of corporate financial decisions. When a firm's objective is to maximize the shareholders' value, it implies that corporate financial decisions have no impact on what the firm seeks to achieve, which is the shareholders' value maximization. Or, rather, corporate financial decisions are "irrelevant" in the sense that they do not affect the shareholders' value, and the firm value remains the same regardless of how the corporate financial decisions would be made. For this reason, the MM theories are referred to as "*irrelevant theorems.*"

We make the following assumptions for the MM theories. Many of these assumptions are perfect capital market assumptions that we presented before in chapter 1. Some of them will be relaxed later.

1. Two firms belong to the same risk class when they have the same risk and the discount rate of their free cash flow is ρ, the cost of capital. Therefore the cost of capital is the same for all the firms in the same risk class.
2. The firm generates a perpetual risky free cash flow, $\widetilde{FCF}$.
3. Stocks and bonds are traded in a perfect capital market, which implies that there are no transaction costs.
4. All debt is risk-free, irrespective of the level of debt held by the firm or by the individuals. The rate on the debt is therefore the risk-free rate of return, r_f.
5. There are no taxes for corporations or for individuals.

Under these assumptions, the MM theory concludes that the firm debt does not matter in determining the firm value. While the assumptions seem unrealistic, the model enables us to focus on the essence of the problem. The proof will show that the basic proposition would not be affected by relaxing some of the assumptions.

The arbitrage argument goes as follows. Suppose that a leveraged firm V_L with a debt, D_L, has a higher value than an unleveraged firm V_U, where two firms are in the same risk class and generate the same risky cash flow. The two firms differ in their capital structure. The total value of the unleveraged firm, V_U, is the same as the value of its equity, E_U. However, the total value of the leveraged firm, V_L, is the sum of the value of its equity, E_L, and its value of debt, D_L. We assume that the perpetual risky cash flow occurs from time 1 on for simplicity.

An investor would buy the unleveraged firm on margin by borrowing D_L, at the same time selling the leveraged firm. Since the leveraged firm has a higher value, the long and short position has a profit, which is $V_L - V_U \geq 0$. This profit is in fact a risk-free arbitrage profit, because the cash flows from the unleveraged firm and the personal debt borrowing is exactly offset by the outflow of funds in the short position of the leveraged firm at time 1. The value of the leveraged firm's equity at time 1 is $\frac{E(\widetilde{FCF})}{\rho} - D_L + E(\widetilde{FCF}) - D_L \cdot r_f$.

The first term, $\frac{E(\widetilde{FCF})}{\rho} - D_L$, represents the present value of the perpetual cash flows[4] and the second term, $E(\widetilde{FCF}) - D_L \cdot r_f$, represents the cash flow at time 1. The value of the unleveraged firm's equity at time 1 is $\frac{E(\widetilde{FCF})}{\rho} + E(\widetilde{FCF})$.

This arbitrage argument is also applicable in the reverse. If the leveraged firm has a lower value than the unleveraged firm, then the individual will sell the unleveraged firm and buy the leveraged firm, and lend D_L at the risk-free rate to retire the debt. Once again, the cash flows at time 1 would be identical in the long and short positions of the trade. Meanwhile, the individual has benefited from the arbitrage profit at time 0. (See table 12.4.)

The main point in the argument is that an individual can borrow or pay down the debt to undo the corporate actions. If corporations can increase shareholders' wealth by corporate financial decisions, then individuals would stand to profit from an arbitrage. From this elegant argument, we have derived the following equation. Let the firm value be V, and since it is independent of the firm's leverage, we have

$$V = S + D = \frac{E(\widetilde{FCF})}{\rho} \tag{12.3}$$

where S and D are the market value of stocks and bonds, respectively.

Let the cost of equity be K_e, as discussed above; then the expected return of the firm $\rho \times V$ is the sum of the expected returns of the equity and debt. Specifically, we have:

$$\rho \times V = K_e \times S + K_D \times D \tag{12.4}$$

Or, by dividing both sides by V,

$$\rho = K_e \times \frac{S}{V} + K_D \times \frac{D}{V} \tag{12.5}$$

That is, the firm's cost of capital (which is well-defined for each risk class) is the weighted average cost of capital, equity, and debt. For this reason, we often refer to the cost of capital as the *weighted average cost of capital* (WACC). (See figure 12.1.)

Equation (12.5) can be rearranged. Substitute $V = S + D$ in equation (12.5) and rearrange by letting K_e be on the left-hand side:

Table 12.4 Arbitrage Process in the Modigliani–Miller Proposition I

	time 0	time 1
If $V_L > V_U$		
Borrow D_L	D_L	$-D_L \cdot (1 + r_f)$
Sell E_L	E_L	$-\frac{E(\widetilde{FCF})}{\rho} + D_L - E(\widetilde{FCF}) + D_L \cdot r_f$
Buy V_U	$-V_U$	$\frac{E(\widetilde{FCF})}{\rho} + E(\widetilde{FCF})$
Net cash flow	$V_L - V_U \geq 0$	0
If $V_L < V_U$		
Sell V_U	V_U	$-\frac{E(\widetilde{FCF})}{\rho} - E_{(}\widetilde{FCF})$
Buy E_L	$-E_L$	$\frac{E(\widetilde{FCF})}{\rho} - D_L + E(\widetilde{FCF}) - D_L \cdot r_f$
Lend D_L	$-D_L$	$D_L \cdot (1 + r_f)$
Net cash flow	$V_U - V_L \geq 0$	0

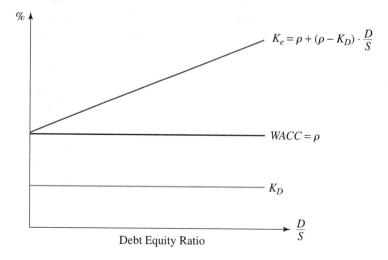

Figure 12.1 Modigliani–Miller theory, proposition I. This figure depicts the cost of equity K_e; the cost of debt, K_D; and the weighted average cost of capital as functions of the debt-equity ratio in the MM proposition I. Proposition I suggests that the weighted cost of capital of the firm (WACC) is independent of the debt level of the firm. Because of this, MM proposition I provides conditions under which financial decisions are irrelevant in determining the firm value.

$$K_e = \rho + (\rho - K_D) \times \frac{D}{S} \tag{12.6}$$

The WACC in Modigliani–Miller Proposition I is ρ, which we expect from the fact that the firm value is independent of the capital structure.

Since ρ is independent of the leverage, an increase in the leverage D/S would result in the increase of the required return of the stock K_e. Often, senior corporate management argues that the increased use of debt will lead to a higher expected net income. This is because when the project's return is higher than the cost of funding it using debt, the use of debt will lead to a higher expected return of the equity capital. The use of financial leverage can increase the expected returns of equity. This proposal is correct to the extent that the accounting formulas lead us to this conclusion. But in the capital market, while the leverage may increase the expected returns to the shareholders, the increase in the discount rate, to compensate for the increased risk to the equity from the higher leverage, will directly offset the increased return. We should bear in mind that the higher leverage will lead to a higher return as well as higher risk. In fact, a higher discount rate will perfectly offset the higher returns because the MM theory hypothesizes that there is no change in the stock value. The shareholders' value has not been enhanced by the increased use of financial leverage in MM proposition I.

Proposition I has important implications for some of the central questions in corporate finance. And these observations are central to the development of the discussion in this book.

First, using the concept of risk class, proposition I shows that the firm's cost of capital is the appropriate discount rate for a new project in capital budgeting only if the new project belongs to a risk class that has the same cost of capital. This is counterintuitive to many financial managers. Often, the cost of capital is interpreted as the cost of borrowing, to ensure that the return on an investment is higher than the cost of borrowing funds. This is unfortunate. When the expected return of an investment exceeds the borrowing cost, undertaking the project does not necessarily enhance shareholders' value. The fallacy of this argument lies in the fact that the risks are not controlled, since the funding cost reflects the risk of the firm, while the discount rate for a project should be related to the risk of the project. When we adjust appropriately for the risk of an investment, the cost of capital for the project's risk class is the appropriate discount rate for the project. The discount rate for the project is related to the risk of the project, and not to the cost of funding. The cost of capital would be more appropriately called the required returns of the investment.

Second, we observe that the weighted average cost of capital can be calculated, since we can estimate the cost of capital for equity and debt. We can also estimate the debt ratio (D/V); then equation (12.5) provides an estimate of the cost of capital (ρ). This analysis can lead us to the firm valuation,

$$V = PV(E(\widetilde{FCF}), \rho) \qquad (12.7)$$

The firm value is the present value of the free cash flows of the firm discounted at ρ. Equation (12.7) is called the *free cash flow discount model*. Notice that the two observations above are related. When projects are independent of each other, their net present value calculation should be treated as valuing a firm. A project, in essence, is a firm.

Intuitive Explanation of the MM Theory

At first glance, MM proposition I seems difficult to grasp, because we resort to fancy machinery like arbitrage and the law of one price to prove the theorem. However, the proposition reveals a surprisingly simple fact. Before we discuss how basic the proposition really is, recall that the value of securities should be determined by the future cash flow and its associated riskiness.

We can apply this basic principle to value firms, since we can treat firms as if they were securities. The reason for this is that firm value is the sum of all the values of all the claims that the firm has issued. Since the MM theory assumes that a firm generates a constant expected perpetual free cash flow (FCF) whether it is a leveraged firm or an unleveraged firm, we can see that the two firms have the same value because their expected cash flow is exactly the same—the constant perpetual free cash flow, FCF. Naturally, it would be no surprise to see that two firms do in fact have the same value, given our assumption.

The only difference between the two firms is their distribution strategy. Each firm has to allocate the same cash flow among claimants. But how is the firm value determined if each firm has different claimants? The unleveraged firm distributes the cash flow among stockholders, whereas the leveraged firm distributes it among both stockholders and bondholders. Therefore, it is obvious that the allocation of the cash flow will not determine the firm value. The firm value should be determined by the firms' investment strategy rather than by their distribution strategy, such as a dividend payout policy. The operating income of the firm should be valued first. Then the firm will know how much money it can distribute to its claimants. However, since only risk-free bonds are available in the MM model, we do not have to worry about wealth redistribution issues between stockholders and bondholders. What MM proposes is that financing decisions and investment decisions are independent of each other by the arbitrage argument, which is the foundation in developing modern corporate finance.

Miller and Modigliani Proposition II

In proposition I, the theory assumes that there are no corporate or personal taxes. But under the U.S. tax code, one important incentive for borrowing is a tax deduction on the interest of corporate borrowing. By assuming no taxes, an important aspect of corporate borrowing is ignored. To remedy this shortcoming, the tax deductibility on interest is incorporated in proposition II, by introducing the corporate tax rate τ_c. Now equation (12.3) is adjusted for the tax shield, and becomes

$$V_L = V_U + \tau_c \times D \tag{12.8}$$

Other equations are adjusted accordingly. For example, equation (12.6) will change as follows.

$$K_e = \rho + (1 - \tau_c) \cdot (\rho - K_D) \times \frac{D}{S}$$

Furthermore, the weighted average cost of capital in the Miller-Modigliani proposition II is

$$WACC = \rho \cdot \left(1 - \tau_c \cdot \frac{D}{S + D}\right).$$

We see that the WACC converges to $\rho \cdot (1 - \tau_c)$ as we increase the leverage, which is exactly the opposite of the Miller-Modigliani proposition I.

The results can be found in appendix A and are not reported here, for reasons that will be provided shortly. (See figure 12.2.)

The Miller Model

In 1977, in his presidential address to the American Finance Association, M. H. Miller proposed the third version of the theory, known later as the Miller model or the Presidential Address (Miller 1977). He showed that proposition II introduced the corporate tax but ignored the personal tax. For a corporate financial theory, how would the personal tax become an issue? In the presence of personal tax, the corporate decision should minimize both the corporate and the personal taxes of the stockholders and bondholders. In other words, the corporate decision should be determined on the after-tax basis rather than on the before-tax basis, because both the stockholders and the bondholders are concerned with the after-tax returns.

Let us assume that the corporate tax is τ_c. The personal marginal capital gain tax rate on equity and the personal marginal tax rate on interest are τ_{pe} and τ_{pb}, respectively. Consider a firm with operating income (EBIT) of \$100. We can think of two cases, depending on how the operating income will be paid out. Case 1 and case 2 will distribute the operating income as interest and as equity income, respectively. If the operating income will pay out interest, the firm will not incur corporate tax on the operating income due to interest tax deductibility. However, the firm should pay its corporate tax if it pays

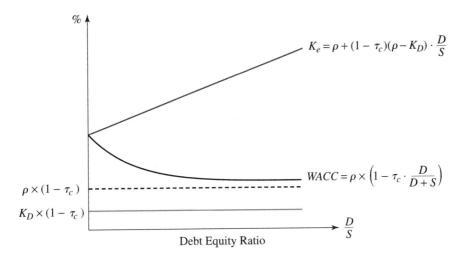

$$K_e = \rho + (1 - \tau_c)(\rho - K_D) \cdot \frac{D}{S}$$

$$WACC = \rho \times \left(1 - \tau_c \cdot \frac{D}{D+S}\right)$$

$\rho \times (1 - \tau_c)$

$K_D \times (1 - \tau_c)$

Debt Equity Ratio $\frac{D}{S}$

Figure 12.2 MM theory proposition II. This figure depicts the cost of equity, the cost of debt, and the cost of capital as functions of the debt/equity ratio in MM proposition II. Since the proposition incorporates the corporate tax, it suggests that the weighted average cost of capital (WACC) decreases with the increase in debt because as the tax shield on the interest payments lowers the cost of debt. The WACC converges to $\rho \cdot (1 - \tau_c)$ as the debt increases relative to the equity.

out as equity income. Consider case 1, where all the operating income is distributed to its bondholders as interest. The total amount received by the bondholders, after the corporate tax and the personal tax, would be

$$X(\text{case 1}) = \$100 \times (1 - \tau_{pb})$$

Now consider case 2, where the operating income is distributed to the shareholders, which can be accomplished only by reporting \$100 corporate taxable income, and the retained earnings are used to purchase shares. The shareholders can sell their shares when they need the funds.

$$X(\text{case 2}) = \$100 \times (1 - \tau_c) \times (1 - \tau_{pe})$$

Whenever $X(\text{case 1}) > X(\text{case 2})$, some firms will increase their debt financing and use the proceeds to buy back the equity, because in doing so, both the stockholders (who pay the personal income tax on the stock and the corporate tax indirectly) and bondholders (who pay tax on the interest income) will pay less corporate and personal taxes combined. As a result, the market will have a higher level of debt and less equity. The converse is also true. If $X\text{case2} > X\text{case1}$, then the firm will issue more shares to repurchase the bonds, such that the market will have more shares outstanding and less debt.

But not all individuals have the same marginal personal tax rate. Let us assume, for the time being, that the marginal tax rate of equity is small. With a small amount of the debt outstanding in the market, tax-exempt institutions will first purchase the bonds, since they will not have to pay tax on the interest. As the debt outstanding increases in the market, more individuals will hold bonds and the marginal tax rate on interest will increase with the increase in the number of bondholders.

If $(1 - \tau_{pb}) > (1 - \tau_c)(1 - \tau_{pe})$, then the total debt amount will increase and equity outstanding will fall. But as the debt increases, τ_{pb} also increases, such that at some point, the inequality does not hold. At that point, equilibrium is reached. Similarly, if $(1 - \tau_{pb}) < (1 - \tau_c)(1 - \tau_{pe})$, then the total debt amount will fall. In this case, τ_{pb} will fall, and reach the equilibrium when both sides of the equation are equal.

This argument shows that the tax codes determine the aggregate amount of corporate debt but not the amount issued by any particular firm. If the personal tax rate on interest payments is high, the aggregate level of the corporate debt will fall, and if the personal tax rate on interest payments is lowered, the aggregate level of corporate debt will rise. The intuition of this result is clear. When the personal tax rate on interest payments is high, more individuals will prefer equity to bonds as investment. This shift of the investment portfolio will lead to a higher yield of the bonds. That in turn will result in increased cost of debt to corporations, which will then refrain from issuing more debt. Hence, in aggregate, the debt amount will fall.

In summary, the Miller model asserts that the firm's value is dependent on the free cash flows generated from the operations, and is independent of the financial management of the firm, which may be the leverage level. The basic argument of MM is that to maximize the shareholders' value, we need to consider the after-tax returns to the investors. Whatever change there is in the firm's leverage, the capital market will trade the firm's stock such that these financial decisions are made "irrelevant" to enhance the shareholders' value. Further, MM asserts that the appropriate discount rate for this operating cash flow depends on the risk class of the cash flow, and not on the borrowing costs of the investors.

Empirically, the MM theories and the Miller model are difficult to refute or prove. The main difficulty is that it is almost impossible to find two identical firms, one of which has debt and the other of which has no debt. Firms are not likely to be willing to participate in a large sample experiment to prove or disprove the theory. But the theory provides a good paradigm with insights into corporate finance. For the purpose of our discussion, we will assume the Miller model, and not proposition II, as a working theory. Proposition II is not used for the subsequent development of our discussion.

The rest of the book will assume the Miller and Modigliani "irrelevant theorems" unless we state otherwise. For this reason, we will not make a particular distinction between the Miller model and the MM theory in our exposition.

12.5   Free Cash Flow Discount Model

The MM theory suggests that we can first determine the value of the firm and then subtract the market value of the debt to determine the firm's capitalization. The firm value should be the present value of the free cash flows of the firm (the cash flows that can be released). The future cash flow is forecast in order to determine the firm value in the future, and then that value is discounted back to the present time. The cash flow begins with net income. Since accounting items have been deducted from profits according to accounting rules, we should add the deducted items, such as depreciation, to the net income to calculate the free cash flow. Interest costs also need to be added to the net income because they are payments to the claimants of the firm.

After the taxes are paid, the cash flows are not "free" to pass to the firm's claimants. Part of the cash has to be used for working capital and part has to be used for capital expenditure. These items have to be deducted from or added to the cash flow to determine the free cash flow every year into the future. Using the free cash flow approach, we do not need to make certain assumptions on the dividend policies of the firm. The model does not have to assume that the firm will pay dividends at a constant payout ratio to the net income or use other dividend payout policies. The calculation of the free cash flow of a firm can best be explained by a numerical example.

Let us consider the free cash flow valuation using table 12.5. We assume that there is no change in the net working capital. We first determine the cost of capital of the firm, ρ. Suppose the beta of the firm is estimated to be 1.30, using S&P 500 as the market portfolio, and the risk premium is assumed to be 2.5%. The risk-free rate is assumed to be the ten-year Treasury bond yield of 3.5%.

$$\rho = 3.5 + 1.3 \times 2.5 = 6.75\% \tag{12.9}$$

We assume that the free cash flows can then be projected, using the projected perpetual growth rate of 1.0 percent. The present value of the free cash flows can then be calculated.

$$V = \frac{E(\widetilde{FCF})}{\text{cost of capital} - \text{growth rate}} = \frac{115}{0.0675 - 0.01} = 2000 \tag{12.10}$$

We have provided two methodologies to calculate the market equity value: discounting the free cash flows and net of the market value of the debt, and discounting the dividends. The two methods should provide the same valuation. The main difference between the two approaches is that the free cash flow approach is concerned with the cash flows for all the claimants: stockholders and bondholders. The discounting dividend approach is concerned with the cash flows only to the stockholders.

Suppose we live in a risk-neutral world where there is no risk premium on any risky assets, so that stocks and bonds both offer risk-free returns to their investors. Then the valuation of the firm and the securities is straightforward. However, when there are risks, we need to determine the distribution process, which is dividing the operating income into interest payments to the debt holders and dividends to the stockholders. When there are risk premiums, the risk of a firm's cash flow has to be allocated to the bondholders and stockholders. Since bondholders bear less risk, the stockholders must therefore bear a higher risk than that of the unleveraged firm. As a result, the cost of equity is higher than the cost of capital of the firm. We need a theory to tell us how to allocate the risk. The MM theory offers us a solution, showing that

Table 12.5 Free Cash Flow Calculation

	FCF
NI	29
Depreciation	20
Interest Cost	86
Cash Flows	135
Capital Investment	20
Free Cash Flows	115

$$K_e = \rho + (\rho - K_D) \times \frac{D}{S}$$

where the cost of equity is K_e; ρ is the cost of capital of the firm; K_D is the cost of debt; and D and S are the market value of debt and equity, respectively.

Discounted Cash Flow Method and Valuation of a Firm

We introduced the discounted cash flow (DCF) method in chapter 1, and we have seen how the method has been used in different contexts. We showed its limitations in identifying all the values in a security. As a result, we showed how a relative valuation model can provide a more appropriate valuation approach.

Specifically, we applied the DCF method to value Treasury bonds and showed that the bond model is a better method to value a bond than the DCF method because the bond model can capture the term structure of interest rates in the bond valuation. We argued that the DCF approach failed to price options because of the difficulties in determining the discount rate for an equity option. The Black–Scholes model was introduced to determine the option value using the relative valuation approach. We used yield to worst, which is a DCF measure, to value corporate bonds with call and sinking fund provisions. We then demonstrated that such bonds should be valued as interest rate contingent claims in order to appropriately value the embedded options of the bonds.

For the high-yield bonds, we used the actuarial approach or the reduced form model in discounting the expected bond payments. They are in essence DCF models. We then showed that the structural model can better capture the value of the put options in the high-yield bonds. For the mortgage-backed securities, the static yield measure was shown to be inadequate to capture the embedded options in the prepayment risk and the extension risk. The yield measure was replaced by an integrated prepayment model and an interest rate model to value these bonds. The use of valuation models to replace the DCF method is also described for convertible bonds and financial institutions' liabilities.

In valuing a firm, the DCF method, as described above as the free cash flow method, is often used. But the following sections will show that it has significant limitations, and that a relative valuation model may be more appropriate.

12.6 Business Model

A firm provides goods and services to the economy. In this real sector process, a firm's returns to its shareholders and claimants depend on the business risks. Each firm has its distinct process in producing the goods and services and, at the same time, generating returns for its investors. This distinctive process is incorporated in a business model.

The MM theory assumes certain free cash flows of a firm without specifying how those cash flows are generated. Its argument depends only on analyzing the firm's value under different corporate financial decisions, such as dividend policy, capital structure, and other decisions that we have already discussed. Similarly, the Merton model (1974) is based on relative valuation, determining any corporate contingent claims relative to the underlying firm value, without mentioning the sources of cash flows. If we want to comprehend the cost of capital of a firm, we need to understand how the free cash flows are generated to further specify their risks. The specification of a business model of a firm is to identify the risks of the firm's cash flows.

In chapters 9 and 10, we have seen that by incorporating the terms and conditions to describe a bond or a liability, we can gain significant insight into the securities. In a similar spirit, a firm is distinct from another firm by its production processes. By modeling the salient features of the production process, we can gain insight into the risk of the firm's cash flows and its appropriate discount rate.

Building a general business model for all firms, such as a general valuation model like the free cash flow model, would be equivalent to proposing a generic model for bonds or liabilities. Making such generalities would overlook salient features of the firm, which may provide important information concerning the firm. However, if the industry sectors have distinct business models, then we can better identify the differences and similarities between two industry sectors. Since the business model can be related to financial reporting, which includes the balance sheets and income statements, we can also better understand how financial reporting is reflected across the firms. For example, we can better appreciate how the reported income relates to a technology firm value versus that of a bank. We will elaborate on this idea in the following sections.

A Business Model

To illustrate the framework of the analysis of a firm, we propose a relatively simple business model for a class of firms. We begin with the retail chain business sector. In order to identify the issues of the analysis, we will start with some restrictive assumptions that do not affect the principles behind the analysis. More details can be added to this basic model when it is used for practical applications.

The business sector of retailing sells goods and services to consumers for personal and household use. It is considered to be the channel of distribution that satisfies the needs of customers all across the nation. If it succeeds in distributing the goods and making profits from them, then the value of the retail firm will be high. The valuation of a retail firm depends significantly on the distribution process—how many sales each store can make of its goods and services. In turn, a retailer needs to understand and analyze the market trends in consumer behavior to determine what goods it should sell, the pricing of the goods, and the quantity of the goods, among other things. The key factors driving consumer spending are the robustness of the economy, the consumer sentiment, and purchasing patterns.

There are many examples of retail chain stores in the market: Starbucks Coffee, Wal-Mart, and McDonalds are just a few examples. They have certain characteristics in common. These chain stores' profitability depends on leveraging on multiple stores to attain economy of scale. They seek to lower the impact of the fixed costs, the overhead costs of managing the chain. Retail chain stores focus on the profitability of each store while keeping the stores similar in management, style, and costs. Therefore the total revenue depends significantly on the revenues of a typical store. The risks of the business are mainly the customers' changing preferences. For example, fast food chain restaurants are scrutinized by health practitioners for their lack of nutritional value to customers. There are researchers who study foods that are detrimental to a person's health. If a study targets a particular food or drink as unhealthy, it may influence a person's behavior to consume that food or drink, which would spell disaster for that company—but is a risk the store has to take. Most retail chain stores actively control costs by ensuring a steady supply of ingredients for the final goods sold. However, since retail chain stores analyze current market trends of consumer behavior, they may want to introduce a new product. Given that customers' preferences change—which is hard to control—the firm must balance the benefit of branding and economy of scale to promote different products.

Model Assumptions

These model assumptions specify the valuation model of the firm. Since there are quite a number of technical details in this formulation of the model, we will present the important aspects of the model here, and its detailed specifications in the appendix to chapter 14.

Market assumptions

In order for the analysis of the model to focus on the business risk of a retail chain store, we ignore the interest rate risks. We will assume that the yield curve is flat and remains constant at r_f, that the firm seeks to maximize the shareholders' wealth, and that the market is efficient.

Corporate finance assumption

We assume the frictionless market of the MM theory, where there are corporate taxes and personal taxes, and the capital structure is irrelevant in the maximization of shareholders' value.

Gross Return on Investment

The business model for the retail chain firm begins with defining the business risk driver. Central to the analysis of the retail chain store business is the sales per store. The most closely watched quantitative indicator is *comparable-store sales* or *same store sales*. This is defined as the change in sales from the previous year for stores open more than one year. This measure avoids any distortion of seasonal effects, since much of the sales for some retail chain stores depend on the Christmas season. It also avoids the increase from opening more stores to generate higher total sales while the sales per store decline. This measure also underscores the major business risk: consumer behavior. The changes of same store sales can detect the changes of consumer behavior that may improve or adversely affect the firm's profitability.

For this reason, we focus on the gross return on investment $(\widetilde{GRI})$, which is

$$\widetilde{GRI} = \frac{\text{sales}}{\text{capital investment}} \tag{12.11}$$

Note that the denominator is capital investment rather than portfolio investment.

The gross return on capital investment is a measure of the same store's sales per unit store value. We can think of the investment as the cost of opening a store. This store then generates sales every year. $\widetilde{GRI}$ measures the sales that \$1 investment can generate. Suppose the chain store has N stores and each store generates the same sales. When we apply $\widetilde{GRI}$ to the chain store, then in the numerator we use the total sales, and in the denominator we use the cumulative investments in stores.

By contrast, a commonly used measure, return on investment (ROI), measures the net income on the investment. It can be affected by the firm's operating leverage, or by changing the business model of the chain store. However, $\widetilde{GRI}$ is not affected by the change of some of the operations of the firm. The sales item is the top line item of the income statement, not the bottom line. $\widetilde{GRI}$ measures the sales generated by capital investments of a store, before taking the cost of goods sold and overhead costs into account.

Following the industry's concerns, we assume that the $\widetilde{GRI}$ is uncertain and is the main source of business risk for the retail chain store. When the store captures the trend in consumers' purchasing behavior, the $\widetilde{GRI}$ will increase, and the chain store will generate significant profits. Conversely, when there is a downturn in sales, $\widetilde{GRI}$ will fall. We think of $\widetilde{GRI}$ as the business risk of the retail chain store. For simplicity, we assume that it is the only business risk. The purpose of the model is to demonstrate the use of relative valuation methodology in corporate finance. Extending to multiple risk sources, using the n factor model descibed in chapter 7, should provide a more realistic model, but may obscure the basic insight in building a business model.

The $\widetilde{GRI}$ binomial process

To model the risk of $\widetilde{GRI}$ to a retail chain store, we assume that it follows a binomial lattice process that is lognormal (or multiplicative) with no drift. It is a martingale process, where the expected $\widetilde{GRI}$ value at any node point equals the realized $\widetilde{GRI}$ at that node point. (See figure 12.3.)

The market probability q is chosen so that the expected value of the risk over one period is the observed risk at the beginning of each step. That is, the risk follows a martingale process, stated below:

$$\widetilde{GRI}(n, i) = q \times \widetilde{GRI}(n + 1, i + 1) + (1 - q) \times \widetilde{GRI}(n + 1, i)$$

$$q = \frac{1 - e^{-\sigma}}{e^{\sigma} - e^{-\sigma}}, \text{ where } \sigma \text{ is the volatility of the risk driver} \qquad (12.12)$$

We assume that the MM theory can be extended to the multiperiod dynamic model described above. In this extension, we assume that all the individuals make their invest-

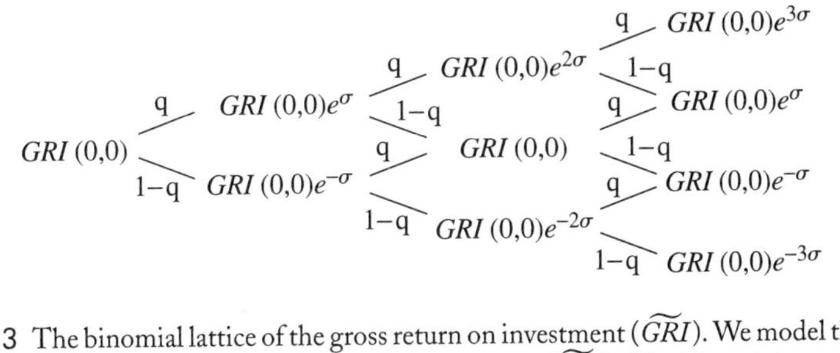

Figure 12.3 The binomial lattice of the gross return on investment ($\widetilde{GRI}$). We model the business risk by a binomial lattice of the gross return on investment ($\widetilde{GRI}$). The binomial process is of the multiplicative form with no drift.

ment decisions and trade at each node on the lattice. These activities include the arbitrage trades described in the MM theory. The results of the theory apply to each node. Therefore, there is a cost of capital ρ at each node dependent on the sector business risk and not the risk of the firm's free cash flows.

The cost of capital ρ of a sector is the required rate of return for that sector's business risk, assuming that the firm has no fixed costs. By contrast, the cost of capital of MM theory assumes a particular business model of a firm, taking the operating leverage as given. The cost of capital of a firm, according to the MM theory, reflects the risk of the free cash flows of the firm. In this chapter, we extend this concept of MM theory to an industry sector and use a firm with no operating leverage as the benchmark for comparison.

Since the firm risk is the same at each node, and the production process is the same at each node on the lattice, we will assume that the cost of capital is constant in all states and time. According to the MM theory, the firm value is the present value of all the dividends along all the paths on the lattice.

Primitive Firm

To apply the contingent claim valuation approach to value the firm, we begin with a definition of the *primitive firm* (V^p) as an underlying security. The primitive firm is a simple corporate entity. We assume that it has no debt or claims other than the common shares, which are publicly traded. To isolate the tax issues from the business risks, the firm does not pay corporate tax.

The firm has the fixed asset CA (or capital asset) as part of its operations. The fixed asset does not depreciate, and the value does not change. We can think of the fixed asset as the stores of the retail chain. This fixed asset is the cumulative capital investment of the firm.

There is cost of goods sold, the variable costs, but there is no fixed cost. The cost of goods sold usually includes the costs of purchasing, warehousing, distribution, freight, occupancy, and insurance. There is a lack of standardization of accounting treatments in this income statement item. For the purpose of the model, the cost of goods sold is the sales cost, such as commission, and the cost of buying the goods from the suppliers. The store simply buys the goods from the suppliers and resells them at a higher price.

The gross profit margin, the gross profit/sales, is an important measure of profitability in retailing. Given that a retail chain store is a distribution channel, gross profit margins determine the profitability of the flow of the business. The gross profit is the net income (or profit) of the firm because there are no other operating and financial costs. Let the gross profit margin be m. All the profits are distributed as dividends to the shareholders.

This primitive firm has several interesting properties.

1. Consider a node of time n and state i. Since CA is the capital invested, the sales at that node are $\widetilde{GRI}(n, i) \times CA$. Since the gross return on investment $\widetilde{GRI}(n, i)$, with $\widetilde{GRI}(0, 0)$ as the initial point, follows a martingale process, the expected sales over any future horizon are $\widetilde{GRI}(n, i) \times CA$. Therefore, at any given time n and state i, the expected profit of the primitive firm is $\widetilde{GRI}(n, i) \times CA \times m$.
2. The gross return on investment is the only risk source of the cash flow. The change of CA or expected cash flows would not change the risk characteristics of the firm. According to the MM theory, there is a cost of capital ρ for this risk. The risk of the

primitive firm does not change from one node to another on the binomial lattice, and therefore the cost of capital for the firm should be the same at all nodes.

3. Then the firm value depends on $\widetilde{GRI}$, CA, and m only. That is, at any node, the firm value is

$$V^p(n, i) = V^p(\widetilde{GRI}(n, i); CA, m).$$

The revenues are always positive, because $\widetilde{GRI}$ follows a multiplicative process and the primitive firm value at each node point on the binomial lattice is

$$V^p(n, i) = \frac{CA \times \widetilde{GRI}(n, i) \times m}{\rho} \qquad (12.13)$$

where we expect that ρ is constant, and does not vary with time n and state i. (See figure 12.4.)

Given the binomial process of the primitive firm, which we will use as the underlying security, we can derive the risk-neutral probabilities, $p(n, i)$, at time n and state i.

The risk-neutral probabilities $p(n, i)$ can be calculated from the binomial tree of V^p by the method described in chapter 4. Let $V^p(n, i)$ be the firm value at node (n, i). In the up state, the firm value is

$$V^p(n+1, i+1) = \frac{CA \times \widetilde{GRI}(n+1, i+1) \times m}{\rho}$$

By the definition of the binomial process of the gross return on investment,

$$V^p(n+1, i+1) = V^p(n, i)e^\sigma$$

Further, the firm pays a cash dividend of $C_u = V^p(n, i) \times \rho \times e^\sigma$. Therefore the total value of the firm V_u^p, an instant before the dividend payment in the up state, is

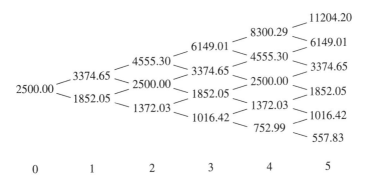

| 0 | 1 | 2 | 3 | 4 | 5 |

Figure 12.4 Primitive firm value lattice. For exposition purposes, we constructed a simplified version of a balance sheet and an income statement in table 12.3. We assume that the number of shares is 100 and the stock price is 5, so that the equity is 500. The risk-free rate is 6 percent. The initial $\widetilde{GRI}$ is 0.5 and the volatility is 0.3. The cost of capital is 10 percent. The time period is 5. The gross profit margin is 0.8333333. The tax rate is 33.33 percent. The long-term debt matures at period 5 and the coupon rate is 8 percent. At period 5 and state 5, the $\widetilde{GRI}$ is 2.24084, the fixed asset is 600, the gross profit margin is 0.8333333, and the cost of capital is 10 percent. If we substitute them in equation 12.13, we have 11204.2 as the primitive firm value.

$$V_u^p = V^p \times (1 + \rho) \times e^{\sigma}. \qquad (12.14)$$

Similarly, the total value of the firm V_d^p, an instant before the dividend payment in the down state, is

$$V_d^p = V^p \times (1 + \rho) \times e^{-\sigma} \qquad (12.15)$$

Then the risk-neutral probability p is defined as the probability that ensures the expected total return is the risk-free return.

$$p \times V_u^p + (1 - p) \times V_d^p = (1 + r_f) \times V^p \qquad (12.16)$$

Substituting V^p, V_u^p, and V_d^p into equation (12.16) and solving for p, we have

$$p = \frac{A - e^{-\sigma}}{e^{\sigma} - e^{-\sigma}}$$
$$\qquad (12.17)$$
$$A = \frac{1 + r_f}{1 + \rho}$$

As long as the volatility and the cost of capital are independent of time n and state i, the risk-neutral probability is also independent of the state and time, and is the same at each node point on the binomial lattice. (See figure 12.5.)

The importance of computing the risk-neutral probability for each node point is clear. Whenever there is another contingent claim on the risk $\widetilde{GRI}$, we can use the primitive firm as a hedging instrument to create an arbitrage-free portfolio. That means we can relatively value the contingent claim based on the primitive firm value. For this reason, we can use the risk-neutral probability p to determine the other contingent claim values.

This argument is a direct extension from the Black–Scholes model. In general, we do not know the cost of capital of the business risk. However, relative valuation enables us to determine the appropriate cost of capital of any contingent claims on the same underlying business risk. By establishing the binomial process of the primitive firm,

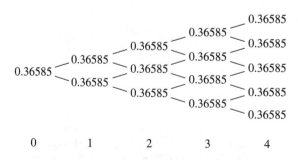

| | 0 | 1 | 2 | 3 | 4 |

Figure 12.5 The risk-neutral probability lattice. According to equation (12.17), A is (1 + 0.06)/(1 + 0.1), which is 0.963636. The risk-free rate, r_f, and the cost of capital, ρ, assumed to be 6 percent and 10 percent, respectively. Substituting 0.963636 and 0.3 (volatility) into A and σ in equation (12.17), respectively, the risk-neutral probability for the upward movement is 0.36585.

using the MM theory that the cost of capital is dependent on the risk of the business, we can relatively value all the other contingent claims on the business risk.

Firm valuation

We assume that the firm has fixed costs, fixed expenditures for operating purposes. The firm value is denoted by V. The fixed cost is independent of the units of goods sold. As an income statement item, fixed cost is an important aspect of the retail chain store. A retail chain store may increase the fixed cost, for example, by increasing the information system budget, in order to result in a higher gross profit margin by obtaining lower acquisition costs from the suppliers. The larger the distribution network, the less important the fixed cost component is. However, many chain stores fail because they cannot reach the critical number of stores that can bear the fixed costs necessary in operations of the firm. In essence, the fixed costs are analogous to the fixed coupon payments of a perpetual debt to the primitive firm. And the firm is a contingent claim on the business risk, $\widetilde{GRI}$.

We assume that the firm pays corporate tax. The government takes a portion of all the profits and losses of the firm, and is considered another claimant of the firm value. We in essence assume that the firm can carry the losses in its tax reporting such that the government also stands to lose when the firm is not profitable. Since the purpose of the model is not to investigate the impact of taxes on corporate decisions, we use the simplifying assumptions to make the model tractable. Under this assumption, we assume that this treatment of tax is equivalent to the government's holding a proportion (τ_c) of the firm's shares.

Hence the firm, assuming no net working capital is required, has the stochastic free cash flow $CF(n, i)$.

$$CF(n, i) = (CA \times \widetilde{GRI}(n, i) \times m - FC) \times (1 - \tau_c) - I(n, i) \qquad (12.18)$$

where $I(n, i)$ is the capital investment made with the firm at time n and state i.

To simplify the exposition, we assume that the firm pays out all the stochastic cash flows as dividends. Negative dividends are interpreted as cash infusion from the stockholders. Now we assume that the firm has an investment plan. $\$I$ is planned to be invested annually as fixed assets. Therefore, the fixed asset increases by the capital investment every year.

$$CA(n + 1) = CA(n) + I \qquad (12.19)$$

The planning horizon and the terminal condition

Following an approach similar to the discounted free cash flow method in valuing a firm, here we also assume that there is a strategic planning time horizon T. We will value the firm at each node at the planning horizon T.

If the firm has not defaulted before reaching the horizon T, we can determine the firm value. As in the discounted free cash flow model, where the valuation of the firm at the horizon is often subject to simplifying assumptions in determining what the firm will do beyond a certain time, we will also make some simplifying assumptions. First we assume that the firm value without taxes and fixed costs follows the risk-neutral stochastic process stated below:

$$dV = rVdt + \sigma_V Vdz$$

The impact of the fixed cost on this firm is analogous to a perpetual debt to an all-equity firm. The bankruptcy condition is same as that described for the structural model. That is, bankruptcy occurs when the firm value is lower than the market value of the perpetual debt.

The valuation formula of the perpetual debt is given by Merton (1974).

$$\Phi(V^p, \infty) = \frac{FC}{r_f}\left\{1 - \frac{(\frac{2FC}{\sigma^2 V^p})^{\frac{2r_f}{\sigma^2}}}{\Gamma(2 + \frac{2r_f}{\sigma^2})}M\left(\frac{2r_f}{\sigma^2}, 2 + \frac{2r_f}{\sigma^2}, \frac{-2FC}{\sigma^2 V^p}\right)\right\} \quad (12.20)$$

where

$$V^p = \text{the primitive firm value}$$

$$FC = \text{fixed cost per year}$$

$$r_f = \text{risk, free rate}$$

$$\Gamma = \text{the gamma function}$$

$$\sigma = \text{the standard deviation of } \widetilde{GRI}$$

$$M(\bullet) = \text{the confluent hypergeometric function}$$

$$M\left(a, 2+a, -\frac{2FC}{\sigma^2 V^p}\right) = \frac{1}{br_f}e^{-\frac{b}{V}}$$

$$\times \left[-(1+a)bFC\left(\frac{b}{V^p}\right)^a + e^{\frac{b}{V^p}}FC\left(aV^p\Gamma(2+a) + (1+a)(b - aV^p)\Gamma\left(1+a, \frac{b}{V^p}\right)\right)\right]$$

where

$$a = \frac{2r_f}{\sigma^2}$$

$$b = \frac{2FC}{\sigma^2}$$

and

$$\Gamma(x) = \int_0^x t^{x-1}e^{-t}dt$$

$$\Gamma(a, x) = \int_x^\infty t^{a-1}e^{-t}dt$$

According to Merton's model, FC is a coupon rate per unit time. In our case, FC is a fixed cost per year. r_f is the (instantaneous) riskless rate of interest, the same for all time. V^p is primitive firm value at the horizon date at each state of the world. σ is the instantaneous volatility of the firm's return per unit time. We have assumed that σ is equal to the standard deviation of $\widetilde{GRI}$. This firm does not pay dividends beyond the horizon date.

Therefore, the before-tax firm value at each node point on the lattice at the planning horizon is the primitive firm value net of the "perpetual debt" value, which is the present value of the fixed costs taking into consideration the possibility of default of the firm at a future date. Since the firm has to pay taxes, which are based on a portion of profits, we make a simplifying assumption that the firm value is equal to a portion of the before-tax firm value. The portion is given by $(1 - \tau_c)$. This assumption requires the government to share the profits and losses in the same proportion as the other claims on the firm value. This assumption is not quite consistent with the tax code. However, for our purpose, since this assumption is used only at the end of the planning horizon, this approximation may be acceptable.

The firm value at time T, at the end of the planning period, at each node, is

$$
\begin{aligned}
V(n, i) \\
= Max \Bigg[\bigg\{ \frac{CA(n, i) \cdot \widetilde{GRI}(n, i) \cdot m}{\rho} - \Phi \left(\frac{CA(n, i) \cdot \widetilde{GRI}(n, i) \cdot m}{\rho} \right) \\
+ \left(CA(n, i) \cdot \widetilde{GRI}(n, i) \cdot m - FC \right) \bigg\} (1 - \tau_c), 0 \Bigg]
\end{aligned}
\tag{12.21}
$$

where $\Phi(V^p(n, i))$ is the present value of the perpetual debt. The value is bounded from 0 because of the limited liability condition. This completes the set of assumptions on the firm.

The valuation binomial lattice

Now we can construct the tree with the nodes representing the joint values of the fixed asset CA. From this tree, we can determine the terminal values at time T for both the fixed asset value and the cash value at each node.

Given the CA values at the terminal nodes, we can determine the firm value, taking default into consideration. Then we use the tree from the primitive firm for relative valuation to determine the firm value at each node point by backward substitution.

The firm value can be determined by the backward substitution construction, as follows

$$
V(n, i) =
$$

$$
\frac{p \times V(n + 1, i + 1) + (1 - p) \times V(n + 1, i)}{(1 + r_f)} \times (1 - \tau_c) + CF(n, i)
\tag{12.22}
$$

where $CF(n, i)$ is the retained earnings as given by equation (12.18). The firm value at the initial node is 935.92. (See figure 12.6.)

Intuitively, we can think of the primitive firm as the "underlying firm" of the Merton model. The fixed costs (or fixed expenses) are equivalent to the interest payments of a perpetual bond of the primitive firm since $\widetilde{GRI}$ is the only risk source, we can formulate the arbitrage-free hedging between the firm and the primitive firm. For this reason,

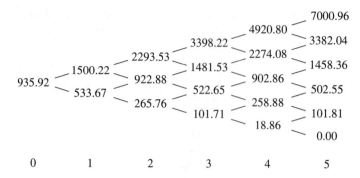

Figure 12.6 The firm value (V^{fc}). To calculate the firm value, we subtract the fixed cost from the primitive firm and multiply by $(1 - \tau_c)$. Since the fixed cost is wages for employees and other fixed costs for the firm to operate as a going concern, we treat the fixed cost as if it were a risky and perpetual cash outflow. We use the Merton model to calculate the present value of the perpetual and risky fixed cost. The fixed cost is perpetual because we assume a going concern and risky because the firm has possibilities of not paying the fixed cost when the firm value is less than the fixed cost. The corporate tax rate is 0.340909 and the fixed cost is 100, according to table 12.3. Furthermore, the primitive firm at period 5 and state 5 is 11204.2 and the present value of the risky perpetual debt (i.e., the fixed cost) is 1602.6. The firm value at period 5 and state 5 is $[(11204.2 - 1602.5) + (1120.42 - 100)] \times (1 - 0.340909)$, which is 7000.96.

we can derive the firm value at each node by conducting the backward substitution procedure. We need to establish the terminal conditions of the firm values at some horizon time T, called the planning horizon.

For the purposes of this explanation, we present a general structure of a business model as a model for retail chain businesses. The model has the standard ingredients of a firm with fixed and variable costs, and with uncertain sales. The revenues are directly proportional to the capital investment. However, this business model may not apply to other business sectors because each sector considers other factors to analyze its firms. For example, the banking sector involves the analysis of the balance sheet of assets and liabilities. We will deal with the business model of banking in chapter 14. In order to focus on the business aspects of the model, we ignore all capital structure and dividend issues by assuming that all free cash flows are paid out.

12.7   Implications of the Valuation Model

A firm's business model can be characterized by five parameters:

The business risk : σ

Gross return on investment : $\widetilde{GRI}$

Investment size : I

Operating leverage : L

Cost of capital : ρ

We have previously defined all the parameters except the operating leverage. Operating leverage, L, is defined as the fixed cost to the revenues. In order to isolate the impact of investment from our present analysis, we assume that there is no investment opportunity ($I = 0$). The above shows that we can use the business model to study the behavior of the firm value as if the firm is a contingent claim on the risk of the $\widetilde{GRI}$. This shows that we can study the performance profile of the option value behavior over a range of values of $\widetilde{GRI}$, following the option analysis presented in the previous chapters to study the impact of the operating leverage on the firm value. This approach is analogous to using the primitive firm as the "stock price" of an option, and the use of different operating leverages L in the analysis is analogous to using different strike prices for simulations to better understand the impact of the in-the-money and the out-of-the-money on the firm value.

The model has the following implications:

1. Comparing with the Merton model—Unlike the Merton model, where the firm value is assumed to follow a lognormal distribution with a constant instantaneous rate of return, firm returns depend significantly on the fixed-cost and variable-cost structure. Indeed, we have shown that the firm with fixed costs can behave like equity to a leveraged firm. The volatility at each node point will not be constant. Taking the business model into account, we can better understand the credit risk of a bond not simply from the viewpoint of Merton's model, but from the viewpoint of the business model: the level of fixed costs, the volatility of the risk source, and the salient features of the firm to generate profits.
2. Market price of risks—The risk source is the $\widetilde{GRI}$. The firm value, stocks, and bonds are contingent claims to this risk source. We can determine the market price of risk implied by the cost of capital (ρ) by using the observed prices of these contingent claims on the firms. That is, our model first assumes the level of the cost of capital for the sector. The model then determines the stock value. But since we can observe the stock price, we can calibrate the model to fit the model stock price to the observed stock price by adjusting the cost of capital of the firm.
3. Performance profile of the firm—By simulating the firm value and also the stocks and bonds for increasing initial gross returns on investment, we can gain insight into the allocation of risk and values of the contingent claims on the firm.

12.8   Analyses of the Business Model

In this model where there is no debt, the firm can still default because of the fixed cost. We now simulate the firm value as the $\widetilde{GRI}$ increases. Further, we show how this firm value relation to the $\widetilde{GRI}$ changes with the sector volatility. Figure 12.7 presents the results.

In particular, we use the income statement and balance sheet in table 12.3 for illustration. We have used the parameters such that the $\widetilde{GRI}$ is from 0.1 to 1, cost of capital is 10%, the risk-free rate is 6%, the coupon rate is 8%, and the period is 5. We have assumed that the high FC is 140, the low FC is 70, high volatility is 0.4, and low volatility is 0.1. (See figure 12.7.)

By comparing the firm values in case 1 (high fixed costs and high volatility) with case 3 (low fixed costs and high volatility), we see that for the firm with high fixed costs, the firm value increases with the increase of the $\widetilde{GRI}$ with a higher curvature and higher

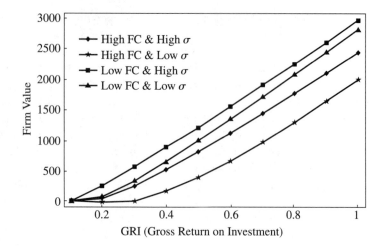

Figure 12.7 Firm value related to the $\widetilde{GRI}$, assuming no investment. The $\widetilde{GRI}$ is from 0.1 to 1 with an interval of 0.1, the cost of capital is 10 percent, the risk-free rate is 6 percent, the coupon rate is 8 percent and the period is 5. We assume that the high FC is 140, the low FC is 70, high volatility is 0.4, and low volatility is 0.1.

gamma. This shows that the presence of the fixed costs leads to the firm value behaving more like a call option.

In cases 2 (high fixed costs and low volatility) and case 4 (low fixed costs and low volatility), the gamma becomes more pronounced. The firm value with high fixed costs behaves like a call option with respect to the gamma and the vega.

12.9   From the Senior Management Perspective

In 1980, as a junior faculty member in the business school at New York University, I was awarded a research scholarship funded by a powerhouse on Wall Street. I was looking forward to the reception for the recipients of the scholarship because I was eager to learn from the senior executives of the firm how in such a short time they had managed to build such a successful company, and what their visions were for their firm in the coming years, when Wall Street seemed to have limitless opportunities. I had so many questions regarding practical corporate finance that my only worry was that I would not have much time to discuss all the topics I wanted to cover. Indeed, the reception was a wonderful opportunity for me to ask my questions.

When the evening arrived, I put on my only jacket and one of my two ties, polished my shoes, and stepped onto the plush executive floor of the firm. I took the first opportunity to ask my questions when I had a chance to meet a partner of the firm.

"With financial innovations going around in Wall Street, how do you see the firm capturing all these opportunities in the near future?" I asked eagerly.

He looked at me as a father would his son, and, to my surprise, he lifted his right foot and starting stamping on the floral patterns of the beautiful Persian rug. He did that repeatedly until all the flowers bore the footprint of his shoes, and withered. "Well, competitors come up like weeds. We have to kill them, kill them, kill them." He then proceeded to stamp on the floral patterns again, as if to say "Just making sure they are all dead."

Unfortunately, the conversation I had prepared did not go much further than watching the dead flowers. The topic drifted to Yankee games that I knew nothing about.

However, I remember those minutes well, not because of words of wisdom that were so profound that they kept me awake, or the idea that beating competition would lead to a new insight in corporate finance. I remember that occasion well because the scene was repeated subsequently in my encounters with the senior management. They all displayed a competitive instinct as the most natural response, at least according to my limited sample of encounters.

"We are the best of the breed," and "We have no equals or peers because we are unique," and "We respect our competition" are all mantras that corporate leaders pronounce in their rallying calls to their troops. However, in their corporate offices, their concern is competition. When their sector does well, the corporate leaders want to do better than the competition. When their sector falls, the leaders want to watch their competitors struggle for survival.

Corporate executives are the first to appreciate the power of "relative valuation" in their competitive ways. But they need a practical tool to exploit the concept of relative valuation, a Black–Scholes model for corporate decisions. They can do well with a tool that can calibrate their business model to the market competition so that they can judge values in a relative sense. This chapter and the following two chapters seek to accomplish this end.

12.10 Summary

This chapter developed a valuation methodology that takes into account the relationship between real sectors and financial sectors. In order to do that, we developed a contingent claim model for the firm by extending the contingent claim models described in previous chapters to determine the appropriate discount rate that should be used to value the firm. We proposed that a firm could be viewed as a contingent claim on its business risks. The uncertainty of the firm, which arises from the business risks, is mainly determined by the nature of its business model. This approach enables us to focus on the relationship of the firm value through the business risk in the business model.

In order to establish our valuation method, we discussed central theorems in corporate finance that motivated our model, the MM theory. This theory suggests that we should first determine the firm value, in order to determine the value of stocks, bonds, and other claims on the firm. This theory provides a consistent framework of analysis of a firm value. Merton took this idea one step further to build the structural model, which is called the Merton model, to show how the value of financial claims on the firm, such as the stocks and the bonds, can be determined for a given risk level.

Each firm has a distinct business model to generate profits. This being the case, we made the assertion that the goal of the management of a firm is to maximize the shareholders' value. Then we described how the MM model claims that financial and investment decisions are independent of each other. Furthermore, we described the use of free cash flows to value a firm. This approach ignores the embedded options in a firm's business model.

The business model of a firm affects the uncertain nature of the firm value. In order to determine the firm value, we showed that the variable costs and fixed costs should be taken into consideration. In the presence of operating leverage, a firm has an embedded call option on the business risk. We showed how the model can be constructed in a lattice framework and that the MM theory can be extended in the multiperiod dynamic framework. In this framework, we view a firm as a contingent claim on the business risks. This way, we relate the business model to the characteristics of the firm in a contingent claim framework, and consider its impact on the stocks' and bonds' values.

This model enables us to study the behavior of the firm's contingent claims as affected by the business model. By way of contrast, the Merton model does not distinguish all the firms in terms of their business risks, and stock and bond values can be affected only by the firm's volatility. A major implication of our approach of viewing the business model of the firm as a way to evaluate its business risks is not incorporated in the Merton model. Therefore, we can develop a model to value corporate strategic investment decisions using our approach. Strategic investment decisions refer to "capital budgeting on a grand scale" (Brealey and Myers, 2002) or "great non-routine financial decisions" (Sametz, 1964). These decisions are important to the firm value, yet they are rarely incorporated explicitly in the valuation of a firm. A theory that builds on a business model enables us to quantify strategic investment decisions. This will be the subject of chapter 13.

Appendix A.   The MM Propositions

We derive the MM Proposition I, the MM Proposition II, and the Miller model by relaxing the tax assumptions one by one. We make the following assumptions by modifying the assumptions we made in the main text to incorporate the personal taxes.

Assumptions

1. Two firms belong to the same risk class when they have the same risk and the discount rate of their free cash flow is ρ, the cost of capital. Therefore the cost of capital of a firm is the same for all the firms in the same risk class.
2. The firms generate a perpetual risky cash flow $\widehat{FCF}$, which means that they make the same capital budgeting decisions.
3. Stocks and bonds are traded in a perfect capital market, which implies that there are no transaction costs.
4. All debt is risk-free, irrespective of the level of debt held by the firm or by the individuals. The rate on the debt is therefore the risk-free rate of return r_f.
5. There are corporation tax, τ_c, and individual interest tax on income received from holding shares, τ_{pe}, and income from bonds, τ_{pb}.

Derivations

To begin, we illustrate a typical income statement to calculate the free cash flows for evaluation purposes. We use parentheses to represent subtracted items.

Income Statement
Revenues
(Variable Cost)
(Fixed Cost)
(Depreciation)
EBIT [Earning Before Interest & Tax]
(Interest on Debt)
EBT [Earning Before Tax]
(Tax)
NI [Net Income]

The free cash flow with the corporate tax rate τ_c, is $(\widetilde{EBIT}-$ interest on debt$)(1 - \tau_c)$ + depreciation $-$ investment expenditure + interest on debt. Since we assume that we maintain the same amount of capital, we replace the depreciation with the same investment expenditure, which means that the free cash flow is $(\widetilde{EBIT}-$ interest on debt$)(1 - \tau_c)$ + interest on debt. If we further apply the personal tax rates on both equity and bond income, $(\widetilde{EBIT}-$ interest on debt$)(1 - \tau_c)$ is subject to the personal tax rate on equity income and the interest on debt is subject to the personal tax rate on bond income.

We can express the cash flow which the stockholders will receive on an after-tax basis as $(\widetilde{EBIT} - r_f \cdot D) \cdot (1 - \tau_c) \cdot (1 - \tau_{pe})$, and the cash flow going to the bondholders on an after-tax basis as $r_f \cdot D \cdot (1 - \tau_{pb})$. Therefore, the total cash flow attributable to the stockholders and the bondholders combined is

$$(\widetilde{EBIT} - r_f \cdot D) \cdot (1 - \tau_c) \cdot (1 - \tau_{pe}) + r_f \cdot D \cdot (1 - \tau_{pb})$$

$$= \widetilde{EBIT} \cdot (1 - \tau_c) \cdot (1 - \tau_{pe}) - r_f \cdot D \cdot (1 - \tau_c) \cdot (1 - \tau_{pe}) + r_f \cdot D \cdot (1 - \tau_{pb})$$

$$= \widetilde{EBIT} \cdot (1 - \tau_c) \cdot (1 - \tau_{pe}) + r_f \cdot D \cdot \left[(1 - \tau_{pb}) - (1 - \tau_c)(1 - \tau_{pe})\right] \qquad (12.23)$$

The first term on the right-hand side of equation (12.23) is exactly the same as the cash flows for the unleveraged firm with exactly the same risk. Therefore, we discount the cash flows from the first term at ρ. The second term on the right-hand side of equation (12.23) is the risk-free cask flows, so that we can discount them at the risk-free rate of return.

$$V_L = \frac{E(\widetilde{EBIT}) \cdot (1 - \tau_c) \cdot (1 - \tau_{pe})}{\rho} + \frac{r_f \cdot D \cdot \left[(1 - \tau_{pb}) - (1 - \tau_c)(1 - \tau_{pe})\right]}{r_f}$$

$$= V_U + \left[1 - \frac{(1 - \tau_c)(1 - \tau_{pe})}{(1 - \tau_{pb})}\right] \cdot D$$

If we assume that the corporate tax rate, τ_c; the personal tax rate on equity income, τ_{pe}; and the personal tax rate on bond income, τ_{pb}; are equal to 0, we have $V_L = V_U$, which is the MM proposition I. If we assume only the corporate tax rate, and not the personal tax rates, regardless of equity income or bond income, we have $V_L = V_U + \tau_c \cdot D$, which is the MM proposition II. Finally, if we assume the corporate tax and two personal taxes, we have $V_L = V_U$, which is the Miller model, because at equilibrium $(1 - \tau_c)(1 - \tau_{pe})$ is equal to $(1 - \tau_{pb})$.

Appendix B.   The Miller Model

Notation

D: Market value of debt

B: Book value of debt

τ_c: corporate tax rate

τ_{pe}: personal tax rate for equity

τ_{pb}: personal tax rate for debt

K_e: cost of equity

K_D: cost of debt

$r_c \cdot B$: interest cost

I: investment

The Value of a Leveraged Firm

$$V^U = \frac{E\left[\widetilde{EBIT}\right] \cdot (1 - \tau_c) \cdot (1 - \tau_{pe})}{\rho} \tag{12.24}$$

Payments to Shareholders of a Leveraged Firm

$$(\widetilde{EBIT} - r_c \cdot B)(1 - \tau_c)(1 - \tau_{pe}) \tag{12.25}$$

Payments to Bondholders of a Leveraged Firm

$$r_c \cdot B \cdot (1 - \tau_{pb}) \tag{12.26}$$

Total Cash Payments to Suppliers of Capital of Leveraged Firm

$$\widetilde{EBIT}(1 - \tau_c)(1 - \tau_{pe}) - r_c \cdot B \cdot (1 - \tau_c) \cdot (1 - \tau_{pe}) + r_c \cdot B \cdot (1 - \tau_{pb}) \tag{12.27}$$

The Value of a Unleveraged Firm

$$
\begin{aligned}
V^L &= \frac{E\left[\widetilde{EBIT}\right] \cdot (1 - \tau_c) \cdot (1 - \tau_{pe})}{\rho} + \frac{r_c \cdot B \cdot \left[(1 - \tau_{pb}) - (1 - \tau_c) \cdot (1 - \tau_{pe})\right]}{K_D} \\
&= V^U + D \cdot \left[1 - \frac{(1 - \tau_c) \cdot (1 - \tau_{pe})}{(1 - \tau_{pb})}\right] \left(\because D = \frac{r_c \cdot B \cdot (1 - \tau_{pb})}{K_D}\right) \tag{12.28} \\
&= V^U + G \cdot D
\end{aligned}
$$

where $G = \left[1 - \frac{(1-\tau_c)\cdot(1-\tau_{pe})}{(1-\tau_{pb})}\right]$

Derivation of the Cost of Equity and the Weighted Cost of Capital

The change in the value of the leveraged firm, ΔV^L, with respect to a new investment, ΔI, is

$$\frac{\Delta V^L}{\Delta I} = \frac{(1-\tau_c)\cdot(1-\tau_{pe})}{\rho} \cdot \frac{\Delta E(\widetilde{EBIT})}{\Delta I} + G \cdot \frac{\Delta D}{\Delta I} \qquad (12.29)$$

ΔV^L can be broken into four parts: the change in the value of original shareholders wealth, ΔS^0; the new equity issues, ΔS^n; the change in the value of original bonds, ΔD^0; and new bond issues, ΔD^n

$$\Delta V^L = \Delta S^0 + \Delta S^n + \Delta D^0 + \Delta D^n \qquad (12.30)$$

Since new investments should be financed with either new equity and new debt, or both,

$$\Delta I = \Delta S^n + \Delta D^n \qquad (12.31)$$

Alternatively, ΔV^L with respect to ΔI is

$$\frac{\Delta V^L}{\Delta I} = \frac{\Delta S^0}{\Delta I} + \frac{\Delta S^n + \Delta D^n}{\Delta I} = \frac{\Delta S^0}{\Delta I} + 1 \qquad (12.32)$$

$$(\because D^0 = 0 \text{ by assumption})$$

From the income statement we have the following identity:

$$NI + r_c \cdot B = (\widetilde{EBIT} - r_c \cdot B) \cdot (1 - \tau_c) + r_c \cdot B$$
$$= \widetilde{EBIT} \cdot (1 - \tau_c) + r_c \cdot B \cdot \tau_c \qquad (12.33)$$

Dividing both sides by ΔI after taking the changes in each term of both sides,

$$\frac{\Delta NI}{\Delta I} + \frac{\Delta(r_c \cdot B)}{\Delta I} - \frac{\tau_c \cdot \Delta(r_c \cdot B)}{\Delta I} = (1-\tau_c) \cdot \frac{\Delta \widetilde{EBIT}}{\Delta I} \qquad (12.34)$$

Substituting equations (12.33) and (12.34) into (12.29) and equating it with (12.32), we have

$$\frac{\Delta V^L}{\Delta I} = \frac{(1-\tau_{pe})}{\rho}\left(\frac{\Delta NI}{\Delta I} + \frac{\Delta(r_c \cdot B)}{\Delta I} - \frac{\tau_c \cdot \Delta(r_c \cdot B)}{\Delta I}\right) + G \cdot \frac{\Delta D}{\Delta I}$$

$$= \frac{\Delta S^0 + \Delta S^n}{\Delta I} + \frac{\Delta D^n}{\Delta I} \qquad (12.35)$$

$$\rho \cdot (\Delta S^0 + \Delta S^n)$$

$$= (1 - \tau_{pe}) \left[\Delta NI + \Delta (r_c \cdot B) - \tau_c \cdot \Delta (r_c \cdot B) \right] + \rho \cdot \Delta D \cdot (G - 1) (\because \Delta D = \Delta D^n)$$

$$= (1 - \tau_{pe}) \left[\Delta NI + (1 - \tau_C) \cdot \frac{K_D}{(1 - \tau_{pb})} \cdot \Delta D \right] + \rho \cdot \Delta D \cdot (G - 1) \qquad (12.36)$$

$$= (1 - \tau_{pe}) \cdot \Delta NI + \frac{(1 - \tau_{pe})(1 - \tau_c)}{(1 - \tau_{pb})} \cdot \Delta D \cdot K_D + \rho \cdot \Delta D \cdot (G - 1)$$

$$= (1 - \tau_{pe}) \cdot \Delta NI + G^* \cdot \Delta D \cdot (K_D - \rho) \ (\text{Let } G^* = 1 - G)$$

Manipulating equation (12.36), we have

$$\frac{\Delta NI}{\Delta S^0 + \Delta S^n} = \frac{\rho}{(1 - \tau_{pe})} + \frac{(1 - \tau_c)}{(1 - \tau_{pb})} \cdot (\rho - K_D) \cdot \frac{\Delta D}{\Delta S^0 + \Delta S^n} \qquad (12.37)$$

If we follow Modigliani and Miller (1963) by assuming that the marginal changes correspond to the long-term target debt ratio, then equation (12.37) should be

$$\frac{\Delta NI}{\Delta S^0 + \Delta S^n} = \frac{\rho}{(1 - \tau_{pe})} + \frac{(1 - \tau_c)}{(1 - \tau_{pb})} \cdot (\rho - K_D) \frac{D}{S} (\because \frac{\Delta D}{\Delta S} = \frac{D}{S}) \qquad (12.38)$$

The cost of equity on the after-tax basis is

$$K_e = \frac{\Delta NI}{\Delta S^0 + \Delta S^n} \cdot (1 - \tau_{pe})$$

$$= \left(\frac{\rho}{(1 - \tau_{pe})} + \frac{(1 - \tau_c)}{(1 - \tau_{pb})} \cdot (\rho - K_D) \cdot \frac{D}{S} \right) \cdot (1 - \tau_{pe}) \qquad (12.39)$$

$$= \rho + \left[\frac{(1 - \tau_c) \cdot (1 - \tau_{pe})}{(1 - \tau_{pb})} \cdot (\rho - K_D) \right] \cdot \frac{D}{S}$$

WACC

$$= (1 - \tau_c) \frac{K_D}{(1 - \tau_c)} \cdot \frac{D}{S + D} + K_e \cdot \frac{S}{S + D}$$

$$= K_D \cdot \frac{D}{V} + \left[\rho + \frac{(1 - \tau_c) \cdot (1 - \tau_{pe})}{(1 - \tau_{pb})} \cdot (\rho - K_D) \cdot \frac{D}{S} \right] \cdot \frac{S}{V} (\because S + D = V)$$

$$= K_D \cdot \frac{D}{V} + \rho \cdot \frac{S}{V} + \frac{(1 - \tau_c) \cdot (1 - \tau_{pe})}{(1 - \tau_{pb})} \cdot (\rho - K_D) \cdot \frac{D}{V}$$

$$= \rho \cdot \left(\frac{S}{V} + \frac{(1 - \tau_c) \cdot (1 - \tau_{pe})}{(1 - \tau_{pb})} \cdot \frac{D}{V} \right) + K_D \cdot \frac{D}{V} \cdot \left(1 - \frac{(1 - \tau_c) \cdot (1 - \tau_{pe})}{(1 - \tau_{pb})} \right)$$

Since an equilibrium condition is $(1 - \tau_c) \cdot (1 - \tau_{pe}) = (1 - \tau_{pb})$,

$$WACC = \rho \qquad (12.40)$$

Notes

1. Much of the information is drawn from a research report on Starbucks Coffee Japan by Hideki Sakura of the Financial Research Center, Nomura Securities, October 24, 2001.

2. We use this balance sheet and income statement throughout the chapter.

3. If we assume that the dividend grows at 5 percent every year, the equity value is

$$S = \frac{\text{dividend}}{K_e - g} = \frac{\$10}{0.1 - 0.05} = \$200 \text{ where } g \text{ is the dividend growth rate}$$

4. The perpetual cash flows are $E(\widetilde{FCF}) - D_L \cdot r_f$. We use ρ as a discount rate for the risky cash flow part of $E(\widetilde{FCF}) - D_L \cdot r_f$, which is $\frac{E(\widetilde{FCF})}{\rho}$. We use r_f as a discount rate for the risk-free cash flow part of $E(\widetilde{FCF}) - D_L \cdot r_f$, which is D_L. Therefore, the present value of the perpetual cash flows, $E(\widetilde{FCF}) - D_L \cdot r_f$, is $\frac{E(\widetilde{FCF})}{\rho} - D_L$.

References

Abernethy, M. A., and P. Brownell. 1995. The role of budgets in organizations facing strategic change: An exploratory study. *Accounting, Organizations and Society*, 24 (3), 189–204.

Bolton, P., and E. Thadden. 1997. Liquidity and control: A dynamic theory of corporate ownership structure. *Journal of Institutional and Theoretical Economics*, 154 (1), 177–211.

Brealey, R. A., and S. C. Myers. 2002. *Principles of Corporate Finance*. 7th ed. Boston: Irwin/McGraw-Hill.

Brennan, M., and E. Schwartz. 1978. Corporate income taxes, valuation, and the problem of optimal capital structure. *Journal of Business*, 51, 103–114.

Brennan, M., and E. Schwartz. 1984. Optimal financial policy and firm valuation. *Journal of Finance*, 39, 593–607.

Brooks, L. D., and D. A. Buckmaster. 1976. Further evidence of the time-series properties of accounting income. *Journal of Finance*, 31, 1359–1373.

Brous, P. A., and O. Kini. 1994. The valuation effects of equity issues and the level of institutional ownership: Evidence from analysts' earnings forecasts. *Financial Management*, 23 (1), 1359–1373.

Chatterjea, A., J. A. Cherian, and R. A. Jarrow. 1993. Market manipulation and corporate finance: A new perspective. *Financial Management*, 22 (2), 200–209.

Chow, G. C. 1996. The Lagrange method of optimization with applications to portfolio and investment decisions. *Journal of Economic Dynamics and Control*, 20 (1–3), 1–18.

Christofferson, P., F. X. Diebold, and T. Schuermann. 1998. Horizon problems and extreme events in financial risk management. *Economic Policy Review*, 4 (3), 109–118.

Copeland, T., T. Koller, and J. Murrin. 2000. *Valuation: Measuring and Managing the Value of Companies*, 3rd ed. New York: John Wiley & Sons.

Copeland, T., and J. F. Weston. 1992. *Financial Theory and Corporate Policy*, 3rd ed. Reading, Mass.: Addison-Wesley.

Duffie, D. 2001. *Dynamic Asset Pricing Theory*, 3rd ed. Princeton, NJ: Princeton University Press.

Franks, J. R., and J. J. Pringle. 1982. Debt financing, corporate financial intermediaries and firm valuation. *Journal of Finance*, 37 (3), 751–761.

Graham, J. R. 1999. Do personal taxes affect corporate financing decisions? *Journal of Public Economics*, 73 (2), 147–185.

Gupta, A., and L. Rosenthal. 1991. Ownership structure, leverage and firm value: The case of leveraged recapitalization. *Financial Management*, 20 (3), 69–83.

Jensen, M. 1986. Agency costs of free cash flow, corporate financing, and takeovers. *American Economic Review*, 76 (2), 323–329.

Jones, E. P., S. P. Mason, and E. Rosenfeld. 1984. Contingent claims analysis of corporate capital structures: An empirical investigation. *Journal of Finance*, 39, 611–625.

Kale, J. R., T. H. Noe, and G. G. Ramirez. 1991. The effect of business risk on corporate capital structure: Theory and evidence. *Journal of Finance*, 46 (5), 1693–1715.

Kaplan, R. S., and D. P. Norton. 1996. Linking the balanced scorecard to strategy. *California Management Review*, 39 (1), 53–79.

Kaplan, S. N., and R. S. Ruback. 1995. The valuation of cash flow forecasts: An empirical analysis. *Journal of Finance*, 50 (4), 1059–1093.

Lamont, O. 1997. Cash flow and investment: Evidence from internal capital market. *Journal of Finance*, 52, 83–111.

Lang, L., E. Ofek, and R. Stulz. 1996. Leverage, investment, and firm growth. *Journal of Financial Economics*, 40, 3–30.

Lee, H. W., and J. A. Gentry. 1995. An empirical study of the corporate choice among common stock, convertible bonds and straight debt: A cash flow interpretation. *Quarterly Review of Economics and Finance*, 35 (4), 397–419

Majd, S., and R. S. Pindyck. 1987. Time to build, option value, and investment decisions. *Journal of Financial Economics*, 18, 7–27.

Merton, R. C. 1974. On the pricing of corporate debt: The risk structure of interest rates. *Journal of Finance*, 29 (2), 449–470.

Miller, M. H. 1977. Debt and taxes. *Journal of Finance*, 32, 261–275.

Minton, B. A., and S. Catherine. 1999. The impact of cash flow volatility on discretionary investment and the costs of debt and equity financing. *Journal of Financial Economics*, 54 (3), 423–460.

Modigliani, F., and M. Miller. 1958. The cost of capital, corporation finance and the theory of investment. *American Economic Review*, 48, 267–297.

Modigliani, F., and M. Miller. 1963. Corporate income taxes and the cost of capital: A correction. *American Economics Review*, 53 (3), 433–443.

Myers, S., and N. S. Majluf. 1984. Corporate financing and investment decisions when firms have information that investors do not have. *Journal of Financial Economics*, 13, 187–221.

Myers, S. C. 1974. Interactions of corporate financing and investment decisions—Implications for capital budgeting. *Journal of Finance*, 29, 1–26.

O'Brien, P. C. 1988. Analysts' forecasts as earnings expectations. *Journal of Accounting and Economics*, 10 (1), 53–83.

Opler, T. C. 1993. Controlling financial distress costs in leveraged buyouts with financial innovations. *Financial Management*, 22 (3), 79–90.

Pindyck, R. 1988. Irreversible investment, capacity choice and the value of the firm. *American Economic Review*, 78 (5), 969–985.

Ross, S. A., R. W. Westerfield, and B. D. Jordan. 2002. *Fundamentals of Corporate Finance*, 6th ed. Boston: Irwin/McGraw-Hill..

Sabour, S., and A. Abdel. 1999. Decision making with option pricing and dynamic programming: Development and application. *Resources Policy*, 25 (4), 257–264.

Sharpe, W. F., G. J. Alexander, and J. V. Bailey. 1998. *Investments*, 6th ed. Englewood Cliffs, NJ: Prentice-Hall.

Shome, D. K., and S. Singh. 1995. Firm value and external blockholdings. *Financial Management*, 24 (4), 3–14.

Stark, A. W. 2000. Real options (dis)investment decision-making and accounting measures of performance. *Journal of Business Finance and Accounting*, 27 (3/4), 313–332.

Taber, C. R. 2000. Semiparametric identification and heterogeneity in discrete choice dynamic programming models. *Journal of Econometrics*, 96 (2), 201–229.

Winton, A. 1993. Limitation of liability and the ownership structure of the firm. *Journal of Finance*, 48 (2), 487–512.

Further Readings

Bartov, E., and G. M. Bodnar. 1994. Firm valuation, earnings expectations, and the exchange-rate exposure effect. *Journal of Finance*, 49 (5), 1755–1785.

Kaplan, R. S., and D. P. Norton. 1996. Using the balanced scorecard as a strategic management system. Working paper, *Harvard Business Review*, January–February, 75–85.

Kaplan, R. S., and D. P. Norton. 2001. Transforming the balanced scorecard from performance measurement to strategic management: Part 1. *Accounting Horizons*, 15 (1), 87–104.

Kaplan, R. S., and D. P. Norton. 2001. Transforming the balanced scorecard from performance measurement to strategic management: Part 2. *Accounting Horizons*, 15 (1), 147–160.

Shoven, J. B., J. M. Dickson, and C. Sialm. 2000. Tax externalities of equity mutual funds. Working paper, Stanford University.

Subramanyam, K. R., and M. Venkatachalam. 2001. Earnings, cash flows and expost intrinsic value of equity. Working paper, University of Southern California.

Winton, Andrew, 1993. Limitation of liability and the ownership structure of the firm. *Journal of Finance*, 48 (2), 489–512.

13

Strategic Value of a Firm: Real Options

Most firms have significant strategic value, the present value of a firm's future (potential) business. Firm valuation must incorporate the strategic value to provide a more complete description of the firm valuation, something that the standard free cash flow discount method fails to do. The validity of the model is supported by empirical evidence in the valuation of corporate high yield bonds. The model has many applications to both corporate finance and capital markets. It can be used for valuing corporate bonds, structuring and pricing, credit derivatives, enterprise risk management, and designs of corporate insurance.

Thus far, we have discussed two aspects of shareholders' value. Chapter 11 described the financial models for the assets and liabilities to determine their fair value, as opposed to the book value. Market equity value, which is the asset fair value net of the liability fair value, is a measure of the value that the shareholders would claim on the firm if the firm were to liquidate by retiring all the debts at the market prices and selling the remaining assets to investors. In chapter 12, we described how a relative valuation model can be used to determine the market capitalization of the firm. Market capitalization of the firm is the shareholders' value of the firm as a going concern.

Having explained several approaches to value market capitalization or the firm value, we still need to take into account an important component that possibly constitutes a major portion of the firm value: the strategic value of a firm. Business opportunities arise in unpredictable ways. Scientific breakthroughs in biotechnology open profitable opportunities for firms that can capture the opportunities. For example, Genetech went public in the late 1970s and grew to a $30 billion company. The $4 billion capitalization of Amazon.com, an internet retail operation, is based on the potential of the business, even though the firm has yet to report a profit. In other words, we cannot explain the $4 billion capitalization of Amazon.com with only the discounted future earnings, which we could estimate based on the current earnings. The *strategic value* of the firm refers to the possible future business opportunities that the firm could capture, without identifying precisely what those projects would be and how the company would undertake them.

Biotechnologies, such as gene splicing, can lead to the discovery of new drugs and may revolutionize the health care industry. The market rewards firms like Genetech and Amgen for their market positions in that area. Yet few analysts can predict the number of patents these firms can produce or the value of those patents. Internet retail commerce may change the way retail businesses are conducted, but few analysts know where Internet technologies will lead in the future. Surely, though, the capitalization of firms like Genetech and Amazon.com show the importance of the value of such market expectation: the strategic value. Therefore, we cannot ignore such value when evaluating a firm.

With large market potential, like that of biotechnology and Internet companies, the firms which stand ready for possible opportunities can accrue significant market value. But how can we assign value to such intangible business potential of a firm? When these firms cannot offer a plan with clear capital budgeting projection to reflect the value of the projects, how do we apply the present-value methodology to determine the value? Since the strategic value strives against uncertainty, how can any method that is based on the expected cash flows be used when the uncertainty is not modeled?

The answer to these questions demands a new approach, the real option valuation. Previous chapters describe options as financial contracts offering the holders the right, but not the obligation, to buy or sell an underlying security. Derivatives are financial contracts whose payoffs depend on the value or characteristics of an underlying security. A contingent claim is a general construct in which the claim is contingent on risk sources on the real sector. Now we continue to extend the concept of a financial option to a *real option*, which is a contingent claim on business opportunities rather than financial securities. The real option can take into account the flexibility of the investment, which is capital budgeting of a corporation on the real sector, not just investment in financial securities.

This chapter has two parts. We will first identify the salient features of these options and describe a broad range of these options. We will describe the real options in capital budgeting and in specific business sectors. We will then discuss the embedded real options in investment opportunities which firms face, and develop a methodology to evaluate the options. We will apply the methodology to our retail chain stores example and show how real options enable us to evaluate the firm's strategic value. In the second part, we discuss some applications of the model. In particular, we apply the model to value high-yield bonds. Our methodology shows that a business model can value high-yield bonds more accurately than the Merton's structural model by testing the model empirically.

13.1 Characteristics of a Growth Company—An Example of Real Options

A growth company is a company that could attain a high growth rate. The growth may not be based on a clear plan of investing in a series of profitable projects. Consider America On Line (AOL).

AOL's business mission is to make the Internet accessible to everyone. However, the mission itself is not a business model because it does not reveal how revenues could be generated, even though the business mission provides many possible business opportunities that may be realized in the future. AOL believes holding a large subscriber base will ensure many business opportunities. For example, by establishing itself as an important portal to the Internet, AOL could build an E-mail system with instant message delivery. At the same time, it could grow to a larger subscriber base through acquisitions by using the high valuation of its stocks, which have been buoyed by the business potential. AOL acquired Time Warner to gain access to customers via cable and also to the media contents. The business strategy was an opportunistic one based on the business prospects of Internet technologies. Such was the sentiment of the explosive growth of the "new economy" in 1997–2000. AOL exemplified the fact that firms have real options or business opportunities that may not be readily specified as a capital budgeting problem, which depends on projected cash flows and net present value calculations. Real options reap profits, which vary in an uncertain way, depending on the future business environment.

Real options are not embedded only in growth companies. Consider a medium-size biotechnology company. Such a company needs to invest in a series of projects to realize future business opportunities. A series of technologies must be developed, and then commercialized. Since the market will determine the real option value at the commercialization stage, we can view the series of technologies as a series of options.

We can consider a software company holding real options. Each version of a particular type of software has a limited shelf life. After each release of the software, new investments have to be made for the next version or new products have to be explored. Many software companies publish software that does not maintain recurring revenues for a period of time. They do not expect all new software releases to be financial successes, and a failure does not usually reduce a company to financial ruin. The market may view a software company as having a portfolio of options staggered over time, since the company has the flexibility of launching a new release only when the release is projected to be commercially viable.

13.2   Salient Features of Real Options

In contrast to the discounted free cash flow approach in valuing a project, the real option approach has two important features which are particularly critical in capital budgeting: (1) capturing the management flexibility in the investment decisions and (2) determining the appropriate discount rate, which varies across time.

Flexibility

The flexibility of doing investment or disinvestment is important to the valuation of a firm. When the business environment changes from the one assumed in the business plan, most firms revise their plans accordingly. For the same reason, firms establish contingencies in the event of unanticipated changes in the market environment when they make *capital budgeting decisions*. Their capital budgeting decisions will be different, depending on whether the projects are flexible. They accept capital projects which might be rejected if they do not capture the investment flexibility.

This can be illustrated by a simple numerical example. Suppose a firm has to make an investment of $40 to initiate a project. This project can be leasing land for exploration of oil, developing the prototype of a software system, or building a management team for the task ahead.

The project has a second phase of development. In this second phase, the firm has to invest $200 to capture the future earnings. Assume that there are two scenarios with equal probability at the second phase. In one case, the market environment is favorable, and the present value of the future cash flows is $400. In the other case, the market environment is unfavorable, and the present value of the future cash flows is 0. For simplicity, we assume that the interest rates are 0.

We could imagine this type of project in reality. For example, a company wants to launch a new product. However, it is not sure the product will be viable in the market. Therefore, the company conducts market research, such as a consumer survey. If the company receives favorable responses from the consumers, it will build a factory to produce the new product on a large scale. Otherwise, it will abandon the new product. The first phase is the market research phase, where the company pays $40. At the second phase, the company commits an investment of $200 for mass production. At the second stage, it has an option to expand, which has been ignored in the traditional discounted cash flow approach.

Let us apply the discounted cash flow approach to this capital budgeting problem. The expected net present value at the second phase is

$$NPV(phase2) = 0.5 \times (\$400 - \$200) + 0.5 \times (\$0 - \$200) = 0$$

However, the first phase investment is $40. Therefore the project has a negative net present value of −$40, and the project should be rejected.

Now, let us take into account the flexibility of taking on a project. At the second phase of the project, if the unfavorable market scenario prevails, there is no incentive to invest $200. We would invest only when the favorable scenario prevails. Therefore, the expected net present value of the project in phase 2 is

$$NPV(phase2) = 0.5 \times (\$400 - \$200) + 0.5 \times (\$0 - \$0) = \$100$$

Taking the initial investment into account, the net present value of the project is $60.

The analysis shows that the firm should undertake the initial investment in the project because the entire project has a positive net present value, contrary to the conclusion of the discounted cash flow method. In taking the flexibility of the decision-making process into account, we can come to a different investment decision based on different scenarios. The main difference between the real option approach and the discounted value approach is that in the former, risks are explicitly modeled; it clearly distinguishes the favorable scenario from the unfavorable scenario. The way the risks are specified directly affects the decisions of the firm because a different decision is made for each possible scenario.

Determining the Appropriate Discount Rate

The example above illustrates the importance of flexibility in the capital budgeting decisions, which are the state-dependent decision rules. We can determine the value of flexibility by using the real option. Another important use of the option pricing model, as we have shown in previous chapters, is the determination of the appropriate discount rate. The following example illustrates how option pricing can be used to appropriately determine the risk-adjusted discount rate.

As we saw in chapter 7, the discount rate of an option depends on the type of option. Given the expected payment of an option, the discount rate of the expected payment has to depend on the expected returns of the underlying stock, the relative value of the strike price, and the underlying stock price. In essence, to determine the discount rate, we need to develop the option pricing model. To decide on the net present value of a project with embedded real options, there is no better approach than to develop an option pricing model of the project. Valuing a project with embedded real options using the net present-value approach is as problematic as pricing derivatives with a discount rate or option-embedded bonds with a bond yield. In previous chapters, we have shown that the appropriate methodology to value the derivatives is to use a relative valuation approach instead of discounting the expected cash flows of a derivative. Similarly, to value bonds with embedded options, such as mortgage-backed securities, we use interest rate contingent claims methods and do not discount the expected payments of the bonds with the yield to maturity.

Consider a project that has a present value of $100. It is expected that both the value of the project and its risks change over time. Let us assume that the value increases or decreases at an equal probability. Let us further assume that the cost of capital is 20%, which is the expected rate of return of the project, and the risk-free rate is 10%.

We have the following binomial lattice of the project value, depicted in figure 13.1. The initial project value goes up to 110 × 1.2 or down to 90 × 1.2. The upward value, 110×1.2, is determined by increasing by 10 from the initial project value and multiplying the increased value by 1.2, which is the expected rate of return. The downward value, 90×1.2, will be similarly determined except for decreasing by 10. The subsequent project values will de defined accordingly. In other words, the project values are determined by a common factor, which is the expected rate of return and an upward or downward factor, depending on a binomial movement. In this example, the upward factor and the downward factor are 10 and −10, respectively. (See figure 13.1.)

At the end of year 2, we have the option to invest in the project for $144, and the initial commitment fee is $0.05.

If we use the discounted cash flow method, the net present value of the project is

$$NPV =$$
$$\frac{(0.25 \times \$120 \times 1.2^2 + 0.5 \times \$100 \times 1.2^2 + 0.25 \times \$80 \times 1.2^2 - \$144)}{1.2^2}$$
$$- \$0.05 = -\$0.05 < 0$$

Under the discounted cash flow approach, we would reject the project.

Now let us apply the option pricing methodology. In option pricing, we take the relative valuation into account; that is, we make use of the information that the present value of the project is $100 and its subsequent uncertain movements are defined on the binomial lattice.

At the end of year 2, the payouts are given as 28.8, 0, 0 (ordering the states from the highest payout to the lowest). Now we calculate the risk-neutral probability, which is given as

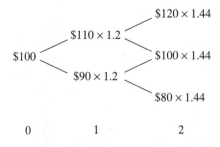

$100 — $110 × 1.2 — $120 × 1.44 / $100 × 1.44 ; $90 × 1.2 — $100 × 1.44 / $80 × 1.44

0   1   2

Figure 13-1 The binomial lattice of the values of the project. The value of the project grows at an expected rate of 20 percent annually over three years. The investment in the project requires a commitment fee initially and an investment at the end of the second year. 1.44 and 1.728 represent 1.2 raised to the second power and third power, respectively.

$$p = \frac{V(1 + r_f) - V_d}{V_u - V_d} \tag{13.1}$$

where V is the value at a node, and V_u and V_d are the values at the up state and the down state from the node, respectively. The risk neutral probabilities are

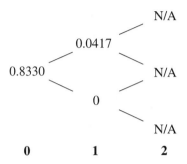

Let the project value be denoted by C, and we can apply the backward substitution defined below:

$$C = \frac{p \times C_u + (1 - p) \times C_d}{1 + r_f} \tag{13.2}$$

The resulting lattice of the project value is

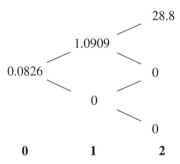

The value of the project, the option value net of the initial cost of $0.05, is $0.0326, which is positive. We should accept the project. This approach shows that we should not use the cost of capital as the discount rate. Instead, we infer the discount rate from the present value of the project.

We have shown that when there are real options embedded in the firm value, the use of the cost of capital to discount the expected free cash flows may be erroneous because it is not apparent what the appropriate cost of capital would be. We apply the contingent claim valuation approach and show that a firm's real option can be valued within the context of a contingent claim valuation model of a firm.

13.3   Examples of Real Options in Capital Budgeting

While we recognize that there are real options embedded in corporations, let us first discuss some of the generic types of real options. Real options are described more often in the context of capital budgeting. Before we discuss how to extend the option valuation methodology to real options, we first provide some examples of generic real options.

Growth Options and Contract Options

Myers (1984a) introduced *growth options*. The real option model refers to the ability of the firm to make an investment only when a project is profitable. The growth is driven by these options. A similar option is a timing option or time-deferring option. McDonald and Siegal (1986) provide a description of such an option where the firm can decide on the optimal time to invest in a project, which follows a risk process.

For example, consider the following numerical example where the firm value follows the binomial movements in figure 13.1. One type of growth option can be formulated by assuming that the firm value at year 2 would double if the management invests at year 2. We can invest only at year 2. The firm value follows the binomial lattice with an equal probability, and the expected value of the firm grows at 20% annually. (See figure 13.2.)

Suppose that the firm has an option to grow such that its value can double with an investment of 100×1.2^2 at the end of the second year. We choose the investment amount at the end of the second year to make the calculation easier. The expansion will be undertaken if the expansion has a higher value than not expanding. Therefore, at each node of year 2, we have $V^* = Max(V, 2V - I)$, where V is the value of the firm at each node of year 2 and I is an investment amount at the end of the second year.

Now consider the net present values at the end of the second year conditional on the firm's investment decision, which are ordered by the state of the world as

$$\text{time 2 and state 2: } Max\left[240 \times 1.2^2 - 100 \times 1.2^2, 120 \times 1.2^2\right]$$

$$\text{time 2 and state 1: } Max\left[200 \times 1.2^2 - 100 \times 1.2^2, 100 \times 1.2^2\right]$$

$$\text{time 2 and state 0: } Max\left[160 \times 1.2^2 - 100 \times 1.2^2, 80 \times 1.2^2\right]$$

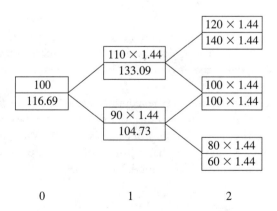

Figure 13-2 Binomial lattice of a growth option. The firm has the option to double its value at a fixed investment cost I at the end of the second year; $V^* = Max(V, 2V - I)$, where V is the value of the firm at each node at year 2. The upper panel is the underlying firm value and the lower panel is the growth option value.

At the end of the second year, the values are 140×1.2^2, 100×1.2^2, and 80×1.2^2, for the three states of the world. Given these values, we can now apply the risk-neutral probabilities calculated in the previous example to determine the value of the firm with the growth option.

By a similar argument, we can evaluate an option to reduce the size of the firm. In this case, at a certain time horizon, the firm is expected to pay out amount I_{payout} as expenses. But the firm has the option to reduce its size by a certain factor (say 50%) by paying a small amount of expenses, I^*_{payout}, where $I^*_{payout} < I_{payout}$. In this case, the terminal condition is given by $V^* = Max(V - I_{payout}, 0.5 \times V - I^*_{payout})$. We apply the same backward substitution procedure to determine the value of the firm with the contraction option.

Investment Series

When companies have to continually invest in irreversible projects and confront the uncertainty of the market or the success of the product, as some software companies have experienced, we can model these companies as having a series of call options. The exercise price is the total amount of investment. To begin the development of a new version of software is to buy a call option. Launching the release of the new version marks the expiration date of the call option. If the new release is not expected to bring a present value of profits exceeding the cost of marketing and supporting it, the project will be abandoned, letting the call option expire. If the new release is launched, the software company will begin the development of another new version; otherwise the company may change its development plan. This is a series of call options. The call option may be related or unrelated, but it defines the future project, whose risks depend not only on the underlying demand for the software but also on the exercise price and the time to expiration.

Abandonment Option

In biotechnology, intellectual properties such as patents have been developed. However, if the commercialization of the intellectual properties cannot be realized, the intellectual properties may be sold, which is the *abandonment option*. Sometimes a company will merge with another company that can make use of the intellectual property. Thus, if the firm cannot exploit the full commercial value of the intellectual property, the full commercial value can still be realized through a merger, and therefore the intellectual property offers the firm an abandonment value.

The real option of abandoning a firm offers the shareholders a put option on the firm value, which is equal to the present value of the firm's free cash flow. The put option has a stochastic strike price, which is equal to the exit value. Berger et al. (1996) empirically investigate the value of this put option in the firm valuation.

The above argument shows that the firm total capitalization should be the sum of the present value of the free cash flows and the put option on the present value of the free cash flows with the exit value as the strike price. Specifically, we have the following equation:

$$V = PV(\widetilde{FCF}) + Put(PV(\widetilde{FCF}), X, \sigma) \tag{13.3}$$

where V is the value of the firm; $PV(\widetilde{FCF})$ is the present value of the free cash flow; Put is the put option on $PV(\widetilde{FCF})$; X is the exit value; and σ is the volatility of the returns of $PV(\widetilde{FCF})$. (See figure 13.3.)

The exit value is estimated from historical values of discontinued operations' fixed assets, inventory, and short-term assets. Using cross-section analysis, the exit value can be estimated from the sample.

The observed total capitalization of a firm net of the present value of the free cash flow, which is an abandonment option value, is shown to be significantly related to the exit value, consistent with the abandonment option theory. Furthermore, the results show that there is a more ready market for the more general or less specialized assets when they are sold, and the abandonment value is higher, which one would expect. In sum, the empirical results support the market pricing of the put options in the firm valuation.

Retainer Option to Defer Investment

Technology development can be often seen as a *retainer option*. Significant investments have to be committed for each stage of the development. The value of the investment depends on the prevailing market valuation when the technology is released. Panayi and Trigeorgis (1998) describe such options more generally as multistage options where there are typically three phases in taking a product from concept to the market. The phases are research, development, and commercialization. Each phase offers the firm a call option. This is a series of compound call options on the valuation of the commercial value of technology.

The concept of a retainer option is commonly used in software development. Prototyping to predict or reduce the uncertainty over the future profitability of a software design choice is a form of a retainer option. In software development, a major revision is expensive. It has been suggested that a prototype of the revision should first be built to simulate the commercial viability of the revision. The software company can make the

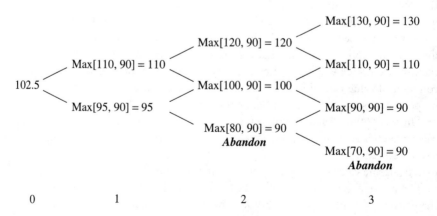

Figure 13-3 Abandonment option. The first argument in the max operation is the firm value and the second argument is the exit price. At the node at time 2 and state 0 or at time 3 and state 0, the firm will exit, because the exit price is higher than the firm value. We assume that the exit price is 90.

Retainer Option Process

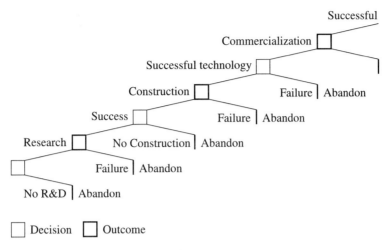

Figure 13-4 Retainer option process. This figure shows the concept of multistage decision options through the familiar example of R&D. Research and development of a new technology can be viewed as a series of sequential decisions, with research as the first stage, followed by decisions on technical construction and commercialization/implementation in sequence stages. Source: Panayi and Trigeorgis, 1998.

decision on the major revision more effectively after the new estimates of the profitability of the revision are made with the prototype. (See figure 13.4.)

Chalasani et al. (1998) consider the problem using a decision tree, where the value of the revised software follows a nonrecombining tree where each node has two outcomes with equal probabilities. They assume that the use of prototyping will change the probabilities assigned to the tree and, as a result, affect the decision to undertake a major revision one period after the prototyping is completed. If the cost of prototyping is less than the present value of the flexibility of decision as a result of prototyping, then the software company should produce a prototype before starting the project of revising the software.

13.4   Examples of Businesses with Embedded Options

We saw in the previous section that the real option approach is a valuable tool in capital budgeting, because the real option approach takes flexibility into consideration and provides with an appropriate discount rate, which is essential for capital budgeting. The growth option or contraction option, the abandonment option, and the retainer option represent a choice of adjusting investments depending on states in the capital budgeting decisions. Since flexibility inherently causes the risks involved in the capital budgeting to change, it is also important to adjust the discount rate to reflect the changing risks over time. On top of capital budgeting, we observe many examples of businesses with embedded options, which shows that the real option approach has broad applications beyond capital budgeting. This section illustrates how we use the real option approach to evaluate a business sector.

Information Technology

Schwartz and Zozaya-Gorostiza (2000) analyze the real options in information technology (IT). Their model asserts that IT assets cannot be developed instantaneously. IT has to be developed over a period of time. And during the development period, the value of the asset V grows at a certain rate until the IT asset is completed. When the IT asset is completed, with value V, it will generate positive cash flows to the firm. By comparison, the firm can acquire the IT asset by not developing, but waiting to acquire the appropriate IT asset at the end of a period, for instance. The advantage of acquiring the IT asset is not committing to a particular technology when the technological uncertainties are high, but acquiring the asset that is most beneficial to the firm at the later date. This value of flexibility has to be balanced against the uncertainty of the cost of acquiring the asset in the future.

Schwartz and Zozaya-Gorostiza then applied their model to a case study on building a banking network expansion described by Benaroch and Kauffman (2000). The banking network expansion problem was posed to an industry leader, who had a three-year lead over the immediate competitor. Using the real option approach, they showed that the optimal decision for the expansion should be delayed so that the expansion could exploit the changing technologies. This analytical result agrees with the actual management decision of the industry leader.

Mining and Exploration: Option to Temporarily Shut Down

Brennan and Schwartz (1985) proposed a mining model that constructs a deferral (alternatively called retainer) option where the mining company considers the spot price of the commodity in order to decide on the expansion of production.

Then Brennan and Schwartz specify the impact of investment on the production. Depending on the level of the prevailing commodity price, the optimal investment decisions of closing and abandonment options can be determined. The difference between the *closing option* and the abandonment option is that in closing, a closed mine can be reopened at a reopening cost in the future, whereas abandonment does not allow any revival of the mine. The firm is then assumed to choose the option that provides the shareholders the highest market value of the firm.

Cortazar and Casassus (1998) extended the model to an ongoing mining company, say, a copper mining company. Specifically, a process of the commodity price movements is proposed. The spot price of copper is defined in a risk-adjusted process:

$$\frac{dS}{S} = \left(r^{real} - cy + b(\overline{S} - S)\right) dt + \sigma_S dW \qquad (13.4)$$

where S denotes the spot copper price; $\overline{S}$ is the long-term average unit price of copper; b is the adjustment speed of the mean reversion process; r^{real} is the constant real risk-free rate; and cy is the convenient yield. The investments lead to increased production. Without any investments, the reserve would be depleted. The multiperiod optimal investment decisions are made by taking the prevailing market price of the copper, as well as all the possible future decisions and past decisions, into account. They use the Bellman optimization method to solve for the optimal decisions.

Cortazar et al. (2001) suggested an exploration model by extending the mining model. In this model, the commodity price follows a process similar to that of mining.

The following assumptions are made in the model:[1]

1. The mine is currently producing copper valued at $W(S, Q)$, where S is the price and Q is the output
2. The mine has flexibility in investing I that will lead to increased production of q with a decrease in unit cost of production. The investment is irreversible.

Since the only risk source is the price of copper, and since copper is a tradable asset, we can assume the copper price will follow a risk-neutral process, and that the mine value is a contingent claim on the copper price. Therefore, the mine value also follows a risk-neutral process. The investment decisions, which must depend on the time and copper price, are then determined to maximize the mine value by the Bellman optimal solution. The solution is the optimal timing of the expansion decision. The real option in this case is a timing option.

Exploration is viewed as a series of compound options, since it is a series of investments which rely on the success of the previous exploration. The model also has a technological risk. In essence, the model assumes that the output or productivity is uncertain. The exploration company seeks to maximize the present value of the revenue, which is the product of the price and the output.

Competitive Model

In practical applications, many capital budgeting decisions must take competition into account. Management has to assume that its competitors will react to its investment decisions. Smit and Ankum (1993) use the binomial lattice framework to determine the equilibrium outcome at each node by taking the optimal strategy of the competitors into account. Unlike other capital budgeting problems, this approach solves for the equilibrium solution at each node point and takes the competitive pricing strategies of the market participants into consideration. Lambrecht and Perraudin (2003) extend the model to a market with incomplete information. In this case, the competitive decision is based on the distribution of the competitive actions, and not on a deterministic observation.

13.5   Strategic Value of a Firm

The real options approach has been introduced for capital budgeting decisions. The concept is then extended to decisions related to a specific industry. This section extends the concept even further to the valuation of a firm. The firm valuation model seeks to determine the strategic value of a firm beyond the value of a project.

In chapter 12, we presented a model of a retail chain store. In this model, we have only one source of risk, the GRI. We assume that the firm has no opportunity to invest or a predetermined investment schedule over time. We now extend the model with growth options by relaxing such investment assumptions.

Specifically, we assume that the firm can invest at most $\$I^*$ each year for the next N years, where N may be ten years. Of course, we do not have to limit an investment period to ten years. Requiring a maximum investment level is reasonable because there is usually a limit to the number of stores that a chain can open in one year, since each store requires significant financial and management resources at the beginning.

We assume that these projects are irreversible. That means that should the gross return on investment (GRI) fall as customers' preferences change, which leads to a fall in revenue per store, the management cannot sell the stores or recover the investment.

This model of a growth option is simple, and has several interesting features. Consider the capital budgeting decision on the store level. When each store is evaluated in a *bottom-up management process*, the business manager can calculate the net present value of starting a new store. In this decision, there is no embedded real option. The store has perpetual cash flows with an expected GRI, which is the prevailing GRI, because the GRI follows the martingale process. Therefore the expected perpetual cash flow is

$$perpetual\ cash\ flow = \widetilde{GRI} \times Investment \times gross\ profit\ margin \times (1 - \tau_c)\ \ (13.5)$$

And the net present value is

$$NPV = \frac{Perpetual\ cash\ flow}{cost\ of\ capital} - Investment \tag{13.6}$$

In capital budgeting, the project will be accepted whenever the net present value is positive. However, investment decisions can be based on a top-down approach.

A *top-down decision* refers to the planning at the headquarters level. The optimal investment decisions are made by seeking the optimal set of investments $I(n, i)$ at each node point such that the firm value is optimized. That is, we seek a set of investments $I(n, i)$ at all the node points within the investment horizon such that the firm value is maximized by using a nonlinear numerical search method. Of course, the investments at each node are bounded by I^*, which limits the investment the firm can make each year.

$$0 < I(n, i) < I^*\quad \text{where } n \text{ is time and } i \text{ is state} \tag{13.7}$$

There are many examples of interdependent capital budgeting decisions. For example, if we can build only a maximum number of new stores over a certain number of years, and not a fixed maximum number of stores every year, then the decision to open a store in any particular year will have to be dependent on optimal decisions on opening the stores in other years. Bottom-up decisions will have to be reconciled with top-down decisions. The method presented in this chapter enables the firm to determine this multiperiod optimal decision.

Another interesting point relates to the cost of capital. In the classical capital budgeting literature, each project can be viewed as a firm, and a firm is a portfolio of projects. In particular, when all the projects belong in the same risk class, the firm also will belong to the same risk class. Consider our example of the retail chain store. If the investments are not state-dependent, that is, if the investment decisions are not affected by the prevailing gross investment return, then the firm belongs to the same risk class as the project. However, when investment decisions are state-dependent, this assertion no longer holds—investment decisions are affected by the prevailing gross return on investment, and therefore, the cost of capital of the firm should reflect the value of the investment flexibility. Because of the real option value from the investment flexibility, the cost of capital of the firm is not same as that of the individual projects that the firm has.

Valuation of the Financial Claims on the Firm: Debt and Equity

Equity with debt behaves like a call option on a firm. The market capitalization of a leveraged company is a complex compound option. Therefore the risk of the debt will also depend on the types of real options of the firm. The real option model can be used to value debt and determine the market value of stocks of the leveraged firm in a straightforward extension, as described as follows. Since we can derive the firm value at each node point on the lattice, we can value the bond at maturity, using a structural model's default condition. We then use the backward substitution approach. Similar to the methodology of valuing a debt package using the concept of a compound option in chapter 9, we can determine the bond value at each node. And we can determine the bond value at the initial node of the binomial lattice.

13.6   Analysis of the Real Option Value

Using the real option approach, we can study the value of the flexibility of investment with the business model presented in chapter 12. Now we assume that we can make optimal investment decisions at each node on the binomial lattice.

Identifying the Real Option Value

We now compare the value of the firm with the growth options against the value of the firm without the growth options by plotting their value for each GRI. Figure 13.5 depicts their values to indicate the impact of the growth option on the firm value.

The results clearly show that the real option value significantly affects the firm value. With the increase in the GRI, the firm value with the growth option increases with a positive gamma exhibiting the curvature. The real option value becomes significant when the GRI is about 0.5.

The maximum investment level I^* represents the scalability of the business model, which means that when business opportunity is favorable, the firm can grow significantly. Within the context of the model, we specify the model with a high value I^*. For a low value I^*, the firm cannot scale up its value even when favorable opportunity arises, because the investment size is constrained to a small amount.

The Shareholders' Value and the Net Present Value of a Project

The model provides insight into strategic investment and capital budgeting decisions. Let V_U be the unleveraged firm (or pure equity firm in MM terminology). Let V_O be the firm without any new investment and with no growth option. Then V_U/V_O measures the relative value of the firm with growth options to that without growth options. Note that there is wealth transfer from the real option value to the "perpetual risk debt" of the fixed-cost firm. The wealth transfer is the flip side of the default premium. When we take on a project, the firm value goes up, but not by the NPV. The NPV does not

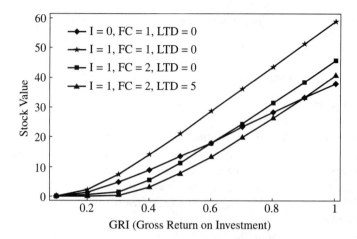

Figure 13-5 The value of the firm with and without the growth options. We assume the long-term debt level to be 5, capital investment 0 or 1, business volatility 30%, risk-free rate 6%, coupon rate 8%, cost of capital 10%, fixed cost 2 or 1 for comparison purposes, and horizon 5 years. The growth option value is significant, and it increases the gamma of the total capitalization with the GRI. Figure 13.3 also shows how the fixed cost (FC), investment level (I), or the long-term debt (LTD) affects the growth firm value. To this end, we increase the fixed cost by 1 and the long-term debt level by 5.

all translate to the increase in firm value. Part of the value is absorbed by the fixed-cost option. There are three main conclusions:

1. The firm value in traditional corporate finance is considered to be the portfolio value of projects. For the contingent claim valuation framework, the firm value includes also the real options, net of the fixed costs, which can be treated as if they are perpetual senior debts.
2. Under this real option model of a firm, the strategic investment decision is not the same as the capital budgeting decision. That is, on the basis of shareholders' value maximization, the two decisions do not agree on accepting or rejecting a project.
3. The contribution of the positive NPV project to the shareholders' wealth is not the same as NPV. Since part of the value is transferred to the present value of the fixed costs, such as employee salaries, the shareholders' benefits are smaller. Almost all the NPV value flows to the shareholders only when the impact of fixed costs is negligible.

Consider a software company. The fixed costs are high in employing programmers. The variable costs are low in downloading software to clients. When the software sells well, gross profits are large. All the employees who are stakeholders are almost guaranteed to receive their compensations. They benefit from the increase in firm value. However, the firm value becomes directly responsive to the NPV when the stakeholders reach their reward limit, with virtual guaranteed employment as a result of the firm's low default on operating expenses. But when the software does not sell well and sales keep decreasing, the staff will increasingly bear part of the present-value loss. The use of real option relates the strategic investment decisions to capital budgeting. Capital budgeting measures the net present value of the project. The real option approach incorporates the wealth transfer of part of the net present value to the fixed cost value, and derives the net increase in shareholders' value in accepting the project.

13.7   A Business Model with Embedded Options: Starbucks Coffee Japan

Yuji Tsunoda, CEO of Starbucks Coffee Japan, contacted Starbucks Corp's CEO Howard Schultz with repeated letters, E-mails, and telephone calls to suggest that Starbucks be introduced to Japan. In October 1995 a joint venture was formed. In 2002, Starbucks Coffee Japan had an initial public offering at ¥ 90.88 billion, a huge valuation when we consider that most of their money was spent on overhead costs (¥ 19.16 billion) and they barely made a profit (¥ 1.44 billion). This prompts us to consider why Starbucks Japan's valuation is so high when we take these factors into consideration.

We will simulate the Starbucks Japan valuation. The results are for illustrative purposes, since we have made many simplifying assumptions. The purpose is to demonstrate how the real option approach is suitable to evaluate a growth firm with high strategic value like Starbucks Coffee Japan.

Sensitivity Analysis

We can use the business model to study the impact of the change in GRI (the business risk) on the firm value, the market capitalization, and the debt. This can be accomplished by simulating the model and calculating the delta of each financial claim on the firm. The deltas are calculated by the ratio of a small change in the security value to a small change of GRI. The change of the security value is induced by the change in the GRI. The sensitivity of each claim changes as the GRI increases. The results are shown in Figure 13.6. Both the market capitalization and the firm value deltas increase with GRI, but the debt's delta falls because the debt has negligible credit risk when the firm value is sufficiently high with the high GRI.

Investment Opportunities: Volatilities and Investment Size

We can use the model described above to analyze alternative business models for Starbucks Coffee Japan. For example, we can analyze the value of scalability. Starbucks Coffee Japan may build a stronger management infrastructure and explore broader geographic expansions. In doing so, they can open more stores in one year, if the market environment is favorable. Within the context of the model, we want to analyze the increase in value of the firm by increasing the annual investments I. With a higher value of the annual investment amount, Starbucks Coffee Japan is more capable of scaling to a larger company in a shorter time.

However, in order to implement a strategy that enables Starbucks Coffee Japan to use a higher level of investment $I^* > I$, the company may first need to improve the management infrastructure, which may include more extensive market research and the capacity to identify the appropriate store locations. The immediate cost of building such an infrastructure should be balanced with the benefits of the scalability. The model proposed can enable us to do such an analysis.

Analysis of the Fixed Cost

Firms are often confronted with the question of how to optimally determine the operating leverage. Maintaining a higher fixed cost can often reduce the variable costs. For

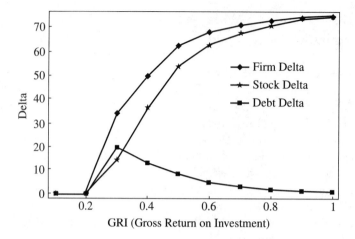

Figure 13-6 Sensitivity analysis—delta. We assume the long-term debt level to be 5.96, the maximum capital investment 1, business volatility 30%, risk-free rate 6%, coupon rate 8%, cost of capital 10%, fixed cost 2, and time horizon 5 years. We calculate the deltas for the firm, the stock, and the bond. Since the firm value is the sum of the stock and the bond, the firm delta should be the sum of the bond delta and the stock delta. The delta is the ratio of the firm value increase by a small GRI increase to the increase in the GRI. The stock delta and the bond delta are similarly defined. The bond delta is larger than the stock delta until the GRI is 0.3. After that, the bond delta rapidly decreases, because the bond value has drawn close enough to the risk-free counterpart.

example, compensation for the staff may be more dependent on the sales of the stores so that the staff can participate in the growth of the company because salespersons' compensations are based on commissions. Given a significant growth option in the company, the analysis seems to be less straightforward. This is because with a higher variable cost, fewer stores may open in the future.

Using the real option model, we can analyze the problem as follows. In the example above, we have calculated the firm value to a range of GRI values. We can consider two types of firms: (1) a firm with low variable and high fixed costs and (2) one with high variable and low fixed costs. Now we can determine the point of indifference as a trade-off between the variable costs and the fixed costs for Starbucks Japan. We can see in figure 13.7 that when the GRI is below the point of indifference, which is 2.89928, the firm with high VC and low FC is more valuable than to the firm with low VC and high FC. (See figure 13.7.)

Strategic Planning and Capital Budgeting

Strategic planning (top down) focuses first on the potential of business on real sectors: the potential of coffee shops in Japan. The strategic plan determines the present value of the financial profitability of a potential market. The value is represented by the real option model. On the one hand, the decision to open each store is a capital budgeting decision (bottom up) where the net present value of opening each store should be positive. On the other hand, the value of the strategic plan is determined by an option pricing model.

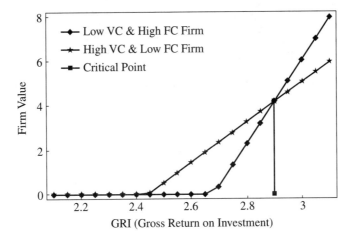

Figure 13-7 Low variable and high fixed costs vs. high variable and low fixed costs. We assume the long-term debt level to be 5.96, capital investment is 0, business volatility 30%, risk-free rate 6%, coupon rate 8%, cost of capital 10%, and the time horizon 5 years. The variable cost is 8.4 and fixed cost 19.16 for the firm with low variable cost and high fixed cost. For high variable cost and low fixed cost firm, the variable cost is 19.16 and the fixed cost 8.4. The critical GRI is 2.89928 where the firm value is 4.12901.

The valuation of Starbucks Coffee Japan is not a capital budgeting problem, because we cannot justify its high IPO price with capital budgeting. Its valuation is not simply based on the present value of the expected cash flow. Using the real options approach, the potential value of the business in the future can be calculated. Starbucks Coffee Japan bets that coffee will still be popular in Japan in the future even though the present cash flow of the firm is relatively low. It is the real option of its strategic planning to provide the value to the company.

Strategic planning and capital budgeting complement each other. Management does not have to choose between a capital budgeting approach and a strategic investment approach. They are both methodologies to add values to the shareholders, but they are clearly different: strategic planning does not begin with specific projects, while capital budgeting begins with specifications of projects. The use of real options to analyze the firm value enables us to separate the roles and responsibilities of the corporate managers and line managers. Corporate managers analyze the market potential of the business and design the business model to maximize the firm value. Line managers deal with the capital budgeting issue, maximizing the net present value of each project they manage.

Another example delineating the difference between strategic planning and capital budgeting is merger and acquisition. Consider an acquisition of a bank by another bank. If the purchase is motivated by capital budgeting analysis where the combined value of the two banks has a positive net present value after the cost of purchase, then the acquisition is a large capital budgeting problem. If the motivation is driven by the belief that the consolidation of banks is inevitable and that the future lies in acquiring a large deposit base, by using a series of acquisitions depending on the state of the world, to support a financial services business, then the acquisition is part of a strategic plan.

Often, *business planning* or *financial planning* in a company is confused with strategic planning. Business planning often asserts that the firm has a determined cost of capital and seeks possible projects that add value to the shareholders. This is no more than a systematic approach to capital budgeting. There is no coherent strategy or business model to exploit a particular opportunity. Financial planning simulates financial ratios and analysis in such a way that the financial performances are benchmarked. For example, the return on equity meets the expectation of 15%, while satisfying a set of target financial ratios. There is no finance in the financial planning in the sense that there is no valuation, discounting, and adjustment for risks. There is no clear relationship between financial planning and strategic planning that will guarantee that satisfying financial targets will maximize shareholders' value. By way of contrast, the real option approach ensures the maximization of the firm. The real option approach is the fair value approach in determining value. It directly relates capital budgeting to the firm maximization.

Not all strategic plans are large-scale. All firms should have strategic planning in the sense that they are positioned to capture any growth in their market sector. The positioning depends on the design of the business model. Any possible expansions are part of the strategic plans.

13.8   A Business Model Approach and the Free Cash Flow Discounting Approach—A Comparison

In chapter 12, we described the free cash flow discounting approach to value a firm. The present chapter describes a business model that uses the real option approach to value a firm with flexible investments. A comparison of the two approaches can provide us with a better understanding of the advantages of using the real option approach in the firm valuation.

Volatility

When projects or firms have embedded options, their values are affected by the change in volatility. Consider a growth option. When volatility increases, the value of the growth option rises. The change in the value of the growth option is relative to the change of the underlying value. Using the dividend discount model or the net present-value model, there is no direct methodology enabling us to adjust the discount rate accordingly with the change in the volatility.

Expected Cash Flows

The expected cash flows of the dividend discount model must take the optimal real option into account. That means we first need to determine the real options in order to apply the dividend discount model. However, there is no direct way to determine the real options without using the option models. We need to use the option pricing models to determine the real option values as well as the discount rate.

Cost of Capital

The dividend discount model assumes one discount rate. As we know, when there are embedded options, the discount rate at each node changes depending on the state of the world. A firm's cost of capital or a project with an embedded option must be a weighted average of many cost of capital numbers, which are dependent on the states.

13.9   Empirical Implications of the Business Model

In this section, we will consider the behavior of the equity value or the capitalization value and the debt value of the firm, which are related to the GRI.

Capitalization

Capitalization of the firm refers to the market value of the firm's equity. The business model can analyze the risks of the capitalization under different market environments.

When the GRI is high, the net income is high. In this case, the firm will always make the capital investment to its limits. In this sense, there is no flexibility to the real option because the maximum investment level is always used. The fixed costs have minimal effect on the capitalization risk because the firm is so profitable that the fixed costs are almost certain to be paid. If the debt level is small, then the capitalization value is quite directly proportional to the GRI. (See figure 13.8.)

It is interesting to examine the impact of fixed costs on the equity risks. Consider a firm with significant fixed costs. As shown by figure 13.8, the equity value would increase with the GRI, with a positive gamma. In this sense, the result seems similar to that of the Merton model, asserting that the equity market value of the firm is similar to a call option of the firm value. However, because of the presence of the fixed cost, the firm can go into default as its value falls. Figure 13.8 suggests that the firm defaults when the GRI is around 0.2.

In the case of the Merton model, the debt is assumed to be a zero-coupon bond and the equity is a European call option on the firm value with a strike price equaling the face value of the debt. When the firm value falls, the equity will remain as an out-of-the-money option and the firm will default only at the maturity of the bond. The Merton model cannot explain why a firm's default is not triggered by coupon or principal payments, but by the fixed cost payments—which is what the business model can capture.

In a way, this model is similar to the Kim–Ramaswamy–Sundaresan (KRS) model, described in chapter 9, in that the firm can default before the maturity of the bond, triggered by the firm's negative cash flow. The difference between KRS and this business model is that the latter allows the firm to borrow to finance the negative cash flows at any time. But the firm value may be so low that the firm does not have the borrowing capacity to finance the negative cash flows at the time of default. In essence, this model solves for the default triggers, which KRS specifies exogenously. (See figure 13.9.)

The market capitalization can be viewed as a security with three types of options: (1) options on the growth, (2) call option of the firm value because of the debt, (3) firm value as an option on the primitive firm because of the fixed costs. The empirical implication of this model is that the market capitalization has a significant gamma value relative to the GRI. This is because each option adds more gamma to the equity value.

Debt Valuation

The firm model suggests that the following features of the business model are important to the valuation of debt. Debt is valued in this model quite differently from the Merton model. The main difference is that the underlying firm for the debt does not follow a

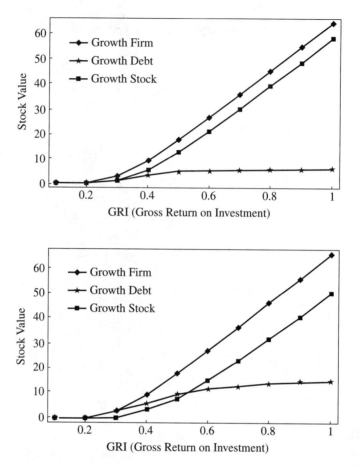

Figure 13-8 Capitalization over a range of GRI. This figure depicts capitalization as a function of GRI. The capitalization exhibits a profile of a call option with positive gamma to the GRI. We assume the maximum capital investment to be 2, business volatility 30%, risk-free rate 6%, coupon rate 8%, cost of capital 10%, fixed cost 2, and time horizon 5 years. The difference between the two panels is that the long-term debt levels of the first panel and the second panels are 5.96 and 15, respectively. We see that the second panel shows more wealth transfer between the bondholders and the stockholders.

random walk. The underlying process for the firm is now dependent on the business model, its fixed cost-structure, and its real options.

One significant implication of this formulation is to show that there is not only a wealth transfer effect between the stockholders and bondholders, but also a wealth transfer of the fixed costs to other claimants on the firm value. Specifically, consider the debt value over a range of the GRIs shown in figure 13.10.

Figure 13.10 shows that the debt has no value when the GRI is less than 0.2. Thus, under the assumption of this numerical example, this firm without growth options cannot be viable because of the high fixed costs. When the GRI is higher than 0.2, the result in the previous section shows that the growth option value begins to impact the firm value, and so the debt increases in value.

In figure 13.8 we showed that the firm defaults at the GRI of 0.4. Within the range of the GRI from 0 to 0.4, the bond behaves like the equity of a firm with a "debt," which is

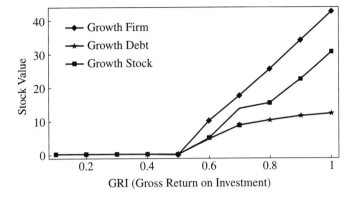

Figure 13-9 Default triggered by high fixed costs. We assume the long-term debt level to be 15, the maximum capital investment 2, business volatility 30%, risk-free rate 6%, coupon rate 8%, cost of capital 10%, and the time horizon 5. We further assume that the fixed costs are twice the second panel in figure 13.8. This figure suggests that the firm defaults even when we assume the large fixed costs and the GRI less than 0.4.

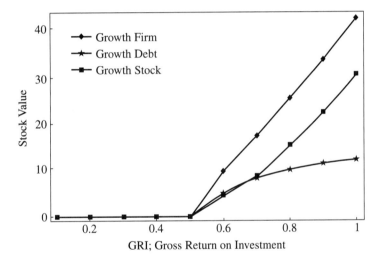

Figure 13-10 The debt value over a range of GRI. This figure depicts the value of the debt as a function of the GRI. Since the debt is a "junior debt" to the operating fixed costs of the firm, the debt value exhibits positive gamma when the GRI is low and negative gamma when the GRI is high. We assume the long-term debt level to be 15, the maximum capital investment 2, business volatility 30%, risk-free rate 6%, coupon rate 8%, cost of capital 10%, fixed cost 2, and time horizon 5 years.

the fixed cost. For this reason, the firm value increases with a positive gamma, a behavior that is similar to the short-term junior debt as explained in chapter 9, about the risk and return allocation between the short-term junior debt and the long-term senior debt. In this case, the senior long-term debt is the fixed cost of the firm and the junior debt is the bond, the financial security.

As the GRI increases beyond 0.4, the debt value exhibits a negative gamma. The value increases with GRI but at a decreasing rate, such that the debt behaves like a fixed asset with a short put option. This characteristic is similar to the Merton model of a risky bond as a contingent claim on the firm value.

In summary, the model shows that the following factors affect a debt value.

Debt leverage

Since the fixed-cost payment has a priority over the bond payment, the fixed cost and the bond can be treated as if they are a senior debt and a junior debt, respectively. Therefore, the behavior of the bond is similar to a junior debt for a firm with a debt package of the senior and the junior debt. That means that the bond value can be sensitive to the firm risk in the sense that the bond payment will be made after the fixed-cost payment.

Operating leverage

The higher the operating leverage, the higher the risk of the debt. When the firm value increases from a low level, a wealth transfer will take place from the bondholders to the recipients of the fixed costs (e.g., employees). Therefore, the bond value will not increase by the same amount as the firm value increases at the beginning. When the fixed-cost payments have been fully made, the firm value increase will accrue to the bond value increase without causing the wealth transfer between the bondholders and the fixed-cost recipients.

In the presence of the fixed costs, the financial debt becomes a junior debt. When the firm defaults on the fixed costs, the financial debt will have 0 recovery value. By way of contrast, in the Merton model of corporate debt, when a firm defaults, the debt holders receive the value of the firm, which is not assumed to be 0. Or, when compared with the reduced form model, the business model approach shows that the recovery ratio is a stochastic number depending on both the financial and the operating leverage of the firm, while the reduced form model assumes some constant recovery ratio number for an industry, an assertion not supported empirically.

Real option size

The real option size, as measured by the maximum capital investment level, is a measure of the growth potential of the firm. The higher the potential growth, the higher the firm value. The increase in the firm value leads to a higher debt value as the likelihood of default decreases.

Volatility

The volatility has a conflicting impact on the debt value. Higher volatility leads to higher real option value. This increase in real option value should lead to higher debt value. But the increase in volatility also increases the likelihood of default because the firm value distribution has a higher variance. Since a distribution has a higher variance, the probability of falling below a certain level will increase, which means that the default probability will increase as the distribution is dispersed. These two conflicting effects may lead to a higher or a lower bond price.

Gross profit margin

Gross profit margin is the ratio of sales net of cost of goods sold to sales. A higher gross profit margin leads to higher income. If the increase of the gross profit margin is the result of the substitution of the variable costs for the fixed costs, then the implications of a higher gross profit margin will have an ambiguous impact on the debt value, depending on whether the firm has significant growth potential or minimal growth opportunities. A substitution of the variable costs by fixed costs may increase the debt value when the firm has significant growth potential. However, the converse is true when the firm has minimal growth potential. The impact of the use of variable costs versus fixed costs on the debt or equity can be analyzed using the business model.

13.10   Implications of the Business Model

As we discussed in chapter 1, the reasonableness of models is judged by their predictions. The value of the theory is based on the insights it provides and on the depth or breadth of its applications. Now we proceed to discuss both the empirical evidence and the applications of the model.

We first discuss how to calibrate the business model, determining the model parameters from observed data. Then we will briefly describe two pieces of empirical evidence of the validity of the business model. Finally, we will explain how to apply the business model in practice.

Calibration of the Model

For clarity of the exposition of the model and to provide clearer intuitions to the readers, we have confined our description of the business model to the retail chain store. However, the model can be used quite broadly. In essence, it suggests that a firm has fixed assets used as capital assets. Such capital assets can generate revenue. The design of the operating leverage and the financial leverage can determine the values of the financial claims of the firm. These assumptions apply to many industry sectors. An important exception to this approach is the financial sector, where the capital asset is not the significant component on the balance sheet; the asset and liability portfolios are. For this sector, we need to adjust the model, and we shall not describe such an adjustment in this chapter.

We have shown that the business model is specified by the following inputs: the investment constraints I, the sector volatility (risk of the primitive firm), σ (sector); the risk premium of the sector risk, ρ; capital asset, CA; fixed cost, FC; the long-term growth rate, g; and the gross investment returns, GRI. We will derive these input data from the firm's financial statements. Specifically, we assume the following:

1. Investment constraints I is estimated by the growth rate in fixed assets in the past five years.
2. Capital asset is estimated to be the total assets net of the current assets. We assume that all the fixed assets not including the current assets are generating revenue.
3. GRI is the revenue generated for each dollar invested in capital assets. Therefore, we use revenue/capital assets to estimate GRI. The revenue is reported in the income statement and the capital asset is derived from the balance sheet.

4. Fixed costs are estimated by the sales and general administration item in the income statement. We assume that this income statement item measures the fixed costs in managing the firm.

Thus far, all the input data can be estimated somewhat directly from the financial statements. However, the risk premium and the risk of a sector are more problematic to estimate. In general we can observe the returns of the stock and the risk of the stock, but not the underlying risk and return of the sector. We need to determine the relationships of the risk and returns of a stock to those of the sector.

Let us first consider the relationship between the stock and the sector volatilities, which can be estimated from the model. For any set of inputs into the model, we can simulate the multiplier α in relating the stock volatility and the sector volatility. Specifically, we calculate the small change of the primitive firm value V^p and determine the resulting small change in the market capitalization S. The multiplier is the ratio of these two changes. We have

$$\Delta V^p = \alpha \Delta S$$

It follows that the multiplier is also the relationship between the stock volatility and the sector volatility.

$$\sigma(sector) = \alpha \sigma(stock)$$

Note that $\alpha = \alpha(\rho, g)$ depends on all the input data to the model. In particular, it depends on the expected returns of the primitive firm ρ and the long-term growth rate of the firm. Using the model for any set of input data, we can simulate the multiplier. Also, the stock volatility can be estimated from the historical data.

Now we turn our attention to the relationship between the expected returns of the stock and that of the sector. To estimate the stock returns, we can rely of the Capital Asset Pricing model, discussed in chapter 2. In assuming the capital asset pricing model, we can determine the expected return of the stock, which is given by

$$R = r_f + \beta(\overline{R}_m - r_f)$$

According to the theory, the equity is a contingent claim on the underlying sector risk (the primitive firm). In chapter 5, we showed that the relative valuation model requires the market price of risk, which is the risk premium to the volatility, to be the same for all the contingent claims on the same underlying risk. Therefore, we have

$$(R - r_f)/(\rho - r_f) = \sigma(stock)/\sigma(sector)$$

In rearranging, we have

$$\rho - r_f = \sigma(stock)(R - r_f)/\sigma(sector)$$

But noting that $\sigma(sector) = \alpha\sigma(stock)$, we have the following equation to determine the expected returns of the sector.

$$\rho - r_f = (R - r_f)/\alpha$$

Now the only input to the model that has not been specified is the long-term growth rate, g. For each value of g, both ρ and σ (sector) can be solved for by equations, noting that α depends on both ρ and σ (sector). Therefore, given any value of g, the model is well specified at this point. But we have one more constraint on the model. We can observe the market capitalization of the firm, and therefore the long-term growth rate g must be determined so that the model value of the market capitalization of the firm is equal to the observed market capitalization. This completes the calibration of the model. We use the observed capitalization to determine the long-term growth rate such that the model is consistent with the market prices. We provide a summary and a numerical example of the business model and its calibration method in the appendix.

Empirical Evidence: The Relationship of the Market Capitalization of the Firm and the Debt Package Value

In chapter 9, we used the example of McLeodUSA to demonstrate empirically the relationship between the market capitalization and the bond package value. We showed that as the market capitalization of the firm falls, the bond package value also will fall. However, the bond value falls more precipitously than the market capitalization as the firm approaches bankruptcy.

We also showed that the Merton model of the corporate bond can explain much of this relationship between the market capitalization and the bond value. But the model tends to understate the acceleration of the fall in the bond price when the market capitalization falls below certain value.

We now use the business model to explain this market capitalization and the bond package value. Specifically, we assume that the GRI declines, leading the fall in the market capitalization and the bond value. It is quite reasonable to make this assumption. A source of the financial problem of McLeodUSA was that the expectation of the demand for communication equipment had been falling together with an excess supply of communication networks. As a result, the market revised its expectations of the returns on the assets of McLeodUSA, and hence the fall of GRI.

We use the calibrated business model of McLeodUSA. The sector volatility and the implied long-term growth rate are estimated to be 0.007 and 0.035, respectively. Further, we add a spread to Treasury curve in discounting the bond. The spread is 500 basis points, so that the bond price equals the observed price initially. The use of a spread is reasonable because we have discussed that bonds tend to be a liquidity spread and a risk premium for the model risks in predicting defaults. In figure 13.11, the results show that the business model provides relatively better explanatory power of the observations than the Merton model. In particular, using the business model, we predict the precipitous fall of the bond value better than the Merton model. The intuition of this result is quite simple. In chapter 9, we show that McLeodUSA has significant operating costs. The debts outstanding do not mature in the next three years, and there is no immediate maturity crisis for the firm in the short run. However, the significant fixed costs and the losses of the operation have to be supported by external financing. When the market revises downward on the returns of the assets, the market capitalization falls, leading to McLeodUSA's loss of access to the capital market. In essence, the firm defaults on its operating costs, something the Merton model would not have considered.

In recent years, there has been a dramatic growth in credit derivatives. In chapter 10, we described different credit derivatives. In brief, for example, a credit default swap is

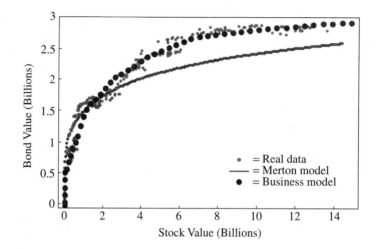

Figure 13-11 depicts the actual market capitalization and the actual bond package value of McLeodUSA. To fit them over time, we use two models. One is the business model and the other is the Merton's model. For the business model, we use the calibrated values such that the sector volatility is 7%, the long-term growth rate is 3.5% and the bond spread is 5%. The business model fits the actual data better than the Merton's model, because the business can incorporate the fixed operating costs.

a swap arrangement between two parties. Suppose ABC corporation has issued some bonds. An asset management company, Corporate Bond Company, holds the bond, and the management wants to protect the investment against a default by ABC. Then Corporate Bond Company can arrange a swap with another company, say Financial Insurance, whereby Corporate Bond Company makes annual payments to Financial Insurance, rather like paying an insurance premium to an insurer. The swap typically has a five-year tenure. In case of a default by ABC Corporation, Financial Insurance will take possession of the bond and pay Corporate Bond Company the par amount of the bond, making whole the ABC Company investment. The valuation of this credit default swap, or determining the appropriate fixed payments for the default protection, can be based on the binomial lattice in a way similar to the approach that we use to value the bond package. In this case, at each node, we determine the make-whole payments of Financial Insurance and determine the present value, using the risk-neutral probability and the risk-free rate for discounting the payments.

The purpose of the above analysis is to indicate the possible applications of the business model. Our analysis has several limitations. For simplicity of the exposition, we do not use the complete information on the debt structure. We do not have the observed OAS for all the debts in the debt structure, and we assume that the bonds with observed OAS are representative of all the bonds. We also assume that the financial statement data properly reflect the economics of the firm. Certainly, in general this assumption is incorrect. But with appropriate equity research, these financial statement data can be properly adjusted. Also, we assume a simple business model for all the sectors. These models can be improved to capture more salient features of the firms. For these reasons, we cannot use the model to determine specific trading strategies. However, the above brief discussion suggests the broad potential applications of a business model.

13.11   Empirical Research on Real Options

Unlike the theoretical work on real options, there are relatively few papers on the empirical verification of the validity of the real option valuation. In part, unlike financial derivatives, the valuation of real options must have much noise in the data. There are very few pure real options with prices that we can observe accurately. The empirical work tends to suggest the existence of real options, but does not empirically verify the pricing of the real options.

Moel and Tufano (2002) collected data on mine closings. They found empirical support for the closing decisions consistent with the results of the Brennan and Schwartz model. Considering that the empirical test seeks to determine the explanatory power of observable parameters, while not testing the valuation model directly, the results are also consistent with other nonoption-based decisions, such as the discount cash flow model.

Mackay (1999) empirically investigated the relationship between flexibility in production and the capital structure. He found that firms with more flexible investment decisions held less debt, while firms with fixed tangible assets had more debt. He interpreted the findings to suggest that the shareholders with real options were more likely to use equity to finance their projects.

Berger et al. (1996) provided indirect evidence that firms' valuation incorporates the abandonment value. Since a firm can always liquidate when the business is unprofitable, the firm value has an embedded option. By estimating the liquidation value of a sample of firms and relating that liquidation value to the firm valuation, they found evidence for the option value.

To empirically verify the real option model, research should test the model directly. Unfortunately, collecting such sample observations is not a simple empirical task.

13.12   What Is Financial Modeling to Senior Management?

At 6:30 pm one evening in 1987, I was tired, standing in the middle of a Yamaichi Securities office in Tokyo with my tie hanging down, like most of my colleagues there. Yamaichi Securities was one of the largest corporations in Japan at the time. We had discussed financial modeling with pension plan clients, arbitrage traders, real estate mortgage groups, and more. The managing director of financial technologies, Morihiro Matsumoto, had just hung up the phone and looked at me, his expression conveying some unease: "Professor Ho, our president wants to have dinner with you tonight." "What does he want to talk about?" "He talks about whatever he wants to talk about."

Our limousine wove through the narrow streets of Tokyo, and when we stepped out, we found ourselves surrounded by ancient trees and meticulously kept gardens. We walked through an arch built in the thirteenth century, taken from Nara. The host greeted me at the door and led me into the hall. In the middle of the spacious hall, there was a low table surrounded neatly by twelve cushions. The president sat on one side with two executive vice presidents sitting next to him. I sat facing the president. Mr. Matsumoto and his deputy sat next to me. A kimono-clad hostess sat next to each of us. The twelve of us had the entire museum to ourselves.

The conversations progressed from the gardens, to the food, and later drifted to the long history of Japan. My listening skills were put to the test. At some point, the president whispered to his deputy, who turned to me and said, "Professor Ho, our president wants to know about financial modeling." Before I could start, our third course came. We toasted ritually. I was going to say, "Financial modeling is about formulating a theory, testing the theory with empirical data, and applying the theory." But why should the master of universe want to know about such a process? I swallowed those words.

The fourth course came, and we had another round of toasting. I wanted to tell the president that financial models could generate trading profits, securitize mortgages, enhance returns in portfolio management, and more. But my mind screamed: "Why would the master of universe want to know the nitty-gritty of daily operations?" I swallowed those words, too.

I decided that the main issue was "global communications." "Global communications," the president repeated after me. Then some subliminal signal caused all of us to turn to the north side of the hall. Two musicians came out and played ancient Japanese music. For the next 30 minutes, the words "global communications" hung in the still air.

When the musicians left, those words once again found their bearings. " Yes, globally, we have different languages, foods, and music, but the mathematical financial models are the same. Using financial models, Yamaichi Securities (London) can buy Eurodollar callable bonds, strip the embedded option to be sold in New York, and the remaining cash flows can be sold in Tokyo." We all chewed on that idea in silence during our fifth course.

"Using the U.S. financial technologies to securitize Yamaichi retail client mortgages, we can create a new market by adapting the U.S. financial models." I proposed another example of global communication using models. We paused as the sixth course came.

"Yamaichi can sell U.S. dollar CMOs to Japanese retail clients for their yields and long durations, and use the financial models to control the risks. Global communication is key to any globalization strategies and to implement a global ambition. Financial models tie Yamaichi Securities global operations in one consistent framework, and that is the infrastructure for the global communications. Indeed, financial modeling is the only rational way to provide performance metrics to Yamaichi's global operations." There were long pauses for thinking. In due course, the president stood up and said, "Thank you."

Back in our limousine, Mr. Matsumoto said, "You had the president listening to you talk about financial modeling the whole evening. That is good." "I know. I am honored," I muttered, feeling drained. We all knew that such meetings rarely fully inform the president about the full capabilities of financial modeling, even in the absence of the distractions of food and music. But an evening is a good start.

13.13 Summary

The main concept introduced in this chapter was the demonstration that there are many embedded options in a firm's value. These options may be growth options, abandonment options, timing options, and other options reflecting the firm's flexibility in its capital budgeting decisions.

These embedded options pose difficulties in using the net present-value approach to capital budgeting or the cost of capital to value a firm, as in the Miller model. The challenge is similar to that of using a discount rate to price a call option or a yield to price an option embedded bond. Even if the expected cash flow of a project or the free cash flow of a firm takes the possible contingencies into account, while not ignoring the possibilities in the alternative capital budgeting decisions, the choice of cost of capital as a discount rate is problematic.

This chapter has provided a step-by-step methodology to show how such embedded real options can be priced. The general methodology is similar to that used by a risk-neutral valuation model. A relative valuation model enables us to value a broad class of firms.

The valuation of a firm provides the key for many applications. Corporate decisions will be affected by the firm value, which is the topic of chapter 14.

Appendix. The Business Model

Building the Model

The business model is built from a series of models. The basic model is the primitive firm lattice, which specifies the stochastic nature of the gross profit of the firm. We then build the firm value lattice, which includes all the considerations of a valuation of a firm: fixed costs, taxes, and investments. Finally, we use the firm value lattice to analyze all the claims on the firm value.

The primitive firm lattice, $V^p(n, i)$, is the value of a firm that bears all the business risks of the revenues. The firm value lattice, $V(n, i)$ is the value of the firm.

Numerical Example

Market Assumptions

The yield curve is the transfer pricing curve, representing the time value of money. It is flat and is constant over time at 4.5% annual compounding rate. The market premium is defined as the market expected return net of the risk-free rate. The market premium is assumed to be 5%. The tax rate of the firm is 30%, which is assumed to be the effective tax rate.

Model Assumptions

The model is based on a five-step binomial lattice. It is a one-factor model, with only the business risk. The model is arbitrage-free relative to the underlying values of a firm that bears all the business risks of the revenues.

Firm Assumptions

We use one example, Hilton Hotels, firm to illustrate the implementation of the model. The evaluation date is October 31, 2002. The sector is consumer and lodging

Equity Data

Market capitalization: $4.9446 billion
Stock volatility (one-year historical volatility of Hilton's stock): 51.9%
beta: 1.255

Financial Data

Revenue: $2.834 billion
Operating costs: $1.542 billion
Fixed costs: $726 million
Capital assets: $7.714 billion.
Long-term debt: $5.823 billion (See table 13.1.)
Interest cost: $357 million

Derived Parameters

Gross return on investment (GRI) = revenue/capital assets = 0.367 (See figure 13.13)
Gross profit margin (m) = (revenue − operating cost)/revenue = 45.58%
Expected rate of return of the stock = 4.5% + 1.255 × 5% = 10.775%

Table 13.1 Debt Package of Hilton Hotels

Observed date	Maturity	Coupon rate	Principal	Price	# of outstanding
20030228	20130228	0.061	1000	100	3473000
20030228	20060515	0.05	1000	96	500000
20030228	20091215	0.072	1000	99	200000
20030228	20171215	0.075	1000	92	200000
20030228	20080515	0.076	1000	102	400000
20030228	20121201	0.076	1000	99	375000
20030228	20070415	0.08	1000	104	375000
20030228	20110215	0.083	1000	105	300000

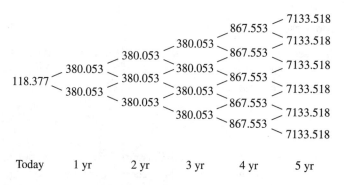

Figure 13-12 Debt cash flow, Hilton Hotels

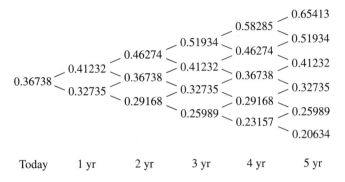

						0.65413
					0.58285	
				0.51934		0.51934
			0.46274		0.46274	
		0.41232		0.41232		0.41232
	0.41232		0.36738		0.36738	
0.36738		0.36738		0.36738		0.36738
	0.32735		0.32735		0.29168	
		0.29168		0.32735		0.32735
			0.25989		0.29168	
				0.25989		0.25989
					0.23157	
						0.20634

| Today | 1 yr | 2 yr | 3 yr | 4 yr | 5 yr |

Figure 13-13 GRI lattice

Primitive Firm

The firm value, the market capitalization, debt, and all other claims are treated as the contingent claims to the primitive firm. The primitive firm is the underlying "security" that captures the business risk of the firm.

Inputs

Observed data: GRI, capital assets

Assumed data: expected excess return = 1.57%, sector volatility = 12.975%. The assumed data is an initial input for the nonlinear optimization procedure. Using the assumed data, we can calculate the expected returns of the sector (ρ): $\rho = 0.045$ +0.0157 = 0.060688. (See figure 13.13.)

Outputs

Lattice of primitive firm value, $V^p(n, i) = \frac{CA \times GRI(n,i) \times m}{\rho}$. (See figure 13.14.)

Lattice of cash flow at each state, based on capital assets of $7.714 billion; $CF^p(n, i)$ = $CA \times GRI(n, i) \times m$. (See figure 13.15.)

Risk-neutral probability: $p(n, i) = \frac{\frac{(1+\gamma)}{(1+\rho)} - e^{-\sigma}}{e^{\sigma} - e^{-\sigma}} = 0.414223$

Fixed-cost Firm

The fixed costs of the firm stay the same. Gross margin also remains constant. The firm defaults when it cannot finance the fixed costs. All excess cash flows are paid out.

Inputs

Observed data: GRI, capital assets, fixed costs, tax rate, gross margin

Assumed data: sector volatility, expected excess sector return, firm value ($10.514 billion)

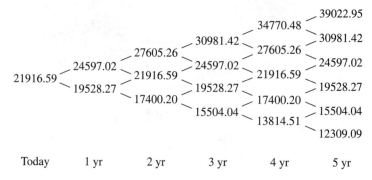

Figure 13-14 Primitive firm value lattice

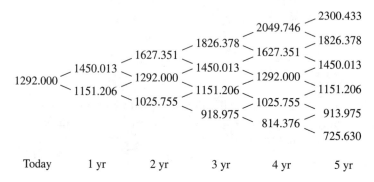

Figure 13-15 Lattice of cash flow of primitive firm

Outputs

Lattice of cash flow at each state: at each node, the cash flow is the revenue net of the operating costs, fixed costs, and taxes; $CF^{fc}(n, i) = (CA(n, i) \times GRI(n, i) \times m - FC) \times (1 - \tau)$. (See figure 13.16.)

Boundary (Default) Conditions and Terminal Conditions

The terminal condition is the primitive firm value net of the present value of fixed costs, operating costs, and taxes. Adjust the value by the long-term growth rate.

Terminal Values

The terminal value at each state has four components: the present value of the gross profit, the present value of the fixed costs that takes the possibility of future default into account, the present value of the tax (which is approximated as a portion of the pretax firm value), and the cash flows of the firm at the horizon time. The present value of the fixed costs is determined as a hypergeometric function, since we assume that the firm can default in the future and the fixed costs are not paid in full.

State (i)	0	1	2	3	4	5
Firm value($mil)	2633.55	5867.18	10635.13	17099.26	25472.04	36115.54

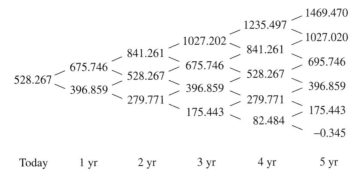

Figure 13-16 Lattice of cash flow of fixed-cost firm

Lattice of Fixed-Cost Firm Value

This is determined by rolling back the firm values, taking the cash flows into account. The firm value at the terminal period at each node is

$$V^{fc}(n, i) =$$
$$Max\left[\left\{\frac{FA \cdot GRI(n, i) \cdot m}{\rho - g} - \Phi\left(\frac{FA \cdot GRI(n, i) \cdot m}{\rho - g}\right)\right.\right.$$
$$\left.\left. + (CA \times GRI(n, i) \times m - FC)\right\}(1 - \tau_c), 0\right]$$

where $\Phi(\cdot)$ is the present value of the perpetual risky fixed cost, and $\Phi(\cdot)$ is the valuation formula of the perpetual debt given by Merton (1974).

$$\Phi(V, \infty) = \frac{FC}{r_f}\left(1 - \frac{\left(\frac{b}{V}\right)^a}{\Gamma(2 + a)}M\left(a, a + 2, -\frac{b}{V}\right)\right)$$

where $a = 2r_f/\sigma^2$ and $b = 2 \cdot FC/\sigma^2$ and $\Gamma(\cdot)$ is a gamma function.

In the intermediate periods, the firm value is determined by backward substitution,

$$V^{fc}(n, i) =$$
$$\frac{p \times V^{fc}(n + 1, i + 1) - (1 - p) \times V^{fc}(n + 1, i)}{(1 + r_f)} +$$
$$(CA(n, i) \times GRI(n, i) \times m - FC) \times (1 - \tau_c).$$

(See figure 13.17.)

The Firm Value Lattice

This lattice allows for capital investment $I(n, i)$ dependent on the state and time. The investments are made to maximize the market capitalization.

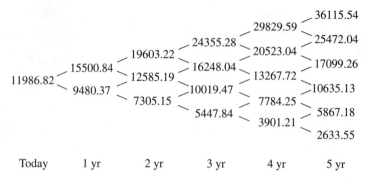

Today   1 yr   2 yr   3 yr   4 yr   5 yr

Figure 13-17 Lattice of fixed-cost firm value

Inputs

In addition to the input data of the fixed-cost firm, we need the observed capital expenditure constraint.

Outputs

Lattice of the binomial coefficients, $B(n, i)$, is the Pascal triangle to determine the binomial coefficients. (See figure 13.18.)

Lattice of capital investment is determined by the nonlinear optimization that maximizes the firm value. We have used a maximum constraint of 0, and hence there is no investment in all periods and states. (See figure 13.19.)

Lattice of capital assets is determined by the forward calculation, which is

$$CA(n + 1, i) = \frac{[B(n, i) \cdot CA(n, i) + B(n, i - 1) \cdot CA(n, i - 1)]}{[B(n, i) + B(n, i - 1)]} + I(n + 1, i).$$

(See figure 13.20.)

Lattice of growth firm cash flow is $CF^g(n, i) = (CA(n, i) \times GRI(n, i) \times m - FC) \times (1 - \tau) - I(n, i)$. (See figure 13.21.)

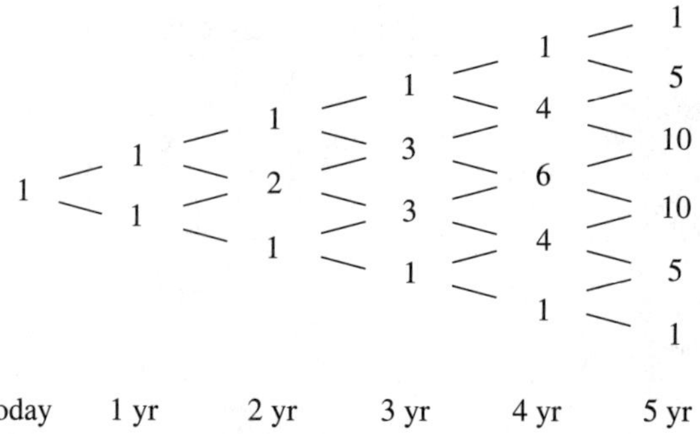

```
                                              1
                                        1
                                  1           5
                            1           4
                      1           3           10
                1           2           6
          1           1           3           10
    1           1           3           4
          1           1           6           5
                1           4
                      1           1
```

Today   1 yr   2 yr   3 yr   4 yr   5 yr

Figure 13-18 Lattice of the binomial coefficients

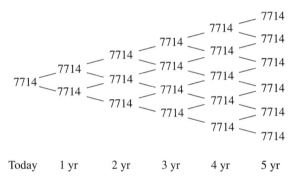

Today   1 yr   2 yr   3 yr   4 yr   5 yr

Figure 13-19 Lattice of capital investment

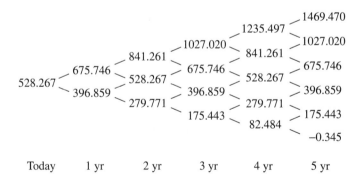

Today   1 yr   2 yr   3 yr   4 yr   5 yr

Figure 13-20 Lattice of capital assets

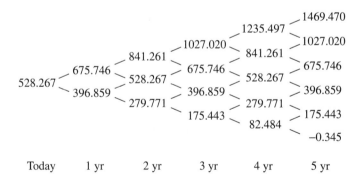

Today   1 yr   2 yr   3 yr   4 yr   5 yr

Figure 13-21 Lattice of growth firm cash flow

Lattice of growth firm value is determined by rolling back the firm values, taking the cash flows into account. The firm value at the terminal period at each node is

$$V^g(n, i) =$$
$$Max\left[\left\{\frac{CA(n, i) \cdot GRI(n, i) \cdot m}{\rho - g} - \Phi\left(\frac{CA(n, i) \cdot GRI(n, i) \cdot m}{\rho - g}\right)\right.\right.$$
$$\left.\left. + (CA(n, i) \times GRI(n, i) \times m - FC)\right\}(1 - \tau_c) - I(n, i), 0\right]$$

where $\Phi(\cdot)$ is the present value of the perpetual debt. In the intermediate periods, the firm value is determined by backward substitution,

$$V^g(n, i) =$$
$$\frac{p \times V^g(n+1, i+1) - (1-p) \times V^g(n+1, i)}{(1+r_f)} +$$
$$(CA(n, i) \times GRI(n, i) \times m - FC)(1 - \tau_c) - I(n, i).$$

(See figure 13.22.)

Leveraged Firm

The firm value is independent of the debt level. Therefore the firm value lattice is the same as the growth firm lattice. The value of the bond is determined by the backward substitution approach. The stock lattice is the firm lattice net of the bond lattice.

Inputs

Same as the growth firm
Observed debt structure: par, maturity, coupon, spread

Outputs

Lattice of leveraged firm value
   Based on the MM theory, the leveraged firm value is the same as the growth firm value. (See figure 13.23.)
Lattice of Growth Debt Value
   We first consider the terminal conditions for the bond to be *Min* [7133.518, firm value at the bond maturity date. We then conduct the backward substitutions, such that we apply the valuation rule at each node point: *Min* [backward substitution bond value + bond cash flow, firm value]. (See figure 13.24.)
   Lattice of market capitalization

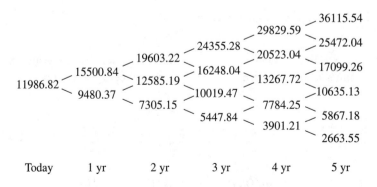

Figure 13-22 Lattice of growth firm value

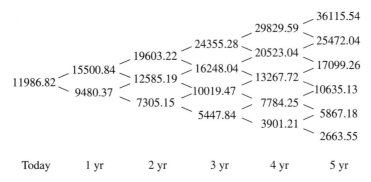

Figure 13-23 Lattice of leveraged firm value

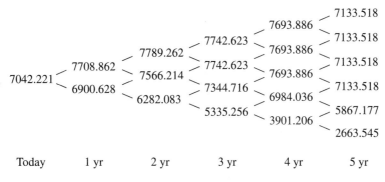

Figure 13-24 Lattice of growth debt value

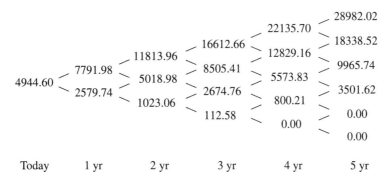

Figure 13-25 Lattice of market capitalization

The market capitalization value is the firm value net of the debt value. (See figure 13.25.)

Debt Cash Flows and Yield Spreads

The debt cash flow is shown below (see figure 13.12):

State (i)	0	1	2	3	4	5
Firm value ($mil)	118.523	380.053	380.053	380.053	867.553	7133.518

Given the bond price to be $5.818 billion, the internal rate of return is 9.26% or the credit risk spread is 476 basis points.

Specific results: stock volatility, debt value

Calibration

Thus far this procedure has assumed the following input data: firm value, sector volatility, sector expected excess return. These are not observed data. They are simply initial data to enable us to proceed with the algorithm in determining the bond value. The model derives market capitalization, stock volatility, and stock expected excess returns. We can directly observe these values. Therefore, we can use a nonlinear estimation procedure in perturbing the assumed data such that the following relationships hold.

1. Market capitalization and stock volatility = observed.

Market Capitalization	4944.6	Given Stock vol.	0.51898
Calibrated Stock Value	4944.6	Estimated Stock vol.	0.51925

Note that the excess return of the stock can be determined by the Capital Asset Pricing model and by the equation below, which is based on the market price of risk of a contingent claim. This provides the third constraint to the nonlinear search.

2. Excess return (stock)= Excess return (sector)×stock volatility/sector volatility

Note

1. The model also assumes the mine can close or reopen at costs. For clarity of the exposition, we will ignore these extensions here.

References

Amram, M., and N. Kulatilaka. 1998. *Real Options: Managing Strategic Investment in an Uncertain World*. New York: Oxford University Press

Arnold, T., and T. Falcon Crack. 2000. Option pricing in the real world: A generalized binomial model with applications to real options. Working paper, Louisiana State University.

Arrow, K. J., and A. C. Fisher. 1974. Environmental preservation, uncertainty and irreversibility. *Quarterly Journal of Economics*, 88, 312–319.

Barraquand, J., and D. Martineau. 1995. Numerical valuation of high dimensional multivariate American securities. *Journal of Financial and Quantitative Analysis*, 30, 383–405.

Benaroch, M., and R. J. Kauffman. 1999. A case for using real options pricing analysis to evaluate information technology project investments. *Information Systems Research*, 10 (1), 70–86.

Benaroch, M., and R. J. Kauffman. 2000. Justifying electronic banking network expansion using real options analysis. *MIS Quarterly*, 24 (2), 197–226

Berger, P., E. Ofeck, and I. Swary. 1996. Investor valuation of the abandonment option. *Journal of Financial Economics*, 42, 257–287.

Brennan, M. J., and E. S. Schwartz. 1985. Evaluating natural resource investments. *Journal of Business*, 58 (2), 135–157.

Busby, J. S., and C. G. C. Pitts. 1997. Real options in practice: An exploratory survey of how finance officers deal with flexibility in capital appraisal. *Management Accounting Research*, 8 (2), 169–186.

Chalasani, P., S. Jha, and K. Sullivan. 1998. An options approach to software prototyping. In *International Conference on Software Engineering (ICSE '98).*

Childs, P. D., S. H. Ott, and A. J. Triantis. 1998. Capital budgeting for interrelated projects: A real options approach. *Journal of Financial and Quantitative Analysis*, 33 (3), 305–334.

Copeland, C., and V. Antikarov. 2001. *Real Options: A Practitioner's Guide*, Texere.

Copeland, T., and P. Keenan. 1998. Making real options real. *McKinsey Quarterly*, 3, 128–141.

Cortazar, G. 2000. Simulation and numerical methods in real options valuation. In *Real Options and Investment under Uncertainty: Classical Readings and Recent Contributions*, Schwartz and Trigeorgis, eds. Cambridge: MIT Press.

Cortazar, G., and J. Casassus. 1998. Optimal timing of a mine expansion: Implementing a real options model. *Quarterly Review of Economics and Finance*, 38 (3), 755–769.

Cortazar, G., E. S. Schwartz, and J. Casassus. 2001. Optimal exploration investments under price and geological-technical uncertainty: A real options model. *R&D Management*, 31 (2), 181–189.

Cox, J. C., S. A. Ross, and M. Rubinstein. 1979. Option pricing: A simplified approach. *Journal of Financial Economics*, 3, 229–263.

Davis, G. A. 1998. Estimating volatility and dividend yield when valuing real options to invest or abandon. *Quarterly Review of Economics and Finance*, spec. iss., 725–754.

Fama, E. F., and K. R. French. 2000. Testing tradeoff and pecking order predictions about dividends and debt. Working paper, University of Chicago.

Fernandez, P. 2001. Valuing real options: Frequently made errors. Working paper, Instituto de Estadios Superiores de la Empresa Business School.

Fichman, R. G. 2001. Early investments in dynamic IT platform innovations: A real options approach. Working paper, Boston College.

Finger, C. 1994. The ability of earnings to predict future earnings and cash flow. *Journal of Accounting and Research*, 32, 210–223.

Friedman, E. J., and S. Johnson. 1997. Dynamic monotonicity and comparative statics for real options. *Journal of Economic Theory*, 75 (1), 104–121.

Kemna, A. G. Z. 1993. Case studies on real options. *Financial Management*, 22 (3), 269–270.

Kim, I. J., K. Ramaswamy, and S. Sundaresan. 1993. Does default risk in coupons affect the valuation of corporate bonds?: A contingent claims model. *Financial Management*, 22 (3),

Kulatilaka, N. 1993. The value of flexibility: The case of a dual-fuel industrial steam boiler. *Financial Management*, 22 (3), 271–280

Lambrecht, B., and W. Perraudin. 2003. Real options and preemption under incomplete information. *Journal of Economic Dynamics and Control*, 27, (4), 619–643.

Lander, D. M., and G. E. Pinches. 1998. Challenges to the practical implementation of modeling and valuing real options. *Quarterly Review of Economics and Finance*, 38 (3), 537–567.

Laughton, D. G., and H. D. Jacoby. 1993. Reversion, timing options, and long-term decision-making. *Financial Management*, 22 (3), 225–240.

Luehrman, T. 1998a. Investment opportunities as real options: Getting started on the numbers. *Harvard Business Review*, 76 (July–August), 51–67.

Luehrman, T. 1998b. Strategy as a portfolio of real options. *Harvard Business Review*, 76 (September–October), 89–99.

Mackay, P. 2004. Real flexibility and financial structure: An empirical analysis. *Review of Financial Studies*, forthcoming.

Mcdonald, R., and D. R. Siegel. 1985. Investment and the valuation of firms when there is an option to shut down. *International Economic Review*, 26 (2), 331–349.

Mcdonald, R., and D. R. Siegel. 1986. The value of waiting to invest. *Quarterly Journal of Economics*, 101, 707–728.

Merton, R. C. 1974. On the pricing of corporate debt: The risk structure of interest rates. *Journal of Finance*, 29 (2), 449–470.

Moel, A., and P. Tufano. 2002. When are real options exercised? An empirical study of mine closings. *Review of Financial Studies*, 15 (1), 35–64.

Myers, S. C. 1984a. Finance theory and financial strategy. *Interface*, 14, 126–137.

Myers, S. C. 1984b. Capital structure puzzle. *Journal of Finance,* 39 (3), 575–592.

Panayi, S., and L. Trigeorgis. 1998. Multi-stage real options: The cases of information technology infrastructure and international bank expansion. *Quarterly Review of Economics and Finance,* 38 (3), 675–692.

Pindyck, R. S. 1988. Irreversible investment, capacity choice and the value of firm. *American Economic Review,* 78 (5), 969–985.

Pindyck, R. S. 1991. Irreversibility, uncertainty and investment. *Journal of Economic Literature,* 29 (4), 1110–1152.

Pindyck, R. S. 1993. Investment of uncertain cost. *Journal of Financial Economics,* 34 (1), 53–76.

Schwartz, E. S., and L. Trigeorgis. 2001. *Real Options and Investment Under Uncertainty: Classical Readings and Recent Contributions.* Cambridge, MA: MIT Press.

Schwarz, E. S., and C. Zozaya-Gorostiza. 2000. Valuation of information technology investments as real options. Working paper, University of California, Anderson Graduate School of Management.

Shackleton, M., and R. Wojakowski. 2002. The expected return and exercise time of Merton-style real options. *Journal of Business Finance and Accounting,* 29 (3–4), 541–555.

Smit, H. T. J., and L. A. Ankum. 1993. A real options and game-theoretic approach to corporate investment strategy under competition. *Financial Management,* 22 (3), 241–250.

Trigeorgis, L. 1993a. Real options and interactions with financial flexibility. *Financial Management,* 22 (3), 202–224.

Trigeorgis, L. 1993b. The nature of option interactions and the valuation of investments with multiple real options. *Journal of Financial and Quantitative Analysis,* 28 (1), 1–20.

Trigeorgis, L. 1996. *Real Options: Managerial Flexibility and Strategy in Resource Allocation.* Cambridge, MA: MIT press.

Weeds, H. 2002. Strategic delay in a real options model of R&D competition. *Review of Economic Studies,* 69 (240), 729–747.

Further Readings

Bernardo, A. E., and B. Chowdhry. 2000. Resources, real options and corporate strategy. *Journal of Finacial Economics,* 63 (2), 211–234.

Berrada, T. 1999. Valuing real options when time to maturity is uncertain. Working paper, JEL.

Bloom, N., and J. Reenen. 2001. Real options, patents, productivity and market value: Evidence from a panel of British firms. Working paper, Institute for Fiscal Studies.

Bloom, N., S. Bond, and J. V. Reenen. 2001. The dynamics of investment under uncertainty. Working paper, Institute for Fiscal Studies.

Bradford, D. F. 1997. Transition to and tax rate flexibility in a cash-flow type tax. Working paper, Princeton University.

Chen, P. F., and G. Zhang. 2002. The role of earnings and book value in equity valuation: A real options based analysis. Working paper, Hong Kong University.

Gamba, A., and L. Trigeorgis. 2002. A log-transformed binomial lattice extension for multi-dimensional option problems. Working paper, University of Cyprus.

Sullivan, K., P. Chalasani, S. Jha, and V. Sazawal. 1998. Software design as an investment activity: A real options perspective. Working paper, University of Virginia.

14

Optimal Corporate Financial Decisions: Corporate Model

Few questions are more fundamental in finance than asking how a corporation should be managed. The Modigliani and Miller model asserts that corporate financial management is irrelevant to shareholders' value in the perfect capital market. Thus, the model shows that corporate management is important when the perfect capital market assumptions fail. Specifically, in the presence of asymmetric information, where investors do not have access to the firm's proprietary information, corporate management establishes goals in terms of its performance metrics and formulates strategies to meet these goals. In essence, a firm must specify its own corporate model to develop a set of consistent corporate strategies, which may include dividend policies, debt structure, capital structure, risk management, and liquidity management. The corporate model provides the framework to determine optimal corporate financial management strategies.

How should a corporation manage its finance? Few questions are more fundamental in corporate finance. One way to begin answering this question is to better understand the responsibilities of a corporate financial manager. There are two main responsibilities of the corporate financial manager: investment and corporate financial management.

As we have discussed before, there are two types of investment decisions: capital budgeting and strategic investment. In capital budgeting, corporate managers have the responsibilities of ensuring that profitable projects are undertaken and unprofitable projects are rejected. A method to determine the profitability of a project is called the discounted cash flow method, which starts with detailed projections of expected future free cash flows of the project, and discounts the expected cash flows at the cost of capital of the project. We accept projects with positive net present value and reject projects with negative net present value.

In strategic investment, corporate financial managers are responsible for positioning the firm to exploit potential growth in a market segment, without any detailed projections of cash flows. The business model is used to determine the strategic value of a project, as discussed in chapter 13. Thus far, we have expressed the importance of investment in enhancing shareholders' value.

In contrast to capital budgeting or strategic investment, corporate financial management is concerned with dividend policy, external funding, capital structure design, and risk and return, allocations of the firm's assets or future income among its claimants. According to the Miller–Modigliani (MM) theory, these decisions do not affect the firm value in a perfect capital market. The MM Theory I and the Miller model in particular hypothesize that all the corporate financial decisions are irrelevant, as explained in chapter 12.

This basic theory cannot explain any casual observation of the marketplace. If a firm's objective is to maximize shareholders' value using the MM theory, then corporate financial management decisions do not have any impact on what they seek to achieve. If these decisions are considered irrelevant, what is the role of corporate financial management? In this case, corporate decisions will be random and there will be no problems for financial managers to agonize over. However, this is not the case. Corporate financial management decisions are important, because how they manage their finances has a significant impact on the corporations.

Theories have been proposed to extend the MM theory to explain the relevance of corporate financial decisions. This chapter will review some of these theories, which mainly incorporate market transaction costs and asymmetric information. However, the empirical evidence fails to provide strong support for any particular theory.

Empirical evidence does support the importance of earnings, return on equity, and other financial performance measures to corporate financial management. This observation suggests that corporate financial management seeks to manage the financial performance measures.

This chapter provides the corporate model, which hypothesizes that a firm uses financial performance measures to provide "signals" or information about the firm to the capital market, where investors do not have full information about the firm. The corporate model enables the corporate financial managers to develop a coherent management strategy to provide optimal information about the firm's value to the capital market.

We will describe the corporate model that will relate the corporate decisions to the financial performance measures. We will use the business model described in chapter 13 to provide the underlying relation of the firm's investment decisions to the performance measures. This approach enables us to have a consistent framework to (1) value firms, (2) analyze a sample of firms in a similar industry, and (3) determine the risk factors to the shareholders' value. It also provides a methodology to determine optimal corporate financial decisions. In essence, this approach enables us to evaluate a firm relative to its peer group, and to formulate optimal corporate financial decisions.

14.1 Corporate Financial Planning—the DFA Approach

To provide a context for the problem of optimal corporate financial decisions, we will illustrate one approach used by corporations. This approach is called *dynamic financial analysis*, or DFA. We will then show how financial models can be used to enhance this methodology.

Problems Posed to DFA

DFA is a financial planning model that is designed to address a broad range of corporate issues. For example, it may be used to estimate the profitability of the firm over a time horizon, to determine the likelihood of meeting the earnings target, or to manage the risk sources, which are often called the risk drivers, so as to avoid missing the earnings target. As a result, the firm can determine its optimal actions to achieve its financial goals by means of DFA. These actions can be change of asset allocation in its investment portfolio, change of its sales distributions, or change of product pricing.

DFA may be used to analyze the liquidity adequacy of the firm. When the firm needs to make significant cash outlays under certain scenarios, DFA may be used to evaluate the ability of the firm to raise the needed cash. In relation to liquidity issues, DFA may be used to study the impact of adverse scenarios on the firm's creditworthiness and its debt rating. Using DFA, the firm may then simulate the business or market risks to determine a financial strategy to deal with these problems.

A Description of DFA

Dynamic financial analysis uses financial projection models to assist in the firm's financial planning. These models begin with the ability to simulate future financial statements. These pro forma financial statements are based on the assumptions of the firm's future businesses and business decisions. These assumptions are provided by the users of the models. Using these assumptions, DFA entails simulating business scenarios on the sales, expenses, business growth, and financial performance measures. The analysis also includes simulating the interest rate, equity, and other market risks that may affect the business.

Beyond the simulations, DFA must have a tax model. Tax codes tend to be complex and detailed. A DFA approach must also have a model of the tax rules to simulate the tax liabilities. And finally, DFA seeks to determine the optimal business decisions such that the firm's objective is maximized. The objective and the constraints on the decisions may depend on the simulated financial statements and the performance measurements. The inputs to the dynamic financial analysis are the initial financial statements of the firm and the business strategies that the firm contemplates in the coming years. Given this information, dynamic financial analysis outputs the projected financial statements at the horizon period, which may be the next quarter or several quarters hence, under multiple scenarios that reflect the market risks and the business risks. The outputs are the distributions of the performance measures of the firm.

For example, from the distributions of the earnings over a year, the system can identify the likelihood of missing the earnings forecast over a time horizon, given the market risks and business risks. Further, alternative strategies can be used to see if other decisions can provide a better solution.

To determine optimal decisions, objective functions have to be specified. There are alternative objective functions to meet earnings forecasts. These are some examples of what firms may do.

Benchmarking to the industry leader

One approach is to use an industry leader in the same market segment as a benchmark. The corporate management strategies are adjusted to attain the performance measures of the leading firm in the market segment. This approach may not lead to optimal corporate management strategies, but it is one way for the investment community to compare the firms and determine the valuation. For example, the industry leader may have no debt, and using a 0 debt ratio as a benchmark may lead its competitors to use less debt in financing their projects.

Average financial ratios and performance measures as the baseline for comparison

The firm may use the industry average of financial ratios and performance measures as the baseline. Then the firm will use financial planning to ensure that it can outperform the industry average.

Balancing the Importance of the Performance Measures

Since the firm's financial performance cannot be measured by only one number (e.g., earnings) the firm can select a number of performance measures and seek to maximize weighted performance measures with different weights.

Advantages and Limitations of the DFA Approach

The DFA approach is an effective decision support tool because it provides intuitive understanding of complex problems. The senior management can use the DFA approach to forecast the possible outcomes and suggest solutions, using their own assumptions on the business risks and market risks. However, DFA is also a way to link the senior management assumptions to the outcomes, where the links are defined by accounting and tax rules, but often not by financial theories such as those (e.g., the arbitrage-free pricing models) we have discussed. Their objective functions in the optimization, as described above, may not be consistent with enhancing the shareholders' wealth. To the extent that some DFAs do not incorporate financial models, they have a number of limitations. These limitations are described in Brealey and Myers (2002), who declare that "there is no finance in financial planning models." More specifically, we provide three limitations.

Defining the corporate objective

If we take "maximizing shareholders' value" as the corporate objective, then the corporate strategies in managing earnings may not be consistent with this fundamental goal. DFA can suggest how new strategies may affect the future earnings, or benchmark the industry leaders, but how should the senior management seek strategies that maximize shareholders' value?

Maximizing the earnings for one year or over two years is not the same as maximizing the shareholders' value, because the shareholders' value depends on all the future corporate actions in different states of the world.

The shareholders' value is a present-value concept. The simulations of future outcomes do not relate to the present shareholders' value unless we know how the market discounts the future values. The determination of the appropriate market discount rate requires the understanding of the market pricing of risks and how payments are made for different outcomes, as we have seen in the "appropriate discount rate" for an option payoff. Only financial theories regarding capital markets can be used to deal with this issue.

Defining optimal strategies

DFA can provide insights into the formulation of optimal strategies because it shows how each of the assumptions of the senior management affects the performance measure. However, the approach cannot determine the optimal strategy. As explained in Bellman's dynamic programming solution, the optimal action taken is affected by future optimal decisions. All decisions are related, and the optimal strategies include all future and present actions. Generally, simulating forward, using rule-based strategies, does not yield optimal strategies that often depend on the state of the world and time in relation to the planning horizon. Typically, the principle of the Bellman optimization is not used to determine the optimal decisions in DFA.

There is another related issue. DFA strategies are typically not "flexible," as the real option describes. While in principle DFA strategies can be specified to be dependent on the state of the world, DFA does not solve for the optimal solution. Users of DFA tend to choose the "best solution" out of a specified set of simulations. The solution does not show how the optimal strategy should be revised as the state has changed or how to discount the payoffs. As a result, DFA often fails to quantify the present value of the real option appropriately by not incorporating financial modeling.

Linkages of corporate finance and capital markets

Corporate finance does not operate in isolation from capital markets. Corporations seek funding from capital markets, and the financing may be in the form of derivatives and other option-embedded bonds. Corporations also invest in instruments that are market contingent claims. The values of these assets and liabilities must be determined by the principles of market valuation, and not by the senior management's subjective view of how the securities would be priced, in order to maintain a coherent and objective analysis.

Financial models that have been presented in the book thus far provide these linkages. For example, we can determine the cost of borrowing by the corporate bond valuation model, taking the credit risk of the firm into account. Therefore, we can appropriately incorporate the change in the firm risk to calculate the cost of borrowing. We have shown how employees' options should be priced and how that pricing affects the firm value. The accounting statements cannot capture such linkages; however, appropriate financial models can capture the impact of the employees' options on the shareholders' value more accurately.

We will deal with these limitations later in this chapter, using a corporate model. We begin with the issue of defining the corporate objective.

14.2   Extensions of the MM theory

Under the perfect capital market assumptions among all individuals, the MM theory shows that individuals can "undo" the firm's financial package. Therefore, all financial decisions are irrelevant. But how can we reconcile the theory with the observations of the real markets, which show that corporate financial management is accepted as important?

There are two approaches in relaxing the assumptions of the MM theory: (1) we may assume that not all agents in the economy have the same information, and (2) there are market frictions, such as transaction costs.

Asymmetric Information and the Pecking Order Theory

Asymmetric information theory asserts that financial decisions are not made on the basis of complete and perfect information, because not all information is accessible to everyone in the world. The financial models thus far have assumed complete information between buyers and sellers.

However, in reality this is not always the case. For example, a used car called a *"lemon"* is a typical case to illustrate asymmetric information. In selling or buying a new car, it would be fair to say that both the buyer and the seller can have the same level of information regarding the quality of the car. But such is not the case with a used car. This is because the seller has better information about his car, for an obvious reason: he has been operating the car. Compared to the seller of the used car, the buyer has no information at all except what the seller says about the car's quality, which the buyer will not take at face value, since the seller has the incentive to describe the condition of the car as better than it really is. As a result of this asymmetric information, a used car may not be sold at a fair price, which is the price that would be paid/received if the buyer has the same information as the seller. The actual price of the used car should be a discounted price to reflect an average quality of the used cars in the market, regardless of the quality of the particular used car. The reason for this is that buyers have no way to tell a good used car from a bad used car.

This "lemon" problem can also apply to corporate finance. Financial managers, shareholders, and lenders may all have different information regarding the values of the assets, securities, and so on. It is common that the financial managers have private information which is not available to the investors. The signaling theory concerns how financial managers with private information about the firm's future cash flows send unambiguous signals to investors if they have the proper incentives to do so. Since the investors know that the financial managers have the tendency to talk up the firm value, they would want to observe the signals of the profitability of the firm, which could not be mimicked by unprofitable firms.

For example, one application of the signaling theory to corporate financial decisions is concerned with the dividend policy of a firm. The MM theory argues that the cost of paying dividends to the shareholders is the personal income tax. Paying cash out as dividends to shareholders must be costly to the shareholders because they have to pay the higher income tax as opposed to the capital gains tax. Yet firms do pay dividends.

In an extensive survey, Lintner (1956) provides insight into how firms pay dividends. Dividends are profits of the firms that are passed on to shareholders in cash. Thus, one would expect the firm to keep some cash or cash equivalents in the company and distribute any excess to the shareholders. Dividends will therefore be related quite directly to the firm's profits over time, with higher profits leading to higher dividends. That is, a firm would follow a constant dividend payout ratio on its profit.

Surprisingly, such is not the case, according to Lintner's research. The results show that a firm tends to have a target payout ratio, which he discovered was a proportion of expected earnings per share. The firm would pay out the dividends, adjusting to the target payout ratio. Specifically, let $D^*(n+1)$ be the target dividend for the next period; then $D^*(n+1) = a \times E(n+1)$, where $E(n+1)$ is the expected earnings at time $n+1$ and a is a target payout ratio. Then the dividend paid at time $(n+1)$ is a partial adjustment to the target dividend:

$$D(n+1) = D(n) + b \times [D^*(n+1) - D(n)], \text{ where } b \text{ is the partial adjustment rate.}$$

For example, if $b = 0.5$, then the dividend payment is always halfway between the target dividend level and the last dividend payment. In this case, the dividend payments fluctuate less than the reported profits. In the case of falling profits, some firms may raise external funds to pay dividends. Lintner concludes that the firm's dividend policy is to decide the target payout ratio and the adjustment rate, and shows that the dividend policy model is empirically robust. This result contradicts the MM theory. Why do firms pay dividends? Kalay (1982), using the signaling theory, argues that dividends are paid as a signal to the shareholders regarding the profitability of the firm.

Another application of the signaling theory concerned with the financing of the firm is called the *pecking order theory*. Myers (1984) uses the incomplete information theory to explain corporate financing behavior. Specifically, he seeks to answer the following question: When a firm needs capital for investment outlay, should it use internal funding, or new equity, or debt?

When a firm needs funds, it has alternative means of securing the funding. Using the incomplete information theory, Myers suggests that the firm should first use internally generated funds, and then short-term debt, followed by the long-term debt to equity.

Let us compare internal funding with issuing new equity. When a firm comes to the market to sell new equity securities to finance a project, potential investors ask this reasonable question: If the project has such a high net present value, why do you want to share the profits with us? The firm has private information regarding the project that investors do not have. Therefore, if the firm issues the equity securities to finance the project, the investors regard the firm as having unfavorable private information about the project. The reason for this is that the firm would not issue the equity securities to share the profits with the potential shareholders. The potential shareholders think that the firm is exaggerating future performance of the project to deceive them. Thus, investors are more likely to discount the value of the project in order to defend themselves as compared to a case where investors have full information about the project. The discount may be too high and the firm will have to use its own internal funds (if it has any).

This same argument holds if we compare short-term debt and long-term debt. Long-term debt requires more private information than short-term debt. The choice of security for external funding depends on the amount of private information involved in the transaction. If there is more favorable private information involved, then the firm is less likely to prefer issuing new equity securities. It will therefore first use its own internally generated funds, and then debt, and finally equity—hence the pecking order.

Trade-off Theory

There is an alternative theory to the funding decision that does not use the signaling theory. In extending the MM theory, the *trade-off theory* takes market frictions such as transaction costs into account. Specifically, the trade-off theory hypothesizes that a firm will increase its dividend payouts or debt ratio until, at the margin, the cost equals the benefit. In the MM perfect capital market world, of course, such an optimal point does not exist. According to the theory, corporate financial management is irrelevant to the shareholders' value, and therefore corporate management is reduced to an irrelevant role. However, this is not true of all firms. The perfect capital market assumptions have to be relaxed.

The trade-off theory applies to capital structure. According to MM proposition II, firms should increase debt financing to benefit from the tax deduction on corporate borrowing, and thus increase the firm value. But there should be a limit to such corporate borrowing.

Specifically, according to MM proposition II, the firm value of a leveraged firm V_L exceeds the unleveraged firm value V_U by the amount of tax shield, $\tau_c \cdot D$, where τ_c is the corporate marginal tax rate and D is the market value of debt.

$$V_L = V_U + \tau_c \cdot D \tag{14.1}$$

However, the theory ignores the present value of bankruptcy costs. In taking such costs into account, denoted by $C(D)$, which increases with the increase in the debt D as the likelihood of the event of default rises, we have

$$V_L = V_U + \tau_c \cdot D - C(D) \tag{14.2}$$

The trade-off theory then hypothesizes that corporate managers should increase the debt level to D^* such that maximum firm value is attained.

$$\frac{dV_L}{dD} = \tau_c - \frac{dC(D^*)}{dD} = 0 \tag{14.3}$$

or

$$\tau_c = \frac{dC(D^*)}{dD} \tag{14.4}$$

That is, the optimal debt level is reached when the marginal increase in the present value of the bankruptcy cost is equal to the marginal corporate tax rate. Suppose that the corporate marginal tax rate is 40%. Then a \$1 increase in debt leads to a \$0.4 increase in the present value of the default cost, and the corporate manager has attained the optimal debt level.

The key issue is how to measure the present value of the bankruptcy costs. We can break the bankruptcy cost into two components: the direct costs and the indirect costs. Direct costs are the tangible payments in the event of default, such as legal fees and court fees. Indirect costs are the possible loss of sales and profits. As explained in chapter 9, during the bankruptcy proceedings, investment opportunities may not be exploited because of the managerial constraints under Chapter 11. However, there is little agreement on the significance of the bankruptcy costs, and hence on the level of debt needed to reach the optimal capital structure.

The main point of the trade-off theory is that a firm has the incentive to increase the debt level for tax deduction up to the point where the present value of the cost of bankruptcy becomes significant and the marginal cost equals the marginal benefit.

14.3   Empirical Evidence on the MM Theory and Its Extensions

The trade-off theory and the pecking order theory deal with similar issues, and they both make significant adjustments to the MM theory. To distinguish the two theories, we consider how they predict a firm's behavior in different situations. Fama and French (2002) tested their predictions empirically to provide a comparison.

In many cases, the pecking order theory is consistent with the trade-off theory. For example, both predict that more profitable firms have higher target dividend payouts. This is because both theories assume that the firms have access to the capital market for external financing. Therefore, there is no need for investing the profits. Since the pecking order theory suggests first using internally generated profits for investment, firms with many investment opportunities exhaust their retained earnings in investment and have little left for dividends. For the same reason, the trade-off theory suggests using the funds for investment instead of paying them out as dividends.

However, the prediction of the pecking order theory differs from that of the trade-off theory in the case of the leverage of a profitable firm. The pecking order theory suggests that the leverage is low (and not high, as predicted by the trade-off theory), since a profitable firm will have internally generated funds to finance investments and will not need to use debt for financing. The trade-off theory predicts that profitable firms, with low expected investment outlay and low volatility in earnings, will have stable future values. In this environment, the management of the firm has a high leverage at which the interest cost deduction on the bonds balances the present value of the bankruptcy cost.

Empirical results support all the hypotheses where both theories have the same predictions. In cases where they differ, the results show that profitable firms tend to have low leverage, as predicted by the pecking order theory. However, the results also show that many firms raise equity capital even when they have no debt. This contradicts the basic premise of the pecking order theory, where equity is the last option to use to raise capital. This particular result has been independently reported by Helwege and Liang (1996), but they have not provided an alternative hypothesis.

The pecking order theory suggests that in a world with incomplete information, firms will seek internal financing first for investment outlay. This hypothesis is supported by empirical research. Firms are considered "conservative" when they hold a significant excess of cash or cash equivalent securities. However, these firms' behavior is transitory. According to prior research, 50% of these firms will hold much less cash within five years, which suggests that they are often stockpiling cash for internally financing a significant investment outlay. Such behavior can be observed across industries. These firms' behaviors do not seem to be motivated by their tax status or by asymmetric information between the management and investors. For example, firms with a high effective tax rate do not in general raise capital by selling debt to increase the tax shield. They ignore it, and use internal funding to finance their investment.

In summary, research has confirmed over a long period of time that firms follow a dividend policy. They try to adhere to the policy even though their cash flows may be volatile. To maintain the dividend policy, they even use debt to finance the dividends. This result contradicts the MM theory. The pecking order theory supports the result of profitable firms having low leverage, since these firms can finance their projects with internally generated funds. The result may also support the Miller model, where the tax deductibility of interest payments for the corporation has much less value than the MM proposition II, ignoring the personal tax, would suggest. But there is no simple answer to why firms raise equity capital before accessing the debt market. Empirical evidence does not provide clear support for the trade-off theory, the pecking order theory, or the Miller theory (or MM proposition II).

Empirical Evidence on the Informational Content in Financial Statements

While empirical evidence does not support any particular theory, it does suggest that financial managers make decisions rooted in financial statements. In this section, we describe what firms do in their management as observed from financial statements and reports. There is also empirical evidence supporting the idea that there is informational content in financial reporting.

Managing liquidity

In sampling several hundred firms, research finds that managing the liquidity of a firm is important, but it is an issue that the MM theory does not address directly. Liquidity is the ability of a firm to have cash and marketable securities to pay for cash outflows. A firm can maintain a line of credit with a bank. In a line of credit, the firm has the right to draw down a borrowing. There is a limit to the amount a firm can borrow. Borrowing is usually short-term, and there are also conditions constraining how the funds should be used.

Firms can have access to the capital market for short-term funding of commercial paper, which consists of money market instruments with maturities as short as one week. Access to the commercial paper market enables the firm to borrow funds to meet its short-term needs.

Short-term borrowing to fund transitory cash requirements, such as to build inventories, is one way to manage liquidity. This approach may have more risk to the firm because short-term borrowings increase the crisis of maturity. When a debt matures, lenders decide if they will continue funding the firm. Default may result from funding negotiations. Money market securities or revolving bank loans are no exceptions.

On the other hand, firms can hold excess cash to meet transitory requirements for funds. According to the MM theory, firms should be indifferent to holding excess cash. The increase in the holding of cash or marketable securities will lower the return on equity, but it will also lower the risk. The "irrelevant" theorem argues that the two effects will exactly neutralize each other's impact on the firm value. The shareholders will be indifferent to the firm's holding excess cash.

Baskin (1987), using a sample of firms in 1972, shows a significant level of cash and marketable securities in a firm's asset portfolio. On average, 9.6% of investable assets are in cash or cash equivalent securities. Kallberg and Parkinson (1992), using a sample in the period of 1979–1981, show the liquidity ratio to be 6.3%. K. John (1993) determines the characteristics of firms that maintain a high level of liquidity. She suggests that these firms have businesses that have a high cost of financial distress. For example, firms with high market value to the liquidation value as measured by the Tobin q, have a high financial distress cost because much of the shareholders' value is based on the firm value as a going concern.

It is important for firms to manage their liquidity because lenders will look at the liquidity ratio in a financial report to determine if the firm can handle the debt and repay it. If a firm has a high liquidity ratio, it is more likely to repay the debt. However, if a firm has a low liquidity ratio, it is more likely to default.

Managing earnings

Economists tend to argue that valuation is based on future cash flows, and the market can decide on the valuation of a firm given the transparency of the information. Considering that firms have much leeway in deciding the accrual basis for reporting earnings, the reported earnings can no longer reflect the firm value.

Empirical results repeatedly support the hypothesis that both the investors and the financial management of the firm focus on the firms' earnings in their valuation of the firm. Clearly, the management is concerned with many other aspects of the company's finances. Similarly, there are many factors investors take into consideration when valuing a firm. However, the single most important attribute of the firm's value is the earnings. This may be the result of the generally accepted accounting principles focusing on reporting firms' incomes and their uses for comparison across firms. This accrual accounting basis will be discussed in more detail later in the chapter. The market desires stable and increasing earnings. Such financial performance signals that the firm has a robust business, and should receive a high valuation.

However, the accounting rules allow financial managers a great deal of leeway in making judgments regarding the reporting of the firm's income value. Since the market rewards firms for stable and growing earnings, management has the incentive to provide such a performance. A number of research results have documented the smoothing of a firm's earning by the management. For example, over 90% of the announced earnings are within one cent of the quarterly earning estimates.

Empirical evidence frequently shows that earnings have strong informational content. That is, when information is made available, it has an impact on the market valuation of the stock. Subramanyam and Venkatachalam (2001) have more recently shown that earnings have informational content over a three-year time horizon. To measure such an impact, research has to hold other factors constant. In particular, the measure of stock returns has to isolate the market effect, when the stock price change is the consequence of a broad market movement but is not related to the release of the information. Typically, the excess returns of the stock over the market are tested for correlations with the release of the information about the announcements of changes in earnings.

There are alternative measures of accrual earnings. For many technology stocks, analysts and firms have argued that their earnings have been understated because the earnings are affected by the goodwill on their balance sheet. If a firm is acquired at a price higher than the equity on the balance sheet, the difference is the goodwill. The goodwill value has to be released as accrual costs, which adversely affects the earnings. Many technology firms may have positive cash flows, and they are profitable in a cash flow sense, and can remain as going concerns without the need for future funding. However, the announced earnings can still be negative, because of the accruals being carried forward for the future. Hence, some firms propose to use an earning measure that is based on cash flows, called *cash earnings*.

Moehrle et al. (2000) tested the informational content of alternative measures of cash earnings, seeking to show whether investors consider cash earnings provide more relevant information for the valuation of the firms. The results show that no measure can provide more informational content than the earnings with accruals. There is some evidence that cash earnings have more importance for unprofitable companies.

Summary

Empirically, the MM theory has not been proved or disproved, as we discussed earlier. The results are mixed, and the extensive empirical research, which has stretched over 40 years, does not support alternatives to the MM theory. This observation leads the researchers to believe that the MM theory is roughly correct. Conducting an experiment to truly test the theory is difficult, since the experimenter has to build two firms with different capital structures but otherwise identical in all respects in order to observe any difference in a firm's valuation. This is implausible in reality.

On the other hand, empirical evidence suggests that corporate financial decisions do take the financial performance measures into account and that there is informational content to the financial disclosures, meaning that the investment community does assign value to the financial reports disseminated by the firm. We will use such empirical evidence as the motivation for the corporate model.

14.4   The Corporate Model

The corporate model hypothesizes that the corporate managers of a firm have an objective function that motivates the corporate management decisions. The objective function is to provide optimal signals to the market on the financial performance of the firm, based on accounting performance measures. The corporate model has five major assumptions.

Maximization of MM Firm Value

We present the financial modeling of a corporation by beginning with an assumption that the goal of the financial manager is to maximize the shareholders' value. To this end, the financial manager should enhance the firm value in the first place by pursuing profitable investment strategies, where the investment may be capital budgeting or strategic in nature. The firm value should be maximized before we can discuss the values of the claims on the firm.

The claimants are the stockholders, bondholders, or other financial claimants. Simply stated, we should first make the pie as large as we can before we worry about how to share it among the parties. We will refer to this firm value under the perfect capital market assumptions as the MM theory firm value. Strategic investment decisions and capital budgeting decisions must seek to maximize the firm value in the sense of MM theory based on the business model in chapters 12 and 13.

Asymmetric Information

We assume that the investors know the business model of the firm, but they cannot see its inputs, such as the gross profit margin, the gross return on investment, and the investment amount. The firm provides the financial statements and performance measures or reveals its corporate financial decisions. From them, investors can conjecture the inputs to the business model. They can then determine the firm value based on their conjectures.

Capital Market Efficiency

The corporate model, however, must be consistent with the efficient functioning of the capital markets. Specifically, the valuation of securities and contingent claims must be consistent with the arbitrage-free assumptions. This way, the corporate model can ensure that the optimal corporate decisions are consistent with the functioning of the capital markets. Without this requirement, corporate planning would become vacuous, not taking the capital market into consideration.

The market is at least semistrong efficient, as discussed in chapter 1, in that the firm value fully reflects the information made available in the financial statements.

Maximization of a Corporate Objective Function

We assume that firms have a corporate objective function that expresses the preferences of the corporate financial management. Corporate strategies are derived from this objective function, given all the market constraints. This corporate objective function may be different across the firms in the same way that different firms have different goals and missions, which may change over time.

Chief financial officers (CFOs) are similar to the traders who continually buy and sell in securities markets, dealing with the market sentiments and frictions. CFOs must be concerned with the financing needs of the firm, investment in projects, acquisitions of businesses, and valuation of their firm's stocks. All these activities are related to the capital markets on a day-to-day basis, and therefore they need to respond to market sentiments and frictions.

As a result of the signaling theory in an asymmetric information market, CFOs must respond to the market preference for the use of performance measures based on financial disclosures or on nonfinancial disclosures. In times of uncertainty, the market demands a low debt ratio, stable income, and other corporate management. In times of optimism, the market rewards growth. These sentiments are reflected by the changing cost of capital. CFOs can choose whether or not they want to respond to market sentiments. Some firms believe the firm's bond ratings are important to the corporate management. Rating agencies' measurements may be considered ad hoc, imperfect tools, but the firms may abide by them. These are market frictions not contemplated by the perfect capital market assumptions. The main point is that the CFO's role is to set the goal for the financial performance of the firm beyond that of enhancing the firm value—the firm value that depends on the investment in the MM theory. Corporate decisions may enhance shareholders' value by seeking the lowest cost of capital through adjusting the firm's financial performance.

The firm has a business model with flexible investment decisions depending on the cost of capital. The firm provides a set of corporate decisions and its resulting financial reporting, including financial performance measures. Using such information, the market determines the cost of capital of the firm. The financial management then determines a set of corporate decisions such that the cost of capital is minimized.

For a fixed-income investment, we have described the bond model that is based on the law of one price. We have shown that, by and large, the bond model provides bond fair values quite close to the market observed prices. But traders on the trading floor must consider many market realities to price the bonds. These market realities are often transient factors. Traders never hesitate to emphasize the importance of market knowledge in bond pricing, as explained in chapter 3, which is the difference between market pricing and valuing a bond. We have also described how the basic financial models are adjusted by the option adjusted spreads and behavioral models to specify the fair value more accurately. These adjusted models can be useful tools in practice.

Similarly, the MM firm value is analogous to the law of one price in corporate finance. But the deviation of the firm value from its fair value within the arbitrage band may result from the corporate financial decisions. The role of corporate financial management is to provide the optimal signals to the market through the financial reporting and performance measures.

14.5   Specifications of the Corporate Model

Given the above general assumptions of the corporate model, this section provides the details for constructing a corporate model. Such a model may be used by the senior management in formulating the optimal corporate decisions.

The Business Model

In chapter 13, we described the methodology used in building the business model. Specifically, we showed that the inputs to the business model for the retail chain store, as an example, are gross profit margin (m), fixed costs (FC), gross return on investment (GRI), capital investment rate (I), and leverage (L).

The firm value is then determined for each state and time on a binomial lattice model, assuming the firm will act optimally in its investment decisions, as described in chapters 12 and 13.

Principles of Financial Statements and Performance Measures

The second part of building a corporate model is determining the financial statements and performance measures. This part is similar to that described for DFA. Using the information from the business model, we can determine the financial statements and the performance measures at each node of the lattice.

Financial statements involve many accounting details. If we formulate a model of the financial statements to capture only the essence of the financial accounting by ignoring some of the details, we need to review the principles of financial statements. Financial reporting discloses two aspects of the firm: financial position and performance. Financial position consists of assets and liabilities. Assets are resources controlled by the enterprise as a result of past events and from which future economic benefits are expected to flow to the enterprise. Liabilities are present obligations of the enterprise arising from past events, the settlement of which is expected to result in an outflow of resources embodying economic benefits. Equity is the residual interest in the assets of the enterprise after deducting all its liabilities.

Performance is measured by matching the income with the expenses. Income increases the economic benefits during the accounting period in the form of inflows or enhancements of assets, or decreases of liabilities that result in increases in equity (other than those relating to contributions from equity participants). Expenses decrease the economic benefits during the accounting period in the form of outflows or depletions of assets, or increases of liabilities that result in decreases in equity (other than those relating to distributions to equity participants).

There are principles behind the design of the generally accepted accounting principles' (GAAP) financial accounting rules, and these are the rules that we will capture in the model. The most important rule is based on the principle of accrual basis. The basic idea of accrual basis is to match the expense with the revenue of any investment. For example, some of the expenditure on research and development may be capitalized—as opposed to expensed. That means the cash spent on the expenditure can be offset with a depreciation item—a wasting asset—such that the income statements for the years in development will not be affected greatly. The cost will be released in later financial reporting when the product begins to realize profits.

Another principle is based on depicting the firm as a going concern as opposed to focusing on the liquidation value of the firm. Since financial statements are designed for the investing public, they have to be usable by the target audience. Therefore, they are designed for public investors to evaluate the value of the firm as a going concern. For this reason, they strive to have four qualitative characteristics: understandability, relevance, reliability, and comparability. But they are also subject to constraints on providing relevant and reliable information: timelines, balance between benefit and cost, and balance among qualitative characteristics.

GAAP accounting primarily focuses on the net income—"the bottom line." The accounting reporting shows, as clearly as possible, how the firm provides returns to the investors. Of course, balance sheets and income statements have to be consistent. The change in the balance sheets over a period has to be reconciled with the income over the same period. For this reason, the GAAP balance sheets are used to keep track of historical incomes.

The objective of financial statements is to provide information about the financial position, performance, and changes in financial position of a firm that is helpful to a wide range of users in making economic decisions. Financial statements are both performance measures and "rearview mirror" tools. They are the report cards of the financial performance of the company and therefore must necessarily be backward-looking, providing the feedback to the investors to determine whether the firm has delivered what the company promised. By contrast, other financial reporting may have other purposes. For example, internal reporting may focus more on the internal profitability measures and risk controls. Industry-specific reporting, such as statutory reporting, may focus on the viability as a going concern. Here, we are primarily concerned with the GAAP accounting.

For illustrative purposes, the simplest accounting model can be described below.

Income statement identities

Income Statement Identities

Gross Profit	= Sales − Cost of Sales
EBIT	= Gross Profit − Fixed Costs − Depreciation
Earnings before Taxes	= EBIT − Interest Cost
Net Income	= Earnings Before Taxes (1 − tax rate)
Change in Retained Earnings	= Net Income − Dividends

Balance sheet identities

Balance Sheet Identities

Current Assets	= Cash + Other Short-term Assets
Total Assets	= Capital Assets + Provision + Other Assets
	= Total Liabilities + Equity
Change in Capital Assets	= Capital Investment

Financial ratios for performance measures

In financial reporting, we can use financial ratios as metrics to compare across the firms. One set of performance measures is used to understand the net income in relation to other items of the financial reports. These items are number of shares (N), equity (E), assets (A), revenues (Rev), and operating income ($EBIT$). From these financial statement items, we can define the following financial ratios:

$$Price\ multiple = \frac{Capitalization}{Equity} \tag{14.5}$$

Equity is an approximate measure of the shareholders' capital invested in the firm. Capitalization is the market valuation of the shareholders' value, including all future returns to the shareholders. The *price multiple* is therefore the return of the shareholders' investment, and it is an important measure of the firm's ability to maximize the shareholders' value. For a firm that can generate profitable future returns for the shareholders, the price multiple will be high.

$$Price/Earnings\ Ratio = \frac{Capitalization}{Net\ Income} \tag{14.6}$$

The *price/earnings ratio* (P/E ratio) is the ratio of the share price to the earnings per share, equivalently expressed as the ratio of the capitalization to the firm's net income. The ratio measures how the market estimates the future earnings of the firm relative to the present net income. For example, if the market assumes that the firm pays out all its net income (earnings) as dividends and the net income does not grow, then the P/E ratio is the payback period. The payback period is defined as the number of years during which the dividends received would cover the initial cost of investments in buying the stock. In chapter 2, we derived the stock pricing model based on the projected dividends. If we assume that the firm pays out all its net income as dividends, then the reciprocal of the P/E ratio is the expected rate of return of the stock net of the constant expected growth of the net income.

$$Coverage = \frac{Net\ Income}{EBIT} \tag{14.7}$$

Coverage measures the ability of the firm to cover its tax and interest obligations. If the coverage ratio is high, then the firm can use its net income to cover any unanticipated increase in the interest costs or the tax liability.

$$Operating\ Efficiency = \frac{EBIT}{Gross\ Profit} \tag{14.8}$$

Operating efficiency measures the impact of the fixed costs on the firm's profitability. The higher the ratio, the lower the fixed cost and the higher the efficiency.

$$Production\ Efficiency = \frac{Gross\ Profit}{Sales} \tag{14.9}$$

Production efficiency is also called the gross profit margin, the ratio of the gross profit (sales net of the cost of sales) to the sales. The higher the gross profit margin, the lower the variable cost is, and the higher the production efficiency.

$$Turnover = \frac{Sales}{Assets} \tag{14.10}$$

Turnover measures the sales generated by each dollar of the assets. The higher the turnover, the more effectively the assets are used.

$$Leverage = \frac{Assets}{Equity} \tag{14.11}$$

The financial managers control *leverage*. They decide on the firm's level of debt; the higher the leverage, the greater the use of debt. When the firm returns are higher than the interest cost of the debt, increasing the leverage will lead to a higher income to the shareholders.

We can express the price multiple as the product of the financial ratios mentioned above:

$$Price\ multiple = P/E\ Ratio \times Coverage \times Operating\ Efficiency$$
$$\times\ Gross\ Profit\ Margin \times Turnover \times Leverage \tag{14.12}$$

Further, the accounting identity in equation (14.12) shows that the elasticity of the price multiple to each of the financial ratios is 1. That means the percentage change of the price multiple is the sum of the percentage changes of all the financial ratios. This relationship seems to suggest that if we can increase each financial ratio, the resulting cumulative percentage changes of the financial ratios will lead to a percentage increase in the shareholders' value.

Financial managers can compare all these performance measures with those of other firms, and understand the underlying relationships among these measures in order to manage the firm.

Optimality: Objective Function, Constraints, and Control Variables

The third part of the corporate model specifies the preferences of the corporate financial management in terms of the firm's financial performance measures. Corporate strategies are then derived from this objective function, given all the market constraints.

The objective function may be to maximize a weighted sum of the performance measures, where the weights may be determined by the firm's corporate strategy. This approach is similar to that practiced by the firms using a "balanced scoreboard." The firms may want a selection of performance measures to attain a certain target, and not focus on one particular performance measure. Since the firm is also concerned with its ability to meet its performance targets, the objective function must minimize the variations of possible future performance measures.

The objective function is multiperiod. Typically, financial planning is determined over multiple periods. For example, firms tend to make five-year plans. The objective function should be concerned with the projected performance measures over the planning horizon. Moreover, the objective function does not necessarily have to be constant over time. At times, the market may apply a significant risk premium to the credit risk. At such times, the firm may lower the debt ratio by changing the weighting on its balance of performance measures.

Now the firm seeks to maximize the objective function. In this optimization process, we also must have constraints. There may be restrictions on the level of debt, excessive cash positions, and other issues. These constraints arise from market frictions. For example, banks may be required to have their equity to total asset ratio above 8 percent, which is the risk-based capital required (to be discussed in chapter 16). These constraints can then be imposed on the optimization.

The final part of the optimization is the specification of the control variables. These control variables are specified in a state-dependent multiperiod context. For example, dividends that are to be paid in the future depend on the prevailing net income. Then the optimal strategy will be to seek to optimize the multiperiod objective function, so there will be flexibility to react to the outcomes of events, and immediate actions are dependent on future optimal decisions in the sense of the Bellman solution.

The objective function may differ from one firm to another. Technology growth firms may focus less on the immediate net income than mature banks do, because the former focus on enhancing the strategic values of the firms, while the latter tend to provide predictable incomes for their investors. Utility firms may emphasize the stability of their income more than mining firms, whose income is highly dependent on commodity prices. Indeed, the role of the corporate finance manager is important. He is responsible for achieving financial performance that satisfies the market preference for the financial performance of a firm. Investors rely on financial managers to optimally maximize the objective function of the firm.

Corporate Decisions

We now discuss in more detail how corporate decisions are related and how they affect the performance measures of the firm within the context of the business model.

Dividend policy

The optimal dividend policy is significantly affected by the cumulative capital expenditure and the gross investment returns. The higher the dividend payout, the lower the net income in the future is, since the lower retrained earnings lead to lower investments that would contribute to income in the subsequent period. The return on equity, however, may increase if the firm's return on capital exceeds the reinvestment rate.

Paying dividends to stockholders may lead to lowering the firm value ex-dividend, and thus possibly lowering the claims for the bondholders. Paying dividends can lead to wealth transfer from bondholders to stockholders. For this reason, there should be constraints on the amount of dividends to be paid to shareholders according to the bond covenants.

Provisions

Provisions are an accrual item in accounting and not a cash item. The firm may set provisions for anticipated losses, for example, in investment. The level of provisions to be reported tends to be subjective; it depends on the management's view of future possible losses. Therefore, optimal provisions can be determined in a multiperiod context, depending on the expectations of future investment loss. The firm may increase or decrease the provisions, and the provisions affect the earnings.

Cash Requirements

If there is friction in raising capital, then the cash requirements have to be managed. If a firm holds excess cash, the return on equity will fall. If the cash level is low, then there may be costs to raising capital, and it could affect the credit rating of the firm.

Debt level

The debt level clearly affects the debt ratio of the firm. A higher debt leads to higher interest costs, resulting in lower net income. Reducing the number of shares with debt may lead to higher earnings per share (EPS) but also higher EPS volatility. However, it may also lead to lower EPS because of the increase of interest costs that lower the firm's earnings.

Each of these decisions may affect the objective function of the corporate model.

External financing

Another corporate decision is determining external financing needs. For example, the firm may require external funding for all its investments and other cash needs are derived from short-term debt financing. Or the firm can issue equity to raise cash. The MM theory ensures that the new equity issuance does not affect the shareholders' value. The converse is also true. The model assumes that the firm can buy back both bonds and shares, using cash. The change of the capital structure does not affect the firm value.

Finally, we can specify the objective function. Based on the simulated financial statements and performance measures in each state of the world, we can determine the expected values and standard deviations of the performance measure over the horizon period based on the initial date. The expected value and the standard deviation should be specified using the real probability of the binomial lattice outcome. Since this represents the expectation of the firm and not the risk-neutral expectation, the market probabilities should be used.

For example, we may assume that the objective function of the firm is

$$\Psi = \sum_{t=0}^{n} \left[E\left[ROE(t)\right] - \lambda \cdot \sigma_{ROE}(t) \right] P(t) \tag{14.13}$$

where $ROE(t)$ is the return on equity at time t, which is a stochastic parameter because the values are different in each state i. E represents the expectation operator based on time 0, and σ is the standard deviation operator. Both E and σ are based on market probability q, which was specified in chapter 12, and not the risk neutral probability p. λ is the risk aversion parameter, showing the preference for stable income relative to the expected value. $P(t)$ is the discount factor, which is the market time value of money. The use of present value shows the preference for optimizing the performance in the near future to doing so in the distant future. Finally, we seek to maximize the preferences over the horizon period, which we assume to be five years.

After the objective function is specified, we can determine the optimal corporate finance decisions for financial planning. The optimization is the nonlinear search for the optimal solution of all the control variables at all the nodes, and therefore the solution is state- and time-dependent, but not path-dependent. This completes the corporate model.

14.6   A Comparison with Previous Research

A firm is an organization with many activities. These activities include production, marketing, sales, general management, financial management, and many others. These activities are often tied together in an organizational chart showing how the firm is managed. The manifestations of these activities are the firm's mission, culture, and other attributes. Service Master, Wal-Mart, and AOL are examples of firms that have different business missions.

ServiceMaster was founded in 1947 with the purpose of serving God. Wal-Mart was founded as a low-cost retail chain. AOL was founded to provide easy access to the Internet for everyone. While the organizational charts look similar across these companies, the companies are different in very tangible ways. Their different business missions affect their corporate strategies and their corporate preferences, as expressed by their objective functions in their corporate model, and their growth strategies, as expressed by the business model. These differences are not apparent in financial statements.

The goal of a firm is to increase the shareholders' value. The traditional approach of valuing a firm via its financial analysis will fail to capture the essential features of a firm because firms are different from each other. Imposing a standard procedure to discount its free cash flows would inevitably fail to measure a firm's value. Recognizing that firms have different business models, our approach can better compare the values across different firms.

The value of a firm begins with a business model. The founders of a firm may design such a model, or the model may have evolved over time and adapted to changing economic realities. However, when a firm is not viable, a business model must exist. A business model has two sets of assumptions. One set pertains to assumptions of the marketplace and describes the clients and their needs, market supply and demand, and competition. The other set of assumptions describes how the firm is organized so that it can generate profits, given the assumptions of the market.

Relative Valuation and the Discounted Free Cash Flow Methodology

Given the business model and the optimal strategies, we can view a firm as a contingent claim on its business risks, such that the firm value rises and falls in step with the changes in the environment according to the specified risks, and the firm's optimal strategies under the uncertainties.

In a way, the valuation approach does not offer a valuation method in an absolute sense. The method is a relative valuation. The model captures the salient features of a firm and translates such a value to other firms that may have different salient features. We can compare the value of a sample of firms and infer whether one firm is cheap or rich relative to the sample.

Valuing a firm entails discounting the future uncertain cash flows to the present value. The traditional method entails discounting the expected cash flows free to the shareholders at an appropriate discount rate. The difficulty of this approach is deciding on the appropriate discount rate.

However, viewing a firm as a contingent claim of risk factors, the discount rate can be derived using a relative valuation method, and the model provides a way to compare the values of the firm relative to each other.

Although this approach has a number of advantages over the standard methodology, it would be inappropriate to consider the proposed method as a straightforward cookbook approach to valuing a firm. The approach offers a way of analyzing a firm that can be viewed as step-by-step extensions of the relative pricing theory from derivatives to the firm. In doing so, we can better understand this methodology's potential applications and limitations. But we must recognize the limitations of the assumptions of the model and the accuracy of the input data to the model. Direct use of data from financial statements without careful evaluation of the information can lead to erroneous results.

14.7   New Perspectives in Viewing Firms as Contingent Claims

Firms are contingent claims on business risks. This statement is not proposed simply as an observation of nature. The statement should provide an alternative perspective for us to manage a business. Some of the implications of this perspective are discussed below.

Cost of Capital Estimation

We have discussed the use of the Capital Asset Pricing model (CAPM) to determine the cost of capital. This approach depends significantly on the estimation of beta in equilibrium. However, for newer companies or growth companies, the estimation of beta using historical information can be difficult.

Instead of using the CAPM, companies can view firms as contingent claims. We can apply the business model to a sample of firms (the peer group) which we believe have similar characteristics. Following the MM theory, we can assume that the implied cost of capital and the implied volatility of the business risk for this sample of firms are the same. The firms differ only in their capital structure and operating leverage. This hypothesis is empirically testable by examining the calculated implied cost of capital and the implied business risk volatilities. For practical applications, the estimation of the cost of capital using the relative valuation model with a peer group has a number of advantages.

For most companies, knowing the competition in the same sector is very important. Therefore, any information on the competition is useful. The proposed approach of using a peer group and the estimate of the cost of capital, enables the financial management of the firm to better understand its firm's cost of capital in relation to its peers.

The methodology is more accurate because we are using the concept of calibration. We can continually adjust the cost of capital to the changes in the market. This approach enables us to use the relative valuation concept to decide whether the firm is priced above or below its peers. This approach does not require any estimation of the expected market return of the market portfolio or any equilibrium theory. Instead, the model is based on the relative valuation model and the observed stock price. The cost of capital using the peer group approach can be more dynamic. When the market shifts, we can dynamically update the cost of capital value. It may not be possible to update the beta number for

CAPM because the estimation of beta requires historical data. Therefore, if the market keeps shifting, it will be futile to keep posting a new beta number.

Competitive Analysis

In contrast to using a financial ratio, we can now calibrate the models of competitors in the same segment of the market. A firm and its competitors are both contingent claims on the same risk factors. The firms may differ in their cost structures, gross profit margins, and capital structures. However, the peers may compete for the same market share. The use of the firm model to consider the competitive advantage of each firm in the marketplace will be very effective. For example, consider a property and casualty company. Suppose the company forecasts that in 18 months, the insurance price premium will have less pressure, and the sales office can raise the price. The insurance company can analyze a change in pricing strategy as well as a lower expense ratio. In doing so, the firm seeks to increase its market share. If the firm further assumes that its competitors cannot lower their expense ratio, the firm can use the firm model to simulate the increase in market share and its impact on the firm's profitability.

Today, however, the common approach to competitive analysis is to compare the financial ratios. Many firms strive to emulate the financial ratios of the industry leader. This approach cannot formulate strategies to execute a plan. The method alone cannot outperform the leader. Furthermore, there is nothing to indicate that the industry leaders' financial ratios can lead to higher shareholders' value. A dynamic approach to simulating ways to compete in a market place can tie shareholders' value to the strategies.

Financial Disclosures: Fair Valuation and Nonfinancial Disclosures

Firms should be encouraged to disclose nonfinancial indicators of value, which are based on their views of managing the firm to achieve profitability. When a firm is viewed as contingent claims on the business risk, the value of the firm is directly linked to the business environment. Often nonfinancial disclosure regarding the business environment can assist investors in determining the value of the firm more accurately than they can with only financial disclosures. For example, an airline's profitability depends significantly on fuel costs. A disclosure of the airline's views on fuel price risk and ways it manages fuel risks will be valuable. Consider an Internet company whose growth depends on the subscription base growth. AOL was the pioneer in disclosing its growth of subscription base and other measures of success as an Internet portal in addition to financial information. Such disclosures better identify the risks and market potential—value of real options.

Corporate Insurance: Identifying the Tail Risks

A main thrust of valuing a firm as a contingent claim is to focus the firm's risks with nonfinancial risks, business risks such as the GRI for retail chain stores. The real-sector risks are incorporated into the firm's uncertain value. The firm may wish to hold insurance for extreme losses in value. To understand its exposure to extreme losses, the business model can provide clear insights. For example, consider the retail chain discussed earlier. Suppose several of its major stores have to be closed for nonfinancial reasons. The loss of revenues from these stores can be significant. The standard approach would be to calculate each store as a stand-alone firm and determine the store value by discounting the free cash flows of the store at the firm's cost of capital. This approach will often lead to some ad hoc approaches to allocating the fixed costs and to determining the cost of capital.

By viewing the firm as a contingent claim, we can value the stores relative to the retail chain firm's capitalization value. Using the model, we can assume that a portion of the capital asset is destroyed. The model can then be used to simulate the change in the capitalization value.

This approach enables us to determine the level of insurance required on the business risk of each store. The model enables us to evaluate alternative approaches to manage the business risks. These alternatives may be (1) holding significant cash so that the firm can be self-insured, (2) holding less debt to avoid default should such an event occur, or (3) buying insurance.

Corporate insurance can be used for changing the business risk profile. Suppose the firm can buy a put option on the business risk. The firm can then be hedged against a significant downturn in the business, enabling it to be more aggressive in an expansion plan. Alternatively, we can think of holding insurance as a capital structure problem. Part of the capital can be released for the use of insurance. The quantification of this approach can be simulated with the firm model. For details see Shimpi (2001).

Credit Risk

The credit risk measure is concerned with the probability of default of a firm. By viewing the firm as a contingent claim on business risks, the model shows precisely how the business risks affect the creditworthiness of the firm.

By contrast, the rating of a bond typically depends on the firm's leverage ratio, market to book ratio, current ratio, or other financial ratio. While there is an effort to identify the sector that the firm belongs to as an important factor that affects the firm's creditworthiness, there is little focus on the assumptions of the firm's business model to determine the credit risks.

The firm model identifies the features of the business model that are important to measure the credit risks. Some examples are given below.

Debt leverage
Operating leverage
Real option size
Real option volatility
Correlation of the book equity and the stock value
Abandonment value of the assets
Growth of the firm
Profitability of the firm

The business model shows how each factor affects the bond price, and the corporate model relates the financial ratios to the inputs of the business model. We have discussed in detail how these factors affect the firm value and the defaultable bond value in previous chapters. Furthermore, these factors do not affect the firm's credit risk in a linear way, as is often assumed in credit scoring models described in chapter 8. The defaultable bond model based on the business risk will enable us to identify the factors to determine the bond value.

14.8   Principles of Risk Management

More than twenty years ago, before any "rogue traders" appeared in the press, I was invited to a fairly large and prestigious commodities trading company to help them solve a problem. The senior executive took me around the trading floor proudly. They had state-of-the-art technologies. There were rows of traders buying and selling with touch screens; they could see the risk measures and their trading positions. They could generate reports while watching prices across the markets. It was impressive. The senior executive knew that most people would be impressed, and summed up the tour: "We can measure everything and we can see all our positions."

So what was the problem? This was how he explained it to me. "Our boss is the CEO and founder. Everyone here is, in essence, trading with his money. He therefore decides what he likes, what he buys, and what he sells. But he can't control all of the traders on this floor, and we, as managers, can't find out what he likes and what he doesn't like. If we don't know his preference—and his preference seems to change all the time—then how can we decide the optimal forward/futures contracts that our traders should be taking?" His expression of pride disappeared. His self-doubt and humility prevailed. There was a long pause.

"Without understanding his risk tolerance, we can't set trade limits and performance measures. Without these measures, our bonuses and compensations depend extensively on his views as well." As his gaze drifted abstractedly toward his shoes, I understood why the problem was close to everyone's heart. It was not just about the firm. It was about everyone's take-home pay.

"We wondered if you could meet our boss, design an experiment or test, and construct his utility function—some regret function. Let us know how much risk he can take as a trade-off against his profits. That way, we can determine his risk preference or tolerance, and that would be most helpful."

That was over twenty years ago. Today, my experience tells me that many risk managers still share the same sentiment. "What is my boss's risk tolerance function? What should I do beyond measuring and reporting risks?" After listening sympathetically to the senior manager's explanation of the problem, I politely declined the project, for reasons best explained by Professor Paul Samuelson in 1997, in one of his letters.

Samuelson, a Nobel laureate and professor of economics at MIT, wrote: "I regard the 1952 Roy shortfall criterion as a determiner of stochastic portfolio decision, to be arbitrary and unappealing. Life is not a vanity-game duel; that is for the sports pages. What counts for me are the different money outcomes that chance will deal out for each choice-criterion I try to maximize, and how I feel about each algebraic increment of money outcomes."[1]

The business model of a firm cannot be as simple as "the boss's risk tolerance function" or an extension of a vanity game. All the salient aspects of managing the business have to be tied together by finance principles. If the CEO/founder could not explain his business objectives to his management team, and his staff did not know their roles and responsibilities, how would a junior faculty member in finance have the solution? What the senior executive was looking for was "arbitrary and unappealing." I did not think I could assist the firm.

This question concerning the role of risk management is more difficult and important than devising risk measures. The answer must go back to the principles of finance, and not just financial engineering. We can (and we should) begin with a premise like "the objective of financial management is maximization of shareholders' value," and we have seen in this chapter how corporate optimal decisions should be derived in a consistent fashion.

14.9 Summary

In the MM world, where every investor has perfect information about the firm, financial statements have no economic role. According to that world, financial statements will be published, but everyone will ignore them because all investors will already know everything about the companies. Of course, that is not the case. There is significant informational content in financial statements that shows financial statements are the media for management to transform private information into public information. The guidelines for financial statements are rules that determine the line drawn between private and public information. The signaling theory is implemented to resolve this asymmetric information problem.

We have discussed that empirical evidence has supported the hypothesis that our capital markets, particularly the stock markets, are efficient. Using historical information and public information will not lead to excess returns. That does not mean financial statements, which are public information, are not important for the price discovery process in the markets. Investors do use the information to establish the prices. Empirical evidence from many studies has confirmed that financial disclosures are important. They have informational content. Because of their importance for the price discovery or price-setting process in the marketplace, firms have devoted significant resources to presenting financial information. Financial statements are important sources of information for the investment community. However, in a market with imperfect information, the signaling theory suggests that financial reporting is important to the valuation of the firm, yet it remains an empirical issue to quantify its importance. In research literature, this demonstration of the economic value is called the "informational content" of financial reporting.

This chapter has described a complete procedure for deriving the optimal corporate decisions within the context of the firm model described in previous chapters. The methodology can be extended to other industry sectors and the model can be empirically tested. The model shows that the traditional approach to valuing growth stocks or high yield bonds is inadequate. A general framework of analysis such as a free cash flow method may be misleading in determining the value and risks of growth stocks or high-yield bonds.

As we have seen in previous chapters, the business models of firms have their own characteristics, similar to the bonds with their own specifications. The behavior of stocks and high-yield bonds is intricately related to the business model of the firm, something that much research and practice have ignored so far. The business model is related to financial reporting, which is dependent on identifying the risks of the cash flows.

Corporate financial decisions are based on financial reports, and we have concluded that it may not be optimal for corporate financial managers only to meet benchmark performance measures. They should use a business model to implement their optimal strategies to maximize their objective function.

Corporate financial decisions affect the financial performance measures and the allocations of the risks across the financial claimants on the firm value. Each financial decision may have a different impact on the performance measures and the risk allocations of the claims. This chapter has described the corporate model that relates the corporate decisions to the financial performance measures and also provides the underlying relationships of all the performance measures. The corporate model and the business model enable us to evaluate the equity risk in relation to its peer group. We then suggest that financial decisions are made to optimize financial planning of a firm. Financial reporting plays an important part in providing signals to a market with incomplete information.

Appendix.   The Firm Model

We explain the firm model in detail in this appendix. The firm model consists of the business model and the corporate model. The objective of the business model is to maximize the firm value by optimizing the capital expenditure. The objective of the corporate model is to optimize dividend payments, provisions, and the level of long-term debt, given the maximized firm value. A systematic summary of the firm model is given in figure 14.1.

The Business Model of a Firm

Business risk factor

In the firm model, the gross return on investment $(\widetilde{GRI})$ is defined as revenue divided by capital investment. We assume that the $\widetilde{GRI}$ is uncertain and is the main source of business risk. The $\widetilde{GRI}$ follows a recombining binomial lattice process with volatility (σ) and no drift. Therefore, the $\widetilde{GRI}$ is a martingale process, which means that the expected turnover value at any node is equal to the current $\widetilde{GRI}$ at that time period.

We define the business risk $\tilde{x}$ such that $\widetilde{GRI}\,[n+1, i+1] = \widetilde{GRI}\,[n, i] \times e^{\sigma}$ and $\widetilde{GRI}\,[n+1, i] = \widetilde{GRI}\,[n, i] \times e^{-\sigma}$ where $\widetilde{GRI}\,[n, i]$ is the business risk at period n and state i. Since the $\widetilde{GRI}$ is a martingale, the real upward probability (q) is $q = \frac{1-e^{-\sigma}}{e^{\sigma}-e^{-\sigma}}$ so that $\widetilde{GRI}\,[n, i] = q \times \widetilde{GRI}\,[n+1, i+1] + (1-q) \times \widetilde{GRI}\,[n+1, i]$. (See figure 14.2.)

The generation of the financial statement

1. Income Statement

$$
\begin{aligned}
\text{Sales}\,[n, i] = {} & \left[\frac{\binom{n-1}{i} \times \text{Capital Assets}\,[n-1, i] + \binom{n-1}{i-1} \times \text{Capital Assets}\,[n-1, i-1]}{\binom{n-1}{i} + \binom{n-1}{i-1}} \right] \times \widetilde{GRI} \\
& + \left[\frac{\binom{n-1}{i} \times \text{Net Working Capital}\,[n-1, i-1] + \binom{n-1}{i-1} \times \text{Net Working Capital}\,[n-1, i-1]}{\binom{n-1}{i} + \binom{n-1}{i-1}} \right]
\end{aligned}
$$

1st Stage	
Data section	Definition of a business risk factor ($\widetilde{GRI}$)
	Generation of financial statements
	Calculation of financial ratios, gross profit margin (m), $\widetilde{GRI}$ and tax rate ( )
Underlying variables	Definition of a primitive firm, a fixed cost firm and risk neutral probabilities

2nd Stage	
Business model	
Objective function	Max Growth Firm Value [0,0]
s.t.	Capital Expenditure is zero at the initial and the terminal period.
	$0 \leq \text{CapExp}[n,i] \leq$ maximum boundary

3rd Stage	
Corporate model	
Objective function	Max [E(ROE) − 0.5 Var(ROE)]
s.t.	$0 \leq$ dividend[n,i]
	dividend[n − 1,i] $\leq$ dividend[n,i]
	$0 \leq$ Provisions[n,i], lower boundary $\leq$ provisions[n,i] $\leq$ upper boundary
	$0 \leq$ LTD level, Long-term Debt[0,0] + Current Liability[0,0] = Debt[0,0], $0 <$ coupon rate < 1, funds raised for cash

Figure 14.1 A systematic summary of the firm model

$\times$ Reinvestment Rate

Gross Profit $[n, i] = $ Sales $[n, i] \times$ Gross Profit Margin(m)

Fixed Costs $[n, i] = $ Capital Assets $[n, i] \times$ FC factor + Fixed Cost

EBIT $[n, i] = $ Gross Profit $[n, i] - $ Fixed Costs $[n, i] - $ Depreciation $[n, i]$

Depreciation $[0, 0] = $ Depreciation (given at I/S)

Depreciation $[n, i] = $ Capital Assets $[n, i] \times$ Depreciation Rate

Depreciation Rate $= \dfrac{\text{Depreciation (I/S)}}{\text{Capital Asset}}$

Interest Cost $[n, i]$

$$= \left[\frac{\dbinom{n-1}{i} \times \text{Long-Term Debt}\,[n-1, i] + \dbinom{n-1}{i-1} \times \text{Long-Term Debt}\,[n-1, i-1]}{\dbinom{n-1}{i} + \dbinom{n-1}{i-1}} \right] \times \text{Coupon Rate}$$

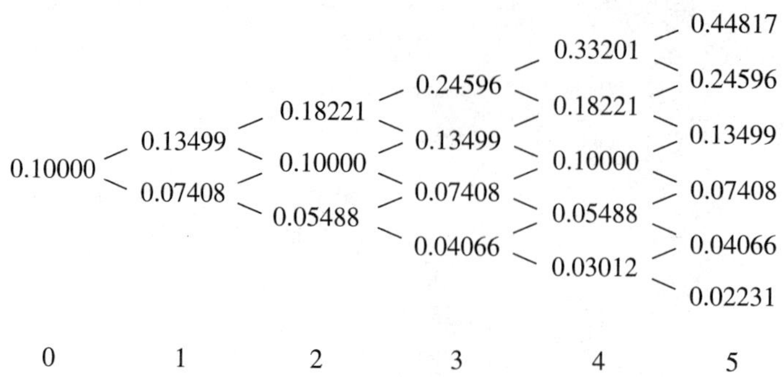

$$
\begin{array}{cccccc}
 & & & & & 0.44817 \\
 & & & & 0.33201 & \\
 & & & 0.24596 & & 0.24596 \\
 & & 0.18221 & & 0.18221 & \\
 & 0.13499 & & 0.13499 & & 0.13499 \\
0.10000 & & 0.10000 & & 0.10000 & \\
 & 0.07408 & & 0.07408 & & 0.07408 \\
 & & 0.05488 & & 0.05488 & \\
 & & & 0.04066 & & 0.04066 \\
 & & & & 0.03012 & \\
 & & & & & 0.02231 \\
\\
0 & 1 & 2 & 3 & 4 & 5
\end{array}
$$

Figure 14.2 The real probability q and the binomial lattice of $\widetilde{GRI}$ when $\sigma = 0.3$. The real probability q is 0.425557 and the $\widetilde{GRI}$ is 0.1 at the initial period by assumption.

$$
-\left[\frac{\binom{n-1}{i} \times \text{Net Working Capital}[n-1,i] + \binom{n-1}{i-1} \times \text{Net Working Capital}[n-1,i-1]}{\binom{n-1}{i} + \binom{n-1}{i-1}}\right] \times R_F[n,i]
$$

Other Income $[n, i]$ = Other Income (given at I/S)

Pretax Income $[n, i]$ = EBIT $[n, i]$ − Interest Cost $[n, i]$ + Other Income $[n, i]$

Tax $[n, i]$ = Pretax Income $[n, i]$ × Marginal Tax Rate(τ)

Provisions $[n, i]$ = 0 (for simplicity)

Net Income $[n, i]$ = Pretax Income $[n, i]$ − Tax $[n, i]$ − Provisions $[n, i]$

Dividend $[0, 0]$ = Dividend (given at F/S)

Dividend $[n, i]$ = 0 in the business model and control variables in the corporate model

Change in Retained Earnings $[n, i]$ = Net Income $[n, i]$ − Dividend $[n, i]$

2. Balance Sheet: Assets

Cash $[0, 0]$ = Cash(given) − Capital Expenditure $[0, 0]$ + Financing $[0, 0]$ + Funds Raised for Cash

$$
\text{Cash}[n, i] = \left[\frac{\binom{n-1}{i} \text{Cash}[n-1,i] + \binom{n-1}{i-1} \text{Cash}[n-1,i-1]}{\binom{n-1}{i} + \binom{n-1}{i-1}}\right] + \text{Change in Retained Earnings}[n,i]
$$

− Capital Expenditure $[n, i]$ + Depreciation $[n, i]$ + Long-term Debt $[n, i]$

Provisions(B/S) $[0, 0]$ = 0(for simplicity)

$$
\text{Provisions(B/S)}[n, i] = \left[\frac{\binom{n-1}{i} \text{Provisions(B/S)}[n-1,i] + \binom{n-1}{i-1} \text{Provisions(B/S)}[n-1,i-1]}{\binom{n-1}{i} + \binom{n-1}{i-1}}\right]
$$

+ Provisions(I/S) $[n, i]$

Other Current Assets $[n, i]$ = Other Current Assets (given at B/S)

Current Assets $[n, i]$ = Cash $[n, i]$ + Provisions(B/S) $[n, i]$ + Other Current Assets $[n, i]$

$$
\text{Depreciation(B/S)}[n, i] = \left[\frac{\binom{n-1}{i} \text{Depreciation(B/S)}[n-1,i] + \binom{n-1}{i-1} \text{Depreciation(B/S)}[n-1,i-1]}{\binom{n-1}{i} + \binom{n-1}{i-1}}\right]
$$

$+$ Depreciation(I/S) $[n, i]$

$$\text{CapitalAssets}[n, i] = \left[\frac{\binom{n-1}{i} \text{Capital Assets}[n-1, i] + \binom{n-1}{i-1} \text{Capital Assets}[n-1, i-1]}{\binom{n-1}{i} + \binom{n-1}{i-1}} \right]$$

$+$ Capital Expenditures $[n, i]$

Capital Expenditures $[n, i]$ = Control variables maximizing the firm value in the business model

Other Assets $[n, i]$ = Other Asset (given at B/S for simplicity)

Total Assets $[n, i]$ = Current Assets $[n, i]$ + Capital Assets $[n, i]$ + Other Assets $[n, i]$

3. Balance Sheet: Total Liabilities and Equity

Current Liabilities $[n, i]$ = Current Liabilities (given at B/S for simplicity)

Long-term Debt $[0, 0]$ = LTD level (control variable) + Long − term Debt (given at B/S)

$$\text{Long-term Debt}[n, i] = \left[\frac{\binom{n-1}{i} \text{Long-term Debt}[n-1, i] + \binom{n-1}{i-1} \text{Long-term Debt}[n-1, i-1]}{\binom{n-1}{i} + \binom{n-1}{i-1}} \right]$$

Other Liabilities $[n, i]$ = Other Liabilities (given at B/S for simplicity)

$$\text{Equity}[n, i] = \left[\frac{\binom{n-1}{i} \text{Equity}[n-1, i] + \binom{n-1}{i-1} \text{Equity}[n-1, i-1]}{\binom{n-1}{i} + \binom{n-1}{i-1}} \right]$$

$+$ Change in Retained Earning $[n, i]$

Total Liabilities and Equity $[n, i]$ = Current Liabilities $[n, i]$ + Long-term Debt $[n, i]$

$+$ Other Liabilities $[n, i]$ + Equity $[n, i]$

3. Cash Flow Statement

Change of Net Working Capital $[n, i]$ = Net Income $[n, i]$ + Depreciation $[n, i]$ + Provisions $[n, i]$

$-$ Capital Expenditure $[n, i]$ − Dividends $[n, i]$ − Tax $[n, i]$

Operating Activities $[n, i]$ = Net Income $[n, i]$ + Depreciation $[n, i]$ + Provisions $[n, i]$

$-$ Change of Net Working Capital $[n, i]$

Financing $[n, i]$ = 0 (assumed for simplicity)

Change of Cash $[n, i]$ = Operating Activities $[n, i]$ − Capital Expenditures $[n, i]$ − Dividends $[n, i]$

$-$ Taxes $[n, i]$ − Financing $[n, i]$

Free Cash Flow $[n, i]$ = EBIT $[n, i] \times (1 - \tau)$ + Depreciation $[n, i]$ − Capital Expenditure $[n, i]$

Notes

1. Moshe A. Milevsky and Michael Posner, *The Probability of Fortune* (Stoddart: Toronto 2000), 187.

References

Amihud, Y., and H. Mendelson. 1991. Liquidity, asset prices and financial policy. *Financial Analysts Journal*, 47 (6), 56–66.

Baskin, J. 1987. Corporate liquidity in games of monopoly power. *Review of Economics and Statistics*, 69, 312–319.

Bellman, R. 1957. *Dynamic Programming*. Princeton, NJ: Princeton University Press.

Black, F., and J. C. Cox. 1976. Valuing corporate securities: Some effects of bond indenture provisions. *Journal of Finance*, 31 (2), 351–368.

Black, F., and M. Scholes. 1973. The pricing of options and corporate liabilities. *Journal of Political Economy*, 81, 637–654.

Brealey, R. A., and S. C. Myers. 2002. *Principles of Corporate Finance*, 7th ed. Boston: Irwin.

Brennan, M., and E. Schwartz. 1984. Optimal financial policy and firm valuation. *Journal of Finance*, 39, 593–607.

Brown, S., and J. Warner. 1980. Measuring security price performance. *Journal of Financial Economics*, 8, 205–258.

Campbell, C., and C. Wasley. 1993. Measuring security price performance using daily NASDAQ returns. *Journal of Financial Economics*, V33, 73–92.

Connor, G., and R. Korajczyk. 1986. Performance measurement with the arbitrage pricing theory: A new framework for analysis. *Journal of Financial Economics*, 15, 373–394.

Datar, S. 2001. Balancing performance measures. *Journal of Accounting Research*, 39 (1), 75–92.

Dechow, P. 1994. Accounting earnings and cash flows as measures of firm performance: The role of accounting accruals. *Journal of Accounting and Economics*, 18 (5), 3–42.

Dugdale, D. 1997. Accounting for throughput: Techniques for performance measurement, decisions and control. *Management Accounting*, 75 (11), 52–56.

Fama, E. F., and K. R. French. 2002. Testing trade-off and pecking order predictions about dividends and debt. *Review of Financial Studies*, 15 (1), 1–33.

Figlewicz, R. E. 1991. An analysis of performance, liquidity, coverage, and capital ratios from the statement of cash flows. *Akron Business and Economic Review*, 22 (1), 64.

Frank, M. Z., and V. K. Goyal. 2003. Testing the pecking order theory of capital structure. *Journal of Financial Economics*, 67 (2), 217–248..

Franks, J. R., and J. J. Pringle. 1982. Debt financing, corporate financial intermediaries and firm valuation. *Journal of Finance*, 37 (3), 751–761.

Garvey, G. T. 1999. Capital structure and corporate control: The effect of anti-takeover statutes on firm leverage. *Journal of Finance*, 54 (2), 519–546.

Geske, R. 1979. The valuation of compound options. *Journal of Financial Economics*, 7 (1), 63–81.

Goldstein, R. S., N. Ju, and H. E. Leland. 2001. An EBIT-based model of dynamic capital structure. *Journal of Business*, 74 (4), 483–512.

Helwege, J., and N. Liang. 1996. Is there a pecking order? Evidence from a panel of IPO firms. *Journal of Financial Economics*, 40 (3), 429–458.

Ittner, C. D. 1998. Innovations in performance measurement: Trends and research implications. *Journal of Management Accounting Research*, 10, 205–238.

Jensen, M., and W. Meckling. 1976. Theory of the firm: Managerial behavior, agency costs, and ownership structure. *Journal of Financial Economics*, 3 (4), 305–360.

John, K. 1993. Managing financial distress and valuing distressed securities: A survey and a research agenda. *Financial Management*, 22 (3), 60–78.

John, T. A. 1993. Accounting measures of corporate liquidity, leverage, and costs of financial distress. *Financial Management*, 22 (3), 91–110.

Jones, E., S. Mason, and E. Rosenfeld. 1984. Contingent claims analysis of corporate capital structures: An empirical investigation. *Journal of Finance*, 39 (3), 611–627.

Kalay, A. 1982. Stockholder-bondholder conflict and dividend constraints. *Journal of Financial Economics*, 10 (2), 211–233.

Kale, J. R., T. H. Noe, and G. G. Ramirez. 1991. The effect of business risk on corporate capital structure: Theory and evidence. *Journal of Finance*, 46 (5), 1693–1715.

Kallberg, J., and K. Parkinson. 1992. *Corporate Liquidity: Management and Measurement*. Homewood, IL: Irwin.

Kim, I. J., K. Ramaswamy, and S. Sundaresan. 1993. Does default risk in coupons affect the valuation of corporate bonds?: A contingent claims model. *Financial Management*, 22 (3), 117–131.

Kothari, S. P. 2001. Evaluating mutual fund performance. *Journal of Finance*, 56 (5), 1985–2010.

Leland, H. E. 1994. Corporate debt value, bond covenants, and optimal capital structure. *Journal of Finance*, 49 (4), 1213–1252.

Leland, H. E., and K. B. Toft. 1996. Optimal capital structure, endogenous bankruptcy, and the term structure of credit spreads. *Journal of Finance*, 51 (3), 987–1019.

Lintner, J. 1956. Distribution of incomes of corporations among dividends, retained earnings and taxes. *American Economic Review*, 46 (2), 97–113.

Mauer, D. C., and G. W. Lewellen. 1987. Debt management under corporate and personal taxation. *Journal of Finance*, 42 (5), 1275–1291.

Mella-Barral, P., and W. Perraudin. 1997. Strategic debt service. *Journal of Finance*, 52 (2), 531–556.

Merton, R. C. 1974. On the pricing of corporate debt: The risk structure of interest rates. *Journal of Finance*, 29 (2), 449–470.

Modigliani, F., and M. Miller. 1958. The cost of capital, corporation finance and the theory of investment. *American Economic Review*, 48 (3), 267–297.

Modigliani, F., and M. Miller. 1963. Corporate income taxes and the cost of capital: A correction. *American Economic Review*, 53 (3), 433–443.

Moehrle, S. R., J. A. Reynolds-Moehrle, and J. S. Wallace. 2000. Are cash earnings disclosures valuable? Working paper, University of Missouri at St. Louis.

Myers, S., and N. S. Majluf. 1984. Corporate financing and investment decisions when firms have information that investors do not have. *Journal of Financial Economics,* 13 (3), 187–221.

Myers, S. C. 1984. Capital structure puzzle. *Journal of Finance*, 39 (3), 575–592.

Opler, T. C. 1993. Controlling financial distress costs in leveraged buyouts with financial innovations. *Financial Management*, 22 (3), 79–90.

Philip, B., and K. D. Miller. 1990. Strategic risk and corporate performance: An analysis of alternative measures. *Academy of Management Journal*, 33 (4), 756–779.

Roll, R. 1984. After-tax investment results from long-term vs. short-term discount coupon bonds. *Financial Analysts Journal* 40 (1), 43–44.

Sangsing, R. C. 1998. Valuing the deferred tax liability. *Journal of Accounting Research*, 6 (2), 357–364.

Sharpe, W. F., G. J. Alexander, and J. V. Bailey. 1998. *Investments*, 6th ed. Englewood Cliffs, NJ: Prentice-Hall.

Shimpi, P. 2001. Integrating Corporate Management. TEXERE LLC, New York.

Smith, C. W., Jr., and L. M. Wakeman. 1985. Determinants of corporate leasing policy. *Journal of Finance*, 40 (3), 895–908.

Smith, C. W., Jr., and R. L. Watts. 1992. The investment opportunity set and corporate financing, dividend, and compensation policies. *Journal of Financial Economics*, 32 (3), 263–292.

Subramanyam, K. R., and M. Venkatachalam. 2001. Earnings, cash flows and *ex post* intrinsic value of equity. Working paper, University of Sourthern California.

Sweeney, R. J., A. D. Warga, and D. Winters. 1997. The market value of debt, market versus book value of debt, and returns to assets. *Financial Management*, 26 (1), 5–21.

Taggart, R. 1977. A model of corporate financing decisions. *Journal of Finance*, 32 (5), 1467–1484.

Tatikonda, L. U. 1998. We need dynamic performance measures. *Management Accounting*, 80 (3), 49–53.

Thomas, H. 1998. Performance measurement systems, incentives, and the optimal allocation of responsibilities. *Journal of Accounting and Economics*, 25 (3), 321–347.

Waddington, B. A. 2001. Performance measurement enhances analytical procedures. *CPA Journal*, 71 (5), 50–51.

Winton, A. 1993. Limitation of liability and the ownership structure of the firm. *Journal of Finance*, 48 (2), 487–512.

Further Readings

Gentry, W. M., and R. G. Hubbard. 1998. Fundamental tax reform and corporate financial policy. Working paper, Columbia Business School, Columbia University.

Gersbach, H. 2001. The optimal capital structure of an economy. Working paper, University of Heidelberg.

Michael, M. S., and P. Hatzipanayotou. 1998. Quantitative import restrictions and optimal capital taxes under a system of tax credits. *Review of International Economics*, 6 (4), 660–669.

Minton, B. A., and K. H. Wruck. 2001. Financial conservatism: Evidence on capital structure from low leverage firms. Working paper, Ohio State University.

15

Risk Management

Risk management is the quality control of finance. It ensures the smooth functioning of the business model and the corporate model in accordance with the design of the business processes. Following the Demming model, a firm should be described as a portfolio of business processes that seek to achieve a business objective. The risks of these processes should be measured, monitored, reported, and managed continually. Risk management fixes the process's defects before they become large, and it should therefore begin with the design of the business process—no different from designing a manufacturing process, where quality control is an integral part of the design.

Today, most trading operations have risk management in place where traders' risk-taking activities are monitored, measured, and managed. So in early February 2002, when Allied Irish Banks PLC (AIB) disclosed that a trader at its subsidiary Allfirst Financial, Inc., a Baltimore-based bank, had lost $691 million in currency trading, the news was a surprise to the financial community. Since this loss hit the financial community, and especially the bank, pretty hard, the news quickly prompted investigations into the possible flaws in the risk management system.

In recent years, there has been an overwhelming amount of activity dealing with the issues of risks. Regulators and industry groups have been making a conscious effort to evaluate possible ways to require disclosures of firms' risks to the investing public. Many firms have started or are considering starting a risk management process, so that a new position, risk manager, is established in the organizational chart. The risk management process puts in place risk management systems. Researchers and consultants are continually proposing new techniques and management approaches for managing risk.

Despite all this attention to risk management, particularly in banks, how can a relatively small bank with little currency exposure report such large financial losses? To underscore the heightened awareness of risk management among the general public, a *Wall Street Journal* report stated, "AIB executives have said that Mr. Rusnak [the trader] had a VaR of $2 million to $3 million a day. In the first half of 1999, Mr. Rusnak had been going over that limit by at most $1 million." Today, risk management and risk management terminologies like VaR, a quantitative risk measure, have come into our daily vocabularies.

Yet, risk as a subject matter was not invented in recent years. The first principle in finance holds risk and returns as inseparable. Recall the Capital Asset Pricing model, the Black–Scholes model, default risk, business risk, and other topics already covered in this book. They are all about risks. If you read this book again and delete all the subjects related to risk, there is not much left—with the exception of a few paragraphs on financial statements. So what are the press and the financial community talking about in "risk management" to indicate that the subject is not finance related? And why is there a separate chapter on risk management in this finance book? How can we be writing this chapter, when the entire book has been written on risk? To answer these questions, we must trace through the historical development of risk management to understand the challenges posed to risk management and the solutions proposed to manage risks. A brief review of some of historical financial losses and their implications is presented in the appendix.

Today, risk management is rapidly becoming a fragmented concept. Risk management seeks to be all-encompassing, but in many ways it has conflicting goals. As a result, the risk management department of a corporation tends to deal with many issues, on a case-by-case basis. Many departments are evolving, meeting the day-to-day demands, and at the same time seeking to define their more global objective.

This chapter takes a more focused approach to risk management. We begin by describing the methods to calculate risk measures. These methods use the financial valuation models described in the previous chapters to simulate financial instruments' values over a range of uncertain outcomes. We then describe how these risk measures may be reported. Reporting provides feedback to the identification and measurements of risks. Reporting enables the risk management to monitor the enterprise risk exposures so that the firm has a built-in, self-correcting procedure that enables the process to improve and adapt to changes.

Finally, risk management would not be complete if no actions were taken to manage the risk exposure. The results of the measurement of risks have to be included in the business decision-making process. Risk management is not confined to protecting the firm from financial distress; it is also concerned with enhancing the shareholders' value.

We view risk management as a quality assurance process monitoring the validity and the effective functioning of the business model and the corporate model. The goal of enterprise risk management is ensuring that the business model and the corporate model are being implemented as planned, and risk management's responsibility is to provide crucial feedback to the senior management on the functioning of the enterprise.

15.1   Risk Measurement—Value at Risk

Risk measurement begins with identifying all the sources of risks, how they behave in terms of the probability distribution, and how they are manifested. Often, these sources of risk are classified as market risk, credit risk, liquidity risk, and legal risk. More recently, there are operational risks and business risks.

To measure the risks, one widely used measure is the *value at risk* (VaR). Value at risk is a measure of potential loss at a level (99% or 95% confidence level) over a time horizon, say seven days. Specifically: 95%–1-day VaR is the dollar value such that the probability of a loss for one day exceeding this amount is equal to 5%. For example, consider a portfolio of $100 million equity. The annualized volatility of the returns is 20%. The VaR of the portfolio over one year is $46.527 million (= 100 − 53.4723) or $32.8971 million (= 100 − 67.1029) for 99% or 95% confidence level, respectively.[1] (See figure 15.1.) The probability of exceeding the loss of $46.527 million over one year is 1% when the current portfolio value is $100 million and the annualized volatility of the returns is 20%. In other words, we have a loss exceeding $46.527 million only once out of 100 trials. A critical assumption to calculate VaR here is that the portfolio value follows a normal distribution, which is sometimes hard to accept. VaR can accept other distributions.

The risk management of financial institutions measures this downside risk to detect

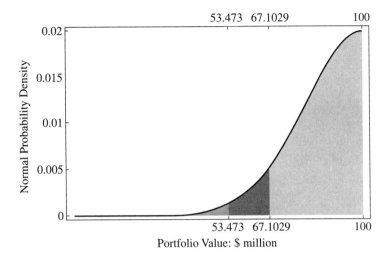

Figure 15.1 The left half of a normal distribution. This figure shows the left half part of a normal distribution, because only the left tail is important to determine the VaR. The probability of the area less than 53.473 is 1%, which means that the maximum loss will exceed the VaR (46.527 = 100 − 53.473) with 1% probability. Note that 1% is the significance level attached to the VaR. The probability of the area less than 67.1029 is 5%. The VaR with 5% significance level is 32.8971 (= 100 − 67.1029).

potential loss in their portfolios. The risk is often measured by the standard deviation or the volatility. A measure of variation is not sufficient because many securities exhibit a bias toward the upside (profit), as in an option, or the downside (loss), as in a high-yield bond, which is referred to as a skewed distribution (as compared to a symmetric distribution, such as a normal distribution). These securities do not have their profits and losses evenly distributed around their mean. Therefore the variation as a statistic would not be able to capture the risk of a position. Volatility is a measure of variability and may not correctly measure the potential significant losses of a risky position.

VaR has gained broad acceptance by the regulators, investors, and firm managements in recent years because it is expressed in dollars and consistently calculates the risk arising from the short or long positions, and from different securities. An advantage to expressing VaR in dollars is that we can compare or combine risk across different securities. For example, we have traditionally denoted risk of a stock by beta and risk of a bond by duration. However, because of different units in measuring the stock and the bond, it is hard to compare the risk of the stock with that of the bond, which is not the case in VaR.

The measure can be used for a security, a portfolio, or a trading desk. Or we can measure the VaR of a balance sheet. The reason for this is that VaR, the commonly used concept to measure risk, has been widely available among practitioners. Furthermore, it has been so general that most people have no trouble applying it to combine various risks in the real world. However, even though people have cited more advantages of VaR over the traditional risk measures, such as beta or duration, VaR has manifested several disadvantages, especially when people have tried to associate it with modern econometric techniques.

15.2   Market Risk

Market risk is often defined as the losses that arise from the mark to market of the trading securities. These trading securities may be derivatives such as swaps, swaptions, caps, and floors. They can be securities such as stocks and bonds. Or they can be the currency exposure in Euros, U.S. dollars, yen, or any currency. Market risk is referred to as the potential loss of the portfolio due to market movements.

While this is the basic idea of the market risk, the measure of the value is a subject of concern. Market risk is concerned with the fall in the mark to market value. For an actively trading portfolio that is managed at a trading desk, the value is defined as the sell price of the portfolio at normal market conditions. For this reason, traders need to mark their portfolio at their bid price at the end of the trading day, the mark to market value. The traders often estimate these prices based on their discussions with the counterparties, or they can get the prices from market trading systems.

Prices for tradable securities of a portfolio are marked to market at values that are often derived from the fair values of the valuation models that have been discussed in this book. For this reason, we can appreciate the importance of the concept and the procedure of calibration. Using calibration, we can approximate the value of any securities to similar securities, and apply the law of one price to infer the appropriate value. Calibration enables us to price the securities relative to other securities that are priced in the market while maintaining consistency, using the arbitrage-free pricing method.

The concepts and the practice of marking to market for the trading portfolios and the investment portfolios had been used for years before risk management procedures became prevalent. Mark to market procedures are important on the trading floor because traders have to report their daily profit and loss. They do so without liquidating their positions every day, but they have to report the change of the mark to market values to the management daily. The daily profit and loss are calculated by the change of the mark to market values.

These daily profit and loss numbers are used in a number of ways. Cumulative profit and loss determines the bonuses of the traders. *Trip wires* that indicate the trading limits are determined such that when the profits and losses or risk exposure exceed certain limits, actions are triggered to control the risk exposure of any one position on the trading floor. Mark to market value is also used for margin calls. When the mark to market value falls to a level that triggers a trip wire, the dealer that is providing the funding for the margin position can call back the lending, which may trigger a liquidation of a position.

For investment portfolios, the applications are similar. The mark to market enables the management to measure the portfolio performance and the risk exposures of the funds. For mutual funds, regulations require the fund management to report the portfolio mark to market value daily, so that investors are updated regarding their asset values. This concept can also extend to the entire balance sheet of a financial institution. In this case, it may not be necessary for the financial institution to mark to market the entire balance sheet daily, but it can do so over regular periods, such as monthly or quarterly.

Now we need to extend the mark to market concept to determine the risk measure, which is the potential loss as measured by the mark to market approach. There are three main methodologies to calculate the VaR values: delta normal methods, historical simulation and the Monte Carlo simulation. In addition to the three methodologies, we explain the extreme value theory to calculate VaR, which takes the fat-tail distribution property in the financial data.

15.3   Delta Normal Methodology

The *delta normal methodology* assumes that all the risk sources follow normal distributions and the VaR is determined assuming that the small change of the risk source will lead to a directly proportional small change of the security's price over a certain time horizon.

VaR for Single Securities

Consider a stock. The delta normal approach assumes that the stock price itself is the risk source and that it follows a normal distribution. Therefore, the uncertainty of the stock value over a time horizon is simply the annual standard deviation of the stock volatility adjusted by a time factor. A critical value is used to specify the confidence level required by the VaR measure. Specifically, the VaR is given by

$$VaR = \alpha \times time\ factor \times volatility \qquad (15.1)$$

α is the critical value which determines the one-tail confidence level of standard normal distribution. Formally, α is the value such that the confidence level is equal to the probability that $\widetilde{X}$ is greater than $-\alpha$, where $\widetilde{X}$ is a random variable of a standard normal distribution.

The time factor is defined as $\sqrt{t}$ where t is the time horizon in measuring the VaR. The time measurement unit of the time factor should be consistent with that of the volatility (the standard deviation of the stock measured in dollars over one year). For example, if the volatility is measured in years, t is also measured in years.

The problem for a portfolio of stock is somewhat more complicated. In principle, we can use a large matrix of correlation of all the stock returns and calculate the value. In practice, that is often too cumbersome. The reason for this is that since we treat each stock as a different risk source, we have the same number of risk sources as that of the stocks constituting the portfolio. For example, if we have a portfolio consisting ten stocks, we have to estimate ten variances and 45 covariances. One way is to use the Capital Asset Pricing model. Then the portfolio return distribution is given by

$$E[R_P] = r_f + \beta_P(E[R_M] - r_f) \qquad (15.2)$$

The distribution of the portfolio is therefore proportional to the market index by beta. By using the CAPM, we have only one risk source regardless of the size of a portfolio, which makes it much simpler to calculate portfolio VaR.

The VaR calculation for bonds requires an extra step. The risk sources for default-free bonds are interest rate risks. These risks do not, per se, directly measure the loss. In the case of stock, the fall in stock price is the loss. But for bonds, we need to link the rise in interest rates to the loss in dollar terms.

By the definition of duration, we have the following equation

$$\Delta P = -\$Duration \cdot \Delta r \qquad (15.3)$$

where *$Duration* is the dollar duration defined as the product of the price and duration:

$$\$Duration = P \cdot Duration \qquad (15.4)$$

$\widetilde{\Delta r}$ is the uncertain change in interest rates over the time horizon for the VaR measure. We assume that this uncertain movement has a normal distribution with 0 mean and standard deviation σ. The interest rate risk is described by a normal distribution. For the time being, we assume that the interest rate risk is modeled by the uncertain parallel movements of the spot yield curve and the yield curve is flat at r.

Given these assumptions, it follows from equation (15.3) that the price of the bond, or a bond position, has a normal distribution given by

$$\widetilde{\Delta P} = -\$Duration \cdot \widetilde{\Delta r}$$

The means of calculating the critical value for a particular interval of a normal distribution is therefore given by

$$VaR(bond) = \alpha \times time\ factor \times \$Duration \times \sigma \times r$$

$$\sigma = Std.\left(\frac{\Delta r}{r}\right) \tag{15.5}$$

Since the standard deviation in equation (15.5) is based on a proportional change of interest rates, we should multiply by r to get the standard deviation of a change of interest rates.

The above formula assumes that the spot yield curve makes a parallel shift and is flat, because dollar duration is derived based on the same assumptions. Further, the above formula assumes that the uncertain changes in interest rates follow a normal distribution, because we use the standard deviation to measure risk. More generally, we can assume that the yield curve movements are determined by n key rates $r(1), r(2), \cdots, r(n)$, as discussed in chapter 3. These uncertain key rate movements are assumed to have a multivariate normal distribution over the time horizon t of the VaR measure with the variance–covariance matrix Ω. Given this multiple risk factor model, the bond price uncertain value is a multivariate normal distribution given by

$$\widetilde{\Delta P} = -\sum_{i=1}^{n} \$KRD(i)\widetilde{\Delta r}(i)$$

where $\$KRD(i)$ is the dollar key rate duration given by $P \cdot KRD(i)$. $KRD(i)$ is the key rate duration as defined in chapter 3. It is the bond price sensitivity to the ith key rate movement. Then it follows that the VaR of the bond is given by

$$VaR(bond) = \alpha \times time\ factor \times \left(\sum_{i=1}^{n}\sum_{j=1}^{n} \$KRD(i)\$KRD(j)\Omega_{ij}\right)^{0.5} \tag{15.6}$$

where the dollar key rate durations of the bond are denoted by $\$KRD$. P is the bond price, or the value of the bond position. Ω_{ij} is the ith and jth entry of the variance–covariance matrix Ω. That is, it is the covariance of the distribution of the ith and jth key rate movements. Here, we calculate the variance–covariance of key rates. Therefore, we do not have to multiply by r.

The use of the key rate duration does not require the bond to be a simple Treasury bond, because the key rate duration allows us to take care of nonparallel shifts of a yield curve. The bond can be complex with embedded options, as in mortgage-backed securities or callable corporate bonds. The valuation of the bond and, hence, the computation of the key rate durations are based on the risk-neutral pricing model. The key rate durations allow us to identify the sensitivities of the bond to each risk source, given all the features of the bond, irrespective of the bond type.

As we have seen, bonds have basis risks. The spread is measured as option adjusted spread (OAS). We have also seen that we can calculate the option adjusted spread duration, $Duration_{OAS}$. The basis risk can be another risk source, and the VaR is given by

$$VaR(bond) = \alpha \times time\ factor \times P \times Duration_{OAS} \times \sigma_{OAS} \qquad (15.7)$$

The assumptions about the interest shifts should be equally applicable to the shifts of the option adjusted spread (OAS) to make equation (15.7) valid.

VaR for a Portfolio

Now we are in the position to determine the VaR of a portfolio of these types of assets. Suppose the portfolio has n securities. Let P_i be the price of the ith security, which may be a bond price or a stock price. Let x_i be the number of the securities in the portfolio. Then the portfolio value is given by

$$P = \sum_{i=1}^{n} x_i \cdot P_i \qquad (15.8)$$

The risk of the portfolio may be measured by the VaR of the portfolio value as defined by equation (15.7). Let $\Delta\theta_i$ for $i = 1 \cdots n$ be the risk sources, with Ω the variance–covariance matrix of these risks. Let $\$Duration(i)$ be the dollar duration (or sensitivity) of the portfolio to each risk source $\Delta\theta_i$. The portfolio uncertain value is given by

$$\widetilde{\Delta P} = -\sum_{i=1}^{n} \$Duration(i)\widetilde{\Delta\theta}_i$$

where P is the portfolio value. Following the above argument, the VaR of the portfolio is given by

$$VaR(portfolio) = \alpha \times time\ factor$$
$$\times \left(\sum_{i=1}^{n}\sum_{j=1}^{n} \$Duration(i)\$Duration(j)\Omega_{ij} \right)^{0.5} \qquad (15.9)$$

We can now calculate the contribution of risk for each risk source to the portfolio VaR. Let us define $VaR\beta_i$ (also called the *component VaR*) to the ith risk source θ_i to be

$$VaR\beta_i(portfolio) = \alpha \times time\ factor \times \sum_{j=1}^{n} \$Duration(i)\$Duration(j)\Omega_{ij}$$

$$\times \left(\sum_{i=1}^{n} \sum_{j=1}^{n} \$Duration(i)\$Duration(j)\Omega_{ij} \right)^{-0.5}$$

$VaR\beta_i$ is the contribution of risk by ith risk source to the VaR measure. It is clear from the definition that

$$\sum_{i=1}^{n} VaR\beta_i = VaR \tag{15.10}$$

That means the sum of the component VaR ($VaR\beta_i$) is equal to the VaR of the portfolio. Since the risk sources are correlated with each other, we have to appropriately identify the effect of correlations and diversifications on the risks to measure the risk contribution of each risk source to the VaR of the portfolio. $VaR\beta_i$ is a way to isolate all these effects.

A Numerical Example

To calculate the VaR of a portfolio of three different stocks (GM, WMT, and IBM), we calculate the daily rate of return for each stock and estimate the variance–covariance matrix of the stocks' returns. The sample period is from January 3, 2001, to May 2, 2002. The total number of observations is 332. For the purpose of calculating VaR, we assume that the expected proportional changes in the stock prices over one day are equal to 0. To calculate the daily rates of return and the variance–covariance matrix, we use the following formulas.

$$r_{i,t} = \frac{S_{i,t} - S_{i,t-1}}{S_{i,t-1}} \ \forall i = \text{GM, WMT, and IBM}$$

$$\bar{r}_i = 0$$

$$\sigma_i^2 = \frac{1}{m} \sum_{t=1}^{m} (r_{i,t} - \bar{r}_i)^2$$

$$\sigma_{i,j} = \frac{1}{m} \sum_{t=1}^{m} (r_{i,t} - \bar{r}_i)(r_{j,t} - \bar{r}_i)$$

where m is the number of days in the estimation period.

We first calculate the individual stock VaR and then the stock portfolio VaR to measure the diversification effect. We assume that the size of the portfolio position is $100 and the invested weights are equal. Further, we assume that the significance level is 1% and the horizon period is five days.

First, we calculate the variance–covariance matrix, assuming that the expected means are 0. From the variance–covariance matrix, we can get the standard deviation of each individual stock as well as the standard deviation of the portfolio with equal weights. To get the standard deviation of the portfolio, we premultiply and postmultiply the variance–covariance matrix by the weight vector. The variance–covariance matrix Ω, the correlation matrix Σ of three stocks, and the variance of the portfolio consisting of three stocks are given below.

$$\Omega = \begin{pmatrix} 0.00050827 & 0.000154099 & 0.000179167 \\ 0.000154099 & 0.00373365 & 0.00013894 \\ 0.000179167 & 0.00013894 & 0.00054746 \end{pmatrix}$$

$$\Sigma = \begin{pmatrix} 1 & 0.353741 & 0.339255 \\ 0.353741 & 1 & 0.306955 \\ 0.339255 & 0.306955 & 1 \end{pmatrix}$$

$$\mathbf{w}^T = \left(\frac{1}{3}, \frac{1}{3}, \frac{1}{3} \right)$$

$$\sigma^2_{Portfolio} = \mathbf{w}^T \Omega \, \mathbf{w}$$

$$= \begin{pmatrix} 1/3 & 1/3 & 1/3 \end{pmatrix} \begin{pmatrix} 0.00050827 & 0.000154099 & 0.000179167 \\ 0.000154099 & 0.00373365 & 0.00013894 \\ 0.000179167 & 0.00013894 & 0.00054746 \end{pmatrix} \begin{pmatrix} 1/3 \\ 1/3 \\ 1/3 \end{pmatrix}$$

$$= 0.000263866$$

Second, since we have the equal weight portfolio, the amount that has been invested in each individual stock is \$33.33. Furthermore, since the significance level is assumed to be 1 percent, alpha is equal to 2.32635.

The detailed derivation of the individual VaR as well as of the portfolio VaR is given as follows.

$$VaR_i = total \; invest \times w_i \times \sigma_i \times \alpha \times \sqrt{days}$$

$$VaR_P = total \; invest \times \sigma_P \times \alpha \times \sqrt{days} \qquad (15.11)$$

where

$$i = \{GM, \; WMT, \; IBM\}$$

$$\sigma_P = \sqrt{\mathbf{w}^T \Omega \, \mathbf{w}}$$

$$= \sqrt{\sum_i \sum_j \omega_i \omega_j \sigma_{i,j}}$$

$$= \sqrt{\sum_i \omega_i^2 \sigma_i^2 + 2 \sum_i \sum_{j \neq i} \omega_i \omega_j \sigma_{i,j}}$$

By plugging the appropriate numbers into equation (15.11), we can get three individual stock VaRs and the portfolio VaR.

$$VaR_{GM} = total \; invest \times w_{GM} \times \sigma_{GM} \times \alpha \times \sqrt{days}$$

$$= \frac{100}{3} \times \sqrt{0.00050827} \times 2.32635 \times \sqrt{5} = 3.9091$$

$$VaR_{WMT} = total \; invest \times w_{WMT} \times \sigma_{WMT} \times \alpha \times \sqrt{days}$$

$$= \frac{100}{3} \times \sqrt{0.00373365} \times 2.32635 \times \sqrt{5} = 3.3505$$

$$VaR_{IBM} = total\ invest \times w_{IBM} \times \sigma_{IBM} \times \alpha \times \sqrt{days}$$

$$= \frac{100}{3} \times \sqrt{0.00054746} \times 2.32635 \times \sqrt{5} = 4.0619$$

$$VaR_P = total\ invest \times \sigma_P \times \alpha \times \sqrt{days}$$

$$= 100 \times \sqrt{0.000263866} \times 2.32635 \times \sqrt{5} = 8.44989$$

Once we have calculated the VaRs, we are concerned with how much each individual stock contributes to the portfolio risk. To this end, we calculate betas of individual stocks. We define beta of the stock here by taking the portfolio as a "market portfolio" of the CAPM described in chapter 2. The method of determining the beta (the systematic risk) of a stock within the portfolio is given by the formula below. The numerator is the covariance of each stock with the market portfolio, and the denominator is the variance of the market portfolio, which is the variance of the portfolio consisting of GM, WMT and IBM.

$$Beta_{Delta\ Normal\ Method} = \begin{pmatrix} \beta_{GM} \\ \beta_{WMT} \\ \beta_{IBM} \end{pmatrix} = \frac{\Omega w}{w^{T} \Omega w} = \frac{\Omega \cdot \begin{pmatrix} 1/3 \\ 1/3 \\ 1/3 \end{pmatrix}}{\begin{pmatrix} 1/3 & 1/3 & 1/3 \end{pmatrix} \cdot \Omega \cdot \begin{pmatrix} 1/3 \\ 1/3 \\ 1/3 \end{pmatrix}}$$

$$= \begin{pmatrix} 1.0631 \\ 0.8418 \\ 1.0951 \end{pmatrix}$$

Component VaR is a product of three parts: the weight ω_i, the β, and the portfolio VaR. The reason to get the β is that β represents the systematic risk or the marginal contribution of each stock's risk to the portfolio risk.

$$Component\ VaR_i = \omega_i \times \beta_i \times VaR_{Portfolio}\ \forall i = GM,\ WMT,\ and\ IBM$$

For example, the GM component VaR is

$$Component\ VaR_{GM} = \omega_{GM} \times \beta_{GM} \times VaR_{Portfolio} = \frac{1}{3} \times 1.0630 \times 8.4498 = 2.9943$$

Since the component VaR is the individual stock's contribution to the portfolio risk, the sum of three component VaRs should be the portfolio VaR. Mathematically, since the sum of each beta multiplied by its corresponding weight is equal to 1, the sum of three component VaRs should be the portfolio VaR. The final results are summarized in the table 15.1.

Portfolio effect is defined as the individual stock VaR net of the component VaR, measuring the effect of diversification on the individual asset risk. When there are many uncorrelated assets in the portfolio, then portfolio effect can be significant. The portfolio effect can also measure the hedging effect within the portfolio if one asset has a negative correlation to another asset.

Table 15.1 VaR Calculation Output by Delta Normal Method

5-day VaR	GM	WMT	IBM	Total
Weight	1/3	1/3	1/3	1
Individual stock VaR	3.9091	3.3505	4.0619	11.3215
Portfolio VaR	—	—	—	8.4499
Beta	1.0631	0.8418	1.0951	—
Beta weight	0.3544	0.2806	0.3650	1
Component VaR	2.9943	2.3711	3.0844	8.4499
Portfolio effects	0.9148	0.9793	0.9775	2.8716

The advantage of the methodology above is its simplicity; it exploits the properties of a normal distribution. Specifically, we can use the additive property of the distribution. In doing so, we can build up the VaR of a portfolio from each single security and we can aggregate the information. Finally, we can calculate the contribution of the risk of each security to the portfolio risk. However, the simplicity comes with a cost.

The main drawback is that the normality assumption precludes other distributions that have skewed distribution as the main source of risks. For example, a short position of a call or put option would be misleading with the use of the delta normal methodology, because the distribution is not normal and the potential losses are much higher than assuming the normal distribution when the time horizon is not sufficiently short. One way to ameliorate the problem is to extend the methodology to incorporate skewness in the measurement. It is important to point out that if security returns are highly skewed (e.g., out-of-the-money options), there will be significant model risks in valuing the securities. In those situations, the error from a delta normal methodology is only part of the error in the estimation. For this reason, in practice, those securities usually have to be analyzed separately in more detail, and they require specific methodologies in managing their risks. Another problem of the normality assumption is the fat-tail effect of stocks, where there is a significant probability for the stock to realize high or low returns. *Kurtosis* of the stock returns, a measure of the fatness of the tails, is empirically significant.

Another drawback of the delta normal comes from the assumption that the risk is measured by the first derivative, called delta. When we cannot adequately measure the risk by the first derivative, we should extend to the second derivative, gamma, to measure the risk. This method is called the *delta–gamma methodology*.

However, for the most part, delta normal does provide a measure of risks enabling risk managers to evaluate the risks of a portfolio.

15.4   Historical Simulation Methodology

Historical simulation is another VaR measure methodology. The method uses a historical period of observed movement of the risk sources: stock returns, interest rate shifts, foreign exchange rate changes. It simulates the portfolio returns over that period as if the portfolio were held unchanged over that period of time. The VaR of the portfolio returns is then computed.

This is a simple methodology, particularly for trading desks. The reason is that for most trading desks, the trading books have to be marked to market daily. The modeling technologies are in place to value the securities and aggregate the reports. Simulating the historical scenarios is a fairly straightforward procedure. As in figure 15.2, we sort the historical return data in ascending order and locate the x percentile to calculate VaR.

Using the historical return data set of each of the stocks in table 15.2, we can find α percentile value of their daily returns to calculate the VaR of each stock and the portfolio. We also use their historical returns to determine their variance–covariance matrix. With the estimation of this variance–covariance matrix, we can determine the securities's from the lowest to the highest beta and the component VaR^2. The results are summarized in table 15.3.

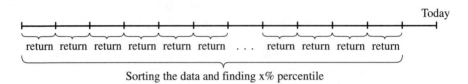

Figure 15.2 The historical simulation methodology. Sorting the data and finding x percentile.

Table 15.2 Historical Return Data Set

Date	(1) GM	(2) WMT	(3) IBM	(1)+(2)+(3) Portfolio
2001,01,03	1.6817	2.8219	3.8557	8.3594
2001,01,04	1.4032	−1.2865	−0.5069	−0.3901
2001,01,05	−1.8240	−1.3321	0.2915	−2.8646
2001,01,08	−0.8871	0.0000	−0.1570	−1.0441
⋮	⋮	⋮	⋮	⋮
2001,10,29	−1.9361	−0.9508	−0.7636	−3.6504
2001,10,30	−0.7170	−0.8306	0.0092	−1.5384
2001,10,31	−0.4152	0.5217	−0.1784	−0.0720
⋮	⋮	⋮	⋮	⋮
2002,04,30	0.5064	−0.2017	−0.0517	0.2531
2002,05,01	0.7067	0.5609	0.2149	1.4825
2002,05,02	0.3714	−0.0880	−0.1740	0.1094
1% percentile	−4.3292	−3.2264	−4.0362	−8.1626
1% VaR	4.3292	3.2264	4.0362	8.1626[1]

Note: Historical return is expressed by $ amount, which is calculated by total investment × weight × return.
[1]8.1626 is not equal to the sum of 4.3292, 3.2264, and 4.0362 because of the diversification effect.

Table 15.3 VaR Calculation Output by Historical Simulation Method

5-day VaR	GM	WMT	IBM	Total
Weight	1/3	1/3	1/3	1
Individual stock VaR	4.3292	3.2264	4.0362	11.5917
Portfolio VaR	—	—	—	8.1626
Beta	1.0631	0.8418	1.0951	—
Beta weight	0.3544	0.2806	0.3650	1
Component VaR	2.8925	2.2906	2.9795	8.1626
Portfolio effects	1.4367	0.9358	1.0567	3.4291

In comparing tables 15.1 and 15.3, the results suggest that the two methods do not provide the same VaR numbers but are reasonably close, within 10% error. One source of error can be the normality distribution assumption. To the extent that in the sample period, the stock returns exhibited significant fat tail behavior, then the discrepancies between the two measures can be significant.

15.5   Monte Carlo Simulation Methodology

The *Monte Carlo simulation* refers to a methodology where we randomly generate many scenarios and calculate the VaR of the portfolio. The method is similar to the historical simulation method, but we now simulate many scenarios using a forward-looking estimate of volatilities rather than the historical volatilities over a period of time.

We use a multivariate normal distribution with the given variance–covariance matrix based on the delta normal method and 0 means of the stocks to simulate the stock returns 100,000 times. (See table 15.4). These returns are then used to calculate the VaR of each stock and the VaR of the portfolio. The variance–covariance matrix of stock returns generated by Monte Carlo simulation is shown below.

$$\Omega_{Monte\ Carlo} = \begin{pmatrix} 0.00050792 & 0.00015374 & 0.00017815 \\ 0.00015374 & 0.00037336 & 0.00013749 \\ 0.00017815 & 0.00013749 & 0.00054419 \end{pmatrix}$$

$$MonteCarlo\ VaR_{GM} = 0.01\ Percentile\ of\ Scenario_{GM} \times total\ invest \times w_{GM} \times \sqrt{day}$$

$$= 0.052593 \times \frac{100}{3} \times \sqrt{5} = 3.9200$$

$$MonteCarlo\ VaR_{WMT} = 0.01\ Percentile\ of\ Scenario_{WMT} \times total\ invest \times w_{WMT} \times \sqrt{day}$$

$$= 0.044945 \times \frac{100}{3} \times \sqrt{5} = 3.3504$$

$$MonteCarlo\ VaR_{IBM} = 0.01\ Percentile\ of\ Scenario_{IBM} \times total\ invest \times w_{IBM} \times \sqrt{day}$$

$$= 0.054149 \times \frac{100}{3} \times \sqrt{5} = 4.0361$$

Table 15.4 Random Numbers Generated from Multi Normal Distribution

	Random number = Return data			
Scenario	GM (1)	WMT (2)	IBM (3)	Portfolio ((1)+(2)+(3))/3
Scenario 1	0.0090	−0.0074	−0.0165	−0.0149/3
Scenario 2	−0.0379	−0.0148	−0.0017	−0.0544/3
Scenario 3	0.0106	0.0022	−0.0081	0.0047/3
Scenario 4	0.0039	−0.0034	0.0073	0.0078/3
Scenario 5	−0.0445	−0.0108	−0.0279	−0.0832/3
⋮	⋮	⋮	⋮	⋮
1% percentile	−5.2593	−4.4950	−5.4149	−3.7629[**]

[**]1% percentile of portfolio return rate.

$$MonteCarlo\ VaR_P = 0.01\ Percentile\ of\ Scenario_P \times total\ invest \times \sqrt{day}$$

$$= 0.037629 \times 100 \times \sqrt{5} = 8.4141$$

Using the variance–covariance matrix of the stocks, which we can calculate from the randomly generated returns, we can then determine the component VaR, as we have done in the examples above. VaR by the Monte Carlo simulation method is given in table 15.5.

The results show that the VaR numbers are similar in all three approaches. This is not too surprising, since the three examples use the same model assumptions: the variance–covariance matrix of the stocks. Their differences result from the use of normality in the delta normal and the Monte Carlo simulation approaches, whereas the historical simulation is based on the historical behavior of the stocks. While we use the assumption of multivariate normal distributions of the stock in the Monte Carlo example here, in general this assumption is not required, and we can use a multivariate distribution that models the actual stock returns behavior best. Another source of error in this comparison is the model risks. The number of trials in both the historical simulation and the Monte Carlo simulations may not be sufficient for the results to converge to the underlying variances of the stocks.

15.6 Extreme Value Theory

The motivation for the use of *extreme value theory* is that the stock distribution is not normal. Empirical observations have shown that the distribution is fat-tail; that is, there are significant probabilities for the stock returns to be high or low, much more so than predicted by the normal distribution. Considering that in VaR, we are more concerned with the extreme left tail of the distribution, the error of modeling the stock returns by a normal distribution may misstate the VaR of a stock quite significantly. Figure 15.3 compares the historical distribution of the stock returns with a normal distribution. The fat-tail effect is quite evident.

The extreme value theory is concerned with the shape of the cumulative distribution function for the value x beyond a cutoff point u. The cumulative distribution functions for x beyond u are given according to the extreme value theory. (See Jorion, 2001. p. 251.)

$$F(y) = \begin{cases} 1 - \frac{N_u}{N}(1 + \xi y)^{-1/\xi} & \text{when } \xi \neq 0 \\ 1 - \frac{N_u}{N}\exp(-y) & \text{when } \xi = 0 \end{cases}$$

Table 15.5 VaR Calculation Output by Monte Carlo Simulation Method

5-day VaR	GM	WMT	IBM	Total
Weight	1/3	1/3	1/3	1
Individual stock VaR	3.9200	3.3504	4.0361	11.3065
Portfolio VaR	—	—	—	8.4141
Beta	1.0656	0.8433	1.0910	—
Beta weight	0.3552	0.2811	0.3637	1
Component VaR	2.9888	2.3652	3.0601	8.4141
Portfolio effects	0.9312	0.9851	0.9760	2.8923

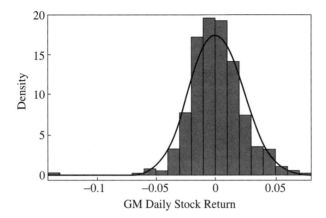

Figure 15.3 Historical return data vs. standard normal distribution. The histogram is the actual distribution of the stock portfolio returns. The smooth line is a standard normal distribution. The figure shows that the actual distribution has fatter tails than the standard normal distribution.

where $y = (\frac{x-u}{\beta})$ with $\beta > 0$. β is a scale parameter and ξ is a shape parameter that determines the speed at which the tail disappears. N_u is the number of observations where the observations exceed the cutoff point u. N is the total number of observations. For simplicity, we assume that y is greater than 0, which means that we are concerned with only positive extreme values.

We use the same sample period as the historical simulation, and the equal portfolio historical return data to calculate the VaR by the extreme value theory.

Step 1. We multiply historical returns by -1 to convert them into positive values. Since the extreme value theory is based on the positive values and we are concerned with left tails of the distribution functions, we multiply the historical returns by -1.

Step 2. We should choose a threshold (u) if we are interested in the cumulative distribution function beyond the threshold. The extreme value theory will show us a parametric distribution of the tail beyond the threshold.

Step 3. We count how many observations are beyond the threshold in the actual data and divide it by the total observations. The ratio is N_u/N. For example, the threshold is 2.5 and total observations are 332. The observations beyond 2.5 are {2.52752, 2.59161, 2.61462, 2.67357, 2.73096, 2.73985, 2.86456, 3.06577, 3.09981, 3.10791, 3.16308, 3.23153, 3.3775, 3.65043, 3.85859, 4.02339, 7.19302}. Therefore, the ratio is 17/332, because we have 17 observations beyond 2.5.

Step 4. Parameters (ξ, β) estimation. Since x follows the probability density function ($f(x)$), we can estimate two parameters, ξ and β, by the maximum likelihood estimation.

$$f(x) = \frac{N_u}{N} \frac{1}{\beta} \left(1 + \frac{\xi}{\beta}(x - u) \right)^{-1-\frac{1}{\xi}} \qquad (15.12)$$

Since the cumulative distribution function ($F(y)$) is $1 - \left(\frac{N_u}{N}\right)\left(1 + \xi \frac{(x-u)}{\beta}\right)^{-\frac{1}{\xi}}$, we can get the probability density function (PDF) by differentiating the cumulative distribution function by (CDF) x.

By taking a logarithm over $f(x)$ and maximizing it in terms of two parameters (ξ, β), we can estimate two parameters. Using the above example, we have the following likelihood function (Π) and the log likelihood function $(\log(\Pi))$, which we maximize to estimate two parameters $(\hat{\beta}, \hat{\xi})$.

$$\Pi = \left(\frac{17/332}{\beta}\right)^{17} \cdot \left(1 + \frac{\xi}{\beta}(2.52752 - 2.5)\right)^{-1-\frac{1}{\xi}} \cdot \left(1 + \frac{\xi}{\beta}(2.59161 - 2.5)\right)^{-1-\frac{1}{\xi}} \cdots$$

$$\cdots \left(1 + \frac{\xi}{\beta}(4.02339 - 2.5)\right)^{-1-\frac{1}{\xi}} \cdot \left(1 + \frac{\xi}{\beta}(7.19302 - 2.5)\right)^{-1-\frac{1}{\xi}}$$

$$\underset{\xi,\beta}{Max}\left(\log(\Pi)\right)$$

Step 5. VaR calculation. By step 4, we get two estimated parameters: $\hat{\xi} = 0.2086$, $\hat{\beta} = 0.6509$. For the calculation of VaR, we should determine the confidence level. Here we choose 0.9995 as the confidence level. Therefore the significance level is 0.0005. The formula to calculate the VaR based on the extreme value theory is given in equation (15.13). (See McNeil, 1999.)

$$VaR_{EVT} = u + \frac{\hat{\beta}}{\hat{\xi}}\left[\left(\frac{N}{N_u} \times (1-c)\right)^{-\hat{\xi}} - 1\right] \times day^{\hat{\xi}} \qquad (15.13)$$

$$\hat{\xi} = 0.2086, \ \hat{\beta} = 0.6509, \ \textit{confidence level } (C) = 0.9995$$

$$VaR_{EVT} = 2.5 + \frac{0.6509}{0.2086}\left[\left(\frac{1}{17/332} \times (1 - 0.9995)\right)^{-0.2086} - 1\right] \times 5^{0.2086} = 9.600$$

VaR at the 0.0005 significance level based on the extreme value theory is 9.60.

15.7   Credit Risk

Credit risk refers to the loss of principal or interest or any promised payments from the borrower for bonds or loans of any securities. For example, credit risk for a swap trade would be the loss of any unrealized profits as a result of a default of the counterparty.

To date, VaR is more concerned with market risk (interest rate, equity, and foreign exchange risk) and less with credit risk. In part, typically used in banks, the definition of credit risk does not specify a time horizon or a requirement of the marking to market value. Credit risk, as conceived by banks, is the loss of coupon and principal payments (often not mark to market value) in the event of default over the life of the loan. Credit risk is measured by internal or external ratings that indicate the likelihood of default, and sometimes the severity of the loss. To maintain an organizational structure within a bank, market risk and credit risk are, traditionally, manage by separate departments. As such, they have different views of risk, and hence different measurements of risk. For this reason, risk analysis tends to make the distinction between credit risk and market risk. Credit risk and market risk are not measured in one coherent framework.

This is unfortunate because credit risk and market risk are intimately related. As the Merton model indicates, the bond value is affected by both the firm risk and the interest rate risk. Further, the firm risk and the interest rate risk are correlated. As a result, the VaR of a bond cannot be derived from knowing the interest rate risk VaR and the credit risk VaR of the bond. Therefore, analyzing the risks separately prevents us from obtaining a complete description of the risk exposure of the bond.

VaR of a Bond

To discuss the credit risk in a value at risk paradigm, perhaps we should begin with determining the VaR of a corporate bond that has credit risks. We have shown that a structural model can determine the bond value by taking the firm's capital structure into account. Further, the bond value is valued relative to the observed equity value. Therefore, if we use a structural model, such as Merton (1974), and specify the firm value process as

$$dV = (\rho V - C)dt + \sigma \, dz \qquad (15.14)$$

then if we simulate equation (15.14) over a time horizon, say one year, we can determine the bond value at the horizon date. If we repeatedly simulate the firm values and calculate the bond price under different market assumptions, we can obtain a distribution of the bond value at the terminal date. From this distribution, we can determine the VaR measure.

This idea can be generalized to determine the bond risk in terms of VaR, taking interest rate and basis risk (the risk of the option adjusted spread of the bond due to liquidity of the market) into account. In this extended case, we can simulate future interest rates and basis risks of the option adjusted spread. For each market scenario (the changes of the firm value, yield curve level and shape, and the basis risk), we can determine the bond value. A large sample of scenarios enables us to determine the VaR of the bond value over a time horizon.

Integrating Credit Risk and Market Risk in a Portfolio Context

In recent years, efforts have been made to integrate market risks and default risks of a portfolio. The importance of this extension is clear. For capital adequacy requirement, hedging strategies, and VaR measures, we are always concerned with the portfolio risk and not the risk of a single security. However, there is no simple formula to aggregate the risk of each security to the portfolio level. The diversification effect can also be significant, such that the portfolio risk can be much lower than the sum of the risks of individual securities. To integrate credit risks and market risks in one approach, current methods tend to use simulations. Barnhill and Maxwell (2002) provide such a methodology.

Their method begins with representing the financial risks by eight correlated (approximately) arbitrage-free term structures of interest rates and a set of 24 equity market indices. They have included the exchange rate. The firm-specific market value of equity, debt ratio, credit rating, and default recovery rates are assumed to be uncertain.

The bond valuation model follows a modification and extension of the Merton (1974) and Longstaff and Schwartz (1995) methods, applied to a multiasset portfolio. Specifically, they assume that the firm value follows the process

$$dV = (rV - C)dt + \sigma V dz \tag{15.15}$$

and the interest rate model is a normal model of Hull and White (1993):

$$dr = (\theta(t) - ar)dt + \sigma dz \tag{15.16}$$

The bond is viewed as a contingent claim of the interest rates and the firm values, such that given a simulated yield curve and the firm value, the bond pricing model can determine the bond price. Next, they determine the market scenarios. They assume that each stock follows a lognormal process with the growth rate equal to the expected returns net of the dividend yields. The equity index returns are assumed to equal the risk-free rate plus a long-term average risk premium of 8% and the equity volatility for the S&P 500 is assumed to be based on the 1998 rate of 23%. The stock risk is assumed to be specified by the Capital Asset Pricing model.

$$k_i = r_f + \beta_i(E(R_M) - r_f) + \sigma \tilde{z} \tag{15.17}$$

where $\tilde{z}$ is the standard normal distribution. The simulated stock return enables us to determine the stock price at the horizon date, and the bond price can be determined.

The Capital Asset Pricing model ensures the correlations of the stock returns. The interest rate risks along with the correlated stock returns specify the correlations of the uncertain bond values at the time horizon. The scenarios projected are used to determine the correlated values of financial assets, and after a large number of simulations, a distribution of portfolio values is generated and analyzed.

The simulation results are interesting, showing the importance of integrating the market risks and the credit risks. They form portfolios of bonds from 24 economic sectors of B rated bonds. They consider the case where all the bonds belong to one economic sector, and another case where the bonds are selected from 24 sectors. Both cases show reduction of volatilities as a portfolio. They also determine the number of bonds necessary to diversify the credit risks away. There is a significant reduction in risk as bonds are added to the portfolio. However, the gains from diversification are relatively small after 15 bonds in different industries.

Currently, many firms are beginning to report risk exposures in market risks (reporting equity risk, interest rate risks, and exchange rate risk separately) and in credit risks. The diversification effect is a complex issue. The crux of the difficulties is the measure of the correlations. Typically, the correlations are determined by the historical data. However, in extreme market scenarios, such as the Asian crisis, the Russian crisis, and other significant unanticipated events, the markets tend to react in the same negative way. As a result, the correlations become significantly positive or negative, and the diversification effect becomes negligible. If the concern is to manage risks in these extreme cases, then we need to take caution in applying methods described in this section, where we assume the correlations are constant, not dependent on the state of the world.

Portfolio Credit Risk

Another approach to specify the correlations of the credit risk of bonds is to study the portfolio credit risk proposed by Wilson (1997a, 1997b), using macroeconomic models. Suppose that we have determined the transition matrix of the credit ratings. If we also have the option adjusted spreads of the bonds for each rating, then we can determine the distribution of the change in bond price by combining the transition matrix and the option adjusted spread. Now we can apply this method to determine the credit risk distribution.

How do we now extend this approach to the portfolio? If we assume that price distributions are uncorrelated, then the risks are diversified and there will be little risk. The main problem with the credit risk of a bond is that risks tend to occur together.

We can use the stock returns to specify the correlations, and then those correlations are used in the structural model. Another approach is to use macroeconomic models. The construction of the model follows the three steps described below.

Step 1. Specify a set of macroeconomic factors that will affect the credit risk of the firms. These variables may be unemployment rates, regional housing price indices, GDP growth rates, government spending, and regional housing indices. The evolutions of their changes in value over time are modeled.

Step 2. Define the default index by measuring the default rate. Wilson suggests using speculative bonds. These historical rates are used as dependent variables. The macroeconomic factors are used as the independent variables.

Step 3. Measure the rating migrations against the speculative default rates. This way, given a change in the speculative default rate, we can determine the change in the rating migrations. The simulations can then be used to simulate the change in value of a bond portfolio.

The results suggest that the function cannot be explained by one factor. For example, we cannot use the stock market index to determine the default rate. This approach can relate the performance of the portfolio to the economic activities. This approach, which does not depend on the stock index, can suggest how the economy affects the credit risk.

Credit VaR—A Numerical Example by CreditMetrics

To calculate credit VaR of an individual risky bond or a portfolio of risky bonds when the holding period is one year, we need a transition matrix, one-year forward spot curves for various ratings, and description of risky bonds (e.g., rating or maturity).[3] We need the transition matrix because the risky bonds will change their rating over the horizon and the value of the risky bonds will depend on their ratings. One-year forward spot curves as well as the bond data set will be used to calculate the present value of the bonds one year hence. The transition matrix and the one-year forward spot curve and bond data set are assumed to be as follows.

Transition Matrix

Initial rating	Rating at year-end (%)							
	AAA	AA	A	BBB	BB	B	CCC	Default
AAA	90.81	8.33	0.68	0.06	0.12	0.00	0.00	0.00
AA	0.70	90.65	7.79	0.64	0.06	0.14	0.02	0.00
A	0.09	2.27	91.05	5.52	0.74	0.26	0.01	0.06
BBB	0.02	0.33	5.95	86.93	5.30	1.17	1.12	0.18
BB	0.03	0.14	0.67	7.73	80.53	8.84	1.00	1.06
B	0.00	0.11	0.24	0.43	6.48	83.46	4.07	5.20
CCC	0.22	0.00	0.22	1.30	2.38	11.24	64.86	19.79

One-year Forward Spot Curves

Category	1	2	3	4
AAA	3.60	4.17	4.73	5.12
AA	3.65	4.22	4.78	5.17
A	3.72	4.32	4.93	5.32
BBB	4.10	4.67	5.25	5.63
BB	5.55	6.02	6.78	7.27
B	6.05	7.02	8.03	8.52
CCC	15.05	15.02	14.03	13.52

Bond Data Set

Bond Number	Credit Grade	Face Value	Maturity	Coupon Rate	Recovery Rate
1	A	100	5	zero	0.60
2	BBB	100	5	0.06	0.55
3	BB	100	5	0.03	0.40

First, we calculate an individual bond credit VaR of the BB grade bond.

Step 1. Bond prices one year hence and corresponding profit/loss calculation. Since we are concerned with how much the bond value will change over one year, we calculate the bond value one year hence. If the BB grade bond retains the same rating, which is the most likely, the bond value one year hence is 88.7654 as shown below. The future cash flow from the bond is determined by the future coupon payments and the time to maturity as of one year hence.

$$3 + \frac{3}{(1 + 0.0555)^1} + \frac{3}{(1 + 0.0602)^2} + \frac{3}{(1 + 0.0678)^3} + \frac{3 + 100}{(1 + 0.0727)^4} = 88.7654$$

In the same way, we can calculate one-year forward prices of all the credit grades. On top of that, we also can calculate the bond price in the case of default, which is the recovery

Table 15.6 One-year Forward Bond Price, Profit/Loss, and Probability

Grade	AAA	AA	A	BBB	BB	B	CCC	Default
Price	95.6241	95.456	94.959	93.928	88.7654	85.0951	71.9208	40
Profit/Loss	6.8587	6.6909	6.1936	5.1626	0	−3.6703	−16.8446	−48.7654
Probability	0.03	0.14	0.67	7.73	80.53	8.84	1.00	1.06
Cumulative Probability	100.00	99.97	99.83	98.16	91.43	10.90	2.06	1.06

Note: The future cash flow from the bond is determined by the future coupon payments and the time to maturity as of one year hence.

rate multiplied by the face value. The resulting prices and corresponding profit/loss are shown in the table 15.6.

Step 2. Bond credit VaR calculation. Since we can assign probability to each profit/loss category, we can draw the probability distribution, which is a basis to calculate the credit VaR. The probability distribution is far from a normal distribution. This is why we cannot apply a delta normal method to calculate credit VaR. Given the distribution and a significance level, we can calculate the credit VaR.

There are two methods to determine the 10% bond credit VaR calculation. First, we can take 16.8446. The position of the 10% cumulative probability of profit/loss is between 10.90% (B grade) and 2.06% (CCC grade). In the conservative view, we can choose 16.8446 as the bond credit VaR. Second, we can take 5.01155. By a linear interpolation,

$$3.6703 + \frac{10.90 - 10}{10.90 - 2.06} \times (16.8446 - 3.6703)$$

we can calculate the bond credit VaR to be 5.01155.

Second, we calculate a bond portfolio credit VaR by the Monte Carlo approach. We assume that the bond portfolio consists of one A bond, one BBB bond, and one BB bond.

Step 1. Given the assumption that the transition probabilities follow the standard normal distribution,[4] we convert the transition probabilities into z thresholds. For example, the A rating bond has 0.09% probability to become AAA and 2.27% probability

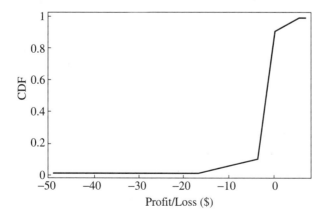

Figure 15.4 Cumulative probability of BB grade bond's profit/loss

to become AA in one year. The corresponding z thresholds are 3.12 and 1.98, respectively. In other words, a variable which follows the standard normal distribution exceeds 3.12 and 1.98 with the probabilities of 0.09% and 2.36% (0.09 + 2.27), respectively.

The calculated Z thresholds are given in the table below.

Thresholds	A	BBB	BB
Z_{AA}	3.12139	3.54008	3.43161
Z_A	1.9845	2.69684	2.92905
Z_{BBB}	−1.50704	1.53007	2.39106
Z_{BB}	−2.30085	−1.49314	1.36772
Z_B	−2.71638	−2.17808	−1.23186
Z_{CCC}	−3.19465	−2.74778	−2.04151
Z_D	−3.23888	−2.91124	−2.30440

Step 2. Estimate the correlation matrix or variance–covariance matrix among the bond returns.

Covariance Matrix	A	BBB	BB
A	0.9	0.7	−0.3
BBB	0.7	2	0.5
BB	−0.3	0.5	1

Step 3. Generate bond return scenarios according to the multinormal distribution. For example, if we generate a triple number {0.415633, −0.621258, −0.252211} from the given multinormal distribution, the first bond downgrades to BBB from the current A rating, the second bond changes from BBB to BB, and the third bond becomes B from BB.

Step 4. Given the ratings one year hence, we can calculate the bond values, because we have the spreads corresponding to the ratings.

Step 5. Repeat the above procedure, say 100,000 times, to generate the distribution of the portfolio values.

Step 6. Given the significance level, we can calculate the credit VaR. Recall that VaR is the maximum loss with a significance level, which means that the actual loss could exceed VaR with the probability of the significance level.

We can get figure 15.5 if we apply the procedure to the bond portfolio.

Table 15.7 shows that the bond portfolio can diversify some of the credit risks. The level of diversification depends on the creditworthiness of the bonds and the correlations of the credit risks across the firms.

15.8   Risk Reporting

The sections above describe the VaR measures. We can now report the risk exposure, and we illustrate it with a bank's balance sheet below (Ho et al., 1999). VaR is defined in this report with 99% confidence level over a one-month time horizon. (See table 15.8.)

The report shows the market value (or the fair value) of each item on a bank's balance sheet and the VaR value of each item. VaR/MV is the ratio of VaR to the market value,

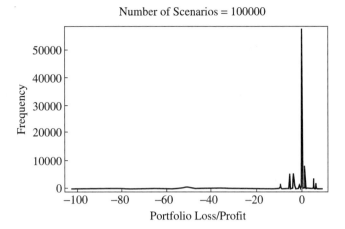

Figure 15.5 Bond portfolio default risk distribution

Table 15.7 Bond Credit VaR and Portfolio Effect

	A-Grade Bond	BBB-Grade Bond	BB-Grade Bond	Portfolio
10% VaR	0.9143	5.3193	5.01155	5.52456
Portfolio effect		11.2448 − 5.52456 = 5.72024		

Table 15.8 Aggregation of Risks to Equity ($mil.) (the VaR Table)

Item	Market Value	VaR	VaR/MV (%)	Component VaR
Prime rate loans	3,286	11.31	0.34	4.5
Base rate loans	2,170	4.92	0.23	−4.3
Variable rate mortgages	625	5.47	0.87	−4.8
Fixed rate loans	1,231	30.49	2.50	−22.5
Bonds	2,854	33.46	1.17	−28.2
Base rate time deposits	1,959	5.83	0.30	3.24
Prime rate time deposits	289	1.56	0.54	0.98
Fixed rate time deposits	443	11.69	2.64	9.55
Demand deposits	5,250	44.62	0.85	36.89
Long-term market funding	1,146	19.85	1.73	15.16
Equity	1,078	10.59	0.98	10.59

measuring the risk per dollar, and $VaR\beta_i$ is the marginal risk of each item to the VaR of the bank (the VaR of the equity).

The sum of the VaR values of all the items is not the same as the VaR of the equity. This is because the sum of the VaR values does not take diversification or hedging effects into account. However, the sum of the component VaR is equal to the VaR of the equity, because the component VaR already reflects the diversification effect or hedging effects. VaR/MV measures the risk of each item per dollar. The results show that the fixed-rate loans and the fixed-rate time deposits are the most risky; the VaR per dollar is 2.5% and 2.64%, respectively.

The results for the component VaR show that demand deposits, while not the most risky item on the balance sheet, contribute much of the risk to equity. All the items on the asset side of the balance sheet (except for the prime rate loans) become hedging instruments to the demand deposit position.

One application of this overview of risks at the aggregated and disaggregated levels is that we can identify the "natural hedges" in the portfolio. The risk contribution can be negative. This occurs when there is one position of stocks or bonds that is the main risk contributor. Then any security that is negatively correlated with that position will lower the portfolio total risk. The report will show that the risk contribution is negative, and that security is considered to offer a natural hedge to the portfolio. This methodology can extend from a portfolio of securities to a portfolio of business units. These units may be trading desks, a fund of funds, or multiple strategies of a hedge fund.

One important application of the VaR is the determination of the capital requirement: the market risk capital charge. We will discuss the risk charge in more detail in chapter 16. The banking regulators adopted a methodology of market risk capital charge different from that applied to credit risk. Instead of using a formula to assign risk weight to each item in the asset portfolio, the regulators agreed to let the banks decide the VaR using the banks' internal model. This approach represents a significant departure from the usual approach of the regulators. Previously, the regulators decided on the measures of risks, as in risk-based capital, and these measures tended to be relatively simple for the bank to compute. However, in reporting the VaR, the implementation of the regulation is now based on complex and often not transparent financial models.

According to the regulation, the banks have to determine the market risk charge, which is given by

$$Market\ risk\ charge = Max\left[VaR,\ factor\ \times\ average\ VaR\ (60\ days)\right]$$

where VaR is defined as 99% ten days holding period. The bank must have capital to support the risk, and the capital must exceed the market risk charge by a specified multiple.

The application of VaR goes beyond the specification of the regulation. It can be used for managing a trading floor: setting limits, trip wire. VaR is used for managing a portfolio and monitoring the risk exposures of funds, particularly the hedge funds. VaR is used for managing a financial institution with a balance sheet. This will be discussed in chapter 16, where we will discuss RAROC (and others) on the issue of capital allocation.

15.9   Risk Monitoring

Backtesting

The purpose of *backtesting* (Jorion, 2001) is to see whether the methods to calculate VaR are appropriate in the sense that the actual maximum loss has exceeded the predetermined VaR within an expected margin. The expected margin depends on which significance level we select when we calculate the VaR.

The basic idea behind the backtest is to compare the actual days when the actual loss exceeds the VaR with the expected days based on the significance level. We calculate the expected and actual VaR violation days.

For illustration, we collect stock price data for the period of 1999.1.4 to 2002.5.3. The number of observation days is 837. We use the delta normal method to calculate VaR. We compare VaR from the period with the actual maximum loss for the period of 2001.5.18 to 2002.5.3. The total backtest days are 238 days.

For the backtest period, if actual returns exceed VaR, then 1 is assigned to the indicator, and 0 otherwise. T_1 is the number of days with indicator= 1 and T_0 is the number of days with indicator= 0. During the sample period, the actual loss exceeds the delta normal VaR nine times. Therefore, the violation ratio $\left(\dfrac{T_1}{T_1 + T_0} \right)$ is 0.038793%. The significance level for the backtest is assumed to be 5%. Therefore the expected number of violations is 11.6 (significance level(0.05) *times* the number of backtest days($238 - 1 - 5$)).

The test statistics are given below. The distribution is $\chi^2 (1)$.

$$test\ statistics_{UC} = -2 \log \left[\left(1 - \textit{confidence level} \right)^{T_0} \left(\textit{confidence level} \right)^{T_1} \right]$$

$$+ 2 \log \left[\left(1 - \frac{T_1}{T_1 + T_0} \right)^{T_0} \left(\frac{T_1}{T_1 + T_0} \right)^{T_1} \right] \quad \chi^2(1) \qquad (15.18)$$

Plugging the appropriate numbers into equation (15.12), the test statistic is 0.662502. Since the critical value is 3.84146, we cannot reject the VaR model. (See figure 15.6.)

15.10   Risk Management

In the previous sections, we have discussed the risk measurement, reporting, and monitoring. Now we discuss the actions that we can take in managing risks.

Much of the impetus for risk management started after the series of financial debacles for some funds, banks, and municipalities. In a few years, much progress has been made in research and development. More financial institutions have put in place a risk

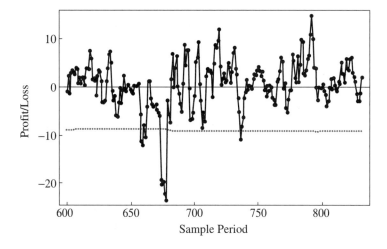

Figure 15.6 Backtesting. The fluctuating line is actual market returns and the dotted line is VaR. The actual market returns exceed VaR nine times out of 232 observations.

management team and technologies, including VaR calculations for the trading desks and the firm's balance sheets.

In reviewing the methodologies and technologies developed in these years, one cannot help noticing that most risk management measures and techniques focus on banks and trading floors in particular. These management techniques are precise about the risk distributions and the characteristics of each security.

In a broader aspect of risk management, we should be concerned with the risk to the value of the firm—specifically the shareholders' value. Risk management is an important aspect of the firm. Under the perfect capital market assumption of Miller and Modigliani, risk management should be irrelevant because all the firms are in the same risk class when they have the same risk, and therefore financial decisions are independent of the firm value.

But risk management can increase shareholders' value if the risk management can reduce transaction costs or taxes, or affect investment decisions. With real options, the cost of capital can change, the strategic investments can be affected by default and other factors, and the firm value can be affected. We also show that in a world with incomplete information, risks affect the signaling that disseminates private information to the public.

Risk management is important to shareholders' value even when the firm has no trading floor. Risk impacts the firm value whether the firm is a manufacturer, a retail chain, or in some other sector. There are many examples of defaults of nonfinancial companies that are not a result of extensive loss in financial securities, and that do not result from the defects in the manufacturing process—rather, the cause is corporate financial management.

Strategic Risk Management

The concept of *strategic risk management* was introduced by Smith and Smithson (1998), who are concerned with the impact of risks on the shareholders' value. They propose to identify the risk sources and to measure their impact on the firm. More specifically, they seek to measure the impact of equity risk, interest rate risk, commodities risk, and currency risk on the shareholders' value. To measure the risk exposure, they propose the elasticity, which is defined as percentage change in the firm value divided by percentage change in the risk source, as a standard of measure.

They show, for example, that the Westinghouse Company share value is sensitive to risk factors of three-year and ten-year key rates for oil, pound sterling, and yen by correlating the stock returns with the returns of a selection of risk sources, using historical data from 1987–1989. They then propose that this enterprise risk exposure can be managed by using financial derivatives of those risk sources to implement a hedging program.

Since the goal of corporate financial management is to maximize the shareholders' value, Smith and Smithson's definition of strategic risk management as managing the shareholders' value seem more appropriate than managing the risk of the firm's equity value or earnings. But there is an alternative approach to managing the risk of the shareholders' value.

Instead of using the historical returns to determine the sources of risks to the shareholders' value, we can study the business processes of a firm in detail. First, formulate the corporate and the business models of the firm. Then we manage the process. This approach will be described in the following section.

Business Process

W. Edwards Deming was a relatively unknown statistician in the United States. However, a documentary on NBC titled *If Japan Can . . . Why Can't We?* thrust him into the spotlight. He was a spokesperson for quality control: to use all given data in making decisions, and to incorporate the views of top management in order to manufacture quality products. His process was hailed in Japan, where they used his methods to value quality over quantity, whereas in the United States at that time, the opposite was true.

Deming has proposed that the central idea of quality control is reducing the problem to a process with phases and observable results. The results are then statistically analyzed as a whole process, not just as a portion of the process. The feedback information from these statistical results is then analyzed to detect defects. The defects should be analyzed and controlled before they become large. This is the essence of the Deming quality control methods that are widely used in industry.

The Deming approach differs from VaR methodologies or other methodologies as exemplified by Smith and Smithson. First, Deming's proposal does not identify the risk sources and measure them directly. On the contrary, Deming focuses on the specification of a process and designs a statistical procedure to measure the defects. Deciding the strategy of management of the defect is the very last step. Second, Deming assumes that there are defects in the process. Quality control eliminates the defects when they are small, and sets the goal of eliminating all possible defects.

This approach is not an alternative to other approaches. It is complementary to VaR and other such methodologies. We began the chapter by stating that the market consensus considers risk management to have four parts: measurements, reporting, monitoring, and management. Deming's approach proposes that risk management begins with the design of the business process, not just the measurements, reporting, and monitoring. The design of the business process should incorporate the reporting of defects and have a feedback loop to the control of risks.

Risk management is the quality control of finance. Financial decisions are made with risk and return trade-offs. However, these are models that must invariably fail in some scenarios. There are defects in our decision-making process. The challenge is to identify any defects ahead of time.

Investment Cycle

To illustrate Deming's approach, we consider an investment process. We argue that an investment process is similar to a manufacturing process. An *investment cycle* describes the process for making investments. It should be clearly organized in order to monitor each business unit's responsibilities to manage the "milestones" of the firm. The milestones are the investment objective, the market outlook, investment strategies, and performance evaluation. There are four phases of the investment cycle that will oversee the milestones: the requirement phase, design phase, test phase, and implementation phase. Each phase will provide the checks and balances for the next phase. The requirement phase establishes goals to meet the client's needs. This in turn will monitor the investment performance and the investment objective. The design phase sets strategies for portfolio managers, who formulate the market outlook from the investment objective. The test phase uses the market outlook to formulate investment strategies. The implementation phase executes the investment strategies that result in trades and portfolio performances, thus completing the investment cycle.

Each phase can be measured separately to assure that each performance ties back to the investment objectives, a process similar to quality assurance management. In the investment cycle, we can break each business unit into its portfolio positions. Using VaR as a risk measure, we can decompose the entire risk of the process so that each risk can be measured separately. Then we can calculate the VaR of each position for each risk source, which is the total risk for all the enterprise risks. Measuring the VaR in an investment cycle will enable risk managers to manage all stages of the investment process rather than just observing a portion of the process.

Risk managers can implement a more complex investment cycle that will include the design phase of all the proposed business strategies to monitor and adjust the business cycle. The business cycle will enable risk managers to provide risk exposures, risk sources, risk limits, and risk policies. Implementing risk management within a business control cycle will benefit the senior management when it comes to making decisions to optimize the shareholders' value using all the measures that impact the balance sheet's risk and profitability. (See figure 15.7.)

The risk management of investment using a process described above illustrates how enterprise management can be implemented by modeling the business processes of the

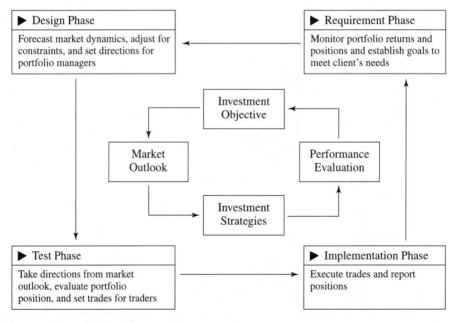

Figure 15.7 An investment process. An investment cycle describes the process for making investments. There are four phases of the investment cycle that will oversee the milestones: the requirement phase, design phase, test phase, and implementation phase. Each phase will provide the checks and balances for the following phase. The boxes for investment objective, market outlook, investment strategies, and performance evaluation indicate that they are actions to take one phase to another.

enterprise. In previous chapters we have discussed the use of business models and corporate models to specify the business processes. We can then apply the risk management methods in identifying, measuring, and monitoring the risks of the processes.

15.11   Boardroom with a View—The Coffin Story

In 1993, I was invited to give a short talk on risk management to the board of directors of an international bank. The board members consisted of executives from various industries, including many from manufacturing businesses. I related the coffin story. Consider a factory that makes coffins. Coffins need to be made strong enough to protect against soil and water. Marketing research has determined that buyers purchase a coffin not only based on the design, but also the strength, to give them a sense of durability.

However, few customers can determine the durability of a casket. Normally, they would not want to see the casket a year or two after it has been buried to check whether or not it is still intact. Nor would they demand to look at it after a rainstorm. On the day of burial, loved ones spend hours looking at the coffin. In a sad and emotional state, the last thing they want to see is a crack on the coffin. They will not tolerate even a hair fracture or dust sealed to the wood. Such imperfections indicate that the product is shoddy and lacks strength.

This actually happened to a manufacturer of coffins. The sales office found that at times, their coffins had dust sealed on the sparkling surface of the coffins. The engineers were put to work to find out the cause. Just the thought of the mourners discovering dust on the coffins and looking at the imperfection for hours drove the engineers into high action mode. They checked the protective materials. They checked the workmanship. They checked the factories, the scheduling, the handling. Nothing came out of the search. They even checked the process for making the protective coating, making sure the entire environment was absolutely free of pollutants while the coffins were being dried after the protective coating had been applied.

The senior engineer lost sleep over the problem. One Sunday, he took a walk in the factory. He wanted to see it when there was no one around. As he walked through the nearly empty factory, he saw the cleaning crew at work. They were responsible for cleaning the entire factory over the weekend. He saw nothing amiss; everything was following the schedules he had designed. Then he looked up. In a ray of sunlight, he saw that dust was rising after it had been stirred up by the cleaning crew. He then realized the problem: After the cleaning crew left, the dust would slowly fall down. When the coffins were put out to dry on Monday, the dust would begin to sprinkle onto the wet paint, and hence would be sealed on the surface when dry.

I suggest that in manufacturing great attention is paid to details to ensure that the process does exactly what it is designed to do because the source of the defects often comes from the design of the process. This idea typically is not appreciated in the financial industry. If we place an advertisement to hire financial engineers specializing in process designs, no one would come to the interview with proper qualifications—because there is no such qualification. Few risk managers would have a diagram of the financial process depicted in the senior manager's office. Sure, there are many systems in place to track the trade tickets (the primary method of recording the basic information relating to a transaction), for instance. That is the operational process. But few have a way of tracking risks and risks transformed from one department to another. I concluded my talk with a design of a business process of a bank.

As I was chatting outside the boardroom, I looked inside and saw that some of the executives from the engineering companies were drawing flow charts and organizational charts of a process while the bankers were watching from their seats. The idea of risk management viewed as quality control of a business process had excited the engineers.

15.12   Summary

Risk management is an integral part of a business process. It is no surprise to students of the subject that the issues are broad, the implications are important, and the approaches are many. In any discussion of risk management, the first challenge is to focus the scope of discussion to keep everyone on the same page.

Risk management involves measurement, reporting, monitoring, and management. We have given an overview of measurements of market and credit risks. The purpose is not to give in-depth descriptions of how to build or how to use the risk measures. The purpose is to provide the principles behind these topics and show how they are related to the principles of finance.

In managing the risk of a firm, we should start with the business process as defined by the firm model. The impact of business risks on the shareholders' value is a cumulative effect of a series of management decisions. The precise relationship is presented in the business process. The risk of each phase of the process can be estimated prospectively. Furthermore, the observations of each phase can be statistically analyzed retrospectively. This is the essence of Deming's quality control. These ideas will be further elaborated in chapter 16.

Appendix A.   Selected Historical Financial Losses

A.1   The Beginning of Rogue Traders: 1990–1992

Making money is the goal of many traders, which of course requires them to take risks on the trading floor. Rogue traders take this attitude to a higher level by taking huge risks. These risks can reap loads of benefits for the investor, as well as for the trader. But they can also lead to huge falls, as we can see in the examples below.

Askin Capital Management

At the beginning of the 1990s, the first large financial loss was first reported by Askin Capital Management in 1990. David Askin was the former head of fixed-income research at Drexel Lambert, which at one time was a highly successful and influential securities firm on Wall Street. After the demise of Drexel, Askin founded a fixed-income asset management company. His management style entailed providing high yields for clients, using mortgage-backed securities. In particular, he developed relationships with major Wall Street firms that repackaged mortgage-backed securities. With his fixed-income research and his quantitative approach, the asset management approach was to acquire complex collateralized mortgage obligations (CMOs) from Wall Street firms.

Firms that were able to place these complex CMO bonds were important to Askin because these placements enabled him to "drive the deal." The simpler tranches, like the PAC bonds or sequential bonds, discussed earlier, could find ready buyers, but the complicated tranches could be placed with more sophisticated firms like Askin Capital Management.

By 1990, interest rates began to climb. There was a lack of liquidity to the CMO bonds, in particular to the more complicated tranches. The result was a widening of spreads, leading to a fall in market price. Part of the Askin fund was buying these CMO bonds on margin. When the bond prices fell, the portfolio value fell even more precipitously. The liquidity problem persisted, and finally Kidder Peabody and other major firms decided to make the margin call. When the margin call occurred, the fund had to be liquidated at a "fire sale," selling at very low prices. With little liquidity in the market, the sales resulted in a loss of $600 million to the investors and Askin Capital Management ceased to exist.

The financial loss caught the market by surprise in a number of ways. Mortgage-backed securities and CMO markets had been growing at extraordinary rates. The reported loss led to concerns about the "riskiness" of these securities. Fixed-income funds could no longer be considered a portfolio that provided stable income.

A.2   The Role of Management: 1992–1994

Although the label "rogue traders" has an ominous tone to it, financial losses should not be blamed solely on their actions. Many times, it is the fault of the financial management that ignores the issues at hand that result in their losses. In the examples below, you can see how these situations will prompt financial managers to assess their roles in the financial market.

Daiwa Bank

In 1992, Daiwa Bank (New York) reported a $1.1 billion loss, and in July 1995 it was reported that Toshihide Iguchi conducted unauthorized U.S. bond trading over an 11-year period. In December 1995, a U.S. District Court sentenced Iguchi, who pleaded guilty to fraud, to four years in prison. He was also ordered to pay a $2 million fine and $70,000 in restitution. Daiwa Bank pleaded guilty in February 1996 to conspiring to help hide Iguchi's losses and agreed to pay $340 million in fines. It was forced to close down its U.S. operation. Two other Daiwa employees charged with smaller roles in the scandal described a conspiracy involving the highest echelons of Daiwa management during their court testimony.

In a way, the Daiwa financial loss was a wake-up call to the financial market—financial losses can happen to any bank. Before the Daiwa case, financial losses tended to be confined to rogue traders in complicated mortgage-backed markets, often called derivatives at that time. Since these markets tended to be confined to sophisticated traders, most investors and regulators considered these losses to be the inevitable trade-off between risk and returns. The events simply heightened everyone's awareness of the riskiness of the mortgage-backed derivatives.

However, the Daiwa case differed from other financial losses in two respects. The trader was trading only Treasury bonds, the simplest and most liquid bonds in the market. And the loss developed over a period of 11 years. Second, the loss was not the result of a rogue trader—it was the result of management that overlooked, and subsequently concealed, the losses from the financial markets that caused Daiwa Bank's massive damage.

Metallgesellschaft AG

In December 1993, Metallgescellschaft AG revealed that its Energy Group was responsible for losses of approximately $1.5 billion. The loss was mainly due to the liquidity problem resulting from the large oil forward contracts it had written.

The Energy Group was committed to sell a specified number of barrels of oil at prices fixed in 1992 every month for up to ten years. To hedge this position, it entered into 154 million barrels of oil in short-term contracts. This level of short-term position is overhedging, since analysis showed that 55% less than this amount is sufficient to hedge the short long-dated position. This overhedging may have been motivated in part by the Energy Group's belief that the long-dated forward prices of oil were well below the expected spot prices.[5]

At the beginning of the program the Group realized a profit margin of $5 per barrel. However, in order to prevent any possible loss, some of the contracts were designed to allow the Group to terminate the contract automatically when the front month New York Mercantile Exchange (NYMEX) futures contract was greater than a specified exit price, a limited cap.

Although it had a limited cap, that didn't prevent the Group from losing money because there was one hitch in the design that it didn't consider—the size of the transactions. By September 1993, the Energy Group had sold forward contracts amounting to the equivalent of 160 million barrels. At this level, the caps were insufficient to limit the risk of rising oil prices. The Group then bought (long) exchange-traded futures to hedge this risk. But exchange-traded futures had a relatively short time to expiration (at most one year).

Moreover, the average trading volume in the heating oil and unleaded gasoline pits usually averages anywhere from 15,000 to 30,000 contracts per day. With the Energy Group reportedly holding a 55,000-contract position in these contracts, the exchange market had to take this outstanding position into account and could not function as a truly perfect capital market. The position resulted in a large reported loss. As a result, Metallgesellschaft decided to liquidate the position, the unrealized losses became realized losses, and the forward contracts were left unhedged. By regulation the unrealized gains and losses of the exchange-traded contracts have to be reported as income, while the mark to market value of the physical goods does not have to be reported. Therefore, the financial reporting does not take the hedging into account. As a result, the financial reporting suggested a highly volatile income for the Energy Group. This became another motivation of the firm to liquidate all the positions. The Energy Group's design of its investment objectives was flawed because it ignored matters such as basis risks, liquidity, and the implications of financial reporting.

Kidder Peabody

In April 1994, Kidder Peabody, a New York investment bank, announced that its Treasury bond desk had lost $200 million. Specifically, its bond trader, Joseph Jett, had made unauthorized trades that resulted in the losses. Jett, the top government bond trader at Kidder Peabody, was accused of generating phony profits of $350 million, an allegation he denied.

This case led to protracted legal disputes. Numerous individuals connected with this scandal were investigated and/or sued. The SEC launched a probe and filed civil administrative charges against many of the parties involved. The New York Stock Exchange conducted its own investigation and levied its own sanctions. The shareholders of GE, which owned Kidder Peabody at the time, brought an action against Kidder, and individuals related to the case sought damages for fraud and deceit. Jett and Kidder went to arbitration. Jett eventually was cleared of civil fraud charges and was never charged criminally. GE sold most of Kidder's assets in late 1994 to PaineWebber for approximately $600 million, after having invested $1.4 billion in Kidder. The financial management obviously did not oversee the activities of Joseph Jett. Perhaps they were assured that he would not engage in criminal activities because he was the top government bond trader. This case shows the social costs of poor risk management. Society must bear all the direct and indirect legal costs.

A.3   Bankruptcies of a Wealthy Municipality and a Major Institution: 1994–1995

Indeed, financial losses can happen to any organization, including an affluent city in Southern California and an august banking institution that had the likes of Queen Elizabeth as a client. What could possibly have brought down these organizations that ranked far above others in their respective nations?

Orange County

In 1994 we witnessed the largest financial loss reported in history to occur to a political subdivision, Orange County, California. The country treasurer, Robert Citron, was overseeing a $7.5 billion investment pool for 187 government participants, including 34 cities and 38 school districts. The county reported a financial loss of $1.7 billion. From January to November 1994, the Orange County investment pool had 24.9–39.8% in inverse floater CMOs that offered a high return in a falling interest rate environment and had 40–50% of the portfolio in fixed-rate securities with a duration in excess of three years. In total, the portfolio had borrowed up to 2.7 times its unleveraged portfolio.

In May 1995, a comprehensive agreement was made. Two hundred government agencies agreed to forgo their rights to sue Orange County and its officials in order to receive better repayments. Fourteen government agencies retained their rights to sue for approximately $40–80 million for their financial losses.

Barings

On February 27, 1995, a rogue trader, Nicholas Leeson, brought down the venerable bank Barings PLC with a reported loss of $1.38 billion. The activities of Nick Leeson on the Japanese and Singapore futures exchanges, which led to the downfall of his employer, are well-documented. The main points are recounted here to serve as a backdrop to the main topic of this chapter—the policies, procedures, and systems necessary for the prudent management of derivative activities.

Mr. Leeson had certain views on the market direction. Over time, he accumulated an outstanding notional futures position on Japanese equities and interest rates of $27 billion: U.S.$7 billion on a Nikkei 225 equity contract and U.S. $20 billion on Japanese government bond (JGB) and Euroyen contracts. Mr. Leeson also sold 70, 892 Nikkei put and call options with a nominal value of $6.68 billion. Compared with the bank's reported capital of about $615 million, these trading positions exceeded any risk limits that the bank could afford.

The Nikkei fell at the same time as the Kobe earthquake—both these events shook up to the Japanese community. However, Mr. Leeson bought more futures contracts, betting that the Nikkei would rebound. Ultimately, his efforts were futile because the Nikkei fell further, resulting in obligations that Barings could not meet. Baring ceased to exist and was sold almost valueless.

A.4   The Record Loss: 1996

When a trader engages in criminal activities, there are expected consequences when regulators catch on to his dealings, especially when the numbers clearly look fudged, as in the case of Sumitomo.

Sumitomo

In 1996, the largest financial loss of the decade was reported. Yasuo Hamanaka, chief copper trader for Sumitomo, engaging in unauthorized transactions for over a decade, had lost a staggering $1.8 billion. Mr. Hamanaka's illicit copper trades cost Sumitomo $2.6 billion in losses. He was sentenced to eight years in prison for fraud and forgery.

Once again, the size of trading was simply staggering. It was estimated that Sumitomo's role in copper trading controlled 8 percent of the world's supply of the metal, excluding what was held in the former East bloc nations and China. Hamanaka was known as Mr. Five Percent because he and his team controlled at least that share of the world's copper market.

Hamanaka's double-dealing began to unravel in December, when the U.S. Commodity Futures Trading Commission and Britain's Securities and Investments Board, which oversee commodity markets in New York City and London, respectively, asked Sumitomo to cooperate in an investigation of suspected price manipulation. Sumitomo later started an investigation of its own.

It took only days for traders around the world to determine that something was wrong at Sumitomo. In mid-May many commodities firms sold their copper holdings in anticipation that Sumitomo would do the same. Prices dropped 15% in four days, leaving the international market in an uproar. Faced with chaos, Sumitomo stepped up the pace of its internal investigation.

Long Term Capital Management

On September 21, 1998, Long Term Capital Management, with more than $3 billion in assets, reported a loss of $300 million in July 1998 and an exposure exceeding $1.25 trillion in derivatives and other securities. John Meriwether, a trader from Salomon, founded the fund, which was known for its sophistication in financial technologies. The loss was reported on the heels of the Russian financial crisis. The U.S. Treasury was involved to assure the trust of the world market and engineered a rescue of LTCM that avoided an outright liquidation of the portfolio. In the end, 14 companies decided to contribute to the bailout, committing sums of $100–$300 million each, infusing an additional $3.65 billion of equity into the fund. Investors' stake was reduced to 10 percent. If the fund had been forced to liquidate, it would have had to liquidate $1 trillion worth of assets.[6]

Appendix B.   Lessons Learned from the Historical Financial Losses

Cost of Risk

What are the implications of these financial losses to the management of a firm? What do these incidents tell us about our society? Are these financial losses the dark sides of all the benefits of financial derivatives discussed in this book? In short, what lessons can we learn from these incidents?

To begin, we must first ask: Why should anyone be concerned with these financial losses? What the issues do they raise that we need to challenge? Should we change the way we do things?

Clearly, management is now concerned with rogue traders who ostensibly have the ability to trigger the demise of an ongoing firm, as in the case of Barings. It was a risk the trader took, but some people view these incidents as part of doing business; there is always a risk factor involved. Can firms establish zero tolerance rules for rogue traders without jeopardizing the risk-taking culture of a firm? Even if we have a satisfactory solution to eliminate any possibility of a rogue trader, financial losses can still occur without a rogue trader, as was seen in the example of Daiwa bank—trades were concealed for over ten years, principally through fraud.

Prime Minister Ryutaro Hashimoto made the distinction in this statement: "There is always the risk of sustaining losses in business. But it becomes a problem when these losses are the result of violating rules." He suggested that the role of government should be confined to legal issues. The role of the government was to ensure securities laws were not violated. Should the society accept these financial losses as part of the process of "survival of the fittest" in the world of business? Should legislation be used to avoid these incidents?

To be sure, these financial losses are undesirable for the firms involved, but also to the society as a whole. There are significant public deadweight costs involved with each incident, as with Kidder Peabody, where legal costs did a significant amount of damage to the firm.

Financial costs aren't the only damages incurred; there are social costs. The loss of public trust is a concern, as demonstrated by Orange County and school systems and municipalities that have suffered significant financial losses. Another social cost is the disruption of the smooth functioning of the capital market. This was demonstrated by the Long Term Capital Management's concern for the orderly functioning of financial markets, where the Federal Reserve Bank was involved to resolve a private sector matter.

In an even broader context, the Japanese government's top spokesman, Chief Cabinet Secretary Seiroku Kajiyama, in 1996 suggested that these financial losses had more profound implications for the society. He argued that the ethical problems go much deeper than breaking a few regulations. "This shows that the moral standards of companies and all Japanese have declined," he said. "I'm very concerned about this numbed attitude people have toward money."

From these experiences, it is important to recognize that large financial losses have broad implications for management, the stakeholders of the firm, the investing public, and the public at large. As long as there are incentives for an individual to accumulate large financial positions, to the point where that is considered the foundation of the risk and return trade-off, large financial losses will occur. When these debacles happen at regular intervals, there will be an impact on the social fabric. It's no wonder that in recent years, not only have firms stepped up their efforts to control financial risks, but governments, industry groups, and regulatory agencies have increased their efforts to identify the issues of risk management and find solutions to the problems. The preliminary results of this effort are called risk management. Thus far, this book has described risks and returns in finance primarily on the basis of how securities are priced and how the valuation leads to financial management. Risk management at present focuses on actual solutions to the problems as illustrated by the historical events. We now proceed to describe such solutions.

Approaches to Managing Risks

We should first note that, in general, risk management is part of a business objective. Risks and returns are two sides of the same coin. Business profits often require taking risks, and not taking risks means not doing business. Managing risk is not eliminating risk. To develop risk management strategies, perhaps we should begin with the question "What went wrong?" and apply the question to these financial losses.

During financial losses in the 1990s, derivatives were considered taboo. For example, after the Orange County default, the use of derivatives was prohibited there. Derivatives in those days were defined broadly. They were not just all the over-the-counter trades in swaps and options; they included all the mortgage-backed securities, as Askin Capital Management, Barings, and Merrill Lynch demonstrated. But we know that derivatives are an integral part of the financial markets. They offer efficient mechanisms to maintain the law of one price, resulting in an efficient and liquid market. Besides, Kidder Peabody and Diawa showed that these financial losses can be the results of trading Treasury bonds, the simplest and the most liquid securities. Eliminating derivatives is neither an adequate solution nor a desirable one.

Some firms called for even more drastic solutions. For example, some called for avoiding all margin trading and leveraged investments. All reported large financial losses are the results of some kind of borrowing, when we include securities that have indirect leverage—forward and futures contracts, options, and many of the securities that we have discussed. But how, then, can we define "unleveraged securities"? If the firm has a high debt position, we have seen that even those stocks are indirectly leveraged! It would be futile to implement such a solution. If we went along with that idea, would that mean we should also eliminate the cash management process? We have seen the importance of being able to borrow and invest in cash management. Reverse repurchase agreements and repurchase agreements are important liquidity management mechanisms. Furthermore, we have seen that many items on the balance sheets have embedded options. To manage these embedded options, a firm does better to use leverage to lower, and not increase, the risk exposure. Leveraging cannot be the source of the problem. It should be seen as a tool used to manage risk—as part of the solution.

Could the culprits be rogue traders? Maybe management should not allow rogue traders to be in a position of risk-taking. However, to identify a person as a rogue trader is challenging. No one will step onto the trading floor and state he is a "rogue trader." Leeson didn't disclose himself as a rogue trader; in fact, he had the confidence of the management for years before he was labeled a rogue trader. There have been many discussions about incentive systems in trading. Traders' bonuses are typically a portion of the profit, and they do not bear the loss. Remember the performance option in chapter 6? Given this embedded option in their employment contract, and given that the option value increases with higher volatility, the traders have every incentive to take risks. In large risk trades, the trader stands to make huge profits if the bet wins, and at worst he will lose his job. Because these risks can highly compensate rogue traders, other incentives and controls need to be established to prevent any trader from becoming a rogue trader. What are these procedures? Will these procedures be helpful? What if the rogue traders are not the only problem?

Could it be the inexperience of professionals that leads to financial losses? If they do not understand the risks involved, this could lead them to make ill-advised decisions. As financial markets and instruments become more complex and when executions of trades involve large transactions at high speed, professionals are not qualified to make rational judgments concerning their organization. At least this was the argument Mr. Citron of Orange County tried to make, and any firm should take that lesson seriously to prevent such loss from occurring as a result of management decisions. However, there are counterexamples of the "unqualified" argument. The cases of Askin Capital Management and LTCM show that the presumed possession of knowledge and technologies is not enough to avoid these unfortunate incidents.

Last, regulators have argued for better financial disclosure to minimize financial losses. They have proposed to change financial disclosures in financial statements in a way that enforces regulations. While financial disclosures will always be refined as the requirements and the nature of businesses keeps changing, changing financial disclosures can be counterproductive if the regulations are ill-conceived. The problem of Metallgesellshaft shows that regulations were part of the problem rather than the solution to the problem. The principles of financial disclosure are sound, but the implementation is difficult. The regulatory issues and the outcomes of regulations can be complex and subtle. As a case in point, we will consider FAS 133 in chapter 16. When firms have to provide fair value of the assets and not the liabilities, their reported value will in essence report more risk if the firm actually conducts appropriate asset and liability management. Or consider FAS 115. When there are such strict rules in the use of derivatives for hedging, firms are forced to take business risks without hedging in their risk management. These are complicated issues of action and reaction between the investing public and the firm's management. In the end, regulators do not manage the companies; the firm's management does. Regulations will be deemed to fall short of solving the problem.

Perhaps there is no one solution to the problems. Or maybe these financial losses represent a broad range of sources of problems that we need to deal with separately. It is clear that all these solutions have significant business and social costs. The costs and benefits have to be balanced. If we consider risk management from the point of view of a firm, then the answer is simpler. Risks and returns are inseparable in business, and our attitude toward risk is important. Risk should be managed as we strive for profits.

Therefore risk management is an integral part of the business process. The following chapters will discuss what it means to integrate risk management into the business process in a systematic fashion.

Notes

1. We will show how to calculate VaR shortly.
2. Since we use the same stock prices as the delta normal method, we have the same variance–covariance matrix, which means that we have the same betas.
3. The example is taken from Gupton, Finger and Bhatia (1997).
4. Even though it is a strong assumption that the transition probabilities follow the standard normal distribution, we make this assumption for simplicity.
5. Rene M. Stulz, "Rethinking Risk Management." In *The New Corporate Finance: Where Theory Meets Practice* edited by Donald Chew, Jr. (New York: McGraw-Hill, 1999).
6. Daniel A. Strachman, *Getting Started in Hedge Funds* (New York: John Wiley, 2000).

References

Barnhill, T. M., and W. F. Maxwell. 2002. Modeling correlated market and credit risk in fixed income portfolio. *Journal of Banking and Finance,* 26 (2-3), 247–374.

Bruce. M. C., and F. J. Fabozzi. 1999. Derivatives and risk management. *Journal of Portfolio Management,* spec. iss., *Derivatives and Risk Management,* 16–27.

Chow, G., and M. Kritzman. 2002. Value at risk portfolio with short positions. *Journal of Portfolio Management,* 28 (3), 73–81.

Christoffersen, P. P, F. X. Diebold, and T. Schuermann. 1998. Horizon problems and extreme events in financial risk management. Federal Reserve Bank of New York, *Economic Policy Review,* 4 (3), 109–118.

Christopher, L. C., R. Mensink, and A. M. P. Neves. 1998. Value at risk for asset managers. *Derivatives Quarterly,* 5 (2), 21–33.

Cummins, J. D., R. D. Phillips, and S. D. Smith. 2001. Derivatives and corporate risk management: Participation and volume decisions in the insurance industry. *Journal of Risk and Insurance,* 68 (1), 51–92.

Dowd, K. 1999a. A value risk approach to risk-return analysis. *Journal of Portfolio Management,* 25 (4), 60–67.

Dowd, K. 1999b. Financial risk management. *Financial Analysts Journal,* 55 (4), 65–71.

Embrecht, P, Claudia Klupperlberg, and Thomas Mikosch. 1997. *Modelling Extremal Events for Insurance and Finance.* Berlin: Springer-Verlag.

Froot, K. A., and J. C. Stein. 1998. Risk management, capital budgeting, and capital structure policy for financial institutions: An integrated approach. *Journal of Financial Economics,* 47 (1), 55–82.

Glasserman, P., and P. Heidelberger. 2000. Variance reduction techniques for estimating value-at-risk with heavy-tailed risk factors. *Management Science,* 46 (10), 604–609.

Gupton, G. M., C. C. Finger, and M. Bhatia, 1997, CreditMetrics™-Technical Document, J. P. Morgan, New York.

Ho, T. S. Y., A. A. Abrahamson, and M. C. Abbott. 1999. Value at risk of a bank's balance sheet. *International Journal of Theoretical and Applied Finance,* 2 (1), 43–58.

Hull, J. and A. White, 1993. One-factor interest-rate models and the valuation of interest-rate derivative securities. *Journal of Financial and Quantitative Analysis.* 28 (2), 235–254.

Hull, J., and A. White. 1998. Value at risk when daily changes in market variables are not normally distributed. *Journal of Derivatives,* 5 (3), 9–19.

Jeremy, B. 2001. Testing density forecasts, with applications to risk management. *Journal of Business and Economic Statistics,* 19 (4), 465–474.

Jorion, P. 2001. *Value at Risk*, 2nd ed. New York: McGraw-Hill.

Kroll, Y., and G. Kaplanski. 2001. VaR analytics-portfolio structure, key rate convexities, and var betas. *Journal of Portfolio Management*, 27 (3), 116–118.

Kupiec, P. H. 1998. Stress testing in a value at risk framework. *Journal of Derivatives*, 6 (1), 7–24.

Kupiec, P. H. 1999. Risk capital and VaR. *Journal of Derivatives*, 7 (2), 41–52.

Lina, E. J, W. Perraudin, and P. Sellin. 1999. Value at risk for derivatives. *Journal of Derivatives*, 6 (3), 7–26.

Longin, F. M, 1996. The asymptotic distribution of extreme stock market return. *Journal of Business*, 69 (3), 383–408.

Longstaff, F. A., and E. S. Schwartz. 1995. A simple approach to valuing risky fixed and floating rate debt. *Journal of Finance*, 50 (3), 789–819.

Lopez, J. A. 1999. Methods for evaluating value-at-risk estimates. *Economic Review—Federal Reserve Bank of San Francisco*, 2, 3-19.

McNeil, Alexander. 1999. Extreme value theory for risk managers. In *Internal Modelling and CADII*, London: Risk Publications, pp. 93–113.

Merton, R. C., 1974. On the pricing of corporate debt: The risk structure of interest rates. *Journal of Finance*, 29 (20), 449–470.

Meyer, D. W. 1995. Using quantitative methods to support credit-risk management. *Commercial Lending Review*, 11 (1), 64–70.

Milevsky, Moshe A., and Michael Posner. 2000. *The Probability of Fortune*. Toronto: Stoddart Publishing.

Modigliani, F., and L. Modigliani. 1997. Risk-adjusted performance. *Journal of Portfolio Management*, 23 (2), 45–54.

Smith, C. W., C. Smithson. 1998. Strategic risk management. In *The New Corporate Finance: Where Theory Meets Practice*, 2nd ed. edited by Donald Chew, Jr., pp. 460–477. Boston: Irwin/McGraw-Hill.

Taylor, J. 2001. Rethinking the credit-loss distribution: The implications for RAROC modeling. *Commercial Lending Review*, 16 (1), 7–12.

Wilson, T. 1997a. Portfolio credit risk 1. *Risk*, 10(9), 111–117.

Wilson, T. 1997b. Portfolio credit risk 2. *Risk*, 10(10), 56–61.

Further Readings

Avellaneda, M., and A. Paras. 1996. Managing the volatility risk of derivative securities: The Lagrangian volatility model. *Applied Mathematical Finance*, 3, 21–53.

Bauer, C. 2000. Value at risk using hyperbolic distributions. *Journal of Economics and Business*, 52 (5), 455–457.

Bennett, W. G., and L. M. Tilman. 1997. Measuring yield curve risk using principal components analysis, value at risk, and key rate durations. *Journal of Portfolio Management*, 23 (4), 72–84.

Brown, K. C., and D. J. Smith. 1993. Default risk and innovations in the design of interest rate swaps. *Financial Management*, 22 (2), 94–105.

Cambell, R., R. Huisman, and K. Koedijk. 2001. Optimal portfolio selection in a value-at-risk framework. *Journal of Banking and Finance*, 25 (9), 1789–1804.

Credit Suisse First Boston International. 1997. *CREDITRISK+, A Credit Risk Management Framework*.

Crouhy, M., D. Galai, and R. Mark. 2000. A comparative analysis of current credit risk models. *Journal of Banking and Finance*, 24 (1), 59–117.

Dong-Hyun, Ahn, J. Boudoukh, M. Richardson, and R. F. Whitelaw. 1999. Optimal risk management using options. *Journal of Finance*, 54 (1), 359–375.

Falkenstein, E. 1997. Value at risk and derivatives risk. *Derivatives Quarterly*, 4 (1), 42–50.

Hull, J. 1989. Assessing credit risk in a financial institution's off-balance sheet commitments. *Journal of Financial and Quantitative Analysis*, 24 (4), 489–502.

Hull, J., and W. Suo. 2001. A methodology for assessing model risk and its application to the implied volatility function model. Working paper, University of Toronto.

Jarrow, R. A., D. Lando, and S. M. Turnbull. 1997. A Markov model for the term structure of credit risk spreads. *Review of Financial Studies*, 10, 481–523.

Kellezi, E., and M. Gilli. 2000. Extreme value theory for tailed-related risk measures. Working paper, Kluwer Academic Publishers.

Lopez, J. A. 1997. Regulatory evaluation of value-at-risk models. Working paper, Federal Reserve Bank of New York.

Madan, D., and H. Dilip. 2000. A two-factor hazard rate model for pricing risky debt and the term structure of credit spreads. *Journal of Financial and Quantitative Analysis*, 35 (1), 43–65.

Morgan Guaranty Trust Company of New York. 1996. *RiskMetrics™—Technical Document.*

Neftci, S. N. 2000. Value at risk calculations, extreme events, and tail estimation. *Journal of Derivatives*, 7 (3), 1–15.

Oldfield, G. S., and A. M. Santomero. 1997. Risk management in financial institutions. *Sloan Management Review*, 39 (1), 33–46.

Rebonato, R., and P. Jackel. 1999. The most general methodology to create a valid correlation matrix for risk management and option pricing purposes. Working paper, Quantitative Research Centre of the NatWest Group.

Rodriguez, G. J. L. 1999. Portfolio optimization with quantile-based risk measures. Working paper, Massachusettes Institute of Technology.

Santomero, A. M. 1995. Commercial bank risk management: An analysis of the process. Working paper, Financial Institutions Center.

Singh, M. K. 1997. Value at risk using principal components analysis. *Journal of Portfolio Management*, 24 (1), 101–112.

16

Financial Institutions: Applications of Financial Models

Banks, insurers and pension funds are important segments in our economy. Conceptually, these financial institutions may be viewed as hedge funds, funded by the liabilities to invest in an asset portfolio in a frictionless market, and the spread between the assets and liabilities generates the revenues. In practice, however, their business objectives and processes have to be formulated, taking the institutional framework into account. For example, the credit rating, performance metrics, STAT/GAAP accounting, and other constraints have to be incorporated into the business model of a financial institution. Therefore, financial modeling of a financial enterprise should incorporate economic valuation models, accounting models, and other models that describe the institutional framework and the business process.

Commercial banks, property and casualty insurance companies, and life insurance companies are examples of financial institutions. Commercial banks sell loans and/or borrow from depositors. They provide the immediacy of borrowing and lending to the markets. Property and casualty companies sell insurance such as workers' compensation, auto insurance, and hurricane and flood insurance, providing financial relief for event risks, as opposed to financial risks or mortality/morbidity risks. Life insurance companies provide mortality/morbidity risk insurance. Financial institutions, in the process of providing financial immediacy in an economy, participate in capital formation and risk transformation.

Financial modeling finds broad applications in financial institutions because of the nature of their business. A significant portion of their balance sheets, assets and liabilities, are financial assets. The financial models discussed in the previous chapters can be used to value and manage the balance sheet items. Further, since their liabilities and some of their assets have scant marketability, the concept of fair value can be used to evaluate them in a consistent fashion with the other parts of the balance sheets. Financial institutions are specially regulated in order to assure their solvency so they can provide the public with confidence to buy their financial products. Financial modeling becomes increasingly important for the regulators to measure risks for solvency reasons. Finally, financial institutions use financial modeling to manage their business processes in transforming the risks of the assets and the liabilities, and the pooling of capital for their investment. In short, financial modeling is fast becoming one of the building blocks of an operational infrastructure of a financial institution.

To underscore the importance of financial modeling to financial institutions, we first consider three current issues confronting management:

1. With the increased use of the mark to market concept, how should financial institutions change their financial disclosures?
2. With the increased awareness of risk management, how should financial institutions manage their assets and liabilities?
3. How should financial institutions define their enterprise risk management and their risk-adjusted performance measures to be consistent with the maximization of the shareholders' value?

To answer these questions, we will describe a step-by-step procedure in building an integrated financial model of the firm. Such a model can provide insights into the questions above. There are four parts in this procedure.

1. We describe a business model of a bank. This model describes the process by which a bank generates profits and the associated risks. It also describes the strategic value of a bank, leading to the valuation of the bank business.
2. We describe fair value financial statements and book value financial statements based on the business model. This section describes the bank's business model in terms of financial statements. The financial statements specify the performance measures of the bank. Both fair value accounting and book value accounting are presented.
3. We specify the corporate model of the bank. Corporate decisions such as dividend policies and capital structure are modeled, and the corporate finance objective function is then specified.
4. Finally, we define the business processes and their performance measures. The operations of the bank are separated into business processes. Financial models are then used to determine the benchmark of each process to measure its performance. In doing so, the risk of the bank is monitored and managed.

This chapter concludes by showing that the appropriate use of financial modeling is also important to regulation. In particular, we give examples of regulations which are inconsistent with the first principles in finance, and show how such regulations can have unintended consequences.

16.1   An Overview of the Financial Sector

In this chapter, we are particularly concerned with a specific group of financial institutions that Merton called "principal financial institutions," as discussed in chapter 11. When a depositor opens an account in a bank, the bank collects the deposit, which is a liability on the bank's balance sheet. The bank must service the depositor with interest and withdrawals. Similarly, when the bank makes a loan, the loan will appear on the balance sheet as an asset, providing the bank's income and principal.

Insurance companies are included in the group of "principal financial institutions." When an insurance company underwrites an insurance policy, reserves are created for any eventual payout for the policyholder. After each transaction, principal financial institutions have to manage the assets or liabilities on their balance sheets. Our discussion does not extend to asset-managing firms, investment banks, clearing corporations, and other financial institutions that do not act as principals in financial intermediation.

Financial institutions differ from corporations in several ways. First, most financial institutions are subject to many sets of regulations. Second, they have a different business model. Their business model is based on managing the balance sheet of financial contracts. As chapter 12 shows, in order to understand the value of a firm, we need to understand the business model. For these reasons, casting financial institutions as corporations and valuing the free cash flow of a financial institution may result in misleading analytical results. The source of possible confusion arises from the discounting of the free cash flows. This is because for the financial institutions, there are two components of the free cash flows: one generated by the new sales and the other generated from the assets and liabilities on the balance sheets. These two cash flows have different risk characteristics and should have different discount rates. We will deal with this problem later in the chapter.

Market Structure of Banks

In the United States, there are two major bank classes: the money center bank and regional banks. Although there are other minor classes, such as thrifts and community banks, our discussion will focus on these two primary classes. Money center banks are major banks, usually based in the financial centers and involved in international lending and foreign currency operations. Regional banks focus on lending and deposit activities in specific areas of the country. According to the Federal Deposit Insurance Corporation (FDIC), there were 8,315 banks in 2000, with Citi Group ($902 billion) and J.P. Morgan Chase Company ($715 billion) being the largest. Within the banking system, there were $3.86 trillion in loans. A significant portion (44%) of these loans were secured or partially secured by real estate.[1]

Market Structure of Insurance Companies

There are two main types of insurance companies: property and casualty companies and life companies. Property and casualty companies sell insurance to policyholders to provide financial relief in the event of an accident, such as workers' compensation, auto insurance, hurricane and flood insurance, and many others. Life companies sell insurance to policyholders to cover their mortality and morbidity risk. *Mortality* is the ratio of deaths to a specific population, and the *morbidity risk* is the frequency and severity of the incidences of disease and sickness of a well-defined group of persons.

The insurance sector is quite concentrated. The ten largest insurance companies have 80 percent of the market share. There are two main types of insurance companies whose corporate entity is defined by its ownership. One group of insurance companies has its stocks traded in the market. These are called *stock companies*, meaning that their stocks are publicly traded. The other group has its policyholders as their shareholders. These are called mutual companies. The *mutual companies* collect premiums from their policyholders, and when the premiums exceed the expenses, the free cash flows are distributed to the policyholders as dividends. Since the policyholders are the shareholders, the stocks are not publicly traded.

Financial Institutions' Regulators

All financial institutions are regulated by several government agencies to ensure that they are making appropriate, fair, and legal transactions in the financial markets. The *Securities and Exchange Commission* (SEC) is the primary regulator for all publicly traded companies. In addition to the SEC, banks are regulated by other agencies because, as financial intermediaries, they provide information services, liquidity services, and transaction cost services. The main regulators are the Federal Deposit Insurance Corporation, the Office of the Controller of the Currency, the Federal Reserve System, and the National Association of Insurance Commissioners.

Federal Deposit Insurance Corporation

Established in 1933, the *Federal Deposit Insurance Corporation* (FDIC) insures the deposits of member banks, both commercial banks under the Bank Insurance Fund and savings and loans under the Saving Association Insurance Fund. The FDIC collects insurance premiums from the member banks, and invests the premiums in the insurance funds. When an insured bank is closed, the FDIC is responsible for receiving and liquidating funds.

Office of the Controller of the Currency

Established in 1863, the *Office of the Controller of the Currency* (OCC) is the oldest regulatory agency. In the United States there is a dual banking system; banks can be nationally chartered or state chartered. The OCC has the responsibility to charter or close national banks. While money center banks are often nationally chartered, some banks may choose to be state chartered.

Federal Reserve System

The Federal Reserve Bank, as the central bank, has direct responsibility over some of the banks and their respective parent companies. All nationally chartered banks are members of the *Federal Reserve System*. When banks need funds and have few lending alternatives left, as members of the system they have access to the borrowing and lending of reserves and to the discount window, which enables banks to borrow at a lower rate.

National Association of Insurance Commissioners

The regulation of the life and property and casualty companies is not centralized on the national level, but is on a state-by-state basis, in all 50 states plus the District of Columbia. Each jurisdiction has a commissioner, who has the primary responsibility of issuing operating licenses. The commissioner must ensure the financial soundness of the insurers. The commissioner also seeks to maintain high professional standards of the insurers in their product offerings and pricing fairness. The commissioners are coordinated under a national organization, the *National Association of Insurance Commissioners*. Its main goal is to develop standardized financial reporting.

Current Market Pressures Confronting Financial Institutions

Banks and insurance companies both have a significant market concentration, although many smaller institutions are also important. They are diverse and nonhomogeneous. They cater to local communities or regional needs. They are also regulated regionally by a diverse group of regulators. All this implies that while smaller institutions should be considered as a group, setting standards for them has become difficult. However, as a sector, they are important because there is a vast amount of assets under their management, affecting financial services and pensions in the economy. Therefore their efficient functioning in the economy should be a major concern in our capital markets.

In recent years, financial institutions globally have been undergoing dynamic changes under different market pressures. Risk management and accounting standards are being established worldwide. International committees in both insurance and banking are evaluating standards to measure the risks of financial institutions in their operations. International committees are also requiring minimum capital for conducting certain businesses or operating financial institutions. Furthermore, accounting rules are being debated concerning businesses' financial disclosures, requiring different approaches and procedures to report financial investments and liabilities holdings.

In particular, the International Accounting Standards Board (IASB) is taking the lead in a global effort to develop a unified set of accounting standards. To accomplish this goal, IASB seeks to bring all the national accounting standards to one approach. The underlying principle of these standards is fair valuation of financial assets and liabilities. We have discussed one approach to fair value of liabilities in chapter 11. The IASB approach will have broad implications for financial institutions globally. Indeed, the European Commission has mandated that all public companies in the European Union must report using IASB standards by 2005. Private companies will have to comply at a later date. The financial sectors are actively engaged in determining the appropriate rules for their businesses.

At the same time, financial institutions are actively seeking to provide integrated financial services. Both banks and insurance companies are expanding into asset management. These new businesses further challenge financial institutions to design new business models to accommodate their changing businesses, including new product offerings and new fee-based businesses, such as ATM processing for banks and new retirement funds for insurance companies.

The financial markets and product innovations also greatly affect financial institutions. The most important aspects for financial institutions are product features that they provide to their customers. These products have many contingencies that lead to selling embedded options. The financial institutions are challenged to appropriately value and manage these options. The purpose of this chapter is to show that a better understanding of the concepts and implementations of financial models is important to deal with these issues effectively.

16.2   Organization and the Business Model of a Financial Institution

A financial institution has five primary business units: asset management, liability management, headquarters, sales distribution, and fee-based business units. These units have specific roles in the organization. Depending on the financial institution, they may have different designations. Banks and insurance companies, while similar as principal financial institutions, have many differences. Many of the differences arise because they are under different regulators.

Asset Management

For a commercial bank, the asset management unit is often thought of as "wholesale banking" because its clients are mainly institutions rather than individuals. Wholesale banking provides loans to clients. In practice, the wholesale bank can be an organization itself—a bank—with deposit funding. But primarily it lends to generate profits, and it funds its lending by significantly using the capital market to borrow funds from other institutions instead of using retail banking channels to gain access to deposits.

For an insurance company, the asset management unit is called portfolio management. This unit manages the assets whose funding comes from the premiums. Historically, portfolio management is a way to manage the premiums collected. The net investment income is the income generated by the portfolio management net of all asset management costs. More recently, portfolio management has become more of a business unit responsible for generating profits for the insurers. The business model of insurance companies is not confined to selling profitable insurance policies to customers and building an effective sales distribution system. Some insurance companies view selling insurance as a means to gain access to funding for their investments, implying that investment incomes are expected to generate a large part of their profits.

Liability Management

For commercial banks, the liability unit is called retail banking. Retail banking is responsible for the deposit accounts, which are used to fund the investments. Managing liability requires understanding the clients' needs and providing them with profitable services. Commercial banks must continually develop new products and services to encourage the customers to bank with them. At the same time, they must manage the costs of serving the clients' needs.

For insurance companies, liability management units are called the "business units." They are responsible for product designs and sales of the products. Product designs include deciding on the appropriate premium and evaluating the risks on the policies. They also must do extensive marketing to understand the customers' needs and competitive pressures. A large part of their responsibilities is managing the sales force, which must be able to explain their products to the customers and to provide services to the policyholders.

Headquarters

For the purpose of our discussion, the headquarters provides the strategic and tactical management of the asset and liability units. The headquarters is the central management of the corporation. For banks, the treasury department provides the transfer pricing between the assets and liabilities units. It lends to asset units so that they can buy loans. The treasury borrows from retail banks, making use of their deposits. It may be viewed as providing the function of a bank to its profit centers, the wholesale and retail banking units. The transfer pricing is usually benchmarked off the market rates. Any shortfall or surplus of funds between the inflows of deposits and outflows of loans will result in the treasury department using the capital market to fill the gap.

The *asset–liability management committee* (ALCO) determines the strategic positioning of the asset and liability portfolios. It is responsible for evaluating the credit exposures in the loan, as well as the duration or key rate duration mismatch of the assets and liabilities to generate profits from the yield curve movements.

Another strategic financial management feature of the financial institutions is debt financing, which differs from the liabilities of retail banking. Debt financing is based on capital market prices. The debts are for managing the capital structure and not for building a market share in funding.

For insurance companies, the organization of the headquarters is slightly different because of their regulations. The business units have to be specified according to their products. The excess assets that are not required to support the liability are reported as surplus. Assets are then assigned to the lines of business. In fact, the investment and the products can be intricately tied together. For example, we have seen in chapter 11 that the SPDA pays a crediting rate that is tied to the yield of the asset portfolio. The portfolio yield is defined as the average book value yields of the assets. In such cases, it is somewhat difficult to measure the profitability of each part of the balance sheet. Historically, asset and liability managements are separate. The liability side is encouraged to sell profitable products, while the asset management provides the highest returns or income to the financial institutions. Managing assets and liabilities together, using transfer pricing, represents a change in the business process. More recently, some insurers have wanted to encourage cooperation of the asset and liability managements in order to provide profitable products for clients. They are concerned that the use of the transfer pricing curve, as in banks, may lead to competitive behavior between the asset management and the liability management.

For the insurers, there is much less emphasis on using derivatives in their funding operations between assets and liabilities, whereas banks use the swap markets to fund investments or generate returns on the deposits. Furthermore, the regulation is such that the treasury is reluctant to participate in the derivative markets in order to hedge or fund any mismatch of inflows and outflows of funds. Therefore, the role of the treasury is relatively insignificant compared to its role with banks. Asset and liability management should be an important part of the operation for a life insurer. Typically, the corporate actuarial department gathers all the information from all the business units to determine the risk exposure of combining assets and liabilities.

Sales Distribution

The branches of banks are responsible to collect deposits and provide funding for the banks' investments. Some banks depend on an extensive network of branches to build a deposit base. They may accomplish that objective by acquiring other banks and building more branches. Some banks build their deposit base by providing services to special markets, focusing on certain communities or certain groups of clients who have special needs. For example, retirees have special needs with investment of their pensions, and foreign workers may need remittance services and other foreign bank relationships. Some customer relationships require more direct meetings, while corporate accounts may require services in liquidity.

For insurance companies, the distribution of personal and commercial policies can be accomplished by using a *direct selling system* (captive) or *agency system* (broker). In direct selling, the insurers' policies are sold by employees. The insurers contact the policyholders to generate new sales or maintain clients. In the agency system, outside agents may sell the products of one insurer exclusively or may sell a number of insurers' products as independent agents.

The trade-off of these two approaches is between cost and control. Building a sales force and maintaining the staff in direct selling requires significant capital investments. However, the insurer has control over their conduct and objectives in their sales efforts. Furthermore, the sales network adds value to the firm. In the agency system, the acquisition cost becomes a variable cost, adding less strain to the insurer's cost structure. But the insurer cannot vertically integrate the product sales with the client relationships.

Fee-Based Business Units

Banks may have asset management as a separate business unit offering ease of transfer of funds from deposit accounts to managed funds, and vice versa. Insurance companies may have asset management as a separate business unit, and they also have part of their balance sheet called the separate account. A general account consists of the assets held by an insurance company that support the liabilities. Separate accounts have assets that belong to the policyholders. The insurance company, as a fee-based business, is managing the policyholders' assets on their behalf. They are assets for some of the annuities and investment where the policyholders bear the investment risks and the insurance company collects fees for managing the assets and providing services as an insurance company. Thus, they are not considered a principal financial institution because they are not acting as financial intermediaries.

16.3   Financial Disclosures on Valuation

Regulators and managers of financial institutions are currently debating the appropriate accounting system and financial disclosures that the financial industry should adopt. The debate centers on two approaches: GAAP accounting and fair value accounting. The crux of the debate focuses on the applicability and feasibility of the use of financial models for accounting purposes. A discussion of this debate can provide us the insights into the usefulness and the limitations of financial models in corporate financial management.

GAAP Accounting

Generally accepted accounting principles (GAAP), the financial reporting standard used by the investment community, seeks to appropriately represent financial situations of the firm. We will use GAAP accounting as the example of the book value accounting in this discussion. Publicly traded insurers (stock companies) use GAAP for their audited financial statements. Mutual companies (insurance companies that are not publicly traded) do not need to provide GAAP financial reporting. One distinctive feature of GAAP is its attempts to match income and expenses. Costs can be amortized over the assumed life of a policy. Another example is the amortization of capital expenditure. GAAP accounting allows for amortization of capital expenditure so that the expenses are matched with the income. In doing so, we can avoid the strain on the reported income when the investment is made.

Perhaps the most significant challenge to book value accounting is the prevalent use of embedded options in the balance sheet. As we have discussed, callable bonds such as corporate bonds with call provisions or mortgage-backed securities with prepayment options have embedded options. These embedded options lower the bond price and increase the bond yield, or the coupon rate. But in book value accounting, the income is based on the coupon received and the bond value is based on the principal amount. This approach is not well suited to treat option-embedded assets in financial reporting.

Similarly, for the liabilities, in book value accounting financial institutions can offer the lenders, depositors, or policyholders contingencies advantageous to them. We have seen in chapter 11 that financial institutions sell a broad range of options to their customers. This way, they can lower their borrowing costs in terms of the interest or other annual payments. In book accounting, the cost of the embedded options is usually not fully accounted for. Financial institutions mostly have only to report the actual payments to their customers. The costs are reported on a retroactive basis and not on a prospective basis.

Therefore, buying callable bonds in the asset portfolio and selling options to customers in the liability portfolio can increase the reported interest margin. This is because the callability of bond increases the book yield of the investment. At the same time, selling options to policyholders lowers the book yield of the funding. This focus on the short-term reported income by corporate managers will lead to holding embedded options in both assets and liabilities in their balance sheets. These financial institutions will have unmanaged option risks that may lead to depleting shareholders' value in the future. In this case, inadequate financial reporting leads to a violation of the corporate goal of enhancing shareholders' value.

Regulating such option risk exposure on the balance sheet is a complicated subject, which we will discuss later. One approach is the use of fair value accounting.

Fair Valuation of Assets and Liabilities

Standards are being sought to determine the fair value of liabilities for accounting purposes. Fair value for accounting purposes is generally defined as the "transaction price" at which the product can be bought and sold. This definition is, of course, somewhat unsatisfactory because the liabilities are defined to be contracts that have no market and cannot be transacted. Not surprisingly, the fair value accounting system is a matter of much debate. In fact, there are two debates. The first debate concerns the desirability of using fair valuation for accounting purposes. At present there is a separation of trading and nontrading activities in financial reporting, but under fair value accounting, there is only one standard. Can fair value accounting be possible? The second debate is how to define "fair value," dealing with the complex implementation issues. Can fair value accounting be implementable?

In the first debate, the camp favoring book value accounting argues that accounting numbers should be reconcilable, objective, and repeatable. For this reason, book value can be more appropriate than the fair value accounting, which depends on financial modeling, an approach they believe may not satisfy these criteria. They also argue that fair value accounting is not appropriate for banks to use in managing risks. Fair values, as we have seen, often depend on complex financial models which rely on many assumptions. Further, these models are more difficult to verify independently than the book accounting approach. For these reasons, financial institutions might misstate their balance sheet value in the financial reports.

Those supporting book value further suggest that fair value accounting should not be used for business transactions unless the banks are subject to performance measures based on fair values. However, most performance measures used by investors today are based on book value. For example, fair value accounting cannot provide relevant information because the profitability of the loans is determined by the interest income and not by the mark to market value of the loans. In some cases, book value supporters argue, fair value information is unreliable or counterintuitive—for example, when a firm's credit rating falls because there is adverse information on its future earnings and its debt fair value is lowered. In this case, the firm's equity, which is the asset value net of the liability value, may in fact increase. The increase of equity value indeed may provide a misleading signal to the market, since the reported higher equity value is a result of adverse information on the firm.

The fair value information also lacks objectivity when assumptions are made. Without an active market, valuations will vary across a range of assumptions underlying the estimates, which does not result in comparability. Therefore, fair valuation lacks comparability of the same balance sheet item across different firms for lack of standard model assumptions. Furthermore, it lacks comparability between financial institutions and non-financial companies because the latter do not have the mark to market concepts for their businesses.

Marking to market will lead to volatility of the equity and discourage the banks from long-term lending. It is argued that banks use the net interest income measure, to develop the relationships with the borrowers. Stable net interest income as measured by GAAP enables them to lend at a fixed interest rate over a longer term.

Supporters of book value accounting argue that the goals of accounting are relevance, reliability, understandability, and comparability—and fair value accounting fails them all. On the other hand, GAAP financial reporting also has its role, as its numbers are more readily verifiable and more amenable to standardization. For these reasons, taxes can be based on these financial statements.

The camp for fair value disclosure argues that book value cannot disclose the true value of the liabilities. When the interest rate level changes, the present value is affected. However, such market reality is not captured by the book value approach. Proponents of fair value accounting standards suggest that the fair value accounting is forward-looking and, therefore, more relevant to the share prices and returns, useful for loans, securities, and long-term debts. We have seen that VaR is determined from fair values; therefore fair value accounting can forecast violations of the bank regulatory capital requirements. Without fair value accounting, as we will see in hedge accounting, in section 8 of this chapter, we have to provide both fair value and book value for a hedging position, misrepresenting the risks on the hedge. Fair value accounting provides a more transparent reporting of the value on the balance sheet than does book value accounting. If apparent volatility of the market equity value is a concern to the investors, then the source of the problem lies in the inadequacy of the financial disclosure. Given appropriate financial disclosure, investors can be informed about the risk of the firm's business. Enabling investors to understand the firm's business should be more relevant and more important than concerns about unintentionally "misleading" the public with correct and appropriate information. Also, fair value accounting can capture the embedded option values on the balance sheet more accurately. As we have seen, the book accounting approach cannot determine the option value easily.

For the second debate, the *International Accounting Standards Commission* (IASC) has proposed that the results of all financial contracts be reported under fair value accounting by all financial institutions. The contingent claim valuation approach is being proposed for its ability to capture the relevant attributes and determine values, which may be used for internal management. Both realized and unrealized gains or losses will be recognized in the income statement. The items must appear on the balance sheet when there are rights or obligations associated with the item. Fair value accounting can provide more transparency.

There are different approaches to defining the discount rate or the appropriate spread off a standardized transfer pricing curve. For a zero spread, the rate is discounted using the Treasury spot curve or swap curve. Insurance companies use an insurance discount curve that is relevant for their firm; for example, an AA insurance company uses an AA insurance company curve. The precise valuation methodology is still being formulated.

The debate underscores the advantages and disadvantages of both approaches. While the accounting standard will evolve over time, the recognition of the importance of fair value accounting for the industry has been established. This debate shows that the management of a financial institution should consider the fair value approach—or financial modeling—as an important tool for managing their business processes.

16.4 Risk Management

Risk management is important to banks, as we discussed in chapter 15. Measures such as value at risk (VaR) and earnings at risk (EaR) are valuable tools in a risk management system, particularly for the trading book, where there is an active market and the derivatives tend to have a short time to termination. However, banks have investments with a longer-term horizon on their structural balance sheet. Is it possible to extend these tools for their situations? Is there such a thing as daily VaR that can be calculated? How should banks manage the risks in their assets and liabilities?

Banks tend to use income simulation as a methodology. They simulate the incomes of the assets and liabilities combined in a large range of scenarios over the next five years. The simulations are designed to evaluate the effectiveness of any strategies that will provide the highest returns to the bank while protecting against the downside risks. The asset and liability mix is then evaluated to obtain the optimal income distribution. This approach is similar to the dynamic financial analysis (DFA) that we discussed in chapter 14. (See appendix A for a review of what commercial banks have done in risk management in recent years.)

Insurance companies' practices in managing the risks of the assets and liabilities on their balance sheets are similar to those of banks. Insurance products are very illiquid. There is no market for reselling the products (except when selling blocks of businesses). To manage the risk of their illiquid portfolios, they are regulated to perform cash flow testing. It is done as follows. The liabilities of a business unit (a portfolio of an in-force business) along with its assigned assets are analyzed according to the regulatory requirement. The cash flows of the block of business are projected into the future under different interest rate scenarios. At the end of the horizon of their simulations, the portfolios are required to show positive assets when all the liabilities are paid down. This analysis assumes appropriate investment returns and investment strategies. The assets have to be classified as "admissible" to support the obligations of the liabilities, since some assets are not qualified to support the liabilities. If there are many scenarios in which the cash flow testing fails—where the remaining value is negative at the terminal date—the firm either has to put in more reserve or change its *asset liability management* (ALM) strategies. Again, the approach is similar to DFA, except that the projection is conducted over a long time horizon, at the time when nearly all the assets and liabilities will run off.

Another difference is that the cash flow testing does not take new sales into account. Historically, these asset and liability management methods were developed to ensure that the insurer always has enough assets to support its liabilities. For this reason, it suffices to show that the cash flows of the (admissible) assets and liabilities can ensure the solvency of each business block on a runoff basis. As a result, we can ignore future sales, long-term debt financing (it is junior in liability priority), other assets in the surplus (we want to be more conservative in our estimates), and taxes, which are more relevant when the block of business is profitable and less relevant for solvency tests.

Yet, using a direct extension of asset liability management methods for solvency to maximize shareholders' value can be erroneous. For example, solvency tests are used to protect the liability. But those tests do not reflect the default risk of the firm. However, if asset and liability management seeks to ensure solvency, while also seeking to maximize shareholders' value, then we must take an extended approach. The discussion of this extended approach of using a business model was discussed in chapter 14, and this discussion showed that financial modeling is important to risk management of the structural balance sheet of a financial institution.

16.5   Capital Allocation and Risk-Adjusted Performance Measures

The balance sheet of a financial institution may be viewed as an arbitrage position. The financial institution funds its position to buy the assets. This risk of this margin position has to be supported by capital. The Basel Committee on Banking Supervision[2] set up a framework to measure the risk capital and the requirement for capital for banks under their jurisdiction. The measure is a percentage of the amount, depending on the type of asset. The 1988 accord concerned the derivatives and credit risks on assets. It specifies the risk weight for each item. These risk weights determine the portion of the assets at risk. The total amount of capital at risk then determines the capital required to remain creditworthy. The Committee believes the core capital (basic equity) should consist of equity capital and disclosed reserves, which are emphasized as the key element of capital. Capital is defined to have two tiers. The first tier, at least 50% of a bank's capital base, consists of equity capital and published reserves from posttax retained earnings. The remaining elements of capital (e.g., preferred stocks) are included in the second tier that is up to an amount that is equal to the core capital. In 1993 the committee dealt with interest rate risks and equity risks. (See appendix B for a more detailed description of the requirements.)

These capital requirements determine the capital that the bank must hold. The bank, in turn, assigns the risk capital to its business units. Thus the risk capital becomes a measure that may be comparable to any investment, where there is an initial investment to calculate the returns. This is the motivation for *risk-adjusted performance measures* (RAPM), which are typified by considering the income relative to the required capital. For example, it the required capital is measured by VaR, then the RAPM is given by

$$RAPM = \frac{revenues - costs - expected\ losses}{VaR}$$

There are alternative risk-adjusted performance measures, depending on the choice of the required capital and the income. For example, the required capital may depend on the level of capital required by the credit rating agency, and not just on the regulatory requirements or on the firm's internal risk control. Some firms may use the maximum requirement of all the agencies.

Earnings at risk (EaR) is the potential loss in earnings over a time horizon at a certain probability level. The definition is similar to that of VaR, but EaR focuses on the earnings and not the value of the position. The required capital may be based on the EaR, which can be calculated on an undiversified, diversified, or marginal basis. EaR at the marginal basis of a business unit can also be calculated as the EaR contributed to the firm by the business units. The EaR of the undiversified business unit is the measurement of the EaR of the business unit as a stand-alone entity, ignoring the diversification effect on the risk of the earnings when all the business units' earnings are aggregated. The diversified EaR is the measurement of the entire firm's earnings in aggregate.

The undiversified business EaR can be used for performance measurements. For example, a *risk-adjusted return on capital* (RAROC) is defined as

$$RAROC = \frac{return}{(total\ available\ equity \times \frac{EaR\ of\ business}{EaR\ of\ the\ bank})}$$

specifying the required capital to be the proportion of the EaR of the business to that of the bank, multiplied by the total equity.

Alternatively, we can adjust the return in the performance measure. For example, *return on risk-adjusted capital* (RORAC) is defined as

$$RORAC = \frac{return - required\ capital \times r_f}{EaR}$$

In this case, the return is adjusted by the income of the required capital, where r_f is the time value of money of the required capital. RORAC is the excess return to the risk-free return per unit EaR risk.

There is a lack of standardization for the risk-adjusted performance measure because there is no consistent measure of performance across the firms and there are conflicting purposes of the measure. The stated purposes of determining a risk-adjusted performance measure are listed below:

1. To set risk limits to each of the business units
2. To distribute the cost of holding the risk capital on the firm level to each business unit
3. To develop a consistent framework to measure the returns of the business units on the risk-adjusted basis
4. To ensure that the business units are enhancing shareholders' value, using market cost of capital for their risks.

Thus far, there is no measure that seems to be able to satisfy all these needs. The practice of assigning the cost of holding capital to each business unit is more like cost allocation, which is determining how to share the cost. For this reason, the usual problem of cost allocation arises in capital allocation. In particular, when the business unit risks are less than perfectly correlated, some of the risks are diversified. Therefore the aggregated risk for the bank is less than the sum of the business unit risks.

Consider an extreme example where a bank has many business units that require capital, for example, securities trading units. These business units have uncertain profits that are uncorrelated. Then, while the risk of each business unit may be significant, the aggregated risk to the bank may be negligible because of diversification. In this case, how should the bank assign capital to each business unit to control the risks?

One solution is that the bank can assign the costs by the marginal contribution of risks to the bank. This approach would encourage business units to take on projects that minimize the contribution of risk to the bank. However, this capital budgeting decision process is not necessarily consistent with enhancing shareholders' value. For example, we have seen from the portfolio theory that the relevant risks to the investor should be beta (β). Projects that lower the risk as measured by VaR may not be consistent with maximization of a bank's value.

Another approach is to view the required capital as the "investment" in the project, and the projected free cash flows as the returns. Each business unit is viewed as a separate investment. In this case, we can apply the Capital Asset Pricing model to determine the performance of the business unit. In particular, we require the rate of return of the business unit to be higher than the risk-free rate plus the business beta times the market premium. This approach still leaves the "required capital" to be defined.

Risk-adjusted performance measures may be applicable to specific purposes or certain businesses and situations. But in general they cannot provide an appropriate measure of profitability of business units. There are pitfalls to this measure as described above. Performance measures should be designed to measure how each business unit enhances shareholders' wealth.

Froot and Stein (1998) state that "RAROC, as currently applied, is not derived from first principles to address the shareholders' value maximization." For performance measures to be derived from the first principles, we need to make assumptions of the firm's objectives. If these measures are not derived from the first principles, then it is not clear what these performance measures will achieve for the firm and how the performance measure aligns the goals of the business units. As we have seen in previous chapters, in order to maximize the shareholders' value, we first need to identify a corporate model, which can then provide a consistent set of performance measures.

16.6   Financial Modeling of a Financial Institution

In the previous sections, we have shown that financial models should be used for determining values on the balance sheet, for risk management, and for performance measures. However, we cannot solve each problem in isolation from the others. We need a coherent framework, which we will call "the financial modeling of a financial institution." We will begin describing this framework by first specifying the business model. For clarity of the exposition, we will use a bank as an example, though the discussion is equally applicable to other financial institutions.

Step 1. Defining the Business Model of a Bank

In chapter 12, we suggest that the business model may differ for each market sector, and the financial institution sector requires its own business model. The approach we take is similar to that described in chapter 12 by first determining a primitive firm valuation model and then determining a bank as a contingent claim on the primitive firm. While we will present only a basic model for a commercial bank, the model is applicable to other financial services companies.

In essence, the business model specifies the sources of profits to the claimants of the firm. For the bank, the main source of income is the interest margin between the deposit rate and the investment rate. The source of risk is the interest rate risk, which may induce the depositor to withdraw or deposit savings. The interest rate risk also affects the deposit rate-setting strategy, which affects the profitability of the firm. There are operating costs in the banking business. We incorporate both fixed costs and variable costs.

Finally, the bank has its strategic value. It has the growth option in buying deposit accounts, expanding its client base. Under different interest rate regimes, the bank may decide to increase its base. The investment will depend on the prevailing state of the world. These investment decisions will be made to maximize the value of the firm.

We will make several assumptions about the commercial bank and the capital market.

Asset valuation

For a clear explanation, we assume that the asset portfolio consists only of marketable securities, although the approach does allow loans and other nontradable assets to be included. All assets are tradable short-term instruments, approximated by "cash" such that its returns are the risk-free rate and the market prices are its cash value. This is a simplifying assumption enabling us to focus our discussion on the corporate measures without being distracted by complicated issues of valuing nonmarketable securities.

Liability valuation

We assume that the bank sells money market deposit accounts. There are no other types of liabilities, such as savings deposits or corporate short-term and long-term debts. For transfer-pricing purposes, the time deposits are discounted by the government bond rates to determine the internal economic value of the liability payments. The deposits are then invested in cash, generating risk-free returns.

Strategic value

The bank has the real option of acquiring a deposit base. We can think of the bank being able to buy other banks, enlarge the branch network, or take other actions. In these cases, they make a capital investment outlay of (I) and the deposit base increases by $\Delta D(I)$, where $\Delta D(I)$ is an increasing function of I. For simplicity, we may assume that the deposit base increases with the investment outlay in direct proportion; that is:

$$\Delta D(I) = \alpha I$$

for some positive constant α

Capital structure of the bank

We are concerned with the impact of the bank's capital structure on the risk of its capitalization. For this purpose, we assume that the bank has one long-term debt of face value *principal* with coupon rate r_{coupon}. The bond matures at the time horizon T. This assumption is similar to the business model presented in chapter 13.

Goals of the bank

The bank seeks to maximize its shareholders' value in its strategic investments in acquiring the deposit base, subject to the regulations on risk-based capital.

Business risk

For simplicity, we consider interest rate risks as the only business risk of the bank. The interest rate uncertainties affect the bank's strategies in setting the interest rate margin, and hence its profitability. The profitability in turn affects the strategic value of the bank, in its strategic investments in acquiring a deposit base. The strategy then determines the firm value. This assumption of using interest rate risk as the only source of business risk is clearly an oversimplification. We noted earlier that the model can be extended to multiple sources of risks (see chapter 7), and therefore more business risk sources can be incorporated. The interest rate risk is modeled by a one-factor, arbitrage-free interest rate model. Therefore, when we are given an observed yield curve, the arbitrage-free interest rate model determines the one-year rate at each node point of a binomial lattice of interest rates.

The model of a bank can be based on the O'Brien (2000) valuation model for the negotiable order of withdrawal account and money market deposit account, described in chapter 11.

Since the only risk source for this simple model of a bank is the interest rate risk, we can assume a one-factor model specified in a binomial lattice. The short-term rate is denoted by $R(n, i)$, for time n and state i, at each node of the lattice.

In order to value these nonmaturing accounts, we need to take two interrelated issues into consideration. They are the deposit rate and the depositors' desired balances. The deposit rates do not move in tandem with the market rates. The model is presented below:

$$R^D(n+1, i) = a\left(b \cdot R(n+1, i) - c - R^D(n, i)\right) \qquad (16.1)$$

$R^D(n, i)$ is the deposit rate determined by the bank. It is based on the competitors' rate, which in turn is determined by the market interest rate $R(n, i)$. The parameters a, b, and c are estimated from the historical data.

Let the level of deposits, also called the deposit base, be $D(n, i)$, and then we assume that

$$\log(D(n+1, i)) = a_1 + a_2\left(R(n, i) - R^D(n, i)\right) + a_3 \log(D(n, i)) \qquad (16.2)$$

$D(n, i)$ depends on the spread between the market rate and the deposit rate, and it is also related to the previous period. At the end of the period and the subsequent periods, the total payments at $t(COF_t)$ are of the form

$$COF(n+1, i) = \left(R^D(n, i) + c(n)\right)D(n, i) - (1 - f)\left(D(n+1, i) - D(n, i)\right) \qquad (16.3)$$

where $c(n)$ is the annual maintenance costs and f is the required reserve rate. The cash outflows of holding a deposit base are the interest costs and the maintenance cost (the first term) net of the deposit inflows after putting up the required reserve.

The firm's revenue is the risk-free returns on the assets. The assets are modeled as cash, $Cash_t$; and therefore revenue, which is the cash inflow denoted by $CIF(n,i)$ at time n and state i, is

$$CIF(n, i) = Cash(n, i) \cdot R(n, i) \tag{16.4}$$

The net cash flow NCF at each node (n, i), is given by

$$NCF = CIF - COF$$

The Primitive Firm V^p   The primitive firm V^p is the present value of the stochastic net income discounted at the stochastic risk-free rate. Implicit in the model is that the bank is considered a pure interest rate contingent claim. The bank is valued such that investors have an option adjusted spread of the returns on the equity investment. The introduction of an option adjusted spread is equivalent to using a cost of capital of a firm under interest rate uncertainties. We now see that the bank is similar to a bond that provides cash flows with embedded options. The development of the model of a bank parallels that of the firm described in chapters 12–14.

The Firm V   Extending the O'Brien model, we now incorporate the bank liability modeling to the business model. V represents the bank with a fixed operating cost (e.g., the expenses of the headquarters).

The fixed cost is independent of the deposit size of the bank and the interest rate level. As an income statement item, fixed cost is an important aspect of the bank, since other items are mainly interest income or interest expenses. The fixed cost captures the cost of a bank's operation.

The larger the distribution network of a bank with many branches operating efficiently, the less important the fixed cost component relative to the bank's revenue.

As in the model of the retail store chain, the presence of fixed costs may result in default on the vendors and suppliers. The employees' salaries and benefits can be a significant part of the drain in the firm's cash position. For these reasons, it is important to model the contribution of the fixed costs of a bank to provide a better understanding of the default risks and valuation of the claims on the firm value.

We assume that the bank grows by acquiring a deposit base with investment outlay of $I(n, i)$ where it depends on the time and the state of the world, defined by the interest rate level. This increase in the deposit base may be the result of acquiring other banks or building a customer base by opening bank branches or acquiring new accounts through product innovations. Of course, investment decisions should depend on many factors other than the interest rate level. The purpose of this exposition is to develop a basic model of a bank to illustrate the use of financial models. We therefore seek to describe a parsimonious model that captures the essential features of a bank. Incorporating other risk sources will be left for future research.

We further assume that the investment outlay $I(n, i)$ is directly related to the deposit base. The larger the deposit base, the more expensive the acquisition. Let $D(n, i)$ denote the deposit base and $\Delta D(n, i)$ the increase in the deposit base as a result of the investment. Then we have

$$\Delta D(n, i) = \alpha I(n, i)$$

where α is a constant such that $0 < \alpha$.

The interest rate level affects the deposit base as described by equation (16.2). We now further assume that the change in the deposit base can also be a result of new acquisitions. Therefore, we have the following equation, specifying the additional change in the deposit base over time and state.

$$D(n + 1, i) = D(n, i) + \Delta D(n, i)$$

Assuming that there is no dividend payout, the change of the cash position $Cash(n, i)$ is the budget constraint:

$$Cash(n + 1, i) = Cash(n, i) + NCF(n, i) - I(n, i) - FC - r_{coupon} \cdot principal$$

where the investment $I(n, i)$ is dependent on the state and time of the world, and will be solved to maximize the bank's value based on the business model of the bank; FC is the fixed costs; and the coupon rate on the debt and face value are r_{coupon} and $principal$, respectively. A firm will be in default if the capitalization value, the market value of equity, falls below 0.

As in the example for the firm model, the shareholders have limited liability, protected from the liabilities of the fixed costs and the long-term debt. In essence, the fixed costs are analogous to the fixed coupon payments of a perpetual debt to the primitive firm. Finally, we assume that the bank does not pay taxes (a marginal tax rate of $\tau_c = 0$).

Terminal Condition   We assume that the bank has a strategic planning horizon T, the same as the maturity of the debt. At the end of the horizon, the bank liquidates its cash position, pays the face value of the debt, and distributes the residual cash as dividends to the shareholders. Therefore the bank value at time T, at the end of the planning period, can be determined using the Merton model as explained in chapter 12, where the fixed costs of the bank are viewed as a perpetual bond, and the bank value is viewed as an option on the primitive firm value.

Though the model is simplistic, it provides some insight into the valuation of a bank. It shows that the real option value of the bank depends on the competitiveness of the pricing. If the price is somewhat sticky, in the sense that the deposit rates do not adjust quickly to the changes of the market rate, the real option value may be higher. Referring to equation (16.1), the coefficients a, b, and c determine the profitability of pricing. Indeed, as described in chapter 11, the speed of adjustment of the deposit rate may depend on whether the deposit rate is being raised or lowered. This kind of pricing strategy affects the bank's profitability and ultimately the bank's value, as described by this model. Further, this model can capture the strategic value of the bank. When the interest rate volatility increases, the opportunity for a bank to increase its deposit-based profits increases. Every registered bank with a customer base has this strategic value. This model provides a methodology to identify this growth option value as it is related to the market risk and the business model of the bank.

Step 2. Integrating Book and Fair Value Accounting

Next we relate the business model to the financial statements of the bank. We will present the model using both the fair value approach of the financial statements and the book value financial statements of the general accepted accounting principles.

To date, much of the discussion on fair value of liability focuses on the equity of the banks, the asset fair value net of the liability fair value. To use the fair valuation for the management of the bank, we must also consider its implication on fair value income. To describe the performance of a bank on a fair valuation basis, we must take both balance sheets and income statements into account.

Further, fair value accounting is not independent of book value accounting. On the contrary, the two accounting systems can be used together to provide a more comprehensive description of the performance of the bank. We now proceed to describe such a system.

We first begin with the fair value accounting.

Balance sheet equation

$$S = A - L \tag{16.5}$$

S is the shareholders' market value of equity; A is the asset market value or fair value; and L is the liability economic value or fair value. Within the context of the model, there are two liabilities: the core deposit and the long-term debt. The core deposit is related to the business and the long-term debt is a capital market instrument.

This equation is often discussed in financial literature. S, the market value of equity, is identified as the shareholders' capital. As we discussed in Part 2 of this book, we can develop valuation models for a broad range of assets and liabilities on a balance sheet and an off balance sheet that consists of derivatives. For the bank model, we have described the valuation model for deposit accounts. There is extensive literature on valuation of life insurance liabilities using this option valuation approach. The approach this book proposes has been explained in Reitano (1997), Girard (1996), and Grosen and Jorgensen (2000). In essence, this approach provides a systematic methodology for determining the present value of all the simulated cash flows over a set of scenarios. One aspect of much discussion on the valuation of liabilities is the spread required in the discounting. This model assumes that the bank establishes a transfer pricing methodology. (See Wallace, 1997, for a discussion of transfer pricing.)

Referring to equation (16.5), when the assets suffer losses in default, asset value A decreases, leading to a loss in the equity value. In another scenario, suppose that the asset has longer duration than the liability, where duration is defined as the value sensitivity to the interest rate movement. When the interest rate rises, the asset value will fall faster than the liability value. As a result, the equity value again falls. Banks tend to have longer asset duration than liability duration. The impact of the loss in economic value with the rise of interest rate is immediately captured. By contrast, using the interest margin of book value accounting, the impact of the rise of interest rates on the earnings will not be recognized before the funding rate has to be revised upward.

Income statement equation

$$y = pv + r_A A - r_L L - FC \qquad (16.6)$$

y is income to the bank on a total return basis, taking the capital gain (whether it is realized or unrealized) and the interest income into account. This income is not the realized income on the accounting basis. It is the added value to the firm's market value of equity over the reporting period.

v is the sales volume over the reporting period (a month or a quarter), measured by the economic value, which is the change in deposit level $\Delta D(n, i)$, as explained above.

p is the profit margin of the time deposits, where the profit margin is defined as the expected proceeds over the reporting period net of the economic value of the time deposits divided by the current economic value of the time deposits. The amount received is $(1 + p)v$. Note that the gain on sale is 0 if we use the required option adjusted spread (ROAS) approach in determining the liability value, as described in chapter 11. This is because the ROAS is determined to ensure that there is no gain on sale at the time of sale. All profits are released over time and are captured by the equations described later. Unlike the balance sheet equation (equation (16.5)), where the liability is considered only to be the runoff business, we incorporate the growth of new sales in the income equation.

r_A is the total return of the assets, where the realized and unrealized capital gains and all the cash flows received during the reported period are taken into account. Total return is a standard performance measure for asset management. This model seeks to maintain consistency of measures between asset management and liability management. The total return approach is discussed in more detail in Ho et al. (1995). One important aspect that this book incorporates is the sales growth model.

r_L is the total return of the liabilities, where the liabilities are marked to market and the total return is the change in market value together with all the liability payouts during the reporting period. Payouts for life insurance include the benefits and the cash value withdrawals. For time deposits, they will be all the interest payouts and withdrawals. The modeling is based on cash flows, so when an incident (or early withdrawal) occurs during the reporting period, the incident will increase the total return of the liability. The increase in the liability is the present value of the future insurance (time deposits) payments plus expenses. This approach does not distinguish between earned and unearned premiums. The model is concerned only with the expected cash flows and current portfolio holdings. For each time interval, the premiums (or time deposits) that have been received as inflows have no effect on the total returns of the liabilities for that time period.

FC is the operating expenses for the period. This model assumes that all operating expenses are fixed costs. Any variable costs that depend on the deposit base are considered part of the cost of funding, a cash outflow of the liability. This book focuses on the financial theory of risk transformation and not on the operational aspects of the insurance or commercial banking business. While expenses are central to the performance of a life insurance company or a commercial bank, the model will assume that these expenses are certain and predictable, in order not to distract from the purpose of this exposition.

Equation (16.6) provides an attribution of the changes in the equity value of the bank's structural balance sheet. Perhaps the most important components are the total returns of the asset and of the liability. With respect to the interest rate risk, if the dollar key rate durations of the asset are matched with the liability, then the asset total return net of the liability total return is the profit release. If the dollar key rate durations are not matched, then equation (16.6) identifies the interest rate risk exposure of the balance sheet.

Retained earnings statement equation

$$\Delta S = y \tag{16.7}$$

where ΔS is the change of the market value of the equity.

Equation (16.7) relates the income statement to the balance sheet. The accounting system ensures that the information on the balance sheet over time must be consistnt with the income statement information.

The sources of funds equation is

$$\Delta L = r_L L + f \tag{16.8}$$

where ΔL is the change in fair value of the liability
r_L is the total rate of return of the liability
f is net funding, where

$$f = b - L_{paydown} + v \tag{16.9}$$

and where b is new borrowing (including loan or bond issuance)

$L_{paydown}$ is paydown of liabilities or benefit payments (early withdrawal or deposit withdrawal) that leads to a fall in the market value of the liability by the same amount.

v is new volume sales

The increase of liability is viewed as a source of external funding while a decrease of the asset value is viewed as a use of funds. When the expected total return of the liability is high, the model concludes that the cost of funding is high. When the interest cost for the deposit increases unexpectedly, the liability value increases. This is not interpreted as an increase in sources of funds but an unexpected increase in the cost of funding.

Uses of the funds equation

$$\Delta A = r_A A + f + pv - FC \tag{16.10}$$

The uses of the funds equation captures all the inflows and outflows of funds to the cash account. Note that this model ensures that the double entry approach is maintained. Combining equations (16.10) and (16.8), we have

$$\Delta A - \Delta L = r_A A - r_L L + pv - FC$$

Using equation (16.6), we can establish equation (16.7) and thus ensure that the retained earnings statement holds. That is, the change in the surplus is the change of asset net the change of the liability value.

This model has ignored taxes and dividends, but the fair value accounting statement can incorporate these two items in a straightforward manner. Both tax payments and dividends are treated as an outflow of funds in the uses of funds statement. The dividend also reduces the change in equity in the retained earnings statement. This completes the description of the fair value accounting.

Book Value Accounting

The description of book value accounting parallels that of fair value accounting. The financial statements consist of the balance sheet, income statement, retained earnings statement, and uses and sources of funds. The description will be brief because it is a standard overview of basic accounting. We will use Euclid letters to denote the corresponding book value item.

Balance sheet equation

$$\mathbb{S} = \mathbb{A} + \mathbb{L}$$

Asset book value is based on the historical cost. The accounting value can be different from the fair value because the market interest rates and other market factors change over time. The fair value is the present value of the expected cash flows and may capture these market changes. Historical cost does not capture market changes.

Similarly, the book value of liability is based on the historical cost and it too, may differ from the fair value. The net value of the book asset and book liability is the net worth, which is the sum of the paid-in capital and the cumulated retained earnings.

Income statement equation

$$y = pv + r_{\mathcal{A}}\mathbb{A} - r_{\mathcal{L}}\mathbb{L} - FC$$

The first term is the portion of the gain on sale (if any) reported as book value gain. The second term is the book value of the assets times the book income rate. This is usually referred to as the asset income. The third terms is the interest costs from all the funding sources. The second and third terms combined are often called the net interest income.

Retained earnings equation

$$\Delta S = y$$

The change in book equity is the book income net of the dividends. The change of the book value of the equity is called retained earnings.

Sources and uses of funds equation

$$\Delta \mathbb{L} = r_{\mathcal{L}}\mathbb{L} + f$$
$$\Delta \mathbb{A} = r_{\mathcal{A}}\mathbb{A} + f + pv - Fc$$

where f is net funding is the same as that defined for fair value accounting.

These two equations complete the double entry format of accounting statements.

Now we apply the financial statements described above to the specific model of the bank. In this model, we assume that all the assets have short term maturity, cash, C. Therefore both the fair value and the book value are equal to $C = A = \mathbb{A}$. L is the fair value of the liability and long-term debt, whereas $\mathbb{L}$ is the book value of the liability, which is the deposit base plus the face value of the debt, $\mathbb{L} = D + F$.

Since there are no capital gains in investing in cash, the book value and fair value of asset returns are the same: the risk-free rate $r_A = r_{\mathbb{A}} = r_f$. The book cost of funding r_L is the deposit rate R^D. The sales volume is the new deposit, $\mathcal{V} = v = \Delta D$.

We assume that there is no gain on sale for the reported income for both book and fair value accounting, and hence $p = p = 0$. The model does not allow any external borrowing, and therefore $b = 0$.

By identifying each item of the fair value and book value financial statements, we have related the business model of a bank to the financial statements, and therefore we can build these financial statements at each node on a binomial lattice.

The purpose of the model presented is two-pronged. First, the model shows how the business model, fair value accounting, and book value accounting can be integrated into one consistent framework. Second, by using the model, we can analyze how fair value and book value accounting can be used for managing a financial institution. There are many accounting details that should be considered that will add complexity to the model, and perhaps insights into how one can integrate the business model with the corporate model. This simple example can provide the basic ideas for future extensions of the model.

We must first note some of the limitations of this model because of the simplified assumptions. We assume that the bank invests only in cash. The model ignores the lending business and the asset allocation issues in optimally deciding the proportion of investments in stocks, long bonds, or short-term bonds. The cost of capital of the financial institution is determined by the implied option adjusted spread. The franchise value is determined by the growth option on the interest rate risk only.

Step 3. Defining the Corporate Model of a Bank

The corporate model specifies the preferences of the corporate financial management and the optimal corporate financial decisions based on the preferences. The preferences are expressed as the objective function, the measure that the corporate management seeks in order to maximize the use of the control variables available. The corporate model consists of both book value accounting and fair value accounting. In this way, we can use the model of the financial institution to relate the management actions to the shareholders' value.

Objective function

The objective function of the corporate model may differ from one firm to another. For illustrative purposes, we assume that the bank's corporate model objective is to increase the shareholders' market value of equity at a stable rate over a planning horizon of, say, five years. This assumption is made to simplify the analysis and description. All banks have to be concerned with regulatory solvency or capital adequacy tests and financial reporting. We will show that the corporate model can be extended to deal with these issues. Incorporating all the other objectives and constraints to the model is important to the implementation, although the explanation will be complex and it will cloud the issues we are trying to explicate.

The bank may have more than one performance measure to maximize. The preferences may depend on a number of performance measures in a multiperiod framework over a certain time horizon. Some criteria for the objective function in a multiperiod framework are discussed below.

Level of Capital—For Regulatory and Rating Purposes   The bank may have a target level of risk-based capital. The minimum level may be determined by the regulators or by the rating agencies. The bank may have a certain preference for attaining a particular rating. The rating can establish the confidence of the customers, which is important for the management.

ROE—For High Returns to Investors   Returns on equity and net income are often cited as the most important financial performance measures. Many banks seek to increase the ROE or earnings.

Volatility of (ROE)—Stable Returns for Investors   Corporate management prefers delivering stable returns to investors. Incomes that are based on opportunistic activities may not lead to a valuation that is attained by incomes generated from the franchise. Investors reward stable and predictable incomes through a lower cost of capital for the firm, and hence higher capitalization value.

Dividend Payout Ratio—"Satisfying the Clientele" Effect   Corporate management may consider a stable dividend payout as important for its investors as we have discussed in Chapter 14.

VaR and EaR—The Risk Measures Are Used for Rating Agencies and Regulators   Capital requirements may depend on the value at risk measure.

The form of the objective function may be a weighted sum of the criteria. Furthermore, the objective function should be appropriate for multiperiod planning. In other words, the preferences should be expressed over multiple periods. For this reason, we need to consider the present values of the preferences, assigning higher weights to the criteria for the immediate future and less for the distant future. The form depends on the business mission of the firm and the business strategies that it is pursuing. The expectation and standard deviation operators are based on the real probability and not the risk-neutral probability.

In contrast to the corporate model presented in chapter 14, the objective function of the bank requires both the fair value accounting and the book value accounting. This is because of the mix of risk measures and performance measures that are based on both economic and book valuations.

Control variables

To maximize the objective function of the corporate model, management may change the mix of management controls. These corporate management controls are the debt ratio (which is the value of long-term bond to the total asset value), the dividend policy, and the capital level. These control variables are specified within the context of the model. With a more extensive model, other control variables may be the asset allocation, tax efficiency, and other corporate actions.

The bank may raise debt to retire some of the equity, resulting in a higher debt ratio. The increase of the debt ratio may raise the ROE, if the ROE exceeds the bond coupon rate. At the same time, the higher the debt ratio, the more volatile the future ROE may be.

Another control variable is adjusting the capital level. When there is excess capital, ROE will be lowered. But if the capital level is low, the credit measures may be affected. The optimal capital level can be determined given the objective function and constraints.

Step 4. Identifying the Business Processes

The process for financial institutions focuses on the specification of roles and responsibilities of all the departments participating in transforming the financial risks. The precise design of the process, of course, should depend on the particular institution's business mission, culture, and other management issues. In general, the process should have four cycle phases: specification, design, test, and implementation.

The senior management is responsible for the specification phase. They must specify the limits of the risk exposure and the expected returns on the shareholders' equity or the embedded value[3] of the financial institution, given the supply of and demand for funds in their marketplace. The asset and liability committee is responsible for the design phase. They are responsible for the planning of the growth and structure of balance sheets that will meet the requirements of senior management. The portfolio management of an insurer or the treasury of a bank is responsible for the test phase. In this phase, current market prices and liquidity are used to ensure that the target balance sheets and profitability can be realized, and that the design is consistent with market reality, the realizable transaction, and transaction prices. Finally, the line businesses and trading are responsible for implementation, where loans are made, deposits are collected, and securities are traded. Performances are then reported to the senior management for feedback control, thus completing the process cycle. A more detailed discussion of such a process is beyond the scope of this book. Ho (1995, 1999) discusses this process in more detail.

The bank has five departments: senior management, the ALM committee, the treasury (portfolio management), line business, and risk management. The responsibilities of each department are listed below.

1. Senior management is responsible for the operations of the bank and setting the bank's performance targets; it includes the management committee, which represents the stakeholders' interests.
2. ALM is responsible for determining the asset and liability structure. For the purpose of this book, asset and liability management coordinates with risk management.
3. The portfolio management (treasury) is responsible for investments, including asset allocation, sector rotation, and securities evaluation and trading. For most banks, portfolio management is separated into trading and other functions. The proposed methodology can be used for drilling down to such disaggregated levels.
4. Line business is responsible for the sale of time deposits and purchases of loans.
5. Risk management is responsible for the management of the process.

The model can be used in a multiperiod context. To simplify the explanation, we will present the model as a one-period model. The period refers to the reporting period, which may be one month or three months. The model will be used on a prospective basis when the model is used for risk management. At the same time, we will use the model on a retrospective basis when the model is used for performance measures. While these assumptions are unrealistic for a bank, such simplifications will enable us to study the process of commercial banking business more effectively.

The model can be used on a retrospective basis for measuring performances of each department in the process of the commercial banking business. This is accomplished by setting up asset benchmark returns (r_A^*) and liability benchmark returns (r_L^*). The benchmark returns are the returns of portfolios (loans or deposits) based on the average performance determined by the senior management. For the assets, this is often accomplished by using some broad-based market index, tilted to reflect the desired risk exposure of that asset and liability management view. Similarly, the liability benchmarks are determined by the liability modeling without assuming significant superiority in knowledge and information of the line of business. The performance of the ALM department depends on the views that it takes and how their views are reflected by the benchmarks that they establish for each reporting period. Therefore, their performance is measured by the difference between the returns of the asset and liability benchmarks. Specifically, we have

$$y(ALM) = r_A^* A - r_L^* L \qquad (16.11)$$

The performance of the portfolio management, $y(PM)$, is measured by the expected return of the asset portfolio net the expected returns of the benchmark on the prospective basis. For return attribution, on the retrospective basis, the performance is the realized returns on the assets net the realized returns of the liabilities. Specifically, we have

$$y(PM) = r_A A - r_A^* A \qquad (16.12)$$

The performance of the line business $(y(LB))$ is measured by the profits generated from new sales and its management of the liabilities, compared to the performance of the benchmarks.

$$y(LB) = pv + r_L^* L - r_L L \qquad (16.13)$$

We can now specify the corporate performance measure by noting that

$$y = y(ALM) + y(PM) + y(LB) - FC \qquad (16.14)$$

The senior management's role is to ensure that the income (y) will enhance the shareholders' value by managing the process and ensuring that the net income meets the shareholders' expectations.

It is important to note that this book proposes a set of performance measures. It does not suggest that management compensations should be directly related to these measures, even though these measures can be part of the input. It also does not propose a management system to deal with human resource issues. It focuses on the process–

engineering aspect of risk transformation and control for a bank or any financial institution.

The senior management should design and specify the process in more detail. Financial modeling is used to describe this process, and provides the following performance measures:

- Identifying the balance sheets and the income statements that incorporate all of the phases (a specific example is given below)
- Measuring risk and performance of each phase against its benchmarks
- Attributing the institution's performances and risks to each phase of the process.

While performances in general are additive, risks are not. Indeed, not only are risks diversifiable, so that they are not additive, but they are often cross-hedged across different business lines. Therefore, risk attribution must take these issues into account to assure coherence in the analysis.

In sum, this process approach provides an integrated framework of risk management to the institutions. By comparison to using risk measures like value at risk, earnings at risk, and others, this approach has three important attributes:

Bottom-up approach

The methodology ties information from the transaction level to the corporate goals, from trading decisions to corporate strategic decisions. In contrast, there is no consistent framework (to date) to relate value at risk and other risk measures to the corporate goals and management actions. For example, some proposed that the VaR be measured in economic values and the earnings at risk (EaR) be measured in book values. These measures are therefore not consistent with each other.

Process-oriented approach

The methodology focuses on the process of risk transformation in a financial institution. To date, value at risk and other measures have focused on the risks of shareholders' equity and returns only. Without identifying the process within the institution, such risk measures fail to identify the sources of the risks. The sources of risks are not confined to market risk and credit risk. Other sources of risk come from the risk transformation process.

These sources of risk include line of business risks (mortality/morbidity risks, disaster risks, depositors' withdrawal risk, and many others), liquidity risks, the timing of inflow and outflow of funds for the institution, and asset and liability mismatch on the structural balance sheet. The senior management, asset liability committee, treasury (portfolio management), and line department are identified to manage part of these risks.

Consistency

The methodology ensures consistency of risk measures. In contrast, VaR and other measures may not be consistent with each other. For example, VaR is economic value-based, while EaR is book value-based. They do not readily tie to a set of consistent corporate actions.

In comparison with the GAAP accounting approach, this proposed methodology is forward-looking, based on future stochastic cash flows, capturing future uncertainties in the measure. We use capital market observations to provide a systematic and consistent present value calculation. In contrast, GAAP accounting must be backward-looking, using deferred acquisition cost, amortization of goodwill, and other accrual bases. Furthermore, the measures of the risks tend to be rule-based and not continually calibrated to market realities.

16.7   Applications: Asset and Liability Management

With the presence of the balance sheet, financial institutions must manage their assets and liabilities. They cannot be managed effectively if they are managed separately. Assets have to perform so that they can support the cash flow obligations of the liabilities.

Total Return Approach

An asset and liability management approach that is consistent with the shareholders' value is the *total return approach*. We can calculate the key rate durations and other risk measures for both assets and liabilities. This approach seeks to match the assets and liabilities risk exposures. This way, we can be assured that any small changes of the market parameters—such as interest rates, equity, and basis risk exposures—of the assets and liabilities will have minimal exposure.

The total return approach proposes that many insurance products can be viewed as contingent claims to interest rates or other market factors. To the extent that lapse risks and mortality risks cannot be dynamically replicated using market instruments, the approach assumes that many such risks can be diversified and the residual risks are paid for by a spread.

A valuation model for a block of new business or in-force business is called the *liability benchmark*, which can then be analyzed and replicated by tradable assets consistent with the arbitrage-free modeling. The replicating portfolio is called the asset benchmark. The asset benchmark is used as a basis for managing the liabilities. In doing so, we can determine an investment process with an appropriate asset–liability performance measurement. Assets and liabilities performance measurements are used for such management.

Pathwise Approach

In cash flow testing, we have seen that in managing assets and liabilities, we may wish to analyze them on a runoff basis. We assume that there is no trading, no sale of assets or liabilities, and no new sales. Using such an approach, we can determine the cash flows at the end of the period when all assets and liabilities have run off. All cash flows in the interim periods are assumed to be reinvested at the risk-free rates. At the end of the period, we can determine the likelihood of the losses.

In chapters 4 and 5, we introduced the pathwise value approach, where we project the interest rate and equity scenarios under the arbitrage-free and risk-neutral models, and discount the cash flows at the risk-free rate along the scenario paths. The resulting present value is the pathwise value. The set of pathwise values for all the scenarios forms a distribution. The discount rate at each period for an option is adjusted according to the equilibrium expected returns of the option at each point. Then the present value of the cash flows discounted at the appropriate rate has a distribution of the pathwise values that is identical to the risk-neutral approach. That means we can determine the pathwise values by discounting both the assets and the liabilities at the risk-free rates. From the distribution, we can determine the potential loss at a certain probability level, holding the portfolio on a runoff basis. Therefore, the distribution of the pathwise value can be used to determine the VaR of a portfolio, not on a total return basis but on a hold to maturity basis. We have shown that the use of the distribution of the pathwise value is a natural extension of the VaR measure for nonmarketable securities. (See figure 16.1.)

Enterprise Risk Management

We must first recognize that financial services companies are in the business of "risk transformation." A well-designed process has to be in place to utilize investors' capital to transform risks to borrowers into risks to lenders. Regional banks take saving deposits and lend the proceeds in the form of loans and mortgages. Commercial banks transform certificates of deposit to corporate loans. Life insurance companies transform life policies and annuities to capital market investments. General insurance companies transform property and casualty policies to capital market investments. These transformations must

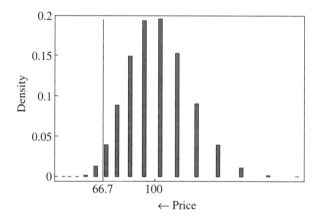

Figure 16.1 VaR calculation by the pathwise approach. We need to theorems to calculate VaR by the pathwise approach. The first theorem is that the option price is the mean of the pathwise values with respect to the risk-neutral probability and real probability. The second theorem is that the distribution of the pathwise values under risk-neutral measure converges to that of the pathwise values under the market measure as the time step Δ goes to 0. We assume that the initial stock price is 100, the stock volatility (σ) is 0.2, the expected stock return (μ) is 0.12, and the risk-free rate of return (r_f) is 0.1. We divide the one period into 15 subperiods (n = 15). We generate 2 raised to the power of 15 paths. The market probability and the risk-neutral probability are calculated by using $\frac{Exp[\mu/n]-d}{u-d}$ and $\frac{Exp[r_f n]-d}{u-d}$, respectively. u is defined as $Exp\left[\sigma \cdot \sqrt{1/n}\right]$ and d as $1/u$. We enumerate the pathwise values in an increasing order and add up the corresponding probability up to 5%. The pathwise value, which falls on the 5% significance level, is $66.7. Therefore, VaR at 5% significance level is $33.3 ($100 − $66.7).

be implemented by well-designed processes. To ignore the risks of these processes in managing the risk of a financial institution is as meaningless as to evaluate an automobile manufacturing firm using all the standard financial analysis while ignoring its process of building cars.

Risk management of a financial services company should begin by evaluating the process of risk transformation, and then measure the risk and performance of each phase of the process. Since an enterprise is the sum of many business processes, the performance of a financial institution should be measured by consolidating the performances of all the major departments or business units of the process, adjusted for their risks.

The new approach is to exploit the financial technologies that have experienced tremendous growth since the 1980s and apply them to the financial services industry. Specifically, the financial models can provide a set of accurate, relevant, consistent measures of performance of all the major departments. These measures should be able to hold each department accountable for its actions. And all their benchmarked actions will be consistent with a common firmwide objective. In doing all this, financial institutions will be able to perform in an economically rational fashion.

16.8 Regulatory Issues

Financial modeling is increasingly important for regulations. It is important to note that some regulations are not consistent with some of the financial theories that we have discussed in this book. The implications of regulations not being consistent with financial theory may have unintended consequences.

Financial Derivatives Disclosures, FAS 133

Financial Accounting Standard Board (FASB) Statement 133 (FAS133), "Accounting for Derivative Instruments and Hedging Activities," requires companies to record derivatives on the balance sheet as assets or liabilities at their fair value. In certain circumstances, changes in the value of such derivatives may need to be recorded as gains or losses. The ruling is concerned with disclosure of hedging. However, if derivatives are qualified as a hedge, they can be reported on a book value basis. The conditions are:

1. Hedge on a product and not a block of business
2. Must be able to show that the hedge is 80% effective
3. The hedge effectiveness can be demonstrated by cash flow matching.

The implications of this ruling can be illustrated by an article in the February 7, 2002. *Wall Street Journal* by Patrick Barta, "Freddie Mac and Fannie Mae Seem More Volatile as Accounting Rule Highlights Hedging Risks."

Fannie Mae reported its hedging position as shown below (in billions of dollars, notional amount)

	Swap	Swaption
2000	202.5	82.5
2001	281.8	219.9

The swaps are assumed to be hedging the interest rate risks of holding the mortgages by managing the mismatch of the assets' and liabilities' interest rate risk profile. In holding the mortgages, Fannie Mae has sold interest rate options to mortgage holders (as we explained in chapter 10). The prepayment options for the mortgagors result in risks to investors like Fannie Mae. Therefore, the swaptions are used as interest rate options to neutralize the effect. The hedging strategy seems straightforward, but the financial reporting according to FAS 133 can be misleading. The swaps and swaptions, which are classified as derivatives, must be recorded at market value because, according to the ruling, they are not qualified as a hedge. On the other hand, the mortgages are reported at book value because they are not traded. When the interest rate changes, the changes in the market value of the swaps must be reported, but the book value of the mortgages does not change. As a result, both Fannie Mae and Freddie Mac have to report the changes of the swaps and swaptions as "income," and the uncertainty of this reported income is perceived as "risk," even though the swaps and swaptions are used to minimize the interest rate risks of the mortgages.

Barta reported that "Freddie Mac's fourth-quarter profit more than doubled to $1.3 billion from a year earlier, but absent that new rule, Freddie Mac's profit would have risen 29%. . . . At Fannie Mae, shareholder equity gyrated as income surged. At the start of 2001, shareholder equity . . . stood at $20.8 billion, then fell to as low as $13.8 billion before ending the year at $18.1 billion."

What are the implications of such reporting to the investment community? A portfolio manager considered the "paper loss" to reflect a fall in shareholder equity that could "one day undermine a company," and had reduced his investment position in Fannie Mae. This is of course unfortunate. If these swaps are properly used as hedging instruments, the "paper loss" will be offset by the unreported gains of the underlying mortgages. When firms make an effort to manage their business risks, accounting rules can in fact deter such efforts.

While Fannie Mae and Freddie Mac are large, profitable firms that can afford to overcome these financial reporting obstacles, most firms cannot, and such accounting rules can have a significantly adverse impact on the management of firms. Appropriateness of the accounting rules in dealing with the fair value of instruments, particularly those with embedded value, should be evaluated more carefully.

Financial Disclosure for Fair Value Accounting for Investments: SFAS 115

The SFAS 115 ruling is concerned with fair value accounting for investments. All investments have to be determined by the criteria of (1) trading, (2) ready for sale, (3) hold to maturity. We will describe these in turn. Note that the liabilities reported on a book value basis are called reserves, and the reserves are calculated by the actuaries under the guidelines, as explained in chapter 11.

When the firm classifies assets as "trading," the assets have to be marked to market. Both realized and unrealized returns have to be reported in the income statements. The mark to market value is reported on the balance sheet. In this case, both the value and the returns are affected by changes in the market. Banks' trading books belong to this classification.

On the other hand, assets can be classified as "hold to maturity." In this case, the assets are held at book value and the income is the interest income, as defined by the accounting requirements. For example, some bonds do not pay interest, but for accounting purposes they may report paying accrual interest. In this case, the asset price and income are not affected by changes in the market. They are reported on a historical basis.

In between these two cases, assets can be classified as "ready for sale." In this case, the asset value is based on the book value. But the asset's unrealized profits and losses have to be reported according to SFAS no. 130, "Reporting Comprehensive Income." Comprehensive income consists of net income and equity adjustments relating to foreign currency conversion, fair value of derivatives, and availability of sale securities, which are all reported in the consolidated statement of stockholders' equity and comprehensive income.

In practice, firms tend to classify most items on the balance sheet as ready for sale. As we have seen, because the assets' value is based on the historical value and derivative prices are determined at the market price, the equity value may become volatile if some of the assets are hedged by derivatives. Similarly, such a classification of assets also leads to misleading performance measures.

Embedded Value

For an insurer, the corresponding equity value is called *embedded value*. Embedded value is reported in the financial statements of all U.K. and many European insurers. The measure may become a standard of valuing an insurer's equity value. At present, equity is a statutory value which is based on historical values. Regulators introduce the embedded value accounting approach to capture the prospective analysis.

The embedded value (EV) is the present value of future profits ($PVFP$) and adjusted net asset value ($ANAV$).

$$EV = PVFP + ANAV$$

ANAV consists of free (unrestricted) capital or capital not tied up in the runoff of the business, after deducting the taxes paid by the company. The determination of the free capital is based on the "going concern" principle, where a continuation of the business activity is stipulated.

PVFP is the present value of future after-tax income and the net value of future changes in capital. The appropriate cost of capital, typically the weighted average cost of capital, as described in chapter 12, is used to determine the present value.

To calculate the free cash flow, it is necessary to adjust for reserves. There are different types of adjustments to reserves. The adjustments are made for expected losses from defaults in bond investments or other unrealized losses, and reserves which are tied up for use in the runoff of the business, as required by regulations or internal management.

The free cash flows are then determined. The cash flows are discounted at the cost of capital, and the present value is the firm value. The firm's capitalization value is the firm value net of the market value of debt. The choice of the discount rate of the free cash flow requires a more detailed discussion. This method is similar to the Miller–Modigliani Theory in the sense that the value of the firm is determined first, and then the market value of the debt is subtracted from the firm value to determine the firm's capitalization.

The discount rate used for the free cash flow to determine the embedded value is usually specified by the weighted average cost of capital (WACC) of the firm, as explained in chapter 12. The WACC has two components, the cost of equity K_e and the cost of debt K_D.

The cost of equity can be estimated from the Capital Asset Pricing model, which was presented in chapter 2. The cost of equity is the sum of the risk-free rate and the excess returns that the management seeks to provide to its shareholders. Alternatively, we may use a required spread off a yield curve of 4% through 10%. This spread represents the risk premium of holding the equity risk of the firm. The cost of debt is the after-tax yield of the bond. WACC is then given by

$$WACC = \left(\frac{S}{V}\right) K_e + \left(\frac{D}{V}\right) K_D$$

However, the free cash flows of the embedded value are based only on the in-force business. We discussed in chapter 11 how arbitrage-free models are used to determine the value of the in-force liabilities by viewing them as contingent claims on market parameters. Consider a simple example. Suppose an insurer sells only a guaranteed investment contact (GIC), a simple liability payment. The equity value of the firm may have significant risks, since the firm value depends on the sales forecasts, profitability of the products, and many other business-related risks. However, the cash flow of the runoff of the business is simple, and may be easily replicated by zero-coupon bonds. In chapter 11, we discussed how the GIC can be discounted using a spot yield curve. The use of WACC to discount a cash flow similar to that of the GIC would not be appropriate, resulting in a misleading valuation of the embedded value of the firm. WACC is the discount rate of the firm's risk and in general not the appropriate discount rate for an in-force business, because the business risks, like sales uncertainties, are parts of the business risk but not the in-force business risks.

Furthermore, since the embedded value is estimated from the expected free cash flow of in-force business of the firm, the methodology has to be adjusted to estimate any embedded options on the balance sheet, since we have shown that the valuation of any embedded option requires stochastic simulations of future scenarios.

When insurers report their equity value by using the embedded value approach, they may be using the discount rate, which is in general not appropriate for the risk of the free cash flow of an in-force business, and they may not value the embedded options. Such reported values will mislead the investors. Further, if insurers use the embedded value as their performance measure, their investment and pricing strategies will be suboptimal. Not using financial modeling appropriately may have significant adverse consequences.

Reserve for Variable Annuities

Reserves are required to ensure that the liability borne by the insurer is reflected on the balance sheet of the firm. In chapter 11, we discussed the significance of the savings product variable annuities in our marketplace. We also discussed the guarantees on variable annuities by the insurers, leading to significant embedded options that the insurers have sold to the policyholders; that is, the insurers are bearing the risk.

We also have discussed that the variable annuity has been sold with different kinds of guaranteed death benefits. While the variable annuity is managed in a separate account and is not a general liability to the insurer, the death benefit guarantees become liabilities to the insurer when the policyholder dies and the account value (the value of the portfolio of the policyholder) has less value than the guaranteed amount. The insurer has to make whole, paying from the general account. This liability occurs when the stock market falls and the policyholder dies. How much should the insurer reserve for this event? What is the conservative estimate of this value (as reserves are supposed to be)?

At present, the NAIC reserve requirement for the variable annuity is described as follows. Reserves can be thought of as the "fair value" of the liability measured in a conservative fashion for the Statutory Statement. The rule to determine this value is to assume that the stock immediately falls 14% and then increases 14% annually. The reserve amount is therefore dependent on the number of policyholders die in the first year, and the rule assumes that the stock market rebounds after an initial fall.

If we follow the arguments presented in this book, we can see that these assumptions are not at all conservative. Why should the stock market rebound? Why should we be confined to one year of stock market loss? When the reserve requirement is inadequate, the regulation inadequately insures the financial soundness of the company. Inadequate reserves also result in misleading financial disclosure of the fair value of the liability of the business.

Conditional Tail Expectation

Conditional tail expectation (CTE) is an approach proposed as an alternative to the use of VaR for assets or liabilities that are not traded and are held to maturity over a long period of time by insurance companies. The methodology is being used in Canada to determine the required reserve for some of the liabilities of insurance companies.

For illustrative purposes, we consider instruments which have equity risk and no interest rate risk. The methodology follows generally the steps listed below:

1. Use historical experience to determine the volatility of the equity risks and expected returns.
2. Simulate the cash flows of the instruments over the life of the instruments and determine the net cash flows at the end of the simulation period.
3. Identify the $x\%$ of the highest losses of the simulations.
4. Discount the estimated highest losses at the cost of capital of the firm, measured by the weighted average cost of capital.
5. The mean of these present values of the losses is the CTE , and is used as a basis of the reserve.

According to the analytical results we have presented, the CTE method must in general mismeasure the risks. For simplicity, consider a special case of measuring the potential losses in writing a put option. As we showed in chapter 2, a put option has a negative beta; the discount rate for the put option should be lower than the risk-free rate, if we assume the stock return to have a positive risk premium to determine the put option's expected payoff, as in the CTE measure. However, the regulation proposes using WACC, a discount rate for the CTE higher than the risk-free rate. As a result, the value of the potential loss is understated by the CTE method. The source of the error is the inappropriate use of the discount rate.

In chapter 3 we discussed the appropriate method to determine present values of the scenarios. We have shown that the distribution of the pathwise values of the scenarios, based on the risk-neutral approach, provides the appropriate measure of risks for financial instruments held to maturity. In particular, the result suggests that the distribution of the pathwise numbers provides a theoretically consistent approach to measure the

VaR and the CTE risk of an asset, liability, or combined position of both. The VaR value using the pathwise values will determine the potential loss of the runoff values of a position at a certain probability level.

CTE may become an important measure of risk for assets and liabilities for financial instruments which are not traded. However, without using the appropriate financial model to discount the potential losses, the present value of the losses may be significantly understated and the consequences may be very significant.

Summary

Financial modeling is important to regulations. When regulations are inconsistent with the principles of the capital market (e.g., the law of one price or arbitrage pricing theory), corporate financial management of the firm is adversely affected. We have seen how such regulations affect the hedging strategies and asset and liability management of financial institutions. Furthermore, since more changes in regulations are pending, and some of the proposed changes still have flaws in their specifications, we should heighten our awareness of the appropriate use of financial models.

16.9   Summary

This chapter has described the use of financial models to manage a financial institution. While we focused our discussion on a bank, the framework can be extended to other financial institutions. The model integrates the business model, fair value accounting and book value accounting, and the corporate management objective function. The model can enable us to determine the optimal corporate strategies by managing the business processes with benchmarks for performance measures.

The analytical approach incorporates the use of the contingent claim valuation model. The model enables us to determine the appropriate discount rate for the real options. The valuation model provides a methodology for determining the firm value. As a result, the model also provides a method to maximize shareholders' value with the firm value optimization procedure.

Using this framework, we evaluated asset–liability management of financial institutions. We discussed the approaches for determining the capital allocation and performance measures. Finally, we proposed the use of process engineering as an approach for implementing risk management strategies.

Perhaps the most important message of this chapter is the emphasis on the importance of the business model for valuing a firm and the corporate model for corporate optimal decisions. The models provide a consistent framework to specify an objective function. This chapter showed how the business model and the corporate model can differ between the retail chains and financial institutions.

Prior to the development of contingent claim valuation models, the Capital Asset Pricing model would have been used to determine the risk premiums of any risk assets, as we discussed in chapter 2. The theory enables us to determine the present value of any risky cash flow, as long as we can estimate the beta. For this reason, the valuation of a firm is based on determining the free cash flows and beta of the firm. This approach is sufficiently general in that it can be applied to any firm of any industry type.

However, firm value has embedded options, and the business risk changes in character over time. Furthermore, corporate management is dynamic. Business decisions, such as investments, depend on the circumstance of the market reality. As a result, assuming the beta of a firm to be stationary into the future, and using historical stock returns to estimate the beta value, can lead to a firm valuation that is too imprecise. As research progresses, the contingent claim theory will enable us to better understand the management of a firm and provide insights into some of our current challenges in financial institutions.

We began this chapter with three questions. We now conclude with the answers to each of them.

1. With the increased use of the mark to market concept, how should financial institutions change their financial disclosures? This chapter suggests that we should have a combined approach with fair value and book value financial statements. The two types of statements disclose different sets of information, and together they can provide a more complete picture of the firm's financial performance. We have provided an example of such a system in this chapter.

2. With the increase in the awareness of risk management, how should an enterprise manage its assets and liabilities? An enterprise should define its business processes and design the business units to operate its business processes optimally. Each business unit has its own benchmark to determine its financial performance, and the performance measures should be based on both book value and fair value financial statements.

3. How should financial institutions define their enterprise risk management and their risk-adjusted performance measures to be consistent with the maximization of the shareholders' value? The risk-adjusted performance measures should be derived from the financial institution's business model and corporate model. The investment decisions should be made to optimize the firm value in enhancing shareholders' value. The corporate financial decisions are derived from the objective function of the corporate model of the firm.

Appendix A. What Actions Have Commercial Banks Taken?

Santomero (1997) conducted a survey of major commercial banks on what they had done in the area of risk management. Commercial banks have been under scrutiny in the area of risk management because, as one can see, many major financial losses came from commercial banks. Also, they have a special role in the economy because they accept deposits which are insured by the government. They are the units in the economy that are directly related to monetary policy and are important to the functioning of the financial system. Thus, risk management efforts tend to be important in this sector of the economy. A review of what they have done can provide examples of risk management practices.

Tools to Manage Risks

Most banks have four tools to manage risks.

1. They try to establish standards of risk measures across units, and standardize the reports.

2. For trading and other business units, the banks establish position limits and rules to avoid risk concentration.
3. For investments, there are formal guidelines for asset types that are acceptable for the portfolio and for strategies.
4. Finally, perhaps the most difficult challenge is to align compensation with the business unit so that, on the one hand, it is encouraged to accept profitable projects and, on the other hand, their attitude toward risk is aligned with that of the firm.

Identification and Measurements of Risk

Traditionally, the most important risk source for banks is the credit risks. They have internal rating systems which provide investors with information regarding the credit-worthiness of the firm. Banks strive to level their rating to market standards to assure that their firm is not risky compared to other companies, so that shareholders would be motivated to invest in them. However, few banks have ways to aggregate the risks to evaluate the effect of diversification. Presumably, in practice aggregating data from all the departments is not a simple matter.

For interest rate risks, banks use gap analysis, cash flow mismatch along the maturity spectrum, to simulate the income under different scenarios. For currency risks, there is less standardization. Much of the management is on the trading floor level.

There are two types of liquidity risks: normal operation and extreme change in business. The former is simpler, since banks would insure themselves to have credit lines and other mechanisms in place. The latter is more complex. When there is a significant change in the scenario, many mechanisms that are usually used to access funding will not be available because the sources of funds are no longer assured. Usually, a plan is developed for such liquidity crises.

Banks are also concerned with regulatory risks, reputation risks, and environmental risks. These risks are not modeled and are measured imprecisely.

Reporting and Management

Research has found that providing an aggregation of risks is challenging. The measures are not consistent across risk types, because they have different purposes for different business units. For example, credit risk is measured in terms of an internal rating; rating agencies do not publicize their methods of evaluating. Then how can we see the diversification effect of credit risk with currency risk exposures in another country? In this chapter, we have described methods that will lead to aggregate risk measures.

What risk management controls have banks put in place? Perhaps capital allocation is the main thrust of control. Bankers Trust's RAROC (risk adjusted return on capital) is one approach that best demonstrates the variations on the theme. Business units are allocated capital based on the risks measured. The performance of each unit is based not only on the profit but also on the risk-adjusted basis. The higher the risk, the higher the capital allocated. The profit is the return per unit of capital employed. The profit probability distribution is estimated from historical observation of the business units' profits. RAROC provides incentives for business units to minimize risk that increases the profit per unit of risk. Another performance measure is earnings at risk. It uses historical earnings data to estimate the distributions of the earnings. In doing so, the risks of the earnings can be estimated.

Appendix B.   Capital Requirements and Risk-based Capital

To ensure that financial institutions have the assets to support their liabilities, capital requirements are imposed on them. Here we outline the capital requirements imposed on banks. The Basel Agreement (1988) was designed to establish minimum levels of capital that cover only credit risks for internationally active banks. In 1996, the Basel Committee amended the Basel Capital Accord to incorporate market risks. This amendment added a capital charge for market risk based on either the standardized method or the internal models method. Banks can calculate the capital charge for market risk by internal models, provided the models and the procedures conform to certain quantitative and qualitative standards. To obtain total capital adequacy requirements, banks should add their credit risk charge to their market risk charge.

Total capital adequacy requirements = credit risk charge + market risk charge

First of all, we need to define capital. Capital is the equity of the firm that supports the banks to take principal positions. It is interpreted more broadly than the usual definition of equity book value, since its goal is to protect deposits. Therefore, we should recognize that provisions are related to capital.

Tier 1 capital, or "core" capital, includes paid-up stock issues and disclosed reserves, most notably from after-tax retained earnings. Goodwill is excluded. Tier 2 capital, or "supplementary" capital, includes undisclosed reserves, asset revaluation reserves, general provisions/general loan loss reserves, hybrid (debt/equity) capital instruments, and subordinated debt with maturity over five years, limited to 50 percent of tier 1 elements. Tier 2 is added up to an amount equal to the core capital.[4]

The Basel Accord requires capital to equal at least 8 percent of the total risk-weighted assets of the bank. In other words, total risk-based capital ratios should be at least 8 percent. Risk-adjusted assets can be calculated by multiplying each asset by the corresponding weight and adding up all the assets. For example, a bank has two types of assets, residential mortgage loans and cash. The weights of residential mortgage and cash are 0% and 50%, respectively. The amounts of residential mortgage and cash are $100 and $500, respectively. The risk-adjusted assets are 0% × $100 + 50% × $500 = $250. Therefore, the bank should have total capital of $20 as credit risk charge, at least $10 of which should be tier 1 capital.

$$Total\ risk\text{-}based\ capital\ ratio = \frac{total\ capital\,(Tier\ 1 + Tier\ 2)}{risk\text{-}adjusted\ assets} \geq 8\%$$

Concerning the market risk charge, two approaches are available. The first is based on a specified "building block" approach, which is sometimes the standardized method. The building block approach was first proposed in April 1993. The problem with this approach is that it is arbitrary, in the sense that the same capital charge of 8 percent is applied to equities and currencies, regardless of their actual return volatilities. Another problem is that it does not account for diversification across risks. In response to industry criticisms, the Basel Committee proposed a major alternative in April 1995. The second approach is that banks have the option of using their own risk measurement methods to determine their capital charge (this is called the internal model approach). Market risk charge obtained by the internal model approach should be set at the higher of the previous days's VaR or the average VaR over the last 60 business days times a multiplicative factor (k). The multiplicative factor should be at least 3. The holding period is ten days, and the confidence level is 99% to calculate VaR for market risk charge purposes.

$$\text{Market risk charge at day } t = Max \left[k \cdot \frac{1}{60} \sum_{i=1}^{60} VaR_{t-i}, \ VaR_{t-1} \right]$$

Notes

1. Anthony Saunders, *Financial Institutions Management,* 3rd ed. (Boston: Irwin, 1999).

2. The Basel Committee consists of representatives of the central banks and supervisory authorities of the Group of Ten (Belgium, Canada, France, Germany, Italy, Japan, the Netherlands, Sweden, the United Kingdom, and the United States), plus Luxembourg and Switzerland. It meets at the Bank for International Settlements in Basel, Switzerland. Some of the specific rules are provided in appendix B.

3. The embedded value is the asset economic value net of the liability economic value.

4.

$$\text{Tier 1 (core) capital ratio} = \frac{core \ capital \ (Tier 1)}{risk\text{-}adjusted \ assets} \geq 4\%$$

References

Altman, E. T., and I. T. Vanderhoof, eds. 1994. *The Financial Dynamics of the Insurance Industry.* Boston: Irwin.

Avery, R. B., and A. N. Berger. 1991. Risk-based capital and deposit insurance reform. *Journal of Banking and Finance,* 15, 847–874.

Berger, A. N. 1995. The relationship between capital and earnings in banking. *Journal of Money, Credit, and Banking,* 27 (2), 432–456.

Berger, A. N. 1997. Problem loans and cost efficiency in commercial banks. Working paper, Office of the Controller of the Currency.

Berger, A. N., R. J. Herring, and G. P. Szego. 1995. The role of capital in financial institutions. *Journal of Banking and Finance,* 19 (3/4), 393–430.

Berlin, M., and L. J. Mester. 1999. Deposits and relationship lending. *Review of Financial Studies,* 12 (3), 579–607.

Bhattacharya, S., A. W. A. Boot, and A. V. Thakor. 1998. The economics of bank regulation. *Journal of Money, Credit, Banking,* 30 (4), 745–770.

Boot, A. W. A., and A. V. Thakor. 1991. Off-balance sheet liabilities, deposit insurance and capital regulation. *Journal of Banking and Finance,* 15 (4/5), 825–846.

Bradley, M. G., C. A. Wambeke, and D. A. Whidbee. 1991. Risk weights, risk-based capital and deposit insurance. *Journal of Banking and Finance,* 15 (4/5), 875–893.

Cordell, L. R., and K. K. King. 1995. A market evaluation of the risk-based capital standards for the U.S. financial system. *Journal of Banking and Finance,* 19 (3/4), 531–562.

DeGennaro, R. P., L. H. P. Lang, and J. B. Thomson. 1993. Troubled savings and loan institutions: Turnaround strategies under insolvency. *Financial Management,* 22 (3), 163–175.

Dermine, J., and F. Lajeri. 2001. Credit risk and the deposit insurance premium: A note. *Journal of Economics and Business,* 53 (5), 497–508.

Deshmukh, S. D., S. I. Greenbaum, and G. Kanatas. 1982. Bank forward lending in alternative funding environments. *Journal of Finance,* 37 (4), 925–940.

Doherty, N. A., and J. R. Garven. 1986. Price regulation in property–liability insurance: A contingent-claims approach. *Journal of Finance,* 41 (5), 1031–1050.

Duffie, D., and M. Huang. 1996. Swap rates and credit quality. *Journal of Finance*, 51 (3), 921–949.

Esty, B. C. 1998. The impact of contingent liability on commercial bank risk taking. *Journal of Financial Economics*, 47 (2), 189–218.

Feldstein, M., and S. Seligman. 1981. Pension funding, share prices, and national savings. *Journal of Finance*, 36 (4), 801–824.

Figlewski, S., and T. C. Green. 1999. Market risk and model risk for a financial institution writing options. *Journal of Finance*, 54 (4), 1465–1499.

Flannery, M. J. 1981. Market interest rates and commercial bank profitability: An empirical investigation. *Journal of Finance*, 36 (5), 1085–1101.

Froot, K. A., and J. C. Stein. 1998. Risk management, capital budgeting, and capital structure policy for financial institutions: An integrated approach. *Journal of Financial Economics*, 47 (1), 55–82.

Girard, L. N. 1996. Fair valuation of liabilities—are the appraisal and option pricing methods really different? *Risk and Rewards*, 25 (March), 5–9.

Grosen, A., and P. Jorgensen. 2000. Fair valuation of life insurance liabilities: The impact of interest rate guarantees, surrender options, and bonus policies. *Insurance: Mathematics and Economics*, 26 (1), 37–57.

Hendricks, D., and B. Hirtle. 1997. Bank capital requirements for market risk: The internal models approach. *Economic Policy Review*, 3 (4), 1–12.

Ho, T. S. Y. 1995. Quality based investment cycle: Toward quality assurance in the investment industry. *Journal of Portfolio Management*, 22 (1), 62–69.

Ho, T. S. Y. 1999. A VaR model of an investment cycle: Attributing returns and performances. *North American Actuarial Journal*, January,

Ho, T. S. Y., A. Scheitlin, and K. Tam. 1995. Total return approach to performance measurement. In *The Financial Dynamics of the Insurance Industry*, E. I. Altman and I. T. Vanderhoof, eds. Boston: Irwin.

Hojgaard, B. 1999. Controlling risk exposure and dividends payout schemes: Insurance company example. *Mathematical Finance*, 9 (2), 153–182.

Houston, J. F., and C. M. James. 2001. Do relationships have limits? Banking relationships, financial constraints, and investment. *Journal of Business*, 74 (3), 347–374.

John, K., T. A. John, and L. W. Senbet. 1991. Risk-shifting incentives of depository institutions: A new perspective on federal deposit insurance reform. *Journal of Banking and Finance*, 15 (4/5), 895–915.

Kane, E. J., and H. Unal. 1990. Modeling structural and temporal variation in the market's valuation of banking firms. *Journal of Finance*, 45 (1), 113–136.

Kraus, A., and S. A. Ross. 1982. The determination of fair profits for the property–liability insurance firm. *Journal of Finance*, 37 (4), 1015–1028.

Lintner, J. 1956. Distribution of incomes of corporations among dividends, retained earnings and taxes. *American Economics Review*, 46 (2), 97–113.

Lopez, J. A. 1998. Methods for evaluating value-at-risk estimates. Federal Reserve Bank of New York, *Economic Policy Review*, 4 (3), 119–124.

Lucas, A. 2001. Evaluating the Basel guidelines for backtesting banks' internal risk management models. *Journal of Money, Credit, and Banking*, 33 (3), 826–846.

Minton, B. A., and S. Catherine. 1999. The impact of cash flow volatility on discretionary investment and the costs of debt and equity financing. *Journal of Financial Economics*, 54 (3), 423–460.

Mitchell, K., and N. M. Onvural. 1996. Economies of scale and scope at large commercial banks: Evidence from the Fourier flexible functional form. *Journal of Money, Credit, and Banking*, 28 (2), 178–199.

Niinimaki, J. P. 2001. Intertemporal diversification in financial intermediation. *Journal of Banking and Finance*, 25 (5), 965–991.

O'Brien, J. M. 2000. Estimating the value and interest rate risk of interest-bearing transaction deposits. Working paper, Board of Governors of the Federal Reserve System.

O'Hara, M. 1983. A dynamic theory of the banking firm. *Journal of Finance*, 38 (1), 127–140.

Reitano, R. R. 1997. Two paradigms for the market value of liabilities. *North American Actuarial Journal*, 1 (4), 104–137.

Santomero, A. 1997. Commercial bank risk management: An analysis of the process. *Journal of Financial Service Research*, 12 (2/3), 83–115.

Saunders, A. 1999. *Financial Institutions Management: A Modern Perspective*, 3rd ed. Boston: Irwin.

Stoughton, N., and J. Zechner. 1998. Optimal capital allocation using RAROC and EVA. Working paper, University of California at Irvine.

Sundaram, S. 1992. The market valuation effects of the Financial Institutions Reform, Recovery and Enforcement Act of 1989. *Journal of Banking and Finance*, 16 (6), 1097–1122.

Wallace, M. 1997. Performance measurements using transfer pricing. Transamerica Insurance Company research paper.

Further Readings

Oldfield, G. S., and A. M. Santomero. 1995. The place of risk management in financial institutions. Working paper, Financial Institutions Center.

17

Structured Finance: Foreign Exchange Models

Financial models are widely used in foreign exchange markets. The basic relative valuation concepts extended to the foreign exchange markets include interest rate parity, the Black–Scholes model, and put–call parity. These concepts, together with their practical relevance, are discussed in this case study. This case study also underscores a theme of this book: financial modeling should begin with stating the business objective and the model assumptions. Failing to understand these may risk financial ruin.

In the previous chapters, we have described some of the financial models used in investment and financing decisions, and we have shown how capital market financial models and corporate finance are often inseparable. We will illustrate this idea further in this chapter by considering a case study of a structured finance deal. We will also describe some of the financial models in foreign exchange markets.

In February 1998, daily newspapers in Seoul reported that SK Securities, Hannam Investment Trust Company, and LG Metal (hereafter SKS) had incurred a loss of $180 million in addition to their original investments of $35 million—shocking news to the Korean securities industry. SKS argued that the Morgan Guaranty Trust Company of New York (hereafter JP Morgan) had misrepresented its expert judgment on the risks of the devaluation of the Thai baht and Indonesian rupiah. The case was finally settled out of court

We will examine the conflict between JP Morgan and SKS.[1] The purpose of this case study is to analyze a seemingly complicated structure, the total return swap. The structured financing of SKS illustrates the close relationships of models of capital market securities and an investment corporation. In this example, we can see how (1) an investment corporation is formed by packaging capital market securities, a process called "structured finance"; (2) how the risk of the derivatives translates to the risk of the investment corporation and to SKS; (3) how risk of the investment corporation should be managed.

17.1 Background

Early in January 1997, JP Morgan (Hong Kong) offered SKS a seemingly attractive investment proposal. According to the proposal, if SKS invested in the fund, it could realize returns of 3% or 4% above the Korean bond yield. In addition, SKS could receive another 3 percent if it utilized a structured derivative trading designed by Morgan.

On January 29, 1997, SKS established a fund called Diamond Fund in Labuan, Malaysia. It raised $35 million denominated in Korean won (KRW) and borrowed $53 million denominated in Japanese yen from Morgan with the redemption paid in a combination of U.S. dollars, Thai baht, and Japanese yen. Diamond Fund invested $88 million in bonds denominated in Indonesian rupiah. In essence, SKS raised the investment fund in Korean won, leveraged the investment by borrowing in yen, and invested the proceeds in rupiah bonds. The structure exposed SKS to significant baht, yen, rupiah, and dollar exchange rate risks relative to the won.

SKS anticipated realizing an annual 20.225 % rate of return on this investment. But that was not the case. The investment had incurred significant losses within one year; Diamond Fund was obligated to pay over $213.6 million to Morgan, threatening the viability of SKS, one of the major investment banks in Korea

How can a deal structure lead to a loss that is so significantly greater than the initial investment? What risks have been involved in TRS? These are the questions we will answer.

17.2   Economics of the Structure

The purpose of the structured finance was to provide high returns for SKS's Korean investment, using the rupiah bonds and taking the rupiah, baht, and yen currency risks. The deal structure had several components, and they should be analyzed separately. Once we do that, we will combine them to see the overall picture.

The basic idea is quite simple. SKS first established an investment vehicle, Diamond. It raised the capital in won and converted to dollars for Diamond. Then Diamond borrowed from JP Morgan (Hong Kong), not in the form of equity participation but in a form of a structured note called total return swap (TRS). The capital, which consisted of the equity investment in won by SKS and the sale of the structured note in yen to JP Morgan, was converted to dollars and then invested in rupiah-linked notes.

However, there were two important features of this structure that made the SKS investment different from traditional investments. The TRS could result in significant profits and losses to the parties, JP Morgan and Diamond. JP Morgan required two guarantees for its funding of Diamond: one guaranteed the profits to JP Morgan in the event of Diamond default, and the other guaranteed that the loss of JP Morgan be capped at its initial investment. SKS provided both guarantees, with the latter provided via Boram Bank.

Boram Bank received $300,000 from Diamond. Boram Bank guaranteed that it would pay if Diamond could not pay whatever Diamond owed Morgan on the termination date. After Boram Bank paid to Morgan, it would demand the same amount from SKS. The reason for this was that according to the contract between Boram Bank and SKS, SKS should put more money into Diamond so that Diamond could pay Morgan. In other words, Morgan had one more backer to make sure that it would be paid the full amount.

We have studied how to evaluate various securities, starting from simple ones such as straight bonds, and progressing to complicated securities like convertible bonds. We have also applied the valuation methodology to evaluate firms. Here we illustrate how various financial models have been used in the real world. This case study shows that in structured finance, we have to analyze not only the derivatives involved but also the guarantees. These guarantees are also contingent claims, and their risks and values are just as important to the investors as the investment portfolio. We now investigate the deal structure in more detail.

17.3   Deal Structure

We analyze the deal in three parts: the equity funding, the structured note funding, and the investment. (See figure 17.1.)

The Equity Investment in Diamond

The first part of the transaction consisted of the equity funding of Diamond. SKS provided 30 billion won to Hannam Fund, an intermediate investment vehicle. Hannam Investment Trust Company and LG Metal each contributed 5 billion won to Hannam

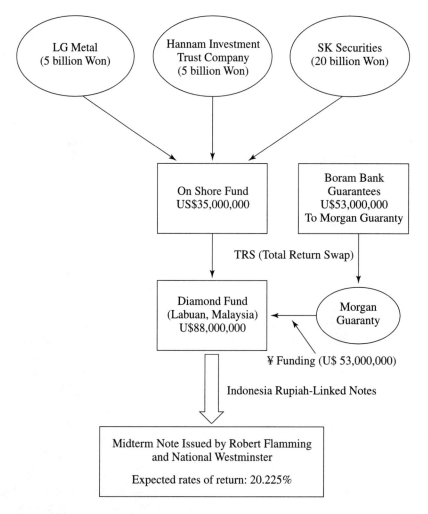

Figure 17.1 The structure of the deal

Fund, which purchased 3,500,000 shares of Diamond for $35 million. $35 million was equivalent to 30 billion Korean won at the prevailing rate of exchange.

A Structured Note Sold to Morgan

Morgan provided $53 million in yen to Diamond. Morgan bought a structured note from Diamond with the redemption in one year, under the terms and conditions agreed on January 29, 1997, described in appendix A.

The key elements of the agreement were Diamond's obligations to Morgan at the termination date and the guarantees. Let us first consider the payment at the termination date. Diamond was to pay Morgan according to the following formula:

$$\$53\text{million} \times \left(97\% - \text{Max}\left[0.00\%, \frac{\text{Yen}_{\text{Mat}} - \text{Yen}_{\text{Spot}}}{\text{Yen}_{\text{Mat}}}\right] - 5 \times \frac{\text{Baht}_{\text{Spot}} - \text{Baht}_{\text{Mat}}}{\text{Baht}_{\text{Mat}}} \right)$$

where Yen_{Spot} is the yen foreign exchange rate, quoted as Japanese per dollar set on the trade date (122.00) and baht per dollar (25.884).

The payment formula consists of the cash payment, the Japanese yen put option, and the baht forward.

Cash payments

The first part is straightforward. Diamond was to pay 97% of the initial investment of $53 million in dollars.

The yen put option

The second part was the functional equivalent of Diamond purchasing a Japanese yen put option from Morgan, which would be an option for Diamond to sell $53 million worth of yen on the payment date. The exchange of payments would be as follows. If the yen depreciated against the dollar during the one-year term of the swap, Morgan would pay Diamond $53 million multiplied by the percent the yen depreciated, and if the yen appreciated, no money would change hands.

To see how it is a put option on the Japanese yen, we manipulate the second part a little bit.

$$53 \text{ million} \times \text{Max}\left[0, \frac{\text{Yen}_{\text{Mat}} - \text{Yen}_{\text{Spot}}}{\text{Yen}_{\text{Mat}}}\right]$$

$$= 53 \text{ million} \times \text{Yen}_{\text{Spot}} \times \text{Max}\left[0, \frac{1}{\text{Yen}_{\text{Spot}}} - \frac{1}{\text{Yen}_{\text{Mat}}}\right]$$

$$= 53 \text{ million} \times \text{Yen}_{\text{Spot}} \times \text{Max}\left[0, \text{Yen}^*_{\text{Spot}} - \text{Yen}^*_{\text{Mat}}\right]$$

Since $\text{Yen}^*_{\text{Spot}}$ and $\text{Yen}^*_{\text{Mat}}$ are Japanese foreign exchange rates, quoted as dollar per yen, the underlying asset is the yen and the money unit is United States dollars. Therefore, $\text{Max}\left[0, \text{Yen}^*_{\text{Spot}} - \text{Yen}^*_{\text{Mat}}\right]$ is a put option on yen. The strike price is $\text{Yen}^*_{\text{Spot}}$ and the maturity date is the termination date.

The baht forward

The third and final part was the functional equivalent of Diamond purchasing $265 million worth of baht forward from Morgan, which was a contract for Diamond to buy $265 million worth of baht on a payment date. The exchange of payments would be as follows. If the baht depreciated against the dollar during the one-year term, Diamond would pay Morgan $265 million multiplied by the percent the baht had depreciated. If the baht appreciated, Morgan would pay Diamond $265 million multiplied by the percent the baht had appreciated.

The Rupiah-Linked Notes

The third and last part of the overall transaction was the securities investment made by Diamond. The rupiah-linked notes are complex derivative instruments because the value of the notes is dependent on the rise or fall of another foreign currency, the rupiah. The rupiah-linked notes might imply that their principal and interest payments would vary by the fluctuation of the rupiah–dollar exchange rate, but would not lose all their value regardless of the exchange rate. However, their value could be wiped out entirely, depending on rupiah–dollar exchange rates. Because of this feature, these were risky leveraged derivative transactions. The terms and conditions of this trade are provided in appendix B.

The interest payment and redemption formulas are as follows.

First coupon: $\left[20.20\% \times \dfrac{2369.5}{\text{IDR\_1}} \right]$ per annum, payable semiannually in arrears

on Act/365 basis in dollars.

Second coupon: $\left[20.20\% \times \dfrac{2369.5}{\text{IDR\_2}} \right]$ per annum, payable semiannually in arrears

on Act/365 basis in dollars.

Redemption: $\left[100\% + \left(\dfrac{2369.5 - \text{IDR\_1}}{2369.5} \right) + \left(\dfrac{2369.5 - \text{IDR\_2}}{2369.5} \right) \right]$

$\times \dfrac{2369.5}{\text{IDR\_2}}$ in dollars

with a minimum of 0%

To understand the rupiah-linked notes, we assume that the rupiah will not change until the maturity date, which means that IDR_1 and IDR_2 are 2369.5. The rupiah-linked notes become straight notes with a coupon rate of 20.20%. However, if IDR_1 and IDR_2 are 2615 and 10550, respectively, as the rupiah exchange rates realized on the first coupon date and the redemption date, the first coupon payment would be 9.13%, the second coupon rate would be 2.26% and the redemption amount would be 0, which clearly shows that the notes depended on the rupiah exchange rates.

On the surface, these notes appear to yield a return equivalent to rupiah-denominated notes with a 20.20% rate of interest. The value of such notes would fluctuate on the basis of the rupiah–dollar exchange rate, but would be protected from ever reaching zero. However, embedded within the redemption formula was a currency derivative, the equivalent of a rupiah forward, which would render the notes worthless if the rupiah depreciated enough. In fact, due to the dramatic decline in the value of the rupiah, these notes had no value on the redemption date.

Boram Bank's Guarantee

There were two important guarantees related to the TRS. First, SKS would be responsible for the full payment to Morgan if Diamond could not pay the amount specified in the terms and conditions, regardless of Diamond's value, which was essential to convert Morgan's $53 million into a loan. Second, in Boram Bank's guarantee as a precondition to the parties entering into the transaction, Boram Bank agreed to guarantee Diamond's obligations to Morgan under the TRS.

17.4 Pricing

We have two structured notes to analyze in this deal. The first is the TRS structure, and the second is the rupiah-linked notes. For pricing purposes, we need a currency option model and the interest parity theorem.

Currency Option Model

To directly apply the Black–Scholes option model in chapter 4 to the currency option, we should take two things into account. First, foreign currency can be treated as if it were known dividend yield paying stock, because by holding foreign currency, we can get a foreign risk-free rate in the same way that we receive a known dividend yield from stocks. Second, the distribution of a stock price at T when the initial stock price is $S^* e^{-qT}$ is equal to the distribution of a stock price at T when the initial stock price is S^* and the stock pays a known continuous dividend yield at the rate q. Since the stock price at T follows a lognormal distribution, a mean and a variance will matter for the lognormal distribution. Since the stock pays the known dividend yield, which is not a stochastic variable, the volatility of the known dividend-paying stock is the same as the volatility of the stock without paying the dividend. Furthermore, the stock price S^* at time 0 will decline to $S^* e^{-qT}$ at time T when we assume that the stock price does not change up to time T other than the known continuous dividend yield payment.

When we replace the initial stock price S^* in the Black–Scholes option model with $S^* e^{-r^f T}$, we have the Garman–Kohlhagen formula to price currency options.[2] Therefore, the Garman–Kohlhagen formula is an extension of the Black–Scholes model, where the "stock" is the cash in the foreign currency and the foreign interest rate is viewed as the "dividends" of the stock.

The Garman–Kohlhagen put option formula is

$$currency\ option = X \cdot \exp\left[-rT\right] N(-d_2) - e_{spot} \cdot \exp\left[-r^f T\right] N(-d_1)$$

where

$$d_1 = \frac{\ln(e_{spot}/X) + (r - r^f + \sigma^2/2)T}{\sigma\sqrt{T}}, \quad d_2 = d_1 - \sigma\sqrt{T}$$

r^f and r are the foreign and domestic risk-free interest rates, respectively; e_{spot} is the spot exchange rate; X is the exercise exchange. The other variables are similarly defined as the Black–Scholes model.

Interest Parity Theorem

Suppose the spot exchange rate is e_{spot} and the forward exchange rate is $e_{forward}$. Let the domestic interest rate be r and the foreign interest rate be r^f. If an investor has \$1, then he can convert \$1 to e_{spot} foreign currency and invest in the foreign rate. At the end of the year T, he receives payoff (1) in foreign currency, $e_{spot} \exp(r^f T)$.

Alternatively, he can first invest in the domestic interest rate and then exchange to the foreign currency by the forward exchange rate. The payoff is payoff (2) in foreign currency, $e_{forward} \exp(rT)$.

Payoff (1) must equal payoff (2) because this is an arbitrage argument. The following equation is the interest rate parity, which determines the forward exchange rate.

$$e_{spot} \exp (r^f T) = e_{forward} \exp (rT)$$

Put–Call Parity

In the put–call parity, the transaction consisting of buying a call on the stock and shorting the stock is the same as the transaction of buying a put on the stock and borrowing the dollar amount of the exercise price. The exercise price of the put should be identical to the exercise price of the call to make the put–call parity hold. In chapter 4, we showed the put–call parity can be stated as

$$C - S = P - PV(X)$$

where C and P are the call and put options, respectively; S is the underlying stock; and $PV(X)$ is the present value of the exercise price. In terms of currency options, the holder of a call (a put) option has the right, but not an obligation, to buy (to sell) \$1 at a strike exchange rate, for example, 120 yen.

Buy a call on \$1 + *Short*\$1 =

Buy a put on\$1 + Borrow yen amount of an exercise price.

To understand the above equation, we should bear in mind that one dollar can be treated as if it were an asset in the exactly same way that we treat a stock as an asset. If we hold a stock, we can have future cash flow and sell it to have another asset. In exactly the same way, we treat \$1 as a risky asset based in yen. The put–call parity enables us to value a currency put option using the call option pricing model.

Model Assumptions

For illustrative purposes, we assume that all the yield curves are flat with the Japanese interest rate 1.2%, the U.S. interest rate 6%, and the baht interest rate 9.2%. The spot yen exchange rate is 122 per dollar, and the baht exchange rate is 25.884 per dollar. The volatility of the log rate of return on yen exchange rates is 11.27%.

Pricing of the dollar fixed payment

Since the discount rate is 6% continuously compounding, we have the present value of $53million × 0.97 × exp(−0.06).

Pricing of the TRS put option

$$\$53 \text{ million} \times \left(\text{Max} \left[0.00\%, \frac{\text{Yen}_{\text{Mat}} - \text{Yen}_{\text{Spot}}}{\text{Yen}_{\text{Mat}}} \right] \right)$$

$$= \$53 \text{ million} \times \left(\text{Yen}_{\text{Spot}} \times \text{Max} \left[0.00\%, \frac{1}{\text{Yen}_{\text{Spot}}} - \frac{1}{\text{Yen}_{\text{Mat}}} \right] \right)$$

We see that the above equation is a yen put option with the excise price of $\frac{1}{\text{Yen}_{\text{Spot}}}$ ($0.008196 = 1/122$). By using the Garman–Kohlhagen formula, we can calculate the yen put option value, which comes to 2.56717%.

The third part of TRS, $\$53 \text{ million} \times \left(5 \times \frac{\text{Baht}_{\text{Spot}} - \text{Baht}_{\text{Mat}}}{\text{Baht}_{\text{Mat}}} \right)$, can be manipulated in a way similar to the second part.

$$\$53 \text{ million} \times \left(5 \times \frac{\text{Baht}_{\text{Spot}} - \text{Baht}_{\text{Mat}}}{\text{Baht}_{\text{Mat}}} \right)$$

$$= \$53 \text{ million} \times \text{Baht}_{\text{Spot}} \times \left(5 \times \frac{1}{\text{Baht}_{\text{Spot}}} - \frac{1}{\text{Baht}_{\text{Mat}}} \right)$$

Pricing of the baht forward contract

To calculate the forward value,[3] we apply the interest rate parity.

Applying the interest rate parity to price the baht forward contract, we have

$$\text{Baht}_{\text{Mat}} = \text{Baht}_{\text{Spot}} \times \exp \left[0.92 - 0.06 \right].$$

The forward value is 0.1482976%.

If we put three parts altogether, the present value of the payment made by Diamond on the termination date is $\exp \left[-0.06 \right] \times 0.97 - 0.0256717 - (-0.148297)$, which is 1.0361. It follows that Diamond receives $1 from Morgan on the trade day and takes on a liability with a present value of 1.0361. To put it another way, Diamond would have to pay back $1.10017 (i.e., $\exp \left[0.06 \right] \times 1.0361$) to Morgan on the termination day.

Pricing of the rupiah-linked notes

Since the notes' value depends on the future course of rupiah exchange rates, using arbitrage-free pricing, the expected future spot rate is the forward exchange rate. The forward prices in the forward contract, expiring six months hence and one year hence, are $2369.5 \times \exp[0.12/2 - 0.06/2]$ and $2369.5 \times \exp[0.12 - 0.06]$, respectively. After plugging the forward prices into the coupon and principal formula and discounting back to the present time, we have \$0.98930 if the principal is \$1. Since Diamond paid \$1 (i.e., the principal) to buy the notes and present value of cash flow from the notes is 0.98930, Diamond paid more than what they should pay to buy them.

17.5   Simulations

Since we have three currency exchange rates which influence the cash flow to see the combined effect of TRS and the notes' investments, we assume for simplicity that the yen is constant and the rupiah exchange rate six months hence is equal to the rupiah exchange rate one year hence. Furthermore, we assume that interest rate is 0.

Let us consider two extreme situations. In one, the baht and rupiah depreciate to the extent that they are converging to infinity. In the other, they are converging to 0. In the first case, Diamond will incur a loss of \$300 million and Morgan will get a fixed cash inflow of \$86.41 million. If IDR_1, IDR_2, $Baht_{Spot}$ and $Baht_{Mat}$ are going to infinity, as we assume in the first extreme situation, Diamond does not receive the coupon payments and the principal from the rupiah-linked notes. On top of that, Diamond will pay to JP Morgan \$265 million, because Diamond bought five baht forward contracts ($5 \times \$53$ million). Since derivative transactions are zero-sum games, we know that one party's loss is equal to the other party's profit. Therefore, the total profit of Morgan will be \$386.41 million. In the second case, where IDR_1, IDR_2, $Baht_{Spot}$ and $Baht_{Mat}$ are converging to 0, SKS will get infinite profit and Morgan will get a fixed cash inflow of \$86.41 million.[4] However, because it is a zero-sum game, Morgan will incur infinite loss, if there is no a cap clause for Morgan's loss in the contract. (See table 17.1 and figure 17.2.)

In figure 17.2, we have drawn the payoff on the part of SKS. When the baht and rupiah approach 60 and 15,000, respectively,[5] SKS will incur about \$232 million loss.

Table 17.1 Cash Flows of SKS and Morgan

Time	SKS	Morgan Guaranty
T_0	$-U\$35,000,000^*$	$+U\$35,000,000^{**}$
T_1	$U\$88,000,000 \times \left\{ \left[20.25\% \times \frac{2369.5}{IDR\_1} \right] \times \frac{Act}{365} + \left[20.20\% \times \frac{2369.5}{IDR\_1} \right] \times \frac{Act}{365} \right\}$	0
	$U\$88,000,000 \times \left\{ \left[20.25\% \times \frac{2369.5}{IDR\_2} \right] \times \frac{Act}{365} + \left[20.20\% \times \frac{2369.5}{IDR\_2} \right] \times \frac{Act}{365} \right\}$	0
T_2	$Max \begin{bmatrix} 0.00\%, \\ U\$88,000,000 \times \left(100\% + \frac{2369.5 - IDR\_1}{2369.5} + \frac{2369.5 - IDR\_2}{2369.5} \right) \times \frac{2369.5}{IDR\_2} \end{bmatrix}$ $+ U\$53,000,000 \times \left\{ Max \left[0.00\%, \frac{Yen_{Max} - Yen_{Spot}}{Yen_{Max}} \right] + 5 \times \frac{Baht_{Spot} - Baht_{Max}}{Baht_{Max}} \right\}$	***

*Since SKS borrowed U\$53,000,000 from Morgan and invested U\$88,000,000 to buy Rupiah Linked Notes, which Morgan Guaranty held, the cash outflow on the part of SKS is U\$35,000,000.

**Since Morgan sold the Rupiah Linked Notes to SKS at U\$88,000,000 and lent U\$53,000,000 to SKS, the net cash inflow of Morgan is U\$35,000,000.

***If the SKS's cash flow is positive (negative), Morgan Guaranty will pay (receive) the absolute value of that amount..

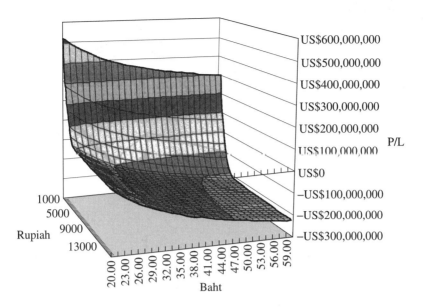

Figure 17.2 Simulation results Data: http://pacific.commerce.ubc.ca/xr/data.html Maximum profit and loss are \$A545, 445, 772 and −\$232, 440, 820, respectively.

However, if the baht and rupiah appreciate against the dollar, SKS will get about \$525 million profit. One thing that this simulation shows is that the payoff is volatile, depending on two exchange rates. We will quantify the riskiness of TRS combined with the rupiah-linked notes using VaR analysis.

17.6   VaR Calculation

We will see the combined risky level of the TRS and the rupiah-linked notes because the SKS position consists of the TRS and rupiah-linked notes. To this end, we used a historical simulation to calculate VaR. We collected daily exchange rates of three currencies over the period Feburary 13, 1996, to February 12, 1998; where the total of observation days is 760.[6] We converted them into daily rates of return on the exchange rates.

   We calculate the historical VaR on three different dates. The first date is the trade date (1997/2/12). The second date is the halfway date (1997/8/12) between the trade date and the terminiation date (1998/2/12). The third date is the termination date. By calculating the historical VaRs on three different dates, we can see how the risk level of TRS is changing across three dates. To this end, we collect the exchange rate data for one year before three different dates. From these one year exchange rates, we draw 100,000 random samples with replacement. Once we have 100,000 exchanges rates of three currencies, we can calculate the value of TRS as well as the Indonesian Rupiah Linked Notes for each set of three currency rates. Since we have 100,000 different values of TRS as well as the Indonesian Rupiah Linked Notes, we can generate the distribution from which we can calculate the historical VaR. The results are summarized in table 17.2.

   From the table 17.2, we can see that VaR does not properly forecast the loss which SKS actually incurred. The reason for this is that we estimate VaR based on past data,

Table 17.2 VaR Results

Period	Significant Level		
	10%	5%	1%
1996/2/13~1997/2/12	75,487,138	72,967,769	70,555,489
1996/8/13~1997/8/12	37,448,936	4,150,706	−5,381,140
1997/2/13~1998/3/12	−163,490,853	−173,741,049	−180,014,133

and the past data do not predict future exchange rates, especially when we experience a volatile situation like the Asian financial crisis. To overcome this VaR problem, we often conduct a stress test in addition to the VaR estimation.

17.7 Remarks

It is interesting to observe that we can construct highly complicated securities such as TRS by combining simple products like a European option or a forward contract. As a matter of fact, if we want to summarize financial engineering in two words, they would be "bundle" and "unbundle." We explain those words through TRS. Morgan has bundled the yen put option and the baht forward contract to create TRS, and SKS should unbundle TRS into three parts to evaluate it.[7]

This case demonstrates the importance of using business processes to manage the investment risk. As the SKS investment demonstrated, the risk analysis of an investment goes beyond the valuation of the derivatives. The source of the problem in the analysis of the case shows that the financial guarantees established in the structured finance led to significant losses for SKS.

Using the investment process to manage the risk, SKS should have begun with the establishment of the investment goal. If one seeks a 20% investment when the interest rate in dollars is only 6%, one may assume that there are risks involved. The goal of the investment should articulate the risk tolerance of the investment clearly.

The next phase of the investment process is the design phase, where the structure of the deal should be analyzed. In particular, the results should be simulated and the economic values (arbitrage-free fair value, as discussed above) calculated. The robustness of Morgan's proposal should have been analyzed and the risks should have been assured to be within the bounds of the investment goal determined in the first phase. Specifically, the effectiveness of the hedge between the baht and the yen would be in question. We have discussed the use of stressed scenarios. These tests would reveal that the guarantees were indeed risky.

The following phase is the test phase. In the test phase, the simulation would be tested with historical data and simulated under different exchange rate scenarios. These tests should verify the results of the design phase.

Finally, in the implementation phase, the investment returns should be marked to market, empirically showing the simulation results are valid. We have discussed how VaR should be used to monitor the risk exposure continually, in order to measure the risk exposure that may be compared with the marked to market realized risks. These analyses should be conducted daily. Thus any flaws in the simulations would have been detected, and actions would have been taken to rectify any miscalculations.

17.8 Concluding Remarks on Financial Modeling

The title of this book, *Financial Modeling,* emphasizes the process of developing financial models. The purpose of the book is not only to provide a collection of financial models, but also to show how to develop and apply them. We show that financial models should be built to provide business solutions, and therefore we often begin with the understanding of the business objective. We then proceed to the phase of specifying the model assumptions. By definition, the assumptions of any model cannot be realistic, and they are only approximations to reality. Nevertheless, these assumptions enable us to provide insights and measurements.

After determining the consistent set of assumptions, we move on to the implementation phase of financial modeling. In this phase, we determine the models in such a way that we can provide input information to the model and derive the output results. These output results can then be used to deal with the business problem.

Using the output results to solve the business problem is the application phase. In this phase we need to interpret the results carefully, taking all the assumptions into account. From these results, we can take decisions to act.

It is important to note that financial modeling is a cycle. We must continue to monitor the model and its applications. The monitoring enables us to minimize the model risk and adjust our assumptions with new information and empirical data. This is an important phase of the process. Often there are securities that we cannot model for lack of information. For example, builders of mortgage-backed securities models in late 1980s lacked the prepayment experiences to determine the prepayment models. Even though at that time we did not have an accurate financial model, we could still build a financial modeling process, with a procedure in place to update the models.

Another important aspect of this phase of financial modeling is to formulate investment or trading strategies. In our modeling, we have assumed efficient capital markets. When the financial model results do not support the efficient capital market hypothesis, we call these situations "anomalies" in the capital markets. In this phase of the financial modeling cycle, we can decide whether the "anomalies" are based on the model risks or market mispricing that can be exploited.

The case study in this chapter demonstrates these phases of financial modeling further. We began with the business objective of using a structured finance vehicle to provide abnormal investment returns. In the specification phase, we use the arbitrage-free framework to value the structures. In the implementation phase we determined the derivatives and the guarantees valuation models. In the application phase, we developed the simulations to show the risks inherent in the deal structure. At this phase, the investors can decide whether the expected returns justify the risks associated with the investment. The expected returns of the investments must necessarily be subject to the investors' view of the market: the uncertain movements of the exchange rates and the interest rates. To conclude the cycle, these models are used to monitor the deal to ensure that the assumptions of the model are valid. Such verification may include the estimates of the volatilities of the risk sources.

Often, financial engineers focus on building financial models. However, managing the different phases of financial modeling is perhaps the most important part of financial engineering.

Appendix A.   Total Return Swap Terms and Conditions as of January 29, 1997

Notional Amount:	US$53,000,000
Party A:	Morgan Guaranty Trust Company of New York
Party B:	Boram Bank, Hong Kong branch
Trade Date:	January 29, 1997
Start Date:	February 12, 1997
Termination Date:	February 12, 1998
Underlying Assets:	5,300,000 shares of Diamond Capital Investment Ltd.
Party A Pays:	US$ liquidation value of the underlying assets
Party B Pays:	Notional Amount × 97%
	$-1 \times \text{MAX}\left[0.00\%, (\text{Yen}_{Mat} - \text{Yen}_{Spot})/\text{Yen}_{Mat}\right]$
	$-5 \times (\text{Baht}_{Spot} - \text{Baht}_{Mat})/\text{Baht}_{Mat}$
Baht_{Spot}:	25.884
Baht_{Mat}:	Thai Baht foreign exchange rate, quoted as baht per dollar set as the midrate at 11 A.M. Singapore time two business days prior to the termination date with reference to Telerate Page 44175
Yen_{Spot}:	122.00
Calculation Agent:	J.P Morgan Securities Asia, Ltd.
Documentation:	ISDA

Appendix B.   Indonesian Rupiah-Linked Notes Final Terms and Conditions

Principal Amount:	US $44,000,000
Issuer:	National Westminster Bank, PLC
Trade Date:	January 29, 1997
Settlement Date:	February 12, 1997
Maturity:	February 12, 1998
Issue Price:	100.00% of principal amount
First Coupon:	[20.20% × 2369.5 /IDR_1] per annum, payable semiannually in arrears on Act/365 basis in dollars
Second Coupon:	[20.20% × 2369.5 /IDR_2] per annum, payable semiannually in arrears on Act/365 basis in dollars
Redemption:	Principal amount [100% + (2369.5 − IDR_1)/2369.5 +(2369.5 − IDR_2)/2369.5] × 2369.5/IDR_2 in dollars with a minimum of 0%
IDR_1:	Indonesian rupiah foreign exchange rate, quoted as the offer side of rupiah/dollar by Morgan at 11 A.M. Singapore time two business day prior to the first coupon date with reference to Reuters page MBRC.
IDR_2:	Indonesian rupiah foreign exchange rate, quoted as the offer side of rupiah/dollar by Morgan at 11 A.M. Singapore time two business day prior to the maturity date with reference to Reuters page MBRC.
Unwind Provision:	Upon request at any time during the life of the note, Morgan will provide an unwind valuation.
Business Days Convention:	Singapore, Jakarta, Tokyo, London, New York
Listing:	Listed in London

Appendix C.   The Put–Call Parity

The implication of the TRS for Diamond is that its portfolio position can be viewed as

Short dollar one-year payment+

put option on yen paid in dollars − baht forward paid in dollars

Now consider cash in yen as a risky asset ("stock") in a dollar account. Then (in chapter 4) we have shown the put–call parity, which states that

$$\text{Call(stock, X)} - \text{Put(stock, X)} + \text{bond(X)} = \text{Stock}$$

where the call and put options have the same underlying stock and a strike price X, which is also the face value of the bond, maturing at the expiration date of the put and call options. Applying the put–call parity to Diamond position, we have

Short dollar one-year payment + put option on yen paid in dollars =

Short yen cash + call option on yen paid in dollars

And if we rewrite Diamond's position, we can describe the portfolio as

Short yen cash + call option on yen paid in dollars + baht forward paid in dollars

In re-expressing the portfolio this way, we can see the initial rationale for the baht forward contracts. At the time of structuring the deal, SKS believed that the baht was the target to a basket of currencies related to Thailand's trading partners. One major component was the yen. With an implied short position in yen cash, it was calculated that the long position of the baht forward contract would hedge the yen currency risks. In essence, if the baht forward contract had been effective in hedging the yen risks, Diamond would have faced no downside risk.

Notes

1. This case is based on "A Study on the Conflict between the JP Morgan and SKS" written by Sang Bin Lee in *Economic Review*, 20, 1999, Hanyang Economic Research Center, Seoul, Korea.

2. Garman, M., and S. Kohlhagen, "Foreign Currency Option Values," *Journal of International Money and Finance* 2 (December 1983): 231–237.

3. Even though Morgan put the cap on their loss in the forward contract, we ignore the cap feature for simplicity. The forward value is the same with or without the cap feature.

4. Since there are no stochastic terms like IDR_1, IDR_2, $Baht_{Spot}$ and $Baht_{Mat}$ on the part of JP Morgan, Morgan will get a fixed cash inflow regardless of two extreme situations.

5. We also assume that the yen is constant, as we do in table 17.1.

6. We collected data from http:/pacific.commerce.ubc.ca/xr/data.html..

7. SKS would not have experienced its nightmare if it had carefully followed the unbundle process in advance.

18

Concluding Thoughts

The potential application of financial models is vast. Modern financial modeling has been built since the 1970s. It is a process that begins with economic theories, proceeds to the formulation of financial models, and ends with their applications to financial markets. Despite the dramatic growth in financial modeling, the subject remains young. Its full implications will be felt only when we can appreciate its potential applications beyond the capital markets. Corporate finance, tax/financial reporting, regulations, equity research, and more will be the new frontiers in the applications of financial models in the coming decades.

Capital markets and corporate finance are two parts that make up a whole; one cannot function completely without the other. Capital markets invest in corporations and can maintain a somewhat complete market for all contingencies by using corporation securities. Corporate finance requires capital markets to determine the optimal values of securities which the corporation holds and issues. This book explains how capital markets and corporate finance are interrelated by describing the financial models of both in one coherent framework.

The previous 17 chapters have taken us from the basic present value concept to the valuation of a firm. This progressive exposition of financial valuation modeling describes the building blocks of financial modeling, from options to exotic options, from bonds to a broad range of financial innovations, from the trading books to the structural balance sheets of financial institutions, and from credit risk valuation to the valuation of a going concern.

We suggest that financial valuation models can be used for financial decisions and for developing trading and risk management strategies. Since these models can be tested empirically, we hope this book offers not just a review of the long and vigorous development of a valuation modeling approach, but also a stimulation for further research and applications of modeling to financial management.

The central premise of the book is to present the contingent claim model to describe the theoretical as well as the practical aspects of capital markets and corporate finance. We believe proposing such an approach is the main contribution of the book. In this chapter, we offer three aspects of financial modeling to highlight the central theme of the book, which is financial modeling.

1. We follow the historical conceptual development of financial valuation modeling. These concepts provide the theoretical foundation for the specifications of the models.
2. We describe a broad range of valuation models and develop a conceptual structure that best expresses the insights in building a valuation model.
3. We describe the applications of the valuation models from capital markets to corporate finance. We show that modeling is an indispensable tool for financial management and will become more important in its evolution. We conclude with our thoughts on the future.

18.1   Conceptual Development of Financial Models

The development of financial models did not occur overnight. Since the 1970s, knowledge and understanding of financial modeling has continually pushed the frontiers of exploration. Many pioneers in theories, empirical testing, and applications have contributed to these achievements. Some of these contributors provided the core principles of finance on which these models are based.

Eugene Fama first proposed the definition of market efficiency and hypothesized that our capital markets were efficient. Without an efficient capital market, the law of one price would not hold and the valuation model would have much less importance to the financial community. When securities' prices do not reflect the information in the marketplace, there is no meaning to "relative valuation."

Prior to the development of relative valuation, value was determined by discounting the expected future cash flow by an appropriate discount rate. Harry Markowitz and William Sharpe developed the portfolio theory, the Capital Asset Pricing model, that determines the appropriate risk premium for discounting to reflect the market risk aversion behavior. The portfolio theory argues that the risk premium should apply only to undiversifiable risks. However, this premium is not easily observable in the capital market. This approach remains an imprecise tool.

Perhaps one beginning of the relative pricing theory is the use of the arbitrage-free argument. The ability for any investor to sell an asset (even though he does not own it) and buy another asset enables the market to develop one price, if the two assets have the same cash flow. Therefore the arbitrage-free mechanism ensures that the law of one price holds.

Merton Miller and Franco Modigliani were the first to propose the assumption of a perfect capital market that leads to the arbitrage argument. In this idealized world, it is possible to grasp the concepts of the arbitrage mechanism and realize the impact it has on securities pricing. They were the first to apply this concept to corporate finance— the Modigliani–Miller theory, which showed that the value of a firm is independent of corporate financial decisions.

Fischer Black and Myron Scholes were the first to propose two important insights. First, they identified a class of securities called derivatives. If a derivative has a price risk directly related to the price risk of another security (the underlying security), then the value of the derivative should be priced relative to the underlying security. Second, the arbitrage mechanism can be used in a dynamic way to determine the derivative value. The Black–Scholes model proposed to neutralize the risk inherent in options. Option risks can be eliminated by taking the opposite position in the stock. There should be a specific ratio between the stock and option positions such that the risks from the stock and the option exactly cancel each other. Then the appropriate discount rate can be determined for the derivative value. The Black–Scholes model is important because it provides insights into the pricing of a broad range of securities. Until this model was devised, the market had no effective way of valuing derivatives. Further, the model can be empirically tested, and results show that it can be a valuable tool for a broad range of financial management: trading, investments, and risk management, among others.

In the late 1970s, U.S. interest rates were no longer targeted, and were adjusted by market forces. Compounded by inflation rates, U.S. Treasury securities rates were volatile. Researchers tried to extend the Black–Scholes model to interest rate risks. However, interest rates are not securities, and the yield curve movements must also be constrained—they are not underlying securities in the same way as stock options. Instead of applying the Black–Scholes model directly to bonds, research introduced interest rate models. These models used the arbitrage argument to determine the movements of the yield curve, viewing a class of bonds as contingent claims to the yield curve. In subsequent years the interest rates were no longer targeted by the central bank, interest rate risks became significant, and we witnessed a growth of research in term structure models and their applications to the bond with embedded options.

Stocks, bonds, and currencies can be considered the bedrock of the securities markets. The natural extension of these theories is to incorporate the currencies. Further, research extended the valuation approach to a broad range of options, called exotic options. They include Asian options, compound options, chooser options, and many others, used in the capital markets or embedded in securities.

Robert Merton was the first to introduce the option pricing (later called the structural model) approach to corporate securities. The structural model suggested using the balance sheet information to value bonds. Thus credit risks could be analyzed along with interest rate risks. That is, the structural model enables us to value the firm's liability as a contingent claim to the firm value.

Based on what the book has discussed, we can further assert that firms can be viewed as contingent claims to some risk factors. Research proposes that real options are contingent claims on business opportunities. The real options approach used risk factors as the underlying security. Here, we present an integrated approach to valuing the firm and formulate the optimal financial strategies.

Financial researchers are not the only main contributors to the success of the valuation models. Richard Bellman's optimization principles are central to specifying the behavior of rational decisions made by option holders, and hence the valuation of myriad options. In addition, Edward Deming's concept of quality control enables us to specify the process engineering for financial risk management.

The core of these principles of finance guides us toward a deeper understanding of building financial models so that we can apply financial models to strategic and tactical financial management. These principles have changed finance as a social science by building a new foundation.

18.2   Overview of Valuation Models

Some corporations and investment companies use the traditional discounted expected cash flow method to value stocks and bonds. They calculate the present value of future cash flows that the securities are expected to generate. But there is a shortcoming in this method; it fails to adjust for the contingency of the cash flows. A slight hitch that is ever so present in valuation models is how to determine the appropriate discount rate for such cash flows.

We unveil the relative valuation model to supersede the discounted expected cash flow method. Not only does it enable us to determine the appropriate discount rate, but it can also be extended to value equity options, which are priced relative to an underlying security. In fact, a broad range of equity options can be modeled by specifying the terminal and boundary conditions. The relative valuation model provides a general solution to the valuation problem when the discount rates are changing over time. The value is determined by continually revising the hedge, using the underlying stocks and bonds so that the equilibrium discount rate is not required. This general model is shown to be consistent with fair value pricing because the model does not permit any arbitrage opportunity.

The relative valuation model for equity options can be extended to interest rate contingent claims. They are contingent claims because these interest rate models are based on interest rate risks such as short-term interest rates rather than stock risk. The relative pricing model is shown to be extendable to any set of risk sources. This solution maintains arbitrage-free conditions, in which the one-period risk-neutral expected rate of return of any maturity bond is the one-period risk-free rate.

When there are multiple risk sources, as in the cases of interest rate options, valuation models can be developed to incorporate them. This general solution can apply to a broad range of derivatives, often referred to as exotic options. Considering that these option models require only no-arbitrage opportunities, which is a necessary condition for a fair valuation of any securities, they can be used to provide fair valuation of financial instruments that do not necessarily have a liquid market. Option adjusted spread can be used as a construct to capture the liquidity or the default spread of the instruments. In doing so, pricing models can be developed for corporate bonds and mortgage-backed securities.

For a firm that is subject to default risk, the equity of the firm can be viewed as an equity option on the firm value, and the corporate bond as a fixed payment with a short position of a put option on the firm value. Applying the option valuation models and calibrating the models to the observed data on a recovery rate, we developed models for high-yield securities. This approach enabled us to extend our general model to securities that have credit risks and interest rate risks, including convertible bonds.

We extend these concepts further to show that financial instruments that lack marketability (or are close to nonmarketable) can be fairly valued. The contingent claim valuation model can be used to value principal financial institutions' balance sheets: deposit accounts of banks and insurance products of insurers. The fair valuation of financial institutions provides effective balance sheet management and risk management.

Financial modeling is further extended from capital markets to corporate finance. We argue that firms are contingent claims on real sector opportunities; each class of firms has its own valuation models, just as each exotic option has its own pricing model. We apply this general valuation approach to value firms, which are characterized by their business models. Business models are used to determine the key sources of business risks, sources of income, and the cost structure of firms' investment. Their investment opportunities are valued as real options—options based not on financial assets but on the uncertain investment opportunities in the real sector. The business model can then be linked to an objective function in the corporate model. The corporate model is introduced to determine the financial decisions and risk management strategies of the firm. Then all the performance measures of the firm can be derived. Financial models, such as the business model and the corporate model, can be applied to principal financial institutions to meet some of their business challenges.

18.3   Applications of the Financial Models

Financial models have a broad range of applications in investments, hedging, fair value analysis, risk management, and corporate finance. All these applications demonstrate that financial models are tools for corporate and investment companies. Traders and portfolio managers use financial models routinely. However, we propose that these financial models will also be a beneficial for corporate managers in making financial decisions that are optimal in maximizing their firm value or the shareholders' value. We hope these applications will encourage corporate managers to use financial models in the future.

Investment

Financial models are used in investment in many different ways. One common application is the cheap/rich analysis. Financial models enable us to compare the observed market price against the theoretical price of a security. The theoretical price is often called the fair value. Such a comparison helps investors to judge whether the security is trading fairly, or if the security is being undervalued (cheap) or overpriced (rich). Modeling is an important tool to benchmark the value of a traded security. Financial models are used to determine the option adjusted spread of bonds. The option adjusted spreads provide a way to compare the relative valuation of bonds across different fixed-income securities sectors.

Another application is the total return analysis. The use of models enables investors to simulate the returns of a security under different market scenarios. We have simulated the returns of a corporate bond if the interest rate falls, as well as the look-back option price change when the underlying security's price falls precipitously.

Financial models are used to enhance index strategies. The performance of portfolio managers is often based on comparing the bond portfolio returns against those of the benchmark portfolio indexes. The portfolio managers seek to outperform the market indices. For fixed-income markets, the benchmark could be the Lehman Index, which consists of a large number of bonds traded in the marketplace. The financial models of bonds enable us to construct a portfolio of a small number of bonds that can replicate the behavior of any broad-based index. The replication allows us to select the bonds that can outperform the index.

Financial models are used in investment processes to calculate the "greeks" of the benchmarks, that is, the sensitivities of the benchmarks such as the delta and the durations. The portfolio managers can manage the risks and returns of the portfolios using such analytics. The portfolio performances are measured using return attributions. The sources of returns can be identified using the financial models. This way, portfolio managers can identify the sources of returns and attribute the returns to their intended actions. They can specify the excess returns due to their bets on the market direction. The return attribution process provides a systematic approach to analyze the performance of a portfolio.

Hedging Strategies

Hedging is a way to control the risk exposure of the portfolio or asset–liability positions. It is a technique that should and can be used in management of hedge funds, the structural balance sheet, trading positions, and delivery of real goods like crude oil.

We have introduced the "greeks" of a derivative, which include delta, gamma, theta, vega, rho, duration, convexity, and key rate durations. The sensitivities of a security enable us to replicate the returns of a derivative by continually adjusting the hedge ratios, using the underlying securities. The financial models provide a systematic approach to hedging a derivative.

Financial models also offer a systematic approach to static hedging of a security or a portfolio. Static hedging does not require a continual revision of the positions of the hedging instruments. The approach is a buy and hold strategy that enables investors to manage illiquid securities.

Related to static hedging is the use of financial models to implement replications of option-embedded financial products, which include insurance products, structured derivatives for institutional clients, and innovative corporate liabilities. The use of path-wise values enables us to decompose a security to its basic building blocks. This decomposition enables us to replicate a financial instrument by marketable assets, which can be bought or sold in the market. Replications use the law of one price (arbitrage conditions) to maintain the pricing relationships across different markets.

Fair Value Analysis

Financial models are used beyond trading floors and asset management. They can provide a systematic and consistent methodology to value securities that do not have a liquid market, if they have a market at all. Financial models are used to provide the fair value, also commonly called the economic value or the market value. Fair values are based on the present value of the future payments; in contrast, book values are based on the historical costs. This concept and the methodology to determine such measures have broad applications.

The fair value approach is central to the pricing of financial products widely available in the marketplace. These financial products lead to continual innovations that make our markets efficient. The exotic options market and collateralized mortgage obligations are examples of financial innovations. Any new financial products by definition have no markets at the beginning. Fair value is used to initiate the price discovery process until the markets become sufficiently liquid. Financial models continue to help the financial market become more efficient and complete during the process.

Even nontraded securities that lack marketability can be analyzed using the contingent claim modeling. There are many examples of financial instruments that have no markets and prices, such as insurance and banking products. The models provide a rational pricing for these products even though there is no secondary market to discover the price. The fair value approach provides a systematic way to measure profitability. The ability to quantify the profitability of these products leads to innovations of financial products in order to meet customers' needs.

High-yield bonds that have significant default risk can be measured using financial models. Although such bonds are often illiquid and complex to analyze or value, contingent claim valuation models relate the credit risks (the measure of the probability of default) to the valuation of high-yield bonds by taking many risk factors into consideration. The model can be used to explain how the firm's operating leverage, business risk, the capital and debt structure, and strategic value determine the high-yield bond value. That is, a high-yield bond value is dependent not only on its terms and conditions but also on the default probability and the recovery ratio. All these factors affect the risk, and hence the discount rate, of the bond. High-yield bond fair value plays an important role in the efficiency of corporate fundings and innovations in corporate liabilities.

Recently, fair value has become the focus of discussions regarding corporate financial disclosures. In the future, fair value accounting will have a significant impact on the management of firms. The acceptance of financial model values in the marketplace enables regulators to consider fair value accounting. Adopting the fair value approach will require two significant departures in the generally accepted accounting principles (GAAP). First, fair value will focus on values with a forward-looking basis and not a historical basis. Second, fair value accounting will focus more on value and less on income, as opposed to the GAAP accounting, which strives to match income with expenses. We have discussed the broad implications of such departures for financial disclosures. The fair value accounting approach offers the investing public a better way to understand the firm's value, but the implementation of such concepts will have to overcome many challenges. The appropriate use of financial models will play an important role in the design of the implementations.

Risk Management

In reviewing the financial losses of the 1990s, we discussed the importance of risk management to the proper functioning of financial systems. Financial models should be used for risk management to regulate the business process of the firm.

First, they should be applied to asset–liability management. Financial models are important tools to asset–liability management in a number of ways. They can determine the transfer pricing between assets and liabilities. Since both assets and liabilities may have embedded options, financial models are used to identify the embedded options and to see how the option risks from the assets can be transferred to the liabilities or vice versa.

In order to build benchmarks for performance measures in asset–liability management, financial models are needed. A block of business of liabilities can be replicated by marketable securities. In so doing, the replication of the liability using these marketable securities can be used as a benchmark for the management of the assets. In this asset–liability management process, we can manage any mismatch of risks between assets and liabilities.

Financial models are used to determine risk measure standards. Value at risk and earnings at risk are examples. We suggest that Deming's concept of quality control, viewing a business as a process built from well-defined phases, can be used to construct benchmarks for risk management and risk measures. Each phase has clear specifications of roles and responsibilities for each business unit. The results of each phase are measured using statistical techniques. We argue that risk management is identifying, measuring, monitoring, and managing the performance of a business process, with appropriate feedback mechanisms. In short, risk management is quality control on a production process that is based on financial risks.

Corporate Finance

In the near future, financial models will have a broader impact on corporate finance. Three areas that will be affected are real options, the business model, and the corporate model.

Financial models are used to determine the value of investment opportunities. Real options are embedded options in the value of a firm. Specifically, a firm with growth potential has significant strategic value that is not based on any capital budgeting decisions or specific financial planning or expected income from the client base. Strategic value is the valuation of the firm based on potential profits that the firm could exploit if such an opportunity is made available. In valuing these real options, we have discussed a methodology to formulate investment strategy, beyond the tactical capital budgeting approach. We show how capital budgeting decisions, based on a bottom-up approach, can be reconciled with strategic investments, based on the top-down approach.

Financial models are not confined to describing financial securities, particularly market-traded derivatives. Financial models can be built to describe the valuation of firms. The specification of such a model is called the business model. We propose that the business model is analogous to the terms and conditions of the financial products or derivatives. It specifies how the firm pays profits to its claimants (stockholders and bondholders, for example) as a contingent claim to its business risks. Firms differ, not just because they have different business risks but also because of how the risks are allocated to their stakeholders (including vendors, employees, and management) and the market price of the business risk. Financial models provide a systematic way to value a firm so that we can see how the financial decisions made by the management can be attributed to the firm value maximization.

We have extended the business model to the corporate model for financial managers. Currently, corporate finance and capital market financial models are quite separate, in that the valuation of the securities (stocks and bonds) is not often directly related to corporate financial decisions. For example, we have shown that financial decision support tools, such as dynamic financial analysis, are often not based on any financial theory of capital markets. They are projections or simulations of the financial statements, based on accounting rules. The corporate model should be specified to link corporate finance with securities valuation that is consistent with the capital market valuation.

We have proposed a corporate model that can relate financial performance measures derived from financial statements to the firm's market values, such as capitalization and fair values of the firm's bank loans, and to other corporate liabilities (public or private). By relating the financial performance measures of the firm to the firm's market values, we can better understand the issues in financial disclosures, showing how financial disclosures are related to market valuation or vice versa. In essence, the corporate model provides the direct link behind the commonly used financial ratios, such as price/earnings ratio (P/E ratio) and market to book ratio (capitalization/book equity). This link has direct applications to stock analysis and investment banking.

18.4   Financial Modeling as a Process

Financial modeling is a process. We begin with financial theories that provide us the assumptions to build the models. The models are then used to provide analytical results. These results are then used to provide solutions to our business problems. Finally, the results are monitored to enable us to adjust the assumptions to our models.

Figure 18.1 summarizes the process. We begin with examples of business objectives and conclude with the applications of the model. The use of the financial model requires us to evaluate the model assumptions continually.

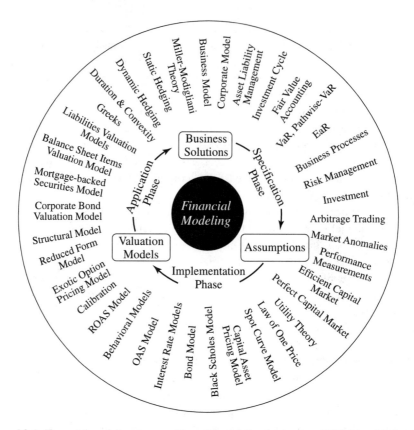

Figure 18.1 Financial modeling process. Financial modeling is a process. We begin with financial theories that provide the assumptions to build the models. The models are then used to provide analytical results. These results are used to provide solutions to our business problems. Finally, the results are monitored to enable us to adjust the assumptions to our models.

18.5   Looking into the Future

Financial modeling has a vigorous past in its developments, conceptual progress, and impacts of its applications in practice. We do not know where the new developments will lead us. We can only predict that financial modeling will have a vigorous future. We would feel enormously rewarded if our exposition of financial modeling can contribute to some changes in the financial community in what we think are the right directions. Below is the authors' partial wish list of six items.

Rational Accounting System

Banks, insurance companies, asset management firms, corporations, venture capitalists, and all market participants would agree on one goal: to maximize the wealth of the stakeholders. However, accounting performance measures based on GAAP accounting principles often do not lead to such a goal. The goals of maximizing earnings and other performance measures often conflict with maximizing shareholders' wealth. We have seen how fair value accounting, which is applied only to assets and not to liabilities, leads to complications in asset–liability management of financial institutions. We have shown how the book value accounting fails to measure option valuation in employee compensation for corporations, and financial guarantees in pension investments. Financial objectives can be distorted by financial performance measures based on book value accounting. As financial innovations continue to impact our capital markets and as global financial systems mature, a more rational accounting system will be necessary for improved functioning of the economy.

We hope this book provides a broad enough description of basic issues to show that companies can be measured and analyzed in one consistent fashion, and at the same time to recognize that different firms and industry sectors have their own distinct business models. Financial reports should be more transparent, with a clearer depiction of the business model in order to see the linkages between the business risks and the financial results.

Some of the concepts described in the book can be used in a rational accounting system: (1) forward-looking accounting that is based on future contingency of payments, thus capturing not just the uncertainties but also the payouts related to the different states of the world; (2) use of an appropriate discount rate that takes the different prices of risks into account; (3) use of calibration to value items on the balance sheet, which will lead to the marking to market approach, thus extending the practice on the trading floor to corporate finance.

Financial Disclosures

Our present financial disclosures to investors are based in large part on accounting disclosures. In testimony before Congress during the investigations of WorldCom's alleged fraudulent financial disclosures, both the external auditors and the stock analysts insisted that the source of the problem was that they were given false financial information. That means both external auditing and analysis of the firm's capitalization depend crucially on financial accounting statements provided by the firm. Clearly, financial disclosures are important. But the present definition of financial disclosure is too narrow in scope and too ambiguous to be used as a source of information.

Our use of the business model suggests a financial modeling approach to link business risks to financial performances. We hope that financial disclosures will include more on the business risks and the business model, such as the projected cost of fuel for airlines, or the advertising rates and subscription base for the dot.coms. A systematic display of the forecast inputs to the firm's business model will provide a transparent picture of the financial health of the firm and accountability of the management to the investors.

Today, a business model is a vague concept; it generally refers to the business plan of a firm, or even just a business concept of the management. There is no rigorous treatment of the business model assumptions or of the relationship of the business model to the profit payouts to the firm's investors. A clearer disclosure of the firm's business model, and a systematic measure of its performance, can lead investors and management to a more efficient allocation of resources and a more robust financial system.

More Finance in Financial Planning

From capital markets to corporate finance, valuation is central to management decisions. We hope this book provides a systematic approach to valuation, irrespective of the decisions made for capital budgeting or for bond trading.

Today, many firms seek to meet earnings targets, stabilize future earnings, and attain steady growth. These are financial performance targets that may not be maximizing shareholders' value. We hope that financial managers will focus more on the enhancement of the economic value of the firm, using the financial valuation models that are derived from basic economic assumptions, as illustrated by the models described in this book.

The use of these financial models should be incorporated into the financial planning that, to date, is based in large part on accounting rules. The use of an appropriate discount rate for risks, the cost of borrowing based on the market pricing of bonds, and the market evaluation of the risk of the projects are not usually considered in these models. We hope that future financial planning will be based on financial valuation in a way similar to that proposed in regard to the use of corporate model.

Uniting Strategic Planning and Capital Budgeting

The discounted cash flow method is used in capital budgeting, yet large investment outlays are made without being based on any cash flow projections. Corporations tend to dichotomize investments to strategic investment (top-down) and capital budgeting (bottom-up). Using a well-specified business model and a corporate model, we can bridge the gap between the two approaches. In establishing the bridge, the strategic planning can be more explicit in its implementations, and capital budgeting can be integrated into a corporate planning framework. We believe the shareholders' value and the net present value of a project have to be related to the business model of the firm, under a specific strategic investment plan. We hope that business models will be more widely used to specify the strategic planning of firms.

Using Financial Process Engineering to Manage Risk

We hope risk management is beyond measuring and monitoring risks. After all, risks and returns are inseparable, and therefore we cannot manage them separately. We hope risk management will be the active part of the design of a business process, and not just the measuring and monitoring of the process when the business model has already been put in place. Risk management is the integral part of the design and its maintenance.

We hope risk management is not simply about managing the financial disclosures and statements. It is forward-looking, and therefore it must integrate the capital markets and corporate decisions in one paradigm. By calibrating the performance of the firm to the market continually, we can detect defects in the process before they grow into large financial losses—the very essence of risk management.

Specifically, we hope risk management can use financial models to develop benchmarks for performance measures for each phase of the business process. There are milestones in the business process where the outputs can be measured. Using feedback mechanisms, risk management strategies can be put in place to correct any problems detected. We hope to see a map on the wall of the risk manager's office that shows how the risks are transformed in the business processes and how actions can be put in place when red lights start flashing.

Growth of Real Sector Contingent Claims Markets

Derivatives do not have to be confined to contingent claims on the financial sectors. They can be extended to be contingent claims on the real sectors. We hope that innovations will continue to make the markets more complete, so that we can have better access to different outcomes of the real sectors. These innovations may be the forward market on national income, housing starts, and other economic indicators. Financial publications need not focus on the stock and bond prices, but on all the output data: agricultural outputs, electricity supply, patents pending, and many others. Financial claims on these economic risks are as valuable to the economy as claims on financial securities.

Corporate insurance is offered in the marketplace for corporations to partially unload their business risks to insurance companies. Innovations of corporate insurance (insurance products for managing business risks) and innovations in capital markets can be one and the same. Risk-sharing can be securitized so that business risks are assured to be more diversified. Business risk can be securitized when firms can define the business models more rigorously, and corporate finance and capital markets are more integrated in the management decision-making process. We hope a real sector contingent claim market will grow and will lead to securitization of the business risks.

18.6   The World of Contingent Claims

In 1987, Mr. M. Hitori of Yamaichi Securities Ltd. (USA) and I were celebrating the joint venture agreement between our two companies at their headquarters in the World Trade Center. I had just flown back from Tokyo after many long, grueling negotiations with the parent company, and we were glad that all the posturing was over and we could talk about our future.

Inside the quiet boardroom, away from the hustle and bustle of the trading floor below, I looked out from the 96th floor. The Hudson River was glistening in the afternoon sun, flowing south, passing the Statue of Liberty, before opening to the Atlantic Ocean. The future awaited us.

After some niceties, Mr. Hitori became serious. His face was stern and his eyes half closed, as if he was carefully choosing his words. He lifted his cup of tea and said, "To World Peace." "Yes, Mr. Hitori. Please explain." "Today, you have a stake in our success and we have a stake in yours. Japanese and Americans are different people, but money is our common numeraire that brings us together. Finance brings people together. We, the finance people, are the workers for world peace."

No one questioned that the contract we had just signed was a contingent claim on our company, GAT. GAT's successes were based on the future growth of the demand for financial services in a specific way, as described in our business model. And in turn, a vibrant economy was the driving engine behind the successes of many financial corporations. Contracts like the one we just consummated, are signed, negotiated, and traded many times over the world, and they maintain the economy for the future.

There may be some skeptical readers who relate finance to greed, which many times has been a basis for war. They find it incredible to argue that finance is in fact the foundation for peace. Cynics may say this is more a view of nations of wealth, and finance is only another way for them to accumulate more wealth. These cynics may be the same readers who find the assumptions of the valuation of contingent claims to be too preposterous to be useful, in turn disregarding the broader meaning of contingent claims: sharing the economic wealth of the world.

"Yes, Mr. Hitori. Maybe one day the contingent claim theory will be extended to geopolitical models. To world peace."

19

Technical Matters: Market Model and Binomial Lattices

The ability to master two art forms—mathematical finance and economic intuition—in using financial modeling is key to delivering optimal business solutions. Mathematical finance simultaneously provides an elegant generalized description of financial theories and a powerful tool to derive financial modeling solutions. But its abstraction should be related to the economic intuitions that remain the bedrock of financial theories.

We have described binomial lattices for modeling a security or interest rate movements, and we have shown how these models are used for valuing securities in the capital markets and for determining optimal decisions in corporate finance. In the capital markets, we can use binomial lattices to value a broad range of securities, such as securities' whose value may depend on multiple risk sources and optimal decisions of the investors or the issuers. In corporate finance, we have shown how the binomial lattice can be used in corporate and strategic investment decisions. This framework provides us with tools to determine optimal corporate decisions, and relate to the capital market by showing how corporate decisions affect the equity and bond prices of a firm. Therefore, this binomial lattice framework provides a flexible and intuitive analytical tool for financial modeling.

Recently, there has been an extraordinary growth of research in continuous time models, some of which we indicated in chapters 5 and 6. The HJM, BGM/J, and other models have shown that by using the continuous time framework, general interest rate models can be developed that satisfy a broad range of requirements. The purpose of this chapter is to relate the binomial lattice approach to the general framework of the continuous time model. This chapter is written for financial engineers with a mathematical background.

The chapter has three sections. The first section describes a formulation of market models using binomial lattices. This approach provides the mathematical foundation and the intuition behind the "change of measures" that derives the Black models from an interest rate model. The second section describes the necessary mathematical tools explains how the continuous time model values securities. The continuous time framework uses much mathematical formalism to determine the martingale measures. The binomial lattice model may provide a clearer understanding of the approach. The third section describes how the discrete time derivation is different from the continuous time derivation for the European call option. In this section we show that two approaches are basically the same.

In appendix A, we provide the derivations of the continuous time models of a sample of interest rate models described in chapters 5 and 6. These derivations show how the continuous time and binomial models are related mathematically. Appendix B summarizes three representations in modeling interest rate risks for a sample of interest rate models. The interest rate movements can be modeled by (1) the spot rate movements, (2) the instantaneous forward rate movement, (3) bond price dynamics. Appendix C shows how to combine a binomial lattice in a way that path-dependent cash flow can be converted to path-independent cash flow.

The exposition of these results enables us to better appreciate the formal mathematics used in much of continuous time financial modeling. The chapter can therefore bridge the gap between the binomial lattice and the continuous time modeling. This chapter is particularly useful for financial engineers who have been exposed to continuous time modeling. Using this chapter, they can understand financial models in an alternative perspective. At the same time, this chapter is also useful for financial engineers trained in binomial modeling. They can use this chapter to tie their intuitive approach in binomial modeling to the mathematics needed for developing complex models.

19.1   Building a Market Model in a Binomial Lattice

Black models for bond options, cap/floors, and swaptions are called market models because the inputs to these interest rate contingent claim models do not require the use of short-term rates or instantaneous forward rates. The inputs to these models tend to be benchmark securities or rates, such as three-month LIBOR or one-year swap. These market models resemble the Black–Scholes model because the valuation is expressed more directly from the underlying asset values.

We now show that the change of numeraire approach can be implemented in a fairly straightforward manner under the framework of a binomial lattice. And we can relate market models to the binomial interest rate models. First we specify the simple Ho–Lee model for illustrative purposes.

The Ho–Lee Model

This formulation is a bit more general than that reported in chapter 5. The formulation does not require the probability to be 0.5, even though in the numerical example we continue to assume the probability to be 0.5. The yield curve is flat at 6 percent and the interest rate volatility is 20 percent.

π: the risk neutral probability (constant)

$P(T) = \exp(-rT)$: initial discount function

$\delta = \exp(-2\sigma r)$: input data

$h(T) = \dfrac{1}{\pi + (1 - \pi) \cdot \delta^T}$: perturbation function lattice

$P(n, i, T) = \dfrac{P(T + n)}{P(n)} \dfrac{\prod_{t=n}^{T+n-1} h(t)}{\prod_{t=1}^{n-1} h(t)} \delta^{T \cdot i}$: a discount function of maturity (T)

at time n and state i

$F(n, i, T^*, T) = \dfrac{P(n, i, T^* + T - n)}{P(n, i, T^* - n)}$: the forward price at time n and state i

where the forward contract delivers a (T) time to maturity bond

at the expiration date T^* (See figure 19.1).[1]   (19.1)

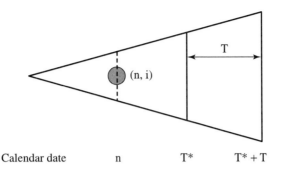

Calendar date   n   T*   T* + T

Figure 19.1 Calendar date versus time to maturity. T is a time to maturity variable rather than a calendar time. Since the forward contract with the forward price of $F(n, i, T^*, T)$ delivers the T time to maturity bond at time T^*, the deliverable bond is the $T^* + T$ period bond at the initial time. n and T^* represent the calendar time, and T represents the time to maturity, which is consistent with the notation of the Ho–Lee model.

To understand the market model from the Ho–Lee model perspective, we can consider using a bond option as an example. Let us consider a bond call option expiring at time $T^*(= 5)$, with the underlying bond of the option a zero-coupon bond with the time to maturity of $T(= 3)$ at the option expiration date, $T^*(= 5)$.

The Ho–Lee model can determine the one-year discount rate lattice $P(n, i, 1)$, as illustrated in figure 19.2.

At time $T^*(= 5)$, the underlying bond prices at each state are $P(5, i, T)$ where $T = 3$ and $i = 0, \cdots, 4$. The price lattice of the underlying bond is given in figure 19.3.

Now we use the recursive procedure with the risk-neutral probability of 0.5 and determine the bond call option price, as we discussed in chapter 5. (See figure 19.4.)

We can reformulate the call option valuation another way. We can determine the necessary change of the risk-neutral probability to the equivalent martingale probability, which is called forward measures, such that the valuation model of the call option is similar to the Black model. That is, the option value is the present value of the expected payoff of the cash flow at the option maturity, where the expectation is based not on the

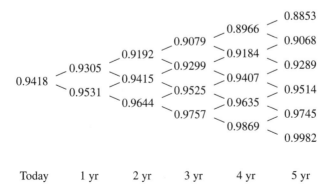

Today   1 yr   2 yr   3 yr   4 yr   5 yr

Figure 19.2 The one-period discount function lattice of the Ho–Lee model

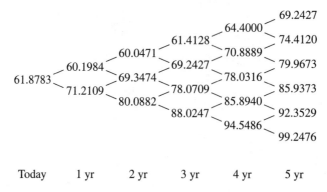

Today   1 yr   2 yr   3 yr   4 yr   5 yr

Figure 19.3 The price lattice of the underlying bond. We assume that the underlying bond is a zero-coupon bond with the face value of 100. The maturity date of the bond call option is year 5. The underlying bond of the bond call option is a 3-year bond at the option maturity date, which is year 5. Therefore, the underlying zero-coupon bond pays the face value (=100) at year 8.

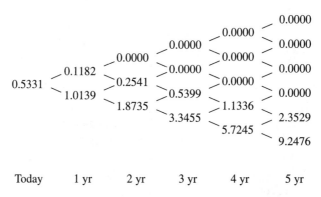

Today   1 yr   2 yr   3 yr   4 yr   5 yr

Figure 19.4 The price lattice of the bond call option by backward substitution. The option payoff condition at maturity date is $Max[P(5, i, 3) - X, 0]$ where the exercise price (X) is 90. Therefore the option payoff in the lower right corner at year 5 is 9.2476 (= $Max[99.2476 - 90.0]$). We can obtain the bond option value (=0.5331) at the initial time by backward substitution where we use the risk-neutral probability of 0.5 and the one-period discount functions given in figure 19.2.

risk-neutral probability but on the forward measure, and the discounting is simply $P(t)$, not requiring a backward substitution procedure. The procedure is as follows.

To build a market model based on an interest rate binomial model, we begin with determining a binomial lattice of the numeraire bond, $P(n, i, T^* - n)$. This lattice is equivalent to setting up a lattice of a risk-free one-period discount function in the backward substitution method. We choose the numeraire zero-coupon bond, which matures at year 5 for illustration purposes. We can choose any zero-coupon bond as the numeraire. (See figure 19.5.)

Next we build a binomial lattice of the underlying bond maturing at time $T^* + T$ (= $5 + 3 = 8$). In this case, we specify the price process of the $T^* + T(= 8)$ year maturity bond, $P(n, i, T^* + T - n)$. The price lattice of the $T^* + T$ year bond is given in figure 19.6.

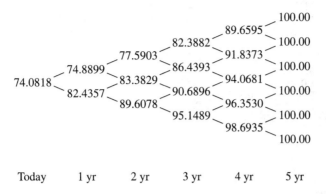

Figure 19.5 The price lattice of the numeraire bond with maturity date of year 5. The numeraire bond matures at year 5, which is identical to the expiration date of the bond option. The maturity of the numeraire bond does not have to be the same as the expiration date of the bond call option. However, it is usual to make a maturity date of the nunmeraire bond the same as the option expiration date where the option payoff occurs.

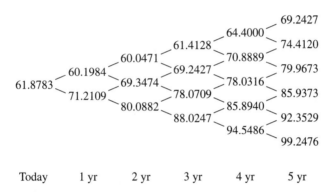

Figure 19.6 The price lattice of the underlying bond maturing at time $T^* + T$ (= 8) The $T^* + T$ year zero-coupon bond pays the face value at year 8. We illustrate the price lattice of the $T^* + T$ year zero-coupon bond during the period from the initial time to year 5. This bond is the underlying bond of the bond call option.

Finally, we construct the market lattice based on these two lattices of bond prices. The market lattice is defined as the relative price of the two bonds.

$$F(n, i, T^*, T) = \frac{P(n, i, T^* + T - n)}{P(n, i, T^* - n)} \text{ for } n \leq T^* \tag{19.2}$$

$F(n, i, T^*, T)$ is the forward contract price defined at each node of the lattice. That is, at each node on the interest rate lattice, we assign three prices: the price of the bond maturing at time T^*, the bond maturing at time $T^* + T$, and the forward price. These three prices form the bundle, as described in the filtration model in chapter 5, assigned to each node of the lattice.

Recapitulating what we have discussed so far, the risk-neutral expected return of any maturity bond over each time step on the lattice is the then a one-period risk-free return on the interest rate lattice to warrant a no-arbitrage condition. Specifically,

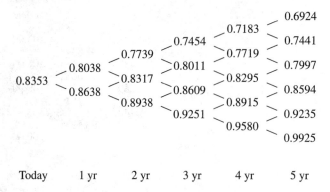

Today   1 yr   2 yr   3 yr   4 yr   5 yr

Figure 19.7 The lattice of the forward prices. We can calculate the forward price by dividing the underlying bond by the numeraire bond at each node. The numeraire bond matures at year 5 and the underlying bond matures at year 8. For example, we can obtain the forward price 0.6924 in the upper-right corner of the lattice by dividing 0.6924 at the corresponding node on the underlying bond lattice in figure 19.6 by 100 at the corresponding node on the numeraire bond lattice in figure 19.5.

$$\{\pi P(n+1, i+1, T-1) + (1-\pi)P(n+1, i, T-1)\}\, P(n, i, 1) = P(n, i, T) \quad (19.3)$$

The above equation holds for all maturities T, and can be verified directly, using the specification of the Ho–Lee model.

There is another way of understanding the arbitrage-free condition. Consider the process of the forward price. The forward contract is a self-financing strategy in that it requires no investment at any time. Therefore, at each node the expected return of holding the forward contract should be 0. That means the forward price should follow a martingale process.

Let us simplify the notation as follows:

$$F = F(n, i, T^*, T), \text{ the forward price at node}(n, i)$$

$$F^u = F(n+1, i+1, T^*, T-1), \text{ the forward price in the up state}$$

$$F^d = F(n+1, i, T^*, T-1), \text{ the forward price in the down state}$$

That is, for some probability value π_f, the expected value of the forward price equals the forward price at node (n, i):

$$\pi_f F^u + (1-\pi_f)F^d = F \quad (19.4)$$

This probability value π_f can be solved by the above equation, and can be shown to be

$$\pi_f = \frac{F - F^d}{F^u - F^d} \quad (19.5)$$

where F, F^u, and F^d have been derived in the forward price lattice. Since π_f is derived from the forward contract prices, which depend on the time n and the state i, they need not be a constant on the lattice, and are defined for all the time which is less than

T^*. Since this probability measure is defined in terms of the forward price process and the forward price process is martingale, we call this measure the forward measure. (See figure 19.8.)

Once we calculate the forward measures at each period in figure 19.8, we can determine the forward measure distribution over the states at each period. At time 0, the forward measure distribution Q is $Q(0, 0, T_1^*, T^*) = 1$ by construction, where $Q(0, 0, T_1^*, T^*)$ is the forward measure distribution at time 0 and state 0. At time 1, the forward measure distribution is

$$Q(1, i, T_1^*, T^*) = Q(0, 0, T_1^*, T^*) \times \underset{1\times 2}{q(1, T_1^*, T^*)},$$

$$state\ i = \{0, 1\}$$

$$\underset{1\times 2}{q(1, T_1^*, T^*)} = \left[1 - \pi_f\left[0, 0, T_1^*, T^*\right],\ \pi_f\left[0, 0, T_1^*, T^*\right]\right]$$

where π_f is the forward measure when a bond which matures at T_1^* is the numeraire and can be expressed as

$$\pi_f\left[n, i, T_1^*, T^*\right] = \frac{\frac{P[n,i,T^*]}{P[n,i,T_1^*]} - \frac{P[n+1,i,T^*]}{P[n+1,i,T_1^*]}}{\frac{P[n+1,i+1,T^*]}{P[n+1,i+1,T_1^*]} - \frac{P[n+1,i,T^*]}{P[n+1,i,T_1^*]}}$$

$P\left[n, i, T^*\right]/P\left[n, i, T_1^*\right]$ is the forward price where the maturity date of the forward contract is T_1^* and the maturity date of the underlying asset is T^*.

At time 2, the forward measure distribution Q is

$$\underset{1\times 3}{Q(2, i, T_1^*, T^*)} = \underset{1\times 2}{Q(1, i, T_1^*, T^*)} \times \underset{2\times 3}{q(2, T_1^*, T^*)}$$

$$= \begin{bmatrix} (1 - \pi_f\left[0, 0, T_1^*, T^*\right]) \cdot (1 - \pi_f\left[1, 0, T_1^*, T^*\right]), \\ (1 - \pi_f\left[0, 0, T_1^*, T^*\right])\pi_f\left[1, 0, T_1^*, T^*\right] + \pi_f\left[0, 0, T_1^*, T^*\right](1 - \pi_f\left[1, 1, T_1^*, T^*\right]), \\ \pi_f\left[0, 0, T_1^*, T^*\right] \cdot \pi_f\left[1, 1, T_1^*, T^*\right] \end{bmatrix}^T$$

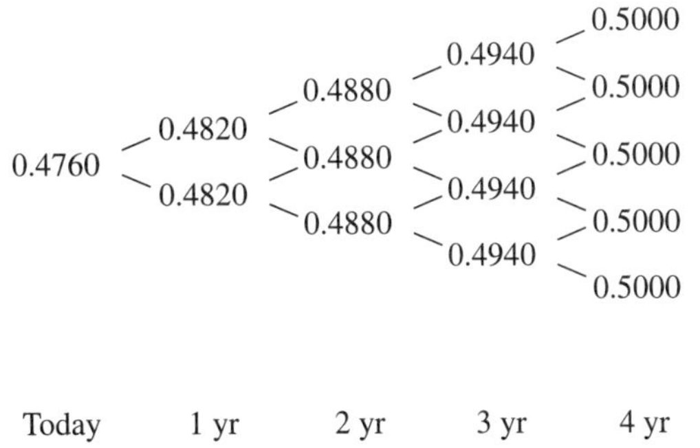

Figure 19.8 Forward measures at each node. We can generate the forward measure lattice by recursively applying equation 19.5. Using equation 19.5 we can obtain the forward measure 0.5 in the upper-right corner by calculating $(0.71827 - 0.74412)/(0.69242 - 0.74412)$. The forward prices are from figure 19.7. The forward measures are only time-dependent.

where

$$q(2, T_1^*, T^*) = \begin{bmatrix} 1 - \pi_f\left[1, 0, T_1^*, T^*\right]\pi_f\left[1, 0, T_1^*, T^*\right] & 0 \\ 0 & 1 - \pi_f\left[1, 1, T_1^*, T^*\right]\pi_f\left[1, 1, T_1^*, T^*\right] \end{bmatrix}$$
$$\underset{2\times 3}{}$$

At time t, the forward measure distribution Q is

$$\underset{1\times(t+1)}{Q(t, i, T_1^*, T^*)} = \underset{1\times t}{Q(t - 1, i, T_1^*, T^*)} \times \underset{t\times(t+1)}{q(t, T_1^*, T^*)}$$

where

$$\underset{t\times(t+1)}{q(t, T_1^*, T^*)} =$$

$$\begin{bmatrix} 1 - \pi_f\left[t - 1, 0\right] & \pi_f\left[t - 1, 0\right] & 0 & 0 & 0 & 0 \\ 0 & 1 - \pi_f\left[t - 1, 1\right] & \pi_f\left[t - 1, 1\right] & 0 & 0 & 0 \\ 0 & 0 & 1 - \pi_f\left[t - 1, 2\right] & \pi_f\left[t - 1, 2\right] & 0 & 0 \\ \vdots & \vdots & \vdots & \vdots & \vdots & \vdots \\ 0 & 0 & \cdots & 1 - \pi_f\left[t - 1, t - 1\right] & \pi_f\left[t - 1, t - 1\right] & 0 \\ 0 & 0 & \cdots & 0 & 1 - \pi_f\left[t - 1, t - 1\right] & \pi_f\left[t - 1, t - 1\right] \end{bmatrix}$$

The forward measure distribution at each node is shown in figure 19.9.

Now we come to the main result of this discussion. Using the forward measure, we can determine an alterative method for pricing the bond call option. Let the price of the option be $C(T^*, T)$, where T^* denotes the expiration date and T the time to maturity of the underlying bond at expiration date T^*. Then, for example, when T^* is 2, the option price is

$$C(2, T) = P(2)\left[X(2, 2) \cdot \pi_f^0 \cdot \pi_f^1 + X(2, 1) \cdot \pi_f^0 \cdot (1 - \pi_f^1)\right.$$

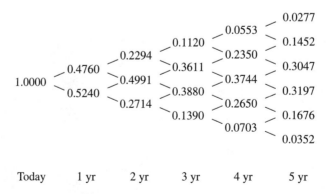

Figure 19.9 Forward probability distribution at each period when a bond, which matures at year 5, is a numeraire. For each time period, the sum of all the probabilities over the states is 1, and each probability is nonnegative. We will use this forward measure distribution to show how the Radon–Nikodym theorem holds on the binomial lattice.

$$+X(2,1) \cdot (1 - \pi_f^0) \cdot \pi_f^1 + X(0,0) \cdot (1 - \pi_f^0) \cdot (1 - \pi_f^1)] \qquad (19.6)$$

where π_f^0 and π_f^1 are the forward measure at time 0 and time 1, respectively. $X(T^*, i)$ is the payoff of the call option at time T^* and state i, and it is given by

$$X(T^*, i) = \frac{Max[P(T^*, i, T) - X, 0]}{P(T^*, i, 0)}$$

where $P(T^*, i, 0) = 1$ by definition, and $P(n, i, T)$ is given in the bundle at each node on the interest rate lattice , and X is the strike price. (See figure 19.10.)

To determine the forward measure, we use the bonds maturing at time T^* as the numeraire and the bond maturing at time $(T^* + T)$ as the underlying bond of the bond call option. In fact, to derive the Black model, other numeraire bonds are possible. For example, we change the numeraire bond from a five-year bond to a seven-year bond, to see whether we have the same bond call option price. We choose the seven-year bond for illustration purposes. We follow the same procedure to calculate the bond option price, using the forward measure except for the numeraire bond. (See figures 19.11–19.15.)

Change of Numeraire Theorem

The change of numeraire theorem presented by Geman et al. (1995) shows that in an arbitrage-free economy, the Radon–Nikodym derivative[1] is equal to the ratio of the numeraire growth rates. That is,

$$\frac{dQ^N}{dQ^M} = \frac{N(t)/N(0)}{M(t)/M(0)} \qquad (19.7)$$

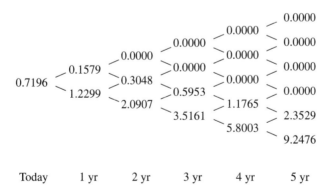

| | Today | 1 yr | 2 yr | 3 yr | 4 yr | 5 yr |

Figure 19.10 The lattice for determining the call option price. We calculated $E^{\pi_f}\left[\frac{Max[P(5,i,3)-X,0]}{P(5,i,0)}\right] (= 0.7196)$ by backward substitution without discounting using the forward measures. The reason for dividing the option payoffs at year 5 by $P(5,i,0)$ is that we should normalize the payoffs with the numeraire. 5.8003 at year 4 can be obtained by $(2.3529 \times 0.5 + 9.2476 \times 0.5)$ where 0.5 is the forward measure at year 4. Once we have 0.7196 at the initial time, we multiply 0.7196 by the 5 year discount function, $P(5)$, which is 0.5331, the same as the backward substitution with the risk-neutral probability in figure 19.4. In other words, we calculate the initial bond option price by $P(5) \cdot E^{\pi_f}\left[\frac{Max[P(5,i,0)-X,0]}{P(5,i,0)}\right]$.

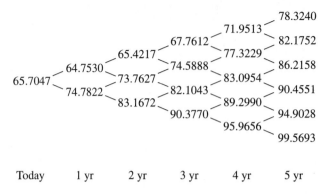

Figure 19.11 The price lattice of the seven-year numeraire bond. The numeraire bond matures at year 7, which is not identical to the expiration date of the bond option. The previous numeraire bond matures at year 5, which is the maturity date of the bond call option.

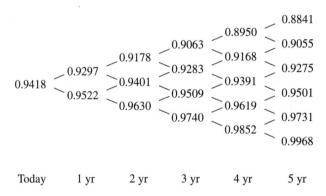

Figure 19.12 The lattice of the forward prices. We can calculate the forward price by dividing the underlying bond by the numeraire bond. The numeraire bond matures at year 7 and the underlying bond matures at year 8. For example, we can obtain the forward price 0.8841 in the upper-right corner of the lattice by dividing 69.2427 at the corresponding node on the underlying bond lattice in figure 19.6 by 78.324 at the corresponding node on the numeraire bond lattice in figure 19.11.

where

Q^N: the equivalent martingale measure generated by a numeraire N

Q^M: the equivalent martingale measure generated by a numeraire M

$N(t)$: numeraire value at time t

In the discrete time bond option pricing model, the Radon–Nikodym derivative corresponding to equation (19.7) is given by

$$\frac{Q(n, i, T_2^*, T^*)}{Q(n, i, T_1^*, T^*)} = \frac{P(n, i, T_2^*)/P(0, 0, T_2^*)}{P(n, i, T_1^*)/P(0, 0, T_1^*)} \tag{19.8}$$

where

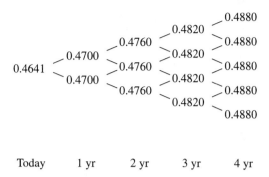

Today   1 yr   2 yr   3 yr   4 yr

Figure 19.13 The lattice of the forward measures. We can generate the forward measure lattice by recursively applying equation 19.5. Using equation (19.5), we can obtain the forward measure 0.4880 in the upper-right corner by calculating $(0.89505 - 0.90553)/(0.884055 - 0.90553)$. The forward prices are from figure 19.12. The forward measures are only time-dependent.

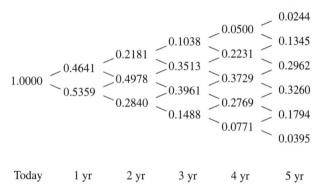

Today   1 yr   2 yr   3 yr   4 yr   5 yr

Figure 19.14 Forward measure distribution at each node when a bond, which matures at year 7, is a numeraire. See figures 19.8 and 19.9 for the pdf calculation methods. For each time period, the sum of all the probabilities is 1, and each probability is nonnegative. We will use this lattice for the change of the numeraire theorem later on.

$$T^* = \text{underlying bond's maturity date}$$

$$T_1^* = \text{1st numeraire bond's maturity date}$$

$$T_2^* = \text{2nd numeraire bond's maturity date.}$$

Let us consider a bond call option expiring at time $T^*(= 5)$. The underlying bond of the bond option is a zero-coupon bond with the time to maturity of $T (= 3)$ at the option expiration date, $T^*(= 5)$. We choose the numeraire zero-coupon bond which matures at year 5 for illustration purposes. We can choose any zero-coupon bond as the numeraire. In this case, the forward probability distribution Q at option maturity date and each state i is generated by (see figure 19.8 for forward measures)

$$(1) \cdot (0.523982\ 0.476018) \cdot \begin{pmatrix} 0.517992 & 0.482008 & 0 \\ 0 & 0.517992 & 0.482008 \end{pmatrix}.$$

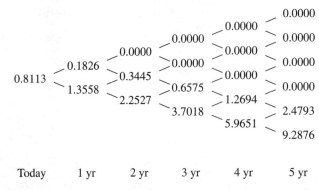

Today   1 yr   2 yr   3 yr   4 yr   5 yr

Figure 19.15 Determining the call option prices. We calculated $E^{\pi_f}\left[\frac{Max[P(5,i,3)-X,0]}{P(5,i,2)}\right]$ (= 0.8113) by backward substitution without discounting using the forward measures. The reason for dividing the option payoffs at year 5 by $P(5,i,2)$ is that we should normalize the payoffs with the numeraire. 5.9651 at year 4 can be obtained by (2.4793 × 0.4880 + 9.2876 × 0.512) where 0.4880 is the forward measure at year 4. Once we have 0.8113 at the initial time, we multiply 0.8113 by the 7-year discount function, $P(7)$, which is 0.5331, the same as the backward substitution with the risk-neutral probability in figure 19.3. In other words, we calculate the initial bond option price by $P(7) \cdot E^{\pi_f}\left[\frac{Max[P(5,i,3)-X,0]}{P(5,i,2)}\right]$.

$$\begin{pmatrix} 0.511998 & 0.488002 & 0 & 0 \\ 0 & 0.511998 & 0.48802 & 0 \\ 0 & 0 & 0.511998 & 0.488002 \end{pmatrix} \cdot \begin{pmatrix} 0.506 & 0.494 & 0 & 0 & 0 \\ 0 & 0.506 & 0.494 & 0 & 0 \\ 0 & 0 & 0.506 & 0.494 & 0 \\ 0 & 0 & 0 & 0.506 & 0.494 \end{pmatrix} \cdot \begin{pmatrix} 0.5 & 0.5 & 0 & 0 & 0 & 0 \\ 0 & 0.5 & 0.5 & 0 & 0 & 0 \\ 0 & 0 & 0.5 & 0.5 & 0 & 0 \\ 0 & 0 & 0 & 0.5 & 0.5 & 0 \\ 0 & 0 & 0 & 0 & 0.5 & 0.5 \end{pmatrix}$$

and the resulting forward probability distribution $Q(5, i, 5, 8)$, $i = \{0, \cdots, 5\}$, at bond
$$\underset{1\times(5+1)}{}$$
option maturity date is given by figure 19.9: {0.0351583, 0.167649, 0.319676, 0.304694, 0.145165, 0.0276565}. The corresponding option payoff at maturity and each state i in the above example is {9.24759, 2.35295, 0, 0, 0, 0} (figure 19.10). We can calculate the expected option payoff by multiplying the option payoff by the corresponding forward probability, which is 0.719599. And then, if we multiply the expected option payoff by the initial discount function $P(5)$, we can obtain the bond option price (= 0.5331), which is the same as the former example (figure 19.10). Now that we have the change of numeraire theorem, we can calculate the bond option price with another numeraire bond, without using backward recursive methods. If we choose a seven-year bond as numeraire, we can directly calculate the forward probability distribution at the bond option maturity date using the change of numeraire theorem. Reshuffling equation (19.8)

$$Q(5, i, 7, 8) = \frac{P(5, i, 7)/P(0, 0, 7)}{P(5, i, 5)/P(0, 0, 5)} \times Q(5, i, 5, 8), \quad i = \{0, \cdots, 5\},$$
$$\underset{1\times(5+1)}{} \qquad\qquad\qquad\qquad\qquad\qquad\qquad \underset{1\times(5+1)}{}$$

we can calculate $Q(5, i, 7, 8)$ = {1.12264, 1.07003, 1.01988, 0.97208, 0.926523,
$$\underset{1\times6}{}$$
0.8831} × {0.0351583, 0.167649, 0.319676, 0.304694, 0.145165, 0.0276565} =

{0.0394701, 0.179389, 0.326031, 0.296187, 0.134499, 0.0244234} (figure 19.14). This time we should normalize the option payoffs at the maturity date, using the seven-year numeraire bond instead of the five-year zero-coupon numeraire bond. Therefore, renormalized option payoffs are calculated by

$$\left(\frac{Max\,[F \cdot P(5, i, 8) - X, 0]}{P(5, i, 5)}\right) \times \frac{P(5, i, 5)}{P(5, i, 7)}, \quad i = \{0, \cdots, 5\}$$

which are {9.28759, 2.47932, 0, 0, 0, 0} (figure 19.15). If we multiply the normalized option payoff by the forward probability distribution, we can get the expected option payoff of 0.811345. And last, we have only to multiplify the expected option payoff by $P(7)$ to get the option price of 0.5331, which is the same as the above two examples.

Implications of the Forward Measure Approach

1. When we use the forward measure π_f instead of the risk-neutral measure π, the valuation model is simplified to using the distribution of the bond price at the expiration date of the option and discounting the expected value by the discount factor $P(T)$, an approach akin to the discounted cash flow approach of the Black–Scholes model, as if we assumed that there were no interest rate uncertainties. By contrast, if we use the interest rate lattice with the risk-neutral measure π, we would need to conduct a backward substitution approach to derive the option value.

2. Suppose, by market convention, bond option prices are based on assuming a Black model, with the bond price distribution at the expiration date being lognormal (as was discussed in chapter 6). The bond price is given by equation (19.1), where the market provides the call option price. $P(n, i, T)$ and π_f are functions of δ. Using equation (19.1), we can determine the value δ, such that the call option price equals the market quoted price. That means we have shown that there is a *delta* in the Ho–Lee model such that the distribution of the bond price at the expiration will have the price distribution derived from the quoted market volatility.

Given such a δ, we have also specified the interest rate model, or all prices of the bond of any maturity at each node point of the lattice. If we use this lattice to price all other interest rate contingent claims, we will be assured that the volatility of the lattice has been calibrated to the market-quoted volatility of the bond options, directly from the Black model. By contrast, if we do not use the forward measure, we will first determine the call option price from the market-quoted volatility by the Black model, and then calibrate the interest rate lattice to the option price. Using the forward measure, we can determine the Ho–Lee model that can fit the market call option price directly.

3. In the capital market, there are many bond options. Therefore, it would be quite limited if we fit the interest rate model to only one observed bond option price. But the methodology above can be extended to bond options with different expiration dates by allowing for a term structure of volatilities. That is, by using the extended Ho–Lee model or n-factor Ho–Lee model, we can build a market lattice from the interest rate lattice, which can then be assured to fit the market-observed bond option prices.

4. A cap or a floor, as we have discussed, is a portfolio of bond options. Therefore, the above methodology is analogous to the BGM/J LIBOR model based on the interest rate binomial lattice.

5. We can build a market lattice based on the distribution of the coupon bond prices, instead of the zero-coupon bond prices, as we have described here. This distribution will enable us to price the bond option on the coupon bonds. In our derivation, we assign the zero-coupon bond prices (using the closed-form discount function) at each node point. By the same token, you can assign a coupon bond value at each node. Now you form the forward measure using the coupon bond, and derive the Black model. Hence we can determine the swaption value in the market lattice. This approach will provide a market model fitting the swaption volatilities.

Generalizations of the Forward Measure

The illustration above can lead to other generalizations. This is an area of much active research in pursuit of an efficient and accurate interest rate model.

In our example, we build the market lattice based on a forward contract. But a forward contract can be viewed as the value of a bond maturing at time T_1^* relative to another bond maturing at time T_2^*, where T_2^* is less than T_1^*. In general, security valuation does not have to be relative to a particular bond. The security that the relative valuation is based on is called a numeraire. We can change the probabilities (or measure) by any choice of the numeraire and the underlying. Using this approach, we can develop lattices that fit certain needs of a market model. For example, the BGM/J LIBOR market model, within the Ho–Lee model context, uses the reset period, say three months, and a LIBOR money market account as the numeraire. More generally, we can use options, callable bonds, and many other items.

We started with a specific Ho–Lee model to determine the market models. However, we can use more general forms of the Ho–Lee model—for example, the n-factor Ho–Lee, Black–Derman–Toy, Hull–White, and other interest rate lattice models described in chapter 5 to fit the market observed prices using the market lattice. Furthermore, the Ho–Lee framework described in this book, for simplicity reasons, assumes that the volatilities depend only on time. That is, the δ depends only on n and not on i. We do not have to confine ourselves to this restriction. Indeed, δ can be dependent on both time n and state i, allowing the recombining binomial lattice to accept a broad range of stochastic processes. The lattice can be nonrecombining and the volatility can be dependent on the states as well. In this general framework, we can solve for the equivalent martingale measures for an appropriate choice of numeraire and the specifications of the delta such that the model can fit the market conventions. The general form of an arbitrage-free binomial lattice can be derived using the methodology of Ho and Lee (1984).

Perhaps the most important generalization is to allow for a broad class of stochastic processes of the interest rates. Under the HJM formulation, for example, the short rate processes, which may be the interest rate processes or the instantaneous forward rate processes, may depend not only on time and prevailing interest rate, but also on history and other information set. Research has shown that under such generalization, the basic ideas presented above still hold.

The formalism to represent the information set that grows with time is called filtration. The concept of a forward measure is generalized to the equivalent martingale measure to allow a class of acceptable numeraire instead of using a zero-coupon bond. The methodology to adjust the equivalent martingale measure for a change in the numeraire is called the Radon–Nikodym derivative. The theorem that ensures that we can always determine an equivalent martingale measure is called the Radon–Nikodym theorem. The theorem that enables us to determine the equivalent martingale measure and gives us a tool to determine the effect of a change of measure on a stochastic process in a general setting is called the Girsanov theorem. We will provide a more detailed description of these concepts in the following section.

These results enable us to build an interest rate model that may satisfy many requirements. However, we should note that in practice, at least for the time being, most models are still based on relatively simple assumptions. This is because in practice, calibrating a multifactor model with the uncertainty based on a complex information set is problematic. A complex interest rate model requires a larger set of benchmark securities that can provide relevant information to calibrate a large set of inputs to the model. Often such a set of benchmark securities is not available. For example, there is no active derivative market from which to infer the correlations of the interest rates. Meanwhile, simpler models can provide the users of the model with better intuitions of its working. Therefore, we should caution against the use of these generalized methodologies. In these cases, useful properties of binomial model may not be used because these generalized models are not recombining. On the other hand, our exposition of the use of binomial models in these more general contexts may lead us to search for a general specification of the lattice model (for example, allowing δ to be time- and state-dependent), which in turn may lead to specifying more general market models within a binomial lattice. This will be left for future research.

19.2   A General Approach to Valuation

The purpose of this section is to provide an overview of the mathematical formalism that enables us to extend the basic model described thus far to a more general context. We will show that the basic ideas can be used in broader setting. For example, the concepts apply to a continuous time world, more complex information is set in the filtration model, and the solutions are assured by theorems in mathematics that we will introduce.

Consider a three-period binomial lattice. We assume that the initial stock price S_0 is positive. Since two positive numbers u and d are assumed to be $0 < d < u$, the stock price will move downward to dS_0 or upward to uS_0 at period 1, and subsequent movements are determined in the same way. The stock price process is depicted in figure 19.16. The stochastic movements of the stock prices will be determined by which side of a coin has landed when we toss a coin. If the coin has landed a head up, the stock price will move upward and vice versa. We assume that the time period is 3 for simplicity. The following numerical examples are based on this three-period binomial lattice. (See figure 19.16.)

Time Convention

In some financial models time is modeled as a discrete object and time instants are denoted by $t = 0, 1, 2, \cdots, n$, where n denotes the last instant of time. Here the actual length of each time interval can be one day, or one week, or even one year. This kind of financial model is called a discrete time model. There are also financial models where time is modeled as a continuous object so time t belongs to an interval $[0, T]$. Here T may be a finite or an infinite number.

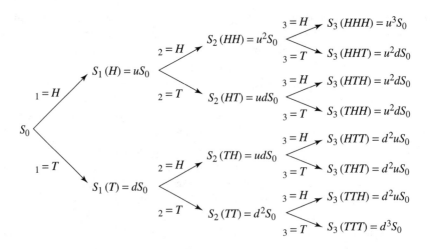

Figure 19.16 A three-period binomial lattice

Function

A function f from a set X to a set Y is a rule which assigns a unique element $f(x)$ in Y to each x in X. "Mapping" is often used interchangeably with "function." We express that f is a function of X into Y by $f : X \to Y$. If a set Y is confined to real numbers, the function is called a real valued function and denoted as $f : X \to \mathcal{R}$. In the three-period binomial lattice, S_1, S_2, and S_3 are functions because once we have H or T, we can assign stock prices to each H or T. S_1, S_2, S_3 should be considered as functions on Ω, as defined below, i.e. S_i maps each triple like (HHH) or (HTH) to some real number.

Probability Space

Financial models usually involve the explicit modeling of future uncertainties, and this is achieved by the use of the tools from standard probability theory. A probability space is a combination of the sample space, the σ algebra of subsets of the sample space, and the probability measure. The sample space is the set of all the possible behaviors (called paths) of the financial variable under consideration. The probability measure assigns relative measure of possibility that each path actually occurs in the future. The σ algebra is a family of subsets of the sample space on which we want to assign probabilities.

Let Ω be a set of all the possible outcomes and $\mathcal{F}$ be the set of all subsets of Ω. In the three-period binomial lattice, Ω is {HHH, HHT, HTH, HTT, THH, THT, TTH, TTT}. Since the set of all subsets of Ω is $\mathcal{F}$, one set which belongs to $\mathcal{F}$ is {$\Omega, 0, \{HHH\}, \{HHT, HTH, THH\}, \{HTT, THT, TTH\}, \{TTT\}$}. An element of $\mathcal{F}$ is called an event.

Definition 19.1 A probability space is a triple $(\Omega, \mathcal{F}, \mathbb{P})$, where Ω is a nonempty (finite or infinite) set, called the sample space or path space; $\mathcal{F}$ is a σ algebra on Ω; and notation: $\mathbb{P}$ is a mapping of $\mathcal{F}$ into $[0, 1]$ with the following properties:

(i) $\mathbb{P}(\Omega) = 1$

(ii) If $A_1, A_2, \cdots$ is a sequence of disjoint sets in $\mathcal{F}$ then

$$\mathbb{P}(\bigcup_{k=1}^{\infty} A_k) = \sum_{k=1}^{\infty} \mathbb{P}(A_k) \tag{19.9}$$

The probability measure $\mathbb{P}$ assigns a nonnegative number to each event such that the sum of all the nonnegative numbers is equal to 1. For example, if $\Omega = \{HHH, HHT, HTH, HTT, THH, THT, TTH, TTT\}$ and all the elements in Ω are equally likely, then the probability of each outcome is 1/8. For any sequence $\{A_k\}_{k=1}^{\infty}$ of disjoint events, the probability of their union is the sum of their probabilities.

Example 19.1 Suppose a coin has probability 2/3 for H and 1/3 for T. For the individual elements of $\Omega = \{HHH, HHT, HTH, HTT, THH, THT, TTH, TTT\}$, we have

$$\mathbb{P}\{HHH\} = \left(\frac{2}{3}\right)^3 \qquad \mathbb{P}\{HHT\} = \left(\frac{2}{3}\right)^2 \left(\frac{1}{3}\right)$$

$$\mathbb{P}\{HTH\} = \left(\frac{2}{3}\right)^2 \left(\frac{1}{3}\right) \quad \mathbb{P}\{HTT\} = \left(\frac{2}{3}\right) \left(\frac{1}{3}\right)^2$$

$$\mathbb{P}\{THH\} = \left(\frac{2}{3}\right)^2 \left(\frac{1}{3}\right) \quad \mathbb{P}\{THT\} = \left(\frac{2}{3}\right) \left(\frac{1}{3}\right)^2$$

$$\mathbb{P}\{TTH\} = \left(\frac{2}{3}\right) \left(\frac{1}{3}\right)^2 \quad \mathbb{P}\{TTT\} = \left(\frac{1}{3}\right)^3$$

For $A \in \mathcal{F}$, we define

$$\mathbb{P}(A) = \sum_{\omega \in A} \mathbb{P}\{\omega\} \tag{19.10}$$

For example, assume that $f = \{\Omega, 0, \{HHH\}, \{HHT, HTH, THH\}, \{HTT, THT, TTH\}, \{TTT\}\}$. Since a subset of f is A, A would be one of $\{HHH\}, \{HHT, HTH, THH\}, \{HTT, THT, TTH\}, \{TTT\}, \Omega$, and 0. If A is $\{HHT, HTH, THH\}$, then

$$P(HHT) + P(HTH) + P(THH) = \frac{4}{9} \left(= \left(\frac{2}{3}\right)^2 \frac{1}{3} + \left(\frac{2}{3}\right)^2 \frac{1}{3} + \left(\frac{2}{3}\right)^2 \frac{1}{3} \right)$$

Filtration

Consider an experiment of tossing a nickel, a dime, and a quarter. The sample space is $\{HHH, HHT, HTH, HTT, THH, THT, TTH, TTT\}$. If we assume that we know only the number of coins which have landed heads up, then the set of subsets of the sample space, $\mathcal{F}$, is $\{\{HHH\}, \{HHT, HTH, THH\}, \{HTT, THT, TTH\}, \{TTT\}\}$. Under the $\mathcal{F}$, we cannot distinguish away HHT, HTH, and THH, because they belong to the same subset of $\mathcal{F}$. In other words, they have the same number as the coins that landed heads up. If the outcome is HHH, everyone knows that this outcome has occurred. However, if the outcomes are HHT, HTH, and THH, we know that one of three outcomes has occurred, but we cannot know which one. Therefore, we can represent information structure by a partition of sample space. The null partition $\mathcal{F} = \{0, \{HHH, HHT, HTH, HTT, THH, THT, TTH, TTT\}\}$ represents no information, because the outcomes in the same subsets are indistinguishable. The discrete partition $f = \{\{HHH\}, \{HHT\}, \{HTH\}, \{HTT\}, \{THH\}, \{THT\}, \{TTH\}, \{TTT\}\}$ represents full information, because each outcome is distinct. When the sample space, Ω, is finite, it is convenient to represent information through partitions of Ω. On an infinite sample space it is convenient to represent information through the σ-field.

Definition 19.2 (σ-algebra) Let Ω be a nonempty set. A collection $\mathcal{G}$ of subsets of Ω is called a σ-algebra on Ω if and only if

The sample space is in $\mathcal{G}$, that is, $\Omega \in \mathcal{G}$

For every $A \in \mathcal{G}$, its complement is in $\mathcal{G}$, that is, $\Omega - A = A^c \in \mathcal{G}$

For a sequence $\{A_k\}_{k=1}^{\infty}$ such that A_k is in $\mathcal{G}$ for every $k \geq 1$, then $\bigcup_{k=1}^{\infty} A_k$ is also in $\mathcal{G}$.

The concept of σ-algebra expresses the set of all information available at an instant of time. Accumulation of the information by the passage of time is modeled by the concept of filtration.

Definition 19.3A Let Ω be a nonempty set. A discrete time filtration is a sequence of σ algebras $\mathcal{F}_0, \mathcal{F}_1, \mathcal{F}_2, \cdots, \mathcal{F}_n = \mathcal{F}$ such that each σ algebra in the sequence contains all the sets contained in the previous σ algebra. If the sample space Ω is a finite set, then a σ algebra $\mathcal{F}$ is generated by a partition $\{A_1, \cdots, A_m\}$ of Ω. That is, for any σ algebra $\mathcal{F}$, we can find a partition $\{A_1, \cdots, A_m\}$ of Ω such that every set in $\mathcal{F}$ can be obtained from $A_1, \cdots, A_m$ by a finite number of set-theoretic operations. Therefore, in the case of finite sample space, a σ algebra can be identified as a partition of the sample space. Such an identification is not possible in a continuous time framework.

Definition 19.3B Let Ω be a nonempty set. A continuous time filtration is a family of σ algebras $\{\mathcal{F}_t | 0 \leq t \leq T\}$ such that $\mathcal{F}_s \subset \mathcal{F}_t$ for any $s < t$.

Example 19.2 Below are some important σ algebras of subsets of the set Ω in the three-period binomial model.

$\mathcal{F}_0 = \{0, \Omega\}$

$\mathcal{F}_1 = \{0, \Omega, \{HHH, HHT, HTH, HTT\}, \{THH, THT, TTH, TTT\}\}$

$\mathcal{F}_2 = \left\{ \begin{array}{l} 0, \Omega, \{HHH, HHT\}, \{HTH, HTT\}, \{THH, THT\}, \{TTH, TTT\} \\ \text{and all sets which can be built by taking unions of these} \end{array} \right\}$

$\mathcal{F}_3 =$ the set of all subsets of Ω

Define A_H and A_T for simplicity to express $\mathcal{F}_1 = \{0, \Omega, A_H, A_T\}$,
where $A_H \triangleq \{HHH, HHT, HTH, HTT\} = \{H \text{ on the first toss}\}$
$\quad\quad A_T \triangleq \{THH, THT, TTH, TTT\} = \{T \text{ on the first toss}\}$.
Further, define A_{HH}, A_{HT}, A_{TH}, and A_{TT} to express

$$\mathcal{F}_2 = \begin{cases} 0, \ \Omega, \ A_{HH}, \ A_{HT}, \ A_{TH}, \ A_{TT} \\ A_H, \ A_T, \ A_{HH} \cup A_{TH}, \ A_{HH} \cup A_{TT}, \ A_{HT} \cup A_{TH}, \ A_{HT} \cup A_{TT} \\ A^c_{HH}, \ A^c_{HT}, \ A^c_{TH}, \ A^c_{TT} \end{cases}$$

where

$$A_{HH} \triangleq \{HHH, HHT\} = \{HH \text{ on the first two tosses}\}$$

$$A_{HT} \triangleq \{HTH, HTT\} = \{HT \text{ on the first two tosses}\}$$

$$A_{TH} \triangleq \{THH, THT\} = \{TH \text{ on the first two tosses}\}$$

$$A_{TT} \triangleq \{TTH, TTT\} = \{TT \text{ on the first two tosses}\}$$

Definition 19.4 Let $(\Omega, \mathcal{F}, \mathbb{P})$ be a probability space. A random variable is a mapping $X : \Omega \rightarrow \mathbb{R}$ satisfying the following measurability condition: for any open interval (a,b) in $\mathbb{R}$, the set $\{\omega \in \Omega | a < X(\omega) < b\} \equiv \{a < X < b\}$ of elements in Ω which are mapped into (a, b) by X belongs to the σ algebra $\mathcal{F}$. In this case we say that X is $\mathcal{F}$-measurable. In a three-period binomial lattice, the stock prices are random variables because we can assign them to each element of Ω.

Definition 19.5 The distribution of a random variable X is a measure $\mathcal{L}_X$ on $\mathcal{R}$, that is, a way of assigning probabilities to real number sets. It depends on the random variable X and the probability measure $\mathbb{P}$. In a three-period binomial lattice, the distribution of the stock prices is binomial, as shown in example 19.1.

Definition 19.6 Let Ω be a nonempty finite set; let $\mathcal{F}$ be the σ algebra of all subsets of Ω; let $\mathbb{P}$ be a probability measure on $(\Omega, \mathcal{F})$; and let X be a random variable on Ω. The expected value of X is defined to be

$$\mathbb{E}X \triangleq \sum_{\omega \in \Omega} X(\omega) \mathbb{P}\{\omega\} \tag{19.11}$$

The variance of X is defined to be the expected value of $(X - \mathbb{E}X)^2$, that is,

$$Var(X) \triangleq \sum_{\omega \in \Omega} (X(\omega) - \mathbb{E}X)^2 \mathbb{P}\{\omega\} \tag{19.12}$$

Definition 19.7 We say that two sets $A \subseteq \mathcal{F}$ and $B \subseteq \mathcal{F}$ are independent if

$$\mathbb{P}(A \cap B) = \mathbb{P}(A)\mathbb{P}(B) \tag{19.13}$$

Example 19.3 In the three-period lattice, we assume that p and $q \ (= 1 - p)$ are a head and a tail probability, respectively.

$$\mathbb{P}\{HHH\} = p^3, \ \mathbb{P}\{HHT\} = \mathbb{P}\{HTH\} = \mathbb{P}\{THH\} = p^2 q \tag{19.14}$$

$$\mathbb{P}\{HTT\} = \mathbb{P}\{THT\} = \mathbb{P}\{TTH\} = pq^2, \ \mathbb{P}\{TTT\} = q^3$$

Let $G_1 = \mathcal{F}_1$ be the σ algebra determined by the first toss: G_1 contains the sets $0, \Omega, \{HHH, \ HHT, HTH, HTT\}, \ \{THH, \ THT, \ TTH, \ TTT\}$.

Let $G_2 = \mathcal{F}_2$ be the σ algebra determined by the second toss: G_2 contains the sets $0, \Omega, \{HHH, HHT, \ THH, \ THT\}, \ \{HTH, HTT, \ TTH, \ TTT\}$.

Let $G_3 = \mathcal{F}_3$ be the σ algebra determined by the third toss: G_3 contains the sets $0, \Omega, \{HHH, \ HTH, \ THH, \ TTH\}, \ \{HHT, HTT, \ THT, \ TTT\}$.

These three σ-algebras are independent. For example, if we choose the set $\{HHH, HHT, HTH, HTT\}$ from G_1 and the set $\{HHH, \ HHT, \ THH, \ THT\}$ from G_2, then we have

$$\mathbb{P}\{HHH, HHT, HTH, HTT\}\mathbb{P}\{HHH, HHT, THH, THT\} =$$

$$(p^3 + 2p^2q + pq^2)(p^3 + 2p^2q + pq^2) = p^2$$

$$\mathbb{P}(\{HHH, HHT, HTH, HTT\} \cap \{HHH, HHT, THH, THT\}) =$$

$$\mathbb{P}\{HHH, HHT\} = p^3 + p^2q = p^2$$

Regardless of which set we choose in G_1 and which set we choose in G_2, the product of the probabilities is the probability of the intersection.

Definition 19.8 The covariance of two random variables, X and Y, is defined to be

$$Cov(X, \ Y) \triangleq \mathbb{E}\left[(X - \mathbb{E}X)(Y - \mathbb{E}Y)\right]$$
$$= \mathbb{E}[XY] - \mathbb{E}X \cdot \mathbb{E}Y \tag{19.15}$$

Definition 19.9 If X and Y both have positive variances, we define their correlation coefficient as

$$\rho(X, \ Y) \triangleq \frac{Cov(X, \ Y)}{\sqrt{\mathrm{Var}(X) \cdot \mathrm{Var}(Y)}} \tag{19.16}$$

Definition 19.10 A stochastic process on the probability space $(\Omega, \ \mathcal{F}, \ \mathbb{P})$ is a function $x : [0, T] \times \Omega \to \mathbb{R}$ such that for every $0 \leq t \leq T, x(t, \cdot)$ is a random variable on $(\Omega, \mathcal{F}, \mathbb{P})$.

Definition 19.11 A stochastic process x on a filtered probability space $(\Omega, \ \mathcal{F}, \ \mathbb{P}, \ \{\mathcal{F}_t\})$ is adapted to the filtration $\{\mathcal{F}_t\}$ if and only if x_t is $\mathcal{F}_t$-measurable.

$$X_t \triangleq X(t, \cdot) : \Omega \to \mathbb{R}$$

Definition 19.12 For an event A on the probability space $(\Omega, \ \mathbb{P})$ and a partition $\mathbf{f}$ of Ω, the conditional probability $\mathbb{P}(A|\mathbf{f})$ is the random variable

$$\mathbb{P}(A|\mathbf{f})(\omega) = \frac{\mathbb{P}\left[A \cap \mathbf{f}(\omega)\right]}{\mathbb{P}\left[\mathbf{f}(\omega)\right]} \tag{19.17}$$

Definition 19.13 Let $(\Omega, \mathcal{F}, \mathbb{P})$ be a probability space. Let $\{\mathcal{F}_k\}_{k=0}^n$ be a filtration under $\mathcal{F}$. Let $\{X_k\}_{k=0}^n$ be a stochastic process on $(\Omega, \mathcal{F}, \mathbb{P})$. This process is said to be Markov if

1. The stochastic process $\{X_k\}$ is adapted to the filtration $\{\mathcal{F}_k\}$
2. For each $k = 0, 1, \cdots, n-1$, the distribution of X_{k+1} conditioned on $\mathcal{F}_k$ is the same as the distribution of X_{k+1} conditioned on X_k.

Example 19.4 The stock price process in a three-period binomial lattice is a Markov process. If we want to estimate the distribution of S_{k+1} based on the information in $\mathcal{F}_k$, the only relevant piece of information is the value of S_k. For example, if we estimate the distribution of S_3 based on the information in $\mathcal{F}_2$, the distribution is $u^3 S_0$ and $u^2 dS_0$ for $\{HH\}$ and $u^2 dS_0$ and $ud^2 S_0$ for $\{HT\}$. The distribution at period 3 is invariant if we add $\mathcal{F}_1$ to $\mathcal{F}_2$, because $\mathcal{F}_2$ already contains $\mathcal{F}_1$.

The Markov property describes the securities prices in the efficient markets. For example, the distribution of future prices based on the current price is the same as the distribution of future prices based on the current price in addition to the past prices. The reason for this is that the past prices are already reflected in the current prices when we assume the weak-form-efficient markets. In this case, we can say that the prices exhibit the Markov property.

Definition 19.14 We have a sequence of random variables $M_0, M_1, \cdots, M_n$ in a probability space $(\Omega, \mathcal{F}, \mathbb{P})$. A sequence of σ algebras $\mathcal{F}_0, \mathcal{F}_1, \cdots, \mathcal{F}_n$ has the property of $\mathcal{F}_0 \subset \mathcal{F}_1 \subset \cdots \subset \mathcal{F}_n \subset \mathcal{F}_{n+1}$. If each M_k is $\mathcal{F}_k$-measurable and for each k, $\mathbb{E}(M_{k+1}|k) = M_k$, then the sequence $\{M_k\}$ is a martingale.

Example 19.5 For $k = 0$, the set $\mathcal{F}_0 = \{0, \Omega\}$ contains no information, and any $\mathcal{F}$-measurable random variable must be constant. By definition, $\mathbb{E}(S_1|\mathcal{F}_0)$ is $(pu + qd)S_0$. If $(pu + qd) = 1$, then $\{S_1, \mathcal{F}_0\}$ is a martingale.

For $k = 1$, the information set is $\mathcal{F}_1 = \{0, \Omega, H, T\}$. By definition, $\mathbb{E}(S_2|\mathcal{F}_1)$ is $(pu^2 + qud)S_0$ for $\{H\}$ and $\mathbb{E}(S_2|\mathcal{F}_1)$ is $(pud + qd^2)S_0$ for $\{T\}$.

If $(pu + qd) = 1$, as before, then $\{S_2, \mathcal{F}_1\}$ is a martingale.

For $k = 2$, we have the same conclusion. Therefore, if $(pu + qd) = 1$, then $\{S_k, \mathcal{F}_k; k = 0, 1, 2, 3\}$ is a martingale.

The martingale process has no specific trend, because the expected value at a certain time in the future is equal to the current value. If the expected value is greater than the current value, the stochastic process has a tendency to go up, and vice versa. This concept is important in the derivative pricing. As we will see, stock prices discounted by the one-period risk-free rate follow martingale processes. To convert a stochastic process into a martingale, we need the Radon–Nikodym derivative.

Theorem 19.1 Let $\mathbb{P}$ and $\widetilde{\mathbb{P}}$ be two probability measures on a space $(\Omega, \mathcal{F})$.[2] Assume that for every $A \in \mathcal{F}$ satisfying $\mathbb{P}(A) = 0$, we also have $\widetilde{\mathbb{P}}(A) = 0$. Then we say that $\widetilde{\mathbb{P}}$ is absolutely continuous with respect to $\mathbb{P}$. Under this assumption, there is a nonnegative random variable Z such that

$$\widetilde{\mathbb{P}}(A) = \int_A Z d\mathbb{P}, \qquad \forall\, A \in \mathcal{F} \qquad\qquad (19.18)$$

Z is called the Radon–Nikodym derivative of $\widetilde{\mathbb{P}}$ with respect to $\mathbb{P}$.

The theorem can be explained intuitively. Suppose $\widetilde{\mathbb{P}}$ and $\mathbb{P}$ are simple functions and not stochastic. Then, in calculus, we often write

$$\widetilde{dP} = \left(\frac{\widetilde{dP}}{dP} \right) dP$$

Equation (19.18) is the extension of the above equation to stochastic calculus, where the Radon–Nikodym derivative is analogous to the term $\left(\frac{\widetilde{dP}}{dP} \right)$. The importance of the theorem is that when we value a derivative, we begin our modeling with a market probability. Suppose that we can determine the risk-neutral probability; then the Radon–Nikodym theorem allows us to replace the market probability with the risk-neutral probability, because formally we can determine the Radon–Nikodym derivative and change the probability measure accordingly. But we first have to determine the risk neutral probability. This is accomplished by using Girsanov Theorem, which we will discuss later.

Example 19.6 Let Ω be the exhaustive set of events $\{HHH, HHT, HTH, HTT, THH, THT, TTH, TTT\}$, the set of coin toss sequences of length 3. Let $\mathbb{P}$ correspond to probability $\frac{2}{3}$ for H and $\frac{1}{3}$ for T. These probabilities are analogous to the market probability q, which has been used throughout the book. Let $\widetilde{\mathbb{P}}$ correspond to probability $\frac{1}{2}$ for H and $\frac{1}{2}$ for T. Let us think of this $\widetilde{\mathbb{P}}$ as the risk-neutral probability. Now we define the Radon-Nikodym derivative to be $Z(\omega) = \frac{\widetilde{\mathbb{P}}(\omega)}{\mathbb{P}(\omega)}$, to be consistent with equation (19.18), where ω is each event in the set Ω. That is, Z is defined to be a stochastic process with outcomes that are the ratio of the probabilities, and the probabilities are the market probabilities $\mathbb{P}$. For this example, the Radon–Nikodym derivative is

$$Z_3(HHH) = \frac{(1/2)^3}{(2/3)^3} = \frac{27}{64}$$

$$Z_3(HHT) = Z_3(HTH) = Z_3(THH) = \frac{(1/2)^3}{(2/3)^2(1/3)} = \frac{27}{32}$$

$$Z_3(HTT) = Z_3(THT) = Z_3(TTH) = \frac{(1/2)^3}{(2/3)(1/3)^2} = \frac{27}{16}$$

$$Z_3(HHH) = \frac{(1/2)^3}{(1/3)^3} = \frac{27}{8}$$

If we multiply Z by $\mathbb{P}$, we can get $\widetilde{\mathbb{P}}$. This means we can convert market probabilities into risk-neutral probabilities.

Under market probabilities, Z follows a martingale process. For example, when the state is $\{HH\}$ at period 2, the expected value is $\frac{27}{64} \times \frac{2}{3} + \frac{27}{32} \times \frac{1}{3} = \frac{9}{16}$, which is equal to $Z_2\{HH\} = \frac{9}{16}$. From the Radon–Nikodym derivative, we can easily convert $\mathbb{P}$ into $\widetilde{\mathbb{P}}$ and vice versa.

State Prices

The existence of the Radon–Nikodym derivative enables us to construct the risk-neutral probability for any stochastic processes under certain conditions. Of course in the case of a binomial process, we can construct the risk-neutral probabilities. As we have shown in chapter 3, the risk-neutral probabilities can be used to calculate the risk-neutral expectation of stock, and this expected value would drift at the risk-free rate. If we adjust the drift of the Radon–Nikodym derivative downward, we can construct a process from the stock process that is martingale. This is what we will do next, by first defining the state price density process ζ_k.

To express the value of a derivative security in terms of the market probabilities rather than risk-neutral probabilities, it is useful to introduce the state price density process.

$$\zeta_k. = (1 + r)^{-k} Z_k, \ k = 0, \cdots, n$$

Once we know $\zeta_k \forall k$, we calculate the stock prices, given the future cash flow. Given the cash flow at period 3 of the stock, we can calculate the initial stock price by multiplying the cash flow by ξ_3 and corresponding market probabilities. For example, $S_3(HHH)$ $\xi_3(HHH)\mathbb{P}(HHH) + \cdots + S_3(TTT)\xi_3(TTT)\mathbb{P}(TTT)$ is the initial stock price.

Therefore the product of the stock process and the state price process is a martingale process under the market probabilities. As a result we can calculate the initial price in two ways. First, we calculate ξ_k and the market probabilities $\mathbb{P}$. Once we have ξ_k and $\mathbb{P}$, we can calculate the initial stock price, as we have shown above. Second, we convert $\mathbb{P}$ into $\widetilde{\mathbb{P}}$. Once we have $\widetilde{\mathbb{P}}$, we calculate the initial stock price by multiplying the cash flow by $\widetilde{\mathbb{P}}$ and discounting it to the present time at the risk-free rate. We will describe the second method below.

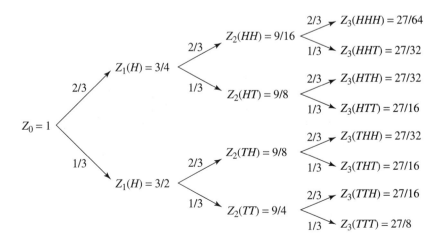

Figure 19.17 The Z_k values in the three-period binomial lattice

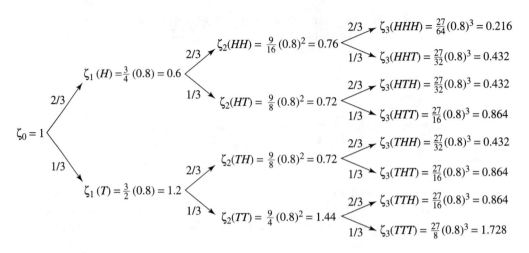

Figure 19.18 The state price value ξ_k in the three-period binomial lattice. The probabilities shown are for P, not $\overline{P}$. We assume that the one-period risk-free rate is 25 percent.

The stock price follows the binomial process with $u > r > d > 0$ and a positive initial price S_0. We assume a money market process, $M_k = (1+r)^k$, $k = 0, 1, \ldots, n$, and a portfolio process, $\Delta_0, \Delta_1, \ldots, \Delta_{k-1}$, which are $\mathcal{F}_k$-measurable. Finally, we assume a wealth process $X_{k+1} = \Delta_k S_{k+1} + (1+r)(X_k - \Delta_k S_k) = \Delta_k(S_{k+1} - (1+r)S_k) + (1+r)X_k$, which is also $\mathcal{F}_k$-measurable. The Discounted wealth process is $\left[\frac{X_{k+1}}{M_{k+1}}\right] = \left[\Delta_k\left(\frac{S_{k+1}}{M_{k+1}} - \frac{S_k}{M_k}\right) + \frac{X_k}{M_k}\right]$.

Definition 19.15 Let $\widetilde{\mathbb{P}}$ be a probability measure on $(\Omega, \mathcal{F})$, equivalent to the market measure $\mathbb{P}$. If $\{\frac{S_k}{M_k}\}_{k=0}^n$ is a martingale under $\widetilde{\mathbb{P}}$, we say that $\widetilde{\mathbb{P}}$ is a risk-neutral measure.

We can easily check that the discounted stock process is a martingale under $\widetilde{\mathbb{P}}$. For example, at the initial period, the expected stock price given $\mathcal{F}_0$ is $4 (= 6.4 \times \frac{1}{2} + 1.6 \times \frac{1}{2})$, which is equal to $S_0 (= 4)$. (See figure 19.19.)

Example 19.7 The portfolio process $\{\Delta_k\}_{k=0}^{n-1}$ given the stock price process in figure 19.19 and a call option on the stock when the exercise price is 5 and the maturity period is 3.

The portfolio process has been calculated so that the portfolio of shorting Δ_k shares of stock and long one share of the call option is a risk-free portfolio.

For example, $\Delta_2(HH) = 1$ can be calculated as shown below.

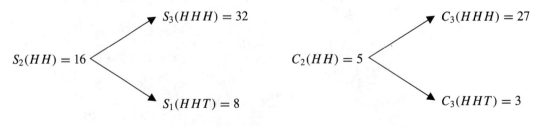

Stock   **Option**

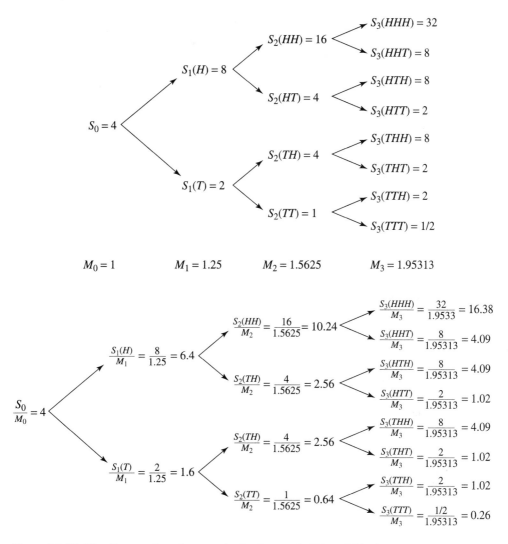

Figure 19.19 The discounted stock process in the three-period binomial lattice

If we formulate a portfolio of longing $\Delta_2(HH)$ shares of the stock and shorting one share of the call option, we have $\Delta_2(HH) \times 32 - 27$ for $\{HHH\}$ and $\Delta_2(HH) \times 8 - 3$ for $\{HHT\}$. If we make the portfolio risk-free, $(\Delta_2(HH) \times 32 - 27)$ for $\{HHH\}$ should be the same as $(\Delta_2(HH) \times 8 - 3)$ for $\{HHT\}$. Since $\Delta 2(HH) \times 32 - 27$ is equal to $\Delta_2(HH) - 3$, we have $\Delta_2(HH) = 1$. (See figure 19.20.)

Theorem 19.2 If $\widetilde{\mathbb{P}}$ is a risk-neutral measure, then every discounted wealth process $\{\frac{X_k}{M_k}\}_{k=0}^n$ is a martingale under $\widetilde{\mathbb{P}}$, regardless of the portfolio process used to generate it. This theorem can be explained quite intuitively. If we live in a risk-neutral world, then all securities have a risk-free return, as would every self-financing portfolio that does not have inflows or outflows of funds. For this reason, the portfolio process relative to the money market fund is a martingale process.

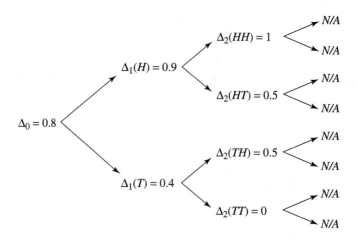

Figure 19.20 The portfolio process in the three-period binomial lattice

Definition 19.16 Let V_n be the payoff at time n, and say it is $\mathcal{F}_n$-measurable. If there is a risk-neutral measure $\widetilde{\mathbb{P}}$, then

$$V_0 = \widetilde{\mathbb{E}}\frac{V_n}{M_n} \tag{19.19}$$

Therefore, when we have constructed the risk-neutral probability, we can use equation (19.19) to determine the security price. The existence of the risk-neutral probability is given by Girsanov theorem, which says that we can define another process (or change the probability from market process to the risk-neutral process) by adjusting the drift term.

Given the cash flow of a European call option at maturity, we can calculate the call option price at period 0:

$$\frac{27}{1.95313} \times \frac{1}{8} + \frac{3}{1.95313} \times \frac{1}{8} + \cdots = 2.304$$

By the Girsanov theorem, we can get $\widetilde{\mathbb{P}}$ from $\mathbb{P}$ using the Brownian motion, which has been used to describe stock prices in finance. Once we know $\widetilde{\mathbb{P}}$, we can price any securities, including options.

$$V_0 = \frac{1}{(1+r)^3}\left[\left(\frac{r-d}{u-d}\right)^3 V_3(HHH) + \cdots + \left(\frac{u-r}{u-d}\right)^3 V_3(TTT)\right] \tag{19.20}$$

Theorem 19.3 (Girsanov Theorem) Let $B(t)$, $0 \le t \le T$, be a Brownian motion on a probability space $(\Omega, \mathcal{F}, \mathbb{P})$. Let $\mathcal{F}(t)$, $0 \le t \le T$, be the accompanying filtration, and let $\theta(t)$, $0 \le t \le T$, be a process adapted to this filtration. For $0 \le t \le T$, define

$$\tilde{B}(t) = \int_0^t \theta(u)du + B(t),$$

$$Z(t) = \exp\left\{\int_0^t \theta(u)dB(u) - \frac{1}{2}\int_0^t \theta^2(u)du\right\}, \tag{19.21}$$

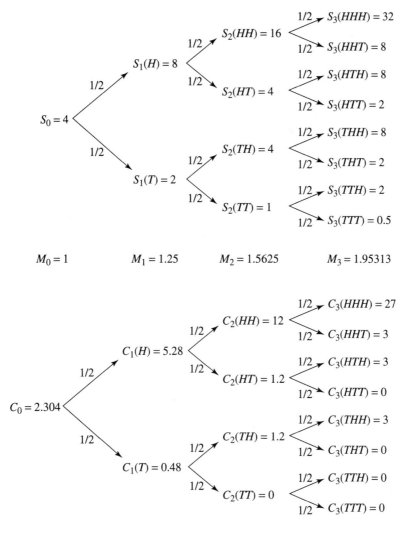

Figure 19.21 The stock process, the call option process, and the discounted wealth process. The probabilities shown are for $\widetilde{P}$.

and define a new probability measure by

$$\widetilde{\mathbb{P}}(A) = \int_A Z(T)d\mathbb{P}, \qquad \forall A \in \mathcal{F} \tag{19.22}$$

Under $\widetilde{\mathbb{P}}$, the process $\widetilde{B}(t)$, $0 \le t \le T$, is a Brownian motion.

We show a systematic diagram in figure 19.22 to summarize section 19.2. As can be seen, we need several concepts to price an option in the risk-neutral pricing framework. We begin with a definition of a function. Then we define a probability space. Based on the probability space, we can represent an information structure. Once we understand the function and the probability measure, we can define a random variable. If we put a time dimension to the random variable, we can construct a stochastic process.

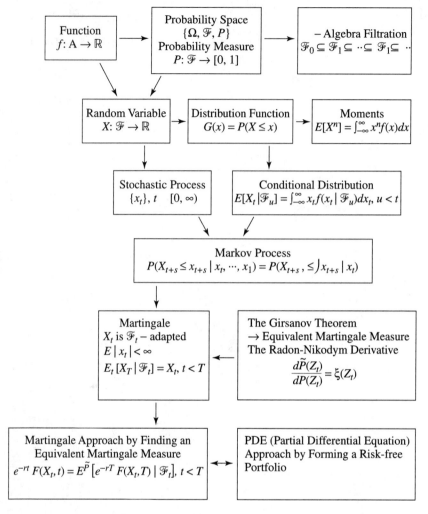

Figure 19.22 A systematic diagram

The Markov process is an important property of the financial stochastic processes because the efficient market hypothesis is a central concept in finance. The Girsanov theorem allows us to convert a stochastic process called a Brownian motion into a martingale. Once we have a martingale process, it is easy to price securities, which follow the martingale process. Another approach in addition to the martingale approach is to solve a partial differential equation. The partial differential equation can be formulated by forming a risk-free portfolio, which consists of an option and the corresponding underlying asset. (See figure 19.22.)

19.3   Comparison of the Option Derivation Between Discrete Time and Continuous Time

We have explained the necessary machinery to derive a European call option in a discrete framework as well as in a continuous framework, in order to show that two derivations go in a parallel manner. Figure 19.23 compares the binomial option pricing model with the Black–Scholes model in several aspects, such as stock distribution and delta. In this section, we derive a European call option.

Discrete Time Model (n − Period Binomial Model)

1. Sample space $\Omega = \{(x_1, \cdots, x_n) | x_j = H, T \}$

2. Filtration $\mathbb{F} = \{\mathcal{F}_0, \mathcal{F}_1, \mathcal{F}_2, \cdots, \mathcal{F}_n = \mathcal{F}\}$

$\mathcal{F}_o = \{0, \Omega\}$

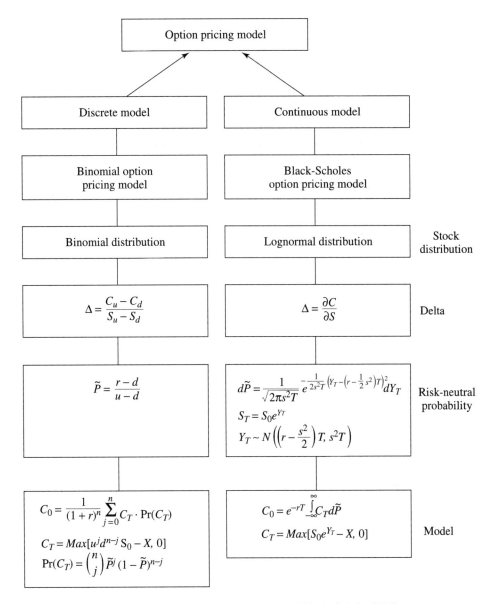

Figure 19.23 Comparison of binomial option pricing and Black–Scholes PDE

$\mathcal{F}_1$ is the smallest σ-algebra containing the two sets

$$A_H = \{(H, x_2 \cdots, x_n) | x_j = H, T \, j = 2, \cdots, n\}, A_T = \{(T, x_2 \cdots, x_n) | x_j = H, T\}$$

$\mathcal{F}_2$ is the smallest σ-algebra containing the four sets

$$A_{HH} = \{(H, H, x_3 \cdots, x_n) | x_j = H, T \, j = 3, \cdots, n\}, A_{HT} = \{(H, T, x_3 \cdots, x_n) | x_j = H, T\}$$

$$A_{TH} = \{(T, H, x_3 \cdots, x_n) | x_j = H, T \, j = 3, \cdots, n\}, A_{TT} = \{(T, T, x_3 \cdots, x_n) | x_j = H, T\}$$

Analogously $\mathcal{F}_k$ is defined to be the smallest σ-algebra containing the 2^k sets determined by the first k tosses of the coin.

3. The probability measure $\mathbb{P}$ is defined intuitively by $\mathbb{P}\{(x_1, \cdots, x_n)\} = \frac{1}{2^n}$.
4. The stock price process is $\{S_k | k = 0, 1, \cdots, n\}$

S_k is the stock price at time k and is a random variable defined as follows:

S_0 is a constant random variable that represents the stock price s today.

S_1 is the stock price at time 1 and is given as one of the two values su, sd depending on the outcome of the first coin tossing (u for H and d for T). Here $u > d > 0$.

S_k is the stock price at time k and is given as one of $(k+1)$ different values, depending on the outcome of the first k tosses of the coin:

$$S_k = su^a d^{k-a} \text{ if the number of heads in the first } k \text{ tosses is } a.$$

$\mathbb{P}(S_k = su^a d^{k-a}) = \frac{k!}{a!(k-a)!} \frac{1}{2^k}$

5. Unconditional distribution of S_k

$$S_k = sd^k (u/d)^{X_k}, \text{ where } X_k \sim Binomial(k, 1/2)$$

6. Conditional distribution of S_k

$$S_k = S_{k-1} d (u/d)^{X_1}, \text{ where } X_1 \sim Binomial(1, 1/2)$$

$$E_{k-1}[S_k] = S_{k-1} \left(\frac{u+d}{2} \right)$$

$$Var_{k-1}[S_k] = S_{k-1}^2 \left(\frac{(u-d)^2}{4} \right)$$

Continuous Time Model

Almost all financial models in continuous time use the Brownian motion as a basic building block.

1. Brownian Motion

A standard Brownian motion is a continuous time stochastic process $B = \{B(t) | t \geq 0\}$ on a probability space $(\Omega, \mathcal{F}, \mathbb{P})$ defined by the following properties:

1. $B(0) = 0$ almost surely
2. For any times t and $s > t$, $B(s) - B(t)$ is normally distributed with mean 0 and variance $s - t$
3. For any times $t_0, \cdots, t_n$ such that $0 \leq t_0 < t_1 < \cdots < t_n < \infty$, the random variables $B(t_0), B(t_1) - B(t_0), \cdots, B(t_n) - B(t_{n-1})$ are independently distributed
4. For each $\omega \in \Omega$, the sample path $t \mapsto B(t, \omega)$ is continuous.

It is a nontrivial fact, but it can be proved that the probability space (Ω, P) can be constructed so that there exist standard Brownian motions.

2. Filtration

The flow of information available at each instance is modeled via the natural filtration $\mathbb{F}^B = \{\mathcal{F}^B(t)|t \geq 0\}$ associated with the Brownian motion. $\mathbb{F}^B(t)$ is the smallest σ algebra containing all sets of the form $\{\omega \in \Omega | a < B(s, \omega) \leq b\}$, where $s \leq t$ and $a < b$ are real numbers.

For technical reasons, however, we should enlarge the σ-algebra $\mathbb{F}^B(t)$ slightly. The standard filtration $\mathbb{F} = \{\mathcal{F}(t)|t \geq 0\}$ of the standard Brownian motion B is defined as follows: $\mathbb{F}(t)$ is the smallest σ algebra containing $\mathbb{F}^B(t)$ and all null sets of Ω. The probability measure P is also extended by defining $P(N) = 0$ for any null sets N. We will always assume this standard filtration $\mathbb{F}$, unless it is explicitly stated otherwise.

3. Ito Integral

Most continuous time financial models describe the behavior of financial variables like stock prices or interest rates in terms of stochastic differential equations, which are defined via the Ito stochastic integral. Here we give only a heuristic description of the Ito integral. Rigorous treatment of this topic can be found in various references. We will closely follow the treatment in Duffie (2001). We assume for the time being that the standard Brownian motion B is the price process of a stock. A trading strategy is an adapted process $\theta = \{\theta_t | t \geq 0\}$ specifying at each state $\omega \in \Omega$ and time t the number of units of the stock to hold. Let L^2 denote the space of adapted processes satisfying the condition $\int_0^T \theta_t^2 dt < \infty$ almost surely for each T. Then for each θ in L^2 there is an adapted process with continuous sample paths, denoted $\int \theta \, dB$, that is called the Ito integral of θ with respect to B.

The value of the process $\int \theta \, dB$ at time T is denoted $\int_0^T \theta_t \, dB_t$, and represents the total trading gain generated up to time T by trading the security with price process B according to the trading strategy θ. Furthermore, for each θ in H^2, meaning that $E\left[\int_0^T \theta_t^2 dt\right] < \infty$ for each T; thus the process $\int \theta \, dB$ is a martingale: $E_S\left[\int_0^T \theta_t \, dB_t\right] = \int_0^S \theta_t \, dB_t$ for $S < T$ and $\text{var}\left[\int_0^T \theta_t \, dB_t\right] = E\left[\int_0^T \theta_t^2 dt\right]$. In fact, $\int_0^T \theta_t \, dB_t$ is the limit in the mean-square sense of the finite sums $\sum_{k=0}^{Tn} \theta_{k/n}(B_{(k+1)/n} - B_{k/n})$, because the number n of trading intervals per unit time goes to infinity and the latter sum is really the trading gain when trading occurs at every $t = k/n$.

4. Ito Process

An Ito process is a process S of the following form :

$$S_t = x + \int_0^t \mu_s \, ds + \int_0^t \sigma_s \, dB_s \tag{19.23}$$

where σ is a process in L^2 and μ is a process in L^1 in the sense that $\int_0^t |\mu_s| ds < \infty$ almost surely for each t. It is common to write the above equation in the informal differential form $dS_t = \mu_t dt + \sigma_t dB_t$; $S_0 = x$. The stock price process is usually defined as an Ito process.

5. Ito Lemma

Suppose X is an Ito process with $dX_t = \mu_t dt + \sigma_t dB_t$, and let $f : \mathbb{R}^2 \to \mathbb{R}$ be twice continuously differentiable. Then the process Y, defined by $Y_t = f(X_t, t)$, is also an Ito process with

$$dY_t = \left(f_X(X_t, t)\mu_t + f_t(X_t, t) + \frac{1}{2} f_{XX}(X_t, t)\sigma_t^2 \right) dt + f_X(X_t, t)\sigma_t dB_t \quad (19.24)$$

6. Black–Scholes Stock Model

The Black–Scholes model assumes that the stock price process S is given by an Ito process of the form

$$dS_t = \mu S_t dt + \sigma S_t dB_t; \quad S_0 = x$$

where μ and σ are constants called the drift and the volatility, respectively. The Ito lemma applied to the function $f(S_t) = \log S_t$ gives

$$d \log S_t = (\mu - \sigma^2/2)dt + \sigma dB_t \quad (19.25)$$

Hence we get

$$S_t = x \exp\{(\mu - \sigma^2/2)t + \sigma B_t\} \quad (19.26)$$

that is, S_t follows a lognormal distribution.

European Contingent Claim

A European contingent claim (or option) maturing at time n is defined by its payoff $C = C_n$, which is an $\mathbb{F}_n$-measurable random variable. In the continuous time case n is replaced by T. We want to determine the no-arbitrage value of the option before maturity. The idea is to construct a portfolio of stock and risk-free bond at time 0 with some initial amount of money and rebalance it at each time instant in a self-financing way so that the liquidized value of the portfolio at the maturity of the option exactly matches the payoff of the option. If such a replication is possible, then the value of the portfolio before maturity should be the value of the option in order to avoid arbitrage opportunity. In fact, such a replication is possible in both the binomial and the Black–Scholes models. In the binomial model the construction of a replicating portfolio is elementary and explicit. In a continuous time Black–Scholes model, on the other hand, we have to develop some sophisticated results from continuous time stochastic calculus.

Pricing in the Binomial Model

1. Replicating Portfolio

Let θ_k and M_k denote the number of shares of the stock and the risk-free bond, respectively, that an investor holds from time k to immediately before time $k + 1$. Then the process $(\theta, M) = \{(\theta_k, M_k) | k = 0, 1, \cdots, n - 1\}$ is called the portfolio process for the market consisting of the stock and the risk-free bond. The value of the portfolio is $\Pi_k = \theta_k S_k + M_k$. The value of θ_k is unknown before time k, and it is decided by the investor after the market value of the stock S_k at time k is known. We have to decide the values of (θ_k, M_k) for $k = 0, 1, \cdots, n - 1$ in such a way that the liquidized value of the portfolio at maturity matches the payoff of the option: $\Pi_n = C_n$. The construction of the replicating portfolio starts from time $n - 1$ and proceeds backward in time.

The procedure works because we know the value of the portfolio at time n (the maturity of the option), which should be the same as the payoff of the option. Thus we can get a complete picture from a one-period binomial tree. We suppose that we are at the starting node (called A) of the one-period binomial tree and the stock price is S at node A. The stock price can go up to Su (node B_1) or go down to Sd (node B_2). The portfolio values at node B_1 and B_2 should be given by V_1 and V_2. The number of shares of stock θ and the cash amount M at node A should now satisfy the following relations:

$$\theta Su + M(1+r) = V_1$$
$$\theta Sd + M(1+r) = V_2$$
(19.27)

It is a linear system of equations whose solution can be determined explicitly. Now the value of the portfolio at the node A is given by

$$V = \theta S + M = \frac{qV_1 + (1-q)V_2}{1+r}$$
(19.28)

where $q = \frac{(1+r)-d}{u-d}$.

We conclude that we can construct a portfolio of stock and risk-free bond in such a way that the liquidized value of the portfolio should be the same as the payoff of the option. Then the no-arbitrage principle guarantees that the no-arbitrage value of the option before maturity should be given by the value of the replicating portfolio.

2. Pricing Formula Using an Equivalent Martingale Measure

An equivalent martingale measure (EMM) is a probability measure Q on $(\Omega, \mathcal{F})$ such that (1) it has the same null sets as $\mathbb{P}$ and (2) the stock price process denominated by the money market acocount is a martingale with respect to the measure Q:

$$E_k^Q\left[\frac{S_{k+1}}{\beta_{k+1}}\right] = \frac{S_k}{\beta_k}$$
(19.29)

for all k, where $\beta_k = (1+r)^k$ is the money market account and r is the one-period risk-free interest rate. Taking q as the probability of upward movement of the stock under the measure Q, we see that Q is a EMM if and only if $0 < q < 1$ and $uq + d(1-q) = 1+r$. Therefore EMM is uniquely determined by

$$q = \frac{(1+r)-d}{u-d}$$

if u and d satisfy the condition $u > 1+r > d > 0$, which will be assumed henceforth, unless it is explicitly stated otherwise. In fact, this condition guarantees that the market consisting of the stock and the money market account admits no arbitrage opportunity.

Now the option value C_k at any time $k < n$ can be written as an expectation of deflated payoff under EMM:

$$C_k = \beta_k E_k^Q\left[\frac{C_n}{\beta_n}\right] = E_k^Q\left[\frac{C_n}{(1+r)^{n-k}}\right]$$
(19.30)

where E_k^Q denotes the Q expectation conditional upon the information at time k. Under the measure Q the risky stock grows only at the risk-free rate:

$$E_k^Q[S_{k+1}] = (1+r)S_k.$$

(19.31)

For this reason, Q is also called the risk-neutral measure and the above pricing formula is also called the risk-neutral pricing formula.

Pricing in the Black–Scholes Model

Pricing by the expectation under an equivalent martingale measure

Step 1: Finding EMM An equivalent martingale measure (EMM) is a probability measure Q on $(\Omega, \mathcal{F})$ such that (1) it has the same null sets as P and (2) the stock price process denominated by the cash account is a martingale with respect to the Q:

$$E_s^Q\left[\frac{S_t}{\beta_t}\right] = \frac{S_s}{\beta_s}$$

(19.32)

for all $s < t$, where $\beta_t = e^{rt}$ is the money market account and r is the risk-free interest rate. The existence and uniqueness of EMM in the Black–Scholes model is guaranteed by the Girsanov theorem.

Note first that

$$\frac{d(S/\beta)}{S/\beta} = (\mu - r)dt + \sigma\,dB = \sigma\left[\frac{\mu-r}{\sigma}dt + dB\right]$$

(19.33)

Defining

$$\lambda = \frac{\mu-r}{\sigma}$$

(19.34)

and

$$\xi_t = \exp\left(-\int_0^t \lambda\,dB_s - \frac{1}{2}\int_0^t \lambda^2\,ds\right) = \exp\left(-\lambda B_t - \frac{1}{2}\lambda^2 t\right)$$

(19.35)

we see that ξ_t is an exponential martingale, so by the Girsanov theorem the process

$$\widetilde{B}_t = B_t + \int_0^t \lambda\,ds = B_t + \lambda t$$

(19.36)

is a standard Brownian motion under the new measure Q, which is defined by

$$Q(A) = \int_A \xi_T\,dP = E^P[\xi_T 1_A]$$

(19.37)

Therefore $\frac{d(S/\beta)}{S/\beta} = \sigma\,d\widetilde{B}$ and thus S/β is a martingale under the new measure Q.

Step 2: Finding a Replicating Portfolio   Next we observe that for any portfolio Π_t of stock of Δ_t shares and risk-free bond, the denominated value Π/β should also be a martingale under Q. In fact,

$$\frac{d(\Pi/\beta)}{\Pi/\beta} = \Delta\sigma\, d\widetilde{B} \qquad (19.38)$$

Finally we define a Q martingale:

$$X_t = E_t^Q\left[\frac{C_T}{\beta_T}\right] \qquad (19.39)$$

Then, by the martingale representation theorem,[3] we can find an adapted process δ_t such that $dX_t = \delta_t d\widetilde{B}_t$. Now we define the portfolio process Π by the following requirements:

$$\Pi_0 = X_0$$

and

$$\Delta\sigma\frac{\Pi}{\beta} = \delta \qquad (19.40)$$

It then follows that $\Pi = \beta X$ and, in particular, $\Pi_T = \beta_T X_T = C_T$, that is, the portfolio Π replicates the payoff of the option in a self-financing way, and therefore, in order to avoid arbitrage opportunity, the option value C_t before maturity should be the same as the value of Π_t:

$$C_t = \Pi_t = \beta_t X_t = \beta_t E_t^Q\left[\frac{C_T}{\beta_T}\right] = e^{-r(T-t)}E_t^Q[C_T] \qquad (19.41)$$

This is the risk-neutral pricing formula in the Black–Scholes continuous time model. Even though we have used some sophisticated machinery from stochastic calculus to find the replicating portfolio, the basic idea of pricing by replication remains valid in the continuous time setting. Furthermore, the final pricing formula in continuous time has the same appearance as the one in discrete time, and the equivalent martingale measures have the same meaning in both cases.

Step 3: Calculating the Expectation   In some simple cases, the expectation in the risk-neutral pricing formula can be computed explicitly. As an example, we derive the Black–Scholes formula for call option value. The derivation is straightforward, yet involves lengthy expressions. It is best to simplify the notation. We make the following simplifications:

Let $t = 0$ and calculate the option price as of time 0.
Accordingly, the current information set $\mathcal{F}_t$ becomes $\mathcal{F}_0$. This way, instead of using conditional expectations, we can use the unconditional expectation operator $E_t^Q[\cdot]$.

There are only a few cases in which we can a get closed-form expression for option value. In general, we can at best approximate the option value given by an expectation for example, using a simulation of relevant random variables. The Monte Carlo simulation is one of the most widely adopted simulation methods for evaluating the expectation.

Black–Scholes PDE

In many important cases, the option value can also be obtained by solving a partial differential equation (PDE), called the Black–Scholes PDE. The best aspect of this approach is that once we have a PDE whose solution describes the option value, the PDE can be efficiently solved (approximately) by well-developed numerical methods like the finite difference method, which is much more efficient in implementation than the Monte Carlo simulation.

Not all European option valuation problems can be attacked using the PDE approach. We have to place some limits on the payoff structure of the option. (In general, we also need to impose a restriction on the nature of the underlying variable process, i.e., the Markovian restriction, which is acceptable in this simple Black–Scholes case.) To illustrate the PDE approach, we assume that the option payoff C_T is function of S_T only, that is, $C_T = g(S_T)$. Then the option value C_t at time t is a function of time t and the stock value $S_t : C_t = f(S_t, t)$. The idea is to construct the portfolio

$$\Pi_t = C_t - \Delta_t S_t \tag{19.42}$$

of the option and the Δ_t units of stock in such a way that, by choosing Δ_t appropriately, the portfolio should be risk-free. Then, using the Ito Lemma, we see, after taking $\Delta_t = f_S(S_t, t)$ that

$$d\Pi_t = \left(f_t(S_t, t) + \frac{1}{2}\sigma^2 S_t^2 f_{SS}(S_t, t) \right) dt \tag{19.43}$$

Thus the portfolio Π is a risk-free portfolio. Then, to avoid arbitrage opportunity, we should have

$$d\Pi_t = r\Pi_t dt \tag{19.44}$$

where r is the risk-free interest rate. It amounts to the Black–Scholes PDE,

$$f_t(S_t, t) + \frac{1}{2}\sigma^2 S_t^2 f_{SS}(S_t, t) + rS_t f_S(S_t, t) - rf(S_t, t) = 0 \tag{19.45}$$

with the final condition $f(S_T, T) = g(S_T)$. Solving this final value problem for PDE gives the no-arbitrage value of the option.

Equivalence of the pricing PDE and the expectation under EMM

The equivalence of the two approaches above is established by the Feynman–Kac theorem, which asserts that under some regularity conditions on the drift and volatility of the underlying variable, the expectation of the type in the risk-neutral pricing formula can be computed by solving a PDE of the Black–Scholes type. (See figure 19.22.)

Appendix A. Continuous Time Versions of the Ho–Lee Models

To derive corresponding continuous time results, we assume that length of time is measured in the unit of year and each time step in the binomial model considered in chapter 5 and chapter 6 has length Δ measured in years. We will investigate the behavior of the bond prices, spot rates, and forward rates as Δ goes to 0. Our model can be viewed as a discrete time formulation on a recombining binomial tree of the Heath–Jarrow–Morton methodology. Therefore we need to find the forward rate volatility in the continuous time limit of our model. Then the continuous time limits of bond prices, short rates, and yields follow from this HJM representation of our model.

Forward Rate

Recall that

$$f_{i,j}^n(T) = -\frac{1}{\Delta} \ln \frac{P_{i,j}^n(T+1)}{P_{i,j}^n(T)}$$

$$= f(T+n) + \frac{1}{\Delta} \ln \prod_{k=1}^n \frac{G_{(T+1)nk}^1}{G_{Tnk}^1} + \frac{1}{\Delta} \ln \prod_{l=1}^n \frac{G_{(T+1)nl}^2}{G_{Tnl}^2} - \frac{(i-0.5n)}{\Delta} \ln \delta_{T+n}^1$$

$$- \frac{(j-0.5n)}{\Delta} \ln \delta_{T+n}^2$$

The forward rate $f^n(T)$ at time n has a stochastic term consisting of two independent binomial random variables. In fact, we can write

$$f^n(T) = \text{deterministic part} - \frac{\ln \delta_{T+n}^1}{\Delta} X_1(n) - \frac{\ln \delta_{T+n}^2}{\Delta} X_2(n)$$

where $X_1(n)$ and $X_2(n)$ are centralized independent binomial random variables with mean 0 and variance $\frac{n}{4}$. We set

$$\sigma_1(n, T) = \sigma_1(n+T) = \frac{f_{i,j}^n(T) - f_{i+1,j}^n(T)}{2\sqrt{\Delta}} = \frac{\ln \delta_{T+n}^1}{2\Delta^{3/2}}$$

and

$$\sigma_2(n, T) = \sigma_2(n+T) = \frac{f_{i,j}^n(T) - f_{i,j+1}^n(T)}{2\sqrt{\Delta}} = \frac{\ln \delta_{T+n}^2}{2\Delta^{3/2}}.$$

Then we get

$$f^n(T) = \text{deterministic part} - 2\sqrt{\Delta}\sigma_1(n+T)X_1(n) - 2\sqrt{\Delta}\sigma_2(n+T)X_2(n)$$

$$= \text{deterministic part} - \sqrt{n\Delta}\sigma_1(n+T)\frac{X_1(n)}{\sqrt{n/2}} - \sqrt{n\Delta}\sigma_2(n+T)\frac{X_2(n)}{\sqrt{n/2}}$$

Let $t = n\Delta$ be fixed while $\Delta \to 0$, $n \to \infty$. Then it is known that $\frac{X_k(n)}{\sqrt{n/2}} \to \varepsilon_k(t)$ for $k = 1, 2$, where ε_1 and ε_2 are independent. Therefore we see that, letting $f(t, \tau)$ denote the instantaneous, continuously compounded forward rate at time t for time to maturity (not calendar maturity!) τ,

$$f(t, \tau) = \lim_{\substack{\Delta \to 0 \\ n, T \to \infty \\ t=n\Delta, \tau=T\Delta}} f^n(T) = \text{limit of deterministic part} + \sigma_1(t+\tau)W_1(t) + \sigma_2(t+\tau)W_2(t)$$

with slight abuse of notation, where $W_1(t)$, $W_2(t)$ are independent 1-dimensional Brownian motions. Let $F(t, M)$ be the forward rate for the calendar maturity M; that is, $F(t, M) = f(t, M - t)$. Then we have

$$F(t, M) = \text{limit of deterministic part} + \sigma_1(M)W_1(t) + \sigma_2(M)W_2(t)$$

Therefore the HJM volatilities that correspond to our model are given by

$$\sigma_k^{HJM}(t, M) = \sigma_k(M)$$

so the HJM volatilities depend only on the calendar maturity M, and not on the current time, t. Now the stochastic differential equation governing the dynamics of the forward rates corresponding to our model is given by

$$dF(t, M) = \alpha(t, M)dt + \sigma_1(M)dW_1(t) + \sigma_2(M)dW_2(t)$$

where the drift is given by the HJM condition on the risk-neutral drift of the forward rate

$$\alpha(t, M) = \sum_{k=1}^{2} \sigma_k^{HJM}(t, M) \int_t^M \sigma_k^{HJM}(t, m)dm =$$

$$\sigma_1(M) \int_t^M \sigma_1(u)du + \sigma_2(M) \int_t^M \sigma_2(u)du$$

Of course, our discrete time model satisfies the discrete time analogue of this HJM drift restriction. In fact, the expectation of $f^n(T)$ is completely determined by the volatility specification $\sigma_k(m)$, $k = 1, 2$, $m = 0, 1, 2 \cdots$. Now we will show that the expected forward rate $E[f^n(T)]$ converges to the value $F(0, t + \tau) + \int_0^t \alpha(s, M)ds$ given by the HJM drift. For any integer m

$$\delta_m^1 = \exp\{2\Delta^{3/2}\sigma_1(m)\} \text{ and } \delta_m^2 = \exp\{2\Delta^{3/2}\sigma_2(m)\}$$

and so for any $n > m$

$$d_{n,m}^1 = \delta_n^1\delta_{n-1}^1 \cdots \delta_{m+1}^1\delta_m^1 = \exp\left\{2\Delta^{3/2}\sum_{k=m}^{n}\sigma_1(k)\right\} \text{ and}$$

$$d_{n,m}^2 = \delta_n^2\delta_{n-1}^2 \cdots \delta_{m+1}^2\delta_m^2 = \exp\left\{2\Delta^{3/2}\sum_{k=m}^{n}\sigma_2(k)\right\}$$

From the expression of $f^n(T)$ we have

$$E\left[f^n(T)\right] = f(T+n) + \frac{1}{\Delta}\ln\prod_{k=1}^n \frac{G^1_{(T+1)nk}}{G^1_{Tnk}} + \frac{1}{\Delta}\ln\prod_{l=1}^n \frac{G^2_{(T+1)nl}}{G^2_{Tnl}}$$

$$= f(T+n) - \frac{n}{2\Delta}\ln\delta^1_{T+n} - \frac{n}{2\Delta}\ln\delta^2_{T+n}$$

$$+ \sum_{k=1}^{n-1} \frac{1}{\Delta}\{\ln(1+\delta^1_{T+n,k}) - \ln(1+\delta^1_{T+n-1,k})\}$$

$$+ \sum_{k=1}^{n-1} \frac{1}{\Delta}\{\ln(1+\delta^2_{T+n,k}) - \ln(1+\delta^2_{T+n-1,k})\}$$

Let $t = n\Delta, \tau = T\Delta$. We will let $\Delta \downarrow 0, n, T \uparrow \infty$ in such a way that $t = n\Delta, \tau = T\Delta$. We want to see the behavior of $E\left[f^n(T)\right]$. To do this, we derive an approximation of

$$\frac{1}{\Delta}\log\left(\frac{1+d^1_{m,k}}{2}\right) \text{ for } m > k$$

Since $\sigma_1(n) = \frac{1}{2\Delta^{3/2}}\log\left(\delta^1_n\right)$, we have

$$\frac{1}{\Delta}\log\left(\frac{1+d^1_{m,k}}{2}\right) = \frac{1}{\Delta}\log\left(1+\frac{1}{2}(d^1_{m,k}-1)\right) \equiv \frac{1}{\Delta}\log(1+x)$$

where

$$X = \frac{1}{2}(d^1_{m,k}-1) = \frac{1}{2}\left(-1 + e^{2\Delta^{3/2}\sum_{i=k}^m \sigma_1(i)}\right)$$

$$= \Delta^{3/2}\sum_{i=k}^m \sigma_1(i) + \Delta^3\left(\sum_{i=k}^m \sigma_1(i)\right)^2 + O(\Delta^{9/2})$$

Using the Taylor expansion of $\log(1+x)$, we have

$$\frac{1}{\Delta}\log\left(\frac{1+d^1_{m,k}}{2}\right) = \Delta^{1/2}\sum_{i=k}^m \sigma_1(i) + \frac{1}{2}\Delta^2\left(\sum_{i=k}^m \sigma_1(i)\right)^2 + O(\Delta^{7/2})$$

From this approximation, it follows that

$$\frac{1}{\Delta}\sum_{k=1}^n \log\left(\frac{1+d^1_{T+n,k}}{2}\right) - \frac{1}{\Delta}\sum_{k=1}^n \log\left(\frac{1+d^1_{T+n-1,k}}{2}\right) - \frac{n}{2\Delta}\log\left(\delta^1_{T+n}\right)$$

$$= \frac{1}{2}\Delta^2 n\sigma_1^2(n+N) + \Delta^2\sigma_1(n+N)\sum_{k=1}^n \sum_{i=k}^{T+n-1}\sigma_1(i) + nO(\Delta^{7/2})$$

$$\rightarrow \sigma_1(t+\tau)\int_0^t \int_s^{t+\tau}\sigma_1(u)\,du\,ds$$

A similar estimation holds for the terms containing d^2.

$$\frac{1}{\Delta}\sum_{k=1}^{n}\log\left(\frac{1+d_{T+n,k}^2}{2}\right) - \frac{1}{\Delta}\sum_{k=1}^{n}\log\left(\frac{1+d_{T+n-1,k}^2}{2}\right) - \frac{n}{2\Delta}\log\left(\delta_{T+n}^2\right)$$

$$= \frac{1}{2}\Delta^2 n\sigma_2^2(n+N) + \Delta^2\sigma_2(n+N)\sum_{k=1}^{n}\sum_{i=k}^{T+n-1}\sigma_2(i) + nO(\Delta^{7/2})$$

$$\rightarrow \sigma_2(t+\tau)\int_0^t\int_s^{t+\tau}\sigma_2(u)\,du\,ds$$

Gathering these, we conclude that

$$E\left[f^n(T)\right] \rightarrow f(t+\tau) + \sigma_1(t+\tau)\int_0^t\int_s^{t+\tau}\sigma_1(u)\,du\,ds + \sigma_2(t+\tau)\int_0^t\int_s^{t+\tau}\sigma_2(u)\,du\,ds$$

$$= F(0,M) + \sigma_1(M)\int_0^t\int_s^{M}\sigma_1(u)\,du\,ds + \sigma_2(M)\int_0^t\int_s^{M}\sigma_2(u)\,du\,ds$$

$$= F(0,M) + \int_0^t\alpha(s,M)\,ds$$

where $M = t+\tau$ is the calendar maturity. Therefore the expected forward rate converges to the right value. In conclusion, the HJM model corresponding to the continuous time limit of our two-factor binomial model is of the form

$$dF(t,M) = \alpha(t,M)\,dt + \sigma_1(M)\,dW_1(t) + \sigma_2(M)\,dW_2(t)$$

$$\alpha(t,M) = \sigma_1(M)\int_t^M\sigma_1(u)\,du + \sigma_2(M)\int_t^M\sigma_2(u)\,du$$

Short Rate

Upon integrating the forward rate stochastic differential equation, we get

$$F(t,M) = F(0,M) + \int_0^t\alpha(s,M)\,ds + \sigma_1(M)W_1(t) + \sigma_2(M)W_2(t)$$

$$= F(0,M) + \sigma_1(M)\int_0^t\int_s^{M}\sigma_1(u)\,du\,ds + \sigma_2(M)\int_0^t\int_s^{M}\sigma_2(u)\,du\,ds$$
$$+ \sigma_1(M)W_1(t) + \sigma_2(M)W_2(t)$$

Hence

$$r(t) = F(t,t) = F(0,t) + \sigma_1(t)\int_0^t\int_s^{t}\sigma_1(u)\,du\,ds + \sigma_2(t)\int_0^t\int_s^{t}\sigma_2(u)\,du\,ds$$

$$+ \sigma_1(t)W_1(t) + \sigma_2(t)W_2(t)$$
$$\equiv g(t, W_1(t), W_2(t))$$

The Ito lemma implies

$$dr(t) = g_t dt + g_{W_1} dW_1(t) + g_{W_2} dW_2(t)$$

because the second partial derivatives of g with respect to W_1 and W_2 are all 0.
Note that

$$g_t = F_M(0, t) + \sigma_1'(t) \int_0^t \int_s^t \sigma_1(u)\,duds + \sigma_2'(t) \int_0^t \int_s^t \sigma_2(u)\,duds + t(\sigma_1(t)^2 +$$

$$\sigma_2(t)^2) + \sigma_1'(t)W_1(t) + \sigma_2'(t)W_2(t)$$

$$g_{W_1} = \sigma_1(t) \text{and}$$

$$g_{W_2} = \sigma_2(t)$$

We introduce the following vector notation for convenience:

$$\sigma := (\sigma_1, \sigma_2), \, \sigma' := (\sigma_1', \sigma_2'), \, W := (W_1, W_2) \text{ and}$$

$$X(t) := \left(\int_0^t \int_s^t \sigma_1(u)\,duds, \int_0^t \int_s^t \sigma_2(u)\,du\,ds \right)$$

Then we have

$$dr(t) = \left\{ F_M(0, t) + t|\sigma(t)|^2 + \sigma'(t) \bullet (X(t) + W(t)) \right\} dt + \sigma(t) \bullet dW(t)$$

where the dots represent the usual dot product of two plane vectors. With this notation, we also have

$$r(t) = F(0, t) + \sigma(t) \bullet (X(t) + W(t))$$

If it were a one-factor model, we would get

$$dr(t) = \left\{ F_M(0, t) + t\sigma(t)^2 + \frac{\sigma'(t)}{\sigma(t)} \left[r(t) - F(0, t) \right] \right\} dt + \sigma(t)dW(t)$$

Hence we see that the model exhibits mean reversion when $\sigma'(t) > 0$. To get a similar interpretation in the case of a two-factor model, we set

$$\sigma(t) \bullet (X(t) + W(t)) = |\sigma(t)| \cdot |X(t) + W(t)| \cdot \cos \theta(t) \text{ and}$$

$$\sigma'(t) \bullet (X(t) + W(t)) = |\sigma'(t)| \cdot |X(t) + W(t)| \cdot \cos \phi(t)$$

where $\theta(t)$ is the angle between the two vectors $\sigma(t)$ and $(X(t) + W(t))$, and similarly for $\phi(t)$.
Thus we have

$$dr(t) = \{F_M(0, t) + t|\sigma(t)|^2 + |\sigma'(t)| \cdot |X(t) + W(t)| \cdot \cos\phi(t)\}dt + \sigma(t) \bullet dW(t)$$

$$= \left\{F_M(0, t) + t|\sigma(t)|^2 + \frac{|\sigma'(t)| \cos\phi(t)}{|\sigma(t)| \cos\theta(t)} [r(t) - F(0, t)]\right\} dt + \sigma(t) \bullet dW(t)$$

Therefore the resulting short-rate dynamics exhibits mean reversion.

Yield

The spot yield $R(t, M)$ for the maturity M at time t is defined by

$$R(t, M)(M - t) = \int_t^M F(t, m)dm$$

Then we get

$$dR(t, M) = \frac{1}{M - t}\left[R(t, M) - r(t) + \sum_{i=1}^2 \int_t^M \sigma_i(m) \int_t^m \sigma_i(u)du \cdot dm\right] dt$$

$$+ \sum_{i=1}^2 \left[\frac{1}{M - t}\int_t^M \sigma_i(m)dm\right] dW_i(t)$$

Hence the yield volatility is given by

$$\sigma_i^R(t, M) = \frac{1}{M - t}\int_t^M \sigma_i(m)dm$$

So for $t < m < M$ we have

$$\sigma_i^R(t, M)(M - t) = \sigma_i^R(t, m)(m - t) + \sigma_i^R(m, M)(M - m)$$

and thus the future spot yield volatilities $\sigma_i^R(m, M)$ are completely determined by today's yield volatilities $\sigma_i^R(t, M)$ and $\sigma_i^R(t, m)$.

Appendix B. Summary of Continuous Time Interest Rate Models

In this appendix we express various term structure models in terms of a spot rate, a forward rate, and a bond price.

Ho–Lee Model

1. Spot (short) rate: $dr(t) = \theta(t)dt - \sigma \cdot dW(t)$ (under risk-neutral measure)
   $\sigma > 0$: constant, $\theta(t)$: deterministic function
   $\theta(t) = \sigma^2 \cdot t + \frac{\partial f(0,t)}{\partial T^*}$
where $f(t, T^*)$ is the (continuously compounded) instantaneous forward rate at time t with calendar maturity T^*.
   2. Forward rate: $df(t, T^*) = \sigma^2(T^* - t) \cdot dt + \sigma \cdot dW(t)$ (under risk-neutral measure)
   3. Zero-coupon bond price: $dB(t, T^*) = r(t) \cdot B(t, T^*) \cdot dt - \sigma(T^* - t) \cdot B(t, T^*) \cdot dW(t)$

Extended Ho–Lee Model

1. Spot (Short) rate:

$$dr(t) = \left\{ t \cdot \sigma(t)^2 + \frac{\partial f}{\partial T^*}(0, t) + \frac{\sigma'(t)}{\sigma(t)} \left[r(t) - f(0, t) \right] \right\} \cdot dt + \sigma(t) \cdot dW(t)$$

where W_1, W_2: independent Brownian motions $\sigma_2(t)$, $\sigma(t)$: deterministic function of time

2. Forward rate: $df(t, T^*) = (\sigma(T^*) \int_t^{T^*} \sigma(u) \cdot du) \cdot dt + \sigma(T^*) \cdot dW(t)$

3. Zero-coupon bond price: $dB(t, T^*) = r(t) \cdot B(t, T^*) \cdot dt - (\int_t^T \sigma(u) \cdot du) \cdot B(t, T^*) \cdot dW(t)$

Two-factor Ho–Lee Model

1. Spot (short) rate:

$$dr(t) = \left\{ t \cdot \|\sigma(t)\|^2 + \frac{\partial f}{\partial T^*}(0, t) + \frac{\|\sigma'(t)\| \cos \phi(t)}{\|\sigma(t)\| \cos \theta(t)} \left[r(t) - f(0, t) \right] \right\} \cdot dt + \sigma_1(t) dW_1(t) + \sigma_2(t) dW_2(t)$$

where

W_1, W_2: independent Brownian motions

$\sigma_1(t)$, $\sigma_2(t)$: deterministic function of time

$\|\sigma(t)\|^2 = \sigma_1(t)^2 + \sigma_2(t)^2$

$$\sum_{i=1}^{2} \sigma_i(t)(X_i(t) + W_i(t)) = \|\sigma(t)\| \cdot \|X(t) + W(t)\| \cdot \cos \theta(t)$$

$$\sum_{i=1}^{2} \sigma_i^1(t)(X_i(t) + W_i(t)) = \|\sigma^1(t)\| \cdot \|X(t) + W(t)\| \cdot \cos \phi(t)$$

$X(t) = (X_1(t), X_2(t))$

$$X_i(t) = \int_0^t \int_s^t \sigma_i(u) \, du \, ds$$

$W(t) = (W_1(t), W_2(t))$

2. Forward rate: $df(t, T^*) = \left(\sum_{i=1}^{2} \sigma_i(T^*) \int_t^{T^*} \sigma_i(u) \cdot du \right) \cdot dt + \sigma_1(T^*) \cdot dW_1(t) + \sigma_2(T^*) \cdot dW_2(t)$

3. Zero-coupon bond price: $dB(t, T^*) = r(t) \cdot B(t, T^*) \cdot dt - B(t, T^*) \cdot \sum_{i=1}^{2} (\int_t^T \sigma_i(u) \, du) \cdot dW_i(t)$

N-factor Ho–Lee Model

1. Spot (short) rate:

$$dr(t) = \left\{ t \cdot \|\sigma(t)\|^2 + \frac{\partial f}{\partial T^*}(0, t) + \sum_{i=1}^{N} \sigma_i^1(t)(X_i(t) + W_i(t)) \right\} \cdot dt + \sum_{i=1}^{N} \sigma_i(t) \cdot dW_i(t)$$

where

$W_1, \cdots, W_N$: independent Brownian motions

$\sigma_1(t), \cdots, \sigma_N(t)$: deterministic function of time

$$\|\sigma(t)\|^2 = \sum_{i=1}^{N} \sigma_i(t)^2$$

$$X_i(t) = \int_0^t \int_s^t \sigma_i(u) \, du \, ds$$

2. Forward rate: $df(t, T^*) = \left(\sum_{i=1}^{N} \sigma_i(T^*) \int_t^{T^*} \sigma_i(u) \cdot du \right) \cdot dt + \sum_{i=1}^{N} \sigma_i(T^*) \cdot dW_i(t)$

3. Zero-coupon bond price: $dB(t, T^*) = r(t) \cdot B(t, T^*) \cdot dt - B(t, T^*)$
$\times \sum_{i=1}^{N} (\int_t^T \sigma_i(u) du) \cdot dW_i(t)$

Hull–White Model

1. Spot (short) rate:

$$dr(t) = (\alpha(t) - \beta \cdot r(t)) \cdot dt + \sigma \cdot dW(t)$$

$\alpha(t)$: deterministic function of time given by

$$\alpha(t) = \frac{\partial f(0, t)}{\partial T^*} + \beta \cdot f(0, t) + \frac{\sigma^2}{2\beta}(1 - e^{-2\beta t})$$

β, σ: constant

2. Forward rate:

$$df(t, T^*) = \frac{\sigma^2}{\beta} \left(e^{-\beta(T^*-t)} - e^{-2\beta(T^*-t)} \right) dt + \sigma \cdot e^{-\beta(T^*-t)} dW(t)$$

3. Zero-coupon bond price:

$$dB(t, T^*) = r(t) \cdot B(t, T^*) dt - \frac{\sigma}{\beta}(1 - e^{-\beta(T^*-t)}) \cdot B(t, T^*) \cdot dW(t)$$

CIR Model

1. Spot (short) rate:

$$dr(t) = (\theta - \alpha \cdot r(t)) dt + \sigma \cdot \sqrt{r(t)} dW(t)$$

θ, α, σ: constants

2. Forward rate:

$$df(t, T^*) = \sigma^2 \cdot r(t) \cdot C(t, T^*) \cdot D(t, T^*) \cdot dt + \sigma \sqrt{r(t)} \cdot D(t, T^*) dW(t)$$

where $D(t, T^*) = \dfrac{\partial C}{\partial T^*}$ and $C(t, T^*)$ is the solution to the Ricatti ODE :

$$\frac{\partial C(t, T^*)}{\partial t} = \frac{\sigma^2}{2} C(t, T^*)^2 + \alpha \cdot C(t, T^*) - 1, \ \ C(T^*, T^*) = 0$$

3. Zero-coupon bond price:

$$dB(t, T^*) = r(t) \cdot B(t, T^*) dt - \sigma \sqrt{r(t)} C(t, T^*) \cdot B(t, T^*) \cdot dW(t)$$

Appendix C. Recombining Lattice

In chapter 13, we discussed the use of the binomial model in valuing the real options of a firm. The real option entails the management's investing I at a node (n, i). When there is a cash inflow or outflow at a particular node, the value of the firm is no longer path-independent. This can be explained more easily by providing a simple example.

Suppose the firm has neither assets nor cash at time 0. At a future date, the firm receives no cash flow other than a \$1 payment at time n^* and state i^*—that is, at node (n^*, i^*). For simplicity, we assume that the interest rate is 0 and the firm keeps the cash in the subsequent periods. Let $V(n, i)$ be the value of the firm's cash position at node (n, i). Clearly $V(n, i) = 0$ for all $n \leq n^*$ and $i \leq n$, except for $V(n^*, i^*)$, which is \$1. However, what are the values of $V(n^* + 1, i^* + 1)$? If we follow a scenario path to the node $(n^* + 1, i^* + 1)$, passing through the node (n^*, i^*), then the cash position will be \$1. However, for cases where the paths do not pass through the node that pays \$1, the value of the cash position is 0. Therefore, $V(n^* + 1, i^* + 1)$ does not have a well-defined value.

An approach to getting around this problem is to consider that value at the node to be the "expected" value. We no longer assign the cash value at each node, because we can assign the expected value. Then the value is no longer path-dependent. To assign the expected values to all the nodes of the lattice, we use a forward induction method.

We have used backward substitution to determine the initial value, given the terminal values on a binomial lattice. We have calculated the present value of the terminal values by backward substitution. In this case of assigning expected values to all the nodes of the lattice, we are concerned with how the future node values will be generated, given a node value at time n and state i. In a similar manner, we generate the future values under the condition that the present value of the future values is equal to the given node value. (See figure 19.24.)

We assume that the upward probability is p and the one-period risk-free rate is 0 for convenience. Furthermore, we assign x to a node at time n and state i, which is denoted Value$[n, i]$, and generate the future node values after period n.

Proposition: Suppose payments $X[n, i]$ are given at the node points and that we have calculated the node values of Value$[n\text{-}1, i]$ and Value$[n\text{-}1, i\text{-}1]$. Then, if we determine the node value at time n and state i, Value$[n, i]$, by forward induction, it is specified by

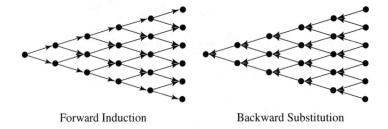

Forward Induction   Backward Substitution

Figure 19.24 Forward induction and backward substitution

$$Value\,[n, i] := \frac{\binom{n-1}{i-1} \cdot Value\,[n-1, i-1] + \binom{n-1}{i} \cdot Value\,[n-1, i]}{\binom{n-1}{i-1} + \binom{n-1}{i}} + X\,[n, i]$$

with the standard boundary conditions:

$$Value\,[0, 0] = X\,[0, 0]\,.$$

$$Value\,[n, n] = V\,[n-1, n-1] + X\,[n, n]$$

Then the expectation of the value of the cash position (integrate over all the states) at the terminal date of the lattice equals the present value of the payments $X[n, i]$, determined by the backward substitution method.

This procedure is used in developing the business model and the corporate model, reducing a nonrecombining tree to a binomial lattice that we use to analyze a firm.

Proof

We prove the theorem when we have a cash flow at period n and state i. Once we prove the one cash flow case, it is straightforward to extend to a multiple cash flow case. When we have a multiple cash flow at various nodes across a binomial lattice, we start generating the binomial lattice as if we had only one cash flow and repeat the procedure for each cash flow. Since we have a different binomial lattice for each given cash flow, we add up the binomial lattices node by node to end up generating the final binomial lattice.

We prove the theorem by induction. Without loss of generality, we have a cash flow, $\$x$, at period n and state i. The present value of $\$x$ at period n and state i is

$$PV \text{ of } V\,[n, i] = \binom{n}{i} \cdot x \cdot p^i \cdot (1-p)^{n-i} \tag{19.C.1}$$

When we apply the forward induction by one period, we have

$$V\,[n+1, i+1] = \frac{\binom{n}{i} \cdot x}{\binom{n}{i+1} + \binom{n}{i}} \text{ and } V\,[n+1, i] = \frac{\binom{n}{i} \cdot x}{\binom{n}{i} + \binom{n}{i-1}} \tag{19.C.2}$$

The sum of the present values of $V[n+1, i+1]$ and $V[n+1, i]$ is equal to $\binom{n}{i} \cdot x \cdot p^i \cdot (1-p)^{n-i}$, which is the present value of x at period n and state i.

Now we assume that the present value of the cash flows at period $n+k$, which have been generated by forward induction, is equal to the present value of x at period n and state i. Then we should show that the present value of the cash flows at period $n+k+1$ is equal to the present value of the cash flows at period $n+k$.

The present value of the cash flows at period $n+k$ is

$$\sum_{i=0}^{n+k} V[n+k, i] \binom{n+k}{i} p^i (1-p)^{n+k-i} \qquad (19.\text{C}.3)$$

The present value of the cash flows at period $n+k+1$ is

$$\sum_{i=0}^{n+k+1} V[n+k+1, i] \binom{n+k+1}{i} p^i (1-p)^{n+k+1-i} \qquad (19.\text{C}.4)$$

Since we generate the cash flows at period $n+k+1$ by forward induction, the relationship between the cash flows at period $n+k$ and period $n+k+1$ is

$$Value[n+k+1, i] := \frac{\binom{n+k}{i-1} \cdot Value[n+k, i-1] + \binom{n+k}{i} \cdot Value[n+k, i]}{\binom{n+k}{i-1} + \binom{n+k}{i}}$$

When we plug this relationship into equation (19.C.4) and simplify it, we can show that equation (19.C.4) is equal to equation (19.C.3).

Q.E.D.

Notes

1. We explain the relationship between T and T* ni figure 9.1. T* denotes the calendar time where as T is tiem to maturity at T*.

2. We will provide the formal definition of the Radon–Nikodym derivative in the following section.

3. $\mathbb{P}$ is market probability, and $\widetilde{\mathbb{P}}$ is risk-neutral probability, which we use for pricing proposes. The reason that $\widetilde{\mathbb{P}}$ is called the risk-neutral probability will be clear later.

4. See Oksendal, B. *Stochastic Differential Equations*, 5th ed. 1998. Springer-Verlag, Berlin, p. 53, theorem 4.3.4.

References

Björk, T. 1999. *Arbitrage Theory in Continuous Time*. New York: Oxford University Press.

Duffie, D. 2001. *Dynamic Asset Pricing Theory*, 3rd ed. Princeton, N.J.: Princeton University Press.

Geman, H., N. El Karoui, and J. C. Rochet. 1995. Change of numeraire, Changes of probability measures and pricing of options. *Journal of Applied Probability*, 32, 443–458.

Ho, T. and Sang Bin Lee. 1984. Term structure movements and interest rates contingent claims pricing. Salomon Brothers Center Series. New York University.

Neftci, S. N. 2000. *An Introduction to the Mathematics of Financial Derivatives*, 2nd ed. San Diego: Academic Press.

Shreve, S. E. 1997. *Stochastic Calculus and Finance*. Lecture notes.

Glossary of Notations

Using consistent notations throughout the book is important. This book is about financial models. An appropriate choice of notations will enable the unambiguous specification of the models and provide clarity for the readers. However, specifying such a set of notations is particularly challenging for this book. The financial models cover both the capital markets and corporate finance. In each subfield of finance, there are standard notations; finding consistency across these subfields can be complex. To accomplish this task, our choice of notations follows some guidelines:

1. We maintain notations accepted in the standard literature as much as possible.
2. We use capital letters to denote securities or present values of cash flows, with subscript u and d denoting up state and down state, respectively.
3. n denotes the period and i the state of the world.
4. Time is denoted by t or n; T^*, t, or n denotes calendar time as it passes. T^* is the maturity date of the expiration date in calendar time. T is the time to maturity.
5. S is capitalization of the firm or the stock price.
6. $F(n, i, T^*, T)$ is a forward contract or futures contract at time n and state i, expiring at calendar time T^*, and delivering a zero-coupon bond with the time to maturity T.
7. $P(n, i, T)$ denotes the nth period, ith state, time to maturity T bond—that is, the discount function at the node (n, i). The par value is \$1.
8. $B(n, i, T^*)$ is a default-free bond that may have a coupon at node (n, i) with a maturity date T^*. $B(n, t, T)$ is the default-free bond that has a time to maturity T. The par value is \$100.
9. $D(n, i, T^*)$ is the defaultable bond with a maturity date at T^*. The convention is similar to B.
10. V is the firm value or project value.
11. $C(n, i, T^*)$ is the call option with a expiration date T^*.
12. P is the put option.
13. A is an asset.
14. L is a liability.
15. CA is a fixed asset on a capital asset.
16. CF is cash flow; FCF is free cash flow; and NCF is net cash flow.
17. $r(n, i, T)$ is the yield of a zero-coupon bond with a time to maturity T at node (n, i). Hence it is the yield curve or the transfer pricing curve. r is the continuously compounding rate. $r_{\frac{1}{2}}$ is a semiannually compounding risk-free rate. r_f is the one-period risk-free rate.
18. r^f and r denote the foreign risk-free interest rate and the domestic risk-free interest rate, respectively.
19. e_{spot} and $e_{forward}$ denote the spot exchange and the forward exchange rate, respectively.
20. $R(n, i, T)$ is the yield of a zero-coupon bond which is not a benchmark representing time value.
21. Fc is the fixed cost.
22. m is for margins (e.g., the profit margin) or the number of subperiods.

23. π is for premiums (e.g., default premium, risk premium).
24. τ is for the tax rate, with subscripts denoting the type of tax.
25. p is the risk-neutral probability.
26. q is the market probability.
27. σ denotes volatilities.
28. Ω is the variance-covariance matrix.
29. $\sum$ is the correlation matrix.
30. $N(\cdot)$ is the cumulative normal distribution function with mean 0 and standard deviation 1.
31. $\tilde{e}$ is random error or noise.
32. dZ is the normal distribution over an (infinitely) short time dt, with mean 0 and standard deviation $\sqrt{dt}$.
33. Bold letters represent vectors.
34. The tilde ($\sim$) over a letter means the stochastic movement.
35. The bar ($-$) over a letter means the expected value.
36. Euclid font type or math type two is used for book values.

Specific Notations

Valuation

VaR_{asset}: VaR of an asset

S: the market capitalization or stock value

S_i: stock price of state i

S_T: the underlying stock price on the expiration date, T

S_u: the up-state movement of the stock

S_d: the down-state movement of the stock

$P_i^n(T)$ or $P(n, i, T)$: the price of a T time to maturity zero-coupon bond, at time n and state i

$P(t, T)$: the T-year bond value at time t without default risk

$p_d(t, T)$: the probability of default at time t for a bond with T time to maturity

$P(T)$: the initial discount function, price of a zero-coupon bond with a face value of \$1 and time to maturity T

$P(t, T^*, T)$: the value of the swaption, which expires at time T^*, on a swap with tenor T at time t

$B(t, T)$: the T-year bond value at time t without default risk

$B^j(n, i)$: the entries in each lattice for a double-up sinking fund where j denotes the jth case; n, the period; and i, the state

$B_c(n, i)$: the callable bond price in the ith state and the nth period

$B(n, i, T)$: bond with time to maturity T at time n and state i

$B(T)$: the price of a zero-coupon bond with time-to-maturity T

$D(n, i)$: the deposit level

D: the market value of the debt

$IO(n, i)$: interest rate option value at time n and state i

coupon: coupon payment

principal: face value

F: the forward or futures price

$F(T^*, T)$: the futures prices or forward prices at the initial period with the expiration date T^* delivering a T-year maturity bond. Here T^* denotes the calendar time and T denotes the time to maturity.

$F(t, T^*, T)$: the futures price or forward price at time t with the expiration date T^* delivering a T-year maturity bond.

C_k: caplet

$PWV(k)$: the present pathwise value where k denotes the index for the path

$PWV^P(k)$: the present pathwise value for the primary decomposition of the security

C: the value of a European futures option, a European call option, or a bond call option

$C(t, T^*)$: the call price or the payoff to a call option on the expiration date T

P: the put option price at the expiration date

CP: conversion price

y: income to the bank on a total return basis

v: the sales volume over the reporting period

I: the investment value of the bond

I^*_{payout}: the payout as expenses

V: the project value or the firm value

V_u: the project value or the firm value at the up state

V_d: the project value or the firm value at the down state

V^p: the primitive firm value

V^{fc}: the fixed-cost firm

V^p_u: the primitive firm at the up state

V^p_d: the primitive firm at the down state

$c(n)$: the annual maintenance costs

$CIF(n, i)$: the cash inflow

NCF: the net cash flow

FCF: the free cash flow

$FCF(n, i)$: the free cash flow at time n, state i

$Cash_t$: cash position at time t

W: the wealth level or the warrant

ω: a proportion of the portfolio

Φ: the market value of the fixed costs

Γ: the value of the growth option

V: firm value

V_L: leveraged firm (value)

V_U: unleveraged firm (value)

V: the market observed value of the financial contract

Ψ: objective function

f: net funding

b: new borrowing

$I_{paydown}$: paydown of liabilities

v: new sales volume

e: operating expenses for the period

κ: present value of bankruptcy costs

PV: present value

$U(\cdot)$: utility function

I: investment size

Rates

$F_{t_k t_{k+1}}$: the forward rate for the period between time t_k and t_{k+1}

$f(t, T^*)$: one-period forward rate or the instantaneous forward rate at time t with the maturity date of T^*

μ_s: continuously compounded stock return

m: the gross profit margin

R_{req}: the required rate of return of the stock

$r(t)$: the yield of the bond

YTM: the yield to maturity

r: continuously compounding risk-free rate

$r(n, i)$: the one-period interest rate or the discount factor

$R^D(n, i)$: the deposit rate determined by the bank

$R(n, i)$: the market interest rate

r_f: one-period risk-free rate

ρ: the discount rate

$\overline{R}_i$: mean of return of asset i

$r(n)$: interest rate at time n

R_A: total return of the assets

R_L: total return of the liabilities

K_e: the cost of equity

R_M: market return rate

$r_f(t)$: the transfer pricing curve

R_t^D: the deposit rate set at time t

R_x: a cap rate

R_t: the market short-term rate at time t

K_D: the cost of debt

ρ: the cost of capital

τ_c: the corporate tax

τ_i: the personal marginal tax rate on interest

τ_e: the personal marginal capital gains tax rate on equity

GRI: the gross return on investment

r^{real}: the constant real risk-free rate

c: the convenience yield

$r(n, i, t)$: t-year interest rate at time n and state i

$r(n, i)$: one-period interest rate for time n and state i

$r(n, i, j)$: one-period interest rate for time n and state i,j

π: risk premium

g: growth rate

R_{coupon}: coupon rate

r: the continuously compounding yield

$r(T)$: a spot curve

r_{t, T^*}: the interest rate which will be applied during the period t to T^* when t and T^* denote calendar time

$r(t, T)$: the yield to maturity of the zero-coupon bond with time-to-maturity T at time t

Time

T^*: swap delivery date

T: the tenor of a swap

T^*: the expiration date of the option

t_k: a reset date

δ_k: the reset period $t_{k+1} - t_k$

T: time to maturity

dt: an infinitesimal time interval

$KRD(i)$: ith key rate duration

t_i: knot point

Statistical Operators

$E(R_i)$: the expected rate of return of an asset i

$E(\widetilde{CF})$: the expected value of a risky cash flow

$\widetilde{X}$: a normal distribution with mean 0 and standard deviation of 1

Ω: covariance matrix of all risk sources

p: the risk-neutral probability

q: the market probability

σ_i: the standard deviation of an asset i

$\sigma(t, T)$: the volatility of the T-year at time t

$\sigma(n)$: volatility at time n

$\sigma(i, j)$: the volatility of the j-year spot rate i years from now, or the volatility surface for i and j as they vary over a range of years

$\sigma^f(n)$: the term structure of forward volatilities

$\sigma^s(n)$: the volatility of the nth year rate of the spot curve

σ_k: annualized volatility for the kth caplet

σ: the instantaneous standard deviation (or volatility or risk) of the underlying asset

σ_p: portfolio risk

σ_M: the market risk

$\sigma(s)$: the term structure of volatilities of proportional changes in a bond price

$\sigma(\cdot)$: a standard deviation over dt

Ω: a variance–covariance matrix

$\sum$: correlation matrix

Δt: increment at time t

$N(\cdot)$: the cumulative normal distribution

$\bar{e}$: the error term

$\mathbf{v}$: an eigenvector

μ: the instantaneous returns or the drift of the underlying asset

dZ: a unit of risk, a normal distribution over an (infinitely) short time interval, which has a 0 mean and $\sqrt{dt}$ standard deviation

α: the critical value

b: the adjustment speed of the mean reversion process

λ: the recovery ratio

π: the default premium

m: profit margin of the time deposits

β_{asset}: beta of an asset

f^*: the reserve ratio

Δ: the hedge ratio

u: upward movement proportion

d: downward movement proportion

λ: the eigenvalue or the market price of risk, $\frac{u-r}{\sigma}$

Indices

N: the number of assets

n: the number of additional shares after conversion

m: the number of outstanding shares

i and j: the state of the world

m: the number of steps in one period

Glossary of Terms

abandonment option: the option if the commercialization of the intellectual properties cannot be realized, the intellectual properties may be sold.

absolute priority rule: a rule to determine the payments to different classes of bondholders, junior or senior debts, according to specifications made by bond covenants when bankruptcy occurs.

acceleration clause: the clause in the indenture requiring the firm to pay, not just the coupon, but the principals in case of any substantial breach of the covenants.

accrued interest: an accounting entity that amortizes the coupon payment over the period between two coupon dates.

Accumulated Benefit Obligation (ABO): the present value measure extended from VBO, which includes the non-vested benefit, but at present pay level.

accumulators: investors who hold the bonds in anticipation of the firm to buy back the bonds.

actuarial model: the methodology, proposed by Pye, of using historical data to help us forecast the future and price the default premium.

Adjusted Net Asset Value (ANAV): an asset value which consists of free (unrestricted) capital or capital not tied up in the run-off of the business, after taxes are paid by the company.

agency deals: the mortgage-pass-throughs that originate from government agencies.

agency system (broker): In the agency system, outside agents may sell the products of one insurer exclusively or may sell a number of insurers' products as independent agents.

Allocated Loss Adjustment Expenses (ALAE): the extent of the expenses that have been allocated already.

Altman's Z score: the scoring system to determine the credit worthiness of a firm with respect to the bond, which uses discriminant analysis to establish important factors that determine the likelihood of a firm to enter bankruptcy in the future.

American option: an option having an early exercise feature that can only be valuable for the holder.

amortization: one component of the charges of the liability, which is used to smooth the reported pension income.

announcement date: the date that dividends are announced.

annuity: an insurance product which pays a monthly benefit as long as the insured person is alive, providing protection against extreme longevity of the insured person.

arbitrage band: a band around the theoretical price in the market places where an arbitrage position cannot be profitable.

arbitrage free interest rate model: the model which uses the relative valuation concepts of the Black-Scholes model and argues that the valuation of interest rate contingent claims is based solely on the yield curve, assuming that the yield curve moves in a way that is consistent with the arbitrage free condition.

arbitrage opportunity: a situation where two or more identical securities are priced differently.

Asian option: an option whose payoff on the expiration date is an index, where the index is the average stock price over a historical period, like last week.

Asset-Backed Securities (ABS): bonds secured by assets such as the securitized account receivables, the lease incomes, and financial securities, etc.

Asset Liability Management (ALM): a management technique that is responsible for determining the asset and liability structure.

Asset Liability Management Committee (ALCO): the committee that determine the strategic positioning of the asset and liability portfolio.

asymmetric information theory: a theory asserting that financial decisions are not made based on complete and perfect information because not all information in the world is accessible.

at the money: a state of the underlying stock being traded around strike price.

atomistic agent: agent with no market power.

back-test: the test to see whether the methods to calculate VaR are appropriate in the sense that the actual maximum loss has exceeded the pre-determined VaR within an expected margin.

backward substitution: the recursive option pricing method by rolling one period back at each iteration.

bank rate: the interest rate offered by the bank to its customers in different accounts.

bankers' acceptances: negotiable, bank-backed business credit instruments typically financing an import order.

barbell position: buying bond positions with short-term bonds and long-term bonds while selling medium-term bonds such that the net portfolio position and the dollar duration are zero.

basis risk: the uncertain changes in the spreads.

basket option: an option where the option holder can choose the highest value of several stocks.

behavioral model: a model which is empirically estimated in order to describe the behavior of the agents in the market that affect the securities value.

Bellman optimization procedure: a procedure which provides a very elegant solution to optimal exercise rule, proposing that if the option price is given by the optimal exercise strategy, then that strategy has to be optimal over any period.

benchmark securities: the actively traded securities that the relative valuation model is based on.

Bermuda option: one common variation of American option, which allows the holder to exercise the option at certain times, for example, at the end of each month or week.

beta: the measure of systematic risk, that is, the covariance divided by the variance of the market portfolio.

bid-ask spread: the difference between the highest bid and the lowest ask prices, which is the cost of transacting to the investor.

binomial distribution: the probability distribution to be observed when the event with two possible outcomes such as the flip of coin is repeatedly tried.

Black model: the pricing model of benchmark securities, which are quoted by the volatilities implied by the adjusted Black-Scholes model for each instrument.

Black volatility: the caplet implied volatility that we can determine if we label the current T month LIBOR as stock and if we apply the Black-Sholes model to theses caplets, assuming that the caplet is a call option for a given caplet price.

boilerplate: some industry standards of the bond indentures, which follow a certain format and language for the ease of interpretation of the intent and implementation of the agreements.

bond factor: the proportion of the principal, which remains outstanding, to the issued amount.

bond option: an option that gives the holders the right to buy an underlying bond at a fixed price on the expiration date.

bond performance profile: the value of a bond over a range of instantaneous parallel movements of the interest rate level.

bottom-up management process: the capital budgeting decision on the store level. In this approach, line managers deal with the capital budgeting issue, maximizing the net present value of each project that they manage.

boundary conditions: conditions imposed on the payoff during the life of the option, from the initial date to the expiration date.

broad based index: an index such as the Lehman index which is compiled by holding all the outstanding bonds.

brokers: middlemen who seek out the buyers and sellers of the stock, providing the services for a fee.

Brownian motion: A random process B_t, $t \in [0, T]$, is a Brownian motion if the process begins at zero and if B_t has stationary, independent increments, and if B_t is continuous in t and if the increments $B_t - B_s$ have a normal distribution with mean zero and variance $|t - s|$.

bullet payment: accrual bond that accrues all the interests to be paid at the terminal date.

bundle: a set of numbers assigned to each node to keep track of the state that the node has passed.

burn-out: A pool that has gone through a low interest rate period.

business planning: a systematic approach to capital budgeting.

business process: a production process, which generates goods and services, and a financial process, which provides financing of projects and distributions of its revenues to its stakeholders.

calibration: the estimation of the term structures of volatilities so that the model can price all the observed prices of the derivatives simultaneously, that is, the estimation of the coefficients of the volatility functions, assuming that the functions take a specific functional form.

call at make whole: the provision which enables a firm to have control over the capital structure but not the option of refinancing the bond when interest rates are favorable.

call provision: the provision represented by a call schedule which allow the corporation to buy back bonds at the call price at a specified date.

call schedule: the schedule stating the call prices at corresponding dates.

Capital Asset Pricing Model (CAPM): a model to value risky assets such as stocks and risky bonds when investors choose their optimal portfolio on the efficient frontier.

capital budgeting decision: the process of planning expenditures on assets whose cash flows are expected to extend beyond one year.

capital gain (or loss): the difference between the price sold and the price originally bought.

Capital Market Line (CML): the tangent line to the efficient frontier from the risk free asset, which should represent the optimal portfolios for all risk averse investors.

capital structure: a structure which specifies the relationships of all the claims on the firm's assets and profits.

capitalization: the claims of the stockholders.

caplet: a series of bond options and each option is called a caplet.

cash earnings: an earning measure that is based on cash flows.

CDD (cooling degree-days): the number of degrees above 67 Fahrenheit.

ceded amount: the premium paid to re-insurer when the insurance company may purchase re-insurance from the re-insurer in order to pass a high severity of loss to them.

cheap (rich) bond: a bond having a higher (lower) OAS than its comparable bonds and the difference cannot be explained by the difference in liquidity premium and credit premiums.

cheap (rich): priced below (above) the fair price.

cheap/rich value: the observed bond price net of the theoretical bond price.

Cholesky Decomposition: Given a symmetric positive definite square matrix X, the Cholesky decomposition of X is the factorization $X = U'U$, where U is the square root matrix of X.

chooser option: an option (the choice) on options such that the holder of which has the right to choose at a pre-specified time to have a call or a put option on the same underlying asset.

closed form models: a kind of interest rate models, which provide the price of benchmark securities given the volatility assumptions and are ideal to use for market convention in quoting benchmark securities in terms of the market volatilities.

closed form solution: a solution that can be expressed in one equation rather than by an algorithm.

closing option: an option to temporarily shut down but to be re-opened at a reopening cost in the future.

closing price: the last transaction price of the trading session.

Collateralized Mortgage Obligation (CMO): a structured security backed by mortgage-backed securities and other collateralized mortgage obligations.

commercial deposit accounts: checking accounts for corporations.

commercial paper: a short term unsecured promissory note issued by corporations.

commissions: fees paid to the broker who sells the insurance contract to the customer.

commodity option: an option on the commodity such as crude oil, wheat, pork bellies, precious metal (like gold) and other non-financial goods.

commodity: another type of tangible asset which is more homogeneous in nature and can be bought and sold more easily, e.g., gold, oil, natural gas, and wheat.

comparable-store sales (or same store sales): the change in sales from the previous year for stores open more than one year.

comparative statics: an analysis to show how each variable affects an option price when other variables are constant.

complete bond market: the market where default free discount bonds in all the maturities are traded such that any default free fixed income security is a portfolio of discount bonds that are traded in the market.

complete market hypothesis: the hypothesis which emphasizes the availability of securities for market participants to trade to reveal their preferences to the market places.

component VaR: the marginal contribution of each stock's risk to the portfolio risk.

compound chooser option: an option which gives the holder the right to choose another chooser option or a call (put) option at an expiration date.

compound option: an option acting on another option.

concentration risk: the risk of investing a significant amount in one sector in managing a corporate bond portfolio.

Conditional Tail Expectation (CTE): an approach proposed as an alternative to the use of VaR for assets or liabilities that are not traded and are held till maturity over a long period of time for the insurance companies.

constant maturity swap: a swap between two parties such that the swap payment is based on the swap rate of a fixed term at each payment date.

contango: the reverse relationship of normal backwardation where the forward price is above the expected spot price.

contingent claim theory (or relative valuation approach): a theory to show us how a security's value is related to other benchmark securities' values, essentially justifies for using this benchmark approach for valuation.

continuous time model: a model where we choose to assume that all individuals trade continuously.

conversion price: the stock price at which the converted equity holding equals the par value of the bond.

conversion ratio: the number of shares that convertible bond holders receive when they convert the face value of the bond into the stock.

convertible bond (CB): a corporate bond that offers bondholders the option to convert their bonds into a specific number of shares.

convexity adjustment (correction): making the interest rate movements adjust upward, so that the expected bonds' returns are equal to the one period interest rate to maintain the arbitrage-free condition, such that the local expectation hypothesis holds.

convexity: a measure of such an acceleration or deceleration rates in a bond value to better describe the behavior of the bond price in relation to the changing yield curve.

corporate bonds: public bonds issued by corporations, available for any investors to buy and sell.

coupon rate: a percent of the principal.

coupons: the payments which are usually regular and periodically paid to the bond holder.

covenant: the first part of the indenture, which is describing specific measure the borrower has obligated himself to and the main concerns of the bond holders. A violation of the covenant triggers the event of default.

coverage: the ratio of net income to the EBIT.

covered call: writing a call option while holding the underlying stock.

credit derivatives: the derivatives which are related to, but not exclusively, credit risk. The credit default swaps, credit linked notes and collateralized debt obligations are typical examples of the credit derivatives.

credit risk: the loss of principal or interests or any promised payments from the borrower.

credit sensitive bond: a bond with a coupon rate which is not fixed till the maturity of the bond but dependent on the bond rating.

crediting rate: the interest rate paid to the policyholders as accruals to their account value.

critical parity value: the parity value at which the firm would optimally exercise the forced conversion.

cross default clause: the clause in the indenture stating that the bond is in default if the firm defaults on any bond in the debt structure.

cubic spline function: a spline function of degree 3, which is a set of polynomials on subintervals joined using continuity conditions.

debentures: unsecured bonds which are perhaps the most common bond type.

debt structure: the portfolio of debt of the corporation.

default premium: the difference between the promised yield to the expected yield.

deferred acquisition costs: costs calculated via accounting means of delaying the recognition of upfront expenses.

defined benefits: one type of pension plans which obligates the sponsor to agreed pension payments into the future.

defined contribution: one type of pension plans where the participants bear all the risks of the performance of the pension fund.

degree-day: the cumulative temperature differences between the average temperature of the day and 67 degrees, which is an objective and verifiable number that financial derivatives can use as a factor for designing contingent claims.

delta (Δ): the sensitivity of the option price to the stock price which measures the number of stocks we need to short to hedge a call option.

delta-gamma methodology: the method to extend to the second derivatives (gamma) to measure the risk which we cannot adequately measure by the first derivative (delta) in the delta-normal methodology.

delta-neutral portfolio: a portfolio with zero value of delta.

delta-normal method: one of the methods of calculating VaR, which considers all the risk sources to follow a normal distribution.

development costs: the expenses that may be the cost of litigations and the settlement.

development pattern of claims: the payout of the claims on average from property and casualty insurance, which actuaries can estimate using a development triangle.

development triangle: a triangle where the loss incurred and the increase in loss over time are recorded.

digital option (binary option): an option which pays $Q if the underlying has value above the strike price on the expiration date. There is no payment if the underlying has value below the strike price.

direct selling system (captive): the insurers' policies are sold by employees. The insurers contact the policyholders to generate new sales or maintain clients.

discount function (factor): the price of a discount bond with maturity T years with $1 principal.

discount rate: the charge on loans to depository institutions by the Federal Reserve Banks.

discount window: the government monetary policy where central banks provide short-term liquidity needs of banks.

discounted cash flow method: a method of calculating the present value via discounting the expected payoffs of an investment with the risk adjusted rates of return.

discrete time model: a model where all trading occurs at regular time intervals (at the end of a period.

diversification: the lowering of risks by holding a multiple risky assets, that is, a portfolio of risky assets may have less risk than that of the individual risky assets.

dividend discount model: a stock valuation model where the value of the stock is the present value of all the dividends that we can receive from the stock.

dividend yield: the total dividends paid during the fiscal year divided by the stock price at the closing of the market.

dollar duration: the value sensitivity of the bond portfolio to the yield curve measured in dollar.

dollar key rate duration: the dollar change in value with a small shift of the key rate.

double up option: a feature of the sinking fund operation, where the firm can retire the stated sinking fund amount or the double amount at each sinking fund date.

dual currency bond: a bond that pays interests in one currency and principal in another currency.

duration (effective duration): the price sensitivity of a bond to a parallel shift of the spot curve, where the spot yield is typically assumed to be semi-annual compounding.

Dynamic Financial Analysis (DFA): a financial planning model that is designed to address a broad range of corporate issues.

dynamic hedging: the continual revision of a portfolio at each node point on the binomial lattice.

early exercise: a feature that allows the holder to exercise the option at any time before and right up to the expiration date, not just at the expiration date.

Earning at Risk (EaR): the potential loss in earnings over a time horizon at a certain probability level.

efficient capital market: a market where the price traded fully reflects all the information.

efficient frontier (efficient set): the set of all the portfolios that have the lowest risks (measured by the standard deviation of returns) for each level of expected returns.

efficient market hypothesis: the hypothesis which emphasizes how much information has been incorporated into prices.

efficient portfolio: the portfolio with the highest returns for each level of risks.

elasticity: the ratio of the proportional changes in value, e.g., the proportional change in the market value of equity or the market value of debt to proportional change in the firm value.

embedded option: options that cannot be detached and traded separately.

embedded value: the corresponding equity value for an insurer.

employee stock options: options, usually call options, issued to a selection of firm's employees as part of their compensation for their work.

enhanced index: an investment strategy (product) where the portfolio manager will try to out- perform the predetermined index by a certain amount.

equilibrium models: a model which determines interest rates under the condition that the supply of funds is equal to the demand for funds in the economy.

equipment bonds: bonds secured by the firm's equipments.

European call (put) option: a financial contract that gives the holder the right to buy (sell) the underlying stock at a fixed price at a specified time.

ex-dividend date: the date after dividends are paid.

exchanges option: an option which offers the holder the higher of the two stocks.

exotic options: options that are neither standard nor commonly used.

expectation hypothesis: the hypothesis that the movement of the yield curve should be dependent on market expectations, which is the relationship between the forward rate and the spot rate.

expense loading on premiums: taking a portion of the premium as revenue.

extreme value theory: the theory to calculate VaR by taking into account the fat-tail shape of the cumulative distribution function for the random variable.

fair value of a bond: the value determined by using the bond model with an appropriate OAS, which is used to indicate the intrinsic value of a bond or the market implied present value of the cash flows.

fallen angels: bonds issued with an original investment grade, but rated downward to the high yield level afterwards.

Federal Deposit Insurance Corp. (FDIC): the corporation which insures the deposits of member banks, both commercial banks under the Bank Insurance Fund (BIF) and the savings and loans under the Saving Association Insurance Fund (SAIF).

Federal Funds: reserves traded among commercial banks for overnight use.

Federal National Mortgage Association (FNMA): a government-sponsored enterprise that functions to increase the availability of mortgage credits for home buyers, which is more commonly known as Fannie Mae.

Federal Reserve System (FRS): the central bank system that has direct responsibility over some of the banks and their respective parent companies.

filtration: the information set that the valuation model requires at any time and state in the world.

filtration model: a model to construct the information set at each node point of a lattice for a particular valuation model.

financial asset (security): a financial claim on real asset or an agreement among parties, such as stocks and bonds.

financial engineering model: a model which is particularly concerned with implementation issues such as efficient algorithms in solving differential equations and numerical methods in solving for optimal solution, etc.

financial planning: a systematic approach to simulate financial ratios and analysis in such a way that the financial performances are benchmarked.

financial process: an activity of a firm, which provides financing of projects and distributions of its revenues to its stakeholders.

firm value: a firm's market total capitalization as a going-concern, which is the present value of the free cash flows of the firm or the value of all the claims on the firm.

first principles: some economic assumptions which are fundamental in describing the basic nature of the people and the markets, e.g., assumption of nonsatiation.

Fisher model: a model providing some indications of the determinants of the yield spread which is the yield of the bond net the yield of the Treasury bond with a similar maturity.

fixed income securities: the securities whose future payments are often specified as a fixed amount as promised payments over time.

fixed rates: a fixed coupon rate.

flight to quality: the behavior of investors seeking to hold liquid and safe bonds such as Treasury securities.

floating rates: short term interest rates which change over time.

floor: a series of bond options and each option is called a floorlet. If at expiration, the current n period rate is below the strike rate, the option pays a difference of the two rates times a factor to scale the actual payment.

forced conversion: a conversion where the company forces the bondholders to convert the convertible bond into stock by calling the convertible bond.

forward contract of a bond: the agreement to deliver a bond with time-to-maturity T in a future date T^* (the termination date) at a price predetermined in the agreement.

forward contract: an agreement between two parties, a buyer and a seller, on a future date, expiration date, and the contract price on the underlying asset. There is no exchange of money or goods at the initial agreement. At the expiration date, when the contract expires, the buyer will take the delivery of the underlying asset at the contract price.

forward rate: the yield of the forward contract calculated from the given spot yield curve, which is the expected rate from the market.

forward volatilities: the volatility of the one period forward rate in year n, for each $n = 1, 2, \ldots$

free cash flow (FCF) discount model: a valuation methodology of a firm by discounting its free cash flows at its cost of capital.

futures contract: an exchange traded contract which is basically the same as the forward contract except that they are exchange traded with daily marking to market.

gain-on-sale: the immediate gain reported in the fair value accounting.

gamma: the ratio of the change of delta to the change in the stock price.

Generally Accepted Accounting Principles (GAAP): the financial reporting standard used by the investment community.

gross profit margin: gross profits (revenues net of cost of goods sold) divided by net gross sales (revenues).

group insurance: insurance issued to a group of people under a master policy.

growth option: the ability of the firm to make an investment only when the projects are profitable.

Guaranteed Minimum Account Value (GMAV): the variable annuity to guarantee the account value at a certain future date to have a minimum level equal to the initial premium.

Guaranteed Minimum Death Benefit (GMDB): minimum guarantees of the payment at death.

Guaranteed Minimum Income Benefit (GMIB): a guarantee which has a ratcheting feature, guaranteeing the highest historical value of the account value at the anniversary dates over the period from the start date to the time of death, akin to selling a look-back option.

Guaranteed Minimum Withdrawal Benefit (GMWB): a variable annuity that allows the policyholders to partially withdraw from their account value at the book value, in essence offering the policyholders an American put option.

HDD (heating degree-days): the number of degrees below 67 Fahrenheit.

heat equation: a partial differential equation to describe the flow of heat in materials where the rate of heat flow is proportional to the temperature gradient.

hedge ratio (Δ): a specific ratio between the stock and option positions such that the risks coming from both the stock and option would exactly cancel each other.

high prepayment efficiency: the value of the mortgage when the mortgage reaches the initial date in the backward substitution procedure. Then the mortgagor's prepayment decision is optimal.

high yield (junk) bonds: bonds with ratings below BBB for S&P or Baa by Moody's.

historical simulation method: the method to calculate VaR, which uses a historical data.

immediate annuity: an insurance contract that pays a specified amount every year until death.

implied spot curve: the curve that represents the time value of money estimated from all the coupon issues of the Treasury markets as opposed to observed from the traded prices of the STRIPS market.

implied volatility surface: the set of volatilities that gives the best fit between the benchmark market quotes (or prices) and the theoretical prices in terms of two dimensions.

implied volatility: a volatility measure which make model option price equal the observed option price.

in the money: a state of intrinsic value being positive.

indenture: the bond contract agreed upon between the bondholders and the shareholders, which has two separate agreements on the obligations of the borrower and the aftermath in the event of default.

index fund: stock portfolios which is constructed to mimic the market portfolios, like S&P 500.

indifference curve: the combination of the risk and return that have the same level of utility.

individual insurance: insurance sold on an individual basis.

intangible asset: an asset that does not have a physical presence and whose value is determined by, for example, branding, intellectual properties such as know-how or knowledge of technologies.

Interest-Only (IO): a contract where investors receive only monthly interests of the mortgage pass-through.

interest cost: one component of the charges of the liability, which is the growth in PBO during a reporting period calculated by the product of the discount rate and the PBO at the beginning of the period.

interest rate derivatives: the financial instruments that are actively traded in over-the-counter markets whose stochastic movements are directly related to the interest rate movements.

interest rate model: the model which specifies how the short term interest rate movements are projected into the future without arbitrage opportunity.

International Accounting Standards Commission (IASC): a commission proposing that the results of all financial contracts be reported under fair value accounting for all financial institutions.

intrinsic value: the value of the option if the option were to be exercised immediately.

inverse floating rate note: a note whose interest payment formula is $a - r$, where a is a constant number and r is a specific interest rate like 3 month LIBOR.

investment cycle: the process for making investment. There are four phases of the investment cycle: the requirement phase, design phase, test phase, and implementation phase.

investment grade bonds: bonds with ratings equal or above BBB and Baa.

investment value: the convertible bond value ignoring the possibility of converting the bond into equity.

invoice price (amount transacted or dirty price): the quoted price plus the accrued interest, which is the true economic value of the bond.

irrelevant theorem: a theory asserting that corporate financial decisions are irrelevant in the sense that they do not affect the shareholder's value, and the firm value remains the same regardless of how the corporate financial decisions would be made.

issue size: the size which indicates the liquidity in the market.

key rate duration: a measure of the proportional change in bond price to a small change in the key rate.

key rate duration profile: the relationship of the key rate durations with the key rates.

knock in option: a European option (put or call) which comes into existence whenever the underlying reaches the barrier any time before expiration.

knock out option: a European put or call option that ceases to exist when the underlying stock reaches the barrier (a pre-specified stock level) any time before the expiration that may be above or below the current stock price.

kurtosis: a measure of fatness of the tail of the distribution function.

lapse risk: the rate at which policyholders voluntarily terminate their contract.

latent warrant: a long dated call option on a stock, which would not be exercised.

law of one price: a statement that if two securities have the same cash flows, then they should have the same price, which results from the availability of arbitrage mechanism.

Lehman index: one common fixed-income benchmark portfolio which is an index compiled by holding all the outstanding bonds in the Treasury, agency, corporate, and mortgage market.

lemon problem: a typical case to illustrate asymmetric information.

leverage: the ratio of assets to equity.

leveraged buyout: the method to replace the management as shareholders buy the shares with their use of borrowed funds to gain control of the firm.

levered portfolio: a portfolio consisting of the stock bought on margin and the option to duplicate the option payoff at the maturity date.

liability benchmark: a valuation model for a block of new business or in-force business, which can be analyzed and replicated by tradable assets consistent with the arbitrage-free modeling.

life insurance: the line of business, which is paid upon the death of the insured person and provides protection against premature death.

liquidity (marketability) spread: a part of a positive option adjusted spread for high rating bonds, which is an additional returns required by the bond holders for liquidity risk (non-marketability).

liquidity premium: additional returns required as a compensation for holding long bonds.

liquidity premium hypothesis: the hypothesis that the yield curve should generally be an upward sloping reflecting the liquidity premium that increases with maturity.

local expectation hypothesis: the hypothesis that the expected future one period spot rate should equal the forward rate.

lognormal process: the process where the volatility term is proportional to the interest rate level $r(t)$.

London Interbank Offered Rate (LIBOR): the British banker's association average of interbank offered rates for dollar deposits in the London market based on quotations at major banks.

Long-term Equity Anticipation Securities (LEAPS): the exchange traded options with longer expiration.

long run interest rate: a theoretical construct, hypothesizing that the economy has a constant long run interest rate that interest rates converge to over time while long-term interest rate continuously make stochastic movements.

long tail of a product development loss: the loss to be expended over time.

lookback option: an option which offers the holder the right to receive the highest historical price of stock or the prevailing stock price at the expiration.

loss frequency: the number of events that are likely to occur some losses within some time interval.

loss severity: the estimate of the severity of losses caused by an occurrence.

Macauley duration: the weighted average life of a bond.

market-observed spot curve: the yield curve observed from the STRIPS market.

market capitalization: the market value of the equity, which is the product of the number of shares outstanding and the share price.

market makers: a brokerage or bank that maintains a firm bid and ask price in a given security by standing ready, willing, and able to buy or sell at publicly quoted prices (called making a market).

market model: the interest rate models that take market prices as inputs to the models.

market order: an order to buy (sell) at the specialist ask (bid) price.

market portfolio: a portfolio which consists of all the stocks in the market, with the portfolio weight of each stock being the proportion of its capitalization (the stock price times the number of shares outstanding) to the value of the market.

market price of risk: the excess return required for a risk factor per unit risk measure.

market risk: the losses to arise from the mark to market of the trading securities, which is referred to as the potential loss of the portfolio due to market movement.

market volatility surface: a set of volatilities based on the Black models.

marking to market: the process of assigning the value of a security where there is an exchange of cash to settle the daily price difference.

Markov property: the property that the conditional distribution of $\widetilde{S}(T)$ given information up until t ($< T$) depends only on $S(t)$.

matrix pricing: using the yield spread of blended yields (the linearly interpolated yields of two on-the-run Treasury bonds) to determine the yield of the bond dependent upon the market prices of actively traded bonds.

maturity: the time to the final payment of a bond.

mean reversion process: the dynamics describing the behavior of interest rate that if the interest rate is low, then the interest rate will be adjusted upward, and conversely, if the interest rate is high, then the interest rate will be adjusted downward.

medium term note: bonds sold to a specific target group without the full disclosure of Securities Exchange Commission.

model: a simplified description of a real situation.

modified duration: the price sensitivity to the changes in the yield to maturity.

Money Market Deposit Account (MMDA): a product introduced at a bank to compete with money market mutual funds.

money markets: the markets where investments with a short time value of money, ranging from daily to annual rates, occur.

Monte Carlo simulation: A procedure for randomly sampling changes in market variables in order to value a derivative.

Monte Carlo simulation method: a methodology to randomly generate many scenarios and calculate the VaR.

morbidity risk: the frequency and severity of the incidences of disease, illness, and sickness of a well-defined group of persons.

mortality table: the compilation of the death experiences of the population.

mortality: the ratio of deaths to a specific population.

Mortgage-Backed Securities (MBS): securities backed by a pool of individuals' home mortgages.

mortgage pool: a portfolio of mortgages collected together under certain guidelines.

mortgages: bonds that use real estate properties, such as collaterals, for securing purpose.

municipal bonds: a municipalities' borrowings.

mutual company: the insurance companies that has policyholders as shareholders.

National Association of Insurance Commissioners (NAIC): Non-profit organization formed to provide national uniformity in insurance regulations.

nearby contracts: those options with a short time to expirations.

Negotiable Order of Withdrawal (NOW) accounts: transaction accounts offered to non-corporate customers.

net premium written: the premium net of the ceded amount.

Net Working Capital (NWC): the short-term assets net of the short-term liabilities.

nominal rates: the yields of the bonds or the interests that we receive in our investments.

nominal yield curve: the plot of the yields to maturity of the Treasury securities outstanding in the market place to their maturities.

non-vested benefits: the obligations to the firm depending on whether the employee remains at the firm.

nonforfeiture benefits (or cash values): premiums that whole life insurance provide in order to protect policyholders who have developed significant reserves by paying premiums, which state laws mandate.

normal backwardation: the relationship between the expected spot price and the forward price where the forward price is less than the expected spot price, i.e., the forward price has an upward drift.

normal process: the process where the volatility is independent of the interest rate level.

normative model: a model which is prescriptive and offer us the most favorable way to achieve our objectives.

notional amount: the principal of a swap which will never result in a payment.

OAS duration: a measure of the sensitivity of the bond price to a parallel shift of the option adjusted spread.

Office of the Controller of the Currency (OCC): the oldest regulatory agency in the US, which has the responsibility to charter or close national banks.

on-the-run issues: the issues that have been recently issued and the market is very liquid, particularly for these issues.

one-factor model: the model assuming that there is only one source of risk, which implies that all bond prices depend on the movements of the rate (r), and that all bond prices move in tandem because of their dependence on one factor.

open interest: the number of contract sold (and bought) for a particular contract.

open market operation: the government monetary policy where central banks buy and sell Government securities in the secondary markets.

operating efficiency: the ratio of EBIT to the gross profit.

option adjusted spread (OAS): the constant spread (in basis points) that we add to the spot curve such that when we apply the bond model based on the spot curve with the OAS, we have the theoretical price or the observed price.

option premiums: option prices.

organization structure: a structure which specifies the business units, the management team, and other business units of the firm.

out of the money: a state of the intrinsic value being zero.

Over the Counter (OTC) market: a market that has no central location and no specialists to maintain the trading of each security, e.g., NASDAQ.

overnight repurchase rate (repo): the dealer's financing rate for overnight sale and repurchase of Treasury securities.

par price: the principal remaining at the time and not 100. By market convention, par is often denoted by 100 to mean 100% of the remaining principal.

par rates: the Treasury notes and bonds yield, which are benchmarks for the market to infer the time value of money since the Treasury notes and bonds are sold at a coupon rate such that the market price is 100% of the principal (that is, the bonds are sold at 100 or par.)

par yield curve: the plot of par rates against their maturities, i.e., the relationship of the coupon rate of a par bond with maturity T and its maturity.

parity value (conversion value): the product of the conversion ratio and the stock price.

participating policy: the whole life policy that returns excess premiums in the form of policyholder dividend because the policyholder participates in the experience of the policy.

pass-throughs: the bonds issued as claims against a mortgage pool. They simply pass the interest and principal collected from all the mortgagors and pass them to the bondholders on a pro rata basis.

passive portfolio management: the asset management which is not seeking actively to provide high returns for the clients but passively reacting to the performance of the benchmark bond index.

path dependent option: an option with the payout depending on the price path that the stock has traversed.

pathwise value: the risk adjusted present value of the payoffs along each scenario which can be determined by discounting the payout at the risk free rate in the risk neutral lattice.

payoff diagram: a diagram for the payments to the option holders on the expiration date.

pecking order theory: an application of the signaling theory to the capital structure, which suggests that the firm should first use internally generated funds, and then short-term debt followed by the long-term debt to equity in order.

Pension Benefits Guarantee Corp. (PBGC): a federal government agency that insures private defined benefit pension plans.

pension plan: a financial arrangement between two parties: the sponsors and the participants. Under the agreement, the sponsors make periodic payments into an investment fund, called the pension fund, which provides the capital for retirement benefits as part of the compensation to the employees.

perfect capital market: a market where many buyers and many sellers exchange their securities in a frictionless.

performance option: an option that pays $Max[X(Y, 0]$, where Y is a stock index and X is a portfolio value.

perpetual bonds (consol bonds): fixed income securities that have no maturity (or infinite time to maturity).

Personal Demand Deposit Accounts (DDAs): checking accounts for individual customers.

Planned Amortization Class (PAC): a CMO bond designed to have negligible prepayment risk.

planning horizon: some horizon time where we need to establish the terminal conditions of the firm value.

policy loads: loans which policyholders can borrow against their cash value.

policy reserves: the fund set aside so that the deficit can be funded from the accumulation of the earlier gains.

portfolio effect: the individual stock VaR net of the component VaR, measuring the effect of diversification on the individual asset risk.

portfolio theory: a theory on constructing an optimal investment portfolio and understanding the implications of the optimal portfolio on the securities pricing.

positive model: a model which describes the financial world that we have as seen through the prism of financial models.

preferred habitat: a segment in the yield curve that each investor occupies.

preferred habitat hypothesis: a hypothesis that different segments of market participants hold different parts of the yield curve.

premium load (front-end load): a charge the insurer deducts to cover a portion of the operating expenses.

prepayment model: a model which explains the mortgagors' prepayment behavior from historical data.

prepayment risk: the risk of the mortgagors' prepaying their loans to the banks.

Present Value of Future Profits (PVFP): the present value of the future after-tax income and the net value of the future changes in the capital.

price multiple: the ratio of capitalization to equity, which is the return of the shareholders' investment.

Price Value of a basis point (PV 01): the change in the bond price or portfolio value by 1 basis point shift of the yield curve.

price/earning ratio (P/E ratio): the ratio of the share price to the earning per share, equivalently, expressed as the capitalization to the firm's net income.

primary decomposition: the path-wise value of cash flow assuming a zero volatility.

primary market: a market where the initial sales of the securities occur.

prime rate: the base rate on corporate loans posted.

primitive firm (V^p): a simple corporate entity which has no debt or claims other than the common shares, which are publicly traded, as an underlying security.

Principal-Only (PO): a contract where investors can be received only the principal of the pass-through monthly.

principal components: the eigenvectors of an $n \times n$ symmetric matrix of the variance—covariance matrix of n key interest rate historical changes over a specified time period, which represent the direction of the interest rate movements such as level, steepness, and curvature movements while eigenvalues represent the amplitudes of the interest rate movement.

principals (face values): the payments that are promised to be repaid by the borrower to the lender.

pro rata sinking fund: sinking fund which is designed so that the repayments are amortized over a period of time on a pro rata basis.

production efficiency: the ratio of the gross profit to sales.

production process: a activity of a firm generating goods and services.

profit release approach: The profit of the sale of the liability is released continuously and the profit is the spread.

Projected Benefit Obligation (PBO): the present value of the pension which requires an estimate of the future pay level.

promised yield: the yield based on the promised coupon and principal payments.

public bonds: bonds available to general investors, which are required to provide a full disclosure.

Public Securities Association (PSA): a market convention adopted by the Public Securities Association in which prepayment rates are assumed to follow a predetermined formula path over time.

put-call parity: the relationship among a European call option, a European put option with the same strike price and expiration date, and the underlying stock.

quoted price (clean price): the price that bond will be bought or sold.

ratchet option: an option such that the payout on the expiration date is an index, where the index is not just the current stock price, as it is in standard options, but the index depends on the highest of the historical stock prices.

rating bucket approach: a crude approach to control credit risk where we assign the same proportion of bonds in each rating group.

rating transition: the probabilities of an upgrade or downgrade of the bond rating.

real asset: an asset including tangible or intangible that may produce products and services to an economy.

real option: an option that is a model of the flexibility of the capital budgeting of a corporation on the real sector — not just investment in financial securities.

real rates: the yields that reflects the real sector where there is no impact of money on the purchase of goods.

real time prices: the continual establishment of the price of the stock through the efficient trading of the stocks.

recombining tree: a tree where an up state followed by a down state equals a down state followed by an up state.

recovery ratio (recovery rate): the proportion of the amount received by the creditor emerging from bankruptcy to the par amount.

reduced form models: the credit risk models which relates bond value to historical estimates. For example, they do not endogenize the recovery rate, but use the historical estimates for the recovery rate.

Required Option Adjusted Spread (ROAS): the option adjusted spread that makes the fair value of the liability equal to the initial premium value at the time of sales.

reserve: the book value of the insurance liability.

reset dates: the dates for the resets of floating rates which reflect changing market conditions.

retainer option: an option to commit significant investment for each stage of the technology development.

retention option (installment option): a kind of compound option with a series of strike prices, which offers the holder the opportunity to buy the asset by installments.

Return on risk adjusted capital (RORAC): a performance measurement defined as (return − required capital $\times$ r) divided by EaR.

Risk Adjusted Performance Measurements (RAPM): measurements that are typified by considering the income relative to the required capital.

Risk Adjusted Return on Capital (RAROC): a performance measurement defined as return divided by total available equity multiplied by the ratio of business EaR to the bank EaR.

risk averse: an individual's risk preference which requires higher returns to compensate for an increase in risk.

risk management: a method of managing risk with VaR and EaR.

risk neutral probability: a probability assigned to each node of a tree such that all interest rate contingent claims have an expected "risk-free return," which is the one period rate.

risk neutral valuation approach: a valuation method based on the risk neutral underlying asset lattice by assuming that the underlying asset has a risk-free return.

risk premium: the additional returns that a risk-averse investor requires for the risk he takes on.

round-trip trade: instantaneous execution of buy and sell trades.

safety covenants: covenants to protect the bondholders for the life of the bond by some conditions that would trigger the firm to accelerate the principal payments to the bondholders.

secondary decomposition: the path-wise value of the security net of the path-wise value of the primary decomposition.

secondary market: a market where the shares are traded after the initial shares replacement.

secured creditors: creditors having the debt secured by some assets of the firm.

Securities and Exchange Commission (SEC): the primary regulator for all publicly traded companies in the U.S.A..

securities market: a network of activities for transactions of securities.

security's characteristic line: the regression of the time-series return data of market portfolio against each security's time series return data.

Security Market Line (SML): the linear relationship between the expected returns and the betas.

semi-strong form efficiency market: a market which reflects publicly available information such as dividend announcements.

senior creditors: creditors having higher priority to the claims than the junior creditors.

Separate Trading of Registered Interest and Principal of Securities (STRIPS): the stripping of designated Treasury securities into its coupons and principal payments; each of them becomes a zero-coupon bond.

Separation Theorem: a theorem which can tell the risky asset composition of an investor without knowing his risk preference.

service cost: one component of the charges of the liability, which is the increase of PBO attributable to employee service during the period.

short selling: selling a security without owning it.

Single Premium Deferred Annuity (SPDA): an insurance product where the policyholder pays a single premium to the insurance company and the insurance company pays a fixed amount every year for rest of the life of the policyholder.

sinking fund provision: the provision that requires bonds to be retired over time according to a specified schedule.

specialist: a person to whom each stock is assigned and who is responsible for the observation of the orderly price movements and the liquidity of the stock.

spot curve: the relationship between the required rate of return of default free one dollar invested over a time period of T which measures time value of money required by the market.

spot market: the market where actual monetary transactions are made by investors who pay for financial or real assets, as opposed to other markets where agreements are made for future delivery of assets.

spot volatilities: the volatility of the nth year rate of the spot curve for each $n = 1, 2, \ldots$

spread option: an option on the yield spread of two bonds.

spread protected debt securities: the securities that can be redeemed on a specified date prior to maturity, at the option of the holders. The redemption price is equal to the present value of the remaining promised payment discounted at a rate equal to a specific Treasury yield plus a fixed spread.

static hedge position: the position which does not have to be revised until the expiration when the entire position can be liquidated.

static yield: the yield of the projected cash flow if the mortgage prepayment speed is quoted along with the PSA assumption.

stock company: the insurance companies that has traded stocks in the markets.

stock volatility: the risk of the underlying stock returns measured by the standard deviation.

straddle: a portfolio of put and call options sharing the same strike price, which pays for both options immediately whereas the chooser option does not pay for both options entirely.

strategic debt servicing: the adjustment of the absolute priority rule via debt holders' acceptance of an immediate loss by giving up a portion of the firm to the equity holders for the longer term gain.

strategic risk management: a process to identify the risk sources and to measure their impact on the firm.

strategic value: the present value of a firm's future potential businesses.

strong form efficiency market: a market which reflects all the information including private information.

structural models: the credit risk models which are concerned with relating the bond value to the firm's business risk and its capital and debt structure at the time of evaluating the bonds.

subjective model: a model which seeks to abstract complex problems to deal with a "purpose in hand." They are derived by some rules or ideas that may even contradict the basic principles in finance or economic theories.

supporting tranches: non-PAC bonds in the deal.

surety bond: a property and casualty insurance contract where the insurance covers the fulfillment of an obligation. The surety bonds guarantee the performance of the obligation (the principal) of a party to the other party (the obliges).

surrender charge: a charge as a penalty which exists during the first years if the policyholder wish to withdraw the money from the account value.

swap: an over-the-counter instrument, which is an exchange of payments between two parties. These payments are interest payments, which may be based on a floating rate or fixed rate, on the same amount of principal and maturity.

swap rate: the coupon rate determined for the fixed payments, i.e., the rate on the notional amount such that if we view the fixed payments as a bond, the market value of the bond is par, which is equivalent to the par rates of the bond market.

swaption: an option on swaps.

systematic risk (market risk): the risk that cannot be diversified away.

tangible asset: an asset that has a physical presence and has been made for specific functions or has the ability to produce physical goods, e.g., buildings, roads, bridges, and factories, etc.

tenor of the cap: the maturity of the last caplet.

tenor of the swap: time to termination of a swap.

term insurance: an insurance contract that pays a death benefit in the event of the death of the insured during the coverage period.

term premium: the excess return over the risk-free rate.

term structure of volatilities: the relationship of the spot rate volatilities with respect to the maturity.

terminal conditions of the options: payout specifications at the expiration date.

theta: the time decay, which is the change in the option price over a short period of time assuming the other variables including the stock price does not exchange.

time value of money: the market participant's preference for returns over a time horizon, which should be a smooth function related to the time to maturity, that is, the discount of a future payment to a smaller present value.

top-down approach: a strategic investment approach in the headquarter level. In this approach, corporate managers analyze the market potential of the business and design the business model to maximize the firm value.

total capitalization: the sum of the market value of the equity and the market value of the debt.

total return approach: an asset and liability management approach that is consistent with the shareholders' value.

total return swap: the credit derivative where the total return payer pays the counterparty (total return receiver), the coupons and the capital gains (loss) of a security over the term of the swap. In return the total return payer receives an agreed-upon spread off the LIBOR rate.

trade-off theory: an theory to determine the capital structure where debt will be raised by comparing its tax deductibility against its bankruptcy cost.

tranche: a segmentation of the bonds into different classes.

transfer pricing curve: the spot curve that determines the internal benchmark for present value calculations.

transition matrix: the table to determine the probability of the credit rating migration from one rating to the other using historical data.

Treasury bills: Treasury discount instruments (which have no coupon payments) with maturity less than one year at issuance.

Treasury bond index: a portfolio constructed by all the Treasury notes and bonds outstanding subject to some liquidity constraints on each bond issue.

Treasury bonds: Treasury securities which are similar to Treasury notes and have a maturity of 30 years at issuance.

Treasury Inflation Protection Securities (TIPS): the bonds recently issued (since 1997) which have the principals linked to the inflation rate such that the principal of the bond is adjusted by the semi-annual inflation rate.

Treasury notes: Treasury fixed income securities with coupons paid semi-annually and with maturity less than 10 years at issuance.

trip wires: the trading limits.

trustee: a representative for all the bondholders in each bond class, who oversees the agreement made between the borrowers and lenders and is also responsible for exerting the rights of the bondholders in the event of default.

turnover: the ratio of sales to assets.

Unallocated Loss Adjustment Expenses (ULAE): the extent of the expenses that have not been allocated already to pay the underwriting, maintenance of the policies, and legal expenses.

underwriters: the insurer's agents who evaluate the risks and determine the premium charged to the customer.

underwriting: the process of determining the insurance rate (or premium) for the specified coverage.

unearned premium: the portion of the premium received by the insurer which has to be retained to cover the remaining term of the contract.

universal life: a flexible premium policy that allows the insured to change the death benefit from time to time, unlike traditional policies that maintain premiums at a given level over a fixed contract period.

unsystematic risk (residual risk): the risk that can be diversified away.

upstairs dealers: dealers who place their orders to the stock exchange for the purpose of providing liquidity to any imbalance of supply and demand of shares, standing ready to buy and sell shares, making a profit in the process.

US STRIPS bond option: a bond option which offers the holder the right and not the obligation to buy a specific US STRIPS bond at the expiration date at a fixed price.

valuation: the process of determining reserves in the whole life contract.

Value at Risk (VaR): a measure of the maximum loss of the portfolio over a time horizon, given a certain significance level.

vanilla swap: a swap where one party pays a standard floating rate (for example, daily LIBOR) and receives a fixed rate.

vega: the sensitivity of the option price to a small change in volatility.

Vested Benefit Obligation (VBO): the present value of the pension benefits assuming the same pay level of the employees.

vested benefits: the employee's right to receive earned pension benefits even if the employee leaves the employment.

volatility surface: the extension of the volatilities of the entire yield curve into the future, that is, the volatility of nth year spot rate volatility at Tth year in the future.

weak form efficiency market: a market which reflects the past information like past prices in the current prices.

wealth transfer: the phenomenon where stockholders' wealth is transferred to the bond-holder or vice versa..

weather derivatives: contingent claims on weather, e.g., temperature, precipitation, or snow accumulation, etc.

Weighted Average Cost of Capital (WACC): the cost of capital of the firm which equals to the weighted average cost of each capital component such as stocks and bonds. The weights are the market value of the capital components.

whole life: an insurance contract that provides protection to the policyholder for as long as the insured lives.

whole loans: the mortgage-pass-throughs that originate from private corporations.

yield curve movement: the change of the yield curve shape over a relatively short time interval, say one month.

yield to call: the yield to the first call price.

Yield To Maturity (YTM): the internal rate of return of a bond.

yield to worst: the lowest yield number for all the possible call prices on the call schedule.

Index